ISBN 978-0-428-96567-9
PIBN 10788102

THE SOUTHERN PRESBYTERIAN JOURNAL

A Presbyterian weekly magazine devoted to the statement, defense and propagation of the Gospel, the faith which was once for all delivered unto the saints.

VOL. XV NO. 1 | MAY 2, 1956 | $2.50 A YEAR

New Educational Building of McIlwain Memorial Presbyterian Church, Pensacola, Florida.
(See Page 25)

ANCHORED—OR ADRIFT? — By L. Nelson Bell
(See Page 3)

LET FREEDOM RING — By Rev. John R. Richardson, D.D.
(See Page 7)

THE SOUTHERN PRESBYTERIAN JOURNAL
The Journal has no official connection with the Presbyterian Church in the United States
Rev. Henry B. Dendy, D.D., Editor..**Weaverville, N. C.**
Dr. L. Nelson Bell, Associate Editor..**Asheville, N. C.**
Rev. Wade C. Smith, Associate Editor..**Weaverville, N. C.**

— LETTERS —

Texas City, Texas
April 11, 1956

Dear Editor:

In response to your question "Do our readers agree with this observation" concerning "Bureaucracy" in the Southern Presbyterian Church I submit the following:

The General Assembly minutes of 1949 (the year prior to reorganization" of Assembly Agencies) show 2,663 ministers in our Church. Last year's Minutes (1954 figures) show 3,196 ministers which is a gain of 533 ministers. In the statistical summaries of each year indicating the type employment of ministers (15 possible categories) 1949 shows 1,619 ministers employed as pastors and last year's (1954 figures) shows 2,139. This represents an increase of 520 ministers serving the Church as pastors. A comparison of 1949 and 1955 Minutes shows in the former 786 churches without any pastoral ministry while in the latter only 547. The number of churches increased 244 in these years.

These same official tables show a gain of 16 ministers in the category of Secretary and a gain of 13 in the category of Presbytery Executive Secretary in these six years. Also shown is a gain of 29 in the category of Foreign Missionary and 19 as Chaplains.

I am convinced that a net gain of 533 ministers in the six years with a gain of 520 in the pastoral ministry does not indicate any trend of pastors into "Secretarial splendor". Also the presence of 46 laymen and women in the 1955 listed Assembly Board positions speaks well of the use of qualified lay people by the Church in "Secretarial capacities."

Sincerely,
Dave Currie
First Presbyterian Church,
Texas City, Texas

Sir:

It may be out of order to send you the attached memorandum, but so many people, mostly church officers, have talked about the change in recent months (years) of sermons from what they formerly were, that I thought maybe you or some of your writers might develop an article for the Journal that would cause both ministers and laymen alike to consider the importance of a "return" to more effective preaching, and a closer relationship between the minister and the Session.

I would not want my name connected with this as I think I have no ambition for publicity, but it's something that I think many ministers need to have their minds refreshed on.

MODERN verus OLD FASHIONED SERMONS

It is a well established fact that a good sermon depends upon two elements, one being the practical reasoning and delivery of the minister, and, the other being its appeal to the mind and heart of the listening congregation. That the mind of many ministers, and the mind of most laymen do not meet as often and as consistently as they should is not news to anyone.

The minister's mind, too often, is steeped in depths of theology far beyond the practical comprehension of the people in the pews. On the other hand, the minds of the people in the pews are steeped in every day considerations of their vocations in which they serve each other and provide for their families and those associated with them in their several business operations.

Apparently our modern sermons, while no doubt based upon the scriptures as the individual minister chooses to interpret them, are delivered in conformity to the way they were taught in the Seminaries. However, too many ministers overlook the fact that the people to whom they are directed have not had this Seminary line of thought, and unless the minister can blend enough practical content in with his theology to inspire the listeners, then it adds credence to the appraisal that what the congregtion gets is more of an oration than an inspirational sermon.

In times past ministers would often discuss with the Session from time to time, some of the aspects of a particular sermon or a series of sermons they planned to develop and deliver to their congregations. This had an excellent effect in more ways than one. So far as the lay mind was concerned, it revealed the thinking of the minister as well as that of the laymen. Oftentimes differences in the thinking could and were reconciled to the benefit of both the minister and his Session without antagonism. Actually, the minister and his Session were drawn closer together in understanding with no thought that either was trying to dictate to the other.

It's different nowadays in many churches. Rarely ever do ministers engage in a friendly discussion of sermons with the Session. Too many sermons have impressed (not inspired) the congregation with the evident feeling that the sermons are of the "canned" variety and are following some line of form- thinking imported from some source alien to what our Southern Presbyterian Church needs. In addition to the too often impractical aspects of such sermons, too many ministers fail to reach the minds and hearts of the listeners because of the unnatural tone of voice employed. Most laymen like to understand, not just to hear an oration. Dr. Stitt's style of preaching over the radio is what appeals to listeners. He talks as if what he says is an individual message to each listener, no frills of oratory, and his voice does not imply any superiority in theology. He makes his points briefly and so plain that a child can understand and receive benefit from what he says.

Finally, the balance of authority between the Minister and the Session would be achieved, as outlined in the Book of Church Order, if each element (clergy and lay) could be drawn closer together in ALL matters, controversies overcome, and a true spirit of unity might once more prevail. Too many laymen may be justified in believing that too many ministers are "captives", receptive to push-button influence and dictation from sources outside the confines of the Southern Presbyterian Church.

An Elder

Anchored --- or Adrift

By L. NELSON BELL

Protestants rightly look with suspicion on authoritarianism in any form. At the same time, they should view with like suspicion an iconoclastic approach to spiritual truth.

It is obvious that there must be some norm, some basis, on which Christian faith must rest and the determination of that basis is of the greatest importance.

Because of the place which the Bible holds in the Christian faith there has been an unending debate as to what the Christian's attitude should be to the Book.

Any who have recently studied in college, university or seminary know how very relevant this question is. In some quarters the Bible is considered merely a human document. In others it is accorded a higher status, revelation being admitted but at the same time the human element in the agents who wrote and compiled the writings being emphasized to the point where error, even wilful distortion, is assumed. To others the Bible is truly the Word of God in all of its entirety.

How shall the young Christian approach this dilemma? How shall he reconcile these differences in attitude to the Scriptures? Can they be reconciled?

Let us state categorically that we are not here discussing who is a Christian, or what makes a Christian. We believe that any person who truly believes that Jesus Christ is the Son of God and that He died for our sins is a Christian. The clear statement of Paul to the Romans is all sufficient: *"That if thou shalt confess with thy mouth the Lord Jesus, and shalt believe in thine heart that God hath raised him from the dead, thou shalt be saved."*

But, we all know in our own personal experience, and have seen in the lives of others, that there are a great many Christians, ordained and otherwise, who have no convincing message, no apparent power with either God or man. When confronted by a sinner and his need of a Savior there is lacking the spiritual wisdom and power needed to bring that seeking one to Christ. When confronted with a congregation of spiritually starved and ignorant people these people still go away hungry.

There are *many* reasons for such lack of spiritual power: unconfessed sin; failure to pray; trust in self rather than in the Holy Spirit; ignorance of the techniques of personal work; etc., etc. Also, we believe, failure to believe God's Word and a failure to use it as the Sword of the Spirit.

It is about the latter that we would write. We have held this article in abeyance for weeks because we are so anxious to write only that which will stand the test of God's clear scrutiny. We write with a compelling urge because we believe this to be one of the gravest problems in Christian circles. We are writing of but one thing—spiritual power and its relationship to faith in God's Holy Word.

Only too often we confuse organizational ability, eloquence, scholarship, an attractive and impelling personality, technical know-how, and many other desirable qualities and accomplishments with something entirely separate from and unrelated—the presence and power of the Holy Spirit.

The Southern Presbyterian Journal, *a Presbyterian Weekly magazine devoted to the statement, defense, and propagation of the Gospel, the faith which was once for all delivered unto the saints, published* every Wednesday by The Southern Presbyterian Journal, Inc., in Weaverville, N. C.

Entered as second-class matter May 15, 1942, at the Postoffice at Weaverville, N. C., under the Act of March 3, 1879. Vol. XV, No. 1, May 2, 1956. Editorial and Business Offices: Weaverville, N. C. Printed in the U.S.A. by Biltmore Press, Asheville, N. C.

ADDRESS CHANGE: When changing address, please let us have both old and new address as far in advance as possible. Allow three weeks after change if not sent in advance. When possible, send an address label giving your old address.

It is our observation that there is an inescapable relationship between what a man believes about the Bible and spiritual power in his work for God. We may earnestly try to camouflage our loss, but it is there, and, deep down in our hearts we know it, just as Samson's physical strength was gone when his head was shorn. Is there not something vital missing when the authorship of the Holy Spirit is questioned or denied as we take up God's Word? Is there not an inescapable link between a simple faith in the Scriptures and the presence and power of the Holy Spirit in the life of the Christian?

Here is the problem: Is the Bible the Word of God or does it merely *contain* the Word of God? Is the Bible completely reliable and authoritative, or must it be read and accepted with reservations?

To a layman the answer is so simple one wonders why so many become confused. *If* the Bible *contains* God's revelation, mixed along with many inaccuracies, deliberate frauds, ignorant statements, pre-dated history palmed off as prophecies, and thought-forms which really mean just the opposite of what they affirm, then *who* will sort out the true from the false? Of course the answer will be that this must be left to the scholars; that we must accept their conclusions.

If such is the case then we are reduced to an amazing situation, - *no longer are we to accept the Word of God for what it claims to be, God's holy and inspired revelation, but, we turn for comfort and instruction to men; to men who are constantly disagreeing among themselves as to facts and meanings; to men whose conclusions and affirmations of yesterday are discarded today for a new set of conclusions and affirmations.*

Or, we may decide that we ourselves will read the Bible and accept that which seems reasonable to us and question or reject the rest.

In either case we find ourselves adrift, subject to the changing whims and conclusions of men, rather than anchored in the assurance that God has given us a fully inspired and authoritative revelation of Himself and His dealings with and plans for His creation.

Anchored or Adrift? - that is the question.

Anchored or Adrift? - that is our problem.

This does not mean that we can explain all that we find in the Bible. It does not mean that there are not apparent discrepancies. It does not mean that at times we are not confused by some minor parts. Nor does it mean that all of the Bible is of equal relevance for us, although equally true.

Is it reasonable to think that God would have given us a revelation, such as the Holy Scriptures, all parts of which would have been equally clear to finite minds? For His Own divine purposes, and for our own good, He has hidden many truths that we might, through the aid of the Holy Spirit, search the Scriptures for their meaning. It was the Holy Spirit Who took Moses and the prophets and the Psalms and made clear to the early disciples and apostles their hidden references to Christ.

Again, is it reasonable to ask ourselves whether God would have given us a Book consisting of multiplied errors, frauds, ignorance and spurious prophecies, along with divine truth? If such had been the case surely our Lord would have called the attention of His disciples to these errors. Instead, all through His earthly ministry there was constant reference to and affirmation of the Old Testament record as being completely trustworthy and authoritative.

Does this mean that scholarly research should be discredited? Or, that we should decry a reverent and critical study of the Bible? Far from it. Such research and reverent study is both desirable and necessary. But, it is incumbent on every Christian to pray that he may distinguish between rationalistic and destructive criticism on the one hand, and that which is reverent and factual on the other.

Is this a plea for a theory that only certain *words* are inspired and that any deviation from these words and phrases is a deviation from faith in the fully inspired Scriptures? It is not. A thought may be expressed in many ways, using many different words. Where the translations are a faithful rendering of the original manuscripts, or those we now have, they can be considered truly the Word of God, whether in German, Chinese, French, English, or any other language.

But, this is a plea for the doctrine of full, or plenary inspiration of the Scriptures. It is revealing that those who most vehemently inveigh against "verbal" inspiration are not primarily concerned with *words* but with *doctrines* which words convey.

Presbyterians are standing on both Scriptural and historic confessional ground when they affirm their belief in the full inspiration of the Scriptures. In those days when men used language and terminology honestly and without double meaning, we find the Westminster divines using phrases about which there can be no question. The Confession of Faith states in Chapter I, "The Holy Scriptures" . . . *"The authority of the Holy Scriptures, for which it ought to be believed and obeyed, dependeth not upon the testimony of any man or church, but wholly upon God (Who is truth itself), the author thereof; and therefore it is to be received, because it is the Word of God."* (Section IV)

Again we read: " . . . *and the entire perfection thereof, are arguments whereby it doth abundantly evidence itself to be the Word of God; yet, notwithstanding, our full persuasion and assurance of the infallible truth and divine authority thereof, is from the inward work of the Holy Spirit, bearing witness by and with the word in our hearts."* (Section V).

And again we read: *"The Old Testament in Hebrew . . . and the New Testament in Greek, . . . being immediately inspired by God, and by his singular care and providence kept pure in all ages, are therefore authentical; so as in all controversies of religion the church is finally to appeal unto them . . . ".* (Section VIII).

And finally: *"The infallible rule of interpretation of Scripture is the Scripture itself; . . . "*

The Confession of Faith could not be clearer than it is in affirming that we are to look to the Scriptures for their interpretation and not to "any man or church."

The Bible itself, on which our Confession of Faith bases its own clear affirmations, also makes it incumbent on man to turn to it, not to men for interpretation. Or, where interpretation is the result of scholarly inquiry, it is only to be received if it is in accordance with Scripture itself.

Why are the Scriptures the subject of such repeated attacks? Is it not because Satan hates and fears the Bible more than anything else? The "Yea, hath God said?" in Genesis is still a favorite question today. Satan has never been able to stand against the Word of God because it is a divinely forged weapon for the use of believers. Paul tells us that the Word of God is the "Sword of the Spirit." It is the only weapon of offense, described with the arsenal for defense. Our Lord used it three times in the wilderness and Satan was thwarted. Today, when we fail to believe and use it as a weapon with which to attack Satan it is he who triumphs. When we undertake a witness for our Saviour without the Bible in our minds and hearts and on our lips our efforts fail miserably. Little wonder the Devil has never ceased to try to discredit God's Word.

But, many young people will find themselves in a quandary. Anxious to believe the Bible, and to have an anchor for their faith, they are told that it is "scientifically inaccurate," "historically muddled," "often sub-Christian in concept," "full of palpable errors," etc., etc. What can they believe? We would suggest that when such statements are made *the one making the statements be asked to give specific illustrations of these errors, etc.* Write them down. *Do not argue.* Then, submit these supposed errors to someone competent to answer them. It will be interesting to see how many of these "errors" are in the mind of the detractor of the Scriptures, not in the Scriptures themselves.

Some honest young people fear that such an attitude to the Bible requires a form of intellectual suicide, or dishonesty. But such is not the case. If one starts with the premise that God has given a faulty and impaired revelation, and that the chaff and the wheat must be separated before one can find the truth, obviously he has left out of account the element of faith. God requires of us, more than anything else, a complete surrender of our entire personalities, including our hearts and wills and minds. When we do this we come humbly to His Word and say, "Lord, I believe, help Thou mine unbelief."

What effect does reliance on man and his interpretations, or denials, have? It is like a ship cutting loose the anchor and drifting to and fro. How often we meet individuals whose beliefs depend on the latest book they have read? How often we find slavish quotations from various authorities, leaving out of account the Book they question, and that it has an answer for its own integrity.

Can one imagine a greater hindrance to faith than to have its concepts and conclusions dependent on some individual, no matter how brilliant or scholarly he may be? It is true that there are some who affirm their faith, because of their trust in and admiration for a true man of God and his conclusions. But again we have the *mistake of personal faith depending on human conclusions.*

It is right at this point that we must face the issue. It is right here that we determine whether our faith shall be anchored, or whether it shall be adrift on the sea of human speculation.

What is the effect of a vacillating and ever changing philosophy towards the Scriptures, a philosophy which depends on man for inner assurance and which rejects the full inspiration of the Word of God? Certainly one of the most tragic effects is a loss of spiritual power. There is no longer full assurance as we undertake to wield the Sword of the Spirit. We believe God the Holy Spirit is grieved when we question His Word and that it can be demonstrated that with such questioning power departs. We can go through the motions of Christian service but something vital and precious has departed.

Those who have made the Bible a part of their lives; who know it and can quote it appropriately, find that God has placed in their hands a weapon which can be used with deadly effect on the enemy of souls. That is why our attitude to the Scriptures is so desperately important.

When our faith is anchored in words such as these we will find that, like Paul we can: *"having overcome all to stand"* . . . *"Thus speaketh the Lord God of Israel, saying, Write thee all the words that I have spoken unto thee in a book."* Jeremiah 30:2.

"All Scripture is inspired by God and is useful for teaching the faith and correcting error, for re-setting the direction of a man's life and training him in good living. The Scriptures are the comprehensive equipment of the man of God, and fit him fully in all branches of his work." II Tim. 3:16-17 (Phillips)

"But we must understand this at the outset, that no prophecy of Scripture arose from an individual's interpretation of the truth. No prophecy came because a man wanted it to: men of God spoke because they were inspired by the Holy Spirit." II Peter 1:20-21 (Phillips)

"For the word that God speaks is alive and active: it cuts more keenly than any two-edged sword; it strikes through to the place where soul and spirit meet, to the innermost intimacies of a man's being: it exposes the very thoughts and motives of a man's heart." Heb. 4:12 (Phillips)

"But the unspiritual man simply cannot accept the matters which the Spirit deals with - they just don't make sense to him, for, after all, you must be spiritual to see spiritual things. The spiritual man, on the other hand, has an insight into the meaning of everything, though his insight may baffle the man of the world. This is because the former is sharing God's wisdom, . . . " I Cor. 2:14-16 (Phillips)

L.N.B.

A Significant Action

The withdrawal of the Bible Presbyterian Church from the American Council of Churches and from the International Council of Churches is but another unhappy episode in a group which seems to have failed to heed the warning of Paul to the Galatians: *"For the law is fulfilled in one word even this; Thou shalt love thy neighbor as thyself. But if ye bite and devour one another take heed that ye be not consumed one of another."*

In taking this step these courageous men have disassociated themselves from a leadership which has all too often seemed to "rejoice in inquity" while proceeding to expose it; a leadership which seems to have forgotten that "defending the faith" requires Christian love if it is to really adorn that faith.

Let us pray that this step may be but the beginning of a new and positive witness for the Christian truth, where truth may be given an opportunity to speak for itself. L.N.B.

MISS LINA E. BRADLEY

A Faithful Steward

When the *Southern Presbyterian Journal* was founded fourteen years ago the first member of the staff employed was Miss Lina Bradley of Bishopville, S. C., a former missionary to China and an experienced and capable secretary and office supervisor.

Since that time Miss Bradley has served this paper with a degree of faithfulness and efficiency rarely attained by one called on to perform so many and important tasks. It can truthfully be said that she has served far beyond the line of duty.

On May 1st Miss Bradley retired and all associated with the *Journal* wish to publicly express to her our deep affection and heart-felt appreciation for her services.

It is our prayer for her that the coming years may be filled with happiness, part of which will stem from the knowledge that she has done a hard job faithfully and well.

The Editors and Staff

Let Freedom Ring

By Rev. John R. Richardson, D.D.

The annual meeting of the Christian Freedom Foundation was held this year in the Great Northern Hotel in New York City on April 11th and 12th. In addition to the transaction of the usual business the meeting was devoted to a discussion of the fundamental problems of economics, especially as related to Christianity and freedom. By Christian economics the Foundation means an economic system operated by Christian men in accordance with their best understanding of the laws of God. The directors of this Foundation believe that the economic laws, like all of God's laws, are immutable. The constitution of the Foundation affirms that man for the attainment of his well-being should respect these laws of economics just as much as the other laws of God.

We believe that the addresses given at this annual meeting of the Board of Directors of the Christian Freedom Foundation will be of interest to the readers of the *Southern Presbyterian Journal.* We are glad to report the highlights of this meeting for the enlightenment and edification of our constituency.

Dr. Alexander St. Ivanyi was the first speaker. He was formerly a Protestant Bishop of Hungary. He fought for freedom in his own country. He was a refugee and later became a citizen of our country. He lost his professorship at the Massachusetts Institute of Technology because of his exposure of Communism in that institution. He is a competent student of economics and the world situation. He has an interesting story to tell.

Despite the fact that it might sound like an exaggeration, Dr. St. Ivanyi stated that he was firmly convinced that the most important event in the struggle between the Western world and Communist Imperialism is at present the official representation of World Protestantism behind the Iron Curtain. In this connection he discussed the large group of the World Council of Churches that represented Protestantism in Budapest, Hungary, September 15-20, 1955, and another group that just returned from Russia. Analyzing the situation he said we cannot avoid the conclusion that the initiative in this undertaking has come from the National Council of Churches in America. To the rest of the world, observed the speaker, the National Council of Churches of this country means American Protestantism. The main part of his message was an analysis and evaluation of the results of these official representations of the World Council from the Hungarian standpoint and of the National Council from the Russian standpoint.

Dr. St. Ivanyi stated that these visits represent a great reversal in the attitude of Protestants toward tyrants. The National Council-led World Council leaders, said Dr. St. Ivanyi, went out of their way to show their sympathy— not to the imprisoned clergymen— but especially to the two most outstanding representatives of collaboration with the Communists. He remarked, "You can imagine—and we who are in constant touch with the Hungarian people; know — how the Hungarians felt seeing these Western Churchmen fraternizing with men whom they regard as worse than murderers."

Summarizing his thoughts, the speaker concluded with this statement, "There seems to be no question but that a great reversal is being effected by these leaders of Protestantism in the historic role which used to place Protestant clergymen on the side of the oppressed and against the oppressor. Now official Protestantism makes friends with the worst tyrants of recorded history hoping to gain concessions from them for the people, for the members of the Protestant churches, for the leaders of one particular Protestant Church, whichever the case may be individually with these visiting delegates. . . .

Knowing the people of Hungary I can safely say that they would not approve of any concessions if those were given only to the Reformed Church or to the Protestants. They would rather share the wrath of their Communist masters together with the Roman Catholic and Jewish Hungarians than to benefit by these alleged concessions by themselves alone. . . . These visits did not and will not help religious people behind the Curtain. On the contrary they harm them. A psychiatrist of the army, Major Wm. E. Mayer, recently published the result of the four year long investigation of more than a thousand brain-washed U. S. prisoners of war in Red China. The Communist 'instructors' and psychiatrists usually 1. destroyed the U. S. prisoner's belief in the values of civilization, and 2. his belief that his country cares for him and his religious beliefs. This brain-washing process 'turned the American prisoners into the most uninformed men we have ever seen' . . . The official visitors in Hungary will achieve about the same result if they insist on going there again. Seeing this large number of Western clergymen fraternizing with the Communist bosses and accepting honorary degrees from them, Hungarians cannot help but come to the conclusion that (1) the West has no moral standards; (2) the West is eager to make friends with those whom Hungarian clerical and lay-martyrs resisted at the cost of their lives in the past and (3) that Christianity caters to power rather than obeys God. These Western visitors might have achieved what the Communist bosses have not yet been able to achieve during their ten years rule in Hungary —a mass brain-washing of the population and a cessation of their spiritual resistance to Communist tyranny."

"A LOOK AT SWEDEN'S 'MIDDLE WAY'"

Dr. F. A. Harper, the second speaker, used as his subject "A Look at Sweden's 'Middle Way'". He has just returned from four months of study in Sweden and had much interesting information about the breakdown of the "middle way" in that country.

Dr. Harper is a well known student of economics and sociology. He went to Sweden to report and find out whether socialism has worked the marvels there that have been reported to us. At the very beginning he stated that he realized that there must be a definition of the meaning of socialism before he could give an intelligent report. He reminded the audience that there have been published in excess of 600 separate and variable definitions of socialism. The definition that he adopted was his own and he defined it thus, "Socialism is the forcing of a centrally controlled economic life upon all persons within some geographic boundary under an authoritarian monopoly that is politically managed."

With this definition in mind Dr. Harper tested it on the basis of its fruits. As a result of this test he learned that socialism has been a great burden on the personal incomes of the costs of government. He found that socialism is economic slavery, since a slave is one whose time and earnings are not his own. He affirmed that the loss of free choice in the spending of incomes has now reached 48 per cent in Sweden. This he illustrated by charts. He pointed out that when Marquis Childs wrote his "Sweden, the Middle Way" in 1938 the corresponding figure was only 28 per cent.; Sweden was only then at the quarter mark. By this test, socialism has doubled in Sweden since Childs wrote his book, suggesting that a better title might have been something like this: "Sweden's Avalanche of Socialism: The Middle Way by 1954." He points out that if the loss of free choice in the spending of incomes in Sweden should continue at the rate of the last third of a century, their enslavement will have become complete within the expected lifetime of young people now of college age. A century ago, Sweden—like the United States—operated its affairs with a high degree of individual responsibility and ownership. The cost of all formalized government a century ago took less than ten per cent of personal incomes at a time when personal incomes were only one-sixth what they are now. In other words, the present cost of government in terms of "real kroner" per person governed is about thirty times that of a century ago.

Dr. Harper further stated his opinions on education in Sweden. He pointed out that Lenin once said, when speaking about education: "Give us the child for eight years, and it will be a Bolshevist forever." (Nikolai Lenin, in speech to the Commissars of Education, Moscow, 1923). The socialist government in Sweden has now essentially accomplished the education control of which Lenin spoke. Practically all children in Sweden now attend schools under the authority of the Ministry of Education and Ecclesiastical Affairs. He said, "A century ago it appears that as many as one child in four was being educated outside of government schools. Literacy even then was at a high level. Education of this one-fourth was in part by schools outside the home and in part by home schooling. The formal home schooling rapidly lost out until little remained by 1915. Non-government schools outside the home continued to expand, however, until the early twenties; they then receded until 1940, when only 1½% of the children were in schools of this type. Schooling of any form other than under government operation is now all but gone for the eight-year period of which Lenin was presumably speaking—roughly ages 7-15." The two great universities of Sweden, Uppsala and Lund, are state operated. State control even reaches far into adult education. Folk High Schools have now become largely public institutions, being a part of the "forward march of the working classes" under a socialist government.

The fruit of socialism is also to be observed in the church and religion. The Church of Sweden is a State Church and every child is born a legal member. All the clergy are trained in the two State Theological Schools. Expenses are met through tax collections rather than through voluntary giving. As a result, participation in church affairs is slight especially in urban centers. Dr. Harper quoted Archbishop Brilioth who said recently that Sweden today could not, with any certainty, be called a Christian country. The Archbishop said, "The Christian clothing it wears is an illusion." He pointed out also that the Swedish Welfare State has dulled the spiritual appetites of the people. He also quoted Rev. Lars Bejerhold who epitomized the condition in Sweden by saying, "the church is generally tolerated but scarcely loved."

Socialism likewise fails to meet the moral test, said Dr. Harper. Abortions are now about one-tenth of all calculated pregnancies. Abortions became legalized in the late thirties, in a way similar to that of Russia in 1920. By the early 1950's legal abortions had risen to about one per twenty births. Homosexuality, if voluntary and involving adults, was legalized in 1955.

The conclusion reached by Dr. Harper through his study of Sweden is that socialism is undermining the sterling character of some of the finest people on earth.

THE TRAGEDY OF SOCIALISM

On the afternoon of April 11th Dr. Harold John Ockenga brought a striking message on "The Tragedy of Socialism."

By way of introduction he explained that it makes a great deal of difference as to what kind of society a Christian lives in. He said that he was greatly concerned regarding the fact that we are very rapidly moving along the road to the Welfare State in America. One of the things endangering our freedom today is Socialism. Human nature cannot take the pressures of Socialism. Socialism panders to the worst in human nature and offends the best in human nature. Socialism breaks up under the Biblical doctrine of human nature. Dr. Ockenga has made several visits to England for the purpose of studying Socialism in operation. One of the claims of Socialism, he said, was that it saved England from Communism. This was an untenable defense, he said, because Socialism in Russia has been no protection against Communism. Neither did Socialism protect Poland from Communism. Some defenders of Socialism claim that it has improved the conditions of the masses. He found that there may be a few facts to justify this statement but there are many others that oppose it. He said that he discovered the British people "under Socialism were undernourished and emaciated." Socialism had not helped to build character in these people. Defenders also say that Socialism has promoted the distribution of wealth more equally than before. To this the speaker retorted, "Perhaps it has in some instances but at the expense of killing incentives and resulting in a bankrupt government."

NATURAL LAW IN SOCIAL SCIENCE

Dr. John Q. Stewart, a full professor at Princeton University, gave a profound discourse on "Natural Law in Social Science."

Dr. Stewart affirmed that there is sufficient basis for belief in natural theology as well as for revealed theology. He cited Romans 1:20 indicating that St. Paul recognized the validity of this contention. He pointed out that when the United States was founded a strong reliance on natural law in social phenomena was far stronger than now among our political and ecclesiastical leaders. We were told that just as physical engineering recognizes natural laws so should social engineering. He deplored the fact that many educational institutions ignore this phase of thought. He said, "The various social sciences in our misnamed 'universities,' which nowadays are really multiversities, have specialized and subspecialized to such a degree that few investigators have the wide sympathies and trainings necessary to discover profound principles common to all human activities. I have the good fortune to be a member of a small but enthusiastic volunteer team of research workers whose combined expertness represents leading fields in both natural and social science. We are much concerned with reducing the gulf which people think they see between natural science and social science."

The group is learning to identify and examine various sorts of "social energies." Among those listed were "action," "feeling," "logical meaning," "conformity," and so on. He affirmed that in due time our principles of social energy can be made fully intelligible to students with little training in mathematics or physics. But first much testing and development lies ahead. Where mass social relations are studied, understanding of social energies and of their transmutations and interplay is a splendid aid to diagnosis and prediction of social events.

The Princeton Physics Professor stimulated his audience to pursue further the implications of social physics.

OUR DANGER IS INTERNAL

The speaker for the evening of April 11th was Dr. E. Merrill Root, Professor of Philosophy at Earlham College and distinguished author of the recent volume entitled "Collectivism on the Campus." Dr. Root's subject was "Our Danger Is Internal."

Dr. Root began by saying America today, and sanity and freedom today, are in deadly peril. Why? His answer to this was, "Is it because a ruthless and brutal enemy is poised to let the tanks and the artillery loose against us; is it because a brutal and ruthless enemy is poised to loose concentrated death upon us from the skies? Such an enemy exists and such a peril is real, and we must be strong to guard the outer gates against treacherous and lethal assault. We must not leave the outer gates unprotected. But though that is true, it is our minor danger: our major peril lies not at the outer gate, but within the inner door."

Dr. Root says that the Communists plan to bring extreme collectivism to pass and conquer the whole world and reduce it to the rigid regimen by 1984.

Dr. Root says that the Communist purpose to dominate—but never to destroy the world. However, if they merely destroyed America, they would negate their own plan. They regard America as a very rich prize to be looted, as pirates looted the treasure ships upon the Spanish Main. America, to them, is a storehouse of incredible riches at present, and a workshop of mighty industrial potential for the future. They wish to possess the riches and to exploit the potential, so that they may enrich the grubby ant-heap collectivism that they call society. Their plan and their purpose is to capture America intact—and to capture it in the only way they can so do, by infiltration and subversion from within. They plan to capture America by destroying America's faith in freedom, in individualism, in initiative and competition; and by hypnotizing America with the lie that collectivism is the way, the truth, and the life. Thus we have to realize the kind of war we face today. Dr. Root would have America to see that in the so-called "cold war," we are fighting the very hottest kind of war. It is more deadly than a military war, a shooting war; and if and when a shooting war comes, it will have been won or lost already in the heart and the mind. It is a war that will be won or lost in the classrooms of America, where the battle of the mind is being fought today. The real war today is a psychological war, a spiritual war; a mighty armada of the air will not save us if we persist in letting collectivism infiltrate our government. Collectivism plans to overthrow us in our minds and in our wills. The method of attack used by the enemy is to brainwash us through our culture. Illustrating this method that is being used by the collectivists, Dr. Root says that when a wasp wishes to destroy a larger, more powerful insect, such as a butterfly, it merely stings the nerve centers of its victim, paralyzing it but leaving it alive, and then devours the doomed creature at its leisure. That is what our enemies, the collectivists, plan to do—that is what our enemies, the collectivists, are doing—they are paralyzing the very nerve centers of American life, especially by infiltrating our education, and especially by brainwashing us through our culture.

"Why should the Communists bother to invade us?" Dr. Root answered his question by saying, "They are already here!" He asked his audience to face this searching question—the most pertinent one can ask—"What use is it to post guards with high powered rifles on the outer walls, if at the same time we invite our enemies in through the inner door to drink vodka with us, and smile tolerantly as we watch them pour cyanide over our children's food?"

If anyone doubts the statement that Communism has invaded us we refer such persons to Dr. Root's book called, "Collectivism on the Campus." An abundance of evidence is presented to substantiate this assertion in the book.

As one example of how the liberals work Dr. Root cited an article written in the Vassar Alumnae Magazine. The Vassar Alumnae Magazine for February, 1950, contained an article written by Prof. Edna C. Macmahon, entitled "Did You Major in Economics?" She says that economics today is grouped around a comparative study of the practice of systems. In naming the systems worthy of study she lists prewar German Fascism, Russian Communism, British Socialism . . . Here comes an awkward hiatus. Capitalism, or free enterprise, as a functioning system, she nowhere names. She lists its antitheses as worthy of study. But where is free enterprise? Dr. Macmahon makes this sapient observation: "At the college teaching level, however, it is still generally taken for granted that an understanding of Marx is essential to an understanding of socialism." She does not, however, add the equally pertinent statement that an understanding of Hayek and von Mises will help one's understanding of free enterprise. Dr. Root adds that one is bewildered by the article into a belief that, if you major in economics at Vassar, you are isolated from the system under which—like it or not—you live. Such is the danger of the inner door. The address left the impression that it does not make sense to pour out futile billions in military preparation for a shooting war, when we do all that we can to popularize and endorse the ideas of collectivism in the battle for the mind.

WHAT RELIGION CAN DO TO DEFEAT COMMUNISM

The first speaker on the morning of April 12th was Mr. J. Anthony Marcus, Russian-born, an escapee, a successful business man and long-time citizen of our country. He is a devoted Christian and a competent student of economics. In the business world Mr. Marcus is an Independent Oil Producer and President of the Institute of Foreign Trade. He has kept in close touch with Russia and since the time he was naturalized as an American citizen he has made sixteen trips to Russia. Today he is telling the story of the Soviet Godless force that is out to destroy everything Christians stand for and everything that the founding fathers of this country fought and died for.

Mr. Marcus has been disappointed at the lack of interest on the part of prominent Americans in their fight against the Communist evil. He illustrated this by stating that he was invited to speak before the members of the Hitchcock Memorial Church in New York and he agreed on condition that they would have in the audience ten leading industrial and financial executives who were residents of Westchester County. They thought his request very modest and assured him that there would be twenty or thirty of these people there. About a week before the meeting was to take place he received a telephone message that they could not induce one of them to come because it was the last football game of the season. Mr. Marcus said, "This is indicative of the tragedy of our time. They who have most at stake in the present emergency care the least. We are pleasure drunk, we are too much steeped in our petty pastimes to see what is happening to us. We don't want to find out why, for example, our taxes are bordering on confiscation; why must our boys do garrison duty all over the world after a victorious war; we do not care to find out who the real culprit is." The speaker made a strong plea for vigorous, courageous, persistent and consistent action against the threat of Communism to our country. He said that, "We have witnessed the murder and enslavement of millions of men, women and children; we have known for years that the Stalinists had murdered tens of thousands of men of God like yourselves, and what have we done about it? Not a single meeting has ever been held in these United States to protest against the outrages. Not a single protest march has ever been recorded since the man-made hurricane was let loose by Lenin and his cohorts on November 7, 1917. No one could truthfully claim lack of information about the true state of affairs behind the iron curtain. We have had hundreds of thousands of escapees in the free world, the living witnesses of the Soviet inferno, and we have made very little use of their knowledge to lay bare the story which we must know for our own good." According to Mr. Marcus we have refused to take the Communists seriously. From the very inception Lenin, the arch-conspirator for world enslavement, had reminded us time and time again: "We have never concealed the fact that our revolution is only the beginning, that it will lead to a victorious ending only then when we shall have inflamed the whole world with its revolutionary fires." "This prediction is rapidly coming to pass," said Mr. Marcus. "One-third of the human race is under the bloody rule of the enemy; the earth is drenched with the blood of millions of men and women resisting enslavement; the Siberian tundras fertilized with the bones of Christian victims. The enemy is cunning and determined. He works day and night against us. A Stalinist anywhere in the world is ready to give his life at the drop of a hat if the Communist party so ordered. Are we as zealous about defending our heritage?"

The idea of co-existence with Communism was discouraged by Mr. Marcus. He said, "Anyone who entertains the illusion that co-existence with evil Stalinism is possible or desirable is not intelligent enough to know what is good for his country or himself. We have had co-existence with the enemy since November 1933, when we became diplomatic bedfellows with him. Has it improved our relations with the Kremlin gangsters? On the contrary, it has worsened. In 1933 the Soviets were economically and industrially impotent. With our recognition came world-wide prestige. That was what the Communists wanted more than anything else. It opened to them unlimited opportunities all over the world, for many governments followed our example and extended recognition to the same power. We failed to realize that anything the enemy wants badly, just as the Chinese bandits now want it, is proof that it is going to benefit him at our expense. Our country became the hunting ground of many thousands of Soviet spying commissions spying on our industries, laboratories, stealing our priceless technology acquired at great cost in labor and money. Our sales to the Soviets actually dropped after recognition. The Kremlin had gotten what it wanted, and we learned that all the talk about orders running into the billions was only a bait to get us into the trap. A little country like Cuba has been buying from us many times the amount we ever shipped to Russia, except for the war years when we gave away our substance to help rescue Stalin and his gangsters from annihilation by Germany and the Russian peoples."

"The New Look" in Russia should not deceive us said Mr. Marcus. He continued, "Kruschev's goal is the same as Stalin's ever was. Khrushchev's crocodile tears at the 20th Congress of the Communist Party last February that even he and his immediate associates never knew if they would come out alive from a conference with Stalin were designed to deceive the Russian people, to deceive the gullible free world. He and his Bulganin and Mikoyan and Molotov and the rest of the camarilla were Stalin's closest satraps. They made Stalin's purges and sadistic actions possible."

Pointedly, Mr. Marcus asked the audience: Is it in our interst to hobnob with such sadists? Is it moral to sit with them at the conference table, knowing in advance that they will never abide by their spoken or written word: What have we ever accomplished by conferring with them in the past? And since our trading with them exchanging industrial, scientific and educational delegations can only benefit the enemy, is it not stupid of us to participate in such exchanges?

Mr. Marcus wrote to Dr. Eugene Carson Blake concerning the mission of Protestant Churchmen going to Russia. He told him, "You are not dealing in Russia with free Churchmen like yourselves. Those who invited you did not do so of their own free will. They have done so by order of the tyrannical, Godless regime out to destroy all religions, all men of God, and all else that is dear to our hearts in America. . . . Your very presence in Russia will be rendering aid and comfort to the bitterest enemy of freedom and religion. The Russian Churchmen will lie to you about everything in Russia. They will have to or face liquidation. The Soviet regime is trying to use you and other religious organizations to confuse our people here to enhance their prestige, to give the impression that religion is free there, but at the same time plotting to destroy religious institutions everywhere. If you really wish to render a service to the people of Russia and to the cause of freedom, you should now hold a meeting and declare to the whole world that you will come to Russia only when the Soviet regime has been destroyed by its own people, when there is the same sort of freedom of religion in Russia as we have in the United States. You will then give the people of Russia inspiration to carry on their struggle until freedom is won. If this warning is not heeded, I am certain that you will regret it to the end of your days."

We all know that Mr. Marcus's advice was not heeded and when Dr. Blake returned with his deputation team, he called the mission "a distinct success."

Mr. Marcus said, "I too consider it a distinct success but not for America and not for the Christian Church. It was a distinct success for the Soviet propaganda machine which staged it and which now has recordings of the conversations held and the answers given by the Russian Churchmen, to be held against them some day, to be used in calling them 'agents of the imperialist Americans, spies and agents of Wall Street,' as they have done in innumerable instances in the recent past."

In explaining what religion can do to defeat Communism, Mr. Marcus stated that one of the things it must *not* do is exchange delegations with the enemy. He said, "Rendering aid and comfort to the enemy is treason."

Mr. Marcus closed his message by saying, "The fervent hope is that the Christians of America will not forsake the Russian people, will not aid the enemy, will stand by them in spirit and belief that with a little effort on our part we can aid them to perform the surgical operation upon their cruel Stalinists which will rid them and the rest of the world of the Lenin-Trotzky-Stalin nightmare."

POLITICAL INTERVENTION: HELP OR HINDRANCE

Mr. Percy L. Greaves, Jr., spoke on the subject "Political Intervention: Help or Hindrance." Mr. Greaves pointed out that there are many ways to destroy wealth but the original Marxist method as outlined in the Communist Manifesto of 1848 was that of Government interventions. Later Marx found this method too slow and advocated the method of violent revolution. The mass myopia of our age is the belief that governmental action can improve the results obtainable by free and moral men, said Mr. Greaves. He made this statement, "Unless this trend is changed it may well lead the United States into a complete dictatorship. Government intervention in the affairs of moral men always makes matters worse never better."

Mr. Greaves observed that many men who made fortunes in America under the free enterprise system and established foundations were not aware of the fact that many of these foundations would be used to undermine the principles that enabled them to earn the wealth to establish the foundation. He cited a number of examples.

At the closing session of the Christian Freedom Foundation Dr. Howard Kershner reported that the Christian Freedom Foundation's influence is growing and more and more Americans are finding the publication "Christian Economics" enlightening.

The Christian Freedom Foundation is doing a great work. In the final analysis every Christian and lover of freedom should be thankful to God for this organization that is out to dispose of every form of modern despotism and to promote Christian libertarian principles.

Overtures

To The 1956 Assembly—Referred to Committees Editor's Comments

TO THE STANDING COMMITTEE ON BILLS AND OVERTURES, 1-9.

(1) The Presbytery of Tuscaloosa overtures the General Assembly as follows:

WHEREAS, the Seal designed by great men of our Assembly in the past, which in each of its component parts, so aptly sets forth the Biblical truths on which our Assembly has been built, and

WHEREAS, no General Assembly in the past has ever made this Seal our official Seal, threfore,

BE IT RESOLVED, that the 1956 Assembly vote to ratify this Seal as proposed, thus making it officially that of the Presbyterian Church in the United States.

(2) The Synod of Florida passed the following overture:

That the General Assembly consider taking action upon the question of providing a uniform church emblem of the Presbyterian Church, U.S., for the purpose of publicizing it along the highways.

(3) WHEREAS, the General Assembly of 1949 effected a radical reorganization of the agencies of the General Assembly; and

WHEREAS, sufficient time has elapsed since such radical reorganization to determine the effectiveness, as well as minor defects, in this reorganized program; and

WHEREAS, it seems expedient that opportunity be given for adjustments which may be needed because of unforeseen situations which have arisen during the past six years:

THEREFORE, the Presbytery of Knoxville overtures the General Assembly to make a study of the existing agencies, appointing for this purpose an Ad Interim Committee to be composed of ministers and ruling elders from local churches.

(4) WHEREAS, there is a certain virtue from the standpoint of economy and administration in locating the several Boards and Agencies of the Assembly at one point within the Church.

The Presbytery of Birmingham overtures the General Assembly to apoint an Ad Interim Committee to study the advisability of such a move and to hear any offers that might be made by interested parties and to report to the 1957 Assembly with recommendations.

(5) The Presbytery of Cherokee respectfully overtures the General Assembly to appoint an Ad Interim Committee to study the possibility of moving the agencies of the General Assembly to Atlanta, Georgia. (In the interest of economy and efficiency).

(6, 7, 8) WHEREAS, at practically no cost to the Church, a valuable property, known as the

Presbyterian Center, has been secured to house the Assembly Agencies now located in Atlanta; and

WHEREAS, it appears that funds outside the Church may be available to erect a new and commodious building, provided all Assembly Agencies are located at the Prsbyterian Center; and,

WHEREAS, a considerable savings in travel and other costs would be effected if all agencies at the Assembly level were located in one place near the population center of the Church;

THEREFORE, the presbyteries of Westminster, Piedmont and Mid-Texas respectfully overture the General Assembly to appoint an Ad Interim Committee, representing each synod, to study every phase related to the possible location of all its agencies at the Presbyterian Center and to report its findings and recommendations to the 1957 Assembly.

(9) WHEREAS, 1958 is scheduled for the program emphasis on "The Church"; and

WHEREAS, much of the division and divergent opinion in our Church results from diverse conceptions of the nature and function of the Church, together with the Church courts; and

WHEREAS, this diversity is evidenced in the crucial question: Shall the Church echo the voice of the people or the voice of God to His people, in questions of Morals, Ethics and Social Actions? and

WHEREAS, we believe that this question is basic to many of the discussions which occupy much of the time of our Church courts; and

WHEREAS, Chapters XX and XXV of the Confession of Faith and Chapters I - IV of the Book of Church Order are and have been variously construed:

THEREFORE, The Presbytery of Fayetteville respectfully overtures the General Assembly of the Presbyterian Church in the U. S.:

1. To appoint an Ad Interim Committee to make a study of and deliverance on the Biblical doctrine of the nature and function of the Church;

2. To recognize the urgency of this question by appointing to this Committee the best scholarship available in our Church, and,

3. To direct this Committee to make as complete report as possible to the 1957 General Assembly, in view of the 1958 year of emphasis on "The Church."

TO THE STANDING COMMITTEE ON JUDICIAL BUSINESS, 10-15.

10) The Presbytery of Atlanta respectfully overtures the General Assembly that there is another parenthesis inserted in the Form of Call immediately after the parenthesis "(and a manse)" to read "(and a ———— vacation)."

(11) The Presbytery of New Orleans overtures the General Assembly to approve the amendments to Paragraphs 115 and 116 to read as follows: 115. A candidate for licensure must be a graduate of a four-year college or university fully accredited by its proper regional accrediting association; and a candidate for ordination must, in addition, be a graduate of the three-year course in a theological seminary under the control of our Church, or of the three-year course in a theological seminary accredited by the American Association of Theological Schools and approved by the presbytery. As evidence of his graduation in either case the candidate shall cause an official transcript of his record to be sent directly from the institution in question to the Stated Clerk of the presbytery.

116. The presbytery shall examine the candidate on his knowldge of any or all of his academic studies, and on his knowledge of his theological studies, including the original language of the Holy Scriptures. Official transcripts from his college and seminary (see par. 115) may be accepted in lieu of examinations on all subjects except Theology, the Sacraments, Church Government, and the English Bible. (The remaining parts of par. 116 to remain unchanged.)

(12) The Presbytery of Brazos overtures the General Assembly to clarify Paragraph 62 of the Book of Church Order, in reference to the question of whether a Session may call and have a meeting of the Session without it being called by the pastor, where there is a pastor, and particularly defining what shall constitute an emergency.

(13) The Presbytery of Red River respectfully overtures the General Assembly to define the status of a retired member in the local church.

(14) The Presbytery of Brazos overtures the General Assembly to define the authority of the presbytery to organize churches in the following particular: In the light of paragraph 38 of the Book of Church Order, may the presbytery commission an evangelist to organize a church?

(15) The Synod of Tennessee respectfully overtures the General Assembly to clarify the answer of the General Assembly to overture No. 12 of 1953, by indicating whether a presbytery can require a Session to make a report directly to a Board or Agency of the Church, or whether the presbytery can only require the report to be sent to itself.

TO THE STANDING COMMITTEE ON THE OFFICE OF THE GENERAL ASSEMBLY, 16-18.

(16) The Presbytery of Florida again respectfully overtures the General Assembly to restore the column of Ministers' Salaries in the statistical report.

(17) WHEREAS, the General Assembly has eliminated the column "Pastors Salaries" in the statistical reports of the Church to the presbytery and the General Assembly, and

WHEREAS, the Home Mission Association of the Assembly's Board of Church Extension has gone on record requesting the Assembly to restore this column, and

WHEREAS, the information formerly contained in this column contained important information for Executive Secretaries and Superintendents of Home Missions, therefore,

BE IT RESOLVED: That Montgomery Presbytery overture the General Assembly to restore this column.

(18) We (the Board of Christian Education) overture the General Assembly to clarify the meaning of the Manual of the General Assembly concerning the length of service of members of Boards and Agencies of the Assembly. Does a service of two terms of three years each, and a fraction of another such term, preclude nomination and election for a third complete term of three years?

The Board of Christian Education would respectfully urge that where a person is elected to fill an unexpired term that he be ruled eligible for additional service of three complete terms of three years each.

TO THE STANDING COMMITTEE ON GENERAL COUNCIL, 19-22.

(19) In view of the wealth of historical materials which have been gathered in the Historical Foundation at Montreat and in our seminary and college libraries, and

In view of the needs for these important and irreplaceable documents to be safely preserved and at the same time made available for a wider use by students and scholars in our churches, and

In view of the difficulty of getting to these records in their present scattered state, and

In view of the ease with which they could be destroyed forever in a moment of time in modern warfare,

The Presbytery of Norfolk overtures the General Assembly to request the General Council to study this need and to make possible facilities in the Historical Foundation for photostating and/or microfilming these documents in their possession and those in the libraries that copies may be placed in the seminary libraries for safe keeping and more accessible use.

(20) WHEREAS, there is a wealth of historical material which has been and is being gathered in various different libraries and historical foundations, and

WHEREAS, there is need for these most important and precious documents to be both safely presrved and at the same time widely used by the students and scholars in our colleges and seminaries,

THEREFORE, the Presbytery of Brazos hereby overtures the General Assembly to request the General Council to study this need and to bring to the succeeding Assembly suggestions as to how the most precious documents in the possesion of the Church may be, by the use of microfilm or by some other method, made more widely accessible to the libraries of our colleges and seminaries.

(21) In view of the increasing need for it, the Presbytery of Lexington respectfully overtures the General Assembly to provide the Presbyterian Historical Foundation with funds for photo-copy equipment with which to micro-film historical records.

(22) The Presbytery of Mid-Texas respectfully overtures the General Assembly to establish an office of Central Treasurer for all of the Assembly's agencies and causes, empowered to allocate benevolence receipts in proportion to the approved budgets of Assembly's agencies, in order that all causes may receive their proportionate part of the Assembly's budget before any cause receives more than its share.

(31) WHEREAS, it is the policy of the General Assembly to formulate a total budget for all its agencies and institutions, and then allow its constituent churches to use the method each feels best for meeting its proportionate share of the Assembly's budget, and

WHEREAS, a specific exception has been made for the past several years in regard to the "Easter

Offering for the Relief of Human Suffering", thus producing confusion and lack of participation in those churches committed to a policy of a unified budget,

THEREFORE, the Presbytery of Mid-Texas respectfully requests the General Assembly to order its General Council to include an amount in the budget of the Assembly for the use of the Department of Overseas Relief and Interchurch Aid of the Board of World Missions to permit all our churches to share in this worthy cause in the manner they deem best suited to the local situation.

TO THE STANDING COMMITTEE ON WORLD MISSIONS, 23.

(23) The Presbytery of Wilmington respectfully overtures the General Assembly to give to the Board of World Missions any authority and encouragement needed to enable the Board to make a personal approach to students in our seminaries and in the Assembly's Training School who are likely prospects for mission service, offering to these prospects definite calls to particular service.

TO THE STANDING COMMITTEE ON CHRISTIAN EDUCATION, 24-27.

(24) WHEREAS, recent studies indicate that about 60,000 boys and girls from homes in the Presbyterian Church, U.S. are in colleges or seminaries, and only 4,000 in our own Presbyterian institutions; and

WHEREAS, many of these would attend our own schools if the financial cost were not greater than at state schools; and

WHEREAS, those who attend state or independent institutions need much better care and spiritual nurture than most synods provide;

THEREFORE, the Synod of Georgia respectfully overtures the General Assembly to take one of the following steps:

1. Appoint an Ad Interim committee to study the whole problem of the Church's responsibility to its young people in the realm of higher education; or 2. Increase substantially the Challenge Fund now administered by the Board of Christian Education so that larger sums may be available for worthy young people who need help in attending our own institutions and better provision for those who will be attending state institutions.

(25) The Synod of Appalachia respectfully overtures the General Assembly to appropriate as much as $200,000 to the Challenge Fund of the Board of Christian Education, this sum to be placed in the "spending budget" of the Board.

(26) WHEREAS, the General Assembly of 1955 granted a final budget appropriation of $50,000 to Montreat College, while reaffirming the statement of the 1952 Assembly that the General Assembly will not make appropriations for Montreat College,

THEREFORE, the Synod of Missouri respectfully overtures the 96th General Assembly to make no appropriation whatsoever for Montreat College.

(27) The Presbytery of Upper Missouri respectfully overtures the General Assembly not to grant any further funds to Montreat College.

TO THE STANDING COMMITTEE ON INTER-CHURCH RELATIONS, 28, 29.

(28) WHEREAS, the Presbytery of Harmony wishes to express its attitude toward membership of the Presbyterian Church, U.S. in the National Council of Churches of Christ in the U.S.A. and the World Council of Churches; and

WHEREAS, continued membership gives tacit approval of public pronouncements and resolutions that have been widely circulated, which do not express the convictions of a majority of the total membership; and

WHEREAS, resolutions above referred to have accused those not in agreement with their social, economical and political views as unchristian; and

WHEREAS, the leadership of both associations above referred to, openly envision the ultimate goal as organic union of all Protestant churches in one world Church:

NOW THEREFORE, the Presbytery of Harmony respectfully overtures the General Assembly for determination of policy as to whether or not the Presbyterian Church, U.S. shall withdraw from or remain in the National Council of Churches of Christ in U.S.A., and the World Council of Churches; same being conducted in accordance with properly constituted authority.

(29) The Presbytery of Congaree respectfully overtures the General Assembly to submit the matter of continued membership in the National Council of Churches of Christ in the U.S.A. to the presbyteries for their advice so that the 1957 General Assembly will have sound and reasonable grounds upon which to act upon this matter.

WE FURTHER SUGGEST, that the question submitted to the presbyteries be: "Shall the Presbyterian Church, U.S. withdraw its membership from the National Council of Churches of Christ in the U.S.A.?"

TO THE STANDING COMMITTEE ON CHRISTIAN RELATIONS, 30.

WHEREAS, the General Assembly of the Presbyterian Church, U.S. has by resolution recommended the opening of our churches, schools and colleges to all races, and

WHEREAS, the action of the General Assembly has been published throughout the United States and elsewhere as the attitude and belief of the Presbyterian Church, U.S.

NOW, we the Presbytery of Harmony declare:

1. That we do not agree with the action of the General Assembly above referred to.

2. That we believe that the action of the General Assembly referred to will cause dissension and hatred between the races.

3. That the action of the General Assembly aforesaid was taken without submitting such issues to the presbyteries composing the Assembly; and it is our conviction that such action does not truly indicate the convictions of its presbyteries or the membership of the Church.

NOW THEREFORE, The Presbytery of Harmony respectfully overtures the General Assembly of the Presbyterian Church in the U.S. to authorize a ballot by each presbytery of the General Assembly of the Presbyterian Church, U.S. for determination of policy as to whether or not Presbyterian Church, U.S. shall have segregation or integration of all races; same being conducted in accordance with properly constituted authority.

Editor's Comments

Overtures 1, 4, 5, 6, 7 and 8

The overtures having to do with the centralization of Agencies of the General Assembly are unfortunate. They are unfortunate for the following reasons:

a. They are not spontaneous but originated from one single source.
b. The General Assembly, at its last meeting, acted overwhelmingly against this suggestion.
c. Acting in good faith the Board of World Missions has already proceeded towards the erection of its own building in Nashville.
d. The reasons against centralization in Atlanta have been amply and effectively documented.
e. Such continued agitation places all of the Boards of our Church in a difficult position which is wholly unjustified.

These overtures should be answered in the negative.

*

Overture 9

We consider this important but not in the way some would hold. The Church unquestionably has the duty to make deliverances on Morals, Ethics and Social Actions. But, unfortunately some would lower the place of the church and make it an agent of controversial political issues.

We would approve of such an Ad Interim Committee provided it is composed of ministers and laymen who represent the spiritual perception and leadership without which it could do much more harm than good.

Overture 11

Will this mean that we continue to be increasingly a class church, reaching only the more educated and socially fortunate? Let us remember that "the letter killeth, but the spirit giveth life." Let us also remember that in our own church today some of our most dedicated and useful ministers have not been the fortunate recipients of the training we are making more and more mandatory.

Overtures 15 and 22

In some quarters there is an ever increasing tendency to regiment the giving of individuals and local congregations. For convenience in book-keeping this may be desirable, but, from the standpoint of Christian stewardship and the right of the giver to send his gifts where he feels the Lord would have them go, there is grave danger for all concerned. The arbitrary philosophy of some with reference to the benevolent giving of the church needs to be thoroughly gone into and a greater freedom left to those who give the money. H.B.D.

ANGLERS

(From *"New Testament Evangelism"* by Wade C. Smith)

Lesson No. 137

Continuing

Three Human Essentials for Personal Evangelism

Essential No. 2—A Real Desire to Win Souls

Startling as the great spiritual need for personal work is, there seems to be a lack of a desire in the hearts of the great majority of Christians to meet it. Most people (Christians or not) will respond to some urgent physical need. A man is entombed in a mine. Scores of other men, moved by compassion for him in his pitiable plight, will work like beavers night and day, barely stopping for food or sleep, even putting their own lives in jeopardy, to rescue him. Yet the poor fellow may not at best have a dozen years to live after he gets out. The same man's immortal soul may be in imminent peril, as he goes back and forth to his work, under the eaves of many Christian homes; a simple word of personal invitation to come to Christ, blessed of the Spirit, would save him to eternal life; but never a word does he get. The merchant, a church member (maybe an officer) sells him his groceries, another his dry goods, another solicits his insurance premiums, and so on down the line - all the industrious church folks take a little toll from this doomed man - but none seem stirred to the point of snatching his immortal soul from the devil. Why is it? It is not because people have no hearts; it is the lack of vision. "Where there is no vision, the people perish." (Prov.29:18). And the lack of vision on the part of God's people is often caused by the mist of selfishness. We are absorbed in our own selfish ends. It takes time and thought and effort to win souls. It takes time and thought and effort to sell insurance, too; but that is another matter. And we have not the *desire* to do personal work. We like to do what we like to do.

What shall we do to get the desire? The answer to this is simple, too. Ask for it. Of all the prayers one could ever make, it would seem that this prayer would most certainly be acceptable to God; that one might *have the desire* to win souls to Christ; that, seeing lost men passing by him every day, working beside them, trading with them, accepting favors of them, befriending them in other ways, his heart might go out in longing for their salvation; that this might become such a burning desire, nothing would satisfy until he made an earnest effort in the God-appointed way to win them to Jesus. (Again see Luke 11:13). Do you want a desire like that? It would cause you to make some sacrifices, to turn loose some things now tightly held, to give up some cherished plan perhaps. Do you want it? If we deal with the question frankly we may find that *we do not even want the desire!* Then let us ask God to make us *want the desire* - enough to cause us to ask for it. We can simply keep going back until we reach bottom, and there get a start, if there is a spark of right motive.

Even after the desire is experienced, it must be nourished by food and exercise, or it will die out. The food is daily devotional reading of God's Word (which will be dealt with more fully in a later lesson) and prayer; the exercise is the *practice* of soul-winning, - and more prayer. It is well to remember that no feature of this business of soul-winning can be set up, once for all, like a picture or a statue, to remain there until taken down. It is a living plant, requiring constant attention.

(Next lesson will describe the third "Human Essential").

Helps To Understanding Scripture Readings in *Day by Day*

By C. C. Baker

Sunday, May 6, Psalm 145:1-5. Read through Psalm 145 with this outline in mind: God's greatness (vv.1-6); God's goodness (vv.7-10); God's glory (vv. 11-13); God's grace (vv.14-21). What idea of permanence is given to God's reign in v.13? See how gracious this eternal God is: He is close to those that fall (v.14), supplies the needs of those who look to Him for sustenace (vv.15-16), answers those who call upon Him (vv.18-19), who preserves those who love Him (v.20). Do vv.14-21 substantiate the Psalmist's statement of the goodness of the Lord in vv.7-10? Little wonder that the Psalmist praises Him (vv.1-6). Do any of the truths of vv.14-21 cause you to give praise to God?

Monday, May 7, Deut. 6:4-9. The God whom the Israelites are called upon to love with their whole beings (v.5) is not a vague non-entity, but the Lord, *their* God - the one who brought them out of Egypt, appeared to them at Sinai, and has watched over them and cared for them for over 40 years. What other attitude are the Israelites called upon to have toward Him (vv.13-15)? To "fear" (v.13) means to "revere with awe." How should this "fear" prevent a Santa Claus or grandfather concept of God? We witness to our love and reverence of the Lord when we keep His commandments (vv.1-3,6-7, 17-18; John 14:21). What commandment did Jesus leave with His disciples (John 15:12)? Do you truly love God for all His blessings and for what He has done for you in Christ? Do you stand in awe of Him - knowing it is by His grace alone that you are saved and that your eternal reward depends on your faithfulness to Him? Does your keeping of His commandments witness to your love and reverence for Him?

Tuesday, May 8, Proverbs 3:1-6. Observe in v.5a that a person is to trust in the Lord with his *heart,* that is, with his whole being. The writer is not saying that we should not use our minds when we are faced with decisions (v.5b), but that, while we use our minds, we should not lean upon them (v.7a) but upon the Lord (vv.5-6). In what practical ways can the promise of v.6 be applied in your life? For a Christian, failure to lean upon the Lord for strength and guidance is sin (v.7). To look to Him and honor Him means spiritual life and nourishment (vv.8-10). Even in times of adversity (vv.11-12) all things work together for good for the Christian who loves God.

Wednesday, May 9, Psalm 136:1-9. Read consecutively the first half of each verse and you will find that this Psalm tells the story of what God did in the early portions of the Old Testament. What particular passages from Genesis and Exodus are brought to mind? How would the response "His mercy endures forever" support the fact that God was behind the acts of creation (vv.4-9)? that God delivers His people from trouble (vv.10-24)? that God supplies the needs of His creatures (v.25)? What is the Psalmist's own response to these facts (vv.1-3, 26)? Can you give thanks that God is in control of the earth, that He supplies the needs of His creatures and delivers His own from trouble?

Thursday, May 10, Psalm 100. Even the Psalmist was missionary-minded (v.1). What knowledge concerning their relations to the Lord did the Psalmist desire for the nations (v.3)? What words in vv.2&4 describe the attitude the Psalmist desired the nations of the earth to have toward the Lord? Is this true of most of the nations of the earth today? If it were true, would many of our national and world problems be solved? How should the facts given in v.5 inspire the attitudes of vv.2&4 toward God? In what ways have the truths of v.5 been true for you - to cause you to worship and give thanks?

Friday, May 11, Psalm 118:24. God has delivered the Jews from 70 years of exile from their homeland. Read the Psalm with this suggested outline in mind: Call to Praise (vv.1-4), Affirmation of Faith (vv.5-9), God's deliverance (vv.10-13), Praise because of deliverance (vv.14-18), Personal dedication (vv.19-29). The Lord, and no man, delivered the Israelites out of their trouble (vv.6,8-9). He is their shield and strength (vv.14,16). Praise and thanksgiving become a part of their lives (vv.19,24). Others are encouraged to worship (vv.1,29). Does the Lord mean so much to you that you want to praise Him and dedicate your life to Him? Are the convictions expressed in vv.5-9 your own personal convictions because of your own personal experience with God?

Saturday, May 12, *II Timothy* 2:15. Paul advises Timothy to charge certain Christians to refrain from conversations that would undermine the faith of others (v.14). Verse 18 gives an example of the false teaching that was being propounded. As the Christian's personal faith is undermined, his moral conduct is also likely to suffer (vv.16,19). Paul feels that the source of spiritual truth is the Bible (3:15b-16) and that it is through a conscientious study of the Bible that the Christian arrives at the truth (2:15). What should our relationship to those who doubt certain tenets of the Christian faith be (vv.14-16)? Honest doubts and questions can usually be clarified by a sincere study of the Bible. To propagate one's doubts is only to harm the lives of others.

SABBATH SCHOOL LESSONS — REV. J. KENTON PARKER

LESSON FOR MAY 13

Preaching To The Gentiles

Background Scripture: Acts 9:32 - 11:18.
Devotional Reading: Acts 10:34-43

The command of Jesus had been very plain; beginning at Jerusalem, they were to go into all the world. This had been in the mind and plan of God from the very first. The call of Abraham included a blessing to the whole world. For a time the revelation of God was confined for the most part to the Jewish nation. To them He gave the Law - both moral and ceremonial - and to them He committed the "oracles of God." They were the Chosen People, but chosen for a purpose; to preserve the true religion of Jehovah, and when the time came, and as opportunities arose, to pass this religion on to others. In other words, they were to be a missionary nation. They, however, failed to do this.

The disciples were slow in obeying Jesus' command. Then persecution scattered the believers and they that were scattered abroad went everywhere preaching, (or talking) the Word. The apostles remained in Jerusalem for a good while. Two of the deacons who had been chosen, Stephen and Philip, became preachers, and Philip, as we have seen, went down to Samaria and preached Christ, and was the messenger sent to the Ethiopian eunuch. Peter and John were sent to Samaria. The Samaritans, being a mixed race, became a connecting link between the Jew and the Gentiles. They had been commanded to go into Samaria.

In our lesson today we have the account of Peter's work as he opened the door to the Gentiles. Peter does not seem to have continued to preach to the Gentiles, but confined his endeavors mostly to the Jews. He was known as the apostle to the Jew, while Paul became the apostle to the Gentiles. Peter steps out of the Book of Acts for the most part after our lesson today and Paul and his companions become the central figures in the spread of the gospel.

I. *Peter at Lydda:* 9:32-35.

Notice the expression, "the saints which dwelt at Lydda." The word "saints," in the plural, is often used in the Bible. The word "saint" in the singular is used only five times, and only once, in connection with a particular man, "Aaron the saint of the Lord (Ps. 106:16). The other times the reference is indefinite: "one saint," "another saint," "certain saint," "every saint." All of God's people are "saints." I believe that it is very foolish and very harmful to single out any one individual and exalt him to a position of "saint." I feel that Paul and Peter and John would reject such a term being applied to them except as it applied to *all* Christians. The only "aristocracy" in God's Kingdom is that based upon humility, service, and sacrifice. All of us, if we are true Christians, are made "kings and priests unto God," and the selecting of a few names to be designated St. is to be deeply deplored. All of us know, of course, that in the original Greek the Gospel writers and Paul and Peter are not prefaced by "St."

At Lydda Peter finds a man sick of the palsy, Aeneas by name, and said to him, Aeneas, Jesus Christ maketh thee whole: arise, and make up thy bed. And he arose immediately. This miracle caused all that dwelt at Lydda and Saron to turn to the Lord. This should have been true wherever miracles were performed, but it was not always so.

II. *Peter at Joppa:* 9:36-43.

Joppa was near Lydda, and when Dorcas, who was known and loved for her good works and almsdeeds, died, they laid her in an upper room and sent for Peter. He put all the mourners outside, and kneeled down and prayed, and then, turning to the body, said, Tabitha, arise. She opened her eyes and when she saw Peter, sat up. He lifted her up and presented her alive. This great miracle became known throughout all Joppa and many believed in the Lord. Again we see a miracle having the desired effect. They were meant to be "signs" to the people. Peter remained at Joppa many days, staying in the home of Simon, a tanner.

III. *Peter and Cornelius:* 10:1-48.

We come now to the main part of our lesson; the conversion of Cornelius, a Roman centurion, and the "Gentile Pentecost" which took place in his home at Caesarea. Our study naturally falls into four parts: The Vision of Cornelius; The Vision of Peter; The Meeting in his House; and Peter's Defense.

1. The Vision of Cornelius.

He was a centurion, an officer in the Roman army. There were several of these centurions who are mentioned, and they seem to be much better men than the Roman officials of higher rank, such as Herod and Pilate, and later on, the ones before whom Paul was tried. There was the centurion whose servant was healed by Jesus, (see Matt. 8:5-13). Jesus marveled at this man's faith, and said, I have not found so great faith, no, not in Israel. A second one was the centurion who had command of the band of soldiers who crucified Jesus. When he heard and saw all that took place, he said, Truly this man was the Son of God. Then we have the centurion who was kind to Paul, (see Acts 27:43): But the centurion, willing to save Paul, kept them from their purpose (of slaying the prisoners).

The centurion named Cornelius, about whom we are studying, was a devout man, and one that feared God with all his house, which gave much alms to the people, and prayed to God alway. With all of these admirable qualities, however, he was still an unsaved man. He needed Christ as Savior from sin. A good man is saved in the same way that a bad man is saved, for "all have sinned," and all must be saved by grace through faith. He saw in a vision an angel of God who said to him, Cornelius. He answered, What is it Lord? The angel told him to send to Joppa and fetch one Simon, whose surname was Peter: and he shall tell thee what thou oughtest to do. God usually uses men to carry the gospel to other men. The angel could have told him what he must do to be saved, but God honors us and uses us to be His messengers. We are the ones who are to "go and tell." Cornelius lost no time in calling for some of his servants, and a devout soldier, and sent them on their way.

2. The Vision of Peter.

Peter had to be prepared for his mission. He had never preached to Gentiles, as far as we know. He was a strict Jew and would have felt defiled by contact with people of another nation. His experience at Samaria had perhaps broadened his outlook somewhat, but he needed further instruction and enlightenment before he was ready for a trip to the home of a Roman officer.

Peter, while waiting for food to be prepared, became hungry, and his vision was in keeping with a feeling of hunger. He saw heaven opened and a vessel descending in which were all manner of creeping things, wild beasts, etc. A voice said, Arise, Peter, kill and eat. He answered, Not so, Lord, for I have never eaten any thing that is common or unclean. The voice said again, What God hath cleansed, that call not thou common. This vision, repeated three times, thoroughly prepared Peter for the work before him. He lodged the men for the night, and the next day went with them, taking certain of the brethren with him.

3. The Meeting in the Home of Cornelius.

Cornelius had called together his kinsmen and near friends. When Peter came in, he fell down at his feet and worshipped him, but the apostle hastened to lift him up, and say, Stand up: I myself also am a man. How different from his so-called "successors," who allow the cardinals to prostrate themselves! Peter explains why he is there, and beginning at verse 34 we have his sermon in which he declares that he perceives that God is no respecter of persons, but in every nation he that feareth Him and worketh righteousness is acceptable to him. This does not mean that such people are saved, as we plainly see from the context. It does mean that God will lead such sincere seekers after truth into full light, as He led this man, Cornelius. Peter preaches Christ to those assembled in the house, saying, through His name whosoever believeth in Him shall receive remission of sins. We see that Christ is necessary to salvation. Cornelius and the others were doing the best they knew, but that best was not sufficient. We have too many false teachers today who try to tell us that "If we do the best we know how, then everything will be all right." Too many are satisfied, or try to be, with "religion." Do we, as the messengers of God, ever allow our hearers to have a false sense of security? Let us never confuse men and women but lead them into the full light and to a personal acceptance of the Lord Jesus Christ as Savior and Master.

While Peter was speaking the Holy Spirit fell on all those that heard the word. Peter commanded them to be baptized with water. They had already received the baptism of the Spirit. Water is a symbol of this real baptism.

IV. *Peter's Defense of his Action.*

It was to be expected that the strict Jews would call Peter to account for what he had done. They brought what they thought was a serious charge against him, but after he rehearses the whole matter, they, for a time at least, seem satisfied.

YOUNG PEOPLE'S DEPARTMENT — REV. B. HOYT EVANS

YOUTH PROGRAM FOR MAY 13

Food For Thought

Hymn: "O Word Of God Incarnate"
Prayer
Scripture Lesson: Psalm 119:9-16
Hymn: "Lamp Of Our Feet Whereby We Trace"
Offering
Hymn: "O Grant Us Light That We May Know"

PROGRAM LEADER:

Horace Greeley is reported to have said, "It is impossible to mentally or socially enslave a Bible-reading people." We need to give special emphasis to the word "reading." It is not enough to possess the Bible as an ornament or a good luck charm. There is no magic virtue in the paper or the ink, the leather binding or the gold edging of the Bible. The Bible makes us strong and free only when we know what it teaches, and we cannot know what is in the Bible until we do some reading and studying of our own.

For our program today we shall study one of the most familiar of our Lord's parables. As we hear the words read once again let us give close attention to the reading and be prepared to join in applying the teachings to our own lives. (Ask someone to read Luke 15:11-32. Make the assignment well in advance of the meeting and urge the person to make careful preparation for the reading.)

FIRST SPEAKER:

This passage is usually referred to as the parable of the Prodigal Son. It might better be called the parable of the Loving Father, because the father is really the most important person in the story. The father in the story represents our Heavenly Father. The main purpose of the parable is to point out the love of God for all His rebellious children. It is clear that the father in the story loved both of his sons, even when they were not very lovable. How do we know that God loves us even though we are not deserving of His love?

While the primary purpose of the parable is to reveal the love of God, we can also learn from it something about ideal family relationships. What can an earthly father give to his children that is more important than his wise love? Is it wise for a loving parent to protect his children from every difficulty and every temptation? Is it wise love when a father forces his children to do what he thinks is right? How much independence and how much protection should a loving father provide?

SECOND SPEAKER:

Surely the most colorful character in the story is the wayward son. In both his departure and his return he attracts our attention. Why do you think this young man left home in the first place? Do you think his idea of living conflicted with his father's idea? Why did the son not want to engage in "riotous living" in the sight of his father? Would we be embarrassed for our parents to observe and hear all the things we do and say? We can conceal some things from parents, but nothing can be hid from God.

When this young man's money and fair weather friends had left him, he discovered that all he had left was the memory of father and home, the person and the place he had tried so hard to forget. What does the Bible mean when it says, "He came to himself"? Does it not mean that he began to develop a new sense of values? At the first he thought only of his own wants and feelings. Now he begins to be concerned about his father's feelings. He is not only sorry for himself, he is sorry for his father. Is a person likely to turn to the Lord seeking pardon until he realizes that his sins have wounded God?

How can selfishness like that described in the parable destroy the happiness of a home?

THIRD SPEAKER:
Sometimes the older brother is left altogether out of the story, but the parable would be incomplete without him. He is especially important to those of us who are in the church. Church people are not often guilty of the obvious sins such as drunkenness and rioting which we usually think of in connection with the younger brother. The older brother had not committed any of these obvious sins, but he was a sinner just the same. We found that the real fault with the younger son was in his attitude toward his father. He really began to live when his attitude changed. The older brother had a bad attitude also. He did not show it in such violent ways, but it was there. He did his father's will out of a sense of unpleasant duty and not because he loved him. If the younger son was selfish at the beginning, what about his older brother? Is there any indication that he ever changed his attitude? He resented the fact that his younger brother had been restored to the family, but was he himself really a part of the family at heart? The younger son "returned" to his father. Did the older son also need to "return"?

We need to remember that we are not being good church members and good family members just because we slavishly obey all the rules. God desires the kind of service that grows from love. Can there be happy homes unless the family members love each other? Can a church be healthy if all its service is done out of a sense of hard duty? Are sins of open rebellion worse than sins of secret resentfulness? If so, why? If not, why not?

(Your group might enjoy dramatizing this story. You could have people act out the parts silently while someone reads the passage, or the characters could memorize their lines and recite them. If you do have a dramatization, be sure to stress the love of the father, the rebellion of the younger son, and the resentfulness of the older son.)

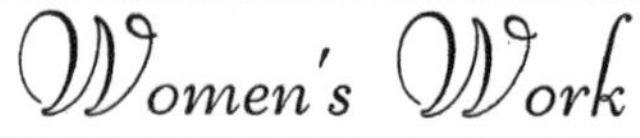

Women's Work

Rev. and Mrs. Armando Rodriguez

Armando Rodriguez thought it would be fun to go to the corner Presbyterian Mission Church on Sunday night and poke fun at the new minister and, in general create some confusion in the young people's meeting. He started out well but soon found himself ejected from the church after being given due warning that his actions would not be tolerated by the new minister. But God had placed His hands on Armando even though he did not know it at the time. The minister visited Armando and invited him to come back, not to again create a disturbance, but to learn of Christ the Savior.

On January 12, 1936, Armando took his stand for Christ and became a worker for the Lord.

As the years went by and Armando grew in "wisdom and stature and in favor with God and Man," this young man offered his life to God for full time service.

His trials before graduating from Columbia Theological Seminary were many, but Armando never gave up. He knew God would stand by him even in the midst of a fierce battle on the Western Front.

Today the Rev. Armando Rodriguez and his lovely wife who also found Christ at the Ybor City Presbyterian Mission Church are serving the Lord in the First Presbyterian Church of Cairo, Ga.

God works in a mysterious way to perform His wonders, and the Reverend Rodriguez is a glowing example of God's Grace operating in the lives of men.

In Gratitude We Give Again

Every woman in our Church is invited to a Birthday Party this month. No matter how old or how young a person may be, all of us love a Birthday Party. There are many ways to have a Birthday Celebration and many different kinds of gifts to be given. Beginning in May 1922, Southern Presbyterian women have brought to their Birthday Party each year an offering with grateful hearts saying, "God hath wrought great things for us whereof we are glad."

Looking back over the list of the objectives to which our gifts have been given through the years, we can see with our mind's eye the individuals who have been touched with these gifts. For it is not the Buildings, Classrooms, Homes, Bible Institutes, Colleges, and Hospitals that are most important but the individual lives which have been brought to Christ and prepared for work in His Kingdom.

The amount given in dollars and cents can accurately be determined but the spiritual values received by those whose lives have been touched as a result of these gifts and who in turn have passed blessings on to others cannot even be estimated. Nor can we estimate the blessings received by those who have been the givers. We know the Lord loveth a cheerful giver and the gifts have been brought with joy and followed with our interest and prayers.

So again comes to us this opportunity of giving out of our abundance to our two objectives this year. What could be more thrilling than to have a part in establishing area schools to train those who teach our children in Sunday schools. God's Word teaches us that if we train up a child in the way he should go when he is old he will not depart therefrom.

Our church's life has already been stimulated by the leadership of those who heard the preaching of the Word in Ybor City. God has richly blessed the work which has been carried on there by the consecrated leaders and devoted workers. Surely out of the abundance of the things we enjoy we can give generously to this great work.

So may we this year bring generous and loving gifts, large enough that we can be happy about the amount we give. Praying about the individual gift we give that it may be sacrificial enough to really mean something to us as we give it and that it may be an expression of the love and appreciation we feel for the blessings we have in our own lives. Most of us could double the amount we gave last year without having to make too great a sacrifice. What glorious returns the Lord gives us in return for the gifts we give Him. As these offerings are presented may we pray God's richest blessing upon them. Let us pray that God will richly bless all of us who give and that our Birthday season this year may be a rich experience for us all and bring Honor and Glory to our Heavenly Father in building up His Kingdom.

—(Mrs. A. R.) Mary B. Craig

Recommend The Journal To Friends

WANTED—Dedicated Young Woman to serve as Church Secretary and Assistant to Pastor. Wm. E. Hill, Jr., West End Presbyterian Church, Hopewell, Virginia.

My Name Is Samuel . . .
My Saviour's Name Is Jesus Christ

Samuel has learned to read. Thanks to you he has a Bible in Malayalam and God speaks to him in his own language.

Each year ten million people in far-flung parts of the world learn to read. In most cases there are few books printed in their own language, so they seize upon any book with eagerness—whether it be Communistic propaganda or the Bible.

Here are ten million newly-opened minds to be reached with the Word of God and won to His cause. Because of your gifts and those of others who care, millions of these people do have the Bible for their first book. With them the race against atheistic reading matter is being won for Christ . . . but other millions are without the Bible. Help us place in their hands a Bible written in their own language.

Your gift this year may be another blow to those who would suppress His Word. Because of you more new readers may learn of God and His love for them.

—American Bible Society
450 Park Avenue
New York 22, N. Y.

Church News

Bible Presbyterian Synod Votes Withdrawal From ACC and ICC

The second largest Synod in the history of the Bible Presbyterian Church met in St. Louis beginning April 5. By an overwhelming majority it voted to withdraw from the American Council of Christian Churches and the International Council of Christian Churches. The withdrawal resolution is as follows:

"Reaffirming its position on the purity of the visible church and its position on separation from modernism and inclusivism, the 19th General Synod of the Bible Presbyterian Church finding sufficient cause for dissatisfaction with its representation by the American Council of Christian Churches hereby terminates the power of that agency to represent said denomination and directs the stated clerk of this Synod to give immediate notification of this action to the American Council of Christian Churches."

A similar resolution was adopted with reference to the International Council of Christian Churches.

Dr. R. Laird Harris was elected moderator of the Synod.—*The Bible Presbyterian Reporter.*

The General Council

Atlanta, Georgia

A new record budget for a church whose membership is at an all-time high was recommended by the spring meeting of the General Council. A total of $6,931,896 for General Assembly benevolence causes is proposed by the Council as the 1957 budget for the Presbyterian Church, U.S. This proposal will be presented to the General Assembly meeting in Montreat, N. C., in early June.

The new budget, as proposed, would give $3,500,000 to World Missions, or slightly over 50% of the total.

The Council acted after hearing that the membership of the Southern Presbyterian Church is now above 807,600—the figure reached by January 1, 1956. Dr. James G. Patton, executive secretary of the Council, reported that this new membership record is the result of the addition in 1955 of 85,502 new members, by far the largest in the history of the Church. Of this number 28,310 were received on profession of faith. Only in one year, that ending March 31, 1951, and including two Easters in the Church year, had the Church added a larger number on profession of faith, Dr. Patton stated.

In another action, the Council set a goal of 1,000,000 members by 1961, the 100th anniversary of the founding of the Southern Church. Declaring that the anniversary should be observed in some fashion, and that "to ignore it would be strained and unnatural," the Council also asked that the General Assembly appoint a 15 to 20-person committee to plan and promote the observation.

A theme of "Our Heritage and Mission" was proposed for the Centennial year. Emphasis should be on heritage and mission of the Presbyterian Church, U.S., as a member of the Presbyterian family throughout the world," the Council stated.

Among other actions, the Council proposed, for General Assembly approval, a calendar of emphases and special days for 1958, and passed on a number of proposals relating to the calendar and program. Among these was the initiation of a group study of possibilities for extensive revision of the special seasons order in the calendar.

By another action, the Council set up a committee to study the possibility of reactivating the Council's Research Committee which was abolished last year.

Dr. Patton, Dr. Bob S. Hodges, associate secretary, and Mr. Bluford B. Hestir, director of publicity, were re-elected to their positions by the Council, and a recommendation that the General Assembly complete their re-election by approving it was made.

In response to an overture from the Presbytery of Nashville, addressed to the General Council, the body recommended to the General Assembly that it appoint an Ad Interim Committee to study the place of Homes for the Aging in the Presbyterian Church. It was also proposed that this same committee be given directives to study Homes for Children and Hospitals.

The proposed budget for 1957 is broken down as follows:

Board of World Missions		$3,500,000
Board of Church Extension		1,518,225
Board of Christian Education		580,000
Board of Annuities and Relief		441,817
The General Fund		868,259
Board of Women's Work	$125,000	
The General Council	180,000	
Assembly's Training School	185,000	
Montreat	118,000	
Stillman College	190,000	
Historical Foundation	23,800	
American Bible Society	40,459	
Administrative Expense	6,000	
Interchurch Agencies		23,595
National Council	10,200	
World Council	8,295	
Geneva Building	2,100	
Lord's Day Alliance	1,000	
Religion in American Life	2,000	
		$6,931,896

The Presbyterian Vacation Fund

This Vacation Fund is made up of voluntary contributions from Presbyterians and Presbyterian Church organizations. The Fund is used to provide periods of physical rest and spiritual rejuvenation to ministers on small salaries at one of the three great conference grounds of our Church, namely, Montreat, North Carolina, Massanetta Springs, Virginia, and Mo-Ranch, Texas.

As the summer approaches again, we desire to call attention of generous Presbyterians to this Vacation Fund, and its importance in the life of many of our hard pressed ministers and church workers. By means of the assistance afforded from this Vacation Fund scores are able to have a vacation who otherwise would not have such a privilege. Many of those thus assisted have written as follows: "Without the help of the Vacation Fund I would not have been able to have attended the conference. It has helped me both physically and spiritually to get back to my duties as pastor with a thankful heart and renewed zeal." We are now screening the recommendations from Presbyteries to determine how many can be sent this summer. The answer to this question will in part depend upon the total amount of contributions received for this purpose.

Any who desire to have a share in this noble work will please send a contribution to Mrs. Ira D. Holt, Treasurer, Box 358, Montreat, North Carolina, so that we shall know how many we shall be able to send this summer through this worthwhile enterprise.

Change of Address

Rev. J. W. Hickman, from Demopolis, Alabama, to First Presbyterian Church, Livingston, Alabama.

McIlwain Memorial Church, Pensacola, Florida

The dedication of the new educational building of McIlwain Memorial Presbyterian Church, Pensacola, Florida, Rev. Donald C. Graham, minister, took place on April 8. Built and furnished at a cost of $100,000, including the refronting of the old educational building, the new structure provides office and study space, a large conference room, a beautifully furnished parlor, and assembly and classroom space for the Junior, Intermediate and Adult departments.

In order to erect this building on property adjoining the church, the former manse had to be razed first and a new manse built which is valued at over $30,000. Half of this total investment has been given and the rest will be covered probably during the next two years. After this the enlargement of the sanctuary, already crowded to capacity, is anticipated.

McIlwain Memorial is a community church but also enjoys a ministry to scores of Navy personnel. Two of these young men received Christ as their Saviour and have come under the care of presbytery for the Gospel ministry. Fellowship dinners and recreational activities help to integrate this Navy group with the Westminster Fellowship young people. Altogether, more than eighty young people are in regular Sunday evening attendance at the four youth groups.

The church's emphasis on Presbyterian doctrinal instruction includes a Week-day Bible School on Monday afternoons throughout the school year. Particularly in the young adult groups, study courses have included distinctively Presbyterian creedal subjects such as Predestination and many have become enthusiastic Calvinists.

The church recently revised its missionary program and assumed the partial support of ten Southern Presbyterian missionaries. On one recent Sunday the congregation provided over $5400 for this World Mission need. This increase in giving is in keeping with the general financial growth of the church which has increased six hundred per cent in six years.

Sunday evening services are largely attended throughout the year but a unique summer feature introduced five years ago has become a part of the permanent program of the church. For five months Sunday evening Waterside Vespers are held at a small stadium at a nearby park, right at the water's edge. A complete worship service is included with hymns sung from words thrown on the screen, a brief sermon, and a thirty minute Christian sound film. Hundreds attend every Sunday evening including many non-church people of the community.

One interesting incident concerns a woman who attended these Vespers and, still unknown to the minister and congregation, placed this church which she had never entered in her will for bequest. More important, before her death she accepted Christ as her Saviour and was received into the membership of the church with radiant confession of her faith.

Southwest Georgia Presbytery

met for its Spring meeting in the First Church of Albany on April 10th. At the request of the retiring Moderator, Elder D. L. Wall of Cuthbert, the opening sermon was preached by William A. Jordan, a senior in Columbia Seminary, who is serving the Cuthbert Church, and will become its pastor upon graduation.

The Lord's Supper was observed with Rev. L. B. Colquitt and Rev. Phil Dunford, both of Albany, officiating. Rev. E. Rowland of Climax was elected Moderator.

The pastoral relations existing between Rev. John R. Howard and the Tifton Church were dissolved as of April 15th.

The Commission on the Minister and His Work announced that four members of this year's graduating class in Columbia Seminary had accepted work in the Presbytery and would be received at the Summer meeting. They are William A. Jordan for Cuthbert and Dickey Churches, Robert J. James for Cordele Church, Kenneth Boyer for Fort Gaines and Cuba Churches, and Saunders Garwood for Elmodel and Pelham Churches.

Rev. Armando Rodriguez was received from Savannah Presbytery and a Commission was appointed to install him as pastor of the Cairo Church; Rev. F. M. Kincaid was received from East Alabama Presbytery and a Commission appointed to install him as pastor of Holt Church, Columbus; Rev. J. W. McQueen was received from Birmingham Presbytery and a Commission appointed to install him as pastor of the First Church of Albany. Three ministers have moved within the bounds of the Presbytery and Commissions were appointed to install them as follows:

Rev. John R. Smith moves from West End Church, Valdosta, to Adel Church; Rev. T. B. McPheeters from Donalsonville Church to Dawson Church; Rev. C. L. McDonald from Dawson Church to Donalsonville Church.

Rev. Phil Dunford of Albany will direct the Senior Conference and Rev. T. C. Bailey of Camilla will direct the Pioneer Camp. Both Camp and Conference will be held at Georgia Southwestern College in Americus during the month of June.

Four Institutes for training Vacation Bible School workers will be held in May, one at the First Church, Quitman, one at the First Church, Bainbridge, one at Westminster Church, Albany, and one at the First Church, Columbus.

Rev. John R. Smith of Adel was named as the Moderator-in-Nomination for the Fall meeting. An adjourned meeting will be held in Moultrie on July 10th.

Columbus, Georgia

A Leadership Training School for the Columbus churches was held in Sherwood Church March 14th to 20th. Miss Neva Delgado, D.C.E. for the First Church was Dean of the school. Dr. D. B. Walthall of Atlanta taught "Leadership Education in the Local Church." Mrs. E. A. Schettler of Knoxville, Tenn., taught "The Church's Program for Youth." Mrs. W. B. Clemmons of Columbus taught "Teaching Primary and Junior Children." Mrs. J. S. Kirkpatrick of Decatur, Ga., taught "Teaching Nursery and Kindergarten Children."

On March 29th the lot in Carver Heights was dedicated and ground broken for the erection of a $36,000 educational building for Negroes. This work is being sponsored by the First Church of Columbus, and aided by the Negro Work Division. Rev. L. W. Bottoms of the Negro Work Division made the address at this special service. The work will be directed by the Rev. and Mrs. W. B. Clemmons until it is fully organized.

The First Church of Columbus has signed a contract to have its morning service televised each Sunday for five years.

Davidson, North Carolina

Congressional Medal of Honor winner Sgt. Jerry K. Crump has joined the staff of the Davidson College ROTC department as rifle team coach and small arms specialist.

A native of Lincolnton, Sgt. Crump earned the Congressional Medal in Korea during September of 1951. He also holds the Purple Heart with cluster, the United Nations ribbon and the Korean service ribbon.

Davidson College senior Jim Beaumont Marshall of Clarksville, Tenn., has been awarded a Southern Regional Fellowship in Public Administration.

The Universities of Alabama, Kentucky and Tennessee and the governments of those regions have combined resources in the program for training and teaching.

The award is valued at $1,950, and is designed to encourage the training of executive leaders and skilled administrators for the public service.

Three prominent leaders in management and business spoke to the Davidson College Business-Economics Association at a banquet here May 1.

Mr. T. Coleman Andrews, Chairman of the Board and Chief Executive of the American Fidelity and Casualty Co., Richmond, Va., Dr. Willard J. Graham of the University of North Carolina and Dr. W. A. Paton of the University of Michigan were present.

In addition to the 75 members of the Davidson Club, other students interested in business and business-relations attended, as did prominent business men from the area. One hundred fifty guests were present. The banquet was given in the ballroom of the David Ovens College Union on the Davidson campus.

In its liberal arts program Davidson offers majors in business and in economics, as well as industrial psychology. It is from these students that the Business-Economics Association draws its membership.

Maxton, North Carolina

At the annual meeting of the Alumni Association of Presbyterian Junior College, held in the McNair Cafeteria on the college campus following a five o'clock supper, new officers were elected for the coming year as follows: The Rev. Samuel N. Thomas, Acme, president; Mr. Mills Kirkpatrick, Maxton, vice president; Mrs. Betty Jean Wood, Maxton, secretary-treasurer. Alumni trustees nominated to the Board were: The Rev. Samuel N. Thomas, Acme; Mr. Murphy McGirt, Maxton; Mr. Glenwood Smith, Norfolk, Va. Action was taken by the Presbyterian Junior College Alumni Association authorizing the president to make an approach to the alumni associations of Peace College and Flora Macdonald College looking to cooperative arrangements in view of the coming consolidation of the three colleges. A nominating committee was appointed to select two nominees in advance for each office and mail out to all alumni before Homecoming Day next year, so as to permit each alumnus to vote.

Clinton, South Carolina

A new scholarship fund has been established at Presbyterian College, President Marshall W. Brown announced recently.

It is the Mildred Johnston Hay Scholarship Fund, given by Mrs. Willis P. Johnston of Asheville, N. C., and named for her daughter, Mrs. Fred Jay Hay of Dillon.

Mrs. Johnston presented Presbyterian College with a check for $3,000 and plans to add to this amount in the future.

Dr. Brown, in announcing the Mildred Johnston Hay Scholarship, said that first preference will be given to aiding ministerial students.

Richmond, Virginia

An installation service for the newly-elected Student Body officers for 1956-57 school year at Union Theological Seminary in Virginia was held Friday in Watts Chapel on the campus. The eleven new officers were elected March 28-29, 1956, at a Student Body meeting with the formal installation being held Friday. The new officers are: James G. Carpenter, of New Orleans, Louisiana, President; David F. Bridgman of Houma, Louisiana, Secretary; Warren L. Moody, Jr., of Richmond, Virginia, Treasurer; E. O'dell Smith of Bristol, Tennessee, Spiritual Life Chairman; Warren C. Brannon of Raleigh, North Carolina, Fellowship Chairman; Hardin W. (Corky) King of Burlington, North Carolina, Athletics Chairman; John D. Garrison of Burlington, N. C., Stewardship Chairman; Verlin A. (Vic) Krabill of Pocomoke City, Maryland, Society Missionary Inquiry Chairman; Eugene D. Witherspoon of Wilmington, North Carolina, Home Missions Chairman; William W. Bloom of Bradenton, Florida, Witness Chairman, and Ernest T. Thompson, Jr., of Richmond, Virginia, Publications Chairman.

— BOOKS —

"THE HEM OF HIS GARMENT." Argye M. Briggs. Wm. B. Eerdmans. $2.00.

Many a young girl becomes a victim of bad circumstances caused by materialistic parents. If she has not found her identity or a root sense of belonging and is thrown back on her unsaved personality, she is doomed to frustration and despondency. Such is the pattern for the heroine during the first part of her life.

Sharon suffered in circumstances brought on by the uncertain riches of oil strikes and by her shiftless, charming rake of a father. Since no one loved her, not even her own mother, she had her own living to make.

After a long struggle of defeats experienced by "Strange Sharon," the Lord Jesus claimed and delivered her. She touched the hem of Christ's garment and was healed like the woman of the New Testament.

Here is a Christian novel for the enjoyment and enrichment of young adults. E.C.S.

"A MAN UNDER AUTHORITY." Raymond Henry Belton. Moody Press. $2.75.

"The world is yet to see what God can do with a life wholly yielded to Him."

What would happen to your family, your Church or community if you knew you only had one month to live? Suppose you believed and acted on the possibility of Christ's imminent return? Would your witness be more effective?

"The Man Under Authority" gives a stirring picture of a British church transformed from a worldly, indifferent organization into a first century congregation.

The reading of this novel could start a soul-saving revival in your Church. Like the pastor and his fiancee, some would forget their pride and love the praise of God rather than the praise of men, if too they were willing to pay the supreme sacrifice—the surrender of their dearest possession.

This book would do any Christian good, and could be the means of salvation to others.

—E.C.S.

AN APPEAL TO OUR SUBSCRIBERS

Let each one try to get one or more new subscribers to The Journal. See Page 28 for Special Award Offer.

THE SOUTHERN PRESBYTERIAN JOURNAL
The Journal has no official connection with the Presbyterian Church in the United States
Rev. Henry B. Dendy, D.D., Editor..........Weaverville, N. C.
Dr. L. Nelson Bell, Associate Editor..........Asheville, N. C.
Rev. Wade C. Smith, Associate Editor..........Weaverville, N. C.

EDITORIAL

Why No Idols?

Many of our readers will know the answer but only recently did this writer discover the specific reason for God's command against images and "likenesses"—against the sin of worshipping something made by the hand of man.

In Deuteronomy 4, beginning with the 15th verse, we find these words: *"Take ye therefore good heed unto yourselves; for ye saw no manner of similitude on the day that the Lord spake unto you in Horeb out of the midst of the fire:"* and there then follows an injunction against idolatry in its many forms.

God who is a spirit, revealed Himself to the children of Israel at Mt. Sinai (Horeb), giving to Moses the Law. There were great physical manifestations on the mount; fire, thunder, lightnings and a thick cloud. But, the people saw no likeness of God Himself.

In his farewell messages to Israel, as recorded in Deuteronomy, Moses recapitulates the experiences through which they had passed and again warns them of God's strict command against the making of images of any kind. That this is based on the fact that they saw no similitude of God when He revealed Himself on Mt. Sinai is of more than passing significance.

With this fact before us; with the fact that one of the ten commandments is directed specifically against idolatry in any form, one wonders why a great Church has debased its own worship through images, relics, pictures, etc., etc.?

Also, one wonders why within Protestantism today there is an increasing emphasis on "aids to worship," pictures, candles, etc., etc.? Can this be an evidence of a lack of spiritual content in the worship and message of the Church? History would indicate that the further a people get from fellowship with God the more they "enrich" their worship with material objects.

The fact is that in such matters we face a strict command from God Himself. Furthermore, any tendency to depend on material or psychological aids can be a confession that the spiritual content of our message has receded.

Moses' parting warning was directed primarily to that new generation who had grown to maturity in the wilderness wanderings. But, it is directed to us too:

"Take heed unto yourselves, lest ye forget the covenant of the Lord your God, which he made with you, and make you a graven image, or the likeness of anything, which the Lord thy God hath forbidden thee." L.N.B.

A Brazen Affront to Christ and Christians

Our attention has just been called to the January page of a large wall calendar advertising a liquor store. The picture, which occupies two-thirds of the page, is Vanderlaan's picture of Christ.

The average Christian has no conception of the ends to which the liquor industry will go to promote the sale of alcoholic beverages. Furthermore, there is apparently no end to which the same interests will not go to attack and discredit individuals and movements looking towards a curtailing of their power. With millions of dollars at their disposal they constitute an influence on American life which is evil beyond words.

The end results of alcohol are never mentioned; the "men of distinction" are paraded on the pages of our magazines; "gracious living" is made synonomous with beer and the alcohol industry is intruded into our homes by radio and television until a new generation is being brought to believe that there is neither sin nor danger in liquor consumption.

There have been sporadic attempts to restrict liquor advertising where inter-state commerce is concerned. Such legislation has never received the serious and united support of Christians which it deserves.

Christians certainly have the right to raise their children so that they are protected from the insinuating influences of the liquor interests. At present this is impossible. It is impossible because these interests have power wielded by few others. It is also impossible because these same interests are utterly lacking in a sense of moral responsibility. When unlimited funds, political power and a lack of moral responsibility combine it is a *serious* situation for the nation.

There is much talk today about the social responsibility of the Church. It is our contention that such responsibility begins with the individual. Christ's emphasis was always directed to the individual and his responsibility; first to God and then towards his fellow men.

If such is the case, how can one expect the church member who is a social drinker to exercise any worthwhile influence against alcohol? How can he inveigh against an industry and its blatant bid for more drinkers when he himself is a supporter of that industry?

Furthermore, how can parents expect a new generation to grow up in sobriety when they themselves set the example of non-temperance in their homes? History shows that the concessions of one generation become the excesses of the next. Because of this the Christian social drinker has a grave responsibility from which he can never escape. *And, this responsibility may go on through eternity.*

The present tendency to classify alcoholism as primarily a disease ignores the fact that the Bible calls drunkenness *sin.* Nowhere is disease even suggested as a bar to heaven's gates. But, we are told God's kingdom is barred to drunkards.

Such being the case, and America being what she is, there seems but one position for the Christian to take and this is expressed in the words of Paul, when speaking of another stumbling block to weak Christians:

"But when ye sin so against the brethren, and wound their weak conscience, ye sin against Christ. Wherefore, if meat make my brother to offend, I will eat no flesh while the world standeth, lest I make my brother to offend."

L.N.B.

Admission of New Members

From time to time, I have tried to call to the attention of readers of the *Journal* customs and things of interest, particularly where there seem to be a useful suggestion in them. One matter that greatly impressed me in the services of St. Columba Presbyterian Church at Cambridge, England, was the reception of members on profession of faith. The first part is substantially the same as ours, the minister in the name of the congregation asking questions of the candidates. The close is much the same as would take place in one of our congregations with the minister and elders giving the right hand of fellowship in behalf of the congregation.

In the midst of the service there is, however, an additional item which is very effective. The minister reads a vow which the candidate or candidates repeat after him, somewhat as the groom and the bride each repeat after the minister their marriage vows. This part of the service reads thus:

Will you now say after me:

I take God the Father for my Father:
I take God the Son for my Saviour and Friend:
I take God the Holy Spirit for my Comforter and Guide.
I take God's Word for my Rule of Faith and Conduct:
I take God's People for my People: and so doing I give myself to Him in the service of His Kingdom.

W.C.R.

The Mystery of Reconciliation

To a large and attentive congregation Pastor Edward Thurneysen preached the Gospel of Reconciliation at the morning service in the Basel Munster, March 11th. The service began with a verse from the fifty-third chapter of Isaiah followed by the Christian salutation, Grace be unto you and peace from God our Father and the Lord Jesus Christ. The Scripture reading was 2 Cor. 5.11-21 and the text verses 18-21. All things are of God and reconciliation is wholly His work. The Apostle repeats the word reconciliation five times in this section to let all possible emphasis fall upon it. Reconciliation is accomplished for us in the death and the resurrection of Christ. As our High Priest He offered Himself a sacrifice to

The Southern Presbyterian Journal, *a Presbyterian Weekly magazine devoted to the statement, defense, and propagation of the Gospel, the faith which was once for all delivered unto the saints, published* every Wednesday by The Southern Presbyterian Journal, Inc., in Weaverville, N. C.

Entered as second-class matter May 15, 1942, at the Postoffice at Weaverville, N. C., under the Act of March 3, 1879. Vol. XV. No. 2, May 9, 1956. Editorial and Business Offices: Weaverville, N. C. Printed in the U.S.A. by Biltmore Press, Asheville, N. C.

ADDRESS CHANGE: When changing address, please let us have both old and new address as far in advance as possible. Allow three weeks after change if not sent in advance. When possible, send an address label giving your old address.

remove the wrath of God and reconcile us to Him. Today the crucified and risen Christ is present speaking through the pleading voice of the Preacher calling each one to enter on this blessed state of reconciliation.

The hymns were all centered in the Passion and work of Christ for us. After hearing the Preacher from the high pulpit beside the pillar in the nave of the cathedral, we reversed our seats and faced the Table of the Lord in the transept. Then we came forward and stood four abreast before the Table while Pastor Thurneysen, standing behind the Table, divided the bread for each four and Pastor Koechlin and another associate administered the cup.

On the way home I visited a communicant of that congregation. She said that she had been reared a Roman Catholic, but that she had come into the Reformed Church because the preaching we had that morning made God so close and accessible to her—not separated off by a host of intermediaries: priest, bishop, cardinal, pope, saints, Virgin, statues, pictures. W.C.R.

ANGLERS

(From "*New Testament Evangelism,*" by Wade C. Smith)

Lesson No. 138

THE THIRD OF "THREE HUMAN ESSENTIALS"

A Surrendered Will. One of the most illuminating instances of personal work recorded in Scripture is that of Philip and the eunuch; and the strength of that incident lies in the fact of Philip's entire submission to the promptings of the Holy Spirit. With the Spirit in full control, all the other potent steps followed. Philip was doing a most successful and conspicuous piece of work in Samaria. He was winning souls by the score. Multitudes were coming to hear him preach the Good Tidings. There was great joy in the city; men and women were being baptized, and it would seem that Philip was, of all places in the world, just where he ought to be. Then all of a sudden the Spirit said to Philip, "Arise and go down into the desert toward Gaza." Well, there were no people living in the desert; only a traveler now and then might be seen trying to get across it as fast as he could. One might travel a whole day without seeing anybody. Who would wonder if Philip had questioned why the Spirit was taking him away from an abundantly productive work, to isolate himself where there would be small chance of doing anything at all? Philip had a will of his own. No man could preach as he did without having plenty of determination, which is just another name for will power. Yet Philip obeyed the Spirit, and he lost no time doing it. "He arose and went." His splendid will power was lost in the will of the Spirit. Later, after he had reached the desert, perhaps wondering what the Spirit would tell him next, he spied the Ethiopian Treasurer driving southward in his chariot. "Then the Spirit said unto Philip, Go near, and join thyself to this chariot." Note, the Spirit usually directs only a step at a time. Sometimes it is simply a matter of "joining oneself to the prospect's chariot." Get interested in "where he is going" - what he is thinking about; the Spirit often uses discoveries here to serve as a "cue" for the next step. So it was with Philip. The man was reading and *pondering* the 53rd chapter of Isaiah, and as Philip ran alongside the chariot and saw what the great man was doing, he knew the next step: "Understandest thou what thou readest"? Of course he didn't. How glad Philip was to help him - and what a happy climax! (Read the story in Acts 8:5-38). The Ethiopian was perhaps the last man Philip would have selected for such an interview - but the Spirit knew. Philip *ran* when the Spirit said "Go." He had this third essential for soul winning: a surrendered will.

(This lesson will be continued in the next issue.)

Helps To Understanding Scripture Readings in *Day by Day*

By C. C. Baker

Sunday, May 13, Hebrews 13:16. The author encourages the Hebrew Christians to copy both the faith and the life of their spiritual leaders (v.7). What kind of behavior is desired in their relations with others (vv.1-3,16)? What attitude toward material things is encouraged (vv.5-6)? Do you believe the promises given in vv.5-6? False teachers were robbing these Christians of their true spiritual food (v.9). What is the real source of spiritual nourishment for the Christian (vv.8,12)? Are you aware of the great damage that false teaching can do to those who are under your care - in cutting them off from their source of spiritual nourishment? Do you present to those around you Christ, the source of all they need for spiritual growth?

Monday, May 14, Ephesians 1:1-6. Ephesians one and two form the Scripture readings for the next six devotionals. As you read 1:3-6, do you receive the impression that one becomes a Christian by one's own "whim" or does God have the "say-so"? What is the source of the resources that the Christian has to live the

great truths presented in chapter one on the sovereignty of God, Paul also stresses the human responsibility of the individual in chapters 4-6. List some of the admonitions Paul gives concerning Christian conduct in chapters 4-6. The Christian who maintains this tremendous concept of an all-powerful God should apply to his daily living the precept of 1:12.

Friday, May 18, *Ephesians* 2:1-7. Notice the condition Paul says you were in before you became a Christian. What word in vv.1,5 appropriately described the spiritual state of your soul? What was the cause of this condition (v.1b)? What would be an example of "following the course of this world" (v.2a)? Who do you think is the "prince of the power of the air" (v.2b)? Does v.3 pretty accurately describe your old nature? What was your standing before God (v.3b)? Did you ever realize how terrible your plight was when you were outside of Christ? What has God in Christ done for the Christian (vv.1,5,6)? Was there anything in you that made you merit salvation (vv.4,7)? Thank God again for His great mercy toward you.

Saturday, May 19, *Ephesians* 2:7-14. How would you explain the teaching of v.8 in your own words? Perhaps Titus 3:5-7 can help you. How is this teaching in harmony with what you found in chapter one? Observe the reason given in v.9 for our not being saved by good works? What is the place of good works according to v.10? Should they flow as a natural consequence of saving faith? As one thinks of the past from which he has been delivered (vv.11-12) by the grace of God, he should remember what it cost God to save him (v.13b). Do you praise God for His grace to you as revealed in the cross?

Recommend The Journal To Friends

LESSON FOR MAY 20

The Church In Antioch

Background Scripture: Acts 11:19 - 12:24.
Devotional Reading: Galatians 6:1-10

There are several verses in our Devotional Reading that illustrate the spirit and life of the Church at Antioch (as well as the church in Jerusalem, and elsewhere). Let us look at some of these verses.

"Bear ye one another's burdens, and so fulfill the law of Christ." This was certainly characteristic of the Church as a whole in these early days. They regarded themselves as a big family, united in love, and shared with each other all their material and spiritual blessings. We have seen how true this was of the Church at Jerusalem, and it was equally true, no doubt, of the church at Antioch. Verse six is also true of this church. It was started by those who were taught in the word communicating to those who were to teach others. They that were scattered abroad went as far as Antioch preaching the word. Barnabas was sent to further instruct them, and he got Paul to come.

Verses seven and eight: "Be not deceived; God is not mocked: for whatsoever a man soweth, that shall he also reap. For he that soweth to the flesh shall of the flesh reap corruption; but he that soweth to the spirit shall of the Spirit reap life everlasting."

While these words do not apply directly to the church in Antioch any more than to all Christians, and all men, they illustrate very forcefully a part of our Background Scripture, (12:20-23) which contains the account of the death of the monster Herod. Herod had certainly "sown to the flesh," and when he died, "eaten of worms," he was reaping just what he had sown.

Verse 9: "Let us not be weary in well doing," can be applied to this church, and is an exhortation needed by us all. It was an untiring church, doing all it could for the spread of the gospel, and became the Missionary Center of the whole church, as we will see.

Verse 10: "Let us do good unto all men, especially unto them who are of the household of faith." (Compare this verse with 11:29 of Acts, and see how it fits this church). This seemed to be the rule among all the churches. The Church of Antioch had the marks of a splendid organization.

I. *The Church at Antioch:* 11:19-30.

This is our Printed Text and the main subject for our study.

The Church at Antioch was founded by some of the Christians who had fled from Jerusalem when the persecution that arose about Stephen waxed strong and bitter. These refugees traveled as far as Phenice and Cyprus and Antioch, preaching the word to none but unto the Jews only. Some of them began to preach to the Grecians. Their efforts brought forth glorious fruit, for a great number believed and turned to the Lord.

When this good news reached the ears of the church at Jerusalem they sent Barnabas to them. He came, and when he had seen the grace of God he was glad and exhorted them all that with purpose of heart they would cleave unto the Lord.

We have a word-portrait of this man which is short, but most revealing: "For he was a good man, and full of the Holy Ghost, and of faith." Where can you find a more attractive picture of a noble man, and a successful worker? Here are the basic qualifications for a successful ministry. "He was a good man": that in itself speaks eloquently. A good man is God's noblest creation, or re-creation, for such a man has been "born from above." It is only by the grace of God that we can be "good men." "Full of the Holy Spirit." He was a God-possessed man, as well as a God-made man. God was living in Barnabas. That made him a man of power. "And of faith"; full of faith, like the heroes of faith in the eleventh chapter of Hebrews. Barnabas, like some other minor characters of the Bible, (Jonathan and Nehemiah, for instance), is one of the most beautiful characters of history. His name means "son of consolation, or encouragement." He lived up to the meaning of that name. He was the "Great-Heart" of the early church. Bunyan must have had him in mind when he portrayed that well loved character in Pilgrim's Progress.

How we need such men in our churches today! They are the ones who encourage the "babes in

Christ," and also those who faint and fall by the wayside. They are the ones who speak "a word in season" to those who are heart-broken and weary and heavy-laden. They are the ones who hold up the hands of the preacher and lift the fallen. A Barnabas is a blessing to any church.

In verse 25 we see another wonderful trait of character in this man, Barnabas: "Then departed Barnabas to Tarsus, for to seek Saul." Barnabas, like John the Baptist, was truly humble. He recognized that there were greater, more capable men than he. When he saw the great work that had begun at Antioch he felt the need of a man like Saul of Tarsus for the work. If he had been a small minded, jealous man, he would have hesitated about bringing a man of Saul's ability to take up the work, for he no doubt saw that Saul would soon take the lead. Barnabas was a noble-minded, generous man who had the good of the church at heart, and not his own selfish interests. The work needed a well-equipped leader, a broadminded leader, who could reach Gentile as well as Jew. So he set out to find Saul and bring him to Antioch, and this was a turning point in the history of the church, and also in the life of Saul. Think of all that would have been missed if Barnabas had not found Saul and brought him to Antioch! Perhaps Barnabas was thinking of Saul himself as well as of the need. The work called for Saul; there was a wonderful opportunity there; and Saul needed just such an opening, for he was a man of action. The work and the man fit together, and there Saul starts his career which turned him into Paul the Apostle to the Gentiles, and the great missionary.

In many crises of Church History, as in the lives of Martin Luther and John Calvin, we see illustrations of this same marvelous Providence of God. Surely, God moves in mysterious and wonderful ways to carry out His plans and purposes!

Barnabas and Saul worked together for a whole year in Antioch, and taught the people. The disciples were called Christians first at Antioch. A Christian is "Christ's man"; he belongs to Christ. It is said that many of the heathen had the name of their special god tattooed on their bodies. This may have suggested to the heathen that they call these disciples "Christian," for, like Paul later says about himself, they bore in their bodies "the marks of the Lord Jesus." These people saw that the disciples were devoted to Christ, talked about Him, worshipped Him, and tried to live like Him. Would men "see Jesus" reflected in our lives, and be constrained to call us after the name of our Saviour, if they had never heard the word "Christian" before? Are we worthy of the "Name"? Is He ever ashamed that we bear His name? Is there any honor so great as to be a "Christian"?

The remainder of this chapter tells of the "great dearth" that should come, and what these Christians did. The prophecy was fulfilled in the days of Claudius Caesar. "Then the disciples, every one according to his ability, determined to send relief unto the brethren which dwelt at Jerusalem." So the young church sends a "love gift" to the mother church. Here we have a sample of what our Savior prays for in John 17; the oneness of the church.

II. *James and Peter:* 12:1-19.

Persecution was now reaching the apostles again. This time it was the Roman authorities that took the lead. Herod the king stretched forth his hand to vex certain of the church. He killed James the brother of John with the sword, and seeing this pleased the Jews, he proceeded to take Peter also.

Peter is put in prison with the avowed purpose of killing him after the Passover season. But God had other plans for Peter, and all the power of the Roman Empire could not interfere with those plans. The angel of God came at night and released him from prison. The story of his release is intensely interesting. It was only after he had been completely freed that the angel left him and Peter fully realized what had taken place. Where should he go? When he considered the matter he decided to go to the house of Mary, the mother of John Mark. When he knocked, a damsel came to hearken, and when she knew Peter's voice, she opened not the gate for gladness, but ran and told them that Peter stood at the gate. They thought she was mad, or that it was his "angel." They finally opened the door. In verse five we are told that prayer was being made for him, but they were astonished when those prayers were answered in such a spectacular manner. Would we be as surprised if some of our prayers were answered in such a way? It is not always God's will to rescue His servants. James was killed while Peter was spared for a time. Peter tells his story and commands them to tell James (the other James). When day came there was no small stir among the soldiers. Herod dealt with the matter in the Roman way. He examined the keepers and commanded that they should be put to death.

III. *The Death of Herod and the Growing Word:* 20-25.

Herod dies; the Word multiplies and grows.

YOUTH PROGRAM FOR MAY 20

The Power Of Words

Hymn: "I Love To Tell The Story"
Prayer
Scripture: James 1:16-26, 3:1-12.
Hymn: "Lord, Speak To Me That I May Speak"
Offering
Hymn: "Take My Life And Let It Be Consecrated" (Be sure to use the stanza which begins, "Take my voice . . . ")

PROGRAM LEADER:

The substance called dynamite is a synonym for power. Used in the proper way it is exceedingly valuable. In a moment of time it can do work that would require days of human toil. If dynamite is used improperly, it can do untold damage. Because it is so potentially dangerous it must be handled with great care. No sane person would think of letting children use dynamite as a plaything. Even those of us who are older and understand its power do not make a practice of toying with dynamite.

While all of us respect the power of dynamite, there is something else which we use every day and which is just as powerful as dynamite in another way. Words are potentially powerful. If we understood their power, it is certain we would use them more carefully. Words, like dynamite, can be used both constructively and destructively. Words can be either harmful or helpful. Since this is true, the way we use words is of great importance to us as Christians. The earnest Christian will endeavor to use his words helpfully and will avoid every harmful speech. Our words are involved in stewardship. Just as we are responsible to God for the use we make of our time, talents, and money, so we are responsible to Him for the use we make of our words. (Read Matt. 12:36-37) This will be no new idea to most of us, but it is a thing about which we are apt to become careless. In this program we want to do some serious thinking about words and the use we make of them. We want to make two lists: one of the useful and helpful ways of using words and the other of harmful or destructive ways of using words. (Have the young people supplied with Bibles and ask them to read carefully the two passages from James, 1:16-26 and 3:1-12, before they begin making suggestions for the lists. While they are reading, write headings for your two lists on the blackboard or on large sheets of paper or cardboard. We offer some suggestions for your lists below, but do not add them to the lists until your young people have advanced all their ideas. As the various suggestions come from the young people, take time to discuss them. Ask why they are helpful or harmful, as the case may be.)

HELPFUL WAYS OF USING WORDS

1. Praising God and praying.
2. Telling others of Christ.
3. Teaching the ignorant.
4. Transmitting worthwhile news.
5. Encouraging the disheartened and comforting the sorrowing.
6. Wholesome entertainment (singing or speaking).
7. Saying good things about people whenever possible.
8. Speaking in defense of those who are wrongly accused.
9. Speaking out for worthy causes.
10. Making people feel at ease through friendly conversation.
11. Expressing our love and concern for others.
12. Speaking forgiveness to those who have wronged us.
13. Clearing up misunderstandings between people and between ourselves and others.

HARMFUL WAYS OF USING WORDS

1. Speaking lightly or disrespectfully of God.
2. Speaking to discourage or hinder others in their faith and spiritual growth.
3. False teaching.
4. Spreading false and harmful reports about others.
5. Telling unwholesome jokes and stories and singing unwholesome songs.
6. Use of profanity or cheap slang.
7. Bitter words spoken in anger.
8. False accusations.
9. Spreading gloom and doubt.
10. Distorting the truth.
11. Cynical speech (making fun of things and people.)

AN APPEAL TO OUR SUBSCRIBERS

(See Page 16)

Women's Work

ADVENTURING FOR GOD

A very timely pamphlet bearing the above title may be secured from the Board of Women's Work for only ten cents a copy. If placed in the homes of our church members it could prove of real value to families as they seek to become more Christian during this year of special emphasis on Christian Family Life. Not only is the pamphlet appropriate for the individual family, but it might be used as the basis of a program for a Family Night meeting or a meeting of the Women of the Church.

It is in the home that the first training is given and lasting impressions are received. There are several things in the home that each of us can do that will set us on the "Road to High Adventure for God." As we travel this road we need to *watch* the signposts, *choose* the right direction and *follow* the road indicated, if we would make progress in Christian Family Life.

The Signposts listed are five in number:

1. "Personal Behavior—Turn to the right and go straight ahead;"
2. "Family Attitudes—Slight Curve Ahead!"
3. "The Way of Love—Straight Ahead!"
4. "Apply the Rule of the Road—Keep Going!"
5. "Keep on Keeping on!"

As a family ask God to keep you alert to see opportunities for showing kindness, consideration and courtesy to all persons regardless of background.

Begin in the family to develop wholesome attitudes and actions toward all.

Seek to have a spirit of understanding and appreciation of the worth of every individual.

Study together the teachings of Jesus in such passages as the Parable of the Good Samaritan.

Avoid anything that might plant in the minds of children a dislike or prejudice toward other persons—"You cannot know the Lord of Love as long as there is any resentment or bitterness in your heart."

Have as guests in the home, missionaries on furlough and students from other countries.

Encourage the reading of biographies of successful people, such as missionaries, scientists, doctors, musicians and others; this will prove to be an enriching experience.

The signposts may prove difficult to follow, but we can succeed, for we are promised the power—for prayer is the greatest steadying power, and "Love is the door through which we pass from selfishness to service, and from solitude and loneliness into fellowship with all mankind." A home founded on real love is a bit of the kingdom of God come down to earth.

Christianity is interpreted to others by our attitudes and acts, therefore we need to make our lives and our homes so attractive that others may catch a vision of Him, who is the Head of a truly Christian Home.

Mrs. John E. Stauffer
Chairman Intergroup Work
Appalachia Synodical

Reverend and Mrs. Herbert Meza

It is a long way from the Latin quarter of Tampa, Florida, known to all as Ybor City, to a Presbyterian Mission outside the busy metropolitan city of Lisbon, Portugal, and yet from our Presbyterian Mission Church in Ybor City, God called two splendid young people - Rev. and Mrs. Herbert Meza - to represent Him in Portugal as ambassadors of Christ.

How did it all start? Many years ago, Herbert Meza was invited to attend the Ybor City Presbyterian Sunday school. He had never attended Sunday school. The Holy Bible was unknown to him. He attended the mission each Sunday and with great interest heard the teacher tell of Jesus who is the Saviour of the world. Gradually Herbert became conscious of the need of a Saviour and on December 31, 1939, he made his public profession of faith in his Lord. This was the beginning of a faith and zeal that saw Herbert graduating from Davidson College with high honors and from Union Theological Seminary in Richmond, Virginia. Now he was offering himself for service to our Board of World Missions. Herbert had wanted to go to China but the doors were closed to this great land and so he accepted the challenge of Portugal. Dalia Santos, now Mrs. Herbert Meza, also found Christ at the Ybor City Presbyterian Mission Church. She too, in the face of much opposition from her own family, offered her life for full time Christian work.

In due time these two young people married and today with their two fine boys, Mark and Scott, they are giving themselves for the Lord in Portugal.

There are others in Ybor City that God will call if we make it possible through the establishment of a stronger work many may very well follow in the footsteps of Herbert and Dalia as servants of the Lord.

Can we do less than pray and give so that the Holy Spirit will lead us to greater efforts for His Kingdom?

Frank Carrera, Jr.

It took fifteen years to win Frank Carrera, Jr., to the Lord. His two sons came as children to the Ybor City Presbyterian Mission Church and while he did not object to his boys attending Sunday school and taking active part in the Mission program, neither did he or his wife show any interest in the church or their spiritual life. The boys grew up to manhood and by their testimony in being faithful to the Lord they were used of the Lord to win first their mother to Christ and then later on their father.

As Mr. Carrera grew in the knowledge of his Lord, he also grew in the service of the church. His ability to grasp the problems of the Mission was amazing. Slowly, but surely, he began to lead the congregation in a program of stewardship. Using his many years of experience as a prominent business man, he was able to increase the giving of time and money for the work of the church nearly 50%.

When the outside hostile world made fun of his stand for Christ and his Church, he stood firm. When the time came to go into the community and present the claims of Christ to the Latin brethren, Mr. Carrera was among the best soul winners.

How the grace of God has worked in this man's life together with that of his wife has become an inspiration both to the minister and his fellow Christians.

Your prayers and your gifts will help us to reach more men like Frank Carrera, Jr.

Prayer for a House

MARTHA SNELL NICHOLSON

Walk thru the rooms of this house, dear Lord,
Making them fair and sweet.
May every wall know the touch of Thy hand,
Each floor the print of Thy feet.

Help us to look through Thine eyes, dear Lord,
To stand at our windows and see
Not commonplace people who walk the streets,
But souls who have need of Thee.

Kindle a fire on our hearth, dear Lord,
Warming all who might come.
Build Thou an altar where prayer shall arise,
For prayer is the heart of the home.

Sit at our table with us, dear Lord,
Making each meal a feast,
Breaking the bread, and pouring the wine,
Our Host and our Guest and our Priest.

Dwell in the rooms of our house, dear Lord,
Making it sweet and fair,
Till even the people passing will say,
"The blessed Lord Jesus lives there!"

Hoover Recommends the Bible

J. Edgar Hoover, Director of the FBI, warns that juvenile delinquency is increasing at an alarming rate, but insists that it can be prevented. "It is not a scourge which rules with an inevitable necessity," he says. "One of the best weapons with which to attack this malady is religious training. The young boy and girl trained in the teachings of the Bible have a moral reliance which serves as a compass for everyday living. They know the difference between right and wrong, good and evil. They are able to conquer the temptations of life."—Exchange.

Church News

Additional Overtures to the General Assembly

(36) The Presbytery of Meridian respectfully overtures the General Assembly to withdraw from the National Council of Churches of Christ in the United States of America.

(37) WHEREAS, The Presbytery of Florida wishes to express its grave concern toward the membership of the Presbyterian Church, U.S. in the National Council of Churches of Christ in the U.S.A. and the World Council of Churches, and

WHEREAS, continued membership gives tacit approval of public pronouncements and resolutions that have been widely circulated which do not express the conviction of a majority of the total membership of our Church, and

WHEREAS, resolutions above referred to have accused those not in agreement with their social, economic and political views as unChristian, and

WHEREAS, the leadership of both associations, above referred to, openly envision the ultimate goal as organic union of all Protestant Churches in one world Church.

NOW THEREFORE, the Presbytery of Florida overtures the General Assembly to authorize a ballot by each presbytery of the Presbyterian Church, U.S., for the determination of a policy as to whether or not our Presbyterian Church should withdraw from the two councils, same being conducted in accordance with properly constituted authority.

(38) The Presbytery of Augusta-Macon respectfully overtures the General Assembly to provide an affiliate membership in our churches for members of our Armed Services and their families.

(39) The Presbytery of East Alabama respectfully overtures the General Aessmbly to authorize a ballot by each presbytery of the General Assembly, Presbyterian Church, U.S., for determination of policy as to whether or not the Presbyterian Church, U.S., shall have segregation or integration of all races; same being conducted in accordance with properly constituted authority.

Commissioner Substitute

At the recent meeting of Norfolk Presbytery one of the commissioners reported his inability to attend the General Assembly this year and the following change was made:

Ruling Elder W. E. Fluker, 1816 Springfield Avenue, Norfolk 6, Va., takes the place of Ruling Elder George E. Walter, Exmore, Va.

Rev. M. Bland Dudley was received from Mecklenburg Presbytery and will be pastor of the Holmes Church. His address is Cheritan, Va.

Rev. John B. Boyd was dismissed to East Hanover Presbytery and he will be assistant pastor at Grace Covenant, Richmond, Va.

W. W. Grover, Stated Clerk.

Atlanta, Ga. — Dr. Manford G. Gutzke, professor of English Bible and Religious Education at Columbia Theological Seminary in Decatur, has just published his third book—his first major work.

The publication, entitled "John Dewey's Thought and Its Implications for Christian Education," is a 241 page volume, published by King's Crown Press at Columbia University. Primarily a student's book, it is a discussion of processes involved in education to show that the method of education now used in schools can be also used in Christian Education. It stresses the value of student-participation as a means of learning and suggests that this method be utilized in the processes of learning in Christian education.

The publication is built around Dr. Gutzke's dissertation for the Ph. D. degree he received from Columbia University in 1954.

Atlanta, Ga. — The Rev. Dwight L. Barker, former pastor of Cameronian and Park Avenue Presbyterian Churches, Rockingham, N. C., has been assigned to active duty in the chaplaincy of the U. S. Army, according to an announcement made here by the Board of Church Extension, Chaplains and Military Personnel Department.

Elberton, Ga.—George McWhorter, Milledgeville, Ga., has been appointed publicity chairman for the Synod of Georgia for the Miami Presbyterian Men's convention to be held Oct. 10-13, 1957. The appointment was announced by J. W. Hyde of Elberton, president of the Georgia Synod Men's Council.

Augusta, Ga. — President and Mrs. Dwight D. Eisenhower, and their son, Major John Eisenhower, were worshipers at Reid Memorial Presbyterian Church in Augusta, Sunday, April 15, and heard Dr. Wade H. Boggs, Sr., former moderator of the General Assembly and supply minister of Reid Memorial, bring a message on "The Sovereignty of God."

This was the president's first visit to Reid Memorial Church since its new building was completed. Two years ago President Eisenhower laid the cornerstone for the sanctuary.

New Orleans, La.—A Christian Family Life Institute was conducted April 16, at Napoleon Avenue Presbyterian Church. Keynote speaker of the institute was the Rev. Frederick W. Widmer, director of Family Life Education of the Board of Christian Education, Richmond.

Mr. Widmer was assisted by the following discussion leaders:

Mrs. L. C. Majors of Richmond; Mrs. Edwin Stock of New Orleans; the Rev. Robert Kilgore of Raceland; and the Rev. George H. Ricks, regional director of Christian Education, Baton Rouge.

This was the first of a series of nine institutes planned by the Committee of Christian Education for the Synod of Louisiana. According to Dr. James Gregory, Pastor of the Napoleon Avenue Church, it was held to develop the ability to meet family problems without fear, and with Christian love.

Christian family life is the special emphasis for 1956 in the "Forward With Christ" movement.

The Synod of Mississippi will meet for its one hundred and twenty-sixth annual session at Belhaven College, Jackson, Mississippi, Tuesday, June 26, 1956, at 7:30 P.M.

R. E. Hough, Stated Clerk

Presbytery of Meridian — The regular spring meeting of the Presbytery of Meridian was held in the Handsboro Church, April 17, 1956. Rev. J. T. Echols, Moderator, presided. The opening sermon was preached by Dr. R. L. Summers, Gulfport, on the assigned subject: "The Fatherhood of God." This was followed with the Communion service.

There were twenty-seven ministers and thirty-four ruling elders present. Also a number of visitors.

A memorial service was held for the late Rev. W. D. Mathis.

Rev. W. B. Hooker was received from the Presbytery of Ouachita. He becomes pastor of the Magee and Sharon churches. Mr. Edward Rosser Wall of Newton was received as a Candidate for the Ministry. Candidate George Carpenter was dismissed to the Presbytery of Louisville. The pastoral relation between Rev. J. T. Echols and the Waynesboro church was dissolved, and he given a certificate of transfer to Granville Presbytery. Calls from the Taylorsville and Calvary churches for the pastoral services of Mr. Oscar H. Welborn, a senior in Columbia Seminary, were approved; also calls from the Wiggins and New Augusta churches for the pastoral services of Mr. Thomas G. Kay of Philadelphia, Pa., were approved.

The Presbytery sent to the General Assembly an overture requesting withdrawal from the National Council of Churches.

Rev. Jack J. Wolf of Ocean Springs was appointed to preach the opening sermon at the next regular meeting of the Presbytery which will be held in the Bailey Presbyterian Church, Meridian, Miss., RFD No. 4, meeting on July 17th.

The Handsboro Church, Rev. John C. Wingard, pastor, was a most gracious host. The Presbytery and visitors were served a delightful fish dinner during the noon recess hour.

L. A. Beckman, Jr., Stated Clerk

Mecklenburg Presbytery in its 212th stated session meeting in the Bethel Presbyterian Church on April 17th received Rev. Claire S. Albright from East Hanover Presbytery and arranged for his installation as pastor of the Marshville Presbyterian Church and ordained Mr. John Richard Crawford as an evangelist. Mr. M. S. Bell was licensed to preach and a Commission was appointed to ordain and install him pastor of the Seigle Avenue Presbyterian Church. (These three are in the Senior Class at Union Theological Seminary.) Presbytery received four men as candidates for the ministry: Mr. David K. Dunn, of the Mulberry Church; Lieut. Kenneth B. Orr, of the Westminster Church; Mr. John Roscoe, of the Watson Heights Church; and Mr. Henry Howard Smith, a member of the Myers Park Church.

The pastoral relations were dissolved as of June 1st between Rev. F. C. Debele, Jr., and the Commonwealth Church. Rev. M. R. Williamson was elected to become Stated Clerk in his stead. Pastoral relations between the Hopewell Presbyterian Church and Rev. Henry S. Schum were dissolved as of May 30th. Mr. Debele goes to the Eau Claire Church in Columbia, S. C., and Mr. Schum becomes pastor of the Princeton Church in Johnson City, Tenn.

A commission was appointed to install Rev. S. Wylie Hogue pastor of the Wadesboro Presbyterian Church.

Dr. R. C. Long was elected moderator to succeed Rev. S. H. Zealy. Revs. G. E. Dixon and T. Duke Williams presided at the Lord's Table.

Mr. Theodore B. Pratt, Promotional Director of the Presbyterian Survey, made an address about the Survey. Revs. W. L. Hall, Lawrence I. Stell and Mr. Voit Gilmore were heard in regard to the Consolidated College Campaign. Approval was given of the movement. Mr. Harvey C. May was heard in an address on the Church and Manse Building Fund. The Commission on the Minister and His Work reported on the dissolution of the pastoral relations between Rev. Andrew Allen and the Amay James Church; of the dissolution of the pastoral relations between the churches of the Belk Parish and Rev. S. Wylie Hogue; of the dissolution of the pastoral relations between the Cameronian and Park Avenue Churches and Rev. Dwight Barker, who has gone to the chaplaincy; of the dissolving of the pastoral relationship between Rev. Geo. Fletcher and the Ellerbe, Mt. Carmel and Norman Churches - (Mr. Fletcher was transferred to Lexington-Ebenezer Presbytery where he becomes pastor of the Wilmore, Kentucky, Presbyterian Church); of the removal of Rev. Bland Dudley to Norfolk Presbytery so that he might be pastor of the Holmes Presbyterian Church at Bayview, Va. - and the dissolution of the pastoral relations with the McQuay Memorial Church. Candidate Edgar Byers was transferred to Albemarle Presbytery.

Mrs. Loyd Ardrey, president of the Women of the Presbytery, presented Mrs. Boyce W. Hunter, former president, who reviewed the work of the women in 1955. She told of 96 organizations enrolling 12,618 women who gave $146,400.00.

Rev. I. Howard Chadwick was nominated for moderator of the next meeting to be held in the Pleasant Hill Church on July 24th. Rev. J. E. Wayland, Jr., host pastor, gave a printed history of the one hundred and twenty-eight year old congregation. There were 81 ministers, 79 elders and 27 visitors enrolled. Rev. F. C. Debele was assisted in his office of Stated Clerk by Revs. A. Leslie Thompson and R. W. Rayburn.

Tryon, N. C. — At a congregational meeting following morning worship on April 15, the Tryon Presbyterian Church officially approved plans for a future building program. The plans call for the erection of a church on a four acre plot of ground opposite the Harmon Field area of Tryon.

The church, built in the contemporary style of architecture, will consist of two separate buildings, constructed of native stone and wood. The sanctuary will be of the modified arena type, with the seating capacity for two hundred twenty, plus a choir of twenty-six voices. The sanctuary will be air-conditioned.

The building fund campaign will begin on May 13, with the guest minister being Dr. Robert Stamper, chairman of the development program of Columbia Seminary. Frank Gallimore is chairman of the building committee; Charles Reakirt is chairman of the finance committee. Rev. Joe Wagner is the pastor.

Davidson, N. C.—Director of Defense Mobilization Arthur S. Flemming will deliver the Davidson College commencement address May 28, highlighting a three day program.

The traditional exercises will begin Saturday, May 26, and will extend through Monday morning as alumni, seniors, parents and faculty join in the feature event of the college year.

Dr. E. Lee Stoffel, pastor of Charlotte's First Presbyterian Church, will give the Baccalaureate Sermon on Sunday.

Events will begin at 11 a.m. May 26 with the annual Alumni Council meeting in the College Union. Three new members of the Board of Trustees will be elected to succeed W. Olin Nisbet, Jr. of Charlotte, Robert W. Gorrell of Winston-Salem, and C. R. Wilcox of Rome, Ga., whose terms expire this year.

The Senior-Alumni luncheon will be held at 1 p.m., class day exercises at 4 p.m. and a concert in Chambers auditorium at 8 p.m. The Davidson Male Chorus and soprano Norma Heyde will be presented in concert.

Faculty homes will be open to seniors, parents, alumni and friends Sunday evening.

Raleigh, N. C.—Three leaders for North Carolina Presbyterians' campaign to raise $3,500,000 for higher education in the Synod have been announced.

Voit Gilmore, mayor of Southern Pines, N. C. was named general chairman of the campaign; Dr. Lawrence I. Stell, pastor of Trinity Presbyterian Church, Charlotte, was selected to be ministerial chairman; and Thornton H. Brooks, Greensboro, N. C., attorney, has accepted the appointment as Special Gifts chairman.

The consolidated Presbyterian College to be erected in Laurinburg, N. C., will receive $3,000,000, and the remaining $500,000 will go to the Campus Christian Life Program of the Synod. The drive will continue until June 1.

Mayor Gilmore's appointment was announced by W. H. Neal of Winston-Salem, chairman of the college's Board of Trustees. During the drive, Mr. Gilmore will use a private plane to enable him to give "vigorous leadership in all areas of the state." The mayor will maintain his office in Southern Pines during the campaign.

Clinton, S. C. — Summer school at Presbyterian College will open on June 12 this year, Academic Dean George C. Bellingrath announced.

Registration is scheduled for that day, beginning at 9 a. m., and classwork will begin on the following morning. The eight-week session will extend through August 11.

Dr. Bellingrath said classes will meet daily six days each week, with a maximum of nine hours granted for the summer work. A total of 23 courses in ten departments will be offered at this session.

These departments include: Bible, economics, psychology, English, fine arts, Spanish, history, mathematics, sociology and biology.

Clinton, S. C. — A Presbyterian College senior has been named to receive a Rockefeller Fellowship to Princeton Theological Seminary, Dr. Nathan M. Pusey, fellowship chairman and president of Harvard University, announced recently.

He is Ray Lord of Dublin, Ga., who this June completes an outstanding career as a scholar and campus leader at Presbyterian College.

The grant, in the form of a full scholarship, was made possible through the Rockefeller Brothers Theological Fellowship Program of the American Association of Theological Schools, Inc. Dr. Pusey is president of the association.

The program is to enable certain selected young men and women of exceptional merit to devote one year to theological study that they may explore the possibility of entering the Protestant ministry. Recipients were selected on the basis of Christian character and personality and proven intellectual ability of the highest order, combined with keen spiritual responsiveness with deep human sympathies. They may attend any fully accredited theological seminary in the United States or Canada.

Memphis, Tenn.—Woodland Presbyterian Church in Memphis recently launched a $130,000 campaign for the church's new Fellowship Hall, second unit in the building program. Inspirational speaker for the kick-off banquet was Dr. W. J. Millard of Evergreen Presbyterian Church. Everett D. Woods, architect, told of the plans for the new structure.

Already Woodland Church has a conditional grant of $30,000 made by the Church Extension Committee of Memphis Presbytery toward the building.

The new building will serve as a temporary sanctuary seating 400, with the ground floor providing Church School space for 300 children. D. Joyce White is finance committee chairman. The Rev. W. Chester Keller is pastor.

Nashville, Tenn.—Construction of a new $350,000 office building here for the Presbytrian, U.S. Board of World Missions will begin this summer, officials announced.

They said purchase of a $42,500 two-acre site for the structure in an exclusive Nashville residential section will be completed shortly.

Progress on the project had been delayed for some months by a taxpayers' suit in the Chancery Court seeking to void a permit for construction of the building granted by the Nashville Board of Zoning Appeals.

Late in February, Chancellor Thomas W. Steele upheld the right of the board to erect the building in the area.

Nashville, Tenn. — Rev. and Mrs. Lewis H. Lancaster, Jr., of our Japan Mission announce the birth of a daughter, Beth Neville, in Osaka, Japan, on April 17.

Zion Church, Columbia, Tennessee—Zion Church was filled with worshippers at the Sunrise Services Easter Morning. Under the ministry of Rev. W. M. Ford, this is the fifth successive year such services have been held at Zion Church. Originally started in 1951 under the combined efforts of the Youth Fellowship of Zion Church and the First Church in Columbia, the first service was held at Geers Memorial Park in Columbia; however, since that year these services have been held at Zion Church which is approximately six miles from Columbia and which will celebrate in 1957 one hundred and fifty years of continuous service to Christ and the community. This year seven other churches in Columbia joining in, came to worship at Zion. Under the direction of Mrs. Robert Armstrong a scene of the resurrection morning was presented. Mr. Ben Alexander of the Methodist Church preached the sermom.

Montgomery Presbytery met in its 240th Stated Session, in the Campbell Memorial Presbyterian Church of Vinton, Virginia, on Tuesday, April 17, 1956, at 10:00 a. m. with 50 ministers and 56 elders present. Rev. J. L. Coppock was elected Moderator.

Rev. John A. Ricks was received into Presbytery from Concord Presbytery and arrangements made for his ordination as an evangelist that he may serve as a Chaplain in the U. S. N. R.

Mr. Robert J. Rock and Mr. Don Carlos Abbott were received under the care of the Presbytery as Candidates for the Ministry of the Gospel.

Plans were made to raise $200,000.00 to build new churches.

Candidate Richard S. Andrews was dismissed to Wilmington Presbytery that he may accept a call to become a pastor of two churches there.

The importance of Sabbath Observance was emphasized.

E. W. Smith, Stated Clerk

YOU CAN WITNESS FOR CHRIST

By George S. Lauderdale

God does not require somebody special to do his missionary work. The Holy Spirit Who rests upon God's servants that they might be witnesses unto Him to the uttermost parts of the earth, makes the difference between Christians and men of the world. Peter and John were ordinary fishermen, but when Christ called and baptized them with the Holy Spirit, the elders of Israel seeing their boldness and perceiving that they were ignorant and unlearned men, "marveled; and they took knowledge of them that they had been with Jesus." Acts 4:13.

Consider Elijah. A man subject to like passions as we are, he prayed earnestly that it would not rain, and for three and a half years it did not rain on the earth! "And he prayed again, and the heavens gave rain, and the earth brought forth her fruit." James 5:18. Nor was that all that this prophet did to show Israel and the nations that the Lord, rather than Baal or any other idol, is God.

Of Like Passions As We

God used Elijah to miraculously feed a starving widow's household many days and to bring back her son from the dead. He heard his prayer and sent down fire from heaven at Mount Carmel in the presence of eight hundred and fifty prophets of Baal and the people of Israel; He gave Elijah and the people courage to slay the false prophets.

Proof that Elijah was no superman is given in I Kings, chapter 19. He became downcast and wanted to die: "It is enough; now, O Lord, take away my life; for I am not better than my fathers." (verse 4). This prayer came from the lips of the man whose mighty pleas to God had shut and opened the windows of heaven! He also moaned, "The children of Israel have forsaken thy covenant, thrown down thine altars, and slain thy prophets with the sword; and I, even I only am left; and they seek my life to take it away." I Kings 19:10.

Elijah A Missionary

So spoke the man who had laughed at Baal's prophets and had put them to confusion and to death, who had bravely condemned wicked King Ahab although the latter sought him in every nation! Surely Elijah was subject to like passions as we are; yet he was a witness for God in all the lands where Ahab looked for him. Everywhere Ahab told the story of the drought caused by Elijah's prayers, and had the foreign kings help him hunt Elijah. Thus the prophet through his persecution was a missionary to that ancient world.

Paul and Barnabas Mere Men

Others who did marvelous mission work for God include Paul and Barnabas. Were they divine that they healed the man at Lystra, a cripple from the cradle? The heathen citizens of Lystra thought so, and said of them, "The gods are come down to us in the likeness of men," and the priest of Jupiter brought oxen to sacrifice to the missionaries. Acts 14:11-13.

Paul and Barnabas protested, tearing their clothes, running and crying out, "Sirs, why do ye these things? We also are men of like passions with you." Acts 14:15. They proceeded then to tell them of the one true God whom all men must worship.

Receive the Holy Spirit'

The question now comes to you and me: Why do we lack power and wisdom, since the men whom God has used before this as His witnesses shared our sinful nature? The answer: we have not prayed as we should, particularly for the Holy Spirit, Who alone can enable us to complete the humanly impossible task of world evangelization.

Let us trust God and not worry about our weakness; instead of frailty's being an excuse for not winning souls, it should cause us to pray the more. Remember Christ's words, "If ye then, *being evil*, know how to give good gifts unto your children, how much more shall your heavenly Father give the *Holy Spirit* to them that ask Him?" Luke 11:13.

AN APPEAL TO OUR SUBSCRIBERS

Let each one try to get one or more new subscribers to The Journal. See Page 15 for Special Award Offer.

Have you remembered Foreign Missions in your will?

There's spiritual satisfaction in knowing that your will—your last earthly business transaction—contains a gift to the Lord's work.

There's a joy in knowing that your gift will live far down into the future, carrying the Gospel to those in need.

Many members of our Church have remembered Foreign Missions in their wills. Our Board of World Missions has not only provided a channel for the careful and efficient use of such gifts, but has frequently been able to assist donors in arranging their legacy exactly as they wish.

If we can be of service to you in this way, please let us know. We have a little folder on wills that we will be glad to mail anyone on request.

CURRY B. HEARN, TREASURER

BOARD OF WORLD MISSIONS

PRESBYTERIAN CHURCH IN THE UNITED STATES

POST OFFICE BOX 330, NASHVILLE 1, TENN.

"To Foreign Missions a Share"

THE SOUTHERN PRESBYTERIAN JOURNAL

A Presbyterian weekly magazine devoted to the statement, defense and propagation of the Gospel, the faith which was once for all delivered unto the saints.

MAY 16, 1956

General Assembly
Standing Committee Chairmen

Bills and Overtures—Rev. B. O. Wood, D.D.

Judicial Business—Mr. George H. Wright

Office of the General Assembly—Rev. Frederick H. Olert, D.D.

General Council—Rev. D. H. Edington, Jr.

World Missions—Rev. Fred J. Hay, D.D.

Church Extension—Rev. E. B. McGukin, D.D.

Christian Education—Rev. Alton H. Glasure, D.D.

Annuities and Relief—Mr. John Wellford

Women's Work—Rev. R. A. Bolling, D.D.

Interchurch Relations—Rev. John F. Anderson, Jr., D.D.

Christian Relations—Rev. George Vick, D.D.

The Minister and His Work—Rev. Joseph B. Mack, D.D.

Let Us All Be Much in Prayer for the Meeting of the General Assembly
The Meeting Will Open on Thursday Evening, May 31st at 7:30 P.M.
All Sessions Will Be Held in the Anderson Auditorium,
Montreat, N. C.

VOL. XV NO. 3

$2.50 A YEAR

THE SOUTHERN PRESBYTERIAN JOURNAL
The Journal has no official connection with the Presbyterian Church in the United States
Rev. Henry B. Dendy, D.D., Editor..**Weaverville, N. C.**
Dr. L. Nelson Bell, Associate Editor..**Asheville, N. C.**
Rev. Wade C. Smith, Associate Editor..**Weaverville, N. C.**

EDITORIAL

Christian Pedagogy

In the general realm of teaching it is recognized that there are various methods of approach. Many will say that the greatest teachers are those who teach their students how to think for themselves.

Admitting such to be the case one would venture the belief that in Christian teaching, as in Christian preaching, there is a central aim to produce *faith*. If I, as a teacher, have a firmly fixed faith in the great verities of Christianity, why should I not labour to produce a like faith in those who come under the influence of my personality and my teaching?

If anywhere along the line, faith is shaken and the student finds himself denied the basis of faith itself and a nebulous basis of reason or hypothesis substituted, is that good Christian pedagogy?

To be specific: by any interpretation is it good teaching to question the historicity of the resurrection? or the virgin birth? or the records of the supernatural in the Scriptures?

Is it good teaching to suggest that, because He was man as well as God, Our Lord was therefore capable of erroneous beliefs and teaching?

Is it good teaching to give to students as *required* reading books which openly and flagrantly deny great sections of the Scriptures; eliminating or explaining away the supernatural, while at the same time these dangers and denials are not pointed out and labeled for what they are?

In very large measure the future of any church or group lies in the hands of those who teach in their colleges and seminaries. If there exists a theory of teaching which leaves the determination of truth or error entirely to the student then that would appear to be a very low concept of the privilege and responsibility of Christian pedagogy.

If those to whom is delegated the responsibility of teaching have themselves had their faith shaken until they are no longer able to give a positive reason for their faith then it would seem that their calling should be elsewhere.

There has rightly been criticism of those who have presented Christianity in terms of negation, for Christ and His Gospel are gloriously positive. In like manner, those who assume posts of teaching in Christian institutions should themselves have a positive faith and glory in the privilege of leading their students into the same positive position. When the positive element is one of "positive uncertainties" it may be "teaching" but it is not Christian teaching.

All of which leads us to say that Christian teachers have a duty and that duty is to strengthen faith, not hinder it. L.N.B.

Can It Be? America, a Second-Rate Power! !

We would not for one instant discount the fact that it is righteousness which exalteth a nation. Nor would we forget for one moment that our strength is in the Lord and not in armaments.

But, in the world in which we live, it is also a fact that lawlessness must be restrained by men of good will and righteous ideals who, when necessary, exercise physical force to curb evil.

This obtains in every community where there are laws and police to enforce those laws. Abolish the power to execute judgment and evil will take over. One is not unduly pessimistic when he admits that it is only the fear of punishment which restrains criminals and those with criminal tendencies and makes life safe for the community as a whole.

What has happened and is happening in America? Ever since World War II we have laboured on the assumption that Communism and those nations dominated by it can be restrained and contained by some measure of good-will, mutual recognition and the hope that the often repeated objectives of Communistic leaders are not to be taken at face value, but that Communism is really willing to go on living on a basis of peaceful co-existence with the rest of the world.

Operating on this basic philosophy we have conferred with, accorded mutual respect to and continued to look on Communism as a bad dream from which we shall awaken some day to find all peace and light.

During this era of wishful thinking, and looking away from realities, an almost unbelievable thing has taken place. Bewitched by Geneva and now lulled further by visits from Moscow to London, *America now finds herself on the verge of being a second-rate power.*

In his news analysis, broadcast over C.B.S. on Friday night, May 4th, Eric Severeid made the flat statement that for the first time in history America is faced with the strong possibility of becoming a military power eclipsed by Russia.

Already Russia has the largest submarine fleet in the history of the world. She has the largest standing army in the world. There is strong reason to believe that her air-power now equals ours and is increasing at a rate far surpassing ours. In the realm of nuclear science and atomic weapons, because of captured German personnel and know-how, she is almost abreast of our latest developments.

But, America has one potential for good to which Russia makes no claim and for which she has made no provision. In America men are still free to worship God and millions of them do put their trust in Him and honestly seek His will to do. It is in this area of life that America's hope lies. It is in God that any and all men may seek refuge.

As true as this is, why, oh why, do we continue on a course which could mean our own national destruction and the plunging of the world into the darkness of a war from which civilization might never recover?

On Sunday, May 6th, Dr. George Gallup, Director of the American Institute of Public Opinion, announced that in answer to the question: (The two leaders of Russia - Bulganin and Krushchev - have recently visited England) "Do you think they should or should not be invited to come to the United States to talk with Eisenhower and Dulles?"

This Gallup Poll revealed that 51% of those questioned thought they should be invited; 31% opposed and 18% had no opinion.

Two weeks ago a group of students at Princeton University invited a convicted perjurer and traitor to speak to them and while the University authorities disapproved of his coming they permitted the students to have their way and Alger Hiss spoke.

Today there is increasing disapproval of attempts to uncover Communistic infiltration in business, labor, government or education. For the first time in a decade a Communist can work with a sense of lessened tension and opposition on the part of those he is plotting to destroy.

What has happened to America? Is this a type of battle fatigue? Is it the soporific effect of repeated propaganda barrages designed to teach that we can do business with Communism; that peaceful co-existence is the only alternative to war?

We are probably affected by a multiplicity of causes, not the least of which is our national determination to have security, prosperity and good times *at any cost*, the surrendering of freedoms or otherwise.

This writer, on his own initiative and without involving this *Journal* as an organization, would affirm again that the only right way to deal with Communism is to *separate from it.* Within the country, where infiltration is proven, those guilty should be treated as spies and traitors. Outside of the nation there should be no diplomatic, political or economic ties whatsoever. *This would not mean war.* But, it would be the greatest single blow which could be aimed at the Communistic conspiracy around the world. Such a move would encourage those dormant and potential forces within Communist - dominated countries, would *discredit* Communism before the world and would open the way for a completely new appraisal of national and international morality.

At the present rate of deterioration and indifference; of complacency and compromise, the future is truly dark. We have changed but Communism has not. We are living in a twilight zone of wishful thinking, Communism is living

The Southern Presbyterian Journal, *a Presbyterian Weekly magazine devoted to the statement, defense, and propagation of the Gospel, the faith which was once for all delivered unto the saints, published* every Wednesday by The Southern Presbyterian Journal, Inc., in Weaverville, N. C.

Entered as second-class matter May 15, 1942, at the Postoffice at Weaverville, N. C., under the Act of March 3, 1879. Vol. XV, No. 3, May 16, 1956. Editorial and Business Offices: Weaverville, N. C. Printed in the U.S.A. by Biltmore Press, Asheville, N. C.

ADDRESS CHANGE: When changing address, please let us have both old and new address as far in advance as possible. Allow three weeks after change if not sent in advance. When possible, send an address label giving your old address.

in a state of alert and active advance, capitalizing on our own blindness and folly.

Or, is it the writer who fails to sense our "improved position"? Are we (and those who think as we do) the ones who fail to grasp the situation? Is our present course in the affairs of the world a safe and realistic one?

If the present trends are all right, then we are wrong. If, on the other hand, our thesis is Christian, and therefore right, our nation is headed for the brink of disaster.

Because of our dilemma, Christians should pray earnestly for guidance. In a year when political parties promise Utopia in exchange for votes, basic issues and concepts are often pushed into the background. We are truly a God-blessed nation. But we have not responded to God's goodness as we should. Nevertheless, within the nation there is a great host of men and women—the salt and the light of our social order—who owe it to themselves and to the world to pray that our eyes may be opened and that we shall determine our national and international policies on a basis of righteousness, and nothing else.

To that end we should pray daily. L.N.B.

Paul and Bodily Resurrection

According to the Easter accounts, the Risen Lord had a body with hands and feet, flesh and bones, Luke 24.39, yes "the same body which had been crucified," John 20.20,25,27. He ate before the eyes of the Apostles, Acts 10.41, and commanded them to handle Him with their hands in order to show them that He was no mere ghost. But these facts are often challenged by inferences drawn from I Corinthians 15, verses 44-46 and verse 50.

Several remarks may be made on this matter. First, some scholars, such as Dr. James Orr, posit a change in the body of the risen Christ at His Ascension to account for any differences between the Gospel of the Forty days and these verses in I Corinthians. While we mention this possibility, we do not endorse it.

Secondly, Paul did not surrender the Jewish doctrine of the resurrection of the body for something like the Greek doctrine of the immortality of the soul. His doctrine was defended by the Pharisees who taught the resurrection of the body, and opposed by the Sadducees and the Greek philosophers who rejected it, Acts 23.6-9; 17.31-32. According to Paul, all the fullness of the Godhead dwells in Christ in a bodily manner, Col. 2.9; and we look for the Saviour to change these bodies of our humiliation into the likeness of *the body* of His glory, Phil. 3.20. Paul starts the fifteenth chapter of First Corinthians with the common primitive Christian testimony to the resurrection, and his use of the figure of the seed and the stalk takes up an illustration much used by Jesus, cf. Jn.12.23f and several of the parables in the Synoptics. I Cor.15.35f looks back to Adam and the first creation, the Resurrection is a mighty act of God bringing in the new aeon in the last Adam. The whole is Christological, not philosophical. From Adam death reigned as a tyrant; through Christ believers reign in life Rom.5.17.

e' Barth, M., *Der Augenzeuge*, p.251.
c so Rengstorf, K.H., *Die Auferstehung Jesu*, p. 74.

Thirdly, Paul's description of the body as sown in corruption, dishonor, and weakness and raised in incorruption, glory, and power indicates the greatness of the change wrought in the Resurrection of Jesus Christ, as God's decisive step on the way to the final erection of His Kingdom. But the body thus described does not thereby cease to be a body; it is not changed from a physical body into a ghost. Paul does not describe the body which is sown as a *physical* body. The use of the adjective physical in the RSV of I Cor. 15.44-46 is an error in the translation of the Greek. The Apostle says: "it is sown a *psychical* (psychological, animate, or natural) body."

In contrast thereto, the resurrected body is not a non-physical or ghost body. It is a *Spiritual* body in the sense that it was raised by the Holy Spirit, Rom.8.11, Jas.2.26, and the Spirit is the life principle thereof. The same two adjectives, *psychical* ('natural') and *Spiritual* are contrasted in I Cor.2.13-15. Further, the adjective *Spiritual* in I Cor.10.3-4 does not mean that the manna in the Wilderness was non-physical or ghost bread, but real food given by the Holy Spirit.

Fourthly, *flesh and blood* in I Cor. 15.50 does not describe the physical side of man as against his mental and spiritual side, but rather it refers to human nature, generally sinful fallen humanity, in distinction from God or His Spirit, cf. Isaiah 31.3: Mt.16.17; Gal.1.16: Eph.6.12: Hebr.2.14. Moreover in I Cor. 15.50, *flesh and blood* is not the predicate but the subject of the sentence. The sentence is not: the resurrected life will not be flesh and blood only spirit or soul. It is: flesh and blood, that is human nature descending from Adam, cannot inherit the Kingdom of God by any worth, value or merit of our own - rather it will be changed by the Holy Spirit. Those who die in the Lord will be made alive at the coming of Christ, the life-giving Spirit. Those who remain will also be changed, and made like unto His glorious body. W.C.R.

Missions and the Mystery of Marriage to Christ

By George S. Lauderdale

"This is a great mystery: but I speak concern-ng Christ and the Church." Ephesians 5:32.

Christians are married to the Saviour. "Turn,) backsliding children, saith the Lord; for I .m married unto you." Jeremiah 3:14. Because he believer belongs to Christ, he is not to for-;et and forsake Him but to abide in Him, and vin many lost souls of the world to salvation. *'aithfulness insures fruitfulness.*

Spiritual wedlock with God's Son is joyful. 'Can the children of the bridechamber fast vhile the bridegroom is with them?" asked 'esus, in defense of His disciples' disregard of he mournful customs of unhappy religionists. Ie is the Bridegroom, as Psalm 45 also states, nd His followers are His bride; in the joy of Iis salvation Christians teach transgressors ;od's ways and sinners are converted to Him! This unhappy world needs such a glad testimony.

A New Life Mate

Before a person is born again he is not mar-ied to Christ but is in an adulterous and fatal mbrace with sin. The Lord sets believers free rom this unholy union by effecting their death, /hich always annuls the marriage tie, and makes ossible a new and glorious life with Him. "Ye lso are become dead to the law by the body f Christ; that ye should be married to another, ven to him that is raised from the dead, that /e should bring forth fruit unto God." Romans 7:4.

Shameful are the offspring of men given to vil who have not through Christ died to sin nd received Him as husband. "For we ourselves lso were sometimes foolish, disobedient, de-eived, serving divers lusts and pleasures, living n malice and envy, hateful, and hating one nother." Titus 3:3. Non-Christians everywhere oday are being enticed by their own lusts, and ust is conceiving, bringing forth sin, which /hen it is finished brings forth death.

Instead, souls can be united to Christ and ring forth fruit unto God. "The fruit of the pirit is love, joy, peace, longsuffering, gentle-ess, goodness, faith, meekness, temperance." ;alatians 5:22,23. "The fruit of the Spirit is n all goodness and righteousness and truth. . . . Iave no fellowship with the unfruitful works f darkness." Ephesians 5:9,11. Preaching :hrist is as proper as it is merciful!

Faith, Purity Become the Bride

The perfect Husband, Christ provides all our needs; let us trust Him therefore and seek first the kingdom of God and His righteousness. We can go into all the world and preach the gospel to every creature, caring nothing for what we shall eat or drink or wear because we are His.

Christ, chiefest among ten thousand and altogether lovely, must have a spouse whose appearance is also comely, particularly in her heart which is open to God's eyes. Sin lurks in the black recesses of the souls of unregenerate men, but Christ loved the church, gave Himself for it that He might sanctify and cleanse it with the washing of water by the Word, which discerns the thoughts and intents of the heart. His blood purges our very consciences! Hebrews 4:12; 9:14.

Submit to Christ

True believer, love your Husband and keep His command to go and teach all nations and baptize them into the same fellowship with the triune God which you enjoy. Honor and reverence Him that His favor may rest on you. "For after this manner in the old time the holy women also, who trusted in God, adorned themselves, being in subjection to their own husbands." I Peter 3:5.

Be clean in order to know His nearness and also to show the world that He is holy. "It is written, be ye holy; for I am holy." I Peter 1:16. Submit to His corrections for He would thus make you the more productive in winning souls. "Every branch that beareth fruit, he purgeth it, that it may bring forth more fruit." John 15:2.

AN APPEAL TO OUR SUBSCRIBERS

Let Each One Try To Get One or More New Subscribers to The Journal

See Back Page for Special Award Offer

ANGLERS

(From "*New Testament Evangelism,*" by Wade C. Smith)

Lesson No. 138

THE THIRD HUMAN ESSENTIAL (*Continued*)

A Surrendered Will. After all, this is the most necessary of all the human processes in personal work: the will surrendered to Christ. As in every other thing His disciples are enjoined to do, our Lord set the example in this. The very Saviour whom we would present to lost men, Himself at the most critical moment in His earthly career submerged His will in the will of the Father. "Nevertheless, not my will, but Thine be done." We may recognize the command, the authority and the urgency; we may have the most earnest desire to be a soul-winner; but if the will is not surrendered we will fail utterly. And, again, a once surrendering is not sufficient; there must be a continual surrender. Not only surrendering our will to Christ, to obey His command, but surrendering to do the thing in the *way* He wants it done. There will be fresh surrender all the way, for it is human nature to be continually getting off the track, and it is necessary that God may be continually getting us back on. The devil delights in planting fresh seeds of wilfulness in already surrendered soil. One subjugation of weeds in the garden will not do for the summer; we are constantly having to chop them down, or the good seed will have no chance to bear fruit.

There is another important thing about the surrendered will to Christ. It makes possible a very necessary and becoming humility. Without humility the soul-winner will make little if any progress. The absence of humility is a sure sign of misconception of one's status. If you are saved and on your way to heaven, it is not because of any merit of your own. "For by grace are ye saved, through faith; and that not of yourselves; it is the gift of God." (Eph. 2:8) "For if a man think himself to be something, when he is nothing, he deceiveth himself". (Gal. 6:3) "God resisteth the proud, but giveth grace unto the humble." (Jas. 4:6).

It is said that on one occasion, when the author of Pilgrim's Progress came upon a poor, drunken sot in the gutter, he paused and said: "But for the grace of God, there lies John Bunyan." We may not have been drunkards, thieves or roues; but if not, why not? God's grace is the only answer. We can claim no credit if we are fairly decent citizens. Who gave you a praying mother and the Christian background, which was denied the habitue of the slums? Surely no man can boast; surely every man who really thinks must be humble.

Here again our Lord leads in example, for He was meek and lowly. (See Matt. 11:29) He called His disciples to follow Him and become fishers of men. Have you ever seen a real fisherman slashing around, making himself conspicuous with a big noise? Far from it. His approach is with quietness—as little fuss as possible. Nothing more unpretentious than a fisherman angling - if he is good at catching fish.

*(The next three lessons will deal with "*THE METHOD*" in soul-winning)*

Helps To Understanding Scripture Readings in *Day by Day*

By Rev. C. C. Baker

Sunday, May 20, John 8:31-36. Jesus is speaking to those who have professed to believe in Him (vv.30-32). What is promised to those who become true disciples of Christ (v.32)? The truth Jesus speaks of is that which He learned from His Father (v.38) and that which was embodied in His Person (15:6). As you analyze the Jews' reaction to Jesus' promise (v.33) what element seems to be lacking in their understanding? To what type of freedom were they referring? What type of slavery does Jesus feel is more real than political slavery (v.34)? Think back to the sins in your life over which Christ has given you victory (v.36) and give Him thanks for true freedom.

Monday, May 21, Romans 8:29-39. God knew who would be His and called them into His family (vv.29-30). It cost Him the life blood of His only Son to accomplish this (v.32). Now, therefore, God will spare no effort to accomplish His purpose in our lives (vv.31,33,34,35-39). His purpose is that we be made into the likeness of His Son, Jesus Christ (v.29). If His purpose for us is also the purpose of our lives, is there any earthly thing that can keep it from being accomplished (vv.35-37)? Is there anything Satan or any of the powers of evil can do to prevent its fulfillment (vv.38-39)?

Tuesday, May 22, Ephesians 3:14-21. "For this cause" (v.14) refers back to the fact that, due to the coming of Christ, Gentiles as well as Jews are included in the promises of God (3:4-6). "For this cause" Paul prays earnestly for the Gentile Christians at Ephesus (v.14). Paul can pray for them because God dwells within their hearts (v.20). What is the channel through which God lives within the Christian (vv.16b-17)? Observe the tremendous resources

does the parable of vv.5-9 teach? What promise is given to those who "ask," "seek," "knock?" (vv.9-10)? What point does Christ make in vv.11-13 about answer to prayer? How do vv.11-13 make plain God's willingness to answer prayer? Verses 2-4 give suggested areas for prayer when coming to the throne of grace. Think of each of the petitions of the Lord's Prayer in terms of the insights into prayer given in vv.5-13. Will the Kingdom come (v.2) if you earnestly pray for it? What about the forgiveness of sins (v.4)? our daily food (v.1)? Are the themes of the Lord's Prayer a part of your prayer life?

Not One — But Seven Surprises!

When you begin to tithe, you'll be surprised at:

1. The amount of money you have for the Lord's work.

2. The deepening of your own spiritual life.

3. The ease with which you meet your own obligations with the 9/10ths.

4. The pleasure you'll find in larger giving.

5. The soul satisfaction in practicing stewardship of time, talent, possessions.

6. A new appreciation of the goodness of God.

7. Yourself . . . for not adopting the plan sooner.

LESSON FOR MAY 27

The Church In Asia Minor

Background Scripture: Acts 12:25 - 15:35
Devotional Reading: Isaiah 49:7-12

In our Devotional Reading from Isaiah we have a very definite prophecy concerning the entrance of the Gentiles into the Kingdom. "And I will make all my mountains a way, and my highways shall be exalted. Behold these shall come from far: and, lo, these from the north; and these from the land of Sinim." Paul and Barnabas were the instruments in God's hands of helping to make this prophecy come true. We study today what is usually called, Paul's First Missionary Journey. Barnabas and Saul had been sent to Jerusalem to carry the "Love Gift" which the Christians at Antioch had collected for the church at Jerusalem. (See 11:30 & 12:25)

I. *The Sending of the First Missionaries:* 13:1-4.

There were certain prophets and teachers in the church at Antioch, and as these ministered to the Lord, and fasted, the Holy Ghost said, Separate me Barnabas and Saul for the work whereunto I have called them. In these three or four verses we have some very important and fundamental principles given for the guidance of the church in its missionary work. The most important fact is the leadership of the Holy Spirit. The Holy Spirit *called* Barnabas and Saul: "whereunto I have called them." All true missionaries, and all true ministers, are called by the Holy Spirit. It is not a ministry or mission which is originated and manipulated by men. The Spirit spoke to men and used men to formally ordain and send the missionaries out, but the initiative was taken by the Holy Spirit. "Ye have not chosen me, but I have chosen you," said Jesus to His disciples. In this case the Spirit chose the two men who were to be sent on this most important mission. He has various ways of calling men, and of making His will known, and it is our business to obey the call when it comes. The Holy Spirit has His part, and the church has her part. Notice the two expressions: "They sent them away," (verse 3), and, "being sent forth by the Holy Spirit." Our Board of World Missions, representing the church, sends out our missionaries. Behind the "Board," however, the Great Head of the church through the Holy Spirit must be the real power working through the church's agencies. These men and women are ordained, as the first missionaries were, by prayer and the laying on of hands. We all know, however, that if they are to be real messengers, they must be equipped for their work by the Holy Spirit.

II. *Barnabas and Saul in Cyprus:* 13:4-13.

They departed from Seleucia and came to Cyprus, that birthplace of Barnabas who was a Levite from this large island. They preached first at Salamis in the synagogue of the Jews, and came on over to Paphos. Here they met opposition in the form of a sorcerer, a false prophet and Jew, whose name was Bar-jesus, or Elymas. This man withstood the two missionaries, trying to turn away the proconsul, Sergius Paulus, from the truth. Then Saul, (from now on called Paul) filled with the Holy Spirit, rebuked him in severe terms and pronounced the judgment of God upon him: The hand of the Lord is upon thee, and thou shalt be blind, not seeing the sun for a season. When the deputy saw what was done he believed, being astonished at the teaching of the Lord. Paul and his company sail from Paphos and come to Perga. John Mark leaves them and returns to Jerusalem.

III. *Antioch, in Pisidia,* (not to be confused with the other Antioch) 14-51, or 52.

From Perga they come to this city in Asia Minor. They went into the synagogue on the Sabbath day and after the reading of the Scripture they were invited to speak. Paul preached to them, giving a short resume of the history of Israel down to the time of David. Of David's seed God promised to raise up a Savior and this promise was fulfilled in Jesus. He shows them how John the Baptist had pointed out this Jesus as the Messiah. To them this word of salvation is sent. According to prophecy, which they read each Sabbath, but did not understand, they fulfilled this same prophecy in condemning Him to death, even when they found no cause of death in Him. Jesus was taken down from the cross and laid in the grave, "But God raised Him from the dead."

With this verse Paul comes to the main part of his sermon, the Resurrection of Jesus from the dead. This fact was proved by His being seen by competent witnesses for many days. His resurrection is also a fulfillment of Old Testament prophecy, which he proves by quoting from Psalm 2, from Isaiah 55, and from Psalm 16, where the psalmist says, "Thou shalt not suffer thine Holy One to see corruption." David died, and saw corruption, But He, whom God raised from the dead saw no corruption.

Having shown them, both from witnesses and from Scripture, that Jesus had indeed risen from the dead, he now proceeds to tell them that, "through this man is preached unto you the forgiveness of sins. All that believe are justified from all things from which they could not be justified by the law of Moses." Here we have the germ of the great doctrine of Justification by Faith, or by grace through faith which Paul elaborates in his epistles, especially Romans and Galatians. This is the heart of the Gospel. The church departed from this basic teaching and almost perished during the dark days preceding the Reformation. It was the rediscovery of this precious truth, and the earnest preaching of it, that revived the church.

He next warns them very solemnly in the words of Habakkuk 1:5, Behold, ye despisers, and wonder, and perish: for I work a work in your days, a work which ye will in no wise believe, though a man declare it unto you. Why do men stumble over the gracious offer of God to pardon all our sins because of the work of Christ? I suppose that pride and self-righteousness play a large part in this refusal. Salvation by grace does humble us, but it is the only sort that is available for a lost and ruined sinner.

This sermon had, at first, a tremendous effect. When the Jews were gone out the Gentiles besought that these words might be preached to them the next Sabbath, and a great many of the Jews and religious proselytes followed Paul and Barnabas, who persuaded and urged them to continue in the grace of God. The next Sabbath day almost the whole city came together to hear the word of God. It looked as though there would be a mighty revival in Antioch. "But when the Jews saw the multitudes, they were filled with envy, and spoke against those things which were spoken by Paul." This phrase, "But the Jews" is to become more and more familiar to us as we follow Paul in his journeys. The same spirit of "envy" which had caused the rulers to oppose and persecute and crucify Jesus, takes possession of the unbelieving and fanatical Jews and shows itself wherever Paul preaches.

Paul makes it plain to them that God's purpose will not be thwarted. It was necessary and fitting that the Jews should be given the first opportunity to accept Christ as their Messiah, and rejoice in that salvation. If, however, they refused to believe or accept the message, counting themselves unworthy of everlasting life, "lo, we turn to the Gentiles, for so hath the Lord commanded us saying, 'I have set thee for a light to the Gentiles, that thou shouldest be for salvation unto the ends of the earth.'" (See Isaiah 42:6 and 49:6). This was indeed "good news" to the Gentiles, and many of them glorified the word of the Lord and entered into eternal life.

"But the Jews" - again we come to that phrase - stirred up the devout and honorable women and chief men and raised a persecution against them and expelled them out of their coasts.

IV. *At Iconium:* 13:51-14:6.

As in Antioch, a great number of both Jews and Greeks believed, but the unbelieving Jews stirred up the Gentiles and evil affected their minds against the brethren. The storm which was gathering did not break at once, and for a long time they were able to speak boldly, and their preaching was attested by many signs and wonders done by their hands. The city became divided, and when an assault was made on them by the Gentiles and Jews and rulers, meaning to stone them, they were aware of it and fled to Lystra and Derbe.

V. *At Lystra:* 14:8-28.

They preached the gospel in all that region. At Lystra there was a man impotent in his feet, who never had walked. Paul, seeing that he had faith to be healed, commanded him to "Stand upright on thy feet." "And he leaped and walked." This miracle astonished the people and they began to acclaim them as "gods" come down in the likeness of men. They brought oxen and garlands and proceeded to worship them. This filled the missionaries with horror, and they ran in and stopped them, and besought them to turn from these vanities to the Living God.

Now the scene abruptly changes. Certain Jews came from Antioch and Iconium, and persuaded the people and they drew Paul out of the city and stoned him. He arose, however, and the next day departed to Derbe. After encouraging the brethren they returned to Antioch (in Syria).

VI. *The Council at Jerusalem:* 15:1-35.

A turning point in the Church.

Her Face Shone

This is a true story about a Japanese woman and the Gospel of Luke. Though it is true, we have never learned her name. We shall call her Mrs. Matsuyama.

We learned about Mrs. Matsuyama from a missionary in Japan. He told us how, during one of his trips into the high mountains of the central part of the Island of Honshu, he met her. It was cold winter, and he had plodded through new snow to a small village. Eight women and one man were sitting on cold straw matting around a tiny charcoal fire in a poor farmhouse. They had come there to worship and to hear the missionary. Together they sang hymns and prayed, and the missionary told us he remembered his sermon was about Jesus' call to Matthew.

There was one face that especially drew his attention. It was the face of one of the women. On her features were written peace and freedom. The simple service of worship ended, and the missionary left the village to walk back through the still cold to the railroad and then to his mission station in Tokyo. The man in the group walked with him, and it was from him that he gained an explanation of Mrs. Matsuyama's radiance and peace.

Her husband had died not long before. She was left with three children. It was 1952, and the collapse of Japan in the war was carved deep into the lives of her people.

The death of a husband was a tragedy immeasurable. Mrs. Matsuyama sought comfort at the Shinto shrine and prayed in the name of her departed ancestors. She went to the Buddhist priest, looking for peace in her heart; she made a pilgrimage to the sacred temples of Kyoto; it was in vain.

On one of the days, as she walked toward the village shrine, a schoolgirl came to her and brought her a booklet, much soiled and ragged. "Take it," the girl said; "I found it on the street. Somebody must have lost it. I read it; there is a wonderful story about a man who helps the helpless . . . "

Mrs. Matsuyama took the booklet. It was the Gospel of Luke.

She read it from beginning to end without stopping. Her life began again. Then she looked for Christians, but her whole district was untouched by the Church. She traveled to another town and learned of a missionary who lived there. He baptized her.

Our friend from Tokyo who told us this story said that the little congregation he found in her village was her congregation, sparked by her knowledge of the truth.

Atheism on Some College Campuses

Not long ago a rather frightening story came to our attention.

A young man, reared in a middle-class, God-fearing home, went away to a famous technical institute in the East. He was a well-balanced, happy, even brilliant boy, with sound and serene religious convictions.

In two years he changed completely. He was no longer calm and happy, but confused and defiant. He told his parents they were wrong about religion. He had learned, he said, that there is no God, and he had learned it from a mathematics professor!

This professor, it seems, was a "good fellow." He wore tweeds, smoked a pipe, and his home was always open to his students. There they gathered and talked things over. And there the professor planted his seeds of atheism.

His tool was ridicule; not blatant, but gentle and "reasonable." Religion, he argues, is a fine thing—for people who need it. But it is rather ridiculous, he insisted, for intellectuals to make something real out of intangible ideas that cannot be proved by physical formulas.

There's no telling how many young men this professor has poisoned. Nor is he alone.

Some time ago a mother called on us, worried about her son who was in a small middle western college. He, too, had become an ardent disciple of a professor. This man, idolized by his students, taught that the Bible is a collection of myths and folk-tales, interesting and valuable in a way, but certainly nothing to base one's life upon.

This young man, too, had become confused and unhappy.

Too often a witty and brilliant professor becomes the idol of his students. His influence is enormous.

Sometimes, we suppose, the professor is sincere in passing along his atheism. Again, he may be a left-winger, proselyting in the cause of godless Communism.

There aren't many such men on our campuses. Most professors are sound, normal people who teach what they're supposed to teach and let it go at that. And most of them are good church people themselves.

But it doesn't take many to do a lot of damage. One professor in a thousand can poison and confuse scores of youthful minds in the course of a semester.

What can we do?

Two things, in our opinion.

First, parents can prepare their boys and girls for such encounters. If a student has his guard up when a professor strays from his subject into religious subversion, he is not likely to get hurt. He might even start an argument with the professor and scuttle the whole thing at the start.

Secondly, we should have some laws that would require any educational institution, supported in any degree by public funds, to fire on the spot any professor or instructor caught teaching directly, or indirectly—on the campus or off it—that there is no God.

—From Amarillo, Texas, *Daily News*

How One Chairman Prepares for the Birthday Season

(A letter to her fellow-chairmen)

Dear Mrs. Livingston:

Your letter was waiting for me when I returned to my home after having had a wonderful visit to Ybor City Presbyterian Mission at Tampa. I wish that I could have received your letter before leaving for Florida and I would have gotten in touch with you via telephone during my visit there.

One of our projects in North Carolina this year is working out an itinerary for a guest Church Extension speaker in each of our nine Presbyterials for the Church Extension Season. Last year we did this in eight Presbyterials, but we have a small mountain Presbyterial that was afraid to try it. We hope that we can be 100% this year. I believe the most effective ways to create interest in the work are: (1) Invite Home Missionaries and Staff Members to speak in our churches and visit in our homes so that our people can learn to know them personally. 2) Plan "go-see" trips to nearby Home Mission fields. I feel that "one seeing" is worth a dozen "readings."

We have just recently had one of these "go see" trips. On February 10-14 we took 37 key women from our Synodical including our Synodical President via chartered Greyhound bus from Charlotte to Tampa for a tour of Ybor City and to learn first-hand of the work that is being done at our Mission there and of the proposed expansion program in West Tampa. We made a tour of a cigar factory to learn something of the working conditions of the people. Rev. Walter B. Passiglia (Director, Ybor City Presbyterian Mission) will speak in Mecklenburg Presbyterial from May 20-25. However, we have been unable to secure speakers for the month of May for the other eight Presbyterials. We are depending on the 37 women who shared in the wonderful experience of visiting the Mission to tell the story in their local churches. I have colored slides that we made at the Mission which I plan to use as many times as is possible throughout the Synodical.

On February 25 the following Synodical officers will meet to work out plans for presenting our Two-Fold Birthday Objective: President, Treasurer, Chairman of Stewardship, Chairman of Christian Education, and Chairman of Church Extension. We are asking each of these Synodical officers to write a letter to her corresponding officer in the local churches, to supplement letters that will be written by Presbyterial officers, concerning the Birthday Offering. For example: I will write to all local chairmen of Church Extension in the Synodical, a total of approximately 600 letters.

With further reference to planning for the women of the Synodical to visit Home Mission fields, you might be interested to know about the trips that we have made during the past few years:

1952-53 Guerrant Presbytery (5 trips) by automobile.

1953 Italian Mission, Kansas City, Mo., by plane.

1954 Indian Presbytery, Oklahoma, by bus.

1956 Ybor City, Tampa, Florida, by bus.

1956 In August a group of our women plan to visit Emmanuel Center, Baltimore, Md., by plane.

I have written this letter hurriedly and am not sure that I have given you anything that will help you in your work. Of course, the most important thing of all is for us to study our Handbook very carefully from cover to cover and try to do as many of the duties that are outlined for us as we possibly can do. It is impossible for us to do everything that is suggested. Then, these other things should follow.

I hope you plan to attend the Church Extension Conference. In the meantime, let me know about some of the things that you are planning to do in your Synodical.

Sincerely yours,

(Mrs. W. W.) Ruth F. McGinn
Chairman of Church Extension
North Carolina Synodical

YOUTH PROGRAM FOR MAY 27

What The Bible Says About Itself

Hymn: "My Hope Is Built On Nothing Less"
Prayer
Scripture: Psalm 19:7-14
Hymn: "Lamp Of Our Feet, Whereby We Trace"
Offering
Hymn: "How Precious Is The Book Divine"

PROGRAM LEADER:

(Supply the young people with Bibles, distribute the references before the program begins, and ask them to read the verses at the proper time.)

The Bible is a special book for us. We look to it for spiritual guidance and accept its teaching as true. What reasons have we for according this book such special honor? Throughout the years God's people have accepted the Bible's estimate of itself. Our experience and the experience of countless others assures us that we have not trusted the Bible in vain. We all have some idea of what the Bible says of itself, but in this program we shall try to put together in a systematic way some of the things which Scripture says concerning Scripture.

FIRST SPEAKER:

The Bible claims to be the inspired revelation of God. (Read II Tim. 3:16) The Bible also gives us a definition for inspiration. (Read II Pet. 1:21) This means that God has made Himself known through the agency of men who have written under the guidance of the Holy Spirit. That the Bible is the message of God is further indicated in the prefaces which many of the Old Testament writers used before their messages, such as: "Thus saith the Lord," "The Word of the Lord came unto me, saying . . .", and "Thus the Lord Jehovah showed me . . ". Christ, in His fifty-five recorded quotations from the Old Testament, evidently regarded them as the words of God. (Read Mark 12:36) Many other New Testament writers refer to Old Testament passages as the words of God or of the Holy Spirit.

All of these references have referred to the Old Testament. What has the Bible to say concerning the inspiration of the New Testament writers? This is what Jesus said of the apostles: (Read Luke 10:16; also John 14:26 and Mark 13:11). In I Corinthians 2:13 Paul speaks of his words as "that which the Holy Ghost teacheth." Concerning his message to the Thessalonians he said, "when ye received the word of God which ye heard of us, ye received it not as the word of men, but, as it is in truth, the word of God . . . " I Thess. 2:13. Regardless of what men may say about the origin of the Bible, the Scriptures themselves claim to be inspired.

The Bible claims to be a lasting and dependable authority in matters of faith and life. (Read II Timothy 3:16-17) In this passage the Bible claims to be able to produce a perfect or complete spiritual product. It makes this claim because it is authoritative in its ideas, "doctrine and reproof," and in practical matters, "correction and instruction in righteousness." In Psalm 19 it is claimed that the Scriptures can "convert the soul, make wise the simple, rejoice the heart, and enlighten the eyes."

Our Lord Jesus used the Scriptures to defeat Satan at the time of the temptations in the wilderness. In the fifty-five references Christ made to the Old Testament there are many appeals to the Bible as an authority. He even proves points by specific words indicating that He considers the very words to be authoritative. His quotations are taken from every section of the Old Testament Scriptures. He evidently considered all of Scripture to be true. Let us hear His exact words about the Scriptures. (Read Matthew 5:17,18) Now let us hear what He said about His own words. (Read John 8:14, 16 and Matthew 24:35).

When the Bible claims to be able to produce a complete spiritual product, it claims to be a fully sufficient guide for the spiritual needs of mankind. We know that the Bible tells us of the way to eternal life through Christ, and that is the most basic matter of all. Jesus warned the Scribes and Pharisees of the danger of substituting tradition for Scripture saying that they taught "for doctrines the commandments of men." Mark 7:7. The warning in the Book of Revelation could well be applied to the whole Bible. (Read Revelation 22:18,19).

THIRD SPEAKER:

The Bible tells us that it is a book which can be understood to those who come to it in faith. This is not to say that everything in the Bible is easy to understand, but it is to deny the idea that ordinary people are unable to interpret the Scriptures for themselves and that the church must tell them what to believe. The clarity of Scripture is indicated by these passages: (Read Psalms 19:86, 119:105, 130). The understandability of the Scriptures and the right of the people to interpret for themselves is implied in the words of Christ. (Read John 5:39) Concerning the Berean people it is written that "they searched the Scriptures daily . . . therefore many of them believed." It is through the hearing and reading of the Bible that faith comes to us. (Read Romans 10:17).

Of course, the church through its teaching ministry has the responsibility of helping the people in their study of the Bible. Scripture makes it clear that God honors the office of teacher, but even so, the people have the right to judge the teacher and his teaching, and the Bible is their standard of judgment. This was one of the great principles of the Protestant Reformation. Read Galatians 1:8. This passage shows that teachers, and even angels, can be wrong, that the people are responsible for measuring the words they hear, and that the standard of measurement is the revelation we have already received in the Scriptures.

PROGRAM LEADER:

Quite naturally, we have not considered everything the Bible has to say about itself. We have chosen to consider some of the clearer statements and have given thought to some of the most important claims the Bible makes for itself. What we have observed should surely heighten our belief in the Bible and increase our devotion to God and Saviour Who is revealed in this Book.

Church News

ADDITIONAL OVERTURES

(34) **Whereas,** Mrs. Kate Bitting Reynolds left a large sum in trust for the relief and support of aged an infirm ministers of North Carolina, and

Whereas, the Board of Annuities of the General Assembly make it a practice to reduce the amounts granted to ministers of North Carolina in proportion to the amounts paid to them by the Reynolds Fund, thus defeating the purpose of the Fund, which was intended by the Will of Mrs. Reynolds to give to the aged and infirm ministers of North Carolina additional support over and above that granted by the Board of Annuities.

Therefore, the Presbytery of Fayetteville respectfully overtures the General Assembly to review the Board of Annuities and Relief in granting aid and relief.

(33) The Presbytery of Winchester respectfully overtures the General Assembly to clarify the reporting of ruling elders and deacons in the statistical reports of sessions and presbyteries as to active or inactive status or both.

Announcement: Rev. and Mrs. J. V. N. Talmage announce the marriage of their daughter Janet Crane Talmage to Dr. Frank Goulding Keller Wednesday, April 25, 1956, in Chunju, Korea. Both the bride and groom are medical missionaries employed in the Presbyterian Medical Clinic in Chunju, Korea.

The ceremony was performed by Rev. R. K. Robinson of Mokpo. The couple are taking a short honeymoon in Japan, will reside in Chunju, and will continue their work in the Presbyterian Hospital there.

THREE MODERATORS: (left to right) — Rev. J. McDowell Richards, D.D., Moderator General Assembly; Rev. O. M. Anderson, D.D., Moderator Synod of Louisiana; Elder J. H. Nelson, Moderator of Red River Presbytery. This picture was taken at the Laymen's Convention recently held at Alabama Presbyterian Church, near Ruston, La., by George Crosby, of Bastrop, La.

Davidson, N. C. — James R. Morrill, III, Davidson College senior from Winston-Salem, has been awarded a $1500 graduate fellowship by Tulane University.

The award is for one year, and will enable him to pursue the M.A. degree in history. It is one of nine such fellowships given by Tulane to applicants from all over the United States.

J. Harold McKeithan, Jr., of Winston, Salem, a senior at Davidson College, has been named a Rockefeller Brothers Theological Fellow following nation-wide competition.

He will study this fall at the Union Theological Seminary of Richmond, Virginia, under the fellowship, which is valued at $1,025.

Report on Meeting of Winston-Salem Presbytery

The Presbytery of Winston-Salem convened for its 75th Stated Meeting at the Glendale Springs Presbyterian Church, Glendale Springs, N. C., May 1, 1956, at 10:00 a.m. 26 ministers and 29 ruling elders were enrolled. The Devotional Service in charge of the retiring moderator featured the singing by the choir of the Glade Valley School.

The Presbytery was called to order by the retiring moderator, the Rev. James R. Jackson, and the Rev. R. E. Hildebrandth was elected Moderator.

The Glendale Springs Church, located in the heart of the Blue Ridge Mountains, is one of a large Home Missions Field served by Dr. John W. Luke. It is doing an outstanding piece of work in this area.

Three ministers were received: the Rev. Ralph L. Underwood from the Presbytery of Fayetteville - he will be installed pastor of the Southminster Church, Winston-Salem, June 3. The Rev. Percy Carter, an ordained minister in the American Baptist Convention, was received upon examination. He takes charge of the new Negro work located in the Dellabrook Community of Winston-Salem. The Rev. Archie W. Jones, an ordained minister in the Moravian Church, was received upon examination and will be installed pastor of the Meadowview Church, Lexington, N. C., June 24.

The Rev. James R. Jackson's pastoral relation with the Jefferson Church was dissolved and he was granted a letter of transfer to Westminster Presbytery to take charge of a church in Tampa, Fla.

Dr. Harold J. Dudley, Executive Secretary of the Synod and Mr. Voyt Gilmore, Director of the Campaign to raise $3,500,000.00 for the Consolidated College, were present; the latter spoke on the progress of the Campaign.

Dr. James M. Carr of the Assembly's Board of Church Extension was present and spoke briefly on the work of his department.

The chairman of the Presbytery's Committee on Church Extension, the Rev. Graham McChesney, and the Rev. P. J. Garrison, Jr., Executive Secretary of Church Extension, spoke on several promising projects for Church Extension in the Winston-Salem area. Presbytery authorized the purchase of several sites for future use.

The next Stated Meeting of the Presbytery will be held at the First Presbyterian Church, Winston-Salem, September 11, 1956.

J. Harry Whitmore, Stated Clerk

Nashville, Tenn. — The Board of World Missions in Nashville announced that it has received word of the April 10 arrival of a son, Nelson Bell, in Chunju, Korea, to Rev. and Mrs. John N. Somerville of our Korean Mission.

Mr. Somerville is the son of Rev. and Mrs. W. G. Somerville of Barnardsville, N. C. He received his education at Presbyterian College and Columbia Theological Seminary. He is a member of Asheville Presbytery.

Mrs. Somerville is the former Miss Virginia Bell, daughter of Dr. and Mrs. Nelson Bell of Montreat, N. C. She is a graduate of Wheaton College, and Johns Hopkins Hospital School of Nursing. She is a member of the Montreat Presbyterian Church.

Memphis, Tenn. — At a meeting of the Memphis Presbytery, held April 24 at Frayser Presbyterian Church, the Rev. Norman B. Gibbs was elected to a three-month term as moderator. Mr. Gibbs is the pastor of the First Presbyterian Church in Jackson, Tenn.

The Presbytery accepted the resignation of the Rev. A. Clarke Dean in order that he might continue his service at another church. Mr. Dean, the pastor of Buntyn Presbyterian Church, will become associate pastor of Myers Park Presbyterian Church in Charlotte, N. C. The resignation of Rev. Charles A. Harper was also accepted at the meeting. Rev. Harper, pastor of the Frayser Church, has reached the church's retirement age of seventy.

The Rev. E. M. Nesbitt, Central Treasurer of the Presbytery, announced that member churches gave $76,000 to benevolent causes during January, February and March.

The next meeting of the Presbytery will be July 17, at Marl Bluff Church near Henderson.

Change of Address:

Rev. John B. Pridgen, Jr., from Statesboro, Ga., to P. O. Box 6065, North Augusta, S. C., Fairview Presbyterian Church.

Nashville, Tenn. — Dr. Marshall Scott, Dean of the Presbyterian Institute of Industrial Relations at McCormick Theological Seminary, Chicago, gave the key address at a Synod-wide young people's retreat in Tennessee.

The Tennessee Synod Spring Retreat for young people was held at Nacome Camp on April 20-22 and had for its theme, "Tall Buildings and Little Men." Some 167 college students attended.

Houston, Texas — A call to make "churches the focal point for seven days a week activity, not just Sunday alone" was sounded in Houston by Hal Hyde, Secretary of the Urban Church Department of the Board of Church Extension. At an April city-wide conference on churches and the changing city, sponsored by the research and survey committee of the Council of Churches, Mr. Hyde said that this could be achieved by proper planning before a church was built.

He gave as examples of proper planning, picking a location near a community focal point, such as a school or shopping center, and building on a site of from three to five acres so that parking, landscaping, and recreation could be provided for.

San Antonio, Texas — The Rev. Joel E. May, Minister of Education of the First Presbyterian Church of San Antonio, Texas, has been called by the same congregation to become the Associate Minister. He will serve in the fields of Education and Administration.

BOOKS

BIBLE DOCTRINE: A Junior High Workbook on the Westminster Shorter Catechism. Unit One; Book Two. Dorothy Partington. The Committee on Christian Education, the Orthodox Presbyterian Church, Phillipsburg, New Jersey, 1955. $1.50, Teacher's edition; $1,25, Student's workbook.

Not long ago our review of Book One of this series of four workbooks appeared. Book Two has now been published and merits every bit of praise paid to the first. The author is well qualified in training and experience to present Bible doctrine based upon the Shorter Catechism that is both true to the Bible and relevant to the needs and problems of young people. The author is not content that the answers of the Catechism be memorized without understanding; therefore the workbook-discussion approach is used.

Book Two follows the same form as Book One. There are fifteen lessons with such titles as: Christ As Our Prophet, The Way to God, Dead Men Live! Growing in Goodness, The Christian's Hope, etc. A question from the Shorter Catechism is printed at the beginning of each lesson, and the pupil is sent to the Bible to find the answer substantiated and to his everyday life to see its applicatio. The pupil is always driven to see the beliefs of the Christian Faith as directly related to his own needs. The workbook supplies space for answers to completion, multiple choice, true-false, and essay type questions. In addition, the fine illustrations attract even the interest of adults.

This workbook carries us through question 38 of the Catechism, completing the section of "what man is to believe concerning God." "The doctrines covered in this part of the catechism are basic to a profession of faith on the part of the children. Every bit of Biblical knowledge and teaching skill which you have should be directed to clarifying each child's understanding of the person and work of Christ and to confront him with the question, 'Have I put my faith in the Savior?' "

We who have so long suffered from the lack of regular catechetical instruction now have no excuse for not presenting our young folks with the best material possible for a vital and intensive study of the basic doctrines of the Reformed Faith. These workbooks could easily be used in communicant classes or vacation Bible school, but the wealth of suggestive material could also be put to use in Senior High Fellowship groups or serve as well as the basis for midweek doctrinal studies for the whole church.

—Albert H. Freundt, Jr.

THE ORDAINED LAMPSTAND. Edwards E. Elliott. 10 cents. **ARE YOU A BIBLICAL BAPTIST?** George M. Marston. 15 cents. The Committee on Christian Education, the Orthodox Presbyterian Church, Phillipsburg, N. J., 1955.

These two booklets represent efforts on the part of the Orthodox Presbyterian Church to give Christians some understanding of their relations to the visible church and its sacraments. Mr. Elliott points to the Biblical teaching that the visible church is present when preaching is based upon the Word of God, when the sacraments are administered with discretion, and when there is a recognized discipline. He gives brief attention to the Scriptural evidence for Presbyterian government, mentioning additional material for further reading. He stresses the obligations and responsibilities for corporate witness and worship involved in membership vows. By demonstrating that the visible church is inescapable, he indicates that those who belittle the organized churches are removed from the Biblical and Presbyterian concept of the nature of the church.

Mr. Marston has prepared an excellent booklet on the Calvinistic view of baptism. After referring to Scripture, he concludes that baptism signifies cleansing from sin and union with Christ and that it is rightly performed by sprinkling. But this is not done without examination of the alleged immersion passages. The right of the children of believers to baptism is based upon the doctrine of children as included in the covenant of grace. The names of more advanced books on the subject are listed for those who wish to do further study. These two booklets are fine examples of tracts that can be put into the hands of members of all Presbyterian churches to give individuals some understanding of their beliefs and supply them with information for those who would oppose the Biblical basis of our church and sacraments. Both are well written and inexpensive enough for wide distribution.

—Albert H. Freundt, Jr.

THE SOUTHERN PRESBYTERIAN JOURNAL

A Presbyterian weekly magazine devoted to the statement, defense and propagation of the Gospel, the faith which was once for all delivered unto the saints.

MAY 23, 1956

BOARD OF WORLD MISSIONS ISSUES STATEMENT ON MEMBERSHIP IN JICU AND JNCC

The following telegram was received just as we were going to press:

NASHVILLE — In a unanimous action the Board of World Missions today approved the following statement:

"We recognize the value of the Japanese International Christian University to the Christian cause in Japan, and we approve of our missionaries unofficially cooperating with the JICU in any way that seems practicable to them.

"Further, we would favor becoming a member of the JICU Foundation in New York when it sees its way clear to put in its constitution the doctrinal basis of the World Council of Churches, which affirms the acceptance of Jesus Christ as God and Saviour." The Board in addition approved the cooperation of its Japan mission with the Japanese National Council of Churches, on the basis of of associate membership. This is the only type of membership open to the missionary group in that country, and is a non-voting relationship.

Both actions came after the Japanese Mission of the Church, reviewing its position at the request of the General Assembly and the Board, voted 27-23 in favor of membership in the National Council, and 26-25 in favor of the JICU.

**Let Us All Be Much in Prayer for the Meeting of the General Assembly
The Meeting Will Open on Thursday Evening, May 31st at 7:30 P.M.**

VOL. XV NO. 4

$2.50 A YEAR

THE SOUTHERN PRESBYTERIAN JOURNAL
The Journal has no official connection with the Presbyterian Church in the United States
Rev. Henry B. Dendy, D.D., Editor....Weaverville, N. C.
Dr. L. Nelson Bell, Associate Editor....Asheville, N. C.
Rev. Wade C. Smith, Associate Editor....Weaverville, N. C.

EDITORIAL

A Significant New Venture

For more than a year plans have been quietly under way for what may well prove to be one of the most significant developments in Protestantism in our generation.

On October 15th a new Christian magazine will begin publication. This is to be called CHRISTIANITY TODAY. The name itself is significant and was chosen because those responsible for it are determined to present Christianity as a vital force relevant to every individual and society as a whole in the day in which we live.

About fifty Contributing Editors in America and abroad have been secured and a like number of world correspondents. An amazing response has come from more than a thousand individuals who were contacted to provide the funds necessary in the formative period. This response has been equally enthusiastic in Christian circles from which articles, editorials and sermons will be drawn.

The format of the magazine is dignified and distinctive. It will be published fortnightly and the annual subscription rate is $5.00 per year. Editorial offices are located in the Washington Building, Washington, D. C., and the magazine will be printed by the McCall Corporation at their Dayton, Ohio, plant.

This *Journal* is particularly interested in this venture because our own Associate Editor has shared in the ground work necessary in such a large task and because he will be Executive Editor of the magazine. Due to his health, and to make this possible he has been led to relinquish his large and successful surgical practice to devote his full time to work for this *Journal* and for *Christianity Today.*

Newspapers across the country have recently carried considerable space with reference to the new magazine and *Time* has also picked up the story.

The Editor is Dr. Carl F. H. Henry, formerly professor of theology at Northern Baptist Seminary in Chicago and currently professor of Christian Philosophy at Fuller Theological Seminary in Pasadena, California. The Associate Editor is Rev. J. Marcellus Kik, Dutch Reformed pastor and author of a number of books. The Managing Editor is Larry E. Ward, formerly Managing Editor of Christian Life and recently associated with the Gospel Light Press, producers of the literature used in the Hollywood Presbyterian Church and many other evangelical churches across the nation.

—H.B.D.

The following news release has been received from the Washington offices:

CHRISTIANITY TODAY

Suite 1014 - Washington Building
Washington 5, D. C.
DISTRICT 7-1753

May 3, 1956

Formation of a new religious magazine with impressive circulation throughout the English-speaking world was announced today in Washington, D. C.

To be known as *Christianity Today,* the new publication will be issued bi-weekly, with initial distribution scheduled for October 15.

Editor will be Dr. Carl F. H. Henry of Pasadena, California, who leaves his post as professor of Christian Philosophy at Fuller Theological Seminary to head the editorial staff. Associate editor will be the Rev. J. Marcellus Kik, well-known Dutch Reformed minister and author. Executive editor is Dr. L. Nelson Bell, Asheville, North Carolina, surgeon and for many years a contributor to church periodicals. Managing editor is Larry Ward, former managing editor of *Christian Life* magazine.

Editorial appointments and publication plans were announced by Dr. Harold John Ockenga, chairman of the magazine's board of directors and minister of famed Park Street Church in Boston. He also disclosed a staff of fifty contributing editors representing major denominations, and the additional names of fifty correspondents stationed around the world.

Editorial, circulation and advertising departments of *Christianity Today* will be located on the tenth floor of the Washington Building, overlooking Pennsylvania Avenue and the White House. The magazine will be printed by McCall Corporation in Dayton, Ohio, and has contracted for an initial distribution of 200,000 copies.

"*Christianity Today* will be designed primarily for the clergy," stated Editor Henry, "but the informed layman will be kept in mind." The magazine will aim to present evangelical Christianity "competently, attractively and effectively," he added. "It will advance the basic truths of Christian faith in a positive and constructive way, applying the biblical view vigorously to contemporary life."

Contributing editors include prominent evangelical leaders from Britain and the Continent as well as the United States. Among them are Professor G. C. Berkouwer, Dutch theologian; Dr. Geoffrey W. Bromiley and Professor Norman Hunt of Scotland; Professor F. F. Bruce, Dr. W. E. Sangster, and Dr. J. C. Pollock of England; Dr. Pierre Marcel of France. Americans on the list include Lt. General William K. Harrison of the Caribbean Command, U. S. Armed Forces; Professor W. Stanford Reid, McGill University, Montreal; Professor Andrew W. Blackwood, Temple University School of Theology; Dr. Edward L. R. Elson, minister of National Presbyterian Church, Washington, D. C.; Dr. Billy Graham, Montreat, North Carolina; Dr. Robert J. Lamont, First Presbyterian Church, Pittsburgh; Bishop Arthur J. Moore, The Methodist Church, Atlanta; Dean Stanley W. Olson, Baylor University College of Medicine, Texas; Professor William Childs Robinson, Columbia Theological Seminary, Decatur, Georgia; Dr. Samuel M. Shoemaker, rector of Cavalry Episcopal Church, Pittsburgh, and others.

Modern in format, and reflecting in title and typography the combination of a rich heritage and contemporary relevance, *Christianity Today* will normally run forty pages, increasing at times to forty-eight. The subscription price will be five dollars a year.

The editors announced the following objectives of the new venture: to articulate competently and fitly the central doctrinal distinctives of historic Christianity; to animate the New Testament sense of the unity of believers in Jesus Christ as the only Savior and God, by setting forth the Bible doctrine of the Church; to proclaim the unity of the revelation of God in nature and Scripture, and hence to exhibit the compatibility of true science and revealed religion; to reaffirm and reinterpret the basic implications of historic Christianity concerning the liberty as well as the value of man in the realm of political economy and societal relations, thus applying the biblical revelation vigorously to the contemporary social crisis; to stress the enduring spiritual and moral qualities contributory to national stability and survival; to exhibit the aggressive world impact of Christian missions, evangelism and education; and to disclose the doctrinal fallacies and weaknesses of the speculative theologies and philosophies of religion.

"Reactionary" or Stable

No one likes to be called reactionary for the word is associated with those who are attached to the status quo and opposed to progress.

It is pleasant to be termed liberal and progressive, but again such terminology can be misleading.

When Christianity is under discussion we all will be wise to clearly define our terms and consider their implications, for it is perfectly possible to advocate changes which have in them no elements of progress and it is also possible to try to shake foundations which must remain steady if the efficiency of the Christian witness is to be maintained.

A Basic Truth

There is urgent need that the content of the Christian message shall not be sacrificed on the altar of ecclesiastical expediency. By this we mean that *at all costs* that which constitutes the Gospel message shall be maintained and proclaimed. To insist on this vitally important consideration is not to be reactionary, it is to be stable where stability means everything.

Strange to say, we have been living in a generation where considerations other than the

The Southern Presbyterian Journal, *a Presbyterian Weekly magazine devoted to the statement, defense, and propagation of the Gospel, the faith which was once for all delivered unto the saints, published* every Wednesday by The Southern Presbyterian Journal, Inc., in Weaverville, N. C.

Entered as second-class matter May 15, 1942, at the Postoffice at Weaverville, N. C., under the Act of March 3, 1879. Vol. XV, No. 4, May 23, 1956. Editorial and Business Offices: Weaverville, N. C. Printed in the U.S.A. by Biltmore ffices: Weaverville, N. C. Printed in the U.S.A. by BiltmorePress, Asheville, N. C.

ADDRESS CHANGE: When changing address, please let us have both old and new address as far in advance as possible. Allow three weeks after change if not sent in advance. When possible, send an address label giving your old address.

actual content of Christianity have often been given the priority. This can only mean that there has been a lessening importance attached to Christian doctrine and a larger emphasis accorded ecclesiastical organization and procedure.

We are frank to admit that strongly held convictions on matters of minor import have been and can be a hindrance to Christian fellowship and progress. But a lack of conviction on the essential elements of Christianity strike at the very heart of an effective witness and add confusion where clarity is so very important.

Effect on Preaching

George W. Cornell, Associated Press writer on religion, recently had a column in which he quoted a number of well-known churchmen who confessed that much of today's preaching is "trivial and trite and feeble." Methodist, Presbyterian and Lutheran leaders were quoted, deploring the lack of preaching of a vital message and characterized by obvious lack of power.

Where does such preaching come from? From a lack of convictions on what constitutes the Christian message. That there are signs that this is changing is encouraging; that there is a need for such a change should be obvious to all.

A Changed Emphasis

Unconsciously but irrevocably there has been a tendency to change the emphasis from man's need for personal redemption (the very heart of the evangel), to a demand that man reform himself and the society of which he is a part. Without realizing it we believe many have preached a humanistic philosophy which has magnified the creature and brought the Creator down to man's level.

Unregenerate man has looked on this kind of religion as hardly worthy of consideration. If this concept is true then man is the master of his own soul and of his own destiny. But there is something which tells him this is a travesty on the demands which Christ would make of him.

A Need for Stability

The Christian faith is a stable faith for it is built on that foundation which cannot be moved - Jesus Christ, the eternal Son of God. To maintain that Christian truth has not changed through the years is to maintain that man's need has not changed and that God's remedy also has not changed. If so to maintain is "reactionary" then God give us more men of that stamp.

This does not for one minute mean that methods and approaches do not change. The church or minister who would carry out its program with the same methods used even a few decades ago would rightly be called reactionary. Every new avenue and method of preaching the Gospel should be harnessed and used. But, the basic message is the same in every generation and to all generations.

Misguided Zeal

In one's determination to maintain the Gospel message in its fullness and purity it is not only possible but it also unfortunately happens that men have and do exercise a misguided zeal which is equally harmful.

Where contending for the faith becomes contentiousness it makes a travesty of Christianity. Where Christian love and fellowship are marred by unworthy words and actions there is something basically wrong, for the Holy Spirit is grieved and the body of Christ made to suffer.

Christian ethics must motivate and control every effort to maintain Christian truth. To have it otherwise is to do untold harm to the very cause one is zealous to promote.

A Needed Clarification

Who suffers when Christian truth is neglected? Those who need that truth for their eternal welfare. Who suffers when misguided zeal leads to loveless words and acts? The same needy souls outside of Christ, *plus* the Church, the body of Christ.

For that reason there is great need that all who name the name of Christ shall distinguish clearly between those things which are an essential part of Christianity itself, and those interpretations on which men of equal piety and spiritual perception may differ.

Also, there is great need that there shall be a clear distinction between policies, methods, objectives and organizations on the one hand and the proclaiming of Christ and Him crucified, for it is the Person and Work of Christ which alone give relevance to preaching and living.

A Needed Authority

Various theories of inspiration have made a shambles of biblical interpretation and preaching. The greatest need in the whole area of Christianity today is a return to faith in the full integrity and authority of the Scriptures. Without such faith preaching lacks something vital. Without such faith man's reason inevitably takes more or less precedence over divine revelation.

But, where there is a wholesome, yes, even child-like acceptance of the divine record, there is found a spiritual power and effectiveness which otherwise is woefully lacking.

hammedans for Christ in the province of a single church in central Java and led to their baptism. Christians are taking vigorous interest in all the concerns of life. The students are being confronted with the Gospel. The new churches are rejoicing to find in the ecumenical movement an opportunity of making their voices heard in the world Church.

The little Church in Kalimantam has grown from 15,000 to 30,000 since the beginning of World War II. The Basler Mission is working in close unity with this young Church, giving financial help, sharing in the theological work and buildings and women's work.

—Translated and summarized by WCR.

THE CHRISTIAN VIEWPOINT

Today there is a medical doctor teaching in a great university school of medicine. Back in the depression that young man finished high school in southeastern North Carolina. He wrote for a college catalog in the spring. Nothing else was heard from him about attending college. One of the faculty members was asked to look him up on a trip to Wilmington and find out if he planned to come to college.

He found the young man working in a little crossroads filling station and store, pumping gasoline, checking oil, and selling fatback and snuff to field hands. "I thought I'd better give up the idea of going to college," he said. "It's depression times. Father doesn't have much money. Many people don't have a job. I do, and I decided I had better keep it."

"If I could get you a scholarship of $100.00 do you think you could make it?" asked the faculty member.

"Yes, I think I could."

So he came to Presbyterian Junior College and today is teaching medicine to future doctors. Not long ago, in an emergency, I called one of the doctors he has taught.

Our young people are our greatest national wealth. We need to use, and not waste, our nation's brain power. The Soviet Union has 4,300,000 students enrolled in post high school courses, while we in the United States this year have only 2,533,000 in colleges. (Benton Reports, p.9) Scholarships which encourage young people to use their talents are a good investment.

"Cast thy bread upon the waters, for thou shalt find it after many days." (Ecclesiastes 11:1)

Department of Bible, Presbyterian Junior College, Maxton, N. C.

ANGLERS

(From *"New Testament Evangelism"*

by Wade C. Smith)

Lesson No. 140

THE METHOD

"I am astonished to know how easy it is to get the people if you really want them. I am yet more astonished at the miraculous way in which a single spark of enthusiasm for souls, once kindled, is able to pass like a flame through a great church, and set it moving in a crusade of love, pity and human service."—W. J. Dawson

Bear in mind these lessons are dealing with the subject from the standpoint of the individual soul-winner. It is not what the Church ought to do nor what the preachers ought to do, but "What I ought to do" that is of first importance. Let one first go into executive session with the Lord and himself on this proposition, to get his bearings.

Every unsaved person my responsibility. Every unredeemed sinner in my community is a liability on my account with God. The only way I can clear the account is by an honest effort to reach each one of them personally with the message, or show a valid reason, acceptable in God's sight, why I did not. It is a large task, requiring time and thought and prayer.

Even if one had nothing else to do, this task would call for some orderly system of procedure. A method (or system) is all the more necessary for folks who have many demands upon their time. Therefore, let each worker organize himself for the most effective soul-winning program. He has recognized the Challenge; he has noted the Equipment at hand; he believes the Holy Spirit has the regenerating power, and that this power can be secured through prayer - and he has viewed the "Three Essentials" which he may possess. Now it only remains for him to proceed - with method. At the same time let us not exalt mere method above its appointed place. There may be times when the earnest soul-winner, impelled by sudden impulse, under the guidance of the Holy Spirit, will do something different, quite apart from any method, apparently. But God has given us minds for planning; and His orderly processes, as well as our own experience, encourage us to train our efforts in some orderly arrangement. Therefore, Method.

Discovering "Prospects." A prospect in this case is an unsaved soul. Usually, when one first faces the challenge of soul-winning, there are one or more prospects already in mind. Sometimes the prospect, himself, constitutes the challenge. Often the prospects are so close by as to be an embarrassment to timid beginners, rather than something to be sought. These ought to be bravely dealt with, without delay. It does not help to be trying to win one over there, while dodging one over here. The very fact of embarrassment is evidence that faith is being tested; and remember, faith is a big factor in this engagement. "Beyond the Alps, lies Italy." The Alps must be crossed first.

However, the soul-winner should have a method for discovering prospects. This is a much simpler matter than the beginner might suppose. Your private list of prospects will include, first, all those unsaved persons of your acquaintance or within your knowledge. It is good to have a written list. Keep it in your private note book, or on cards in a place with your intimate belongings. You need not label it. Then, if misplaced, and picked up by someone else, no harm would be done. The list will figure in your daily intercession; it will give character and purpose to prayer. But that is a phase of the subject for treatment at another time. We will continue "finding prospects" in the next lesson.

Helps To Understanding Scripture Readings in *Day by Day*

By Rev. C. C. Baker

Sunday, May 27, *Luke* 4:16-21. A home-town boy who makes good comes back to Nazareth to preach. Observe how He had been received in other places (vv.14-15). What is the theme of His message in vv. 18-21? Is verse 22 a typical reaction of home-town folk? What were the people of Nazareth looking for Him to do (v.23)? Because they thought they knew Him so well, they had little genuine faith in His miraculous power (Mark 6:2-3), and Jesus was unable to perform any miracles among them (Mark 6:5-6). Even Gentiles had more faith than they (vv.25-27). What does vv.28-29 reveal of their real attitude toward Jesus? Have you become so familiar with the great Biblical truths that you are no longer appreciative of their true greatness and power?

Monday, May 28, *Luke* 3:8-14. John the Baptist used some very strong language in talking to the crowds (v.7). The people to whom he spoke were overly proud of their religious heritage (v.8). What did he call upon them to do (vv.8a,13,14a)? He threatened judgment if they did not repent (v.9), yet notice the response of the people (vv.7a, 10). What was

Friday, June 1, James 3:10-18. There were evidently those in the churches to which James was writing that were primarily interested in getting ahead of everyone else (vv.14,16), lording it over others as teachers (v.1). While pretending to be authorities on religion, they were reviling each other (vv.9-10) and setting a very poor Christian example (vv.14-15). Observe the power of the tongue (vv.3-5). It can do terrible damage to the church if it is not controlled (vv.6-10). James presents the need for the wisdom that is from above, that is, the wisdom that is a fruit of the Spirit (v.17). How would the qualities of v.17 meet the need of the congregations to which he wrote? What Christian qualities would replace the jealousy and selfish ambition existing in the lives of these Christians (vv.13,18)? Is there anything in your conversation resulting from jealousy or selfish ambition that hurts the life of your church? Pray for more of the wisdom of v.17.

Saturday, June 2, Luke 12:15-34. The main point of the passage is found in v.15. How does Jesus make this point real in the parable of vv.16-21? Why did God call the man a "fool" (v.20)? Are there times when the sin of covetousness causes you to be a "fool" in this respect? What does Jesus say a person should put first in his life (vv.31-34)? What advantages does heavenly treasure have over earthly treasure (vv.20,21,33)? What promises are there in vv.22-31 of God's concern for our physical needs? Are the illustrations used in vv.24-29 valid? Has God provided for your physical needs? What kind of "riches" do you prize the most?

"I Charge You . . ."

By Rev. Albert G. Harris, Jr.

(Charge given to young minister on the occasion of his ordination and installation as pastor).

Paul spoke in Ephesians 6 of the armor of the Christian soldier with which he is able to fight the hosts of wickedness.

I would like to speak of the man of God within the armor and of his life with the saints. It is necessary to fight militant evil, but our daily task is to live with imperfect good.

However, I would not tell you to do great things or to exhibit vast virtues. I would simply charge you to pray certain prayers. These prayers are my own and I charge you to share in them.

First, I charge you to pray that God would give you strong teeth in order that you may bite your tongue when you are tempted to speak but should remain silent. Preachers talk a great deal. Oftentimes they talk so much that they do not take time to listen to other people.

And it is extremely difficult to talk much without saying wrong things.

The Bible lays great emphasis upon the tongue. In the third chapter of James the tongue is compared to a fire. A small fire, out of control can do great damage. So with our tongue. "With it we bless the Lord and Father and with it we curse men who are made in the likeness of God" (James 3:9).

Bite your tongue when on the tip of it are words which would wound and alienate. We must speak the truth but we can always speak the truth in love (Ephesians 4:15).

I charge you also to pray that God will give you steady hands to hold the Bread of Life out to hungry people. Jesus said, "I am the bread of life" (John 6:48). It is your highest privilege to share Him with others. There are many people who are spiritually hungry all around you. But strangely enough many of them do not want to eat. I understand that people can be physically undernourished in the midst of abundant food. They eat enough but the food they eat does not contain sufficient vitamins and minerals for their physical needs. So it is with many who are spiritually starving. They may reject the Bread of Life, but it is still your task to hold Him forth to them. God has chosen us as "Ambassadors of Christ, God making His appeal through us" (II Corinthians 5:20). On the one hand, God's appeal; on the other hand, frail men. We have this treasure in earthen vessels. But let not the vessel fail to contain the message. Pray God for steady hands to hold forth the Bread of Life.

Third, I charge you to pray for a sensitive nose to smell trouble before it becomes tragic. The pastor's task is to care for the flock which God has given him. The purpose of God's grace in his own life is that it may be used. Our God is the "God of all comfort, who comforts us in all our affliction, so that we may be able to comfort those who are in any affliction, with the comfort with which we ourselves are comforted by God" (II Corinthians 1:3, 4).

Think particularly of the timeliness of your presence. In the New Testament there is a word "Kairos" which means "the right time," "the particular moment of need or fulfillment." There are times when you can help others and times when you cannot. Pray that you may be there at the right time. Opportunities which pass sometimes never return. There is no one who has not missed such opportunities, but if we are alert and ready to go in spite of previous plans and in response to present need, we shall miss few opportunities to help.

Finally, I charge you to pray God for stout toes which may be stepped on without a squeal of protest. After all, it was Christ who endured revilings without reviling back. This quality of life is the one quality most insisted upon in the New Testament. We pray "Forgive our debts," and we immediately must add, "as we forgive our debtors." Jesus pointed out that we are to love our enemies and to expect nothing in return. This is to be "sons of the Most High; for He is kind to the ungrateful and selfish" (Luke 6:35).

The most celebrated word of all is defined by such kindly actions. "Love does not insist on its own way; it is not irritable or resentful" (I Corinthians 13:5). It is easy to identify one's own way with God's way and refuse to admit that it ever could be wrong. Yet this is not the manner of love. Irritation and resentment are too often twin boulders in the path of progress in the life of churches. Pray that it may not be so with your work.

Pray for strong teeth with which to bite your tongue when you should not speak.

Pray for steady hands to hold forth the Bread of Life to men who seem to refuse it.

Pray for a sensitive nose to smell trouble before it becomes tragic.

Pray for stout toes which may be stepped on without a squeal of protest.

And you will be bound by the golden chain of prayer unto the Throne of God and unto the hearts of all God's people who are praying with you. You will never be alone. You will be with God. And you will share His victory.

In The Church

P. Dickson

2—Some "get around" this explicit prohibition of the ordaining of women as elders and preachers by saying that in these passages the Bible is not inspired. A few years ago a certain minister in my presbytery arose, addressed the moderator and said: "I move you, sir, that this presbytery overture the General Assembly to permit the ordaining of women as elders." Another minister spoke up and said, "But that would be contrary to the teaching of God's Word." The maker of the motion replied: "But you know, some of Paul's writings are not inspired." But it is noteworthy that the great Apostle is careful, in writing on this matter of women's preaching or speaking in the church, to claim that what he says is expressly by inspiration (I Cor.14:37). I do not recall that he makes that explicit claim anywhere else.

After forbidding women to exhort, teach, preach, or pray in public mixed assemblies, he says, "Let all things be done decently and in order." (I Cor.14:40). And evidently it was because of signal disorders in the church at Corinth that the Apostle writes this directive. For the church at Corinth was marked by glaring disorders in its public worship, such as: profanation of the Lord's Supper, obtrusiveness of those who had the gift of "tongues," too many speakers at the same meeting, confusion of more than one speaker trying to speak at the same time, and the disposition of women to speak in public.

The Apostle's injunction for women to keep silent in the church also, of course, includes women's leading in public prayer in mixed assemblies. It would necessarily have to follow, from the very language he uses. But it is further enforced in I Timothy 2:8, though in our King James Version it is obscured. "I will therefore that men pray everywhere . . . " In the original Greek the article *the* is before *men*. So, what he really says is: "I will therefore that *the men* pray everywhere . . . "; Of course he is speaking of public services. Also, the Apostle here is not using the generic Greek word, *anthropos,* man, which would mean the race of man, both men and women, but the word *aner,* which means man as contrasted with woman, as in the expression "man and wife."

Now, the Bible does not say that women shall not speak, in public, to other women or to boys and girls. So, she has about two-thirds of the human race to minister to, and that ought to satisfy the ambitions of any woman.

Also, she has the privilege of doing personal work with individual men.

All appointments to office, in the Old Testament and in the New, were of men only. (Deaconesses or female helpers, or servants, merely had the care of the poor and sick among them, and never among needy men.) And so, all arguments based on so-called "Women's Rights," the changed status of women in 20th Century Western civilization, or on woman's ability, consecration and devotion to the church, fade away as a snowflake on a hot stove when laid alongside the blazing light of God's divine revelation. It would seem that after all the sin and suffering of our poor, sad humanity since the Garden of Eden the world, and certainly the Church of Christ, would have learned by now that you CAN'T IMPROVE ON GOD. Grandmother Eve was the first one to try it, and she did not exactly make a "howling success" of it. Said Satan: "Yea, hath God said, Ye shall not eat of every tree of the garden? Well now, He didn't really mean what He said; you can't take that literally, for Ye shall not surely die."

And when God said that women shall not be elders and preachers, if He did not mean what He said, then what did He mean? Those who are advocating the setting aside of God's command in this matter seem to say: "Oh yes, I know God said this thing is black, but He really means that it is white." If He did not mean what He said in this matter then language ceases to have any meaning, and when He said, for instance, "Thou shalt not steal," what He really means is, If your neighbor has something you need or want, go ahead and take it. And by the same fallacious line of reasoning when He said Thou shalt not kill, He did not mean that at all, but if someone crosses your path and it suits your purpose better, go ahead and take his life, for "times have changed."

Ah my brethren, this rejection of the plain teaching of God's inspired Word in this very important matter is "wresting the Scriptures:" yea, it is more: it is "will-worship" and it is apostasy, and, as for me, I'll have none of it. And let no one say it is because we admire and respect womanhood less, but rather that we respect and honor God's divine Word more. Basically and fundamentally men and women are the same in their relations to each other now as when they were created and when they were expelled from the Garden of Eden, or when the Holy Spirit gave these injunctions to His Church through His apostles. For the basic force of the injunctions is that the woman is "not to usurp authority over the man," (I Tim. 2:12). The church will set aside the plain teachings of the Sacred Scriptures in this vital matter at its peril.

woman is safe from Satanic hate and the subtlety of the enemy when she goes unprotected, as she always does when refusing to recognize man as her head.

"As I write, one of the saddest things I recall is the spirit with which women have received this teaching, for, disobeyed, it invites demon possession or insanity. A Christian worker came to me saying: 'I am afraid I shall go insane. You little know what awful things I am suffering.' Another showed by her spirit and manner the blackness of darkness through which she was passing. No relief came to them until they saw the divine order in the church and took their places. After that the transformation in them was so marked that I want to go all over the world and tell women who call themselves leaders in Christian work, in order that they may be saved from awful peril, and no longer hinder the very cause they love. My heart was made sad as I met three persons who had pressed forward in other movements on the highest lines of truth until they came up to the divine order in the Church as God's Word represents it. They refused it, reasoned over it, compared men they knew as leaders, and at the last interview I had with them were baffled, defeated, overcome, and out of fellowship with God, attacked by disease, the brightness once seen on their faces changed to perplexity, the freshness of their testimony ended, for 'the glory had departed' from their spiritual lives, and could never return until they had rendered the obedience that God says is 'better than sacrifice!' "

Some who would disregard the guidance of the Bible in this matter say that many people have been converted through the preaching of women evangelists and pastors. Lack of space prevents our going fully into this point here, but suffice it to say that this is the age-old fallacy of "Let us do evil that good may come," or "The end justifies the means."

People have been saved by the preaching of men evangelists who later confessed that they themselves were not even saved. It simply shows the power and efficacy of God's truth; the power is in the Seed rather than in the sower. And so this argument is invalid in the face of God's "Thou shalt not." It is tantamount to saying "Lord, since people are converted under the preaching of women, you made a mistake in saying that they must not preach, and since women are faithful and capable in the work of the church, you made a mistake in saying they must not be elders, and we propose now to rectify your mistakes."

In conclusion let us open our Bibles and once again reverently listen as God speaks to us His will in this matter of women's place in the church. We shall read from the American Revised Version of 1901.

"As in all the churches of the saints, let the women keep silence in the churches: for it is not permitted unto them to speak; but let them be in subjection, as also saith the law. And if they would learn anything, let them ask their own husbands at home: for it is shameful for a woman to speak in the church. What? was it from you that the word of God went forth? or came it unto you alone?

"If any man thinketh himself to be a prophet, or spiritual, let him take knowledge of the things which I write unto you, that they are the commandments of the Lord. But if any man is ignorant, let him be ignorant . . . Let all things be done decently and in order.;—(I Corinthians 14:33-39).

"I desire therefore that the men pray in every place, lifting up holy hands, without wrath and disputing. In like manner, that women adorn themselves in modest apparel, with shamefacedness and sobriety; not with braided hair, and gold or pearls or costly raiment; but (which becometh women professing godliness) through good works. Let a woman learn in quietness with all subjection. But I permit not a woman to teach, nor to have dominion over a man, but to be in quietness. For Adam was first formed, then Eve; and Adam was not beguiled, but the woman being beguiled hath fallen into transgression."—(I Tim. 2:8-15).

"Faithful is the saying, If a man seeketh the office of a bishop, he desireth a good work. The bishop therefore must be without reproach, the husband of one wife, temperate, sober-minded, orderly, given to hospitality, apt to teach." (I Tim. 3:1-2).

Let it be noted here that the Apostle Paul uses the term bishop interchangeably with the term elder, and he is not speaking of bishops such as some churches have today. The word in the Greek literally means overseer.

"Rebuke not an elder, but exhort him as a father; the younger men as brethren. (I Tim. 5:1).

"For this cause left I thee in Crete, that thou shouldest set in order the things that were wanting, and appoint elders in every city, as I gave thee charge; if any man is blameless, the husband of one wife, having children that believe, who are not accused of riot or unruly. For the bishop must be blameless, as God's steward . . ." (Titus 1:5-7).

REV. J. KENTON PARKER

LESSON FOR JUNE 3

The Church In Europe

Background Scripture: Acts 15:36 - 18:22
Devotionaal Reading: Acts 17:22-31

This is Paul's Second Missionary Journey. In the First he and Barnabas had carried the Gospel into Asia Minor; in this one, Paul and Silas take the Gospel into Europe.

Paul's intention was to visit the brethren in the cities where they had gone on their first trip and see how they were getting along. Barnabas determined to take John Mark with them but Paul, remembering that Mark had turned back and left them on the first journey, did not think it good to take him this time. The contention was sharp between these two friends and the result was that Barnabas chose Mark and sailed for Cyprus, while Paul chose Silas and set out for Syria and Cilicia. It seems a pity that these two great men, and close friends, Paul and Barnabas, should have had such a sharp disagreement, but God overruled it all for the advancement of His work. Paul became reconciled to John Mark later and asked that he be brought to him. (See 2 Tim. 4:11.) It seems a pity that leaders in the church cannot always "see eye to eye," but there have been these sharp disagreements, not only in the early church, but when the Reformation came, and later in the days of the glorious Revival under the Wesleys and Whitefield and others. God made good to come out of this separation of friends, and He is able to make good come out of seemingly unfortunate occurrences.

I. *From Derbe to Troas:* 16:1-8.

A very important addition was made to the party at Derbe. A certain disciple was there named Timothy, his mother a Jewess, his father, a Greek. This young convert had a fine reputation and became Paul's "son in the faith," to whom he wrote two of his Pastoral Epistles which have been of such tremendous value to the church, and especially to preachers. Paul and his party went through the cities, delivering the "Decrees" of the Council at Jerusalem. The churches were strengthened and encouraged and increased in number daily. The Holy Spirit forbade them going on further into Asia; and when they tried to go into Bithynia again, the Spirit suffered them not. So they came to Troas, a city on the Aegean Sea.

II. *In Philippi:* 16:9-40.

1. The Vision at Troas; The "Man of Macedonia."

Macedonia was a province of Greece, just across the Aegean Sea from Troas. The vision was easily understood, for the "man of Macedonia" was saying, "Come over into Macedonia and help us." They immediately endeavored to go into Macedonia, and loosing from Troas came to Philippi, after passing through some minor places. Philippi was a chief city of that part of Greece and a Roman colony. Paul always struck for strategic places, and usually for large cities.

2. The Conversion of Lydia.

It is noteworthy that the first convert to Christianity in Europe was a prominent business woman. She became the first-fruits of that glorious company of Christian women who have done great things for the Christian church. The gospel of Christ has meant more to women than to any other class of people. During the ministry of our Lord upon earth a band of loyal, devoted women followed Him and helped all they could. Out of Mary Magdalene He cast seven demons, and it was in the home of Mary and Martha of Bethany that He spent some of His most restful hours. None of the women of that company ever betrayed, or denied, or deserted Him. They were "the last at the cross and the first at the empty tomb." Christ and His gospel have liberated and honored women. Not only has that gospel done great things for them, but women have done marvelous deeds for the cause of Christ. This has been true all down through Church History, and is true today. In our own denomination the "Women of the Church" are making the "Men of the Church" ashamed of themselves. "Help those women which labored with us in the gospel," says Paul. He found them to be the best of workers in the kingdom of God.

The conversion of Lydia is a very quiet conversion, but no one can hint that it was not genuine. A company of godly women were accustomed to gather in a prayer-meeting by a riverside. Perhaps the apostle felt somewhat disappointed that there was no synagogue of the Jews where he could go and begin his preaching, and speak to the men, but he took the opportunity which presented itself and spoke to these women. A "seller of purple," of the city of Thyatira, a woman who worshipped God, heard his message. Her conversion is described in beautiful words: "whose heart the Lord opened." This is a fine description of what takes place when we are "born again." "As many as received Him, to them gave He power to become the sons of God, even to them that believe on His name." Lydia received Jesus Christ into her heart as her personal Savior, and immediately urged the party to make her home their headquarters. This is what all of us need to do; receive Him into our hearts and into our homes!

3. The Afflicted Slave Girl: 16-24.

A damsel with a "spirit of divination" followed "Paul and us." (We know that Luke was with the party because of the frequent use of the pronouns "us" and "we.") She kept crying, These men are the servants of the Most High God, which show unto us the way of salvation. Paul was grieved with this sort of testimony, and said to the spirit, I command thee in the name of Jesus Christ to come out of her. And he came out. We have instances in the life of our Lord where the demons cried out in similar language, We know Thee Who thou art, the Holy One of God. Her masters, who had been using this girl for their own purposes and profit, finding her no longer profitable to them - their hopes of gain were gone - caught Paul and Silas and drew them to the market place unto the rulers, charging them with troubling their city by teaching customs unlawful for Romans. This aroused the multitude, and the magistrates commanded to beat them. After they had laid many stripes upon them they cast them into prison charging the jailor to keep them safely. He thrust them into the inner prison and made their feet fast in the stocks.

4. The Conversion of the Jailor: 25-34.

There was a new noise in the prison at midnight. I doubt if anything like it had ever been heard there before. Paul and Silas were praying and singing praises to God; "And the prisoners heard them." What a testimony!

We have next the miracle of the earthquake which not only shook the foundations of the jail, but opened its doors and loosed the bonds of the prisoners. The keeper of the prison, awakened out of his sleep, and seeing the prison doors open, he drew his sword and would have killed himself. (He knew the rigid Roman law!) Paul hastened to tell him that they were all there.

All of these strange happenings had a tremendous effect upon the jailor. He called for a light, came trembling and fell down before Paul and Silas. He brought them out and said, Sirs, what must I do to be saved? Had he heard Paul preach, or had the testimony of prayer and song and the miracle brought conviction to his soul? Of course, conviction is the work of the Spirit, but had the Spirit used these methods and occurrences? Paul gives the simple answer, so often quoted; Believe on the Lord Jesus Christ, and thou shalt be saved, and thy house.

The conversion of the Philippian jailor is very different from that of Lydia, or the slave girl. In one respect all conversions are alike; they all mean a turning away from sin and a turning to God. Some, however, may be very spectacular, others very calm and quiet. The conversion of Lydia was just as genuine as that of the jailor; the conversion of James and John and Peter, just as genuine as that of Saul of Tarsus, but the outward circumstances were very different. Let us beware of trying to make all conversions conform to one type. We must be "born again," but this new birth comes in different ways. The Spirit works like the wind; sometimes there is a tornado; at other times, a gentle breeze.

III. *In Thessalonica:* 17:1-9.

There was a synagogue of the Jews in this city, and as usual, when such was the case, Paul went there to worship and to reason with those who came. He had good results at first, but "the Jews which believed not," caused trouble, and Paul and Silas went on to Berea.

IV. *At Berea:* 17:10-14.

These were "more noble" than those in Thessalonica. They received the Word with all readiness of mind and searched the Scriptures daily, whether these things were so. Therefore many of them believed. An open mind and a searching of the Scriptures will cause people to believe. They had to leave because of the Jews.

V. *In Athens:* 15-34.

Paul had but little success in Athens where the atmosphere was full of idolatry, skepticism, and scoffing. It is hard to reach people like these.

VI. *At Corinth:* 18:1-22.

Paul stayed in this city for some eighteen months and founded one of his strongest churches. See I and II Corinthians.

YOUTH PROGRAM FOR JUNE 3

What The Bible Says About God

Hymn: "Great God, How Infinite Art Thou"
Prayer
Scripture: Isaiah 40:9-31
Hymn: "Our God, Our Help In Ages Past"
Offering
Hymn: "Joyful, Joyful, We Adore Thee"

PROGRAM LEADER:

(You can have audience participation in this program, if you will ask the young people to bring their Bibles and be ready to read the references as they are needed in the program. You can note all the references that are to be read, jot them down on slips of paper, and distribute them before the program begins. As the various speakers come to the references, in their speeches, they can ask for them to be read aloud.)

The Bible gives us no systematic definition of God. There is no one passage which tells us everything we need to know about God. On the other hand, the Bible has so much to say about God that it would be virtually impossible to discuss all of its teachings in a large book, much less in a brief program like this one. We do have some well known definitions of God, and these definitions are Biblical. One of the best known is found in the opening words of the Apostle's Creed: "I believe in God the Father Almighty, Maker of heaven and earth . . " This description of God does not tell us everything about Him, but it suggests a great deal. These truths concerning God are not only taught in the Scriptures, they are amplified. The Bible tells us what is meant by these terms which are used to describe God. Our speakers will call attention to some of the outstanding passages which increase our knowledge of God.

FIRST SPEAKER:

We do find one very basic definition of God in the Bible, and that is in the words of Jesus. (Read John 4:24.) All the other Scriptural teachings with respect to the nature of God are consistent with this basic fact. God is essentially spirit. From our own experience we know that man is also basically spirit. This too is consistent with Christ's definition of God as spirit, because it is written that man was created in the likeness of God. There is a vast difference between God and His spiritual creatures. God is infinitely perfect and His creatures are not. (Read Isaiah 55:8,9.) Our spiritual God is exalted above all other beings. (Read Exodus 15:11.)

SECOND SPEAKER:

The Creed speaks of God as the Almighty, and this suggests to our minds those qualities which are possessed by God alone. In many places the Bible refers to God as the Almighty. His limitless power is spoken of by the prophets. (Read Jeremiah 32:17.) The Bible speaks often of the eternity of God, describing Him as "the Alpha and the Omega, the beginning and the end." (Also read Psalm 90:2.) Scripture tells us that God is unchangeable, speaking of Him as "the Father of lights, with whom is no variableness, neither shadow of turning." James 1:17.

THIRD SPEAKER:

The Creed refers to God's power when it speaks of His being "Maker of heaven and earth." This suggests to us the wonderful works of God and the knowledge of Him which we receive as we behold His works. (Read Psalm 19:1.) God alone has power to create from nothing. (Read Hebrews 11:3.) God works to preserve and uphold His creation. (Read Psalm 103:19.) God's most wonderful work of all is that of redeeming His lost creation. (Read Isaiah 62:12.)

FOURTH SPEAKER:

Finally the Creed suggests to us the personal nature of God when it calls Him "Father." This means that God has a fatherly relation to His people, and that He possesses all the qualities of fatherhood to perfection. The Bible is uniformly consistent in describing God as a person rather than an impersonal force. The reference to Him as our Father is the richest and most beautiful of all these personal references. The personality of God is revealed most perfectly in Christ. (Read John 14:9.)

In the First Epistle of John we find two other suggestive definitions of God which describe for us the essential nature of our heavenly Father. (Read I John 1:5 and 4:8.) Jesus said to His disciples, "If ye then, being evil, know how to give good gifts unto your children, how much more shall your Father which is in heaven give good things to them that ask Him?" Matthew 7:11. Our heavenly Father gives us the best gifts because He is both "Light" and "Love."

Light is the symbol of a number of spiritual qualities which belong in perfection to God. Knowledge, wisdom, righteousness, holiness, and truth are all elements which go to make up spiritual light. God possesses all these qualities in their fullness. (Read Colossians 2:3; Psalm 145:17; and Deuteronomy 32:4.) These are representative passages which bear witness to God's qualities of spiritual light.

Many religions claim power, wisdom, and might for their gods, but the Scriptures are unique and unanimous in pointing to our heavenly Father as a God of love. Because of His love He is merciful to us. (Read Psalm 103:10, 11 and Psalm 116:5.) God's mercy and love do not require Him to violate His sense of right. God the righteous judge says, "The soul that sinneth, it shall die." Ezekiel 18:20. In order that God could be both just Himself and justifier of sinners, it was necessary that He make a great sacrifice. He sent His righteous Son into the world to die in the place of sinners. (Read or recite John 3:16.) That is the measure of God's love, and it is surely the most wonderful thing the Bible has to say about God.

Women's Work

Excerpts of Letter From Estelle and E. H. Hamilton

This morning Hola and I went across a very high swinging bridge, and then walked a couple of hours along a cliffside trail. Sometimes we could look straight down 1000 feet. At one place a landslide had wiped out the trail, but there was a narrow ledge remaining, and we each clung to the side of the mountain not daring to look down as we went across. We soon came to a waterfall of wonderful beauty, with tiers of mountains above it. Then on, an hour longer, to a village, named E-shing, high on the side of the mountain.

We went to this village I never knew existed and dedicated a church I didn't know was being built. Moreover, all the afternoon we examined 22 new believers - men, women, and young people - and that evening we baptized them, and preached, and held communion. And I was the first missionary ever to go to that village. Can you beat that? (Don't feel we were too hasty in baptizing them. All had believed at least a year, and attended services there in an elder's house. And you ought to have seen the flame that came into their eyes when I asked each one, "Are you willing to suffer for Christ?")

Then came some more fun. At 10 o'clock at night, with a little torch, we took a trail right down the side of the mountain to a wide mountain river, and the water was cold and swift. My clothes were tied about the neck of my Taiyal guide, and we held on tight to each other, because although it was only waist-deep the current was swift and the rock-bed was slippery. Once across, I took a voluntary bath there in the river; then we climbed to the opposite road and by 11 p. m. reached Lohao, where our Japanese "bed" was awaiting us. And so we called it a day.

These mountains of Taiwan are a wonderful missionary challenge. Some of you young people who can drive a jeep with a steady hand, cross a high swinging bridge with a steady foot, and preach the everlasting Gospel with a steady joy - come on out here to this glorious work among these erstwhile "headhunters" of Formosa.

Our student work at "Friendship Corner" in Taipei is also growing wonderfully, and so is our English worship service there every Sunday morning. Recently, I baptized seven new believers one Sunday morning. All but one had attended a Communicants' Class which I held one night a week for six weeks. The one that didn't attend the class was an American airman, a fine lad who turned to Christ from a life of sin, and now is witnessing for Him every chance he gets. Of the six Chinese baptized (four men and two women) *five were members of the Legislature of Free China.*

And now this week we are starting another Communicants' Class. Digging in for another crop!

You Can Have Part in The 1956 General Assembly

The 1956 Assembly will convene in Montreat, N. C., on the evening of May 31 and continue in session until it has completed its work, probably through June 5.

Prior to this, opening May 30, there is to be an important pre-Assembly Conference on Evangelism, designed to give instruction in the immediate emphases in the developing program of Evangelism, but primarily to create an atmosphere in which God's Spirit may work to rekindle the flames of evangelistic fervor in the men of the Assembly.

Only a representative group of ministers and elders, plus a few responsible leaders from the Boards and Agencies of the Assembly will actually attend the General Assembly. It may be as it once was, that these persons, because of the prayers of people of the Church, be so completely under the control of God's Holy Spirit that they will do things they themselves never knew they would do. We, of the Church, may have just as large a part in that Assembly as we will to have, by our prayers for those who are there to make the decisions that will affect Christ's work through us and through His Church for another year. If we could really see from God's point of view, might we not discover that those of us who pray—really pray—are more determinative in the decisions than those present in the Assembly. May it be, however attained, that people remembering the power of prayer to reach the Almighty will say: "The men were moved by the Spirit of God" and of that which is done: "This is the doing of God."

Remember, every member of our great Church can have a part, who wills to pray.

The Eleventh Annual Training School

of the Synodical of North Carolina will be held at Peace College, Raleigh, N. C., on June 4th through the 9th, 1956. An excellent faculty will develop the general theme for the school of "Facing Life With Christ."

The following are members of the faculty:

Dr. Paul Leslie Garber of Agnes Scott College, Decatur, Ga.
Dr. Ben L. Rose, First Presbyterian Church, Wilmington, N. C.
Dr. John L. Miller, Snow Hill, N. C.
Dr. William H. McCorkle, Atlanta, Ga.
Mrs. C. Darby Fulton, Nashville, Tenn.
Mrs. John W. McQueen, Birmingham, Ala.

Besides these teachers of classes there will be special addresses each evening by the following:

Dr. Fred H. Olert, Second Presbyterian Church, Richmond, Va.
Dr. M. C. McQueen of Clinton, N. C.
Dr. James M. Carr, Board of Church Extension, Atlanta, Ga.
Dr. James A. Jones of Union Theological Seminary, Richmond, Va.

Mrs. Ralph Holt of Burlington, N. C., is the Director of the School and Mrs. R. A. Willis of Monroe, N. C., the Dean.

The Bible in 1,092 Languages and Dialects

BLIND GET MORE EMBOSSED SCRIPTURES

The total number of volumes of Scriptures distributed throughout the years by the American Bible Society is rapidly approaching the half-billion mark and will be passed early in the Spring of 1957, the Society's annual Board of Managers report revealed on May 10.

The society, the most widely-supported Protestant organization in the country, held its 140th annual meeting at the Fifth Avenue Presbyterian Church, New York City.

Distribution of Scriptures during 1955 totaled 14,918,353 volumes in the United States and abroad. This, when added to 466,231,012 distributed since 1816, brings the 140-year total to 481,149,365.

Contrasting sharply with the first year, when only 6,410 volumes were distributed, the past six years have never dipped below the ten million mark and have totaled more than 81 millions by themselves.

During 1955, parts of the Bible were translated into languages in which it had never been known before. The number of languages and dialects into which at least one book of the Bible has been published is now 1,092. The whole Bible has now been published in 207 languages and dialects; the New Testament only, in 265 more, and at least one complete book of the Bible in 620 more.

Among the new publications were the first Gospels in the Tiruray language used in the Philippines; in Tzutujil, used in Guatemala, and Chinantec, Oaxaca, Chontal, and Mezquital Otomi, used in Mexico.

Other noteworthy publications included an English Illustrated New Testament with nearly 600 pictures; the first Old Testament in Luvale (Africa); the first New Testament in Conob

(Guatemala); a new revised Bible in Tshwa (Africa), and the Bible in colloquial Japanese. The last, the first Bible the average man in Japan can read easily, effected impressive new interest in Scriptures and resulted in distribution of 1,872,313 volumes, more than a half-million ahead of 1955. The new Bible won the literary prize for the best book of the year.

The Society also participated in revisions of translations of the whole Bible in Spanish, Portuguese, Arabic, modern Armenian, Bulu, Luba-Lulua, Thai, Hiligaynon, Cebuan, Bicol and Tagalog.

Special attention was given to the needs of the blind in this country and other parts of the world. The 53,371 volumes and Talking Book records brought the all-time total past the half-million mark to 533,653. The embossed Scriptures have now been supplied in 41 languages and systems to finger-tip readers.

Other highlights from the report include:

The Society supplied nearly 150 tons of paper for Scripture printing in Eastern Europe.

Chaplains of the Armed Forces and the Veterans Administration received 1,397,100 volumes of Scriptures in response to specific requests.

Scripture circulation in Latin America again broke all previous records - with 3,540,770 volumes distributed during 1955 - and once more demand exceeded supply.

The Society adopted a budget of $2,899,000 for 1956, the largest in its history, to meet increasing needs for Scriptures.

Church News

Additional Overtures to General Assembly

(40) The Presbytery of Louisville respectfully overtures the General Assembly as follows:

WHEREAS, there are inadequacies in the Directory for Worship of the Presbyterian Church, U. S. and the Book of Common Worship of the Presbyterian Church, U.S.A., such as:

1. The exclusive use of the King James translation of the Bible in its materials;

2. The antique, difficult-to-understand language used in the suggested prayers;

3. The failure to be realistic in orders of service as to time and volume of content;

4. The lack of notice of the importance of music in worship, specifically, failure to include suggestions for wedding and funeral music;

5. The absence of good installation services for use in the Sunday school, with Youth groups and Women's groups;

6. The exclusion of suggested services to be used by laymen who conduct public worship;

WHEREAS, the Presbyterian Churches, in the past year, have produced a joint hymnal of note and good taste to overcome these same types of handicaps in Presbyterian hymn books;

WHEREAS, the leaders of worship in all branches of Presbyterianism would find much value in a joint Book of Worship, such as:

1. A unifying result in the modes of worship in the three Churches;

2. An instrument for the exchange of worship ideas of the three Churches;

WHEREAS, worshippers in the congregations of the three Churches would profit in like manner, and would find the services more meaningful;

NOW, THEREFORE, the Presbytery of Louisville respectfully overtures the General Assembly to take immediate steps to inaugurate the beginning of a joint Book of Worship with the Presbyterian Church, U.S.A. and the United Presbyterian Church.

(41) The Presbytery of Louisville respectfully overtures the General Assembly as follows:

WHEREAS, the Board of Christian Education does not have funds available for capital investment in local book stores in Louisville, Kentucky, or other areas throughout the Church, and

WHEREAS, the Board of Christian Education has declined to make Vacation Church School material available through existing local book stores, and

WHEREAS, materials of all of our other Boards of the Church are available through local book stores, and

WHEREAS, there is a notable reluctance on the part of individual churches to order Vacation Church School material from the Board in Richmond, Virginia, and

WHEREAS, it appears that some of our churches are obtaining material for their Vacation Church School from other sources, which material is Presbyterian, and otherwise, and

WHEREAS, local book stores offer discounts on books to church libraries and ministers that the Board of Christian Education in Richmond does not allow, and

WHEREAS, Presbytery of Louisville is deeply concerned lest the present policy of the Board result in increased reluctance of individual churches to avail themselves of Vacation Church School material through the Board of Christian Education,

NOW, THEREFORE, the Presbytery of Louisville respectfully overtures the General Assembly of the Presbyterian Church, U.S. to direct the Board of Christian Education to reinstate its former policy of making material and supplies available through local religious book stores.

(42) WHEREAS, the total of 921 children in our Church memorizing the Shorter or Child's Catechism last year is far short of the 4,059 in 1922, when our Church membership was 411,854 as compared with 780,853 in 1954, and

WHEREAS, this is a decrease exceeding 75% while membership has increased nearly 100%, indicating marked decline in catechetical instruction, and

WHEREAS, recent growth has brought to our Church many fine people of different religious backgrounds, numbers of whom are interested in learning more about our Reformed doctrine, and

WHEREAS, our Book of Church Order, section 345, states that "the Bible, together with the Catechisms, shall be the chief textbooks of the Church School, the center of every course of instruction; . . . ",

NOW, THEREFORE, the Presbytery of Central Mississippi respectfully overtures the General Assembly as follows:

(1) To instruct the Board of Christian Education:

a. To make an early and thorough study of this problem;

b. To promote an effective program looking to greater emphasis and increased use of the Catechisms in the homes and Church schools of our Assembly;

c. To commend presbyteries and churches with records worthy of special mention in this important matter;

d. To include a special report on progress in the Annual Report to the General Assembly each year.

(2) To instruct the General Council to supply full support to the Board of Christian Education in this important matter.

Overture 43 is identical with 32 (in Blue Book) except for name of seminary — in 4th line of first "whereas".

(43) The Presbytery of Louisville respectfully overtures the General Assembly meeting in Montreat, N. C., on May 31, 1956, as follows:

WHEREAS: The original records and early publications of the Presbyterian Church in the U.S. are now to be found not only in recognized depositories (such as the Historical Foundation in Montreat and the Library of Union Theological Seminary) but also in state archives, college and university libraries, and individually owned collections scattered over a wide area of the United States, so that these historical materials are nowhere available in a single center; and

WHEREAS: It is to be hoped that these materials would be sent to the Historical Foundation if authentic copies were available to these archives, libraries, and individuals; and

WHEREAS: Some of these materials exist in only one or two known copies, many of which are in such condition as to suffer from handling; which handling would be eliminated if microfilm copies were available; and

WHEREAS: Those records that are in private hands are frequently irrecoverably lost by fire or other destruction; and

WHEREAS: These documents ought to be reproduced and made available to church courts, officials, and agencies in their work; to seminary faculties and students that our Presbyterian heritage might be better known and appreciated; and to historians and research workers who wish access to these hitherto inaccessible records for use in their historical studies; and

WHEREAS: Equipment for photographic reproduction is now obtainable that would make authentic copies of these priceless documents and records from our past, these photographic copies then being made available at strategic centers; and

WHEREAS: The Historical Foundation of the Presbyterian Church in the United States is the agency of the General Assembly designated to assemble and house a complete collection of the official documents and publications of the Presbyterian Church; and

WHEREAS: Few of our Presbyterian institutions or church courts are able to have photographic reproductions of materials made at economical prices, but must rely upon expensive commercial photography for necessary duplication of materials; and

WHEREAS: The Library Section of the Presbyterian Educational Association of the South, composed of librarians of all Presbyterian seminaries and colleges of our denomination, has unanimously agreed to recommend this project to our church courts;

NOW, THEREFORE, The Presbytery of Louisville overtures the General Assembly to appropriate $25,000 to establish a photographic Reproduction Center at the Historical Foundation. Of this amount up to $10,000 shall be used for the purchase of equipment and supplies, and up to $5,000 per year shall be available for three years to provide adequate personnel to initiate the project.

Done by the Presbytery of Louisville
meeting at Shelbyville, Kentucky
on April 24, 1956

Edwin N. Rock, Stated Clerk

(44) The Presbytery of Suwannee humbly overtures that the General Assembly request all of its Boards, institutions, and recommend to all of its associated institutions, to allow at least 25% of their endowments, to be invested in church loans, for construction purposes. It is understood these loans are to be placed only on the strictest business principles.

(45) The Presbytery of The Everglades overtures the General Assembly, through the Office of the Stated Clerk, to restore the salary listings of ordained ministers in the Assembly Minutes.

(46) In view of the financial saving that might result if all Boards and Agencies of the General Assembly were located in one central place, the Presbytery of Lexington-Ebenezer respectfully overtures the General Assembly to appoint an Ad Interim Committee representing each Synod to make a thorough study of locating all of its Boards and Agencies in one place and report its findings and recommendations to the 1957 General Assembly.

(47) The Presbytery of East Alabama respectfully overtures the General Assembly as follows:

Whereas, a great number of churches across our General Assembly use the Uniform Lesson Series, and

Whereas, the Uniform Lesson Series does not provide guidance or material for Second Sessions, and

Whereas, the only literature available from our Board of Christian Education for those churches using Uniform Lessons is made up of three books, all copies from another denomination press, and

Whereas, our churches to meet evident needs are in increasing numbers organizing our Juniors into vesper and fellowship groups, and

Whereas, our sister denominations have organized Junior Fellowships or their counterparts, published literature to guide them, and achieved an acceptable degree of success with this age grouping, and

Whereas, many presbyteries of the General Assembly are launching programs of Junior Camps, similar to our present programs for Pioneers and Seniors:

Therefore, the Presbytery of East Alabama respectfully overtures the General Assembly to request the Board of Christian Education to reevaluate its position on Junior Vesper Groups, and that the Board, to aid churches in setting up such groups, publish appropriate literature which will enable our churches to enlist those children who are so eager to be led into paths of service.

THE GENERAL FUND AND INTERCHURCH AGENCIES

Statement of Receipts

January 15 - April 30, 1956

The General Fund Agencies

Budget for 1956	$846,581.00
Received from January 15th through April 30, 1956	117,231.74
Percentage of annual budget received to date	13.85
Balance needed for the year	729,349.26

Interchurch Agencies

Budget for 1956	$21,495.00
Received from January 15th through April 30, 1956	3,753.82
Percentage of annual budget received to date	17.46
Balance needed for the year	17,741.18

E. C. Scott, Treasurer

The Presbyterian Church, U.S. has eight members on the Board of Managers of United Church Women attending the annual session of the Board in Colorado Springs, Colorado, April 24 - 26. A total of 140 women from 40 states were present for the meeting.

The Presbyterian, U. S., women members of the Board of Managers who attended were: Mrs. Leighton M. McCutchen, Atlanta, Ga.; Mrs. F. R. Crawford, Farmville, Va.; Mrs. A. R. Craig, Rutherfordton, N. C.; Mrs. John T. McCall, Nashville, Tenn.; Mrs. J. P. Walker, Murfreesboro, Tenn.; Mrs. R. G. Martin, Pensacola, Fla.; Mrs. Chris Matheson, Gainesville, Fla.; and Mrs. Paul B. Thomas, Baltimore, Md.

These were selected either by the United Church Women's Assembly-at-large, by their respective State Council of Church Women, by the Board of Women's Work in Atlanta, or by the Board of United Church Women.

DR. GUTZKE HONORED

Atlanta — Dr. Manford Gutzke, professor of English Bible and Religious Education at Columbia Theological Seminary, and widely known for his unusual Bible study courses conducted each Monday evening at Atlanta's North Avenue Presbyterian Church, was honored Tuesday, May 15, with a reception at the Presbyterian Book Store in Atlanta.

Occasion of the reception in honor of the Decatur professor is the publication of his first major work, "John Dewey's Thought and Its Implications for Christian Education." The book is the result of doctoral study and dissertation, and it examines many of the techniques and philosophies of education as advocated by John Dewey, in their application to the educational efforts of the Christian Church.

BOARD OF DIRECTORS OF LOUISVILLE SEMINARY PASSED RESOLUTION OF CONGRATULATION TO DR. FRANK H. CALDWELL

We, the members of the Board of Directors, want to congratulate you, Frank H. Caldwell, on this anniversary of twenty years as president of Louisville Seminary. You have led the Seminary through some dark hours into prominence and excellence in service to the Church. As a dedicated leader, you have done the Seminary and the Church much good. As a Christian man, you have been good for all of us who serve with you. We rejoice in your leadership in this Board, in the Seminary faculty, and in the Church at large.

As a token of our appreciation in this anniversary year, we want to tell you that we are planning to designate some fitting portion of the new campus in your honor.

May God richly bless you in your labors in this joyous and crucial time in the life of the Seminary.

LOUISIANA

Red River Presbytery — Belcher Presbyterian Church, Belcher, Louisiana:

Presbytery was convened and Moderator's Sermon was preached by Elder J. H. Nelson "Hear What The Spirit Saith To The Churches." 29 Ministers and 32 Elders enrolled with 10 guests.

Moderator Wm. E. Giddens, Jr., of St. Joseph and Waterproof Churches was elected Moderator. James W. Anderson, Benton, Temporary Clerk.

Memorial to Dr. W. A. Alexander was read, prayer offered; Tom Duncan.

Fall Meeting September 11, 1956; 9:30 A. M. Highlights 250th Anniversary of First Presbytery in America; 100th of Trinity Church Jonesville where meeting will be held.

Presbytery Enters Travel Pool to send Stated Clerk to Clerk's Association, Montreat, N. C., August 16-17.

Haynesville Presbyterian Church U.S.A. at the request of their Elder W. D. Martin, with proper release from New Orleans Presbytery U.S.A.; was received into Red River Presbytery at the recommendation of the Church Extension Committee.

Candidates Dismissed: William Mitchell to Durant Presbytery to Broken Bow, Okla.; Robert

J. Stewart to East Arkansas Presbytery, Searcy, Ark.

Commissions for Installations of Rev. John M. Wilson at the John Knox Church and Rev. Paul Currie, Trinity Presbyterian Church, Jonesville, La., were commended and dismissed, reports adopted.

Commissions to General Assembly 1956 were awarded by Clerk.

Committee on Meetings of Presbytery (Ad Interim) report adopted. Winter meeting second Tuesday February; Spring meeting second Tuesday May; Fall meeting second Tuesday September. All to begin 9:30 A. M. (3 one day meetings instead of two one-day and one two-day meetings.)

Nominations: Moderator-Designate Rev. Leonard R. Swinney; Trustees all re-elected except J. W. Head - replaced by R. G. Lawton, Jr., W. O. C. Section of Evangelism and Outreach Chairman of Y. P. to aid in 1957 Evangelism plans.

Stated Clerk Rev. W. R. Gage, Box 302 Winnfield urged Church Treasurers to pay Presbyterial tax. Also set up committee to revise Standing Rules.

Davidson — Five recent graduates of Davidson College have won graduate scholarships and fellowships for the 1956-57 academic year.

They are William V. Porter, Jr., of Charlotte, a 1954 graduate; L. M. DeVane, Jr., of Jennings, Fla., 1954; 1st Lt. Norman M. Johnson of Rocky Mount, 1954; John Y. Fenton of Rolling Fork, Miss., 1955; and Thomas A. Langford of Charlotte, 1951.

NORTH CAROLINA

Davidson — Dr. George E. Staples, pastor of the Highland Presbyterian church of Winston-Salem, will join the Davidson College staff in August as Minister to Students.

The announcement of Dr. Staples appointment was made by Dr. John R. Cunningham, president of Davidson.

"We welcome Dr. Staples to the college," said Dr. Cunningham. "His appointment is in keeping with an effort to add to the staff a person with overall responsibility for the religious life and activities of the campus.

"Our personnel committee and the Board of Directors of the Y. M. C. A. believe Dr. Staples to be extremely fitted for this responsible task at Davidson. We are fortunate to obtain the services of a man of his experience and ability."

Dr. Staples, a native of San Antonio, Texas, has served the Highland church since it was formed in 1950. Under his leadership the church has grown to a membership of approximately 500, and last June dedicated a new physical plant designed by architect Harold E. Wagoner of Philadelphia.

OKLAHOMA

Oklahoma City — More than 150 men attended the Spring Rally of Mangum Presbytery of the Oklahoma Synod at the Central Presbyterian Church at Oklahoma City April 21. Dr. C. Ralston Smith of the First Presbyterian Church of Oklahoma City was principal speaker. C. A. Tackett, president of the Synod, reported on plans for the Summer Conference. The men were welcomed by J. E. Clary, Presbytery president. Earnest Nunley reported that the men were reminded of the 1957 Miami convention.

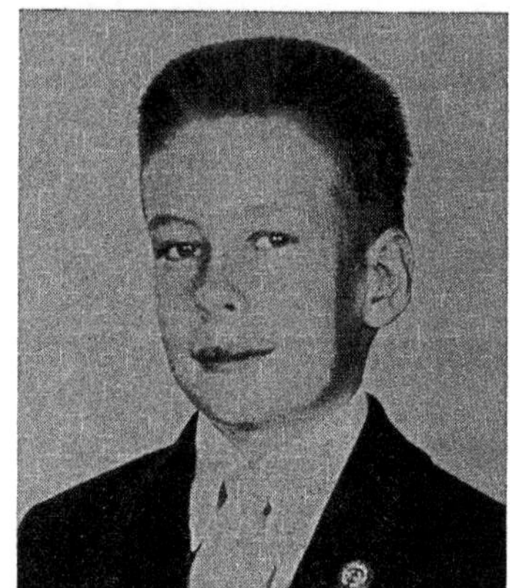

Seven Years Perfect Attendance

Cato Holler, Jr., son of Mr. & Mrs. Cato Holler, of Marion, N. C., was recently awarded a 7-year pin for perfect attendance at Sunday School in the First Presbyterian Church of Marion. His mother was also presented with a similar award.

SOUTH CAROLINA

Iva — Presbyterian chairmen for the promotion of the Miami convention were announced by E. W. Evans, of Iva, Synod chairman. The Presbytery chairmen were: Bethel, George H. Estes, York; Charleston, W. R. Baldwin, Orangeburg; Congaree, Lawrence C. Newton, West Columbia; Enoree, Harold Thompson, Greenville; Harmony, Irwin McIntosh, Kingstree; Pee Dee, not yet appointed; Piedmont, Holmes Simons, Anderson; South Carolina, Roy A. Smith, Donalds, S. C.

Rev. W. Ted Jones, Columbia, was named secretary of the Synod convention committee, and Rev. Robert L. Alexander, Greenwood, advisor.

Clinton — Two outstanding Presbyterian leaders will speak at the 75th commencement exercises of Presbyterian College on June 3-4, President Marshall W. Brown, announced today.

They are the Rev. Robert Strong, pastor of the First Presbyterian Church of Augusta, Ga.; and the Rev. Marshall C. Dendy, executive-secretary of the Board of Christian Education of the Presbyterian Church, U.S.

Dr. Strong will preach the baccalaureate sermon on Sunday morning, June 3. Dr. Dendy is scheduled to deliver the commencement address on the morning of June 4.

UNION THEOLOGICAL SEMINARY

Union Theological Seminary will graduate forty-two members of the Senior class at the Commencement exercises Tuesday, May 22, at 11:30 A. M. in Schauffler Hall. In addition to the graduating

BOOKS

"THE GOSPEL OF THE SPIRIT." Samuel Eyles Pierce. William B. Eerdmans. $1.50.

More than 100 years ago this treatise was published in England. It received a hearty reception when first produced and was called "an epitome if not the masterpiece of all the author's writings." The first part of the book compresses valuable material on "The Person and Office of the Holy Spirit." The second part presents the entire work of the Spirit of grace upon the persons of the redeemed from their regeneration to their glorification both in body and in soul. The author states, "The Holy Ghost has His influence and puts forth His divine energy in everything which concerns the people of God from their regeneration to their glorification. . . . He is the Christian's most divine Comforter in the hour of death. He sanctifies their last moments with His presence and everlasting consolations. He admits them into the state of glory and therefore puts forth the influence and glory of His indwelling in their souls and fills them with all the fullness of God. He leads the soul into glory and to fellowship with the God-man, so that the elect are as truly dependent on the Holy Spirit for all the enjoyment of the Father's love and the blessings of glory as they were in a time-state for all the blessings of grace and salvation. He indwells in their souls and will throughout eternity. He will fill the Christians and all the faculties of their souls with increasing knowledge and enjoyment and communion of all the blessings of the Father's love and the glories of Christ which are essential, personal, relative, and mediatorial."

There is a devotional tone in this entire volume that will be difficult to ever surpass. To the Christian who wants to know more about the Holy Spirit and how to live the Christian life more effectively here is a volume that we unhesitatingly commend. J.R.R.

"KNIGHT'S MASTERBOOK OF ILLUSTRATIONS." Walter B. Knight. William B. Eerdmans. $6.95.

Sometime ago Dr. Knight published a volume called, "Three Thousand Illustrations for Christian Service." It has been used widely. This volume is in no way a duplicate of the former volume. Rather it is a companion volume. The power of illustrations and anecdotes is known to all. The author has again arranged the contents into a convenient alphabetical system. Here are illustrations presented from a great number of famous speakers, preachers, magazines, books and sermons. In fact, the coverage is so wide that no one man could hope to cover the same area unless he spent as the author has many years at the task. Much of the material is original and therefore unpublished. It is fresh and up-to-date. The illustrations number more than four thousand. This volume will be helpful to Christian workers and Sunday School teachers or in the pulpit.

"THE APOSTOLIC PREACHING OF THE CROSS." Leon Morris. Wm. B. Eerdmans. $3.50.

This volume is an effort to understand what exactly was in the apostles' minds when they used such words as "redeem,. covenant, propitiate, reconcile, and justify." Mr. Morris studies these great themes against the background of the related Old Testament passages, for here we have one of the major influences on the thinking of our New Testament writers. Having completed this initial consideration of the background material, the author then goes on to examine these great doctrinal words in their own New Testament setting. The result is a most rewarding study of one of Scripture's major themes.

"CALVIN'S DOCTRINE OF LAST THINGS." Heinrich Quistorp. John Knox Press. $3.00.

Sensible theologians are again listening to the voice of John Calvin. His theology is exegetical and expository as well as systematic. Many books have been written on Calvin's theology but few have ever stopped to consider his teachings concerning eschatology. Dr. T. F. Torrance of Edinburg explains in his introduction that Calvin's main teaching concerning eschatology can be formulated by saying that eschatology is the application of Christology to the work of the Church in history. It is the understanding of the Church in all creation - in terms of the reign of Christ. Calvin's teaching here pivots upon the doctrine of union with Christ. Because we are united to Christ and participate in His risen humanity, eschatology is essential to our faith.

Although the Reformers were primarily concerned with the matter of justification, nevertheless Luther and Calvin both treated the last things from time to time as relevant points in their Scriptural exegesis and preaching. Both Luther and Calvin had a strong expectation of the return of Christ. Both believed that the hour of death becomes decisive for our eternal future. Both Reformers held to a two-fold issue—either acceptance to an eternity of bliss or rejection to eternal damnation.

In this volume we see how Calvin endeavored in his eschatology as in his whole teaching and preaching to bring out the witness of the Bible—the witness that Christ is the central truth of the Word of God. The author shows, however, that Calvin did not deal with certain aspects of eschatology and today the church will be wise in filling in the gaps.

He concludes this volume by saying, "In the confusions and distresses of the present the Church of Jesus Christ needs clear teaching and persuasive preaching about the coming of its King and His Kingdom which is alone eternal so that it may give out its message as a herald to a slumbering or mad world whether it be for salvation or for judgment. The Church which lives by this confession may in the woes of our time joyfully look upward to its coming Saviour and mid every increasing oppression, pray to Him with growing longing as Calvin did, and indeed still more fervently than did he; 'quosque Domine?' "

The author has rendered a fine service in presenting this clear and carefully documented statement concerning Calvin's teaching in regard to the last things. Here we see that the Reformed Faith is a theology that deals with all of life here and that which is to come. J.R.R.

"THE TEACHING OF THE EPISTLE TO THE HEBREWS." Geerhardus Vos. Eerdmans. $2.00.

This volume presents Dr. Vos's lectures on the teaching of the Epistle to the Hebrews. From time to time they appeared in mimeographed form. Sometime ago they were issued in duplicated form by the Theological Seminary of the Reformed Episcopal Church in Philadelphia. His son, Rev. Johannes Vos, has edited the material throughout

PUBLISHED FORTNIGHTLY

Announcing A Significant Development In Protestant Journalism

STATEMENT OF POLICY AND PURPOSE

There is a growing conviction among ministers and laymen that a magazine is needed to present evangelical Christianity competently, attractively, and forcefully. It is felt that evangelical Christianity has often been misrepresented by both liberal and fundamentalist. Some liberals have not taken time to study the works of evangelical scholars; some fundamentalists have been so busy attacking others that they have failed to present adequately the positive aspects of historical Christianity.

The main thrust of CHRISTIANITY TODAY will be to present in a positive and constructive way the basic truths of the Christian faith as clearly taught in the Scriptures. Mindful of the great creeds of the historic evangelical churches, it will be neither reactionary nor static. The magazine will seek to present the content of the Christian faith on a high ethical plane, undergirded by Christian love, and empowered by the Holy Spirit. Designed to *win* men to the evangelical faith, the magazine will request all contributors to keep this specific aim prayerfully in mind.

The policy of CHRISTIANITY TODAY will be to apply the Biblical revelation vigorously to the contemporary social crises, by presenting the implications of the total Gospel message in every area of life. Fundamentalism has often failed to do this. Christian laymen are becoming increasingly aware that the answer to the many problems of political, industrial, and social life is a theological one. They are looking to the Christian Church for guidance in these spheres. We have the conviction that a consecrated and gifted evangelical scholarship can provide strategic answers.

The list of evangelical scholars is growing. This is evident in America, Great Britain, and the Continent. The magazine will provide a medium of scholarly exchange of viewpoints by the publication of articles from such sources. This should prove helpful to the busy minister, who usually has little access to the works of scholars in other lands.

The magazine will seek to avoid controversial doctrinal discussions growing out of distinctive denominational differences, while defending the great emphases of the historic creeds. It does not intend to concern itself with purely internal problems and conflicts of the various denominations. If significant enough, there will be objective reports of such.

CHRISTIANITY TODAY will be a reading *must* for laymen and pastors.

Subscription Rates — $5 for one year, $8 for two years, $10 for three years

AN INVITATION

CHRISTIANITY TODAY is happy to extend a special introductory subscription opportunity to those subscribing between now and the first publication in October. Your subscription now will entitle you to receive free of charge the six issues to be published in the fall of 1956, in addition to the full one, two or three year period for which you subscribe.

CHRISTIANITY TODAY

1014-22 Washington Building **Washington, D. C.**

THE SOUTHERN PRESBYTERIAN JOURNAL

A Presbyterian weekly magazine devoted to the statement, defense and propagation of the Gospel, the faith which was once for all delivered unto the saints.

MAY 30, 1956

VOL. XV NO. 5 $2.50 A YEAR

THE SOUTHERN PRESBYTERIAN JOURNAL
The Journal has no official connection with the Presbyterian Church in the United States
Rev. Henry B. Dendy, D.D., Editor..........Weaverville, N. C.
Dr. L. Nelson Bell, Associate Editor..........Asheville, N. C.
Rev. Wade C. Smith, Associate Editor..........Weaverville, N. C.

EDITORIAL

"Like Unto the First"

That which we are pleased to call the American way of life did not just happen. It has its roots in freedoms inherent in the Christian faith and is based upon a concept of life where every man was given an opportunity to exercise his right to make of his opportunities the best which talent and energy might produce.

Back of this concept was the recognition that man is responsible to God and also to his fellowman and that the government was the umpire to see that the rules were observed.

Today we are enamored with the fruits of our civilization and the fruits of the Christian principles which have largely dominated our way of life, but strange to say we often seem content to pull up the roots which bear the fruit while at the same time expecting the fruit to perennially remain.

We Christians know that Christian character, with its disciplined attitudes and behavior, is not superimposed on life. If real it must be the result of an inner Christian faith. This faith in turn is the result of an experimental knowledge of Christ and His Word.

Our particular generation is disturbed and confused as we see on every hand evidence of crumbling moral concepts. The home, the Church and our secular institutions are not having their influence and impact on a new generation which they did in the past.

Can it be that we have paid more attention to the fruits of Christianity than we have to the roots which produce that which we all want in our lives and the lives of others?

The story is told of a man who served hamburgers with all the trimmings. After a while he asked those who were eating whether they noticed anything peculiar. Then he told them the hamburgers had everything usually present except the meat.

In our homes and in our church life is it not often true that we have had all of the trimming but have left out the meat? We have homes with multiplied gadgets for convenience and comfort. We have church programs and activities galore. But, whether we are willing to admit it or not there are often lacking those basic elements of the Christian faith—prayer, Bible study, consistent Christian living—without which Christianity is a name rather than a fact.

Centuries ago the children of Israel had fallen into gross sin. They had turned from God to idols, from disciplined lives to gross immorality. In his hot anger Moses threw down the tablets on which God had given him the law. There is an interval of judgment and renewed turning to God.

Then God said unto Moses: *"Hew thee two tables of stone like unto the first: and I will write upon these tables the words that were in the first tables, which thou brakest."* Do we not have here an indication of the way back to the things which count?

Juvenile and adult delinquency is a scandal in American life. Both restraint and discipline are breaking down and we continue in the very things which have brought these conditions into existence.

A minister recently confessed: "I have been so wrapped up in the ritual and the program of my church that I had forgotten the message." It is the *message* which is the root of Christian faith and living, the message of sin and man's lost condition and of God's redeeming love in Christ Jesus which *must* be preached and lived. Life with its pressures and complications is more complex than in past generations. But the living Christ can and will give to each individual that turns to Him all of the resources necessary for Christian living. Our days will not exceed our strength; our problems will not be greater than the wisdom He offers; our needs will never be greater than His inexhaustible supply.

Nevertheless, to receive these all-important things from the hand of an ever-loving God man nust place himself in the way of receiving them. ?rayer as a part of everyday living is as impor-ant as the air we breathe. Bible study as a 'egular part of our daily program is as necessary ıs the food we eat. Walking in the conscious ›resence of the living Christ, trying to know and lo His will is more important than the sunshine ›n which life itself depends.

Have we lost the way? Are we enmeshed in ι whirl of Christless living? Do we see crum-›ling about us those values which come from Christ and His church and which alone make ife worthwhile? If such is the case then we ıeed to return to the *source* of true life and in ıumble confession and dependence on the Christ ›f Calvary we will find that eternal life is not ;omething to be looked forward to after death ›ut that we possess it now and that it is life ıbundant. L.N.B.

Youth Crusade

One of the most significant movements in :eligious circles in Charlotte in recent years was :he Youth Crusade held in the Caldwell Me-norial Presbyterian Church, April 22-28. The :rusade was the culmination of much thought ınd prayer on the part of a group of students in the Myers Park High School. These young people felt a deep concern for their fellow stu-lents, who were showing no fruits of faith, even though many were members of local churches, ınd for those students who had never made a profession of faith in Christ. Out of this con-:ern, and much prayer, came a conviction that :hey should sponsor a series of evangelistic serv-ces, conducted by young people, and primarily :or young people.

The small committee was enlarged as other young people showed interest, and later three local ministers were asked to counsel with the :ommittee from time to time. Several churches ›ffered their plants for the crusade, but the :ommittee finally selected the Caldwell Church. Four young men, three in college, and one in ıigh school, were selected as the main speakers. Young people from the six high schools in the :ounty were invited to participate in the serv-ces, and the response was very encouraging. An ›rder of service was finally agreed upon, and ncluded group singing, testimonies by two young people each night, Scripture reading and :he message.

The messages were simple Gospel messages, and the results were amazing, humanly speak-ing. The invitation to accept Christ as Saviour and Lord, or rededicate life to Him, was given each evening, and around 35 to 40, on an aver-age, responded each night. Included in this number were boys who had been expelled from athletic squads in the local schools for drunk-enness, and others, who to say the least, were juvenile problems. These young people were given special instruction in Christian faith and Christian living, and invited to counsel person-ally with any of the young people or ministers present in the inquiry room.

The crusade demonstrated most conclusively that many young people of today are taking their Christian religion seriously, and are sin-cerely concerned about their young friends. These young people should be encouraged in every way possible, and religious leaders should capitalize on this unprecedented opportunity that has come to our day through this spiritual awakening in the hearts of young people. The crusade was truly an answer to prayer. C.G.M.

Serving One's People

In a recent issue of the Readers' Digest, there is a beautiful story of Dr. Laurence Jones who so served his own people, the Negroes in the piney woods section of Mississippi, that he re-ceived from Governor White of Mississippi the accolade "the first citizen of Mississippi." The story reminds one of the even more famous name of Booker T. Washington who also greatly served his people. Tuskegee Institute of Ala-bama adds the name of Professor George Wash-ington Carver. These able Negro educators gave their lives and talents primarily to the service of their own people and thereby won a niche in the hall of fame in the minds both of the Negro and of the white people of our country.

These three examples came into my mind as I talked with Dr. A. B. DuPre, professor of systematic theology in the University of Pre-toria, South Africa. Dr. DuPre is touring the universities on the Continent talking with men in the same chair of theology as his own on the race question. From such conversations and his own mature thought as a fine Reformed theologian there emerge some tentative positions.

DuPre does not care for *partheid* or *segrega-tion* on legal bases. For him the Church has

The Southern Presbyterian Journal, *a Presbyterian Weekly magazine devoted to the statement, defense, and propagation of the Gospel, the faith which was once for all delivered unto the saints, published* every Wednesday by The Southern Presby-terian Journal, Inc., in Weaverville, N. C.

Entered as second-class matter May 15, 1942, at the Postoffice at Weaverville, N. C., under the Act of March 3, 1879. Vol. XV, No. 5, May 30, 1956. Editorial and Business Offices: Weaverville, N. C. Printed in the U.S.A. by Biltmore Press, Asheville, N. C.

ADDRESS CHANGE: When changing address, please let us have both old and new address as far in advance as possible. Allow three weeks after change if not sent in advance. When possible, send an address label giving your old address.

no use for secular terms. He favors brotherly consideration of other races, and occasional visits, on invitation, by white groups to Negro Churches and of Negro groups to white Churches. He does not speak of any superior race. Since the distinctive Christian virtue is humility he does not care to speak of himself or his race as better. But he does recognize that Providence has made differences between races and believes that this variety ought to be continued that each people may make its own fullest contribution to the glory of God.

When the Apostle said that in Christ there is neither male nor female, neither Jew nor Greek, he did not mean that Christians are devoid of sex nor that the facial appearance of the Greek is the same as the Jew.

Dr. DuPre would learn from Providence what the cases of Drs. Washington, Jones and Carver have illustrated in America. He says that it is generally better for the educated, gifted, persons of one race to serve their own people. Let them come to the top there and any inferiority complex will thereby be erased.

At this writing he sees no occasion for a Negro minister to serve a white congregation in South Africa. There are so many more white than Negro Christians at this writing that the whites ought to and are serving as missionaries to the Bantu. But each of these white ministers and teachers is obligated to raise up Negro leaders to take his place so that the end shall be a Negro Reformed Church thoroughly autonomous. In this Church, as elsewhere in society, the Negroes are to hold the top places in the service of their own people. If the conditions are ever reversed and the white people lose the Gospel, then he prays that Negro ministers may come to them with the Gospel until white ministers are raised up for the white people.

DuPre was greatly put out at the account in *Newsweek* of the South African Government's turning down a plan to set aside 300 million dollars to promote the industrial, commercial and agricultural development of the Bantu people. He is all for the parallel development of each race, and for the stronger one financially helping the other in that respect, even as he is for the one with the larger percentage of Christians sending the Gospel to the other.

This is the thinking of one in a different country with a different setting. But the illustrations drawn from our country show that it may have in it elements worthy of our consideration. W.C.R.

"Your Time Is My Time"

An old love song employs the above phrase. Most accurately God can say this (and does) to each of us: "Your time is My time."

Time is a priceless commodity. It is given of God to be used judiciously. We hear the expressions: "Just killing time," or "Just passing the time of day." Viewed in the light of the Scripture, such expressions are profanely offensive to God. Time is not given to be destroyed, nor to be dissipated. Rather is it to be impregnated—every moment of it—with God-honoring activity.

We do not have to "pass away the time." The tremendous thing about this phenomenon is that it passes away without our cooperation. Our job is to seize the fleeting moments, cram them with fruitful employment, and return them with the dividends of honest toil to Him who gave them. Is not this something of the meaning of Paul's words when he speaks of "redeeming the time, because the days are evil"? (Ephesians 5:16).

Dr. John R. Mott, that world-renowned Christian layman, in speaking on this subject said: "The best unit of time is the day. The key to triumphant living is to take one day at a time and live as though it were our last. And let us be sure that we begin each day with God. If a man begins the day with God, I am ready to take chances on what he does the rest of the day."

The Scriptures have much to say about the use of time. A study of the many references makes abundantly plain that the days God gives us are to be captured and capitalized upon for the glory of Christ.

In order to accomplish better this purpose we might do well to follow the example of a prominent American minister who is also a physician. As a young man, although busy as the proverbial one-armed paper-hanger, the Holy Spirit convicted him of wasting time. By way of checking up on himself he devised a plan whereby he could chart his activities for every 15-minute period from 6:30 A. M. to 11:30 P. M. daily for three days. At the end of that time he applied this test to each period:

1. Did it bring glory to God?
2. Did it bring blessing to others?
3. Was it profitable to me?

Crossing off everything which did not pass the muster of this three-fold standard, he was amazed to find 50% of his former activities eliminated. With diligence he began to pray in the words of the Psalmist: "So teach us to number our days, that we may apply our hearts unto wis-

The German speaking students gave a parody on *A Mid-summer Night's Dream,* the American students gave a cake with 70 candles and sang "Happy Birthday."

As one listened to the addresses and skimmed through the largest of the festschrifts, *Antwort,* several things stand out as significant contributions by Barth. The first is that one must not start his thinking, as Kant and the idealists do, with man, but with God. We can only reflect on what the Word itself says and speak out of the Revelation itself. Therefore, "exegesis, exegesis, exegesis." God speaks His Word in the miracle of the Incarnation of Jesus Christ. The true God Who became the servant, the true man Who was exalted to be Lord of all is the key by which to understand the Bible and to measure all our theology. We cannot talk about God without at the same time talking about man. But this does not mean starting as the existentialists do with man's understanding of himself. One starts properly with Jesus Christ Who died for me: in presenting Christ first one is also to think of man, for He became man and represents man.

Thirdly, Barth, with such colleagues as the late K. L. Schmidt, brought back the Church as the place where God speaks and made it a renewed power on the Continent of Europe. Again the Good Shepherd spoke His Word and the sheep heard. Barth testified against euthanasia as murder: the Confessing Church pastors took up the charge when Hitler had the invalids in the sanatoriums executed, some pastors such as E. Wilm going to concentration camp for their courageous testimony to the sanctity of human life.

The largest Festschrift, *Antwort,* carries articles from all parts of the world and sundry denominations, including the Roman Catholics. It was a pleasure to note there Niesel's commendation of Barth's appreciative treatment of the Heidelberg Catechism—he closes his discussion of Justification with its questions and answers. Also Wilhelm Vischer of Montpelier has a timely word, "Thou shalt not make unto thee any images." Professor F. Lieb insists on the historicity of the life and death of Jesus of Nazareth as the basis of our faith in distinction from Bultmann's treatment thereof. The subjects treated range from music to medicine: the writers are in friendly relations with but often in considerable theological difference from Barth. And your reporter would similarly classify himself. There is much to learn from this distinguished theologian. There are places where one differs. For example, I do not agree that the thought of Isaiah 53.5 (Kirchliche Dogatik Iv.i.279) is limited to the Old Testament, cf I Peter 2.24. On the other hand, I am unable to classify as a modernist, one who heartily affirms every article in the Apostles'

Creed, and who has mightily called the Church back to the study, the teaching, and the preaching of the Bible.

The serious note in the festive evening came in Barth's grateful references to close friends who had died in the last twelve months: the cousin who painted the portrait: the publisher who handled the large Festschrift: the esteemed colleague, Karl Ludwig Schmidt: the French friend Pierre Maury whose sermon, Our Times are in Thy Hand, closes the *Antwort.*

W.C.R.

ANGLERS

(From *"New Testament Evangelism"* by Wade C. Smth)

Lesson No. 141

METHOD (*Continued*)

Finding "Prospects." Look upon every person you meet as a possible "prospect" - until you have ascertained otherwise. Get the habit. You can do it. The writer knows a soul-winner who asks the Lord every morning before he leaves his bedroom to make an engagement with a "prospect" for him that day. He usually finds one or more. If you are making this a matter of daily prayer you will find yourself watching to see who comes across your path, sent by the Lord. You may see him across the counter in the store, or beside you in the train or on the bus. Another friend of the author has a habit of picking out his seatmate in the coach with a view to traveling with a "prospect." He will pass a whole vacant seat sometimes to drop in by a fellow who looks lonesome, or shows some other indication of an "opening." It is surprising how many people will come across one's path during the day, who are ripe for approach on the subject of their own spiritual need. Like a vast unexplored territory this fertile field for sowing and reaping lies all about us. Men do not go about begging Christians to talk to them. Those who most need help are apt to appear most indifferent and repellant. That is why the territory is unexplored. It is closed; but the barrier can be broken down, and sometimes it will simply come tumbling down. Christians are so rare who are willing to push in with the remedy. This pushing in is the hardest thing a personal worker has to do. If he is selling Fuller brushes or magazines he may put his foot in the crack of the cautiously opened door; but he has the marvelous "Pearl" to *give* without price and he has not the courage to tap on the door. To "push in" he must give first place to God's kingdom.

Another friend made this interesting confession to the writer: "I am amazed to discover something about myself which I never realized until now. It is the extent to which I can be absorbed in a certain thing to the exclusion of all others. My great grandfather was a cobbler. My grandfather was a shoe merchant; so was my father, and I have inherited the shoe business. Shoes - men's shoes, women's and children's shoes go walking through my daily program. Shoes have been bred and born into my very nature. Shoes are my meat and drink. I rise in the morning thinking shoes; I go to bed at night with my brain shelves stocked with shoes, all styles. As I walk along the street I don't see people; I see first and last their feet. The crowd to me is just so many pairs of shoes. I can tell almost at a glance the quality, approximately the price, and in many cases the name of the manufacturer. If a stranger meets me, introduces himself, tells where from, where going, and his business (if it is not the shoe business) I will within a few minutes after his departure forget everything about him except the shoes he was wearing. Them I cannot forget. Today, I recognize my fault. I am an avowed follower of the Lord Jesus Christ and I am an officer in the church. My first business is not shoes; it is rather the work that God wants me to do for Him. My first thought about a stranger or an acquaintance should not be his shoes, but his soul; not the quality of leather in his s-o-l-e but the measure of hope in his s-o-u-l."

No, it is not difficult to discover "prospects" if we are interested. We are very apt to find what we are looking for. A dead-in-earnest searcher will find the North Pole, though his quest carry him through perils and indescribable hardships. The main thing is to make it a matter of purpose and deep concern; not a passing thought or a momentary endeavor, but a daily life practice, saturated with prayer. It makes a big difference when we decide upon a course as a life policy. It is thus invested with a dignity and importance which impels.

More about prospect finding in the next lesson.

Helps To Understanding Scripture Readings in *Day by Day*

By Rev. C. C. Baker

Sunday, June 3, Matt. 14:22-27. Notice carefully each of the events that occurred in vv.22-25. Try to imagine the situation of the disciples out on the lake (v.24). How would you have felt if you had seen someone walking out on the water in the storm (v.26)? What

This boldness was in direct answer to the prayer of v.29), and existed in the face of persecution (vv.27-28). What do you suppose onlookers thought of these Christians as they beheld the actions of vv.32-34? Pray that God's Spirit may be poured out on our Church, that there may be a manifestation of genuine love for each other on the part of all groups.

Friday, June 8, *Galatians* 1:10-11. False teachers were upsetting the faith of the Galatian Church, teaching a gospel contrary to Paul's gospel (vv.6-7). How sure was Paul of the accuracy of the message he preached (vv.8-9)? "Let him be anathema" (vv.8,9) means "Let him be accursed." What was the source of Paul's gospel (vv.11-12,15-17)? What was the reaction of the apostles when they heard his preaching (1:24;2:9-10)? From reading 2:6-10, does there appear to be any contradiction between what Paul preached and what Jesus taught His disciples. (Notice also Peter's respect for Paul's writings in II Peter 3:15-16.) Do you realize that though there be a variety of denominations, there is only one central message that is valid to proclaim. Is the message of Gal. 2:16 the message you proclaim (vv.10,11)?

Saturday, June 9, *I John* 4:7-12. Verse nine contains the very heart-throb of the New Testament. The great aim of God's sending Christ to die (v.10) was that in Him we might have life. It is His design that this new life in us might radiate itself out to others (v.7a). This love for others is the result of the very life of God (v.8) living within us (v.12). God's love for us as manifested to us in the cross (v.10) is an example of how we ought to love one another (v.11). What are the implications of v.8? To what extent have you found God's life and love flowing through you to others?

When The Holy

By James E. Bear

(A personal interpretation and testimony by t

It may be symptomatic of a low spiritual ebb when we feel surprised at seeing God take over, bringing about results none of us felt possible.

We would mention a recent happening in the Board of World Missions which gave to all present the uplifting consciousness of God's guidance and help. We report this with the belief that God can use it for His Own glory all across our church.

For some years there has existed within our church a wide difference of opinion regarding the Japan International Christian University and the wisdom of our active participation in this venture.

Much of this difference has resulted from misunderstanding. To some the JICU has been a symbol of ecumenicity and a willingness to co-operate. To others it has been a concrete illustration of a loose use of the term "Christian," without any indication as to the meaning of the term and without any doctrinal safeguards whatsoever.

The former group, grounded in the modern concept of ecumenical approach, has keenly resented the failure of the Board of World Missions to approve of our church's participation.

On the other hand, the Board earnestly tried to secure from the Foundation of the University some simple statement of its Christian position, but without success.

It is not overstating the case to say that there has been, in some quarters, a seething discontent with the Board over this issue.

This difference of viewpoint naturally became evident on the mission field, and, as the number of younger missionaries increased the time inevitably came when the mission would reconsider its own attitude.

A few weeks ago the Japan mission voted, 26 to 25, to participate in the activities of the JICU, subject to the approval of the Board of World Missions.

It was this decision which confronted the Board at its recent meeting. Reports had come from Japan telling of the wonderful spirit of restraint and mutual love which had obtained at the meeting of the mission, despite the strong difference of opinion.

Furthermore, there were reports of the work of God's Holy Spirit in the University itself.

To Evangelize
e Today

Lauderdale

written that the king's favor is toward a wise servant; be wise and pray to God, and then men will be moved into His kingdom!

PRAYERFUL ZEAL THRIVES ON DISCOURAGEMENTS!

Threats and scorn could not quench the zeal of tireless Nehemiah as the walls began to rise again from the rubble he found in Jerusalem. The sight of the broken wall, which he surveyed alone with God one night did not discourage him, but rather challenged his valor, and made him the more determined to take away Israel's reproach.

Those quiet hours with God insured the response of the people in Jerusalem. "Then I told them of the hand of my God which was good upon me . . . And they said, Let us rise up and build." Nehemiah 2:17,18. Nehemiah did not put off his clothes, except for washing, until the work was completed, and his zeal was matched by his men; they stayed dressed and on duty day and night, too!

LOVE OF CHRIST CONSTRAINS

Love for God and the people motivated Nehemiah to make his great sacrifices. When wicked men including the Arabians, Ammonites, and Ashdodites, conspired to stop the work and the people complained, Nehemiah prayed and said, "Be not ye afraid of them: remember the Lord, which is great and terrible, and fight for your brethren, your sons, and your daughters, your wives, and your houses." Nehemiah 4:9,14. When Satan's servants sent false peace-feelers, he replied that he was doing a great work and could not come down to them.

Zealous Nehemiah knew like the apostle Paul, both of whom were inspired to labor by the Lord Jesus Christ, that though he bestowed all his goods to rebuild Jerusalem, and give his body to be burned, and lacked love, he would have been profited nothing. Because he loved God and labored as he did, Nehemiah's reward is great; his oft-repeated prayer of faith, and the words which close the book bearing his name are: "Remember me, O my God, for good." Nehemiah 13:31.

May the love of Christ and the certainty of eternal glory rekindle our zeal to preach Christ to the world! "For God is not unrighteous to forget your work and labor of love, which ye have showed toward His name . . . show the same diligence to the full assurance of hope unto the end . . . be not slothful, but *followers of them* who through faith and patience inherit the promise." Hebrews 6:10-12. Nehemiah is a God-given example for all missionaries to follow in zeal, prayer, love, and perseverance!

SABBATH SCHOOL LESSONS — REV. J. KENTON PARKER

LESSON FOR JUNE 10

The Gospel Overcomes Paganism

Background Scripture: Acts 18:23 - 21:16; Ephesians 5:15-18
Devotional Reading: Proverbs 23:1-5, 29-32

Our Background Scripture contains the account of Paul's Third Missionary Journey. In 18:23 we have a brief outline, or summary, of that journey : "And after he had spent some time there (Antioch), he departed, and went over all the country of Galatia and Phrygia in order, strengthening all the disciples."

The lesson today has a temperance application. Paganism was noted for its terrible excesses; its degrading immorality, together with drunkenness, debauchery, and greed. Heathen religions encouraged such intemperance rather than restraining it. In our Devotional Reading from Proverbs we are warned against three kinds of intemperance: over-eating, "dainties and deceitful meat"; riches; and drunkenness. These are three very common forms of intemperance. There are others. It is a wonderful victory to have self-control in all things. "The fruit of the Spirit is . . . Temperance," or Self-control. Only the Holy Spirit can enable us to be "temperate in all things."

In our lesson we see how "mightily grew the word of God and prevailed"; (19:20). This verse is selected as the Memory Verse for the younger groups. It might well be taken as a text for the whole lesson. We see how the Word of God triumphed over men's minds and hearts; over evil spirits; over false religions, and over bad business.

I. *Apollos: "Mighty in the Scriptures"*: 18:24-28.

He was an eloquent and learned man, a disciple of John the Baptist, and he was preaching and teaching the things of the Lord, knowing only the baptism of John. Aquila and Priscilla took him and expounded to him the way of God more perfectly, and he began to preach Jesus Christ. Sometimes humble disciples can teach those who are "learned." It speaks well for Apollos that he was willing to listen to those who were not as well educated as he was, but who knew the "way of God" more perfectly. God forbid that our "pride" in our own learning should ever hinder us from hearing and heeding those who have had a deeper life and experience than we have had in spiritual matters. There are some so-called learned men who are "ever learning and never able to come to the knowledge of the truth", and there are others - sincere seekers after truth - who are ever learning new and deeper truths. I am afraid that we have some men today - even leaders of the church - whose "pride of learning" is a barrier and hindrance. I am sure that they could learn much from ordinary Christians, both in the realm of faith, and spiritual power.

II. *Paul at Ephesus:* 19:1-41.

This section contains the larger part of our study for today, and I wish to divide it into several parts:

1. The Baptism of the Holy Spirit. When Paul came to Ephesus he asked the disciples whether they had received the Holy Spirit. They replied that they had not so much as heard whether the Holy Spirit was given. They had been baptized only with John's baptism. He explained the matter to them, laid his hands upon them, and the Spirit came upon them and they spake with tongues and prophesied.

2. Miracles performed by Paul. For three months Paul spoke boldly in the synagogue, and then the disciples were separated and he continued to preach in the school of Tyrannus for two years. All those that dwelt in Asia heard the word of the Lord Jesus, both Jews and Greeks. And God wrought special miracles by the hands of Paul, so that the sick were cured and evil spirits were cast out.

3. The Burning of Books: 13-20. There were seven sons of one Sceva, a Jew, exorcists, who took upon themselves to call over those who had evil spirits, "We adjure you by Jesus whom

Paul preaches." The evil spirit answered, Jesus I know, and Paul I know; but who are ye? The man who had the evil spirit leaped on them and overcame them. This made a deep impression on the people and they brought their books together and burned them (books of sorcery). "So mightily grew the Word of God and prevailed." The only way to cast out evil spirits is through the power of the Holy Spirit, in the name of Christ, The best way to destroy bad books - and we have plenty of them today - is through the power of the Best Book; the Word of God.

I am afraid that we have many people in our day who are as foolish as these seven sons of Sceva. They are attempting to cast out evil spirits in the power of man. So much of our work among juvenile delinquents and among drunkards and alcoholics is superficial. We have our camps and our recreations and other things to try and reform, when we should bring young people face to face with Christ and the Gospel. I believe the devil laughs at many of our man-made schemes. I believe that a genuine conversion, a "born again" experience, is the only cure that will stand the test of time and eternity. Why do so many of our social workers seem to be afraid of the only real remedy?

4. The Uproar at Ephesus: 21-41.

Paul planned to go over into Macedonia and Achaia and then on to Rome. In the meantime he sent Timothy and Erastus over into Greece while he remained in Asia for a time. Then came the "no small stir" which we have described in the balance of this chapter. The "stir" came when Paul's preaching began to interfere with "Bad Business." A thing like this will always arouse selfish and greedy men. They do not like for us to interfere with their money-making schemes. The whisky and beer "barons" have always feared and fought real preaching of the gospel for they know that such preaching is "bad for their business."

The trouble started at Ephesus when Demetrius, a silversmith, called together his fellow craftsmen and told them that Paul was ruining their business. The demand for silver shrines was rapidly decreasing as Paul preached about the One True God. These men had their wealth by making these images of Diana, and now Paul was threatening their business and the very worship of the "great goddess Diana" whom all Asia and the world worship. These words stirred up the mob and for the space of two hours they cried out, "Great is Diana of the Ephesians." The town-clerk, who seems to have been a capable man, appeased the crowd and dismissed them.

The preaching of the gospel is bound to affect all forms of bad business, if we preach a pure gospel and the whole gospel. There is also bound to be a conflict between the gospel and all false religions, unless we are prepared to compromise and surrender. I know that there is a strong movement today to seek to combine all the religions of the world into a "World Religion." Take the best, these people say, in all religions and form a religion which all can accept. Dr. Lenski, in his fine Interpretation of Revelation, suggests that much of the symbolism in that Book is related to movements of this kind, and Paul warns us of the dangers of these "latter days," when all sorts of false teaching will abound. This attempt to harmonize and combine all false religions would seem to be the "devil's masterpiece." To "believe the lie" is one mark of these works of Satan.

III. *Paul at Troas:* 20:1-12.

Paul now makes a trip over into Macedonia, remaining there some three months. He then returns to Asia and came to Troas where he stayed several days. They came together on the first day of the week to break bread, (the Lord's Supper), and Paul preached. (Notice the clear indication of the change from the Jewish Sabbath to the first day of the week, the Lord's Day as it was called). Paul continued his preaching until midnight and a young man fell down from the third story and was taken up dead, but was restored to life.

IV. *Paul at Miletus:* His Farewell to the Elders from Ephesus: 20:13-38.

Paul arrives at Miletus and sends for the elders of the church at Ephesus. When they come he gives them a very solemn charge. He reminds them of his preaching while among them, that he had kept nothing back, but had declared to them all that was profitable, testifying both to Jews and Gentiles repentance toward God and faith toward the Lord Jesus Christ.

He also tells them that he is going to Jerusalem where "bonds and affliction abide me." None of these things, however, would keep him from his purpose. He knows that they will see his face no more, and very solemnly declares that he is "pure from the blood of all men." For I have not shunned to declare unto you the whole counsel of God. Can all of us who preach make such a statement?

He warns them that "grievous wolves" will enter in among them not sparing the flock. He urges them to watch, and reminds them again of his own example. He had coveted no man's silver or gold, or apparel, but supported himself. He takes a most touching leave of them, as they weep, and embarks for his voyage to Jerusalem.

V. *Journey to Jerusalem:* 21:1-16.

On his way he found certain disciples at Tyre

who said to him that he should not go up to Jerusalem. Again, one Agabus, a prophet, took Paul's girdle and bound his own hands and feet and told him that the Holy Spirit said, So shall the Jews at Jerusalem bind the man who owns this girdle. Paul is determined to go on.

YOUNG PEOPLE'S DEPARTMENT — REV. B. HOYT EVANS

YOUTH PROGRAM FOR JUNE 10

Meet The Hymnbook

Hymn: "I Sing The Almighty Power of God"
Prayer
Scripture: Psalm 98 and Ephesians 5:18-20
Hymn: "Joyful, Joyful, We Adore Thee"
Offering
Hymn: "Take My Life" (Stanzas 1, 3, 6)

PROGRAM LEADER:

In October 1955 a new book called *The Hymnbook* made its appearance and caused considerable excitement among three and a half million members of the Presbyterian family in America. Committees from five different Presbyterian bodies worked three years to produce a joint hymnal, and *The Hymnbook* is the result of their labors. The cooperating denominations were these: Presbyterian U. S. A., Presbyterian U. S., Associated Reformed Presbyterian, United Presbyterian, and the Reformed Church in America.

The editor of *The Hymnbook* was Dr. David Hugh Jones, Professor of Church Music at Princeton Theological Seminary. Dr. Jones writes that *The Hymnbook* differs from existing hymnals "in the addition of about fifty psalms desired by the United Presbyterian Church and the Associate Reformed Presbyterian Church, and about twenty-five so-called Gospel hymns which were requested by all the denominations. There are several Negro spirituals and several songs from the Orient which have never appeared in one of our standard Presbyterian hymnals. Furthermore, a good number of the more recent hymns culled from at least twenty-five contemporary hymnals have been included. These hymns have been out long enough to prove their worth and I think are a worthy addition to *The Hymnbook*."

Concerning the popular reception accorded *The Hymnbook* Dr. Jones states, "The sale of the book has gone far beyond everyone's expectation. Although we ordered books for the Princeton Seminary Chapel about the first of December, we have not received them yet."

The first speaker will describe some of the outstanding features of the new *Hymnbook*, and the second speaker will tell us some of the ways to use this book, or any hymnal, more effectively.

FIRST SPEAKER:

The denominations represented in *The Hymnbook* have "somewhat different hymnological backgrounds" according to Dr. Jones, so it would be virtually impossible to include all the favorite hymns of all the people. One of the very commendable features of this new book, however, is the wide variety of hymns it contains. It is also pleasing to find that the music had been arranged so that the tunes can be sung with greater ease and satisfaction by ordinary, untrained voices.

Another praiseworthy feature of *The Hymnbook* is its very fine index. This index includes topical and alphabetical listings of the first lines, alphabetical and metrical listing of the tunes, listing of authors, composers, and sources, and most commendably, a list of all the Scripture passages to which the hymns refer.

The hymns, of course, make up the major portion of the book, but there are three other helpful sections. (1) In "Aids to Worship" we find a number of suitable prayers and calls to worship, the Ten Commandments, and the early creeds of the church. (2) In the section of "Service Music" we find a wide selection of chants and responses. These are helpful in churches which have more formal, or liturgical, services. (3) In the section of Scripture Readings there are 67 passages from the Old and New Testaments appropriate for public reading. Some of these passages are arranged for responsive reading and some for unison reading. The divisions for responsive reading are made with greater intelligence and understanding than in many hymnals. All except two of the readings are from the Revised Standard Version of the Bible. The change from the King James Version was made at the suggestion of two-thirds of the ministers who were questioned. It is likely that many people will miss the stately wording of the older version.

When all requirements are considered, it is surely true that *The Hymnbook meets more* needs than any one hymnal that has yet appeared in our churches.

SECOND SPEAKER:

Some of the churches in our denomination have already made *The Hymnbook* their official hymnal. Others will be taking this step as the books become more readily available and as the need arises. Still other churches will continue to use the books they have for many years. Regardless of the particular book we use in our church, it is likely that we do not know as much about it as we should. A knowledge of our hymnal will add richness to our spiritual life and to our worship.

One of the big problems in many churches is that the people know relatively few of the hymns in the books they have. The index can help us to use more hymns. Nearly every hymnal has an alphabetical list of hymn tunes. You will notice that many of the tunes are used with more than one set of words. Let us now look in our books at some familiar hymns. Is there an unfamiliar hymn with the same tune? (Allow time for looking up the hymns. You can speed it up by giving the page number of the tune index.) Now let us sing this new hymn with the familiar tune. (A good pianist will make this part of the program more profitable and enjoyable.)

Most hymnals also have a metrical index. Tell the young people where to find it. You will notice that many of the hymns have the same metrical arrangement. Hymns can be alternated if they have the same metrical arrangement. Now, find a hymn which has an unfamiliar tune. Notice its metrical arrangement, such as 7.6.7.6.D.. If you can find a familiar tune with the same arrangement, you can use the words with that tune. Let us choose a hymn and try it.

Another way to increase our appreciation of the hymnal is to learn to use the topical index. How many times when we were responsible for a program have we paged hurriedly through the book trying to find some suitable hymn? Suppose, for instance, that we were having a program about the Church, and we wanted to sing some fitting hymns. All we need to do is to look under "Church" in the topical index, and we find a list of appropriate hymns.

Let us endeavor to be more thoughtful in our use of the hymnal, and we shall find that our singing will mean more to us and to our programs and services.

Women's Work

A Calm and Quiet Inner Spirit

Your beauty should not be dependent on an elaborate coiffure, or on the wearing of jewelry or fine clothes, but on the inner personality—the unfading loveliness of a calm and gentle spirit, a thing very precious in the eyes of God. —I Peter 3:3-4 (Phillips Translation)

In so much of today's striving, there is a great deal of activity and "business." With the acceleration that has come in the speed and mode of travel, in the scope and means of communication, in scientific inventions and discoveries, we are faced with the danger of being so busy that we lose the integrity of our own souls.

This characteristic of our age has very definite repercussions on our homes and our children. Pressure that often results in frustration is the parent of bad temper and tension. "The King's daughter is all glorious within!" Could it be that as women we have too often struggled for superfluous things and in so doing have paid the price of a calm and gentle spirit? Do folks meeting us sense the presence of the One who walked the hills of Galilee; who went often into the mountains to pray; who healed everyone who came to Him? When you walk into a difficult situation, do you become a part of the problem or a part of the solution? Much will depend on to what degree you have this inner beauty; what your spiritual resources are.

Is the implication, then, that as a Christian, one is to sit quietly and let the rest of the world go by? It would be best for Christ to speak his own word to us in regard to this. "Why call me Lord, Lord, and do not the things that I say?" The inner resources which make for a developing beauty are also the empowering for the sharing the heart of the compassionate Christ with our next door neighbors, and with all the world. Nothing will send you on his errands faster and with greater joy than the reality of His presence within you.

Prayer:

Dear Lord and Father of mankind,
Forgive our feverish ways;
Reclothe us in our rightful mind,
In purer lives Thy service find,
In deeper reverence, praise.

—Ruth Youngdahl Nelson

From *The Church Woman*

World Day of Prayer
Highlights from 1956 Report

Alabama

Grove Hill: An interracial service was held at 8:45 in the morning. Church chimes called everybody to a minute of prayer; 705 took part in a twenty-four hour vigil.

Arkansas

Hot Springs: Army and Navy Hospital broadcast sacred music during the noon hour over loud speaker. Traffic lights all over town were held red for one minute at 2:00 o'clock for silent prayer.

Florida

Vero Beach: Announcement of service was made on movie screen. Six windows were decorated in important places, and the service was broadcast.

Louisiana

Shreveport: Traffic was stopped for one minute. Special services were held at home for blind, for aged, and at business girls' hostel. A TV panel was heard before the day and movie theatres showed trailers.

Oklahoma

Cookson: Cherokee County, entertained two Indian churches.

New Kirk: Business houses and bank closed.

Shawnee: Theater was offered for hour of meditation. Chimes played for fifteen minutes preceding each meeting.

Texas

Gainesville: A covenant of prayer at 9 a. m. by members of committee for two weeks before World Day of Prayer.

Iowa Park: All grades in elementary school used children's service.

Taylor: Fire Department sounded siren at noon for prayer. Two high schools observed prayer at their morning assemblies.

Teague: Prayer committee visited the sick with the service.

—From **The Church Woman**

Church News

Additional Overtures to the General Assembly

(48) The Presbytery of Potomac respectfully overtures the General Assembly to consider the advisability of setting up a Division of Welfare Agencies, to be under the direction of the Board of Annuities and Relief, to study the problems, give guidance and set up standards for homes for children, homes for the aging, hospitals and similar agencies.

(49) Whereas, the General Assembly of the Presbyterian Church, U.S., has by resolution recommended the opening of our churches, schools and colleges to all races, and

WHEREAS, the action of the General Assembly has been publicized throughout the United States and elsewhere as the attitude and belief of the Presbyterian Church, U. S.,

Now, we the Presbytery of Charleston, declare:
1. That we do not agree with the action of the General Assembly referred to above.

2. That we believe that the action of the General Assembly referred to above will cause dissension and hatred between the races.

3. That the action of the General Assembly aforesaid was taken without submitting such issues to the presbyteries composing the Assembly, and it is our conviction that such action does not truly indicate the convictions of its presbyteries or the membership of the Church.

Now therefore, the Presbytery of Charleston respectfully overtures the General Assembly to authorize a ballot by each presbytery of the General Assembly for determination of policy as to whether or not the Presbyterian Church, U.S., shall have segregation or integration of all races; same being conducted in accordance with properly constituted authority.

(50) WHEREAS, the Presbytery of Charleston wishes to express its attitude toward membership of the Presbyterian Church, U. S., in the National Council of Churches of Christ in the U. S. A. and in the World Council of Churches, and

WHEREAS, continued membership gives tacit approval of public pronouncements and resolutions that have been widely circulated, which do not express the convictions of a majority of the total membership, and

WHEREAS, resolutions above referred to have accused those not in agreement with their social, economical and political views as un-Christian, and

WHEREAS, the leadership of both associations, above referred to, openly envision the ultimate goal as organic union of all Protestant Churches in a one World Church:

Now Therefore, the Presbytery of Charleston respectfully overtures the General Assembly for determination of policy as to whether or not the Presbyterian Church, U.S., shall withdraw from or remain in the National Council of the Churches of Christ in U.S.A., and the World Council of Churches; same being conducted in accordance with properly constituted authority.

World Mission Receipts

Budget for 1956	$3,300,000.00
Receipts to date	942,680.64
Percentage of annual budget received for 1956	28.56%
Balance needed for 1956	2,357,319.36

Curry B. Hearn, Treasurer

GEORGIA

Cherokee Presbytery met in an all-day session Tuesday, at the Westminster Presbyterian Church, Rome, Ga.

The Rev. Charles Moffatt, pastor of the First Presbyterian Church, Cedartown, Ga., served as moderator.

An address on the subject of Presbyterian History was delivered by Dr. E. C. Scott, Stated Clerk of the General Assembly of the Presbyterian Church U.S.

Following a sermon by the Rev. H. Paul Currie, pastor of the Calhoun Presbyterian Church, the Lord's Supper was observed under the leadership of the Rev. L. Samuel Magbee, host pastor and the Rev. Dan A. Dunaway, pastor of the Rockmart Presbyterian Church.

The Rev. David Lehman, pastor of the Atcooga Presbyterian Church, Dalton, Ga., resigned his pastorate in order to accept an appointment by the Board of World Missions to Brazil. Mr. Lehman and his family will spend the better part of the summer in training at Montreat, N. C. before leaving for their new assignment. Mr. Lehman will continue to be a member of Cherokee Presbytery, which now has three missionaries in Brazil. The others are the Rev. Stephen J. Sloop and the Rev. Paul B. Smith.

Presbytery announced that the summer camp and conference program will again be held at the Rabun Gap - Nacoochee School, Clayton, Ga. The Rev. J. Clyde Plexico, Jr., pastor of the First Presbyterian Church, Cartersville, Ga., will direct the Senior Conference to be held June 25-30. The Rev. David Boozer, pastor of the Parkview Presbyterian Church, Marietta, Ga., will direct the Pioneer Camp, to be held July 2-7.

Presbytery accepted the invitation of the Beersheba Presbyterian Church, Route No. 3, Summerville, Ga., for the next meeting to be held September 18th, and nominated the Rev. Boozer, to serve as Moderator for that meeting.

Robert C. Pooley, Jr., Stated Clerk

LOUISIANA

The Presbytery of Louisiana met on April 17 in the Baker Church. Judge John T. Hood of Lake Charles was elected Moderator. Some high lights of the meeting were the presentation of the Louisiana Moral and Civic Foundation by Mr. Earl Hotalen, Secretary; the presentation of Christian Campus life by representatives of the different Westminster Fellowship Groups; the examination for ordination of Mr. Keith Wright who is to be Assistant Minister in Charge of Education in the Lake Charles Church; and the appointment of a Commission to organize the Broadmoor Church in Baton Rouge. The Presbytery recessed to meet at the Meeting of Synod on July 17.

Robert D. Earnest, Stated Clerk

MISSOURI

Cape Girardeau — Dr. Mark Scully, superintendent of schools at Dearborn, Mich., and a Presbyterian elder, was named early in May to be president of Southeast Missouri State College.

Dr. Scully, a native of Charleston in southeast Missouri, was an elder in the Paducah, Ky., First Church, when he was superintendent of schools for that city. He is a graduate of the college which he will head beginning July 1, and holds an M.A. from Peabody College, Nashville, Tenn., and a doctorate from Columbia University, New York. Mrs. Scully is the former Pearl Irene Golden of Anniston, Ala. The couple has two sons.

Buffalo Presbyterian Church Celebrates Its Bi-centennial

Greensboro, N. C.

In celebration of its bicentennial, Buffalo church is presenting a historical pageant on the evenings of June 15th and 16th, on the church grounds. On Sunday the 17th at the regular 11 o'clock service the preacher will be a descendant of pioneer families of the church. After dinner on the grounds a sacred concert will be rendered by the Greensboro Oratorio Society, Don Trexler directing. Soloists will be Mrs. John Russell, soprano; John Medearis, bass, and Erlu Neese, tenor. All descendants of pioneer families of the church, wherever located, are especially invited to this bicentennial, as are all other persons who are interested. The title of the pageant is "Let Freedom Ring." It will emphasize colonial and Revolutionary War history and the part played by members of this church in that momentous struggle for religious and civil liberty, and other matters pertaining to the history of this congregation.

Greenville, S. C.—An evangelistic series was held during the week prior to Easter Sunday by the Rev. John Knight, pastor of the Smyrna Presbyterian Church of Smyrna, Georgia. A prayer session was held each night before the services. There was evidence of a planting of the Seed which will be reaped as time passes. There were seven public professions of faith as a result of God's Spirit blessing the services. Cottage Prayer meetings and visitation evangelism were preparatory exercises. The Pastor and Session wish to publicly thank the Lord for sending Rev. Knight.

Rev. L. T. Newland, D. D.,
of Blowing Rock, N. C., has been honorably retired because of age, and has adopted Black Mountain, N. C., for residence, as of June 1st this year.

School. The presentation was made by Paul Fulton, superintendent of the Sunday School, who called attention to the fact that in the case of Anne Ford this bar represented attendance every Sunday for eight consecutive years.

Nashville — Rev. and Mrs. Clarence M. Bassett of our Mexico Mission announce the arrival of a daughter, Betty Ruth, on March 24 in Mexico.

Mr. Bassett was born in Greenville, Texas, though he now considers Amarillo, Texas, his home. He is a member of Dallas Presbytery. He received his education at Austin College, Austin Theological Seminary and Union Theological Seminary.

Mrs. Bassett is the former Miss Katherine Myers, daughter of former Mexico missionaries of our church, Mr. and Mrs. Z. V. Myers. She is a member of the First Presbyterian Church of Kingsville, Texas. She received her education at Austin College and the Assembly's Training School.

Rev. and Mrs. Howard Cameron of our Congo Mission announce the arrival of a daughter, Grace Ann, on May 2 in Bulape. Mr. Cameron is from Eastman, Georgia, and is a graduate of Maryville College and Columbia Theological Seminary. He is a member of Augusta-Macon Presbytery. Mrs. Cameron is the former Miss Wilma Davis of Etowah, Tenn. She is also a graduate of Maryville College, and is a member of the Presbyterian Church of Eastman, Ga. Miss Nan Fulson of our Congo Mission arrived in this country in April for her regular furlough in the United States.

A native of Atlanta, Miss Fulson received her R.N. degree from the Crawford W. Long School of Nursing. She is a member of the North Avenue Presbyterian Church in Atlanta, and she plans to make her home in Atlanta while she is in this country.

On June 1st, Miss Martha Getsinger will become the Director of Youth Work in the First Presbyterian Church of Florence. Miss Getsinger, a native of Anderson, South Carolina, has for the past few years been assisting in Young People's Work in the West End Presbyterian Church of Hopewell, Virginia. Miss Getsinger completed her academic work at Montreat College.

In the beginning Miss Getsinger will mainly confine her efforts to revitalizing our Young People's work with special attention to the Vesper Programs on Sunday evening.

Due to the work of some of our Deacons and the cooperation of the Session and Board of Deacons, Mr. Archie L. McNair, a member of this Church and a student at Columbia Theological Seminary, will be in our Church to assist in the work of the ministry throughout the months of June, July and August.

Mr. McNair will conduct the Evening Services each Sunday and will be in charge of the full program during the Pastor's vacation in the month of August.

— BOOKS —

"GOD - THE SUPREME STEWARD." John E. Simpson. Zondervan. $.50.

Many have written on stewardship from the human side and the place that it occupies in Scripture. The author believes that there should be more teaching about giving from the divine standpoint. This phase has been left almost untouched in our thinking and writing. "God so loved . . . that he gave" transcends all other gifts. This little book has a great message in reminding us that God is the supreme example in the realm of stewardship.

"WHITEFIELD'S SERMON OUTLINES." Geo. Whitefield. Edited by Sheldon B. Quincer. Eerdmans. $2.50.

Here are thirty-five sermon outlines from the best of George Whitefield, the famous eighteenth century evangelist. These outlines have been taken from rare books of Whitefield sermons and they are fine examples of the spiritual power wielded by this man of God. With the publication of this volume a significant group of Whitefield's sermons are available to today's preacher in suggestive and readily adaptable outline form.

"TEENAGE RAMPAGE." Jim Vaus. Zondervan. $1.00.

The author points out that there are many teenagers today who are running rampant in the community bringing havoc upon society. They need to be reached for time and eternity. This book is written in order to help others to understand these lost youths and how to reach them for Christ.

"THE BLESSED HOPE." George E. Ladd. $3.00.

In this volume Dr. Ladd sets forth and defends the statement that "The blessed hope is the second coming of Jesus Christ and not a pre-tribulation rapture." The author affirms His belief in the personal premillenial second advent of Christ and he subscribes to the general pattern of prophetic truth. At the same time Dr. Ladd argues that premillenialism and pretribulationism are not necessarily the same. The author seeks to encourage careful study of the Bible, to bring a better understanding to a difficult subject and to promote Christian liberty in the interpretation of prophetic truth.

"STUDIES IN COLOSSIANS." Richard Sturz. Moody Press. $.35.

Here is a book on the preeminence of Christ in which to steep the soul. The author shows how Colossians reveals its treasures to those who desire to put into practice the basic principles of the new life in Christ.

"NEO-ORTHODOXY." Charles Caldwell Ryrie. Moody Press. $.75.

The purpose of this book is to tell what neo-orthodoxy is and what it does. The author shows that the danger of neo-orthodoxy is that much of its terminology is the same as that of the conservative theologians. Because of this similarity many do not readily discern the differences in content. The author shows as simply as possible the errors to be found in the theological movement that goes by the name of neo-orthodoxy.

"THE CAMBRIDGE SEVEN." J. C. Pollock. Intervarsity Christian Fellowship. $1.00.

The Cambridge Seven emerged from British universities and was stirred to the depths by the work of D. L. Moody, the American evangelist. The story is told of seven Cambridge men of high social position and noted athletic ability who gave themselves to the work for Christ in difficult fields of labor. The seven men were Montagu Harry Proctor Beauchamp, William Wharton Cassels, Dickson Edward Hoste, Author T. Polhill-Turner, Cecil Henry Polhill-Turner, Stanley P. Smith, and Charles Thomas Studd.

"WITNESS TO THE CAMPUS." Roger Ortmayer. Methodist Student Movement. $1.50.

This little volume is an attempt to think about the prior questions that must be asked if we want to explore the Christian witness to the contemporary academic community. It is the result of a seminar sponsored by the division of educational institutions of the Methodist Board of Education. These papers were read and discussed, each addressed to one of the questions such as, "What can we find out about evangelism from the Gospel?" "What happens in conversion?" What does one think about evangelism in the university context?" There are seven chapters some of which are adaptable to any campus. Others deal with campus activity from the liberal point of view. This book will have to be read with discernment.

"CLINICAL TRAINING FOR PASTORAL CARE." David Belgum. Westminster Press. $3.00.

This volume is a guide for students of pastoral care whether they are in theological schools, in clinical training centers, or actively engaged in the parish ministry. It offers an orientation to the nature of the hospital and the functions performed in it. Resources of the pastor are discussed and suggestions made for using them to communicate with the patient and to meet his needs. The pastoral call is thoroughly analyzed as well as the adaptation of the call to the situation.

"REST FOR THE WEARY." Vance Havner. Fleming H. Revell Co. $2.00.

Not cessation of labor but learning how to rest while we work is Vance Havner's answer to the tension of our time. The real rest, he writes, for now and through eternity is service through the strength of Christ within. These meditations will help weary souls to find Balm in Gilead and rest for all.

"FOLLOWING GOD THROUGH THE BIBLE." Alexander G. Patterson. Christopher. $2.50.

The author holds that the Bible consists of a series of events and these events form a chain, and no link in the chain can be left out. One link gone and the story can never be complete. The absence of one link causes confusion instead of clarity. This book, therefore, is based upon a method of Bible study that the author calls "The Succession Of Events." The idea is that when God starts something He carries it on. With this idea the author shows that each event dovetails into the other.

"INVESTING YOUR LIFE." W. J. Werning. Zondervan. $.75.

The author is assistant stewardship counsellor of the Lutheran Church, Missouri Synod. He tells here how to invest life and means where they will count for the most.

You Are in BIG Business

Presbyterian higher education, although small in proportion to all such education in the South, looms large in the finances of our Church. It represents $1,303,125 (1955) in the giving of local churches to this cause. For the synods which finance and control most of our institutions, this is big business.

- Our 28 institutions enroll 9,507 students.
- There are 779 faculty members.
- On the 28 campuses there are 534 buildings.
- The value of buildings and equipment is $41,351,263.
- Endowments total $40,526.263.
- Our program of higher education also includes work with Presbyterian students and faculty members in other church schools, private schools, and tax-supported institutions. It is estimated that there are 60,000 Presbyterian students in the South, and more than 5,000 Presbyterian faculty members.

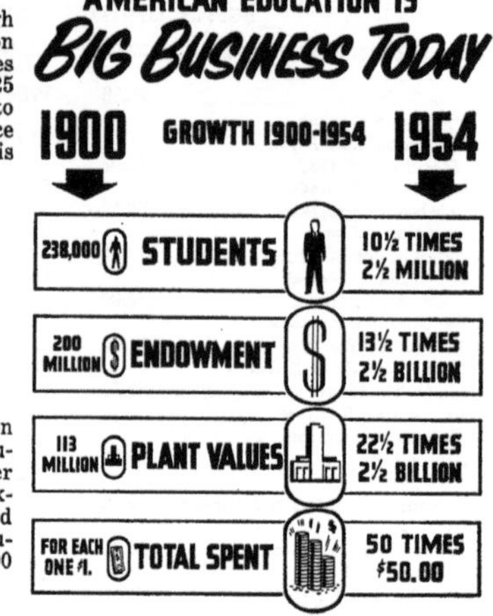

Role of the Liberal Arts College

A liberal arts education of the type offered by our church colleges is not, and should not be, vocational education. The tremendous cost of professional and specialized education usually is paid for on a tax-support basis.

Liberal arts education, on the other hand, is designed to impart to all students, regardless of professional preference, an understanding of all the forces which make up our civilization. It gives meaning and purpose to the events which we observe in our generation. Church colleges concentrate on learning to live, which their officials believe should come before learning how to make a living. It should be remembered that most of the professions require a bachelor's degree as a condition of entrance into specialized training. Increasingly, business is seeking men and women with the liberal arts education.

It should be understood, also, that a church college is first of all a college. It is not characterized by narrow denominationalism. Church colleges furnish a channel through which our denomination serves mankind and honors God.

Providing leadership for the Church is a by-product of the educative process, although a very important one.

Quality Education in a Christian Setting

PRESBYTERIAN EDUCATIONAL ASSOCIATION OF THE SOUTH

Box 1176, Richmond 9, Virginia

THE SOUTHERN PRESBYTERIAN JOURNAL

A Presbyterian weekly magazine devoted to the statement, defense and propagation of the Gospel, the faith which was once for all delivered unto the saints.

VOL. XV. NO. 6 JUNE 6, 1956 $2.50 A YEAR

DR. W. TALIAFERRO THOMPSON

Moderator of the 1956 Assembly Meeting at Montreat, North Carolina

THE SOUTHERN PRESBYTERIAN JOURNAL
The Journal has no official connection with the Presbyterian Church in the United States
Rev. Henry B. Dendy, D.D., Editor......Weaverville, N. C.
Dr. L. Nelson Bell, Associate Editor......Asheville, N. C.
Rev. Wade C. Smith, Associate Editor......Weaverville, N. C.

EDITORIAL

Faith Working in Love

In our church courts, in our personal relationships, in our homes, wherever men come into close association with others there are inevitable clashes of opinion and of personalities.

These differences can be a fruitful area of Christian witness for God can use those yielded to Him to take these very things and use them for His Own glory.

In the churches in Galatia a deep controversy had arisen over circumcision and legalism. Many had been drawn back from the freedom of the Gospel into the legalistic concepts of the Jewish Christians.

Paul enters this controversy with a letter designed to clarify the situation and to magnify the freedom which men have in Jesus Christ.

In the fifth chapter, verse 6, he sets forth a principle which should guide our thinking and our actions today: *"For in Jesus Christ neither circumcision availeth anything, nor uncircumcision; but faith which worketh by love."*

Does our faith express itself in arrogance? in a determination to have our own way? in selfishness? in an inability to try to see the other's viewpoint? How often we have to admit that it does just that.

But, if with our faith, our strong convictions, our deep interest, we have the God-given grace to express our position in love, what a blessed experience for all concerned.

The work of God's kingdom will go forward when our faith is worked out in love; when our convictions are tempered with that fruit of the Holy Spirit, love, which softens, constrains and wins.

This is not theoretical but practical, not imaginary but effective. By God's help we too may be Christians known by our *work of faith, labour of love and patience of hope.*

It makes a tremendous difference. L.N.B.

Sharper Than Any Two-edged Sword

There is quietly developing in America a controversy which is of the greatest significance, one which can and should develop. It is not a controversy between personalities except in so far as they represent divergent viewpoints. Rather it is a controversy having to do with the basic concept of the content and authority of Christian doctrine.

There are only a few who would care to champion the theological liberalism of fifty years ago. Two world wars have effectively shattered the easy optimism of a theology which anticipated human progress in terms of man's innate goodness and his own inherent ability to improve himself and the society of which he was a part.

Amidst the confusion resulting from the disillusionment of these humanistic optimists there came a voice of conviction in the person of Karl Barth and for nearly forty years he has been the most influential personality in the theological world.

The innate sinfulness of man and God's redemptive work through Jesus Christ as man's only hope have been declared and stressed. It is probable that Barth's own strong convictions and his prolific writings have intensified his influence, and at a time when such a clear-cut stand was sorely needed.

At the same time, he is one of the most difficult men in the world to follow because he has fluctuated so widely in his own teaching and also because he is both confused and confusing, at the same time being both logical and illogical.

Because of the influence of Barth, more than any other one individual, there has emerged a new system of theology known as neo-orthodoxy. Like its author, neo-orthodoxy varies from time to time and with the individual who has espoused it.

The theological world, conservative as well as liberal, owes a great debt to Barth. He forced many to see the untenable and illogical (as well as the impracticable) position of modernism. He unqualifiedly accepted many of the basic positions of the conservative theology of an earlier generation.

At the same time, while veering sharply away from modernism, the turn has never been complete. While confusing the pale equivocations and vacillations of many liberals by stating his firm belief in such doctrines as the virgin birth, there has been a baffling unwillingness to accept Scriptural affirmations as the basis of authority and a reaching out into the thin air of human reason to come up with a doctrinal belief. This is well illustrated by one of his followers who has said: "I believe in the virgin birth, not because the Bible says so but because it seems a logical explanation of the incarnation."

It is at this point that neo-orthodoxy is weak and will continue to be weak until it makes a further turn back to the historical evangelical position. The inherent weakness is this nebulous basis of authority for faith and its resulting lack of convictions on the part of many of its followers, a lack which is all too evident in the use of the Bible itself.

Furthermore, this lack of an authoritative basis has resulted in a doctrinal instability by many and strange and compulsive emphases on the part of others. Men of strong minds and broad scholarship have taken sharp issue with Barth where he is conservative and joined with him where he is himself uncertain or liberal. Men such as Paul Tillich and Reinhold Niebuhr are in this category and have wielded great influence, particularly in American circles.

The developing controversy which we mentioned in the beginning stems from those proponents of neo-orthodoxy who resent the statement "the Bible says," as a basis of final authority, and who deplore the "literalism" which they find inherent in it.

On the other hand, they find themselves baffled by the obvious fact that such reference back to a divine authority carries a weight and produces results for which they have no adequate explanation.

One of America's outstanding secular journalists recently remarked to the writer: "The liberals are scared to death, because if those whose ministry is based on the finality of the divine record are right then they, the liberals, are dead wrong and they know it."

The dilemma of the neo-orthodox position is its own affirmation that the Bible is only a *partial* authority, that it only *contains* the word of God. This one fatal premise opens up the entire gamut of individual interpretations which have always characterized liberal thinking. Each man becomes his own authority; each individual mind takes or rejects that which his own reason (or that of the fellow-traveler in neo-orthodoxy who he is following), may dictate. That this results in a certain degree of theological anarchy is a foregone conclusion.

No matter how much one may extoll the fruits of the Christian faith, if the fruits are separated from their root in the integrity of the Biblical record there is no life with which to pass them on to others.

This same lack of a Scriptural basis produces the strange philosophy that corporate sins may be rectified without the personal redemption of the individual sinner; Christianity then becomes primarily a matter of social adjustments and not of a sinner before a righteous and holy, but also loving and personal God.

Admitting to the fullest that there is a total *influence* of the Church and of the Christian on the social order, we must never forget that the inescapable sequence of God's plan is that individuals must be saved personally before they can live as Christians in the society of which they are a part.

This controversy will vary in the degree with which men accept or reject Biblical integrity and authority but it is an inevitable consequence of the elevation of reason over revelation. Those who now reject the "incredible" stories of Scripture such as the virgin birth, the miracles of our Lord, His vicarious and blood-bought sacrifice on Calvary, His bodily resurrection, etc., etc., would do well to ponder the words of a former unbeliever: *"Why should it be thought a thing incredible with you, that God should raise the dead?"*, and to rejoice in his experience with the risen Lord Who told him: *"I have appeared unto thee for this purpose, to make thee a minister and a witness both of these things which thou hast seen, and of those things in the which I will appear unto thee."* From that day the scriptural record be-

The Southern Presbyterian Journal, *a Presbyterian Weekly magazine devoted to the statement, defense, and propagation of the Gospel, the faith which was once for all delivered unto the saints,* published every Wednesday by The Southern Presbyterian Journal, Inc., in Weaverville, N. C.

Entered as second-class matter May 15, 1942, at the Postoffice at Weaverville, N. C., under the Act of March 3, 1879. Vol. XV, No. 6, June 6, 1956. Editorial and Business Offices: Weaverville, N. C. Printed in the U.S.A. by Biltmore Press, Asheville, N. C.

ADDRESS CHANGE: When changing address, please let us have both old and new address as far in advance sa possible. Allow three weeks after change if not sent in advance. When possible, send an address label giving your old address.

came an unswerving basis of authority for the apostle Paul. Shall we regard it with less confidence?

Begging the question with the straw men of "literalism" or "individualism" does not clarify the situation. Men have and do make mistakes in attitudes and interpretations. It is true that historical settings, local contexts and cultural differences must be recognized for a clear understanding of the Scriptures. But such an understanding lessens not one whit either the integrity or the authority of the Word of God.

Fortunately, this controversy can be settled by the simple process of seeing how the two viewpoints work out when applied to individual lives, and to society. Which shows the presence and the transforming power of the Holy Spirit? Which brings men to grips with their own personal problem of sin? Which turns men in repentance to the foot of the cross - to the blood-bought redemption of Calvary? Which has the power to transform men (instantaneously or gradually) into new creatures in Christ?

Let this controversy continue because on its right solution rests the present and future power and usefulness of the Church. L.N.B.

Drugs Available for Mission Hospitals? ? ?

In several of our Southern cities local physicians have become interested in collecting samples and larger consignments of drugs for transmission to our mission hospitals abroad. In a few instances the quantity and value of these drugs have assumed major proportions.

This is to ask you to pass on this word to physicians in your locality, telling them of the need and asking them to join in this activity. They will find many of their retail drug men interested and cooperative.

The Board of World Missions has appointed the undersigned a committee to head up this project. You can choose the mission hospital you wish to receive these drugs. We will advise you as to the best method of packing and shipping.

One doctor has already collected and shipped over $7,000.00 worth of drugs to Africa and Korea. If this idea is developed on a large scale it can bring great blessing to all of our mission hospitals - and to the people they serve.

L. Nelson Bell, Chairman
Montreat, N. C.

Peggy Boggs
1338 East 53rd St.,
Savannah, Ga.

Sam F. Bissett
1015-17 West Platt St.,
Tampa 6, Florida

Amazing Grace

There is an old song we Presbyterians sing only too rarely. Some one has facetiously said it is the "National Anthem of the Baptists." If that is true let us appropriate it to our own uses too for it applies to all Christians.

Our concern in this matter is a practical one. Too few Christians are amazed by God's grace. We are proud and feel that in some measure we deserve God's grace. There is a sophistication today which makes many feel that they are doing God an honor to join the church.

Not until we realize what we really are and from what Christ has saved us can we possibly realize anything of the depths of God's love and grace.

The veneer of respectability, of education, of social position and correctness confuses us and we think we are pretty good folks. Only when God's Holy Spirit convicts us of our sins and shows us how black they really are can we hope to praise God for His marvelous grace.

The sinfulness of man and the awfulness of that sin can only be evaluated in the light of what God found necessary to do to solve the sin problem. If the Son of God Himself had to come into this world to redeem men then that truly is amazing grace.

John Newton knew by experience when he wrote:

Amazing grace! how sweet the sound,
That saved a wretch like me!
I once was lost, but now am found,
Was blind, but now I see.

'Twas grace that taught my heart to fear,
And grace my fears relieved;
How precious did that grace appear
The hour I first believed.

Thro' many dangers, toils and snares,
I have already come;
'Tis grace that brought me safe thus far,
And grace will lead me home.

When we've been there ten thousand years,
Bright shining as the sun,
We've no less days to sing God's praise,
Than when we first begun.

L.N.B.

Primarily a Teacher?

By Gordon H. Clark

This summer there is to appear a volume by E. E. Tilden, Jr., entitled *Toward Understanding Jesus.* The advance notice indicates that one of the author's assumptions is that Jesus was primarily a teacher. Although no review can be written before the book is seen, and though therefore what follows does not directly envisage this book, one can ask independently whether Jesus was in fact primarily a teacher. Would this presupposition tend to produce an accurate study of Jesus or would it tend to distort the picture?

Of course, Jesus was a teacher to some extent. He taught certain moral principles as exemplified in the Beatitudes. He also taught some profound theology: his concept of Messiah, and the sovereignty, which he shared with his Father, of selecting the recipients of revelation (Mt. 11:25-27). But though he taught, can it be said that he was primarily a teacher? Does his fame, does his significance, depend chiefly on his teaching career?

To answer this question, comparison might well be made between Jesus and some acknowledged great teachers. Plato, Kant, and the grand old man of many a small college have been great teachers. Characteristic of them all is their length of service. They taught several generations of students. And if some teacher enjoyed a shorter span of life, it is still clear that men do not achieve fame in teaching with only three years to their credit.

In the next place, a great teacher manages to get his instruction across to the majority, if not to the dullest, of his students. Judged on this basis, Jesus was not altogether a success. His disciples rather uniformly misunderstood what he said. Nor can he be defended by the excuse that he was unfortunately stuck with duller than average pupils: he had chosen them himself. Had he been a great teacher, he would have selected more intelligent material. But to the end Jesus upbraided his disciples for their failure to understand.

But above all, to say that Jesus was primarily a teacher is to contradict his explicit statements. Such an assumption ignores the expressions of purpose that Jesus himself made, and thus leads to distortion. How can an author expect to be historically accurate if he disparages the sources?

Note these claims made by Jesus himself: the Son of Man came . . . to give his life a ransom for many; the Son of Man is come to seek and to save that which was lost; I am not come to call the righteous, but sinners to repentance. And if Christ's words continue to verse 16, we may add, God so loved the world that he gave his only begotten Son that whosoever believeth in him should not perish but have everlasting life. If perchance these words are not Christ's own, but John's comment, the verse nonetheless testifies to the original and uniform Christian position. Cf. Gal. 4:4; Heb. 2:14-17; I Jn. 3:8. For further profitable and interesting study, see *The Typology of Scripture,* by Patrick Fairbairn, 1900 edition, Vol. I, pp. 98 ff, and *The Christian View of God and the World,* by James Orr, sixth edition, pp. 276 ff.

Undoubtedly Jesus taught; but he came to die. His primary purpose was to purchase redemption by his blood. The main burden of teaching could safely be left to Paul; but no one else could bear our sins in his own body on the tree. Any contrary view not merely distorts, but rather obliterates the Jesus who came to save his people from their sins.

ANGLERS

(From "*New Testament Evangelism*"
by Wade C. Smith)

METHOD (*Continued*)

Lesson No. 142

Finding Prospects. Following up one prospect will sometimes turn up others in a surprising way. A church member with many misgivings as to her fitness, at the request of her pastor undertook to visit a woman prospect whose name had been handed to the pastor by another worker. A knock at the door failed to get any response. The house was closed up. A neighbor working in her flowers next door stepped to the fence and volunteered the information that Mrs. A. had gone away for the day. The visitor thanked her and incidentally mentioned that she had called to invite Mrs. A. to special services being held at the church. This naturally led to an invitation extended to the neighbor, whereupon she frankly informed the visitor that she and her entire household had no connection with any church. There were five children and they attended no Sunday school. There were two grown sisters of the husband living with them. They were business women. The interview extended into several other visits, resulting in all the adults attending the services, three of them making a profession of faith, and the five children enrolled in the Sunday school. That was a recent occurrence at this writing. The oldest of the five children has since made a profession of faith and joined the church, and the blessed work of the Holy Spirit goes on, ultimately, we have a right to hope, resulting in the saving of the whole household. Prospects beget prospects.

One way to start a private prospect list is to mentally call a roll of your acquaintances as you may be able to think of them, beginning at home, then your neighborhood and your intimate and not so intimate friends. Think of the people with whom you have business contact and those who serve you in one way and another. The circle may widen and enlarge as you have time to put your mind to the matter. As each one comes up in thought try to decide in your own mind just what the spiritual status of each one is. You may be surprised to discover how little you know of their soul's welfare. You know their politics, their views about education, music, art, merchandise, automobiles, chickens, golf, servants, the threat of war, United Nations, bobbed hair and the market; but, come to think of it, you could not state just how they stand in relationship to Jesus Christ. You are not exceptional in this, though you may be a steady church member, even considered as a good church *worker.* The president of Women of the Church in one of our large churches said to the writer: "In all my acquaintance, I do not know a soul who is not a member of the church." Then she explained that all her contacts were with church people. She leads a busy life for her Master, a tireless worker in her church and Sunday school. Her whole time and interest are thus spent, except such as is necessary for home responsibilities. When she was asked if she could say confidently that every person she knew had accepted Jesus Christ as Saviour, she was obliged to admit that she was very ignorant of the spiritual condition of many of them. She had simply taken that as a matter of course; but on serious reflection she had doubts about some. Then the following questions and answers came:

"Is your 'clean up woman' a Christian?"

"I do not know; I never asked her."

"Is the laundry man a Christian?"

"I do not know."

"Are the school teachers who work with your children five days in the week Christians?"

"I do not know. Yes, I have met each one of them, but I had not thought of that."

"Are the sales-persons who wait on you in the department store Christians?"

"I really have not inquired."

Then she said, "Please stop," for she had caught the point. She had been satisfying herself with the thought, if she thought at all, that she had no outbreaking evidence that these were bad people, or that they were not Christians. Thus she could truthfully say that of all her acquaintances she knew of none who were out of Christ. She had not inquired, and of course she did not know. Here is the fatal defect in the program of most Christians, so far as soul-winning is concerned; they are taking a lot for granted and making no effort to make certain, while a great tide of unredeemed lives is sweeping by and eddying around their own Rock of Safety.

Still more about "prospects" in next lesson.

Helps To Understanding Scripture Readings in *Day by Day*

By Rev. C. C. Baker

Sunday, June 10, *John* 15:14-15. The disciples were coming into a new relation with Christ (v.15). Up till now they had merely been the recipients of His teaching and instruction (v.15), but now they were to enter with Him into the work of the Father. What was the part they were to play in the work of the Kingdom (v.16a; Matt. 28:19-20). Observe that their work was to be no fly-by-night accomplishment (v.16). What resources has Christ given His disciples for their work (14:26; 15:16b)? What does He expect of them in their relations with each other (vv.12,17)? Why (17:21b)? Friendship with Christ is no cheap and easy relationship (vv.13-14), but think of the wonder of being a friend of God!

Monday, June 11, *Mark* 10:13-16. As the crowds gathered about Jesus (v.1), He taught them, answering various specific questions (vv.2,17) and teaching lessons to His own disciples (vv.10-11,14-15). Observe the different ways in which He taught His disciples. What prompted Him to talk to them about divorce (vv.10-12)? How did Jesus teach a spiritual truth that grew out of an actual situation in vv.13-16? What truth did He teach (vv.14-15)? How did Jesus relate the incident of vv.17-22 to the instruction of His disciples (vv.23-31)? Do you see in these pictures of Jesus as a teacher any examples of methods you might use to get spiritual truths across to others.

Tuesday, June 12, *John* 2:1-11. One purpose of this and all of Jesus' miracles is expressed in v.11. What had Mary known about her Son ever since the angel Gabriel had spoken to her before Jesus' birth (Luke 1:31-35)? What do you think the motive behind her request in v.3 was? The reply of Jesus in v.4 is a rebuke, but the original text does not carry the harsh tone of the English translation. How was the host saved from a social embarrassment through this miracle (vv.6-10)? How was the cause of the Kingdom of God advanced (v.11)? Are there ways in the normal course of your daily activities in which you can help promote the cause of Christ?

Wednesday, June 13, *John* 8:1-11. Why did the Pharisees and Sadducees bring the woman taken in adultery to Jesus (vv.3-6)? Jesus gained the victory over them, not by argument, but by the sheer moral force of His personality. What effect do you imagine the silence of Jesus in v.6 and again in v.8 had upon the consciences of the Pharisees? How do you explain the remarkable result (v.9) of the one penetrating remark Jesus made (v.7)? Notice who left the group first (v.9). How often do we find ourselves behaving as did these Pharisees—ready and eager to condemn the sin of others? What practical effect ought the words of Jesus in v.7 have upon our daily conduct? How often do we, as followers of Jesus, exhibit His mercy and compassion (vv.10-11) in our relationships with others?

Thursday, June 14, *Luke* 5:1-7. Thus far Peter seems to have followed Christ at a distance. In this passage see how Jesus wins his complete allegiance. First He asks a small favor - that Peter row out from shore (v.3). Notice Peter's reaction to the request of v.4 (v.5). Do you think Peter expected to catch anything? Observe the extent of the catch (vv.6-7). What must Peter have seen in Jesus to cause him to react as he did in v.8? Contrast what Peter called Jesus in v.5a and v.8b. What new allegiance did Peter show in v.11 as he received this new realization of who Christ was. As the Lord Jesus reveals more of Himself to you through certain life experiences, do you respond with a deeper allegiance to Him?

Friday, June 15, *Luke* 9:10-17. When we consider the number of people who sought after Jesus (v.14) when He was trying to rest (v.10), we obtain some idea of the impact of His ministry. Notice who the people said He was (vv.7,8,19). What was Jesus' attitude toward the crowd He was temporarily trying to escape (v.11; Mark 6:34)? What seemed to be the attitude of the disciples toward the crowd (v.12)? It is remarkable that Christ, though weary, taught and cured the people (v.11) and then welcomed them to stay for dinner. After witnessing this miracle (vv.13-17), what conclusions did the disciples reach as to who Jesus was (v.20)? Are you able, even when physically and emotionally exhausted, to express genuine Christian concern for those who look to you for help or guidance?

Saturday, June 16, Luke 23:33-38. Try to imagine something of the suffering Jesus endured on Golgotha's Hill: The physical pain of the crucifixion itself (v.33); the shame of being classed with common criminals (v.33); the humiliation of becoming a spectacle of horror for curious onlookers (v.35); the heart break that must have come from the open ridicule of His deity and all that He had lived for and stood for on earth (vv.35-38). What was Jesus' response to His enemies (vv.42-43)? Do we, as followers of Christ, ever turn from taking a stand for the right when such a stand might cause us to become the objects of misunderstanding or ridicule or even physical persecution? We are not to seek persecution, but we are to believe the words of Christ, "Blessed are ye when men shall persecute you . . . Matthew 5:11-12.

The 1956 Assembly Retiring Moderator's Sermon

God's Commandment for His People

By Rev. J. McDowell Richards, D.D.

I John 3:23—*"And this is his commandment, that we should believe on the name of his Son Jesus Christ, and love one another, as he gave us commandment."*

The Lord's day had come once again in the city of Ephesus. The Christians of the metropolis were gathering according to custom for prayer and praise and for the declaration of the Gospel. This time, however, there was a particular sense of expectancy which permeated the group, and a subdued excitement which could not be mistaken. It had become known that the Apostle John, the well-loved and now ancient disciple of Jesus Christ was to be present and that, in all probability, he would be preaching his last sermon. Already the signs of his approaching end had become unmistakable, and it was evident that his remaining days on earth were few. Surely in this valedictory message there would be great truths set forth which no believer could afford to miss.

At last the great moment arrived. The old man, now too weak to walk, was borne in and placed before the assembly. His hair was snowy white and his face radiant with something of the light of another world. When the time came and he had arisen to speak, however, he delivered no lengthy discourse, but only said, "Little children, love one another," lifted his hand in benediction, and was done.

So runs a familiar story concerning the last days of the disciple whom Jesus loved. It is in keeping with another tradition related by Jerome, who said that in his later years John was accustomed to repeat again and again the same injunction, "Little children, love one another," until some of the believers became weary of it and asked, "Master, why do you always say this?" "Because," he replied, "it is the Lord's commandment, and if only it be done, it is enough."

The traditions mentioned accord well with the writings of John and we may accept them as an accurate clue to the spirit and the emphasis of his later ministry. It is well for us to remember, however, that this man had not always been characterized by sweetness and light. It was not for nothing that his Lord had given to him and his brother James the name, "Boanerges"—"Sons of Thunder." These were men of emotions so strong that they wanted to call down fire from heaven upon the Samaritan villagers and to consume them, because they would not receive their Lord. It was this same John who forbade a man to cast out devils in the name of Christ, because he followed not with the disciples, and who was doubtless amazed and dismayed at his Master's rebuke, "Forbid him not: for he that is not against us is for us." A man of enthusiasm, of passion, of temper, he must quite evidently have been. The change that was wrought in this disciple was doubtless as great as that in Peter, though it is not so clearly set before us in the Gospel narrative. He was no person of patience, of sympathy, and of compassion in the beginning. It was the transforming power of Christ, and the sanctifying work of the Holy Spirit through the years which made of him the great Apostle of love, even as they made of Simon Peter a Rock for righteousness and for the Kingdom of God.

For this reason one may doubt the full correctness of the tradition concerning John's last message. He would not have preached the obligation without pointing to the power by which it might be performed. If indeed he was accustomed to repeat the words, "Little children, love one another," it was to those who knew the Gospel, and had accepted Christ as their Lord and Saviour. Their obligation was implicit in their faith. This is the note which recurs again and again in the First Epistle of John, and which is stated in our text: "And this is his commandment, That we should believe on the name of his Son Jesus Christ, and love one another, as he gave us commandment."

Saving faith in Jesus Christ was the heart of John's message as it was of all the New Testament. Unless the Christian life begins with him it does not begin. The uniqueness of Christ's place as the Son of God, the fact that God's love manifested itself in the sending of his Son into the world that we might live through him, the good news that the "blood of Jesus Christ cleanseth us from all sin", — these are truths which are essential to the Apostle's writings and the presupposition of all his exhortations. A decisive act of faith is essential to the righteousness of life which is emphasized throughout John's epistle, and to the abiding work of love.

It is an interesting fact that the literal translation of the Greek phrase used here is not "believe *in* the name" but "believe the name" of his Son Jesus Christ. In commenting on this, Dr. B. F. Westcott says that it is equivalent to "believe as true the message which the name conveys." The full title, "His Son Jesus Christ" is itself a compressed creed. In the word Son we find suggested the Deity of our Lord and the love of God the Father, who gave his only-begotten Son that we might have everlasting life. In the name Jesus we are reminded of the perfect humanity of the Master, with all the winsome grace of his personality, the clarity of his mind, and the flawlessness of his character. In the title Christ or Messiah we find implicit the divine mission for which he was appointed and the nature of his atoning work. It is a title which looks back into the long preparation for his coming and finds in him the fulfillment of God's promises to Israel through the prophets, but which looks forward also to a glorious culmination of God's plan in the future.

Here as always, however, the concept of faith set forth is not one of intellectual acceptance alone but also of active and vital commitment. The salvation offered to man in the New Testament is the gift of God. Justification is by faith and by faith alone. The desire of the Christian is to "be found in him, not having mine own righteousness which is of the law, but that which is through the faith of Christ, the righteousness which is of God by faith." At the same time the New Testament knows nothing of faith divorced from life, but only of faith which issues in life. It is Dr. Charles Hodge who suggested that we might understand the word "believe" more accurately if we wrote it as "be-live", — that is to base all of our lives and actions upon our acceptance of Christ as Lord and Saviour. We have no power to live as we ought apart from our commitment to him. If our lives give no evidence that he is at work in us, that fact is itself an indication that we do not truly believe.

It is a futile thing for a man to say to a doctor, "I believe in your skill and in your ability to cure my disease, but I will not follow your prescription." It is idle for one to declare to a candidate for office, "I believe that you are a leader who could solve our problems and you have my full support — but I cannot go to the polls to vote." It is mockery for one to assert his belief in democracy and his faith in the "American Way of Life" and then to scoff at the laws of his land or to avoid the discharge of his duties as a citizen. So is it meaningless for a person to declare his faith in Christ and then to disregard the precepts of the Master in the attitudes which he manifests and the deeds which he commits day by day. Belief in Christ assuredly implies that we will love him, who first loved us and gave himself for us. Because it issues in love for him, it will inevitably lead, John says, to the keeping of his commandments. The duty which he emphasizes here is that in which all other commandments concerning our fellow men are summed up — it is that we should love one another. "Love," as the Apostle Paul had said, "is the fulfilling of the law."

It is not of Paul that John is thinking, however, but of Christ. His mind goes back to that upper room where only the eleven are now left with their Lord. The shadow of the cross is upon him. Only a little while ago he has girded himself with a towel, taken a basin and washed the disciples' feet in an example of humility and of service which we can never forget. "A new commandment I give unto you," he says, "that ye love one another; as I have loved you, that ye also love one another."

What was there new about this commandment. The Old Testament had said, "Thou shalt love thy neighbor as thyself" and Christ had added his own authority to the obligation thus set forth. Yes, but there are occasions when we do not love ourselves very much; times when we are sick and ashamed of ourselves, and when we would be rid of our own personalities if we could. But when Christ said, "As I have loved you" he made this a new commandment because he gave a completely new and different standard. The love of Christ—utterly pure, absolutely unselfish, determined to seek and to save that which was lost, not counting the cost, willing to endure the cross, praying forgiveness for those who nailed him to the tree—that is our standard now. It is this new commandment of Christ that John is emphasizing in our text, for he uses almost the identical words of the Lord as recorded in his Gospel.

New Testament scholars will not need to be reminded of the fact that the word which is here used for love is "Agape", not "Eros". This word describes a love "which is an expression of character, determined by will and not a thing of spontaneous emotion. In this sense 'love' is the willing communication to others of that which we have and are; and the exact opposite of that passion which is the desire of personal appropriation." We cannot always direct our emotions; we are not equally attracted to all men, but we can assuredly will that which is good for all men; we can unstintingly give of ourselves for their welfare.

How much we need to heed this command in the church today, and how much the world needs to see this kind of love in us! Tertullian bears witness to the impression which the attitude of Christians toward their fellow-believers made upon the pagan world. He reports the people of his day as saying: "Behold how these Christians love one another . . . for they are even prepared to die for one another." Men have not been speaking thus about Christians in our day. Sadly enough, they have had little occasion to do so. We rejoice that the days of denominational strife and enmity have so largely passed; yet there is still a need for improvement in the relationships between denominations. The Churches need increasingly to see themselves not in the competitive relationships of the business world, but as members of the same family, as partners in the service of Christ. Somehow we must learn to avoid costly duplication of efforts, to be statesmanlike in our planning so that we shall not be competitors to win the same few in one community, while the multitudes elsewhere go unreached. We must learn to love and understand one another so well that we can present a common front to the world. The differences among us should increasingly be those of organization only, as we plan and work together in affection and in trust because we own a common loyalty to Christ.

Our primary responsibility here, however, is for conditions within our own Church. We have been passing through days of controversy and debate. Great issues have divided us, and even today there are many questions before us on which we are not agreed. In loyalty to conscience and to duty we must bear our witness to truth, as God gives us to see the truth. When differences arise, however, we need to remember the limitations of our own wisdom, and to respect the motives of those who, with equal sincerity, and an equal right to seek God's will for their lives and for our Church, are constrained to take a different view. It is very easy in the course of our debates for tempers to become strained; for unkind words to be spoken; for bitterness to be aroused; for pride and a determination to carry the day for our side to displace charity and good will as our ruling passion. "Little children, love one another." "Put on therefore as God's elect, holy and beloved, a heart of compassion, kindness, lowliness, meekness, long suffering; forbearing one another, and forgiving each other, if any man have a complaint against any; even as the Lord forgave you, so also do ye: and above all these things put on love, which is the bond of perfectness, and let the peace of Christ rule in your hearts."

The spirit which is needed in our Church courts is needed also in local churches. Sadly enough there is never a year which comes that does not find some congregations divided within themselves by differences between good men. Too often party is set against party, one individual becomes alienated from another, and bitterness prevails. Church quarrels are always a reproach to the name which we bear and a hindrance to the work of Christ. It is possible to be technically right and to win one's argument, while at the same time sacrificing that which is essential and doing injury to the cause of the Kingdom. Let us remember that "love suffereth long and is kind, love envieth not, love vaunteth not itself, and is not puffed up, doth not behave itself unseemly, seeketh not her own, is not easily provoked, thinketh no evil."

In the spirit of love must be found also the solution of our social problems. Our section, and to some extent our Church as well, are torn today by the question of racial relationships. It is not likely that we shall soon be able to agree on all of the policies which should be adopted, the practical steps which must be taken. On one point, however, we should be able to agree. No policy can be right which is not based upon love and upon an honest desire for the good of our brethren—whether they be white or black, yellow or brown.

The man of any race who accepts Christ is truly a child of God and the brother of every other believer. No policy, no attitude, no word which is based upon hatred, or scorn, or a desire to humiliate, or a willingness to keep any other person from attaining the fullest development of which he is capable can be in accord with the mind of Christ. Christians, white and black, in the Southland or in any other part of the world today, need to be much in prayer that they may understand the will of God, that they may know what Christ would have them do, and that they may be given the grace to obey. "For this is the message which we heard from the beginning, that we should love one another . . . He that loveth not his brother abideth in death . . . If a man say, I love God, and hateth his brother, he is a liar: for he that loveth not his brother, whom he hath seen, how can he love God whom he hath not seen?"

In love is the motive which will lead us to a new concern for the needs of the suffering, the sorrowful and the needy about us. "But whoso hath this world's good, and seeth his brother hath need, and shutteth up his compassion from him, how dwelleth the love of God in him?" We have not begun to do what we should for the widows, the fatherless, the displaced, the needy and the suffering of the world.

In love, too, is the only power which can send us out in a great forward movement of Evangelism and Missions both at home and abroad. It is true that the new commandment of Christ was directed especially to the relationship between those who were already his servants. By implication, however; by what we call "good and necessary inference," it deals with our obligation to all men. Christ died for all. In every individual we see a soul in need of him; one, who, by his grace and through his redeeming power, is potentially a child of God. If true love is inconsistent with closing our hearts to the physical needs of men, how much less can it be reconciled with indifference to the spiritual state of those who are lost apart from Him; who are perishing because they have not received the Bread of Life.

We rejoice in the rapid growth of our Church in recent years; we thank God for that which has been accomplished on our mission fields. At best, however, we have scarcely touched the fringe of that which is possible for us and demanded of us. We have not begun to labor as we ought, we have not in any real sense sacrificed for Christ, we have not understood what it is to love. We need to come again to the foot of the cross, to see the broken heart of God in Christ, to catch something of the passion of him who loved us and gave himself for us. In penitence and in devotion we are called to dedicate ourselves anew to the fulfillment of his Great Commission. Constrained by his love, forgetting our differences, united by his Spirit, we must move forward in the work to which he has called his people.

"And this is his commandment, that we should believe on the name of his Son Jesus Christ, and love one another, as he gave us commandment." Lord, we believe. Help Thou our unbelief! Lord, we do love. Teach us to love, in fullness and in truth!

SABBATH SCHOOL LESSONS — REV. J. KENTON PARKER

LESSON FOR JUNE 17

Ambassador In Bonds

Background Scripture: Acts 21:17 - 26:32
Devotional Reading: II Timothy 1:8-14

These are exciting and dangerous days for Paul. We have seen in the first part of chapter 21 that he was repeatedly warned not to go to Jerusalem. In verse 4 we are told that the disciples at Tyre said to him "through the Spirit", that he should not go up to Jerusalem. In verses ten and eleven a certain prophet named Agabus took Paul's girdle, and bound his own hands and feet, and said, Thus saith the Holy Ghost, So shall the Jews at Jerusalem bind the man that weareth this girdle, and shall deliver him into the hands of the Gentiles. Hearing these words, "We, and they of that place besought him not to go up to Jerusalem." Luke was evidently one of those who urged him not to go. Paul answered that he was ready not only to be bound but to die at Jerusalem for the name of the Lord Jesus. Did the apostle make a mistake here? He could, as we know, be somewhat "hardheaded," if we can use that expression about so great a man. If he did make a mistake the Lord overruled it and gave him the opportunity of bearing witness before kings and rulers and even Caesar himself. We see the courage of Paul and his sincere conviction that he must go to Jerusalem. It would seem, however, from the account, that the Holy Spirit was speaking through all these friends who advised him not to go.

Another question comes to mind. Did Paul err in yielding to the suggestion of James and the brethren that he conform to the Mosaic Law? It seems a bit strange that the apostle who stood so firmly for freedom from the Ceremonial Law should do what he did in verses 22-26. It did not keep him from being seized by the fanatical Jews but rather furnished them with an excuse and occasion for the outbreak that is described in verses 27-29.

All of these unfortunate occurrences gave Paul a fine opportunity to bear witness to the Gospel and relate the story of his own conversion. In II Timothy 1:8-14, (Our Devotional Reading), he urges Timothy "not to be ashamed of our Lord, nor of me his prisoner," and says of himself, "Nevertheless I am not ashamed." He certainly lived up to those words.

I. *The Uproar in Jerusalem:* 21:17-40.

The brethren received Paul gladly and he related to them—to James and all the elders—what wonderful things God had wrought among the Gentiles through his ministry. They made the suggestion that he take four men who had a vow on them, and purify himself with them, etc., in order to show the multitudes that he was still a loyal Jew and kept the Mosaic Ceremonial Law. Paul complied with their suggestion, but instead of keeping him out of trouble, it led to the uproar. A question comes to me at this point. Why did not the "brethren," or the Church at Jerusalem, not try to do more to protect and help Paul? From the record it appears that he was "on his own," to use a modern expression. Was the church so weakened from persecution that it was unable to do anything? The unbelieving Jews seemed to have things their own way in the city where three thousand had been converted at Pentecost, and many more soon afterwards. Did there still exist a feeling of lukewarmness or even jealousy toward the "apostle to the Gentiles"?

The Jews which were of Asia, (had they followed Paul?), when they saw him in the temple, stirred up all the people and laid hands on him. It was not long before the whole city was aroused, and they went about to kill Paul. Tidings came to the chief captain that all Jerusalem was in an uproar. He came with soldiers and commanded him to be bound with two chains and demanded what he had done. He took Paul to be a certain Egyptian who had formerly led a band of murderers. Paul explained who he was and asked permission to speak to the people.

II. *Paul's Defense "on the Stairs":* 21:40 - 22:30.

Paul spoke to the crowd in the Hebrew tongue, and this kept them quiet for a time. His defense consisted of a short account of his personal background as a Jew, his zeal as a persecutor of the Christians, and his marvelous vision and conversion on the road to Damascus. He adds the account of his trance in the temple and the command to "Depart : for I will

told Paul who got one of the centurions to take the young man to the chief captain. When he was told of the plot the chief captain immediately called two centurions and ordered them to get two hundred soldiers and some horsemen and spearmen and conduct Paul down to Caesarea. Then he wrote a letter to Felix explaining the case, and making it appear to his advantage (the chief captain's). So Paul was conducted safely to Caesarea and presented to the Governor Felix.

V. *His Trial and Defense Before Felix:* 24:1-27.

In five days his accusers came down with a "certain orator" named Tertullus who made quite a speech, beginning in a flowery and flattering manner, and accused Paul of being "a pestilent fellow, and a mover of sedition among all the Jews throughout the world, and a ringleader of the sect of the Nazarenes: who had gone about to profane the temple, whom we took and would have judged according to our law, but the chief captain came upon us and with great violence took him away out of our hands." Here is a typical speech of a shrewd lawyer who twists the facts to suit his own ends and pays no attention to the truth. We have the same kind in our day. The Romans prided themselves upon "law" but we get a good picture of a Roman tribunal and of the corruption of Roman courts.

Paul defended himself in a masterful way, showing clearly that he was innocent of all the charges brought against him. Felix was so impressed that he deferred judgment until the chief captain should come down and allowed Paul to have a large degree of liberty and the privilege of having his acquaintances come and minister to him. When his wife Drucilla was come, who was a Jewess, he sent for Paul and heard him concerning the faith in Christ Jesus. Felix "trembled" as Paul spoke, but put off the matter. He was convicted but not converted.

VI. *Paul Before Festus and Agrippa:* Chapters 25 and 26.

Festus succeeded Felix. He went up to Jerusalem and the Jews desired him to send for Paul, planning to kill him. Festus, no doubt suspicious of this course, answered that Paul should be kept at Caesarea, and told them to come down and accuse him. Paul appealed to Caesar.

While he was waiting King Agrippa came down to visit Festus and Paul had the opportunity of defending himself, and witnessing for Christ and the Gospel before King Agrippa and others. The result was acquittal, but since he had appealed to Caesar, to Caesar he had to go. (Study Paul's speech before Agrippa.)

YOUNG PEOPLE'S DEPARTMENT — REV. B. HOYT EVANS

YOUTH PROGRAM FOR JUNE 17

The Land Of The Pineapple

Hymn: "The Morning Light Is Breaking"
Prayer
Scripture: Isaiah 42:1-12
Hymn: "O Love Divine, That Stooped To Share"
Offering
Hymn: "In Christ There Is No East Nor West"

PROGRAM LEADER:

(You can make this program richer and more interesting by securing additional information on Hawaii from an encyclopedia or from magazine articles.)

Mark Twain described Hawaii as the "loveliest fleet of islands that lie anchored in any ocean." The impression of the islands which we gain from our reading is certainly consistent with his description. In the title of this program we refer to Hawaii as "The Land of the Pineapple" because it is through the pineapple that we in the United States are most familiar with the islands. The growing and canning of the pineapple is one of the principal industries of Hawaii. Practically all of the pineapple consumed in the United States is produced there.

Our main interest in Hawaii, however, is not with the beauty of the land or the lusciousness of the pineapple, but with the progress of the church there. Our speakers will give us some background information about the land, and then tell us how the Christian church came to be, how it has grown, and what influence it has had.

FIRST SPEAKER:

Hawaii lies about 2200 miles southwest of San Francisco and about 1400 miles north of the Equator. There are twenty islands in the group, only eight of which are inhabited. The combined area of the eight is not quite as large as the state of New Jersey. The climate is truly delightful, never cold and never too hot.

The rainfall is variable. Honolulu, the capital, averages 32 inches a year, and the city of Hilo, less than 300 miles away, averages 100 to 150 inches a year. The islands are very mountainous. On the largest island, Hawaii, are two mountains which tower over 13,000 feet above sea level. On one of them, Mauna Loa, is the largest active volcano in the world.

SECOND SPEAKER:

The islands are said to have been first discovered in 1555, and rediscovered by Captain James Cook in 1778, who named them the Sandwich Islands in honor of the English Earl of Sandwich. Captain Cook met his death at the hands of natives who were quite savage until missionaries came in 1820. The government of the islands was a simple despotism until 1840 when a new constitution was granted which provided for a government consisting of a king, an assembly of nobles, and a representative council. A queen, who came to the throne in 1891, desired to have absolute powers of monarchy restored, but a revolution broke out and the kingdom era was ended. An effort was made to have the islands annexed to the United States as a territory, but it was not until 1898 that this was accomplished. Three years later the new territory sought to be admitted as a state, and the same admission is still being sought.

The half million people of the islands are made up of original islanders and people of nearly every Asian and European nationality. Their history of peaceful living together provides a commendable demonstration of cooperation and neighborliness. Regardless of their national origins, they have always been strictly loyal to the United States.

The islands have shown a very rapid and sound development. Fine modern buildings are to be seen everywhere. There is a very adequate system of highways and railroads, and airfields dot the islands. There are at least six excellent harbors which will accommodate the largest ships afloat. Public and private schools number 320, and the students enrolled in them total over 25% of the population. The tax supported University of Hawaii at Honolulu has an enrollment of 6000 students.

Agriculture is the principal industry, and sugar is the principal product. It is estimated that over half the population is engaged in sugar production. Next in importance is the pineapple industry, which has already been mentioned. Quite a number of other agricultural products are being grown in Hawaii, but none of them in really important quantities. The delightful climate, scenic beauty, and fine accomodations of the islands make the tourist trade next in importance to agriculture. Many of the people who go as visitors remain as citizens of the territory.

FOURTH SPEAKER:

As has already been indicated, the culture of Hawaii was primitive and pagan when Captain Cook first landed there. It is truly marvelous that such tremendous progress has been made in so short a time. Now we find a prosperous, well educated civilization in the place of the paganism that existed little more than a hundred years ago. How is it to be explained? In 1820 Congregational missionaries from New England landed in Hawaii. The truth they taught was gladly received in place of the dying pagan religion of the natives. Today, the original Hawaiians are nearly all Christians, and that fact explains the cultural and economic progress they have made. Wherever Christianity goes, all of life is improved. In the "Land of the Pineapple" we find one of the most encouraging examples of missionary fruits. Perhaps God has not blessed every land with the beauty and charm of Hawaii, but any land, no matter how bleak and barren it may be, can become spiritually rich when it chooses to receive the Son of God and to walk in His ways.

She Has Served Well

As the gracious lady entered the auditorium her fellow town people rose in her honor. Later she stated she had never before felt like a celebrity. The Parent Teachers Association had invited the people of Maxton to do her honor and they came out in force, to express appreciation of a great teacher, Marguerite Townsend. They called it "her night."

Back in 1910 she graduated from Columbia College and began teaching children. There were a few years elsewhere and a time of graduate study at Columbia University, but for forty years she has started the boys and girls of Maxton upon their educational careers, presiding over the first grade. There were an invocation and a benediction that night and two musical selections, but most of the time was taken in just saying "Thank you" to one who had served well. Many of the more than 2,000 children she has taught were back for the occasion. A medical doctor gave a sketch of her life. One of her girls, now a matron, read a poem on "To - morning." One presented a life membership in the National Congress of Parents and Teachers. Another presented a gift, sent in by former pupils so readily that the original goal of five hundred dollars was almost doubled. The names of those who had written a stack of letters and telegrams carrying greetings were read. One of her boys, now head of a multi-million-dollar corporation, sent a hundred shares of stock worth over a thousand dollars. After the postlude the several hundred of her alumni and the multitude of her friends gathered round to express their love for one who had loved and served little children.

"And they that are wise, shall shine as the brightness of the firmament; and they that turn many to righteousness as the stars for ever and ever." (Daniel 12:3)

Department of Bible,
Presbyterian Junior College,
Maxton, N. C.

Where Are You Going To Spend Your Vacation?

If you want to go to the mountains where it is cool and delightful and where you can get refreshment of soul, mind, and body why not plan to attend one of the summer conferences at Montreat?

For your convenience, in choosing a conference date that will fit in your summer schedule, and prove specifically helpful to you, we are listing here some of the conference dates that may be of interest to Women of the Church:

June 25-29 — Young Adults - For young women (and their husbands)

July 3-12 — Leadership School - For Sunday school workers

July 18-25 — Women's Training School - For all women

July 26 - Aug. 1 — World Mission Conference - Chairmen of World Missions and all especially interested

Aug. 2-8 — Music Conference - For all lovers of music

Aug. 9-16 — Church Extension Conference - Chairmen of Church Extension and all concerned with reaching people at home

Aug. 16-26 — Bible Conference - For Chairmen of Spiritual Growth and for Bible leaders, especially.

Montreat is a good place for families to vacation, offering opportunities in clubs to children and to all age youth, while these fine conference opportunities are offered adults and interested and thoughtful young people.

A MISSIONARY BOOK

The four evangelists, Matthew, Mark, Luke and John drew a composite portrait of Jesus when on earth, which has been and is the inexhaustible study of the ages. An average of one new life of Christ is issued every month, not to mention the millions of sermons, hymns and meditations which that portrait has inspired.

Then Luke, whom Paul called the "Beloved Physician," goes on with a historical instinct, a personal touch and a deep humility, to write about the Church of which Jesus was the Founder and against which He said no enemy could prevail. This is the only authoritative history we have of the first generation of the Christian Church. And in influence it is unsurpassed by any brief history ever written. The theme of the Book is found in Acts 1:8, in a passage in which the writer linked the narrative of the Gospel with that of Acts:

"And ye shall receive power, after that the Holy Ghost is come upon you and ye shall be witnesses unto me in Jerusalem and in all Judea and in Samaria and unto the uttermost part of the earth."

And, like a good preacher who keeps to his text, Luke proceeds to develop his story along four lines: (1) the receiving of the Holy Ghost, chapters 1 and 2; (2) the preaching of the Gospel in Jerusalem and in all Judea, chapters 2 to 7; (3) the Gospel in Samaria, chapter 8; (4) the great transition of the offer of salvation to the Gentiles and the preaching of the Gospel to the whole world, chapters 9 to 28.

When I was a boy in school, text books of history were about as dull as could be made. The print was small. There were no pictures. The facts were told with lots of dates and the student was expected to remember and which he promptly proceeded to forget, except one or two. Important documents were put in the appendix where they received little attention. The writers of those histories might have taken a lesson from the Acts of the Apostles, where there are word pictures which are vivid and unforgetable.

Take, for instance, that man crippled from his birth, carried daily to the Beautiful Gate of the Temple, where he was miraculously healed in the name of Jesus of Nazareth, his shrunken ankle bones all new again and he walking and leaping and praising God. What a picture for the artists!

Or look at Stephen being stoned to death by the mob and dying with a prayer on his lips for man. This story has passed into poetry: "The martyr first whose eagle eye could pierce beyond the grave; who saw his Master in the sky and called on him to save." Read these and other word pictures, let your imagination play about them, tell them to somebody else, and see how they live again.

Consider too the way in which important documents are often handled by historians, set apart by themselves for further reading. They may be speeches or statements of policy. Some standard church historians have a running account of facts and then in a separate chapter they discuss the history of doctrine. Not so our historian Luke. He records many important documents but he weaves each into the body of the history with its proper setting, making a continuous narrative.

The Acts of the Apostles record the great sermon of Peter at Pentecost and some of his lesser discourses; Stephen's sermon before the Sanhedrin; the Bible study of the evangelist Philip, with the eunuch of Ethiopia; the outline of Peter's sermon in the house of Cornelius; three sermons of Paul, at Antioch in Pisidia, before a superstitious audience, in Lystra, and to the cultivated audience on Mars Hill in Athens. Also three of Paul's defenses are recorded: his defense before the great crowd in Jerusalem, Chapter 22; before Felix, the Governor, Chapter 24; and before Agrippa, Chapter 26. Each of these important discourses is given its own setting and effectiveness. In the Book of Acts, which is a story of the early progress of the Christian Church, there are smaller stories within the main story, all full of thrilling interest, making a continuous narrative with a new interest on every page.

The Book of Acts answers a missionary's inquiries: How shall I begin? What shall I say to a new audience? How nurture new believers? How receive them into the Church, and organize the Church with what officers? These and many other questions are answered in Acts.

The Book of Acts is the fulfillment of the Lord's promise of the Holy Spirit to convince the world of sin and to guide the worker into all truth. There is also a fulfillment of the promise, (John 14:12) "Greater things than these shall ye do."

The Book of Acts closes, as it were, abruptly with Paul a prisoner, preaching in Rome, but the kind of work described there goes on and on, for the Lord had said, "Lo, I am with you alway, even unto the end of the world."

—Source Unknown.

Reading With a Purpose

The summer months make a wonderful time for reading those mission books that sometimes get crowded out when time is limited, so "be sharp" and get this reading done, that you may tell some others about the books and encourage them to enjoy the reading too.

The subject for study this fall is Mission Field U.S.A. Two books for adults are:

Missions U. S. A. by James Hoffman. With a reporter's skill in presenting facts, Mr. Hoffman explores the many mission fields that exist in the United States. He shows how the church is handling some of the problems in new ways. In pointing out where the church's forces are urgently needed, he makes clear that every church member is part of these forces and has a direct responsibility in helping to bring America nearer to God's will.

This Is Your Neighbor by Louisa Rossiter Shotwell is a documentary photographic and pertinent text record of the current mission crises in the United States and the response churches are making to them, giving the reader a sense of direction for Christian action in his own community.

And a special book for Presbyterians U. S. is *Bright Future* - a new day for town and country church by James M. Carr.

The subject for study for World Missions in February 1957 is Southeast Asia. What is it? Where is it? Who are its people? Southeast Asia is as far around the globe as you can get from the United States. Read the following books and find out all about Southeast Asia:

The Church in Southeast Asia by Thomas and Manikam, is about the problems and opportunities facing the church in Southeast Asia, a vast and important area of the world that is too little known to most Americans. The significant fact brought out by the authors is that the church is coming of age in Southeast Asia. American church members, understanding what this new maturity means, will know better how to work with fellow Christians across the Pacific toward mutual goals.

East From Burma by Constance M. Hallock. Here the author provides a wealth of information about the political, economic, social, and religious life in the diverse countries that make up Southeast Asia. Burma, Taiwan (Formosa), Indo-China, the Philippines, Indonesia, Malaya, and Thailand are the countries brought into focus. Emphasis is on the people - their characteristics, their contributions to Christian leadership in their environment - and on the many ways in which the church enters their lives.

Order all books from the Presbyterian Book Stores, Box 1176, Richmond 9, Va., Box 6127, Atlanta 8, Ga.; Box 1020, Dallas 21, Texas.

Dr. Ben Lacy Rose, D.D.

Union Theological Seminary in Virginia
Richmond, Virginia

Dr. Ben Lacy Rose,
pastor of the First Presbyterian Church of Wilmington, N. C., has been elected to the Faculty by the Board of Trustees of Union Theological Seminary, Dr. Jas. A. Jones, President of the Seminary, announced. He will occupy the newly created chair of Pastoral Leadership and Homiletics. Dr. Rose is expected to begin his teaching at Union Seminary in September, 1956.

Dr. Rose was ordained by Wilmington Presbytery in 1938 in the Kenansville Presbyterian Church, and from 1938 to 1941 was pastor of the Chinquapin, Bethel, and Beulaville Presbyterian Churches in Duplin County, North Carolina. From 1941 to 1946 he was a chaplain in the Army, serving with the 113th Mechanized Cavalry Group in the European Theatre of Operations. He was twice decorated with the Bronze Star Medal and with the Legion of Merit, and received five battle stars for the major campaigns in Europe.

For nine years Dr. Rose was pastor of the Central Presbyterian Church of Bristol.

Since February, 1955, Dr. Rose has been pastor of the First Presbyterian Church of Wilmington, North Carolina.

Dr. Rose was born in Fayetteville, North Carolina. His father, the Hon. Charles G. Rose, was at one time Moderator of the General Assembly of the Presbyterian Church in the U. S., and was division counsel for the Atlantic Coast Lines Railroad. His mother was Irene Lacy of Raleigh, North Carolina. He is a nephew of Dr. Benjamin Rice Lacy, Jr., President Emeritus of Union Theological Seminary.

After graduating from the Fayetteville High School, Dr. Rose received his A.B. degree from Davidson College in 1935, and graduated from Union Theological Seminary in Virginia with a Bachelor of Divinity Degree in 1938. He returned to the Seminary to earn his degree of Master of Theology in 1950, and the degree of Doctor of Theology in 1955. In May 1952, King College of Bristol conferred the honorary degree of Doctor of Divinity upon him.

He is a member of the Board of Church Extension of the General Assembly of the Presbyterian Church in the U. S., and of the Board of Trustees of the Consolidated Presbyterian College, Synod of North Carolina. His civic activities have included work with the Boy Scouts, the Community Chest organizations in various communities, the Veterans of Foreign Wars and the American Legion. In 1955 community leaders and city officials elected him to receive the Bristol Lifetime Citizen Award, "in recognition of his achievements as a citizen of Bristol . . . and as a token of the esteem in which he is held."

Twice the Office of the Chief of Chaplains has appointed Dr. Rose to preach to servicemen in military installations. The most recent preaching mission was made in 1954 to the scattered bases of the U. S. Air Force in Labrador, Greenland and Newfoundland.

Dr. Rose is married to the former Miss Anne Claiborne Thompson, daughter of the Rev. Dr. and Mrs. William Taliaferro Thompson of Richmond, Virginia. They have four children: Anne, Margaret, Lucy, and Ben, Jr.

George Matthew Lindsay

George Matthew Lindsay died at his home in Tutwiler, Mississippi on January 10, 1956, after having been in ill health for some time. He was born in Amite County, Mississippi near Capel on September 11, 1890, the son of Mr. and Mrs. L. P. Lindsay. His father was an elder in the Rose Hill Presbyterian Church.

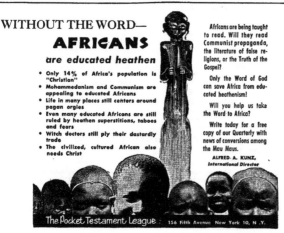

Mr. Lindsay moved to Tutwiler, Mississippi, in 1913 where he lived during the remaining years of his life. In 1929 he was ordained an elder in the Presbyterian Church of Tutwiler, and in 1942 he was made Clerk of the Session. He had served as a member of the Church Choir, as Superintendent of the Sunday School, and as a Commissioner to the General Assembly. He is survived by his widow and his son—Jos Pugh —besides a sister and several brothers.

Missionary News

Nashville

Mr. and Mrs. James A. Halverstadt and their son, Hugh, will arrive in this country about June 7 for their regular furlough.

Mr. Halverstadt, who serves as Treasurer of the Congo Mission, considers Decatur, Ga., home. He is a graduate of Davidson College, and Columbia Theological Seminary, and is a member of the North Avenue Presbyterian Church of Atlanta.

Mrs. Halverstadt is the former Miss Charline Fleece of Decatur, Ga. She attended Converse College, and received her A. B. degree from Agnes Scott College. She, too, is a member of the North Avenue Presbyterian Church in Atlanta. The Halverstadts will proceed to Atlanta upon their arrival in the United States, and will make their home there during this furlough year.

Rev. and Mrs. Joseph H. Spooner of our Congo Mission announce the birth of a daughter, Susan Rebecca, on March 20 in Congo.

Mr. Spooner is a native of Junction City, Arkansas. He received his education at the Louisiana Polytechnic Institute, Arkansas College, and Columbia Theological Seminary. He is a member of Ouachita Presbytery.

Mrs. Spooner is the former Miss Maxine Westmoreland of Sidney, Arkansas. She also attended Arkansas College. She is a member of Scotland Presbyterian Church in Junction City. The Spooners have four other children, three daughters and a son.

A daughter, Linda Bell, was born to Rev. and Mrs. Thomas Dwight Linton in Korea on March 22.

Mr. Linton is the son of Rev. and Mrs. W. A. Linton, long time missionaries of our Church in Korea. He is a graduate of the University of Richmond, and Columbia Theological Seminary. He studied for one year at the University of Edinburgh, in Edinburgh, Scotland.

Mr. Linton is a member of Atlanta Presbytery.

Mrs. Linton is the former Miss Marjory Potter of Orlando, Florida. She is a graduate of Florida State University and the Assembly's Training School. She is a member of the First Presbyterian Church of Orlando. The Lintons have one other child, a son.

Rev. and Mrs. Jack Brown Scott of our Korea Mission announce the arrival of a son, Edward Allen, in Korea on March 22.

Mr. Scott is a native of Greensboro, North Carolina, and is a graduate of Davidson College and Columbia Theological Seminary. He is a member of Orange Presbytery.

Mrs. Scott is the former Miss Eleanor Caslick of Paris, Kentucky. She attended the University of Kentucky and graduated from Vanderbilt University. She also studied for one year at the Assembly's Training School. She is a member of the First Presbyterian Church of Paris, Ky.

Mr. Scott is engaged in evangelistic work, and Mrs. Scott serves as a medical missionary. The Scotts have one other child, a daughter.

Nashville — The arrival in the United States of six missionaries for the Presbyterian Church, U.S., from Brazil to begin a year's furlough is announced by the Board of World Missions here.

Two of the six are already in America; the others are expected by June 1.

From Garanhuns, in the North Brazil mission, have come the Rev. and Mrs. W. G. Neville. They reached this country May 15 to begin a regular furlough that will be spent chiefly in Decatur, Ga., and Montreat, N. C. Mr. Neville is a native of York, S. C., although he considers Clinton his home. He is a graduate of Presbyterian College and Columbia Theological Seminary, and is a member of Enoree Presbytery. Mrs. Neville, the former Miss Mary Lindsay Tennant of Augusta, Ga., is a graduate of Shorter College, Rome, Ga., and is a member of Greene Street Church, Augusta. The Nevilles have four children, all of whom are living in this country.

From Uberlandia, in the West Brazil Mission, the Rev. and Mrs. John G. Viser are returning about May 31. They plan to make their headquarters during furlough in Greenville, S. C., except during the summer months when they will be at Mission Court, Richmond, Va. Mr. Viser is from Greenville, a graduate of Columbia Bible College, Presbyterian College, and Union Theological Seminary, Richmond. He also is a member of Enoree Presbytery. Mrs. Viser, the former Thelma Louise Allen of Greenville, attended Columbia Bible College, and is a member of Northminster Church of her native city. The Visers have four children ranging from 15 months to 10 years.

Latest to reach this country among the six will be the Rev. and Mrs. Donald E. Williams of Recife, in the North Brazil Mission. They plan to spend June and July at Black Mountain, or Spray, N. C., the homes of Mr. and Mrs. Williams, respectively. The remainder of furlough will be spent in Mission Court, Richmond. Both attended Columbia Bible College. Mr. Williams is a graduate of Columbia Theological Seminary, and is a member of Asheville Presbytery. Mrs. Williams also attended Wheaton College. They have four children, two sons and two daughters.

Four missionaries of the Presbyterian Church, U.S., are on their way, or will go shortly, to their stations in Mexico and Africa, after a year's furlough in the United States.

Already returned to Mexico, preparatory to resuming their work at Ometepec in deep Southwest Mexico, are the Rev. and Mrs. John B. Wood. They left this country in early May.

Mr. Wood, a member of Southwest Georgia Presbytery, is a graduate of Wheaton College and Columbia Seminary in Decatur, Ga. Before going to Mexico, he served the Glen Haven Presbyterian Church of Decatur, and was chapel minister of First Church, Valdosta, Ga. Mrs. Wood, the former Madge Vander Mey of Chicago, Ill., is also a Wheaton graduate, and taught in high schools in Chicago and Decatur. The couple has three boys ranging from four to eight years.

Returning to the Belgian Congo are Mr. and Mrs. Walter D. Shepard, educational and industrial missionaries at Lubondai station. Mr. Shepard serves the mission in preparing architectural plans when needed, but his chief task has been as principal, teacher and property manager at Central School for missionaries' children. A native of New Orleans, he is a graduate of Tulane University, and studied at Austin Theological Seminary one year before going out as a missionary. Mrs. Shepard teaches pre-school children and classes in the Central School. She is a native of Houston, and attended the University of Mississippi. The Shepards have a boy and two girls, ranging in age from nine to three years. The missionaries are members of Napoleon Avenue Presbyterian Church in New Orleans.

With the appointment of 14 new missionaries and the re-appointment of two others by the Board of World Missions in early May, the missionary force of the Presbyterian Church, U.S., has passed the 500 mark for the first time in 29 years.

The Board, in announcing its appointments following the May meeting, also pointed out that resignations and retirements effective between now and September 1 will cause a sizeable reduction in the total, so that the final total for 1956 may be under 500 unless a number of additional candidates can be found ready for appointment.

The Board points out that a large number of missionaries will shortly complete their years of service and their qualifications for Social Security, and will retire this summer. Already 13 retirements and one resignation have been accepted, effective during the summer.

Nashville — The Board of World Missions of the Presbyterian Church, U.S., has voted to begin missionary work in Iraq, bringing to nine the number of countries in which the Southern Presbyterians are working.

At the invitation of three other Presbyterian-order denominations now cooperating in the United Mission to Iraq, the Board voted to become a part of the 32-year-old missionary enterprise. Cooperating in the United Mission are the Presbyterian Church, U.S.A., the Evangelical and Reformed Church, and the Reformed Church in America. The three churches are currently maintaining a staff of more than a dozen missionaries in the booming, oil-rich country which is predominantly Moslem.

The Presbyterian Church, U.S., already is at work in mission fields in Korea, Japan, Taiwan, Mexico, Brazil, Ecuador, Portugal and the Belgian Congo.

First step in the new venture will be the appointment of three members of the U.S. Board to membership on the Joint Committee for the United Mission. As soon as missionary volunteers for service in the area can be found, the Board will then recommend them to the Joint Committee for appointment.

This action, together with the unanimous approval of a statement on the Japanese International Christian University, and the appointment of 16 missionaries, constituted the high points of the May meeting of the Board.

Others actions included:
Taking notice through discussion and special prayers of intercession for the Protestant Christians of Colombia, whom the Central Committee on Latin America reports as now undergoing the most severe persecution in the history of the fanatical attacks launched during recent years. All mission work has been ordered closed in the South American country, and the Evangelical Fellowship throughout the world was asked to join in special prayer for these brothers in Colombia.

Hearing a special report by Board member Lamar Westcott of the Westcotts' visits, just concluded, to mission fields in Portugal and Africa. Mr. Westcott told the Board that they found work in Portugal to be highly impressive, and expressed his conviction that the Board has reason to be proud of the work being done by its missionaries in both areas. He pointed out his impressions on the rising cost of living in Africa, the rising spirit of nationalism, and urged: "We should do all possible to train natives to take over the Christian work as rapidly as possible. Our days there in Africa seem to be numbered."

As a result of the Board member's report on high costs, the Board voted that its Business and Finance committee should make a thorough special study of the cost of living in all fields in which the Board maintains missionaries.

Hearing a report of progress on the Board's new building in Nashville. Contract on the building was to be let soon.

Approving a recommendation by the Home Base Committee that the 1957 General Assembly in Birmingham be encouraged to give special attention to missions. It will mark the 50th anniversary of the 1907 General Assembly in Birmingham which adopted a great forward-looking statement on missions, with emphasis on the layman's part in it. Recommendation will be made by the Board that the 1957 Assembly put special emphasis on the layman's part in world missions, and by a special pre-assembly conference, take note of the role of the layman in world evangelism.

Hearing a report that the receipts to date for the Easter Offering for Overseas Relief and Inter-Church Aid total $63,989, well ahead of the same date in 1955.

Voting expressions of deep appreciation for the services rendered by missionaries whose retirements will become effective during the next few months. These are:

Miss Katheryne L. Thompson, formerly missionery to China, and for the last few years a missionary to Japan, who will end 35 years of service effective September 1, 1956.

Dr. and Mrs. Martin A. Hopkins of China, who finished more than 39 years of service June 1, 1956.

The Rev. and Mrs. G. R. Womeldorf, former missionaries to China, who closed 33 years service June 1, 1956.

Mrs. A. A. Talbot, formerly of the China mission, who closed 33 years service June 1, 1956.

Resignations of Miss Ruth Farrior, formerly of the China mission, and Mr. B. Gayle Rider, short-term missionary to Mexico, were accepted with regret, and expressions of appreciation of their services.

Refund of Income Tax Paid on Manse or Rental Allowance

Through the kindness of Mr. G. B. Strickler, Treasurer of the Board of Church Extension, I am able to give you the following information:

The Internal Revenue Code of 1954, Section 107 (2), provides that rental allowance paid to ministers, to the extent used to rent or provide a home, is exempt from Federal Income Tax. We are now in receipt of information that Revenue Ruling 56-58 of the Commissioner of Internal Revenue, dealing with manse allowances to clergymen, revokes prior rulings of the Commissioner and states that it will accept certain court decisions and will follow these decisions, which held that rental allowance paid to ministers, to the extent used to rent or provide a home is exempt from Federal Income Tax.

It is our understanding that under Revenue Ruling 56-58 ministers may claim a refund of tax paid as a result of reporting rental or manse allowance as income in the year 1953 to the extent that it was used to rent or provide a home. The years 1954 and 1955 are covered under the Internal Revenue Code of 1954, as previously set out, and claims for years prior to 1953 are barred in view of the three year statute of limitations for filing a refund claim. The Federal Income Tax return for the calendar year 1953 being due on March 15, 1954, the statute of limitations for filing a claim for refund of 1953 taxes will not expire until March 15, 1957.

Anyone making a claim for refund should understand that the Internal Revenue Department will make a careful review of the Income Tax refund of the claimant for any year in which a refund is claimed and should, therefore, be fully prepared to answer any questions with regard to such return.

Claim form number 843 may be obtained from the Internal Revenue Department and when completed, should be filed with the District Director of Internal Revenue where the tax was paid. Instructions for filling out the form are printed thereon.

E. C. Scott, Stated Clerk

Religious Statistics — Korea

Recent figures published by the Republic of Korea Ministry of Education indicate the following membership in religious bodies in South Korea (as of April 15, 1956).

Protestant	849,608
Roman Catholic	166,732
Buddhist	3,458,520
Chun-do-kyo	1,495,723

The population of South Korea is roughly twenty-five million.

These figures cannot be considered strictly accurate since methods of reporting vary widely even among the Christian churches. If one parent is a Roman Catholic, the entire family may be listed as members. Some Protestant churches report only baptized members, others include catechumens and Sunday School children. The Buddhist figure is probably the least realistic, because whole villages and families are nominally followers of this religion which has been active in Korea for centuries. The Chun-do-kyo is a cult of Korean origin, and at times has been virtually a political organization which has borrowed freely from other religions, including Christianity, without being any one of them.

At best not more than three or four out of every one hundred Koreans is a Christian, while 75% hold to spirit and ancestor worship or have no religion at all. Pray for the unfinished task of bringing Christ to Korea! (Figures from the *Hankook Ilbo*, prominent Korean newspaper.)

The Presbyterian Church of Brazil Has:

350 ordained ministers
13 licensed preachers
100 ministerial candidates
18 lay evangelists
1877 elders
1752 deacons
76307 communicant members
60927 non-communicants
437 organized churches
58 organized congregations
609 congregations under the supervision of churches
1520 preaching points
45 day schools with 5887 scholars
1248 Sunday Schools with 6214 classes, 8799 teachers & officials, 94691 scholars
262 juvenile societies with 7974 members
454 Young People's Societies - 13906 members
558 Women's Societies with 18490 members
316 other societies, with 8372 members
801 churches (worship buildings)
161 manses
435 other properties

During 1955 -

4486 persons were received into church fellowship
421 adult members died
4783 children were baptized.

There are thirty-three presbyteries, which meet annually.

There are six synods, which meet biennially.

The General Assembly meets once in four years. In 1950 it met in Presidente Soaros, in the State of Minas Gerais. In 1954 it met in Recife, in the State of Pernambuco.

These statistics are of the national church only. Those of the American Presbyterian Missions are sent to their respective Boards.

Harold H. Cook, Statistical Secretary

GEORGIA

Atlanta — Dr. Wade H. Boggs, consultant to the Board of Annuities and Relief, and moderator in 1954 of the General Assembly of the Presbyterian Church, U.S., recently announced his acceptance of a call to join the staff of Druid Hills Presbyterian Church here, as one of the ministers. The call will be effective September 1, 1956.

At the same time, Dr. Boggs announced that he has tendered his resignation to the Board of Annuities and Relief, which he has served for 13 years—11 as executive secretary and two as consultant. Dr. Boggs' resignation has been made effective as of September 1.

After June 1, Dr. Boggs will be in Montreat, N. C., most of the summer, managing the Vacation Fund and Geneva Hall, before returning to Atlanta to begin his duties at Druid Hills.

Dr. Boggs' acceptance of the call to Druid Hills Church means that he will return after an absence of 21 years, to the church of which he was pastor from 1926 through 1935. After leaving the Atlanta church he served as pastor of the First Presbyterian Church of Shreveport, La., from 1935 through 1943 when he became executive secretary of the Board.

Winder — Climaxing a year of progress, the First Presbyterian Church of Winder observed a week of evangelistic services recently. Dr. Felix B. Gear of Columbia Theological Seminary was the evangelist during the pre-Easter week services.

The Rev. William A. Bodiford became pastor of the Winder Church in June of 1955, after his graduation from Columbia Theological Seminary. He was ordained on August 7, 1955. Before he came to Winder, the church had suffered a series of setbacks in the resignation of the pastor and the loss of a number of members.

Now there is a total of 120 members, with 24 of these being new communicants, and six by letter of transfer.

Three new deacons were installed and today the diaconate is an active one. The diaconate is striving for one hundred per cent efficiency. All members are becoming more interested in the program and progress of the church.

The current project is a building program which was initiated in December 1955. Now, six months later, the fund amounts to over $3,000.00. This amount has been contributed by the congregation, over and above the regular budget.

NORTH CAROLINA

Kings Mountain Presbytery — A highlight of the May meeting of Kings Mountain Presbytery in the First Presbyterian Church, Belmont, was the visit and challenging appeal of Mayor Voit Gilmore of Southern Pines, the General Chairman of the Presbyterian Consolidated College Campaign, now being conducted by the Synod. Other speakers in behalf of the Campaign were: Mr. R. Dave Hall, of the First Church, Belmont, and Chairman of the Campaign in the Presbytery.

Mr. Hall reported that Kings Mountain Presbytery has been asked to raise $265,000.00 as its "Fair Share" of the needed 3½ million dollars. Already churches have accepted quotas that total $214,000.00, and over $115,000.00 of this already has been raised. Four churches: Linwood, Spindale, Shiloh, and Belmont First, already have met their asked quota.

Rev. C. D. Patterson, pastor of the Cramerton Presbyterian Church, was elected Moderator.

Rev. John S. Brown preached the sermon as retiring Moderator. Rev. W. Priestly Conyers, pastor of the host church, and Rev. Jas. T. Womack, Jr., pastor of the Lincolnton Presbyterian Church, presided at the Communion Table and were assisted by eight members of the Session of the host church.

Rev. Jas. N. Brown, Chairman of the Committee on Candidates, reported three Candidates were completing their theological studies this month and had requested letters of admission to other presbyteries in order that they may be examined for ordination and be installed as pastors of churches. Mr. Jas. B. Harrison, Jr., member of Olney Presbyterian Church, was received as a Candidate under the care of this presbytery.

An overture that the General Assembly instruct the Board of Annuities and Relief to discontinue the practice of reducing appropriations made to aged and infirm ministers of the Synod of North Carolina, and that the Board be directed to pay to these ministers amounts equivalent to amounts paid to the men of the entire church, was approved and ordered sent to the General Assembly.

The Rev. J. S. Johnson, pastor of the Bessemer City and Longs Creek Presbyterian Churches, was chosen Moderator-Nominee for the next Stated Meeting to be held in the Lowell Presbyterian Church, Tuesday, September 18, 1956, 9:30 A. M.

Maxton — An earnest purpose to continue in strengthening the educational program on the campus of Presbyterian Junior College in order that the college may more fully contribute to the forward movement in Christian education contemplated in the consolidated college to be erected in Laurinburg was expressed by resolution of the Board of Trustees of Presbyterian Junior College at the semi-annual meeting held at the college in Maxton.

In reports to the Board attention was called to the progress toward the consolidation. Synod has approved the plan. The trustees, elected by Presbyterian procedure, have chosen the site. A great financial campaign is now in progress. "We must, asking God's blessing, do all we can to make it a success," it was stated.

The presidents of the three colleges which will unite are already meeting as a committee. Dr. William C. Pressly, president of Peace College, is chairman. An action taken at the first meeting of the cooperating presidents as a committee was read, expressing gratitude to the members of the consolidated Board for their faithful, devoted, and sacrificial service in the large amount of time and labor they have given to their difficult and de-one year. He plans to study Biblical theology as well as to observe the Student Christian Movement in Germany.

An outstanding seminarian, Mr. Meeks won the Austin Presbyterian Seminary's highest honor in January when he received the $1,000 Alumni Fellowship for scholastic achievement.

Mr. Meeks is the son of Mr. and Mrs. B. L. Meeks, Route 1, Carrollton, Ala. He attended Aliceville High School where he was valedictorian of his graduating class, editor of the annual and a member of the football squad.

Austin — **William O. Walker,** rising senior from Grandfalls, Texas, was named president of the student body for the 1956-57 school year in student elections held at Austin Presbyterian Theological Seminary late in April.

Seminary students elected Sam Junkin, Kerrville Middler, to the Vice Presidency. Other administrative officers, both from the Junior class, are Holly Mitchell, Shreveport, Louisiana, Secretary; and Jack Bennett, Palestine, Texas, Treasurer.

VIRGINIA

Richmond — Dr. James D. Smart, pastor of the Rosedale Presbyterian Church in Toronto, Canada, delivered the address to the graduating class of the Presbyterian Training School, here, on Monday, May 21.

The baccalaureate sermon was delivered by the Rev. Albert Edwards, pastor of the First Presbyterian Church, Harrisonburg, Va., Sunday, May 20. Both services were held at 8 p.m. in Schauffler Hall.

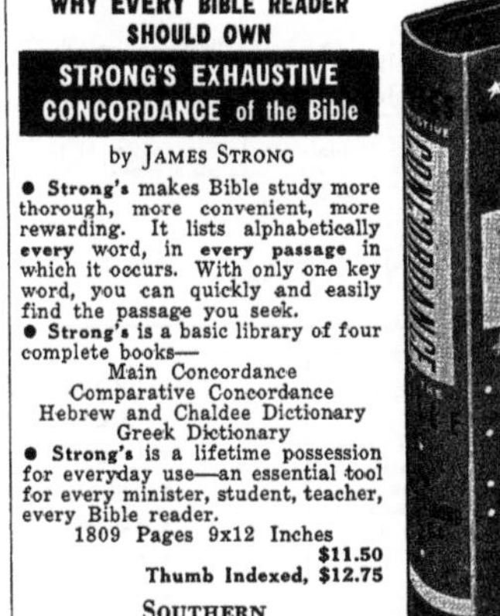

THE SOUTHERN PRESBYTERIAN JOURNAL

A Presbyterian weekly magazine devoted to the statement, defense and propagation of the Gospel, the faith which was once for all delivered unto the saints.

JUNE 13, 1956

EDITORIAL

The 1956 Assembly Meeting at Montreat

By Rev. John R. Richardson, D.D.

In the last issue we carried the picture of the newly elected Moderator, Dr. W. T. Thompson. We also carried in that issue the sermon delivered by the retiring Moderator, Dr. J. McDowell Richards.

In this issue we are carrying the report of the Pre-Assembly Conference on Evangelism.

In the next issue (June 20, 1956) you may look forward to reading Dr. Richardson's detailed report and analysis of the 1956 Assembly.

H.B.D.

VOL. XV NO. 7 $2.50 A YEAR

THE SOUTHERN PRESBYTERIAN JOURNAL
The Journal has no official connection with the Presbyterian Church in the United States
Rev. Henry B. Dendy, D.D., Editor........................**Weaverville, N. C.**
Dr. L. Nelson Bell, Associate Editor........................**Asheville, N. C.**
Rev. Wade C. Smith, Associate Editor........................**Weaverville, N. C.**

EDITORIAL

Can Man Love More Than God?

There is an ominous development in theological circles today. Universalism has existed for centuries but the Universalist Church has been outside the pale of recognized Protestantism.

Now, all over the Church we find universalism being embraced, not by men outside the Christian circle but by some in positions of great confidence and influence.

To the unwary it sounds so plausible to affirm that God's redemption extends to all men and whether they accept Christ or not that still somehow, somewhere, everyone will be saved.

To the unwary it seems honoring to God to say that His love is so great that He could never permit men to suffer eternal punishment or separation from Him.

That this man-made theory strikes at the very heart of the Scriptural record; that it does violence to the revealed will and plan of God; that it makes a mockery of the Gospel of Jesus Christ is enough to make men pause and shudder and this because it offers a false hope to men who wilfully reject the love of God in Christ Jesus.

A few days ago the President of the American Association for the Advancement of Atheism reported that his organization had dwindled in recent years because so few ministers preached eternal punishment and had changed the Christian message to one of doing good to others, thereby undercutting their chief reason for being organized.

This in itself should give some pause, but our chief concern is that the love of God (which can never be exhausted or overstated), should be used as a pretext to promulgate a doctrine which overlooks not only the depths of God's love and mercy but also His holiness and justice.

The Russellites of a past generation (now called Jehovah's Witnesses), had scant recognition in recognized theological circles. Today his counterpart is legion and he moves in the most select circles of Protestantism and his concept of Agape - the love of God - is extolled to the skies.

But what saith the Scriptures:

"And many of them that sleep in the dust of the earth shall awake, some to everlasting life, and some to shame and everlasting contempt." Daniel 12:2.

No one in all of the Bible says more about eternal punishment than our Lord. It was our Lord who spoke these words: *"to destroy both soul and body in hell"* . . . *"everlasting fire"* . . . *"Then shall he say also unto them on the left hand, Depart from me, ye cursed, into everlasting fire, prepared for the devil and his angels."* . . . *"And these shall go away into everlasting punishment but the righteous into life eternal"* . . . *"But he that shall blaspheme against the Holy Ghost hath never forgiveness, but is in danger of eternal damnation."* . . . *". . . . and they that have done evil, unto the resurrection of damnation."*

The references to *eternal* punishment are many. The question is not one of whether it is *real fire;* that is of minor importance. The question is that the Bible plainly teaches that death determines the future for all eternity. Hell is separation from God and that is the fire of God's judgment regardless of how its literal application is applied.

Why did Christ come into the world? To show the love of God and to redeem mankind. John 3:16 declares the love of God in its fact and in its magnitude and it states that faith in Christ is the *alternative* to "perishing" and the guarantee of "everlasting life."

John 3:36 could not be more specific: *"He that believeth on the Son hath everlasting life: and he that believeth not the Son shall not see life; but the wrath of God abideth on him."*

Why give this the lie? Why twist the clear statements of Scripture? Why pose as having a higher moral concept than God Himself?

This neo-universalism, in some cases is prompted by a deep love of humanity and a high concept of God's love. But it runs directly counter to God's revealed attitude to sin and the enormity of sin itself. It also runs directly counter to the revelation of God's provision for man's redemption from sin. It is only when we see the Son of God dying on the cross for sinful man that we begin to have even a remote understanding of what sin and its consequences really are.

Furthermore, it is a dangerous philosophy which confuses God's universal *offer* with a salvation which will be universally applied. "Whosoever" means just what it says - that all who will accept God's free offer of saving grace are saved. The distinction between God's saving grace for the elect and man's own free agency to accept God's offer is one into which we will not try to enter. Our concern is rather that violence shall not be done to the entire structure of the plan of salvation and the ultimate fate of those who reject that plan.

Nor do we intend to discuss the end of those who have died in ignorance. These we can well leave in the hands of a loving and all-knowing God.

The chief concern of this editorial is that Christians, and those who stand in positions of influence in particular, shall not develop a doctrine which can do inestimable harm to those who espouse it, a doctrine which cannot be sustained by Scripture and one which does violence to the entire structure of the Gospel message.

Sin and righteousness and judgment to come are not popular subjects. Hell is considered old-fashioned by some. The fact of and the effect of sin for all eternity are awful to contemplate. How much more awful if these things are obscured through a false concept of God and His holiness.

A physician who happily tells his patient with cancer that all will be well may give that patient a few moments of false security but he is unfaithful to both his profession and to his patient.

Where the *eternal* destiny of man is involved we will be faithful preachers of the Word and faithful to those who come under our ministry if we stick to *revealed truth* and not to wishful thinking. Hebrews 10:26-31. L.N.B.

Hell in Colombia

A bigoted government, urged on by fanatical priests, are persecuting Protestants and the Protestant Church in days reminiscent of the Inquisition.

The writer recently talked with a man who had just returned from a conference with the State Department. He said: "All hell has broken loose in Colombia."

Religious persecution has been rampant in Colombia for years. It has now gotten worse. Protestant missionaries have been ordered to desist from their work. Some have been arrested. Nationals, members of Protestant churches, have been beaten and imprisoned. Property of churches and missions has been damaged.

Religious freedom, guaranteed by the Constitution, does not exist and the result is a reign of terror, so far as Protestants are concerned.

Protestant organizations are protesting but so far to little avail. One wonders why the silence of the Church which has been dominant in that country for centuries? Can it be that where given the opportunity and backed by a dominated government the days of the Inquisition would be repeated?

We would commend to the readers of the *Journal* the following communication from the Board of World Missions:

"The Board of World Missions, in session here on Tuesday, May 15, was greatly concerned over a communication from Dr. Howard W. Yoder, Secretary of the Committee on Cooperation in Latin America, telling of new persecution in Colombia, South America. Dr. Yoder wrote:

> 'We have just received an authentic word from Colombia that the religious persecution has taken a bad turn for the worse. All forms of Protestant work have been ordered closed in the Mission territories which make up three-fourths of the area of the country. Thirty churches have been closed in the last two weeks and seven Colombian pastors thrown into jail.

"The Evangelical Confederation of Colombia has issued an urgent call to prayer and fasting. It is suggested that we pass this information on

The Southern Presbyterian Journal, *a Presbyterian Weekly magazine devoted to the statement, defense, and propagation of the Gospel, the faith which was once for all delivered unto the saints,* published every Wednesday by The Southern Presbyterian Journal, Inc., in Weaverville, N. C.

Entered as second-class matter May 15, 1942, at the Postoffice at Weaverville, N. C., under the Act of March 3, 1879. Vol. XV, No. 7, June 13, 1956. Editorial and Business Offices: Weaverville, N. C. Printed in the U.S.A. by Biltmore Press, Asheville, N. C.

ADDRESS CHANGE: When changing address, please let us have both old and new address as far in advance as possible. Allow three weeks after change if not sent in advance. When possible, send an address label giving your old address.

to other interested people or groups so that many might join with our Colombian fellow-Christians in special prayer.

"The request for prayer, which is signed by Juan A. Dyck, Executive Secretary of the Evangelical Confederation of Colombia, is as follows:

'WE INVITE ALL EVANGELICAL BELIEVERS OF COLOMBIA TO JOIN IN PRAYER:

'*First:* For the many Evangelical Churches closed in the country. Thirty churches have been closed in two weeks.

'*Second:* For the pastors and believers who suffer in the prisons for the Cause of Christ. Seven pastors have been placed in prison in two weeks.

'*Third:* For the gatherings that are to celebrate the Centenary of Evangelical work in Colombia in different places in Colombia.

'*Fourth:* For freedom to hold evangelical meetings throughout the country to worship and glorify God.

'*Fifth:* For a new dedication on the part of each one of us to serve and glorify God.'

"While our Church has no work in Colombia, this information is sent to you on instructions from our Board in the hope that you may have opportunity in Synods, Presbyteries, or local congregations, to tell our people of the sufferings of fellow-Christians in Colombia and to join with them in prayer."

C. Darby Fulton"

THE CHIEF OBSTACLE

On a Home Mission report recently sent out was this question: "What is the chief obstacle with which you have to contend?" One reply was received that gave a brief and informative answer. It was this: "TV." There are numerous churches other than Home Mission churches, where the lament is heard: "People stay away from the evening service to watch television." Nor is it infrequent that an officers' meeting has to be cut short so everyone can get home to see a fabulous give-away.

To be sure the Lord means for all to have some recreation and relaxation—but He does not mean that a man should take it all sitting on his neck.

TV is a symptom of the ill, it is not the malady itself. When one foregoes the opportunity of worship or the call of the kingdom service to watch some comedian perform, the fault is not in the television, but in the individual's lack of spiritual maturity. It is symptomatic of the fact that the member does not have a sense of what is vital in life. It demonstrates an unwillingness to put first things first. It is an effort to evade the discipline of discipleship. It is very evidently a lack of Christian commitment.

The unfortunate part about this disease is that it is not corrected when the favorite program is over, or the set is broken. When the individual gets to Church or the officers' meeting, the trouble still persists. It expresses itself in half-hearted participation, and a pessimistic view toward larger realization of Christian concern and activity.

Television is the scapegoat, it is heart trouble that is causing the difficulty.

—Associate Reformed Presbyterian

IT CAN BE DONE

By Rev. Frank A. Brown

When a church jumps, in four days time, from an annual gift of $200.00 to an annual gift of $2500.00 to world missions, that is news. It is all very well for our big churches, like Chattanooga First, to tell us how they climbed to the eighty thousand dollar mark, but the church wants to hear what the little churches can do.

When the three tiny churches of Piney Flats, Tenn., called a new pastor in March 1956, they little expected that the first project he would lead them to would be a missionary conference —a school of missions with PLEDGES. They had been without a regular pastor for nearly two years. Many things clamored for attention at once. Many needs cried for money. How natural to have said, "Wait for a year or two until pastor and people can get together and work on local needs first, and then we will do something for the world missions."

No. As soon as a team could be secured from Nashville, they held nineteen meetings and launched the canvass, with magnificent results. The pastor, Rev. Carl Wilson, was on the team and spoke effectively on "The Meaning of the Missionary Call" and "Seek Ye First the Kingdom of God." I am begging him to tell the story and "to make known to you the grace of God which hath been given in the churches of Piney Flats."

1956 Montreat Assembly

By Rev. John R. Richardson, D.D.

It was not unusual to hear new Commissioners to the Assembly ask: "What is the Assembly about anyway?" It is perfectly natural for a question like this to arise and readers who have not attended an Assembly might ask the same question.

The answer to the question put in official language would be:

"The General Assembly shall have power to receive and issue all appeals, references, and complaints regularly brought before it from the lower courts; to bear testimony against error in doctrine and immorality in practice, injuriously affecting the Church; to decide in all controversies respecting doctrine and discipline; to give its advice and instruction, in conformity with the Constitution, in all cases submitted to it; to review the records of the Synods; to take care that the lower courts observe the Constitution; to redress whatever they may have done contrary to order; to concert measures for promoting the prosperity and enlargement of the Church; to erect new Synods; to institute and superintend the agencies necessary in the general work of the Church; to appoint ministers to such labors as fall under its jurisdiction; to suppress schismatical contentions and disputations, according to the rules provided therefor; to receive under its jurisdiction, with the consent of three-fourths of the Presbyteries, other ecclesiastical bodies whose organization is conformed to the doctrine and order of this Church . . . and in general to recommend measures for the promotion of charity, truth, and holiness through all the churches under its care."

The aim of the Assembly set forth in these expressive words covers a lot of territory but, as a matter of fact, an Assembly transacts a great deal more business than is found in this list of duties. Recent Assemblies have added to this list a dynamic program of Evangelism always scheduled just prior to the opening day. This feature is steadily growing in influence upon an increasing number of Commissioners.

Pre-Assembly Conference on Evangelism

Dr. William H. McCorkle, Secretary of the Division of Evangelism, convened the conference on Evangelism Wednesday afternoon at 3:00 P. M. He explained the primary obligations on the part of Christians in this sphere and indicated that there is a growing momentum of interest in many parts of our Church. More Southern Presbyterians, he said, are realizing at the present time that the first business of the Church is to reach the un-reached for Christ.

Dr. William C. Mebane, prominent physician of Wilmington, N. C., led the opening devotional. He used the example of Philip to show that a layman has a responsibility to preach Jesus. He insisted that Philip did not preach philosophy or literature, but Christ. He warned that opportunities are fleeting and that Christians must, like Philip, "run" to seize the opportunities to witness for Christ.

A stimulating seminar was conducted by Dr. Elton Trueblood, Professor of Philosophy at Earlham College on the subject, "The Small Group Program in the Local Church." Dr. Trueblood observed that there is an increasing desire for a closer fellowship and a sense of community in our day. Because of this desire small groups can be units of evangelistic warmth and power. Together with others of common concern, Christians discover there is vitality and meaning in their faith. Through such groups the spiritual life of the Church is being developed.

This is a re-discovery, said Dr. Trueblood, of what the early Church knew; that the most effective group is the small group. He declared: "Fellowship is central in the Christian idea. The fashionable notion of trying to be religious without the Church is passing."

Dr. Trueblood also observed: "Many churches are too big. There is no sense of responsibility on the part of many members in a big church."

After raising the question, "What can the small group mean to you in your Church?", this speaker had some fine things to say. He stated that this innovation was not to add to other meetings because we have too many meetings already. He also indicated that there are evident dangers in groups of the kind that he was advocating. It is very easy, he averred, for such a group to become subjective, increasingly concerned with its own local problems. Another danger to watch for is that such a group can become sentimental, forgetting that its aim is to equip for service. Still another danger is found in the fact that such a group can become a center of spiritual pride, looking askance at less interested Christians. Lastly, another danger that must be guarded against is that such a group sometimes becomes independent and isolated from the main program of the Church, and therefore becomes a liability instead of an asset.

These dangers, said Dr. Trueblood, are real, but every good thing has difficulties. The question must be asked whether vague religiosity, continued lethargy, and spectator religion are not to be feared more. Leaders in the group must be on the alert to be kept from cliquishness by insistence on the necessity of working with and within the Church.

In the conduct of these group meetings, Dr. Trueblood advised that each meeting should start on the dot, and there should be no lagging. If any member is absent, his absence should be investigated by an interested member of the group. At each meeting each one should tell what he has done for Christ and His Church since the last meeting. This should be at the report period. There should also be a report on recent insights gained from Scripture reading. At each meeting there should be a plan for future service. Finally, there should be a period of prayer, both silent and vocal.

Later in the afternoon, Dr. Trueblood spoke on the importance of a sense of vocation in the Christian life, especially as related to un-ordained men. He said that even though there is evidence of more religious vitality in America, this is not enough. Too many Christians in all of our Churches give too little money and too little time to the work of the Church.

When men join the Communist cause, said Dr. Trueblood, they have to tithe. For example, Whitaker Chambers once confessed that out of $1600.00 a year, he gave $160.00 to the Communist cause when he was a card-carrying Communist. No little change, he affirmed, is good enough. There must be a change in a big way that will result in sacrificial giving to promote the cause of Christ.

Total evangelism was advocated by the speaker as the only thing that can meet the needs of our day. This total evangelism, he declared, should include all Christians. The task is too big for professional evangelists. There must be a division of labor in the Christian enterprise but this does not apply to the task of evangelism. It was brought out that today it takes twenty-eight Southern Presbyterians an entire year to bring one lost person to Christ. The sense of vocation for all Christians is a New Testament doctrine. He asserted that in the Bible the word "layman" cannot be found and neither can the word "clergy," but all Christians are embraced under the doctrine of the priesthood of believers and all Christian priests should exercise their priestly functions.

Total evangelism should include all parts of a person's personality, said Dr. Trueblood. We should put our hearts into it for without emotion we are not going to do much good. But there must also be the application of our minds. The Communists use their minds: their minds are sharpened to be used and to "out-think" their opponents.

Total evangelism must also include the use of our time. It is easier to write a check than to give time to the Lord. The Christian in the factory, and the school, and wherever people may be found, must seek to witness for Christ. The Christian must never consider himself as "off duty."

This message was concluded with some helpful observations on "Vocational Evangelism." The speaker referred to a recent retreat where Christian doctors came together to study how to reach other doctors for Christ. Christian lawyers, he said, should come together to be trained as to how to reach other lawyers for Christ. This procedure should be applied to every vocation.

Dr. William M. Elliott, pastor of the Highland Park Presbyterian Church of Dallas, gave an inspirational message on "Evangelism, the Supreme Function of the Church." He said that Christians must be convinced that evangelism is the greatest business in the world. Our danger is to spend our time talking about it while, at the same time, dodging the performance of it. Evangelism is essential for the Church. According to the speaker, it is also essential to society. He remarked, "Society cannot be altered until people are changed." The Church, he said, in the New Testament is a life-changing institution. The Church must be engaged in getting men into a right relationship with God. No other institution is doing this. People must be inwardly changed and this is the Church's responsibility.

Dr. Elliott's second message dealt with the subject, "Conversion Ought to Mean Something." This was based on the experience of Zacchaeus. Conversion, he said, must issue in better people. Zacchaeus' manner of living was altered. It reached his pocketbook, and it gave him a concern for other people. He became a different person. Dr. Elliott declared, "Too many church members are like the rest of the world." Becoming a Christian, he continued, should be a revolutionary experience. "Life is never the same after conversion. Becoming a Christian, therefore, is more than accepting Christ's forgiveness. It is much more."

Dr. Elliott quoted an English writer who recently said: "The Church is a field for evangelism rather than a force for evangelism." He remarked, "There is much truth in this statement, because Christianity claims eight hundred million Christians but a large number of these are not really Christians."

The third address by Dr. Elliott was on, "Ye shall be witnesses." A witness was described as one who relates what he knows first hand. This, said Dr. Elliott, any Christian can do and witnessing is the duty of all Christians: all believers who have heard the good news must pass it on. This is not the business of specialists but of all Christians who have met Christ along any Damascus road.

Dr. John L. Casteel, Professor of Homiletics at Colgate-Rochester Divinity School, spoke on, "The Marks of Christian Prayer." He indicated that the kind of prayer we should be concerned with is *Christian* prayer. The resurgence of instinctive or natural prayer we hear a great deal about today, said Dr. Casteel, is not enough. When people speak of "the Man Upstairs," it shows that the sense of God is very vague, and people then begin to pray merely because "it is the thing to do." He described Christian prayer as "redeemed prayer." Prayer demands a change of heart before it can be efficacious. Christian prayer must also have a living sense of God. To the Christian, God must be personal, present and powerful at the time of prayer. Further, he said, Christian prayer makes moral demands; our hands must be clean and we must be willing to do the will of God when we approach Him in prayer. Prayer must be linked with evangelism and Dr. Casteel said that "when we engage in evangelism we must do a great deal of hard praying." Unless we pray, we shall be short-winded on the track. To have staying power, we must have praying power. Dr. Casteel failed in his message, however, to state that the paramount factor that distinguishes Christian prayer is its mediation through Jesus Christ. The New Testament tells us that there is only one Mediator between God and man. The speaker said many fine things but it is regrettable that this important Christian truth was overlooked in a message on "The Marks of Christian Prayer."

Dr. Harry Denman conducted a seminar on "Visitation Evangelism." He began the seminar by raising some probing questions. He asked, "Suppose I come to your Church Sunday morning as a visitor. What would happen?" Many answers were given to this question. The next was: "How long would it be before an invitation to become a Christian would be given to me?" He said that insurance men are eager to sign up prospects as quickly as possible but many Christians are not so eager. He asked one insurance man present, "If I came to your office and I wanted $50,000.00 insurance, what would you do?" The man answered, "I would have you at the doctor's office within thirty minutes." An embarrassing question was: "How many in your Church go out each week to seek some soul for Christ?" Business, he said, doesn't sit down and wait for people to come and neither should Christians. The last question was: "How many people in your city do you know who are un-converted and lost in sin, and are you sad because of their lost condition?"

ANGLERS

(From *"New Testament Evangelism"*

by Wade C. Smith)

Lesson No. 143

METHOD (continued) - Finding "Prospects"

This writer has traveled up and down our land for the past forty years - south, west, north, east and across the seas - and he has never yet had a stranger to ask him if he was a Christian! He has been thrown with strangers in hotels, boarding houses, railroad stations, Pullmans, coaches, buses and steamers; many of them he had reason to believe were church members, some afterward proving to be church officers, elders, deacons, stewards, vestrymen and even pastors. Yet not one of them tried to ascertain if he was a saved man. This was not because they hesitated to intrude upon his private affairs, for they asked about every other kind of a personal question: where was he from, where was he going, what was his name, was he married, any children, how many boys, how many girls, what was it he had in that square package so heavy (stereopticon slides!), borrowed his paper, got change from him, told him all their ills - offered him a cigar - but never offered him Christ. And many of these had found for themselves the Pearl of Great Price. It is a sad commentary on the missionary spirit of church members; and if the reader is asking if this is an indictment against *him*, he can answer his own question by reviewing the contacts and conversations he has had with strangers where ample opportunity was afforded to broach the only really vital subject. Did he? Or did he not?

Getting Contact. It is obvious that thousands of church members whose sails are now flapping in the calm of inertia would pilot hapless voyagers into port if they could only get a start. If they could once break the ice! That seems to be the hardest thing to do - and perhaps it is. So many church folks know perfectly well the plan of salvation, have a fair knowledge of the Bible and some desire to do this vital service, but their timid souls falter before the first step of witnessing.

As a matter of fact, the first step, or getting contact, is very simple. It is as simple as asking for a drink of water. Indeed, our Lord, Himself, used this very means on one occasion, and His asking for a drink was the entering wedge to a thrilling episode in soul winning. We will do well to study and *imitate* His *method.* Getting contact is beginning at a point where your prospect is thinking or working. It is throwing yourself "into gear" with him, though for the moment it may be throwing yourself "out of gear" with yourself. It is always a sympathetic approach. It makes capital out of the aims and desires and employments of the person sought.

Paul laid down the principle for getting contact in his first letter to the Corinthians (9:19-23). "I am made all things to all men," he said, "that I might by all means save some." Motte Martin, missionary to the Congo, secured his sure place in the hearts of the natives by sitting down on the dirt floor in their thatched hovels and eating with them the casava batter bread out of the one pot, the entire family reaching the food with fingers - doubtfully washed. It took a strong stomach to do that; but he had a stomach for saving souls. Perhaps no man on the missionary field has ever been more greatly beloved by the people among whom he worked, than this man.

"Are you a Christian?" Often, however, the time is short and it is desirable to bring matters quickly to an issue with your prospect. There is a very simple and practical question which can be effectively used without giving offense. It is this: "Are you a Christian"? If he is, he will be glad to affirm it. If he is not, you will find him immediately on the defensive, and the answer will indicate the line of presentation. If your prospect, as a rare exception, should be irritated by the question, just keep cool and sympathetic (praying!) and the matter will likely work around your way again, even improved by the riffle. Remember, this is God and you working together; and that is a guarantee of your peace in the outcome - no matter what the outcome may be.

Personal work is not without its surprising come-backs, which sometimes provoke a smile. The writer drew up at a garage in a Virginia village and asked the young man to repair a broken connection. He smilingly lifted the hood of the car to examine the "disconnection" and we both peered in upon the situation. He was so nice and pleasant about it that, there under the hood our heads so close together it seemed to afford an opportunity to learn what might be his spiritual "status." So I remarked, "You must be a Christian." He looked a little embarrassed, and replied apologetically, "No sir, I'm a Presbyterian." And that was that.

But the question, "Are you a Christian," is direct and to the point. There can be no misunderstanding of it. It cuts off a lot of "whipping the devil around the stump," and clears the atmosphere at once for real business. Prayer, of course, is the prime factor in discovering prospects and in securing the point of contact. Prayer must precede, accompany and seal every step in the whole program of soul-winning.

(Next lesson, "Fishing with the Word")

Helps To Understanding Scripture Readings in *Day by Day*

By C. C. Baker

Sunday, June 17, *Gal.* 5:13-15. The keynote of the letter to the Galatians is the "freedom" that the Christian experiences as a result of salvation by grace (5:1a,13a). In what way were the Galatians in danger of losing this freedom (vv.1-3)? Do you know of any Christian group that insists on the keeping of certain outward regulations to guarantee salvation? While Paul insists that the Christian is free from the restrictions of the law, what would he say to the Christian who feels that his freedom entitles him to live as he pleases (vv.13,15)? What is the law to which the Christian must submit (v.14)? What exhortation do you find in these verses that you can apply to your life?

Monday, June 18, *Gal.* 5:16-26. Make a list of words that are opposite in meaning to the words listed as the fruit of the Spirit in vv.22-23. Which list represents your basic nature? The characteristics of your old nature are diametrically opposed to the fruit of the Spirit (v.17). Verses 19-21 list other works of the flesh. Do you think that it is possible to replace your old nature with the qualities of vv.22-23 by your own efforts? What is the true source of these qualities (vv.16,18,22a,25)? What must the Christian be willing to do with the old nature (vv.16,24)? Living the Christian life is turning from sin and yielding yourself to God, allowing God, the Holy Spirit, to put in your life the qualities of the Person of Christ. In what ways do you need to be more like Christ (vv.22-23)?

Tuesday, June 19, *John* 8:31-38. A profession of faith in Christ is merely the beginning of one's spiritual journey (v.31). What condition (vv.31-32) does Christ lay down for the Jews to find true freedom? What was obviously lacking in the reply of these Jews who professed belief in Christ (v.33)? What was their basic attitude toward Christ (vv. 48, 52,57)? How would you interpret the statements of Jesus in vv.31-32,36? Are you one who professes to believe in Christ and yet does not understand the true meaning of His coming? Are you progressively finding victory over temptation in your Christian life, as you grow in the true freedom that results from full fellowship with Christ? (vv.31-32).

Wednesday, June 20, *Romans* 7:4-6. Before Christ came, God's people lived under the Old Testament law. What was one of the accomplishments of these Old Testament regulations (vv.7-11)? Study the analogy of the relation of the wife to the husband in vv.2-3. How is this analogy applicable to the Christian's relation to the law (v.4)? What new power does the Christian possess that was not available under the law (v.6b)? What event in the life of Christ frees the Christian from the penalty of breaking God's law (v.4a)? What event in Christ's life gives the Christian power to live a different life (v.4b)? Do you recognize the full significance of the cross and resurrection in delivering you from the bondage of the law and giving you power to live the Christian life?

Thursday, June 21, *Colossians* 2:16-3:4. The Colossians were being taught that spiritual growth was the result of abstaining from certain foods and worldly practices (vv.16,21). What limitations does Paul say such rules and regulations have (v.23)? What does Paul say is the source of such regulations (v.22)? Do you tend to base your spirituality on the fact that you refrain from certain worldly practices in which others engage? Real spiritual growth comes from fellowship with Christ Himself (v.19; 3:1-3). What does Paul feel the Christian's primary concern should be (3:1-2)? Does your spiritual growth result from a positive seeking of the presence of Christ?

Friday, June 22, *Galatians* 6:1-6. There are two very real dangers into which a Christian can fall in his relation to a fellow-believer. He can withdraw and be unconcerned about the other's life, or he can sit in judgment on the other's conduct. If a Christian slips in his conduct, what is the purpose of another's going to him (v.1)? In what spirit should he go (v.1)? Do you go to fellow Christians in need with the spirit of v.2? What message in vv.1b, 4,5, should prevent us from sitting in judgment upon others? Each Christian is to carry his own load (v.5) and to help carry the burden of a fellow Christian when that burden is too heavy for him to carry alone (v.2).

Saturday, June 23, *1 John* 4:13-21. The facts connected with the Christian faith are often simple to state, but profound in meaning. God has demonstrated in a simple and understandable way that He loves the sinner (vv.9,10). The believer's salvation is wrapped up in one who is very close to God's heart - His own Son (v.14). Contact with God can be established simply by faith in Christ (v.15). Faith in Christ draws one into a unique relation with God - God's very nature dwelling within (vv.15,16). The Christian has proof within himself that he is a child of God (v.13). The Christian faith changes one's outlook concerning the future (v.17). It affects one's relations with others (vv.20-21). Is the marvelous reality of these simple facts present in your life?

SABBATH SCHOOL LESSONS — REV. J. KENTON PARKER

LESSON FOR JUNE 24

The Continuing Mission Of The Church

Background Scripture: Acts 27 and 28
Devotional Reading: Psalm 67

The Continuing Mission of the Church might be stated concisely in the concluding words of the book of Acts: "Preaching the kingdom of God, and teaching those things which concern the Lord Jesus Christ." In the first chapter of this book Jesus had told His disciples that they were to be His witnesses . . . "unto the uttermost part of the earth." In the book of Acts we find Paul reaching for that "uttermost" as he presses on and on until he finally lands at Rome. After his first imprisonment there, which was rather mild, he is believed to have gone into Spain, or even further. The Mission of the Church has been, and is, to continue to preach the Gospel until all the world has heard the message of Salvation.

Psalm 67 is a beautiful expression of this desire and hope: "That they way may be known upon earth, thy saving health among all nations." We live in a sick world. Body, mind, and soul are all contaminated by sin. The world needs "saving health"; not merely cured bodies, but cured souls. Christ is the only Physician who can minister to this deep need. When He shall reign as King and Judge, then, and only then, can the nations "be glad and sing for joy." The Church's mission is to hasten that glad day, so that the world can be happy and prosperous. This is the continuing mission of the church.

Our lesson today divides itself simply and naturally into these two parts: I. Paul's Voyage to Rome, and II. Paul's Preaching in Rome.

I. *Paul's Voyage to Rome:* 27:1 - 28:15.

This is the larger part of our lesson and contains most interesting and instructive material.

1. The voyage to Crete (Fair Havens) : 27:1-12.

Since Paul had appealed to Caesar he had to be taken to Rome as a prisoner. They delivered him and certain other prisoners to a centurion named Julius, of the band called Augustus' band. In this officer we have another fine centurion who treats Paul kindly and considerately. They set sail and come first to Sidon where Paul was allowed to visit his friends and refresh himself. Sailing by Cyprus they came to Myra. There they find a ship going to Italy. They came to Crete, and to a place called The Fair Havens. Much time was spent there and sailing became dangerous, so Paul admonished them with these words: Sirs, I perceive that this voyage will be with hurt, and much danger, not only of the lading and ship, but also of our lives. The centurion made the mistake of believing the master and owner of the ship rather than Paul, and since the haven was not commodious to winter in, and the more part advised to depart, they set sail again. The majority vote is not always the safe vote. We see this illustrated many times in the Bible and history. One man who lives close to God has more wisdom than a multitude who live out of touch with Him.

2. *The Shipwreck and Escape:* 13-44.

"When the south wind blew softly" they supposed that they were going to have fair weather, and sailed from their safe haven. A softly blowing south wind may precede, and even point to a terrible storm. We sometimes have days in the Winter which we call "pet days." I have seen such days followed by snow and ice. A calm precedes a storm. This is true in Nature; it is often true in the experiences of life. It was not long before the tempestuous wind called Euroclydon bore down upon them. The sailors did all they could to save the ship, but finally, "all hope that we should be saved was taken away."

It was in this crisis that Paul emerges as the leader and encourager of both sailors and passengers. He had seen a vision of an angel of god, "Whose I am, and Whom I serve," saying, Fear not, Paul: thou must be brought before Caesar: and lo, God hath given thee all them that sail with thee. A few good men will often save a city or a ship or a nation. Paul states his short "creed" to all those aboard: *"I believe God."* This is a splendid "Confession of Faith." If we can say it with sincerity, and without reservation, we are standing on a firm foundation. In its full meaning it would include all the other parts of the "Faith once delivered to the saints."

God had promised to save their lives but this promise was conditional, as we see from verses 30-32. When the shipmen were about to flee from the ship, under color as though they would have cast anchor out of the foreship," Paul said to the centurion, Except these abide in the ship, ye cannot be saved. Then the soldiers cut the ropes and let the boat fall off. From his position as prisoner Paul now comes forth as virtual commander of the vessel. He also persuades them to eat some food and thus strengthen themselves for the ordeal through which they were still to pass. He took bread and gave thanks to God in the presence of them all. In this emergency he was a good witness for the God he served. They ran the ship aground and it was broken to pieces by the violence of the waves. The soldiers wanted to kill the prisoners, but the centurion, willing to save Paul, kept them from their purpose. They cast themselves into the sea, and all that could swim, and others who could not, were saved by clinging to boards and broken pieces of the ship. The whole company of two hundred and seventy-six were saved as God had promised.

3. *Experiences on the Island of Malta:* 28:1-10

The island upon which they were cast was Malta, (the now famous Malta, the most bombed spot in World War II).

The "barbarous" people showed them no little kindness, for they kindled a fire and received them because of the rain and cold. I will always remember verse three of this chapter. Dr. Graham, who was our beloved pastor when I was in Davidson College, used the first half of this verse one Wednesday night for the text of his talk. He applied it in a very practical way. Each one of us can gather our "bundle of sticks" and lay them on the fire. How can we keep the "Home Fires Burning," in our homes, in our nation, in our churches? Each one of us can do his or her part. We can gather our bundle of sticks and lay them on the fire. Do you wonder that I never forgot that prayer-meeting talk?

The latter part of this verse, taken with the next two, illustrates a common experience in dealing with human nature. One moment Paul was taken to be a murderer; the next, a god. When the viper came out of the heat and fastened upon him the people thought it was a judgment sent upon a murderer, and looked on him, expecting him to fall dead, but when he shook the viper off, they changed their minds and thought that he was a god.

The shipwrecked persons were received courteously by the chief man of the island, Publius by name. His father was sick and Paul healed him. Then they brought others and they were also cured. Naturally the people of the island were grateful, and showed their gratitude by giving them such things as they needed.

II. *Paul Preaches at Rome:* 11-31.

"I must see Rome also." That had been the burning desire of the apostle. He was a city man, and he knew the strategic importance of outstanding cities. Of all the cities of that day Rome, as the seat of the Empire, was the most important. At last, this desire of the apostle was to be gratified.

After three months they left Malta, and landing at Syracuse, came on to Rhegium, and then to Puteoli. There they found brethren and were desired to tarry some days. Even on land, Paul seems to have assumed leadership. It was no longer a centurion and some soldiers leading a prisoner, but the prisoner doing pretty much as he pleased. I like to think of this centurion, and many of those with Paul, as converts to Christianity. I do not see how it could have been otherwise. Some of the brethren came to meet the party, who were an encouragement to Paul, for he thanked God and took courage. We can imagine how he felt as he approached the great heathen city of Rome, where there were but few Christians, and the unbelieving Jews with the idolatrous Romans. Most of the prisoners were delivered to the captain of the guard, but Paul was suffered to dwell by himself with a soldier that kept him. These soldiers that kept Paul were probably those whom he mentions in his letter to the Philippians as "the saints of Caesar's household." (Phil.4:22)

After three days Paul called together the chief of the Jews and explained to them why he was in Rome. These Jews seemed not to have heard of him, but they had heard of Christians, and knew that "this sect" was everywhere spoken against. They desired to hear him, and when they had appointed a day, he expounded and testified the coming of the kingdom of God, proving from the Old Testament that Jesus was Christ, their Messiah. Some believed, and some believed not, and when they agreed not among themselves he warned them very solemnly in the words of Isaiah, "For the heart of this people is waxed gross, and their ears are dull of hearing and their eyes they have closed: lest they should see with their eyes, and hear with their ears, and understand with their heart, and should be converted, and I should heal them." This warning was given also by Christ. (see Matt. 13:15). Paul tells them that God will send the gospel to the Gentiles and they will hear it. He dwelt two whole years in his own hired house, preaching the kingdom of God and the things concerning Christ with confidence, no man forbidding him. Under the providential protection of God he was given this wonderful opportunity.

YOUNG PEOPLE'S DEPARTMENT — REV. B. HOYT EVANS

YOUTH PROGRAM FOR JUNE 24

The Land of The Eskimo

Hymn: "From Greenland's Icy Mountains"
Prayer

Scriptures: Acts 1:1-8

Hymn: "From Ocean Unto Ocean"

Offering

Hymn: 'O Zion, Haste, Thy Mission High Fulfilling"

PROGRAM LEADER:

(Supply the young people with pencils and slips of paper, and give them this brief true-false test about Alaska. Let them check their own answers as you proceed with the program. It will be necessary to write the questions on the blackboard or a large sheet of paper.)

1. Alaska is the oldest and largest territorial possession of the United States. T

2. It is one tenth as large as the United States. F

3. Alaska was once owned by Russia. T

4. The highest point in North America is to be found in Alaska. T

5. Alaska is altogether unsuitable for farming. F

6. The majority of the inhabitants are Eskimos. F

7. The discovery of gold called attention to the importance of Alaska to the United States. T

8. The mining of gold is no longer of any great importance in Alaska. F

9. Alaska is a strategic military base. T

10. Alaska is now seeking admission to statehood. T

LEADER'S INTRODUCTION:

Alaska is the oldest and largest territorial possession of the United States. It was discovered in 1741 by Vitus Bering a Danish navigator in the service of the Russian Navy. The territory was acquired from Russia by the United States in 1867 for $7,200,000 - a penny an acre. Even at that price many people thought it was a foolish purchase. Alaska was practically forgotten until the gold rush of the 1890's called attention to it again. Gold mining continues to be a very important Alaskan industry. The United States has received four billion dollars since acquiring this territory, or 555 times the purchase price.

Alaska is almost one fifth as large as the United States and is separated into three geographic divisions. Two ranges of mountains running east to west mark off these divisions. The southern section, being protected by a high range of mountains and favored with warm Pacific winds, has a surprisingly mild climate. This fact plus heavy rainfall and long hours of summer sunlight makes this area highly suitable for farming. Quite naturally, the largest concentrations of population are to be found in the south.

The central section lies between the Alaska mountain range on the south and the Brooks range to the north. Incidentally, Mount McKinley is located in the Alaska range, and at 20,300 feet is the highest point in North America. Alaska's two great rivers, the Yukon and the Kuskokwim, flow westward through this section to the Bering sea. The most important town of this area is Fairbanks.

The northern section lies for the most part within the Arctic Circle. Its few towns are accessible by sea only during the months of midsummer. This is the least productive section of the territory and the most sparsely inhabited.

Especially since World War II the population of Alaska has increased tremendously, having more than doubled since 1940. Now the Eskimos and Indians make up only about a fourth of the population. The larger cities are quite modern. There is the tax-supported University of Alaska near Fairbanks, and the Northern Presbyterian Church supports Sheldon Jackson Junior College at Sitka. The great rivers, the air strips, and the new Alcan highway now make most of Alaska's cities accessible by three kinds of transportation.

Alaska is strategically located in relation to all of the Northern Hemisphere. Its location is more central to the great world powers than any other civilized place. From Fairbanks, Alaska, it is 3249 miles to New York, 4381 miles to London, and 4335 miles to Moscow. This makes it very important from a military standpoint. Recognizing their new position of importance, the people of Alaska are very anxious to have their territory admitted as a state of the union.

It is not our purpose to conduct a geography and history lesson on Alaska. We are concerned for the people who live there and their need of Christ. Let us now hear about these people.

SPEAKER:

When we speak of Alaska we think of Eskimos, but you have already heard that they make up a very small proportion of the total population. There are about 20,000 of them including related people. There are also about 12,000 Indians. These original inhabitants of the territory have welcomed missionaries, and many of their villages are almost 100% Christian.

These people also gladly welcomed other white men who came with evil influences. The result has been that their primitive life has been further corrupted by civilized vices. There is still much Christian work to be done among them.

There are also the people who came during the gold rush and remained to make their homes. There are Europeans and Asians who came to trap furs and to fish. The land to which these people came was physically and spiritually desolate. Their lives and homes were very largely without Christ. They too need the church and the saving Gospel which it proclaims.

In the 1930's when dust storms devastated great areas of farm land in the midwest many of these farm families moved to Alaska to begin again. They left their homes in bitterness and discouragement. It was most important for the church to follow them to their new homes with the encouragement of Christ.

As has already been indicated, Alaska has experienced its greatest growth since World War II. This growth is of a more permanent nature than that of the gold rush days. Many young people see in this great country a place of opportunity, and they are hopefully establishing their homes there. The church must not forget them and their children.

Our own church has no work in Alaska, but we can all see the importance of extending the work of Christ there, and we can pray for the churches which are serving these many types of people in the land of the Eskimo.

Women's Work

Do Little Children Need To Be Saved?

By Annie Ludlow Cannon
(Mrs. J. F. Cannon, Blowing Rock, N. C.)

Have you ever won a boy or a girl to our Savior? Nine years ago, my answer would have been "no." At that time it had not occurred to me that they needed a Savior. The blessed Word says: "For all have sinned." (Romans 3:23). Does that refer to adults only? When He says **'all,'** He means **'all'!** And the need of the children was placed upon my heart.

During the years, it has been my privilege under the guidance of the Holy Spirit to introduce Jesus to children; invite them to accept God's love GIFT and then to teach to them the Bible.

Everywhere, the children are eager and ready to accept the free GIFT of salvation. Only our heavenly Father knows the number who have been saved through the ministry of The Child Evangelism Fellowship.

The Fellowship is a group of "believers doing together what we have failed to do alone." The weekday GOOD NEWS BIBLE CLUBS do not take the place of our Sunday Schools but supplement that part of the Church's ministry.

For more than thirty years, the writer has been a Sunday School addict so she, too, is guilty of failing to place soul-winning ahead of Bible teaching. Since entering this field of service, it is my earnest conviction that if our Sunday School teachers placed upon soul-winning the same emphasis that our lovely Lord placed upon it, they would not only be soul-winners but better teachers. And, contrariwise, if they strived to be better teachers they would become soul-winners.

The supreme passion of our Lord was " to seek and to save." Let us not forget that He said, "It is not the will of your Father which is in heaven, that **one** of these **little ones** should perish." (Matt. 18:14).

May you know the joy of leading boys and girls to a saving knowledge of our Lord and Savior Jesus Christ!

Spread of the Gospel in Print

Over one million copies of the Gospel of John, in six languages, have been supplied to Africa by The Pocket Testament League during the past six months. Thousands upon thousands of Africans have also heard the Gospel preached over loudspeakers by PTL evangelists.

Three hard-hitting evangelistic teams, made up of PTL evangelists, African interpreters and missionary co-workers, traveling out of Nairobi, Kenya, in PTL sound trucks have been averaging six meetings a day with daily attendances in the thousands. At the conclusion of each meeting, Scripture portions in their own languages are distributed to those attending. These evangelistic efforts are being conducted in four strategic areas: Kikuyu reserve villages (where nearly a million Kikuyu tribespeople have been gathered since the Mau Mau crisis began), schools, Mau Mau detention camps and Kenya's large cities.

A recent bulletin from one PTL: team holding city-wide campaigns in Kenya's port city of Mombasa, reports: "15,000 packed Mombasa Stadium rally. God moved mightily. Thousands in after-meeting. Over 500 decision cards so far!"

PTL teams are now moving into the Belgian Congo, to begin the same type of large-scale Scripture distribution and Gospel evangelism there. Missionaries throughout this central part of Africa report a critical need for the Scriptures. The need has been greatly accentuated by the millions of newly literate Africans. Says Alfred A. Kunz, International Director of The Pocket Testament League: "Never before have there been so many people in Africa who could read. Never before has there been such a hunger for th Word of God in printed form. This is a tremendous new missionary challenge. And it is one which must be met NOW."

Church News

David Holt Appointed Assistant to President U.T.S.

Rev. David R. Holt of Richmond, Virginia, has accepted a call to become the Assistant to the President of the Seminary beginning July 1, 1956, President James A. Jones announced recently. A native of Nashville, Tennessee, he grew up in Jacksonville, Florida, where his father, Rev. Albert C. Holt, was pastor of the First Presbyterian Church. After serving in the U. S. Navy during World War II, Mr. Holt graduated in 1949 from the University of Florida with the degree of Bachelor of Science in Business Administration. After employment in Miami, Florida, he entered Union Seminary in Richmond where he graduated in 1955.

At the Commencement exercises he was awarded the degree of Master of Theology for this year of graduate work and his thesis: "Stewardship and the Professional Fund Raiser."

Mr. Holt is married to the former Miss Luella Scoggins of Nashville, Tennessee, and they will reside at 3511 Brook Road in Richmond after July 1st.

Mr. Holt succeeds the Rev. Henry McKennie Goodpasture who has resigned in order to do graduate study in Edinburgh, Scotland, in preparation for world mission service.

U.T.S. Commencement

Union Theological Seminary graduated forty-two members of the Senior Class at the Commencement exercises Tuesday, May 22. In addition to the graduating seniors, eleven ministers received the Master of Theology Degree, and five ministers received the Doctor of Theology Degree.

The speaker for the Commencement exercises was Rev. Harry M. Moffett, Jr., D.D., a member of the Board of Trustees of the Seminary and pastor of the First Presbyterian Church, Gastonia, North Carolina.

President James A. Jones announced the awards to the following students: The E. T. George Awards for improvement in the speaking voice were granted to: Claire S. Albright, a member of the Senior Class from Paducah, Kentucky; Finley C. Patton, a member of the Middler Class from Lexington, Virginia; Robert B. Dunbar, a member of the Middler Class from Rock Hill, South Carolina; and John C. Kepley, a member of the Junior Class from Roanoke, Virginia. These awards were established by the late E. T. George, an Elder of New Orleans, Louisiana, and are continued through a legacy from him.

The William Monroe Wicker Award was given to M. Stanyarne Bell, a member of the Senior Class from Greenwood, South Carolina. The Wicker Award is given annually to the student "whose fidelity to duty, love of others, and devotion to Jesus Christ are an abiding inspiration," and is made possible by the Adult Fellowship Class of the First Presbyterian Church, Charlotte, North Carolina. Mr. Bell will serve as pastor of the Seigle Avenue Presbyterian Church of Charlotte, North Carolina.

The Henry W. McLaughlin Rural Church Award by the New Providence Church was given to Edgar Dean Byers, from Cornelius, North Carolina. This award is given to the student who has shown marked interest in and aptitude for the rural church ministry. The award was established in 1953 by the congregation of the New Providence Presbyterian Church, Raphine, Virginia. Mr. Byers will serve the George Kirby and Antioch Churches just outside of Goldsboro, North Carolina.

The Campbell Scholarship was awarded to Bryan Clinton Childress of Montgomery Presbytery, a member of the Middle Class.

Seven students were named to the Mattie Glover Hocker Memorial Scholarships. These scholarships were established by a bequest from the estate of Mattie Glover Hocker and a gift from her brother, Mr. Joseph Glover of Roanoke, Virginia. Scholarships on this foundation are awarded to able men preparing for the Gospel ministry with the expectation that there will be at least one Mattie Glover Hocker Scholar graduating from the Seminary each commencement. This year students receiving these scholarships are: Seniors - M. Stanyarne Bell, Greenwood, South Carolina; John R. Crawford, Milledgeville, Georgia; John Edwin Stanfield, Hot Springs, Arkansas; Wayne P. Todd, Miami, Florida; Middlers - William W. Bloom, Bradenton, Florida;

John W. Dozier, Macon, Georgia; Juniors - John M. Handley, Charleston, West Virginia; Charles R. Kennon, Memphis, Tennessee; and Clifford A. McKay, Clearwater, Florida.

The Baccalaureate sermon, "God Is Love," was preached at 11:00 A. M. on Sunday, May 20, in Schauffler Hall, by the Rev. William Taliaferro Thompson, D. D., Robert Critz Professor of Christian Education, and Dean of Instruction, who is retiring after thirty-six years on the Faculty of Union Theological Seminary in Virginia.

Board of World Missions

Newly appointed by the Board are the following 14 persons:

To Brazil: Dr. Verlin Arnold Krabill, as an agricultural-educational missionary in East Brazil. Dr. Krabill, a doctor of veterinary medicine, is currently a student at Union Theological Seminary, Richmond, and has been teaching veterinary pathology in Ohio State University and the University of Delaware since 1953. He is a native of Frederick, Md., and holds degrees from the University of Maryland (B. S. in Agriculture) and University of Georgia (D.V.M.). He is a member of the Pitts Creek Presbyterian Church, Pocomoke City, Md.

Miss Edna Bryan Quinn, as a teacher of missionaries' children in North Brazil. Miss Quinn, of Washington, D. C., received her education in George Washington University and the Duke University School of Nursing. She is a member of the Blacknall Memorial Presbyterian Church, Durham, N. C.

The Rev. and Mrs. Robert Murray Marvin, as evangelistic missionaries in Brazil. Mr. Marvin is the pastor of Lake Norfolk Presbyterian Church, Henderson, Ark. He is a graduate of Bob Jones University and Columbia Theological Seminary, with a background of work in industry prior to entering the seminary. As a student he supplied the Roberts Presbyterian Church, Anderson, S. C. He is a member of East Arkansas Presbytery. Mrs. Marvin is the former Phyllis Elain Yates of Pennington, N. J. She is a graduate of Bob Jones University, and taught school in Decatur, Ga.

To Mexico: The Rev. and Mrs. Ernest Alfred Joseph Seddon, Jr., of San Saba, Texas, as educational and evangelistic missionaries. Mr. Seddon is pastor of the San Saba First Church. A native of Fort Worth, Mr. Seddon is a graduate of the University of Texas and Austin Theological Seminary. He has a long record of service to the Mexican people of Texas, having served Mexican churches in Gulf, Bay City, and Palacios, Texas, in evangelistic work; the Tex-Mex Institute as principal and minister; the Mexican churches of Gonzales and Austin, and as executive secretary of Latin American work for the Synod of Texas. Mrs. Seddon, the former Ruth Mary Wehmeyer of Milwaukee, Wis., and El Paso, Texas, is a graduate of the University of Texas. The couple have a son and a daughter.

To the Far East: Mr. Robert Simpson Gould, of DeLand, Fla., as educational missionary for a three-year term, in a Far Eastern field to be decided by the staff of the Board of World Missions. Mr. Gould is a 1956 B.C.E. graduate of Georgia Tech, and has been working during the summers for the Georgia State Road Department and Westcott Construction Company of DeLand. He is a member of the First Church in DeLand.

Miss Sarah Evelyn Jeffrey of Jeanerette, La., as an educational missionary to Japan. She is a graduate of Belhaven College, Jackson, Miss., and has been teaching in French Camp Academy, French Camp, Miss., since 1951. She is a member of the French Camp Presbyterian Church.

The Rev. and Mrs. David Lewis Parks, as evangelistic missionaries to Korea. Mr. Parks is now the assistant pastor of the First Church in Jackson, Miss. He is a native of Weaverville, N. C., and a graduate in electrical engineering at Georgia Tech, and received his B. D. from Columbia Theological Seminary. He served, as a seminary student, at Fort Lauderdale Presbyterian Church, Brittain's Cove Presbyterian Church near Weaverville, N. C., and Calvary Church, Elberton, Ga. He is a member of Central Mississippi Presbytery. Mrs. Parks is a native of Hendersonville, N. C., and attended Montreat College and Belhaven College.

Miss Anna Ruth Perry, as educational missionary to Japan. She is of Logan, W. Va., and is to receive her M. A. degree from Assembly's Training School, Richmond, this month. She has served as student assistant at Union Seminary Library, and as a Greenbrier Presbytery worker and director of vacation church schools. She is a member of First Church, Logan. She is expected to teach music and English at Kinjo College.

To the Congo: Mr. Maurice Edmund Marlette, Jr., as teacher of missionaries' children, for a three year term. A native of Montgomery, Ala., Mr. Marlette is now child welfare worker for the Alabama Department of Pensions and Security for Montgomery County, and makes his home in Hayneville. He is a member of the Hayneville Church, and is a graduate of both Davidson College and the University of South Carolina.

Miss Ann Shirley Anderson, as educational missionary in the Congo. She is now attending Peabody College for Teachers, Nashville, Tenn. She holds a B. A. degree from Agnes Scott College, Decatur, Ga., and a M.R.E. from Assembly's Training School. She has served as a DCE for Napoleon Avenue Church, New Orleans, and First Church, Fayetteville, N. C. Miss Anderson is a member of the latter church.

Miss Lucretia Walton Stevenson, as a medical technologist in the Congo. She is now completing a year's work at Assembly's Training School. Miss Stevenson is from Camilla, Ga., and holds degrees from Wheaton College and Emory University Hospital School of Medical Technology. She has served as medical technologist in Tampa, Fla., St. Charles, Ill., and Elmhurst, Ill. She is a member of Camilla, Ga., Presbyterian Church.

In addition to the 14 named above, the Board appointed two others who have been in missionary service before. Dr. and Mrs. J. K. Levie of Ringgold, Ga., will go as medical (dentist) missionaries to Korea. About 15 years ago the Levies were forced by poor health to give up missionary service. Dr. Lewis has been practicing dentistry in Ringgold since that time, and the couple have now asked to be allowed to serve for three years, carrying their own dental equipment with them.

ARKANSAS

Monticello — Officers for the Presbyterian Children's Home Association have been announced for the current year and the 1957 meeting set for April 23-25 at Goodland Indian Orphanage near Hugo, Oklahoma.

The Rev. William C. Sistar, superintendent of the Palmer Orphanage, Columbus, Mississippi, is the new head of the Presbyterian Children's Home Association. Other officers include Dr. Fred A. Walker, superintendent of the Presbyterian Home in Farmington, Mo., as vice president of the Association; and the Rev. Jerry Newbold, Jr., superintendent of the Vera Lloyd Presbyterian Home in Monticello, Ark., secretary.

At the Association's meeting here in late April, twelve of the sixteen Homes were represented.

Among those who attended the sessions in Monticello were: the Rev. and Mrs. Allen C. Jacobs, Talladega, Ala.; the Rev. and Mrs. Nelson R. Hawkins, Itasca, Texas; Mr. Harry Barkley, Black Mountain, N. C.; Mr. and Mrs. R. E. Moore, Cleveland, Tenn.; Dr. and Mrs. M. A. Macdonald, Clinton, S. C.; Dr. and Mrs. Fred A. Walker, Farmington, Me.; the Rev. Albert McClure, Barium Springs, N. C.; Miss Ann Bryan, Banner Elk, N. C.; Dr. Hunter B. Blakely, Richmond, Va.; the Rev. and Mrs. William C. Sistar, Columbus, Miss.; the Rev. Oscar Gardner, Hugo, Okla.; the Rev. Jerry Newbold, Jr., Monticello, Ark.; and Mr. R. D. Kauffelt, Lewisburg, West Virginia.

Among guests attending were Mr. and Mrs. W. A. Hethcox, of the ARP Children's Home in Brighton, Tenn.; Mr. and Mrs. Robert Pomeroy of Assumption, Ill., representatives from Presbyterian Church, U. S. A.; and Miss Mildred Arnette, Dallas, Texas, representing the Child Placement Service of the Synod of Texas.

LOUISIANA

The Synod of Louisiana will convene in the Ruston Presbyterian Church, Ruston, La., July 17 at 2:30 P. M.

New Orleans — Miss Nancy Gregory, member of the First Presbyterian Church in New Orleans, has been elected president of the Pioneer Council of New Orleans Presbytery. She succeeds Miss Ann Hiller, member of the Napoleon Avenue Church.

The Council is composed of junior high school students who are members of churches within New Orleans Presbytery.

New Orleans—The strategy committee of New Orleans Presbytery has announced that plans have been made toward the purchase of a site for a Presbyterian Church in the Carolyn Park area in New Orleans.

The congregation in this area is at present holding its services in an elementary school. The worship services are under the leadership of the Rev. Max Ecks, Jr., and Charles W. Schneider is superintendent of the Sunday School, also held in the school building.

New Orleans — Ground-breaking for the new education wing of Oak Park Presbyterian Church, New Orleans, recently marked the beginning of the $66,000 structure which is expected to be ready for use at the end of six months.

NORTH CAROLINA

A Well Earned Honor

Davidson

Davidson College has awarded the Algernon Sydney Sullivan Medallion to Early B. Eldridge, beloved superintendent of the Glade Valley, N. C., high school.

The Sullivan award recognizes fine spiritual qualities practically applied to daily living, and has at Davidson usually been given persons whose unselfish service has not received due recognition.

Mr. Eldridge went to the Glade Valley school in 1918, when it was a home mission of the Presbyterian Church, U.S., and has served it for 40 years.

He spent 32 of the 40 years living in a small, three-room apartment in one of the dormitories, denying himself and his family the comforts of a separate home because he felt the school needed the money for more useful purposes, largely in giving less fortunate mountain children a chance for a high school education.

At times when the school could not pay his salary, he worked for the love of the school and used salary funds to pay the institution's debts. He has pushed the program of expansion of the facilities and seen several buildings added in recent years.

The Glade Valley school was established in 1909 by Orange Presbytery, which was later divided into Orange and Winston-Salem Presbyteries. The school has since been under the control of both.

Mr. Eldridge has kept it out of debt even though his budget was limited, and has acted as farm supervisor, treasurer, "errand boy," buyer and professor, as well as Clerk of the Session in the Glade Valley Presbyterian church.

Charlotte — Members of Tenth Avenue Presbyterian Church broke ground for a new sanctuary during ceremonies Sunday, April 27. Tenth Avenue Church was destroyed by fire January 23, 1955, and since that time the congregation has had no building of its own in which to worship.

The new structure will be erected on a four and one-half acre site in a new location, and eventually the church will be renamed.

The plant, consisting of a sanctuary, education building, and fellowship hall, will cost approximately $110,000.

At the ground-breaking services a check for $5,000 from Mecklenburg Presbytery was presented to the church building fund.

Taking part in the ceremonies were Joe M. Bradley, member of the church since 1890, who turned the first spadeful of dirt; Rufus Grier, chairman of the home missions committee for Mecklenburg Presbytery who presented the check from the presbytery; Dr. R. C. Long, moderator of Mecklenburg Presbytery; Frank H. Kimbrell, chairman of the building committee; Clarence Brumley, clerk of the session; J. N. Berryhill, chairman of the board of deacons; and T. E. Gray, a member of the church since 1901.

The session of the Hazelwood Presbyterian Church wishes to take this opportunity to thank the Rev. W. Creed Cooper for the fruitful spiritual revival he has recently concluded in our church. Through visitation and preaching we have seen the visible results of six who joined the Church by profession of faith in our Lord Jesus Christ and baptism and one by reaffirmation of faith. We are certain that the messages he brought will bear fruit for the years yet ahead, and we highly recommend our brother to other churches as an effective evangelist and a man being used of God.

W. H. Marquis, Moderator

TENNESSEE

Morristown — The Rev. Samuel H. Hay, D. D., LL.D., pastor of the First Presbyterian Church, Morristown, has retired from the pastorate after 36 years here. His home will now be in Columbia, S. C.

Morristown's First Church has made him Pastor Emeritus and Holston Presbytery presented him with a gold watch and gold pen.

Memphis — Southwestern College conferred honorary doctorates upon three Presbyterian leaders June 5, when the college graduated its 1956 class of about 100 students.

Rev. Wave Hunter McFadden, pastor of First Presbyterian Church in Monroe, La., will be called back by his alma mater for a Doctor of Divinity degree.

Dr. Warner L. Hall, also a graduate of Southwestern, will receive the hood of Doctor of Divinity. Dr. Hall is the pastor of Covenant Presbyterian Church in Charlotte, N. C.

Mrs. William Andrew Dale, another outstanding leader in our Church, will receive a Doctor of Humanities degree from Southwestern at the commencement.

Newport — Rev. J. Graham Spurrier, Pastor of the Newport Presbyterian Church, was the Guest Minister for Revival Services at the Estatoa Presbyterian Church, of Celo, North Carolina, Hershey J. Longenecker, Pastor.

From thirty to sixty minutes before the evening meetings, Mr. Spurrier taught the book of First Peter. During the evening services there were three professions of faith. The meetings were a very real blessing and inspiration to the Estatoa Church and to many in the community.

Memphis — Dr. Turney B. Roddy, pastor of Highland Heights Presbyterian Church, Memphis, was honored by the Men of the Church, May 10, and was presented with a new automobile.

Approximately 500 people attended the program honoring Dr. Roddy. Wheaton Ennis, president of the Men of the Presbytery, and member of Highland Heights Church, presided over the program which included the history of the life of the pastor.

Harry Cosby presented the automobile on behalf of the members of the congregation.

Dr. Roddy has spent all of his ministry in this church. When he was a candidate for the ministry he was instrumental in organizing it and has served as pastor since his ordination in June 1924.

Dr. Roddy is also Stated Clerk and Treasurer of Memphis Presbytery.

TEXAS

Austin — The Rev. William I. Boand, instructor in the Biblical department of Austin Theological Seminary, Austin, Texas, has accepted a call to be assistant minister of St. Charles Avenue Presbyterian Church, New Orleans.

He succeeds the Rev. Arch McD Tolbert, associate minister, who leaves the last of May to become minister of the First Presbyterian Church, Sherman, Texas.

Mr. Boand is a native of San Antonio, Texas, and received his education at Davidson College, Davidson, N. C.; New College, University of Edinburg, Scotland; and Austin Seminary.

A New Departure — Houston — Something new in the field of theological education began for three students from Austin Presbyterian Theological Seminary on June 4. They, together with students from four other Protestant seminaries in Texas, began that day a course in Pastoral Clinical Education at Texas Medical Center here.

The course is one of several which will eventually be offered by the brand new Institute of Religion in the $70,000,000 complex of schools and hospitals that make up the Texas Medical Center. The first of its kind in America, the Institute will seek to train medical personnel, pastors, and ministerial students to work together as a health team.

Enrolled in the first course are three Presbyterian students in their middle year at the Austin seminary: Jack Rorex of Kingsport, Tenn; Van Shaw of Austin; and William Murchison of Crockett, Texas. The course which these young men will be taking will run for 12 weeks during the summer and will cover administrative, nursing, medical and theological aspects of pastoral care in a general hospital.

The Institute works independently of the five seminaries, but its courses are part of the curricula of the seminaries, and the staff members of the Institute hold positions on the faculties of the seminaries.

VIRGINIA

Richmond — The Assembly's Youth Council of the Presbyterian Church, U. S.; Westminster Fellowship National Council of the Presbyterian Church, U. S. A.; and the United Presbyterian National Youth Council, will for the first time meet simultaneously and will hold (some) joint sessions at Hanover College, Hanover, Indiana, August 11-18.

According to the announcement by the Rev. John B. Spragens, who heads the Department of Youth Work of the Board of Christian Education in Richmond, officers of these three youth groups have been meeting together each fall for several years in order to share each other's ideas and programs. About a year and a half ago at such a meeting they decided that it would be helpful to have the three complete Councils meet together. This decision, plus the desire of the young people for the joint sessions, and the request of the 1955 General Assembly that various agencies and groups consider and develop ways of closer relationships and understanding with the other Presbyterian bodies in this country, has led to arrangement of the Hanover meeting this summer.

— BOOKS —

"SEVEN WORDS OF LOVE." G. Hall Todd. Baker Book House. $1.50.

These sermons demonstrate in a striking way that the seven sayings of Christ on the Cross have a timely relevance. This book is characterized by a freshness and originality. Each message has real value of background reading for ministers in the preparation of a series on the seven words from the Cross.

"NAUGHT FOR YOUR COMFORT." Trevor Huddleston. Doubleday & Co. $3.75.

For the past twelve years the author of this book has lived in South Africa. He is a South African citizen. He has been responsible for a parish and a secondary school. He has also been publicized a great deal recently because of his opposition to the South African government's policy in regard to segregation. The author confesses that he does not write from an impartial standpoint and it is evident that he is honest in making this confession. He presents his own private opinions forcefully and he will be read with interest by those who share his views. One thing is certain and that is that he offers no solution to this complicated question. It is very doubtful if there is a solution to it here on this earth. J.R.R.

"SELECTED LETTERS OF JOHN WESLEY." Frederick C. Gill. Philosophical Library. $4.75.

This volume has been compiled from the original 1931 standard edition that contains 2,700 letters of Wesley. The author believes that John Wesley's letters provide the most intimate portrait of him that we possess. In them we may listen to him talking on paper about all the experiences of his life. Whoever his correspondent and whatever his subject Wesley was always direct, concise, and full of common sense.

"CHURCH AND CAMPUS." Dewitt C. Reddick. John Knox Press. $2.00.

In this volume Presbyterians look to the future from their historic role in Christian Higher Education and ask some searching questions about what we are doing in higher education. The gist of this book is to be found in the thesis that the student needs the Church and the Church also needs the students. As Dr. J. J. Murray has put it, "If we want Christianity to become an effective force in the life of our nation and of the world we need these students." Each chapter points out the need for a thoughtful and aggressive program on the part of the Church to reach the student for Christ.

"THE CUP OF FURY." Upton Sinclair. Channel Press Inc. $3.00.

Upton Sinclair has written "The Cup of Fury" as a warning to his nation. In his book are the intimate, personal, revealing stories of men and women like Jack London, Sinclair Lewis, O. Henry, and many others whose "moderate drinking" became uncontrollable alcoholism.

Sinclair writes, "I was raised in a virtual sea of liquor. First, it was my father and then no fewer than three of my uncles. Then one friend after another, all of them destroying themselves. I put before the public this tragic record of a half-century of genius twisted and tortured by drink and I ask that it be read with one fact always in the back of the reader's mind; three out of four of today's college students are drinkers."

This volume is a documented searching exposure of the whiskey industry and its attempt to make drinking "a social grace." It should be put in the hands of young people to show them the despair and degradation caused by drink.

"THE CHURCH SECRETARY." Virginia S. Ely. Moody Press. $2.50.

Efficient church secretaryship is not as easy a vocation as one might think. It has singular opportunities in it for service, but it also makes exacting demands. The author has been trained in this field and taught the subject and is familiar with the position. The information is first-hand. Every church secretary will welcome this book of guidance. It points the way to more effective and practical service in the church. There are numberless tips to the businesslike yet friendly cooperation that may and should characterize the position of church secretary. Things are noted that may never have been thought of as part of church-office routine—things that will smooth out the interruptions that so often upset the plan and schedule of the day.

"MORAL PRINCIPLES IN THE BIBLE." Ben Kimpel. Philosophical Library. $4.50.

This is a study of the contribution of the Bible to moral philosophy. Using the Bible as a source book and employing the methods of philosophical analysis the nature of moral judgment is interpreted. A moral principle is defined as an invariant relation between a type of acting and a quality of life. Such a relation is the basis for moral judgment whose invariance is esteemed in Scripture as evidence for the justice of God. The author is Professor of Philosophy in Drew University.

"THE LIFE AND TIMES OF ELIJAH." John R. MacDuff. Baker Book House. $3.00.

This is a dramatic book even as Elijah was a dramatic character. It is practical even as Elijah's message was practical. The warnings of Elijah are as timely today as when God breathed His message into the prophet's soul. Here is a book that is rich in counsel, instruction, and inspiration. All Christians will read it with genuine pleasure and satisfaction. It will appeal to readers of all ages, to clergymen and laymen alike.

"FIFTY-TWO COMPLETE YOUNG PEOPLE'S PROGRAMS." George F. Santa. Zondervan. $2.50.

The programs in this volume are suggestive and are intended to serve as "pump-primers" for young people's leaders in arranging a year of young people's programs. The ideas and plans are not untried theories. The author is an expert and recognized authority in the field of young people's work and conducts a clinic to aid young people's workers. All of these ideas have been tried and tested to prove their practical worth. Each program is illustrated.

Our Presbyterian Heritage

Last year the Southern Presbyterian Journal sponsored a symposium on the Reformed Faith. Addresses were made by a group of outstanding Presbyterians and all who attended gave enthusiastic response.

Without in any measure competing with any other program in our church a similar symposium will be held this year, again placing its emphasis on our Presbyterian heritage.

THE TIME—August 15th — 10:00 A. M.

THE PLACE—Weaverville, N. C.

DR. C. GREGG SINGER—*"The Reformed Faith and the Contemporary Crisis in Education"*

DR. GORDON H. CLARK — *"The Reformed Doctrine of Verbal Inspiration of the Scriptures."*

DR. FLOYD HAMILTON — *"The Reformed Doctrine of Infant Baptism"*

DR. AIKEN TAYLOR — *"The Reformed Doctrine of the Means of Grace"*

DR. W. C. ROBINSON — *"The Reformed Doctrine of the Bodily Resurrection of Christ"*

DR. R. F. GRIBBLE — *"The Reformed Faith as Related to the Virgin Birth Foretold in Isaiah* 7:14"

MR. GEORGE BURNHAM—*"To the Far Corners"*

Make Plans Now To Attend This Meeting

THE SOUTHERN PRESBYTERIAN JOURNAL

Weaverville, N. C.

THE SOUTHERN PRESBYTERIAN JOURNAL

A Presbyterian weekly magazine devoted to the statement, defense and propagation of the Gospel, the faith which was once for all delivered unto the saints.

VOL. XV NO. 8 | JUNE 20, 1956 | $2.50 A YEAR

MUNDY BASS HUNT THORINGTON ADAMS

HONOR GRADUATES COLUMBIA THEOLOGICAL SEMINARY

Five seniors were awarded Graduate Fellowships during graduation exercises at Columbia Theological Seminary, June 4, 1956. The Fannie Jordan Bryan Fellowships in the amount of $750 each were awarded to Mr. William A. Adams, Seneca, South Carolina and Mr. Chilton Thorington, Signal Mountain, Tennessee. Three Alumni Fellowships in the amount of $700 each were awarded to Mr. John Richard Bass of Lyons, Georgia, Mr. Francis Hunt of Greenville, South Carolina and Mr. Luther M. Mundy of Abbeville, South Carolina.

THE SOUTHERN PRESBYTERIAN JOURNAL
The Journal has no official connection with the Presbyterian Church in the United States
Rev. Henry B. Dendy, D.D., Editor....................Weaverville, N. C.
Dr. L. Nelson Bell, Associate Editor....................Asheville, N. C.
Rev. Wade C. Smith, Associate Editor....................Weaverville, N. C.

EDITORIAL

Censored Religion?

Freedom - of assembly, of the press, of expression - all are a part of the American heritage and its basis is found in the ideals which have always been a part of Protestantism.

The recent action of the "governing body" of the National Council of Churches, opposing the sale of religious radio and television time to individuals carries in it a threat to the basic religious freedoms which we all hold so dear. One wonders if Bishop Donald H. Tippett and his committee really considered the implications of their action?

That the National Council of Churches, or any religious group, should become the arbiter of religious propaganda is a thought from which most Americans will recoil.

If this recommendation from the National Council should be acted upon favorably by the radio and television companies it would mean that Dr. Norman Vincent Peale, Bishop Fulton J. Sheen, evangelist Billy Graham and others would be denied the privileges of their present paid broadcasts. It would mean, in effect, a censoring of religious radio and television programs by an organization which could well fail to represent the entire spectrum of religious thought in America.

We do not believe this action of the National Council will be favorably received. What disturbs us is that they should have taken it at all.

—L.N.B.

"Because God has not abandoned this world, because He rules and overrules its tangled history, and because we have been given a share in the power of His Spirit, we can with confidence hope and expect that what is built upon the foundations which He has laid will stand."—Quoted by David Lawrence in U. S. News & World Report, May 25, 1956.

"Fund For The Republic" Makes Grant To United Church Women

The following news release has just been received from the Office of Public Relations of the National Council of the Churches of Christ U. S. A.

New York, N. Y., June 8 — A grant of $10,000 has been made by the Fund for the Republic to United Church Women for "educational work in race relations." Mrs. T. O. Wedel of Washington, D. C., president of United Church Women, a General Department of the National Council of Churches, made the announcement in connection with a meeting of the department's Administrative Committee, in session at the Grosvenor Hotel, 35 Fifth Avenue, New York City.

"The grant will make possible a series of workshops in key communities," Mrs. Wedel said, "with the purpose of (1) alerting and educating women of the churches on civil rights and civil liberties; (2) uniting the strength of church women to a more potent force in obtaining the rights which our Christian faith seeks for all people; (3) helping to make the total community aware of the implications and dangers in the denial of rights to any persons; (4) studying how to deal with controversy, how to work with people who differ without alienating them, and how to create fellowship and understanding between those who hold opposite views."

The workshops will have trained and dedicated leaders skilled in the area of civil rights and civil liberties and will be carried out in cooperation with member denominations who are also giving special attention to this aspect of Christian Social Relations, some of whom likewise have received grants from the Fund for the Republic.

The following AP article appearing in the June 10 daily papers of our Nation should give the United Church Women pause in accepting the donation from the Fund for the Republic.
H.B.D.

House Group Will Probe Fund For The Republic

Washington, June 10 (AP) — Chairman Walter (D-Pa.) announced today the House Committee on Un-American Activities will investigate the Fund for the Republic at public hearings starting June 27.

Walter said the committee is seeking "the objective facts" on whether the fund—set up with a grant from the Ford Foundation—is a "friend or a foe in our nation's death struggle against the Communist conspiracy."

The fund was set up with a 15-million-dollar endowment from the Ford Foundation. Hutchins said it has assumed independent status.

Walter said in a statement that the fund is financing "a number of activities which have aroused criticism and doubt on the part of members of Congress, prominent patriotic organizations and individuals including Henry Ford II himself who has publicly described some of the actions of the fund as 'dubious in character.' "

"Is this foundation, with its vast reservoirs of funds and power, a friend or a foe in our nation's death struggle against the Communist conspiracy?" Walter asked. "Are its extensive and diverse activities strengthening or weakening our security structure in the Communist cold war? Are the leaders of this force, which enjoys the benefits of tax immunity, serving an interest inimical to our basic American traditions?"

In our February 15, 1956 *issue, page* 7, *we called attention to the fact that THE FUND FOR THE REPUBLIC had granted* $15,000 *to the Division of Christian Relations of the Presbyterian Church, U. S., "for educational work in racial and cultural relations." We also pointed out that this same foundation had recently given larger sums to the NAACP and other radical organizations for the same purpose.*
H.B.D.

The 1956 Montreat General Assembly

by

Rev. John R. Richardson, D.D.

Opening Night

Dr. J. McDowell Richards, the out-going Moderator, used as his text for the opening sermon I John 3:23; "And this is His commandment, That we should believe on the Name of His Son Jesus Christ, and love one another, as He gave us commandment." At the very beginning, Dr. Richards explained the importance of Christian faith. He said: "Saving faith in Jesus Christ was the heart of John's message as it was of all the New Testament. Unless the Christian life begins with Him, it does not begin. . . . A decisive act of faith is essential to the righteousness of life which is emphasized throughout John's Epistle and to the abiding work of love. . . .

At the same time, the New Testament knows nothing of faith divorced from life but only of faith which issues in life. . . . So it is meaningless for a person to declare his faith in Christ and then to disregard the precepts of the Master and the attitudes which he manifests and the deeds which he commits day by day."

After recognizing the vital importance of faith, he then emphasized the thought that this faith must be indissolubly bound up with love. He remarked: "How much we need to heed this command in the Church today and how much the world needs to see this kind of love in us.

"The spirit which is needed in our church courts is needed also in local churches. Sadly enough, there is never a year which comes that does not find some congregations divided within themselves by differences between good men. Too often, party is set against party and one individual becomes alienated from another and bitterness prevails. Church quarrels are always a reproach to the Name which we bear and a hindrance to the work of Christ. . . . Love is the motive which will lead us to a new concern for the needs of the suffering, the sorrowful and the needy about us. . . . In love, too, is the only power which can send us out in a great forward movement of evangelism and missions, both at home and abroad. . . ."

The Southern Presbyterian Journal, *a Presbyterian Weekly magazine devoted to the statement, defense, and propagation of the Gospel, the faith which was once for all delivered unto the saints,* published every Wednesday by The Southern Presbyterian Journal, Inc., in Weaverville, N. C.

Entered as second-class matter May 15, 1942, at the Postoffice at Weaverville, N. C., under the Act of March 3, 1879. Vol. XV, No. 8, June 20, 1956. Editorial and Business Offices: Weaverville, N. C. Printed in the U.S.A. by Biltmore Press, Asheville, N. C.

Address Change: When changing address, please let us have both old and new address as far in advance as possible. Allow three weeks after change if not sent in advance. When possible, send an address label giving your old address.

Before the election of Moderator, Dr. Richards submitted his Moderator's report. In this report, he pointed out that it is necessary for a Moderator "to remember that under our system of government *the man who holds this office possesses no actual authority and his work carries no weight other than that which may be inherent in its content.*" The retiring Moderator should be congratulated upon having observed this so scrupulously during the past year. Some recent Moderators have not been as careful to practice this historic Presbyterian principle. Dr. Richards concluded this report with an analysis of our Church. He closed with these words: "There are numerous signs of encouragement. We have made real advances in recent years. Our Church is vibrant, growing and capable of tremendous achievements in the service of Christ. Far more is demanded of us than we have ever done before. God grant that we may be faithful in our task."

The Election of Moderator

Dr. John F. Anderson, pastor of the First Presbyterian Church, Dallas, Texas, placed in nomination the name of Dr. W. T. Thompson, Professor of Christian Education in Union Theological Seminary, Richmond, Virginia. This nomination was seconded by Dr. Marion S. Huske, of Reidsville, North Carolina. When no other nominations were made, Dr. Huske moved that Dr. Thompson be elected by acclamation and a standing vote. Upon his election Dr. Thompson stated that this was the third time he had been nominated. On two previous occasions the Church felt he was too young, but he was glad that on this occasion the Church did not feel he was too old for this responsibility. The new Moderator is a graduate of Davidson College and Union Theological Seminary. Before going to Union Seminary, he served pastorates in Lexington, North Carolina; First Presbyterian Church, Knoxville, Tennessee; Government Street Presbyterian Church, Mobile, Alabama. He is the author of a new volume, recently published by John Knox Press, entitled "Adventure in Love."

Two Memorials

The Ninety-Sixth Assembly took time out from its published agenda to participate in two memorial services. A bronze plaque was presented to the Assembly to be placed in Howerton Hall in memory of Dr. J. R. Howerton, the virtual founder of Montreat. The inscription on the plaque read: "He envisioned the value of Montreat to the Kingdom of God, inspired and led the movement to acquire the property for the Presbyterian Church, U. S., and served as the first President of Montreat, 1906-1907."

Following the close of business, Friday afternoon, the Commissioners attended a special service for the unveiling of the memorial to Dr. R. C. Anderson, for thirty-six years the Manager of Montreat. His widow, Mrs. R. C. Anderson, Mr. F. L. Jackson, and Dr. Tom Spence took leading parts in the unveiling. Dr. Spence, Curator of the Historical Foundation, declared: "Dr. Anderson provided the physical tools for Montreat's spiritual mission." The creation of the R. C. Anderson scholarship fund in Montreat was announced by Mr. Jackson.

Christianity and Health

An Ad Interim Committee was set up in 1954 to explore the subject of Christianity and health. A progress report was made to the 1955 Assembly. This year the following affirmations were adopted:

1. We believe in the power of God to heal the whole man in body, mind and spirit.
2. We believe in the responsibility of man to do all possible to prevent and to heal sickness of body, mind or spirit. Our faith in a sovereign God does not deliver us from personal responsibility before Him to act upon our present knowledge of health and cure.
3. We believe in a cooperative ministry of those professions concerned with healing, such as medicine and the ministry. Such a cooperation is a part of man's responsibility in preventing illness and in effecting cure.
4. We believe that it is necessary for every generation to affirm the power of God in human life and, at the same time, to advance in the understanding of God's ways of working through His creation in healing. Thus increased understanding of the sciences, undergirded by faith, may enable man, more and more, to meet his own responsibilities in securing and maintaining health.
5. We believe the soundness of health is not necessarily a measure of righteousness and also that sickness is neither an indication of unrighteousness nor absence of saving faith.

6. We believe that if we neglect our faith in the power of God, or, on the other hand, if we neglect our human responsibilities, we fall into error.

7. We believe that the interpretations of faith in the area of healing rising out of the distortions mentioned above which are receiving wide credence find no support in the Scriptures when rightly interpreted: hence, our people are cautioned to take care concerning promises which may have considerable appeal but which have no foundation in Scripture, or are not in the spirit of Jesus Christ, or are based on isolated texts in the Bible which are not interpreted in the light of the Biblical message.

8. We believe that the Christian Church can and should offer that love and fellowship and strength to every person under its influence which reveal the redeeming power of God in the growth of the individual. We believe this constitutes a preventive ministry in the sense of sustaining the person in hours of crisis so that the disintegration of body, mind or spirit will not occur and that this also serves a healing purpose as the Church functions as a channel for divine grace.

The Position of Women in the Church

The report of the Ad Interim Committee on a Biblical study of the position of women in the Church was presented by Dr. Edward G. Lilly, Chairman of the Committee. The Assembly adopted the first recommendation of this Committee which approved Overture No. 58, stating that it is not out of accord with the teaching of the Bible to have women speak in the courts of our Church. The second recommendation relating to Overture No. 69, that came from the Presbytery of Fayetteville, asking that the proper and necessary steps to amend the Book of Church Order to provide for the eligibility to hold the offices of Ruling Elder and Deacon in the congregations of the Presbyterian Churches of the United States, on a permissive basis, was answered in the affirmative by a close vote of 234 to 226.

The Assembly debated approximately two hours before the vote was taken on this recommendation. Dr. Guy T. Gillespie, former President of Belhaven College, was the first speaker to oppose the recommendation. He said that it placed the opponents in a false light. It also presented a serious conflict between our convictions concerning the Word of God and our appreciation of the marvelous work the women have been doing in their devotion to Christ. He declared that this move was a radical departure from the position of the Church.

The Rev. Gabriel Abdullah, of Suwanee Presbytery, also opposed this recommendation. He asserted: "Never has there been in the Bible a woman Elder. Let us not fear to follow Scripture."

Dr. Daniel Iverson, speaking against the recommendation, said: "The Scripture is consistent in giving to man the leadership in the Church of Christ. When the Word of God was completed that was the pattern for us to follow. We must not be governed by what other denominations do, or do not do. Our Church would be making a grave mistake if we depart from our established practice."

The Rev. James G. Spencer declared that "electing women Elders and Deacons will not solve our problems and that when the women begin to move forward to occupy the official places of the Church now held by men, the men will begin to move backward and let the women bear the burden of responsibility."

Dr. Fred H. Olert, of East Hanover Presbytery, spoke for the recommendation and affirmed: "Scripture does not support discrimination on any level. I have served churches where we have had women officers and the practice has proved successful."

Ruling Elder, Tom Johnson, of Central Texas, spoke in favor of the recommendation. He argued: "Women helped win the World War. I am in the telephone business and we employ women. The same thing is true in other businesses. We need women on our official boards."

According to the Book of Church Order, before such a change as this can be made in the Constitution of the Presbyterian Church, U.S., a majority of eighty-five Presbyteries must ratify the Assembly's actions during the coming year and then be approved by the 1957 Assembly. The Assembly turned down a motion to send the Committee's statement down to the Presbyteries with recommendation that it be read aloud when the question comes up for action.

Marriage, Divorce and Re-Marriage

For several years, an Ad Interim Committee has been studying the subject of marriage, divorce and re-marriage. This study has proved to be a complex problem as far as agreement was concerned. The Committee reported certain areas of agreement and also a number of areas of disagreement. The Assembly voted to delete from Chapter 26 of the Confession of Faith paragraphs No. 5 and No. 6, thus making the divine intention of marriage as set forth in the Bible without any exception. The Assembly also answered Overture No. 26, from the Presbytery of Dallas, in these words: "In the judgment of this Committee, a minister should not perform any marriage where there is not a clear intention to establish a Christian home. Whether this involved actual membership in some true Christian church should be left to the discretion of the minister."

The question of common law marriage was assigned to the Committee to be studied in the light of Scripture, especially what constitutes marriage as relating to the State and the Church. The Assembly approved the Committee's statement: "It is the judgment of the Committee that in the light of Scripture what constitutes marriage is neither the act of the State, nor the Church, but the mutual consent of the parties to live together as man and wife. Therefore, in the sight of God a common law marriage is a valid marriage. Nevertheless, in the light of a Christian's obligation as a citizen he should obey the laws that govern marriage in the State where he lives."

Sunday

The Commissioners to the 96th General Assembly and their guests listened attentively to a deeply challenging address by the Rev. Stephen Sloop, a dynamic missionary to Brazil. "The Greater Works to the Greater Glory of God" was the topic of his message. The speaker called upon the Assembly to acknowledge "the debts of love we owe to all men everywhere all the time." In payment of these debts he said we promote the greater glory of God. Christians must give themselves unstintingly for the welfare and conversion of all men, he told the Assembly. With word-pictures of various Brazilian converts, the missionary illustrated the strength of the Gospel of Christ in creating new men and new women.

Many Commissioners were surprised to learn that "today there are more Protestant Brazilian ministers preaching the Gospel to their own people than there are Brazilian Roman Catholic priests." Dr. Sloop said that there is a growing desire on the part of influential Brazilians to have our Church send more missionaries to their country. He related the fact that Dr. Vincente, President of a large bank in Brazil, said to him last August: "I am not a Protestant: my wife is a Presbyterian. I should like to make one request. Ask your mission board to send us more missionaries."

During the afternoon, the Inter-Church Relations Committee presented the fraternal delegates. The Rev. L. T. Knox, pastor of the Second A.R.P. Church of Gastonia, North Carolina, brought greetings from his communion. Speaking on the meaning of Christian greetings, he said: "It is the courteous thing to do. We express our appreciation to you for the many contributions you have made because of Christ. We are neighbors and we can be helpful to one another."

The United Presbyterian Church was represented by the Rev. Robert H. Mayo, pastor of the First United Presbyterian Church in New Castle, Pennsylvania. Mr. Mayo spoke with a note of bitterness and practically all of his address was filled with rancor. He criticized severely the members of his own Church who were seeking to conserve it. Mr. Mayo evidenced no sense of propriety and abused his fine privilege. Apparently, he was intent upon opening old wounds. He did great injury to the cause of real Christian fellowship.

For the past few years, several representatives of the United Presbyterian Church have spoken in such a manner. Many feel that if such representatives continue to offend the Assembly, the interchange of fraternal delegates should be terminated.

Dr. Glenn Moore, Executive Secretary of the General Council of the Presbyterian Church, U.S.A., conveyed a formal letter to the Assembly. He expressed fraternal esteem of the U.S.A. Church. Dr. Moore reported: "We have just had a good Assembly. It was not an exciting one. We made a good record this year and a new unity is expressing itself in our Church." On the subject of segregation, Dr. Moore declared that at the recent Assembly this statement was officially made: "Whatever you say on the subject of segregation you must be ready to apply it to your own local congregation." This counsel evidences a note of sincerity not always found in such pronouncements.

The Assembly was informed by Dr. Moore that negotiations for a merger with the United Presbyterian Church were making rapid progress. He said that the U.S.A. Assembly voted to unite with the United Presbyterian Church and there were less than half a dozen negative votes. Then Dr. Moore affirmed: "Our Assembly voted to send this action down to the Presbyteries. Our Church would be glad to unite with any Church that would like to unite with us."

The evening service featured an address by Dr. Frontis Johnston, Professor of History at Davidson College, on the subject, "Woodrow Wilson - the Realist." "Woodrow Wilson," Dr. Johnston stated, "was a member of a small group of great men whose religion far transcends the normal. He firmly believed and lived by his words; 'The Bible is the Word of life. I do not understand how any man can approach the duties of life without a faith in Jesus Christ.'" In this scholarly address Dr. Johnston followed the great Presbyterian President through his entire career and drew out of his life wisdom that needs to be applied to our national life today.

"To interpret Woodrow Wilson properly," Dr. Johnston said, "four factors which molded the man must be kept in mind." These were: "He was Scotch-Irish; a Southerner; a Christian

report of the Board of Christian Education affirmed. "The highest nature of man cannot be satisfied by bread; it is satisfied by God who has given Himself and His daily blessings to man," continued the report.

The major purposes of the Board of Christian Education are set forth in this statement: "To teach the Gospel of Jesus Christ, to lead man to put his faith in Christ, and to teach man the full responsibilities of Christian faith."

To assist the Board in fulfilling its mission a Curriculum Study Committee has been appointed to make an extensive study of the question of curriculum. The committee is now engaged in this study. The study will include theological content that should go into Sunday School materials and description of the methodology to be used. An appraisal of the present curriculum will be made to determine what improvements or changes should be made.

The financial statement of the Board indicated a healthy condition. Total receipts amounted to $2,732,867.32.

Some of the days recommended by the Assembly for observance include the following days and seasons: Religious Education Season, September 1-30, 1956; Rally Day, September 30, 1956; Laymen's Sunday, October 21, 1956; and Christian Family Week, May 5-12, 1957. Pastors and Sessions are requested to acquaint the men of their congregations with the purpose, program, and leadership of the Presbyterian Men's Convention to be held in Miami, Florida, October 10-13, 1957, which is Laymen's Sunday.

The Standing Committee on Christian Education stated that the Mountain Retreat Association had a successful 1955 conference season and listed twenty-six conferences to be held in Montreat during the current season. The Association has paid $45,000.00 on the Howerton Retirement Fund and is now ready to pay $25,000.00 on the water and power extension program. It has received $32,000.00 more than spent last year. The fiscal year the college has a balance of approximately $22,000.00.

The Standing Committee expressed appreciation to Dr. Marshall C. Dendy for his fine spirit of co-operation, and to his entire staff for their work in ministering to the increasing needs of our Church.

Board of Annuities and Relief

"Fulfilling of Seven Opportunities" was the subject of the attractive presentation of the 1955 Annual Report from the Board of Annuities and Relief. This Board is charged with the responsibility of handling the Ministers' Annuity Fund, Employees' Annuity Fund, Ministerial Relief, Group Insurance, Gift Annuity

Agreements, Wills, and the Management of the Presbyterian Center.

The Board reports that through prompt and constant endeavor, and through promotion and consistent endorsement, the Ministers' Annuity Fund is fast becoming accepted not only as a "good thing to have," but as a necessity. During the year 1955, the Board made grants to 320 minister annuitants and widows of annuitants totaling $284,472.14. The assets of the Fund have been increasing in a gratifying way during the sixteen years it has been in operation.

In 1955, Ministerial Relief was forwarded regularly to 56 ministers, 230 widows of ministers, and 14 orphans of minister's homes. To 315 homes a total of $196,812.86 was sent in the form of Ministerial Relief grants. In addition, $287,912.34 of the Fund of Ministerial Relief was used by authorization of the General Assembly to supplement the inadequate annuities of 320 annuitants. The total Ministerial Relief funds disbursed during the year to both beneficiaries and annuitants was $484,725.20. The funds with which Ministerial Relief is administered are secured from three sources: income on Endowments made to the Board; the Joy Gift each December; and the proportion received from the Church budget.

The Board reported also that as of December 31, 1955, 2,293 are enrolled in the Life Insurance feature, and that 1,678 of these are included in the hospitalization and surgeon's fee coverage.

The Standing Committee commended the diligence of the Staff of the Board of Annuities and Relief and expressed its continued confidence in the leadership of the Board.

Board of Church Extension

The purpose of the Board of Church Extension is to lead in the expansion and strengthening of the home Church. As an evidence of the fact that this responsibility has been discharged, the Board shows that our Assembly's net growth in membership has gone from 227,-000 to 255,000 or a net gain of 39 per cent and the giving has increased 220 percent. In this relatively short period, they have organized 569 new churches, for an eleven year average of 4.31 new congregations per month. These new churches now have a total membership of 92,615. During the year 1955 these new churches contributed a total of $7,726,276, of which $3,050,-833 was for building, $3,878,833 was for current expenses, and $797,312 was for benevolences. From the above figures we learn that our investment in new Presbyterian churches is already returning over three-quarters of a million dollars per year in giving to Benevolences. The Board of Church Extension is happy to have had some part in bringing almost every one of these 569 new churches into being.

During the year 1955 the six Departments of the Division of Home Missions have functioned at full capacity in their efforts to carry out the tasks assigned by the General Assembly.

The urban church department points out that the population of our country is moving ever-increasingly to our cities and their suburban environs and this is indeed true in the area covered by our church. The population in our Southland in 1950 was almost equally divided between the rural and city classifications. The prediction is made that by 1975, if the present movement cityward continues, approximately 60 per cent of our people will be living in the cities of over 10,000. The Urban Department offers its assistance to any church or groups desiring that a study be made.

The Town and Country Church Department conducts four Town and Country Pastors' Institutes. With the perennial shortage of pastors, resulting in an inadequate program in literally hundreds of churches throughout the Assembly, it was emphasized and we are urged to adopt a new strategy in grouping our churches. Our policy of grouping churches will never solve this problem. It can only result in more vacancies.

The Church Architecture Department explained that sixteen million dollars was spent on church building. Another ten million could be added that, no doubt, has been borrowed. This amount nears the twenty-nine million spent on current expenses and is about twice the amount the Church gave to the total benevolent program. It is the highest amount spent on church building in the history of our church. This department offers advice and assistance to groups planning new church buildings.

The Radio and Television Department presented a report indicating progress. The Assembly was told that perhaps never before has there been so wide a coverage by any Protestant denomination. The Protestant Radio and Television Center makes possible the most effective use of electronic communication for mass evangelism and Christian teaching.

The Assembly approved the Standing Committee's recommendation that during the Week of Prayer and Self-Denial for Church Extension in 1957, our people be asked for a one million dollar supplemental offering to help meet the pressing need for capital funds to build churches in this day of marvelous opportunity. Dr. E. B. McGukin, Chairman of the Standing Committee, explained that eighty per cent of all funds so raised in a Presbytery should be retained by it for church building within its own bounds and twenty per cent remitted to the

Board of Church Extension for distribution to areas of greatest need and opportunity. Dr. P. D. Miller and his staff were thanked for their faithful services.

Board of World Missions

The Presbyterian Church in the United States has the responsibility for evangelizing at least 40,000,000 people in Mexico, Ecuador, Brazil Belgian Congo, Portugal, Formosa, Japan, and Korea. All of these areas are wide open to our missionaries today. Never have the people been more willing to listen. Despite the dire need and this unprecedented opportunity our Church does not have enough missionaries to do more than a small part of what is demanded by the dignity and dimensions of the task. We have only 477 missionaries to reach these forty million people.

That there is some unrest in Africa is recognized, but it is said to be primarily of the kind that can be attributed to "growing pains." The year 1955 was marked by a significant number of forward steps which gave great promise of fruitfulness in the years ahead. A new work was opened in the capital city of Leopoldville and the first dental school in the Congo was established at Lubondai Station.

The Presbyterian Church in Brazil continues to command the respect and admiration of all those who are familiar with its work and program. The Church has kept pace with its goal and has grown from a communicant membership of 50,000 to 80,000 and the effort is continuing with cumulative success. Our own three Missions in Brazil, now at the peak of their strength with 110 missionaries, are cooperating with and assisting the national church in this effort.

Formosa is a key place. It is in the hearts of the missionaries as a strategic portion of the far-flung battle line of the Kingdom of God. The variety, extent, and effectiveness of the work of the Mission has grown during the past year. The report said, "There is the work with the Aborigines, or high mountain people. Originally they were head hunters fiercely independent and were never fully conquered by the Japanese during all the fifty years they dominated the island. This work has been one of the miracles of modern missions, but it sprang up so rapidly that there was not enough trained leadership to direct its growth and development." Formosa with all of its difficulties and problems and complications, with all its encouragements and opportunities of preaching Jesus Christ the Saviour, is in the hearts of the missionaries.

The Protestant Church in Japan will soon celebrate its one hundredth birthday. After a century of growth the church finds itself in the midst of great opportunity as well as complex problems. In order to more adequately meet the urgent need of evangelizing its territory, the Japan Mission is calling for nineteen evangelistic and educational workers immediately. Particularly acute is the need for ordained ministers.

There is evidence everywhere in the work in Korea of an intensive forward movement. The churches are bursting at the seams with overflow attendance, and are having to tear down and build, or add to old buildings in order to accommodate the crowds who wait on the steps or remove sliding windows in order to take part in the services. The missionaries have been maintaining the pioneer evangelistic work to which they had been called by the Korean Church.

Our mission in Mexico, in common with others in our several fields, finds itself dealing more and more with a new and happy factor in our work. That is the presence alongside itself of a growing and vigorous national church. In the last ten years the Mexico Mission has received 24 new missionaries, 4 of whom will be in language study through the year 1956. During the same period, 3 have died, 4 have retired, and 11 have resigned for health or other reasons. This year several more reach retirement age. The need, therefore, is urgent in this field.

During the year 1955, the Presbyterian Church in Portugal, while assiduously strengthening her inner life, moved once more in the direction of answering an importunate need within the Protestant community. After four years of study, survey and planning the first Protestant hospital, known as the Clinica de S. Lucas, was inaugurated in January. It is administered by four Protestant physicians and surgeons, in cooperation with Presbyterian fraternal workers and representatives of the Lisbon churches.

The Board reports with gratitude that the regular receipts for 1955 totaled $2,932,052.80, and were sufficient to cover the actual expenditures, although they fell short of the approved spending budget by $117,947.20.

Included in the Standing Committee's report on World Missions was information in regard to the unanimous decision of the Board of World Missions concerning the Japanese International Christian University. The Board's decision was: "We would favor our Board accepting membership in the Japanese International Christian University Foundation in New York *when it sees its way clear to put in its Constitution the doctrinal basis of the World Council of Churches which affirms its acceptance of Jesus Christ as God and Savior.*" A

Commissioner from Potomac Presbytery moved that this requirement be eliminated and that we begin to support the Japanese Christian University regardless of what it believes. This amendment was voted down by a large majority.

Christian Relations

The Standing Committee found portions of the report of the Permanent Committee on Christian Relations to be unsatisfactory. The following statement was added to the Permanent Committee's report: "We face this problem with the realization that the basic cause of all delinquency in both adults and young people is human depravity expressing itself in rebellion against the sovereign will of God for society. Underlying this report is our profound belief that the regeneration of the individual by divine grace is the foundation of all true reformation of social relationships."

Dr. George H. Vick, Chairman of the Standing Committee, reported that the actions of this Committee were unanimous and a fine spirit of harmony prevailed throughout all discussions.

Interpretation

1. The 1956 Assembly was not as glamorous as some Assemblies in recent years, but it will be remembered as one characterized by a fine Christian spirit in all discussions. Few discordant notes were heard. The removal of agitation on behalf of an ecclesiastical merger has tremendously improved the attitudes of Commissioners in their relationships with each other. Differences still exist but they are faced with a greater measure of understanding and courtesy.

2. Dr. W. T. Thompson, the new Moderator, was eminently fair at all times. Elected by acclamation, he served impartially as the Moderator of the entire Assembly. His calmness and winsomeness were contagious.

3. The Worship Programs added much to the spiritual atmosphere of the sessions. These programs were built around the great hymns of the Church.

4. As one observes the operations of the Assembly he is impressed with the efficiency of our Boards and Agencies and the progress our Church is making in every department. No one will claim that our Communion is "without spot or wrinkle or any such thing," but it is obvious that we are marching forward in the Southland and in eight foreign countries.

5. For our continued success in the ministry of Christ we must constantly bear in mind that the message we are to speak to the perplexities and confusions and anxieties of our day is of paramount significance. Out of the depths of a vital Christian faith and a profound Christian love let us pray that we may be faithful in delivering the whole counsel of God. Our concern at this point is not academic but practical, "Man shall not live by bread alone but by *every* Word that proceedeth out of the mouth of God." This truth we need to underline heavily.

ANGLERS

(From *"New Testament Evangelism"*
by Wade C. Smith)

Lesson No. 144

"Fishing" With The Word

Angling. In "fin" fishing, successful angling is inducing the fish to swallow the hook. This of course involves the matter of "bait" for the hook. The keen point of the hook with its securing barb might *partially* represent the Holy Spirit, for it is He who penetrates and engages. Bait is essential in "fin" fishing. Its counterpart in soul fishing is the Word of God.

At the very beginning of the effort to win souls to Jesus Christ, the personal worker must be under strong conviction as to the verity of God's Word, for this will be the most effective equipment he can hold *in his hand.* (You see this leaves room for *prayer* as of equal importance, if not of first importance). To be a successful soul winner—and a happy one—he must be ready to stake his all on the integrity, the veracity and the infallibility of the inspired Word. No use to start out with a Bible for which you must apologize—in any part of it, Old Testament or New Testament. A piece of goods with a flaw in it (or a suspected flaw!) takes all the pep out of a salesman. An automobile dealer, in explaining to the writer why his agency had shifted from one make of car to another, said, "The car I was handling had one weak feature in it, and though it was excellent in every other respect, that one weakness so persistently forced itself into my thinking that it took the edge off my sales talk, and I made the change at a great sacrifice so that I might represent to the public an automobile whose every feature I can be enthusiastic about to the last degree."

The Bible is invincible. As the "Sword of the Spirit," inspired of God and guaranteed by Him not to fail, the personal worker for Christ can proceed with it in entire confidence. Moreover, it has been tested through the centuries and has been found all sufficient for the soul's every need. Stop right here and read Isaiah 55:10-13 and Hebrews 4:12.

The Word of God, weapon and food. God's Word is both weapon and food for the Christian soldier, and he must know it as food before he can use it as a weapon. It is not an uncommon thing for new converts in their enthusiasm over their discovery of the new life, to start out giving testimony of their experience. They grow bold and are ready to tell their story in meetings; but after a time the narrative wears smooth and loses its freshness. Then they become discouraged and languish, if indeed they do not lapse altogether into the old uselessness. Ninety-nine times out of a hundred the cause of this is the lack of nourishment in the Word.

They have failed to put fresh fuel to their blazing fire, and it burned out. The reason Moses' burning bush did not fail was because the Spirit of God was in it. The Holy Spirit is in His Word. "The sincere milk of the Word" is not only necessary for the very life of "newborn babes," but it is the essential food for every redeemed soul that would be of service to the Master. The soul winner must daily and regularly feed upon the Word of God just as surely as the physical man must have bread and meat and drink in order to stay alive. In the failure of God's people to take daily nourishment of the spiritual food which is provided in His Word, lies the secret of the Church's weakness and ineffectiveness before her great task today. If all Christians were even half as intent upon getting the spiritual diet for their souls as they are to regularly and amply supply their stomachs, a revolution would come in the Church unparalleled by any that has gone before. Such a heart searching and such a rise in spiritual power would occur in the Church as to make the world stop and rub its eyes in wonderment. A great wave of evangelism would sweep around the earth and multitudes would be brought to the Lord—*by Bible reading Christians.*

(More about the Word as food and weapon in next lesson.)

Helps To Understanding Scripture Readings in *Day by Day*

By Rev. C. C. Baker

Sunday, June 24, II Peter 1:3-11. God's divine election must be supplemented by the Christian's desire to grow in grace (v.10). The Christian is able to grow because of the divine power of God that dwells within him (v.3). However, the Christian must choose whether or not he will avail himself of the divine resources and turn from sin to God (v.4). Thus the Christian decides what is to be the nature of his eternal inheritance (vv.9-11). Is there any particular virtue listed in vv.5-7 that is lacking in your life and causing you to be unfruitful for Christ (v.8)? Is it your desire to turn from the appetites of the flesh and become a partaker of the divine nature (v.4)?

Monday, June 25, I Corinthians 11:23-32. One of the most sacred experiences in the Christian's life is the celebration of the Lord's Supper (vv.23-26). What was the attitude of the Corinthian Christians toward this sacred institution (vv.20-22)? What are the terrible consequences that can come upon those who treat this service lightly (vv.27,29-33)? Though your behavior is in no way comparable to that of the Corinthian Christians, are there times when you approach the Lord's Table without the deep reverence it deserves? Read vv.23-26 again, meditating on the meaning of the communion service. What does it mean to you personally?

Tuesday, June 26, *Psalm* 32. David may have written this Psalm following his confession of sin with Bathsheba (Psalm 51). The terrible ordeal of harboring unconfessed sin (vv.3-4) has been relieved by a confession of sin to God (v.5). Detect the tremendous release (vv.1-2,11) that comes with making things right with the Lord. What new relation did the Psalmist find with God after his confession (vv.6-7)? What lesson did he learn according to v.10? What counsel does God have for you if you are harboring unconfessed sin in your life (vv.8-9)?

Wednesday, June 27, *Jeremiah* 31:31-34. Jeremiah lived in the days just before Judah was sold into exile for 70 years. Through Jeremiah God promised that following Judah's destruction and exile there would be a day when the country would prosper again (vv.27-28). Jeremiah also prophesied that there would be a time when God would have an entirely new relation to his people above and beyond the Old Testament covenant (vv.31-32). Though God's people utterly fail Him (v.32b), His mercy and love toward them cannot be destroyed (vv.28b,31-34). How is the New Covenant superior to the Old (vv.32-33)? What hope do God's people in this age have for a better time to come (v.34)?

Thursday, June 28, *Luke* 24:13-32. Jesus was the master teacher of history. What concept of Christ did the men on the Emmaus road have (vv.20-21)? What did they know about the resurrection (vv.22-24)? Observe the series of questions Jesus put to them when he first talked with them (vv.15-19)? What was the actual purpose of the questions? Must a teacher know what the feelings and thoughts of his students are before he can really teach them? Is good rapport important to good teaching? Following these questions, Jesus began to teach them directly (vv.25-27). How did they come to recognize the risen Christ (vv.30-31)? Is it more effective for a person to discover truth for himself than to have someone simply tell it to him? What lessons from Jesus' methods of teaching can you apply to your teaching?

Friday, June 29, *John* 16:4-14. Jesus has been warning His disciples that after His departure, persecution would come upon them (15:18-21; 16:1-3). This warning was designed to prevent them from being surprised when the enemies of Christ turned their wrath upon them (v.4). Yet, observe that Christ's departure was to their advantage (vv.6-7). What relation would the Holy Spirit have to the disciples (v.13)? What relation does He have to the world (vv.8-11)? Why do you think the Holy Spirit reveals himself one way to the world and another way to the Christian? Is His main task in your life the rebuking of sin (vv.8-10) or is He able to lead you into deeper spiritual truth (v.13)? What relation does He have to the Lord Jesus (v.14)? Could a desire to persist in sin rather than to glorify Christ be one reason for the Holy Spirit's not revealing more of Christ to you?

Saturday, June 30, *John* 6:51-59. Jesus was speaking to those who followed Him for the dole of bread they might receive (vv.24-26). In stressing the point of v.27, He mentions the truths of vv.51-59. Did the crowd have any discernment of spiritual truth (vv.41-42,52)? What do you think Jesus hoped to accomplish by proclaiming spiritual truth to this group? Notice the disciples (v.60). What did the twelve see in Christ that the others missed (vv.66-68)? Do you know the spiritual nourishment that comes from Christ's own presence in your life (vv.53,56)? This abiding presence of Christ in a person's heart is eternal life (vv.54,58).

REV. J. KENTON PARKER

LESSON FOR JULY 1

Nine Letters Of Faith And Encouragement

Background Scripture: Luke 9:28-36; Hebrews 13:9, 18-25; I Peter 1:1, 2; 2:19-25; II Peter 1:1, 2, 15-18; Jude 3:17-25.
Devotional Reading: Psalm 20

"In the name of our God we will set up our banners" (Psalm 20:5). In the Song of Solomon, 6:10, we have some words which are usually taken as referring to the Church, the Bride of Christ: "Who is she that looketh forth as the morning, fair as the moon, clear as the sun, and terrible as an army with banners?" Victorious armies have flags waving, and bands playing. The Church is an army. It is marching to victory. Our banners are not man-made: "In the name of our God we will set up our banners." The Cross of Christ is our "banner", and we march forth in the name of the Conquering King of Kings and Lord of Lords. In Revelation 19:11-16 we have a striking description of our Great Commander: "And he hath on his vesture and on his thigh a name written, KING OF KINGS, AND LORD OF LORDS."

If we are to be victorious in our fight against all the mighty hosts of sin and Satan, we must have FAITH in our Leader and Commander. It is in His Name that we go forth to battle. In our lesson today we have some selections from the Word of God that will strengthen our faith and encourage us. The Golden Text from Jude 3 is an exhortation to "Earnestly contend for the faith which was once delivered unto the saints." These words are badly needed in our day when so many attacks are being made upon our faith and so many forces are seeking to discourage us in our battle against "principalities and powers and spiritual wickedness in high places." These attacks of our enemies have never been more subtle or more dangerous than in these "last days," when, as Paul warns us, there will be a fearful "falling away" from the faith, and the preaching of "another gospel" which is not "another," and is characterized as having a form of godliness without its power. The real gospel is the power of God unto salvation. No other is worth believing or preaching.

I. *The Transfiguration:* Luke 9:28-36.

Verse 27 reads, "But I tell you of a truth, there be some standing here, which shall not taste of death, till they see the kingdom of God." About eight days after this Jesus took three of His disciples up into a mountain to pray, and as He prayed, He was transfigured: "the fashion of His countenance was altered and His raiment was white and glistering."

The disciples had seen Him daily as He preached and taught and healed, but His Deity had been veiled by His humanity. They had made a noble Confession of Faith in Him as the Christ of God. He had told them of His approaching sufferings and death and warned them not to be ashamed of Him. Peter especially had not liked this talk about His suffering and death, and had said impulsively, Be it far from thee, Lord; this shall never be unto thee. He now allows the three disciples to see "His glory," as Peter afterwards speaks of it. The Transfiguration comes at this critical time in His ministry and reveals to them a triumphant Christ and His coming Kingdom. Peter remembered this scene and refers to it in II Peter 1:16; they were eyewitnesses of His majesty. It gave them a solid basis for their faith and hope, and a much needed encouragement. It is well for us to keep in mind that the Christ we serve is a glorified Christ, risen from the dead, reigning at the right hand of His Father, from whence He shall come to judge the living and the dead. Our faith is not built upon "cunningly devised fables," as some unbelievers and scoffers would tell us today, but upon the Word of God; upon the Christ Who is the Son of God, "My beloved Son," whose kingdom is an everlasting kingdom.

II. *The Blood of the Everlasting Covenant:* Hebrews 13:9,18-25.

Why is so much said about "Blood" in both the Old and New Testaments? Read and study the Epistle to the Hebrews and you will get a clear answer to that question. God made a Covenant with His People in the Old Testament and this Covenant was signed and sealed with blood. The blood of beasts on Jewish altars slain could not take away sin; it could only tell the story in symbol, type, and illustration, of the coming Lamb of God Who takes away the sins of the world. He bore our sins in His own body on the tree; He was made sin for us Who knew no sin; the blood of Jesus Christ cleanses from all sin. This is the blood of the New Covenant which is shed for the remission of sins.

There are many "divers and strange doctrines" today and the most dangerous of them all is the teaching of the Unitarians, which at one stroke would destroy the Deity of our Lord and the

"Blood of the everlasting Covenant." The proclaiming of such "another gospel" which is not another, but a counterfeit, is very common. Let us never swerve from our faith in the precious blood of Christ, by which we have been redeemed. Only such a faith can make us perfect in every good work. Only through the Risen Shepherd of the sheep can we have peace and grace: "To whom be glory for ever and ever. Amen"!

III. *"Because Christ also Suffered for us":* I Peter 1:1,2; 2:19-25.

Peter is writing to the "sojourners of the dispersion" who have been scattered abroad and who are suffering for the sake of Christ. They were to remember that Christ suffered for them before they were called upon to suffer for Him. He left them an example of suffering. They were to follow in the steps of One Who did no sin, and yet suffered for sin. He bore His suffering patiently: "When he was reviled, reviled not again." He did far more than this, however: "Who his own self bare our sins in his own body on the tree, that we, being dead to sins, should live unto righteousness: by whose stripes ye were healed." Our sufferings are not even in the same category with His. Let us remember that no matter how much we suffer, He suffered far more than we can ever suffer, and *His sufferings were vicarious:* He suffered, the just for the unjust, that He might bring us to God. Here is great encouragement for the "suffering saints" of the First Century, and for suffering saints of the Twentieth Century also. I suppose that the memory of that terrible agony of the Shepherd and Bishop of our souls has strengthened the faith and encouraged more saints than any other thing. Because Christ suffered for us, we need never be ashamed to suffer as a Christian, but rather rejoice that we are counted worthy in a small degree to be a partaker of His sufferings. What a tonic for our faith is found in this passage from Peter's Letter to the Christians of his day!

IV. *"Precious Faith":* II Peter 1:1,2; 15-18.

This "precious faith" is founded on the righteousness of God, and our Savior Jesus Christ, and leads to multiplied grace and peace. A faith that is "precious" must be based upon a precious foundation. How firm a foundation ye saints of the Lord, is laid for your faith in His excellent Word! This is the Word which tells us of the salvation which we have in Christ. What a chasm separates our precious faith from the faith of ignorant and misguided and darkened minds of those who put their trust in "cunningly devised fables." This phrase aptly describes all the false religions of the world. Millions upon millions are blindly following such "fables." Added to these there are many "counterfeit gospels" which assume the name "Christian." They flourish even in our enlightened country. Satan is never as shrewd as when he pretends to offer something dressed up in the garb of Christianity. The "beast" often pretends to be a "lamb."

Our "precious faith" is built upon the Solid Rock, the Lord Jesus Christ, whose power and coming were seen by the apostle Peter when he was with Him in the "holy mount." Only when we catch a vision of such a Christ, Who is worthy of all glory and honor, can we have a sure word of prophecy which is as a shining light in a dark world. We are living in "dark and dangerous days." Evil flourishes on a big scale. We have need for our "precious faith."

V. *"Kept":* Jude 3, 17-25: "Keep you from falling."

Jude urges us to "earnestly contend for the faith which was once delivered unto the saints." Why? There have always been "mockers," and in these "last days" they will abound. These people walk after their own ungodly lusts. The world is full of such men and women. How can we be "kept"? How can we "keep ourselves" from these subtle and dangerous enemies?

First, we must build up ourselves in our most holy faith. We must be able to really "contend" for our faith; to give an answer to those who make fun of our faith. Sometimes people criticize "doctrinal preaching." How else can we proclaim the great fundamental facts of our faith? I can think of nothing more important than the preaching of such truths: the deity of our Lord, His Atonement, His resurrection, His coming in glory. The Church can only stand when these foundation stones are laid for our faith. Real revivals have always come from the preaching of truth.

Second, Praying in the Holy Spirit - Prayer and the presence of the Spirit.

Third, Save souls; pull them out of the fire.

Fourth, Keep yourselves in the love of God.

Fifth, Commit ourselves to Him; He is able to keep us from falling.

Something To Sing About

It is said that in a wealthy residential section of Richmond, some new owners complained that the singing at a small Christian church nearby disturbed them. They therefore circulated a petition to be presented to the city council asking that the church be silenced.

The solicitors brought the petition to a Jewish resident and asked him to sign. He read it and said, "Gentlemen, I cannot sign it. If I believed as do these Christians that my Messiah had come, I would shout it from the housetops and on every street of Richmond, and nobody could stop me."—Evangel.

YOUTH PROGRAM FOR JULY 1

Literature For Sunday Schools

Hymn: "My Dear Redeemer, And My God"
Prayer
Scripture: Psalm 19
Hymn: "O Love Divine, That Stopped To Share"

PROGRAM LEADER:

It is likely that most of us take our Sunday school literature for granted. When we receive our quarterlies, do we ask ourselves who had provided them for us? Do we not usually assume that it is the responsibility of the Sunday school itself to provide literature for its members? How would you feel if your teacher announced at the beginning of the quarter that there was no material to be distributed because there had not been money enough to pay for it? What would you think if the superintendent announced that there would be no more literature because the Sunday school officers and teachers did not think it was important or helpful? If either of these things happened in our Sunday schools, it is quite certain that most of us would be very startled.

It so happens that there are Sunday schools which are not able to purchase necessary literature. Most of these are newly organized and have not had opportunity to "get on their feet" financially. The Board of Christian Education of our church offers a three months supply of free literature to new Sunday schools. The Senior High young people of the Presbyterian Church U. S. have decided to share in this provision of free literature as one of the financial objectives for 1956. It is suggested that 20% of the benevolence budget be set aside for this work. In some groups it is the practice to receive a special offering for these financial objectives, but in any case, we shall see that this particular objective is a very worthy one in which we may have a part.

Our speakers will seek to point out some of the ways this free literature serves so importantly in the life of a new Sunday school.

FIRST SPEAKER:

Our leader has suggested that some new Sunday schools cannot afford to buy the literature they need to make a beginning. You may be wondering if this is really true in many places, and if so, why. Some of our new Sunday schools are being organized in very poor communities, and in many instances those who are most interested at the first are small children. In the 351 outpost Sunday schools of our denomination about two thirds of the members are children and young people. These persons have very little, if any, income. If provision of the literature depended upon them, it might not be provided.

It is true that many outpost Sunday schools are sponsored by established churches, and it is also true that these churches are able to buy the literature to get started. There are other new Sunday schools being organized in isolated communities where there are no established churches to share in the cost of buildings, materials, and supplies. In these communities the free literature is most helpful and most important.

SECOND SPEAKER:

The gift of free literature from the official board of the church is a source of encouragement to any new Sunday school. This is true even if the people are able to buy their own materials. Many people, especially those who are not very well acquainted with the church, have an idea that the church is "out to get all the money it can" from its people. It is altogether possible that people who are reached for the church by new Sunday schools will have this suspicion. It will be a real revelation to any who have such ideas to find that they are associated with a church which is concerned about giving as well as getting. It is encouraging to all people to know that the church is interested in them.

THIRD SPEAKER:

There are many times when the officers and teachers of a new Sunday school are at a loss to know what kind of literature to secure and where to order it. In other cases it may be felt that one quarterly or one hymn book is as good as another. There also may be an unwise attempt to "save money" by ordering insufficient amounts or by ordering "cheaper" books instead of the better ones. The gift of free literature solves all these difficulties. Sufficient quantities are provided. The literature is properly graded. In short, the school is provided with the very best tools for teaching and learning. Getting these schools off to a good start is one way of insuring continued success. Through our contributions to this project we young people can have a share in the numerical and spiritual growth of our church through its new Sunday schools.

Offering
Prayer of Dedication (For the special offering or for the portion of your benevolence budget which is designated for this objective.)
Hymn: "Seal us, O Holy Spirit"

Women's Work

New Life in Our Circle Meetings

Feeling that the different phases of the circle program of the Women of the Church should be closely correlated in order to attain rightful spiritual significance, I have worked with the general chairman of circle chairmen to activate interest in and undergird all activities with prayer.

Before the first circle meeting of the new year the general chairman of circle chairmen and I met with the circle chairmen, circle program chairmen, circle Bible leaders, and circle chairmen of Spiritual Growth to make plans and come to a common agreement for the circle program. In this meeting it was agreed that women in circles could be closely knit in their interest and activities by the following procedure:

First: *Calendar for each month* — That the general chairmen of circle chairmen and the general chairman of Spiritual Growth compile a calendar to be given to every member of the circles. This calendar to give some information about the special church-wide emphasis for the month, some prayer suggestions and list of the activities and other special items and actions from the Executive Board. These calendars to be mimeographed in the church office on Friday before the circles meet on Monday in order for the circle chairmen and the circle chairman of Spiritual Growth to consult together in advance and work effectively when the circle meets.

Second: *The Circle Meeting* — The circle chairman to call the meeting to order and recognize the chairman of Spiritual Growth. The chairman of Spiritual Growth calls attention to the Calendar of the month, listing the special emphasis, the activities for the month, and suggests prayer needs to undergird the program for the month. She then leads the circle in a season of prayer (this can be done in different ways—she can even call on some other member to lead in prayer — it should be changed from time to time). The circle chairman then emphasizes the need for keeping the calendar as information and urges members to participate in the activities and to be united in prayer for the needs of the program for the month and for the personal needs of others. Circle chairman then calls on the one who is to lead the "Let's Talk About" discussion.

After the circle members have discussed the special emphasis for the month — the "Let's Talk About" — the circle chairman conducts the business of the circle. After the business, the circle chairman presents the chairman of Bible study, who at the conclusion of her lesson, closes the meeting with prayer.

Third: *Each Circle Sends Copies of the Calendar* for the month to their absent members. This helps to keep them in touch with the ongoing program of the Women of the Church and enlists their interest in it.

After the first circle meeting another joint meeting of all the different chairmen of the circles was held to evaluate the meetings. It was agreed that new life had been brought to our circle meetings through this advanced planning with the circle chairmen, circle program chairmen, circle chairmen of Spiritual Growth and circle chairmen of Bible study. Each one understands the unity of the program and feels a responsibility for the time element of the whole. The different general chairmen meet with their respective groups all during the year, but getting the groups together before the first meeting and then off and on during the year helps to pull the different phases of the program together and give it the proper spiritual value. As some of the new circle chairmen expressed it, "Nothing has helped me so much as 'this sharing' as we evaluate together our circle meetings in the light of their real purpose."

Mrs. Rufus D. Wilson
Burlington, N. C.
Chairman, Spiritual Growth

Prayer for a Time of Mission

That God lead us in wisdom and into knowledge of the truth;
That God revive His Church, beginning with ourselves;
That we realize how far below the level of God's promises we have been content to live;
That we put away from ourselves all pride and be willing to be taught by God and used by Him
That we consent together to let God do in us and for us what He is willing to do;
That each congregation of our Church be a fellowship of love, service and devotion into which we gladly welcome others;
That God bring us back to a living faith by which alone we can walk humbly with God and in love and charity towards all men;
In the strong Name of Jesus we offer this prayer. Amen

My soul, wait thou only upon God.
For my expectation is from Him.

—*The Presbyterian Herald* (Ireland)

From Strength to Strength

O Living Christ

O living Christ,
 Live Thou in me;
Through,life, through death
 I'll go with Thee—

To Galilee,
 And Bethany,
Gethsemane,
 And Calvary:

Thy joy to see,
 Thy peace in me,
Thy power to be
 My victory.

To Oregon,
 Or to Iran,
To old Nippon,
 Or Turkestan:

Wherever souls
 Are needing Thee,
And men are dying
 Needlessly.

O living Christ,
 Live Thou in me;
Through life, through death,
 I'll go with Thee.

—E. H. Hamilton

Prayer

Prayer is so simple,
It is like quietly opening a door
And slipping into the very presence of God,
There in the stillness
To listen for His voice,
Perhaps to petition,
Or only to listen;
It matters not;
Just to be there,
In His presence,
Is prayer!"

—Author Unknown

Church News

NORTH CAROLINA

Charlotte — The 1956 Algernon Sydney Sullivan Awards were presented by Queens College to Miss Rena C. Harrell, retiring librarian of the college, and to Miss Peggy Brice, an outstanding member of the graduating class. These awards, the highest bestowed by the college, are presented through the New York Southern Society in a number of selected colleges; and the basis of selection is unselfish service. The Queens awards were made during the commencement convocation.

The Reverend John Selden Whale, M. A., D. D., of South Devon, England, will be Visiting Professor next year at Union Theological Seminary in Virginia, President James A. Jones announced recently. An outstanding educator, lecturer, preacher, and author, Dr. Whale will teach Christian Theology during the third quarter of the Seminary session of 1956-57. His classes and seminars will discuss the theme: "The Christian Faith in the Modern World."

Davidson, N. C. — Two Davidson College seniors from Missouri were among the most distinguished graduates in Commencement exercises May 28.

Jason D. McManus of University City and Donald H. Stewart, Jr., of Kirkwood were graduated Cum Laude and were members of Omicron Delta Kappa, national honorary leadership fraternity.

Both were members of Phi Delta Theta social fraternity, with McManus serving as president and Stewart as the organization's representative on the Interfraternity Council, the second highest elective position.

Two Davidson College graduates have been awarded scholarships to the Duke University Law School.

They are Hurley N. Seaford of Concord and Archie B. Joyner, Jr., of Greensboro. They will both enter the law school in September.

The scholarship won by Seaford is valued at $1,000 for one year, and Joyner's at $750 for one year.

Columbia Seminary Graduates

Columbia Theological Seminary graduated fifty-four members of the senior class at Commencement exercises held on Monday, June 4, in the Druid Hills Presbyterian Church. The speaker for the Commencement exercises was the Rev. Dr. J. E. Cousar, Pastor of the Independent Presbyterian Church, Savannah, Georgia. In addition to the graduating seniors one minister received the degree Master of Theology.

The Baccalaureate sermon was delivered in the Morningside Presbyterian Church at 11:00 o'clock A. M., June 3, by the Rev. Dr. Stephen T. Harvin, Pastor of the South Jacksonville Presbyterian Church, Jacksonville, Florida. The sermon before the Student Society of Missionary Inquiry was delivered in the Decatur Presbyterian Church at 8:00 P. M., June 3, by the Rev. Dr. Tom Frye, Pastor of the Druid Hills Presbyterian Church.

The following seniors received the degree Bachelor of Divinity:

Adams, William Anderson, Box 509, West Point, Ga.

Archibald, Donald Lewis, 1733 Cornell Drive, Augusta, Ga.

Baker, John Lewis, Route 5, Huntsville, Ala. Ebenezer Pres. Ch.

Bass, John Richard, Route 5, Lyons, Ga. (Sept. U. of Edinburgh).

Bodiford, William Allen, Winder, Ga. First Pres. Ch.

Boyer, Kenneth Elmer, Fort Gaines Pres. Ch., Fort Gaines, Ga.

Bridges, Arthur Charles, Files Valley Pres. Ch., Itasca, Texas.

Brown, Charles Samuel, Nettleton First Pres Ch. US, Nettleton, Miss.

Browning, Edward Huie, Belle Glade, Fla.

Campbell, John David, Jr., Henry Memorial Pres. Ch., Dublin, Ga.

Craven, Charles Eugene, Haines City, Fla.

Crowther, Curtis Fennell, Brainerd Pres. Ch., Chattanooga, Tenn.

Daugherty, Lawton, Sullivans Island Pres. Ch., Sullivans Island, S. C.

Donaldson, William Jay, Jr., Columbia Seminary, Decatur, Ga.

Durham, Clarence Gunn, 214 Lumpkin, Thomson, Ga. (Sept. U. of Edinburgh).

Elyea, Charles Dwelle, Jr., Chaplain's Office, Elgin State Hospital, Elgin, Ill.

Estey, C. Phil, Route 4, Athens, Ga.

Floyd, Robert W., 2411 Young Drive, Augusta, Ga.

Fortson, Samuel Donald, Jr., First Pres. Ch., Gadsden, Ala.

Freundt, Albert Henry, Jr., Forest Pres. Ch., Forest, Miss.

Fuller, Harold Edwin, Jr., Dallas Ch. Manse, Route 5, LaGrange, Ga.

Garwood, Saunders Bernhard, Mother's Memorial Pres. Ch., Pelham, Ga.

SOUTH CAROLINA

Clinton — Presbyterian College conferred 100 baccalaureate degrees and five honorary degrees and heard addresses by two prominent Presbyterian leaders as the highlights of the 75th commencement exercises on June 3-4.

Dr. Robert Strong, pastor of the First Presbyterian Church of Augusta, Ga., preached the baccalaureate sermon on June 3.

The commencement address the next day was delivered by Dr. Marshall C. Dendy of Richmond, Presbyterian College alumnus who serves as head of the Board of Christian Education of the Presbyterian Church US.

The honorary degrees, all doctor of divinity, were conferred upon four alumni and one friend. Alumni recipients were: the Reverends Isaac Bagnal of Bennettsville, S. C.; James McDowell Dick of Raleigh, N. C.; Bonneau Dickson of Atlanta; and William J. Hazelwood of Decatur, Ga. The fifth honorary degree went to the Rev. Ted Jones of Columbia.

VIRGINIA

Salem — At a called meeting of Montgomery Presbytery held in the Salem Presbyterian Church on May 29, with 30 ministers and 7 ruling elders present, Montgomery Presbytery dismissed Candidate Bertis E. Downs, III, to Kanawha Presbytery that he may accept a pastorate there.

Presbytery dismissed also Rev. John E. Richards of the First Church of Roanoke, Virginia, to Augusta-Macon Presbytery that he may become pastor of the First Church of Macon, Georgia.

Rev. G. P. Whiteley of the Glasgow Church was dismissed to Bluestone Presbytery that he may become pastor of the First Church of Bluefield, W. Va.

The campaign to raise $200,000.00 to establish churches in growing communities of our Presbytery has already reported $264,095.00 pledged and there are still 23 churches to be heard from. It is expected that over $300,000.00 will be pledged before the campaign closes.

One new church has already been started from this fund. It is in the Starmount section of Roanoke. Rev. B. E. Bain is the pastor.

Rev. Mr. Richards, the Chairman of the $200,000.00 fund campaign reported that the Presbytery hopes to begin at least 6 new churches in the near future.

Rev. W. W. Williamson of the Westminster Church of Lynchburg was nominated to be the Moderator of the next Stated Meeting (the 241st), which will be held in the Pearisburg Presbyterian Church on July 24, 1956.

E. W. Smith, Stated Clerk

TEXAS

Commerce — Dr. John F. Anderson, pastor of the First Presbyterian Church of Dallas, Texas, was the baccalaureate preacher at the commencement exercises of East Texas State Teachers College May 27. Degrees were granted to over two hundred and fifty graduates in the subsequent commencement service. Dr. D. C. Butler, professor of English, filled the pulpit of the Commerce church for two Sundays in June in the absence of the pastor, Rev. Walter Lazenby, Jr. Dr. Butler is a member of Paris Presbytery and a former missionary to China. A Boy Scout troop, broadening the ministry of the church to its youth, has been recently chartered with Tom Morris scoutmaster and M. D. Parham assistant. Ruling Elder Tom R. Young is institutional representative and Kenneth Michels is chairman of the troop committee.

— BOOKS —

"STAND BY, BOYS!" K. Norel. Wm. B. Eerdmans. $1.00.

The author who visited Zeeland just after the storm to survey the flooded polders in the human plight writes for boys and girls in moving and vivid account of both the tragedy and heroism brought on by the flood. This is absorbing reading for ages 8-14. Even older young people will enjoy reading this true story about Holland's fight against the sea.

"YOUNG PEOPLE'S PROGRAMS." Doris Louise Seger. Scripture Press. $1.00.

Thirteen original program suggestions which have been awarded first prize in the recent Scripture Press Idea Contest. These programs will be helpful in encouraging strong Christian living and livable Christian truths:

"ST. PAUL'S JOURNEYS IN THE GREEK ORIENT. Henri Metzger. Philosophical Library. $2.75.

The background of the journeys of St. Paul in the eastern part of the Roman Empire is described vividly by the author who has himself lived in the Near East and traveled along the routes of St. Paul. The author is a former member of the French School in Athens and of the French Institute at Istanbul, and lecturer at the University of Lyons.

"SHORT SKITS AND GAMES FOR WOMEN'S GROUPS." Carolyn Howard. Zondervan. $1.00.

This book is divided into chapters dealing with such subjects as baby showers, bridal showers, and general occasions. All material can be used at almost any kind of women's gatherings. Emphasis is on children and home life.

"IT'S TOUGH TO BE A TEENAGER." Bob Cook. Zondervan. $1.00.

Bob Cook understands teenagers. He lives with them, prays for them, and here offers information that will be helpful in reaching them. The book is designed to help teenagers in their transition from childhood to adulthood.

"FORTY RAINY DAY GAMES." Lora Lee Parrott. Zondervan. $1.00.

This booklet covers games, handcraft activities, and miscellaneous activities adapted to junior age children.

"FIFTY-TWO VARIETIES OF PROGRAMS FOR ALL OCCASIONS." T. C. Gardner. Zondervan. $.35.

This book offers suggestions on how to vary programs in order that each program will be interesting, inspiring, and dynamic. They are Bible-connected and evangelistically under-girded.

THE SOUTHERN PRESBYTERIAN JOURNAL

A Presbyterian weekly magazine devoted to the statement, defense and propagation of the Gospel, the faith which was once for all delivered unto the saints.

JUNE 27, 1956

EDITORIAL

VOL. XV NO. 9 $2.50 A YEAR

THE SOUTHERN PRESBYTERIAN JOURNAL

The Journal has no official connection with the Presbyterian Church in the United States

Rev. Henry B. Dendy, D.D., Editor........Weaverville, N. C.
Dr. L. Nelson Bell, Associate Editor........Asheville, N. C.
Rev. Wade C. Smith, Associate Editor........Weaverville, N. C.

EDITORIAL

Power for Living

What does the average individual need most; to be told his duty, or, to be told where he may find the power to do his duty?

We do not question that a part of the so-called prophetic ministry is to declare to man what his duty to God and his fellow-man may be. But, that is but part of such a ministry for man's greatest need is the transforming presence and power of the living Christ in his heart.

Years ago we heard a Chinese pastor use the following illustration; an allegory but a truth we all need to recognize: "A man fell into a deep pit from which he found himself unable to escape. After many futile attempts to climb out he saw a man standing above him. It was Buddha who said: 'Poor man, if he will come up here I will help him.' Then he went on his way. After that Confucius came along and looked down into the pit and said: 'Poor fellow, if he had listened to me he never would have gotten down there.' Then he too went his way. After that Christ came along and looked down into the pit. 'Poor fellow,' He said, and with that He leaped down into the pit and lifted him out."

How true it is that the religion of Jesus Christ is the religion of power. What man could not do for himself Christ did for him.

In the practical, every-day life of the Christian, we all need to be reminded that we are still impotent, that it is Christ Who dwells in us Who has the power and on Whom we must lean.

To know our duty is important. To know the *sole source* of power whereby we may do our duty is probably the central need of men and should have a central place in all preaching.

Our reason for this emphasis is the firm belief that our sinful hearts constantly lead us off into a sense of false security - a feeling that we are within ourselves sufficient for our problems. We need the constant reminder that we are *not* able to cope with life alone. Christ must be lifted up not only as Savior but also as Lord. He will show us our duty and He will also give us the power necessary.

If there has been undue emphasis on declaring what God requires of man without an equal emphasis on man's need for divine power, this unbalanced message can easily be rectified. The Gospel of Jesus Christ meets every phase of man's need. Let it be preached in all of its fullness! —L.N.B.

The Social Drinker

The following communication has been received from a Mother who has now come to see the terrible evil of serving alcoholic beverages to her guests. May many others heed this sincere warning.—Ed.

I have been through many different phases of thinking concerning liquor — Having been reared by devout persons who felt that Christians could not drink or serve liquor, I did neither — Then, I, too, weak, stupid and immature in my Christian thinking, served it to my friends and joined in drinking high-balls myself. Several years ago, I woke up to realize that I could not put myself in the position of a Sunday school teacher to young people or as a mother to my fine children and continue to indulge, even if casually, in anything as potentially dangerous, as completely insidious as alcohol; so I quit — but, coward that I am, I have continued to serve it to my friends who drink, trying to compromise with the Devil's best weapon that "you are *not* your brother's keeper" — But somehow a stronger, clearer voice has been ringing in my heart — "whatsoever causeth thy brother to stumble" — and as I have grown older and seen the stark, bleak and ugly tragedies that this *"harmless, little social habit"* has brought upon thousands of innocent people, — as I have read newspaper accounts of the countless crimes committed by persons under the influence of liquor, I am convinced that at least ninety percent of the murders, assaults, broken and shattered homes have been caused directly by drunkenness.

Even among my friends, I have seen misery brought by this fashionable and seemingly innocent custom. Now, I *hate* liquor. No longer can I condone it in any way. I see the horrible "Monster" for what it actually is—I look past the glass into the suffering faces of hundreds and thousands of little children—I see a terrified six year old boy struggling, begging, pleading for his life as a drunken maniac attempts to strangle him and finally shoots him through the head. I see a sweet little girl being beaten unmercifully by a drunken mother until her maimed and broken body lies still and quiet — I see pitiful, pleading childish faces that should be happy but are full of misery and frustration as they watch one parent murder the other in a drunken fit of temper. I see other little babies neglected and weeping piteously for the mother who is sitting in a drunken stupor at some cocktail lounge.

I see these pictures—Yes, I see sin in action! I see sin, stripped of all its glamour, its sophisticated charm. I see it ugly, base, cruel, loathsome. I see it through the high-ball glass. No, I can never again offer the stuff to anyone. My conscience rebels. God forgive me for ever being "fooled" by it. His Word through the ages has warned — "at last it biteth like a serpent and stingeth like an adder."

Christ's Technique in Winning Men

By Rev. Saml. McPheeters Glasgow, D. D.

"Come ye after me, and I will make you to become fishers of men."

"Come ye . . . " We can only bring an empty hand and a willing heart, but we must come.

"I will make . . . " Infinite power playing upon human life and its limitations.

"After me . . . " As My devoted, committed, obedient servant.

"You to become fishers of men . . . " It's a process; it's a school. They were fishers of fish. He wants to turn their talents uphill, into the heights. Under God the Holy Spirit one can become a fisher of men.

There are three personal imperatives here. *I Must Believe Something.* There must be a final conviction in my heart that men without Christ are lost. Some say "it makes no difference what you believe, so long as you do right." They might just as wisely say, "It makes no difference whether you put gas in your car or not, so long as it runs." What we believe in our hearts controls what we do and can do.

I Must Be Something. What we are, really are, limits our life and its contribution. If we want to be able to lead men to Christ as Saviour and Lord, we must be in fellowship with Him as our personal Saviour and Lord. It was after Andrew had found Him that he could lead Peter to Him.

I Must Bestow Something. Simon Peter's experience with Christ is arresting. He had much to say, but little to give until Christ was really crowned as King in his heart and life. Then, when Christ entered as Lord there was power and there were great issues in his witness and work.

Being fishers of men is the primal business of the Church of Christ, and the children of God in Christ. Every Christian belongs in this service.

A Dangerous Principle

By The Rev. Floyd E. Hamilton

On page 28 of the General Assembly Blue Book the ad interim Committee on a Biblical Study of the Position of Women in the Church makes the following statement: "From our study of the Bible we are led to believe that the Holy Spirit will progressively lead God's people into a new understanding of the practice of the will of God."

This, taken by itself, is a very skilful wording of a truth which is or should be precious to every student of the Bible. We have every right to expect that God's Spirit will help us to understand better how to practice what the Word of God says.

But that is not what the Committee apparently means, for in the immediately following sentence we read: "This is the promise of Jesus

The Southern Presbyterian Journal, *a Presbyterian Weekly magazine devoted to the statement, defense, and propagation of the Gospel, the faith which was once for all delivered unto the saints,* published every Wednesday by The Southern Presbyterian Journal, Inc., in Weaverville, N. C.

Entered as second-class matter May 15, 1942, at the Postoffice at Weaverville, N. C., under the Act of March 3, 1879. Vol. XV, No. 9, June 27, 1956. Editorial and Business Offices: Weaverville, N. C. Printed in the U.S.A. by Biltmore Press, Asheville, N. C.

Address Change: When changing address, please let us have both old and new address as far in advance as possible. Allow three weeks after change if not sent in advance. When possible, send an address label giving your old address.

(John 16:12-14)." What is this promise? "Howbeit when he, the Spirit of Truth, is come, he shall guide you into all truth: for he shall not speak of himself; but whatsoever he shall hear, that shall he speak: and he shall shew you things to come. He shall glorify me: for he shall receive of mine, and shall show it unto you."

These words of Jesus were spoken to the apostles, and the church has always interpreted them as meaning the promise of the Holy Spirit to them in writing the New Testament, and the predictive prophecies found in it, *not as a promise to all Christians that they shall receive new truth and predictive prophecies from the Holy Spirit.* Our church teaches that "the Word of God, which is contained in the Scriptures of the Old and New Testaments is the only rule to direct us how we may glorify and enjoy him." Does this Ad Interim Committee believe that? One wonders, for they apparently have interpreted their first sentence above quoted in terms of the John 16:12-14 passage, and seem to hold that the church today can receive new truth from the Holy Spirit, even when it is contrary to the plain teaching of the Bible. Paul lays down the requirements for eldership (bishops) and for deacons, and says among other things, "the bishop therefore must be without reproach, the husband of one wife,' '(I Tim. 3:2). A little farther down he says, "Let deacons be husbands of one wife."

Nothing could be plainer than that Paul is forbidding women from being elders or deacons. The Ad Interim Committee wants women elders and deacons. Therefore on their principle of the interpretation of Scripture they can change Paul's command to read "bishops and deacons can be women." Conditions and circumstances have changed, say the committee, and we can expect that the Holy Spirit will, "progressively lead God's people into a new understanding of the practice of the will of God."

Now this matter of having women elders and deacons, important as it is, fades into insignificance in comparison to the importance of the principle of interpretation of the Bible used by the Ad Interim Committee. According to the principle they have used. the church may receive the leading of the Holy Spirit to teach doctrines directly contrary to those taught in the Bible, if the circumstances and conditions of society demand such a change! This is the principle Harry Emerson Fosdick used in his book "The Modern Use of the Bible." If that principle were adopted we would no longer have an authoritative Bible, but a book which would change as conditions and circumstances change.

Now I am perfectly aware that some things Paul said applied a general, unchanging principle, to temporary, local conditions. He applied the principle, "Let all things be done decently and in order" to the local conditions in Corinth, where only loose women went about with their heads unveiled, so he said, "Judge ye in yourselves; is it seemly that a woman pray unto God unveiled?" (I Cor. 11:13). That was applying the unchanging principle to local conditions. When conditions change, it has become proper for women to pray with unveiled heads, but they must still do things "decently and in order," the unchanging principle.

But this matter of having women elders and deacons is different. Paul grounds his commands on the principle of headship. "The head of every man is Christ; and the head of the woman is the man; and the head of Christ is God." (I Cor. 11:3). When he says, "I permit not a woman to teach, nor to have dominion over man," (I Tim. 2:12) there is every indication that this was a basic principle, not the application of an unchanging principle to temporary and changing conditions.

But if the Ad Interim Committee had confined itself to trying to prove that the ordination of women was the application of an unchanging principle to temporary and changing conditions, their argument would not be as disturbing, (though I for one would disagree with them). What is so dangerous about their position is that they are in effect saying, "Though the Bible teaches one thing, conditions have changed, so we can disregard what the Bible says, even when it teaches apparently unchanging doctrine!" May our church never adopt such a principle in undermining the Word of God!

Three Visions

By Rev. James O. Reavis, D. D.

Two of the former presidents of the United States were members of churches which continue to do a good work in the Presbyterian Church in the U.S.: Andrew Jackson was a member of the Hermitage Presbyterian Church in the Presbytery of Nashville. Woodrow Wilson was a member of the Central Presbyterian Church in Washington, D. C., in the Presbytery of Potomac.

For thirty-seven years Rev. James H. Taylor, D. D., was the pastor of the Central Presbyterian Church and pastor and close friend of President Woodrow Wilson during the President's residence in Washington.

By invitation of Dr. Taylor, President Wilson addressed the Presbytery of Potomac at its meeting in the Central Presbyterian Church, April 20, 1915. In his address to the Presbytery the President said, in part:

"When I hear men like Dr. Stuart (Dr. Warren H. Stuart, at the time Professor of Religion in Hangchow Christian College) pleading for means to introduce this great influence of Christianity into a part of the world, now for the first time, feeling its connection with the rest of mankind, now first awaking to the possibilities of the power that lies latent in it, I wonder if it is possible that the imagination of Christian people will fail to take fire.

"Why this is the most amazing and inspiring vision that could be offered to you - this vision of that great sleeping nation, suddenly cried awake by the voice of the Christ. Could there be anything more tremendous than that?"

Now forty years and more have passed since President Wilson spoke these words to the members of the Presbytery of Potomac.

Today there is offered to the followers of Christ another vision - not "inspiring" but "amazing" and "tremendous." A vision of the six hundred million people of China, dominated, demoralized, and doomed in Spiritual darkness by the Atheistic and Materialistic forces of Communism.

Yet true Christians throughout the world refuse to be discouraged by this distressing vision of China. They are encouraged and strengthened by the inspired vision which was given to the Apostle John on the Isle of Patmos (Rev. 7:9, 10) and by the assurance that their Divine Lord and Redeemer is alive forevermore, everpresent and "working with them" as they press forward to the work of "making disciples of all nations."

"After this I beheld, and, lo, a great multitude, which no man could number, of all nations, and kindreds, and people, and tongues, stood before the throne, and before the Lamb, clothed with white robes, and palms in their hands; and cried with a loud voice, saying, Salvation to our God which sitteth upon the throne, and unto the Lamb."

One Gospel for Our Lost Race

By George S. Lauderdale

Because all men are descended from Adam, all are sinners. Pride fills every heart, God's laws are broken hourly, and He says it is a shame even to speak of the things which sinners do in secret. Due to universal sin, death awaits all; the men of every generation go to the grave, their bodies returning to dust.

God was not pleased that Adam rebelled against His Word, and continued loving him after his fall. By sending Jesus Christ into the world, He has opened the way for our lost race to be redeemed: whoever believes on God's Son will not perish but have everlasting life. This good news is to be proclaimed in all the world to every creature!

To show the dying and ignorant, fighting and unhappy children of Adam how to be reconciled to God by faith in the Lord Jesus Christ is God's own work. Missionary visiting, praying, and giving by Christians displays the very same love which led the Saviour to die on the cross as a sacrifice for sins; the Holy Spirit sheds abroad God's love in our hearts and directs world evangelization.

BE A HUMBLE, TRUE WITNESS

Missionaries cannot afford to be proud and haughty, for they are partners of Adam's sinful nature the same as those to whom they minister! Nor should we underestimate the power of Satan over the nations, and pretend that men are not in dire need of the cleansing blood of the Lord Jesus Christ. "The Cretians are always liars, evil beasts, slow bellies. This witness is true. Wherefore rebuke them sharply, that they may be sound in the faith." Titus 1.12,13. So came the Word of God to a missionary on Crete, and applies everywhere.

None need be deceived by false doctrine if he realizes that every human heart is desperately wicked. The truth is that man cannot save himself, but must trust solely in the Lord Jesus Christ. There is one gospel of God: "As we said before, so say I now again, If any man preach any other gospel unto you than that ye have received, let him be accursed." Galatians 1:9.

HOW SATAN DECEIVES

Satan brought about the fall of our race, and he is now doing all he can to keep men from being restored to God's fellowship and favor through faith in Jesus Christ. "You are too wicked," he tells men, and they despair of being saved; "You are good enough already in God's sight," he lies to others, and they think they are going to heaven as they travel to hell. He even tells the same persons at different times each of these falsehoods.

The true religion is that salvation is a gift of God, received by faith in His Son Who received the wages of sin, death, for guilty men. Salvation cannot be by works, therefore; men must be born again before he can see the Kingdom of God. His works are not pleasing to God, much less acceptable to purchase his pardon.

ANGLERS

(From *"New Testament Evangelism"* by Wade C. Smith)

Lesson No. 145

FISHING WITH THE WORD (Continued)

It is well for us to remember that as soul-winners we are endeavoring to make Jesus Christ known to men in His saving power. We cannot do it unless we know Him ourselves in that way. Jesus is revealed to us in His Word. If we lived a thousand years we could never exhaust what the Word has to teach us about Jesus. Day by day, in its application to, and interpretation of, our ordinary experiences, the Word, if permitted, gives us clearer visions of Christ and stronger conviction as to the verity of all His claims about Himself. As He becomes more and more necessary to us in this way, more and more satisfying to every craving of the soul, the more convincing is the manner of our telling others about Him. The Word, the Living Bread, makes us strong to do His will. Neglect of the Word renders us aenemic and unusable.

This point of feeding daily upon God's Word for oneself cannot be overstressed. It is not enough to study the Bible to feed others. That is not the best way to *feed. The writer* had an idea that when he became a pastor there would nevermore be any danger of his own undernourishment, for would he not have to be daily searching through the Word to feed his congregation twice on the Lord's day and at least once on a week night? To his great surprise he found it possible to pore over Scripture day and night and come to the week-end jaded and utterly depressed in spirit. His sermons went flat. What was the matter? Hadn't he prayed enough? Possibly not. But that was not the main trouble. He had neglected to read the Word for himself - to find there the rebuke to his own waywardness and to see there the Saviour who had died *for him;* to read afresh those precious promises for the reviving of his own spirit. He was like a hotel waiter carrying in large trays of food for the guests, day and night, and never taking the time to quietly sit down and eat a square meal himself. A preacher may not starve to death, for he could hardly handle the Word for others faithfully without catching a few crumbs; but he can become very sickly and pale, while his congregation begins to think about giving him a vacation - maybe an indefinite one. This preacher resolved upon a radical step. He would let the sermons go; they seemed not to be getting anywhere much anyhow. But he would take time each day to find in the Word, with the Spirit's help, some precious truth just fitted for his own hungry heart. The spark was revived and fanned into flame, and the truth most refreshing to himself was the one which "struck fire" when he preached it.

The first essential about the Word is to feed upon it and love it for ourselves.

(More about fishing with the Word in next lesson)

Helps To Understanding Scripture Readings in *Day by Day*

By Rev. C. C. Baker

Sunday, July 1, *Jeremiah* 1:4-10. When the fortunes of the people of God were about to change, God always sent a servant to prophesy of coming events (vv.1-5). What was the nature of the message Jeremiah was to preach (vv.10, 16)? The armies of Babylon were coming as God's instrument of judgment upon Judah (vv.14-16), and they were coming soon (vv.11-12). How did Jeremiah feel about his task (vv.6,17b)? What kind of response could he expect (vv.17,19)? What figures are used to describe God's provision for his needs (vv.9,18, 19)? Do you think God has a plan for your life as He did for Jeremiah's life (v.5)? Will He give direction and help to any who is willing to follow His plan (vv.7-8)?

Monday, July 2, *Jeremiah* 2:1-3,9-13. The Lord now brings indictment against Judah. What attitude did the people have toward God in their early days (vv.2-3)? God calls upon His people to witness to other nations (v.10). They do not change the worship of their false gods from one generation to another (v.11a), but Israel, who knows the true God, is fickle (v.11b). What does v.12 add to this thought? What two sins are involved in forsaking the true and living God (v.13)? According to v.13, what damage do we do to ourselves when we forsake the Lord? Do you find that when you turn from God you lose contact with that which truly satisfies your inner needs (v.13)?

Tuesday, July 3, *Jeremiah* 18:1-6. God teaches His lessons in terms that man can understand (vv.1-4). What happened to the clay with which the potter was working (v.4)? How was the relation of the potter to the clay analagous to the relation of the Lord to Israel (v.6)? How does the behavior of a people toward sin affect their relationship with God (vv.8-10)? How did the spiritual lesson of the potter and the clay (v.6) apply to the Jewish people of Jeremiah's time (v.11)? Are you aware of the fact that the extent to which you play with sin directly affects the extent to which God will use you in His service? What wonderful promise is there for the penitent in vv.7-8?

Wednesday, July 4, *Jeremiah* 8:4-9. A rather shallow religiosity pervaded the country (7:4; 8:8-11). The people would not heed the word of the Lord (v.9) and refused to repent of their sins (vv.4-6). How does the figure of v.6b dramatize their condition? God's other creatures do not rebel in this manner (v.7). All groups of people were guilty (v.10); no one was concerned about his sin (vv.6,12). Hence terrible judgment was the only recourse (vv.1-3). Pray that the present religiosity in our land may not blind us to our need of repenting of our sins, that God's judgment may not have to fall on us because we are blind to our real needs.

Thursday, July 5, *Jeremiah* 32:6-12. As the armies of Nebuchadnezzar are beseiging Jerusalem (v.2), and its fall, as a witness of God's judgment (vv.3-5), is imminent, God holds out hope for the future (v.15). Jeremiah is instructed to buy a piece of property at Anathoth (vv.6-12). As you read vv.6-15 closely, observe that this transaction is no ordinary business deal, but a sign from God to His people. Would a person normally buy land out in the country (vv.7-8) when the capital city was under siege? The transaction took place publicly (v.12). What message concerning the future would be conveyed by a prophet of the Lord committing such an act? Though the outlook for your future may at times seem dismal or discouraging, God is still in control of tomorrow.

Friday, July 6, *Jeremiah* 31:31-34. God encouraged His people by the words as well as the deeds of the prophet. Through Jeremiah God promised that following Judah's destruction and exile there would be a day when the country would prosper again (vv.27-28). Jeremiah also prophesied that there would be a time when God would have an entirely new relation to His people above and beyond the Old Testament covenant (vv.31-32). Though God's people utterly fail Him (v.32b), His mercy and love toward them cannot be destroyed (vv.28b, 31-34). How is the new covenant superior to the old (vv.32-33)? What hope do God's people in this age have for a better time to come (v.34)?

Saturday, July 7, Jeremiah 17:5-8. A contrast is drawn between the worldly man (v.5) and the godly man (v.7). Contrast the attitude of each toward the Lord (vv.5,7). In these same verses, what is the source of the strength of each? Study the figures used to describe these two kinds of men (vv.6,8). Both the shrub (v.6) and the tree (v.8) are planted in a climate that is hot and dry. What will happen to the shrub (v.6)? What will happen to the tree when heat and drought come (v.8)? What makes the difference (v.7)? Have you found the Lord a very present help and strength in time of trouble and difficulty?

SABBATH SCHOOL LESSONS

REV. J. KENTON PARKER

LESSON FOR JULY 8

Jesus Christ Is The Son Of God

Background Scripture: Matthew 3:13-17; Hebrews 1:1 - 2:8; 6:1-3.
Devotional Reading: John 14:1-11.

In John 14 we have the "Cure for Troubled Hearts," and that cure is FAITH: "Believe in God"; "Believe also in me"; "Believe me"; "Believest thou not"? He was going to prepare a place for them; He was coming back to receive them unto himself. Whither I go ye know, and the way ye know. Thomas saith unto him, We know not whither thou goest, and how can we know the way? I am the way, the truth, and the life: no man cometh unto. the Father but by me. Philip saith unto him, Lord, show us the Father, and it sufficeth us. He that hath seen me hath seen the Father. Believe me that I am in the Father, and the Father in me. Jesus is stating here what he states over and over again, the great fact that *He is the Son of God.* The only cure for Troubled Hearts, and for Sinful Hearts, is found in a Savior Who is God Himself: a Savior Who is no more than a man can never meet the need of our burdened, broken, and sinful souls.

It is difficult to see how anyone can be as unbelieving and as blind as the Unitarian. The "Leaven of the Sadducees" - Unbelief - is the most deadly of all sins. It has about it an air of respectability, self-exaltation, and superiority which is unpardonable. As long as it has control of the heart and mind it is impossible for a man to be saved. These may seem like very strong words, but I am sure that they are fully warranted by the plain teaching of Scripture. The only way of salvation is through Christ, the Divine Son of God. If we reject Him, refuse to believe in Him, then our case is hopeless. He that believeth on Him is not condemned; But he that believeth not is condemned already, because he hath not believed in the name of the only begotten Son of God.

•

Faith in Jesus Christ as a mere man dishonors both the Father and the Son, making them both liars, for the Father testifies to the fact that Jesus Christ is His Son, and Jesus makes that claim again and again. In John 8:58 we have this word; "Verily, verily, I say unto you, Before Abraham was, I AM." As we study these selected passages today may our faith in Him as the Son of God be confirmed that no doubts will ever enter our minds on this vital point. These verses are but a few of the many that could be given. The whole gospel of John, for instance, is written for this specific purpose; "These are written that ye might believe that Jesus is the Christ; the Son of God; and that believing ye might have life through His name." (John 20:31). May the Holy Spirit use our lesson this day to firmly establish our hearts in this most important matter, and turn many unsaved souls to the only Savior Who can save us from our sins; the God-man; the eternal Son of God Who became man in order that He might save man. Let the Church cast out with scorn and loathing the destroying leaven of the Sadducees - Unitarianism - with its deadening effect upon the Church, and upon men.

I. *The Trinity:* Matthew 3:13-17.

"In the unity of the Godhead there be three persons of one substance, power, and eternity; God the Father, God the Son, and God the Holy Ghost. The Father is of none, neither begotten nor proceeding; the Son is eternally begotten of the Father; the Holy Ghost eternally proceeding from the Father and the Son." (Confession of Faith, Chapter II, paragraph 3) "There are three persons in the Godhead: the Father, the Son, and the Holy Ghost: and these three are one God, the same in substance, equal in power and glory." (Shorter Catechism, Q 6) One of the proof-texts for these statements from the Confession of Faith and the Catechism is this selection from Matthew which we are studying today: "And Jesus, when He was baptized, went up straightway out of the water; and lo, the heavens were opened unto Him, and He saw the Spirit of God descending like a dove, and lighting upon Him: And lo, a voice from heaven, saying, This is my beloved Son, in whom I am well pleased." Certainly no clearer proof is needed. We have all three persons of the Godhead present and taking part in His baptism. We have Jesus, the Son of God, being baptized by John; we have the Spirit in the form of a dove descending upon Him; we have the voice of the Father proclaiming the divine sonship of the Son. We hear this voice again at the Transfiguration, (see Luke 9:35). Peter refers to this in II Peter 1:17. In John 12:28 we hear the voice again: There came a voice from heaven, saying, "I have both glorified it, and will glorify it again."

The Unitarian denomination is small, but when you think of the millions of unbelieving Jews and Mohammedans, we have a lot of Unitarians in the world. I cannot regard these as "Christians," for they deny the basic requirement for being a Christian. The influence of this pernicious "leaven" is felt in many denominations of the Christian Church. There are Unitarians in some Protestant pulpits. I was interested in the attitude of certain Communists who were being questioned in Charlotte the other day. They claimed to be loyal citizens of the United States, and yet refused to answer some simple questions. They took refuge under the very Constitution they were seeking to destroy. Is not this what the Unitarian does? His attitude of unbelief strikes at the foundation of the Christian Church, for Jesus said, after Peter's Confession of Faith in Him, "Upon this rock I will build my church and the gates of hell shall not prevail against it."

II. *Many Proofs of His Deity:* Hebrews 1:1 - 2:8.

I want to look at some of the verses used in this section:

1. Jesus is contrasted with the prophets. These prophets were great and good men; none greater in history; but *they were men;* good men, great men, inspired men; but they never once claimed to be anything but men. God spoke through them and used them. But now, in these last times, God has spoken by *His Son: the Son.*

2. This Son is the "heir of all things." In the parable in Luke 20:8-18 we have the same expression used: "This is the Heir: come, let us kill him." This "heir" is "my beloved Son." (Verse 13)

3. "By whom he made the worlds." In John 1:3 we read, "All things were made by him; and without him was not anything made that was made." All three persons of the Godhead had a part in Creation. In the beginning God created the heavens and the earth . . . And the Spirit of God moved upon the face of the waters. (Genesis 1:1-2). In Hebrews and in John we see that Jesus Christ, the Son of God, was also active in creation. As Dr. Lenski so well says, "What is done by one person of the Godhead, is done by all three persons." For instance, I say, "I built this house," when there were several people helping to build it.

4. "Who being the brightness of His glory." There are many ways in which the glory of God is manifested in the world. The heavens declare it. The most marvelous way in which God is glorified is in His Son. When we see Him we see the Father. No man hath seen God at any time: the only-begotten Son, Who is in the bosom of the Father, He hath revealed Him.

5. "And the express image of his person." (the very image of his substance) We state this by saying, "same in substance."

6. "Upholding all things by the word of his power." "Equal in power and glory." We see this almighty power manifesting itself in the marvelous "works" He did while here. "Believe me for the very work's sake," He said to the Jews.

7. "Had by himself purged our sins." It was impossible for the blood of bulls and goats to take away sin. Only a nobler Name and richer blood could.

8. "Sat down on the right hand of the majesty on high." He finished His atoning work and entered into His exalted position as our Great High Priest, to make continual intercession for us.

9. "A more excellent name" than angels: 4-14.

"Better than the angels." Angels are created beings. He is the Son, begotten of the Father. The relationship of Father and Son is very much better and closer than that of Creator and Creature. We can realize that, those of us who are parents. We can adopt a child but it is not exactly like having one who is bone of our bone and flesh of our flesh. We can "create" a machine, (using that word loosely), but a child of ours is entirely different. We become "sons of God" when we are born of His Spirit, but the Sonship of Christ is unique.

The angels must worship Him, for He has a more excellent name than they. "But unto the Son he saith, thy throne, O God, is for ever and ever." He is God.

10. "So great Salvation": God-planned; God-executed; God-applied; God-attested. No won-

der we are solemnly warned about neglecting so great salvation. There is a two-fold application. It is usually applied to unsaved persons who neglect to receive it. But Christians can "neglect", or "drift away" also. We may forget that we are "bought with a price." Do we Christians appreciate the greatness of our blood-bought salvation, or are we careless and "let it slip"?

III. *"Let us go on unto perfection"* Hebrews 6:1-3.

A foundation is to be built upon; principles must lead to practice. The end and aim of salvation is PERFECTION. Are we making progress toward the goal? True orthodoxy is never dead. It is a living principle. Are we alive and growing?

YOUNG PEOPLE'S DEPARTMENT

REV. B. HOYT EVANS

YOUTH PROGRAM FOR JULY 8

Who Is A Success

Hymn: "Stand Up, Stand Up For Jesus"
Prayer
Scripture: Mark 10:35-45
Hymn: "More Holiness Give Me"
Offering
Hymn: "Jesus Calls Us: O'er The Tumult"

PROGRAM LEADER:

(Distribute slips of paper and pencils to the young people and ask them to prepare two lists: (1) Marks of success from a Christian standpoint, (2) Marks of a successful life according to the world's way of judging. Make two columns on a blackboard or a large sheet of paper and list all the different ideas suggested.)

From our experiment here we have seen that there is not always agreement between the worldly idea of success and the Christian idea. We can see the same failure to agree in the passage of Scripture which was read. The sons of Zebedee were sure that they would be successful, if only Jesus would promise them places of importance in His kingdom. Their idea of success was to be in a position where they could "lord it over" other people. Jesus refused their request, and at the same time explained to them that their idea of success was altogether wrong. Then Jesus explained His own formula for success. He did not merely give them advice about the matter, but He made it clear that this was the way He was proceeding toward success Himself. Jesus said His way to success was not through being served, but through service . . . not through saving His life, but through giving it as a ransom for others. This is not only Christ's way of success, it is the only way which is open to His followers . . . to all of us who call ourselves Christians.

I am sure that all of us realize that this idea of being servants is not very acceptable to ordinary human nature. By nature we would rather receive service and honor from others than to render it to them. We would rather have others look up to us than to look up to them. We enjoy being important more than recognizing the importance of others. In short, Christ's idea of success is not very popular with human nature.. This is perfectly natural, because human nature is always seeking to satisfy itself. Before a person can honestly accept Christ's formula for success he needs to have this nature changed. He needs to be made a new creature in Christ. The only person who can follow the Christian way of success is one whose life has been transformed by Jesus Christ, and the only way a person can have his life transformed is by accepting Christ as his Lord and Saviour.

FIRST SPEAKER:

We need to remember that the service which makes a person successful must be Christian service. In order to lead to success the service we render must be genuinely helpful to others and it must be done in the name and for the sake of Christ. It would be possible for a person to give himself in service in a bar room or a gambling hall, but you would hardly expect this kind of service to lead to success because it is harmful rather than helpful to the people who are being served. If what we do for people does not serve to make them better, then our service will not result in success, because the thing which they serve is wrong. Sometimes young people think that if they only give themselves to the service of some great cause, success is sure to come. This is true only if the cause is a part of the greatest cause of all, the cause of Jesus Christ.

SECOND SPEAKER:

If we sometimes have the wrong ideas about what is required to make a successful life, we may also have the wrong ideas about who are the truly successful people among our acquaintances. The world insists so loudly on its own terms of success that Christians are apt to be wrongly influenced. We are tempted to think, along with the world, that the person with a great deal of wealth or in a high position is truly successful simply because of his wealth or his position. We are also tempted to think that the person who has not attained these things is unsuccessful. If we find ourselves yielding to such temptations, we need to read again what Jesus said about His own life . . . that He came to serve and to give His life. He was the most successful man who ever lived on earth, yet He had none of the things which the world insists are necessary for success.

THIRD SPEAKER:

There is another danger which we need to avoid in our thinking about the true nature of success. The last speaker made it clear that wealth, position, and worldly importance are no guarantees of genuine success, but neither do they make success impossible. Sometimes our attitude toward the rich and important is like that of the fox toward the "sour grapes." Some of the most successful people in the history of the world, judging by the formula of Jesus, have been those who were wealthy and important. We also need to realize that being poor and insignificant in the eyes of the world does not insure being successful in the eyes of Christ. The fact is that neither wealth nor poverty, importance nor insignificance have anything at all to do with the success which is open to those who walk in the way of Christian service. Not every person is a success, but everyone can be. All that is required is that we yield all that we have to Jesus Christ.

— LETTERS —

Sir:

"Two or three times I've started to write the *Journal* and usually decided it would be better to talk rather than write.

"At any rate I do not think I ever read a better one that was so little known. It was less than two years ago that I got the first copy.

"It seems to me that its light is too much under the bushel and I would judge that there are thousands in our Church that would like to have it if they knew of it."

J. W. McClung, Jr.

Regular readers of the *Journal* are urged to pass the word on to others. New subscriptions are always welcome.

Women's Work

An Open Letter

Women of the Church

Dear Friends:

This note is written to you who spent yourselves - your money, and your prayers in White Cross Gifts for us in 1955. I do not have the names and addresses of all who sent gifts, so would appreciate your help in getting my message to others you may know I have missed. I would like to write every one of you a personal letter for I am the one who gets the greatest joy out of White Cross. It is the source from which many needs are supplied. It is not only sheets to make a clean bed that lightens the day's tasks!

We have used a few of the baby things as gifts, and those have been a special satisfaction. Occasionally a new-born arrives at the day of discharge with nothing to put on (wrap them in an old garment, or a not too clean rag.) We have dressed these infants from our White Cross gifts. Twice we have given a gift for other reasons—Jean Landsborough (Dr. Connan) asked me to fix something for her to give the hundredth infant she delivered in hospital in 1955. Forty odd in the years was the record previous to 1955's 103 obstetrical deliveries. We gave our Changhua preacher's wife a gift when her second baby was born at Christmas time just because she is young and badly wants nice things for her infant girl. Another item was used for a wedding gift - someone sent a double bed candlewick spread which did not suit for hospital use. The day I unpacked it, P'an Ah Liang was announcing her engagement at a little service in the nurses' classroom. (Ah Liang was fifty-three years old, had never been married, of course, and no longer had expectations.) Suddenly someone as "middleman" introduced her as helpmeet for a Presbyterian elder living in the southern end of the island whose wife had died, his children were all grown and away from home. He had two "hospitals" (not in the same town) and just could not manage without help. They were married about three months ago. I hope it is a happy arrangement for Ah Liang, and I think it is. She got the candlewick bedspread! All the nice little sundries (rubber bands make traction dressings for harelips, and finger injuries, etc., applicators and gauze squares in packets suit the out-call bag), I hoard for Dr. Wilkerson's use which is quite all right since he is the only one in surgery who knows about nice supplies. The little sewing woman got the needles, but I happen to know she promptly had a run of nurses and doctors needing to "borrow a needle!" It's all right for they are very expendable in wet heat - cannot save them. The linen in Dr. Wilkerson's clinic, the sheets on the operating room table, most of the bed linen in the wards, the garments on the patients who get changed before coming to surgery (some day we will change them all) - everywhere one looks White Cross. I am hoarding the "cream of the crop" for the new operating room which is today only a blue print, but we hope will be a reality before long, thanks to our Board of World Missions who started the fund and JCRR (U.S. relief agency) who has added handsomely to it.

The city is noisy with native music today—little itinerant bands roaming the streets with mobs of children following them. Stands and peddlers are selling gaudy (some pretty - some fantastic) paper lanterns, and the temple in front of us is being set up as are all the others in the island. Tomorrow is the 15th of the lunar first month, and lantern festival - the last of the New Year celebrations. They do it in a big way in Taiwan! Most of our patients went home for the New Year, February 12, but we did not have a bed for a woman who wanted to come in this morning. Our hospital buildings and equipment would astonish you, but a lot of sick get well here, and they have the Gospel preached to them. I wish I could tell you what our White Cross Gifts mean to us and to the work, but you'd need a Changhua Christian Hospital background to understand. Your gifts have brought joy, better care to sick, and a flash of sunshine to others along the way. I thank you for us all, and pray the Lord will bless you for this work done in His name.

Sincerely,

Charlotte A. Dunlap

Just For Today

Just for today I will try to live through this day only, and not tackle my whole life problem at once. I can do something for 12 hours that would appall me if I felt that I had to keep it up for a lifetime.

Just for today I will be happy. This assumes to be true what Abraham Lincoln said, that "Most folks are as happy as they make up their minds to be."

Just for today I will try to strengthen my mind, I will study. I will learn something useful. I will not be a mental loafer. I will read something that requires effort, thought and concentration.

Just for today I will adjust myself to what is, and not try to adjust everything to my own desires. I will take my "luck" as it comes, and fit myself to it.

Just for today I will exercise my soul in three ways: I will do somebody a good turn, and not get found out. I will do at least two things I don't want to do - just for exercise. I will not show anyone that my feelings are hurt; they may be hurt, but today I will not show it.

Just for today I will be agreeable. I will look as well as I can, dress becomingly, talk low, act courteously, criticize not one bit, not find fault with anything and not try to improve or regulate anybody except myself.

Just for today I will have a program. I may not follow it exactly, but I will have it. I will save myself from two pests: hurry and indecision.

Just for today I will have a quiet half hour all by myself, and relax. During this half hour, sometime, I will try to get a better perspective of my life.

Just for today I will be unafraid. Especially I will not be afraid to enjoy what is beautiful, and to believe that as I give to the world, so the world will give to me.

—From An Eatshop Card.

One Minute Messages on Stewardship

Stewardship is entering into all phases of our church. We want to become better informed stewards. Nothing will take the place of our Bible, certainly it comes first. We can read tracts, books on stewardship - and make them alive.

We can attend some conference during the summer.

There are really only two answers to the call of Christian service - "I will and I will not!" Many of us, like Moses, at first try to interject an "I cannot" but self-examination will usually prove that the trouble is not of ability, but of will. Many seem to think only of self, not what they are doing, certainly not for the glory of God. Shyness is not a Christian virtue. Not all of us can be fluent speakers, but in spite of human weakness, we can have the quiet poise of selflessness, the assurance that it is "not I but Christ in me." And there is nothing more rewarding to personal spiritual life than learning by leading others to understand, or by leading others in the doing of God's will.

Does your Stewardship life have a fresh, joyful quality? Will you be "On Tiptoe," expectant for Christ?

—From "On Tiptoe" by Elena Reisner,
Board of Women's Work

Nation Needs Dual System of Education

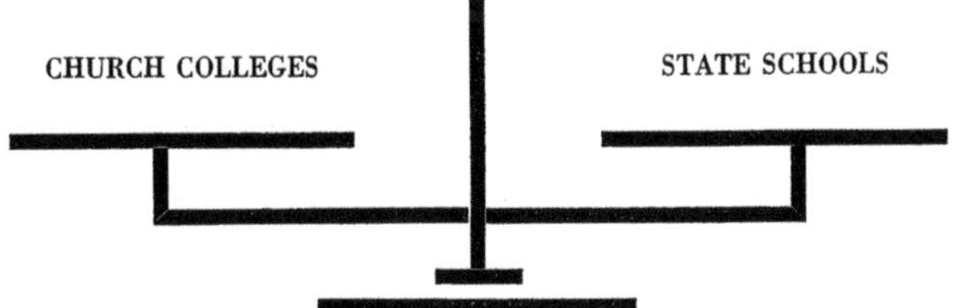

One of the great strengths of America has been its dual system of controls in education.

The churches first lighted the lamps of learning in this country as churchmen also lighted the torches of liberty. Until 1947, more than half of the college students were in church-related and private institutions. Now the pendulum has swung the other way; 56 per cent of the students are in tax-supported institutions.

Privately financed colleges, including our church institutions, have freedoms not enjoyed by public institutions—freedom to include religion in the curriculum, freedom to select students more carefully, freedom to discuss all forces which bear upon civilization. These freedoms constitute important safeguards for all education.

Population Trend Points to Crisis

More and more young people are going to college. With one-third of our youth on the campuses, the total enrollment is 2 2/3 millions. At present population growth rates, college enrollment will reach nearly three millions by 1960 and total more than four millions in 1970. It may go higher.

The public schools have been going through crises imposed by this growth—teacher shortages, too few buildings, too little money. Now the crisis is moving toward the colleges, including our own.

Presbyterian colleges desire to remain small (under 1,000) in order that campus environment may be controlled and that instruction may be more personal. But most of our colleges would be more efficient in operation if they were larger than they are now. They need more Presbyterian students.

Above all, our Presbyterian colleges must have more buildings, more teachers, better pay for teachers, more scholarships, bigger endowments, and more giving by local churches.

It has been well said, "Quality education is the only kind with which the Church should be associated." Better support is the price of such education.

PRESBYTERIAN EDUCATIONAL ASSOCIATION OF THE SOUTH

Hunter B. Blakely, Secretary • Box 1176 Richmond 9, Va.

Church News

Change of Address: Rev. J. David Simpson, from Ft. Smith, Ark., to 22 Wesley Place, Tuscaloosa, Alabama. Now Executive Director of Tuscaloosa Presbytery.

World Mission Receipts

Budget for 1956	$3,300,000.00
Receipts to date	1,301,883.72
Percentage of annual budget received for 1956	39.45%
Balance needed for 1956	1,998,116.28

THE GENERAL FUND AND INTERCHURCH AGENCIES

Statement of Receipts

January 15 - May 31, 1956

THE GENERAL FUND AGENCIES

Budget for 1956	$846,581.00
Received from January 15th through May 31, 1956	162,856.97
Percentage of annual budget received to date	19.23
Balance needed for the year	683,724.03

INTERCHURCH AGENCIES

Budget for 1956	$21,495.00
Received from January 15th through May 31, 1956	5,100.00
Percentage of annual budget received to date	23.6
Balance needed for the year	16,395.00

E. C. Scott, Treasurer

Pastor's Workshop on Alcoholism

A workshop designed to aid parish ministers in understanding and helping the alcoholic will be held at Emory University, July 9-11. Jointly sponsored by the Candler School of Theology, the School of Medicine of Emory University, Columbia Theological Seminary, and the Georgia Commission on Alcoholism, the program will outline how the combined therapies of religion and medicine are providing heartening success in rehabilitating the alcoholic. Faculty members of the various schools will combine with the staff of the Georgian Clinic (state clinic for rehabilitating the alcoholic) to explain the causation and cure of alcoholism. Actual case histories will be utilized to make clear the scope and application of the principles of rehabilitation. The aim of the workshop is to provide the pastor with the insights necessary for giving constructive pastoral care to the alcoholics in his community. The number of participants is limited and pre-registration is advised. Write to WORKSHOP ON ALCOHOLISM, Georgia Commission on Alcoholism, 1260 Briarcliff Road, NE., Atlanta 6, Ga., for further information. Low cost dormitory housing and meals will be available on the Emory University campus adjacent to the classrooms where the workshop sessions will be held.

Ten Nine-Hundred-Dollar Scholarships Awarded Montreat College

This is an eventful experience in the history of Montreat College—the gift of ten scholarships of $900.00 each. $500.00 is to be awarded the selected student and $400.00 of each scholarship to cover the balance of the approximate expenses of educating one student per year.

The student winning one of the scholarships may have it renewed each year for four years . . . so that it amounts to $2,000.00.

The basis of awarding these scholarships — character . . . need . . . ability . . . high school record . . . promise of effective Christian living and service to the Church as a Church Musician, Church Secretary, or Church Worker.

We earnestly invite ministers and others to help us find the worthy young women for these splendid awards.

Write: George A. Anderson, Vice-President, Montreat College, Montreat, North Carolina.

ARKANSAS

Fort Smith — Second Presbyterian Church — The Rev. J. David Simpson, the Pastor of this Church for more than six years, resigned to take up the work as Executive Director of Tuscaloosa Presbytery, Synod of Alabama. During the Pastorate of the Rev. Mr. Simpson, the Second Church was re-located with a beautiful Gothic Cathedral style church. This church which was formerly in what is now an industrial zone of the city with little housing, was moved under the leadership of the Pastor into a new Church plant which conservative appraisal would fix between $85,000 to $100,000. A new manse was also built along with the new church in the Park Hill section of the city. The church and the manse have been cleared of all indebtedness, and the church as a whole is without debt.

The membership has been virtually doubled during the pastorate of Mr. Simpson, and the Sunday School attendance has doubled. The church faces the future in a rapidly growing section of the City of Fort Smith. The opportunity is ripe for growth in membership in this beautiful southside section of Fort Smith.

FLORIDA

Miami — Eight automatic phone-answering machines that take care of sixty calls an hour are almost constantly in use at Riviera Presbyterian Church, Miami, since that church began its Dial-A-Prayer service some time ago.

The Rev. John D. Henderson says the tremendous response to the project seems to show that people "are anxious to have contact with God." "The Minute of Prayer may teach them how to pray. It will at least be a guide to them and in their approach to God," he said.

Not long after the Dial-A- Prayer was started, calls began coming in and at the present they average about 200 calls an hour. Sometimes many callers have to wait their turn because of busy circuits, and calls come in during the night as well as day hours.

On April 10th there were 3,395 calls that these phones couldn't handle, with more than 5,000 calls coming in during that one day alone.

Riviera Church has more than 800 members and a Sunday School enrollment of 790. A new sanctuary was erected last year.

LOUISIANA

Alexandria — The Synod men's conference and convocation of ministers, elders and deacons was held at Silliman College, Clinton, La., June 1-3. Speakers included former Governor Robert Kennon, first president of the Assembly Men's Council; Walter Humphrey, Fort Worth Press editor and president of A.M.C. last year; J. E. (Chink) Dews, Forrest City, Ark., a former A.M.C. president; Dr. Louis Patrick, of St. Louis; Dr. Thomas H. Talbott, Longview, Texas; Rev. Lloyd O'Neal, of Red River Presbytery; Rev. George Ricks, regional director; Dr. Ed Grant, of Baton Rouge; Rev. Ray Riddle and Rev. W. A. Crosland, New Orleans.

The program was declared to be one of the finest the Synod Council has ever presented. Ralph Brewer, Council president and chairman of the Miami convention publicity committee, told the conference about convention plans. He introduced members of the Council.

Officers elected for 1957 were: Hal Baird, New Orleans, president; B. B. Romine, Shreveport, vice president; Reed Gardner, Baton Rouge, treasurer; H. T. Sheppard, New Orleans, secretary.

Next year's conference will be held at Silliman May 25 and 26.

MISSISSIPPI

Belhaven College — Recent Commencement exercises at Belhaven College in Jackson, Mississippi saw the beginning of a new era in the history of the College as two features in the Graduation Program made their appearance for the first time.

Among the candidates for baccalaureate degrees were two men, the first to complete their work at Belhaven since the college became co-educational. These young men were John Campbell and George Elliott, both of Jackson, Mississippi. Mr. Elliott's degree was awarded in absentia inasmuch as he is now serving with the U. S. Marines.

The other new milestone in Belhaven's history consisted of awarding of honorary degrees for the first time. While the charter of the College has long given Belhaven the authority to confer honorary degrees, this is the first year in its history that it has actually done so. Appropriately, the first honorary degree to be conferred was that of Doctor of Letters upon Dr. Guy T. Gillespie, for many years a leading citizen, churchman, and educator of the State of Mississippi. For thirty-three years Dr. Gillespie served as President of Belhaven, he being now the President Emeritus of the College.

The degree of Doctor of Divinity was conferred upon the Rev. J. Wayte Fulton, pastor of the Shenandoah Church of Miami, Florida, upon the Rev. Thomas Russell Nunan, Pastor of the First Presbyterian Church of Greenville, Mississippi, and upon the Rev. Van Arnold, Pastor of the First Presbyterian Church of Greenwood, Mississippi.

Baccalaureate degrees were conferred upon the graduating class of twenty-eight in the Commencement Exercises in which an address by Dr. Roland Sims was the subject, "The Hand Behind the Headlines," was delivered. The baccalaureate sermon was delivered in the First Presbyterian Church of Jackson by the Rev. J. Wayte Fulton of Miami.

VIRGINIA

Bristol — Dr. Irby D. Terrell, Pastor of the McIver Memorial Church in Bristol, Virginia, passed away June 9, in Atlanta, Georgia. Dr. Terrell served as Assistant Director of the Massanetta Bible Conference for a number of years. He is survived by his wife, one daughter and three sons.

Richmond — On June 18 Rev. Robert P. Davis will become the first Director of Camping and Conference Program for the Board of Christian Education of the Presbyterian Church, U. S.

Announcement of his acceptance of the post was made by Dr. John L. Fairly, secretary of Religious Education for the board, at its Richmond headquarters.

The new director, now pastor of First Presbyterian Church, Virginia Beach, Va., has nineteen years of conference experience in two major Presbyterian denominations.

For fourteen years he has served in young people's conferences at Massanetta Springs, Va., and for seven years has been director of the Jamestown Young People's Conference for Norfolk Presbytery.

Ordained in New Castle Presbytery of the Presbyterian Church, U. S. A., he served as pastor of Makemie Memorial Presbyterian Church at Snow Hill, Md., and then at Towson Presbyterian Church in Baltimore before accepting the call to his present pastorate in 1945.

A graduate of Davidson College, he received the B. D. and Th. M. from Union Theological Seminary in Richmond.

Mrs. Davis is the former Lila Ross Norfleet of Winston-Salem, N. C. They have two daughters, Lila Ross and Rebecca Cooper.

Hampden-Sydney — Honorary doctor of divinity degrees were conferred on the Rev. Charles H. Gibboney, of Atlanta, Ga., and the Rev. Paul W. Hodge, of Danville, Va., during Hampden-Sydney College's 180th commencement June 4.

President Joseph C. Robert also conferred the honorary doctor of laws degree on Harold Holmes Helm, New York banker and member of the Board of Foreign Missions, Presbyterian Church, U.S.A. He is an elder in the church at Montclair, N. J.

Rev. Mr. Gibboney is secretary of promotion of the Board of Church Extension, Presbyterian Church, U. S. He served pastorates at Norfolk, Va., and in West Virginia before taking the post at Atlanta. Rev. Mr. Hodge is pastor of Shelton Memorial Presbyterian Church at Danville.

Both degree recipients are graduates of Union Theological Seminary at Richmond, Va.

Rev. Dr. Kelsey Regen, pastor of First Presbyterian Church at Durham, N. C., preached the baccalaureate sermon to the college Class of 1956 at a morning service in College Church on the campus June 3. Dr. Ben R. Lacy, Jr., pastor and college chaplain, conducted the service.

— BOOKS —

"THE BIBLE IN STORY AND PICTURES." (2 volumes) Arranged by Harold Begbie. H. S. Stettman Co. $5.95.

The new pictorial edition of the Children's Story Bible by Harold Begbie is intended to help people understand the timeless truths of the Word of God. The Bible is more than ancient history. It has a message for our own day. Stories such as those which Begbie has selected illustrate the moral and spiritual principles which need to be learned anew in every age. The creation of the world and the origin of life as an act of God, Adam and Eve's unhappiness because they refused to obey God, Job's patience in affliction and sorrow, the forgiving love of Joseph for the brothers who tried to kill him and his concern for his aged father, David's repenting of his sin, the courage of the prophets in declaring unwelcomed truth—such stories strengthen and enrich the lives of those who read them.

The basic facts in the life of Christ are told by Begbie in simple sincerity. Many of the great passages from the Gospels are quoted directly from the King James Version of the Bible. Delightful character sketches are given of the twelve apostles.

The pictures in this book constitute an attractive feature. It is significant that Christ never lost an opportunity to get people to use their eyes. The full color art reproductions, photographs, and drawings in this book show the settings and backgrounds of Biblical events and make it easier to understand the words which God is speaking through the Bible. Boys and girls gladly listen to a story but remember it longer when it is accompanied by pictures which help to create a greater sense of reality. These two volumes will help young people to understand the Bible more clearly and follow it more closely.

"THE DECLINE OF THE AMERICAN REPUBLIC." John T. Flynn. Devin-Adair Co. $3.00.

For twenty-five years the author has watched the course of events in America with growing apprehension. He points out that during a century and a half, despite endless differences about policy at any given time, certain definite principles of organized life were accepted by practically our whole population. These principles involve a collection of moral, social and political concepts. No matter how leaders and groups might differ, there was no important repudiation of the great fundamental concepts themselves. Since the depression, he believes a new generation has been offered a wholly new society and its views of society corresponds with the Fabian philosophy of the British Socialists. The promise of the Fabian philosophy is a new and better world. "The Good Society" that will assure to all mankind the essentials of the "Good Life" along with leisure and a new kind of freedom—freedom from want. The author believes that the Fabian philosophy of the British Socialists is a very perilous phenomenon in America and because of its inherent dangers this volume defends the system of free enterprise. The author believes it to be the only system in which man can live in freedom. He affirms that this freedom can survive only if it is managed within the framework of the social order and a government dedicated to preserving it. He recognizes the defects in the free enterprise system, but he also recognizes the beneficial energies in it and that it insures freedom to all.

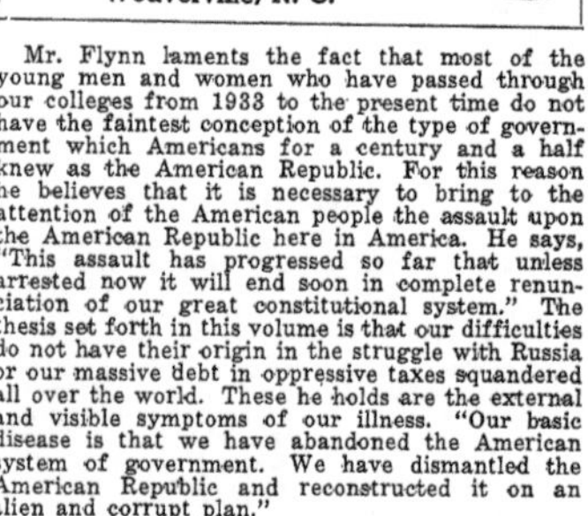

Mr. Flynn laments the fact that most of the young men and women who have passed through our colleges from 1933 to the present time do not have the faintest conception of the type of government which Americans for a century and a half knew as the American Republic. For this reason he believes that it is necessary to bring to the attention of the American people the assault upon the American Republic here in America. He says, "This assault has progressed so far that unless arrested now it will end soon in complete renunciation of our great constitutional system." The thesis set forth in this volume is that our difficulties do not have their origin in the struggle with Russia or our massive debt in oppressive taxes squandered all over the world. These he holds are the external and visible symptoms of our illness. "Our basic disease is that we have abandoned the American system of government. We have dismantled the American Republic and reconstructed it on an alien and corrupt plan."

The positive aspect of the book is found in chapter 17. Here the author explains "How to Build the Republic." One of the first essentials, he maintains, for the restoration of our country is to return the federal Constitution to its historic limits as construed by the Supreme Court for 145 years. Then, he holds that there should be a complete repudiation of the United Nations and the removal of that organization from this hemisphere. He further advocates the repeal of the Sixteenth Amendment. He believes that this amendment has brought many abuses and much distress to our country. He comes out strongly in favor of the Bricker Amendment and feels that it would help to safeguard our Republic.

All readers would not agree with Mr. Flynn or with his views but here is a voice that needs to be heard and it is stimulating. Even though some may sneer at what is called "the American way of life," it has values that must be preserved and

Mr. Flynn points out the dangers of losing them and what we must do to retain them. J.R.R.

"THE MINISTER'S COMPLETE GUIDE TO SUCCESSFUL RETIREMENT." Norman B. Lobsenc. Channel Press.

Here is advice on the financial, emotional, physical, geographical and spiritual aspects of the minister's retirement. It aims to show how the minister can get the most out of his later years. The author believes that despite the great strides mankind has taken in making life healthier and happier for older persons, the pitfalls of the retirement years are still many. This book will assist the minister in making necessary adjustments to retirement. The counsel given here will enable the minister to look ahead to retirement as a period for new achievements and a new kind of happiness and to rise above the perils of a mere retirement status.

"THE ACTS OF THE APOSTLES." David Thomas. Baker Book House. $3.95.

David Thomas was a 19th century preacher. He was for many years editor of the "Homolist." He is well known for his expository commentaries. He has given us here an unusually complete and satisfying commentary on the Acts of the Apostles. It is a systematic work of the entire book of Acts treating every passage with careful analysis and enlightening comment with pertinent application.

"SWEETER THAN HONEY." V. R. Edman. Scripture Press. $1.50.

This little book is one of personal devotion to the Saviour, with poems from John Oxenham's "Bees in Amber," and meditations from Bible references to honey. The author tells us "Honey is indeed sweet to the tongue but the Bible is sweeter to the heart of man, because the heart is capable of deeper delights and finer sensibilities than is the tongue. .. . Sweetness is the last word in excellence for personality and character as it is for food, and the same is true for the Bible. It is the honey of God to the human spirit."

"STAND FAST." John J. Arnold. Society for Reformed Publications. $.35.

This booklet is written by a successful Army chaplain. It discusses various phases of the Army life and relates it to the Christian life.

"GOD'S COMFORT FOR SICK FOLKS." William W. Orr. Scripture Press. $.25.

This booklet shows that God has good news for sick people. It also shows what a perfectly marvelous book the Bible is. The Christian who is sick will find inexhaustible treasures for the needs of the human heart.

"PROGRAMS FOR THE JUNIOR HIGH FELLOWSHIP, NUMBER SIX." Tom Smith. Warner Press. $.75.

Twenty programs are presented here for junior high age. The programs are suggestive and should be appraised by the adult advisor before given before the group.

"UNITED NATIONS." V. Orville Watts. Devin-Adair Co. $3.00.

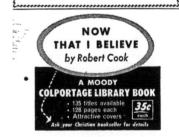

Dr. Watts argues in this volume that the United Nations organization as presently constituted is a step away from freedom and not towards it. He also affirms that it is actually a blueprint for world tyranny. Each chapter in this volume contains valuable information. One of the most illuminating is chapter four called "Behind the Scenes." Dr. Watts states, "Anyone who knows about the U. N. only what he reads in newspaper headlines is likely to think that it is mainly a place for American and Soviet delegates to exchange insults. The fact is that the speeches of delegates in the General Assembly are no more important in the total work of the U. N. than a steam whistle in the work of a factory. The U. N. is a big and busy organization. Even the General Assembly gets things done, but the 'town meeting of the world' is not the place where the Assembly does most of its work and its tub-thumping is one of the least important of all U. N. activities."

It might be surprising to the reader to learn that most governments employ Communists in their work in the U. N. Dr. Watts writes, "The Socialist Government of France, for example, is heavily infiltrated by Communists. The Constitution of their country bars discrimination against Communists in government jobs and the administration does not try to make security checks of its employees. It employs a known Communist to head its research on atomic energy and recently made him advisor to the European Center of Nuclear Research. Therefore, we should expect many of the French Court of Officials and the U. N. Secretary to be Communists . . . Communists of all nations find U. N. posts particularly attractive for two reasons. First, they can cooperate wholeheartedly in U. N. efforts to build a World Welfare State. Second, U. N. employees including Communists have special opportunities for foreign travel and communication even for foreign trade. This is partly because the U. N. subsidizes the international activities of its agents."

The author is the son of a North Dakota minister, a Harvard Ph. D. in Economics and History. He is a former college professor, and now serves as an economic consultant.

"GREAT NEGLECTED BIBLE PROPHECIES." Merrill F. Unger. Scripture Press. $2.50.

Holding that much of the Bible is predictive, the author says that some of these predictions have become history but there are also large segments of the prophetic Word which still remain unfulfilled. He says that there are certain aspects of unfulfilled prediction that have been commonly bypassed by students of Bible prophecy, and these neglected themes are discussed in this volume.

"THE RELIGION OF NEGRO PROTESTANTS." Ruby F. Johnston. Philosophical Library. $3.00.

This is a book of objective presentation of religious beliefs and actions of church men today. With detachment the author analyzes the Protestant religions in terms of types of religious men in the church and relates these types in the general system of action. The analysis is based upon extensive observations and investigations of the religious objectives and experiences of Protestants in rural and urban areas. It concretely presents factors in the changing process of religious action and relates the extent of change with the socio-economic status and the social environment.

PATHS OF SHINING LIGHT. Vera Idol. Abingdon Press. $2.50.

Each chapter of these meditations opens with appropriate Scripture quotations in a beautiful full-page photograph illustrating the subject that adds meaning to the meditation. In every one there is guidance for better living and inspiration for deeper appreciation of the great works of God's hand. The author is professor of English at High Point College.

"CHILDREN'S SERMONS, OUTLINES AND ILLUSTRATIONS." James Stalker, Richard Newton, and others. Baker Book House. $1.75.

This book has been prepared as an aid to those who are called upon to speak and preach to children. The messages come from preachers who understand children and are able to hold their interest. The volume presents an excellent variety. There are long and short messages complete in brief outline as well as story-illustrations of varying lengths and for varying purposes. Anyone called upon to present a religious message to children will treasure this book for its Scriptural messages.

THE CROWN. Robert F. Truesdell. Christopher Publishing House. $4.00.

The title of this religious novel refers to the crown of thorns worn by Christ at the time of His trial and crucifixion and the marked effects of the people who came in contact with it. The setting is in the First Century, A. D., shortly after the death of Christ. The story begins with the visit of the Apostle Paul to Athens on his second missionary journey. The book is divided into five parts with each action-filled part dealing with the experiences of the characters in one of the cities which they visited while devoting their lives to this career.

Any Three of the Books Listed Below Sent Postpaid for $5.00

SUPPLY LIMITED — ORDER NOW

The Basis of Millennial Faith $2.00
By Floyd E. Hamilton

Why 1000 Years? $2.50
By Wm. Masselink

Crucial Questions About The Kingdom of God $3.00
By George E. Ladd

John Calvin: Expository Preacher $2.50
By Leroy Nixon

The Trial of Jesus Christ $2.00
By Frank J. Powell

Supreme Authority $2.00
By Norvel Geldenhuys

The Gospel of The Spirit $1.50
By Samuel Eyles Pierce

Studies in Theology $3.50
By Loraine Boettner

The Reformed Doctrine of Justification $3.00
By Boehl

The Reformed Doctrine of Adoption $2.50
By R. A. Webb

The Faith of Christendom $3.00
By Vander Meulen

Christianity and Liberalism $2.50
By J. Gresham Machen

The Presbyterian Conflict $1.50
By Edwin H Rian

What Presbyterians Believe $2.00
By Gordon H. Clark

The Impact of Christianity on the Non-Christian World $2.50
By Dr. J. H. Bavinck

Pilgrims Progress $1.00
By John Bunyan

The March of Truth $2.50
By Dr. Stephen Szabo

The Called of God $3.95
By A. B. Davidson

Twenty Missionary Stories From India $1.50
By Basil Miller

The Reformed Doctrine of Predestination $4.50
By Loraine Boettner

Christianity Rightly So Called $2.00
By Samuel G. Craig

Who Say Ye That I Am $2.50
By Wm. Childs Robinson

Christ the Bread of Life $2.50
By Wm. Childs Robinson

Christ—The Hope of Glory $3.00
By Wm. Childs Robinson

Knowing The Scriptures $3.95
By A. T. Pierson

Lord of Glory $3.50
By B. B. Warfield

The Plan of Salvation $1.50
By B. B. Warfield

Progress of Doctrine $1.75
By Thomas Dehany Bernard

Does God Answer Prayer $1.50
By Louise Harrison McCraw

God Transcendent and Other Sermons $2.50
By Gresham Machen

Christianity and Existentialism $3.00
By J. M. Spier

The Lord From Heaven $1.50
By Sir Robert Anderson

The Doctrines of Grace $3.95
By George S. Bishop

The Infallibility of the Church $3.00
By George D. Salmon

Successful Church Publicity $1.00
By Carl F. H. Henry

The Covenant Idea in New England Theology $2.50
By Dr. Peter Y. DeJong

The Servant of Jehovah $2.95
By David Baron

Opening Doors $1.50
By R. G. McLees, D.D.

Edward O. Guerrant $1.00
By J. Gray McAllister and Grace Owings Guerrant

Manual of Reformed Doctrine $2.50
By Prof. W. Heyns

Israel and the New Covenant $3.75
By Roger Campbell

Order From

THE SOUTHERN PRESBYTERIAN JOURNAL

Weaverville, North Carolina

Our Presbyterian Heritage

Last year the Southern Presbyterian Journal sponsored a symposium on the Reformed Faith. Addresses were made by a group of outstanding Presbyterians and all who attended gave enthusiastic response.

Without in any measure competing with any other program in our church a similar symposium will be held this year, again placing its emphasis on our Presbyterian heritage.

THE TIME—August 15th — 10:00 A. M.

THE PLACE—Weaverville, N. C.

DR. C. GREGG SINGER—*"The Reformed Faith and the Contemporary Crisis in Education"*

DR. GORDON H. CLARK — *"The Reformed Doctrine of Verbal Inspiration of the Scriptures."*

DR. FLOYD HAMILTON — *"The Reformed Doctrine of Infant Baptism"*

DR. AIKEN TAYLOR — *"The Reformed Doctrine of the Means of Grace"*

DR. W. C. ROBINSON — *"The Reformed Doctrine of the Bodily Resurrection of Christ"*

DR. R. F. GRIBBLE — *"The Reformed Faith as Related to the Virgin Birth Foretold in Isaiah 7:14"*

MR. GEORGE BURNHAM—*"To the Far Corners"*

Make Plans Now To Attend This Meeting

THE SOUTHERN PRESBYTERIAN JOURNAL

Weaverville, N. C.

THE SOUTHERN PRESBYTERIAN JOURNAL

A Presbyterian weekly magazine devoted to the statement, defense and propagation of the Gospel, the faith which was once for all delivered unto the saints.

JULY 4, 1956

VOL. XV NO. 10

$2.50 A YEAR

THE SOUTHERN PRESBYTERIAN JOURNAL
The Journal has no official connection with the Presbyterian Church in the United States
Rev. Henry B. Dendy, D.D., Editor........Weaverville, N. C.
Dr. L. Nelson Bell, Associate Editor........Asheville, N. C.
Rev. Wade C. Smith, Associate Editor........Weaverville, N. C.

EDITORIAL

Beyond Reason — Revelation

That which man could not do for himself God did for him. That which man could not know God revealed to him. In insisting on the vital importance of revelation we are stressing a point which is being minimized today, and a point on which so much hinges.

God has given us minds with which to reason. He has given to mankind the ability to search out truth. He has endowed him with the intellectual capability of experimentation until in our time amazing new discoveries are being made, discoveries which can lead to the transformation (or destruction) of life on this earth.

In all of these discoveries it should ever be kept in mind that man is only finding out what God has already locked up in the wonders of His universe. Man has not created one single atom, nor has he done more than to discover keys which unlock doors leading to the hidden marvels of the Creator.

The Psalmist proclaimed the visible evidences of this Power when he said: *"The heavens declare the glory of God; and the firmament sheweth his handiwork. Day unto day uttereth speech, and night unto night sheweth knowledge. There is no speech nor language, where their voice is not heard."*

Paul, writing to the Roman Christians, makes the same point: *"For the invisible things of him from the creation of the world are clearly seen, being understood by the things that are made, even his eternal power and Godhead; so that they are without excuse."*

In other words, by *reason* man can and should come to a speculative knowledge of God and of His marvelous power. But man needs to know more than this about God; he needs to know of His love and mercy, of His redemptive work and of the One Who makes it possible for sinners to stand in His holy presence.

It is by *revelation* that we learn these things. From beginning to end the Scriptures tell us that God has given us such a revelation. Moses, we are told, *"called for the elders of the people, and laid before their faces all these words which the Lord commanded him."* On down through the Bible we find God speaking to men through His prophets, telling them truths they could never have discovered for themselves. Paul, in defending his preaching of the Gospel, says to the Galatian Christians: *"For I neither received it of man, neither was I taught it, but by the revelation of Jesus Christ."*

What is the basic difference between reason and revelation? If our powers of reasoning come from God why are they not on a par with revelation which is also from God? Perhaps the best way to answer this is to say that reason is a human endowment, varying with each individual, and therefore fallible, while revelation is a matter of divine inspiration and is infallible.

Let us illustrate: One sees an apple by the side of the road. *Reason* says: "There is an apple; somewhere there is an apple tree and it may be close at hand." But, *revelation* goes much deeper than this; it tells us where the tree came from and how it propagates its fruit: *"In the beginning God created the heaven and the earth. . . . And God said . . . let the earth bring forth . . . and the earth brought forth . . . and the tree yielding fruit, after his kind, whose seed is within itself, after his kind."*

Or another illustration: One takes up his morning newspaper and reads of war, murder, thefts, rape, sickness, suffering, death, and *reason* immediately says: "There is something radically wrong with the world and those who live in the world." Again *revelation* goes much deeper, right to the root of the matter, not only telling the cause but also the cure: *"Nevertheless, death reigned—from Adam to Moses . . . and the wages of sin is death, but the gift of God is eternal life through Jesus Christ our Lord."*

It is difficult for man to understand or accept revelation for it runs counter to the normal human processes. In fact, unregenerate man cannot accept revelation for it is a foolish concept. Paul, writing to the Corinthian Christians says: *"But the natural man receiveth not the things of the Spirit of God; for they are foolishness unto him: neither can he know them, because they are spiritually discerned."*

It is obvious that reason and revelation must be combined if we are to have the wisdom God wishes for His children, and *faith* steps in to bridge the gap. For man to live in an intellectual vacuum is folly, for there is so much to know. For man to attempt to live in the realm of reason alone is also folly. *"The fear of the Lord is the beginning of wisdom,"* is a scientific fact ignored by too many in this world.

All of which leads to this conclusion: without God's revealed truth, found in His Word, personified in His Son and made effective daily by His Holy Spirit, our lives are incomplete and ineffective. Man needs and must have *more* than reason.

"For after that in the wisdom of God the world by wisdom knew not God, it pleased God by the foolishness of preaching (Christ crucified), *to save them that believe."*

Beyond reason - revelation. L.N.B.

Degenerate Music

The writer has recently driven over four thousand miles, from the Atlantic to the Rockies. With a car equipped with a radio with automatic station finder we sampled the music of scores of radio stations over a period of ten days.

We love music and enjoy a variety ranging from some of the catchy tunes of today to the classical productions which have stood the test of time.

With all of the wonderful music available for use on radio stations today we express it as our considered opinion that the *majority* of the musical programs heard over the *average* radio station in America today is a disgrace, both to the stations which broadcast it and to Americans who enjoy it, or at least tolerate it.

Much of this so-called music is *dishonest,* in that it is lacking in every quality which makes music a joy and a blessing. Much of it is *degenerate* in that it is designed to excite and amplify the lowest passions. It is not accidental that police are guarding, and in some cases, closing down public halls where the latest rock 'n' roll is played. There is a strange similarity of reaction recently in Washington, D. C., and Accra, on the Gold Coast in Africa when "hot" music was being played. Only stern police action prevented spontaneous rioting in both places.

Allowing for the passing fads, so characteristic of Americans in particular, and for the exuberance of youth which expresses itself one way today and another tomorrow, the fact remains that a candid analysis of popular American music will reveal that as music it is extremely poor; that the words are often moronic; that the orchestras play with a frenzy and a disregard for quality; the result being a sorry and disturbing cacaphony of sound and words which are disgusting.

Fortunately, one usually is in a position to turn off one's radio, or tune in another station. But, unfortunately if the latter is done there is usually little relief to be had either down or up the band.

We do not believe this is a minor problem. To dismiss the radio from our way of life does not solve the problem. To forbid its use to our children could be most unwise. But, as individuals, as groups, as organizations we could well notify our local radio stations that we are sick and tired of the music being broadcast much of the day. We can also compliment them on good programs. All of us have experienced the sense of relief and of real satisfaction when a blaring jazz program shifts to Guy Lombardo, Fred Waring or a time of classical music.

One wonders why some of the sponsors of programs do not set up certain standards for the music they use and tell their hearers why they have done so? Why do not more local business houses sponsor fifteen minutes of wholesome modern or classical music? Why does not some firm announce: "The next fifteen minutes of music, fit for you and your children to hear, comes to you through the courtesy of ——————"!

Does not a nation's music reflect something of the spiritual and moral standards of its people? If such is the case in America today then we have come near plumbing the depths in depravity. That modern American music is so popular abroad brings little comfort; rather it must establish in the minds of those living in

The Southern Presbyterian Journal, *a Presbyterian Weekly magazine devoted to the statement, defense, and propagation of the Gospel, the faith which was once for all delivered unto the saints,* published every Wednesday by The Southern Presbyterian Journal, Inc., in Weaverville, N. C.

Entered as second-class matter May 15, 1942, at the Postoffice at Weaverville, N. C., under the Act of March 3, 1879. Vol. XV, No. 10, July 4, 1956. Editorial and Business Offices: Weaverville, N. C. Printed in the U.S.A. by Biltmore Press, Asheville, N. C.

ADDRESS CHANGE: When changing address, please let us have both old and new address as far in advance as possible. Allow three weeks after change if not sent in advance. When possible, send an address label giving your old address.

others countries that our musical standards are of the lowest.

It is not that we do not have cute, tuneful and attractive current music. The trouble is that along with so much which is wholesome and enjoyable there is a plethora of jazz, blues and rock 'n' roll which crowds out the good music. The comparison is much of that to be found between genuine art and the bizarre and nightmarish blobs and blotches of surrealistic paintings.

Christians have remained quiet far too long in the face of that which is taking place today. The radio is here to stay but radio musical programs need a thorough revamping and if enough people are concerned and vocal about the matter a change can soon be effected.

L.N.B.

Wanted: Good Samaritans

From the ashes of Secession and Reconstruction, Henry W. Grady caught a vision of a new South with "her two races walking together in peace and contentment." He did not envision the two being amalgamated into one, but he did see both walking together in peace and contentment.

Recently I read a volume discussing missionary work in a multi-racial situation, in which there is considerable difference of opinion on race relations. But the best article in the collection is one in which a Christian editor says, in effect: Let us not get so concerned about race relations that we forget the Christian admonition to do good to all men, especially to those who are of the household of faith. The best way to lessen tensions is to find individual occasions to do justice and show kindness to those who are of another race.

And is not that what our Lord taught us in the parable of the Good Samaritan? What has kept our two races walking together in such peace and contentment as we have enjoyed is Good Samaritanism. It is cases in which Negroes have played the Good Samaritan to white neighbors, and in which white persons have acted as Good Samaritans to Negroes. May their tribe increase!

Moreover, one wonders whether the wisecrack about accepting the Negro as a brother but not as a brother-in-law has not been used with the emphasis on the negative part of the statement. In Christ Jesus we are brothers with all those who believe in Him. At the General Assembly and at the Synods we sit at the Lord's Table together. To the celebration of the Communion at the Seminary all those on the Campus, including the families and all who work there, are invited, and generally come. W.C.R.

The Gracious God and the Ungracious Preacher

This was the theme of the sermon delivered last Sunday in the Chapel of St. Leger to the Presbyterian Congregation of Geneva by the Reverend A. G. MacAlpine, Jr., of Tain, Ross-shire, Scotland. Dr. MacAlpine read most of the book of Jonah, and the New Testament comment theron in Matthew. The old Chapel which was used by the Crusaders was filled to capacity and mightily sang the paraphrases and hymns selected from the Church Hymnary with Mrs. Robert Clark, formerly of Signal Mountain, Chattanooga, at the organ. Here is a line from one of those hymns sung:

No earthly Father loves like Thee
No Mother e'er so mild
Bears and forebears as Thou hast done
With me Thy sinful child.

The text for the message was Jonah 4.2, "For I knew that thou art a gracious God and merciful, slow to anger and abundant in lovingkindness, and repentest (relentest) thee of the evil."

The preacher showed that one's primary business with Jonah was not with the difficulty of the story, either rationalizing or defending it (though his sympathies were plainly with those who hold its historicity). As God's Word, Jonah brings us face to face with the living God and He deals with us. In this book we have the fleeing man and the pursuing God, cf. Psalm 139 and the Hound of Heaven. More than that, we have here the ungracious man, even the ungracious preacher, and the Gracious God. God revealed His graciousness to Moses in promise; and to us, in fulfillment of the promise, Grace and truth came by Jesus Christ.

After the service of worship we visited the Calvin Auditorium beside the Cathedral of Saint-Pierre. Here John Calvin delivered his lectures and here John Knox preached to the English refugees. We visited this historic spot, that is, we visited it as much as we could. The building is being restored by the Pan-Presbyterian alliance to be a center of World Presbyterianism and to provide more adequate quarters for the worship of those English speaking Presbyterians who live in and who visit Geneva.

This fall, the Scottish Church will send a full time minister to this congregation, and already the little Chapel of St. Leger is crowded to capacity. It was a pleasure to learn that our Presbyterian Church in the United States has pledged toward this important enterprise and that part of our pledge has been paid. There are today more than 7,000 Americans in Geneva and many more of these would worship at the Presbyterian service were there room.

Then it was, as always, an experience to stand in Calvin's Cathedral of St. Pierre. The high pulpit he used is to one side in the transept with seats facing it on four sides. Below it is the modest table where the small communion is held monthly. When I worshipped there at Pentecost some years ago we took communion at one of the five yearly large communion seasons. In doing that, we formed two lines and walked up to the table in the Choir or Chancel. Four at a time we faced the Table and received the bread from one and the cup from another minister. When I took communion here in Basel at Pauluskirche this Pentecost, the Pastor administered the bread, while two elders, one on either side of him, gave us the cup, the ministers of the elements being behind and the communicants before the Table of the Lord.

W.C.R.

Of Women As Ministers And Church Officers

By Rev. Harold H. Leach

God is witness that His Word is full, a complete guide to His people for faith and service, so that "the man of God may be complete, furnished completely unto every good work" (2 Tim. 3:17 ARV), God would have His people do for Him, in His name. The Greek for "man" (anthropos) all persons, men and women. Jude spoke of revelation as complete: "the faith that was *once for all* delivered to the saints"—finished, ended, no more to follow; same word applied to Christ's sacrifice: "Christ also hath *once* suffered for sins" as He cried on the cross: "It is finished." Because His revelation is complete, full, finished, God warns at the end: "If any man shall add unto them, God shall add unto (Gk., *upon*) him the plagues that are written in this book . . . " (Rev. 22:18).

As to electing or ordaining women to any office in the church, minister, elder or deaconess, there is a *total absence of any instruction for such in the Bible;* while there is full and detailed and repeated instruction for "laying hands on" *men* for these offices.

"Whatsoever is not of faith is sin" (Ro. 14:23b). "So belief cometh of hearing, and *hearing by the word of Christ"* (Ro. 10:17 ARV). Put together we have: Whatsoever is not of faith (that rests on the Word of God) is sin. Election of a woman to office of ministry, elder or deaconess, is without faith that rests on the Word of God; such election is therefore sin.

"Without faith (that rests on the Word of God) it is impossible to be well-pleasing unto Him" (Heb. 11:6). Woman's holding office (over men) in the church is without faith that rests on the Word of God; therefore a woman's holding office in the church is not well-pleasing unto God, though she may be good as an angel. See Prov. 30:6; Deut. 12:32; Ex. 23:2.

Salvation And Predestination

By Hugh E. Bradshaw, D.D.
Pastor
Memorial Presbyterian Church
West Monroe, Louisiana

These two words are closely related. Some might call them twins. If they are, Salvation is of more importance because of the thing it does to our nature. Yet, without Predestination, this Salvation would never be possible. The two are vitally connected. Salvation means life and immortality. Predestination is the route by which we achieve life and immortality. That we may understand Predestination a little better, let us first consider Salvation. Salvation, as God's gift of life to us, is spoken of in Ephesians 2:1-10. We were dead spiritually. God has "quickened" us. That is, He has made us alive where before we were dead. Through Christ we are to "sit together in heavenly places." But before Paul tells us of all this, he sings of this salvation in what some have chosen to call "the Hymn of God's Redeeming Grace" (Ephesians 1:3-14). In this "Hymn" we are told that we are "predestinated" unto the adoption of children and that this predestination is "according to Him who worketh all things after the counsel of His own will." May we first consider

The Nature of Salvation

We have already referred to salvation as meaning *life* and *immortality*. This has deeper significance than mere words when we think of these terms as the opposite of mortality and death. Fallen man is not merely diseased, or anemic, or atrophied spiritually; he is dead. This death involves the knowing, feeling and willing faculties. Salvation brings a new creation in the form of a new life capable of knowing, loving, choosing and obeying God as He is revealed in Christ. Read what Jesus said to

Nicodemus concerning this new birth and the Kingdom of God in John 3:1-18. No wonder Paul sang of God's redeeming Grace!

The second characteristic of salvation is that it brings *complete pardon* and forgiveness for all sin and wrong-doing. This removes the burden of guilt in all its destroying powers as it would reproduce a little hell in each breast. For guilt is relentless and drives its victims past the psychopathic ward to the insane asylum and into hell itself. And there is no penance, good works or atonement men can make for the guilt of sin. However, there is a Saviour who has paid the penalty of sin for us and thus bears away its guilt. It is a great relief to know one is fully pardoned. It is a great thing, they say, to stand pardoned before a human bar of justice. It is an infinitely greater thing to stand before the bar of God's infinite justice as fully pardoned and forgiven. "There is therefore now no condemnation to them which are in Christ Jesus who walk, not after the flesh, but after the Spirit." When you realize the full meaning of God's pardoning grace as told in Romans 8:1 ff, you, too, will sing with Paul and the great host of redeemed saints, this song of God's Redeeming Grace!

A third thing to be said about salvation is that it *"clothes" us with a goodness* that is not our own. For God takes the righteousness of Christ from His back, so to speak, and clothes us with it. But do not be afraid that Christ will be impoverished. He has a cloak of righteousness for every son of Adam who has the faith to reach out his hand and accept this "beautiful garment." We may be, and are, basically, as guilty before God as ever; but, having accepted the righteousness of Christ by faith in Him as Saviour, His glorious robe of righteousness hides our "filthy rags." Surely Paul must sing! For he and all who, like him, accept this salvation are the best dressed creatures in creation.

Salvation, in the fourth place, involves *growth into the likeness of Christ.* We sometimes say that a son is the "spit image" of his father. A Christian man or woman will grow into the "spit image" of God, his Father in Heaven. It may and does take a long time to do it; but it will surely be done. It has to be that way; because we who wear the "righteousness of Chirst" cannot go on being hypocrites forever. That cloak of righteousness we wear looks like we belong to the family of God with Christ as our Elder Brother. And so we do; but our hearts and lives have not been made to conform to the outward appearances. So, by the help of God's Holy Spirit, the old man of sin is made to die and the new man is made to live more and more in keeping with the law of righteousness of Christ. In other words, the inner life is made to conform more and more to the holiness and goodness of that "garment" of Christ's righteousness we wear. This is a process or work of God's Holy Spirit called Sanctification—a very necessary part of salvation. At last, when this work is finished in eternity, the inner life has been made completely perfect as Christ is perfect. This comes about because Christ takes over every faculty of His obedient believers and so enables them to live as they can say with Paul, "I live, yet not I but Christ liveth in me . . . " You do not see how Paul could keep from singing, do you?

One more observation needs to be made concerning the end or purpose of salvation. *Its purpose is that of glory.* Many passages tell us this—such as that one telling us that believers go from "glory to glory"; the command to be perfect as God is perfect; the statement concerning Christ's resurrection glory as revealing Him as the "first fruits" of those who are in Him; and the assurance that believers are partakers of the glory that shall be revealed in Christ. This glory will not be a glory of uniformity. Each believer's individuality will be preserved, transformed, perfected; and in his own way he shall interpret divine glory for the admiring gaze of angels and the universe. God's glory, then, as it is imparted to His children, will be as the beautiful glory of the rainbow rather than the dazzling glory of the sun. This is the end, the goal—in a word more expressive, the destiny of salvation. This is why Paul sang his song of God's redeeming grace. Read it in Ephesians 1:3-14 and you, too, will sing.

So you see salvation is a glorious thing. The half of it has not been told nor could be in such a brief sketch. Even the brilliantly inspired mind of Paul could only say " . . . Eye hath not seen, nor ear heard, neither have entered into the heart of man, the things which God hath prepared for them that love him . . . " The unspeakable gift of God to us brings unspeakable glories.

Predestination the Way to Salvation

Presdestination is God's plan for leading believers into the possession of that glorious salvation. Predestination means to purpose, plan or determine beforehand. The very word plan carries with it the idea of designing or drafting beforehand. Before a journey is made it is or should be planned. The coming of a new life into the world should be, and in most instances is, planned for. Is it strange, then, that God makes His plans and works toward the accomplishment of them beforehand? This is what Paul says has been done. God chose us in Christ "before the foundation of the world." And we are glorified, having been "predestinated according to the purpose of Him who worketh all things after the counsel of His own will." (Ephesians 1:3-14). The word "predestinate" will also be found in Romans 8:29,30. Here we are told that God purposes beforehand that believers shall be made to conform to the "image of His Son" and that, in this planning, the end will be a "glorified" person. In I Corinthians 2:7, Paul speaks of the wisdom of God as having been "ordained before the world unto our glory." God planned to reveal His wisdom to us even before He created the world!

Indeed, the fact that God planned His work of redemption before the subjects of redemption —you and I and all the saved—were born, recurs over and over in the Bible. The Bible tells us that God made His plans before the birth of Esau and Jacob to choose Jacob and make him to become a prince of God—"Israel."

This was predestination. Before Abram became the father of the faithful, and while he was living among the idolatrous peoples of Chaldea, God had His plans to call him out and make him to become what he did become, Abraham, father of the faithful. This was predestination.

Joseph's brethren committed a great crime against him and sinned against God when they sold Joseph as a slave to the Egyptians. This is plain when, years later, after they had lived with Joseph in Egypt and after Jacob had died, the brethren came to Joseph to ask that he not vent his anger and vengeance on them for this crime now that the father was dead.

Joseph readily forgave them as he recognized God's plan for their lives. He said: "As for you, ye thought evil against me; but God meant it unto good, to bring to pass, as it is this day, to save much people alive." (Genesis 50:20). The idea of predestination is in the very term "covenant-salvation." As this wonderful plan is studied throughout the Bible, we learn that God the Father entered into a covenant with Christ, who is God the Son, to assume sinful human nature by being born into the world, and to die for the sins of the whole world. Conditioned on Christ's doing this, God the father would give Him a great host of redeemed people which no man could number. In fulfillment of this covenant, Christ came to earth and died as the Lamb of God. God's predestination of this event is recorded in Acts 4:26-28 as follows. "The kings . . . and rulers were gathered together against the Lord, and against His Christ . . . Thy holy child Jesus . . . for to do whatsoever Thy hand and Thy counsel determined before to be done." Instead of thwarting God's purposes, these evil men, in their rebellion and rage against God, fulfilled the purposes of God the Father to give us a Saviour!

Predestination, then, is the plan by which God works out His purposes. These are of necessity hidden from us except so much as it pleases God to reveal to us. And even in those things revealed, the limitations of our finite minds cannot grasp the things even on the fringe of the infinite—to say nothing of those truths within the realm of the infinite itself. We should not try to penetrate the infinite. It is dangerous not only because the finite mind staggers at such infinity but because these things come under the head of God's business. And people get in trouble trying to mind the business of other persons! In Deuteronomy 29:29, we are told "The secret things belong unto the Lord our God: but those things that are revealed belong unto us and our children forever . . . " Let us tread very cautiously as we think of God's purposes and plans; for we are indeed on holy ground. But ground on which God has seen fit to give us a tantalizing glimpse of His loving purposes to save us and of His ability to carry out that purpose through His predestinating love.

Presdestination is in order to salvation. In other words, the destination is salvation; while predestination is the predetermined way of that salvation. If we keep this clearly in mind it will help greatly. God's most glorious salvation for your and my enjoyment could and would miscarry, humanly speaking, had it not been for the fact that God made plans also by which that salvation would be your real possession.

In this sense, predestination emphasizes the reality of divine grace and the unmerited favor God bestows on us. Predestination is your guarantee and mine that we shall actually possess this unspeakable gift of God in spite of all the efforts of the combined hosts of Hell!

We get into deep waters when we begin to think of predestination as a philosophic explanation of human life and destiny. This takes us into the realm of speculation and philosophic vagaries. Perhaps our thinking has been too long in this realm. Let us put this phase of predestination out of our minds altogether and think of it only as a religious truth emphasizing the reality of divine grace. In this respect, it is a guarantee that this priceless possession called Salvation shall be for those who exercise faith —the true believers. It is a guarantee from God that the process of redeeming love begun with faith shall be brought to a complete, perfect and triumphant fulfillment in a completely redeemed and glorified humanity.

When we complete our plans and work them out for a maturing flower, we enjoy its beauty, fragrance and glory. When we complete our house according to plans and specifications, we enjoy the comfort and 'glory' of our "purchased possession." Why should it seem strange that God and the angels of heaven should rejoice over one sinner that is saved? For that sinner is God's "purchased possession" and will surely be made perfect in holiness according to the redeeming love of God working in us to will and do according to His purposes for our lives. God's predestinating love which makes us "new creations in Christ Jesus" also never lets us go until we are made perfect in His likeness.

The reasonableness of predestination is shown by two illustrations. The first has to do with the gardener and his habits. The skilled hand of the gardener holds a tiny seed. His faraway look takes in the beauty of the perfect flower as he has predestinated it to unfold from that tiny seed. But there are many steps to be taken before this is to be fulfilled. The soil must be mulched, when the suitable kind of soil is found; the seed must be planted; the moisture and sunshine must be right; and there must be more mulching when the tender plant comes up. At last the beautiful flower will bloom—maybe. All elements necessary for a healthful plant must be present at the proper time and in the proper proportions. This is where the predestinating skill of the gardener comes in. He sees to these things as far as his skill and ability will permit. But even if all goes well, a wandering animal or an ignorant vandal may uproot the growing plant so that the flower will never bloom. This is because the gardener is not all-wise, nor all-powerful, nor all-knowing. But God's predestinating plans for the development of His children's lives do not miscarry because He is all-wise, all-powerful, and all-knowing.

The second illustration is that of the architect. He carefully makes his plans for a building or temple. Every detail is carefully worked out on the draftsman's table—the doors, the windows, the arches, the ceilings and floors, the foundations and the roof, the homely strength of its supports and the beauty of its spires and cupolas. Its designs must first be in the mind of the architect, then on the draftsman's table, then in the hands of a construction engineer and the skilled workmen who build by specifications.

The workmen may mar the plans because their lack of skill or unwillingness prevents the architect's plan from materializing. But not so with God. He as the Almighty God is able both to design and to "construct" our lives as temples in which His Spirit may dwell. He it is that works in and through us to do His will. He it is whose perfect work issues in the perfect man as he is in Christ Jesus. He is the Architect and the Construction Engineer for your life and mine and He will build according to specifications if we will let Him.

SABBATH SCHOOL LESSONS — REV. J. KENTON PARKER

LESSON FOR JULY 15

Jesus Christ Is The Saviour Of Men

Background Scripture: John 4:39-42; Hebrews 2:9 - 5:14
Devotional Reading: John 3:14-21

Jesus Christ is the Saviour of men. This Salvation is sufficient for all men. It is efficient for all who believe. He became the Author of eternal salvation unto all them that obey Him. The faith that saves is a living, active faith which results in obedience. The first commandment for us is to *believe* on Him Whom God has sent as the Saviour of the world.

In our Devotional Reading (John 3:14-21 we see this very plainly: "Whosoever believeth in Him should not perish, but have everlasting life"; "He that believeth on Him is not condemned; but he that believeth not is condemned already, because he hath not believed in the name of the only begotten Son of God". Nothing could be plainer than these repeated statements.

I. *The Samaritans Believe:* John 4:39-42.

To understand these verses we will have to read the entire story of Jesus' interview with the woman of Samaria. It is such a well-known story that most of us remember it. These two personal contacts in John 3 and 4 with Nicodemus and the Samaritan woman differ in many ways, but the main point is the same. Jesus told Nicodemus to "believe," if he was to have eternal life; He led the woman of Samaria to "believe" in Him so she could have the water of life. She went to the village and reported to the people. Some believed because of her testimony, and many more believed because of His own word; and said to the woman, Now we believe, not because of thy saying: for we have heard Him ourselves, and know that this indeed is the Christ, the Saviour of the world.

Salvation by grace through faith is one of the foundation stones of the Protestant Church. It was the rediscovery of this plain teaching of Scripture, and the preaching of it, that brought about the Reformation. The preaching of this "Good News" is at the basis of every real Awakening. Men have tried to cover up this precious truth and put in its place a man-made scheme of salvation by works or by character, or in some other way, but this great truth revives and comes to light again in all its glory and power. Redeeming Grace, Amazing Grace, becomes the theme of saved and rejoicing souls as they Sing of "My Redeemer" and His wondrous love to them. The greatest hymns are along this line.

Everywhere the true gospel is preached, *sinners believe,* and are saved. This was true in the days when Jesus spoke to the proud Pharisee and the woman at the well; it was true after Pentecost when they that were scattered abroad went everywhere talking the good news; it has been true in all ages of the history of the Church; it is true now. Stop right here and ask your own soul, Have I believed: am I saved?

II. *More About Believing:* Hebrews 2:9-5:14.

1. We are to believe in a Saviour Who suffered : the Author of eternal salvation had to suffer and die before He could save: Except a corn of wheat fall into the ground and die, it abideth alone : but if it die, it bringeth forth much fruit. This is made clear in these verses from Hebrews. Hebrews tells of the priestly work of Christ, and this priestly work consists of two parts, (1) to make atonement, and (2) to make intercession. He once for all perfectly atoned for our sins by His death on the cross, and is now making continual intercession for us. He tasted death for every man. He became a perfect Saviour through His suffering. It was only thus that He could destroy Him who had the power of death, even the Devil, and deliver those who through fear of death were in bondage. Jesus had told the Jews, "If the Son therefore shall make you free, ye shall be free indeed. He suffered, and therefore He can succor those who are tempted. He became our perfect High Priest, able to save all those who come unto God by Him.

2. We are to believe in a Saviour Who was faithful to the One Who appointed Him. Moses was faithful as a servant in all his house. He was the greatest man, many of us think, in the Old Testament. He was the great Law-giver and Leader who spoke with God face to face, and received from Him instructions as to the way to approach God and worship Him. Christ was more than a servant: He was the Son; the Apostle and High Priest of our confession. He was made like unto His brethren. God had promised that a Prophet should arise like unto Moses (see Acts 7:37). He was greater than Moses, just as a son is more to be honored than a servant. When we think of all that Jesus Christ went through with in the days of His humiliation, from Bethlehem to Nazareth, and then through His ministry of healing, preaching, and teaching, and then on to His death on Calvary, we can begin to see how He was fitted to be a faithful and merciful High Priest. He did always those things which pleased His Father. He came, not to do His own will, but the will of the Father. The plan of salvation was faithfully executed by the Son of God.

3. We are to believe in a Saviour who leads us into "rest." (3:7-4:13) This is illustrated by the Old Testament experience of Israel entering the land of Promise. The one thing which kept the Israelites out of the Promised Land - the "Rest" which had been promised to them - was unbelief, an unbelief which led to disobedience. We are familiar with the story. When Israel was on the border of Canaan they sent out the twelve spies. When these spies came back they gave two "reports"; the majority report, and the minority report. All the spies agreed that it was a good land. Ten of them said that the Israelites could not go up and possess it for they were too weak. The other, a minority report, by Caleb and Joshua, urged the people to go up, trusting in Jehovah. The Israelites accepted the report of the ten, and because of this unbelief and disobedience were kept out of the land until all that generation died. They could not enter in because of unbelief.

The writer of Hebrews urges us over and over again in these verses to enter into our "rest" through a greater than Joshua, even Jesus Christ Who is our Leader and Commander. The urgent word, "Today" is used frequently; "Today, if ye will hear His voice, harden not your hearts." The Holy Ghost saith, Today. Our hearts, hardened and deceived by sin, may keep us out of salvation, even as Israel's heart of unbelief kept them out of Canaan for forty years. We are to give diligence to enter into that "rest" — a rest that remains for the people of God. We are to cease from our own works and rely upon our Leader. Believe Today; accept Him NOW!

See here again the vital importance of *Believing.* It all depends upon this. There is a rest - a heavenly Canaan - but the door can be closed through unbelief. Martin Luther says, The only sin that condemns is unbelief. The only sin which shuts the door to heaven is unbelief, but this is a very common, and a very subtle sin. "Hardened through the deceitfulness of sin" is common experience. The sin of unbelief is not looked down upon like some of the grosser forms of sin. It has an air of respectability. In fact, some people seem to be proud of it. The fact remains, however, that unbelief is the worst of sins, for it makes God a liar.

Let us never fool ourselves into thinking that we can escape the searching eyes of Him with Whom we have to do. All things are naked and open to Him. Let us beware of unbelief. Let us pray the prayer of the disciples, Lord, increase our faith. Only as we rest upon Christ alone for salvation can we enter that rest.

4. *Our Great High Priest:* 4:14-5:14.

In the worship of the Old Testament the high priest was the central figure. Aaron was appointed as the first high priest. He has been called "The Best Dressed man" in the Bible. All of his beautiful garments were symbolic of his office and pointed to the Real High Priest Who should come. He needed beautiful garments to cover him, for he was but a man. Jesus needed no such covering for He was the One altogether lovely, the Perfect High Priest.

Aaron is not taken as the real type, but that strange figure, Melchizedek. (See Genesis 14:18). This priest of the Most High God, "king of righteousness," the king-priest of Salem, (Jerusalem), whose genealogy is not recorded in the Bible, met Abraham and refreshed him with bread and wine, received tithes from him and blessed him. This endless priesthood is declared to be the type of the priesthood of Christ. I wish to notice some of the features of this priesthood.

(1) Christ, our High Priest, has been appointed to this office by God, Who said, (Psalm 110:4) "Thou art a priest forever after the order of Melchizedek." So, He is "called of God." Christ as our Redeemer, is Prophet, Priest and King.

(2) He was touched with the feeling of our infirmities, and tempted in all points like as we are, yet without sin. Just as the high priest under the Mosaic Law, had to be "one of them," so Christ became a real Man so that He could save men.

(3) He suffered and died for us and became the "Author of eternal salvation" unto all them that obey Him. The Author of salvation was "made perfect through suffering." This does not mean perfect in character, for He was sinless, but perfection of experience. The offering He brought to God was a perfect atonement. (See Question 25 in Shorter Catechism). Let us not be "dull of hearing" when we read these marvelous chapters describing the Priestly work of our Blessed Redeemer!

HELP US GET NEW SUBSCRIBERS

Any Book listed on page 19 will be sent you free and postpaid as an award for one New Subscription sent us before August 1st. Earn as many books as you will send in new subscriptions.

YOUTH PROGRAM FOR JULY 15

What To Be - That Is The Question

Hymn: "Come, Thou Fount Of Every Blessing"

Prayer

Scripture: Acts 9:1-6

Hymn: "I Am Thine, O Lord, I Have Heard Thy Voice"

Offering

Hymn: "Take My Life, And Let It Be Consecrated"

LEADER'S INTRODUCTION:

The title of our program is an altered form of a famous quotation from Shakespeare's play "Hamlet.". When Prince Hamlet found himself in an exceedingly perplexing situation he said these words, "To be, or not to be—that is the question." With Hamlet it was a question of whether he should continue living or end his own life. We are certainly not raising such a morbid question as Hamlet's. We know life is worth living, but how shall we live it? That is our question.

The problem of what to do and what to be is a very important one among young people, and sometimes it can be a very perplexing one. Some of us may already know what we are going to be—what we are going to do with our lives. It is likely that others of us are still very much undecided. In this program we shall suggest some principles which we hope will be helpful as our young people try to answer the question of what to be.

We are Christian young people. We have accepted Jesus Christ as Saviour and Lord of our lives. This means we must take Him into consideration as we try to settle the problem of what to be. No decision regarding the use of our lives will ever be satisfactory, unless it takes into account the will of Christ. The most important question a young person can ask with respect to what he is to be is "What is the will of Christ for my life?" Now we shall proceed to the matter of how to discover the will of Christ.

FIRST SPEAKER:

The will of Christ is largely to be found in the Bible. It is true that the Bible does not decide for a particular individual whether he is to be a doctor or a farmer. The Bible does not tell a girl that she should enter training to be a nurse instead of a teacher. The Bible was never intended to give this particular kind of guidance, but the Bible does have something to say to us when we consider the question of what to be. The Bible makes it clear that our chief end is to glorify God and His Son Jesus Christ. Any kind of work that will prevent a person from glorifying God cannot be considered by a Christian. For instance, the Bible charges us to keep the Sabbath day holy. That is one of our ways of glorifying God. The Christian will be doing the kind of work that will enable him to keep this commandment and to glorify the Risen Christ thereby. For another example, the Bible tells us that we serve God and glorify Him as we serve our fellow men in His name. This means that a Christian will use his life in service to others for the sake of Christ. We can see from these considerations that while the Bible does not pinpoint our task in life, it certainly sets forth some principles which narrow down the field of endeavor for the Christian.

SECOND SPEAKER:

God's will is not always consistent with what we call "common sense," but most of the time it is. There are times when God calls on us to do things which seem unreasonable to us, but most of the time His will seems quite reasonable to His people. There have been occasions when God has called young men with speech impediments to become preachers, but ordinarily He calls preachers from the ranks of those who can speak fluently and who enjoy doing so. According to this we should bear in mind two things as we deal with the question "What to do!"

In the first place, we should examine very carefully our own abilities and the circumstances in which we find ourselves. God often speaks to us concerning His will through our abilities and circumstances. Our skills and talents have come from God, and He is the One who controls the circumstances of our lives. He can use these things to lead us in His will, if we will pay attention to them. In this respect the Vocational Guidance centers maintained by our church are very helpful as they enable young people to understand themselves and to measure their abilities.

The other matter which we should bear in mind in this connection is that God is not bound by the abilities He has given us and the circumstances in which He has placed us. Both Moses and Gideon were sure they were unqualified for the work to which God called them. It seemed that God had not taken into account their limitations, but He had, and He knew exactly what He was doing. We need to remember always that God may call on us to be or to do something which seems unreasonable to us, and we must be willing to follow His leading, even when we cannot understand His purposes.

THIRD SPEAKER:

Still another way God uses to make known to us His will is our own inner feelings. It is obvious that this applies only when our inner feelings are guided by the Holy Spirit. If a person who is not a Christian trusts his conscience for guidance, he may be very seriously misled. A Christian, on the other hand, is one who has surrendered his life and will to Christ. He is one who earnestly seeks to know and do the will of His Saviour. Any person who is so yielded to the Lord and who prays faithfully to know the Lord's will, can put some confidence in his inner feelings. When our inclinations fit in with the principles of the Bible and with our abilities and circumstances, we can be quite confident that God is making His will known to us.

FOURTH SPEAKER:

In this question of "What to be" we have been thinking mainly about our chief callings. The main stream of our time and talents should be directed into one channel, and we want to know first of all which channel God has chosen for us. This is our vocation. There is also a thing called avocation. It is a secondary calling or occupation, and all of us will have one or more in addition to the primary vocation. Sometimes we call them hobbies, but whatever we call them, we must let God have His way in the ones we choose to follow. Some of the richest service to God is rendered through avocations.

Some types of work are less suited to the service of God than others. A research chemist may not have many opportunities in his work to speak to people about Christ because his contacts are so limited. He could overcome that limitation if he should choose as an avocation to lead a Boy Scout troup or some other such service. If we let God call us into our avocations as well as into our vocations, we can be sure of rendering acceptable service to Him. As we discovered last week, the way of service is the way of success.

Helps To Understanding Scripture Readings in *Day by Day*

By C. C. Baker

Sunday, July 8, *II Thessalonians* 3:6-13. Some of the Christians in the Thessalonian Church had evidently become so pre-occupied with the imminent return of Christ (2:1-2) that they had stopped working (v.11). How did their idleness affect their daily conduct (v.11)? Do you think Paul's command concerning them was too drastic (v.10)? How did Paul tell the other Christians to act toward those who would not work (vv.5-6)? Do you think the Church of today ought to bring discipline on members who are able but unwilling to work? In his own life Paul exemplified the honorableness of work (vv.7-8). Do you find in your own life that you are much more prone to yield to temptation when you are idle than when you are busy? Make v.13 your watch word for today.

Monday, July 9, *Numbers* 13:25-33. Read the whole of this familiar story of the sending out of the twelve spies to the Promised Land in 13:12,14:10. Each spy was the head of a tribe (13:3). What information were they to gather (vv.17-20)? What answer as to the nature of the Promised Land did they give (13:25-29)? What recommendation did 10 spies make (13: 31-33)? Joshua and Caleb (13:30;14:6-9)? What facts about God did Joshua and Caleb see (14:8-9) that the others did not see (13:33)? What choice did the people make (14:1-3,10)? What should they have remembered from their recent past (14:22)? When faced with seemingly unsurmountable problems, do you lay your plans in the confidence that the Lord will go before you in the future to lead you just as He has in the past?

Tuesday, July 10, *Matt.* 25:14-30. Two whole chapters (24-25) are devoted to teachings on Christ's Second Coming. The believer's responsibility in the light of the Second Coming is stressed in 24:36-25:46. What is the main point in each of the parables in 24:36-25:13? The parables in 25:14-30 illustrate how the Christian can be ready when Christ comes. What were each of the servants to do with the talents while their master was gone (vv.15-17)? Each was given according to his ability (v.15). Of what sin was the unworthy servant guilty (vv.18,25-26)? What things are listed in vv.31-44 that an ordinary Christian can do to use his talents for God? Are there things in this list within your ability to do that you are failing to do? Would you be ashamed if Christ should return in your lifetime because you are not using your talents for Him?

Wednesday, July 11, *I Samuel* 16:14-23. Saul continually did that which was evil in God's sight, until God finally rejected him as King in Israel (15:17-23). God had David anointed to replace Saul's line at his death (16:11-13)—hence the misery of Saul (vv.14-17) and the success of David (v.18). What need could David fulfill in Saul's life (vv.22-23)? Observe the relation that developed between Saul and David (v.21). When one is deep in sin or has fallen away from God it may be of tremendous help for him to form a friendship with a consecrated Christian. How much better it would be, though, if he would confess and repent of his sin as did David after his transgression (Psalm 51).

Thursday, July 12, Psalm 100. The "Lord" (vv.1,2,3,5) is Jehovah, the covenant God of Israel, the one who delivered His people from Egypt, gave them the Law and led them into the Promised Land. He has continually watched over His people. List the exhortations of vv.1-2,4. Are the reasons given in vv.3,5 for the praise of vv.1-2,4 adequate? How are the truths about the Lord as stated in vv.3,5 applicable to what we know of Him in Christ? When you think of what God has revealed to you of Himself in Christ, is the praise of vv.1-2,5 in your heart? The Psalmist desires that all nations know and love the Lord he knows (v.1). Does your knowledge of God cause you to desire that others know Him, too?

Friday, July 13, Job 1:13-19. There was once a devout man of great wealth whose name was Job (vv.1-3,5) in whom God had great confidence (v.8). What was Satan's challenge (vv.9-12)? List the catastrophies that came upon Job in vv.13-19. Would any one of them be a major blow? How would the average person react to such catastrophies? Account for Job's behavior (vv.20-22). Is his philosophy one that should be characteristic of a devout Christian? The story of Job illustrates the truth that a person's sufferings are not necessarily the punishment for sins he has committed. Though Job passed through very deep waters, God was still on the throne (1:12;2:6) and eventually all things worked together for good for Job because he loved the Lord (42:10-17).

Saturday, July 14, Jonah 4:6-11. Jonah was a prophet of the Lord, but he was not all that he should have been before Him. The Lord instructed him to go to Ninevah and preach against its sins (1:1-2), but Jonah fled in the opposite direction (1:3). He was swallowed by a great fish (1:4-17) and through this experience was led to repentance (chapter 2). Though he responded to God's second commission (3:1-2), the fact that Ninevah, a Gentile city, repented did not please his soul (3:10-4:1). What lesson did God teach Jonah through the gourd (4:6-11)? What was basically lacking in Jonah's heart? When you think or speak of the condemnation of God that will fall upon some sinner because of his sin, is it with a heart filled with love that he might repent?

ANGLERS

(From "*New Testament Evangelism*" by Wade C. Smith)

Lesson No. 146

FISHING WITH THE WORD (Continued)

"I spent a Summer with my friend. We were much together. I knew that he was ignorant of Christ and therefore not a Christian. He was a lovable companion, always ready to do more than his share in our rough camp life. Again and again I wanted to speak to him about my Saviour - but this morning he died. My heart is broken with grief and shame. How can I face my Saviour, if, through my neglect, Frank is not there"?

—A Presbyterian Elder's Confession.

In soul winning there are certain parts of Scripture better adapted than others. One must start somewhere, anyhow, and it is well to discriminate here. The first thing the personal worker should know is the PLAN of Salvation. In the helps to personal workers given in the forepart of *The Testament For Fishers Of Men,* on page XVI there is a brief but comprehensive outline of the plan of salvation worked out by Rev. O. E. Buchholz, D. D., of the General Assembly's Training School, Richmond, Va. It is as follows:

1. All of us are sinners. Rom. 3:23, Gal. 3:22.
2. Unbelievers are under condemnation. John 3:18.
3. Yet God loves sinners. John 3:16.
4. And Christ died for sinners. Rom. 5:6, I Peter 2:24,25.
5. He is the sinner's only hope. Acts 4:12.
6. Believe on Him. Acts 16:31.
7. Confess Him. Rom. 10:9,10.
8. Live for Him. Rom. 12:1.
9. A Summary. Rom. 6:23.

The personal worker in the beginning could hardly do better than to con this outline in the order given, with its supporting Scripture passages, until thoroughly familiar with it as an authentic statement of the Plan. Appropriate it afresh as your own. Memorize it. Let it be the Scripture meditation for your "Morning Watch" until you have thoroughly committed it.

Early Feeding. The suggestion of the Morning Watch may as well apply to all your study and meditation on Scripture to be used in personal work. If your day is already blocked out in such compactness that there is no space for this, set the alarm clock for at least a half-hour earlier to make provision for it. There is no time like the fresh first moments of the day for the daily interview with the Master Fisherman.

("Fishing with the Word" continued in next lesson.)

The article following is very pertinent to the one just ending above.

Women's Work

"Be Still and Know That I Am God"

Jesus, our ever practical example, found the quiet hour needful to His well-being. We are told frequently in the Scriptures that "He went apart." We, His handmaidens, have a like need in our daily living. This is a personal matter which concerns our own relationships with our Lord and Saviour. No one can have this quiet hour for us. We must plan and execute it ourselves. There are many helps for us, but we must experience this ourselves.

How shall we meet this personal need? First there must be a *time* to be quiet before Him. Many of God's saints have found early morning best for quiet- before the day has brought its press of household and business duties upon us. One dear old lady, after rearing her own large family, opened her home to many boys and girls in order to help them acquire an education. She met her Master in the early morning - at five-thirty, to be exact. A busy school principal sets her alarm a half hour earlier than necessary so that she might have her quiet time in the early morning. Perhaps later on in the day will suit some best, and others will find the even-tide more suitable to commune alone with God. We will remember that it was at evening that Isaac had his meditations. Let us find the time that is best for us, and let us go apart daily to be still before our Saviour.

Next we must settle on a *place* that is apart and quiet, Perhaps your bedroom, your breakfast room, your library, den, porch or garden will be your chosen place - just any place where you can be quiet and alone with God. David Brainerd found the woods his place. Suzanna Wesley, mother of Charles and John, had nineteen children. She always observed her quiet hour and it is said that not even the youngest child transgressed her closed door. All knew that their mother was spending an hour with God.

How shall we come to this quiet *time* in this quiet *place?* We shall come with a heart open before Him for cleansing, confessing our sin and our unworthiness. We shall come with a heart for filling - claiming His promises. With a heart full of praise for His blessings to us and ours. With a heart seeking His will and His wisdom. Like Hezekiah, of old, we shall "spread it out before the Lord." We shall come with a heart that expects great things from God; a heart and mind that will attempt great things for God.

Our arch enemy Satan will not let us come to our quiet hour without a struggle. He will seek to distract and divert us. Let us be steadfast in the power of the Holy Spirit and keep our quiet hour before our Lord. Then we shall return to our family, church and business duties with peace, poise and serenity.

(Mrs. A. K.) Frances T. Dudley
Concord, N. C.

Did you ever stop to think

that you are never with any woman—friend, relative, stranger, white or colored—that you are not witnessing for or against the Christian way of life? Witnessing is not something we can choose to do, or not to do. The only choice we have is "What shall my witness be? If Christ is in you - has His rightful place - first place - in you, for He will have first place or none, woman to woman evangelism is as natural as breathing." Mrs. Donald W. Richardson

desire to tell the good news of salvation with a happy glowing example of Christian living.

Suppose Jesus, when He was here dwelling in the flesh, had lived a life filled with "excuse giving." Instead we find Jesus constantly in readiness and willing always to do His Father's will.

There is a job for each hour of the day for you and me to do. Do we accept this and try, or do we fight against it with *don't have time, I cannot talk in public, cannot lead a lesson like she did, I work and am just too tired, I'm not too well and must conserve my strength, or I have given of my time through the years, now let the young blood take over*. We, in our weakness, cannot overcome these things, but what is impossible with man is possible with God.

Are these legitimate excuses for failing our Father in Heaven who gave His only Son that we might have everlasting life? How little we are asked to do in return. *He so loved us.* We did not merit this love.

How wonderful if we could blot the little word "excuse" out of our thinking because we had ceased to have the desire to use it and in its stead had written the words "Christian Service" with indelible ink.

(Mrs. W. M.) Eula J. Board
Pulaski, Virginia

One Minute Messages on Stewardship

Undergirding all other weapons is prayer, which unlocks the storehouse of God's Power. What blessings are missed through its neglect. Yet, He could say to each of us as He did of old, "O' Woman, great is thy faith. Be it unto thee as thou wilt." "Do we act as if we believe this?"

Much more important than the method of witnessing is the life of the witness. Only the life that is Christ-centered and Spirit-controlled will bear lasting fruit. "It is dying, not doing, that produces spiritual fruit." (Dying to self, forgetting self). And, only as we die to self and allow Him to live out His life in us, will there be fruitfulness. This happens only after Calvary becomes a reality to us.

Mrs. W. B. Audrey, Jr.

RELIGION IN AMERICAN LIFE

An Expression of Our Gratitude

Faced as we are with difficult times, confronted with much uncertainty, we are beginning to recognize that we are no more self-sufficient than our forebears were. More frankly, perhaps, than in less disturbed times, we are beginning to acknowledge that, like them, we need God's help.

One of the undertakings dedicated to such revival of faith is the movement known as Religion In American Life. I should like to feel that, in every American family, some place is made for an expression of our gratitude to Almighty God, and for a frank acknowledgment of our faith that He can supply that additional strength which, for these trying times, is so sorely needed.

—President Eisenhower.

FORTIFYING OUR FAITH

As the body must be regularly cleansed and recharged, so must the soul. This can be accomplished best by worship, and by public worship, when the fellowship of others fortifies our faith.

Religion is the attempt to close the gap between what we are and what we can be. If we want to raise the level of our moral status as well as our usefulness within our families, our neighborhoods, and our communities, we must return often to the source of our inspiration. These are to be found in Holy Writ, and in our sanctuaries. The cultivation of the worship habit, therefore, can lead us to inner security and simultaneously make us worthier instruments in the attainment of divinely-mandated goals. —Maurice N. Eisendrath.

Down to His Last Palace

By G. J. Peterson,
Moody Bible Institute, Chicago

No one knows exactly how rich India's 72-year-old Nizam of Hyderabad is, although he has been said to be the richest man in the world. For one thing, rats recently chewed their way through more than $8,000,000 in currency stored in the palace vaults, leaving its value in doubt. And the old Nizam immediately fired the man who was hired to appraise his trunks full of jewels when he heard the job would take a full year. "Why the man's salary would have been fabulous," he said.

Then too, times have changed in India since the Nizam's heyday when he was absolute monarch of Hyderabad, and dressed in encrusted brocade bedecked with jewels as he rode around and collected his due from the 19 million population of the area. As a civil servant now subservient to the New Delhi government, he has to struggle along on a tax-free stipend of only $1,000,000 a year, plus an expense account of half that much. In tune with the tight times, the penny-pinching Nizam has delegated his fleet of Cadillacs and other expensive cars to the garage, and rides around in a 23-year-old remodeled Ford. With a family of three wives, 42 concubines, 33 children, 40 grandchildren and an estimated 3,400 servants, he carefully and personally plans the household menus each day.

The Nizam's son, Prince Azam Jah, has no such money-saving qualms. He gives no thought to economy, and passes his days playing polo, studying the racing forms, and frolicking with the 50 ladies of his harem. He now has to struggle along on a monthly allowance of $10,000, and local creditors have been warned that the Nizam will no longer settle his son's debts. Father Nizam recently paid off some $5,500,000 to get his son out of debt. Then he promptly disinherited him and made his 23-year-old grandson the Nizam's heir.

"I am no longer a rich man," complains the poor old Nizam; "everything I have is tied up in trusts. I am practically down to my last palace!" But all things being equal, the fact remains that the Nizam is still, if not the richest man in the world, certainly close to it.

However, the Nizam's great wealth in currency, jewels, trusts and palaces cannot even be compared to the treasures which have been lavishly bestowed by a generous heavenly Father upon every person who has found all in the Lord Jesus Christ by faith; for in Him are hid "all the treasures of wisdom and knowledge" (Colossians 2:3). This same Jesus, who owns all the wealth of heaven and earth, once became poor for our sakes, that we through His poverty might be made rich (II Corinthians 8:9).

Believe and Receive

Have you made the step of faith which transfers you from your place as a condemned son of Adam to a freely justified child of God, and transforms you from a slave of fleshly passions to a conquering saint? You can be a joint heir with Jesus Christ to fabulous treasures in glory. By believing on Christ for salvation, you receive the Holy Spirit, Whom Adam's unregenerate sons cannot receive, and He works in you those things which are well pleasing in God's sight.

Let all men hear the saving gospel of Jesus Christ, for all are under the curse of the law of God. None can keep His requirements and so be worthy of eternal life; the law only shows man his sins. But "what the law could not do, in that it was weak through the flesh, God sending his own Son in the likeness of sinful flesh, and for sin, condemned sin in the flesh, that the righteousness of the law might be fulfilled in us, who walk not after the flesh, but after the Spirit." Romans 8:3,4.

World at the Cross roads

"The western world is standing at the crossroads," says Billy Graham. "Never was the picture darker. Never was the need of divine intervention so desperate. We are facing a political crisis. You can see it in every country. Many of us are going along just as we have in the past. Christian, this is a different age! I believe God is giving the nations an opportunity to repent. If they fail they will be destroyed. The answer for the nations is an old-fashioned Holy Ghost revival in which God can speak once again as by fire."

Church News

DEATH OF REV. W. P. CHEDESTER

Rev. William Pierce Chedester, of Asheville Presbytery, died in Asheville, N. C., on April 29. Mr. Chedester was born in Asheville, September 28, 1879. He studied at Davidson College and at Union Theological Seminary, Richmond, Va., and was ordained by Asheville Presbytery in 1906. He became pastor of the Brevard church and most of his pastoral service was given to the Brevard, Franklin, Andrews, and Ora Street churches in his home Presbytery. An exception was his service in the Pageland group of churches in Mecklenburg Presbytery for three years. He was also for a year a chaplain in the armed services and was for a time associated with Mountain Orphanage, then at Balfour, N. C.

Funeral services were conducted by Rev. Paul N. Gresham. Mr. Chedester was married to Miss Elizabeth Stevenson, of Asheville, March 26, 1919, and is survived by his daughter, Mrs. Mary Elizabeth Guy, of Mt. Juliet, Tenn., and three grandchildren.

DEATH OF REV. SAMUEL B. LAPSLEY, D. D.

Rev. Samuel Baxter Lapsley, D. D., pastor since 1949 of the Cedar Springs church, Knoxville, Tenn., died in Abingdon, Va., on May 31. Dr. Lapsley was born in Vine Hill, Alabama, January 12, 1889. Graduated from Union Theological Seminary, Richmond, Va., in 1923, he was ordained to the ministry by Lexington Presbytery of the Synod of Virginia. Before coming to the Cedar Springs church, he had served the following fields: Pastor at Craigsville, Va., 1922-1930; Aiken, S. C., 1930-1933; Marlinton, W. Va., 1933-1938; field executive and superintendent of home missions of the Synod of West Virginia, 1938-1943; director of the home mission emergency fund campaign, 1943-1944; pastor at Bedford, Va., 1945-1946; educational secretary of the Executive Committee of Home Missions, Atlanta, Ga., 1946-1949; pastor of the Cedar Springs church, Knoxville, since 1949.

DEATH OF REV. WILLIAM L. WALKER

Rev. William Lowry Walker, pastor of the church at Iowa Park, Texas, was killed in an airplane accident in Texas on May 31. Mr. Walker was born in Cleburne, Texas, February 22, 1911. He studied at Georgia Tech, Austin College, and Columbia Theological Seminary, Decatur, Ga., and was licensed and ordained in 1938 by the Presbytery of Paris. Before coming to Iowa Park church only a few months ago, he had served the following fields: Rose Hill and Moores Chapel churches, Texarkana, Texas, 1938 and 1939; First church, Lovington, New Mexico, 1939 to 1942; West Point, Ga., 1942 to 1948; and after a long illness at Mt. Pleasant, Tenn., and then Iowa Park, Texas.

Change of Address: Rev. George A. Hudson, Th. D., from Formosa, to 235 Inman Drive, Decatur, Georgia.

Rev. Thomas McLelland Stevenson was called to his eternal home on May 31 last, after an extended illness in Danville Memorial Hospital, Danville, Va. Mr. Stevenson was born in Loray, Iredell County, N. C., January 14, 1889. He was a graduate of Columbia Theological Seminary. He served as pastor of the Presbyterian churches in Barnesville, Ga., Kershaw, S. C., Craigsville, Va., and Hamer, S. C. He is survived by his widow, residing in Danville, and by two sons, Thomas M. Stevenson, Jr., of Baltimore, Md., and Edward W. Stevenson, M. D., of New Orleans; and one daughter, Mrs. Harold L. Vaughn, of Danville, Va.

GEORGIA

Brunswick — The crash of a four-passenger Cessna plane near St. Simons cost the lives of four Atlanta Presbyterians June 13. They were R. Hays McKinney, H. D. Osner, William Newton, and V. A. Vincoli, all deacons in the Rock Spring Presbyterian Church in Atlanta. Mr. McKinney was serving also as the Superintendent of the Junior Department of the Church School.

The crash took place about 5:00 a.m. in the sound between St. Simons and Jekyll Island shortly after the takeoff. Cause of the crash was not determined.

The four men, on vacation with their families at the coast, took off from the St. Simons airport to fly McKinney to Savannah, where he planned to board a commercial plane for Atlanta.

LOUISIANA

New Orleans — A campaign for $105,000, to be used in church construction, was inaugurated May 17 by the Presbytery of New Orleans at a dinner at the Saint Charles Avenue Presbyterian Church. Representatives of churches in the South Louisiana area attended the meeting, directed by Fred Dykhuizen, chairman of the finance committee of the Presbytery.

Speakers included Dr. John S. Land, pastor of the St. Charles Church; the Rev. Alex Hunter, pastor of First Presbyterian Church; and Calvin Williams, vice-chairman of the finance committee.

$30,000 of the goal had already been raised. The first project will be a new church in Airline Park, expected to be around $100,000. The funds will also be used for the construction of additional churches in Algiers, Houma, Chalmette and Franklin.

NORTH CAROLINA

Davidson — Davidson College graduate Linny M. Baker of Kannapolis has been chosen for the Thomas A. Clark Award by the Alpha Tau Omega social fraternity.

The award is the highest that the fraternity can bestow, and selection is made from the thousands of fraternity members all over the United States. It includes an all-expense trip to ATO's Mackinac, Mich. Congress September 5-8 and a specially designed ring.

Baker was president of the ATO chapter at Davidson during the past year, and one of the outstanding all-round students. He was a member of Phi Beta Kappa and Omicron Delta Kappa, and was salutatorian of the class that graduated May 31.

Linny is the son of Mrs. Bertha Baker of Route No. 5, Kannapolis, and is a graduate of J. W. Cannon High, where he was president of the student body. He attended Davidson on a George F. Baker scholarship.

This fall he will enter the Duke University school of medicine.

Waxhaw — Old Waxhaw Presbyterian Church — This historic old church, the oldest in Bethel Presbytery, celebrated its 200th anniversary last year and sent up the best report in its history. This congregation has always been small but has contributed much to the life of the church at large.

The future of this church looks brighter today than ever before. In the last six years they have grown numerically, physically and spiritually. Each year we have had an evangelistic meeting. This spring the Rev. John H. Knight, Pastor of the First Presbyterian Church, Smyrna, Ga., came to us. He preached the word of God with power for one week and our people were built up in their faith. There were three additions to the church on profession of faith in Christ. We wish to thank the Smyrna Church for the services of this man of God.

We thank God for our past, but we look to the future and the future looks bright for this church. With the coming of an industrial plant nearby, we view the future with hope and are preparing to meet the challenge.

Waxhaw — Tirzah Presbyterian Church is completing a beautiful $40,000 Sanctuary and Education building. This church is 152 years old and has contributed wonderfully to the life of the church at large. We have six sons now preaching the Word of God.

The present building is about 122 years old with few facilities for Sunday School or recreation. In our new building we plan for the future the sanctuary has ample seating capacity. The Educational wing has sufficient classroom space, also a Men's Fellowship Hall and a modern kitchen.

The Synod of Texas

will meet July 17, 18, and 19, 1956 in the First Presbyterian Church, Dallas, Texas, at 7:30 P. M.

The First Church, Dallas, will be entertaining the Synod in connection with its celebration of its Centennial."

Our Presbyterian Heritage

Last year the Southern Presbyterian Journal sponsored a symposium on the Reformed Faith. Addresses were made by a group of outstanding Presbyterians and all who attended gave enthusiastic response.

Without in any measure competing with any other program in our church a similar symposium will be held this year, again placing its emphasis on our Presbyterian heritage.

THE TIME—August 15th — 10:00 A. M.

THE PLACE—Weaverville, N. C.

DR. C. GREGG SINGER—"*The Reformed Faith and the Contemporary Crisis in Education*"

DR. GORDON H. CLARK —"*The Reformed Doctrine of Verbal Inspiration of the Scriptures.*"

DR. FLOYD HAMILTON —"*The Reformed Doctrine of Infant Baptism*"

DR. AIKEN TAYLOR — "*The Reformed Doctrine of the Means of Grace*"

DR. W. C. ROBINSON — "*The Reformed Doctrine of the Bodily Resurrection of Christ*"

DR. R. F. GRIBBLE — "*The Reformed Faith as Related to the Virgin Birth Foretold in Isaiah 7:14*"

MR. GEORGE BURNHAM—"*To the Far Corners*"

Make Plans Now To Attend This Meeting

THE SOUTHERN PRESBYTERIAN JOURNAL

Weaverville, N. C.

THE SOUTHERN PRESBYTERIAN JOURNAL

A Presbyterian weekly magazine devoted to the statement, defense and propagation of the Gospel, the faith which was once for all delivered unto the saints.

JULY 11, 1956

HONORED FOR LONG SERVICE—Dr. J. S. Brown (left) and J. T. Fain, Sr. (right), elders in the First Presbyterian Church of Hendersonville, North Carolina were honored last month by the Session of the Church. Dr. Brown has been an elder since September, 1908 and Mr. Fain since June, 1907. In the center is the pastor, the Reverend Warren Thuston.

VOL. XV NO. 11 $2.50 A YEAR

THE SOUTHERN PRESBYTERIAN JOURNAL

The Journal has no official connection with the Presbyterian Church in the United States

Rev. Henry B. Dendy, D.D., Editor..Weaverville, N. C.
Dr. L. Nelson Bell, Associate Editor..Asheville, N. C.
Rev. Wade C. Smith, Associate Editor..Weaverville, N. C.

EDITORIAL

The General Council

As a supplement to our report of the 1956 Montreat General Assembly, we desire to present a few facts that will be of interest to our readers in regard to the General Council.

The "Forward With Christ" Program was launched January 1, 1955. It has had a large part in enabling our church to report the best year in its history. At the present time 1,672 churches have officially adopted this program. This means that sixty per cent of the churches of over twenty-five members are in the program, and these churches have some seventy per cent of the membership of our entire church. It has stimulated the organization of seventy new churches during the year, which set a new record of achievement. It inspired the giving of our church to reach a new height for benevolences, current expenses, and building. The per capita giving reached the figure of $81.76, an increase of almost $6 over any previous year.

The General Council and its staff have been busy in promoting the stewardship of possessions. The secretaries have spent a large part of their time in answering calls to present stewardship in individual churches. Seven new pieces of printed stewardship material have been released during the year.

The new approach of the Pre-Budget Canvass was highly commended by the Council. Under the old plan the budget was first made and the Every Member Canvass was an attempt to raise the budget. In most cases the budget, generally fixed as low as possible, became the ceiling of giving, and stress was laid on money raising rather than stewardship. Under the Pre-Budget Canvass Plan the canvass is made before the budget is presented. Stewardship is stressed, proportionate giving emphasized, and one's obligation to Christ rather than a budget becomes the norm of giving. The almost universal testimony of the churches using this plan has been greatly increased gifts and a spiritual revival. 1,019 of our churches used this plan in the 1955 Canvass.

The publicity department has continued to develop and render an increasingly valuable service to the church. We desire at this time to express appreciation to Mr. Bluford Hestir, Director of Publicity, for the fine work he and his staff did at the General Assembly. At all times this corps of workers was alert and efficient.

The Stewardship Emphasis Season is scheduled to begin October 1, 1957, and continue through November 17, 1957. November 10 is designated as Every Member Canvass Day, and the theme of the Canvass is "For the Glory of God."

Among the calender recommendations for 1957, we note the following: February 24 - March 3 for Week of Prayer and Self Denial for World Missions; March 4 - April 21, special evangelistic season; October 13 is Laymen's Sunday; and October 27 is Reformation Sunday. Another significant date is the meeting of the General Assembly at Birmingham, Alabama, April 25-30.

The General Council is making plans for the observance of our Centennial in 1961. The Council believes that the One Hundredth Anniversary of our Church's birth is an event of first importance, and any attempt to pass it without notice would be strained and unnatural. We feel that an observance emphasizing the distinctive doctrines espoused by our Southern Presbyterian Church, coupled with a constructive program for the future could do much toward the stimulation of a new enthusiasm for the days ahead. We approve, therefore, of the theme of the Centennial as "Our Heritage and Mission."

J.R.R.

Softness

There is genuine alarm among our national leaders as they face up to the situation which has developed in America during the past decade, - *we are becoming a nation of softies.*

Only recently we spent the night in an ultramodern motel in Texas. Let us compare our quarters with the accomodations our own fathers would have found in the same spot fifty years ago:

Then there would have been shelter from wind and storm but probably a hard bed, sweltering heat, lukewarm water to drink and a basin and pitcher for necessary ablutions.

What did we have to enjoy? A large air-conditioned room, indirect lighting, two large beds, one of them with a gyromatic mattress which lulled the weary traveler to sleep by electricity-induced vibrations, a television set for amusement, abundance of tiny ice cubes, tub and shower and latest luxurious equipment for modern toilet making. Outside was a large swimming pool with temperature-controlled filtered water, and next door an air-conditioned dining room with everything to tickle the palate.

In a number of places across America we found the same type accomodations except for the lack of the gyromatic mattress (these are coming too). Delightful? Yes. But here is the sobering thought: Americans are living in such luxury and ease that we are developing a generation of young people who know nothing else. Luxurious living has always been accompanied by degeneration of muscular *and* spiritual tone. It *can* lead to national disaster.

It is now a known fact that the young people of every European nation are far more fit physically than are American young people of corresponding groups and age. The automobile, the television, delicate foods, undisciplined homes and individual lives are already taking their toll.

The natural question would be: "Would you then have us return to the primitive living of our fathers"? That is not easy to answer. The developing situation may be within the path of God's judgment upon us as a nation. We are no longer a nation of people who have learned the disciplines of necessity. Materialism with its lulling charms has sapped from us the will to be hard and to live by the sweat of our brow. More and more we look to the government for our decisions and for material help and when a people depends on others for such things it takes something out of them; something which is very precious and very important.

Recently we were talking with a friend who has lived abroad for many years. In the course of our discussion we mentioned the strange phenomena of the Scandinavian countries and their spiritual and moral decline. Immediately he replied: "With the development of their socialistic concept and its practical application in government and individual life a sense of dependence on others has been developed. With this security there has come a corresponding increase in the materialistic concept and decrease in a sense of need for God."

This can happen in America. Already we are getting soft to the place where there is being sounded a warning of alarm by top leaders. The trend is here. The question is, are we as a people willing to endure the hardness which contributes to national greatness?

Paul, writing to his spiritual son, Timothy, warned him that the Christian life and profession demands a certain type of hardness and concentration on spiritual values: *"Thou therefore endure hardness, as a good soldier of Jesus Christ. No man that warreth entangleth himself with the affairs of this life; that he may please him who hath chosen him to be a soldier."*

Being a Christian should still entail a certain hardness and a life of discipline from which many of us recoil. Can we change before it is too late? L.N.B.

The Arab Nations and Israel

The bitter attitude of the Arab nations to the little nation of Israel is not hard to understand, but its significance and potentialities cannot be overestimated.

Much of this bitterness stems originally from the displacement of Arab settlers from the area now occupied by Israel, and their continued pitiful state as homeless refugees living in almost unbelievable squalor.

But, this resentment goes much deeper. The Arab nations have stated categorically that they now refuse and shall continue to refuse to rec-

The Southern Presbyterian Journal, *a Presbyterian Weekly magazine devoted to the statement, defense, and propagation of the Gospel, the faith which was once for all delivered unto the saints,* published every Wednesday by The Southern Presbyterian Journal, Inc., in Weaverville, N. C.

Entered as second-class matter May 15, 1942, at the Postoffice at Weaverville, N. C., under the Act of March 3, 1879. Vol. XV, No. 11, July 11, 1956. Editorial and Business Offices: Weaverville, N. C. Printed in the U.S.A. by Biltmore Press, Asheville, N. C.

ADDRESS CHANGE: When changing address, please let us have both old and new address as far in advance as possible. Allow three weeks after change if not sent in advance. When possible, send an address label giving your old address.

ognize Israel as a nation and her right to occupy a part of Palestine.

More than that, the Arabs are fearful of this vigorous little nation because they know by experience that one Israeli soldier is a match for ten of their own.

On the other hand, Israel today has demonstrated to the world its willingness to work, its ability to develop and its determination to succeed. One has but to consider the area now under the control of Israel and compare it with thirty years ago. Amazing industry, dogged determination and brilliant planning has made the desert blossom like a rose. A melting pot of Jews from all parts of the world, many of them knowing little or nothing of their ancient religion and background, they have been motivated by a consuming desire to become a nation, a people with a land and a government of their own. They have succeeded and they intend to continue to succeed.

Geographically, except for the Mediterranean on the West, Israel is surrounded by Arab nations. These Moslem lands are also passing through a phase of extreme nationalism and, so far as Israel is concerned, they are united by a consuming hatred and they are bound together as well by ethnic and religious ties.

In these troubled waters Russia is now fishing. Egypt, led by President Nasser, (probably the most dangerous man in that part of the world) is feeling the heady experience of taking over the Suez Canal from the British and of assuming a role in world affairs for which she has not one single qualification.

Receiving arms from the Communist bloc and undertaking to speak for the Arab world, Egypt is a potential danger. It is also of significance that all of the Arab nations refuse to admit any justification for Israel as a nation and to note that their only restraint against Israel is a wholesome respect for the men and women who comprise the effective fighting force of their hated neighbor.

That Israel must have sufficient arms to maintain a balance is the feeling of many informed world leaders. That this armament must not be sufficient to tempt aggression is also recognized.

Many Christians feel that there is a prophetic significance in this emergence of Israel as a nation. Others discount this aspect of the situation but all students of world affairs agree that the Middle-East is potentially the most dangerous spot on the globe. Palestine, the so-called "navel of the world," lies close to the greatest known oil deposits on the globe. All over the world today national life and military planning are projected on oil. This significant combination of circumstances makes the events developing in that part of the world of the gravest import.

The Old Testament repeatedly states that the attitude of peoples and nations to the Jews is often a determining factor in their own existence. History, both Biblical and secular, would indicate that none have ever prospered who have mistreated the Jews. Regardless of the future role Israel may be destined to play in world history it is certainly worthy of note that this small, virile and struggling national entity has again become the center of controversy, hatred (and possibly of destiny) in the affairs of the entire world.

In the Scriptures Christians are enjoined to pray for all men. It is therefore our duty to pray for those nations and leaders whose center of interests are there in the Middle East. One wonders if as we pray for the peace of the Church, the spiritual Jerusalem, there should not also be a heeding of David's psalm of old: *"Pray for the peace of Jerusalem: they shall prosper that love thee."* ? L.N.B.

"Out of the Mouth of Babes"

I have just heard this story, related to me by the mother of a little boy three years and eight months old today.

They were enroute to Asheville by plane. In the next seat back of them sat two women, one elderly, the other quite young. They were smoking. The little boy, attracted by the fumes, coming over the back of his seat, climbed up and looked at them with that open-eyed frankness of a child. Presently he said to them, "Jesus doesn't like that." The elderly woman leaned forward and said, "What did you say, little boy?" "I said Jesus doesn't like that," he replied. "Why," she asked. "Because it will give you a dirty heart," the little boy answered. After a brief pause, she asked, "How old are you, little boy?" "I'm free years old," he answered.

That was all. A minute of silence in the back seat. The mother touched the little boy on the arm and suggested that he eat his cookie now. He may become a great preacher someday - likely will; but it is doubtful if in all his career he will ever pack as much sound wisdom in so few words. W.C.S.

Why Some People Take Prayer Seriously

By Rev. Henry S. Schum
Johnson City, Tenn.

"Confess your faults one to another, and pray one for another, that ye may be healed." (Jas. 5:16-19) · "The effectual, fervent prayer of a righteous man availeth much." (Dan. 9:1-9)

Some people take prayer seriously. The Bible says, "Elijah was a man subject to like passions as we are, and he prayed earnestly that it might not rain; and it rained not on the earth by the space of three years and six months. And he prayed again, and the heavens gave rain, and the earth brought forth her fruit."

Ezra, the man God used to lead the people from Babylon back to Palestine, upon realizing the sins of the people did this: "And at the evening sacrifice I arose up from my heaviness; and having rent my garment and my mantle, I fell upon my knees, and spread out my hands unto the Lord my God, and said, "Oh my God, I am ashamed and blush to lift up my face to thee, my God; for our iniquities are increased over our head, and our trespass is grown up unto the heavens." . . . And the rest of his recorded prayer is overwhelming evidence that he took prayer seriously.

Joel knew the value of prayer when he said, "Sanctify ye a fast, call a solemn assembly, gather the elders and all the inhabitants of the land into the house of the Lord your God, and cry unto the Lord." Joel 1:13,14.

We read in the biographies of our forefathers who were most successful in winning souls, that they prayed for hours in private. The question therefore arises, can we get the same results without following their example?

Finney said, "I once knew a minister who had a revival 14 winters in succession. I did not know how to account for it until I saw one of his members get up in a prayer meeting and make a confession: 'Brethren,' said he, 'I have been long in the habit of praying every Saturday night till after midnight, for the descent of the Holy Ghost upon us. And now, brethren, and he began to weep, I confess that I have neglected it for two or three weeks.' The secret was out. That minister had a praying church." (From O. J. Smith: *The Revival We Need)*

We do not have to limit our observations to men of the Bible or to our forefathers. There are some people today who take prayer seriously. The only real answer to the overwhelming success of revival in Scotland is effectual, fervent prayer on the part of literally thousands of people who took prayer seriously.

But why do some people take prayer seriously? I think the answer is to be found in a knowledge of and love for God. Some people take prayer seriously because they want to. They want to because they have been changed in their hearts by the operation of the Holy Spirit.

No one takes true prayer seriously who has not repented of his sins and been born into the family of God. When a person comes to know God and to love him, then he becomes anxious to do the will of God.

People who take prayer seriously do so because they know and love God and because they realize that God does His work in answer to effectual, fervent prayer. These people recognize that prayer is a vital key in the plans and purposes of God, and it is for us to use the key to open the windows of heaven so the blessings can come.

"If my people which are called by my name, shall humble themselves, and pray, and seek my face, and turn from their wicked ways; then will I hear from heaven, and will forgive their sin, and will heal their land." II Chron. 7:14. The same principles of prayer still work today.

By now, the purpose of my message must be clear to you. I am anxious to increase the number of people in our church who will take prayer seriously.

I know that many of you pray upon arising in the morning, at meals and before you go to bed at night. Some of you pray in public. That is good. Some of you even come to the one meeting of the week set aside for the purpose of prayer for your church and its activities. That is exceptional in our age when people think that all it takes to keep a church going is organization, money and friendliness. But I am talking about some real spiritual work that can only be done by true Christians who have a real concern.

Would you like to become a real prayer warrior in the biggest war of the ages? Would you like to take prayer seriously because you really want to. Would you like to enter into something really big and have your whole life take on a new significance?

Are you tired of a weak, watered-down Christian experience with no spiritual vision or power? If so, then perhaps I can help you.

First, you must really desire a change from weakness and indifference to power and vision that will result in effectual, fervent prayer.

But you say, "What is there to be so concerned about?"

Just this: The Church of the Lord Jesus Christ is entering into the final days of the greatest world-wide battle for truth that history has ever known. It doesn't take a prophetic student to see that America and the free nations of the earth are being overrun by the greatest Satan-inspired, atheistic world-revolution of all time. The fanatic zeal of God-denying, God-hating Communism is spreading faster than any revolutionary force the world has ever seen. America is fast becoming an island of freedom surrounded on every side by the slave forces of Communism.

These are self-evident facts. I need not go further. Every intelligent person knows that our country is in the gravest danger of its entire history.

And the Christian people of America, the only ones who can really do anything about it—are asleep. We are busy with our organizations, our socials, parties, our nice, but not really necessary activities, and have forsaken the one great task of the church. We have quit praying and have taken a defeatest attitude regarding the evangelization of the world. We have closed our ears to the awful warnings of men in high places. We have closed our eyes to the needs of the heathen to hear the Gospel and be saved. We have closed our hands to the support and help of those who have gone in our stead to represent us to the lost on foreign soil. Some have never started. Others have started and quit.

But you say, "Preacher, show me some Scripture that will clearly indicate that I have a responsibility to pray for the lost and for world conditions."

Here is your answer. Turn to Daniel 9:1-19. "In the first year of Darius the son of Ahasuerus, of the seed of the Medes, which was made king over the realm of the Chaldeans; In the first year of his reign I Daniel understood by books the number of the years, whereof the word of the Lord came to Jeremiah the prophet, that he would accomplish seventy years in the desolations of Jerusalem."

Daniel first looked in the Word of God. He read Jeremiah 25:11,12 "And this whole land shall be desolation, and an astonishment; and these nations shall serve the king of Babylon seventy years, And it shall come to pass, when seventy years are accomplished, that I will punish the king of Babylon, and that nation, saith the Lord, for their iniquity, and the land of the Chaldeans, and will make it perpetual desolations."

Then what did Daniel do? He said, "Well, God's program is going on time all right. I knew the time was about up. We'll soon be going back to Jerusalem. I'm a good Presbyterian and know that what's to be will be. We can't change God. Three cheers for the return of the saints to Jerusalem!"

He did no such thing! Listen to parts of Dan. 9:3-19 "And I set my face unto the Lord God, to seek by prayer and supplications, with fasting, and sackcloth, and ashes: And I prayed unto the Lord my God, and made my confession, and said, O Lord, the great and dreadful God, keeping the covenant and mercy to them that love him and to them that keep his commandments; We have sinned, and have committed iniquity, and have done wickedly, and have rebelled, even by departing from thy precepts and from they judgments; Neither have we hearkened unto thy servants the prophets, which spake in thy name to our kings, our princes, and our fathers, and to all the people of the land. O Lord, righteousness belongeth unto thee, but unto us confusion of faces as at this day; to the men of Judah, and to the inhabitants of Jerusalem, and unto all Israel, that are near, and that are far off, through all the countries whither thou hast driven them, because of their trespass that they have trespassed against thee. . . . O Lord, hear; O Lord, forgive; O Lord, hearken and do; defer not, for thine own sake, O my God; for thy city and thy people are called by thy name."

Daniel took prayer seriously. He wanted to. He had to. He knew God, and knew that God works in answer to prayer — effectual, fervent prayer.

But you say, "Preacher, we know Communism is real and that total war may come to America. Show us Scripture we can use as Daniel did. Here it is in Ezekiel 38 & 39. God says to the northern powers, "And say, thus saith the Lord God; Behold, I am against thee; O Gog, the chief prince of Meshech and Tubal: And I will turn thee back, and put hooks into thy jaws, and I will bring thee forth, and all thine army, horses and horsemen, all of them clothed with all sorts of armor, even a great company with bucklers and shields, all of them handling swords."

It is clear as to the land and people and also the time. "After many days thou shalt be visited; in the latter years thou shalt come into the land that is brought back from the sword, and is gathered out of many people, against the mountains of Israel, which have been always waste: but it is brought forth out of the nations, and they shall dwell safely all of them."

God also says why He is ordering the godless hosts to come upon the people in the Promised Land in the last days. "And thou shalt come up against my people Israel, as a cloud to cover the land; it shall be in the latter days and I will bring thee against my land, that the heathen may know me when I shall be sanctified in thee, O God, before their eyes."

But are there Americans in this picture? Look at Ezek. 39:6 "And I will send a fire on Magog, and among them that dwell carelessly in the isles; and they shall know that I am the Lord."

God is going to judge us with fire that we may come to know that the Lord is God.

Now, as a good, Bible-believing Presbyterian, what can you do? God has a program. He is following it out exactly. Judgment is coming. What can prayer do?

We can do exactly as Daniel did. Continue to examine the Scriptures. Know the way God is going and then pray accordingly. Our prayer will not be to try to avoid disaster, but that we might do the will of God in the days ahead.

Remember, judgment isn't the end. God can keep us in time of judgment and He will lead us through it to the glorious days of eternity promised to every believer.

But He will do all this in answer to the effectual, fervent prayer of His people. God can do anything He pleases—with or without our prayers or help. He has chosen to work in answer to and in connection with believing prayer.

So - do you want to take prayer seriously? Then acknowledge your sins, humble yourself before God, seek his face, ask for a new outpouring of His Spirit upon you. Learn God's plans and His ways. Then you will be a Christian with power and vision and you will take prayer seriously.

Helps To Understanding Scripture Readings in *Day by Day*

By C. C. Baker

Sunday, July 15, *II Corinthians* 7:5-13a. In his first letter Paul rebuked the Corinthians for their immorality (I Corinthians 5). He then sent Titus to carry through disciplinary action (vv.5-15). What results did Titus report as a result of his mission (vv.7,9,11)? What effect did the grief of the Corinthians have on their behavior (vv.9-10)? Observe how Paul felt toward them, even when he wrote the first letter (vv.8,14). What was Titus' attitude toward them (vv.7,13,15)? Do you think the results of vv.7-11 would have been acquired if love had not motivated the actions of Paul and Titus? Love should always motivate Christian discipline; its primary purpose is not to punish but to restore.

Monday, July 16, *Leviticus* 19:33-34. Verse 18b summarizes the whole Old Testament concept of social conduct. How do vv.17-18 show that this principle of conduct should come from the heart? Notice the practical ways in which this principle is carried into every-day life (vv.9-10,11,13-15). Is there anything one should expect in return from the poor of vv.9-10? Observe how vv. 33-34 carry this precept into one's relations with strangers. Should there be any difference in the way we treat strangers as compared to our own people (v.34)? Every injunction in the chapter closes with the phrase, "I am the Lord, your God," showing that these things should be done because of our relationship with God. Review the chapter for practical applications for yourself.

Tuesday, July 17, *Deut.* 6:4-9. According to Jesus, verse 4 contains the greatest commandment of the Old Testament (Matthew 22:37). Remember that the phrase "The Lord our God is one Lord" is a part of that command (v.4a). Loving God supremely means worshipping him alone. We cannot love the Lord and worship other gods (vv.14-15). Loving God involves the keeping of His commandments (v.2) and our holding of Him in reverential awe (vv.2,13). Our love for God involves our worship, obedience and consecration. In what different circumstances of home life can a child be taught this kind of love for God. What do we, as earthly parents, teach our children about their heavenly Father, if we are weak in our discipline or overly-indulgent in our dealings with them? What concept of God are you teaching your child?

Wednesday, July 18, *Luke* 1:26-38. Shame in Mary's own generation (vv.26-27,34) turned to honor in generations to come (v.48). The possible shame of giving birth to a child out of wedlock was something that came from the Lord (v.35), and Mary was willing to submit to it. (v.38). From these circumstances came untold blessings from God (vv.48-49), and praise and gratitude on Mary's part (v.46). The very purposes of God were carried forth (vv.32-33,54-55) because Mary was willing to submit herself to the will of God. Would you be willing to submit yourself to God in the face of shame and scorn by the world if God wanted to use you in a unique way to further His Gospel?

Thursday, July 19, *Luke* 10:38. There was a home just outside Jerusalem where Jesus often found a welcome haven among close friends. This was the home of Mary, Martha and Lazarus. Turn over to John 11:1-5,28-41 and pick out the phrases that describe Jesus' feelings toward Lazarus. What resulted among the Jews as a consequence of Jesus raising Lazarus from the dead (v.45)? Among the Pharisees (vv.47,53,57)? What effect did it have on the faith of Jesus' own disciples (vv.4,15,40-42)? How might the raising of Lazarus have been a help to the disciples' faith when they beheld Jesus, Himself, put to death? God is able to use the affliction of one whom He loves to deepen the faith of others who face crises in their lives.

Friday, July 20, *Luke* 10:39-42. Christians who are weak in faith sometimes try to make up for their lack of faith by a multitude of activities. Observe in John 11:20-27,39 Martha's lack of faith in Jesus' ability to raise Lazarus from the dead. Mary, simply because she loved Christ, anointed His feet with ointment (John 12:1-3) and sat at His feet as He taught (Luke 10:39). It was Martha who was distracted with much activity (Luke 10:40-41; John 12:2). When hard-pressed, she fretted (Luke 10:40). Jesus loved them both (John 11:5) but who did He feel had deep spiritual discernment (Luke 10:41-42)? Could a shallow faith be the cause of our spending much time in church activities and little in the habit of daily prayer and meditation in the presence of Christ?

Saturday, July 21, *Acts* 9:36-43. There is a difference between fretful, dutiful activity done for the church, and acts of charity done because of the constraining love of God in our hearts. Dorcas' deeds were evidently of the latter type. Are your Christian activities the fruit of the love of Christ within you, or the result of a nagging conscience saying you are not doing enough? Observe that Dorcas' good works (vv.36,39) were not beyond the average person's ability. It is often the comparatively insignificant deeds that are the most important in the sight of God (Matt. 25:31-46).

ANGLERS

(From "*New Testament Evangelism*"
by Wade C. Smith)

Lesson No. 147

Continuing "Fishing With The Word"

This story comes from Arizona. It was told by an electrical workman to Hugh D. ("Shine") Smith, missionary to the Navajos and brother of the author. A mountain-climbing party included a plucky lad who slipped and broke his leg and had to be carried back to the hospital. Later, one of the party visited the boy while convalescent and found him still determined to make the climb to the top, so he offered to accompany him on a second effort. All went well until about half way up, the wounded leg which evidently had not fully healed, collapsed, and again the lad lay helpless on the mountainside. But his rugged companion shouldered him and by the greatest effort managed to reach the top. The boy looked at his friend and said, "I wouldn't be here if it were not for you!" The electrical worker who was repairing a nearby power line then said to my brother, "I wonder if when we get to heaven anyone will walk up to us and say, 'If it weren't for you, I wouldn't be here' ".

A comforting discovery to the soul-winner might just as well be made at the beginning of the effort. It is that his task is immensely simplified by the fact that all his line of persuasion is laid down for him in clear print in the Bible. He does not have to resort to his wit, nor skill in debate, for he may not have either. These would, at best, be only a secondary service to him, if any. An unbeliever who is unwilling to confess or relinquish his sin is a most obstinate person to deal with on spiritual matters, and argument, no matter how skillful, gets nowhere. It sometimes makes matters worse. But "the Word of God is quick and powerful, and sharper than any two-edged sword" and it "is a discerner of the thoughts and intents of the heart." The Holy Spirit has supplied this Word and endued it with unfailing power. It will bring conviction. It is folly to lay aside this invincible "sword of the Spirit" and turn to your own words in argument. Use the Word. (see Heb. 4:12).

Using the Word. This does not mean a slavish repetition of Scripture to the exclusion of any thought of your own. But every statement made and every answer given should be truth which can be supported with God's Word, and, of course, actual quotation of the Word is best. If you are faithfully looking to the

Holy Spirit for guidance, and asking for it, you will not go amiss in this. The point is, you do not have to go outside Scripture truth. And you must not allow yourself to be drawn into argument away from it. One of the Devil's favorite lines of "interference" is to shift the conversation away from Bible statements. Note the woman at the well in Samaria. The mention of her five former husbands and her present illicit relationship stung her, and she tried to shift the subject by raising the question of where men ought to worship, in this mountain or at Jerusalem. Jesus, the Master Fisherman, was too wise to allow it, but quickly brought her back to the main line. Often, in introducing the subject, when you ask a "prospect" if he is a Christian, he will begin telling you how he pays his debts, how he never took anything from anybody wrongly, nor drank, nor swore, nor chewed. He may even tell you what a good woman his mother was; or he will bring up the different modes of baptism, or the hypocrites in the church - anything to get away from that searching question. Let him run on awhile; be patient. But when he pauses for breath, quietly ask him if he has accepted Jesus Christ as his Saviour, if he feels assured of the safety of his own soul.

Late one night at a hotel desk the writer was closing the day with a letter to the homefolks. On the opposite side of the desk a traveling salesman was also closing his day with a letter to his firm. He was evidently in a bad humor, for his brow was clouded and as he sealed his letter and stamped it he banged his fist down on it with a half suppressed oath. Our eyes met across the table and he began to tell of the irritations he had suffered during the day. It had rained the whole day; business had amounted to nothing; merchants were blue and wouldn't buy; it was a nasty town anyhow; he never liked to come here; and this hotel! well, it was about the bummest in all his territory. The writer was thinking that if this man were a Christian he would take life more calmly; so when he paused for breath, the question was asked him: "Are you a Christian"? That opened the floodgates. A Christian? He guessed not; and never would be, if he kept his mind. With that he began to relate some things "he knew about Christians." He had been in partnership with a Presbyterian deacon, and the deacon had stripped him of everything he had. Later, after a long struggle to get ahead again, he had foolishly cast his lot in business with a Methodist steward, and through him he had lost his second fortune. Both these, he claimed, had swindled him. Since then he had steered clear of church people, except where he could "tie them up" to their contract so they couldn't get away. He had a contempt for these "hypocrites." Continuing with increasing speed and vehemence, he said he was one of seven brothers. The other six were all members of the church and he was the only honest one in the bunch. That last remark helped to place this poor fellow where he belonged, but there was no chance to get in a word edgeways. He talked a blue streak for 20 minutes. Several times the writer endeavored to ask a question, but he would not be interrupted. Finally, the Sword of the Spirit was drawn. Turning to Romans 14:12 the writer placed his finger at the verse and reaching it up beneath the low hanging bulb that furnished light for both sides of the desk, under the eyes of the tormented man, he was obliged to pause and read it: "So then every one of us shall give account of himself to God." The effect was instantaneous. His jaws snapped together as he jumped to his feet, snatched his letter off the table and with a blunt "Good night!" went to his room. It was the last I saw of him. Next morning the clerk said he had left on the six o'clock train. I do not know all that Romans 14:12 did for him; but one thing is certain, it stopped his line of talk about hypocrites in the church that night as effectually as though a thunderbolt had struck the hotel and split it in two. If we Christians would take the Word at its face value and believe the claims it makes for itself, *and use it,* maybe someday it would be recorded of us, as of the heroes of faith, "who through faith subdued kingdoms, wrought righteousness, obtained promises, *stopped the mouths of lions,* quenched the violence of fire, escaped the edge of the sword, out of weakness were made strong, waxed valiant in fight, turned to flight the armies of the aliens"! by carrying the Word to every fortress that held out against God - *in our own day!*

(More about using the Word, in next lesson)

LESSON FOR JULY 22

We Belong To A Great Company

Scripture: Acts 2:44-47; Hebrews 10:19-25; 11:1 - 13:8
Devotional Reading: Ephesians 4:1-13

In our Devotional Reading we have a beautiful description of this "Great Company" to which all Christians belong: the Church. Every Christian has a "vocation", or "calling"; the upward calling of God in Christ Jesus. We are called out of sin into salvation; out of the world and its wicked ways into a heavenly walk and life. To walk "worthy of that calling" should be the aim and ambition of all those who belong to the "Great Company" of redeemed men and women, described in Revelation 7:9 as a "great multitude ,which no man could number, of all nations, and kindreds, and people, and tongues." In Ephesians Paul is emphasizing the "walk," or manner of life which should characterize those who have been called to follow Christ. We are to walk in all lowliness and meekness with long-suffering, forbearing one another in love. (See Ephesians 4:17; 5:2; 5:15).

He proceeds in 4:1-13 to stress: (1) The Unity of the Church, and (2) its Diversity. We hear a great deal of talk about the Church being divided into so many denominations, and some people criticize us for that obvious fact. When we come to rock-bottom facts, however, the Church is ONE; "We are not divided; all one body, we." This is true of the real Church. There are certain bonds which unite us. Paul tells us what they are: "There is one body, and one Spirit"; one "hope of your calling." The Church is the "Body of Christ". This "Body" is not separated into a hundred different bodies, even though we call the different branches "bodies of Christians" sometimes. Every true Christian is born of one Holy Spirit, and led by that Spirit and filled with that Spirit. We have "one Lord, one faith, one baptism". We are all believers in Christ; He is our Saviour and Lord. We are saved through grace, by faith in Him, and baptized into One Body, when we are baptized in the name of the Father, Son and Holy Ghost. We have "One God and Father of all." We belong to the One Family, and we are all His children. So we should always think of the Church in terms of Unity, not Disunity.

In this Unity there is Diversity. We are not all alike, any more than the trees of a forest, or the leaves on a tree. There are diversities of gifts, and differences of operation. The Church is a real "Body," having members which differ, just like the eyes and hands, and feet of a human body. We cannot all be eyes, or hands, or feet. Our ideal is the "measure of the stature of the fullness of Christ." We are to grow up into Him in all things, built up in truth and love. Every true Christian is a vital part of this One Body; none excluded.

We who live in the United States should understand this analogy. We have one great Country with our Capital, Washington; one President; one Congress; one Flag. In this Union there are many States; some small, some large; some one shape, some another. These States have certain "rights." Why not think of the Church in a somewhat similar manner? Our many Denominations do not destroy the Unity of the Church any more than our many States destroy the Unity of the United States. It is a good thing to have different States.

"We acknowledge one universal church, the same in all ages, of which Christ is the Head." "The church consists of all the redeemed." (Brief Statement of Belief). In our lesson today we get some pictures of that church.

I. *The Church Right After Pentecost:* Acts 2:44-47: Fellowship, Sharing.

The Church takes on new life and a new form at Pentecost. It existed in its Jewish form in the Old Testament. Now it breaks the bands of Judaism and becomes what is commonly called the "Christian Church." Let us never forget, however, that the church of the Old Testament was "Christian" too, for Christ is the Saviour of the Old Testament saints as well as of New Testament saints. They were saved by faith in Him. They had but the "shadow of good things to come." They looked forward to a Coming Messiah; we look back at One Who has come. There was a marvelous Revival at Pentecost, a "Re-birth," one might say, of the One Church.

The glimpse we get is very striking and very lovely. It includes doctrine, or teaching, and fellowship and sharing, or we might change that a bit and say that it is a picture of fellowship based on love, manifesting itself in teaching and sharing. There were certain great facts which they believed, and this united them in a family. The rich sold their possessions and divided their goods and there was a spirit of joy which was contagious; "Praising God, and having favor with all the people." This picture was soon spoiled by the deceit and punishment of Ananias and his wife, (chapter 5) and we find the church changing its methods in caring for the poor. (Chapter 6).

II. *Holding Fast and Encouraging One Another:* Hebrews 10:19-25.

The Book of Hebrews treats especially of the High Priestly work of the Lord Jesus Christ. In the first part of chapter ten His sacrificial work is stressed. "For by one offering he hath perfected forever them that are sanctified." God makes a new covenant with us and will remember our sins and iniquities no more. This is the "new and living way" which is made for us so that with boldness we can enter the holy place by the blood of Jesus.

Having stated this vital and precious truth, we are urged to "Draw near with a true heart in full assurance of faith" . . . "Let us hold fast the profession of our faith without wavering." This is the very heart of the gospel, a rallying point for all true believers. We are to encourage and help each other,provoking unto love and good works, and assembling together for worship. This is needed today. The church must never drift away from the Cross and the atoning death of Christ; His priestly work. The tendency is to stress His life and example and teaching, and neglect the other. Our only hope is in a Saviour Who has opened this "new and living way" by the sacrifice of himself. Only as we draw near the throne of grace through Him and hold fast to Him as our Substitute and Sacrifice for sin can we encourage and help other Christians.

III. *Faith:* Hebrews 11:1 - 13:8.

This extensive section may be divided into two parts: 1. Faith as we see it in the Old Testament, and 2. Faith for us today.

1. Faith as seen in the lives of Old Testament Heroes.

We are given a very striking definition of faith : Now faith is the substance of things hoped for, the evidence of things not seen. I may be sent a deed to property in another state which I have never seen. This "title-deed" is evidence that I own the property. I believe I own it, even though I have not seen it. So we believe God and His promises and by faith lay hold upon our eternal possessions, and our home in the heavens. By faith we also believe that this universe was created by the Word of God and we trust Him Who called it into being.

The main part of chapter eleven is taken up with a list of the outstanding heroes of faith who belong to that "Great Company" of all ages. It was faith that saved Abel, as he by faith, offered a more perfect sacrifice than Cain.

Faith enabled Enoch to walk with God when the world as a whole was walking away from Him. He was translated that he should not see death. He left this testimony, "that he pleased God." Faith always pleases God.

It was faith that made Noah believe the warning of God and build the ark, to the saving of his whole household. He was not only a builder, but a preacher of righteousness, and for one hundred and twenty years preached and built.

Abraham's faith is known far and wide. It led him to leave his country and kindred and venture out on the promise of God. We might call it "Faith of the Pioneer." His faith wavered at times and he made some bad mistakes, but as a whole it showed a complete surrender to God. It was strong enough to stand the test which we find described in Genesis 22.

The faith of Isaac was of a quieter kind. He came between Abraham and Jacob and is overshadowed by them. Jacob's faith finally triumphed and he became a prince with God, but his life is a sad and disappointing one in many ways.

When we come to Moses, "the greatest man in the Old Testament," as many believe, we have a marvelous faith exhibited. As a young man he made a great choice. He refused the crown of Egypt and chose to suffer affliction with the people of God. His faith enabled him to "endure as seeing Him Who is invisible."

Then follows a list of lesser heroes whose faith did great things for them and through them. They were men and women of whom the world was not worthy.

2. *The Faith We Need Today:* Hebrews 12:1 - 13:8.

The heroes above are like a "cloud of witnesses" watching us as we run the race set before us. We are to run with patience, even as they did. We are to endure chastening and hardship and encourage one another. Study these verses.

YOUTH PROGRAM FOR JULY 22

Everyday Greatness

Hymn: "O For A Heart To Praise My God"

Prayer

Scripture: Philippians 2:1-11

Hymn: "O Jesus, I Have Promised"

Offering

Hymn: "A Charge To Keep I Have"

LEADER'S INTRODUCTION:

It is most important for young people to make careful plans for the future. As we discovered in our program last week, we should consider carefully what we are going to be and what we will do with our lives. It is also important to make the right preparation for our vocations. While these things are very true, we must not give ourselves over to living in the future altogether. We must remember that the course we follow in the future is determined very largely by the kind of living we do now. We are not likely to be successful in the future unless we are successful in our present jobs.

Just what are our present jobs? It may be that we do not think of ourselves as having jobs at all. We may think of ourselves as being unemployed. The fact is, however, we all have employment, whether we are aware of it or not. Many of us are high school students. There is a job in itself, and a very important one. Our studies and our other school activities call for a great amount of our time and energy. We also have responsibilities in our homes and churches. These responsibilities make up another phase of our present job. There are many young people in our age group who do part-time work for pay. This too, is a part of our present job. Leisure time and recreation are important for all people, and especially for young people. Even these are meaningful in determining the successfulness of our lives.

As we go about our present tasks or jobs, we ought to be striving for success. Doing daily tasks well is the way to attain the "everyday greatness" spoken of in the title of this program. Let us look at some of the qualities we ought to be developing day by day . . . qualities which will lead to success and "everyday greatness."

FIRST SPEAKER:

One of the basic ingredients of success is dependability. This is a quality which we should develop and practice in everything we do. Can our teachers always depend on us to turn in our papers when they are due? Can our parents count on our doing regular home chores without having to remind us the second and third times? When we agree to have a part on the program at the youth meeting can the leader depend on us to be present and well prepared? Can our friends always depend on us to keep our promises and to do our part? Dependability is one of the roads to "everyday greatness." We ought to walk it every day.

Closely related to dependability is honesty. We are not referring to obvious violations of honesty, such as lying and stealing, but to some more generally accepted forms of dishonesty. A boy who is being paid by the hour and who loafs on the job is being dishonest. A student who "borrows" information which he was supposed to work out for himself is guilty of dishonesty. Any kind of sham or pretense is a form of dishonesty. Some dishonest people seem to be successful, but they could never be called great in the true and pure sense of the term.

SECOND SPEAKER:

Every person who is truly successful is thorough in the work he does. Thoroughness is something we need to practice in everything we do. If we want to get to the top, we must learn to put our very best into whatever we do. There are many times when it is easier to take "short cuts" and do a job in a shoddy manner, but sloppy work can become a habit very quickly, and sloppiness is a sure barrier to success. If we are already in the habit of doing things in a slipshod fashion, it will be difficult to overcome the habit. The best way to overcome this bad habit is to practice being thorough in some very small matters. There is real personal satisfaction in doing a job well, and when we learn thoroughness in small things, we shall find it easier to be thorough in all our work.

THIRD SPEAKER:

Another very important ingredient of success is the attitude we have toward other people from day to day. A person can be very well informed, skilled, thorough, dependable, and honest in his work, and still be a failure if his attitude is unwholesome. Are we always pleasant, friendly, and unselfish in our school, home, and social contacts? We may think this has little bearing on our future in the business or professional world, but personality determines success to a very large measure. Our attitudes shape our personalities, and now is the time our attitudes can be changed if need be. There can be no "everyday greatness" in us unless we begin now to develop and practice these wholesome attitudes.

FOURTH SPEAKER:

In our program two weeks ago we noted that Christ's formula for success called for service. Jesus said, "For even the Son of Man came not to be ministered unto, but to minister, and to give his life a ransom for many." Mark 10:45. Service and helpfulness certainly ought to have a large place in our plans for future life and work. If these characteristics are to be found in us in the future, we must begin to practice them faithfully now. Do we seek to be genuinely helpful to our teachers and fellow students at school? Do we think of our homes as needing our services, or do we think of them only as institutions to minister to our needs? Unselfish service is one of the marks of "everyday greatness."

FIFTH SPEAKER:

There is one simple way to make sure that all these necessary marks of greatness and success will be found in us. If we will unreservedly dedicate our lives to Christ, we shall find ourselves steadily growing in dependability, honesty, thoroughness, friendliness, and helpfulness. These qualities are the natural outgrowth of the new nature . . . the new heart . . . that Christ gives us when we give ourselves to Him. The sure way to "everyday greatness" is complete dedication of all that we are and have to Jesus Christ.

Search the Scriptures

"Let us search and try our ways and turn again to the Lord."

If you desire knowledge, if you would like to grasp the full meaning of Christianity, go to the Bible. Read it chapter by chapter and mark each verse of interest. Eventually you will be able to answer most of your own questions. You will go back to certain passages over and over and years from now they will be as fresh and as powerful as on the day you discovered them.

There are thousands of verses with messages in them for men upon every subject. Whole chapters and whole books will appeal to you. No one has been able to consume and absorb the Bible; it will take more than a lifetime of serious and detailed study. Select subjects like Faith, Prayer, Sin and with the aid of a concordance enjoy hours of worship.

God speaks to man through His Word and the greatest blessing you can receive will come through a careful and prayerful study of His Word. I recommend a seven-year course in the Bible, verse by verse. Ralph Brewer

Women's Work

The Book of the Year

By Tsunetaro Miyakoda
General Secretary of the Japan Bible Society

The special recognition gained by the New Kogotai (colloquial) Bible in Japanese is a great forward step for the Bible cause and evangelism in Japan. The book awards of the Mainichi Shimbun, one of the world's largest newspapers, are similar to the Pulitzer prizes in the United States.

During each of the last nine years on November 3 - Japan's "Culture Day" - an award to the best book of the year has been announced. This annual award is given to a book on its merits as the best reading in its class. Points are also given for excellence of manufacture.

The Japan Bible Society submitted its medium-sized Bible in "Kogotai," colloquial Japanese.

Over 20,000 books covering almost every phase of the life of the nation were submitted. The judges were leading men in every walk of life. Thirty were from Tokyo and twenty-two from Osaka. Some of the best-known men in science, education, art, drama, and literary criticism were among the judges.

It soon became known that among the 350 books announced as not eliminated prior to the day of decision, the Kogotai entry was a leading favorite.

Finally the Mainichi Shimbun, "The Daily," which sponsors the contest, handed down the final judgment of the more than fifty men who carefully examined all the book entries. The Kogotai Bible, they decided, should be awarded special first-place recognition in every way equal to the regular first prize.

The first prize carried with it 50,000 yen ($150) and a bronze tablet. The cash was to go to the author and the tablet to the publisher. In the case of the Bible the cash prize could not go to the author, so a special category was created. The author of the next-best book received the cash award, but the Japan Bible Society received the bronze tablet.

The value of this award will be tremendous. Imagine the effect it will have on missionary distribution for the colporteurs to be offering a book judged "the best of the year." One morning after the award was presented, it was like an answer to prayer to stand on the pavement near the Bible House in Tokyo and watch the passers-by stop and scrutinize the certificate of merit and the first-prize bronze plaque which were on display.

Miss Florence Walvoord, a missionary in Japan of the Foreign Board of the Reformed Church in America has written: "Last spring the Kogotai translation was selected by the National Library Association of Japan as one of its 'recommended books.' This means that its three thousand member libraries all over the nation will be urged to put this edition of the Bible along with other books for special display and recommended reading."

—From the American Bible Society.

Christian Adventure

If you want to get a real thrill out of going to church, follow a few off-hand suggestions culled from remarks of a fellow-pastor. From what may have been but a boring duty — a matchless adventure will be realized.

1. Never miss. That's fundamental. Occasional church-going is like occasional practicing on a musical instrument. It never gets beyond the stage of painful awkwardness. Go regularly and soon you will enter a glorious stage of freedom. Church-going will become an exciting adventure.

2. Study to know the worship pattern. The Pastor can help you. Each organization of the Church would profit much by setting aside an evening to a special study of it. For joyous church-going — know the service and the meaning of each part.

3. Be receptive - not critical. Face the panorama of spiritual values which a church service brings you just like you would watch a sunset or listen to music. Be receptive. "Incline thine ear." Surrender yourself calmly to the glorious experience and respond hilariously.

Don't sit stiffly and severely as if daring God to get anything by the door of your heart. Relax. Surrender to the worship mood.

4. Don't expect the sermon to please you every time. Even .300 is a good batting average in baseball. No pastor could please all his worshippers every time he preaches. If he did he would not be worth his salt. Even in human relationships Jesus commented "beware when all men speak well of you." We may go to church for comfort and strength but sometimes we need to be stabbed awake spiritually and morally. It's when a sermon hits you that God is getting something across to you!

5. Give as well as receive. There are many ways you can contribute: tithes and offerings for the Gospel work of congregation, at home and in other mission fields. But you can also pray for the pastor, the organist, the choir director, choir, ushers, the worshippers about you and especially for those who didn't come — God only knows why. Surprising what this can do for a service - and you. Let your worship be others-centered rather than self-centered.

6. Tell others. If you would keep the blessings of worship - share them. Say to your neighbor over the fence or to your friends over the phone, "Say, I wish you had been at church with me yesterday. The anthem was so helpful - the message so fine and in the prayer we came face to face with God. There was a radiance on the face of those who worshipped."

Church-going need not be boring - it can be a spiritual adventure. Make the most of this privilege while it is still ours. Come to Church every Sunday. And give your *whole self* in the service of our Lord.

—Dr. Paul Luther Wetzler

One Minute Messages on Stewardship

Our stewardship begins at home, and these are Mrs. Askew's thoughts: Home is the first and most precious, the most potent responsibility of a Christian steward. The next most precious are the children.

In what habit of living can our stewardship be best expressed - through our homes?

A true reverence for a happy use of God's Book, God's Day, and God's House of Worship, with the habit of prayer at meals and also at some regular period each day. But equally - this every day living from a sincere devotion to the Lord. Does everything in our homes point heavenward to Christ? The rightly ordered Christian home will always find right places and proportion of time and money for service to Church and community.

Your children's sense of Christ's real and beloved Presence in your home depends on the atmosphere of your home more than anything else. You must make this atmosphere. Three essentials are:

How SINCERE is your home - especially in its religious forms and customs?

How HAPPY is your home - especially in its inner chambers of family intimacies?

How PURE is your home, especially in its habits and thought and speech?

It is well to consider here - your child's abilities, as well as your own - for whose sake are they being used? Is your child using the skill, with his own particular instrument, whether it be piano, typewriter, or pen for Christ?

Does your home, as it is known to Jesus, make Him glad? Remember, He is the abiding guest in every Christian heart and home.

Church News

REV. CHARLES H. GIBBONEY

Atlanta—

The Rev. Charles H. Gibboney, Secretary of Promotion for the Board of Church Extension, June 24 accepted the call to become pastor of Reid Memorial Presbyterian Church in Augusta.

Dr. Gibboney will assume his new duties on September 1.

The six-hundred-member church is the one President and Mrs. Eisenhower attend when they are in Augusta.

Dr. Gibboney goes to the Reid Memorial pastorate after seven years with the board.

He is a native of Roanoke, Va., where he received his early schooling. His undergraduate work was begun at the University of the South, Sewanee, Tenn., and completed at the University of Virginia, Charlottesville. He received the B. D. degree from Union Theological Seminary, Richmond, Va., in 1938, and was awarded the Salem Fellowship. The following year was spent in graduate study at the University of Edinburgh, Edinburgh, Scotland.

After ordination by West Hanover Presbytery, in the fall of 1939, Dr. Gibboney served a group of churches in that area for the following three years and taught Bible at Hampden-Sydney College, Hampden-Sydney, Va. He held a pastorate at Keyser, West Virginia, for two years and for five years was pastor of the Second Presbyterian Church, Norfolk, Va.

In the summer of 1949 Dr. Gibboney became Educational Secretary of the Executive Committee of Home Missions and upon reorganization of the Church's agencies a year later, became Secretary of Promotion for the Board of Church Extension, his present position.

DEATH OF DAWSON TROTMAN

Christian friends around the world have been shocked and saddened by the sudden Home-going of Dawson Trotman, Director of the Navigators, who was drowned in Schroon Lake, New York, Monday, June 18.

During the Navigators East Coast Conference at Schroon Lake, Dawson Trotman was with Jack Wyrtzen, director of Word of Life Camp, and a group of young people in a speedboat, when the boat struck a wave and he and Allene Beck, 21, were thrown out. The girl could not swim, but he held her above the surface of the water while the boat circled back to them. Just as she was pulled to safety he sank beneath the waters. His body was found two days later by a skin diver, Alfred Popp, at a depth of fifty feet.

Mr. Trotman's intimate friend and associate Billy Graham spoke both at the private funeral and public memorial service in Colorado Springs on Wednesday, June 27. In a letter to friends of The Navigators the evangelist said, "I can think of no one with whom I have had closer fellowship and to whom I am more deeply indebted spiritually than this man of God . . . There could not have been a more dramatic and characteristic way to die. He who spent all of his life in bringing salvation and upbuilding to others . . . spending his last moments in saving the life of one who could not swim."

The last thirty of Dawson's fifty years had been spent in vigorous discipleship for his Lord. Converted at the age of twenty through some Scripture passages he had memorized, he immediately began to reach others with the gospel of Christ and help them grow in the Christian life through Bible study and prayer. This dual purpose continued throughout his ministry as he imparted to thousands of Christian and missionary leaders the vision of follow-up and training of laymen to win and teach others.

Putting these principles into action in 1932 in intensive individual training of a few sailors of the USS West Virginia in the San Pedro harbor, he later saw the fruit of their application as the work spread from sailor to sailor, to other ships throughout the fleet and other branches of the service, and later to civilian life.

In 1948 he made his first survey of missions around the world and sent the first representative to spearhead the Navigators' work in a foreign country, Roy Robertson, ex-Navy pilot who set up headquarters in Shanghai, China. Since then "Daws" had traveled hundreds of thousands of miles and worked tirelessly to answer the demands of mission boards, churches and other agencies who have asked the Navigators for help in follow-up. Best known of the helps and correspondence courses he designed to instruct and help the young Christian are "Beginning With Christ" (The Initial Bible Rations), Introductory Bible Study and the Topical Memory System.

Today twelve countries overseas and fourteen U. S. areas have Navigator headquarters. On the very day of their leader's death another of his goals was fulfilled as a team of Navigator missionary representatives entered Africa to assist other missions in the evangelization and training of former Mau Mau terrorists.

Directing the Navigator work as well as continuing the responsibility for follow-up and personal counseling with the Billy Graham Team is the organization's vice president Lorne Sanny. As far back as 1948 Dawson had recognized God's direction in designating Sanny to succeed him in leadership of the Navigators work. Throughout these years and more especially in recent months Daws had trained and prepared him for this task. The heartbeat of Dawson Trotman's teaching and one of the basic principles upon which the Navigators have moved forward is illustrated in the fact that a man trained and equipped of God is ready to assume leadership.

Said Billy Graham, "I believe that the Navigators will continue; I believe that they will expand. And the young man that is to head the Navigators from now on, Lorne Sanny, is one of the best equipped men for the task that I know."

No change in the board of directors is anticipated.

ALABAMA

Birmingham — Two Presbyterian churches in this area are moving ahead with their building and expansion plans.

South Avondale Presbyterian Church announced that workmen have begun laying the concrete foundation for the first two units of a $125,000 building program. The Rev. David Park, pastor, said that the initial units, an educational building and a temporary sanctuary, should be finished by the middle of August. The last two units planned by the congregation, which has purchased a nearly five-acre site for the building, will be the permanent sanctuary, and the youth building. They plan to convert the temporary sanctuary into an Adult Fellowship building.

The Forest Hills Presbyterian Church in Fairfield is planning an expansion of the present plant. Dr. Alva Gregg, pastor, said that the membership was seeking financial assistance. Members have requested a $10,000 grant from the General Assembly, and a $3,000 grant from the local Presbytery, he said.

The congregation wants to build a two-floor educational unit which will have Sunday School departments in the basement, and a temporary sanctuary, fellowship class and Adult Bible classes on the first floor.

With the excavation already completed, the congregation has raised $3,300, and received a grant of $3,910 from the General Assembly and a grant of $3,200 from the Atlanta Presbytery.

The Synod of Florida

The 65th annual session of the Synod of Florida, Presbyterian Church U. S. was held at the Peace Memorial Presbyterian Church, Clearwater, June 19th and 20th, 1956. Retiring Moderator the Rev. Walter B. Passiglia presided at the Communion Service preaching the moderatorial sermon on the topic "Hold Fast."

The Rev. Dr. W. H. Kadel, Pastor, First Presbyterian Church, Orlando, and Vice-Moderator, was unable to attend the meeting of Synod being enroute to the Holy Land with Mrs. Kadel, having been honored with the trip as an expression of appreciation by their congregation.

The Rev. Paul Milburn Edris, Pastor, First Presbyterian Church, Daytona Beach, was elected Moderator by acclamation as was Elder Judge Julian L. Alford of Tallahassee as Vice-Moderator. The clerks of the Synod elected to three year terms included the Rev. Russell F. Johnson, Pastor, Springfield Presbyterian Church, Jacksonville, Stated Clerk; the Rev. Stewart H. Long, Pastor, Bel-Mar Presbyterian Church, Tampa, Permanent Clerk and the Rev. Arthur W. Rideout, Pastor of the First Presbyterian Church, Bradenton, Publicity Clerk.

Synod adopted a benevolent budget of $618,520 for 1957 and assigned this amount to the five Presbyteries of the Synod. A special challenge fund of $5,000 matched by the Board of Christian Education, Richmond, Va., will be used to study the possibility of a Presbyterian Church related College for Florida.

Synod accepted the invitation of the First Presbyterian Church, Ocala, to meet with them in May 1957 during the 100th Anniversary of the Ocala Church of which the Rev. Fred L. Turner is Pastor.

Mrs. F. M. Womack, President of Synodical, The Women of The Church, reported on the outstanding work of the 28,459 members of the 828 circles which were responsible for the raising of $253,-673.00 in 1955.

Representatives of the Synod related institutions reporting to the Synod included the Rev. Dr. John R. Cunningham, President of Davidson College, Davidson, N. C., the Rev. Dr. Felix Gear for Columbia Seminary, Decatur, Georgia; the Rev. A. G. McInnis, Pastor, First Presbyterian Church, Sanford, Fla., as a Trustee of Thornwell Orphanage, Clinton, S. C.; and Miss Patricia Gatlin, Campus Christian Life Worker assigned to the Westminster Foundation, University of Florida, Gainesville, reporting for the Assembly's Training School for Lay Workers, Richmond, Virginia. The report of Agnes Scott College, Decatur, Georgia, was presented by Dr. W. E. McNair, Assistant to the President of Agnes Scott College. A request that one dollar per communicant member of the churches of the Synod be placed in a special fund for Davidson College support was approved by the Synod and recommended to the member Presbyteries.

A special Judicial Commission of the Synod sustained the action of St. Johns Presbytery against the Rev. Arthur A. Froelich, Pastor and the Elders and Deacons of the Maitland Presbyterian Church in the dissolution of the pastoral relation and the removal of the church officers. The Rev. Mr. Froelich gave notice to the Synod of his intention to register a complaint against this action to the General Assembly meeting in Birmingham, Alabama, in April 1957. The Rev. Dr. Stephen T. Harvin, Pastor of the Southside Presbyterian Church, Jacksonville and Chairman of Synod's Special Judicial Commission on this matter was elected by the Synod as respondent to represent the Synod before the Judicial Commission of the General Assembly.

The success of the pre-budget method of church canvassing was reported by several churches of the Synod.

The Rev. Dr. E. D. Brownlee, Pastor of the Presbyterian Church of Inverness, oldest member of the Synod in point of service was recognized by Synod on the 50th anniversary of his licensure, to the Gospel Ministry.

The Men of the Church of the Synod were entertained at a dinner presented by the Peace Memorial Church of Clearwater of which the Rev. Dr. D. F. McGeachey, Jr., is Pastor. The Peace Memorial Church is celebrating its 65th anniversary in the completion of a complete remodeling of the Sanctuary and of Roebling Hall. Dr. Lester Hale of the Speech Department University of Florida, a deacon of the First Presbyterian Church, Gainesville, presented the main inspirational address on Christian Higher Education at the men's dinner.

The closing session of Synod was addressed by the Rev. Dr. Hunter B. Blakely, Secretary of the Division of Higher Education, the Board of Christian Education, Richmond, Va., on the subject "The Christian College — The Dream."

Memorials were received in the passing of the Rev. E. B. McGill, Jacksonville, the Rev. Alva Hardy, Orlando, the Rev. Robert H. Visor, Clearwater and the Rev. Dr. W. T. Martin, Tallahassee.

GEORGIA

Savannah — At the spring rally of the Men of Savannah Presbytery held in Vidalia, Ga., the men voted unanimously to have as their main project, the building and development of a presbytery camp at Hilton Head. Main development will begin immediately and continue through 1956 and 1957. It is hoped that enough facilities will be available by July so that daytime groups can use the site.

Sometime in May, twenty-eight men, at the invitation of G. H. Achenback and Major General Joseph B. Fraser, met to plan for the promotion of the camp to be located on twenty wooded acres given last year to the presbytery by the Hilton Head Company, of which Gen. Fraser is president. The site is 125 yards from the beach.

Dan P. Stearns of Statesboro, treasurer of the Camp Fund, reports that $6,562.31 in cash receipts from churches and individuals has already been received. Disbursements to date for bulldozing, building roads, and clearing the ground, amount to $1,413.75. This leaves a balance of $5,148.56 on hand with $5,795 in unpaid pledges from churches and individuals.

This will be the first conference ground of Savannah Presbytery.

At the meeting of Savannah Presbytery, September 20, 1955, the Camp Finance Committee was authorized to borrow $7,500 from the bank to complete the first phase of the camp. When the presbytery met in Hinesville, May 15 of this year, it reaffirmed this authority and twenty-six men have indicated that they would endorse the bank note with the understanding that individual liability would not exceed $500.

The Rev. Ewell L. Nelson, pastor of McRae Presbyterian Church and G. H. Achenback of Vidalia, past president of the Men of the presbytery, are co-chairmen of the Finance Committee of the camp. The Rev. J. Walton Stewart, pastor of First Church, Savannah, is chairman of the camp's Planning Committee.

Jackson — At impressive ceremonies Sunday, May 27, ground was broken for the new Sunday School Annex of the Jackson Presbyterian Church, marking the first major building program of the Church in the last 65 years.

Attending the ground-breaking rites was a committee from Atlanta Presbytery, including Dr. F. C. Talmadge, secretary of the Committee of Church Extension for the Atlanta Presbytery; Elder Robert Head, of the Druid Hills Presbyterian Church, chairman of the Church Extension Committee, and Dr. Bonneau Dickson, pastor of Atlanta's Rock Springs Presbyterian Church.

The new annex will contain approximately 2,850 sq. ft. with a basement space for fellowship hall, kitchen and storage room and a first floor divided into four classrooms and toilet facilities. Tied onto the right rear corner of the sanctuary, the annex will blend into the architectural designs of the church and will be framed with white clap boards to match the church structure.

Rev. W. H. Bell, Jr., is now in his third year as pastor of the Jackson Presbyterian Church. He is a graduate of Brown University and Columbia Theological Seminary and a native of Atlanta, Georgia.

TENNESSEE

Nashville — Rev. and Mrs. William R. Reily and family of our Congo Mission are scheduled to return to that country on June 27 after their furlough in the United States.

Mr. Reily will begin his second term of service in the Belgian Congo where he is engaged in evangelistic work. He is from Tyler, Texas, and is a member of Paris Presbytery. Mr. Reily attended Tyler Junior College, and is a graduate of George Washington University and Union Theological Seminary.

Mrs. Reily is the former Miss Patsy Miller who is the daughter of Congo missionaries, the Rev. and Mrs. A. Hoyt Miller. She attended the Central School for Missionaries Children in Congo and then came to America where she studied at Erskine College in Due West, S. C. She received her B. A. degree from Queens College, Charlotte, N. C. Mrs. Reily also attended Assembly's Training School in Richmond. She is a member of Myers Park Presbyterian Church in Charlotte.

The Reilys have three small sons age five, two and four months.

Nashville — Rev. and Mrs. Paul Blake Smith of our West Brazil Mission announce the birth of a daughter, Margaret Grace, in Brazil on May 1.

Mr. Smith is from Orlando, Florida, and is a graduate of Maryville College and Columbia Theological Seminary. He is a member of Cherokee Presbytery.

Mrs. Smith is the former Miss Janet Giffen of Marietta, Georgia. She is a member of the First Presbyterian Church of Marietta. They first went to Brazil in September 1948, and are engaged in evangelistic work.

The Smiths have two other children, sons, aged 6½ and 4.

Knoxville — Vice President Richard M. Nixon has accepted an invitation to be principal speaker at the men's convention of the Synod of Appalachia, at Montreat, N. C., August 5.

Announcement of the Vice President's acceptance was made here by Mack Blackburn, president of the men of the synod, and a member of Little Brick Church in Knoxville.

The convention will start August 4 and will last two days, having as its theme, "Man's Place in the Household of God."

H. H. McCampbell, Jr., Knoxville lawyer and Presbyterian leader, will keynote the conference.

Included in the Synod of Appalachia are presbyteries from four states: Knoxville Presbytery in Tennessee and Kentucky; Holston Presbytery in Tennessee; Abingdon Presbytery in Virginia, and Asheville Presbytery in North Carolina.

Any Three of the Books Listed Below Sent Postpaid for $5.00

SUPPLY LIMITED — ORDER NOW

The Basis of Millennial Faith ______ $2.00
By Floyd E. Hamilton

Why 1000 Years? ______ $2.50
By Wm. Masselink

Crucial Questions About The Kingdom of God ______ $3.00
By George E. Ladd

John Calvin: Expository Preacher ______ $2.50
By Leroy Nixon

The Trial of Jesus Christ ______ $2.00
By Frank J. Powell

Supreme Authority ______ $2.00
By Norvel Geldenhuys

The Gospel of The Spirit ______ $1.50
By Samuel Eyles Pierce

Studies in Theology ______ $3.50
By Loraine Boettner

The Reformed Doctrine of Justification ______ $3.00
By Boehl

The Reformed Doctrine of Adoption ______ $2.50
By R. A. Webb

The Faith of Christendom ______ $3.00
By Vander Meulen

Christianity and Liberalism ______ $2.50
By J. Gresham Machen

The Presbyterian Conflict ______ $1.50
By Edwin H Rian

What Presbyterians Believe ______ $2.00
By Gordon H. Clark

The Impact of Christianity on the Non-Christian World ______ $2.50
By Dr. J. H. Bavinck

Pilgrims Progress ______ $1.00
By John Bunyan

The March of Truth ______ $2.50
By Dr. Stephen Szabo

The Called of God ______ $3.95
By A. B. Davidson

Twenty Missionary Stories From India ______ $1.50
By Basil Miller

The Reformed Doctrine of Predestination ______ $4.50
By Loraine Boettner

Christianity Rightly So Called ______ $2.00
By Samuel G. Craig

Who Say Ye That I Am ______ $2.50
By Wm. Childs Robinson

Christ the Bread of Life ______ $2.50
By Wm. Childs Robinson

Christ—The Hope of Glory ______ $3.00
By Wm. Childs Robinson

Knowing The Scriptures ______ $3.95
By A. T. Pierson

Lord of Glory ______ $3.50
By B. B. Warfield

The Plan of Salvation ______ $1.50
By B. B. Warfield

Progress of Doctrine ______ $1.75
By Thomas Dehany Bernard

Does God Answer Prayer ______ $1.50
By Louise Harrison McCraw

God Transcendent and Other Sermons ______ $2.50
By Gresham Machen

Christianity and Existentialism ______ $3.00
By J. M. Spier

The Lord From Heaven ______ $1.50
By Sir Robert Anderson

The Doctrines of Grace ______ $3.95
By George S. Bishop

The Infallibility of the Church ______ $3.00
By George D. Salmon

Successful Church Publicity ______ $1.00
By Carl F. H. Henry

The Covenant Idea in New England Theology ______ $2.50
By Dr. Peter Y. DeJong

The Servant of Jehovah ______ $2.95
By David Baron

Opening Doors ______ $1.50
By R. G. McLees, D.D.

Edward O. Guerrant ______ $1.00
By J. Gray McAllister and Grace Owings Guerrant

Manual of Reformed Doctrine ______ $2.50
By Prof. W. Heyns

Israel and the New Covenant ______ $3.75
By Roger Campbell

Order From

THE SOUTHERN PRESBYTERIAN JOURNAL

Weaverville, North Carolina

Our Presbyterian Heritage

Last year the Southern Presbyterian Journal sponsored a symposium on the Reformed Faith. Addresses were made by a group of outstanding Presbyterians and all who attended gave enthusiastic response.

Without in any measure competing with any other program in our church a similar symposium will be held this year, again placing its emphasis on our Presbyterian heritage.

THE TIME—August 15th — 10:00 A. M.

THE PLACE—Weaverville, N. C.

DR. C. GREGG SINGER—*"The Reformed Faith and the Contemporary Crisis in Education"*

DR. GORDON H. CLARK — *"The Reformed Doctrine of Verbal Inspiration of the Scriptures."*

DR. FLOYD HAMILTON — *"The Reformed Doctrine of Infant Baptism"*

DR. AIKEN TAYLOR — *"The Reformed Doctrine of the Means of Grace"*

DR. W. C. ROBINSON — *"The Reformed Doctrine of the Bodily Resurrection of Christ"*

DR. R. F. GRIBBLE — *"The Reformed Faith as Related to the Virgin Birth Foretold in Isaiah 7:14"*

MR. GEORGE BURNHAM—*"To the Far Corners"*

Make Plans Now To Attend This Meeting

THE SOUTHERN PRESBYTERIAN JOURNAL

Weaverville, N. C.

THE SOUTHERN PRESBYTERIAN JOURNAL

A Presbyterian weekly magazine devoted to the statement, defense and propagation of the Gospel, the faith which was once for all delivered unto the saints.

VOL. XV NO. 12 | JULY 18, 1956 | $2.50 A YEAR

Today's Diversions

This is no mere theoretical dilemma but actually our Church faces a single continuous problem — How to adapt or give unity to the never changing principles of God's plan of Salvation, with the ever changing conditions in both habits and conventions in today's race for diversions.

THE SOUTHERN PRESBYTERIAN JOURNAL
The Journal has no official connection with the Presbyterian Church in the United States
Rev. Henry B. Dendy, D.D., Editor....Weaverville, N. C.
Dr. L. Nelson Bell, Associate Editor....Asheville, N. C.
Rev. Wade C. Smith, Associate Editor....Weaverville, N. C.

EDITORIAL

"Christian" — Do We Honor the Name?

"And the disciples were called Christians first in Antioch." Acts 11:26.

"Thou shalt not take the name of the Lord thy God in vain; for the Lord will not hold him guiltless that taketh his name in vain." Exodus 20:7.

"Therefore say unto the house of Israel, Thus saith the Lord God; I do not this for your sakes, O house of Israel, but for mine holy name's sake, which ye have profaned among the heathen, whither ye went. And I will sanctify my great name, . . . which ye have profaned in the midst of them." Ezekiel 36:22,23.

* * * * *

How many of us *act* like Christians when confronted with the exasperating situations which arise as a part of daily living? How many show by our reactions that we are Christians when confronted with evil? How many of us live like Christians when we are alone?

These questions are directed to our own consciences because we believe for entirely too many of us there is a vast difference between profession and action.

We may be familiar with the prayer of the little girl: "Oh Lord, please make more people Christians and make more Christians nice." This childish prayer is the reflection of a situation all too common, because in daily contacts so often we are not as sweet and "nice" as Christians should be.

All of us who call ourselves Christians should engage in a prayer-directed searching of our hearts. Let us consider our *actions* and *reactions* in the light of what we know Christ would have us do.

How did I react when that thoughtless driver splashed mud on me? What did I say when that neighbor let his dog damage my flower bed? What did bystanders hear when I was treated discourteously on the street? How did I react to those complaints, justified and unjustified, about the work I had done? What did I *feel* and retort when a busybody told me of the unkind remark of someone?

These and dozens of other questions can be asked by us, depending on our own personal situation. And, if we are honest with ourselves and with our God we must answer that only too often that which we have said and done has dishonored that Holy Name which we as Christians bear.

For instance, the writer believes that true Christian race relations will be furthered by all Christians, white and Negro, reacting to each other with exactly the same love, consideration and courtesy which we ourselves would appreciate from others. From such *basic* mutual attitudes of Christian love it is not difficult to go on to the solution of more complex social problems.

Probably the surest (and the easiest) way to proceed in the matter of acting and living like Christians is to start each day saturated with prayer and a reading of some portion of God's Word. From that beginning we should ask His presence and help and then as different problems and contacts with others arise to ask our hearts what Christ would do in similar circumstances. If we do this we believe others will see His likeness in our lives.

If all of us act as Christians should act the world will see a winsomeness in the name Christian which is only too often lacking today and it would be a wonderful witness for the transforming power of Christ in our lives.

But, even in this Satan will place a pitfall. Our Lord has told us to let our light so shine before men that they may see our good works and then *glorify Him*. God forbid that we should ever try to steal His glory. We believe there is a "Satanic sweetness" to be found in the world - a definite bid to win the acclaim of man under the pretext of personal goodness.

Let us beware of this as we would the plague, and let us pray that those with whom we come in daily contact may see reflected in our lives the fruits of the Spirit—those things which we do not have of ourselves—things which glorify the living Christ Whose Holy Name we bear.

L.N.B.

What Do You Think?

One of the gravest problems confronting the Church is *how* her influence shall be exercised in the world for righteousness.

With considerable variations there are two main philosophies having to do with this problem.

The first is that the Church should concentrate on winning souls to Christ and in developing them in their Christian living so that they as redeemed men and women shall then exercise their influence on society as Christian citizens.

The second, while not ruling out the first, would go much further and insist that the Church, as the Church, should enter the lists on social, ethical, moral and spiritual issues.

This *Journal,* holding chiefly to the first philosophy, recognizes at the same time that there may be issues having to do primarily with moral and spiritual problems where a corporate witness is needed.

But, we have the profound conviction that there are limits, both as to objectives and methods, beyond which the Church should not pass.

What are those limits? Is there not some sound basic policy which should guide the Church? Should the Church ever use agents to lobby for specific legislation? What are the limits beyond which Protestantism would find herself using the Church as a political bludgeon? Should the "constituted authorities" of the Church, or her organizations, speak authoritatively for the Church on matters not delegated to them?

These and many other implications need discussion, particularly as our last General Assembly has referred this matter to our Permanent Committee on Inter-Church Relations for study.

We are opening the columns of this *Journal* to a general discussion of this matter. Letters should be limited to 100 words. If articles are submitted they *must* be short.

What do you think?

The Editors.

ANGLERS

(From *"New Testament Evangelism"* by Wade C. Smith)

Lesson No. 148

FISHING WITH THE WORD (Continued)

Our human reasonings are throttled down by many limitations, "but the Word of God is not bound," as Paul, with shackled hands and in prison, wrote to Timothy. Every soul-winner should read frequently the 2nd chapter of 2nd Timothy; it is teeming with richest help and counsel for those who would learn how to deal with lost men to save them.

There is another reassuring thing about the use of Scripture in soul-winning: it is definite and positive. It is direct affirmation. There is a forthright answer for every objection or excuse or question. Nor does one have to be thoroughly versed in all the Bible to wield this invincible weapon. Of course, the more familiar the soul-winner is with his Bible the more readily he can bring its incisive passages to bear fittingly upon the case in hand; but a few well-chosen statements of Scripture are sufficient to begin with. The clear outline of the Plan of Salvation was given in Lesson No. 146, covered by only a dozen verses. Answers to practically all objections can also be covered by a few selected passages. On page XVII of the *Testament For Fishers Of Men* appear seventeen objections which are commonly offered by those resisting the Gospel invitation, these practically covering the whole range of excuses one may encounter. They are copied here, with "God's answers" (not man's), as shown by the passages noted. It is recommended that these also be read in the daily "Morning Watch" until the soul-winner is perfectly familiar with them.

God's Answers To Objections

1. I would have to give up too much.
Mark 8:36 - Rom. 8:32

The Southern Presbyterian Journal, *a Presbyterian Weekly magazine devoted to the statement, defense, and propagation of the Gospel, the faith which was once for all delivered unto the saints,* published every Wednesday by The Southern Presbyterian Journal, Inc., in Weaverville, N. C.

Entered as second-class matter May 15, 1942, at the Postoffice at Weaverville, N. C., under the Act of March 3, 1879. Vol. XV, No. 12, July 18, 1956. Editorial and Business Offices: Weaverville, N. C. Printed in the U.S.A. by Biltmore Press, Asheville, N. C.

ADDRESS CHANGE: When changing address, please let us have both old and new address as far in advance as possible. Allow three weeks after change if not sent in advance. When possible, send an address label giving your old address.

2. I fear I could not hold out.
1.Cor.10:13 - Heb.4:15,16

3. I will wait a little. Jas.4:13,14

4. I am waiting to "feel right."
John 5:24 - Matt.9:9

5. I have sinned away my chance.
Mark 2:17 - John 6:37

6. I have tried but failed.
1.John 1:9 - Phil.1:6

7. I am better than some church people.
Luke 16:15 - Jas.2:10

8. There are hypocrites in the church.
Rom. 14:12 - Rom. 2:1-4

9. How can I learn to believe?
John 7:17 - John 1:12

10. How may I know that I am saved?
1.John 4:13 - Rom.8:16

11. Scientific theories have troubled me.
1.Tim.6:20 - 1.Cor.2:5

12. My relatives oppose it. Mark 10:29,30

13. I am afraid I will come to want. Phil.4:19

14. I cannot believe what I cannot understand.
1.Cor.2:9-16 - John 7:17

15. I cannot make a full surrender to Christ.
Luke 9:24.25

16. The Christian life is too hard.
Matt.11:30 - 1.John 5:3

17. When no reply is made. Heb.2:3 - Rom.6:23

As you read these passages, many of which you may have been familiar with since childhood, they may not seem to have the striking power necessary to meet the situation. They may not thrill or startle you as you feel they ought to do if they are going to work such a change in your prospect. Remember, however, that your prospect hears these words from a status different from your own. The words "condemned already" in John 3:18 do not make you shrink with fear, because you have confessed your Saviour; but they must strike terror to the man who is refusing to believe. Remember, too, that the power of the Holy Ghost is in them. Your part is simply to repeat them, or to see that they get under the eye of an unsaved man. It is the Holy Spirit's part to drive the truth into his inner consciousness with convicting power.

(Next lesson: "Group organization for Personal Evangelism).

Helps To Understanding Scripture Readings in *Day by Day*

By Rev. C. C. Baker

Sunday, July 22, Acts 16:13-15. On Paul's second missionary journey God providentially led him to Troas (vv.6-8). From there the Lord called him to Europe (vv.9-10). In what way can you see God's providence at work after Paul arrived in Philippi (vv.11-15)? Have you ever had the Lord open and shut doors in your life that you might be placed in a position where you could be of special help to someone else? What facts can you gather about Lydia from reading vv.13-15? Does she seem to be the kind of person God would use to help establish a new Christian work (vv.13-15,40)? What qualities that you see in the life of Lydia has God put in your life that you might further His cause in your church?

Monday, July 23, II Timothy 3:14-17. Underline each of the characteristics in vv.2-5 that represent too much of our church life today. Timothy's early training seemed to buttress his faith as he faced unbelief and indifference in his ministry (vv.14-15). What was it in Timothy's training that held him true (vv.15-17)? Is the study of the Scriptures part of the regular training of your child? Is a failure to read the Bible regularly one reason for your slipping into temptation (vv.16-17)? While being a true Christian is not an easy life (vv.10-12), it is a sane and happy life (1:7).

Tuesday, July 24, Romans 16:1-2. Paul, the theologian and thinker, had many friends from the ordinary walks of life. Read through the 16th chapter and list the various titles given to each of the people mentioned. Who were they? What relation did they have to Paul? to his work? How many of them were women? How did Paul feel toward them? Phoebe (16:1-2) was probably the one who delivered this letter to the Roman Church. The duties of deaconesses were evidently about the same as those of deacons. Compare I Timothy 3:11 with I Timothy 3:8-10. What functions could deaconesses fill in the Church today?

Wednesday, July 25, Romans 16:1-2. Notice the two facts that are stated about Priscilla and Aquila in vv.3-4, and then turn to Acts 18:1-3, 18,26 for more information about them. What relation did they have to Paul in his work? Paul mentions them as companions in I Cor. 16:19. He thinks of them when in prison and about to die (II Tim. 4:19). Observe Priscilla and Aquila's relation to each other (Acts 18:2). There is no place in the New Testament where one is mentioned without the other. In what ways can you and your wife, husband, child, etc., work together as a team in the Lord's service?

Thursday, July 26, *Hebrews* 11:8-12. Turn back to Genesis 12:1-9; 15:5-22:1-13 and review the three incidents that reveal Abraham's faith. What observation does Hebrews 11:15 make about Abraham's departing to the Promised Land? What seems to have been a basic characteristic of the men of faith mentioned in vv.10,13,14,16? Life became meaningful to Abraham and Sarah as they kept their eyes on God (vv.8-12, 17, 19). This attitude is well-pleasing in God's sight (vv.2,6,16). Do you find your Christian life meaningless because you fail to look upon yourself as a sojourner in this life and do not keep your eyes upon your permanent home?

Friday, July 27, *Psalm* 103:13-19. The Psalmist is speaking of God's mercies to those who sincerely love Him (vv.13,17-18) but who are also only too conscious of their own sins and shortcomings (vv.9-12). Formulate a statement that summarizes the central thought of vv.8-19. Could v.13 be a key verse? How do vv.8-10 point up the concept of God as a heavenly Father? Consider the dimensions mentioned in vv.11-12. When God forgives sins, He forgets them. What does God remember about our natures (v.14)? How is God's mercy contrasted to the brevity of man's life (vv.15-17)? The mercies and kindnesses of God have been purchased for us through the life blood of His own Son. If God forgets our confessed sins and remembers only that we are made of dust what should our attitude be toward those that sin against us?

Saturday, July 28, *Matt.* 24:42-51. A chief emphasis in the New Testament's teaching on Christ's return is that it will be sudden and unexpected. It is compared to the day of Noah (vv.37-39). With vv.37-39 read Genesis 6:5-7:10 and picture how life was moving and the suddenness of the deluge. What do the pictures of vv.40-41 add? What, then, should be the attitude of the Christian (vv.42-43)? How should the Christian's expectancy of the return of Christ affect his daily behavior (vv.45-51)? What attitude tends to cause a Christian to behave unseemly (v.48)? What is the disposition of the Christian who is ready for Christ's return (v.46)? Does the expectancy of Christ's coming affect your daily behavior?

God's Omnipresence and Christian Missions

By George S. Lauderdale

God is living today! The Giver of Life to others, He also preserves men from perishing: that we are alive shows that He is not dead. The heathen must be told that God is due their thanks, "seeing he giveth to all life, and breath, and all things." Acts 17:25. God's message to vain Greeks at Athens, who ignorantly worshipped idols, was that in Him man lives, moves, and has his being.

God *is* everywhere: men therefore cannot hide their sins. David did the only sensible thing after transgressing the law, when he said, "Against thee, thee only have I sinned, and done this evil in thy sight." Psalm 51:4. God loves to hear sinners confess, for in this way they not only affirm belief in His holiness, willingness to forgive and ability to do so through the Lord Jesus Christ, but also in His being in all places and seeing all things.

Idol Worship Wicked

Idolatry is sin inasmuch as God is spirit, present everywhere. *Every fact God has shown us about Himself is a call to missionary activity!* If God were, or were pictured by, images which millions are worshipping, He could not be everywhere, as the Bible declares. "If I ascend up into heaven, thou art there: if I make my bed in hell, behold, thou art there. If I take the wings of the morning, and dwell in the uttermost parts of the sea; even there shall thy hand lead me, and thy right hand shall hold me." Psalm 139:8-10.

No locality can claim the true omnipresent God, as Ephesus did Diana. His being in every place is constant evidence that He loves all men equallv, and is no respecter of persons. "But will God in very deed dwell with men on the earth?" exclaimed Solomon. "Behold, heaven and the heaven of heavens cannot contain thee; how much less this house which I have built!" II Chronicles 6:18.

God No Man's Property!

When men forget the words of the Lord Jesus Christ that God is a Spirit and must be worshipped in spirit and in truth, they erect shrines and entice the gullible to these places. Pilgrims pay high fees, false prophets and local merchants grow rich, and God is dishonored. He refuses to be bartered with: He will *give* blessings to penitent men anywhere, but is under no obligation to be the patron deity of Jerusalem, Sychar, Rome, Salt Lake City, Mecca, Guadalupe! God has made the Ganges River not one whit more sacred than the waters of the Mississippi, nor the Jordan holier than the Congo.

Christ said His Father is seeking true worshippers, men who will not try to localize Him. John 4:23. Again, it is written that the eyes of the Lord run to and fro throughout the whole earth, to show Himself strong in the behalf of them whose heart is perfect toward Him. If God were not as He is, there would be no basis of Christian missions.

Salvation Offered All

World evangelization is rooted in the being of God, and since He cannot change, the task is perpetually binding! Witnessing for Jesus Christ is the work awaiting Christians their every waking hour.

Because God is everywhere, He can invite all, whether they be in the eastern or western hemispheres, northern or southern, to draw near to Him and He will draw near to them. In this truth then is comfort for men in jails, hospitals, far-flung military or missionary posts: believe what the Bible says about God for the best life! "The Lord is nigh unto all them that call upon him, to all that call upon him in truth." Psalm 145:18. *Whosoever* shall call upon the Name of the Lord shall be saved.

Billy Graham Crusade In Oklahoma City

The Greater Oklahoma City Billy Graham Crusade closed July 1 in Owen Stadium at Norman, Oklahoma. Owen Stadium, located just twenty miles South of Oklahoma City, is the home field of the University of Oklahoma football team. 50,000 persons were in attendance at this great closing service in spite of a near-100 degree temperature and intense traffic congestion on all highways leading to the massive football stadium. There were 1,335 decisions for Christ at the final meeting.

All told during the four-week crusade, attendance totalled 501,000 and there were 7,148 recorded decisions for Christ. Mr. Graham also spoke to 6,500 on the steps of the State capitol, 4,000 at a special Indian day service, 5,000 in the Capitol Hill high school stadium and 28,000 in Tulsa, Oklahoma on one of his Monday "rest nights."

Unique in the history of Billy Graham Crusades and also in the history of the State of Oklahoma, was the presentation of Bibles by Mr. Graham to 20 judges in Oklahoma City. Early in his crusade he spoke on the steps of the State Capitol and state employes were released from their jobs for one hour to hear him.

During his talk, he mentioned that "this Nation was founded under God and that there is a Bible to be found in every courtroom in America. As it turned out—to the embarrassment of Oklahoma City and State leaders—there weren't Bibles in every courtroom in America—at least not in most Oklahoma City courtrooms. Two of the City's lawyers, O. A. Cargill, Jr., and George Miskovsky, immediately started plans to get Bibles for every courtroom. They were joined in this endeavor by Dr. C. Ralston Smith, Chairman of the Crusade and Pastor of First Presbyterian Church, and his co-chairman Dr. Max Stanfield, pastor of the Putnam City Baptist Church. The Bibles were purchased for six state district courts, three federal district courts, two common pleas courts, two county courts, the state supreme court, the state criminal court of appeals and five justice of the peace courts.

Mr. Graham presented the Bibles to the judges in a special ceremony in the Oklahoma County Courthouse. Miskovsky, who is a State Senator, said he plans to introduce a bill in the next legislature to make it mandatory that witnesses in Oklahoma courts be required to swear with their hand on the Bible. The current practice demands only the raising of the right hand when taking the oath.

"There is no profession more dependent upon the Word of God than the law profession," Mr. Graham told the jurists at the presentation ceremonies. Each decision of a lawyer or judge is a moral one, and is a problem that must be faced. Everything in the Lord's universe is dependent upon laws—the first of which were the Ten Commandments." At the conclusion of his message the 20 judges marched by the platform of the Court's largest courtroom to receive the Bible for their respective rooms.

Speaking to the ministers of the area at a final Friday morning "Workshop on Evangelism" June 29, the evangelist told them that the responsibility of following-up these "babes in Christ" is now in their hands and that the success or failure of the crusade results depends entirely on them. Of those making decisions for Christ during the crusade, eighty per cent recorded that they do attend church regularly. This is higher than is true in most cities where crusades have been held.

Another interesting facet of the Oklahoma City crusade was the translation of the evangelist's sermons for the deaf. Each Tuesday and

Friday evenings as well as on Sundays, Rev. and Mrs. Eugene Meader were on hand to perform this special service for the scores of deaf and these people would sing with their hands right along with everyone else during the opening song services.

Police Sgt. John J. Byrd, in charge of the 27-man traffic detail directing traffic to and from Mr. Graham's services noted that the motorists were "almost 100 per cent courteous." He has spent 14 years on the Oklahoma City police force, handling most major fairgrounds projects. "I'd go so far as to say it's the safest place in the world during these meetings," he said, "I've never seen a more polite group of drivers in my life." Sgt. Byrd added: "It's a pleasure to be out here because if a man has lost his faith in human nature, he can regain it. People don't shout or cuss at one another and they wait for pedestrians."

Merchants noted an increase in business, and Pal Barnhart, comptroller for the local hotels, said registrations during the month of June had increased by at least 20 per cent with at least 2,000 more guests this June coming to hear Billy Graham.

Special trains came from all over the State and from Fort Worth, Texas, came a special that carried 375 passengers; from 20 to 60 chartered buses were at the services each night. Sales of books by Mr. Graham and of Bibles were up about 1,000 per cent from a usual month according to the department store book section heads.

What Man Needs Is Not Self - Confidence

By Rev. Kennedy Smartt

Living in a cave all alone, Benedict, for whom the Benedictine monks are named, sought to conquer the temptations of the world, only to find that even there he was at their mercy. In order to take his mind from them he made a bed of briars and thorns in which he would roll until his body was one great sore of pain and misery. Godric used to stand all night in an icy river seeking to calm his fiery temper, and a man named Cirita burned his flesh to the bone with red hot iron seeking to overcome his desire for a very beautiful woman, after he had sworn himself to a life of celibacy.

These men were all deeply sincere in their attempts to conquer their temptations, and yet they failed as have so many others, because of a basic misunderstanding of the Word of God. The Bible does not teach that a man is able by the power of his own will to conquer the problem of sin. The secret of overcoming victory in the Christian life is not in the bolstering of a man's confidence in himself to try a little harder, but rather in his confidence in Jesus Christ as a Saviour who redeems not only from the guilt of sin, but its power as well.

Self-confidence is deceptive. It actually is nothing more than trust in man. Hitler's great mistake was that he rejected God and staked his hope in the power of man's wisdom and strength to create a master race that could subdue the rest of the world. The Bible says, "Cursed be the man that trusteth in man, and maketh flesh his arm, and whose heart departeth from the Lord." (Jeremiah 17:5). And again it says, "Woe to the rebellious children, saith the Lord, that take counsel, but not of me; and that cover with a covering, but not of my spirit, that they may add sin to sin:" (Isaiah 30:1). Paul speaks of Christians as those who ". . . . rejoice in Christ Jesus, and have no confidence in the flesh." (Philippians 3:3).

Self-confidence may also be mere confidence in the security of material riches or power. We lament to see so much of this in our nation today. So many seemingly self-confident people go all to pieces when their petty god of money fails them in a time of accident or illness, or family difficulty. "Lo, this is the man that made not God his strength; but trusted in the abundance of his riches, and strengthened himself in his wickedness." (Psalm 52:7). ". . . . How hard it is for them that trust in riches to enter into the Kingdom of God." (Mark 10: 24b.)

The Bible discourages self-confidence. "Seest thou a man wise in his own conceit? There is more hope of a fool than of him." (Proverbs 26:12). "Wherefore let him that thinketh he standeth take heed lest he fall." (I Corinthians 10:12). When Jesus told his disciples that soon they would all turn against him, Peter self confidently took him to task, denying that he would ever leave him. And Jesus, instead of commending him for the victory of self-confidence, gently humbled him with the news that before the third crowing of the cock, he would have denied the Son of Man three times. (Matthew 26:31ff.) Jesus did not exhort Peter to an exercise of more self-confidence. The answer to Peter's problem was to be found in Peter's complete self-failure which would in turn result in a faith-confidence relationship to the risen Lord Jesus Christ. Peter's ego had to be destroyed before the power of the Holy Spirit could be manifest in him.

When a man is seeking help to overcome some difficult problem in his life, such as alcoholism for instance, an exhortation to more self-confidence is as absurd as telling a picture to paint itself. Alcoholics Anonymous will not even try to help an alcoholic unless he recognizes the existence of "a power greater than himself" upon whom he can rely for strength. Man's help is not found in man himself, and were he left to his own devising, even though he attempt such things as did Benedict, Godric, and Cirita, he would surely fail. Self-confidence is not the answer.

Jesus has told us the story of two builders, one whom he called "wise," the other "foolish." The difference between them was not in their craftmanship, their education, nor their standing in society. It was far more basic than that. The foolish man had built his house upon the sand, while the wise man had built his house upon a rock. The first put his confidence in his house, the second in the foundation that supported the house. And when the wild deluge of this world's tempest beat upon the two houses, it was the house built upon the rock that was able to withstand the stormy blast. And likewise it is not the life that is built upon self-confidence that shall be able to overcome, but rather that life which is anchored in faith in the overcoming power of Jesus Christ, the Rock of Ages.

When temptations beset us and we seem powerless in our struggle against their wiles, when the weakness of our flesh discourages us to the point of despair, and when we have wearied of our vain trying to overcome through more confidence in self, we shall rejoice to hear that true victory comes through faith-confidence in Jesus Christ, who has redeemed us not only from the guilt of sin, but from its power and dominion as well.

"To him that o'ercometh, God giveth a crown;

Through faith we shall conquer, Though often cast down;

He who is our Savior, Our strength will renew;

Look ever to Jesus, He'll carry you through."

What Is Modernism

By Rev. Floyd E. Hamilton

Centerville, Alabama

"In the last days mockers shall come with mockery, walking after their own lusts, and saying, Where is the promise of his coming? for, from the day that the fathers fell asleep, all things continue as they were from the beginning of the creation." II Peter 3:3-4.

An article in a popular magazine recently said that the most irritating thing about the Russians today was their smugness. They had certain preconceived ideas about the West that were so deeply imbedded in their minds that it was impossible to make any impression on them with the truth. They had been told lies so consistently that the lies had become the truth to them, so that any attempt to contradict their false notions met with tolerant, smug, unbelief. They were sure that Westerners were lying about conditions in the West through patriotism, no matter how vehemently the truth was told them.

A somewhat similar condition exists in America regarding Modernism. The Modernist has a smug complacency about his beliefs. The Modernists in the theological seminaries have taught him that theological conservatives are old-fashioned, ignorant, Bible-believers who either do not know the views of modern scholars, or who close their minds to the evidence against the Bible. When Conservative scholars write books in defense of the Bible these Modernists either ignore them or say that they are just ignorant of the results of "Modern scholarship!" The smug superiority of their certainty that "all reputable scholars are agreed that the newer views of the Bible (that is, the view that the Bible is filled with error and is just like any other human document) are the only views possible for educated people," can be very irritating at times. It seems just impossible to break through their smug complacency with the evidence that the Bible is the trustworthy Word of the living God.

On the other hand there is an equally irritating smugness among great sections of the evangelical churches about the theological situation in the world today. They refuse to believe that Modernism offers any serious threat to the established churches in America. When we try to tell them that the official machinery of the churches is largely in the hands of the Modernists, and that the control of most of the church organizations has already passed into the hands of the Modernists and those who vote with the Modernists, such people refuse to be alarmed. "Are they not good men?" they ask, "Are they not advocating Christian education and foreign missions and establishing new churches? Isn't there a greater interest in religion in America today than ever before? Aren't these leaders in the churches advocating evangelism? Have they not all taken ordination vows to uphold the Bible as the Word of God? How can you say that such good men are either Modernists or under the control of Modernists?" It seems almost impossible to arouse the church to the terrible danger of Modernism in the Christian Church in America today.

But what do we mean by Modernism? It is difficult to define because there are so many varieties and shades of Modernism. Perhaps we could give an inclusive definition of Modernism by saying that it is any departure from the teaching that the Old and New Testaments are the Word of God. Such a definition means very little, however, because most Modernists would deny that they have departed from such a belief. They interpret their ordination vows to uphold the Scriptures as the Word of God, very broadly, and claim that they have a right to broad interpretations of the Word of God, broad enough to include most shades of Modernist belief. They will tell us, for example, that they hold to the spiritual meanings of the first chapters of Genesis, even though they do not believe the events recorded there ever actually happened, and they will say that they still believe the Bible is the Word of God. It is necessary, therefore, to pinpoint their beliefs or lack of beliefs, in order to understand just what Modernism is.

Broadly speaking, Modernists differ from evangelicals in their beliefs on the following subjects: (1) The inspiration of the Bible. (2) The nature of man. (3) The character of the religion of the Old and New Testaments. (4) The way of salvation. (5) The Person of Christ. (6) The question of the Virgin Birth of Christ. (7) The nature of the resurrection of Christ. (8) The meaning of the other Biblical miracles. (9) The matter of the atonement of Christ. (10) The question of the brotherhood of man and the fatherhood of God. (11) The question of the future state of man after death. (12) The question of denominations, and church union. There are other points of difference besides these twelve points, but there is one fundamental question that underlies all these and other points of difference, namely, the question of *the validity of the higher critical views of the Old and New Testaments.* This last question is all important, because a Modernist is a Modernist largely because of a certain view of the claims of destructive higher criticism.

Now let no one think that these questions are matters of indifference. It may be a matter of indifference to me whether my neighbor buys a fur coat but if she charged it to my account and expected me to pay for it, it would not be a matter of indifference to me. I may think it is a matter of indifference whether the Book of Genesis was written by Moses or by Nehemiah until I realize that the Modernist is trying to convince me that the story of Adam and Eve is a myth and that my ancient ancestor was an anthropoid ape or a similar animal, and then I suddenly realize that these matters concern my soul's eternal destiny.

You see if the Bible is unreliable mythology as the Modernists claim, then I may be kidding myself about life after death and eternal life. If the Bible is not trustworthy history, and Jesus Christ did not really rise from the grave, then as Paul said, we are of all men most pitiable because we are facing an eternity without the pledge of Christ's knowledge of life after death. If I should become convinced that the stories of the New Testament are idle tales, my religious faith would evaporate and humanly speaking I would become a materialist.

With religious faith would go ethical standards, for if the Bible is merely the same as any other work of literature, its ethics would be a human invention, not the divinely revealed law of God. So if I did not like the ten commandments there would be no reason why I should keep them if I could get away with breaking them. Is it not plain that these matters are all important to us? They concern our soul's eternal welfare.

In the following articles it is my purpose to discuss these questions which are matters of dispute between the Modernist and the evangelical Christian. The Word of God tells us that we should be ready to give a reason for the hope that is in us. I will try to give reasons for the hope that is in us. It can't be done in one article, so in this article we will just make a beginning.

The evangelical believes that the Holy Spirit so guided and controlled the writers of the Old and New Testaments that what they wrote was true and the truth God wanted His people to have. The Bible as it was written in the original languages had no errors of any kind in it. The different writers used their own vocabulary, their own knowledge and their own style of writing, but the Holy Spirit kept them from writing what was untrue, and kept after them until they wrote all that God wanted them to write. After the Bible was written in the following centuries it was copied again and again. The copyists were honest and tried to make exact copies, but a few mistakes of copying crept into the text. Today, by the science of textual criticism we can eliminate almost all such errors of copying, and can be sure that the Hebrew and Greek texts of the Old and New Testaments respectively, are substantially the Word of God.

The Modernists, almost to a man, hold a lower doctrine about the inspiration of the Bible. Some would say that the religious parts of the Bible are inspired, but the rest of it is full of errors. Others, like the Barthians, would say that God can use any portion of the Bible as the occasion for giving to a man His direct revelation, so that that part of the Bible becomes the Word of God to him. The same portion, however, might leave another man cold and untouched, so it would not be the Word of God to him. They would reject the view that the Bible is the Word of God whether it is believed or not, whether it "finds" a person or leaves him cold. It only is the Word of God when it "finds" a person and inspires him. I think you can see that with such a view of the Bible it would be an item of no importance whether it was true or not. The Holy Spirit according to such a view might use falsehood as the vehicle by which the Word of God could 'come'" to a man.

We reply to such a view of the Bible, that if we come to believe any part of the Bible to be false, that part will never "find" us, or be the Word of God for us. Only as long as it is believed to be true will it have any religious value to us. If we cannot trust the Bible when it speaks of historical events, how can we trust it when it speaks of heavenly things? Praise God, we can trust the Bible throughout, and we can believe it when it declares that "all Scripture is given by inspiration of God and is profitable for doctrine, for reproof, for correction, for instruction in righteousness." (II Tim. 3:16). Search the Scriptures, for in them ye think ye have eternal life.

SABBATH SCHOOL LESSONS

REV. J. KENTON PARKER

LESSON FOR JULY 29

Witnessing Through Suffering

Background Scripture: Acts 12:1-5; I Peter 1; 4:12 - 5:14
Devotional Reading: II Timothy 2:1-13

It takes strength to be a Christian. The devil tries to make people believe that religion is for weaklings; women and children; not for manly men. (Some women are stronger than men, however). Paul, in II Timothy 2:1 exhorts Timothy to "Be strong in the grace that is in Christ Jesus." Some old saint said, "It takes all the grace that God can give, simply to live, my brother, simply to live." To live in a time of persecution as these early Christians had to live, requires courage of the highest type. Many weak women proved their strength and courage in those trying days. Men and women of the Church of the Living God, the Church of Christ, must be brave, and train others to be brave.

Paul illustrates this by three simple illustrations. First ,the Soldier : we must "endure hardness," or "suffer hardship with me," as a good soldier. The soldier does not expect an easy, soft time. When you enroll in the army you expect to obey orders; live in camp; train and drill daily; fight on the battlefield; be wounded, suffer, perhaps die. Second, the Athlete: in whatever sport he may engage he has to endure hardness, if he expects to win any prizes, or help win any games. He, too, must deny himself, keep fit, train daily, and contend earnestly, putting everything he has into the race or contest. Third, the Farmer: farming is no easy business. In the harvest field there is work to do. The hours are long; the sun is hot. Plowing and preparing the soil, planting the seed, reaping the grain, is no work for weaklings. It takes both brains and brawn to be a farmer.

So it is with the Christian. Paul endured hardship after hardship. He gives us a list of these in II Corinthians, chapter eleven. He was a great worker and a good soldier, and ran the race as few have run. He had a crown awaiting him, won through being a good witness for Christ through the things which he had suffered. We know little or nothing of this in our land. In some places Christians have to suffer persecution. About all we have to endure are the common ailments and disappointments of life, and sometimes we murmur and complain when they come upon us. What would most of us do if we really had to suffer hardship as a good soldier of Jesus Christ? We live in comfortable, even beautiful homes; we ride to our work and to church in warm automobiles; we worship in lovely churches and listen to soft music and eloquent preaching: we do not know what real hardship is - most of us. When we are stretched upon a bed of sickness are we good witnesses for Christ? If we suffer, we shall reign, Where will be our crown, if we have no cross?

I. *James is Killed, and Peter Imprisoned:* Acts 12:1-5.

Here is a sample of the sort of persecution which came upon the church. There were thousands who were killed and many more imprisoned and persecuted. James, the brother of John was one of these martyrs. We know of Stephen and others. In fact, all the apostles were killed, or exiled, according to history and tradition. Peter had been in prison before, with John. Persecution became even worse later on when Christians were burned at the stake and thrown to wild beasts.

II. *Trial of Your Faith:* I Peter: 1.

Peter is writing to the "elect of the dispersion." The Roman Empire under Nero and others became the instrument of terrible persecutions. She was exerting all her mighty power to exterminate Christianity. Many of the Christians were being put to death. Would those who remained alive become discouraged and give up their faith? He is encouraging them to have faith and a living hope of an eternal inheritance reserved for them in heaven. He salutes them with the words, "Grace and peace be multiplied." If any people needed "grace and peace" they certainly did. He tells them that they are "kept," or guarded by the power of God through faith and can even rejoice in the midst of their grief and suffering.

In verse seven we have the expression, "trial of your faith." Faith must be tested to prove whether it is genuine or not. It is easy to say, or imagine, we have faith when everything is pleasant, but it is a tested faith that becomes "precious." Think of how the faith of many of the "heroes of faith" was tested. Abraham's faith received its severest test when he was told to offer up his son Isaac.

When faith is tested it results in praise and honor and glory at the appearing of Jesus Christ. In Christ, Whom they love, they have joy unspeakable and full of glory. He suffered, too, and the glory which followed His suffering should encourage them in their sufferings. Their hope is in Him. While waiting for Him to appear they are to have hope and live lives worthy of their Saviour and Example. They were to be holy in all manner of living; "because it is written, Be ye holy; for I am holy."

In verse eighteen he reminds them of the cost of their redemption; "Forasmuch as ye know that ye were not redeemed with corruptible things, as silver and gold, from your vain conversation received by tradition from your fathers; but with the precious blood of Christ." Our salvation is costly. It results in our being "born again," not of corruptible seed, but of incorruptible, by the Word of God, which liveth and abideth forever. Man is a creature whose flesh is as grass. It withers and dies, but the Word of God abides forever. Our faith and hope must be in God. His character and His promises furnish the foundation for faith.

Peter is trying to get their minds off of themselves and centered upon Christ and eternal things. What a lesson for us! We are apt to let our minds dwell upon our trials and troubles and suffering and forget the greater and more precious things which concern our glorious salvation and the living hope which we have in Christ.

III. *Suffering As a Christian:* I Peter 4:12 - 5:14.

To suffer as a Christian is no "strange" experience; many of God's people have been great sufferers. This was true in Old Testament times; it has been true ever since. There have been periods of especially severe persecution, but there have been those who have been called upon to suffer in all ages.

We should rejoice because we can share in the sufferings of Christ. Our joy will be even greater when His glory shall be revealed. If we suffer we shall reign with Him and share in the glory which will be His. We are "blessed," or happy when we are reproached for the name of Christ. Is Peter thinking of the two Beatitudes which state this? Certainly we find ourselves in company with many heroic men and women who have lived in the past. Let us be good witnesses for Him, suffering "as Christians."

Suffering in itself may be neither a "blessed" nor profitable experience; we must "suffer as a Christian." Many people today are suffering on account of their crimes. Our jails are full of such people. To suffer as an evildoer brings neither profit nor blessing. The phrase "as a Christian" may be looked at in two ways. It may mean, "because we are Christians." These early Christians suffered because they were Christians. If we suffer for the sake of Christ, we are blessed. To suffer "as a Christian" may mean, to bear our suffering with Christian fortitude. Peter and John and Paul rejoiced that they were counted worthy to suffer for His name's sake. When we bear our trials with patience we give a strong testimony to the power of Christ in our lives. Paul and Silas singing and praying while their backs were bleeding and their feet in the stocks was a striking testimony in the Philippian jail.

Sometimes our suffering takes the form of chastisement. The church needs to be purified; we need correction. No chastisement is pleasant, but it can and should be profitable. Is it always so with us?

Verse eighteen does not mean that there is any doubt about the righteous being saved. A good translation is, If the righteous be saved "with difficulty." It is not easy to save anybody. It cost the life-blood of the Son of God. To accept "free salvation" is difficult for a proud self-righteous man. To be saved a man must be born again. This is supernatural work.

If it is the will of God for us to suffer, then let us commit ourselves to Him. He is our Creator and Redeemer. He loves us with an everlasting love. Let the suffering child find refuge in the arms of his Heavenly Father, Who understands, Who pities, and Who remembers that we are but dust.

We should live for Him Who died for us, feeding the flock of God and be examples to all who believe. We are shepherds, and the Chief Shepherd is looking for faithful undershepherds. We should "gird ourselves with humility to serve one another." Was Peter thinking of the Master girding Himself with the towel and washing the feet of the disciples?

Satan is at the bottom of many of the evils which befall the Christian. He is our "adversary." We are to resist him in the faith.

Peter exhorts us to cast all our care upon Him, (God), for He cares for us.

YOUNG PEOPLE'S DEPARTMENT — REV. B. HOYT EVANS

YOUTH PROGRAM FOR JULY 29

"Heroes In The Fight For The Lives Of Men"

Hymn: "We Have A Story To Tell To The Nations"
Prayer
Scripture: Matthew 7:7-12; 9:1-8
Hymn: "Am I A Soldier Of The Cross"
Offering
Hymn: "O For A Faith That Will Not Shrink"

NOTE TO PROGRAM CHAIRMAN:

(We are beginning a unit of four biographical programs. It will not be possible in the space we have available to give more than a brief sketch of the lives of these people whom we shall be considering. You can make the programs much more interesting and helpful by securing additional information from books, magazines, and well-informed persons. *Presbyterian Youth* contains an abundance of interesting and helpful material for these programs.)

LEADER'S INTRODUCTION:

It has been demonstrated many times that an effective way to reach people for Christ is to minister to their physical sicknesses in His name. As a result of this truth we have medical missions. Mission hospitals and medical missionaries are to be found throughout the earth . . . both in our homeland and in foreign countries. In this program we shall look into the lives of two living heroes. Their heroism is in the field of medical missions, and their geographic field is the continent of Africa.

FIRST SPEAKER:

Our first hero, or more properly, heroine, is Ellen Moore of Liberia. Miss Moore, who is now Mrs. Hopkins, is a home missionary, because she is a native of Liberia. Perhaps you know that Liberia was settled largely by freed

Any of his outstanding accomplishments would have established him as a great man in the eyes of the world, but the thing that has made him a hero is his dedication to healing the sick bodies of Africans in the name of Christ. His reason for giving himself in this service, according to his explanation, is his "reverence for life."

Women's Work

One Minute Messages on Stewardship

"There is a power, more recently acquired by man and very new to woman, through which Christians must learn to express their responsibility as stewards. This power is the full citizenship, the franchise which is rapidly becoming the universal power of all human beings, and its instrument is the ballot - every member of every Christian Church can make his Christian faith and practices effective by his stewardship, as a Cristian citizen, over his or her own ballot. This tremendous power may, like others, be laid away in the napkin of neglect, and so lost to the Kingdom of God on earth; or it may be surrendered to selfish and even evil needs, by casting it on Satan's side. But it may be made a silent and mighty power, for righteousness in the hands of good Christian stewards, both men and women. What are you doing habitually with your ballot? Are you trying to use it rightly?"

—From Mrs. Askew's STEWARDSHIP FOR TODAY

Our Home — Their Home

(Shared With Two Students From China)

I received a card last Mother's Day from a Chinese girl. She came to the U. S. in (I think) 1949 to get her Masters Degree at L. S. U. Our oldest daughter was in graduate school there. Through her we met Wen Yuen. She spent her time between semesters and many week ends in our home. She is now married, and they own their home in New Orleans. When they were married we had a duplicate of our oldest daughter's wedding for her in the Metairie Church—she married in our daughter's wedding dress. Well, we love her and her husband. We keep in touch with them and visit them just like our own children. They do not have any children, but they want to have a family. She went to a Presbyterian Mission School in China and joined the church when she was a little girl.

From another one of our foreign student friends we received a picture with this notation on back: To dearest Grandma and Grandpa Blake, Eugene, 15 months old, January, 1956.

I just didn't know how to put into words what I wanted to say, but I do thank God that He gave me the opportunity to have her in my home when she first came to this country and needed friends; we have had this baby's mother in our home lots, in fact, she stayed with us one summer instead of going to summer school while she was working on her Masters Degree, but the joy and pleasure she has given us just can't be put into words. She is from Shanghai and has not heard from her family in some time. We like to think our home is her home and try to make her feel that way.

Mrs. George J. Blake
Jasper, Texas, former president,
Women of the Church,
Synod of Louisiana

SOME REASONS WHY
I Must Be About My Father's Business

Because I committed myself to doing His business when I accepted Christ as My Saviour and Lord.
I delight to do thy will, O my God.

Because Christ gave His life that all men might be saved.
The love of Christ constraineth me.

Because it is imperative that a man knows and accepts Christ as Saviour, if he is to be saved.
Neither is there salvation in any other.

Because I have an appointed task to do in the Kingdom which no other can do for me.
I have chosen you . . . that ye should go and bring forth fruit.

Because there is an unprecedented hungering for God's Word, and Christ has said to me -
Give ye them to eat.

Because the very urgency of the times demands that I be at my Father's business. I am sure of having only today.
Ye know not what hour your Lord doth come.

Because of my responsibility to my home, and of my desire for the best for all who are in my home.
As for me and my house, we will serve the Lord.

Because I must set a Christian example to those who will follow, so that I may say —
Be ye imitators of me, even as I am of Christ.

Because Christ commanded it.
Go ye into all the world, and preach the Gospel to every creature.

Because doing His will strengthens my faith and gives me courage to stand fast in His love.
They go from strength to strength.

Because our world, our nation, and our Church are crying out "Advance!"
Speak unto the children of Israel that they go forward.

Because I must meet crisis with advance, answering His call —
"FOLLOW ME."

Facing Criticism

Abraham Lincoln once said, "If I tried to read, much less answer, all the criticisms made of me, and all the attacks leveled against me, this office would have to be closed for all other business. I do the best I know how, the very best I can. And I mean to keep on doing this, down to the very end. If the end brings me out all wrong, then ten angels swearing I had been right would make no difference. If the end brings me out all right, then what is said against me now will not amount to anything."

Church News

THE GENERAL FUND AND INTERCHURCH AGENCIES

The General Fund Agencies

Budget for 1956	$846,581.00
Received from Jan. 15th through June 30, 1956	200,394.04
Percentage of annual budget received to date	23.7
Balance needed for the year	646,186.96

Interchurch Agencies

Budget for 1956	$21,495.00
Received from Jan. 15th through June 30, 1956	6,253.62
Percentage of annual budget received to date	29.00
Balance needed for the year	15,241.38

E. C. Scott, Treasurer

Our Flying Doctor of the Congo

Yesterday (July 1) when I noticed Dr. and Mrs. Mark Poole's names in Day By Day, I reached for the latest number (July) of the *Readers' Digest*, to verify my guess. Yes, there it is, a four page article, with illustrations, enthusiastically describing the work of OUR Dr. Poole in the Congo. The writer mentions by name our five well known missionaries who are on the staff, and the names of the givers in our home church who made this great work possible. But what captures most the imagination of the author, is the fact that Dr. Poole navigates his own plane.

Presbyterians who never read a missionary's letter (too dry), nor a missionary's report in our church papers (not important) may sit up and take notice, when they see a secular magazine, with a circulation of ten million, considering as NEWS the medical missions of their own church. Frank A. Brown.

Missionary Furloughs

Nashville — Rev. and Mrs. William T. Mulcay and family of our Congo Mission arrived in this country on June 18 for their regular furlough.

Mr. Mulcay is a native of Augusta, Ga., and is a graduate of Columbia Bible College and Columbia Theological Seminary. He is a member of Augusta-Macon Presbytery.

Mrs. Mulcay is the former Miss Jean Blackwell. She was born in Atlanta, Ga., but she considers Augusta, Ga., her home. She is a graduate of Columbia Bible College.

Rev. and Mrs. Lachlan C. Vass, Jr., and family of our Congo Mission are now in the United States for their regular furlough. They arrived in this country June 27.

Mr. Vass considers Chattanooga, Tenn., his home, though he was born in Germantown, Tenn. He received his education at Davidson College and Louisville Seminary, and is a member of Knoxville Presbytery.

Mrs. Vass is the former Miss Winifred Kellersberger, the daughter of former missionaries of our Church in the Congo. She is a graduate of Agnes Scott College and is a member of the Second Presbyterian Church of Richmond, Va. The couple have four daughters whose ages range between 14½ to 3 years of age. They plan to make their home in Decatur, Ga., during this furlough year.

Miss Willodene Smith of our North Brazil Mission arrives in the United States about July 5 for her regular furlough.

Miss Smith is a native of Charlotte, N. C. She attended Montreat College, and is a graduate of Queens College.

Dr. and Mrs. William Rule and family of our Congo Mission are scheduled to arrive in this country about the middle of July for their regular furlough. Upon arrival in New York the Rules will proceed to Athens, Ga., where they will stay during July and August. After September 1, they will make their home in Knoxville, Tenn.

Miss Mary Elizabeth (Betty) Tenley of our East Brazil Mission is scheduled to arrive in this country the end of this month for her regular furlough.

Miss Tenley is a native of Pineville, Ky., and is a member of the Moore Memorial Church there. She will make Pineville her home during this furlough year.

Mr. and Mrs. Eric S. Bolton and family of our Congo Mission are expected to arrive in the United States July 9 for their regular furlough.

Upon arrival in New York the Boltons will proceed to Wooster, Ohio, where they will be during the year of their furlough.

Miss Marion Wilcox of our Formosa Mission expects to arrive in this country for her regular furlough at the end of this month. Upon her arrival in California, she will go to Charlotte, N. C., where her friends will find her during this furlough year.

Dr. and Mrs. James Boyce and their family of our Mexico Mission are scheduled to arrive in this country by July 1 for their regular furlough. Dr. Boyce considers Dade City, Fla., home.

Miss Margaret Archibald of our Japan Mission is due to arrive in this country in July for her regular furlough. Upon her arrival in the United States she plans to proceed to Tuscaloosa, Ala.

Miss Margaret Pritchard of our Korea Mission is scheduled to return to this country in July for her regular furlough. After September 1 she will make her home at Mission Court during her furlough year.

Following their regular furlough, Mr. and Mrs. Jule Spach and family of our North Brazil Mission expect to return to the field in July. While on furlough the Spachs were in Durham, N. C., where he was doing graduate work at Duke University.

Rev. and Mrs. Milton Daugherty of our East Brazil Mission are scheduled to leave this country July 10 for Brazil following their furlough here. The Daughertys direct the Language and Orientation School for missionaries in Campinas, Brazil.

Rev. and Mrs. T. K. Morrison of our Congo Mission are scheduled to return to the field in July following their furlough in the United States.

Mr. and Mrs. A. M. Shive of our Congo Mission expect to return to that country in July after their regular furlough in the United States.

ALABAMA

Birmingham — World mission opportunities in Korea were discussed May 29 by Dr. John E. Bryan, Birmingham Chamber of Commerce manager, when he was guest speaker at Third Presbyterian Church.

The congregation of First Presbyterian Church enjoyed a Family Retreat May 28, at Fresh Air Farm on Shades Mountain.

The Caravan Class of the Woodlawn Presbyterian Church recently honored its teacher Edgar Van Keuren for more than 20 years of service. The name of the class has been changed to the Edgar Van Keuren Class, and a framed portrait of "Mr. Van" has been hung in the Sunday School room. Mr. Van Keuren is an elder in the church and is a senior partner in the architectural firm of Van Keuren, Davis and Co. of Birmingham.

Shades Valley Presbyterian Church was the host for the May rally for the Men of the Birmingham Presbytery. At a dinner meeting, John J. Deifell of Greensboro, N. C., president of the executive committee of the Assembly Men's Council, spoke on the subject "Christ in Your Home and Business."

U. S. Marine Corps Reservists of the Third 105 millimeter Howitzer Battalion were addressed June 10 by the Rev. J. Ernest Somerville, who spoke on "The Faith That Conquers." Rev. Somerville is minister of the Central Park Presbyterian Church. There are approximately 130 Reservists.

GEORGIA

Augusta-Macon Presbytery, at its adjourned meeting, at Milledgeville, Ga., June 11, 1956, took the following action concerning Rev. H. E. Iverson:

Be it resolved, that,

Whereas the Rev. H. E. Iverson has honestly and forthrightly declared his inability to comply with the instructions of Presbytery given at its Winter Meeting on January 17, 1956, at which time he requested that 'presbytery accept my resignation';

Whereas there is no provision in our Book of Church Order for such action by Presbytery;

Whereas there has been no question raised regarding the morals or character of Mr. Iverson;

Therefore: in accordance with Paragraph 263 of our Book of Church Order, be it known that as of this date that the Rev. H. E. Iverson is divested without censure of his office as a minister in the Presbyterian Church in the United States."

The "instructions of Presbytery" above referred to were:

1. That Presbytery take recognition of the fact that Rev. H. E. Iverson has refused to deal with the Commission on the Minister and His Work, charged by Presbytery on October 18, 1955, to study the work being done by Mr. Iverson and to bring in recommendations concerning it.

2. That Presbytery grant Mr. Iverson an additional extension of time to labor outside the bounds of Presbytery for two months (until March 17, 1956) with the understanding that no further extension will be granted by Presbytery.

3. That Presbytery direct Mr. Iverson not to conduct any religious services in the general locality of a Presbyterian, U. S., Church within or without the bounds of Augusta-Macon Presbytery without the expressed invitation or approval of the Session of that Presbyterian, U. S., Church.

Vernon A. Crawfard,
Stated Clerk

Synod of Mississippi

The Synod of Mississippi met June 26th through 28th, and the following outstanding events transpired.

The Rev. T. T. Williams of Tunica was elected moderator at the Tuesday evening session. The other officials of the Synod of Mississippi were the Rev. R. P. Richardson, Jr., temporary clerk; the Rev. E. G. Boyce, permanent clerk; the Rev. R. E. Hough, stated clerk; and the Rev. B. I. Anderson, publicity clerk.

Reporting were the following committees:

The Hon. Frank Everett reported on the Palmer Orphanage; Dr. G. T. Gillespie, Higher Education and Church Relations; the Rev. Thomas S. Jones, Council of Higher Education; the Rev. W. E. Pleasants, Montreat Association, and Dr. John Reed Miller, Stewardship and Finance.

The Synod was pleased to receive the morning sermon, which was preached by the Rev. T. H. McDill, Professor of Practical Theology, Columbia Theological Seminary, Decatur, Georgia.

The Synod of Mississippi relinquished its control of the Palmer Orphanage and conveyed all its interests in the Palmer Orphanage to the First Presbyterian Church of Columbus, with no strings attached. This conveyance is to be executed on or after October 1, 1956. The Synod commended the Rev. William Sistar for his devoted, courageous and dedicated service as superintendent of the orphanage for the past five years.

On behalf of the Belhaven expansion program, Dr. McFerren Crow, President of Belhaven, presented at the Wednesday evening session Dr. Theodore A. Distler, Executive Director, Association of American Colleges, who spoke on the subject "Christian Higher Education."

The closing session of Synod included the receiving of the resignation of the Rev. R. E. Hough, stated clerk for the Synod of Mississippi. Dr. Hough has been in continuous active service, having held, in addition to his pastorate, duties in the Presbytery and Synod continuously from 1917.

The Synod of Mississippi received an invitation to hold its 1957 meeting at Southwestern in Memphis. The invitation was gratefully received and unanimously accepted.

International Exchange — An exchange of pulpits will take place with an Arkansas minister in Nova Scotia and a minister of the Canadian Presbyterian Church, in Forrest City, Arkansas for a month this summer.

The Rev. and Mrs. Henry E. Acklen and their sons, Andrew and John, of Forrest City will be the guests of the St. Andrew's Presbyterian Church, Sydney Mines, Nova Scotia from mid-July through mid-August. During that same period the Rev. Douglas Wilson and his family will visit the mid-South area and the Rev. Mr. Wilson will supply the pulpit of the Graham Memorial Church of Forrest City, July 22 - August 12.

LOUISIANA

New Orleans — Elected to serve on the Presbyterian Synod of Louisiana Youth Council were: Miss Emma Leah Young, treasurer; William Burge, president; both of New Orleans. William Bradford, Moderator, Shreveport; Warren Williamson, vice-moderator, Baton Rouge; Florence Beatty, stated clerk, Abbeville; Annette Van Peene, historian, Minden. They were named at the 32nd annual Young People's Conference held at Silliman College, Clinton, La. It was also announced that 47 Presbyterian young people from Louisiana will attend a leadership training school in Texas this week.

TENNESSEE

Memphis — Southwestern at Memphis, which college has long focused interest on studies of international affairs, will receive a grant of $35,000 from the Carnegie Corporation of New York, the foundation announced.

The Southwestern grant, to be used for furtherance of the college's program of international studies, is one of 10 grants amounting to almost three quarters of a million dollars.

Dr. Peyton N. Rhodes, president of the college, said that the Carnegie grant recognizes the strategic location of Memphis in international trade as a world center of cotton and hardwood lumber, along with the advantages of the existing International Center.

"This is the second time the corporation has furnished funds to implement an outstanding beginning at Southwestern. Many years ago the college received a substantial grant which enabled us to initiate the tutorial system of instruction. This has been expanded and continues effectively.

"Southwestern is the only college in the South and one of the few in the nation offering this type of instruction. It will also be a leader in a new undergraduate international studies program."

Professors who will direct the program will be Ralph Hon, professor of economics; Thomas M. Lowry, Jr., professor of History and Government; David M. Amacker, professor of political science; and Ross Pritchard, professor of international studies.

Pity the Children

J. Edgar Hoover recently issued the following statement:

"After reviewing the thousands of case histories which have poured into the FBI, I am firmly convinced that there are two factors in our outlook which if not checked will plunge us headlong into national decadence.

"The first is the failure of the home itself as the first classroom and second, our national indifference toward evil influences in our life which are beyond the immediate control of parents.

"Criminals are not born. They are the products of neglect, the victims of indifference, the results of an age which has tossed morality in the junk yard. Moral chaos and crime run hand in hand as they eagerly attempt to destroy peace, order and happiness.

"Unhappily, there are many homes where parents are untrained in their obligations to their offspring; . . . where unguarded talk is as regular as three meals a day; . . . where respect for authority and criticism of officials are common occurrences; . . . where childish independence is encouraged and refractory conduct is condoned; . . . where breaches of discipline and antisocial whims are overlooked; . . . and where God and religion are considered too old-fashioned in an age dedicated to materialism.

"The children of such homes need help. The Sunday Schools can do much and are doing much to bring God and religion into the starved souls of these youngsters."

Mania for Double Earnings

Dr. Henry Schultze, former president of Calvin College, wrote a thoughtful article in *The Banner* on the above subject. He said:

"There are women who go out of the home to work for the support of those economically dependent upon them. Various situations may call for such a program. And we must take off our hats to those who engage in a kind of work that enables them to maintain their homes. . . . But I am interested here primarily in the program of women who leave their homes in an effort to secure double earnings for the family. This, of course, is far more disastrous for the home. . . . We want to have the latest and best in cars, television sets, and so on. We must keep up with the Joneses that we and our children may not develop an inferiority complex. But we are paying altogether too much for our costly homes, cars, and television sets, if they cost us the price of real home life. And, it is feared, is precisely the cost of this craze for double earnings."

Neglecting the Children

According to *Washington Religious Report,* child neglect is one of the growing problems of the day. There are reported to be 40,000 mothers in Washington, D. C. who leave children to come to the city and work in government offices. They do not see their small children for three days in a row. There are 60,000 pre-school children who are neglected in this fashion due to the fact that there are day-care for only 1,795. This situation is serious in its effect on the rising generation. In many cases it seems unavoidable. Mothers find it necessary to work because the fathers are away in military service, or there is divorce, sickness, or some other problem. In some cases, however, it is merely a desire for additional family income beyond actual requirements that causes mothers to take a job and neglect their children. One day they may discover there are some things more important than dollars.

OUR WEEKLY SERMON

An old photographer who is an earnest Christian loves to tell the story of a field trip he made back in the 1920's.

Together with other amateur photographers, he set out one afternoon to get some views of Pontoosuc Lake, a lovely sheet of water nestling between the hills north of Pittsfield, Mass.

Reaching a good vantage spot, they placed their cameras in position and took some pictures. At first they noticed a strange spot on the lake, which at that distance looked like a small island, but when they looked again it had disappeared.

When they returned to their hotel and developed the pictures, the little spot was distinctly marked. Being curious to understand its nature, they examined it through a powerful magnifying glass, and there saw a complete reproduction of a drowning scene. There was an overturned boat, and a man clinging to the stern, while the head of another man was just visible above the water nearby.

While they were examining the picture a man arrived at the hotel and reported that a boating accident had occurred that afternoon and two men had been drowned. The photographers had been too far away from the lake to distinguish the incident, but the camera had made all clear to them afterward.

"And," continues the photographer, "it is so in moral and spiritual things also. The meaning of events that puzzle us now and lead skeptics to dispute the existence of a loving God, will beyond the grave be made plain to the man who trusts where he cannot understand now because he is too far away."

Many things were hidden even from the companions of Jesus so that they perceived them not (Luke 9:45), but afterward the Holy Spirit taught them, and brought "all things to their remembrance" (John 14:26).

Our Presbyterian Heritage

Last year the Southern Presbyterian Journal sponsored a symposium on the Reformed Faith. Addresses were made by a group of outstanding Presbyterians and all who attended gave enthusiastic response.

Without in any measure competing with any other program in our church a similar symposium will be held this year, again placing its emphasis on our Presbyterian heritage.

THE TIME—August 15th — 10:00 A. M.

THE PLACE—Weaverville, N. C.

"EASTWARD TO ASIA" brings you scenes never before on any screen . . . Filmed against a background as wide as the world itself . . . amid settings as timeless as the unchanging East.

The story of
BILLY GRAHAM'S
world tour
in the July Reader's Diges
is now yours to see
in a thrilling new
motion picture

DESTINED TO BECOME
The Most Significant Evangelical Film Of Our Day!

SPECIAL NOTE TO DIRECTORS OF BIBLE CONFERENCES AND SUMMER ASSEMBLIES:

It is not too late to add "EASTWARD TO ASIA" to your program. Through special arrangements, it can be available to you immediately. Write or phone today.

★ **Travel with Billy Graham and the Team through 30,000 miles of modern missionary miracles.**

★ **Witness heart stirring proof of the power of Gospel Evangelism in lands half a world away.**

★ **See Billy Graham preach to multiplied thousands in India—Hong Kong—Philippines—Formosa—Japan—Korea—Hawaii.**

WATCH FOR "EASTWARD TO ASIA" IN YOUR CITY SOON

Feature Length

FOR IMMEDIATE BOOKINGS: *Write—Wire—Phone*

Billy Graham EVANGELISTIC FILMS, INC
2627 Connecticut Ave., N.W.
Washington 8, D.C. COlumbia 5-1070

THE SOUTHERN PRESBYTERIAN JOURNAL

A Presbyterian weekly magazine devoted to the statement, defense and propagation of the Gospel, the faith which was once for all delivered unto the saints.

VOL. XV NO. 13 JULY [illegible] 1956 $2.50 A YEAR

Our Presbyterian Heritage

Last year The Southern Presbyterian Journal sponsored a symposium on the Reformed Faith. Addresses were made by a group of outstanding Presbyterians and all who attended gave enthusiastic response.

Without in any measure competing with any other program in our church a similar symposium will be held this year, again placing its emphasis on our Presbyterian heritage.

See back cover of this Journal for full day's schedule.

THE TIME—August 15th — 10:00 A. M.
THE PLACE—Weaverville, N. C.

Lunch will be served for all those attending but please let us hear from you so that we may make provision for all.

THE SOUTHERN PRESBYTERIAN JOURNAL
The Journal has no official connection with the Presbyterian Church in the United States
Rev. Henry B. Dendy, D.D., Editor....................Weaverville, N. C.
Dr. L. Nelson Bell, Associate Editor....................Asheville, N. C.
Rev. Wade C. Smith, Associate Editor....................Weaverville, N. C.

EDITORIAL

Dr. Bell Goes to Brazil

Dr. Bell, our Associate Editor, left Miami by plane on July 19th and plans to spend two weeks or more visiting a number of our mission stations.

His reports of this trip are due to begin in the August 15th issue of this *Journal.*

Those who have followed his articles written from abroad - (Brazil, Africa, Formosa, Great Britain, and a round-the-world tour), will look forward with keen anticipation to these new reports from areas where God is working so marvelously today.

SUBSCRIBE TO THE SOUTHERN PRESBYTERIAN JOURNAL AND RECOMMEND IT TO OTHERS. BEGIN WITH THE AUGUST 15TH NUMBER.

THE EDITOR

"Ecclesiastical Michals"

Now and then a phrase is coined which is exquisitely expressive. Recently Rev. David H. C. Reed, pastor of the Madison Avenue Presbyterian church in New York did just that.

Speaking of those who stand aloof and critical when a work of God is being done he said:

"And this leads me to say a word about campaigns and evangelistic activities. There has been a tendency, particularly perhaps in Presbyterianism, to despise the popular expression of religious emotion. We have our ecclesiastical Michals looking through a window at the crowds attending Billy Graham's campaigns and 'despising them in their hearts.' Here again surely the answer is to come in and work from the inside, without abandoning our convictions. It was discovered in Scotland that the churches which benefited as a result of the All-Scotland Crusade were those that had been committed rather than those that had criticized. It does not follow that every religious crusade must have our uncritical support but Dr. Graham has proved that he welcomes, indeed looks for, the active cooperation of the churches."

Evangelicals have for too long looked askance at some worth-while work being promoted by those of a more liberal trend, while liberals have discounted or ignored the work of evangelicals because they did not wish to be associated with their more conservative brethren. Both are thereby missing a blessing.

May God deliver us all from being "ecclesiastical Michals" ! L.N.B.

Two Perspectives

The Bible tells us that man looks on outward appearances while God looks into the heart. It tells us that God's thoughts are not man's thoughts, nor His ways man's ways.

There is a striking statement in Jeremiah which shows up the abysmal difference between the outlook of unregenerate man and that which God gives to those who have been redeemed:

Thus saith the Lord, Let not the wise man glory in his wisdom, neither let the mighty man glory in his might, let not the rich man glory in his riches: but let him that glorieth glory in this, that he understandeth and knoweth me, that I am the Lord which exercise lovingkindness, judgment and righteousness, in the earth: for in these things I delight, saith the Lord." Jeremiah 9:23-24.

The world around us *does* glory in intellectual attainments; in demonstrations of power and in material things. If we search our own hearts we know that these things loom large in our estimate of ourselves and of others. But God commands that we should revel in something far different.

God has created us to have fellowship with Himself and has opened the Way for that fellowship - His Son. Our greatest joy should be a single-hearted knowledge of and fellowship with Him through faith in the Lord Jesus Christ.

Little wonder that this transaction is called being "born again," because it opens up an entire new life to us, one where things are given their true value; where people look at things in God's perspective.

Instead of wisdom surrounded by human limitations, a trust in earthly power and a glorying in earthly possessions God gives those who are new creatures in Christ to see that He delights in lovingkindness, judgment and righteousness. All of these are gracious results of a new perspective, a perspective which comes from seeing ourselves and others in the light of God's holiness and love. Also, these same ideals become the ideal of our own personal lives.

The world worships at the feet of three idols - intellect, power, wealth. The Christian worships at the feet of the One Who is all wisdom, all power and everything which is precious.

Only the transforming power of the Living Christ can turn our hearts from worshipping these things which perish to a true understanding of and seeking of those things in which our God delights and which last for all eternity.

L.N.B.

What Happened?

Genesis 1:1—*"In the beginning God .... "*

Genesis 50:26—" . . . *in a coffin in Egypt."*

What happened after that majestic beginning when God created the universe and this world with its marvels? What happened—man in sweet communion with his Creator—then dead, in a coffin in Egypt?

"Who-dun-its" are popular today but the greatest stories in the world are found in the Bible. In Genesis we have the story of generation, degeneration and regeneration. Yes, it's a thriller and although it shows us how sinful we are it points the way to the coming Redeemer.

. . . . .

Genesis 3:17-18—" . . . *cursed is the ground for thy sake; in sorrow shalt thou eat of it all the days of thy life; thorns also and thistles shall it bring forth to thee. . . . "*

Isaiah 56:13—*"Instead of the thorn shall come up the fir tree, and instead of the brier shall come up the myrtle tree: and it shall be to the Lord for a name, for an everlasting sign that shall not be cut off."*

Why the great difference in outlook? Was there any significance to the fact that when our Lord was crucified He wore a crown of thorns? Was he not bearing the full penalty of the curse of sin? Did not His death (and resurrection), open up an entirely new vista for all who have believed down through the ages?

. . . . .

Malachi 4:6—" . . . *lest I come and smite the earth with a curse."*

Revelation 22:20—" . . . *Even so, come, Lord Jesus."*

The curse of sin has been paid in full between those two verses. The first shows fear and judgment; the second a glorious hope to which all who trust Him may turn.

. . . . . .

If you are missing the joy and the teaching to be found in God's Word alone you are missing something of transcending importance - and something very precious.

Of course Christians do not worship a Book; nor do they trust in a Book for salvation. But in this Book we learn of Him. Our Lord says: *"Search the scriptures; for in them ye think ye have eternal life: and they are they which testify of me."*

Search - Learn - Find Him.

L.N.B.

— LETTERS —

Sirs:

Regarding your editorial "Degenerate Music" (issue of July 4th) — That delicious comparison:

"The comparison is much of that to be found between genuine art and the bizarre and nightmarish blobs and blotches of surrealistic paintings."

Whoops and Hooray! ! !

Bob Matthews

Editors Note—Mr. Matthews, now living in Canton, N. C., was for many years pianist for Billy Sunday.

The Southern Presbyterian Journal, *a Presbyterian Weekly magazine devoted to the statement, defense, and propagation of the Gospel, the faith which was once for all delivered unto the saints,* published every Wednesday by The Southern Presbyterian Journal, Inc., in Weaverville, N. C.

Entered as second-class matter May 15, 1942, at the Postoffice at Weaverville, N. C., under the Act of March 3, 1879. Vol. XV, No. 13, July 25, 1956. Editorial and Business Offices: Weaverville, N. C. Printed in the U.S.A. by Biltmore Press, Asheville, N. C.

ADDRESS CHANGE: When changing address, please let us have both old and new address as far in advance as possible. Allow three weeks after change if not sent in advance. When possible, send an address label giving your old address.

What Is Man?

By Floyd E. Hamilton

Centreville, Ala.

"What is man, that thou art mindful of him? And the son of man that thou visitest him? Psalm 8:4.

Last week I started a series on Modernism by asking the question, What is Modernism? The answer I gave was that it is any departure from the teaching that the Old and New Testaments are the Word of God. Then I listed thirteen points on which Modernism and evangelicalism differ, but discussed only one of these points, reserving the others for future articles. The point I discussed was regarding the inspiration of the Bible. The evangelical believes that the Holy Spirit so guided and controlled the writers of the Bible that what they wrote was true and the truth God wanted his people to have. The Modernist departs from this belief in some way. The most important departure today is that of the Barthian who holds that the Bible is not a deposit of God's revelation and truth, so that it is God's Word whether we like it or not, but that God may use any part of the Bible to give God's Word to any particular individual, though to another individual reading the same part of the Bible it would not be the Word of God at all, and thus the question of the truth of any portion of the Bible would be unimportant. Last week we saw that such a position really destroys the Word of God, for if we think the Bible is not true at any point, that point cannot possibly become the Word of God to us while we believe it to be false.

In this article I want to discuss the second question on which evangelicals and Modernists differ, namely, the question of the nature of man. The Word of God teaches that man was created holy, in the image of God, sinless and without any imperfection, but that by his disobedience to the revealed commandment of God, man became spiritually dead, and plunged the whole race into spiritual death, so that in his own strength man can do nothing to get back to God. Only God's Spirit by giving the new birth can make man spiritually alive.

The Modernist, on the other hand regards man entirely differently. He regards man not as having been created in the image of God, but as an animal, the product of evolution in both body and mind. As an animal the Modernist holds that man is a descendant of a branch of the family of anthropoid apes, a distant cousin, so to speak. To the Modernist, sin is either not sin at all or else is a minor imperfection which will be sluffed off in time as the race improves through natural selection. Sin is merely the clinging to man of his animal instincts, not something that breaks the law of God and separates him from God. To the Modernist sin needs no atonement, and therefore the death of Christ was not as a Substitute to atone for sin and to reconcile us to God. To the Modernist, man is a pretty fine organism, able to conquer nature, and capable of improving his own character with possibly a little help and encouragement from God, but if he needs any saving at all he is perfectly capable of saving himself by his own efforts. To the Modernist man needs no change such as the new birth in order to get to heaven (if there indeed is one). Education and "spiritual influences" are perfectly sufficient to give man all the help he needs in his struggle against a malignant nature around him.

It should be plain that this whole idea of the nature of man is directly opposed to the teachings of the Word of God. First of all man is not an animal, even a *higher* animal. Man is a living soul, created in the image of God, not evolved from the beasts. Man as he is today is fallen and dead in sin except as God gives him the new birth and eternal life. Man did not derive either his body or soul from the animals by a process of evolution. Now I am perfectly aware that the schools and colleges today teach organic evolution not as a theory, but as a proven fact of science. The textbooks almost without exception teach that man originally lived in caves, that he was a hairy- ugly-looking being with a low brow, and carrying a heavy club with which to fight his enemies and get his food. In other words that man has climbed a long way up the evolutionary ladder, but that he has evolved from the beasts nevertheless. If you saw the issues of the magazine "Life" dealing with the history of man, you got a pretty good picture of what is taught in school today about the origin of man.

Now this is an extremely important matter. If this evolutionary teaching is true, there is an almost inevitable conflict with the Bible, particularly with the first chapters of Genesis. If the body and mind of human beings are derived from the lower animals by inheritance, it is difficult to see how his relationship to God could come logically into the picture. Personally I am convinced that much of the alienation of the educated classes from Christ and the church is due to their belief in evolution and consequent rejection of the Bible teachings about man.

It would be impossible to deal with the question of evolution in a single article, and I shall not attempt to do so. I have dealt with it briefly in my book THE BASIS OF CHRISTIAN FAITH and in another book now out of print, THE BASIS OF EVOLUTIONARY FAITH in which I show that the evolutionary theory is just an article of faith on the part of the believers in evolution. Here I want only to show that the belief in evolution of the body and mind of man from lower animals is contrary to the teaching of the Bible, and should be rejected by those who believe that the whole Bible is the Word of God.

In the second place, contrary to the position of the Modernists, the natural man, before he is regenerated by God's Spirit, is dead in trespasses and sins, and unable to save himself by his own efforts. He cannot save himself by his good character, or by good works or by turning in his own efforts to Christ. It takes God's power to turn him and to save him after he has been given the new birth of the Holy Spirit. That means that man does not naturally love God and want to obey him. Naturally he is either actively opposed to God or at best indifferent to God and His claims. It takes the omnipotent power of God Himself to change this enmity or indifference of man to God, to Christ and to the work of the kingdom of God.

It follows from this, in the third place, that men cannot be educated into the kingdom of God. Education which takes the natural man and simply improves him and increases his knowledge, will never in itself save any man. In any church preaching may be used by the Spirit in the providence of God to bring the new birth to the hearers, but unless the Holy Spirit does so work the hearers may be just as lost as the people outside any church. In the last analysis it is the Spirit who adds to the church such as are being saved. Organizations, new methods, new plans all have their place in the program of the church but let it never be forgotten that unless they are used in reliance upon the Holy Spirit to carry on the work of regeneration and sanctification, the natural man who is unregenerated may be in the church but not one who has eternal life.

Now in contrast to this the Modernist takes man as he is and makes no effort to change him from his total depravity to a regenerated child of God. He holds that man does not need changing, so he places great emphasis on programs of social betterment and on external organizations. Such programs in themselves do not make their advocates Modernists, but when the spiritual training of the church and the preaching of the true gospel are neglected or ignored, it is pretty good evidence that the minister has Modernist sympathies. Because the Modernist regards man as not needing to be converted or regenerated, he has little sympathy with evangelistic campaigns or evangelistic appeals to accept Christ as Saviour and Lord of life. He holds that man is not at all dead in sin and that all that man needs is to get together with other men in a church which is mainly a social club rather than an instrument established by God for the saving of souls from eternal punishment. Joining a church for the Modernist is pretty much like joining another club, except that it meets regularly on Sunday morning when man's "religious nature" can find expression in a beautiful program of music and pageantry. The sermon is to be one of the presentation of high ideals and ethical culture, ignoring man's need of salvation from the curse and presence of sin, and ignoring the necessity of repentance and faith in the substitutionary death of Christ and his resurrection life.

May God grant that our churches may become awake to this terrible peril of Modernism in the church, and that Christians everywhere may realize the necessity of repentance from sin and faith in the shed blood of Jesus Christ the only Saviour for time and eternity, the only way of salvation.

"Praise the Lord, All Ye Nations"

By George S. Lauderdale

All nations whom thou hast made shall come and worship before thee, O Lord; and shall glorify thy name. Psalm 86:9.

God is great, ruling the world. "Behold, the nations are as a drop of a bucket, and are counted as the small dust of the balance: behold he taketh up the isles as a very little thing . . . . All nations before him are as nothing; and they are counted to him less than nothing, and vanity." Isaiah 40:15-17. All the inhabitants of the earth are as grasshoppers to God, who has stretched out the heavens like a curtain or tent-covering, so that they declare His glory.

All men must worship God. "Lift up your eyes on high, and behold who hath created these things." Isaiah 40:26. Not to properly revere God is to become blind to facts; worship of idols is a wilful closing of the eyes and the choosing of ignorance to understanding. God is not hurt by unbelief, but wicked men are; He takes no delight in watching them walk into blazing wrath lasting throughout eternity. "They shall be greatly ashamed, that trust in graven images, that say to the molten images, ye are our gods." Isaiah 42:17.

The Missionaries' Hope

Scattered bands of believers in God dot the globe who have come to know Him through

Jesus Christ His Son, revealed to man in the Bible. At some future time a higher percentage of the nations will love and serve God, and at the judgment day every knee shall bow and every tongue confess, willingly or otherwise, that Jesus Christ is Lord to the glory of God the Father. Heaven's citizens will hail from every kingdom, according to Psalm 87:4-7, in meter:

"Heathen lands and hostile peoples
Soon shall come the Lord to know;
Nations born again in Zion
Shall the Lord's salvation show;
God Almighty shall on Zion strength bestow.

"When the Lord shall count the nations
Sons and daughters He shall see,
Born to endless life in Zion,
And their joyful song shall be:
'Blessed Zion, all our fountains are in thee.' "

God's Word Good For All

That all nations will not only share in the glory of God's celestial Kingdom, but also contribute to the same is set forth in Revelation 21:24: "And the nations of them which are saved shall walk in the light of it: and the kings of the earth do bring their glory and honor into it." The leaves of the tree of life in heaven are for the healing of the nations. How much better that a nation be healed in this way than to be corrupted by illicit traffic with the wicked city Babylon! The mother of harlots and abominations of the earth, with her the "kings of the earth have committed fornication, and the inhabitants of the earth have been made drunk with the wine of her fornication. Revelation 17:2.

Pray for your native land, that it might become Christian. Do not relax unconcerned as the servants of Satan, intent only on making money, even at the expense of the morals of the nation's youth, are permitted to market and advertise their evil wares. Beer belongs in the gutter and open Bibles in our homes! Let gospel preaching replace crime and sex stories on radio and television; may the prayer meetings among government officials become better attended than their senseless cocktail parties; Christian literature must outsell the shameful offerings of Babylon at every newsstand.

God is calling *the nations* to cease to do evil and to learn to do well. Jesus said, "Go ye . . . teach all nations." Matthew 28:19.

ANGLERS

(From *"New Testament Evangelism"*

by Wade C. Smith)

Lesson No. 149

GROUP ORGANIZATION FOR PERSONAL EVANGELISM

"The church that is not evangelistic ceases to be evangelical. The ideal of every church ought to be inspired by the experience of the Apostles after Pentecost, when they 'added to the church daily such as were being saved'".— William E. Biederwolf.

The preceding lessons treat the subject from the standpoint of the individual soul-winner, the object being to get the reader, or student of Evangelism, to place himself *first* in the line of privilege and responsibility. After that, to consider matters of organization by which he may be yoked with others in winning unsaved men to Christ. It seems that one great hindrance to a world-sweeping movement of Evangelism up to this time has been the reverse of this order in the thinking of Christians. They have considered the challenge as to the Church-at-large, or to groups, as to the clergy and Church leaders; and not as to the individual. It has been a fatal misconception; untold millions have died unsaved because of it.

Satanic Opposition.

Dr. J. E. Conant, in his book "Every-Member Evangelism" has handled this fault in an unusual way. He gives the devil full credit as the author of it, devoting a whole chapter to what he calls "Satanic Opposition." Referring to the marvelous spread of Christian faith following the Pentecostal revival, he says: "The one thing, aside from the divine power, that made the program such a sweeping success was that *every disciple was a witness;* they were all propagandists. It was right here that Satan struck his blow. The first thing he did was to overemphasize the distinctions in the divinely appointed division of service, as finally to get an entirely equal witnessing brotherhood divided into two companies, with the great majority in one, and the small minority in the other. The small company came to be called 'clergy' and the large company 'laity.' And then he worked the witnessing out of the hands of the 'laity,' until it was finally regarded as the exclusive responsibility of the 'clergy.' Then came the Devil's Millenium which history calls the 'Dark Ages'! This was the most terrific blow Satan ever dealt the Church, and one from which she has never recovered."

Is it not possible that even in this generation this sinister plan of the Devil, which has proven so disastrous to the progress of the kingdom, may be overthrown—and that the church may return to the Apostolic program whereby "every disciple was a witness"?

Important as it is that we should consider Soul Winning first of all as an individual and personal responsibility and privilege, yet group organization is necessary to cope with the overall task.

The next lesson will deal with how to form groups in the church for personal work.

Helps To Understanding Scripture Readings in *Day by Day*

By Rev. C. C. Baker

In this issue we are running two weeks Helps in order to get on the same schedule with our S. S. Lessons and Young People's Programs. Some of our readers have been receiving the Journal too late to use these Helps on the date named.—H.B.D.

Sunday, July 29, *Luke* 11:14-23. Those that interpreted Christ's miracles as the hand of Satan (v.15) were the Pharisees (Matt. 12:24). Trace through the logic of Jesus' argument in vv.17-22. Would it be logical for Satan to defeat one of his own cohorts (vv.17-19)? What happens to any country that engages in Civil War (v.17)? If Christ had done this miracle by the hand of God what is the only possible conclusion to which one could come (v.20)? In v.14 one who was stronger than the demon cast him out (v.22). It was the attitude of the Pharisees that provoked Christ's remark about the unpardonable sin (Matt. 12:31-32). There were others who evaded the question at point by asking for further evidence (v.16). Though your heart is not like that of the Pharisee toward Christ, do you still try to evade issues when confronted with some challenge to follow Him?

Monday, July 30, *Matthew* 18:1-4. A person with a child-like faith is very precious in the sight of God. It is this type of faith that makes one a Christian (v.3) and brings eternal rewards (v.4). How does Christ identify Himself with such an one (v.5)? What place does he have in Heaven (v.11)? Observe the terrible consequences to the person who is a stumbling block (vv.6-7). Are there practices or attitudes in you that cause other Christians to stumble? If a sincere Christian stumbles God will not rest until he is brought back into the fold (vv.12-13).

Tuesday, July 31, *Matthew* 6:24-34. Satan will do everything to cause a Christian to be anxious concerning his physical needs. What facts about God and nature make this temptation fallacious (vv.26,28-29)? If God cares thus for His creatures in nature, are the questions of vv.26,30 logical? What does v.32 add? What are the obvious answers to the questions in vv.25 & 27? What must the Christian do in order not to yield to the temptation of anxiety (v.33)? When a Christian is more concerned about his own needs than the work of the Kingdom, what god is he serving (v.24)? Do you yield to the temptation of anxiety over physical needs or do you heed the words of Jesus in this passage?

Wednesday, August 1, *Matthew* 5:1-16. "Blessed" means "oh the happiness of". Pick out the qualities of those who are considered "blessed" (vv.3-11). Are these qualities those the world usually associates with happiness? Notice the various rewards of the "Blessed" in vv.3-11. Do they have much of an appeal to the man of the world? The Christian who cannot be satisfied with these rewards has lost his usefulness in the world (vv.13b,15). Are you content to desire to possess the qualities of the Beatitudes? It is the happy Christian who is the salt of the earth (v.13) and the light of the world (vv.14,16).

Thursday, August 2, *John* 14:25-27. Jesus was going to the cross and the disciples were about to face the darkest hours of their lives. Knowing the difficulties that were before them, Jesus gave the repeated exhortation of 14:1a & 27b. How does the peace of which Jesus speaks differ from the peace of the world (v.27)? Must we strive after His peace, or is it given to us (v.27)? Who is the giver (v.27)? To whom does the peace that He gives us belong (v.27)? What is the connection between the peace that Jesus gives and the Holy Spirit (v.26)? the words of Christ (v.26)? our belief in God (v.1b)? What truth do you find in 16:33 that gives great force to Jesus' offer of peace? How have you responded to Jesus' tender assurance that you need never be afraid?

Friday, August 3, *John* 16:19-24. The disciples were puzzled by Jesus' saying of v.16 (vv.17-19). Jesus knew that an understanding of His departure would bring them great sorrow, and He tried to prepare them for it. Did Jesus try to keep them from sorrowing or tell them that their sorrow was wrong (vv.20-22)? What was the comfort that He offered (vv.20-22)? Do you think American Christians need to learn to accept sorrow and tribulation as a part of their lives in the world (v.32)? We cannot always avoid sorrow but we can learn to endure it and serve God through it as we set our hearts upon the joy that is to follow (Heb. 12:2).

Saturday, August 4, *Rev.* 22:12-21. Part of the wonder of the Christian faith is the fact that the future is in the hands of the Lord Jesus (vv.2-13,16,20). The Second Coming of Christ is the great hope of the Church (vv.17, 20). His Coming is imminent (vv.12,20) in the sense that it is the next even in the program of the Kingdom. It can happen at any time. What will be His office when Christ returns (v.12)? What should be the attitude of the Church toward His Coming (vv.17,20b)? How is she to prepare for His Coming (vv.14,17b)? Do you look and prepare daily for Christ's return?

Sunday, August 5, *Psalm* 105:1-5. *The Psalmist* is able to look back in the history of his nation and see the hand of God at work (vv.5-7) - The Covenant with Abraham (vv.9-11); Sojourn in Egypt (vv.16-25); Wilderness experiences (vv. 39-41); Conquest of the Promised Land (vv.44-45). There was purpose in God's dealings with His people (vv.7-9,11,44-45). He made promises which He kept (compare vv.11&44). Therefore the Psalmist gives thanks and praise to God (vv.1-2). He seeks God's presence with all his heart (vv.3-4). Can you look back and see God's hand in your life, working things out according to His purposes? Does this knowledge encourage you to continue to serve and love Him?

Monday, August 6, *Psalm* 95:1-6. Meditate upon each of the phrases introduced by "Let us" in vv.1-2. The Psalmist says we should enter into God's presence because He is our Creator (vv.3-6), our God (v.7), our Shepherd (v.7b), and our Salvation (v.1b). He warns of the danger of hardening one's heart (v.8a) and receiving the displeasure of God (v.11). This happened on a previous occasion (vv.8-10). (See Exodus 17:1-7; Number 20:1-13). When you come to points in your life when spiritually you are at a turning point do you have a tendency to enter into deeper fellowship with God or continue to live on a lower spiritual plane?

Tuesday, August 7, *Psalm* 29. Praise is ascribed to the Lord for the revelation of himself in the thunderstorm (vv.1-2). "First we hear it rolling in the sky (vv.3,4) and in the North (v.5-6) . . . There is a terrific lightning flash (v.7). During that flash the storm sweeps over the whole length of the land; and now we see it in the desert region of the South (vv.8,9)." The God of the Psalmist is a God to be worshipped (vv.1-2,9b). He is all powerful and exists from all eternity (v.10). He watches over His people and supplies their needs (vv.10-11). When you think about the storm allow these truths about God to sink home, and worship Him for who He is.

Wednesday, August 8, *Psalm* 8. The Psalmist views the heavens and beholds the glory of God (v.1). When he views the vastness of God's creation he questions the significance of man in God's sight (vv.3,4). Verses 5-8 are the answer to the Psalmist's questionings. He finds his answer in the Scriptures in Genesis 1:26-30. Could he have known this apart from the Scriptures? What place does man have in relation to God (v.5; Gen. 1:26)? In relation to His Creation (v.6-8)? Truly when one puts the facts of vv.1,3 together with the truths of vv.5-8, he says "How excellent is thy name in all the earth (v.9)."

Thursday, August 9, *Psalm* 145. God is all powerful (vv.3-6,11). His Kingdom is eternal (v.13). His deeds are terrifying (vv.4-6). His character is Holy (vv.17,20b,21b). Yet, He deals gently and mercifully with His creatures (vv.8-9). List the ways in vv.14-20 that the Lord deals mercifully with His people. What conditions must His creatures meet to find help (vv.14-15,18,19-20)? Does God play favorites with those who look to Him for help? (Observe the word "all" in vv.14-20). What is the response of God's creatures to His graciousness (v.10)? The response of the Psalmist (v.1-2,21)? Do you realize who it is to whom you pray? Do you praise Him for His graciousness to you?

Friday, August 10, *Psalm* 32:1-5. It is a blessed relief when one has sinned to confess that sin (v.5) and find forgiveness (vv.1-2). How did the Psalmist feel when he held unconfessed sin in his soul (vv.3-4)? How does the figure of summer heat dramatize that condition (v.4b)? Since his confession of sin, notice what the Lord has come to mean to him personally (vv.6-7). God has promised to teach and guide us (vv.8, 10b) if we are teachable and are not deliberately obstinate about sin (v.9). To deliberately walk in sin is misery (v.10a), but to walk with God is sheer joy (v.11).

Saturday, August 11, *Psalm* 27. The Psalmist is in desperate straits. His enemies have almost over-whelmed him (vv.3a,11). People are spreading lies about him (v.12). His own family forsakes him (v.10). What does the Lord mean to him personally (v.1)? What is the confidence he has in God (vv.1,5,10)? The confidence and personal strength (v.1,5) the Psalmist possesses in time of trouble comes from (a) a deep personal desire to have fellowship with God (v.4); (b) a willingness to wait upon the Lord in prayer for strength (v.14); (c) a confidence that somehow God is going to work things out (vv.6, 13). What particular points or verses in the chapter do you find especially helpful in times of distress or difficulties?

LESSON FOR AUGUST 5

A Call To Christian Living

Background Scripture: Luke 2:40, 51, 52; I Peter 2:1-3; 4:1-11; II Peter 2
Devotional Reading: Philippians 4:4-9

In order to live and enjoy the Christian Life it is necessary for all to be tranquil within; that there be peace and joy in our hearts. A man cannot live the Christian Life as he should when his mind and soul are restless and disturbed. So, in our Devotional Reading Paul tells us to "Rejoice"; to be anxious about nothing, but to rest ourselves completely upon God and with thanksgiving make our requests known to Him. If we do this, then the peace of God which passeth all understanding shall guard our hearts and minds through Jesus Christ. With the center of our lives thus protected, we can live to the glory of God.

Then, in Philippians 4:8 we have one of those great recipes for real Christian Living. "As a man thinketh in his heart, so is he," and if we "think on these things"; the true, the honest, the just, the pure, the lovely, things of good report, of virtue and praise, as Paul tells us in this verse, then we are prepared for real Christian Living. I am afraid that many of us are so busy thinking of frivolity and crimes and the terrible news which occupies the head lines of our newspapers, or which we see on Television, or hear over the Radio, that our minds become all "cluttered up" with trash and worse than trash. We do not take the time to "think on these things"; the good and beautiful and noble things of life.

A "Call to Christian Living" might well be described as a Call to fix our minds on God and Christ and the higher and nobler things. It is indeed an "Upward Call" of God in Christ Jesus, or as someone has expressed it, "Set our hearts on heaven", for we are citizens of a heavenly Kingdom. Bunyan, in his picture of "The Man with the Muckrake," has vividly illustrated this. There are multitudes of people who are so busy raking all sorts of ugly and disgusting things out of the mire of this world that they pay no heed to the angel holding a crown which he is anxious to place upon our heads. I am writing these words to myself first. It is so easy for us to let the base, or worthless, take possession of our minds and hearts. May God give us grace to allow Him to "keep our hearts and minds through Christ Jesus." A Christian Life must flow from a pure fountain which is yielding clear, fresh water, and not from a spring contaminated with all the disease germs of a filthy world. Allow me to use a crude illustration. We usually turn on our radio while we are eating breakfast so that we can get the news. If we tune in a few minutes early we get an avalanche of "Rock and Roll" songs which are disgusting, to put it mildly. Why not have some of the beautiful songs of former days? I believe that most listeners would enjoy them more.

I. *Christian Living means Growth:*
Luke 2:40,51,52; I Peter 2:1-3.

Jesus furnishes a pattern for Christian Living, and Jesus *grew:* "And the child grew — and Jesus increased in wisdom and stature, and in favour with God and Man." We think of His growing in body and mind, in spiritual and social life. This fourfold growth is what we look for in our children and in ourselves. Jesus was a perfect Child, and so His growth was phenomenal. He is our Perfect Pattern in all things. Let us never be satisfied unless our growth, and the growth of those in our family, develops along all four sides. In this way we get a well-rounded personality. While Jesus was the Son of God, he was also a real boy and real man. There is mystery here, but we see similar miracles every time we cast seed into the ground: "first the blade, then the ear, and then the full corn."

In I Peter 2:1-3 Peter suggests two requirements for growth: (1) the laying aside of all evil that retards growth, and (2) the desire for the sincere milk of the Word. How simple, and yet how true! A child cannot grow as long as its body is full of disease germs. Take your child to a specialist and ask him, What is the matter with my child? He is thin and listless and weighs no more than he did a year ago. The doctor will look for two things. First, is there some disease? Second, What about the food? So with us in the spiritual realm. We cannot grow spiritually if we are all clogged up with malice and guile and hypocrisies and envies and evil speakings. These germs will destroy all chance of growth. Neither can we grow without feeding ourselves on spiritual food, and the Word is like milk, the perfect food for the soul. The Bible is also called "the finest of the wheat," "strong meat," "honey out of the Rock." For an all-around diet, both for babes and for grown men and women, you cannot beat the Bible. If we want to grow, let us feed on the Word!

II. *Christian Living Means Glorifying God:* I Peter 4:1-11.

In verse eleven we may find a summary of these verses: "that God in all things may be glorified through Jesus Christ." Paul puts it in these words, Whatever ye do . . . do all to the glory of God, and our Catechism says, Man's chief end is to glorify God and enjoy Him forever.

We are not to follow "the will of the Gentiles, the lusts of the flesh," but the *will of God.* He describes "the will of the Gentiles" in verse three. It is a very sad, but very true picture of the world as it was in Peter's day, and as it is in our day, for the world has changed but little except in external and material ways. It is still walking "in lasciviousness, lusts, excess of wine, revellings, banquetings and abominable idolatries." Our world is an intemperate world in more ways than one. The whole picture is one of utter absence of self-control over appetites, passions, and desires of the flesh.

Christians must turn away from such indulgence of the lower nature. There may be some who call themselves "Christian" who indulge in such excesses, but they are destroying themselves and bringing reproach upon the holy name by which they are called; upon both the Church and the Saviour Who bought them with His own precious blood. The world may "think it strange" that we do not follow its example and run to the same excess of riot. People may speak evil of us. Judgment is coming upon them, however, and they will have to give an account to Him Who will be the Judge at that Day. Suppose the Judgment Day finds us in company with such people. Suppose the Judge should ask the question, What do these Christians here? If the servant should say, My Lord delays His coming, and should fail to watch and be ready; if he should even be indulging in these sins, and be mistreating his fellow servants, what can the Judge do? He can only appoint him with the hypocrites and cast him out into outer darkness. And Peter says later, in verse 17, "For the time is come that judgment must begin at the house of God: and if it first begin at us, what shall the end be of them that obey not the gospel of God"?

Turning now to the positive side, what are some of the outstanding characteristics of Christian Living? We have space to but make a list of these as outlined by Peter. The end of all things is at hand, be ye therefore sober, (of sound mind) and watch unto prayer. How often Jesus said Watch and pray! Then we are to have "fervent love"; a love that covers a multitude of sins. It is like the green grass that covers the bare ugly soil when Spring comes. Use hospitality one to another without grudging. Eastern people put us to shame in this respect. Then we are to be "good stewards of the manifold grace of God. In our speaking; in our ministry, we are to glorify God in all things. Peter thus presents both sides of Christian Living; its negative and positive side.

III. *Christian Living Means Escaping Terrible Judgment:* Peter 2.

This is a Fearful Chapter; a chapter of warning to us; a picture of judgment upon a wicked world. Would that all of us might hear and heed these warnings! Would that all Christians would see and feel the danger and be sure that we escape the pollutions and pernicious ways of this wicked world!

1. False prophets and false teachers. Jesus warned against them when He said, Beware of false prophets, which come to you in sheep's clothing, but inwardly they are ravening wolves. Peter says they even deny the Lord that bought them. They bring destructive heresies into the church; their conduct is characterized by lasciviousness and covetousness. Upon them shall come "swift destruction." I believe with Lenski that these are symbolized in the Book of Revelation under the term, "Beasts," and also under the false prophet and wicked woman.

2. Peter illustrates this coming Judgment, and the certainty of it, by several Old Testament events: the Flood; the overthrow of the cities of Sodom and Gomorrha. Some try to tell us that God will not punish sinners. Peter shows that He has done this very thing in a most spectacular way. Judgment is called "His strange act." He is not willing that any should perish, but that all should come to repentance, but Judgment becomes absolutely necessary at times. When a boil is ripe, it must be lanced. When "the cup of inquity is full," then judgment, swift and terrible, must fall, as it fell upon Jerusalem.

3. God knows how to deliver the just out of these "temptations," even as He delivered Lot from Sodom.

4. Sins of presumption and self-will, like the "way of Balaam."

YOUTH PROGRAM FOR AUGUST 5

"Heroes In The Battle For The Minds Of Men"

Hymn—"In Christ There Is No East Or West"
Prayer
Scripture—Luke 13:10-22
Hymn: "O Grant Us Light That We May Know"
Offering
Hymn: "Holy Ghost, With Light Divine"

NOTE TO PROGRAM LEADER: (Again we remind you that these biographical programs can be more helpful and more interesting by supplementing the basic material given here with additional information to be found in books and magazines.)

LEADER'S INTRODUCTION:

Christianity has always been the companion of learning. Wherever the church has gone, education has advanced, but it has been difficult to get the church established where people are engulfed in ignorance. Christian missionaries have found it necessary to enlighten men's minds before they can make much progress in spreading the Christian faith. It is also hard to gain a hearing for the Gospel among people who are starving. As a matter of fact, the mind does not function very well when the body is terribly undernourished. Our missionaries have discovered that it is easier to nourish the soul of their people when they are well fed physically.

In our program today we are considering two living heroes of the faith. One of them has been amazingly successful in stamping out ignorance and illiteracy. The other has become famous for helping the starving people of India to feed themselves.

FIRST SPEAKER:

In 1915 Dr. Frank Laubach and his wife went to the Philippine Islands as missionaries of the Congregational Church of America. In recent years Dr. Laubach is thought of as a missionary to the whole world. He is the originator of the famous world-wide campaign against illiteracy which has as its motto "each one teach one."

Realizing from experience how terribly difficult it is to win people to Christianity who cannot read, and recognizing that over half the inhabitants of the world are illiterate, Dr. Laubach became consumed with a passion to teach people to read. He developed a brilliant, yet very simple method of teaching, so that it is possible for the most backward adults to learn to read in a very short time . . . often in a matter of an hour. The very simplicity of his system makes it possible for those who have learned to teach others.

The Laubach method of teaching involves the use of pictures, words, and sounds, all of which are familiar to the people being taught. Charts of these "picture-word-syllable" devices must be carefully thought out for each language and cultural group. The preparation of the charts is most important to the success of the teaching, and Dr. Laubach's brilliance has shown itself in the many charts he has invented and in the success they have met.

It is no accident that this marvelous invention was revealed to a Christian missionary, who has used this opportunity to the glory of God and for the spreading of the Gospel. Dr. Laubach has seen to it that those who learn to read by his method are introduced to the Bible and its message very early in their instruction. We should be deeply grateful to God for this hero whose life has been used so wonderfully not only to enlighten men's minds but their souls as well.

SECOND SPEAKER:

Our second hero is a close friend of the first. He is Dr. Sam Higginbottom, who prefers to be known as a farmer. Sam Higginbottom went to India as a missionary of the Presbyterian Church after graduation from seminary in 1903. During his first term on the field his duties were varied, and his assignment was changed several times. Everywhere he went he was made aware of the desperate poverty of the people and their consequent hunger. He soon discovered that both poverty and hunger were the result of misuse of land and labor. He taught gardening to the boys who were students in one of the mission schools. Better nutrition made them better students. It was obvious that one way to win a hearing for Christ among the people was to lead them to a more abundant physical life in His name.

On his furlough in 1910 Missionary Higginbottom entered the Agricultural College of Ohio State University to learn how to be Farmer Higginbottom. Armed with his new knowledge Farmer Higginbottom returned to India, acquired some land at Allahabad, and established a Christian Agricultural Institute. Through the Institute he began to teach the Indian farmers to improve their crops, their livestock, and their land. It was a slow and tedious process at first, but as results were seen, the idea caught fire. It would be impossible to measure the value of Dr. Higginbottom's work, but the numerous honors he has received bear witness to his genuine success. The most wonderful part of all his service is that his great contributions and accomplishments have been made in the name of and for the glory of Christ. He is a Christian hero to the people of India.

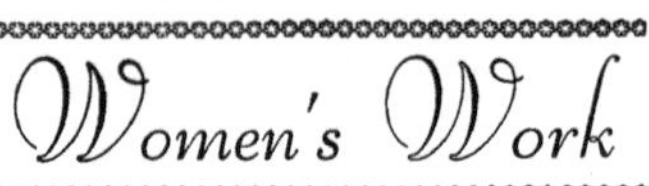

When You Pray

"When you pray, pray to your Father in secret."

Most of us find it hard to do as Jesus did and as He admonished us to do. Perhaps it has always been hard to draw apart from the crowd and pray. In olden days when families were larger and more effort was involved in caring for the family needs it must have been hard to find time to withdraw and seek a quiet spot. Today with our labor-saving devices and smaller families, it would seem that for the present day Christian there would be time to command. But there is the crowd of activities that leaves no time to draw apart.

It leaves us as Christians on time unless we are determined to let nothing separate us from the joy of being in His presence each day, that come what may we will take the time to sup with Him and have Him sup with us. Once we have established this hour, it is our daily bread, we feel that to fully live we must have it and we arrange our schedule to let nothing interfere.

Other times there are for the Christian to draw apart. "In the morning, rising up a great while before day, He went out and departed into a solitary place and prayed." These early morning vigils must have been the glory time for Jesus, the times when the creation seemed good and perfect and the times when He could remember what Heaven had been. The quiet morning stillness, the sparkle of the dew in the sunlight, the sound of the sleepy birds stirring, the world slowly waking, all of this is ours when we do as Jesus did and rise up early in the morning to pray. We are convinced that God is in His heaven and all is right with the world that He made, even though the existing conditions are disquieting.

Another time Jesus drew apart, "And they came to a place called Gethsemane and He saith to His disciples, "Sit ye here while I pray!" The hard time had come to Jesus, an hour to be faced. He withdrew and sought help and comfort and strength from His Father. If we have been in communion with God daily, it is natural for us to do as Jesus did and He gives us, as He did to His Son, that something we need to face our Gethsemane.

These times of drawing apart are necessary to fit us for our real function as Christians. That function is to "Pray without ceasing," the work that Jesus left us to do.

It is the work of the Christian, the work every Christian can do and the work every Christian must do to grow and to make the Kingdom grow. The future of the spreading of Christianity depends upon whether the Spirit of God can persuade us to take up this work of praying without ceasing.

(Mrs. W. T.) Elizabeth K. Nichols
Florence, Alabama

Thermometers and Thermostats

A small boy was trying to explain the difference between a thermometer and a thermostat to his younger sister.

"They are alike," he said; "they both tell the temperature. But the thermostat *"does something* about it."

That is true. While the thermometer is a very useful instrument, its function and only purpose is to indicate the temperature. When the temperature rises, the thermometer goes up; when the temperature drops, it goes down. It merely adjusts itself to its surroundings, it cannot change the temperature in the slightest degree.

All too often this illustrates how we react to circumstances. When something happens, we are aroused with the rest of our family or community. But as the memory dims with the passage of time, our temperature often recedes to normal again without doing anything about it.

The thermostat, on the other hand, is a very sensitive instrument which is electrically connected with the heating unit of the building. When the room gets cold, this little gadget sends messages to the source of heat and sets power in motion for the comfort and wellbeing of the persons in the building. The thermostat differs from the thermometer in that when the temperature goes up or down it *does something* about it.

Yes, you have guessed the application. Every Christian is either a thermometer or a thermo-

Christ's Moment of Supreme Triumph

I Corinthians 15:27

Weymouth translates this verse as follows: And when He shall have declared that "All things are in subjection," it will be with the manifest exception of Him who has reduced them all to Him.

In confirmation of this translation G. G. Findlay in Expositor's Greek Testament says: "All things are subdued!" is the joyful announcement by the Son that the grand promise recorded in the 8th Psalm is fulfilled. Christ proclaims the victory at last achieved; He reports that with the abolition of death, His commission is ended and the travail of His soul satisfied.

What a wonderful moment it will be in the life of the Son of God when all His enemies are conquered, and He can announce to His Father: "All things are subdued!" The all things include Satan, sin, and death—all that has ever lifted its head in rebellion against God and His sovereign rule of the universe. This truly is the moment prophesied by Isaiah in Isa. 53:11. This is the moment when Christ shall see the full results of the travail of His soul and be eternally satisfied. It will be the Moment of His SUPREME TRIUMPH.

Martin A. Hopkins.

Do Your Hinges Creak?

By Jack Kytle

A college youth had become very popular after several months of lukewarm, and sometimes chilly, relations with other students.

"How did you manage it?" asked his roommate. "Only a short time ago, you were a very sad sack."

"It was simple," said the young man of new friendships. "I just did something about my hinges."

When the roommate's face mirrored bewilderment, he went on, "You know how people avoid opening a creaking door. They'll stay out of a room that has such a door as much as possible, just to spare themselves the unpleasantness of hearing it creak.

"Well it finally dawned on me that my tactlessness, irritability, selfishness, and conceit were my creaking hinges. I simply oiled them, and then people began opening my door."—*The Presbyterian Messenger.*

Give God Time

Let us learn to give God time. God needs time with us. If we only give Him time - that is, time in the daily fellowship with Himself, for Him to exercise the full influence of His presence on us, and time, day to day, in the course of our being kept waiting, for faith to prove its reality and to fill our whole being—He Himself will lead us from faith to vision; we shall see the glory of God. Let no delay shake our faith. Of faith it holds good: first the blade, then the ear, then the full corn in the ear. Each believing prayer brings a step nearer the final victory. Each believing prayer helps to ripen the fruit and bring us nearer to it; it fills up the measure of prayer and faith known to God alone; it conquers the hindrances in the unseen world; it hastens the end. Child of God! give the Father time. He is long-suffering over you. He wants the blessing to be rich, and full, and sure; give Him time, while you cry day and night.—*Andrew Murray in* THE TREASURY OF ANDREW MURRAY (Revell).

Recommend The Journal To Friends

Church News

World Missions Receipts

Budget for 1956	$3,300,000.00
Receipts to date	1,502,574.20
Percentage of annual budget received for 1956	45.5
Balance needed for 1956	1,797,425.80

Curry B. Hearn, Treasurer

ROBERT LYNN PETERS

Robert Lynn Peters was born at Ebenezer, Knox County, Tennessee, January 8, 1893. He was called from a life of service here to his eternal home at midnight, May 26, 1956.

His fellow members of the Session, in dedicating this page of the minutes to his memory, desire to record their appreciation of his fellowship and service through the years and their sense of loss at his departure. At the same time they would record their gratitude for the memory of his untiring efforts to build the Kingdom of God in this community and throughout the entire South, and his faithful service to the Church, to which he was most generous in his contributions of talent and substance.

Mr. Peters united with the First Presbyterian Church in Kingsport, by Certificate of Dismission from the First Presbyterian Church in Morristown, Tennessee, September 19, 1926. He served faithfully in the Church and Sunday School and was ordained as a Ruling Elder on January 13, 1935.

Mr. Peters was a faithful Presbyter. He often represented his Church at meetings of Holston Presbytery and the Synod of Appalachia. Twice the Presbytery called upon him to represent it as a Commissioner to the General Assembly - 1942 and 1949.

He served on the local Church Extension Committee and had an active part in locating and organizing the numerous Churches and Chapels in and around Kingsport.

He had served as a member and as Chairman of the Home Mission Committee of Holston Presbytery. He served on Synod's Christian Education Committee as Treasurer and was active in the Assembly's Negro Work, being Chairman of the Board of Stillman College, Tuscaloosa, Alabama, at the time of his passing.

God blessed Mr. Peters in permitting him to be active in all of his work up to the last moment of his life. He had just completed his study and plans for a service which he was to hold at one of the Chapels the following day when his call came.

We extend to his dear wife and sons and their families our deep and heartfelt sympathy and direct them to the Giver of all good and perfect gifts where they may find comfort and peace.

Mr. Peters was used of God in many ways to promote His Church, and by his life he has set an example of Christian living in his Church, home, business and public life, thereby sowing seed which will continue to bear fruit in the years to come to the upbuilding of Christ's Kingdom on earth.

Arthur J. Doggett, Chairman
D. F. Ridings, Sr.
Ross N. Robinson
First Presbyterian Church
Kingsport, Tennessee

PASSING OF REV. O. M. WHITENER

Rev. Olin Marsh Whitener, 44, pastor of the Euphronia, Pocket and White Hill churches of Orange Presbytery, died suddenly of a heart attack on July 5th. A funeral service was conducted in the White Hill church at 10:00 A. M. on July 6th by Rev. W. O. Nelson and a graveside service at 1:00 P. M. in Lakeland Cemetery, Monroe, N. C., was conducted by Dr. Roy F. Whitley.

Mr. Whitener was born in Marshville, N. C., on August 17, 1912 - the son of Mr. Grover J. and Mrs. Nellie Gabriel Whitener. On July 5, 1935, he was married to Miss Alice Boyte of Charlotte. He is survived by his parents, his widow and seven children: Patricia Ann, Nancy Helena, Alice Juanita, Olin Marsh, Jr., Rebecca Jane, Sue and Grover.

He attended Davidson College and Columbia Theological Seminary. He was ordained by Meridian Presbytery, Feb. 3, 1946, and was pastor of the Leakesville, Miss., Presbyterian Church. Other pastorates have been at Orlando, Florida, Carolina Beach, N. C., and Camp Greene Church of Charlotte.

NORTH CAROLINA

Davidson — One of the 50-year-old landmarks of Davidson College, Georgia dormitory, has been razed to permit landscaping of the college's campus in front of W. H. Belk Hall, the 150-room dormitory which was completed last year.

Another old dormitory, Rumple, was torn down last summer. A new dormitory, yet unnamed, will be ready for use in September, and will house 94 students. Three older dormitories, East, West, and Watts, will be renovated this summer at a total cost of more than $80,000.

Davidson — Davidson College has received checks for $225,000 from the Ford Foundation, the first installment on a grant that will total at least $411,400.

It is part of the Foundation's mammoth allocation announced last December to raise faculty salaries in the nation's privately supported colleges and universities.

But Davidson's president Dr. John R. Cunningham warned today that the Ford grant hasn't solved Davidson's financial problems.

"Its main usefulness will be in the purpose announced by the foundation: to stimulate other donors—corporations, foundations and individuals—to make the large and small gifts needed by Davidson and other institutions.

"According to the terms of the grant," said Dr. Cunningham, "we must invest $145,000 of the $225,000 and use its income to raise salaries. This is one of the grants made to 630 privately-supported colleges in the United States.

"The other $80,000 payment is part of an Accomplishment Grant, and we may spend it in any way that we see fit. However, we were one of 126 colleges awarded such a grant for pioneering in the raising of faculty income, and we plan to invest this money as permanent endowment for faculty salaries and academic needs.

"Pay raises for the college totalling $65,000 were announced in March, so it is obvious how great are the needs of Davidson in this area.

"We expect that the total grant will yield about four per cent annual interest. This means that we should be able to add about $18,000 to the faculty salary budget when the entire gift has been received."

Since the March increase was authorized Davidson Trustees have voted to increase the annual salary scale of a full professor to $8,000. This is compared with $6,500 for the 1954-55 academic year.

Dr. Cunningham called attention to the statement of Ford Foundation president H. Rowan Gaither, Jr. last Sunday. Gaither said that "these grants are only an approach to, and not a solution of, the problem. It is hoped that the grants will be interpreted as a challenge by the thousands of alumni, friends, and institutions whose support is vital to private education and to our society."

Mecklenburg Presbytery in a called session held in the Myers Park Presbyterian Church on June 15th approved the merger of the St. Andrews and the McQuay Memorial Presbyterian Churches of Charlotte. The new name will be that of the latter church and their facilities will be used. Rev. Clifford Caldwell will be the pastor of the merged congregations.

At this meeting three ministers were received: Dr. Albert Clarke Deane from Memphis Presbytery and a Commission was appointed to install him as associate pastor of the Myers Park Church; Rev. John Rufus King was received from East Hanover Presbytery and he is the Assistant Pastor of the First Presbyterian Church of Charlotte; Rev. M. A. Cochrane, Jr., was received from Catawba Presbytery, U. S. A. and a Commission was appointed to install him pastor of the Amay James Church.

R. H. Stone, Secretary

SOUTH CAROLINA

Clinton — Just short of $600,000 has been subscribed to the Presbyterian College Diamond Jubilee Development program thus far, President Marshall W. Brown announced recently.

The total now stands at $596,260.90 from 3,575 subscriptions for an average of $167 per subscription.

Presbyterians of the Synods of Georgia and South Carolina which control PC and its alumni everywhere are being asked to support this program which seeks $750,000 for Presbyterian College during 1956 and $2,000,000 over a longer period.

Eleven of the 24 regions within the two states had completed special campaigns for PC by July 1. The program will be resumed in the fall, with a campaign schedule to cover the remainder of the regions.

South Carolina Presbyterians, friends and alumni have subscribed $368,358.80 to date toward the program. The Georgia total stands at $204,302.10, and $23,600 has been subscribed from outside these two states.

A roll call of the regions campaigned to date and their amounts read:

Synod of South Carolina

Region 1 (Laurens & Newberry counties) and students—$156,882; Region 3 (Greenville County)—$72,454.30; Region 4 (Spartanburg, Union and Cherokee counties)—$58,000; Region 5 (Aiken, Edgefield and Saluda counties)—$21,054; Region 8 (Chesterfield, Darlington and Marlboro counties)—$31,272; Region 10A (Florence County)—$8,637; and Region 10B (Dillon, Horry and Marion counties)—$15,504.50.

Synod of Georgia

Region 15 (Atlanta and vicinity)—$110,028; Region 17 (Rome and vicinity)—$31,836; Region 18 (LaGrange and vicinity)—$18,650; and Region 21 (Augusta and vicinity)—$22,733.

"Fugitives From God"

Judge Julius H. Miner of the Circuit Court in Chicago, Ill., says that criminals are "fugitives from God," and that America desperately needs a great religious revival to combat both adult and juvenile crime.

"Criminals are not born," he says. "They are reared in an era which has discarded morality. They are victims of spiritual starvation. Irreligion has obviously become the major contributing factor to our national juvenile crisis."

Judge Miner, an authority on divorce and crime problems, says that a spiritual resurgence is needed to draw the American people to God and prayer. He pointed out that while home religious training is important, "home training can never offer an adequate substitute in the religious education of a child for the planned instruction of the Sunday School."—Exchange.

Smoking on the Increase

Government reports show that smoking is on the increase again. It is estimated that one and a half million Americans who were smoking cigarettes have quit within the past eighteen months. Medical reports as to the harmful influence of tobacco helped many of these to make the right decision. But thousands of others have joined the ranks of smokers in their place. The Government says that cigarette smoking jumped 4 per cent by the end of 1955, reversing a two-year decline. Americans smoked about 383 billion cigarettes in 1955, some 15 billion more than the previous year and only 11 billion short of the all-time peak in 1952.—Exchange.

Pastor's Affidavits Accepted by Income Tax Officials

The pastor of a suburban church at Houston, Texas, has prevailed upon the U. S. Internal Revenue Service to accept his affidavit regarding contributions by members of his church.

Houston internal revenue officials said the refusal to accept the exemptions had been a mistake of an employee in the department, and from now on pastors' affidavits will be honored.

Livingstone's Passion for Christ

When the motion picture, *With Stanley in Africa,* was being filmed in Hollywood, the director said, "We're having trouble with this picture. It's not hard to build up scenes of jungle life, or to create native atmosphere. But here's our main problem—how are we going to get across to the public the power that sent David Livingstone out to Africa and kept him there?"

Perhaps the answer which Hollywood couldn't fathom can be found in Livingstone's entry on his second-to-last birthday: "My Jesus, my King, my Life, my All! I again dedicate my whole self to Thee!"

Offers Reward To Quit Smoking

J. S. Bridwell of Wichita Falls, Texas, owner of a big ranch and oil company, has offered to pay his employees $50 each if they will quit smoking. In a letter to his 250 employees, Mr. Bridwell said that he had been reading "with great interest what some of our great medical men have had to say regarding smoking. Doctors tell us that we are on a great increase in lung, throat, and stomach cancer and many other troubles. I have watched some of my very good friends become seriously ill and some to their death, all because of smoking."

Looking for the Antichrist

Despite the warning of the Scriptures against accepting false Christs, many people are being deceived by pretenders to that title today. The Negro in New York, known as "Father Divine," continues to draw an amazingly large following.

Recently four people were arrested in New Britain, Connecticut, on a charge of blasphemy because one of their number claimed to be Christ. He exhibited wounds in an attempt to prove his identity. He also wore a crown of thorns which he pressed down on his head until the blood flowed. A huge wooden cross was found in the man's home. All four of the people, Polish refugees, claimed to be two thousand years old.

In France a man named Georges Roux has appeared, claiming to be the reincarnated Christ. He lives at Montfavet (Vaucluse) and is planning the conquest of the world. He pretends to healing powers, denies the existence of evil or of Satan, and declares salvation comes from our own unaided effort.

"The crowning sorrow," says D. M. Panton, "is that all the false religions are awaiting a Messiah. The Moslems look for Mahdi, the Buddhists for the fifth Buddha, the Zoroastrians for Shah Bahram, the Hindus for the reincarnation of Krishna, the Jews for a Messiah (other than Jesus Christ). They will all find their 'Messiah' in the Antichrist."—Exchange.

— BOOKS —

THE OFFICE OF CLERK OF SESSION. Frank M. Beatty. John Knox Press. $1.50.

Mr. Beatty is the clerk of session of the First Presbyterian Church of Abbeville, Louisiana. He has spent a great deal of time and energy in research in order to present in this volume suggestions for clerks of session to carry out in the performance of their responsibilities.

One wonders why no one has ever produced a volume of this kind before. New clerks of session certainly need this information, and even those who have served for years could profit by the author's contribution in this volume.

The author, writing to the clerks of session, says, "Your task of keeping the records of your church is a sacred charge not to be lightly esteemed. You have the opportunity to assemble, analyze, and evaluate information from the church records such as would be beneficial to the life of the church. There is something to be treasured and to be responded to with all wisdom as are the opportunities of service made possible through the contacts you are privileged to make in the exercise of your office. Indeed the office of clerk of session affords unique possibilities for you to contribute to the welfare and advancement of your church."

The author discusses the organization and function of the session and the relation of the clerk of session to the local church pastor and higher church courts. He clearly defines the duties of the clerk and has excellent advice concerning the proper care of church records. He gives examples of minutes of session and also minutes of the congregational meeting.

An excellent chapter is devoted to "Opportunities of the Clerk of Session." Here the clerk is shown how he can fulfill and even go beyond the letter of the Book of Church Order and the minimum rules laid down by presbytery. The clerk is urged to have on his heart the membership of his church, to be acquainted with the program of the church at large, have a working knowledge of the Book of Church Order, and maintain contacts in presbytery and the church as far as possible.

Our communion has been greatly benefited by this fine contribution from the pen of Mr. Beatty. We earnestly hope that a copy of this work will be placed in the hands of every clerk of the session within the bounds of our General Assembly.

J.R.R.

"THE WISDOM OF THE TORAH." Edited by Dagovert D. and Runes. Philosophical Library. $5.00.

This present selection from the great Hebrew Book of Guidance or Torah aims to present the philosophical and poetical works of ancient Israel's sages and poets. It is edited by Dr. Runes. The editor believes that the Torah must be considered as one of the world's greatest collections of pure literature. Conservative Christians will not share his high critical views. Included with the writings of Moses, David, Solomon, Job, Isaiah, and Jeremiah are the writings of Jeshu and Ben Sirah, a philosopher of Palestine in the second century B. C. whose writings are kept outside the Canon but rank high as literature.

GENES, GENESIS, AND EVOLUTION. John W. Klotz. Concordia Publishing House. $5.00.

One of the gratuitous assumptions in many educational circles of our day is that all intelligent people believe in organic evolution. This volume disproves such an unwarranted notion.

The author received his Ph.D. in biology and is listed in **American Men of Science.** He is at home in the field of science and is well-versed in Scripture. He begins this brilliant volume by stating that scientists pride themselves on being fair, objective, open-minded, and unprejudiced. Yet science has its sacred cows, and one of these is the theory of evolution. He points out that any attack on the theory as such is regarded as a part of the cult of antiscientism. It is the author's thesis that evolution in the general sense of the term has not taken place. He does not believe that life as we know it is a result of a gradual process of development, that man, for instance, is the descendant of simple, unicellular forms. He holds that, in general, organisms have remained relatively constant and have reproduced after their kind.

While not denying the fact of change and admitting that mutations have occurred in the past and still occur at a fixed, measurable rate, he contends: "But all of this change, insofar as the organic world is concerned, has taken place within limits fixed by the Creator when He fashioned the different 'kinds' in the beginning. In summary, it is the thesis of this book that what has occurred is not the development of higher organisms from lower organisms but rather a finite amount of changes within a fixed and closed system."

It is quite refreshing to read from this distinguished scientist that he believes in the full trustworthiness of the Scriptures in all of their utterances. He writes, "The Bible is true in its every word. Jesus, who declared that He is the Way, the Truth, and the Life, said of the Bible, 'Thy Word is truth.' The Bible asserts that all its statements are true and correct, and this declaration applies to the historical, anthropological, sociological, and scientific statements. Nor need we apologize for this teaching of the Scriptures. Time after time the Bible has been vindicated and its critics put to shame . . . the Bible's claim of absolute truthfulness applies also to the account that it gives us of the origin of the world. It tells us that the world in which we live, the plants and animals which are found on it, and man himself were all created by God. They did not come into existence by chance. They did not develop gradually. But they were created in a wide variety of forms, many of them very complex, and all of them 'very good.' "

This volume is the most satisfactory treatise this reviewer has seen on the subject under discussion. Scientific data is presented accurately and attractively. The author's attitude toward the Scripture is reverent and intelligent. It will be difficult for any honest reader to escape the author's conclusion that though the Christian faces difficulties, the evolutionist faces greater difficulties.

Freely conceding that there are still many things that we do not understand and there are some observations which are present that are difficult to reconcile with the Biblical account of Creation, the author closes with this high note of assurance: "As Christians we know that in the Bible we do not have a theory which is subject to all sorts of changes and modifications, a theory which has come about as a result of the restricted reasoning abilities of human beings, but we have the inspired account of the only Being who was present at Creation." J.R.R.

Any Three of the Books Listed Below Sent Postpaid for $5.00

SUPPLY LIMITED — ORDER NOW

The Basis of Millennial Faith $2.00
By Floyd E. Hamilton

Why 1000 Years? $2.50
By Wm. Masselink

Crucial Questions About The Kingdom of God $3.00
By George E. Ladd

John Calvin: Expository Preacher $2.50
By Leroy Nixon

The Trial of Jesus Christ $2.00
By Frank J. Powell

Supreme Authority $2.00
By Norvel Geldenhuys

The Gospel of The Spirit $1.50
By Samuel Eyles Pierce

Studies in Theology $3.50
By Loraine Boettner

The Reformed Doctrine of Justification $3.00
By Boehl

The Reformed Doctrine of Adoption $2.50
By R. A. Webb

The Faith of Christendom $3.00
By Vander Meulen

Christianity and Liberalism $2.50
By J. Gresham Machen

The Presbyterian Conflict $1.50
By Edwin H Rian

What Presbyterians Believe $2.00
By Gordon H. Clark

The Impact of Christianity on the Non-Christian World $2.50
By Dr. J. H. Bavinck

Pilgrims Progress $1.00
By John Bunyan

The March of Truth $2.50
By Dr. Stephen Szabo

The Called of God $3.95
By A. B. Davidson

Twenty Missionary Stories From India $1.50
By Basil Miller

The Reformed Doctrine of Predestination $4.50
By Loraine Boettner

Christianity Rightly So Called $2.00
By Samuel G. Craig

Who Say Ye That I Am $2.50
By Wm. Childs Robinson

Christ the Bread of Life $2.50
By Wm. Childs Robinson

Christ—The Hope of Glory $3.00
By Wm. Childs Robinson

Knowing The Scriptures $3.95
By A. T. Pierson

Lord of Glory $3.50
By B. B. Warfield

The Plan of Salvation $1.50
By B. B. Warfield

Progress of Doctrine $1.75
By Thomas Dehany Bernard

Does God Answer Prayer $1.50
By Louise Harrison McCraw

God Transcendent and Other Sermons $2.50
By Gresham Machen

Christianity and Existentialism $3.00
By J. M. Spier

The Lord From Heaven $1.50
By Sir Robert Anderson

The Doctrines of Grace $3.95
By George S. Bishop

The Infallibility of the Church $3.00
By George D. Salmon

Successful Church Publicity $1.00
By Carl F. H. Henry

The Covenant Idea in New England Theology $2.50
By Dr. Peter Y. DeJong

The Servant of Jehovah $2.95
By David Baron

Opening Doors $1.50
By R. G. McLees, D.D.

Edward O. Guerrant $1.00
By J. Gray McAllister and Grace Owings Guerrant

Manual of Reformed Doctrine $2.50
By Prof. W. Heyns

Israel and the New Covenant $3.75
By Roger Campbell

Order From

THE SOUTHERN PRESBYTERIAN JOURNAL

Weaverville, North Carolina

Our Presbyterian Heritage

Last year the Southern Presbyterian Journal sponsored a symposium on the Reformed Faith. Addresses were made by a group of outstanding Presbyterians and all who attended gave enthusiastic response.

Without in any measure competing with any other program in our church a similar symposium will be held this year, again placing emphasis on our Presbyterian heritage.

THE TIME—August 15th — 10:00 A. M.

THE PLACE—Weaverville, N. C.

DR. C. GREGG SINGER—*"The Reformed Faith and the Contemporary Crisis in Education."*

DR. GORDON H. CLARK — *"The Reformed Doctrine of Verbal Inspiration of the Scriptures."*

DR. FLOYD HAMILTON — *"The Reformed Doctrine of Infant Baptism."*

DR. AIKEN TAYLOR — *"The Reformed Doctrine of the Means of Grace."*

DR. W. C. ROBINSON — *"The Reformed Doctrine of the Bodily Resurrection of Christ."*

DR. R. F. GRIBBLE — *"The Reformed Faith as Related to the Virgin Birth Foretold in Isaiah 7:14."*

MR. GEORGE BURNHAM — *"To the Far Corners."*

Make Plans Now To Attend This Meeting

THE SOUTHERN PRESBYTERIAN JOURNAL
Weaverville, N. C.

THE SOUTHERN PRESBYTERIAN JOURNAL

A Presbyterian weekly magazine devoted to the statement, defense and propagation of the Gospel, the faith which was once for all delivered unto the saints.

VOL. XV NO. 14 | AUGUST 1, 1956 | $2.50 A YEAR

THE ANNUAL FEAST AT WEAVERVILLE

This Year Will Be As Rich As Ever
AUGUST 15 IS THE DATE
BEGINNING 10 A.M.

The speakers will be:
DR. C. GREGG SINGER DR. GORDON H. CLARK
DR. FLOYD HAMILTON — DR. AIKEN TAYLOR
DR. W. C. ROBINSON — DR. R. F. GRIBBLE
and MR. GEORGE BURNHAM

Lunch will be served at noon for all who attend.

It will help in preparation if you will mail us a card saying you are coming.

THE SOUTHERN PRESBYTERIAN JOURNAL
WEAVERVILLE, N. C.

THE SOUTHERN PRESBYTERIAN JOURNAL
The Journal has no official connection with the Presbyterian Church in the United States
Rev. Henry B. Dendy, D.D., Editor..........Weaverville, N. C.
Dr. L. Nelson Bell, Associate Editor..........Asheville, N. C.
Rev. Wade C. Smith, Associate Editor..........Weaverville, N. C.

EDITORIAL

Is Patriotism Wrong?

One of the by-products of the present "one-world" philosophy which is so popular in some quarters today is the playing down of patriotism.

Conversely we see the strange phenomenon of an over-consideration for the nationalistic feelings of others with a corresponding lack of emphasis on our own national rights and the moral duty of American citizens to be proud of and concerned for the good name and welfare of our own land.

In the July 20th issue of *U. S. News & World Report,* Robert C. Hell of our State Department calls attention to the present drive against patriotism and how it is playing directly into the hands of the enemies of our country.

No one would defend the flag-waving of those "patriots" whose chief aim seems to be the glorification of self, or the grinding of some particular axe. Such is shallow and even obnoxious.

On the other hand, every American citizen should be proud of this land in which we live and a zealous guardian of those things for which she stands. That this will at times involve a clear-cut stand for our national rights and prestige is inevitable. Such is both a duty and a privilege.

As a Roman citizen the apostle Paul found his rights disregarded in Phillipi. Did he yield to the indignities heaped upon him without protest. A reading of the incident shows that he rightly demanded an apology, and got one.

The day of the big stick and of sword-rattling may be gone but along with them has also gone a willingness to stand for rights which often involve moral principles. A firm stand and a bold assertion of national integrity has often nipped incipient trouble in the bud. It may do it again in the future.

As Americans we should be proud and thankful for our country and for our national heritage. Such patriotism is greatly needed today.

L.N.B.

Overgrown Trails

"Let us search and try our ways, and turn again unto the Lord." Lamentations 3:40.

One Sunday morning many years ago, in the course of the sermon in the Westminster Church in St. Louis, I remarked that somebody might possibly be there that day who had not darkened the door of any church for maybe twenty years. After almost the entire congregation had departed, I saw a lone man standing in the far end of the middle aisle. I went to him and found him shaking with emotion. "I am the man you're talking about," said he. "It's been far more than twenty years since I have been inside any church till today, and I don't know why I came here, unless it was to be reminded of what I have been losing."

That incident leads me to write a paragraph about Overgrown Trails. The story just recited is not unusual. A boy, for instance, may have grown up in a Christian home. If so, the church may have been the goal for his feet every Sabbath. The daily practice of Christian virtues may have been his manner of life. And yet new associations in adulthood may have neutralized his interest in the training that was most worthwhile. Therefore, the pathway to the House of God became overgrown with weeds. His religious conviction suffered frustration. High moral and spiritual values fell into eclipse. He may later wake up to what has been happening to him—or he may not. In case he does, however successful he may be in business or in his chosen profession, he has a haunting feeling that he has let something go that was vital to his growth, and that promised contentment for his maturity. And there he stands alone in the aisle of some strange church, his heart flooded with commingled emotion and regret. The people who enjoyed the hour of uplifting fellowship are gone. And there he stands a lonely man. A pathetic figure he is, admitting that he has nobody to blame but himself. Underbrush now chokes the trail that he had deserted.

How easily the wilderness takes over! The convictions that are real in one's impressionable days, together with the duties appertaining thereto become bedimmed, and finally cease to operate. The weeds have choked the ambition that was the heritage of a Christian parentage. Temporary success in things material perchance has thrown bigger gains into eclipse.

What to do? Stand alone in an empty church and bemoan his loss? No! The invitation stands: "Let us search and try our ways, and turn again unto the Lord." That is the sole prescription for relief, but the result is guaranteed. C. H. Spurgeon, great man that he was, prayed every day: "Lord, remember not my sins, but remember me." There it is!

William Crowe, Sr.

"All That Glitters . . ."

There is much which makes appeal to the reading public. Not a little relates to religion. A goodly amount touches the Christian Faith. Too much has to do with erroneous, though glittering, notions. All of this leads us to the Bible.

How are we to look on the Book of Books? Many are the gilded theories launched by men of note, which bid for acceptance by the unwary, fancies that are of the same stripe, and particularly with reference to Scripture viewed in a "new and appealing sense," as not being true in its words but only in its ideas, not propositions, but events, not revelations from God Himself, but tales around the camp-fire, not finality but floundering, not literal but legendary, not sacred but saga.

To wit, - we quote from a sister denomination's Board of Education brochure entitled, "I Believe": "Regarding miracles, men are puzzled: they do not see God acting that way today. (Aside: This might be remarked about a number of facts). Stories were repeated orally for many generations and finally written down by folk without any notion of science like we have. Bible writers gave religious turn to everything they said. We might say: 'It rained this afternoon.' They would be inclined to say: 'The Lord sent rain.' We would say: 'It seems best for me to do so and so.' They would say: 'The Lord told me to do it' . . . Whatever you believe about the details of these narratives, the important thing is to catch the spiritual truth behind them."

Now the people who put out bed-time stories like this, seem quite unaware of the spiritual nightmares they would cause for those who should take them seriously. The general idea seems to be just anything to avoid the plain sense of the Bible. And particularly the learned, - in their own conceits, frown upon anything that looks like the "propositional" method in understanding the Word of God. It should be well-considered that any other fashion of approaching Scripture will make havoc of it!

The proof-text method, the propositional use, the direct guidance approach, - these we are warned against, as we seek to have a word from God. We wonder why this deep concern. And we also wonder who are the concerned.

It requires little examination to see that these are in general the folk who reject some of the cardinal doctrines of Scripture, deny some of its historic facts, spurn the thought that there is a supernatural revelation in the first place. And the conclusion is that this "new method" of dealing with the Word of God is in the nature of a rationalization, a subterfuge, a concealed process of denying inspiration and authority and finality touching the Book.

Of course the propositional method may be, has been, abused. But after all, "Christ died for our sins" *is* a proposition. And however embarrassing it may be to confess the fact, "Believe on the Lord Jesus Christ and thou shalt be saved," *is* a proposition. And so is "On this rock will I build my Church." Also, "Thou wilt keep him in perfect peace whose mind is stayed on Thee."

And, in passing, it may be added that the back-bone of our theology, which is Scripturally-based, is of the proof-text variety. And our advice to those who scorn the "direct guidance" attitude, is to have a care lest in some tight spot they may seek in vain for that everlasting consolation which so many of the saints have found in the Word that liveth and abideth forever!

Also those who are guilty of using the proof-text procedure, seem to be in very good company. We note that the Apostle Paul employed it rather often. And the Apostle Peter did the same, not once, nor twice. And we read how that the Lord Jesus Christ Himself did not think it improper: He fell back on it over and over again. The practice may not have the glitter of the specious advice of men of

The Southern Presbyterian Journal, *a Presbyterian Weekly magazine, devoted to the statement, defense, and propagation of the Gospel, the faith which was once for all delivered unto the saints,* published every Wednesday by The Southern Presbyterian Journal, Inc., in Weaverville, N. C.

Entered as second-class matter May 15, 1942, at the Postoffice at Weaverville, N. C., under the Act of March 3, 1879. Vol. XV, No. 14, August 1, 1956. Editorial and Business Offices: Weaverville, N. C. Printed in the U.S.A. by Biltmore Press, Asheville, N. C.

ADDRESS CHANGE: When changing address, please let us have both old and new address as far in advance as possible. Allow three weeks after change if not sent in advance. When possible, send an address label giving your old address.

letters; but on the whole, we rather choose the time-honored and quite satisfactory method. And we imagine that, after all, the objection is not so much to the *method,* as to the *Book Itself,* to its propositions, doctrine, dogma, fact.

R.F.G.

WHO IS JESUS?

The book of Hebrews says - "Jesus is above all." It reveals the essential preeminence of Christ.

The first chapter gives us an amazing and glowing pen-portrait of the Saviour. (Heb. 1)

He emerges as God's "Son," appointed as 'heir,'" inheriting the universe which He created. (v.2).

He reveals God as the rays of the sun reveal its glories for He is the exact "image" of God. He is carrying the universe to its goal. He is the sin-bearer cleansing the heart. He occupies the "right hand" position of "the Majesty on high." (v.3).

He is far above "Angels" who worship Him. (vv. 4-6).

The tall climax of the "Portrait" lets us hear God the Father calling Him "God" - who has an eternal "forever and ever" Throne. An unending Throne because no hidden source of corruption or evil: the scepter of His Kingdom is a scepter of "Righteousness," which "Righteousness" He loves. (vv.7-9).

Therefore He abides - "Thou remainest" - all else ages and crumbles but "Thou art the same" - His years never run out - "Shall not fail." (vv. 10-12).

There He is - seated at God's "Right Hand" until the consummation of the plan of the ages. (v. 13).

The word was made flesh and dwelt among us. (And we beheld His glory - the glory as of the only begotten of the Father). Full of grace and truth." (John 1:14).

S. McPheeters Glasgow.

Preachers in Politics

IT SEEMS THAT THE FATHER OF OUR COUNTRY showed real concern over the political use of the pulpit in his day. The Evening Star, Washington, D. C., on January 6, 1956, carried the following letter written by Genevieve Clark Thompson of Gaylord, Clarke County, Va.:

No act of our founding fathers was wiser than the firmness with which they separated church and state in our republic.

Therefore, as a Christian, imperfect indeed, and "standing in the need of prayer," I deeply deplore the clergy, in their clerical character, taking part in political controversies.

I do not suggest that ministers should be deprived of their civil rights. But their political activities should be carried on in the hurly-burly of the political arena, not from the sanctuary of the pulpit or ecclesiastical guilds, and as American citizens, not ministers of God. They should not use the pulpit as a barricade and the priestly cloth as a shield but should stand forth and take blow for blow even as other men. It would be a more manly posture.

It is unfair to impose their political views upon people who go to church to worship God and who are unable to reply unless our churches are to be turned into debating societies, which would be an unseemly spectacle indeed.

A friend of mine, a devout woman, daughter of one of the most eminent clergymen of his time, is so disturbed by the political gyrations of her pastor concerning the Gray report that she says she feels like worshiping in the fields. And in another congregation close by, financial support has been withdrawn already by at least one member. These are ominous signs in the wind which wise men would do well to heed.

The clergy, of all people, should remember the beautiful passage from Ecclesiastes beginning, "To everything there is a season, such a time to every purpose under heaven." And surely no man of the cloth can forget the response made by our Lord when the Pharisees sought to entangle Him in the politics of His time, "Render, therefore, unto Caesar the things which are Caesar's, and unto God the things that are God's."

To expound their political philosophy and denounce the civil authorities in their priestly character is a gross impropriety serving neither church nor state. The most likely result of their political effort will be to split their churches asunder, a consequence which all Christians must contemplate with dismay.

With all due respect, I should like to remind these reverend gentlemen that as the source of ultimate power of our Republic is in its citizens, so the ultimate power of the churches is in their members. A shepherd without a flock is a sorry figure.

As an Episcopalian (dues-paying and church-attending) I have been shocked and mortified by the conduct of some clergymen on political matters. Another Episcopal layman, George Washington, so objected to his pastor's political preaching prior to the Revolutionary War that he absented himself from church for some time. Incidentally, if the politics of the majority of the Episcopal clergymen had then been followed we would still be colonial subjects of the British Crown.

The question presently before the voters is not a religious question. It is a civil one. And in political or governmental questions no churchman, high or low, speaks for me.

God Has Spoken

By Rev. Wil R. Johnson, D.D.

That is at once the wonder and the glory of our Christian faith. God has spoken to His people. Jehovah, the self-existent, self-revealing One, is the God who speaks to men. From the beginning this has been so, and is still so. He has consistently and persistently unveiled Himself through five special channels, which taken separately is each one tremendously arresting, and altogether are absolutely convincing.

From before the beginning God has spoken through the Living Word. John 1.1, which says "In the beginning was the Word," could perhaps better be translated "Before the beginning," because the word "beginning" is in our thinking associated with the idea of time. The Word was before time began, for He was with God, and was God. From Him came the word that brought the universe into being. He spake and it was done. He commanded and it stood fast. All things were made by Him, and without Him was not anything made that was made. In all the unfolding through the ages of the Eternal purpose He was the Spokesman of the Godhead. His message was brought to a climax when "the Word was made flesh, and dwelt among us," and redemption as well as creation came from and through Him. He is the tap root, or the bubbling spring of all revelation—the Living Word.

The Pictured Word of creation has also been a channel through which God has spoken to men. His finger prints are on all that He has made. The heavens declare the glory of God and the firmament showeth His handiwork, day unto day uttereth speech and night unto night showeth knowledge. There is no speech nor language where their voice is not heard. Their message has gone out to the ends of the earth. Through them has come a clear revelation of His eternal power and Godhead, leaving all men without the excuse of ignorance. Hence all men, be they ever so savage and barbarous, instinctively worship some conception, too often pitifully crude, of their Maker.

The Whispered Word of His Spirit in the hearts of men has been evident from the first man, until this day with its myriads of people. With an ever-present Conscience as a sounding board; this monitor of the soul, the voice of God in the heart, has never ceased to speak in the still small voice, saying "This is the way, walk ye in it," and as men have followed, they have been led into the Light that shineth more and more unto the perfect day.

The Spoken Word of His prophets has been clothed with moving and transforming power from the beginning of history. As holy men of God have risen to speak as they were Spirit driven, their words have burned and blessed in miracle working power. It was so in the cradle days of the race, and it is still so in these closing days of a dying age. God uses human instruments, now as always, to unveil His heart and mind.

Last and in a sense most important of all, God speaks through His Written Word, and it is this which gives meaning and authority to all the four just named. Its testimony is conclusive in each connection. If any man declares himself to be a prophet of God, and speaks that which is contrary to the Scriptures, he can be at once dismissed as a false prophet. If any spirit speaks to our hearts, be it ever so persuasively, suggesting something which is contrary to the law and the gospel, it is a seducing spirit, and not the Spirit of God. God or creation is very obscure, until the scales have been brushed from our eyes by the new birth. Until then any revelation of Him through His pictured word creates little more than a groping wonder at the best, and frequently nothing but a deep-rooted fear and awe. We are born again, not of corruptible seed, but of incorruptible, by the Word of God, which liveth and abideth forever. It is through this Written Word that our eyes are opened to the transfiguring power of the Living Word:

"Heaven above is softer blue, Earth around is sweeter green,
Glory shines in every hue, Christless eyes have never seen;
Birds with gladder songs o'erflow, Flowers with brighter beauty shine
Since I know, as now I know, I am His and He is mine."

Then:

"Earth's crammed with heaven, and every common bush's afire with God."

Most startling of all is the fact that but for the Written Word, we would long since have lost our Christ! The Living Word would have faded into the fogs of mythology! That is the reason why an adviser of a persecuting Roman Emperor told him all his bloody work would be in vain, even if he slew the last Christian, so long as there was one copy of the Scriptures left on earth. The Church is reborn in every generation because the Living Word, who alone can give life to a soul dead in trespasses and sin, is unveiled through the Written Word, and the longing eyes of lost souls catch a glimpse of the glory of God in the face of Jesus Christ, in these sacred pages, and rise to newness of life.

The Way of Salvation

By The Rev. Floyd E. Hamilton
Centreville, Ala.

"And in none other is there salvation: for neither is there any other name under heaven, that is given among men, whereby we must be saved."
Acts 4:12.

For the past two weeks we have discussed the question of theological Modernism and Evangelicalism. Two weeks ago we mentioned thirteen points in theology among many in which Modernism and Evangelicalism differ. We then discussed the inspiration of the Bible. The Evangelical believes that the Holy Spirit so guided and controlled the writers of the Bible that what they wrote was true and was the truth God wanted his people to have. Modernism rejects the whole Bible as the inspired Word of God so that it is God's Word whether we like it or not, and the Barthians hold that only when God's Spirit uses the Bible portions as the means of giving a direct revelation of God does the Bible in that part become the Word of God to us. As others read the same portion it may not be the Word of God to them.

Then last week we saw that the Modernist and Evangelical regard man quite differently. The Evangelical regards man as a created living soul who has fallen into sin, so that apart from the work of the Spirit of God, he is spiritually dead in sins and must be regenerated by the Holy Spirit in order for him to believe in Christ and be saved. The Modernist regards man as having ascended from the higher animals by evolution, so that he does not need regeneration or need to get right with God in order to have eternal life. Modernists regard man as good by nature, so that he can be taken into the church and the kingdom of God with no change such as the New Birth.

It follows from this that there is a total difference between the Modernist and the Evangelical regarding the way of salvation. The Bible teaches that there is only one way of salvation, namely trust in the substitutionary death of Jesus Christ alone for salvation.

The Bible teaches that because man is dead in trespasses and sins he can do nothing to save himself, and without the regeneration of God's Spirit he cannot even believe unto salvation.

The Modernist rejects the belief in Christ as the only way of salvation. Some Modernists would hold that man does not need to be saved at all. In his natural state he is already in the kingdom of God and needs only a little teaching and help to be all the man that God wants him to be. He holds that sin has not separated between man and God, and therefore holds that man can come to God at any time he wants to. There is a popular song today that expresses the Modernist's idea of the relationship between man and God, when it says that though God is grieved to see the way we live, He will always forgive us, with no trust in the atonement of Christ, but simply by arbitrarily forgiving us, apparently not even with repentance!

Other Modernists would hold that there are many ways to God, and that other religions such as Mohammedanism, Buddhism or Confucianism are equally good ways to God, though possibly Christianity has a few advantages over other religions. Such Modernists would hold that Christianity is far from being an *exclusive* way of salvation, as the Bible teaches, but that any sincere religionist, no matter what his beliefs may be, is acceptable to God if he leads a good life, or at least a respectable life. The Modernist would hold that good character and good deeds are the passports to heaven, for strangely enough, most Modernists would hold that there is a heaven where everybody is going.

Modernists would all deny that there is a place of eternal punishment for unrepentant sinners, as the Bible teaches. Evangelicals might not agree as to the *nature* of eternal punishment for unrepentant sinners, but all evangelicals would agree that there is eternal punishment for those who reject Jesus Christ as their Saviour and Lord.

The Modernist would hold that men are to follow the example of Jesus Christ in Christian living in order to earn salvation if any salvation is needed at all by man, but they would hold that many people who are not even believers in following the example of Christ will be in heaven because of their good lives. In other words, goodness or Kindliness, or respectability are the passports to heaven, though when pressed about it, they would deny that there

Christ on the cross, and there is no other name given among men whereby we must be saved. That means that all other religions are *false* ways of salvation, and lead only to dead ends, not to eternal life in heaven. It makes not a bit of difference whether man is respectable, kindly to his family, liked by his neighbors and friends, and regarded as good by all his acquaintances. Unless he comes to God by Jesus Christ alone, and trusts in His atoning work, he is still a sinner, and still a member of the kingdom of Satan.

When Nicodemus came to Christ, he came as an honest, respectable Pharisee, well-thought of by all his friends, yet Jesus told him "Ye must be born again!" The gate to eternal life is small and narrow, but it is the gate to *life,* and it is the *only* gate to life.

The Modernist can be indifferent to doctrinal issues because they are not important to him, but to the evangelical, doctrinal points concerning the way of salvation are all-important, for an error in the teaching about the way of salvation will send men to hell not to heaven.

Of course, this is a narrow view, but it is the only *true* view of the way of salvation. It is easy to see why evangelicals are opposed to church union with churches where Modernism is dominant. It is because the souls of men and women and boys and girls are at stake. The fact that God so loved the world that he gave his only begotten Son that whosoever believeth on him should not perish but have everlasting life, is the reason we cannot trifle with the message of the way of salvation to a dying world.

If God loved his people enough to come in the person of God the Son and die for them, what a tragedy it would be if those for whom Christ died were to be given the idea that they did not need to trust that Saviour in order to be saved! We love Him because He first loved us, but if our message does not include the reason why we must love Him, or if we do not tell how much He loved us: enough to die in our place, then we will be betraying our Lord and Saviour. That is why we cannot make peace with the Modernist. He betrays the Lord who bought us with his blood, and we would join in that treachery if we become tolerant of his message that leads men to think they do not need to trust Christ for salvation.

Helps To Understanding Scripture Readings in *Day by Day*

By C. C. Baker

Sunday, August 12, *Psalm* 33:8-22. The strong nations of the earth need to recognize the mighty power of the Lord. Simply by His spoken word the Universe came into being (vv.6,9). Not only is the word of the Lord able to create, but it is holy and righteous (v.4). God's very creation bespeaks of this fact (v.5). His thoughts and ways stand forever (v.11). He beholds the ways of men (v.13-15). What becomes of the nation that worships Him (v.12,18-19)? of the nation that acts as if He did not exist (v.10)? of the nation that depends on its own resources (v.16-17)? Do you as an individual recognize that you fare in accordance with your relation to the Almighty God? Allow vv. 20-22 to be your prayer for this nation as she faces the difficult days ahead.

Monday, August 13, *Psalm* 37:1-9. The Psalmist is troubled with the problem of the prosperity of the wicked. What negative admonitions are listed in facing this problem (vv.1,7,8)? Why is the reader thus admonished (vv.2,9,10)? Do you find it difficult not to fret over injustices which cannot be corrected (v.8b)? The positive admonitions of vv.3-7 form the cure for the sin of fretfulness. What is involved in the "trusting" and "committing" of vv.3,5? What does God promise to do when these conditions are met (vv.3,5,6)? The Christian should also learn to wait upon the Lord in prayer (vv.7,9), and delight in His fellowship (v.4). Does a placing of your eyes upon a just God replace the fretfulness of v.1 in your life?

Tuesday, August 14, *Psalm* 139:1-18. Few of us realize how intimately God is acquainted with us (vv.1-6). There is no place we can go where God is not (vv.7-12). He knew us even before He created us in the womb (vv.13-16). These thoughts about God become very precious to the Psalmist (vv.17-18) and knowing God's holiness and hatred of sin, he prays God's judgment upon evil doers (vv.19-21). The Psalmist then closes by asking God to root out sin in his own life (vv.22-24). While aware of the evil that is in the world are you aware also of the sinfulness that is in your own heart? Do you know how keenly aware God is of what is in your heart?

Wednesday, August 15, *Psalm* 135:13-21. The Hebrew was often full of the praises of God (vv.1-4,19-21) because the God whom He worshipped was not made of silver and gold (vv.15-18), but was the living God (vv.5-7) who worked in history in behalf of His people (vv.8-12). Study each of the characteristics of the gods of the heathen (vv.15-17) and find a contrast with what the Psalmist says of the God of Israel (vv.1-14). It creates a sense of wonder to know that the God we worship is alive and active in the life of this world. He is not dead! Join with the Psalmist in the praise of vv.1-4, 19-21.

Thursday, August 16, *Psalm* 130. Even from the depths of despair (v.1) the Psalmist sounds the song of hope. The Psalmist has sinned (v.4), but his real love and trust is the Lord (vv.5-6). Picture the watchman standing guard over the city in the early morning hours searching for the dawn (v.6). So, the Psalmist yearns for the Lord (vv.5-6). From his sin, what confidence does he express in the Lord (vv.3-4, 7-8)? The Psalmist takes God at His word (v.5b) in claiming forgiveness and restoration of fellowship. By faith, too, from I John 1:9 the sincere Christian can claim complete forgiveness and cleansing from his sin.

Friday, August 17, *Psalm* 103:6-12. The message of the Hundred-and-third Psalm needs little comment. The Psalmist begins with praise to God - "Forget not all His benefits" (v.2). His benefits are listed in vv.3-5. Verses 6-18 give further evidences of God's mercies. He vindicates His own (vv.6-7); He is merciful to those who "fear" Him (vv.8-11); He is forgiving toward the repentant sinner (vv.12-18). How do the mercies of God as described in vv.9-12, 14-18 substantiate the picture of Him as a father (v.13)? Meditate upon the figures used to describe: the depth of God's mercies (v.11); the width of His forgiving grace (v.12); the duration of His compassion. (Contrast vv.15-16 with v.12).

Saturday, August 18, *Psalm* 19:7-14. The glory of God is proclaimed by the heavens themselves (vv.1-6). Though they speak no tongue nor language (v.3), the message they proclaim is universal (vv.1-2,4). In beholding the heavens in vv.2,5-6 what message is proclaimed to you concerning God (v.1)? However, it is the Word of God (vv.7-13) that speaks to us of our relation to the Creator. List the words in v.7-10 that describe the Law of God. What effects does it have on the Psalmist (vv.7-14)? How does it satisfy his soul (v.10)? Keep him from sin (vv.11-13)? Give him a spirit of dedication (v.14)? What effect has the Word of God had in your life?

ANGLERS

(From "*New Testament Evangelism*"
By Wade C. Smith)

Lesson No. 150

By Groups — the Pastor the Leader

We come now to see how the individual may be grouped with others in the church organization for greater effectiveness in reaching all the unsaved people in the community. And as we begin to touch the organic life of the church, we first recognize the Pastor's position of leadership. He is responsible for preparing, in plain terms, a constructive plan of action. It should be considered by the Session, who upon approval will adopt it as "official." Then the matter is in shape for presentation to the congregation. The congregational phase, however, will be treated in a later lesson. In this lesson we are dealing with groups within the congregation. It will be noticed that the dominant idea in all of this study is to begin with the individual and work outward. Thus, the individual first, groups second, then larger bodies. The ultimate thought is not merely for the congregation, but for the whole denomination - and the entire Christian forces of the world. The point, however, is to never for an instant lose sight of one's own personal privilege and obligation. That is the fatal pitfall for a movement like this. The larger the groups with which we are associated, the greater the danger of shrinking our own responsibility.

Natural Groupings. There are several methods suggested for group organization in the church. One is to group in four divisions: the men - the women - the young people - the Sunday School. Some may wish to add the officers as another group. There would necessarily be some overlapping, but that can be adjusted. What we want is a minimum of organization, consistent with greatest efficiency. In a large congregation these groups should be sub-divided. Ten men can work together more effectively in this plan than fifty. The same applies to the other divisions. Each group should have a leader, and the Pastor should be ex-officio member of each, also acting as the director general.

It may be objected that we are multiplying organizations and sapping valuable time. Almost any progressive proposition will meet that cry. Sometimes it is the spokesman of wisdom, sometimes of just pure laziness. But it would be well to consider that if bringing the unsaved to Christ, or more properly, taking Christ to the unsaved, is not the all-important mission of the church; and that present methods, with all the present organization are falling far short of the task. This being the case, may it not be well to do some shifting in organization that will give a plan of organized personal evangelism a chance to show its possibilities? It is quite probable that existing departmental organization may not be disturbed, but that the grouping here suggested may be so welded as to inoculate them all with the spirit of evangelism in a personal way. At the same time, caution is advised, lest the plan get sunk into the old ruts which have already blocked progress. For instance, there is a "Spiritual Life" committee in some of the departments mentioned. If this plan is "referred to the Spiritual Life Committee" make sure that it is not misunderstood to be an assignment of the personal work of that department to that committee. To the Spiritual Life Committee, if thoroughly alive, may be charged the *promotion* of the personal evangelism plan for that department; but let it be clearly understood that the plan is to engage every member of the department in soul-winning, and in all the activities connected with the soul-winning program.

Remember, we are working at a plan here to save sinners - the one thing which lay closest to the Master's heart. May it not be that we can depend upon Him to show the way through any difficulties of organization which may arise? Perhaps these very difficulties are the challenge to our faith, which, if met in the power of the Spirit, will make the victory all the more complete!

A program for the group - in next lesson.

Recommend The Journal To Friends

LESSON FOR AUGUST 12

The Way Of Christian Fellowship

Background Scripture: John 13:3-15, 34, 35; I John 1 - 2:17; II John; III John
Devotional Reading: Philippians 2:1-11

There would be no difficulty about "Christian Fellowship" if we would heed the words of Paul in our Devotional Reading: "Fulfill ye my joy, that ye be like-minded, having the same love, being of one accord, of one mind. Let nothing be done through strife or vainglory; but in lowliness of mind let each esteem other better than themselves. Look not every man on his own things, but every man also on the things of others. Let this mind be in you which was also in Christ Jesus," etc. Here we have a perfect recipe for Christian Fellowship and the Supreme Example. What a wonderful place of fellowship the Church would be if we would follow this recipe and His marvelous life! The whole lesson period could be most profitably used in the study of this great selection from Paul's letter to the Philippian church. It forms a most fitting introduction to this study.

I. *Christian Fellowship at the Lord's Table:* John 13: 3-15,34,35.

This beautiful scene takes place in the upper room where the feast of the Passover was kept and the Lord's Supper instituted. John supplements the accounts in the other Gospels by giving us this incident. It is so closely connected with the Sacrament of the Lord's Supper that some denominations observe it as a part of that Feast.

Back of it we find the love of Jesus for His disciples.: "having loved his own which were in the world, he loved them unto the end." (13:1). The whole incident is unsurpassed as a picture of love manifesting itself in humility and service. Compare verse 3 with Philippians 2:6 and you have another bit of background for your picture. Verse 3 reads, "Jesus knowing that the Father had given all things into his hands, and that he came from God, and went to God." Philippians 2:6 reads, "Who, being in the form of God, thought it not robbery to be equal with God." Continue the comparison through the passage. Here we have Amazing Love, Amazing Humility, Amazing Grace! When we think of how rich and glorious He was, and how low He stooped, as He took the towel and girded Himself, and washed the disciples' feet, we begin to realize the beauty of this picture, and its lesson for us.

"If I then, your Lord and Master, have washed your feet: ye also ought to wash one another's feet. For I have given you an example, that ye should do as I have done to you." Some, as I have said, take these words literally and observe a "Foot-washing" ceremony. We feel that Jesus is stating a great principle which should guide us in our attitude toward others. No service is too small or too humiliating or menial, for us to perform if in doing it we can serve someone, and we will be willing to do it if we have sufficient love one for another. We are all equal, as Lord Wellington said, around the Lord's table, and it is a good place for each to esteem others better than themselves, and to be ready to serve rather than be served. "If ye know these things, happy are ye if ye do them" (verse 17). Verses 34 and 35 explain what Jesus means: A new commandment I give unto you, that ye love one another. By this shall all men know that ye are my disciples, if ye love one another." Love is the great "solvent" for all our problems in connection with Christian Fellowship."

II. *Christian Fellowship and the World:* I John 1 - 2:17.

The first epistle of John might be called, "The Christian in the World." Jesus had prayed in John 17, "I pray not that thou shouldest take them out of the world, but that thou wouldest keep them from the evil (one)". "In the world . . . but not of the world," is His ideal for the Christian. We are living in a world full of darkness, of sin, of hatred. We are not to love this wicked world except with the same sort of love that God has for it—the love of compassion, that seeks to save it. There are many beautiful things in the world, of course, like the flowers and other beauties of nature, but John is thinking of the world as it is largely "in the lap" of the god of this world, the devil, and the command of John 2:5 is very plain; "Love not the world, neither the things that are in the world. If any man love the world, the love of the Father is not in him."

We cannot have fellowship with such a world. It would defile us and do the world no good. We can never "win the world" by any such method. The world would only have contempt for us. What do these Christians here? would be the question that it would ask. "Come out from among them and be ye separate, saith the Lord." "What concord hath Christ with Belial, or the temple of God with idols?

Our fellowship is characterized by freedom from sin, by victory over sin, by walking in the light, by a love of the brethren, which the world does not know, and cannot know. By adorning the doctrine of Christ we are to show the world what real Christian Fellowship is, and in this way attract and influence the world to turn to Christ. That was the reaction of the people at Pentecost. When they saw the Christians loving each other and sharing all they had, many of them turned to the Lord and were added to the Church. I believe very firmly that if the church as a whole would show these same characteristics that more men and women of the world who have been trying in vain to satisfy their craving for "fellowship" in the ways of the world would turn to the "better way" of life in Christ. We have something far better to offer than night clubs and dance halls and road houses and gambling dens. Many in the world are like Lord Byron, drinking of every cup which the world has to offer, and then dying of thirst. The souls of men can never be satisfied on the husks of the hog pen.

III. *Christian Fellowship in the Home:* II John.

A Christian home is the nearest thing to heaven that we will find on this earth. Heaven is a place of blessed fellowship, where we will enjoy God and the companionship of the saints throughout the ages of eternity. Home is a place where we enjoy the fellowship of those we especially love for the few years that we spend during our pilgrimage.

In the second epistle of John he is writing to "the elect lady and her children." The natural meaning of these words is that he is writing to a mother in her home. It is thought that the husband and father is dead and that the whole responsibility of the home rests upon the widow and mother.

What are some of the marks of this home where there is a fine atmosphere of fellowship? Certain words are prominent in the epistle. The first is "Truth." No home can be strong without truth as a pillar. The second is "Love." Truth and love go hand in hand in every Christian home. Truth makes the home strong, and love makes it sweet. The third is Obedience, or as John expresses it, "walking after his commandments." Obedience makes the home beautiful. It is disobedience which has made the world ugly. The sky is beautiful because the sky obeys the laws of God. Nature is beautiful because nature obeys. "Only man is vile" and ugly, and it is because he disobeys. The fourth is "Joy." A Happy home is a magnetic home.

John does not minimize, or try to hide, the dangers which threaten the home. There are many "deceivers" who have gone out into the world and they are bent on destroying the home. We must "look to ourselves" that we do not lose our homes. It takes "grace and mercy and peace," and our homes must be "wrapped up in prayer" if we preserve these heavenly places of fellowship.

IV. *Fellowship in the Church:* III John.

One of the greatest privileges and blessings of the church is Fellowship. All churches do not have it. In some there is a "coldness" which can be felt; in others there are "factions" and feelings which spoil the picture.

What does John have to say on this vital subject?

He urges us to be "Healthy Christians." "Beloved, I wish above all things that thou mayest prosper and be in health, even as thy soul prospers." In other words, I pray that your body may be in as good health as your soul. Healthy bodies are good; healthy souls, better. Gaius was a Christian with a healthy soul.

He would have us to be "Helping Christians" : "That we might be fellow-helpers to the truth." The church has all kinds of Christians in it; old and young, rich and poor, weak and strong. When we help one another, we are also helping ourselves, and we are helping Christ. Inasmuch as ye have done it to one of the least of these, my brethren, ye have done it unto me.

We must be "Humble Christians." Diotrephes was about to ruin the church. He wanted too much for himself; he talked too much about others; he was harsh in his attitude and dealings. A Diotrephes is a menace to any church and will destroy its fellowship.

We should be "Heard-from Christians." Demetrius had a good report of all men. This good report was like a bell sounding forth an invitation to outsiders to "come to church." Such a Christian is the best advertisement a church can have. If our churches are filled with such Christians we will enjoy blessed fellowship.

YOUTH PROGRAM FOR AUGUST 12

A Hero In The Struggle For The Souls Of Men

Suggested Devotional Outline:
Hymn: "Take The Name Of Jesus With You."
Prayer
Scripture: John 14:1-14
Hymn: "Wonderful Words Of Life"
Offering
Hymn: "Rescue The Perishing"

PROGRAM LEADER'S INTRODUCTION:

The hero of the faith we are considering in this program is well known to most of us now, but seven or eight years ago very few people had heard of him. Today, there are not many Americans whose names are more familiar throughout the world than his. It is not unusual for a soldier or a statesman, or even a sportsman to become world famous, but it is very unusual when a preacher is known all over the world. Our hero has become famous for his faithfulness and success in the struggle for the souls of men. This hero is the Rev. William Franklin Graham, who is generally known to the world as Billy Graham.

Many of us are already familiar with the facts of his life and his ministry, but as we consider the living heroes of the faith, it is only fitting that we review the life and work of this man whom God has used in such a wonderful way.

FIRST SPEAKER:

Billy Graham was born in 1918 on a dairy farm just outside of Charlotte, N. C. His parents were faithful members of the Associate Reformed Presbyterian Church, and his early life was very typical of any farm lad in a Christian home. He went to Sunday School and church, but was not overly impressed with religion. By the time he was seventeen he had begun to enjoy a rather reckless, thoughtless way of living. He was not a bad boy, he just had nothing important to live for. At this time he yielded to the urging of his parents and attended a revival in Charlotte. He gave his life to Christ and became truly a changed person.

After high school he attended Bob Jones College (then in Cleveland, Tenn.) for a brief period. Leaving Bob Jones, he went to the Florida Bible Institute in Tampa, Florida. It was at this point that he began to preach. In 1939 he was ordained to the ministry of the Southern Baptist church. The following year he entered Wheaton College from which he was graduated in 1943. While at Wheaton Billy met Ruth Bell, the daughter of Dr. and Mrs. L. Nelson Bell, missionaries of our church to China. Two weeks after graduation they were married in Montreat.

Soon after his marriage Billy began to work in the Youth for Christ Movement which had been only recently organized to win young people to Christ. During this time he met and worked with many of the young men who make up the Billy Graham team today. Together they traveled over the United States and the British Isles holding evangelistic meetings among young people. In 1949 the young evangelist really began to attract the attention of the American public in general. He was preaching in Los Angeles and the meetings started lasting weeks longer than planned. It was here that the converts made headlines as their number included movie stars and famous athletes. After this there were tremendous campaigns in major American cities, and more recently in the great cities of Britain and of continental Europe.

SECOND SPEAKER:

What is Billy Graham's message? He would be the first person to insist that his preaching is not eloquent or intellectually brilliant. A few people have criticized his messages for the lack of these qualities. The thousands of people whose lives have been transformed through his preaching make the best defense for the effectiveness of the message he delivers. Billy strives for two things in his preaching: for it to be Biblical and for it to be simple. He insists that sin is the cause of all our real problems, that all men are sinners who cannot save themselves, that Christ the Son of God died for sinners, that sinful men can have forgiveness and life when they accept Christ by faith as Saviour and Lord. He sticks closely to these fundamental facts, avoiding all controversial matters, and the Lord has greatly honored his work.

THIRD SPEAKER:

If there is nothing extraordinary about the man or his message, what is the secret of his power? There is no denying the fact that power is there. In the recent Scotland crusade one prominent minister said that Graham's power is the power of God. If you ask Billy to give an explanation for all that has taken place, he will tell you that God is the only explanation. The real secret seems to be the complete dedi-

"Through her gifted ministry in this area of service, she has been used to lead thousands to a new understanding and appreciation of history as 'His Story' of work wrought in His Name. The Board of Women's Work would express gratitude for Mrs. Fowler's consecrated service, given all the twenty-five years, without remuneration, and for her radiant Christian life and influence which shall live on to His glory."

At the request of the Board of Women's Work there has been prepared and will appear in the August 1956 issue of *The Presbyterian Survey* an article, entitled *A Tribute,* which gives more information about the work done by this friend and talented servant of our Church.

Florida School for Children of Migrant Workers

Thirty-one Mexican-American children began their formal education in the first Hendry County school for children of migratory farm laborers.

The students, children of migrants in the rich Devil's Garden truck farm area deep in the Everglades, will be instructed by Floyd O. Raines, who is living in a house trailer parked next to the school.

The one-room school building acquired by the county school board late in 1955, was moved to its present remote location and completely renovated.

Stewardship

Stewardship is a principle, a plan and a power.

The principle that gives direction to life and behavior is the acceptance of God's entrustment to us.

The plan makes provision for the continuous flow of our gratitude to him and our responsible concern for our fellow man.

The power rests in the multiplied increase of the gift when dedicated to God.

Church News

Tragic Refugee Problem

Montreat — "No solution whatsoever" has been found for the tragic refugee-problem in the Near East, one of the important factors in the tense situation there, the Rev. Paul B. Freeland of the Presbyterian Church, U. S., Board of World Missions declared here recently.

In a report to the members and staff of the Board, the secretary of the Department of Overseas Relief and Inter-Church Aid also stated that he found, in visiting Spain during a tour of eleven European and Near Eastern countries, that misguiding reports have been made from that country concerning the Protestant seminary in Madrid.

The seminary, closed by government order in February, was reported "open" after Protestant protests had been made to the Franco government. Press reports circulated throughout the world announced the seminary was re-opened.

"The 're-opening' consists of removing the official seals from the doors, but a continuing ban on the holding of any seminary classes or activities," Mr. Freeland revealed. "All classroom doors and the doors to the library, as well as the street doors, had been sealed. Now the seals are removed." He was allowed to visit the empty seminary.

Chief purpose of the churchman's trip was to participate in the Second Beirut (Lebanon) Conference on Refugee Problems. More than 60 church and governmental welfare and relief workers were present from throughout the world for the five-day conference.

The group reported that no progress in solving the refugee problem has been made during the eight years since hundreds of thousands of Arabs were dispossessed by the Israeli during the Israeli war. The conference found that:

1. The number in the refugee camps has now passed 1,000,000, and is increasing at the rate of more than 25,000 a year. Additional thousands - estimated as high as half a million . . . are living in Arabian villages along the Israeli border, having lost farmlands from which they derived their living.

2. Of the more than 1,000,000 refugees, almost one-half is under 16 years of age.

3. In most refugee camps, unemployment is 97%, and hope of employment non-existent.

4. More than 10% of the total are Arabian Christians, the rest Moslems.

5. The refugees are living entirely off gifts of food supplied through Church World Service and other church and international relief agencies. Even so, the average daily calorie count is 1,500 per person.

The conference, in reporting the apparently hopeless situation, noted that only political adjustments can alleviate the problem, and noted these points at issue:

1. The right to repatriation. 2. The adjustment and guarantee of frontiers. 3. The just claim to compensation. 4. The status of Jerusalem. 5. The equitable utilization of land and water resources.

During his stay in the Near East, Mr. Freeland was one of a party of 15 permitted to enter the Gaza Strip. This was the first party to visit the Strip in recent months, and movies taken of the group were televised throughout the United States and Western Europe.

"The Gaza Strip," Mrs. Freeland reported, "is five by 20 miles in area, and had a normal population of 100,000 before the Israeli war. Now, 250,000 to 300,000 additional persons, refugees from what was southwest Palestine before it became Israel, have poured into the Strip."

Concerning the situation in Spain, Mr. Freeland revealed that persecution of Protestants is becoming progressively worse.

"Protestants generally are not aware that at the same time that the seminary was closed, the British Bible Society and all other Bible societies working in Spain were closed, and their stocks of Bibles seized and destroyed," he reported.

During the trip, Mr. Freeland also represented the Presbyterian Church, U.S., at the annual World Council of Churches Conference on Inter-Church Aid, held this year in Les Rasses, Switzerland. More than 150 persons attended.

ALABAMA

Dr. Kingsley Morgan to London

The Rev. Kingsley J. Morgan, minister of the Handley Memorial Church, of Birmingham, Alabama, will go to London, England, in July to preach for three Sundays in the historic Westminster Chapel made famous by his father, Dr. G. Campbell Morgan.

In addition, Mr. Morgan will have the honor of delivering the Campbell Morgan Memorial Lecture. This Lectureship was inaugurated in 1949 in memory of the great Bible expositor, and is delivered each summer. Because Dr. Morgan spent many years in the United States, and carried on an itinerant teaching and preaching ministry throughout this country and in Canada, it seemed fitting to the Board of Governors to invite lecturers alternately from England and from North America, and when possible this has been done. The lectures cover a wide territory of interest, but all have as a central core, the Bible - this in keeping with Dr. Campbell Morgan's ministry which was essentially that of Biblical exposition.

For the lecture this year Mr. Morgan will take as his subject "The Bible in the Life of the Missionary."

Birmingham — Lebanon was described as one of the Christian strongholds of the Near East by the Rev. Gavriel Abdullah, pastor of Westminster Presbyterian Church in Jacksonville, Fla., in an interview here. Mr. Abdullah was in Birmingham to attend the sixth annual convention of the American Syrian and Lebanese clubs, and to speak at Third Presbyterian Church.

Mr. Abdullah said that the Christian missionaries are doing a great work in Lebanon, particularly at the American University in Beirut. In addition, many Lebanese are members of a Christian community going back to apostolic times.

Mr. Abdullah spoke Sunday evening, July 8, to the Third Church congregation. The Rev. Mitchell Alexander, a local radio minister who also is of Lebanese descent, had part in the service.

Birmingham — The South Highland Presbyterian Church, to be host to the General Assembly in 1957, began preparations for the occasion with the first meeting of its official planning committee early in July.

Approximately 200 laymen attended this meeting. S. R. Carson is general chairman of the planning and arrangements for the host church.

The General Assembly will hold its next meeting April 25 - May 1, 1957.

Birmingham — Dr. James M. Gregory, whose present pastorate is the Napoleon Avenue Presbyterian Church in New Orleans, La., has accepted the call from Woodlawn Presbyterian Church in Birmingham, Ala. He will assume his duties as minister of the Birmingham church on Sept. 1, it was announced by church officers.

GEORGIA

Cornelia — Rev. Fred Clark, pastor of the First Presbyterian Church here, has been given a trip home to England by members of his congregation. He leaves July 24, and will return August 25.

Mr. Clarke, who is a native of Yaddlethorpe, Lincolnshire, will visit brothers, sister, and friends whom he has not seen in 33 years.

LOUISIANA

New Orleans — Dedication of the new $150,000 TeSelle Educational building adjoining Canal Street Presbyterian Church took place Sunday afternoon, July 8.

The two-story brick and concrete structure is named for Mr. W. J. TeSelle and the late Adriana TeSelle, his wife, both of whom have been faithful and supporting members of the Canal Street Church since 1906. Mr. TeSelle is the senior elder of the church. A portrait of Mr. and Mrs. TeSelle was unveiled in the new building during the program by Mrs. Emily Johnston representing the Women of the Church.

Those taking part in the dedicatory program were the Rev. Pat N. Easterling, the new church pastor; Louis T. Frantz, chairman of the building committee; C. D. Smith, church elder; W. J. TeSelle, leading elder; David Remont, moderator of New Orleans Presbytery, and the Rev. G. H. Wilson, secretary of the New Orleans Federation of Churches. The Rev. Alcee Martin, pastor of Westminster Presbyterian Church of Memphis, Tenn., preached the dedication sermon.

Alexandria — Four churches in northeast Louisiana, three Presbyterian and one Methodist, held a joint meeting at Delhi Sunday evening, July 8, with Ralph Brewer, of Alexandria, president of the Louisiana Synod Men's Council, conducting the service. Brewer spoke on men's work to the ministers and congregations of the Delhi, Winnsboro and Rayville Presbyterian Churches and the Delhi Methodist church.

NORTH CAROLINA

Greenville — Albermarle Presbytery — The following men have been received into our Presbytery and are Pastors of the Churches indicated:

Leslie C. Robinson (a graduate student from Union Seminary, from the Presbytery of Enoree) - Assistant Pastor, First Presbyterian Church, Rocky Mount, N. C.

Edgar D. Byers (a graduate of Union Seminary) - Pastor of the George Kirby Memorial - Antioch field of Goldsboro, N. C.

Edward C. Thornburg (a graduate of Westminster Seminary) - Pastor of Meadowbrook Church, Greenville, N. C.

E. L. Willingham (who has spent a year in graduate study at Westminster Seminary) has been called to the Hollywood and Chicod Churches, which he formerly served.

VIRGINIA

Richmond — The appointment of seven persons to the Ad Interim Committee on Mass Communications for the General Assembly of the Presbyterian Church, U. S., has been announced here by the Moderator of the Assembly, Dr. W. Taliaferro Thompson.

Dr. Arthur Vann Gibson, pastor of Morningside Presbyterian Church, Atlanta, and a member of the National Council of Churches Broadcasting and Films Commission was named chairman. The committee, as directed by the 1956 General Assembly, will study the Church's use of radio and television, in all its phases and through all the agencies of the Church.

Other members of the committee are Dr. R. W. Kirkpatrick, Union Theological Seminary, Richmond, Va.; Dr. D. J. Cumming, Board of World Missions, Nashville, Tenn.; Mr. Cameron D. Deans, Board of Christian Education, Richmond, Va.; Mr. John Hart, station WBIR, Knoxville, Tenn.; Mr. Kenneth I. Tredwell, Station WBTV, Charlotte, N. C.; and Mrs. Wilson C. Wearn, Station WFBC-TV, Greenville, S. C.

Richmond — Rev. Donald O. McInnis has been named as the new regional director of Christian education for the Synod of Alabama, Presbyterian Church, U. S.

Formerly pastor of the First Presbyterian Church, Mt. Holly, N. C., Rev. Mr. McInnis took up his duties as field representative August 1, it was announced by Dr. Marshall C. Dendy, executive secretary of the Presbyterian Board of Christian Education.

The new director replaces Rev. James Alexander, who joined the staff of the Church's Board of Church Extension two years ago.

Headquarters for the new director will be at 5624 First Avenue, North in Birmingham, Alabama. Rev. Mr. McInnis and his family will live in a manse recently purchased by the Synod of Alabama.

Theological Medical Clinic at U.T.S.

Dr. Paul E. Scherer, Professor of Homiletics, Union Theological Seminary in New York, and Dr. David L. Stitt, President of Austin Presbyterian Theological Seminary, Austin, Texas, will be co-lecturers in a Preaching Clinic to be held at Union Theological Seminary in Virginia, July 30 through August 10, 1956.

Their lectures will be given at 10:30 A. M., July 30 - August 3, and August 6-9. Also on the distinguished faculty of the Clinic will be Dr. Warner L. Hall, Pastor of the Covenant Presbyterian Church, Charlotte, North Carolina; Dr. James A. Jones, President, Union Theological Seminary in Virginia; Dr. Robert White Kirkpatrick, Professor of Preaching, Union Theological Seminary in Virginia; Dr. Julian Lake, Pastor of the First Presbyterian Church, Winston-Salem, North Carolina, and Dr. Donald G. Miller, Professor of New Testament, Union Theological Seminary in Virginia.

Open to ordained ministers of all denominations, this annual Clinic is the only one of its kind in the United States. Its uniqueness stems from its similarity to a medical clinic. The Preaching Clinic's purpose is to give the participating ministers opportunities to improve their preaching abilities by personal diagnosis of their pulpit weaknesses. Remedies are offered which will make the minister more effective in his delivery of sermons and his conduct of public worship. Each sermon preached by a student at the Clinic will be discussed by two members of the faculty in the presence of the assembled group. There will follow a period of discussion and questions from the group.

Each night at 7:15, July 30 - August 3, and August 6-9, there will be a worship service led by one of the faculty members of the Clinic. These services as well as the morning lectures are open to the public.

THE SOUTHERN PRESBYTERIAN JOURNAL

A Presbyterian weekly magazine devoted to the statement, defense and propagation of the Gospel, the faith which was once for all delivered unto the saints.

VOL. XV NO. 15 | AUGUST 8, 1956 | $2.50 A YEAR

OUTGOING MISSIONARIES

Front Row, left to right—Miss Pauline Harrop, Taiwan; Mr. and Mrs. William J. Rawlins, Brazil; Rev. and Mrs. Lamar Williamson, Jr., Congo; Rev. and Mrs. James L. Moss, Brazil.

Second Row—Rev. and Mrs. John M. Reagan, Jr., Japan; Rev and Mrs. David B. Lehman, Brazil; Rev. and Mrs. Robert M. Marvin, Brazil; Miss Anna Ruth Perry, Japan.

Third Row—Rev. and Mrs. David L. Parks, Korea; Miss Sarah E. Jeffrey, Japan; Mrs. Frank T. Lemmon, Jr. (Mr. Lemmon not able to be present for picture), Mexico; Rev. and Mrs. Frank M. Kepler, Taiwan; Rev. and Mrs. Edward C. Langham, Jr., Brazil.

Fourth Row—Miss Lida E. Knight, Brazil; Miss Ann S. Anderson, Congo; Miss Lucretia W. Stevenson, Congo; Miss Marjorie Hoffeld, Congo; Miss Dawn Aoto, Brazil; Dr. Verlin A. Krabill, Brazil; Rev. and Mrs. E. A. J. Seddon, Jr., Mexico; Mr. Robert S. Gould, Korea.

THE SOUTHERN PRESBYTERIAN JOURNAL
The Journal has no official connection with the Presbyterian Church in the United States

Rev. Henry B. Dendy, D.D., Editor............Weaverville, N. C.
Dr. L. Nelson Bell, Associate Editor............Asheville, N. C.
Rev. Wade C. Smith, Associate Editor............Weaverville, N. C.

EDITORIAL

Israel Asking a King!

In First Samuel, chapters 8 through 12 there is an account of Israel asking for a King, and of the LORD allowing their request to be granted. An analogy has been drawn from this incident to the effect that since some of our people want women elders therefore God will permit it. No doubt the gracious and long-suffering God and Father of our Lord Jesus Christ remains faithful to His people, even though they prove faithless to Him in many things and in many ways. For in many things we offend all. In the matter of women elders, however, let each one be persuaded in his own heart as the Spirit opens to him the Word. But let everyone take heed lest he misuse Holy Scripture. Let us re-read these chapters ere using them as an analogy supporting women elders. God permitted the choice of Saul as the King of His people Israel, but not without testifying His disapproval of it.

Through the mouth of Samuel, His judge, prophet and priest, God repeatedly indicated His displeasure. In First Samuel 8.6, we read, "But the thing displeased Samuel", margin "was evil in the eyes of". 8.7, "They have not rejected thee (Samuel), but they have rejected ME (the LORD), that I should not reign over them." 12.17 "Your wickedness is great which ye have done in the sight of the LORD in asking you a king." 12.19 "For we have added unto all our sins this evil, to ask us a king." 12.20. "Ye have done all this wickedness."

As our representative and substitute the Lord Jesus was crucified publicly as a malefactor. He shall come publicly as the King of Glory. Today it is our duty to believe in and testify to our Saviour as the invisible King of His Church and the Lord of each believer. Few denominations have phrased this so explicitly as our founding fathers have expressed it in the second chapter of our Book of Church Order. May the God of our Fathers give us grace to recognize and attest the King of Kings in our decisions as to Church government and governors as in worship, doctrine and life. W.C.R.

A Word to Rookies

The young theologian has a difficult position, - so he thinks. So is he right. He must be "up-to-date." The Church expects a "well-rounded leader." One must "know philosophy" and have "quoting acquaintance with present-day theologians." "Systems of thought" are very valuable. First-hand conversational touch with books of note is a *must.* And of course there is sociability and Church-statesmanship and culture and tact, and a reasonable ability to speak in public, and a fair (!) knowledge of the Bible and . . .

In Scripture we read the expression: "Looking unto Jesus": Regarding general problems, His time was not radically different from ours: yet these seemed to have been of no great concern for Him. Not that He was uninterested; for all that interests men, surely interested Him. Not that He was uninformed; he knew what was in man. Not that they were unimportant: sparrows and head-hair, - think on that! No.

No matter how vital these matters might have been, they were side-issues. There were concerns, then, as now, of far more vital import. Whereas we have no injunctions from Him regarding philosophy and theologians and systems of thought, as necessary armamentaria for the preacher, we do note: *Search the Scriptures,* and *Preach the Kingdom,* and *Call to repentance,* and *Seek the Lost.* He advised to tell men *What God is doing.* He fell back on *What is written.* He urged to let the Holy Spirit's power control the life. Some things were absolutes, - and are still such: others were neglible in comparison, and *still* are!

Then, there were the unlearned and ignorant men of the early Gospel era, who were quite able ministers of the New Covenant, despite most unfortunate shortage in certain large-looming matters, perhaps in the eyes of that day, as well as now. They did not choose the story of philosophy: they had a better story. They never relied on the books of the great Rabbis:

they had ONE BOOK. They gave little thought and less time to the then-lauded theological systems: they preached the Gospel of God's love and salvation for sinners, through the crucified and risen Lord Jesus Christ. They set small store by worldly forces: they had the power of God. They were not phased by human greatness, nor dismayed before worldly might: they turned the world upside down! And they never thought of their Bible as the "instrument" of revelation: it was, and is, THE revelation; nor did they understand the Book to be a man-made, editorially confused, trial-and-error record of man's search for God: they understood that all Scripture is inspired of God and profitable . . .

On the oppositely other hand, it must be rather embarrassing to the dignified, historic, intellectual and cultured Churches who now go after fads and fancies of men, that the fastest growing ecclesiastical bodies of this present time are those who take the plain, unrevised Bible, as the very Word of God, believe it, preach it, practice it. Is there no connection here? They seem, with all of their pitiful poverty in the things of world wisdom and human estimation, to have the one thing needful.

Calling all rookies, all theological tadpoles, all novices, all who desire to do the work of the Lord in His great Harvest Field! Wisdom is the principal thing. The fear of the Lord is its beginning. According to a tradition, when the young scholars asked the Rabbi when they could study the sciences and art and philosophy, he advised them to find some time other than day or night, for, he said, "It is written in the law: 'Thou shall meditate therein day and night' ". And we recall from the record, that to Joshua, upon whose shoulders, the impossible task of leading Israel fell, it was enjoined: "This Book of the Law shall not depart out of thy mouth . . . *Then* shalt thou make thy way prosperous, and *then* shalt thou have good success." Those who have marching orders would do well to follow them. To faithfulness, not fame, is the promised crown. R.F.G.

Are Ruling Elders Laymen!

In the accounts of the several Presbyterian General Assemblies it is disconcerting to find the Chairman of an important Committee described as a layman, or even to read that the Moderator of the Presbyterian Church, U.S.A. is a layman. Is the highest office in the largest Presbyterian body in the world held by a layman?

The distinction between clergy and laity is not New Testament. In First Peter the believers are described in 2.9 as a royal priesthood, a holy nation, a peculiar people (laity). And the same people here denominated priests and laity are expressly called in 5.3 "the clergy," "not as lords over God's heritage, literally, the clergy." In the New Testament, then all the living members of the Church are priests, laity, clergy, even as all received the gift of the Holy Spirit on Pentecost, Acts 2.

The distinction between laity and clergy appears in the early Church about 200 A. D., partly from the Old Testament usage. Thereafter there developed a sevenfold order of the clergy: priest, deacon, sub-deacon, acolyte, exorcist, lector (reader), janitor (door-keeper). Now this profusion of officers kept the line between the presiding official and the unordained members from becoming too sharp. For example, a moderate sized congregation of the fourth century might well have fifty persons in these several orders of the clerical militia. The Roman Catholic theology recognizes all these as clergy. It defines as clergy all those who are ordained by a high or a lower ordination to a higher or lower office in the Church. If we are going to borrow their distinction at all, why not borrow it correctly? Dabney was nearer right than our current usage when he described the ruling elder as a clergyman.

Current Roman Catholic practice, however, sharpens the line between the priest and the people by allowing the other six orders to become almost invisible in the typical congregation. That is, as the local priest informed me, the several offices are all concentrated in the person of the priest. He receives and holds all seven of these offices.

But we Presbyterians are doing almost as badly as the current Roman Catholic practice when we recognize only one person in the congregation as a clergyman, that is, we are widening the gap too much between the Pastor and the people. Sometimes this gap is expressed in our worship when a Pastor permits only himself to come to the Lord's Table and places himself between the Table and even the ruling elders. (Probably this is often done unconsciously by the Minister, but it can make or in-

The Southern Presbyterian Journal, *a Presbyterian Weekly magazine, devoted to the statement, defense, and propagation of the Gospel, the faith which was once for all delivered unto the saints*, published every Wednesday by The Southern Presbyterian Journal, Inc., in Weaverville, N. C.

Entered as second-class matter May 15, 1942, at the Postoffice at Weaverville, N. C., under the Act of March 3, 1879. Vol. XV, No. 15, August 8, 1956. Editorial and Business Offices: Weaverville, N. C. Printed in the U.S.A. by Biltmore Press, Asheville, N. C.

ADDRESS CHANGE: When changing address, please let us have both old and new address as far in advance as possible. Allow three weeks after change if not sent in advance. When possible, send an address label giving your old address.

crease a cleavage). In the Presbyterian Churches in England, France and Switzerland one or more elders serve with the Pastor behind the Table of the Lord.

In the old Scottish "Bukes" of Discipline, the preachers, ruling elders and deacons are all called ministers for they are all ordained for serving the Church. Dr. Oscar Cullmann, distinguished New Testament scholar and ruling elder in a French-speaking Church, says this is the true New Testament and Presbyterian way to think of the ruling elder.

In American Presbyterianism, Charles Hodge thought of the Preacher as the presbyter appointed by the Lord in Scripture, and of the ruling elder as only the delegate of the people. Our Southern Presbyterian Book of Church Order, however, was written by the disciples of J. H. Thornwell who taught that the presbyter ordained by Christ in Scripture was the shepherd or ruling elder, like the elder in the Jewish synagogue. Accordingly, the ruling elder has his appointment, his equipment, his call to office, his functions as the gift of the ascended Christ even as does the preacher. Because the ruling elder is the servant of the Lord, only those who have the qualifications given in Scripture ought to be chosen to that office. W.C.R.

"I Have Chosen You"

Do you remember the words Jesus spoke on His way to Gethsemane? After reminding His disciples, "Without me, ye can do nothing," He said, "If a man abide not in me, he is cast forth."

We can accomplish nothing without the permission, the help and the blessing of our Lord. And if we do not abide in Him, we will be cast forth, miserable failures.

Our Lord made another profound remark when He said, "Ye have not chosen me, but I have chosen you." It should spur us on to renewed energy to realize we have been chosen for a particular task. We have accepted the privilege of being CHRIST-ian men and at times we forget the responsibility that goes with this honor.

Sometimes we face difficulties and become discouraged. That is the time to remind ourselves that Christ has selected us. He has trusted us. Woe be to us, men, if we fail Him at this hour. Christ has selected every man who calls himself a CHRIST-ian. You have been designated for some special service. Our Lord depends on you.

Jesus impressed on His followers the idea that they were picked men. Perhaps some thought they were unprepared, not good enough to face a hostile world. We see the same situation today, we hear men say they are untrained and unworthy to accept the task.

The disciples did not choose the task. Christ chose them for the task. God is calling many men to serve Him. Whatever your talent, God intends for you to use it. To serve Him in any capacity is the greatest honor a man may have.

In doing the simple things, we grow in grace, and if your service is acceptable for His honor and glory, you may rest assured the Master has spoken, "Ye have not chosen me, but I have chosen you."

Ralph Brewer, Alexandria, La.

Has Protestanism Lost Its Conscience?

By Gordon H. Clark

The Protestant Reformation was both a doctrinal and a moral movement. And to this day predominantly Protestant countries have maintained a higher standard of morality than the Romish nations. But inasmuch as ecclesiastical organizations deteriorate, especially when they become rich and have need of nothing, one may wonder whether it may not be possible for Protestantism to lose its conscience.

Consider an article published in *Foi Education* (January - March 1956), the periodical of the Federation Protestant de l'Enseignment.

The author writes on Education in the New China. He holds that the key to the understanding of the new China is its agricultural reform. Along with this goes a great cultural effort — schools, universities, museums — which is no merely secondary aspect of socialistic construction. Public service needs men and women who are not robots, but who are responsible individuals capable of developing popular democracy. Culture is at the center of socialism, and the new China has taken seriously these imperatives which determine socialistic policy.

The author continues by praising the introduction of an alphabet to take the place of the ancient characters. Then he sketches the (alleged) workings of primary and secondary education, distinguished, he says, by attention to good health, good instruction, good morality, and good character. The children are taught patriotism, internationalism, and love of peace.

The author then concludes with praise for the Universities, the system of adult education, the socialist edification of the peasants, the building of libraries, and all the marvelous instruments of culture.

But the author in this Protestant periodical has not one word of adverse criticism. There is no suspicion of the brutality, the torture, the massacre of fifteen or twenty million people. All is sweetness and light.

In the United States also there are Protestants who seem to admire Red China. They want it seated in the United Nations. They dislike to hear it criticized. Can it be that Protestants are losing their conscience? Can liberalism preserve any sense of social responsibility? Or does lax theology tend toward a callous disregard of human rights? Could it be that the tendency toward a centrally controlled ecclesiastical organization finds its blood brother in the totalitarian state?

More Corruption

By Rev. R. D. Littleton
Hattiesburg, Mississippi

The men who compiled the Confession of Faith foresaw that there was a tendency of men to bring forth arguments in favor of many grounds for divorce and remarriage except those stated in the standards of our church. The sixth paragraph of Chapter XXXVI states it in these words . . . "Although the corruption of man be such as is apt to study arguments, unduly to put asunder those whom God hath joined together in marriage . . . yet nothing but adultery, or such wilful desertion as can no way be remedied by the church or civil magistrate, is cause sufficient of dissolving the bond of marriage . . . "

The foresight of the writers of the Confession of Faith has been literally fulfilled among ministers in our church, especially those who have been associated with the Division of Christian Relations. These men once swore before Almighty God that they believed the teachings of the Confession of Faith, and promised their brethren that they would defend these teachings at any cost to themselves.

It is admitted that there are difficult cases to handle, but it is also true that the Word of God discourages divorce in every instance, only adultery and irremediable desertion being sufficient grounds for divorce for the Christian.

It is also admitted that it is not easy for some people to live clean lives outside the married relationship, but this is true of people facing continuously certain other types of temptation. The person guilty of causing a divorce, if he is a Christian, has promise of the help of the Holy Spirit in living obedient to the law of God. God sent His Son to die for us that the Holy Spirit might come to us . . . "That the righteousness of the law might be fulfilled in us who walk not after the flesh, but after the Spirit" (Romans 5:4). We can point men and women to the aid of the Holy Spirit who will assist them in being obedient under difficult circumstances. Those who advocate remarriage for those guilty of causing a divorce usually speak of it adding to his happiness, and he may have some pleasures of sin for a season, but the Christian goal is not happiness but righteousness and acceptance with God.

For those who have assumed the office of ministers, it is only cowardice not to defend the truths of the Christian religion. To fail may add to the numbers of the church, but it will only add tares to the kingdom of God within the church.

This sometimes happens too that when a minister has been true to his calling those whom he has warned of sin and its consequences will return to him when they begin to reap the consequences of following their own lusts instead of heeding the warnings of the Word of God.

The phrase which those who advocate other grounds for divorce among Christians than the above mentioned causes is found in I Corinthians 7:15. These are the words, "But if the unbelieving depart, let him depart. A brother or sister is not in bondage *in such cases:* but God hath called us to peace." In this connection Paul had said that a Christian married to an unbeliever, and deserted by the unbeliever, was not bound to the marriage contract. Some argue that this was a case of injustice and that there are many other equally as bad, and that all of them could be included in this phrase "in such cases." Study of the Greek shows this to be in error, and the precise meaning is "in cases such as this," referring only to the cases mentioned above, where either a brother or a sister is deserted. The writers of the Confession of Faith were great students of the languages in which the Bible was written.

The real origin of this effort to delete from our Confession of Faith the teaching with regard to divorce and remarriage is to be found among those who are so greatly in favor of the ecumenical movement that they are willing to desert strongholds of faith to accomplish their goal. Fellowship on a broad scale is to them more important than the defense of the truth. Fellowship in the truth is the real ecumenical movement, and it is the only one God will bless. Let us support true ecumenicity by defending the heritage left to us by God and His apostles.

Shall Women Be Ordained As Elders And Deacons In The Presbyterian Church U. S.

By Rev. G. T. Gillespie, D.D., Litt.D.

By a vote of 235 to 226 the General Assembly has referred to the presbyteries the proposal to change our Form of Government, so as to provide for the ordination of women to the offices of elder or deacon, on a permissive basis.

Obviously, this involves a revolutionary change in our standards and a radical departure from the historic traditions of the church. But that is only half the story. If the Ad Interim Committee which submitted this proposal to the Assembly had been logically consistent and entirely frank, they would have included a provision for the *ordination of women to the ministry;* for the same arguments which were advanced to support ordination of women to the eldership and diaconate apply with equal force to the ministry. The experiences of other churches indicates that adoption of the first innovation is promptly followed by agitation for the admission of women to the ministry, which usually follows in short order. So let us not close our eyes to the fact that we are virtually facing a decision on both questions at this time. For only the first step in a new direction really counts, the others follow naturally and inevitably.

PERSONAL OBSERVATIONS

To guard against wrong impressions and misunderstanding, the writer, in undertaking to discuss this difficult but important subject, wishes to make certain personal observations:

1. In taking sharp issue with the findings of the Ad-Interim Committee, let it be said, with all sincerity, that no reflection is intended upon the personnel of that committee, all of whom are esteemed by the writer for their high Christian Character and ability, and whom he is happy to count as friends.

2. In opposing the ordination of women to official positions in the church, because he believes it to be without Scriptural warrant, the writer wishes to re-affirm his profound respect for Christian womanhood, and his conviction that there is ample room for the use of all of women's God-given talents and graces in the service of Christ and the church, without seeking or assuming those responsibilities which God in his wisdom, has reserved for men.

3. It was particularly gratifying to have the statement from the Chairman of the Ad-Interim Committee that the demand for this change has not come from the leaders, or from the rank and file, of the women of the church. This is not only a fact, but many of the *spiritually-minded women of the church have strongly condemned the proposal,* and are actively exerting their influence to prevent its adoption by the church.

The question therefore naturally arises, "Whence comes the demand for this change"? The obvious answer is, that the real sponsors of this movement, are that increasingly aggressive group of liberals in the church, who, at times seem half ashamed of their Presbyterian heritage, and always like the Areopagites, interested in "some new thing," and who seem to be obsessed with the idea that progress consists in following the fashion set by some of our sister churches, lest we commit the unpardonable sin of being out of step with the ecumenical procession.

THE REAL ISSUE — THE AUTHORITY AND ADEQUACY OF THE SCRIPTURES

The real issue involved in this proposed change, is not a question as to the wisdom, or expediency, from our human point of view, of admitting women to ordination in the Church, but it is far deeper and more vital. Essentially it has to do with our whole attitude with respect to *the authority and adequacy of the Scriptures.*

The basic principle underlying our Presbyterian System, is that the warrant and pattern for the Government of the Church is clearly set forth in the Word of God, the only infallible rule of faith and practice; which principle is stated in our Form of Government Chapter II, Par. 10, as follows:

"Christ as King, has given to his church, officers, oracles, and ordinances; and especially has he ordained therein his system of doctrine, *government,* discipline and worship; all which are either *expressly set down in Scripture,* or by good and necessary inference may be deduced therefrom; and to which things he commands that nothing be added, and that from them naught be taken away."

It is *indeed remarkable, and perhaps not without significance, that this statement which sets forth the historic and distinctive position of the Southern Presbyterian Church, and which is the very crux of the whole matter at issue, was not quoted or even referred to, in the lengthy report of the Ad-Interim Committee.*

Those of us who loyally support this principle have frequently been represented as contending for a strict literalism in the interpretation of Scripture, and for the imposition of inflexible rules which take no account of changed conditions, or exceptional circumstances. Whereas our contention is that *Scriptural statements ought to be interpreted in their natural and obvious meaning, without evasion or mental reservation;* and that Christ has laid down in His Word, not hard and fast rules to bind and hamper His church, but broad principles which are to be applied with spiritually enlightened reason and sanctified common sense.

WHAT SAITH THE SCRIPTURES?

The Old Testament Record

According to the story of creation in Genesis, Woman is accorded a position of *partnership* with man, but *definitely subordinate* to his authority in the social order. No evidence is available to show that this ordinance, established by the Creator, and based upon the natural characteristics differentiating men and woman, has ever been repealed. The Apostle Paul invokes it in support of his contention that men are to be vested with the chief authority in church as well as in the family.

In a few isolated instances, according to the Old Testament record, women assumed, or attempted to assume, positions of leadership or authority, but close examination of the record will show that in each of these cases the *circumstances were extraordinary,* and that, at most, they could only be classed as *exceptions which prove the rule.* But in no sense did they set up a precedent for the elevation of women to positions of supreme authority in either old, or the new dispensations.

In this connection it is worthy of note, that under the Mosaic economy, women were more highly esteemed, and enjoyed a more liberal status than was true of women among other oriental peoples. However *the exclusion of women from any official connection with the Tabernacle or Temple worship was doubtless providential, since it saved Judaism from the immoral practices and degrading influences which characterized the worship of practically all pagan peoples in ancient and modern times.*

The Attitude Of Our Lord

If it was the desire and intention of Our Lord, that the way should be opened for women to serve the church in an official capacity, there is nothing to indicate it in the record of his life and teaching in the New Testament. On the contrary, there are many positive indications that he had no other thought or purpose than that *these weighty responsibilities should rest on the shoulders of men.*

When, after a night spent in prayer, Our Lord chose the twelve disciples, who were to be his constant companions and helpers, and whom he later designated and ordained as Apostles, *it is significant that all twelve chosen were men.* Even though he was at times accompanied by certain women, including his own mother, "who ministered unto him of their substance," there is *no recorded instance in which he recognized or used women in any official capacity, or invested them with authority to preach or to teach in his name.*

The attitude of Jesus toward his own mother was always respectful, but on more than one occasion he made it clear that he did not recognize her right to counsel or influence him with respect to his ministry and the work of his kingdom.

Jesus had a deep understanding of the needs of women of all classes and conditions, and it was in keeping with the compassion of his heart, and his redemptive mission, to stoop to be gracious to her, upon whom the curse of sin had fallen first, and heaviest. He often paid generous tribute to woman's superior faith and devotion, and yet it is worthy of note, that it was in every instance *the ministry of women in the field of personal or private relationships, which called for the Master's commendation.*

The Holy Spirit and The Early Church

Our Lord had promised The Twelve that he would send the Holy Spirit, who would *guide them into all truth.* One important segment of that truth had to do with the *organization and government of the church,* and the Book of Acts is largely the record of the successive steps in the development of the new type of organization, under the leadership of the Apostles and the special guidance of the Holy Spirit.

Just as the Holy Spirit had fashioned the body of the child Jesus in the womb of the Virgin Mary, so it seems fitting that the *Holy Spirit should give substance and form to the new body of Christ, which is His church,* which came to birth at Pentecost. And *just as he guided the Apostles infallibly in preparing and certifying to the church the New Testament Scriptures which completed the sacred canon, so he guided them with the same infallible wisdom, in developing and perfecting the pattern of organization and government, which Christ designed to be the model for his church in succeeding ages.*

The principle of the choice of their leaders by the people, was instituted at the first meeting of the disciples after the Ascension of the Lord, when the one hundred and twenty members of the group gathered in the upper room, and Peter stood up in their midst and pointed out the necessity of choosing one to take the place of Judas who had taken his own life, after betraying his Lord, as recorded in Acts 1:12-26.

In the same connection, it is quite significant, and pertinent to the issue now before us, that *Peter definitely limited the choice to men,* although there were several devoted women present in that company, including the mother of Jesus, who were worthy of all honor.

Again, when the church faced an emergency, because of the neglect of the Greek widows in the daily ministration, as recorded in Acts 6:1-7, *Peter called the congregation together and directed them to choose seven men* to take charge of these temporal matters; and when the seven had been chosen they were set apart to their offices by prayer and the laying on of hands, by the Apostles. Insofar as we have any record this marks the institution of the office of deacon in the church, and since women were certainly not considered eligible in that instance, it would seem to follow as a natural inference that this principle was intended as *a definite feature of the permanent polity of the church.*

We have no record in Acts of when, or how the first elders were chosen, but at an early period they appear to be associated with the Apostles in the supervision and direction of the church at Jerusalem. A similar group functioned in the church at Antioch, and it is definitely stated that Paul as a missionary evangelist "ordained elders in every church." It is also recorded in Acts 20:17-38 that Paul called the elders of the church of Ephesus to meet him at Miletus, where he addressed them as "brethren," and bade them an affectionate farewell. *In each of these references to the eldership it is clear, either from the names listed, the use of the masculine gender, or from the context, that only men were included in the groups.*

Pertinent Statements in The Epistles of Paul

The Apostle Paul, in his first letter to Timothy, after discussing at length the status and conduct of women in the church, solemnly declared; Chapter 2:12, *"But I suffer not a woman to teach, nor to usurp authority over the man, but to be in silence."* Closely following this, in Chapter 3:1-7, he states the qualifications for the office of bishop, which is just another title for the elder, as follows: "If a *man* desire the office of a bishop, he desireth a good work" . . . A bishop then, must be blameless *the husband of one wife* . . . one that ruleth well *his own house,* having *his children* in subjection with all gravity; for if a *man* know not how to rule *his own house,* how shall *he* take care of the church of God?"

Then follows a similar statement concerning the qualifications for the office of deacon, emphasizing also the requirement that *they* should be *"husbands of one wife' "ruling their children and their own houses well."*

The same general requirements for the eldership are set forth by Paul in his letter to Titus, Chapter 1:5-9, as follows:

> "For this cause left I thee in Crete, that thou shouldest set in order the things that are wanting, and ordain elders in every city as I had appointed thee: if any be blameless, *the husband of one wife,* having faithful children, not accused of riot or unruly, for a bishop must be blameless as the steward of God; not self-willed, not soon angry, not given to filthy lucre; but a lover of hospitality, a lover of good men, sober, just, holy, temperate; holding fast the faithful word as he hath been taught, that *he* may be able by sound doctrine both to exhort and to convince the gainsayers."

Assuming as we do, that Paul spoke by inspiration, and with authority as he claimed as "An Ambassador of Christ," *it is difficult to understand how any honest student of the Bible can ignore, evade or liberalize the plain statements of Paul, so as to justify or defend the ordination of women to the offices of elder or deacon.*

The Case of Phoebe

Much has been made by the advocates of the ordination of women, of the incidental reference by Paul in Romans 16:1, to Phoebe as a *"diakonon"* of the church at Cenchrea. It is contended that this word which is sometimes translated *"deacon,"* should be so translated in this case, and it means that Phoebe held the office of deacon in the church at Cenchrea.

In this connection it should be noted that the Authorized version translates the word as *"servant of the church at Cenchrea,"* evidently assuming that the expression was used by Paul in its general and usual sense. By an actual count, it is found that this word is used in the New Testament thirty times; in twenty-seven cases it is translated in its general sense as "servant," or "minister," and *in only three cases where the context evidently requires, it is translated with the special meaning as "deacon."* The weight of evidence therefore would seem to be about nine to one against the possibility that Paul referred to Sister Phoebe as a deacon of the church in the special sense of an ordained official, but far more likely that he was simply commending her as an exceptionally active and devoted worker. Surely, even if the remote possibility of the correctness of such a translation should be granted, *that would provide a slender thread indeed on which to base a divine warrant for the ordination of women as deacons* and elders, in the absence of any corroborating circumstances, and especially, in the face of overwhelming evidence, from numerous Scriptural passages, that *the ordination of women to official positions in the church, was not contemplated, or provided for* in this formative period, when the church was under the personal supervision of the Apostles, and the special guidance of the Holy Spirit.

A FINAL WORD

To all who have studied this question carefully and prayerfully, and have reached different conclusions, the writer cheerfully accords the right of private judgment, and the respect which is due to Brothers in Christ.

To those who have formed opinions casually, and without due consideration, the writer appeals for a reconsideration of this important question on its merits, and a fresh, first hand, study of the teaching of the Bible, until a convincing and satisfying answer has been found.

Let each of us, as *presbyters,* when we come to vote on this question, base our decision, *not on what is expedient, or in keeping with the spirit of this modern age; not on what other denominations are doing, or are planning to do; not on what may be pleasing to the women or to any other group in the church; but on what Christ has clearly revealed in His Word, as the divinely given plan for the government of the church, which he purchased with His blood; and of which He was, and is, and will ever be, the SOLE KING AND HEAD.*

Helps To Understanding Scripture Readings in *Day by Day*

By Rev. C. C. Baker

Sunday, August 19, *Philippians* 2:5-11. Christ's relation to His disciples is the example of our relations with other Christians (vv.5,7). What incidents of humility and service do you think of in the ministry of Christ? Christ's relation to the Father while here on earth is the example of what our relation to God should be (vv.5-6, 8). What is the ultimate example of obedience in the life of Christ? Observe in vv.9-11 the Great Reward for Christ's humility and obedience. God is at work within you to cause you to follow in the footsteps of Christ (v.13). What qualities does Paul call for in the Philippians' lives that you feel you need in your life (vv.2-8, 12-15)?

Monday, August 20, *I John* 3:14-17. One of the greatest commands Christ has given his disciples is that they love one another (John 13:34; 15:12). In fact what does John say of the person who does not love (vv.14b,15)? What does he say about the person who says he loves but does not practice it (vv.7-18)? God has demonstrated His love to us by something that He actually has done for us (v.16a). Love for the brethren is the actual test of our new life in Christ (v.14a). It is no marvel if Christians are hated by the world (v.13), but it is a wonder if they fail to love one another.

Tuesday, August 21, *I Corinthians* 15:20-23. The Resurrection of the body of the believer is directly related to the bodily Resurrection of Christ (v.20). Our hope of the Resurrection is based upon this fact (v. 20). Just as a result of Adam's disobedience death entered into the world - and upon all individuals - so new life comes to every believer because of Christ's Resurrection (v.22). Christ at His coming (v.23) will destroy that which Adam caused (v.26). Observe in the light of the tremendous authority and power which Christ has (v.24), the depth to which He stooped to save us from the powers of death (v.20). Would there have been any hope for us if He had not done this (vv.17-19)? Give thanks to God that He Who is all-powerful stooped to die and be resurrected that we might be raised.

Wednesday, August 22, *John* 13:31-35. The Last Supper has been celebrated (vv.1-2); the traitor has been announced (vv.21-30): the cross is at hand. Observe that Jesus does not mention the cross but prepares His disciples for His departure (13:31-14:4). Where is Jesus going (14:2-3)? Why cannot the disciples follow Him (vv.33,37)? Will Jesus come back again (14:3)? What provision does Jesus make for His disciples while He is gone (14:16-19,26-27)? Study the various ministries of the Holy Spirit in 14:16-19, 26-27. Is Christ's provision for His disciples adequate? What one commandment does He leave them (13:34)? Faced with a traitor in His midst and crucifixion on a cross, Jesus' sole interest at this point is in His disciples. In times of stress and strain can you be concerned for problems and needs of others?

Thursday, August 23, *Matthew* 28:16-20. The Gospels portray Christ as the Lamb of God; the Book of Revelation reveals Him in His Kingship. In giving the Great Commission the risen Christ manifests Himself in His Kingship (vv.18,20). His disciples give Him worship (v.17). He equates Himself with the other two members of the Trinity (v.19). He holds the future in His hands (v.20b). Compare this picture of Christ with that given in Revelation 1:5-7,17-19. Revelation 1:12-16,20 pictures Christ standing in the midst of His Churches clothed in all his regal authority. Meditate upon what Christ says about Himself in the Great Commission with the portrayal of Him in Revelation

1. Do you have a new sense of the authority and presence of the One Who has given you The Great Commission?

Friday, August 24, Matthew 26:26-30. We are not given any description of the deep emotions that must have been present in that last night before the cross. The traitor had been announced (vv.20-25); the disciples were soon to forsake Him (vv.31-35). One can tell from the words of Institution (vv.26-28), that Jesus knew exactly why He was to die. Notice that Jesus in this hour had His eyes not only on the cross, but on that day when He would return in power and great glory (v.29). The Lord's Supper was for the benefit of the disciples —to remind them of what He did for them on the cross; to assure them of His continual presence after His departure; to cause them to look forward to the Final Consummation. In the face of your darkest hours can you see hope beyond?

Saturday, August 25, Ephesians 5:25-27. The husband-wife relationship is compared to Christ's relation to His Church. In vv.21-33 study the relation of Christ to His Church. What verbs in vv.25,29 describe Christ's attitude toward Her? His purpose in His relationship with Her is to strengthen, nourish, and honor her (vv.26-27,29). The Church is subject to Christ because of His love for her (vv.23-24). This subjection on her part is voluntary and is because she loves Him. Think through the relation of Christ to His Church in terms of the relation of a Christian husband and wife. Is this a picture of a happy, harmonious home? How could this picture improve your home life?

ANGLERS

(From "*New Testament Evangelism*"

by Wade C. Smith)

Lesson No. 151

SUGGESTED PROGRAM FOR PERSONAL WORK GROUPS

Let us take for example a group of six, or eight, or ten. We will assume they have enlisted to do personal work. One of the number is chosen as leader, if not already appointed by the church's governing board. They are banded together as a unit in the church's forces to share in the accomplishment of the church's evangelistic objective. Their work may be described under three heads:

1. To pray for the unsaved in the community;

2. To carry the Gospel invitation to the unsaved;

3. To study how to increase in effectiveness as soul winners.

Prayer. They will pray as a group and in private for the salvation of those whom they seek, and also for the evangelistic objectives of the whole Church.

Carrying the Gospel to the unsaved. There should be a list of prospects for the group to definitely work upon. This list may be made up by the members of the group, or it may be supplied by the Pastor (he usually has such a list) - or the two lists combined. How individuals may discover prospects, and how to approach them, was dealt with in Lesson No. 143.

Cards bearing the names of prospects should be divided among the group. Here will come a real test of faith. It is the writer's firm conviction that the prospects should *not be chosen by the worker,* but be *assigned.* This can be safely done under the guidance of the Holy Spirit. Let the group pray that He will direct their hands as they draw them from the lot, (this is scriptural - see Acts 1:24-26), without looking at the names. If left to choose, it is but natural that one will endeavor to select the prospect whom he may think may be most easily approached. This would be shifting the effort into a merely human process. But it is the work of the Holy Spirit. The very one whom you would shrink most from approaching may be the one whom the Lord is going to give you a great blessing in winning. It may be safely said *there is no one in the community* whom you may not, under the guidance of the Holy Spirit, properly invite to accept Jesus Christ. That person may be your worst enemy. Then, this is the occasion of humbling yourself to win a soul to Jesus.

In a certain group the foregoing plan was adopted. Every man pledged beforehand that he would interview any prospect he might "draw" from the prospect cards, after asking the Holy Spirit's guidance. One man, a manufacturer, drew the name of his foreman. They had been friends, but through some labor troubles in the plant growing into a strike threat, which the manufacturer had reason to suspect his foreman had instigated, they had become enemies. The manufacturer dared not discharge the foreman, for fear of precipitating a tie-up. Imagine his feelings when that foreman's name fell into his hands as a prospect for evangelistic effort - the last man in the world he would have chosen to approach on such a subject. But he was game. He went back to his office, praying, and sent for the foreman. The man entered with a defiant air; he thought of course the interview would be on factory matters; but he was quickly disillusioned. The boss said, "Sit down, Jim; there are two things I want to tell you. The first is that I am a sinner in the sight of God, (Jim's face was covered with astonishment; his boss acknowledging *to him* that he was a sinner) but," continued the boss, "Jim, thank God I am a *saved* sinner, because I have accepted the Lord Jesus Christ as my Saviour; and the second thing I want to say to you, Jim, is that I want you to accept Him as your Saviour, too. You need Him, Jim, and I need Him; we are both sinners - the only difference is that I am a saved sinner, and without Christ you are a lost sinner. But it need not continue so. You can settle it right now; won't you take Him?" The boss told me about this, himself. He said that for a moment or two, Jim sat there like a man in a daze. Then his face brightened and he held out his hand to his boss, saying in his crude way, "It's a deal - I'm taking Him for mine, too; thank you, sir." Needless to say, there was no strike. The labor trouble vanished into thin air. The Holy Spirit knew what He was doing.

What a world of ill-feelings and misunderstandings would be dispelled between men and between nations if all who call themselves Christians would begin really trying to win souls to the Master, in the power and under the guidance of the Holy Spirit!

(More about the group program in the next lesson).

SABBATH SCHOOL LESSONS — REV. J. KENTON PARKER

LESSON FOR AUGUST 19

The Grounds Of Christian Assurance

Background Scripture: Matthew 6:25-34; I John 2:28 - 5:21
Devotional Reading: Psalm 46

Our Scripture selections suggest two kinds of Assurance: (1) The assurance that God will take care of us in this life, and (2) the assurance that God will take care of us in the world to come. The first passage teaches us not to be anxious and worried about the "things" we need here on earth, and the second, how we can "know" that we have eternal life. If we possess these two kinds of assurance we will be happy indeed.

The ground of our assurance—both kinds—is found in God; God's character, and God's promises. Our Devotional Reading (Psalm 46) makes this very clear. It starts with a cure for fear: "God is our refuge and strength . . . Therefore will not we fear." This earth is a stormy place. Nature sometimes gets on a "rampage," and nations are in constant turmoil and strife and war. We can "Be still, and know that I am God." There is a simple little picture which illustrates this comforting thought. It is the picture of a storm, and a little bird sitting on its nest as it sways back and forth in the gale. So our "nests" sometimes seem threatened with destruction. If the "God of Jacob is our refuge," we need not fear.

I. *The Assurance that God will take care of us in this life:* Matt. 6:25-34.

First, let me say, that these verses do not teach or encourage us to be idle or lazy. The Bible plainly commands us to work with our hands (and brains), in order to provide for those who are dependent upon us, and to have to give to those that need. Those who do not provide for their households are worse than the unbelievers. The Bible holds the lazy and idle man up to scorn: "Go to the ant, thou sluggard, consider her ways, and be wise," etc. God's saints are busy people; diligent in business, fervent in spirit, serving the Lord. Men like Joseph and Daniel stood before kings because they were diligent. The Saviour Himself sets us an example of honest toil. He was a Carpenter before He was a Preacher. When He began His ministry He said, I must work the works of Him that sent me while it is day.

These verses do teach us not to worry, or be anxious. Let us do our best to provide the "things" we need, and then trust our heavenly Father to take care of us and our loved ones. Even when we work hard and do our best there are many things which are beyond our control. I used to be a truck farmer. We would prepare our soil, plant our seed, work hard to make sure that we had a good yield, but sometimes a dry spell came and all our toil seemed in vain. One day we set out a thousand beautiful tomato plants, and that afternoon there came a terrible hail storm which destroyed them all. There are times when we need these verses badly. Let us see if we can find some reasons, given by our Great Teacher, which will help.

1. The life is more than food, and the body than raiment. Material possessions, however necessary and valuable, are not as precious, or as important, as spiritual possessions. A man can live a good while without food, and can live to a ripe old age on very simple food. Think of Elijah and John the Baptist, and the periods of fasting by Moses and Jesus. The body does not have to be clothed in beautiful garments; John had camel's hair and a leather girdle, and no man was greater than he. Our Master wore the simple robe provided by His friends. In these days we stress our "High Standard of Living." Is our "Standard" a mere material standard? No one ever had a higher standard than Jesus Christ, and He had none of the "things" we consider indispensable. Many of our modern conveniences add nothing to real life, and some of them shorten and hamper our lives. Many of us would be better off if we lived more simply. So our first lesson would suggest that many of the "things" we worry about are neither important or essential.

2. We are more valuable than birds, and God takes care of the birds. Birds are neither idle or lazy. They build their nests and hunt for their food. They do not expect their Creator to do these things for them; to bring their food to them or provide ready-made nests. Yet you never saw a bird die of worry. They expect their food to be provided, and it is.

Now Jesus says, Are ye not much better than they? If God, the Great Provider, sees to it that the fowls of the air have food, will He not look after His children? There have been famines caused by the sins of men, and at other times men starve because of greed, or cruelty, or indifference. There is plenty for all if properly distributed, or not destroyed by men. He even provided for the rebellious and evil; He sends rain upon the just and unjust. Will He not care for us?

3. God provides beautiful garments for the lilies of the field. Will He not provide clothing for the men and women He created? Flowers last but a few hours. We live for a long time.

4. Worry does not help. It hurts. It never adds one cubit to our stature; it does not lengthen life; it shortens it. It is a common saying that worry kills more people than hard work.

5. It is unbecoming in a child of God to be anxious and worried. Gentiles, or heathens, or unbelievers, might be excused, but surely we, His children, those who believe in Him, ought to trust Him. He is our heavenly Father.

6. He knows that we have need of these "things." He created us and is fully aware that we need food and clothing.

7. If we "put first things first"; if we seek first the kingdom of God and His righteousness, then all these "things" will be added to us. Here is His specific promise.

8. Let us not try to carry the burden of tomorrow, only the burden of the day in which we are living. "Give us day by day our daily bread," we ask in our familiar prayer. Life one day at a time, and all our days will be happier.

II. *Assurance for the Life to come:*
I John 2:28 - 5:21.

How can we know that we have eternal life? Surely, that is the most important of questions, and the man who can answer in the affirmative is a happy man. Paul is very fond of this word, "know" : I know whom I have believed and am persuaded that He is able to keep that which I have committed unto Him; We know that we have a tabernacle not made with hands eternal in the heavens; etc.

John, in this first Epistle, is telling us how we may be sure that we have eternal life. I would like to point out three "Tests" which we find in these verses. They form three contrasts. They are mingled together, overlap, and supplement each other.

1. The Test of Righteousness in contrast with Sin. In verse 29 of chapter 2 we find these words: "If ye know that he is righteous, ye know that every one that doeth righteousness is born of him." This is the same test that Jesus suggests when He says, By their fruits ye shall know them. In verse 9 of Chapter 3 it is put in even stronger words: "Whosoever is born of God doth not commit sin; for his seed remaineth in him: and he cannot sin, because he is born of God. In this the children of God are manifest, and the children of the devil." Let us ask ourselves the question, Am I living a life of sin, or a life of obedience to God? The man who is continuing to live the same old life of sin can have no assurance that he is a child of God. If you are a child of God, then you have a new nature; old things are passed away, all things are become new. You hate sin. You turn from it. You grieve over it and confess it and seek immediate forgiveness. The "seed" within you cannot sin, and will enable you to conquer the "old man," and put the "new man" in control. Look for fruit in your life, the fruit of the Spirit. Fruit, more fruit, much fruit, fruit that endures unto eternal life. The Spirit gives you victory over sin.

2. The Test of Love in contrast with Hatred: "We know that we have passed from death unto life, because we love the brethren." He that loveth not knoweth not God; for God is love. Do we love sin? This is a sure sign that we are not "born again." Do we love God? Then

we have the witness of the Spirit that we are children of God. Do we love our fellow men, and especially our brethren? If a man say, I love God, and hate his brother, then he is a liar, for how can we love God, Whom we have not seen, if we do not love our brother whom we have seen? Hatred has no place in the Christian's heart. It is the mark of the world.

3. The Test of Faith in contrast with Unbelief.

In 5:1 we read: "Whosoever believeth that Jesus is the Christ is born of God." In verse 10: "He that believeth on the Son of God hath the witness in himself." In verse 13: "These things have I written unto you that believe on the name of the Son of God: that ye may know that ye have eternal life, and that ye may believe on the name of the Son of God." Do we have a living Faith, not merely an intellectual assent, but a faith that works by love, and brings forth the fruits of righteousness.

Here are three "Tests" that we may apply to our hearts and lives. Let us never be content or satisfied until "we know that we have eternal life."

YOUNG PEOPLE'S DEPARTMENT — REV. B. HOYT EVANS

YOUTH PROGRAM FOR AUGUST 19

What The Bible Says About Christ

Suggested Devotional Outline:

Hymn: "O For A Thousand Tongues To Sing"

Prayer

Scripture: Acts 2:14-36

Hymn: "Jesus, The Very Thought Of Thee"

Offering

Hymn: "There Is A Green Hill Far Away"

Suggested Procedure:

(Write all the Scripture references contained in the program on slips of paper. Ask the young people to bring their Bibles to the meeting. Distribute the references among them, ask the speakers to call on them to read the verses at the appropriate places.)

Program Leader's Introduction:

The Bible is the source book for Christianity. The basic reason for its occupying this important place in our religion is that it introduces us to Christ and tells us what we need to know about Him. What we know about Christ is the heart and soul of Christianity, and the Bible supplies that knowledge. Both the breadth and the depth of Scriptural teaching about Christ is so great that we could not begin to deal with all of it in one program. Our purpose here is to consider some of the central truths about Christ as they are found in the Bible.

First Speaker:

A fundamental part of the knowledge of Christ which we need to have concerns His nature. What does the Bible have to say about the nature of Christ? In brief, the Bible tells us that Christ has a two-fold nature. He is both God and man. There is abundant evidence in Scripture to throughly establish these basic truths.

The Bible clearly claims that Christ is God. (Read John 1:1). "The Word" surely refers to Christ, for in the same chapter (v. 14) we read, "the Word was made flesh and dwelt among us." (Read Matthew 16:16). Jesus not only permitted this statement of Peter's to stand, but said that it was divinely revealed. (Read John 10:30). Here we have Jesus' own clear claim that He is God.

There are many other words and ways by which the Bible establishes that Christ is God. Scriptures ascribe to Christ divine qualities. God alone is eternal, but hear what the Bible says of Christ: (Read John 1:1.) Only God is all-powerful, but this is what Jesus said of Himself: (Read Matthew 28:18.) Unchangeableness belongs to God alone. Hear what the Bible says of Christ: (Read Hebrews 13:8.)

There are some works which can be done only by God, and many of these are ascribed by Scripture to Christ. Only God can create. Hear what the Bible says of Christ: (Read John 1:3 and Col. 1:16.) No one but God can forgive sins, but Jesus forgave the sins of the palsied man as recorded in Matthew 9:2 and Mark 2:5. No one but God has the right to judge or the power to raise the dead, but consider what the Bible says of Jesus: (Read John 5:21,22.) All of these considerations make it plain that the Bible claims a divine nature for Christ.

One of Christ's favorite names for Himself during the days of His earthly ministry was the "Son of man." This name tells us of His human nature, and that He is the representative of humanity. The genealogy recorded in Luke traces His human ancestry back to Adam. Scripture tells us that He was born of the Virgin Mary, that He grew and was subject to His earthly parents, that He became weary, that

He ate food, that He drank water, that He was saddened, that He suffered at the hands of the Romans, that He died on the cross, and that He was buried. All of these are clearly taught in Scripture, and all these are very human things. A careful reading of the New Testament, and especially of the Gospels, will convince any thoughtful, reasonable person that Christ possesses a very real human nature.

Second Speaker:

Another fundamental teaching of the Bible concerning Christ has to do with the reason for His coming to earth as a man. The Scripture makes a very clear statement of the reason. (Read Luke 19:10 and Mark 10:45.) The Bible tells us that Christ came to save His human creatures from their sins, and that He came because of the love of God. (Read Romans 6:23 and John 3:16.)

The purpose of Christ's coming makes it clear to us why it was necessary for Him to have two natures. It was needful for Him to have the human nature so that He could be our true representative. He had to share our nature before He could bear our sin. It was necessary for Him to have the divine nature in order to be an acceptable sin-bearer before God. Every sinful person must die for his own sin, but Christ the Son of God had no sin. The Bible explains it so fully in these passages: (Read II Corinthians 5:21, I Peter 1:18,19, and I Peter 2:24.) The Bible tells us that in Christ we find the righteous God taking the place of His sinful creatures and dying for them that they might live for and with Him.

Third Speaker:

There are many other important truths about Christ taught in the Bible, but one demands our attention because it is so basic. It is the resurrection. (Read Acts 2:32.) It is said that there is no better attested fact in all ancient history than the apostle's belief in the resurrection, and they came to this conviction out of great doubt. Not only does the resurrection prove Christ's victory, but it is the seal of hope for those who believe in Him. (Read I Corinthians 15:20, 22 and Hebrews 7:25.)

What the Bible says about Christ is so clear and so convincing that we can well understand that the best way of leading a person to believe in Jesus is to let him hear and read what the Scriptures say.

Women's Work

The Women's Birthday Gift

Montreat—

Two checks, totaling more than $175,000, were presented to officials of the Presbyterian Church, U. S., here July 19th when the Women of the Church brought in their annual "Birthday Offering" to specific projects of the Church.

The gift, presented during the annual Women's Training School, is the largest ever given by the Women of the Church for a project inside the borders of the Church, and additional donations will be coming in for some time. The gift has been exceeded only by the $200,000 Birthday Offering of 1955, which went to a missionary project—the building of the Yodagawa Christian Hospital, Osaka, Japan.

Largest check presented, for $100,549.35, went to Dr. P. D. Miller, executive secretary of the Board of Church Extension, Atlanta, for use in expansion of the Ybor City Mission work among Latin Americans in Tampa, Fla. The other check, for $75,000, was given to Dr. Marshall C. Dendy, executive secretary of the Board of Christian Education, Richmond, Va., for use in Area Laboratory Schools, in which Sunday School teachers are given training.

Presentation of the Birthday Offering was made by Miss Mary S. Quidor, treasurer of the Board of Women's Work, Atlanta; Mrs. A. R. Craig, chairman of the Board, from Rutherfordton, N. C.; and Mrs. L. M. McCutchen, executive secretary of the Board, Atlanta.

Dr. Miller, in accepting the large check, declared that "Those who are responsible for Ybor City Mission are most grateful for this magnificent gift from the Women of the Church. It will be used immediately for the erection of the West Tampa Presbyterian Church, as an extension, in a new area, of the Ybor City work which has been so successfully directed by the Rev. Walter Passiglia.

'A large and well-located lot has been secured," Dr. Miller explained, "for this new mission and plans are already drawn for the building to be erected. This building will house a full-time operation, including kindergarten, scouting, recreation, and preaching services. The building should be ready for occupancy early in 1957. Because of early and wise planning by the people of Tampa, assisted by the Rev. O. V. Caudill of the Board of Church Extension, there will be no delay in getting this new project under way."

Dr. Dendy told the representatives of 339,000 women in 17 states that the Board of Christian Education has already begun to spend the gift for laboratory schools, in anticipation of receiving it.

"Children do not wait for the Church to provide a teaching ministry before they grow," Dr. Dendy explained. "There is such a vast host of children in our Church now that your Board of Christian Education felt it wise to begin to use the Women's Birthday Fund in 1956. Already, therefore, six Area Laboratory Schools have been established. The total enrollment as of this date numbers 299, with the number continuing to grow.

"Let me thank you on behalf of the thousands of children who are going to be benefitted by the teachings of the leaders who will be attending these schools. Eleven synods are being served by these schools. Every teacher who attends a laboratory school will return to the Sunday School better prepared to guide children, better informed about methods of work, and with new vision and renewed inspiration for the task.

"We believe the Women of the Church are going to find great joy in knowing that your children and your grandchildren are going to receive the finest kind of instruction in our Christian faith and life as a result of your gift. What we are able to do for our children today will pay dividends for Eternity," Dr. Dendy concluded.

In presenting the $175,000 gift, Women of the Church officials revealed that the largest single synod gift came from Texas, with a total of $25,678.88, but that per capita gifts from the Synods of Louisiana and Mississippi, both leaders last year, out-ranked all others. Louisiana, which trailed Mississippi in 1955, took the lead this year with an average of 67.4 cents, compared with 67.1, for Mississippi. The Synod of Appalachia was third with a 61 cent per member average.

REPORT TO DATE —
1956 BIRTHDAY OFFERING FOR YBOR MISSION EXPANSION AND AREA LABORATORY SCHOOLS

Synodical	*Total Offering*	*Per Capita*
Alabama	$7,181.70	.47
Appalachia	10,509.46	.61
Arkansas	4,901.17	.56
Florida	13,465.40	.49
Georgia	12,450.76	.45
Kentucky	5,966.89	.51
Louisiana	7,554.00	.67
Mississippi	8,481.49	.67
Missouri	5,565.47	.51
North Carolina	24,291.23	.44
Oklahoma	1,301.24	.56
Snedecor Region	411.50	.41
South Carolina	12,827.55	.54
Tennessee	7,885.58	.60
Texas	25,678.88	.57
Virginia	20,329.79	.44
West Virginia	5,747.24	.45
	$174,549.35	
Individual gifts	38.00	
Total Offering	$175,587.35	

Texas leads all Synodicals with largest gift—$25,678.88.

North Carolina — $24,291.23.

Louisiana leads all Synodicals in per capita giving — .674.

Mississippi — .671.

Appalachia — .61.

Mary S. Quidor, Treasurer

Christian Stewardship

On the shores of a northern lake away from traffic and telephones a family of six are spending a month of happy holidaying together. The young sons are discovering that Dad is not just a professional man on call day or night to relieve pain, but another "boy grown up," who welcomes this chance to build camp-fires, fish and study nature lore with his family.

It is well that society recognizes the need of respite from work and school and tensions and that in camp or cottage we may turn for a time at least to life's simplicities. Here we may take time off to know those for whom we care the most, our sons, our daughters, our husbands or wives. Best of all in this holidaying together we discover that life can be rich in the things that money cannot buy, that much of the high standard of living can be an empty thing unless it is accompanied by a high standard of life.

The cleverly engineered radio emanating raspy so-called music, the television emphasizing the urge to win at all costs, the beautiful car, the house that has everything except a book—is this the culture we desire for our coming generation? Was it not a wise person who wrote "Help me to live content with small means, to seek elegance rather than luxury, refinement rather than fashion . . . ?"

In my mail a while ago came a card to which was fastened an intriguing key. Underneath was the caption, "Unlock the door and a super de luxe model is yours." Here was just another means of chasing "the something for nothing." Few magic keys unlock doors without a price.

We have all heard it said many times that a real home can only be built on love. This key, if any, has magic in it. Yet we today are so anxious to give our children, our grandchildren things rather than principles or standards that we lose sight of that most important of all gifts. Through our blundering rather than our children's, they lose all sense of values and appreciation.

Gratitude, the psychologists tell us, need not be expected to any noticeable degree in youth. It is not until later years of discretion that adolescents realize what denials have been necessary to parents in order to give them the privileges of today. It is nevertheless not right that we should delay in teaching them what stewardship means—giving their time without pay and that in their receiving they should learn that it costs in time or money or energy.. May it not be that we are today reaping the unfortunate results of days when mothers doing double duty had neither the energy nor inclination to teach the value of two of the most wonderful words in the English or, in fact, any language—"Thank You?"

It is not alone children who accept without appreciation. Adults are equal offenders. Because we pay well today for work done, is no reason to omit the smile or word of gratitude. And how many a voluntary worker in our Society would be inspired to further efforts by a kindly "thank you" or "well done?"

The simplicity of cottage living gives greater time to show our families that St. Paul was right in his description in I Corinthians, 13 of the spectrum of love which has nine ingredients. The place we call home requires all of them to make it happy. They are patience . . . kindness . . . generosity . . . humility . . . courtesy . . . unselfishness . . . good temper . . . guilelessness . . . sincerity.

This lovely paraphrase by an author unknown illustrates the Stewardship of everyday living.

Blessed is she whose daily tasks are a labor of love for she translates duty into privilege.

Blessed is she who mends stockings and toys and broken hearts, for her understanding is a balm to humanity.

Blessed is she who serves laughter and smiles with the meals for she shall be blessed with goodness.

Blessed is she who preserves the sanctity of the Christian home, for hers is a sacred trust that crowns her with dignity.

(Mrs. Gordon) Estelle H. Watts

Printed with permission of the editor of The Missionary Monthly

They Care Enough

This is "a taleof two cities," two cities in Texas whose citizens care enough about migrant workers to treat them as people should be treated in a Christian society.

First, community action in El Campo—

El Campo is a farmers' town. It has a population of about 7,000 to 8,000, a town square that serves as a park, two weekly newspapers, a chamber of commerce known as "Chamber of Commerce and Agriculture," and a generous share of good rice and cotton farm land. For years El Campo has been a key town in the movement of migrant labor.

As many as 10,000 have been in town on one weekend, and 15,000 to 18,000 travel through this town during the harvest season. It is a town the migrants like to go to because "they turn the town over to them." Nevertheless, last year a Migrant Ministry project was the first effort to do anything for the migrants on a community or church level.

The project was a Welcome Center under a tent in the center of the town square. Equipment was donated and young people volunteered, newspapers gave good publicity, a profound impression was the result. A staff member showed a set of slides at a church service which a City Councilman attended. When he saw pictures of showers at a camp in another community, he went into action and the City Council and Chamber of Commerce and Agriculture cooperated to set aside money to double the sanitary facilities at the park and to install showers.

Second, the case of a girl with cerebral palsy—

There was a week of rain in Lubbock just as the harvest was beginning. Crews could not go to work, and many were out of money and food. One family at the Migrant Ministry reception center told a staff member of another family with no food.

A visit to the family also disclosed a five-year-old girl who could not walk. The family said she had polio, but the staff worker suggested a visit to the public health nurse. The nurse suspected cerebral palsy and recommended a visit for the child to the local Treatment Center. Examination confirmed the nurse's opinion that it was not a severe case. The girl could learn to walk with the help of braces and training.

The doctor in charge took a genuine interest in the girl and arranged for the braces from public funds. A member of the local committee volunteered to provide transportation for weekly treatments. The child's mother sold tamales each weekend to make up for the money she

Church News

World Missions

Montreat — The appointment of three new missionaries and the election of officers for the coming year were highlights of the annual summer meeting of the Board of World Missions here in early July.

All three new missionaries will serve in Brazil. The Rev. and Mrs. Ernest Herbert Mellor, Jr., of Guntersville, Ala., and Miss Lida Edmonia Knight of Columbus, Ohio, are the appointees.

Miss Knight, who is now attending the Institute for Outgoing Missionaries here in Montreat, will work in the East Brazil Mission on a five-year short-term appointment. She will serve as an itinerant choir director in an effort to improve the quality of choir and congregational music in mission and National Presbyterian Churches. Miss Knight is a graduate of Muskingum College, and has been attending Assembly's Training School. She has exceptional linguistic ability and has been designated to take an intensive course in Portugese even though given a short-term appointment. Short-term missionaries are not normally required to take heavy work in the native language. Miss Knight has had experience in mission work, having served the United Presbyterian Church, of which she is a member, as a missionary at Pressly Memorial Institute, Assuit, Egypt, on a short-term appointment. She will go to the field in the fall of this year.

Mr. and Mrs. Mellor, however, will not go out until the fall of 1957, after they have attended the Institute for Outgoing Missionaries in that year. He is pastor of the First Church of Guntersville, and a native of El Dorado, Ark. Mrs. Mellor is the former Lalla Brown of St. George, S. C. Mr. Mellor is a graduate of Centenary College of Louisiana and Columbia Theological Seminary, and his wife holds a degree from Converse College, Spartanburg, S. C.

Dr. Wm. M. Elliott, pastor of Highland Park Presbyterian Church, Dallas, was re-elected chairman of the Missions Board, and first and second vice-chairman were also re-elected. These are Dr. Jas. A. Jones, president of Union Theological Seminary, Richmond, and Mr. Wm. H. McCord, Nashville, Tenn., businessman, respectively.

Committee chairman elected by the Board are Mr. McCord, for Business and Finance; Dr. James E. Bear, of Richmond, for Candidates and Recruits; Dr. Jones for Fields; Dr. Harry M. Moffett of Gastonia, N. C., for Home Base; and Dr. H. E. Russell of Montgomery, Ala., for Overseas Relief and Inter-Church Aid.

During its session the Board also heard two special presentations, one by its secretary of Overseas Relief and Inter-Church Aid, the Rev. Paul B. Freeland, and the other by Athens, Ga., businessman Mr. C. A. Rowland.

Mr. Rowland, for 23 years a member of the Board, reported to the Board on his presentation of a copy of the film "Martin Luther" to the Rev. Milton Daugherty, head of the Language School in Campinas, Sao Paulo, Brazil. Mr. and Mrs. Daugherty are just returning to Brazil after a year's furlough. Mr. Rowland offered to supply additional copies of the film for any other mission field in which it might be shown. Mr. Rowland also stressed his belief that there is much need for printed Gospels in native tongues, and suggested that the Board put offset presses in Brazilian and African fields.

Mr. Freeland, in the other special report, told of his just-completed trip to Europe and the Near East, taking part in the Second Beirut (Lebanon) Conference on Refugee Problems, and in the annual World Council of Churches conference on Inter-Church Aid in Les Rasses, Switzerland.

In the course of the trip, Mr. Freeland visited 11 countries where the Presbyterian Church, U. S., has had a part in mission, relief, or inter-church aid work. By special permission, Mr. Freeland and others of the group studying refugee problems was permitted to enter the Gaza Strip, the first such group to do so.

An increasingly serious problem in Korea was considered by the Board, and action was taken authorizing Dr. Hugh Bradley, Field Secretary, and Mr. Curry B. Hearn, Treasurer, to attempt to work out a solution to the problem. The difficulty is that the mission has been doing all its money exchanging through the Bank of Korea at a fixed rate which has become increasingly unrealistic, compared to the exchange rates on the open market. The result has been that mission dollars have had a steadily decreasing purchasing power as the value of the Korean currency decreases. Other missions are experiencing the same difficulty. Mr. Hearn and Dr. Bradley were asked to work with representatives of the Presbyterian, U. S. A. Board of Missions, and that of the Methodist Church, in attempts to obtain U. S. Government sanction to an improved official exchange rate.

The retirement, effective June 1, 1957, of the Rev. and Mrs. J. V. N. Talmage from service in Korea was accepted by the Board. Deep gratitude for the more than 40 years of service given by this couple was expressed by the Board, and special notice was taken of the contributions they have made, both in their own work, and through their children, three of whom are now in active missionary service in Korea.

The Missions Board also heard the report of a special committee, headed by Board member, Dr. L. Nelson Bell of Montreat, N. C., on distribution of free drugs to mission doctors. The committee has been able to contact several doctors who are giving for missionary use thousands of dollars worth of drugs. These drugs for the most part have been provided the doctors as samples, and cannot be sold. Dr. Bell reported that one doctor had already sent more than $15,000 worth of drugs to mission hospitals in Africa, and several additional thousands have gone from other sources to Korea and Mexico. Additional assistance in this work, from doctors, is being sought.

On the recommendation of the Home Base Committee, for cooperation with the Men's Convention in Miami in 1957, the Board approved bringing three outstanding native Christians from mission fields served by the Church. One each from the Congo, Brazil, and Mexico are to be invited.

At the recommendation of the Fields Committee, three persons were named to represent the Board on the Joint Committee for the Iraq mission. The Board voted in May to cooperate with three other Presbyterian churches in a mission work in that Moslem land. Named to sit on the joint committee were Mrs. H. D. Haberyan of Shreveport, La.; Mr. T. M. Barnhardt, Jr., of Charlotte, N. C.; and Dr. C. Darby Fulton, executive secretary, Nashville. The committee will hold its first meeting with the U. S. Church representatives present on Oct. 17. The Board further voted $2,500 for the last quarter of 1956 for support of the work in Iraq, even though no missionaries from this Church are yet on the field.

Montreat — The Board of World Missions of the Presbyterian Church, U. S., has asked that the Rev. Eugene Daniel, candidate secretary of the Board, and Mr. Bluford B. Hestir, director of publicity for the General Council of the Church, make a six-weeks trip to the mission fields in the Orient.

Mr. Daniel was asked to make a special survey of needs for missionaries, and of the requirements for personnel serving in Korea, Japan and Taiwan. Mr. Hestir will work with missionary personnel to help them develop skills in reporting the work of the missions to the Church, will prepare stories on the work in progress, and will take pictures for use with publicity and educational promotion of the three mission fields.

The pair were asked to go out in September and return in time for a report to the November meeting of the Board.

GEORGIA

The first sermon in the new $200,000 air-conditioned Vineville Presbyterian Church of Macon, Georgia, was delivered on July 15, 1956, by the pastor, Dr. Wade P. Huie, Jr. His topic was "The Doors of Thanksgiving." The dedication of the new church building will not be held until September 23 when special services will be held during that week. Dr. Marc C. Weersing, pastor of the First Presbyterian Church of Spartanburg, S. C., will be the guest speaker.

The Vineville Presbyterian Church has long been a spiritual leader in its community and the City of Macon as a whole. The idea of the church originated with the late Messrs. G. T. Kinnett and T. B. Lowry and the first sanctuary was occupied on Nov. 12, 1904, with a membership of 39. This building was later moved and used as a manse, and at present is serving as a Sunday School Annex. The second sanctuary, which was demolished to make room for the present new building, was occupied on July 26, 1910.

Cherokee Presbytery met Friday, July 13th at the First Presbyterian Church in Rome, Ga., in a called meeting.

Mr. Bronson Matney, Jr., recent graduate of Columbia Theological Seminary, was examined for the Gospel Ministry. He was received as a member of Cherokee Presbytery, pending his ordination, which will take place at the First Presbyterian Church, Rome, Ga., Sunday July 22nd, at 7:30 P.M. Members of the commission to ordain Mr. Matney include Dr. L. R. Scott, pastor of the First Church, Rome, Ga. Dr. S. Wilkes Dendy, pastor of the First Presbyterian Church, Dalton, Ga., the Rev. Dan Dunaway, pastor of the Rockmart Presbyterian Church, the Rev. Sam Magbee, pastor of the Westminster Presbyterian Church, Rome, Ga., and the Rev. H. Graham Keys, pastor of the Reynolds Miller and Silver Creek Presbyterian Churches, Rome, Ga. Mr. Matney has been called to serve as assistant minister of the First Church, Rome, Ga.

Mr. Jack Cushman, son of Mr. and Mrs. Edward A. Cushman, of Smyrna, Ga., was received as a

---

Progress report of the Presbytery's success in the Consolidated College - Campus Christian Life campaign was made by Mr. J. W. McLaney. A resolution was passed that the campaign be pressed to a conclusion.

The call of McQuay Memorial Church for the pastoral services of Rev. Clifford D. Caldwell was approved and a Commission was appointed to install him.

Presbytery's Council through its chairman, Rev. A. Leslie Thompson, presented a budget for all causes of $610,760.00. The Presbytery united with the First Presbyterian Church of Charlotte in extending an invitation to the General Assembly to hold its 1958 sessions in the historic downtown church of which Rev. E. Lee Stoffel is pastor.

The Fall meeting will be held on September 8th at Camp Stewart - the host being the Committee on Christian Education. Mr. J. W. McLaney, Sr., is Moderator - Nominee. Stated Clerk Rev. Malcolm L. Williamson was assisted by Revs. A. Leslie Thompson and Robt. W. Rayburn.

R. H. Stone, Secretary

TENNESSEE

Columbia — The Congregation of Zion Church in a regularly called meeting on May 27, 1956, elected four additional Deacons. They are Messrs. John A. Bryant, Stanley Jewell, Billy R. Leach, and Dan Parsons. They accepted the office and were duly ordained and installed on June 17, 1956.

Columbia Presbytery at a called meeting at Na-Co-Me on June 12, granted the request of Zion Church for the full time service of the pastor, Mr. W. M. Ford, beginning July 1, 1956. Under the ministry of Mr. Ford Zion Church is carrying on a full program of the activities of the church. In 1957 a celebration of 150 years of continuous service since 1807 is planned at Zion Church.

RURAL "MINISTERS OF THE YEAR"

Atlanta — Four Presbyterian ministers were selected "Rural Minister of the Year" in their respective states, at the annual Church and Community Workshop at Emory University, July 18. The awards are sponsored jointly by Emory and the Progressive Farmer Magazine.

Dr. John T. Barr, Sr., of Norman , Arkansas; the Rev. Thomas M. Dews, McIntosh, Fla.; Dr. James M. Carr, Atlanta, Ga.; and the Rev. James W. Newton, Burnet, Texas, are the four Presbyterians from a total of eleven Southern ministers receiving awards.

Since 1949, sixty-seven persons from the eighteen denominations have been so honored. They were selected for their outstanding contributions to the development and progress of the support of rural church program in all its phases, and to their overall support of the community activities in their towns. Alexander Nunn, editor of the Progressive Farmer Magazine, made the award presentations.

All four Presbyterian winners received congratulatory telegrams from the governors of their respective states, and all but Dr. Barr were at Emory for the award presentation.

Dr. Barr, a Presbyterial home missionary for Ouachita Presbytery in the Synod of Arkansas, is serving a fluctuating number of rural churches. At one time he was serving eleven, eight of which he himself had founded. These are growing churches and the number which he is serving personally is now declining. He has pastoral duties at the Lake Village, Norman, and Caddo Gap churches, and serves Good Hope Churches near Big Fork; Mazarn Church, Bonnerdale; Oak Grove Church, Caddo Gap; and Owley Church near Norman. Dr. Barr is a native of Hope, Arkansas. He is a graduate of Arkansas College, from which he also holds the honorary degree of Doctor of Divinity, and of Union Seminary in Richmond. He has been the stated clerk for Ouachita Presbytery for 35 years, and for the Synod of Arkansas for the past 32 years.

Mr. Dews is now serving a Larger Parish out of Gainesville, Fla., including Kanapaha Presbyterian Church in Gainesville, and the Fairfield, Reddick, McIntosh, and Micanopy Presbyterian Churches in the towns by those names. He is a graduate of Presbyterian College and Columbia Theological Seminary and before going to Florida, he served as assistant pastor at the First Presbyterian Church, Albany, Ga.

Dr. Carr, who for the past seven years has headed the Town and Country Church Department for the denomination, was named Rural Minister of the Year in the state of Georgia. He is a native of Wallace, N. C., and a graduate of Davidson College and Union Seminary, Richmond. Following pastorates in Virginia, he became Regional Director of Religious Education for the Synods of Georgia, South Carolina, and later for the Synod of Appalachia. In 1945 he was moderator of the Synod of Appalachia. Dr. Carr is author of the current Home Mission Study Book, "Bright Future —A New Day For the Town and Country Church." As Secretary of the Town and Country Church department, with headquarters in Atlanta, Dr. Carr conducts and plans Town and Country Church convocations, conducts summer classes for lay workers in the small churches, helps obtain and direct Sunday School Extension workers in the synods, and speaks throughout the General Assembly on town and country church activities.

Mr. Newton, award winner in Texas, has been serving Burnet, Ilano, and Leander Presbyterian Churches. He recently organized, with the permission of his presbytery, and at the request of resort area businessmen and retired persons living there, the First Union Church of Buchanan Dam, which had a charter membership of 23 persons from six denominations. Two additional ministers are being called to serve the Larger Parish (including these four churches), with Mr. Newton, since the churches are growing so rapidly.

Bishop Arthur J. Moore, resident bishop of the Atlanta Area, delivered the principal address at the banquet at which the ministers of the year were announced. The Church and Community Workshop, an interdenominational group, met for a three-weeks session of work and study at Emory, with the banquet and announcement of citations climaxing the meeting on the evening of July 18.

— BOOKS —

I WAGER ON GOD. Hunter B. Blakely. John Knox Press, Richmond, Virginia. $3.00.

The text of this volume is taken from Pascal's **Pensees.** Writing on the necessity of the wager, Pascal said, "You must wager. It is not optional . . . Let us weigh the gain and the loss in wagering that God is."

This book, the author tells us, is written as a kind of self-confession of how across the years one individual has sought to build a more satisfying faith through the hard process of doubting, searching, reading, and thinking. He holds that faith is God's gift, but as most of God's gifts, it comes only by full cooperation as we labor with the great Giver.

There are fifteen chapters in this volume. The author discusses such themes as "What Christ Means to Me," "God's Word to Man," "That Unique Community," "The Daily Business of the Christian," and "Faith Brings Power."

Dr. Blakely defines faith as "something that is sure and certain enough for one to fasten to for keeps." He has some excellent things to say about faith, but unfortunately he does not always make clear that by faith he is thinking of the Christian faith. Many people today seem to have faith in faith and, for the most part, use the term "faith" ambiguously.

The first chapter of this book puts the emphasis upon the Blakely view of faith rather than the New Testament doctrine of faith. The author is right in insisting that there should be such a thing as "my faith," but we must never forget that there is also such a thing as **"the faith."**

The finest chapter in this volume is called, "That Unique Community." He describes the Church of the New Testament as a society of humble penitents who claimed God's forgiveness day after day and looked to God for power to become better men and women. The early Church, he said, was a fellowship of hope seeking that perfection which they knew they had not yet attained.

The author makes this timely appeal. "The members of the Body of Christ should attempt great things for their Head. He calls them to high standards of personal conduct. They can no longer live as children of this world; they are now children of God, princes and princesses of Heaven. Their conduct must be in accord with this high expectation of their Saviour. They can have no other goal than Christ-likeness."

It is regrettable that Dr. Blakely's view of the Bible does not conform to the views held by our Southern Presbyterian Church since its inception. Writing concerning the book of Job, he said, "The book of Job, for illustration, is built around the story of a good man who experienced fearful suffering. Doubtless such a story of the suffering Job has been told and retold across the years until it became embedded in the traditions of the people of the East. Finally a supremely great thinker with artistry of literary genius took up the old story. Sophocles did the story of Antigone and Shakespeare the tale of Hamlet, Prince of Denmark, and wove into it some of man's finest thinking about the fundamental question, What is the meaning of faith for the time of suffering? The author of Job lived probably in the Sixth Century B. C. when the world had crashed in for the Hebrew people; their nation was conquered, Jerusalem in ruins, and many of their kinsmen either dead or in captivity."

This quotation indicates that the author has adopted the higher critical view of the Bible held by liberals without offering a particle of evidence to support this position. He does not intimate the existence of the conservative position. Granted that the question of the authorship of the book of Job is complicated, it should be pointed out that conservative scholars have held that this book was written not later than during the reign of Solomon. This view has antiquity to commend it. It was advanced by Martin Luther, and during the Nineteenth Century defended by such able scholars as Haevernick, Keil, and Delitzsch. Furthermore, Dr. Blakely's view makes no mention of divine and plenary inspiration, and the implication is, the authorship must be put on a par with Sophocles and Shakespeare.

Writing concerning the book of Jonah, Dr. Blakely affirms, "Whether the book of Jonah is a short story with a powerful moral or a narrative of factual history is of secondary importance." We disagree with this notion since the imprimatur of Christ Himself is placed upon the historicity of this book. We do not think that we have any right to put it into the category of a mere short story. (Matt. 12:39, Matt. 16:4, Luke 11:29-30).

Again the author is quite loose in his thinking on the book of Daniel. He writes, "The reader may find this message, whether he decides on the basis of evidence that Daniel is a tract written for the underground movements of Palestine in the time of Antiochus Epiphanes or considers it to be a bit of history from Babylon."

There are certain features of this book that are worthy of commendation. The author's desire to sound a note of reality is a refreshing one. In our final evaluation of this volume, however, we must frankly confess that certain sections of it are disappointing. For example, take a statement like this, "The Christian thinks of man as a child of God" (p.163). This idea is not Biblical. It is not in harmony with Chapter XIV of the **Confession of Faith.** The Christian thinks of the believer in Christ as a child of God, but not man as man. (John 1:12). Frankly, we have a right to expect a better quality of theology from one who holds the office of Secretary of the Division of Higher Education of the Presbyterian Church, U. S.

This reviewer has always made it a policy to be as generous as the elasticity of his conscience would allow in making an honest appraisal of a book produced by a brother minister in our Communion. It is, therefore, a source of real regret that we find it necessary to point out such weaknesses as are found in this volume. It seems that one who holds an official position in our Church should show greater interest in and respect for the official theology of our Church. There is no index to this volume, but in all of the references and footnotes, and they are numerous, we can find only one reference to our Westminster Standards.

We are convinced that the concessive Apologetics found here must be considered faulty and not in the best interest of full-orbed Christianity. It is logically easier and safer to defend the high truths of Christianity set forth in the Westminster Standards than the lower views expressed in some of these chapters. Christianity is objectively real, and we must be careful lest in our anxiety to appeal to "the modern mind" we fall into the bottomless pit of subjecticism. J.R.R.

JESUS OF YESTERDAY AND TODAY. Samuel G. Craig. Presbyterian and Reformed Publishing Co. $2.75.

Dr. Craig, former editor of **The Presbyterian,** is an able writer and a profound theologian. He has the ability to express theological concepts in understandable language. In this volume he gives us an explication of the statement found in the Epistle to the Hebrews that "Jesus Christ is the same yesterday, and today, yea, and forever."

The main thrust of this volume is to get the reader to realize that Jesus Christ is the same as He ever was, that there is nothing that He has been to any past generation that He may not be to this generation—the generation of which we are a part.

The author insists, "that there is nothing that He has ever been to the most outstanding of His saints that He does not stand willing to be to the weakest and most insignificant of those who would fain call themselves His . . . Since He abides the same through every change and chance of time, we need only repeat their faith in order that we may repeat their victory." There will never be a generation, says Dr. Craig, whose needs Jesus Christ is not able to meet and satisfy.

The fact of Christ's immutability, says Dr. Craig, is that which separates the Gospels from all other biographies. Other biographies tell us what men once were but give us no dependable knowledge of what they are like today. The Gospel biographies, however, not only tell us what Jesus was like 1900 years ago, they tell us what He is also like today. It is this that makes them the most living, the most up-to-date of all books. This is why the Christianity of today is essentially one with the Christianity of the first century. This is true because the Christ who makes it what it is abides the same as age succeeds age.

Due to this fact, Dr. Craig remarks, "No doubt much that is called Christianity today is radically different from the Christianity of the New Testament. But that merely advertises the fact that much of what is called Christianity today is Christianity falsely so-called. There are, of course, unessential changes, but since the object of the Christian faith is the unchanging Christ, genuine Christianity in the nature of the case remains essentially the same as the years come and go."

"Was Jesus a Christian?" is the subject of the first chapter. This question is concerned with whether Christ was merely an example of faith or whether He is its object. If Jesus was merely an example of faith, His uniqueness lies in the fact that He was the first Christian. If, however, He is primarily the object of our faith, His position is radically different. Then He was not the first Christian but one whom we should worship and obey and on whom we are constantly dependent.

"Whence Came Jesus?" is the subject of chapter two. Here the problem of Christ's parentage, or more broadly speaking, His origin, is discussed. The conclusion reached here is that in Christ we have an extraordinary irruption of the Divine into the sphere of the human.

"The Purpose of Christ's Incarnation" is the third topic presented in this volume. We are brought face to face with the Pauline statement that Christ came to save sinners. Dr. Craig writes, "Whatever may prove to be the ultimate account of Christ's coming into the world, this at least is certain—the proximate account of His Coming is to be found in this world's need of a Saviour. Everywhere in the Scriptures the Coming of Christ is grounded in sin. Everywhere we are taught that it was the needy condition of men that led Him to forsake for a season His throne of glory . . . We should permit nothing, therefore, to conceal from us the fact that Christ's coming into the sinful world was motivated by the desire to seek and to save the lost."

Succeeding chapters discuss Christ as Lord, as Redeemer, as the Regenerator of Character, as our Example, as a Man, and as a Friend, as a Teacher, as a Worker of Miracles, as a Social Reformer, as a Judge, and finally, His place in the Cosmos. The book comes to a grand conclusion in pointing out that we must think of Christ in cosmical terms; that is, as one who sustains vital relations not only to the human race but the whole universe of created things visible and invisible. He believes that we cannot think too highly of Christ. Any honest reader will be stimulated to ever entertain a more exalted conception of Jesus Christ.

Dr. Craig has given us in his latest work a volume that is characterized by mature scholarship and penetrating insight into the person and work of Jesus Christ the Redeemer of God's elect. Dr. Clarence E. McCartney read this work in its manuscript form and commented, "I wish that a book like this had fallen into my hands when I was commencing my ministry." In this statement he expresses the reviewer's feeling. The Christian minister will find abundant inspiration in these chapters for helpful homiletical productions. J.R.R.

BRIGHT FUTURE. James M. Carr. John Knox Press, Richmond, Va. $1.25.

The Board of Church Extension commissioned its secretary of Town and Country Church to prepare this volume. Dr. Carr is eminently qualified by experience to write this book. He was reared in a small town church. In his first pastorate he served in a town church and a country church for almost ten years. For twelve years he was regional director of religious education. Since 1949, he has occupied the position of Secretary of Town and Country Church for our communion.

There has been a tendency to write off the country church. The major emphasis of this book is that there is dawning a new day for our rural and small town churches, and, therefore, it would be unwise to feel that the country church is a thing of the past.

Since 1952 the Presbyterian Church has used five thousand and under as the figure in determining what should be designated as a rural and town population. Our nation was once predominantly a rural people depending almost wholly upon agriculture. At the time of the American Revolution 180 years ago we were ninety per cent rural. Dr. Carr tells us that now as a nation we are about two-thirds urban and only one-third rural. We are becoming more and more an urban people. In the sixteen states that constitute the Presbyterian Church in the United States the author finds that in using five thousand as the population dividing line, 53.8 per cent must be designated as rural. Therefore, in our Southland, the geographical distribution is about equally divided. Dr. Carr believes that the future of the entire Church may be at stake in the country church. On the average one-half of our young people reared in town and country is moving to the cities. They naturally go to a church of the same denomination that trains them in their rural community. A denomination with a strong rural constituency grows by natural increase. A denomination which permits her town and country churches to languish away and die faces two possibilities. One is to become a dying church; the other is to grow at the expense of other denominations which remain active in rural areas. Dr. Carr points out that the best situation is a happy balance of urban, larger town, village, and open country churches.

The author's final appeal is for the rural church to adjust its methods to changing attitudes and changing needs of the community. Rural life, he says, is dynamic. It is constantly changing. The rural church cannot be static. If so, she will die. The church must accept the fact of change and adjust herself to it.

Southern Presbyterians would welcome this volume and profit by its information and inspiration. It is indeed encouraging to note that the future of the Town and Country Church is bright. J.R.R.

LET THERE BE LIGHT. Benjamin P. Browne. Fleming H. Revell. $1.95.

Here is new, fresh material for illustrating and highlighting sermons and talks. From his years of experience as a pastor and public speaker the author offers advice on developing original material and how to use illustrations most effectively.

Our Presbyterian Heritage

Last year the Southern Presbyterian Journal sponsored a symposium on the Reformed Faith. Addresses were made by a group of outstanding Presbyterians and all who attended gave enthusiastic response.

Without in any measure competing with any other program in our church a similar symposium will be held this year, again placing emphasis on our Presbyterian heritage.

THE TIME—August 15th — 10:00 A. M.

THE PLACE—Weaverville, N. C.

DR. C. GREGG SINGER—*"The Reformed Faith and the Contemporary Crisis in Education."*

DR. GORDON H. CLARK — *"The Reformed Doctrine of Verbal Inspiration of the Scriptures."*

DR. FLOYD HAMILTON — *"The Reformed Doctrine of Infant Baptism."*

DR. AIKEN TAYLOR — *"The Reformed Doctrine of the Means of Grace."*

DR. W. C. ROBINSON — *"The Reformed Doctrine of the Bodily Resurrection of Christ."*

DR. R. F. GRIBBLE — *"The Reformed Faith as Related to the Virgin Birth Foretold in Isaiah 7:14."*

MR. GEORGE BURNHAM — *"To the Far Corners."*

Make Plans Now To Attend This Meeting

THE SOUTHERN PRESBYTERIAN JOURNAL
Weaverville, N. C.

THE SOUTHERN PRESBYTERIAN JOURNAL

A Presbyterian weekly magazine devoted to the statement, defense and propagation of the Gospel, the faith which was once for all delivered unto the saints.

VOL. XV NO. 16 AUGUST 15, 1956 $2.50 A YEAR

Breaking of Ground for New Sunday School Building at The Austell Presbyterian Church in Austell, Ga. (See Page 15)

Be Sure To Read:

"SLANDER IN BRAZIL"

By L. NELSON BELL

(See Pages 5, 6 and 7)

THE SOUTHERN PRESBYTERIAN JOURNAL
The Journal has no official connection with the Presbyterian Church in the United States
Rev. Henry B. Dendy, D.D., Editor..........Weaverville, N. C.
Dr. L. Nelson Bell, Associate Editor..........Asheville, N. C.
Rev. Wade C. Smith, Associate Editor..........Weaverville, N. C.

EDITORIAL

The Sufficiency of Scripture and Women Elders

The Reformation in general and our Confession in particular stresses the sufficiency or completeness of Holy Scripture. Thus,

> "The whole counsel of God, concerning all things necessary for His own glory, man's salvation, faith, and life, is either expressly set down in Scripture, or by good and necessary consequence may be deduced from Scripture: unto which nothing at any time is to be added, whether by new revelations of the Spirit, or traditions of men."

In full accord therewith, our Book of Church Order declares:

> "Christ, as King, has given to His Church officers, oracles, and ordinances; and especially has He ordained therein His system of doctrine, government, discipline, and worship: all of which are either expressly set down in Scripture, or by good and necessary inference may be deduced therefrom; and to which things He commands that nothing be added, and that from them naught be taken away.
>
> "The exercise of ecclesiastical power, whether joint or several, has the divine sanction, when in conformity with the statutes enacted by Christ, the Lawgiver, and when put forth by courts or by officers appointed thereunto in His word."

Now are these principles being honored in the arguments put forward for women elders, or are we assuming there that the voice of some leaders, the practice of other communions, or the expediency of the hour is the leading of the Holy Spirit even though it is not in accord with Holy Scripture? If we are using the reasoning that befits James' pragmatism or Dewey's instrumentalism, what is to keep our people from using similar reasoning to justify pictures and statues as means of worship in contradiction to the teaching of our Church on the Second Commandment? Or on what basis can we condemn the Roman Catholics who have used the same kind of arguments for their doctrines of infallibility of the Pope and the assumption of the body of the Virgin into heaven?

The Holy Scripture sets forth both the general principle or rule of the government of the Church by men and the specific assertion thereof positively and negatively. First the general principle, "But I would have you know that the head of every man is Christ; and the head of the woman is the man; and the head of Christ is God." I Cor. 11.3. So also Eph. 5.21-24,33.

Secondly, the elder is positively set forth in Titus and Timothy as "the husband of one wife," "one that ruleth well his own house, having his children in subjection with all gravity," Titus 1.6-8: I Tim. 1-7.

Thirdly, negatively, the Apostle specifically forbids women to "usurp" or "to have authority" over men, I Tim. 2.12, I Cor. 14.34-35. The Greek word translated "usurp authority" or "have authority" etymologically means one who acts on his own authority, so Thayer and The Expositors' Greek New Testament. If on mere human authority we put into this office those whom God has not authorized us to place there, can we continue to say that their actions meet the requirements laid down in our Book of Church Order for those acts which have the Divine sanction, namely, that that be by officers appointed THEREUNTO IN HIS WORD, par. 19?

In writing the above we are not denying that the Bible richly recognizes women and the gifts and callings that God has given them. The influence of the Bible has elevated womanhood to the high place she has. We also declare that in Christ they have the same access and nearness to God by grace through faith which the men have. We do not understand that this teaching by the Apostle contradicts his other teaching of the order God has established for the man and the woman in the home and in the Church. This matter goes to the root of our recognition of the sufficiency and the authority of the Word of God which we have accepted as our infallible rule of faith and practice. The Word of God is the sole sceptre of Christ's reign in the Church. W.C.R.

The Sort of Expert Most Needed

The writer recently came upon the following words of the late Dr. James Denney, expositor, theologian, and author of two notable books on the death and the atonement of our Lord. They were first spoken in lectures at Chicago Theological Seminary and later published in his book, "Studies in Theology." In the forty-odd years since, the need of such a reminder of the true mission of the church has become all the greater, and Dr. Denney's fine statement is peculiarly timely now. In part, it is as follows:

"People cry out fiercely that the church ought to mediate, that the church ought to be on the side of the poor and oppressed, and so on. The church ought certainly to be on the side of justice and mercy; but it needs more than sympathy with justice and mercy to decide on the merits of a given dispute; it needs an accurate knowledge of the whole circumstances of the case, and that it is impossible and unnecessary for the church to have. It is no part of my business as a Christian man, or even as a Christian minister, and therefore it is no part of the business of the church, which is the assembly of Christian men, to understand mining, docks, engineering, railways, or any industry, so as to be able to give sentence in cases of dispute.

"To do that is the work of Christian men who in God's providence are called to live the Christian life under the conditions in question; and it should be left for them to do. When representative Christian ministers interpose in economic disputes, in their character as ministers, it tends to put the church in a false position . . . . All life has to be Christianized; but the process is to be accomplished, not by dragging everything under the scrutiny and sentence of the church as it exists among us, but by sending out into all the departments of life men to live and work there in the spirit of Christ . . . There were things He refused to do; there are things that the church and the ministers of the church should refuse in His name. We shall speak often of money, if we speak as He spoke; but we shall not divide the inheritance among rival claimants. We shall not assume that because we are Christians we are experts in economy or in legislation, or in any branch of politics, any more than in science or in art. We shall believe that the church which cultivates in all its members the spirit of humanity, the spirit of liberty, justice, generosity, and mercy, will do more for the coming of God's kingdom than if it plunged into the thick of every conflict, or offered its mediation in every dispute.

"The church does nothing unless it does the deepest things; it does nothing unless it prevails on sinful men to have peace with God through our Lord Jesus Christ, and to walk in love even as He loved us. Let us fix our minds on this as the first and supreme interest, and everything else will come out in its proper place."

As these weighty words of Dr. Denney make clear, the supreme need in these confused times is not for a church expert in sociology and statecraft and business ethics and educational technique and curriculum, but for a church the members of which are expert in the Gospel of our salvation and who practice and preach and propagate it in all the contacts of their lives.

W.T.W.

Arrested Development

Paul's Plaint Gal. 4:19

"My Children, I am again undergoing child birth (for you) until Christ (and His likeness) be (fully) formed in you."

When birth has been accomplished the normal expectation is for growth; evident, healthy growth. The mother weighs the baby daily and the father watches and checks the development. When Paul failed to find this growth in his spiritual children, he declared he is again in the throes of child-birth for them.

Arrested Development! Oh, how many there are who have named the name of Christ as their Saviour, but who do not evidence growth in devotion and active, clear cut, Christian living. What has happened to them?

SUFFOCATION due to *Prayerless Worship*

"Prayer is the soul's sincere desire, unuttered or expressed

The Southern Presbyterian Journal, *a Presbyterian Weekly magazine, devoted to the statement, defense, and propagation of the Gospel, the faith which was once for all delivered unto the saints*, published every Wednesday by The Southern Presbyterian Journal, Inc., in Weaverville, N. C.

Entered as second-class matter May 15, 1942, at the Postoffice at Weaverville, N. C., under the Act of March 3, 1879. Vol. XV, No. 16, August 15, 1956. Editorial and Business Offices: Weaverville, N. C. Printed in the U.S.A. by Biltmore Press, Asheville, N. C.

ADDRESS CHANGE: When changing address, please let us have both old and new address as far in advance as possible. Allow three weeks after change if not sent in advance. When possible, send an address label giving your old address.

The motion of a hidden fire, that trembles in the breast.

Prayer is the Christian's VITAL BREATH, the Christian's NATIVE AIR,

His watchword at the gates of death, he enters Heaven with prayer."

Not enough fresh, invigorating, tonic, air for the soul's healthy growth. Paul in Ephesians, 6:18—"Praying always with all prayer and supplication in the Spirit." Also in 2d Chron. 7:14 that royal verse—"If My people, which are called by My Name, shall humble themselves, and pray, and seek My face, and turn from their wicked ways; then will I hear from Heaven, and will forgive their sin, and will heal their land."

What has happened to the professing Christian? His prayer life has withered, has become unreal, has been neglected, and the fire within is flickering. No wonder the Disciples cried in Luke 11:1 "Lord teach us to pray!"

In Jacob's Bethel Dream prayer appears as a two-way ladder, with angels ascending and descending. They carry the heart's cry to God and return with the answer: vital, unbroken connection. Gen. 28:12-13. The distressing defeat that we see about us displays panting Christians, out of breath and weak. Arrested Development; Prayerless Worship, Christ not being fully formed within them.

STARVATION due to the *Neglected Word*

"My meat (daily food)," says Jesus, "is to do the will of Him that sent Me and to finish His work." Obedience to God's Word is our Daily Food. (Jno. 4:34)

And Peter urges (I Peter 2:2) "As new born babes, desire the sincere milk of the Word, that ye may grow thereby, if so be that ye have tasted that the Lord is gracious."

Runted Christians, under-nourished, therefore thin blood, weak bodies, feeding their spirits upon neither milk nor meat. How can they fight the good fight of faith? How can they endure hardness as a good soldier of Jesus Christ? How quickly they faint and fall in the struggle! How they misrepresent Our Lord and His Salvation!

STRANGULATION due to the *Choking World*

"And others are they that are sown among the thorns. These are they that heard the Word, and the cares of this world, and the deceitfulness of riches, and the lust of other things, entering in, choke the Word and it becometh unfruitful." (Mk. 4:18,19)

Weymouth translates it thus — "Worldly cares and the deceitfulness of wealth and the excessive pursuit of other objects, come in and stifle the message and it becomes unfruitful."

Christian health and growth are crowded out, are choked to death; the competition of "other things," "other objects"; excessively "pursued"; they conquer, they win in the soul. Riches deceive and defeat, the thorns and the weeds and the briars preempt the soil and the strength in the heart, and the good seed's stork turns pale and white and there's no golden grain. Arrested Development in God's Garden.

"O Lord of life, and love, and power, how joyful life might be

If in Thy service every hour, we lived and moved with Thee,

If youth in all its zeal and might, by Thee were sanctified,

And manhood found its chief delight, in working at Thy side.

'Tis ne'er too late, while life shall last, a new life to begin:

'Tis ne'er too late to leave the past, and break with self and sin:

And we this day, both old and young, would earnestly aspire

For hearts to nobler purpose strung, and purified desire."

S.M.G.

Slander In Brazil

By L. NELSON BELL

EDITOR'S NOTE: The following article is the first written by Dr. Bell telling of his recent investigations in Brazil. He has amassed a large volume of material from which to draw, should further articles be indicated. Dr. Bell traveled over 6,000 miles in Brazil, conferring with missionaries and national church leaders from all sections of the country. H.B.D.

A situation has developed in Brazil which is of grave importance to the Brazilian Presbyterian Church as a whole and particularly to the Seminary of the North and the church in that area.

For some time the *Christian Beacon* has been publishing reports of "modernism" in Brazil and of the "brave fight" being waged by Rev. Israel Gueiros to maintain a conservative witness in that country. Dr. Gueiros has made several trips to the United States, the most recent being this spring.

The June 28th issue of the *Christian Beacon* tells of the "historic stand which he (Dr. Gueiros) is making for the faith," and openly solicits contributions for Dr. Gueiros and his work and for a new seminary which he is establishing in Recife.

Believing this agitation to be the dying gasp of a discredited and disgraceful movement to confuse a stand for true conservative evangelical Christianity with a schismatic contentious orthodoxy which knows little of true Christian love the writer has, *as an entirely private enterprise*, made a fifteen day trip to Brazil during which he has visited the main cities and talked with the recognized leaders of Presbyterianism in that country. He has consulted with Brazilian pastors individually and in groups; he has talked with members of the Board of the Seminary of the North; with the dean and faculty members of that institution, and with many missionaries who are representatives of both the Presbyterian Church U.S. and U.S.A.

After a careful and reasonably thorough investigation of the entire situation he would state that it is his considered opinion that *this is the most flagrant case of untrue and unjust accusations against Christian brethren and Christian institutions that he has ever heard of.*

We yield to no man in our loyalty to the historic faith as it has always been interpreted by conservative Presbyterianism. Within the bounds of our own church (Presbyterian U.S.) we have been characterized as "reactionary," etc., etc., because of our insistence on the maintaining of the conservative theological position as consistent with biblical theology, with the standards of our church and with proven effectiveness where preached, taught and lived.

Because of our known position with reference to historic evangelical Christianity, as opposed to liberal trends and beliefs which rob both the message and its application of spiritual power, we are all the more concerned because there are those who, in the name of "conservative Christianity" are engaging in actions, attitudes and movements which can only discredit the cause of Christianity itself.

The socalled "battle for the faith which centers in Recife" is actually a one-man attempt to discredit an entire church and institution and to cast doubts on the Christian faith of Brazilian pastors and teachers and of American Presbyterian missionary personnel.

This is done by the grossest *distortion* of facts, coupled with *multiplied misstatements*, that the writer has ever seen. He could have written the entire sentence above in one short three-letter word; but, it never looks good in print and it is an ugly word to hear.

At this point it may be profitable to inject the observation that despite the statements of Dr. Gueiros, Dr. Carl McIntire and the *Christian Beacon*, the Seminary of the North, the Presbytery of Pernambuco, the Board of the Seminary of the North and the Presbyterian missionaries of that area are as conservative a group of Christians as we have ever met. They stand *unequivocally* for the truth.

We do not use the word "conservative" in an unfavorable sense. Rather we would state that the individuals who make up these different groups, and the groups acting as such, come more nearly representing what we believe to be the historical evangelical Presbyterian position than any comparable individuals or groups we have met in the world.

These individuals and groups are the ones under attack, and that attack comes from a handful of people who base their action on allegations that these people are not worthy of Christian confidence and support. Never have we heard of a greater travesty in the name of "defending the faith."

Six years ago this writer passed through Recife on his way to Africa for a hurried visit. At that time we heard of the discord which had been sown within the Presbyterian Church by a recent visit of Dr. Carl McIntire. Into a church where neither theological liberalism nor modernism was known he had scattered seeds of suspicion and raised issues which had no relevance to that church or area.

One prominent Brazilian pastor was deeply affected. Prior to that time he had been a problem. From that time he became an increasing source of discord, openly boasting of his "intolerance" and seeing in every attitude and action of his Christian brethren a tendency to deviate from orthodoxy and more and more assuming a martyr complex.

It should be noted that missionaries have no official connection with the Brazilian Presbyteries and do not even attend their meetings. It should also be noted that the Board of the Seminary of the North consists of nine men—seven Brazilians and one representative (the Rev. Dr. Langdon Henderlite), from the Presbyterian Mission, U.S., and one representative (the Rev. Dr. Richard Waddell) from the Presbyterian Mission, U.S.A.

It should further be noted that after meeting and conferring with a large number of Brazilian Presbyterian ministers we came to the conclusion that these men would be leaders in their Presbyteries if transplanted to the United States. They are men of *great* ability, spiritual power and insight, character and personality, and, they are Presbyterians of the heritage of Warfield, Hodge, Johnson, Strickler, etc. In fact, they are *superior* men who are an honor to the church in which they have been trained and in which they are so ably serving.

These are the men and this is the church under attack by Dr. McIntire, Dr. Gueiros and a small group of followers, some of them certainly misguided and acting under an impulse and in a way they would *surely* repudiate if they knew the facts.

Dr. Gueiros attributes the failure of the Seminary six years ago to continue him as a teacher to his "fighting for the faith." After reading records from the Seminary and conferring with men who had been in close touch with the situation throughout the years we do not see how he was continued as long as he was.

He now claims there is "modernistic influence" in this Seminary. Let the reader judge from the following incident and we would *urge* a careful reading of the *sequence* of events as they unfold:

Some two years ago a new member joined the faculty of the Seminary of the North in Recife. (We see no useful purpose in giving names because we are here discussing a *principle*, NOT a personality).

After a time students in the Seminary complained to the Dean, a Brazilian, that this professor was teaching destructive critical views of the Scriptures. The Dean told the students to confine their criticisms to written quotations from the class room, on which the merits of the criticism would be judged.

Before long, it was obvious that such teaching was going on, the students reporting to the Dean, to other members of the faculty, and to Dr. Langdon Henderlite, missionary member of the Board of the Seminary living in Recife.

A few days later Dr. Henderlite was due to go to Sao Paulo on mission business and the Dean asked him to confer with Dr. Richard Waddell, the other missionary member of the Board, residing in Sao Paulo. The Dean made it plain to the writer that Dr. Henderlite was requested to have this conference, not only because of his membership on the Board of the Seminary, but also to represent the Seminary in said conference with Dr. Waddell. Prior to this, Dr. Henderlite's reaction has been that the member of the faculty in question should be released at the first possible moment. On conferring with Dr. Waddell, the reaction of Dr. Waddell was identical - that this man should leave the Seminary as quickly as arrangements could be made for him to do so.

Soon after this, the Dean (a Brazilian), also was in Sao Paulo on business for the Brazilian Presbyterian Church. He, too, conferred with Dr. Waddell and told him the faculty was also of the unanimous opinion that this man should leave.

The Board of Directors of the Seminary took unanimous action to effect the dismissal of the professor in question. It should be noted that this Board is responsible directly to the General Assembly of the Presbyterian Church of Brazil, but they also notified the Synod of their action and the Synod voted to concur in and approve of said action. Dr. Gueiros was a member of this Synod and did not say one word but voted to approve the action of the Board.

While the faculty of the Seminary had no power to act they had, with the Dean, in private conversations agreed unanimously that the professor in question should leave. During the interval between these decisions and the termination of his contract four months later he was assigned other subjects to teach and a close check was made on his teaching. During that period there was no cause for complaint.

From the above, we see that the Seminary which is accused of harboring "modernistic influences" got rid of a liberal professor with the unanimous approval of the faculty, the active cooperation of the Dean, the unanimous action of the Board, the approval of the synod and the confirmation of the Executive Committee of the General Assembly.

If a seminary like the Seminary of the North is harboring "modernistic influences," then all the writer has to say is - may God give us many similar seminaries in America! We can use them.

But, Dr. Israel Gueiros has been busy in America trying to raise thirty thousand dollars to start a new seminary in Recife, one to "defend the faith" and to be "true to the Bible." In light of the actual conditions in Recife it is our considered judgment that there could not be a greater travesty in the name of promoting Christianity.

How well the campaign has succeeded we do not know. That such a seminary will be supported only by the schismatic and independent groups in Brazil is certain. That it will continue to sow discord, if eventually organized, is also a certainty. One Brazilian pastor said to the writer: "Stop American dollars from flowing into this project and it will dry up and wither very quickly."

In conclusion, it should be clearly stated that the writer did not take this trip to Brazil because he is a member of the Board of World Missions of the Presbyterian Church in the U.S. However, he *is* a member of that Board which has been characterized as "modernistic" by Dr. Gueiros. He went to Brazil because of this blatant attack on our Missions, our missionaries and on our Christian brethren of the Brazilian Presbyterian Church. He went because he believes such actions, attacks and movements do irreparable harm to the cause of a true witness for the evangelical Christian faith, a witness which is desperately needed where liberalism and modernism are *actually* to be found.

As for Brazil, we would categorically state that our missionaries, the Presbyterian Missions, the Brazilian Presbyterian Church and its institutions are unequivocally worthy of our *fullest support.*

Brethren, pray for this situation; that out of it God may cause even the wrath of man to praise Him.

. . . .

After writing the above in Rio, and reviewing the copious notes made while interviewing a large number of individuals, and, after considering this trip in retrospect we feel that we have been restrained and reserved to a degree which cannot be warranted by the facts.

Also, we have now read two subsequent issues of the *Christian Beacon.* We simply cannot understand how the situation in Brazil can be so persistently *misrepresented.*

Spiritual vigilance and a forthright stand for those things which are basic in the Christian faith have never been needed more than they are needed today. We have no illusions as to the unbelief and compromise to be found currently in many places in Protestantism.

But, here we have the *Christian Beacon* and a few individuals, attacking as theologically unsound a group of Christians as conservative as are to be found in any place in the world.

Such a deliberate campaign of slander and falsehoods must be exposed for what it really is.

This is a beginning. Next week we will cite specific incidents.

The Missionary's Self-Respect

By George S. Lauderdale

One of the things which makes hell's anguish great is remorse. Constant regret is making many men and women miserable during their days on earth also, but God shows us in the Bible that by His grace we can be rightly proud of ourselves! Jesus Christ died to remove our guilt, and has sent His Spirit into the world that we might work with Him to put our talents to the greatest possible use. Remorse and regret are of the devil; witnesses for Jesus Christ can say with the confidence of Paul: "I have therefore whereof I may glory through Jesus Christ in those things which pertain to God." Romans 15:16.

All men want attention, from childhood abhorring the idea of being ignored or regarded as unworthy. Little ones do not have to be taught to show off, and plenty of older persons have but one goal in their speech, to be considered clever.

Listen: what man's soul craves is the approval of God, and *this the gospel of Christ freely offers him.* Faith in Jesus Christ elevates the believer to the rank of a son of God; faithful service in obedience to Christ in making His saving grace known to all the world brings to the human heart such assurance of divine favor that feelings of insecurity, uselessness, and guilt vanish.

CHRIST THE ANSWER FOR YOU

Are you one of those unfortunate souls who want so desperately to be noticed that you will describe your sicknesses to anybody you can corner? Have you ever tried listening to Jesus Christ? First, He will assure you that He knows and is concerned about you, and does not get bored as you lay bare your sins and disappointments before Him. "Trust in him at all times; ye people, pour out your heart before him: God is a refuge for us." Psalm 62:8. Jesus says, "Come unto me, all ye that labor and are heavy laden. . . . Take my yoke upon you, and learn of me . . . and ye shall find rest unto your souls." Matthew 11:28,29.

A second thing Christ will do for you is give you useful employment which you consciously long for as much as for sympathy. His blood purges the conscience from dead works to serve the living God, as the inspired record has it in Hebrews 9:14. Self-respect is just around the corner for each person who believes on Christ for forgiveness and obeys this Word: "Work out your own salvation with fear and trembling; for it is God which worketh in you both to will and to do of his good pleasure." Philippians 2:12,13.

LET CHRIST USE YOU

The Holy Spirit entemples Himself in the bodies of saints to use their brains, feet, and tongues to preach the gospel to every creature under heaven. What a joy it is to labor daily with Him! It is little wonder that those who will not participate in God's global search for souls are gripped by feelings of frustration, despair, futility. "The backslider in heart shall be filled with his own ways: and *a good man shall be satisfied from himself.*" Proverbs 14:14.

God gives His co-laborers independence. They do not fear to come to the light and have their deeds made known, since these are wrought in God. Because God is free of spirit, well-pleased with all He does, His children get this same attitude of inner pleasure from their attainments in His Name.

JUSTIFIED PRIDE THROUGH CHRIST

Although he earned them when he rescued Lot, Abraham refused the battle spoils offered him by the king of Sodom, lest he should say that he had made Abraham rich. Paul deserved pay for his preaching, but turned it down with these words, "For it were better for me to die, than that any man should make my glorying void." 1 Corinthians 9:15. This same man of God would not dare speak of those things which Christ had not done by Him in saving the souls of the Gentiles: "Yea, so have I strived to preach the gospel, not where Christ was named, lest I should build upon another man's foundation." Romans 15:20.

Think of Paul's black past. If any man were ever tempted to give in to remorse and not try to serve God, lock himself away from needy humanity and waste his days in cowardly self-pity, Paul was he. But God made this man one of Jesus Christ's mightiest missionaries! Paul made full proof of his ministry, was able to cite whole congregations of transformed sinners as the seal of his apostleship in the Lord, and before his "departure," as he delighted to term death, the king of terrors, he stated with assurance, "I have fought a good fight, I have finished my course, I have kept the faith: henceforth there is laid up for me a crown of righteousness, which the Lord, the righteous judge, shall give me at that day." 2 Timothy 4:7,8.

ANGLERS

By Wade C. Smith

Lesson No. 152

More About Grouping for Personal Work

There will doubtless be many situations in which one must humiliate himself to approach acceptably his prospect - not in any way to compromise his own convictions, but to exercise that humility in which the Lord Jesus has set the example. It might very properly involve the confession of sin on the part of the worker. Surely no Christian could think himself above it! And it opens up a sympathetic contact with the poor sinner being sought. This is always one sure best way to approach a prospect, if you can show by God's Word the way to be forgiven and The Way to overcome sin.

Prospects should be assigned, to be interviewed *and reported upon.* To provide for these reports and accept new assignments, the group should meet once a week, if possible — not less often than once every two weeks. (Remember, this is an all-year-round program; during a revival meeting the group should meet once a day). This will involve sacrifice; but *Sacrifice* to this end was begun at Calvary! and it was for you as much as for anyone; don't forget that. A way will be worked out if the matter is laid before the Lord in prayer; it is the Lord's business and He makes it possible as we look to Him for guidance.

The reports made to the group on the interviews with prospects will be exceedingly interesting, and often illuminating. A man who had never in his life talked to one about his soul, came to the group meeting one night and told of going to his neighbor to invite him to the church service that night, praying as he went that the Holy Spirit would bless the effort to the man's salvation. The man's wife met him at the door and said that her husband was in the bathroom shaving. Her husband heard the conversation and came out with his face covered with lather, but received the invitation graciously and agreed to come. He did come, and when the invitation was given, a clean-shaven man, but a poor sinner, walked up to the pulpit and made his profession. One interesting feature of this personal work business is that something different is always taking place. There are surprises at almost every turn, mostly happy ones.

Each report to the group meeting of a visitor's experience stimulates to further effort, even though the report seems to indicate failure. A man got up at the group meeting one night when reports were called for, and made a confession. He said, "Men, I started out to see my prospect this morning and I got cold feet and turned back. I'm ashamed of it, and by the grace of God I'm going through with it tomorrow!" Encouraged by this, two others made a similar confession and a similar resolution. All three of them saw and interviewed their prospects next day.

If a prospect has been won, the next step is to get him in touch with the pastor and follow the matter close up until the convert has been before the session (or proper board) and before the congregation in a public profession of his faith in Christ. Further steps for this new member will be suggested in a later lesson, but it may be found desirable to start him to work in your group.

New Assignment of prospects should be made at each group meeting. Sometimes the same assignments re-committed, if it appears desirable - after prayer. Always prayer. A former assignment under the solicited guidance of the Holy Spirit may be transferred to new hands, or exchanged. The point is to keep these prospects in live hands and not allow them to become shelved or forgotten. Every worker, as he goes about his task, will be discovering new prospects (Lesson No. 142 gave an instance of this). Make a note of the new prospect's name and address and turn it in at the next group meeting. Of course this does not mean that a soul winner is not at liberty to approach any one at any time whom he regards as a prospect. It is merely to systematize the work so that all prospects may be "covered." It is conceivable that the group would be so active in discovering new prospects' names that it would be necessary to refer some of them to the pastor for distribution in other groups.

The Census Method of securing prospects has been in vogue for a number of years with more or less satisfactory results, several denominations taking part at the same time and dividing the lists according to denominational preferences; but some have found it better for a single congregation to canvass its own prospect territory.

(More about Group Work in next lesson)

Helps To Understanding Scripture Readings in *Day by Day*

By Rev. C. C. Baker

Sunday, August 26, *II Chronicles* 34:9-13. Josiah was one of the best kings Judah ever had (vv.1-2). Trace the steps of his reform movement in his eighth (v.3), twelfth (vv. 3b-7), and eighteenth (vv.8-13) years in chapter 34. Is it a sign of progress when the House of God is repaired and rebuilt (vv.9-13)? However, even more important, was the discovery of the Word of God (vv.14-18), its reading (vv.18,29-30), and the effect of its reading on the people (vv.19-21,31-33). Josiah humbled himself at the reading of the Word (v.19) because his heart was seeking the Lord (vv.2-3). As he matured and continued to seek God, God revealed more of Himself to him. The climax came in vv.31-33, when the whole land turned back to God. Unless the Word of God brings about repentance in the heart of the people of America, the present advance in church interest in our country will be a sham.

Monday, August 27, *I Chronicles* 28:20-21. Throughout his reign it was upon David's heart to build a temple to the Lord (v.2). It was Solomon, however, whom God chose for this task (vv.3,5-6). To what extent did David give the plans for the temple Solomon was to build (vv.11-19)? To what extent did David provide the raw materials (29:2)? the necessary finances (29:3-9)? the needed personnel (28:21)? What spiritual advice did David give his son (28:9-10,20)? One of the factors that might have caused Solomon later to fall away from God was the over-indulgence of his father. What damage can a parent do, however sincere and devout he may be, when he over-indulges or over-protects his children, so that they never learn the meaning of hard work or how to depend on the Lord for themselves?

Tuesday, August 28, *Luke* 12:22-34. Contrast the context of Luke 12:22-34 with a similar passage found in Matthew 6:25-34. What precedes each passage? Were the Matthew and Lukian accounts given on different occasions? Is the point of each passage the same? Are the same arguments developed? How is the attitude of the Christian contrasted to that of other peoples of earth toward material things (Luke 12:29-31)? Do any of God's other creatures fret and worry about physical needs (vv.24-28)? Perhaps one reason Jesus used this material on a number of occasions was that He knew what a universal and powerful temptation anxiety over material things could be. Where the Christian lays up his treasure, there his heart is also (vv.33-34). Where is your treasure?

Wednesday, August 29, *Luke* 19:12-17. The following questions should be applied, consciously or unconsciously, to every narrative portion of Scripture we study. Apply these questions to today's passage and see if you can discover any new insights into the story. To whom is the story told? *Where* does the action take place? *When* does the action take place? *Who* are the characters involved? *What* do they do? *Why* do they act as they do? (Do not neglect this last question.) Now sum up in your own words the truth you believe Jesus is trying to communicate to His listeners through this story. In what practical, specific ways can you apply this truth to your life today?

Thursday, August 30, *Luke* 9:23-27. The servant walks in the footsteps of his master (v.23). After the disciples have recognized Him as the Messiah (v.20), Jesus points toward the cross (v.22). He also points out the conditions of discipleship (vv.23-26). Verses 25-27 shed light on the meaning of denying one's self and taking up one's cross (vv.23-24). Whoever would follow Christ must be willing to die to those things of the world that bring fame and acclaim (v.25) and openly confess and follow Christ before men (v.26). It involves putting first the things of the Kingdom (v.27). Does working for and looking to the coming of the Kingdom have uppermost place in your life?

Friday, August 31, *John* 6:25-35. Shortly after Jesus had fed the five thousand (vv.5-14), the Jews attempted to make Him their king (v.15). Jesus withdrew from them (v.15b) but the crowd continued to seek Him (v.24). What motivation did Jesus attach to the crowd for seeking Him (vv.26-27)? In reading the following conversation (vv.27-66) remember that Jesus is trying to separate the "rice" Christians from those who were truly seeking spiritual enlightenment. How did He do this (vv.35, 41,48-51,53)? How did the Jews react (vv.42, 52,60,65)? What else did Jesus teach about Himself (vv.39-40,62-63)? How did the twelve react (vv.67-69)? Had they come to the point where they were concerned for spiritual things? How much of your service to the church do you perform for some gain that comes back to you from it?

Saturday, September 1, *Romans* 14:7-12. God is the Christian's only judge (vv.10-12), and no material thing in itself is evil (v.14). A Christian, however, does not live apart from others (v.7). What standard, therefore, does Paul give the Christian for determining what practices he should engage in (v.13)? What should our attitude be toward those who differ with us on Sabbath observances or certain worldly practices (vv.1-4)? What should motivate the decisions we make for ourselves on these matters (vv.6-8)? Is there some practice or attitude in your life that is making another Christian stumble? Do you consciously seek to honor the Lord in all that you do?

LESSON FOR AUGUST 26

Strength Through Trial

Background Scripture: Matthew 4:1-11; James 1
Devotional: Ephesians 6:10-20

I was reading an interesting article the other day about "The World's Strongest Man," and I found that he had built up his strength from his youth by lifting heavier and heavier things. The strongest Christian is not the one who has never had any trials or temptations, but the one who by the grace and power of God has overcome, and is "more than conqueror" through Christ. In the Letters to the Seven Churches of Asia there is a constant refrain, "To him that overcometh."

Our Devotional Reading is the familiar exhortation of Paul to "be strong in the Lord and in the power of his might." The strength to stand trials, either in the form of temptations, or of affliction and persecution, is found "in the Lord." The man who trusts in his own wisdom or power will be overcome. So Paul tells us to "put on the whole armour of God." Our adversaries are powerful. The "wiles of the devil" are too much for mere human wisdom. He is an exceedingly cunning enemy. He knows how to tempt, to worry and vex us, to make life almost unbearable, as he did in the case of Job. We are wrestling with world rulers of the darkness of this world. We hear much in our day about the well-organized hordes of criminals of the worst type who prey upon society. I have been reading lately about the vicious Narcotics Ring which is doing its utmost to ruin the youth of our land. I could mention others like the Whiskey and Beer Rings and the White Slave traffic. Paul used the right words when, under the inspiration of the Holy Spirit, he describes them in these verses.

To meet such temptations and trials we must have supernatural power; the "power of His might." We will have to be clothed in the whole armour of God. We need truth and righteousness and the gospel of peace, the shield of faith, the helmet of salvation and the sword of the Spirit. Every part of our body, mind, and soul must be protected, and we must have offensive weapons also, like the Sword of the Spirit.

Each piece must be "put on with prayer." We will have to be on the alert, watching with all perseverance and prayer. Living in this world is dangerous, both physically and spiritually. We will require all the grace and strength that God can give, simply to live, my brother; simply to live. If we are to live victoriously, be "more than conquerors," we will have to stand in the strength of the Lord God.

I. *Temptations of Jesus:* Matthew 4:1-11.

"Tempted in all points like as we are, yet without sin," says the writer of Hebrews. In this way He becomes the very High Priest that we need when we have to face our temptations. He is able to succor those that are tempted. He knows how to sympathize with us and help us.

These are sample temptations. Satan leaves Him "for a season." I feel that there were more of these temptations, even while He was in the wilderness. Later we know that the devil used Peter to suggest another, and Jesus rebuked that disciple, saying, Get thee behind me, Satan: thou art an offence unto me : for thou savourest not the things that be of God, but those that be of men. Perhaps when He spent all night in prayer, He was wrestling with temptation.

The first one given by Matthew would seem to be a temptation to doubt His father's care, or to use His supernatural power as the Son of God for his own preservation. He answers the tempter by quoting from Deuteronomy 8:3: "Man shall not live by bread alone, but by every word that proceedeth out of the mouth of God."

It was a swift thrust of the Sword of the Spirit, the Word of God. This is the same Sword that we have. If we have an arm to wield it and the skill to use it, as Bunyan so aptly words it, this Sword will enable us to conquer too. I was reading just today some instances where the verse in Proverbs, "My son, if sinners entice thee, consent thou not," had been the means of keeping several young people from yielding to subtle suggestions of the devil.

The second temptation seems to be the other extreme, presumption. The Israelites committed both on the border of the land of promise. First there was unbelief, then they presumed to go up alone and were defeated. The

devil takes Him to the Holy City, and setteth Him on a pinnacle of the Temple, and said to Him, If thou be the Son of God, cast thyself down, for it is written, He shall give his angels charge concerning thee: and in their hands they shall bear thee up, lest at any time thou dash thy foot against a stone. Jesus answers by another thrust of the Sword: It is written again, Thou shalt not tempt the Lord thy God. I think a good illustration of presumption is found today in the case of those who handle poisonous snakes to prove that they have a superior sort of religion. It is one thing to trust God when we are in the path of duty. It is an entirely different matter to needlessly and foolishly risk our lives. If I rush out in front of a car to snatch a child from certain death, I might trust God to save me, but if I throw myself in front of a car to prove that God will take care of me, then I am presuming upon His promises and have no right to expect His protection.

The third temptation would seem to be in the form of Disloyalty; to turn traitor to His Father in heaven. The devil takes Him up into an exceeding high mountain and shows Him all the kingdoms of the world and the glory of them, and says, All these will I give thee, if thou wilt fall down and worship me. God, in the second Psalm, had promised Christ the kingdom. He was to obtain it, however, by the way of the cross. Here Satan suggests a much easier way. Just change allegiance; submit to the devil, the god of this world, who has the world "in his lap," so to speak, and the world will be His. Jesus scorns the traitorous suggestion, by commanding, Get thee hence, Satan; for it is written, Thou shalt worship the Lord thy God, and Him only shalt thou serve. Then the devil leaves Him and angels came and ministered to Him.

We learn from this "Battle in the Wilderness" a great deal about our Saviour, and we also learn how to meet our own temptations. If we know our Bibles, we can have an answer to all the evil suggestions of the tempter. The Word of God and Prayer form a strong combination of weapons.

II. *What James Says About Trials and Temptations:* James 1.

The word means to make trial of, to test, to tempt, and the context will show which of these apply in a particular case. Satan tempts us, and our sinful nature is a fruitful source of temptation. God tests His children as He made trial of Abraham when He commanded him to sacrifice Isaac. God sometimes allows Satan to make trial of us, even as he allowed him in the case of Job. God never tempts to evil: "Let no man say when he is tempted, I am tempted of God : for God cannot be tempted with evil, neither tempteth he any man : But every man is tempted, when is drawn away of his own lust, and enticed." If we keep these differences in meaning in mind, it will help us understand this chapter.

"Count it all joy when ye fall into divers temptations" (or trials). Our trials do not seem a source of joy, either in the form of affliction or of temptation. These things are a test of our faith, and a faith that stands the test, leads to greater growth in grace. One result is patience, or steadfastness. The tree that is out in the open where the wind and rain beat upon it, will strike its roots deeper into the earth than the sheltered tree. So it is with the man or woman who is in the midst of trials. Patience leads to a full grown character.

It takes a heavenly wisdom to understand this. We get this wisdom from God. Verse five is a wonderful promise: "If any of you lack wisdom, let him ask of God, who giveth to all men liberally, and upbraideth not; and it shall be given him." Claiming this promise, none of us need to be ignorant or foolish. Many of us show little wisdom when it comes to our trials and temptations. We cannot see their value unless we have been taught of God. James and Peter and Paul all try to teach us the meaning and worth of trials.

Our trials may be in the form of poverty, and we are tempted to envy the rich. James reverses this and tells us that we should rejoice in our "low degree." Jesus teaches the same truth in the Beatitudes. The rich man will "fade away," but the man who endures temptations will receive a crown of life. Let us be "rich toward God" and not be too worried or anxious about the wealth of this world.

Let us beware of the temptations which come from within, and if not resisted and overcome, will result in sin and death. We have the promise; God is faithful, who will not suffer us to be tempted above that we are able, but will, with the temptation, provide a way of escape. Paul, in describing the struggle which he had with the "flesh," exclaims, Who shall deliver me from the body of this death? He answers, "I thank God through Jesus Christ our Lord." He Who conquered in the wilderness, will enable us to be "more than conquerors through Him that loved us."

God is willing to bestow every good and perfect gift. He will give us the strength we need to meet temptation. James wants us to practice our religion; be doers of the Word, and not hearers only. His definition of "pure religion and undefiled" is a practical way of looking at it. It is a partial definition, part of the fruit which comes from deep roots. Pure religion and undefiled is to visit the fatherless and widows in their affliction, and keep himself unspotted from the world. To do this we must grow strong by overcoming temptations and trials.

YOUTH PROGRAM FOR AUGUST 26

Can You "Win" Salvation?

Suggested Devotional Outline:

Hymn: "Come, Thou Fount Of Every Blessing"

Prayer

Scripture: Romans 5:1-10

Hymn: "There Is A Green Hill Far Away"

Offering

Hymn: "Alas! And Did My Saviour Bleed"

Program Leader:

Can you win Salvation? The word "salvation" suggests that something is done for us. It suggests a Saviour. When we speak of Salvation we have in mind a deliverance from sin and death unto eternal life with God. When we speak of Salvation we think of the One whom we call Saviour, Jesus Christ. The Salvation of which we speak is brought to us by Christ, our Saviour. It is very obvious that we do not save ourselves. Christ saves us. The question now is this: Is there anything we can do to earn or merit the Salvation of Christ?

First Speaker:

The first problem every person faces is the problem of sin and its consequences. The Bible says, "The wages of sin is death." Rom. 6:23. We may not be able to win Salvation, but we can win death. Spiritual death is what we receive in payment for being sinners. In another place the Bible speaks of our being "dead in trespasses and sins." Ephesians 2:1. It seems very unlikely that we could win pardon of our sins, if we are already spiritually dead because of them.

As a matter of fact, we do not win forgiveness. God freely pardons all who come to Him through faith in Christ. We cannot earn pardon, but Christ earned it for us when He died in our place. The Scripture explains it in these words, "When we were yet without strength, in due time Christ died for the ungodly." Romans 5:6. "If we confess our sins, He is faithful and just to forgive us our sins, and to cleanse us from all unrighteousness." I John 1:9.

Second Speaker:

Salvation has a negative and a positive side. We are saved from sin and its punishment. We are saved to everlasting life. We have already discovered that there is nothing we can do to merit forgiveness of our sins. We are freely pardoned by God for the sake of Christ who suffered in our stead. Is there anything we can do to earn or win eternal blessedness with God?

The Scripture says, "The gift of God is eternal life through Jesus Christ our Lord." Romans 6:23. If this eternal life is a gift, then it is not something we win but something which is freely given to us. The eternal life which we have is not our own. It is the life which Christ has given us. Jesus said, "Because I live, ye shall live also." John 14:19. Paul explained it this way: "I am crucified with Christ: nevertheless I live; yet not I, but Christ liveth in me: and the life which I now live in the flesh I live by the faith of the Son of God, who loved me, and gave Himself for me." Galatians 2:20.

Third Speaker:

Some people, who readily recognize that we cannot win forgiveness and life, still maintain that we have a part in winning salvation through our faith. The Bible teaches very definitely that we are saved by believing. "He that believeth on the Son hath everlasting life: and he that believeth not the Son shall not see life; but the wrath of God abideth on him." John 3:36.

It is very clear that belief in Christ makes the difference between life and death — between Salvation and destruction, but is it to our credit that we believe? Can we say that we have a part in winning Salvation because of our faith? The Bible says, "By grace are ye saved through faith; and that not of yourselves: it is the gift of God: not of works, lest any man should boast." Ephesians 2:8,9 — Jesus said, "No man cometh unto the Father but by me." John 14:6 and, "No man can come unto me, except the Father which hath sent me draw him." John 6:44. From these passages it appears that even the faith with which we receive God's Salvation is itself a gift of God.

Program Leader:

There is no sense in which we "win" Salvation through our own efforts. Christ has won it for us through His obedience, death and victorious Resurrection. Let us be careful lest in our speaking and thinking we take credit for what God has done in Christ.

Women's Work

U. S. Churches Rush Relief to Greek Quake Victims

Emergency relief for many hundreds injured and left homeless and destitute by the earthquake and giant tidal wave which swept the Greek Islands in the Aegean Sea on July 9 has been sent by the American churches in the amount of 122,400 pounds of food and supplies valued at $65,000.

The supplies sent immediately upon news of the disaster included U. S. surplus cheese and other dairy products, sugar, cocoa, cottonseed oil and soap, and a carload of corn oil collected by CWS-CROP.

Also immediately dispatched by Church World Service, acting for the major Protestant and Orthodox denominations, were 240 bales of clothing and 159 bags of shoes from stocks in its Athens warehouse.

At the request of CWS representatives in Athens, who rushed to the scene the day of the disaster, expenditures of $2,000 were authorized for purchase of additional relief supplies, including canned milk for babies, canned meat which could be eaten without cooking and 500 blankets.

"The emergency shipments were made possible by the Share Our Surplus program of the churches," stated Paul B. Freeland, Secretary of Overseas Relief and Inter-Church Aid, "in addition to funds provided by the Presbyterian Church, U.S. through the Easter Offering, and other denominational relief programs."

Thus Speaketh Christ Our Lord

Ye call me Master and obey me not,
Ye call me Light and see me not,
Ye call me Way and walk me not,
Ye call me Life and Desire me not,
Ye call me wise and follow me not,
Ye call me Fair and love me not,
Ye call me rich and ask me not,
Ye call me eternal and seek me not,
Ye call me gracious and trust me not,
Ye call me noble and serve me not,
Ye call me mighty and honor me not,
Ye call me just and fear me not;
If I condemn you, blame me not.

—Author Unknown)

(Engraved on an old slab in the Cathedral of Lubeck, Germany.)

"I hereby give and bequeath to the Board of Directors of The Southern Presbyterian Journal Company (incorporated under the laws of the State of North Carolina) $________ for the use and benefit of said company."

Some Reasons Why I Must Be About My Father's Business

Because I committed myself to doing His business when I accepted Christ as Saviour and Lord

I delight to do thy will, O my God.

Because Christ gave His life that all men might be saved

The love of Christ constraineth me.

Because it is imperative that man know and accept Christ as Saviour, if he is to be saved

Neither is there salvation in any other.

Because I have an appointed task to do in the Kingdom which no other can do for me

I have chosen you . . . that ye should go and bring forth fruit.

Because there is an unprecedented hungering for God's Word, and Christ has said to me -

Give ye them to eat.

Because the very urgency of the times demands that I be at my Father's business. I am sure of having only today

Ye know not what hour your Lord doth come.

Because of my responsibility to my home, and of my desire for the best for all who are in my home

As for me and my house, we will serve the Lord.

Because I must set a Christian example to those who will follow, so that I may say —

Be ye imitators of me, even as I am of Christ.

Because Christ commanded it

Go ye into all the world, and preach the gospel to every creature.

Because doing His will strengthens my faith and gives me courage to stand fast in His love

They go from strength to strength.

Because our world, our nation, and our Church are crying out "Advance!"

Speak unto the children of Israel that they go forward.

Because I must meet crisis with advance, answering His call —

Follow me.

Montreat—Election of Mrs. Vernon L. Dyer of Petersburg, W. Va., as chairman of the Women's Advisory Council of the Assembly's Women of the Church, was announced here during the annual Women's Training School.

Mrs. Dyer, who is president of the Virginia Synodical, was elected by the WAC during its week-long session which preceded the training school, but new officers were not announced until the school was well under way.

Serving with Mrs. Dyer as vice-chairman is the president of the Women of Florida, Mrs. Francis M. Womack of Jacksonville, and as secretary, the president of the Women of Missouri, Mrs. Leonard L. Dillon of Independence.

More than 1,110 paid registrations for the school made it one of the largest in recent years.

Other outstanding events of the annual training school, in addition to the announcement of the 1956 $175,000 Birthday Offering, was the announcement of the Birthday Offering Objective for 1957. A dual foreign-mission objective was chosen by the Women's Advisory Council, and announced by a combined verbal and art presentation as Student Work in Mexico and Medical Work in Korea.

Miss Sara Dixon, missionary to Toluca, Mexico, presented the needs for support for the Student Work in Mexico, and the Rev. Bruce Cumming, missionary to Kwangju, Korea presented the Medical Work needs in that country. Miss Claire Randall, of the Educational Department of the Board of World Missions drew background art to illustrate the presentations, as the missionaries talked.

A train derailment caused one unexpected alteration in the program. Dr. Louis Evans, minister-at-large for the Presbyterian Church, U.S.A., was the Bible teacher for the school, but derailment of a freight train blocked the line on which he was traveling to Montreat, and caused him to miss the Opening Bible hour. The Rev. William B. Oglesby, of Union Seminary, Richmond, substituted for Dr. Evans. His Bible study on the temptations of Jesus was delivered when it became evident after the Bible hour began that Dr. Evans could not reach Montreat in time. Dr. Evans' series dealt with studies of women in the New Testament.

The 1956 Women's Training School was the first for the new executive secretary of the Board of Women's Work, Mrs. L. M. McCutchen. She was presented to the more than 1500 attending the opening session, but did not address the school until the second night, when she spoke on "The Forward Look".

The forward look for the Christian, Mrs. McCutchen said, "is not a matter of style but of the attitude of the spirit." It consists of several factors that express themselves in the way that the Christian lives, she explained.

"One of the factors in the forward look is faith," Mrs. McCutchen stated. Another is the "look and habit of discipleship" wherein the Christian puts his mind and spirit to work for his Lord. "This includes assuming the responsibilities that discipleship entails," the executive declared.

"And the forward look includes the growth in love as one of its aspects." This love must find expression in all phases of social and business contacts as well as in the environs of the Church. With faith, discipleship and love, the Christian can look into the future with confidence, but "only in the Lord and Savior Jesus can we find the reality of the Forward Look."

Church News

ALABAMA

Gadsden—A master plan for the development of the conference grounds for North Alabama Presbytery, Presbyterian Church, U.S. will be made. The site, on Guntersville Lake, was purchased earlier this year by the Men-of-the-Presbytery and presented to the Presbytery.

W. Glenn Wallace of Minneapolis, Minn., a nationally known camp site architect has been retained by the conference grounds development committee to prepare the master plan. Mr. Wallace devotes his time to camp-site development and has rendered this type of service to church groups of all denominations as well as to the various character building agencies throughout the nation.

Mr. Wallace has already made a preliminary study of the site and met with the development committee to discuss general plans. After his first visit to the property he was high in his praise of the site for camp and conference purposes.

The Presbytery Men's Council adopted the project of purchasing and developing the conference site for the Presbytery in January, 1955. Funds for the purchase of the site were raised by a committee headed by Judge J. S. Stone, Guntersville.

A committee to study ways and means of financing the development is composed of W. B. Whitfield, Huntsville, chairman; O. L. Majure, Guntersville; Philip Shank, Decatur; and Forrest W. Crowe, Albertville.

Pea River—This old church in East Alabama Presbytery has had a series of revival services, beginning the fourth Sunday in July. The preacher this year was Rev. John H. Knight, pastor of the Smyrna Presbyterian Church, Smyrna, Georgia. The preaching and the fellowship were of a very high order, and the life of the church has been greatly enriched. There were three additions on confession of faith.

A. R. Cates, Pastor

Clio—The three churches of our town, Methodist, Baptist, and Presbyterian, have joined in union revival services for the past twenty-five years. This was Presbyterian year, and our preacher was Rev. David E. Boozer, pastor of the Parkview Presbyterian Church, Marietta, Georgia. Mr. Boozer's message was well received, and the churches were strengthened in their faith through his efforts.

A. R. Cates, Pastor

GEORGIA

Austell—At an impressive ceremony Sunday, July 22, ground was broken for the new Sunday School Building at the Austell Presbyterian Church in Austell, Ga.

Mr. Ernest Perkerson, senior member of the congregation, and his grandson, Van Treadaway, youngest member of the congregation, turned over the first soil for the new structure.

Representatives from each organization of the church took part in the service: Mr. H. A. Shacklett, Sunday Schol superintendent; Mr. Leland Withers, chairman of the Board of Deacons; Mr.

Harold Morris, Men's Club president; Mr. W. L. Little, general chairman of the building program; Mrs. Henry Sanders, Women of the Church president; and Miss Polly Joyner, Youth Fellowship president.

The ceremonies were led by Elder L. P. Williams, who is chairman of the construction committee. Mr. Robert Heal, elder from the Druid Hill church in Atlanta, and chairman of the Church Extension Committee of the Atlanta Presbytery., was the guest speaker.

The new building will be erected at a cost of $30,000 and will be approximately 3100 sq. feet in size. It is designed by Mr. George Yates, architect of Atlanta, to match the existing 60 year old sanctuary. The building will house all of the classrooms for the children and youth of the church, as well as a nursery, pastor's study, and a Sunday School office. Adjoining the building will be a well equipped, fenced in play yard.

The Rev. Forest Taylor, Jr., came to the Austell church four years ago and has seen the interest of its people revived in the church's work and a 119% increase in the church membership.

Rev. John Thomas Newton, Jr., pastor of the Smyrna Presbyterian Church near Conyers, Ga., led his first evangelistic meeting in mid-July at the Loyd Presbyterian Church. His father was born and reared within a mile of the church and two of his uncles are still here.

Mr. Newton is a clear thinker—a good preacher —with a good witness. He is also a good pianist while his wife is a consecrated vocalist. The combination makes an effective team. We believe the hand of God is on this youthful couple and that the Church will find many uses for their gifts.

LOUISIANA

New Orleans—New officers of the Presbyterian Laymen of Louisiana for 1956-57 have been announced.

Hal Baird, of New Orleans, was elected President. He will serve with Reed Gardner, Baton Rouge, vice-president; and Theodore H. Shepherd, New Orleans, secretary. Neal Jeffery, also of New Orleans, was elected vice-president of Sunday School superintendents.

Metaire Presbyterian Church has recently signed a construction contract for the new sanctuary to adjoin the educational building erected in 1951.

Construction is expected to begin as soon as the present building, known as the Metaire Ridge Presbyterian Church, is demolished. Pastor of the church is the Rev. John W. Bracy. The building committee consists of Warren H. Schoner, chairman; M. V. Higbee, vice-chairman; and Dr. S. S. Lewis, C. C. Schaller, John Kennedy and W. B. Nourse.

SOUTH CAROLINA

Seneca—The Rev. Charles Robert Tapp, pastor of the Seneca Church has been called by the Board of Trustees of the Presbyterian Home for the Aged of the South Carolina Synod to become Superintendent of the Home. Mr. Tapp will assume his duties on November 1st.

Contract for the building of the Home has been awarded and construction will begin immediately.

Mr. Alfred Scarborough of Sumter is Chairman of the Board of Trustees and Dr. W. M. Frampton of Central Church, Anderson, S. C., is President and Vice-President.

Mr. Tapp is married to the former Miss Mary Louise Evans of Chattanooga, Tenn., and they have three children.

Union—This church has gone forward in real spiritual blessing under the capable leadership of the pastor, The Rev. Robert G. Balnicky. Blessing has come through an increased interest and attendance at the mid-week prayer service, with an average attendance of 78, the highest at any one service being eighty-six.

Another special blessing, as a result of a Bible teaching ministry, is that 85% of our people bring their Bibles to both the morning and evening services as well as for the special Bible Study on Wednesday evening.

For a number of years now a special "World Mission" offering has been received through the Sunday School and now this project has grown until we have taken on a partial support of a missionary family, The Rev. and Mrs. John N. Somerville, Korea.

Beginning March 24th of this year the church began supporting a Saturday morning radio broadcast "Chime and Bible Time" over the local radio station. The pastor is teaching a series of studies in I Corinthians.

The youth work in this church is one of the high lights of her ministry. The Senior High Fellowship conducts the Evening Worship each 5th Sunday. This service, under the supervision of the Director of Christian Education, is handled completely by the youth; one young man doing the preaching, others praying, presiding, singing, preparing their own bulletins and ushering. We also have an active Junior and Pioneer Fellowship group. We begin work with our youth when they are quite young. For the past two years the church has sponsored a Week Day Kindergarten, under the direction of Mrs. William M. Gettys. This fall the enrollment of this school is expected to double and Mrs. Robert G. Balnicky will be assisting Mrs. Gettys.

This fall, November 4 through 11, Evangelist C. W. Solomon, Montreat, North Carolina will be with us for a series of services. Then in April, 1957 The Rev. John L. Fain, Jr., Pastor of The First Presbyterian Church, Kannapolis, North Carolina will conduct evangelistic services.

VIRGINIA

Norfolk Presbytery met in the First Presbyterian Church, Portsmouth, Virginia, yesterday with 48 ministers and 38 ruling elders present. Rev. Joel B. Whitten was elected Moderator.

Rev. Charles H. Gibboney, D.D., was dismissed to the Presbytery of Augusta-Macon and Rev. Robert J. Wilkins to the Presbytery of Wilmington.

Rev. M. Bland Dudley from Mecklenburg Presbytery has been installed in the Holmes Church, Bayview, Va. Rev. Irving R. Stubbs from the Congregational-Christian Association is assistant pastor of the Royster Memorial Church serving the Lansdale Chapel. Reports from various Commissions reported the ordination of the following Licentiates: Robert Horace Fernandez, pastor of the Jamestown Church, Williamsburg, Va.; James

Jefferson Monroe, pastor of the Bethany Church, Zuni, Va.; James Henry Allen, assistant pastor of the Lafayette Church, Norfolk, Va.; John Robert Hewett, assistant pastor of the First Church, Norfolk, Va.; Ross Broadnax Kirven, assistant pastor of the First Church, Newport News, Va., and Richard Sydney Ruggles, assistant pastor of the Royster Memorial Church, Norfolk, Va.

Four candidates were received and taken under care of presbytery from the Knox Church of Norfolk, Va.: J. Davis Whitesides, James H. McGill, Richard Park and Philip N. Libby, the largest number from one church at one time.

At the April session the presbytery decided to establish the office of Executive Secretary and at this meeting Rev. Donald E. Neel, pastor of the Norview Church, was by unanimous vote called for a period of three years.

The Stewardship Committee reported that $377,-271 had been contributed to all benevolence causes during the year 1955 and recommended a budget of $331,168.00 for the calendar year 1957, which was adopted.

The presbytery will meet in adjourned session in the Ocean View Church on September 6th and in regular stated session, October 16 in the Naomi Makemie Church at Onancock, Va., and in commemoration of the 200th anniversary of the organization of the first Presbytery in this country under the leadership of Rev. Francis Makemie, for whose wife Naomi this church was named.

W. W. Grover, Stated Clerk

Salem—On July 24, 1956, Montgomery Presbytery met in the beautiful new church at Pearisburg. There were present 38 Ministers and 40 Ruling Elders. Rev. W. W. Williamson was elected Moderator and Ruling Elder Arthur B. Richardson was nominated to be our next Moderator.

Presbytery appointed a commission to organize the **"Green Ridge"** Church in the "Starmount" section of Roanoke.

Rev. B. F. Sperow was honorably retired from the Ministry, having reached the retirement age.

Mr. John Charles Kepley of the Second Presbyterian Church of Roanoke was received under the care of the Presbytery as a Candidate for the Gospel Ministry.

The next Stated Meeting of Montgomery Presbytery is to be held in the Blue Ridge Presbyterian Church of Avartal, Va., on October 30, 1956.

E. W. Smith, Stated Clerk

Appomattox—The Presbytery of West Hanover met in stated session in the Amherst Church, July 24, 1956, present 12 ministers and 27 ruling elders, with 15 visitors, including student pastors in Old Providence Rural Parish, Deacon L. N. Warren (President Men of the Presbytery), and Rev. W. C. Jamison, Executive Secretary of Lexington Presbytery.

At the request of the Moderator, F. R. Crawford, M.D., the sermon was preached by Rev. W. Twyman Williams.

Commissioners to the General Assembly, Ruling Elders F. H. Calhoun and J. L. Lancaster, made their reports.

Candidate Gale D. Lammey was received from Memphis Presbytery, and his examination for ordination having been approved, the following Commission was appointed to ordain him, July 29, in the First Church, Charlottesville, where he is to be Minister of Education: Revs. D. H. W. Burr, Jan W. Owen, J. R. Keever, Jr., with S. S. Day as alternate, and Ruling Elders J. L. Lancaster and H. R. Richardson.

Rev. J. W. Orders requested the dissolution of his pastoral relationship with the Cumberland Group and his dismissal to Kanawha Presbytery, which was granted. He is to be pastor of the Elk Hills Church, Charleston, W. Va.

By recent action of the Synod of Virginia, assigning to West Hanover all of Roanoke Presbytery except Henry County, which is to go to Montgomery, and taking from Montgomery part of Campbell County with the City of Lynchburg which is to go to West Hanover, this Presbytery, although losing by this re-assignment nearly all of its territory north of the James River, will have 81 churches and over 12,000 members instead of its present 37 churches and nearly 5000 members.

W. Twyman Williams
Stated Clerk

BOOKS

CALVIN AND AUGUSTINE. Benjamin B. Warfield. Presbyterian and Reformed Publishing Co. $4.95.

From 1887 to 1921 Dr. Benjamin Breckinridge Warfield served as professor of Didactic and Polemic Theology in the Theological Seminary of Princeton, New Jersey. During this time he published a number of volumes relating especially to the Reformed Faith. Dr. Warfield was an extraordinarily gifted theologian, and the literature from his pen was widely read by top-flight theological thinkers.

In recent years there has been a growing demand for republication of a number of the volumes by this distinguished scholar and dynamic theologian. In the foreword to this recent volume prepared by Dr. J. Marcellus Kik, Associate Editor of **Christianity Today**, he affirms, "Because of this lucid and stately style of writing, his penetrating gift of analysis, his knowledge of the works of Calvin and Augustine, and his firm grasp of Reformed theology, there was no one better qualified to estimate and express the unique place of Calvin and Augustine in the history of the Christian Church than Warfield." Editor Kik is also correct in stating that the Evangelical movement of today needs a theology which is true to the Scriptures, and in Calvin's and Augustine's doctrine of the majesty and sovereignty of God, there is found a theology that will inspire the Evangelical movement to greater depth and permanence.

In Part One Dr. Warfield discusses "John Calvin: The Man and His Work," "John Calvin's Doctrine of the Knowledge of God," "Calvin's Doctrine of God," "Calvin's Doctrine of the Trinity," and "Calvinism."

Recognizing that Calvinism is an ambiguous term in many places, Dr. Warfield conceives of it as the entire body of conceptions, theological, ethical, philosophical, social, political, which under the influence of the master-mind, John Calvin, raised itself to dominance in the Protestant lands of the post-Reformation age. The fundamental principle of Calvinism according to Dr. Warfield lies in a profound apprehension of God and His majesty with the inevitably accompanying poignant realization of the exact nature of the relation sustained to Him by the creature as such, and particularly by the sinful creature. The author insists that above everything else God in His Son Jesus Christ acting through the Holy Spirit who He has sent shall be recognized as our veritable Saviour. This is the root of Calvinistic soteriology and Calvinistic soteriology is the heart of Calvinism.

In a stimulating address on "John Calvin the Theologian," Dr. Warfield conveys some idea of what manner of theologian John Calvin was. He depicts Calvin as preeminently the Biblical theologian of his age. It is acknowledged that Calvin was a speculative genius of the first order, and in the cogency of his logical analysis he possessed a weapon which made him terrible to his adversaries. But it was not on these gifts that he depended in forming and developing his theological ideas. Warfield writes: "His theological method was persistently, rigorously, some may even say exaggeratingly **a posteriori.** All **a priori** reasoning here he not only eschewed but vigorously repelled. His instrument of research was not logical amplification, but exegetical investigation. In one word he was distinctly a Biblical theologian, or let us say frankly by way of eminence **the Biblical theologian of his age.** Whither the Bible took him thither he went: where Scriptural declarations failed him, thither he stopped short."

It might be surprising to some—who have not read Calvin first-hand to learn that Warfield describes Calvin as preeminently the theologian of the Holy Spirit. He remarks, "It is probable, however, that Calvin's greatest contribution to the theological science lies in the rich development which he gives — and which he was the first to give — to the doctrine of the work of the Holy Spirit. . . . In the same sense in which we may say that the doctrine of sin and grace dates from Augustine, the doctrine of satisfaction from Anselm, the doctrine of justification by faith from Luther, we must say that the doctrine of the work of the Holy Spirit is a gift from Calvin to the Church. It was he who first related the whole experience of salvation specifically to the working of the Holy Spirit, worked it out into its details, and contemplated its several steps and stages in orderly progress as the product of the Holy Spirit's specific work in applying it to the soul. Thus he gave systematic and adequate expression to the whole doctrine of the Holy Spirit and made it the assured possession of the Church of God."

The second portion of this volume is a study of Augustine and his writings. Dr. Warfield seems to agree with the appraisal that Augustine was incomparably the greatest man whom between Paul the Apostle and Luther the Reformer the Christian church has possessed.

It is pointed out that it was through Augustine's voluminous writings by which his wider influence was exerted that he entered both the Church and the world as a revolutionary force and not merely created an epoch in the history of the church but has determined the course of its history in the West up to the present day.

Although Augustine was an author before he became a Christian, the author reminds us that his amazing literary productivity began with his conversion. Dr. Warfield states that the writings of Augustine entered the Church as a leaven which has ever since wrought powerfully towards leavening the whole mass.

Certainly to no other doctor of the Church has anything like the same authority been accorded. Thus Warfield writes, "In point of fact the whole development of Western life in all its phases was powerfully affected by his teaching."

The author continues, "Thus, his unique ascendancy in the direction of the thought and life of the West, is due in part to the particular period in history in which his work was done; in part to the richness and depth of his mind and the force of his individuality; and in part to the special circumstances of his conversion to Christianity. He stood on the watershed of two worlds—the old world was passing away; the new world was entering upon its heritage; and it fell to him to mediate the transference of the culture of the one to the other."

As a thinker Augustine is highly esteemed by Warfield. He writes, "Augustine brought with him into Catholic Christianity not only a sufficient equipment of philosophical knowledge, but a powerful and trained intelligence and an intellectual instinct which had to find scope. It was in the role of Christian philosopher, seeking to give form and substance to fundamental verities from the Christian standpoint, that he first came forward in the service of faith; and though later the religious teacher and defender of the faith seemed likely to swallow up the philosophical inquirer that he never really did so, but his rich and active mind kept continually at work sounding all the depths. Thus, not only was there imparted to all his teaching an unwonted vitality, originality, and profundity, but the activities set in motion were not confined to the narrow circle of theological science but extended directly or indirectly to all forms of human life.

"In every department of philosophical inquiry he became normative for the succeeding centuries; and until the rise of Aristotelianism in the Twelfth Century and its establishment in influence by the advocacy of such teachers as Albertus Magnus and Thomas Aquinas, Augustinianism reigns supreme." But it was in the spheres of psychology and metaphysics that the dominion of Augustine was most complete, says Warfield. "He aspired to know nothing, he tells us, but God and the soul; but these he strove with all his might to know altogether."

It is of interest to note that Dr. Warfield believes that it was Augustine who gave us the Protestant Reformation. He writes, "For the Reformation inwardly considered was just the ultimate triumph of Augustine's doctrine of grace over Augustine's doctrine of the Church.

This doctrine of grace came from Augustine's hands in this positive outline completely formulated: sinful man depends for his recovery to good and to God entirely on the free grace of God; this grace is, therefore, indispensable, prevenient, irresistible, indefectible; and being thus, the free grace of God must have lain, in all the details of his conference and working, in the intention of God from all eternity."

In our judgment this volume gives us the best summary of Calvinism and Augustinianism in existence. It is truly a magnificent work by a magnificent writer. The type is large, clear, and readable. Any Christian who desires to become better informed concerning the finest intellectual presentation of Christianity will find this volume rewarding reading. J.R.R.

DEVOTIONS FOR JUNIORS. Aver Leach James. Zondervan. $2.00.

Here is a delightful book for Junior boys and girls by a well-known author. Each devotion consists of a brief, clear comment on one thought from the Word of God. Written in simple language, each devotion is designed to help young hearts grow in grace and knowledge of Christ. The author seeks not only to teach but to inspire the hearts of young people and lead them to know and accept Christ as Saviour. Nearly 150 devotions are presented. These appealing devotions will help young hearts to remember and love the Word of God.

LIVING TOGETHER IN CHRISTIAN HOMES. Frederick W. Widmer. John Knox Press. $.75.

This is a teaching guide written to help instructors lead a study group on the Christian home. It deals with how families may improve their Christian living. The author believes that it is possible for individual members of the family to be professing Christians and members of the church and yet in the home lack the Christian qualities of life. This work will help to influence the development of Christian character within the home.

HEAVEN AND HELL. John Sutherland Bonnell. Abingdon Press. $1.00.

Since thoughtful people are asking many questions about the future life, Dr. Bonnell prepared these messages to provide satisfactory answers. He discusses five aspects of the future life. The first is "Is Death a Blind Alley or an Open Road?" Number two has to do with "The Modern Christian Concept of Hell." "Is Recognition Possible After Death?" is the subject of the fourth message. The final one features "The Resurrection of Christ."

Dr. Bonnell affirms that rarely is a sermon preached these days on the subject of hell. He finds that in the past records of the Fifth Avenue Presbyterian Church of New York no sermon has been preached on this theme within forty years. He says that Henry Howard, John Kelman, and John Henry Jowett all ignored it, and in nineteen years ministry he himself never preached a sermon specifically on this subject. This is a terrible indictment of the Fifth Avenue pulpit. May God have mercy upon the souls of preachers who are commissioned to represent Christ, to preach what He preached, and yet ignore the subject of hell. We have suspected for some time that this tragic failure is more or less typical of modern metropolitan pulpits. Here on page thirty-one of this volume it is recorded in black and white that it is an actual fact.

No reasonable excuse or valid defense can be made for this criminal negligence. Dr. Bonnell writes, "Ministers who have ventured to speak on this theme have often times received not thanks but denunciation. Consequently, they have concluded that the wisest course is to avoid the subject altogether."

One who is ordained to preach the **whole** Gospel of Christ should not preach a message because he will receive thanks or refuse to preach it because of denunciation. He should preach it because it is true, because it is Biblical, because it is a part of God's revelation.

In the chapter where Dr. Bonnell discusses hell he presents the various views entertained on the subject in church history. He fails to clearly affirm the Biblical view as being his view and for the most part is exceedingly vague and hazy.

There is a great need for a new book on **Heaven and Hell,** but unfortunately Dr. Bonnell has not filled this need. He has left much to be desired. The trumpet he blows has an uncertain sound. We are thankful, however, that he has brought these great themes into the open because they are not on the periphery of Christianity but at the very heart of the four Gospels. Dr. Herrick Johnson in his monumental book called **"The Ideal Ministry"** declared that there are two everlasting sanctions of Gospel preaching—everlasting life and everlasting death.

It is a colossal mistake to create the impression that hell is the invention of Jonathan Edwards or Cotton Mather. Many preachers would be surprised if they should go through a Gospel harmony and note the passages dealing with the blessedness and the misery in the future life. They will find as one eminent New Testament scholar expressed it, "It is not an element which can be removed by any critical process, but suffuses the whole of Jesus' teaching and Jesus' life." J.R.R.

LIFE AND LOVE—A Christian View of Sex. Clyde M. Narramore. Zondervan. $2.50.

The author discusses such questions as, "How can I rate on a date?" "What is important in marriage?" "How does my body develop?" "What can be done about special sex problems?" "Is marriage in God's plan for man?" The answers are sane, satisfying, and Scriptural. The author is an outstanding authority in the field of Christian education and psychology. He gives wholesome information that will be very helpful for young people and counselors of young people.

YOUR VACATION CHURCH SCHOOL. Arlene S. Hall. Warner Press. $.75.

The author discusses the purpose of the Vacation Church School, its values and goals, and how to improve this phase of Christian education in the local church. An interesting chapter is devoted to how to evaluate the school and conserve the values.

Any Three of the Books Listed Below Sent Postpaid for $5.00

Any Book listed below sent free and postpaid for one NEW Subscription to the Journal sent us before September 15. Earn as many books as you will send in NEW Subscriptions. Send for Sample Copies, free, postpaid.

SUPPLY LIMITED — ORDER NOW

The Basis of Millennial Faith — $2.00
By Floyd E. Hamilton

Why 1000 Years? — $2.50
By Wm. Masselink

Crucial Questions About The Kingdom of God — $3.00
By George E. Ladd

John Calvin: Expository Preacher — $2.50
By Leroy Nixon

The Trial of Jesus Christ — $2.00
By Frank J. Powell

Supreme Authority — $2.00
By Norvel Geldenhuys

The Gospel of The Spirit — $1.50
By Samuel Eyles Pierce

Studies in Theology — $3.50
By Loraine Boettner

The Reformed Doctrine of Justification — $3.00
By Boehl

The Reformed Doctrine of Adoption — $2.50
By R. A. Webb

The Faith of Christendom — $3.00
By Vander Meulen

Christianity and Liberalism — $2.50
By J. Gresham Machen

The Presbyterian Conflict — $1.50
By Edwin H Rian

What Presbyterians Believe — $2.00
By Gordon H. Clark

The Impact of Christianity on the Non-Christian World — $2.50
By Dr. J. H. Bavinck

Pilgrims Progress — $1.00
By John Bunyan

The March of Truth — $2.50
By Dr. Stephen Szabo

The Called of God — $3.95
By A. B. Davidson

Twenty Missionary Stories From India — $1.50
By Basil Miller

The Reformed Doctrine of Predestination — $4.50
By Loraine Boettner

Immortality — $2.50
By Loraine Boettner

Christianity Rightly So Called — $2.00
By Samuel G. Craig

Who Say Ye That I Am — $2.50
By Wm. Childs Robinson

Christ the Bread of Life — $2.50
By Wm. Childs Robinson

Christ—The Hope of Glory — $3.00
By Wm. Childs Robinson

Knowing The Scriptures — $3.95
By A. T. Pierson

Lord of Glory — $3.50
By B. B. Warfield

The Plan of Salvation — $1.50
By B. B. Warfield

Progress of Doctrine — $1.75
By Thomas Dehany Bernard

Does God Answer Prayer — $1.50
By Louise Harrison McCraw

God Transcendent and Other Sermons — $2.50
By Gresham Machen

Christianity and Existentialism — $3.00
By J. M. Spier

The Lord From Heaven — $1.50
By Sir Robert Anderson

The Doctrines of Grace — $3.95
By George S. Bishop

The Infallibility of the Church — $3.00
By George D. Salmon

Successful Church Publicity — $1.00
By Carl F. H. Henry

The Covenant Idea in New England Theology — $2.50
By Dr. Peter Y. DeJong

The Servant of Jehovah — $2.95
By David Baron

Opening Doors — $1.50
By R. G. McLees, D.D.

Edward O. Guerrant — $1.00
By J. Gray McAllister and Grace Owings Guerrant

Manual of Reformed Doctrine — $2.50
By Prof. W. Heyns

Israel and the New Covenant — $3.75
By Roger Campbell

Order From
THE SOUTHERN PRESBYTERIAN JOURNAL
Weaverville, North Carolina

THE SOUTHERN PRESBYTERIAN JOURNAL

A Presbyterian weekly magazine devoted to the statement, defense and propagation of the Gospel, the faith which was once for all delivered unto the saints.

VOL. XV NO. 17 | AUGUST 22, 1956 | $2.50 A YEAR

. EDITORIALS .

THE SOUTHERN PRESBYTERIAN JOURNAL
The Journal has no official connection with the Presbyterian Church in the United States
Rev. Henry B. Dendy, D.D., Editor...............Weaverville, N. C.
Dr. L. Nelson Bell, Associate Editor...............Asheville, N. C.
Rev. Wade C. Smith, Associate Editor...............Weaverville, N. C.

EDITORIAL

Jesus Taught the Messianic, Not the Universal, Fatherhood of God

In a scholarly study of the four gospels, Dr. H. F. D. Sparks, Oriel Professor in Oxford, concludes that "there is no ground whatever for asserting that Jesus taught a Doctrine of 'the Fatherhood of God and the brotherhood of Man.' . . . There is no hint anywhere, either that He Himself believed, or that he taught, a Doctrine of Universal Fatherhood. For Jesus, we may say, men were not sons of God by nature, although they were capable of becoming so by Grace."

"Accordingly, the distinctively Christian Doctrine of the Divine Fatherhood, as evidenced by the Gospels and supported by the rest of the New Testament, is that God is the Father of those, who acknowledge the Messianic Sonship of Jesus, who are incorporated into His new Messianic community, and who are thereby entitled to claim that they are the sons of God through Him."
—From *Studies in the Gospels edited by Dr.* D. E. Nineham.

Some thirty-five years ago, Dr. G. Vos, Professor of Biblical Theology in Princeton, taught us this same doctrine from the Gospels, and to it we have tried to bear testimony, from time to time, in the *Southern Presbyterian Journal.* W.C.R.

Paul and the "Prophetic Ministry"

In theological circles today one of the greatest accolades to be accorded a preacher is that he has a "prophetic ministry." In lay terms this means that he has a vision, a social passion, a concern for the world situation with all of its multiplied inhumanities and injustices and because of this deep concern he writes and preaches of how such ills should be faced and liquidated.

No one questions the validity of such concern for one has but to look around him or read one single edition of a daily newspaper to admit that conditions in the world; whether they be individual problems, local group maladjustments or international tensions; all cry to high heaven of something being wrong.

While we are pleased to think of our own times as having problems peculiar to the industrial age and not existing before, nevertheless the fact remains that today's problems stem from the same sources as have those of each succeeding generation: hate, greed, lust, selfishness, etc.

To the basic moral and spiritual standards of the Ten Commandments our Lord added the implications of love in all of its fulness and as the perfect example of all that love implies He gave us the gospel of His Own transforming and redemptive work of atonement for the sins of mankind.

In the light of that gospel and of the conditions existing in the world where that gospel was first preached it is enlightening to study the messages of the first great apologist for the Christian faith, Paul.

The writer has carefully studied all of Paul's letters and has been impressed with this fact: for the apostle Paul the gospel message was central. It was a message of man's sinfulness and hopeless state; of God's divine intervention; of man's one hope to be found in accepting that which God, in His infinite love and mercy, had done for him.

With slavery on every hand Paul did not inveigh against slavery. With political corruption within and despotic imperialism without, Rome is mentioned only to claim the rights and privileges inherent in Roman citizenship. With impurity and carnality of every kind rampant they are mentioned only as they affected the individual.

Was Paul afraid of the consequences of "prophetic preaching"? Personal fear was certainly not a characteristic of this great apostle.

Was he willing to compromise his message for the sake of expediency? There is nothing to indicate such a willingness. True, he submitted to the urgings of his Jewish friends in the matter of

:aking a vow on his last trip to Jerusalem but he ìid not compromise his message.

Was he oblivious to the social, moral and po-.itical problems all around him? On the other hand ıe was keenly aware of each of them.

Why then do we find so little of the so-called 'prophetic" in Paul's writing? Was he lacking in ⁄ision, in concern for the welfare of those about ıim and to whom he ministered?

Could it be that Paul's vision was far clearer ınd more all-encompassing than some today? Did ıe not look down to the heart of these problems ınd recognize their source work for their true ınd *lasting* solution?

One cannot read the writings of Paul without :oming to the conclusion that he passionately felt hat world problems, whether social, racial, eco-ıomic, political or what have you, all must be met ınd solved at the personal, individual level before hey can be solved on any other.

Apparently Paul's concept of the Church was hat it is a witnessing organism, not primarily a :onquering organization. If such is true then one vonders whether some of the present-day activities ıf the Church are not rather far afield?

Not for one minute would we imply that the in-lividual Christian and the Church should not be oncerned about world problems. Our point is hat our concern should be implemented in ways vhich will truly help solve those problems. As Christians we know that the gospel of Jesus Christ ; still the power of God unto salvation to those vho believe. We also know that such faith must e on an individual basis.

The writer has no illusion that he knows the nswers. Nor would he discourage the application f moral and spiritual pressures against the mani-estations of human depravity all around us. All hat he asks is that we shall act with a vision vhich sees far enough and be motivated by a oncern which would treat the disease itself rather han the symptoms of the disease. L.N.B.

Satisfaction

Since God's love is stronger than His anger, Ie does not destroy the sinner, but has mercy pon Him. On the other hand, He does not arelessly overlook sin, but makes satisfaction or it in the death of His Son. It is easy to sneer at this crude conception of an angry God and to compare it unfavorably with a more refined philosophical theory of God. The weight of sin is not considered. At the Cradle and at the Cross of Christ we stand in the presence of something happening to God, to sin and to ourselves. And though our words of the anger of God and the repentance of God are the stammerings of fools, say them we must unless we would take Christ out of His Cradle and down from His Cross. "For God was in Christ reconciling the world unto Himself."

T. H. L. Parker

A Prayer for the Forgiveness of Great Sins

Peter thrice denied his Lord, and went out and wept bitterly, crying for forgiveness. Later, as Cullmann is now showing, it was Peter who taught the primitive Church the meaning of the Cross as Jesus had expounded it to the disciples from the fifty-third chapter of Isaiah.

Four hundred years ago, Thomas Cranmer, sometime Archbishop of Canterbury, was burnt at the stake in Oxford. Before his death Cranmer had signed several recantations of his evangelical convictions. At the end, he recanted his recantations and burned first the hand which had signed them. Moreover, he offered this poignant penitential plea for pardon:

O Father of heaven, O Son of God, Redeemer of the world, O Holy Ghost, three persons and one God, have mercy upon me most wretched caitiff and miserable sinner. I have offended both against heaven and earth, more than my tongue can express.

Whither then may I go, or whither shall I flee? To heaven I may be ashamed to lift up mine eyes, and in earth I find no place of refuge or succour. To Thee therefore, O Lord, do I run; to Thee do I humble myself, saying, O Lord my God, my sins be great, but yet have mercy upon me for Thy great mercy. The great mystery that God became man, was not wrought for little or few offences.

Thou didst not give Thy Son, O Heavenly Father, unto death for small sins only, but for all the greatest sins of the world, so that the sinner return unto Thee with his whole heart, as I do here at this present. Wherefore have mercy, O God, whose property is always to

The Southern Presbyterian Journal, *a Presbyterian Weekly magazine, devoted to the statement, defense, and propagation of the Gospel, the faith which was once for all delivered unto the saints,* published every Wednesday by The Southern Presbyterian Journal, Inc., in Weaverville, N. C.

Entered as second-class matter May 15, 1942, at the Postoffice at Weaverville, N. C., under the Act of March 3, 1879. Vol. XV, No. 17, August 22, 1956. Editorial and Business Offices: Weaverville, N. C. Printed in the U.S.A. by Biltmore Press, Asheville, N. C.

ADDRESS CHANGE: When changing address, please let us have both old and new address as far in advance as possible. Allow three weeks after change if not sent in advance. When possible, send an address label giving your old address.

have mercy; have mercy upon me, O Lord, for Thy great mercy. I crave nothing for mine own merits, but for Thy name's sake, that it may be hallowed thereby, and for Thy dear Son Jesus Christ's sake. W.C.R.

The Revelation of Redemption

The work of Christ did not lie simply in showing the Father to men able, and perhaps willing, to behold Him. The liberal interpretation of the revealing office of Christ as merely showing men the character of God obscures His central mission as the one who made reconciliation between God and men. He does not show God to men capable of the vision of God, but opens their eyes that they may see Him. He is not a mutual acquaintance bringing into renewed fellowship two friends who have lost touch with each other, but a Mediator of the grace of God to rebellious sinners, destroying that rebellion, and as a good Mediator leading them back to God and reconciling them to Him. We cannot consider the revelation of God in Christ apart from, or indeed, in any way as different from the reconciliation of God in Christ . . .

Jesus revealed in His preaching the gracious mercy of God, shown in Himself: He preached the Gospel of forgiveness and redemption. Hence, His preaching was a part of His redemptive activity - as necessary a part as His "office" of priest and king. Jesus is the revelation of the grace of God.

T. H. L. Parker, in
The Doctrine of the Knowledge of God

Christian Love

"Only Luke is with me. Take Mark and bring him with thee: for he is profitable to me for the ministry."

These words of Paul, shortly before his martyrdom, abound in Christian love. There is sadness in this final letter of the Apostle to the Gentiles, and I regret that we do not have a record of Mark going to Paul in prison in Rome. I am sure their reconciliation was one of the happiest moments in their lives.

Christians often disagree just as Paul and Barnabas did when Mark left them years before and returned to Jerusalem.

I do not pass judgment on that regrettable incident although, according to one legend, Mark, a young man at the time, left the first missionaries to sit at the feet of Peter in Jerusalem in order to secure the facts to write the first Gospel. A few even suggest that the Gospel was dictated by Peter. Whatever the cause of Mark's alleged desertion, Paul, at that time, could not accept Mark's excuse, but years later Paul may have felt that he had misjudged Mark, and this appeal to Timothy to bring Mark to him, revealed Paul's great heart. Mark had become a valuable asset to Christianity and Paul recognized this and in Christian love had forgiven him.

How many years of coolness existed between Paul and Mark no one knows. When and where they were reconciled no one knows. But here we see Paul had either already made peace with Mark or was authorizing Timothy to appeal to Mark for him.

The only way brothers in Christ, who do not understand each other, can restore normal relations is in Christian love. Too often we see flaws in our friends and co-workers in the church, whereas we should realize they are "profitable" in the promotion of the Gospel and receive them as brothers. This was the basis on which Paul reversed his opinion about Mark. It is an example for Christians who fall out among themselves, it conforms with Christ's commandment, "Love one another."

We do not have the complete story of Mark's "walk out" but we have the happy ending, proving once again that love overcometh all things.

Ralph Brewer

Slander In Brazil

By L. Nelson Bell

(*Continued*)

Last week we told in generalities something of the situation which has developed in Brazil through the seeds of discord sowed by Dr. Carl McIntire and his able ally, Rev. Dr. Israel Gueiros. At the conclusion of that article we promised to give specific instances of how the *Christian Beacon* and some of those who have written in behalf of Dr. Gueiros have deliberately misrepresented the facts.

Herewith are *some* of the misrepresentations:

1. *"Dr. Gueiros is backed by the overwhelming majority of one of the five Synods of the Presbyterian Church of Brazil."* (Letter from Miss Margaret Harden soliciting funds for Dr. Gueros).

Dr. Gueiros has the support of 4 of the 49 pastors in his Synod. The majority is "overwhelming," but it is *against him.*

2. *It is due to the compromising attitude of Southern Presbyterian missionaries . . . that this condition and necessity has arisen."* (Same letter).

The writer can say after *careful* investigation that our missionaries in Brazil are as conservative a group of Christians as we have ever met anywhere. They represent historic evangelical Presbyterianism *at its best.*

3. In a "Personal Testimony" Dr. Gueiros gives the impression that his Synod, under his leadership, took action protesting the presence on the faculty of the Seminary at Recife of a man who was teaching liberalism.

Actually, action was taken by the faculty, the Dean, the Board of Trustees and the Executive Committee of the General Assembly of the Presbyterian Church in Brazil without any reference to Dr. Gueiros. The Synod was informed of the action already taken and voted unanimously to concur in and approve of the Board's action.

4. Dr. Gueiros states in a letter dated March, 1956, *"As soon as I began to fight modernism within my denomination along with the leaders of the I.C.C.C., I was compelled to resign my position in the Seminary. This was due to pressure of the Board of Missions."*

The fact is that there is no "modernism" in the Presbyterian Church in Brazil. Dr. Gueiros began a campaign of villification of his own Christian brethren, boasted that he was "more tolerant than McIntire," and made a consummate nuisance of himself. Furthermore, one has to study the situation in Brazil to realize that the Boards do not bring "pressure" on the Brazilian Presbyterian Church. No where in the world is there a more independent and self-governing body. Let the Boards begin to bring "pressure" for some objective and the very opposite is apt to eventuate.

5. In this same letter Dr. Gueiros says the Brazilian pastors in the north *"lost confidence in the Seminary."*

The writer found the very opposite to be the case. One Brazilian pastor told the writer: "This whole distressing matter has drawn us together as never before."

6. Dr. Gueiros states that his *"colleagues and fellow-pastors have asked me to start a new Seminary."*

Even in his own Presbytery the largest number of votes he could muster is four, two of them his own kinsmen. We did not find one man who approves of the proposed "Seminary."

7. Dr. Gueiros says the Seminaries are *"undermining the faith of our students."*

Please read our first article, appearing last week. There one will see how *vigorously* the Seminary under condemnation *reacted against liberal teaching.*

8. The *Christian Beacon* of March 15th, 1956, states that the Seminary in Recife, *"is under the control of the missionary boards of the Northern and Southern Presbyterian Assemblies."*

This is untrue. The Seminary is controlled by a Board of Trustees consisting of nine men, seven from the Brazilian Presbyterian Church, one from the U.S. and one from the U.S.A. missions. This Board is responsible directly to the General Assembly of the Presbyterian Church in Brazil and all administrative offices in the Seminary are held by Brazilians.

9. In a letter dated April 16th, 1956, Dr. Gueiros, speaking of a liberal teacher in the Seminary said: *"his fellow missionaries were not ready to close his mouth."*

This statement is false. His fellow missionaries instituted *immediate* steps to effect his withdrawal from the Seminary.

10. In a letter of the same date Miss Margaret Harden speaks of the $15,000 asked for as *"a very small amount to do such a great work as saving so many Brazilian churches and a great evangelistic field from modernism and apostasy."*

But, in the June 28th issue of the *Christian Beacon* Dr. Gueiros says the *"majority of the pastors in the Church . . . are as fundamental as I am . . . but not as well informed."*

The writer marvels that Drs. McIntire and Gueiros should have chosen the Brazilian Presbyterian Church as the object of their attacks. Seeds of discord and suspicion have been sown in a field as untouched by modernism as any in the world.

11. In the *Christian Beacon* of June 28th Dr. Gueiros states: *"The Presbyterian Church in Brazil took decision to withdraw from the World Council of Churches only to avoid a split which was about to take place if the Church did not do that."*

The Presbyterian Church of Brazil has *never been a member* of the World Council of Churches and Dr. Gueiros knows it. At the first meeting of the World Council a Brazilian pastor, living in America, attended and his name was listed as a representative of the Brazilian Church. The World Council carried the name of the Brazilian Presbyterian Church without authorization and later dropped the listing when informed the *individual* who attended did so as an individual and had no authority to represent his church.

12. In the same article in the *Christian Beacon* Dr. Gueiros states: *"Once more modernism has succeeded in dividing a strong and fundamental denomination."*

It is not "modernism" but Dr. Gueiros who has divided his church. Several years ago, under the evangelistic preaching of Dr. Edwin Orr, Dr. Gueiros confessed that he had greviously sinned in speaking against and attacking his fellow ministers and that these attacks were not justified. Since then he has returned to the "mire."

13. Dr. Gueiros says: *"I need some material help in a hurry to face the problems over here."*

The writer believes that if American money stops, this "valiant defense of the faith" will also stop. There are financial aspects of this whole case which need clarifying.

14. In this same letter Dr. Gueiros says: *"Modernism has infiltrated every part of our church life."*

This is said in connection with an appeal for MONEY to *"throw off the modernist yoke."* We hope the reader sees the full significance of this. It is NOT true that modernism has infiltrated the Brazilian church. This appeal for MONEY goes on to say: *". . . it becomes impossible for the faithful remnant to support their pastors without some outside aid."*

Actually the "faithful remnant" consists (so far as Presbyterians are concerned), chiefly of Dr. Israel Gueiros himself.

15. Miss Harden writes that the proposed Seminary is *"evidently going to be a great instrument in the hands of the Lord."*

Actually it will not be a "Seminary" but some kind of Bible School and it will certainly cater to the schismatic and non-Presbyterian elements in Brazil.

16. The *Christian Beacon* appeals to Southern Presbyterians to *"quit supporting the enemies of such an able, stalwart leader and give their money instead to the Independent Board for Presbyterian Foreign Missions."*

One of the distressing things that we heard in Brazil is of missionaries who are working, not to evangelize the lost but to proselyte from the Presbyterian church those who already believe. This may be "missions" but it is hardly worthy of the support of those who would follow the Great Commission.

17. The July 19th issue of the *Christian Beacon* editorializes: *The Presbyterians of Brazil are confronted with an increasingly serious situation as it concerns the taking over of their church by modernistic influences."*

No such "situation" exists, except in the minds of a few misguided and obsessed individuals. Let the reader judge from the following.

In Recife we met Rev. Victor Pester, an ordained minister in the Brazilian Presbyterian Church, and a member of the Presbytery of Pernambuco. Mr. Pester comes from England and has lived in Brazil many years. He volunteered the following statement to the writer: "I came from a Plymouth Brethren background and you know how rigidly we hold to the conservative theological position. In my association with my fellow Brazilian pastors, and without one iota of compromise on my part, there has never been one time when I have not found myself in the most complete accord with them in doctrine and in practice. There simply is no modernism here."

The writer was in Recife when the Presbytery of Recife met to consider the case of Dr. Israel Gueiros. Neither he nor any missionary attended the meeting of Presbytery, but two days after the conclusion of the meeting he met with and talked to a number of the members of Presbytery. Nothing but *sorrow* was expressed over the situation. They were most unwilling to proceed against Dr. Gueiros but he had left them no alternative. The American Council and the International Council under the leadership of Dr. Carl McIntire has become his goal and his obsession. That these two organizations have been repudiated by the Bible Presbyterian Church is already known in Brazil but the significance of this repudiation has not yet seeped in.

It is a tragic situation and one which must make the enemy of souls rejoice. But, the gospel *is* being preached and God is working in that land, despite the frailties and follies of man.

One of our own missionaries, now on furlough, writes as follows:

"Let me state that the Presbyterian Church of Brazil is preaching and teaching the TRUTH, the WHOLE TRUTH and nothing but the TRUTH . . . in its Seminaries, in its churches, in the cities, in the country . . . and people are turning to Jesus Christ . . . The Bible in its entirety, the Westminster faith in its simple purity, the Catechisms of our Church, and her hymns are being broadcast, protected (when necessary), hallowed and revered on every hand and every minute of the hour."

We know no better ending for this report on the situation in Brazil than (with our missionaries in mind) to quote Paul's words to the Christians in Thessalonica:

"We give thanks to God always for you all, making mention of you in our prayers; remembering without ceasing your work of faith, and labour of love, and patience of hope in our Lord Jesus Christ, in the sight of God and our Father; knowing brethren beloved, your election of God."

The Reformed Faith And The Contemporary Crisis In Education

By C. GREGG SINGER, Ph.D.
Belhaven College Jackson, Mississippi

This is the first of the series of articles carrying the messages given on the program on OUR PRESBYTERIAN HERITAGE given at Weaverville, N. C., on Wednesday, August 15th, 1956. *The other addresses are to follow in succeeding issues of the Southern Presbyterian Journal.* H.B.D.

A. INTRODUCTION.

One of the more encouraging signs on the educational front today is the growth of criticism of nearly every aspect of current educational endeavor from many quarters. This critical attitude toward an institution which has long regarded itself as sacrosanct and immune to the judgment of ordinary mortals is as healthy as it is long over due. The awakening of many segments of the public to the tragic plight of education in this country is encouraging, but it is regrettable that much of this criticism is directed toward the symptoms of the disease rather than toward its causes. It is unfortunate that so much of this growing furor is concerning itself with the more obvious and peripheral problems with which education is beset, with the problem of more and better teachers, of higher salaries, of more and better buildings and with segregation. I would not imply that these are unimportant, but I would suggest that they are merely symptoms of a deadly disease which is striking at the very heart of our educational system at all levels.

It is also regrettable that many of the remedies which are proposed to meet the problems of the day are the property of those who fail to understand the nature of the issues with which they are seeking to cope. Arising from an improper diagnosis, these remedies are doomed to failure, and some of them, like federal aid to education, may well intensify the illness.

II. THE NATURE OF THE CRISIS

The real crisis which confronts education today does not lie in these peripheral problems which are merely the outward symptoms of the disease. In fact, the undue emphasis which is placed upon these outward symptoms serves to screen and to hide from the public the true nature of the crisis before us. The issues are far deeper and more fundamental than most discussions on the subject indicate. They concern the nature and purposes of education, and of man's purpose in life under God. The tragedy lies in the fact that American education has cut itself off from the Bible and has lost its sense of direction. To overcome this loss of inward assurance and achievement it has taken refuge in external trappings and substituted costly programs of "life adjustment" for the older curriculum and activities. But this retreat to the trivial has finally been discerned for what it really is; it has been tried and found wanting in this world of the twentieth century. The crisis has manifested itself in at least three different ways.

In the first place, American education, on the whole, no longer educates and no longer seeks to educate in the older meaning of this term. Rather has it fallen victim to the rampant anti-intellectualism of our day and many educators are seemingly quite content with a curriculum which has a minimum of solid subject matter and a maximum of courses which are usually called social or life adjustment experiences, whatever these phrases may mean.

It is now rather commonplace to hear the complaint that high school graduates can neither read nor spell well. It is equally true that they show even less proficiency in mathematics, the sciences and other subjects which require disciplined minds for their mastery. Indeed, it is quite true that in all too many cases the average high school graduate is less educated than the grammar school product of 1900. But these charges fail to convey the depths of that intellectual degradation which is so characteristic of contemporary educational activity. The average high school graduate of today has little intellectual enthusiasm or desire and he has earned his diploma by taking only those academic courses which are still required for either graduation or college admission. For many of them the peripheral and less exacting courses are far more attractive and in most high schools there is an increasing tendency to decorate the curriculum to an excessive degree with such attractions.

Inevitably the colleges are affected by this rising tide of anti-intellectualism and increasingly they are finding it necessary to use the first two years to give to their students that degree of adequate preparation for the more advanced work which was at one time the prerogative of the high schools. This lowering of the academic standards on the part of the colleges is regretted by many professors and administrators of the universities and liberal arts colleges, but it has been cheerfully accepted and even defended by the professional educators who regard it not as an evil to be corrected, but an educational advance of great merit. For them education is no longer to be regarded in the historic sense of the term, but as an instrument for enlarging social experiences of the students and advancing a democratic way of life. One is tempted to ask how a democratic way of life can be sustained in the midst of such intellectual carelessness and confusion.

This intellectual debasement of the American schools and colleges can be correctly attributed to the pervasive influence of the educational philosophy of John Dewey and to the fact that Instrumentalism has captured nearly every department of education in our great universities and has penetrated to a greater or lesser extent every state department of education in the nation. There are very few local school systems which have not felt the devastating effects of the influence of Teachers' College of Columbia University. Hundreds of thousands of teachers since 1920 have been infected with this deadly virus of the mind and the fact that most of them were not aware of the implications of this educational philosophy has made it no less dangerous.

Its danger lies in the fact that it was not merely a philosophy of education of dubious value, but that it was actually a philosophy of life, an interpretation of God, man, truth and human destiny which at every point was a negation of the historic Christian faith. Dewey's denial of the existence of absolute truth and his pragmatic approach to the meaning of man and human experience made a mockery of those assumptions which had the life blood of education in America since its inception. What his disciples failed to realize was the fact that if Dewey was correct, then there was not suitable foundation or purpose left for the educational activity in which they were engaging. The logical conclusion to his position was the "child centered" curriculum and this meaningless phrase became the stock in trade of all the curriculum planners who wanted to be progressive.

In this new curriculum the accumulated wisdom of the past, the priceless heritage of western culture preserved from previous eras, was quietly cast to one side in favor of more attractive courses of study which would focus the attention of the student on the problems and promises of his own way. These progressive educators, drifting aimlessly themselves with the currents of pragmatism, forgot that without the light of the past and without a Biblical frame of reference the present defied interpretation. The inevitable result of such a program has been the creation of a generation of students which neither knows or appreciates its heritage and sees little value or of promise in the present.

Caught in this groundswell of anti-intellectualism were not only the social sciences and the humanities, but the sciences and mathematics as well. It was no longer regarded as desirable for students to acquire a mastery of subject matter. The learning of facts was replaced by the development of attitudes. But attitudes which have no factual basis must of necessity be erroneous and dangerous.

Inescapably this anti-intellectualism affected the training of teachers. Methods rather than knowledge became the order of the day and courses in methods have so cluttered up most departments of education that their offerings have become the laughing stock of intelligent people and an insult not easily endured by serious students.

Until this grave defect in the training of teachers is removed, the shortage of desirable teachers will continue. I grant that in many cases salaries are too low and no one will deny that the teacher is worthy of his hire. But it is most unlikely that increased salaries will be a sufficient inducement to attract scholarly minds to the teaching profession as long as they are required to enter it through such educational wastelands. Most of the courses which are required in the preparation of teachers constitute an unwarranted insult to which most serious students are unwilling to expose themselves. And it is a matter of professional knowledge that in most colleges the weakest students gravitate toward a major in education. Inescapably the

lic schools is important and such teaching is highly desirable, but it is not the real issue and a policy which would permit released time for Biblical study would not in any way remove the basic problem. It would simply bring it into a sharper focus.

The dominant philosophy in American education is totally and irrevocably opposed to the whole system of Christian doctrine. Its fundamental assumptions concerning education negate those of orthodox Christianity at every point. It denies the Christian views of God, truth, man, sin, redemption and human destiny, and it is very difficult to find a standard text book in psychology which in any way makes a place for the Christian view of the soul. There is no paragraph in the Westminster Confession of Faith which is acceptable to those who consciously accept contemporary educational philosophy. Fortunately in the South there are many convinced evangelicals who see this fatal contradiction and who teach accordingly, but in many sections this is not the case.

For the great majority Christian doctrine must be reinterpreted in the light of pragmatism. They are alarmingly optimistic in their dedication to the proposition that human sin and evil can be corrected by appropriate injections of knowledge and an increased social awareness. They are also convinced that it is within the power of education to bring about a millennial society in which man will achieve a type of righteousness compatible with the findings of modern science and psychology. There is no social ill that cannot be cured nor problem that cannot be solved by education.

The cleavage between Presbyterianism and modern education is not confined to a few basic issues such as the authority of the Scriptures, the nature of evil and the theory of organic evolution. Rather does it involve two mutually exclusive world and life views, the one of which finds its source and authority in the Scriptures and the other of which looks to man for its frame of reference. It is a conflict between humanism which is intrenched in our schools and Christian theism.

In summary then, the crisis in education is not to be construed in terms of a rampant anti-intellectualism, nor even in terms of the affinity of its dominant philosophy with that of Communism. Essentially the crisis finds its deepest expression in the conflict with historic Christianity. It is a crisis of such depth and extent that its consideration may well cause thoughtful Americans to wonder whether such a system of education is worthy of his support, whether it should be maintained and whether it may not be a national liability instead of a national asset.

III. THE ANSWER OF REFORMED THEOLOGY

It is my profound conviction that the Reformed Faith has much to say to contemporary education and educators who refuse to heed its message do so at their peril. Indeed, if our schools persist in their present folly they will be soon facing a bankruptcy so hopeless and yet so obvious that the citizens of this country will refuse to support an institution which is betraying those very ideals it was created to preserve.

Today education is a house divided against itself. Its philosophy is at war with the heritage it is called upon to perpetuate and enrich and not only is it at war with the past, but it is equally confused and uncertain in regard to the future. In educational literature there is much discussion of aims and goals, but its pragmatism logically does away with the possibility of such conceptions. One hears much concerning the necessity of educating the whole person for life in a democracy, but there is no agreement on the meaning of either of these two terms, nor can there be within the frame of Dewey's philosophy. The empiricist is the least able of all men to grapple with the future.

Education is a house divided in its practices as well as in its philosophy. The philosophical deficiencies inevitably bring in their wake failures in accomplishment and this is precisely the case today. Our schools are not producing the kind of trained citizenship which the nation has the right to demand. There is abundant evidence that their products are neither ready to take their part in the economic and political and intellectual life of the nation nor do they show any ability to live in a democratic society. In short, they are not being educated as they should be to live in the world of the twentieth century.

The solution to this crisis is to be found in the Reformed theology and its application to education and the intellectual life of the nation. The key to the situation lies in the loss of certainty and security which has engulfed the modern mind. The sense of certainty must be recovered, a certainty that God and truth exist and that God can be known and that He has revealed Himself infallibly to man in the Scriptures. Education has lost itself in a morass of uncertainty because it has cast itself adrift from the Scriptures.

It is at this point that the Reformed Faith offers the only hope. Education must accept

cational psychology teachers are being called upon to teach the unteachable in their class rooms what is hardly worth teaching them in the first place.

From this impasse education can be rescued only by a return to the Reformed and Biblical view of man. In the Scriptures it finds a meaningfulness and purpose afforded by no philosophy. The Reformed doctrine of man brings educational effort into the proper perspective.

Not only does it affirm that there is a realm of truth which must be taught to men, but it also affirms that man is teachable, that he is worthy of being taught, and that the cultivation of his mind is a divinely imposed obligation and privilege.

Since man is created in the image of God, it is his high duty to think the thoughts of God after Him and to seek to find that meaning which God by creation has given to the world of nature and that prior interpretation which He has given to all human experience. God made both the knowing mind of man and the knowable world of nature. Man as God's vice regent is entrusted with the great privilege of developing a culture which glorifies the Father. An educational system which fails to recognize this divine mandate as the only valid foundation for its existence is a contradiction in terms and must inevitably fail.

Although the Scriptures place education on a very high pedestal they also surround it with strict limitations and never expect more from it than can be accomplished. The Bible never confuses knowledge with righteousness, learning with regeneration or culture with sanctification and it never calls upon education to produce these Christian fruits. This recognition of the limitations of education stands in sharp contrast to the democratic philosophy which dominates the educational picture today. Although it takes a very low view of truth, culture and of man, it actually places around the educational process a halo of which it is utterly unworthy. There is then within contemporary educational philosophy an ironic contradiction which does much to explain why the friends of the present pattern are so concerned with the trends and failures which are so evident.

Dewey and his disciples looked on the schools as an instrument for human betterment and social progress, although within the framework of their own philosophy the meaning of these terms was quite elusive. But in general they equated social progress with the spread of the democratic way of life, the elimination of war and other major social ills and they sought to enlist the schools in the achievement of a socialistic society. Many of the progressives in educational circles have equated the democratic way of life with socialism, and they would dedicate the schools of America to the attainment of this goal of a humanistic and democratic Utopia, the realization of the Kingdom of Man on earth.

The Reformed Faith would never allow education to fall into such pernicious errors. If it exalts man on the one hand as being created in the image of God, it with equal clarity asserts the awfulness of human sin and the doctrine of total depravity. This Biblical doctrine must be a living reality for those who engage in the great calling of education. Educators who keep before them the Biblical doctrine of sin and evil will never confuse learning with justification by faith nor the achievement of a democratic society with the eternal reign of Jesus Christ as Lord of Lords.

They will never expect more from education than the Bible allows and they will remember that our schools and colleges must remain as the servants of the Church and never pose as its equals or superior. Christian educators will never regard the school as substitutes for either the church or the home, but as the instrument by which the redeemed will be more effectively trained for Christian service and their own particular vocations. Discarding the impossible and hopelessly frustrating goals which humanism has dictated for our schools and colleges, they will set forth those purposes and aims for education which are truly in accord with the Scriptures.

With this anchorage in the Bible as the Word of God they will not fall into that dull despair into which instrumentalism and all its many cousins must inevitably lead on the one hand, nor into the charmingly deceptive snares of humanism on the other. If they will not conclude that all serious intellectual training and activity are in vain, neither will they insist that the schools must rebuild American society. Rather will they agree that the role of education is to enable men to serve and glorify the Living God more effectively and to bring their cultural activity and development into subjection to a sovereign God and His revelation of Himself in the Scriptures.

Christian educators will banish from their thinking every concession to humanism, to the doctrine of the sovereignty and essential goodness of man and the perfectability of man and his society, for these are the rocks which have nearly wrecked the American school system.

In the light of these Biblical goals for educational activity, these Christian educators will then rebuild the curricula of all the schools, from the elementary grades through the colleges, for these must be brought into an essential harmony with the Biblical view of culture. Humanism has almost destroyed the curriculum of the high schools as it once existed and many of our colleges and universities have not escaped its baneful influences. The liberal arts and Biblical emphases, once generally accepted as essential for a sound education, have given place to a multiplicity of so called practical and peripheral courses which have contributed so much to the general intellectual debasement of our day. The Reformed faith can no more tolerate anti-intellectualism in the schools and colleges than it can in theology and Christian thought. It abhors the one even as it rebukes the other.

In conclusion, I would suggest that the Reformed Faith has everything to say to education today. It is the one remedy for those maladies of the soul and mind which beset American education. If our schools fail to heed its message they will continue to drift from one new cult to another. Having already lost their vision as to what constitutes a genuine education, they will gradually lose that respectable mediocrity of which they now boast and usher in a new day of spiritual and intellectual darkness the end of which can be only national destruction.

ANGLERS

By WADE C. SMITH

Lesson No. 153

The Whole Church Working At It

"Activity for the salvation of the world is absolutely necessary for the church, necessary to the development of the preacher and the Christian people, necessary to express the principle of life, and also the spirit of Jesus. It is essential to the development of the life of the individual Christian, and the kingdom of our Lord."

—Charles Herbert Rust

"The example of my own church is sufficient to teach that there is no insuperable difficulty in transforming the normal church into an evangelistic center. The difficulties in the way are class feeling, parochialism of idea, and the fastidiousness of a false culture." —W. J. Dawson

"The best evangelistic work is that form which enlists the largest number of helpers. Using a synthesis of methods, in which all talents and officers are recognized and employed, it puts greatest emphasis on personal work. Personal work to be most effective must be systematized, giving attention to training in methods and leading those who undertake it to co-ordinate their efforts, uniting their endeavors in order to secure better and quicker results. The idea should obtain, moreover, that the evangelistic efforts of the church and of the individual should be continuous, knowing no intermittance, carrying their loving zeal into all seasons of the year, into all localities, including those of temporary residence or even of recreation, and throughout life from the dawn of Christian existence to its attainment of the final "well done" which will be the highest reward of every sincere spirit. And it cannot be too strongly emphasized or too often reiterated that it should never be the case that the interest of the worker ceases when some formal confession of Christ has been obtained."

—Bishop Leete.

This is a challenge on a high level. It will require a high type of faith to meet it. Here is the picture of an all-the-year-round soul-winning church, its entire membership imbued with the evangelistic spirit and all departments making evangelism the chief objective. It is reasonable. It is according to the will of God. It is feasible. And it can be demonstrated by any church that will rise to the point of vision and faith to honestly try it. One main weakness of the church in this line lies in the fact that with rare exceptions congregations have depended upon a periodical "revival" or "protracted meeting," led by some outside evangelist, to promote their evangelistic programs where, if indeed, they have a defined policy. These revivals are usually held in the Spring or Autumn (or both) and often more with the purpose of recruiting membership than to rescue dying souls. Such meetings are by no means to be despised, though often questionable methods creep in. A church that is in a "slow dying state," its spirituality at a low ebb, calls for the help of the professional evangelist like the sick man calls for a surgeon. Surgeons are necessary to save our lives at times, but none will claim that living by surgery is a normal state of existence. Yet we make here the confident claim that the best "surgeon" for a dying church is the Holy Spirit, and it is nowhere stated in God's Word that His coming is dependent upon any mortal outside the congregation, not even though that mortal be a high-priced evangelist, with a whole troupe of salaried workers and musicians.

All honor is accorded here to those consecrated men and women in evangelistic parties who have taken to the road for Christ and have conducted great revivals in our communities, doing much good and winning many souls. Though they came high they were worth the price (as in the case when a skilful surgeon comes to our relief and saves a life); but it does not follow that any church should be in the slightest dependent upon such visitations, either in the community-wide method or for the local congregation alone. It is not unusual to see a congregation lapse, after a "protracted meeting" into its former paralysis, while it complacently waits for the next Spring revival to come around - and that may not be the fault of the evangelist. It can be readily seen that a church whose evangelism springs from within and functions steadily the year round will have a spiritual vitality that not only

pletely unaware of the spiritual gifts that are available to us (12:1). Notice each of the spiritual gifts mentioned in vv.8-9,28. Count the number of times the word "Spirit" is mentioned in vv.8-11. What is said about the Spirit in each case? Did you think that you could choose the work you do in the church simply on the basis of your own preference? God desires to give each of us a gift that will enable us to fit into His overall plan for the Church (vv.4-7,12,18). What principle is laid down in vv.21-24 concerning one's attitude toward the lesser gifts? toward the higher gifts (v.31a)? How eager is your desire for spiritual gifts?

Thursday, September 6, *Ephesians* 4:1-7. What is the general exhortation given in v.1? How is this general exhortation made specific in vv.2-3? What is the central drive of these specific exhortations? What does Paul say about your Christian life (v.1) if you find you cannot get along with fellow-believers (vv.2-3)? Do all Christian people have enough in common to enable them to live harmoniously with each other (vv.4-6)? Can this harmony exist despite any adverse circumstances life may thrust upon us (v.1a)? Does harmony mean uniformity (vv.7-8)? Pray that the several factors mentioned in vv.4-5 may become so all-important in your daily living that those factors which have created friction between you and fellow-Christians may seem trivial and unimportant.

Friday, September 7, *Ephesians* 4:11-16. There are so many diverse voices speaking with "authority" on religious subjects today that many lay-Christians, in their confusion, believe it is impossible to discern truth from error. What does Paul have to say concerning such a position (vv.14-15)? Is maturity in our Christian convictions something we inherit when we become Christians or something we must work for and grow into (vv.14,15-16)? To whom must we pay diligent attention if we are to grow into mature knowledge (vv.11-12)? Paul points out that a lack of ability to recognize spiritual truth can also be due to the presence of sin in our lives (vv.18b,22-23). What specific steps can you take to deepen your spiritual discernment?

Saturday, September 8, *Ephesians* 6:5-9. Substitute your own occupation for the word "slave" in v.5 and see how many of the exhortations of vv.5-8 could apply to you. What changes would be brought about in your work attitude and performance if you conscientiously lived by the principles in these verses? Do these principles apply to the more respected as well as to the lowlier types of work (v.9)? Pray for the strength (v.10) to do your daily work, not as a "man-pleaser" (v.6), but unto the Lord (v.7), looking to the wages God has promised (v.8).

LESSON FOR SEPTEMBER 2

The Royal Law Of Love

Background Scripture: Luke 6:27-30; 10:30-37; James 2
Devotional: I Cor. 13

The Law of Love is rightly called, "The Royal Law," for God is the Sovereign Ruler of the universe, and any Law that comes from Him is a "Royal Law." God is love. God so loved the world that he gave his Son. Our Saviour has been appointed King, and the law of His kingdom is the royal law of love.

Our Devotional Reading is the great Hymn of Love, written by the apostle Paul. We usually think of Paul as a great missionary, a great theologian, a great writer, and the exponent of Faith; salvation by grace through faith. Paul was also a "Heart-Giant," and out of his great heart of love, inspired by the Spirit, he wrote this matchless description of Christian Love: "The Greatest Thing in the World." This thirteenth chapter of First Corinthians has always been considered one of the supremely beautiful chapters of the Bible.

In it he shows that without Love all the other Christian graces or "Gifts" are worthless.

Love is "the more excellent way," one of the best "Gifts" which we are to covet earnestly. We may be as eloquent as an angel, as wise as the greatest of the prophets, have faith enough to move mountains, be kind to the poor, and willing to die for our faith, but if we are not motivated by Love, all these will amount to nothing; be a zero.

Then he breaks Love up into its component parts, like the colors of the rainbow in the sky. In verses 4-7, this is done. "Love never faileth." Of the three abiding graces, Faith, Hope, and Love, "the greatest of these is Love." Let us consider this Royal Law, (1) As given in a sermon, (2) As illustrated in a parable, and (3) As applied by James.

I. *As Given in a Sermon:* Luke 6:27-31.

This Law is given in both Matthew and Luke. In Matthew it is a part of the Sermon on the Mount, and in Luke, what is sometimes called, The Sermon in the Plain. This was a Law which He often repeated and emphasized in different forms, for it was a Law which He wished to get into the hearts of his disciples.

He puts the Royal Law in its most difficult form. Ordinary men love those who love them. It takes extraordinary men — born-again men — Christian men, to fulfill the Law as stated here. Loving our enemies, doing good to those that hate us, blessing those that curse us, praying for those who despitefully use us; these things can only be done by people who belong to the "Royal Family." It is not easy, even for them.

Turning the other cheek to those who smite us, and giving to every man who asks of us, are traits of character found in true followers of the One Who turned His back to the smiters, and allowed vulgar men to spit in His face, the face of a King. The "Golden Rule," (verse 31), rightly interpreted, can only be used by people who have "Golden Hearts" which have been touched and transformed by the grace of God. Who can read these words uttered by Jesus in His sermon and not blush for shame as he measures himself by this rule? Oh that God would give us the grace to really live by the Golden Rule! Men of the world sometimes thoughtlessly and rather flippantly say, I live by the Golden Rule; I think I will be all right; I have no need of a Saviour. I want to challenge such men to examine their hearts. I firmly believe that no one but a regenerated person can even approach the keeping of the Royal Law of Love.

II. *As Illustrated in the Parable of the Good Samaritan:* Luke 10:30-37.

Let us go back and see the occasion for this parable. A certain lawyer had asked Jesus a question, tempting Him; Master, what shall I do to inherit eternal life? Jesus had referred him to the law. The lawyer was not satisfied,

used as our Topic: "If ye fulfill the royal law according to the Scripture, Thou shalt love thy neighbor as thyself, ye do well. He shows us how we can fulfill it.

1. The Royal Law of Love is never partial; it shows no respect of persons. This can have a broad application. He applies it to two classes of people; the rich and the poor. Do we honor the rich and despise the poor? It is easy to fall into this error. Most of us have great respect for wealth. Sometimes we envy those who have more than we have. We are tempted to flatter them, and show them special regard, to fawn upon them. We forget that there are two kinds of riches; one is material, the other moral and spiritual. We can see the "gold ring and goodly apparel," but we cannot see the wealth of character which may be possessed by the man in poor raiment. The poor man may be "an heir of the kingdom," destined to inherit all the riches of Christ, while the rich man may be an outcast. Remember that James is speaking of wicked rich men. There are rich men who have both kinds of wealth, like Abraham and Job. The Royal Law would have us love all alike, and treat all alike. This is the real law of liberty. It sets us free from prejudice and faulty judgments in relation to our neighbor.

2. It shows itself in "Works."

There has been a great deal of discussion over this passage - verses 14 to 26 - and some have tried to say that Paul and James teach different kinds of Justification; one by Faith, the other by Works. The difficulty can be dissolved by one expression of Paul, "Faith that works by Love." Both James and Paul would agree that it takes a "Living Faith" to save. Faith must show its vitality by expressing itself in deeds.

James uses a very plain and simple illustration. Suppose a brother or sister is naked or hungry. We can say, Depart in peace, be warmed and filled, but such a faith would be mockery. Faith needs to follow the Law of Love. "I feel so sorry," said a man, as he watched a house burn down. "How sorry do you feel," said another, as he reached in his pocket and drew out a ten dollar bill. Deeds prove the genuineness of both Faith and Love.

His second illustration is that of Abraham. Paul uses the same man. Paul says, Abraham was justified by faith. James says he was justified by works. Both are right, and there is no difficulty, if we remember the rule, Faith works by love. Abraham showed that he had a living faith by his obedience. He was justified by faith, and he was justified by works. His works proved that his faith was not dead, but a living faith. Rahab also believed, but she hid the spies. Her faith was living faith.

YOUTH PROGRAM FOR SEPTEMER 2

Can You Explain The Trinity?

Hymn: "Come, Thou Almighty King"
Prayer
Scripture: John 16:1-15.
Hymn: "Ancient Of Days"
Offering
Hymn: "Holy, Holy, Holy!"

Program Leader:

If you can explain the Trinity, you are a rare person indeed. The doctrine of the Trinity is immensely important to Christianity, but it remains a mystery that we shall not understand fully until we see God face to face. We believe it not because it is taught in the very nature of things or because we have been able to reason it out, but because it is clearly taught in the Scriptures. Belief in the Trinity is a very distinctive Christian belief, and our only authority for believing it is the Bible.

Briefly stated, the doctrine is this: God exists in three persons, "and these three are one God, the same in substance, equal in power and glory." The three persons of the Trinity are the Father, the Son, and the Holy Spirit. They are not three separate Gods, but three forms of the one God. When we speak of the persons as forms, we do not mean that God is Father at one time, Son at another time, and Spirit at another. He is all three at the same time. Neither do we mean that the essence of God is divided into three equal parts. The fullness of God is in each person at all times. It is easy to see why this doctrine is beyond human comprehension. We believe it because it is taught in the Bible, and as we believe it, we find that it answers to our experience with God.

First Speaker:

Some people seem to think that the Old Testament contains no indications of the Trinity, but this is incorrect. In Genesis 1:26 and 11:7 God speaks of Himself in the plural, indicating more than one person in God. Isaiah 48:16 the Spirit is spoken of as a separate person. These are but samples of Old Testament passages which point to the Trinity.

It is only natural that the New Testament should contain clearer teachings concerning the Trinity. There are several passages where all three persons are explicitly mentioned, such as the records of Jesus' baptism. Matthew 3:16,17; Mark 1:10,11; Luke 3:22; and John 1:32-34. Another such passage is the one which has been read to us from the sixteenth chapter of John. Perhaps the clearest teachings of all are found in the great commission (Matt. 28:19) and in the Apostolic benediction (II Corinthians 13:14).

Our next three speakers will consider the three persons of the Trinity separately.

Second Speaker:

The name "Father" as applied to God is not always used in the same sense in the Bible. Sometimes it may denote the Triune God as (1) the originator of all created things, (2) as the Father of Israel, or (3) as the Father of believers who are His spiritual children. In a more fundamental sense the name is applied to the First Person of the Trinity indicating His relationship to the Second Person. (Read John 5:25 and 8:54.) Many works are ascribed by Scripture to the Father, but in many of them the other Persons of the Godhead have a part. The distinctive property of the Father is that He generates the Son from all eternity. There never was, is, or will be a time when the Father is not generating the Son. This is the original Fatherhood of God.

Third Speaker:

The Second Person of the Trinity is the eternal Son of God. We make a serious mistake in thinking that the Son had His beginning at the first Christmas. The Bible is speaking of the Second Person of the Trinity when it says, "In the beginning was the Word, and the Word was with God, and the Word was God." John 1:1. What actually happened on that first Christmas was that the eternal Word "was made flesh, and dwelt among us."

The error most frequently committed with regard to the Son is to deny that He is really and truly God. Anyone who makes this denial must set aside the clear teachings of the Bible because Scripture leaves no doubt that the Son is very God of very God. The Bible calls Jesus God in so many words, it gives Him divine names, and ascribes to Him divine works, divine qualities, and divine honors. There is no question in the Bible that the person Jesus Christ is equal with God and is indeed God Himself.

Fourth Speaker:

The Third Person of the Trinity is the Holy Spirit. He proceeds from both the Father and the Son. He is called the Spirit of God and the Spirit of Christ. Jesus said His Father would send the Spirit, and at other times He said He Himself would send the Spirit. In this way the Spirit is related to both Father and Son. (Read John 14:26 and 15:26.)

The mistake most commonly made in our thinking with regard to the Holy Spirit is to think of Him as an influence rather than a person . . . as an "it" instead of a "He". The Bible indicates the deity of the Holy Spirit in much the same way that it indicates the deity of the Son, by ascribing divine names, qualities, works and honors. The Bible also makes it very clear that the Spirit is a real person. He is given personal names, and personal works and qualities are ascribed to Him. (Read John 14:26 and 16:7-15.)

Program Leader:

We cannot fully explain the Triune God, but we can believe what the Bible teaches concerning Him, and we can pray for more light that we may understand Him better and honor Him more acceptably.

Women's Work

BACK TO OUR PROMISES

Promises Made on Profession of Faith in Christ:

1. Do you acknowledge yourselves to be sinners in the sight of God, justly deserving His displeasure, and without hope save in His sovereign mercy?

2. Do you believe in the Lord Jesus Christ as the Son of God, and Saviour of sinners, and do you receive and rest upon Him alone for salvation as He is offered in the Gospel?

3. Do you now resolve and promise, in humble reliance upon the grace of the Holy Spirit, that you will endeavor to live as becometh the followers of Christ?

4. Do you promise to support the Church in its worship and work to the best of your ability?

5. Do you submit yourselves to the government and discipline of the Church, and promise to study its purity and peace?

Promises Made by Parents When Dedicating Their Children to God in Baptism:

1. Do you acknowledge your child's need of the cleansing blood of Jesus Christ, and the renewing grace of the Holy Spirit?

2. Do you claim God's covenant promises in (his) behalf, and do you look in faith to the Lord Jesus Christ for (his) salvation, as you do for your own?

3. Do you now unreservedly dedicate your child to God, and promise, in humble reliance upon divine grace, that you will endeavor to set before (him) a godly example, that you will pray with and for (him), that you will teach (him) the doctrines of our holy religion, and that you will strive, by all means of God's appointment, to bring (him) up in the nurture and admonition of the Lord?

Missions *in your* Living Room

Coming home on the train from the first meeting of the Administrative Committee of United Church Women, my seatmate was a student who had that day arrived in New York from Pakistan. In reply to my word of welcome to this country, he inquired if he could ask some questions. I was more than happy to be of service and gave advice from how he could get to the diner for food to whether he should live in a dormitory or a private home. Nobody had met him at the plane in New York, for he had come on his own to the United States, heading for Ohio State University to study engineering.

As I talked with him, I remembered that I was carrying out one of the emphases of United Church Women for this year: befriending overseas students. I had had slight contact with this service at Christmastime when foreign students were placed in homes in Indianapolis. One night at a dinner table with students from Thailand, Japan, and Venezuela we brought the four corners of the world into our discussion. The students liked it as well as we.

A tourist going abroad often says, "If I could just get into some homes and know the people as they live, rather than doing just the regular sightseeing." Students from abroad also want to be in our homes and to know us as we live in them day by day.

Friendship extended to a student pays dividends not only to the person who gives but in a special way to the one who receives. Particularly is this true in the field of international friendships. These students go back to be the leaders of their country and to influence a trend either toward or against good-will and understanding. A conversation around a dinner table in an American home may very well be the deciding factor in a national crisis some 15 years from now.

Truly missions is right at our front door and an overseas student befriended in America may mean more in the extension of the kingdom of God than a dozen people converted in his native land. Our service abroad may lie within our own living and dining rooms. Is there an overseas student in your community?

Mae Yoho Ward
From *The Church Woman*

One Minute Messages of Stewardship

TIME - my time is a gift from God and so it is very precious. May my prayer be - "Lord, let me be alive for Thee as long as I live." I must not slump - I have not time. My responsibility as a Christian woman is just as imperative as ever. I have time for real, consistent, regular, believing prayer for others. I have time to visit, not party calls, nor tea calls, but to folks who are glad to be visited - the shut-in, the lonely, the harried young mothers.

I must want to share my time and home with those who are less fortunate. What would I enjoy most if I were they? I may help a woman, whose time is limited, take a place in a circle or some phase of Women's Work in the church, not taking the program over, but in the background, making it possible for her to do it, that she may enjoy the sense of accomplishment.

May my prayer be - "Lord, let me not be selfish nor a spendthrift with my time and home, for my times are in Thy Hands. I wish them there.

—From "I Am A Homemaker, TOO."

Woman and The Tithe

Your Responsibility. Statistics reveal that women control practically one-half of the individual wealth of the country. Husbands and wives should be real partners in the administration of the family income. It is up to the women in many cases to see to it that the family enters into partnership with God. The woman by virtue of her position in the home can see more deeply into the truth that "man does not live by bread alone," and she realizes that the income must be used in providing for spiritual as well as physical needs.

Your Guidance. The question, "How much should I give to God?" is one that can be decided only by the individual. Giving to God is an act of worship, therefore our giving should be acceptable and pleasing to Him. In His Word we find the principles to guide us in deciding how much to give. Lev. 27:30; Deut. 14:22; Mal. 3:7-10. The tithe is the minimum.

Your Example. When Christ came into the world He set for us that supreme example and motive in giving: "God so *loved* . . . that He *gave* . . ." Jesus had much to say about earning, keeping, spending, and giving. We can be sure that Jesus tithed, for if He had failed, the Pharisees would have been quick to accuse Him. To be sure that our giving comes up to that standard, the tithe will have to be the starting point in our giving; and love will lead us beyond.

Your Testimonies. To those who have never adopted the principle of the tithe as a method of giving, we would say, "Ask the person who tithes." When you get tithers to talking, here are some of the things they say:

"One of the most glorious Christian experiences that I have known has been to accept the challenge of the tithe."

"The first and greatest value we have received from tithing is joy."

"For years I have practiced tithing, for the practice of tithing gives recognition to God as Owner and Giver of all things."

"When I tithe the supply never runs out. God's providing hand never fails."

Let us bring our tithes "into the store-house" that we may have an abundant spiritual, as well as financial blessing.

Report to District Conference

As president of the Women of the Church of the First Presbyterian Church, Wauchula, Florida, I am supposed to give a report of our accomplishments for the year. Who knows what was accomplished? Only God.

There were seventy of us women who represented seventy different families, some larger than others, including all ages, whose members probably touched every phase of life in our community. Most of our women attended either circle meetings or general meetings throughout the year where they were exposed to the Forward with Christ program stressing Personal Christian Faith.

At each meeting they took part in the reading of Paul's definition of Love as found in I Corinthians 3:4-8. If each woman became conscious of just one lack in her own life in the expressing of Christian love and made a prayerful effort to express God's love, as He intended, to her own family and friends, who knows what was accomplished.

As the programs for circle and general meetings and intensive Bible study were thought about and prepared by individual women, who knows what latent thirst for a better understanding of Christ's teaching became a conscious need of that person, satisfied only by further reading of God's Word.

As each woman became responsible for her prayer partner when she talked with God about her own needs—who knows what love for her fellowwoman was instilled in her heart?

During our Presbyterian Hour of each morning, in which everyone was invited to be a part, who knows how many hearts were joined in spirit in the Presence of Christ? Who knows what effect that prayer had on our homes, the various phases of work of the church at home and in foreign lands?

A life membership pin will also be presented at this time.

Special music will be given by the Peace College Choir at the evening meeting.

Mrs. Ernest Hunter of Charlotte, N. C., a member of the Governor's Youth Service Committee, will address the group. A message will follow by a representative of the Westminster Fellowship.

Installation of officers will be held. At the conclusion the sacrament of the Lord's Supper will be administered by the minister and officers of the First Presbyterian Church.

Church News

THE GENERAL FUND AND INTERCHURCH AGENCIES

STATEMENT OF RECEIPTS
January 15 - July 31, 1956

The General Fund Agencies

Budget for 1956	$846,581.00
Received from January 15th through July 31, 1956	247,673.97
Percentage of annual budget received to date	29.26
Balance needed for the year	598,907.03

Interchurch Agencies

Budget for 1956	$21,495.00
Received from January 15th through July 31, 1956	7,560.26
Percentage of annual budget received to date	35.1
Balance needed for the year	13,934.74

E. C. Scott, Treasurer

Invitation for 1958 General Assembly

All invitations to the General Assembly for its 1958 sessions should be in my hands by October 1, this year. The Permanent Committee on the Office of the General Assembly will decide on place and date of the 1958 meeting when the Committee meets on October 16, 1956.

This action must be taken 18 months in advance because of the necessity for reserving space in hotels.

Any church that contemplates extending an invitation should write to me at once, requesting detailed information concerning requirements that must be met by entertaining church.

E. C. Scott, Stated Clerk

GEORGIA

Atlanta—Statistics released here August 2 by the Treasurer of the Presbyterian Church, U.S., reveal a sizeable increase in giving to two benevolence causes of the Church during the first seven months of 1956.

Dr. E. C. Scott, Stated Clerk and Treasurer, announced that for both the General Fund Agencies and the Interchurch Agencies, receipts are running higher, both when compared with last year, and when compared with the budgets for each year. Despite a budget increase of about 9% in each case between 1955 and 1956, the proportion of the budget received in the first seven months is about 7% higher now than last year. In terms of dollars received, both funds are running slightly better than 17% higher than last year, Dr. Scott noted. His figures are

For the **General Fund Agencies:**

	1956	1955	
Budget	$846,581.00	$777,378.00	(8.9% up)
Received from Jan. 15 through July 31, 1956	247,673.97	210,400.94	(17.7% up)
Percentage of annual budget received to date	29.6%	27.00%	(2.26% up)
Balance needed for the year	598,907.03 (70.74%)	566,977.06	(73%)

For the **Inter-Church Agencies:**

	1956	1955	
Budget	$21,495.00	19,700.00	(9.1% up)
Received from Jan. 15 through July 31, 1956	7,560.26	6,452.14	(17.17% up)
Percentage of annual budget received to date	35.1%	32.7%	(2.4% up)
Balance needed for the year	13,934.74 (64.9%)	13,247.86	(67.3%)

Atlanta—Harold F. Jackson, chairman of the Board of Deacons at Druid Hills Presbyterian Church and general secretary of the Church School, has been elected president of the Georgia State College of Business Administration Alumni Association.

Mr. Jackson is the Assistant Sales Manager of the A and P Company's Southern division. Mrs. Jackson is treasurer of the General Council of the Presbyterian Church, U.S.

VIRGINIA

An Unusual Tour

Pulaski—Ten Virginians, all members of the First Presbyterian Church of Pulaski, were Mexico City bound in July.

The 7 youngsters, with the Rev. George Ogilvie, Mrs. Ogilvie, and Mrs. Ferd Harvey chaperoning and leading them, went to Mexico City to observe the work in Presbyterian Missions nearby. Just outside Mexico City there are four missions, located in Cuernavaca, Taxco, Toluca, and Morelia.

The travelers also visited the Rev. and Mrs. C. J. Hollandsworth who left the United States last fall for the Mexican mission field. The Rev. and Mrs. Hollandsworth, of Virginia, are at present studying Spanish in Mexico City in preparation for mission work. They are being supported by the First Church of Pulaski.

En route, the travelers stopped overnight in various Presbyterian churches along the way. They carried their own equipment with them in two cars loaded with sleeping bags, food, and portable camping stove. The churches visited by the group included Lookout Mountain Church in Chattanooga; South Highland Church, Birmingham; First Church in Hattiesburg, Miss., and Canal Street Church in New Orleans. Other towns visited were Beaumont, and Corpus Christi, Tex., and various Mexican towns.

NORTH CAROLINA

Maxton — Presbyterian Junior College has announced that Joseph Orrin Payne has been elected as head of the Department of Social Science at the college, beginning with the fall semester opening September 10.

Mr. Payne is at present working upon his doctorate at the University of North Carolina. He is expectd to move to Maxton with Mrs. Payne and their four children during August.

Winston-Salem—The first service was recently held in the new Dellabrook Presbyterian Church here, the most recently completed Negro church.

A few days following the first service an open house was held for the friends of the church. At that time the program included the acceptance of the building and keys by the Building Committee; presentation of the building and keys to the Committee on Church Extension; presentation of the keys to the Rev. Percy A. Carter, Jr., minister of the church, and presentation of the petition requesting the Presbytery to organize the Church. Rev. Lawrence Bottoms and Rev. James Alexander, Associate Secretaries of the Division of Negro Work, Board of Church Extension, Atlanta, Ga., were present to participate in the service.

Further programs for the Church, either underway or to begin operation in the near future include: Vacation Bible School; Kindergarten for ages 4 through 6, self-supporting, and operated by qualified local leaders; and a Day Care Nursery, for ages 2 and 3. The Nursery is also self-supported, operated by local leadership with qualified attendants, and a dietician.

TENNESSEE

Bristol, Tenn.—John V. Matthews, outstanding Presbyterian layman of Fayetteville, Tenn., was the speaker here Sunday, July 29, for the Religious Emphasis Service which launched the final week of the centennial celebration of the Twin Cities.

Mr. Matthews, former president of the Presbyterian Church, U.S., Assembly Men's Council, and now chairman of the planning committee for the 1957 Men's Convention in Miami, spoke on "Building for the Future". More than 1500 people attended the open-air service despite rain. Protestant, Catholic and Jewish congregations in the Twin Cities took part in the services, which had as its theme, "Faith of Our Fathers."

TEXAS

Dallas—At the closing of the 101st session of the Synod of Texas, which was held in Dallas the latter part of July, two elders of the Highland Park Presbyterian Church of Dallas were elected to high office in the Synod in recognition of outstanding ability and service to the Church.

Mr. Toddie Lee Wynne, Sr., was elected Moderator-nominee to be presented to the Synod at the 1957 meeting for election as moderator. Mr. L. R. Klein was elected chairman of the Synod Council which is the steering committee of the Synod, and the governing body between meetings. Mr. Klein succeeds Dr. C. Ellis Nelson, a professor at Austin Theological Seminary.

THE SOUTHERN PRESBYTERIAN JOURNAL

A Presbyterian weekly magazine devoted to the statement, defense and propagation of the Gospel, the faith which was once for all delivered unto the saints.

VOL. XV NO. 18 — AUGUST 29, 1956 — $2.50 A YEAR

. EDITORIALS .

Plans are under way for many improvements in the Journal. Definite announcements will be made soon. For a limited time we can still begin new subscriptions **on request** with the August 15th issue which carried the first installment of **Slander in Brazil** and the splendid article by Dr. C. Gregg Singer—THE REFORMED FAITH AND THE CONTEMPORARY CRISIS IN EDUCATION. See page 20 for special New Subscription Offer.

THE SOUTHERN PRESBYTERIAN JOURNAL
The Journal has no official connection with the Presbyterian Church in the United States .
Rev. Henry B. Dendy, D.D., Editor..........Weaverville, N. C.
Dr. L. Nelson Bell, Associate Editor..........Asheville, N. C.
Rev. Wade C. Smith, Associate Editor..........Weaverville, N. C.

EDITORIAL

Slander in Brazil

The two articles by Dr. Bell under the above title, which have just appeared in this *Journal* are being reprinted in pamphlet form because of the large demand for extra copies.

Order from The Southern Presbyterian Journal, Weaverville, N. C.

10 cents per copy or
$6.00 per 100 copies postpaid.

The Reformed Faith

(Report on the Symposium Held August 15th)

Due to the strong emphasis being placed on the "Ecumenical Church" today there is grave danger of a generation arising which knows little and cares less for the great doctrines which are a part of the Reformed Faith.

It has been said that the doctrines of the Reformation were "strong meat." Actually they are those elements found in the Word of God on which strong faith and godly lives are built and we all are wise to learn more of them.

For two years a symposium on the Reformed Faith has been held in the Presbyterian Church Weaverville, N. C. in August. Last year a great blessing came to those who attended. This year those who came had additional reason to thank God for our Presbyterian heritage.

The first address was given by Dr. C. Gregg Singer, Vice-President of Belhaven College, Jackson, Miss., and his subject was *The Reformed Faith and the Contemporary Crisis in Education.* This address was carried in last week's issue of the *Journal* and is a long-needed expose' of the shallowness of much present-day education and a ringing challenge to the holders of our Reformed Faith to lift up the standards of true education, so much a part of our heritage.

The second address, by Dr. Gordon H. Clark, Professor of Philosophy at Butler University, Indianapolis, Ind., was a masterly defense of the *Reformed Doctrine of Verbal Inspiration.* This will be printed in the September 12th issue of this *Journal* and is commended as a much needed antidote for some of the faith-fragmenting theories of inspiration so popular today.

Dr. Floyd Hamilton, pastor of the Presbyterian Church at Centreville, Ala., had as his subject, *The Reformed Doctrine of Infant Baptism.* Dr. Hamilton has been described as one of the greatest theologians in our church today and we look forward to much from his pen in the future. His address is printed in this issue.

The next address was by Dr. G. Aiken Taylor, pastor of the First Presbyterian Church, Alexandria, La., and was on the subject, *The Reformed Doctrine of the Means of Grace.* Dr. Taylor who wrote his doctor's thesis at Duke University on *John Calvin and Christian Education,* presented a fresh and challenging view of the Bible as God's divine means of grace. This address will appear in an early issue.

Dr. William C. Robinson, Professor at Columbia Theological Seminary, Decatur, Ga., spoke on *The Reformed Doctrine of the Bodily Resurrection of Christ.* In this he clearly showed that this is an essential part of the gospel message and of our own Presbyterian doctrines. It is an emphasis greatly needed in our day when there is so much hazy thinking on this all-important truth.

In the same vein Dr. Robert F. Gribble, Professor at the Presbyterian Theological Seminary, Austin, Texas, spoke on *The Reformed Faith as Related to the Virgin Birth Foretold in Isaiah* 7:14. Again the minds of the hearers were brought to bear on a cardinal doctrine of the Church. The integrity and authority of the Scriptures were magnified and the importance of this truth again emphasized.

The final address of the day (luncheon was served the middle of the day), was by Mr. George Burnham, famous feature writer for the

Chattanooga *News-Free Press,* on the subject, *To The Far Corners.* In this address Mr. Burnham who is slated to become News Editor of the new international religious journal, *Christianity Today,* told of some of his experiences on his Far-Eastern tour with Billy Graham in January and February. These reports were carried in 600 daily newspapers in America, but hearing some of them by word of mouth carried a special blessing to the hearers.

Subsequent issues of this *Journal* will carry these various addresses and it is our firm conviction that again we have enjoyed a stirring reminder of the heritage which is ours. L.N.B.

Your King Will Oppress You You Will Cry Out in That Day, and the Lord Will Not Hear You

I Samuel 8.9-18

This is the solemn protest that the Lord directed Samuel to make to ancient Israel for its sin in rejecting God Who had delivered them out of the hand of the Egyptians. Because they rejected Him Who had delivered them from all their oppressors 10.18-19; therefore, when the king for which they cry oppresses, God will neither hear nor deliver them from the oppressions of their king. This is the serious judgment that their sin has brought upon Israel.

Professor Wm. J. Mueller of the Southern Baptist Theological Seminary cites with approval the interpretation of this story given by B. Vyschelavzeff in *Der religioese Sinn der Macht,* thus:

> In the whole Bible, the idea of the sinfulness of power may be traced from the first Book of Kings to the Apocalypse. Samuel the prophet in ancient Israel, knew that the people might reject God as he instituted an earthly king (I Sam. 10.19). Israel was committing a grave evil in imitating other nations and desiring a king. The prophet warned the people against the fate that awaited them as they put themselves into the keeping of an earthly ruler. When they cry to God for deliverance from the tyranny of kings, God would not hear them.

If there is an analogy between Israel's choosing a king and the Presbyterian Church in the United States in choosing women as elders, what analogous judgment will this act bring upon our Church?

Cardinal Sadoleto appealed to the people of Geneva to return from Protestantism to the obedience of the Pope. In the course of his argument he insisted that the Holy Spirit guided the Roman Church in all her actions and worship. In reply John Calvin wrote that the Holy Spirit is present where the Word of the Lord is, that it is dangerous to boast of the Spirit without the Word. "The Church is indeed governed by the Holy Spirit, but in order that that government might not be vague or unstable, Christ annexed it to the Word." "Those who are of God hear the Word of God." "The Spirit goes before the Church, to enlighten her in understanding the Word, while the Word itself is like the Lydian Stone, by which she tests all doctrines." "It is no less unreasonable to boast of the Spirit without the Word, than it would be absurd to bring forward the Word without the Spirit." "You have paid the penalty of that affront which you offered to the Holy Spirit, when you separated Him from the Word." The Church is made holy to the Lord by the washing with the Word of life, people are regenerated unto God by that incorruptible seed. "It is the sceptre by which the heavenly King rules His people."* Ought it not to be shown that the Word teaches women elders before it is asserted that such a step is the leading of the Holy Spirit? W.C.R.

*Calvin, *Tracts,* I. pp. 35-37

Mrs. Wagner Has Left Us

The *Journal* office "family" has recently been greatly saddened by the death of one of its members, Mrs. Louise Wagner. Mrs. Wagner came to the *Journal* six years ago, and through faithful service has handled many thousands of letters in the correspence that is continually going out from this office. Her buoyant, friendly spirit and keen appreciation of the finer things of life was a definite contribution to the morale of the force and did much to brighten the routine of the daily round. This notwithstanding she was much of the time under the handicap of ill health and great physical discomfort.

We shall sorely miss our friend and co-worker; but rejoice in the thought that she has entered into the "new life" which is free from pain.

The Southern Presbyterian Journal, *a Presbyterian Weekly magazine, devoted to the statement, defense, and propagation of the Gospel, the faith which was once for all delivered unto the saints,* published every Wednesday by The Southern Presbyterian Journal, Inc., in Weaverville, N. C.

Entered as second-class matter May 15, 1942, at the Postoffice at Weaverville, N. C., under the Act of March 3' 1879. Vol. XV, No. 18, August 29, 1956. Editorial and Business Offices: Weaverville, N. C. Printed in the U.S.A. by Biltmore Press, Asheville, N. C.

ADDRESS CHANGE: When changing address, please let us have both old and new address as far in advance as possible. Allow three weeks after change if not sent in advance. When possible, send an address label giving your old address.

The Reformed Doctrine of Infant Baptism

By The Rev. Floyd E. Hamilton

The question of infant baptism is one that concerns every Christian, but particularly Christians in the Southland, because we are so surrounded by those who reject this doctrine. A Presbyterian must know what he believes about infant baptism or he will find that he is in difficulty with fellow Christians, especially the young people of the church who are constantly thrown together with Baptists and others who reject infant baptism.

One of the principal objections raised against infant baptism is that there is no command in the Bible to baptize infants. Since infants are too young to believe in Christ, the Baptists therefore claim that they should not be baptized. This objection is based on the assumption that infants are not members of the church in the New Testament.

Now in the Old Testament times there is no doubt whatever that the children of Jewish believers were considered to be members of the Jewish church (see Acts 7:38, Rom. 11:24) which was identical with the Jewish nation. Infants were considered to be partakers of the covenant blessings promised to Abraham and Moses. Children had all the rights and privileges of the covenant, for "the promise is to you and to your children." Children born in Jewish homes were circumcized and considered to be members of the covenant relationship to God, and therefore members of the church in the Old Testament.

Now when we come to the New Testament period, the New Testament church was simply a projection of the Old Testament church, and there was no change recorded in the organic relationship of the members to the church which Paul in Romans 11 calls the root of the olive tree.

The case for infant baptism rests largely upon the validity of our claim that the church of the New Testament is identical with the church of the Old Testament; that it is not a new organism started apart from the old. In this passage in Romans 11, the figure of the olive tree represents the church of the Old Testament. Paul declares that the Jews, who were the natural branches, had been cut off from that olive tree by their unbelief, and that the Gentiles through belief in Christ had been grafted onto the root of the old olive tree, contrary to nature. It was thus the same olive tree after the grafting in of the alien Gentiles. It was the same church in the New Testament as it had been in the Old Testament. The root of the olive tree bore the branches, the Gentiles, who had been grafted in, thus showing that the New Testament Christians entered into a living organism, a church already in existence. In the New Testament times it simply blossomed forth with increased foliage.

Now under such circumstances we would not expect that there would be a command to perform infant baptism apart from the general command to baptize believers. In the Old Testament church the children, infants eight days old, were circumcized and were then members of the Jewish church. Since the church of the New Testament did not regard itself as something new, naturally the children would be regarded as members of the church, and when baptism became the recognized rite of entry into the New Testament church, naturally the infants would be baptized with adults. Had there been a difference in their status from their status in Old Testament times, the command would have been given *not* to baptize them. Since there is no record of such prohibition, it follows that the status of infants was the same as in the Old Testament and that means that they would be regarded as members of the church, and therefore baptized, even as they had been circumcized.

We must remember that at the first there was no abrupt break with the law of Moses and the temple worship. "Day by day, continuing steadfastly with one accord in the temple," (Acts 2:46) the Christians joined with other Jews in the temple worship. Naturally the children of believers would be circumcized, just as were the children of unbelieving Jews, since they were considered to be members of the covenant, and just as naturally, when the parents were baptized, as in the case of the household of Cornelius, the infant children would be baptized with the adults. With our non-Jewish background, it is hard for us to realize the psychology of the early Jewish converts. We must remember that every male Jew had been circumcized on the eighth day, and that all Jewish children were without question members of the covenant relationship with God. Only when the parents showed unbelief by *not* circumcizing the boys were these children considered outside the visible church.

With such a background the Jewish children of Christian believers at first would have been circumcized and would have been regarded as members of the Christian church just as they had been of the Jewish church. As soon as the rite of baptism began to be recognized as the sign of church membership and of belonging to Christ, just that moment parents would want their children to be baptized as a sign that they were children of believers. Up to the time of Paul's arrest in Jerusalem there is every reason to believe that the Jewish Christians continued to keep the law, including circumcision, though they reluctantly recognized that the Gentiles did not need to be circumcized. If their children were circumcized, of course they were considered members of the Christian church, and as baptism was recognized as an additional ceremony to mark off Jewish Christians as Christians, just as naturally the mark would have been bestowed on the children of Christian families.

Now if God had intended that the children were *not* to be considered to be members of the Christian church, it would have taken a very clear command of God himself to the Jewish Christians to keep the children out. At the very least we would expect that there would have been a record of a conference on the subject as there was over the matter of requiring the Gentiles who became Christians to be circumcized. Just as it took a miracle of the bestowing of the gifts of the Holy Spirit upon the family of Cornelius to convince the Jews that the Gentiles who became Christians should not be required to be circumcized, so it would have taken a miracle to convince them that their Jewish children who had been circumcized, were not members of the Christian church, and therefore that they should not be baptized. Since there seems to have been no such controversy or command against the baptism of infants, they would naturally have been baptized.

If the arguments of the Baptists that only those old enough to believe in Christ were members of the New Testament Church were valid, it would be such a reversal of Old Testament custom and such an innovation that the Jewish Christians inevitably would have protested against the innovation. As Dabney says (Page 787): "The sacred narrative in Acts 15 approaches so near the topic of this innovation, that it is simply incredible an allusion to it should have been avoided, had the revolution been attempted.

"The question which agitated the whole Christian community to its core was: shall Gentile converts, entering the Church under the new dispensation, be required to be circumcized, and keep the ceremonial law? The very arguments by which this question was debated are given. Now, how inevitable would it have been, had the change in membership been made, which the Immersionist supposes, to say: 'Whether you circumcize adult Gentile converts or not; you cannot circumcize their children; because Jewish children and Gentile, are no longer admitted with their parents.' But there is no whisper of this point raised. I cannot believe that the innovation had been attempted."

"When a society undergoes important modifications, its substantial identity yet remaining, the fair presumption is, that all those things are intended to remain unchanged, about the change of which nothing is said . . . Infant membership was esteemed by the Jews a privilege . . . Consider this in the light of the Apostle's language: eg. in Rom. 11:20; Acts 3:23. In these and similar passages, the Jews are warned that unbelief in Christ, the great closing Prophet of the line . . . will be accompanied with the loss of their church membership. According to the Immersionists, the meaning of this warning would be: 'Oh, Jew; if you believe not on Jesus Christ, you (and your children) forfeit your much valued visible Church membership. But if you believe on Him, then your innocent children shall be punished for your obedience? by losing their privileges!' " (Page 786, in Syllabus and Notes).

Not only was there no prohibition of infant baptism recorded in the history of the New Testament church, but we have specified examples of family baptism, in the case of the family of Cornelius, the family of Stephanus, and the family of the Philippian jailor. Of course we cannot *prove* that there were infants in those families, but knowing the customs and marital conditions of that age, with children and their wives and grandchildren all living under one roof as a single family unit, it is highly probable that there were infants in at least some of those families, and if so, they would have been included among the members of the family who were baptized. As long as there were Jewish Christians, their infants would naturally have been circumcized, since they were members of the Jewish church, and just as naturally, since the parents were baptized Christians, they would want their infants baptized also as a sign that they were children of Christian parents.

In the Old Testament period, the blessings of the covenant were promised to believers and their children. That included the sign of the covenant, circumcision. In the New Testament church, since Peter in his Pentacostal sermon said that, "the promise is to you and to your children and to all that are afar off, as many as the Lord our God shall call unto him," (Acts 2:39), it inescapably follows that the New Testament sign of the covenant, baptism was bestowed on the children, infants as well as older children.

The International Standard Bible Encyclopedia has a very pertinent comment on this point:

"In the old patriarchal days each family was complete within itself, the oldest living sire being the unquestioned head of the whole, possessed of almost arbitrary powers, house and household were almost synonymous. God had called Abraham that he might command his children and his household after him. (Gen. 18:19). The passover lamb was to be eaten by the household. The households of the rebels in the camp of Israel shared their doom. David's household shares his humiliation. (II Sam. 15:16.) The children, everywhere in the Old Testament, are the bearers of the sins of their fathers. Life is not a conglomerate of individuals; the family is its center and unit."

Now as we consider the covenant itself, the New Testament covenant is certainly the extension of the privileges and blessings of the Old Testament covenant. As years went by, the blessings of the covenant were amplified and explained in more detail in the Old Testament, with various items added to it, but the covenant itself continued to be the same covenant, though enriched as the years went by. Now when we come to the New Testament, are we going to claim that our present covenant with God is any less rich in privileges and blessings than the Old Testament covenant? Is anyone going to claim that the privileges which were inherent in the Old Testament covenant were not included in the New Testament covenant? If we say that the New Testament covenant simply added to and amplified the privileges which were inherent in the Old Testament covenant, certainly we must say that nothing that was genuine of blessing and privilege would have been taken away in the New Testament covenant. The ceremonial law, it is true, was fulfilled in Christ, so that we do not need to fulfill it today, but the moral law is still our rule of life, and the blessings of the covenant, including membership in the body of Christ, the church, were not abrogated.

That means, therefore, that in the New Testament dispensation the infants of believers would have at least as many privileges and blessings as they had in the Old Testament church. In the Old Testament there is no question but that infants of believers were included in the visible church. They were given the sign of the covenant, circumcision. The promise was "to you and to your children." In the New Testament, therefore, we can expect that the infants of believers will have at least these same blessings and privileges. They will certainly belong to the visible church as they did in Old Testament times. In the Old Testament times if an infant died in infancy the parents would certainly believe it was saved. David simply assumed that his child by Bathsheba was in heaven and that he would go to him. Of course we recognize that not all infants who grow up to adulthood are saved, but that possibility did not prevent them from being circumcized, and should not prevent us from baptizing the children of believers. Baptism is the sign of claiming the covenant relationship for the child by the parents, who take upon themselves the pledge to bring up the child in the fear and admonition of the Lord.

We cannot emphasize too strongly the thought that if infants were to be excluded in the New Testament from the church and from baptism, it would be a complete reversal of all that was included in the Old Testament covenant relationship. Then, infants who were not old enough to believe in God and his promises were nevertheless circumcized and regarded as members of the covenant church. If God intended that in New Testament times this was to be reversed, it would have taken a definite command by God to effect such a change. No such command is recorded.

But what were the principal blessings of the Abrahamic covenant? First, it was the knowledge that they belonged to God. "I will be your God and ye shall be my people."

The Hebrew father recognized that his whole family belonged to God, and as the sign and pledge that he accepted this covenant relationship to God, he circumcized his children.

Second, circumcision was the sign of the removal of the total depravity and corruption into which the child was born. That does not mean that the parents were sinful in bringing the child into the world, but that unless God's power removed the curse of original sin through regeneration, the child was dead in sin. Circumcision was the symbol of the removal of this curse.

In the third place, circumcision was the sign and seal of the righteousness by faith which they had through believing in God and his covenant promises. Abraham believed God's promises and it was reckoned unto him for righteousness. Circumcision was then given as the seal of that faith which he already had.

Now these same three notions we find emphasized in the New Testament, and symbolized in baptism: union to God by faith, the removal of the curse of total depravity by regeneration, and justification by faith in the atoning work of Christ. The Christian is united to Christ through faith, cleansed from the curse of sin and defilement through the new birth, and declared righteous, not because of what he is or has done but simply because of the righteousness of Christ imputed to him and received through faith alone. Notice that these three notions are practically identical with the blessings of the covenant in the Old Testament. Since these blessings of the covenant were claimed by the parent in the rite of circumcision, should not the New Testament parent have the right to claim the same blessings and the sign of the covenant, baptism, for his infant as well as for himself?

The position of the Baptists, who claim that baptism should be given only to believers, not to their infants, if followed to the logical conclusion would mean that their infants are not in the covenant relationship to God, so that the promises to "you and to your children" do not apply to their children until they reach the age of accountability.

If that is so, it would logically mean that if their infants died in infancy, they would not be saved—a horrible conclusion. If salvation is only possible through active belief in Christ, it would seem to follow that infants who cannot intelligently believe would be lost.

Of course the Baptists do not recognize the logic of their position, and therefore have a rite, the rite of dedication of the infants to the Lord, though there is no more a Scriptural command for such dedication than there is according to their claim for the baptism of infants. But if they are claiming the blessings of the covenant for their children in this right of dedication, why not baptize them, for baptism is the very symbol of claiming those blessings for the children? As circumcision was the rite and symbol of entrance into the Old Testament church, so baptism is the symbol of entrance into the New Testament church, and in both instances should be given to infants.

As we have said, parents in the Old Testament period who refused to give the rite of circumcision to the children, thereby cut them off from the blessings of the covenant. If believing parents today do not give this sign of baptism, the symbol of entrance into the church, to their infants, are they not in reality cutting them off from the covenant relationship to God?

Now let it not be claimed that since only males were circumcised by the Jews, and since baptism is given to females as well, the rites do not have a similar meaning. We must not forget that the males were the representatives of the females in the family, in the Old Testament. We do not know why God saw fit to make females go through the rite of baptism in order to be included in the Christian church. Logically it would seem that males could represent them as in Old Testament times. But whatever the reason, females must now undergo baptism. Since adult females are to be baptized, infant females are likewise to be baptized.

But what is the real *ground* for the bestowal of infant baptism? Do we baptize children because we believe they are saved and regenerated? Well, we certainly *hope* they are regeneratd or will be later, and we would not bestow the sign of baptism on them if they did not have at least one parent who was a believer. However, as Professor John Murray points out, the real ground for baptism is in the fact that the parent claims the covenant relationship for his child, and claims that it is a member of the visible church.

In the Old Testament in some cases the sign of circumcision was given to those who apparently were not saved, as in the case of Ishmael and Esau, though they were included in the visible church, and were therefore given the sign of circumscision. In the same way, in the present dispensation, the real reason we baptize our infants is that we claim them to be members of the visible church, and heirs of the covenant.

Now it is perfectly true that the blessings of the covenant can only come to those children whose parents are faithful to their pledges to bring them up in the fear and admonition of the Lord. I want to emphasize this point particularly. Many parents feel that if they baptize their children, that is what will secure their salvation, and in too many families, from that time on, they just ignore their pledges to bring them up in the fear and admonition of the Lord. We must remember that the blessings of the covenant come *through* the training of those children in the fear and admonition of the Lord. Those blessings cannot be expected to come apart from such training by the parents.

If the parents fail in that respect, then the children will not automatically receive the blessings of the covenant simply because they are members of the visible church. But if the parents are faithful to their covenant pledges, then the children will be taught to believe in Jesus Christ and the Triune God, taught to trust Christ as Saviour and Lord, taught to pray, to read the Bible and to be faithful in church attendance, and taught to accept and follow the system of Christian ethics taught in the Bible. In other words, they will be taught to be true Christians. When the proper time comes they will ratify for themselves the vows made in their behalf by their parents at the time of baptism.

When we baptize infants, therefore, we are obeying the command of Christ to preach the gospel to every creature, baptizing them in the name of the Father and of the Son and of the Holy Spirit. We believe the infants of believers were included in that command, though Christ did not specifically mention them then. Since he did not forbid the baptism of infants, and since infants had been previously in the church and had been given the sign of such membership in the Old Testament, we believe they should be given the sign of such membership, i.e., baptism, today.

Let us now consider some of the New Testament passages which imply that infants are in the church of God in this dispensation. The first passage is in the Synoptic Gospels, in Matt. 18:16, 19:13-14; Mark 9:36-37; Luke 18:15-17. "Suffer the little children to come unto me and forbid them not, for of such is the kingdom of heaven." In the Luke passage the word used is BREPHE, little infants. In the Matthew passage it says they were "brought."

This indicates that someone probably carried or led them to Jesus as too small to go to Jesus by themselves. Jesus said, "Of such is the kingdom of God." He was not speaking of the childlike characteristics necessary to entrance into the kingdom of God, but speaking of the specific infants he had taken into his arms. The disciples were trying to prevent them from being brought to Jesus, regarding it as a waste of time since they could not intelligently believe in Jesus. Jesus was indignant, and told the disciples to let them come to him, for "of such is the kingdom of God."

Now while we admit that this does not give us any certain warrant for baptizing infants, it does teach that children as well as adults were among Christ's people. It teaches that infants, as well as older children and adults were in the kingdom of God, and therefore that they were already or would become regenerated. It implied that little infants were in the visible church. If that was so, why should anyone forbid them the sign of such membership, baptism?

In I Cor. 7:14, Paul tells the Corinthian Christians that believing wives and husbands sanctified their unbelieving spouses, "else were your children unclean, but now they are holy." Paul does not argue the point that children were in the visible church, but just assumes that since one parent was Christian, their children were also "holy," i.e., belonging to God. If so is it not probable that they were baptized?

The most important passage is Acts 2:38-39. "And Peter said unto them, Repent ye, and be baptized every one of you in the name of Jesus Christ unto the remission of your sins; and ye shall receive the gift of the Holy Spirit. For to you is the promise, and to your children, and to all that are afar off, even as many as the Lord our God shall call unto Him."

Certainly this implies that their children and all others who were called by God, were to be baptized just as they were to be baptized. Infants, as well as adults, who were called of God, were to be given the sign of the covenant.

Now this means that infants should be baptized. They are part of the church. The church was the same in the Old Testament as it is in the New Testament. And because it is the same, and because the covenant of redemption is the same, through Jesus Christ and him alone, just as in the Old Testament the infants were circumcized, so now, the children of believers should be baptized.

The Silence of Communion

By David Eugene Rule
Esperance, New York

People often wonder what to do during the Communion service. There is so much silence. While the ritual may differ slightly in many of our Presbyterian churches, there are certain principles which may be observed in almost every service.

One's advance preparation is of great importance in his approach to the Sacrament of the Lord's Supper. The Preparatory Service, once the usual, is now the unusual in Presbyterian churches. It served a useful purpose in preparing the soul for fellowship at the Lord's table. With its gradual disappearance the need is becoming apparent for a personal preparation in the home. The observance of the Sacrament is announced in advance, thus providing one with an opportunity for such planning. As the day of observance nears, each person should, through family or private devotions, examine his soul and seek a proper spirit for the service. This experience is reinforced in most of our churches by there being a time for general confession of sins during the service itself. All of these experiences help to make the silence of Communion more meaningful.

Regardless of the method of partaking of the elements—each person as he receives them or everyone at the same moment—the act is followed by silence, broken in some churches only by quiet organ music. Since there are two elements, there are two periods of silence. It is this silence which so many persons wonder how to utilize.

When the bread is distributed, the minister says words to this effect: "This is the body of

upon the meaning of Jesus' death, the love of God, the love which God desires him to have towards others, the blessings of the Christian life.

This is how one may spend the silence of Communion: Remembering Jesus Christ—His body broken for him and His blood shed for all. He prays for himself and then for others. Thereupon, silently, he joins in prayer with his minister who audibly thanks God for this Sacrament.

Above all, one should remember that this is a very personal moment. In many ways it is our most intimate fellowship with the Lord. This is His table. We are His guests. He is the Host. We come, not because we are Presbyterians or members of some other denomination, but because we are Christians. We are welcomed, not because we are members of the church, but because we belong to Jesus Christ by right of redemption. Let us be sure in our hearts that we are welcomed as His redeemed ones. Let us be sure of our relation with Christ when we come. Let us be sure that we have confessed our sins, repented of our wrong-doing, believed in Jesus Christ, and that we are endeavoring in His strength to live a consistent Christian life. Then let us approach His table, for then are we welcomed. And then we shall find the greatest blessing and the deepest meaning in the silence of Communion.

ANGLERS

By WADE C. SMITH

Lesson No. 154

PROGRAM FOR THE CONGREGATION IN PERSONAL EVANGELISM

"Responsibility for working out the program for the whole work of the church belongs to the minister. When he is clear in his own mind what the church should undertake, he should write it out in every detail. He and his elders should review the plan with utmost care, and after agreement is reached, call into conference with the session all the boards and organizations of the church. They too should study the plan with the session and come into agreement at every point.

"With this backing the minister and session are ready to bring the congregation into full conference — repeated conferences if necessary — until all the people understand the purpose of the pastor and session, and are ready for a congregational vote pledging full co-operation." (From report of a Committee on Evangelism in the Presbyterian Church, U.S.A.)

Dr. Charles F. Beach says, "Ministers must no longer be mere preachers, in the sense of preparing and delivering sermons from the pulpit. They must educate their people for the work of Christ, and become their leaders and guides in their efforts to win the unconverted. And the laity must learn to take up the message of the sacred desk and convey it to the families and individuals who are either standing aloof from the ministrations of the sanctuary or are living beyond the sphere of its influence. It is only in this manner that the mass of the unregenerate will ever be brought to Christ."

Thus when through a vision of the need, the power and the method, the pastor by his messages from the pulpit, and the orderly process through various departments of the church, arouses his congregation to a sense of privilege and responsibility in this matter, he is ready to proceed with group organization as described in lessons 149 to 152.

The Places for Prayer. A Committee on Evangelism has made these suggestions about prayer. "Prayer for an Evangelistic campaign ought to be offered in Christian homes that the people may know the spirit and plan of the church, and be prepared to take their places.

"Prayer ought to be carried on by groups, perhaps under the leadership of the four main groups in the church, i.e.: men, women, Sunday school and young people.

"Prayer should be offered in neighborhood meetings, in the homes of members. There is something peculiarly sacred in such a neighborhood prayer association.

"Prayer for a spiritual awakening, very definite and importunate prayer, should be magnified in all the church services.

"Individuals should be led to give more time to prayer in the secret place, where God meets his children, and builds His life into them. It is here that the Holy Spirit falls upon the solitary man of prayer with a new and irresistible impact, clears away the things which have dimmed his vision, weakened his faith and destroyed his power to be a true Christian. All other prayer plans have additional power when men and women thus pray alone."

(*Next Lesson — A program for Study Classes in Evangelism*)

Helps To Understanding Scripture Readings in *Day by Day*

By Rev. C. C. Baker

Sunday, September 9, I John 2:3-14. To walk in close fellowship with God involves a complete committment of ourselves to Him. We must keep His commandments (vv.3-5), especially that of loving our neighbor (vv.7-11). To walk closely with God involves overcoming temptation (v.14) and having His Word abide in our lives (v.14). It means loving Christ more than the allurements of this world (vv.15-17). Above all it involves allowing Christ Himself to dwell wholly and completely in our lives (vv.6-10). Thus to abide in Christ means to have a character that is a likeness of that of Christ Himself (v.6). Are you willing to commit your life completely to Christ for this day, to walk in complete fellowship with him, loving Him more than anything else?

Monday, September 10, *Deuteronomy* 6:20-25. There was purpose in the ordinances and ceremonies that the Old Testament Jew was taught to perform. What effect must they have had on a child growing up in a Jewish home (v.20)? What facts about the Lord's relationship to His people would the child have learned through them (vv.21-25)? Observe that a child's religious training was to be conducted primarily in the home (vv.6-9). How important were the lessons the child learned in his home to his future welfare (vv.24-25)? To what extent does one's personal well-being depend upon his relation with God (vv.24-25)? Do you feel that your home should be the primary instrument of Christian education in the life of your child?

Tuesday, September 11, *I Samuel* 1:28-28; 2:18-19. The Levitical priesthood had fallen into corruption (2:22-25) and the word of the Lord was seldom spoken in Israel (3:1). Through a devout mother, full of faith (1:11) and gratitude (1:26-28), the Lord began to use new means of speaking to His people (2:35-36). Look in 1:9-28, 2:18-19 for different aspects of Hannah's life that contributed to the development of Samuel's spiritual life. Was her religious zeal simply a momentary experience? Was she faithful in her religious vows? What place did prayer have in her life? What fruit of her labor was eventually to result in Samuel's life (3:19-21)? Is there someone under your influence whom God could use if you were faithful in your Christian responsibilities toward him?

Wednesday, September 12, *Daniel* 1:3-15. From time to time God gives His servants unique opportunities to witness for Him. What was Daniel's opportunity (11. 1-6)? With the opportunity to witness often comes some temptation that must be overcome. What was the nature of Daniel's temptation (vv. 8-15)? If in the company of high dignitaries, would you put obedience to Christ above conformity to the conduct of men? How did God use Daniel in a unique way to serve Him (v. 17-21)? Is a yielding to temptation one reason God is not using you more as a witness to Him?

Thursday, September 13, *I Corinthians* 12:27—13:1. Paul teaches some of his deepest truths as he endeavors to cope with the most distressing situations. This is the only letter in which Paul deals with the subjects of the unknown tongues, gifts of healing, and the working of miracles. It is the Corinthian Church that is the most divided and the deepest in sin. In meeting the situation Paul did not minimize the importance of those things with which the Corinthians were concerned (12:27-31). In fact, the whole of chapter 14 is devoted to untangling some of the specific problems of the church. However, notice the approach Paul uses in presenting the real need of this congregation (12:31b). How does he show the comparative emptiness of those things with which the Corinthian Christians were primarily concerned (13:1-3)? How is love superior (13:8-9)? Are you concerned more with your place and position in the church than you are with the harmony of the church as a whole?

Friday, September 14, *I Corinthians* 28:2-10. Have you ever longed to do some particular work for the Lord, and then discovered that He did not want you to do that particular task for Him? This was David's disappointment (vv. 2-3). Notice the two-fold way in which David met the frustration of his plans (vv. 4-10): (a) He thought upon those things which God *had* enabled him to do (vv. 4-5) and (b) he then did all he could to aid and encourage the man God had chosen for the coveted task (vv. 9-10ff). It is important that we do not aim our plans above the plans God has for us (vv. 2-3), and equally important that we accept and carry out God's plans for others as well as for ourselves with all our hearts (v.9). Are you carrying out God's plans for your service to Him in the spirit of v.9?

Saturday, September 15, *Joshua* 14:6-12. God had made a promise to Caleb forty-five years before the events of today's passage (Deuteronomy 1:36, Joshua 14:7-10). Today's passage sees that promise fulfilled (vv.13-14). God has made many promises to us as Christians (promises of guidance Prov. 3:5-6, of victory over temptation I Cor. 10:13, of power in service Acts 1:8, etc.) but for many Christians these promises are never fulfilled. Observe the secrets of Caleb's success in his walk with God: What was the outstanding characteristic of his life (vv.8,9,14; Deut. 1:36; Numbers 14:24)? How enduring was his faith (vv.7-10)? How practical was his willingness to do his part in claiming the promise (vv.11-15)? What lesson is there here for your spiritual life?

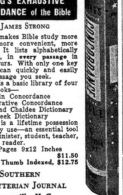

LESSON FOR SEPTEMBER 9

The Source Of Human Conflicts

Background Scripture: Luke 22:31-34; 54-62; James 3 and 4
Devotional Reading: Psalm 34:13-22

Our tongues; our troubles; good and evil; these are the matters which concern the psalmist in verses we have for our Devotional Reading. David's tongue was often at fault. The "Sweet Singer of Israel," whose lips spoke such wonderful poetry and sang such beautiful psalms, could be a source of evil. He had to pray, Set a watch, O Lord, before my mouth; keep the door of my lips. The same fountain sent forth both salt water and fresh, both sweet water and bitter. This ought not so to be. How is it in your life and mine? Then, troubles, trials and affliction were the common experiences of David's life. His enemies were many, and cruel. His own heart was a strange mixture of good and bad. The "man after God's own heart" was guilty of adultery and murder. His good and evil natures were in conflict. His soul was a battlefield.

In our lesson today we are studying about the "Holy War," as John Bunyan so aptly and vividly describes it. Mansoul is an armed camp. All the forces of hell are combined for its overthrow. The Lord is on our side, and we can gain the victory in His Name and by His power. Paul describes this conflict in Ephesians 6:10-18, and also in Romans 7:7-25, and closes the chapter with a question and answer: Who shall deliver me from the body of this death? I thank God through Jesus Christ our Lord.

I. *The Conflict in Peter's Soul:* Luke 22:31-34 and 54-62.

Peter, like David, was very weak and human. Before Simon, the man of sand, could be transformed into Peter, the rock, there was a conflict, and he had to be changed by the power of God. The struggle is seen as it comes to a climax in the verses above. May we get some helpful lessons from his bitter experience!

The first act is seen in the upper room where the Lord's Supper has just been instituted. The strife among the disciples as to which one of them would be the greatest in the kingdom, had again manifested itself, and Jesus had spoken His words of warning and promised that they should eat and drink in His Kingdom and sit on twelve thrones judging the twelve tribes of Israel.

He turns to Peter with a special word of warning: Simon, Simon, behold Satan hath desired to have you, that he may sift you as wheat. But I have prayed for thee, that thy faith fail not: and when thou art converted, strengthen thy brethren. Peter is confident - over-confident - —in his ability, and replies, Lord, I am ready to go with thee, both into prison, and to death. Jesus warns him, I tell thee, Peter, the cock shall not crow this day, before that thou shalt thrice deny that thou knowest me. The sequel is found in verses 54-62, ending in these sad words, "And Peter went out and wept bitterly." What can we learn from the bitter tears of Peter. How can men like Peter and David, who love God, fall so low? These experiences are written for our good. If such men could sin so grievously then each of us would do well to take heed to the warning words of Paul, Let him that thinketh he standeth, take heed lest he fall, Or the words of Jesus, The spirit indeed is willing, but the flesh is weak. Then, on the other side of the picture; if they could be forgiven, restored, and used so greatly, we need not despair, even though we fall. How much better it would be, however, if we did not fall, but were kept by the power and grace of God! John B. Gough, whose record was his shame, expressed his feelings in a most telling way, when, with the tears rolling down his cheeks, he said, "Young men, keep your record clean!" What would David and Peter have given if they had kept their record clean?

Now for some additional lessons. Beware of boasting about, or in, our own strength, of feeling that we are able to keep ourselves from falling. Paul said, I have no confidence in the flesh, and by "flesh" he meant his old human nature. Sin has so weakened us that we are no match for our adversary, the devil, when he starts his "sifting" of our souls. Satan desired Peter, and he almost succeeded in getting him. Only the prayers of his Master saved him. Satan wants you and me; especially if we are leaders in the church. Every now and then he "sifts" someone who has been very prominent in the Lord's work, and causes the enemies of Christ to blaspheme. There was a case very recently in the newspapers. If Peter had been less boastful; if he had showed more humility; if he had

earthly, sensual, devilish. The world is full of this latter sort of wisdom which comes from beneath, from the bottomless pit. The devil is cunning and shrewd, and he imparts his shrewdness, his "smartness" to his followers. Our number one criminals, our most fearful enemies of mankind, are not ignorant men and women, but those who have been "educated" in the ideologies of the "god of this world." He would like to "brain-wash" us all and fill our hearts and minds with this earthly, sensual, devilish wisdom, full of envy, strife and confusion, of which Communism is one example. Another example is the "Narcotics Ring." It takes brains of Satanic cunning to organize such a "Ring" which reaches into all the world, and is like an ugly octopus dragging our young people down to hell.

The wisdom from above is first pure, then peaceable, gentle, and easy to be entreated, full of mercy and good fruits, without partiality, and without hypocrisy. Oh that our world might be permeated with this sort of wisdom! It can only be found in those who have been taught of God, and belong to the Body of Christ. I need not remind you that there is deadly conflict between these two kinds of "wisdom."

3. There are two kinds of "lusts," (pleasures or desires). There are the desires of the "flesh," and there are the desires of the spirit. There is a conflict — an awful conflict — between the two. Paul uses the terms, "old man," and "new man." He describes this conflict very vividly in Romans, chapter seven, and then in chapter eight, he tells how we can have victory and peace and joy. We must yield ourselves to the Spirit, if we would conquer.

4. There are two kinds of people; two attitudes. There are the proud and the humble. Pride and humility may struggle in the same heart and life. God resists the proud, but gives grace to the humble. Pride in the heart opens the door to the devil. If we humble ourselves in the sight of God, He will lift us up. To kneel at the cross and trust in His atoning blood, is to find salvation. To kneel before the throne of grace in humble reliance upon Him will bring comfort and peace and joy in the Holy Ghost.

In all these "Human Conflicts" let us look to the One alone Who can give us victory. The Victorious Life is the radiant, Happy Life!

YOUTH PROGRAM FOR SEPTEMBER 9

Who Is A Christian?

Suggested Devotional Outline:
Hymn: "Am I A Soldier Of The Cross?"
Prayer
Scripture: I John 5:1-13
Hymn: "Blessed Assurance; Jesus Is Mine"
Offering
Hymn: "I Am Thine, O Lord, I Have Heard Thy Voice"

Leader's Introduction:

Who is a Christian? More to the point, are you a Christian? Am I a Christian? Are you sure that you have eternal life? Am I certain that I am a child of God? It may seem foolish to raise such questions among young people in a church organization, but the fact is that many church people are not at all sure about the answers to those questions. It is altogether possible to be a member of the church without having assurance that you are a Christian.

One of the significant revelations coming out of the Billy Graham campaigns is that as high as sixty per cent of the decisions are made by church members. This indicates that many of the church members are very unsure about their spiritual standing. Spiritual life is so important and the alternative is so terrible, that we cannot afford to be uncertain about it. For this very reason we are always justified in asking, "Are you a Christian?" and "Are you sure that you have eternal life?"

John's First Letter was written to meet this very problem we have been discussing. He stated the purpose of the letter in these words: "These things have I written unto you that believe on the name of the Son of God; that ye may *know* that ye have eternal life, and that ye may believe on the name of the Son of God." I John 5:13. If we will read this book carefully and apply its teachings to our lives, we can know for certain whether or not we have eternal life. Our first two speakers will outline for us two of the most important tests suggested in the letter.

First Speaker:

John says that a person who has eternal life is one who "walks in the light." If you want to be sure that you are a Christian, then be sure to walk in the light. What does it mean to walk in the light? First of all, it involves knowing the truth . . . the truth about ourselves and the truth about God. We know the truth about ourselves . . . that we are lost in our sins . . . when we see ourselves in the light of God's righteousness. We know the truth about God when we come to know Him in the person of His Son, Jesus Christ. Walking in the light also involves believing the truth as it is revealed to us in the Bible and in Christ. It is not just a matter of receiving information, but of believing it. That belief involves personal committment to Christ. Having learned the truths that we are dead in our sins and that God loves us and gave His Son to save us, we must trust our lives to Him. We are not walking in the light unless we prove our faith in it by trusting our lives to it.

Second Speaker:

John says that those who have eternal life should be like obedient children. As we walk in the light we come to know the will of God for our daily living, and we must obey it. Obedience is a thing which can be easily observed. John says we are being obedient to the will of God, if we "walk in love." The Bible tells us explicitly and demonstrates to us practically that "God is love." This means that love characterizes the life of God. The life of God is a life of love. There is no eternal life except the life of God. If we have eternal life, it is because the life of God is in us. If we have the life of God in us, we will be loving, because He is love. Love is the distinguishing mark of a genuine Christian because it is a distinguishing mark of God. John says a person cannot be a possessor of eternal life unless he loves God, and that a person cannot love God without loving his brothers also. This is the second important test for proving our Christianity.

Third Speaker:

In the privacy of our own thinking let us submit ourselves to these two tests. Do we honestly walk in the light which God has given us? Do we truly love Him with heart, soul, mind, and strength, and our neighbors as ourselves? Let us hope that we can pass these tests in all fairness, but what if we find ourselves to fail. Is there any word in this letter for those who examine themselves and come to the conclusion that they definitely do not have eternal life? This letter tells them that "God is love." I John 4:8. We also read, "My little children, these things write I unto you, that ye sin not. And if any man sin, we have an advocate with the Father, Jesus Christ the righteous: and he is the propitiation for our sins: and not for ours only, but also for the sins of the whole world." I John 2:1,2. "If we confess our sins, he is faithful and just to forgive us our sins, and to cleanse us from all unrighteousness." I John 1:9. If any person does not have eternal life, let him receive it now by trusting his life to the Son of God who loves us and gave Himself for us.

Because I Belong There—

I believe that God wants us to stand together in His name in His House of Worship. I am rewarded many times over for my humble part in worshiping Him. I find in the church comfort and such solace as come to me from no other source. I seek and obtain His guidance there. I shed my troubles there. I meet my brothers there because I am at home. Yes, I go to church because I belong there.

—A State Governor

I Make Public Acknowledgement—

I recognize my complete dependence on God. I am too human to avoid a deep desire for the well-being of my loved ones and myself, and I know that these things depend upon His sufferance and assistance.

I go to church to make public acknowledgement of these personal beliefs and to worship God in the company of others of like mind.

—Another State Governor

I Find It Makes Life Noble—

I consider the church my best friend because it glamorizes the present and glorifies the future. It constantly reminds me of the dignity of man and of his labor. It makes eminently worthwhile every decent thing I do; it holds forth the promise of fulfillment of immortality.

—A Prominent Writer and Journalist

I Find Companionship—

Being in the Church all my life, I find a companionship and peace of mind in the serenity of a church service. I feel that with all the blessings God has bestowed upon me, certainly I should attend His Church and show my love and appreciation for all He has done.

—A Young Person

From TIDINGS

The Churches Give Wings to the Word

To American Indians, migrants and other groups who are reached by the national distribution office and supplied with inexpensive Scriptures. The Navajo New Testament will be available in 1956.

To the Middle East from Aegean Sea to headwaters of the Nile the Society distributes Scriptures in 34 languages. 65,000 New Testaments are distributed annually to Armed Forces in Greece. Circulation in Iraq increased almost 100% in 1955. Poverty of the masses requires large subsidies to keep selling prices within reach of the average countryman. In Israel the Scriptures in Hebrew will probably need to be printed locally. The Society will furnish the stock and plates.

To Europe where 150 tons of paper were sent to East Germany for Bibles; 50 tons to Hungary. 20,000 refugees per month are still pouring into West Germany.

To Africa where the Bible Society is following the millions who are on the move. The new Liberia office provided 19,000 volumes in 1955.

To Asia where the great new factor is literacy. 10,000,000 people a year are learning to read. The new colloquial Kogotai Bible was released in Japan in April, 1955. More than 75,000 copies had been sold by the end of the year. The Scriptures are distributed in more than 20 languages in the Philippines. In Korea the Bible Society again functions rather normally. 20 million Chinese living outside the China mainland are open to the Gospel.

And Yet There is Much to do! Despite the efforts of our American Bible Society working in cooperation with 24 other national Bible Societies there are still millions who wait for the Word of God.

In Japan, where a missionary edition of the colloquial Bible is needed to meet the needs of students, farmers, and other low-income groups.

In Hong Kong, where large numbers of refugees need the Scriptures.

In Southeast Asia, where the Scripture needs of 20 million refugee Chinese are largely unmet.

In India, where the number of new literates is increasing daily, and where the Bible must be their first book.

In Europe, where the supply of paper will make Bible publishing possible in Eastern European countries.

In the Middle East, where Scripture distribution to military forces, prison inmates, and Arab refugees is a pressing opportunity.

In Latin America, where the evangelical churches are cooperating whole-heartedly in Scripture distribution and where the increasing demand for Scriptures must be heeded.

You and Your Church Can Help — Mindful of the great need, the Advisory Council of 1955 unanimously adopted a report which said in part: "We call attention to the fact that the American Bible Society is related to the denominations in a unique manner and is in a real sense the agency of the denominations in the task of translating, publishing, and distributing God's Word. We recognize, also, the indispensable service which the Society renders to the denominations in their respective missionary tasks. We recognize that, if the churches were to do this work individually, the costs would be immeasurably higher. Hence, we acknowledge the responsibility of the denominations in supporting the Society and in accepting the increases which come in the budget of the Society due to emergency needs and expanded program."

—From The American Bible Society.

Search The Scriptures

"Let us search and try our ways and turn again to the Lord."

If you desire knowledge, if you would like to grasp the full meaning of Christianity, go to the Bible. Read it chapter by chapter and mark each verse of interest. Eventually you will be able to answer most of your own questions. You will go back to certain passages over and over and years from now they will be as fresh and as powerful as on the day you discovered them.

There are thousands of verses with messages in them for men upon every subject. Whole chapters and whole books will appeal to you. No one has been able to consume and absorb the Bible; it will take more than a life-time of serious and detailed study. Select subjects you like—Faith, Prayer, Sin —and with the aid of a concordance enjoy hours of worship.

God speaks to man through His Word and the greatest blessing you can receive will come through a careful and prayerful study of His Word. I recommend a seven-year course in the Bible, verse by verse.

Ralph Brewer

Church News

Montreat — Richard M. Nixon, vice president of the United States, was highlight speaker at the Men's Conference of the Synod of Appalachia held here August 4 and 5. The vice president, a Quaker, was introduced by evangelist Billy Graham whose home is in Montreat.

Nixon addressed the conference at the Sunday morning service in Anderson Auditorium. In his address to the Presbyterians, Nixon urged that churches and "men of God" take their influence to areas "where political policy and moral ideals converge." In his message he appealed for Christian influences in the areas of world peace, labor-management, and race relations.

Also on Sunday, new officers of the Synod's Men's Council were installed.

Saturday morning the conference opened with an address by Herbert H. McCampbell, Jr., Knoxville, Tenn., attorney, and elder in the First Presbyterian Church there.

Later Saturday three seminars were held: "Stewardship," led by Ennis Jackson from Gastonia, N. C.; "Visitation Evangelism," led by S. H. McCall, Jr., president of the Men's Council of Mecklenburg Presbytery; and "Good Programs for Men," led by the Rev. I. M. Ellis, regional director of Christian Education for the Synod of Appalachia.

Saturday evening the Appalachia men heard an address by Dr. W. G. Neville, missionary from Garanhuns, Pernambuco, Brazil, now in the States on a year's furlough. Dr. Neville spoke at a banquet at the Assembly Inn.

Some 400 attended the conference which adjourned Sunday afternoon. Theme under consideration during the two-day meeting was "Man's Place in the Household of God."

GEORGIA

Atlanta — The Rev. Stuart Dickson Currie, formerly pastor of First Presbyterian Church, Fulton, Mo., and now completing doctoral studies in Emory University's Institute of the Liberal Arts here, has accepted a call to become professor of Bible at Queens College, Charlotte, N. C.

Mr. Currie announced August 4 that he has accepted the Queens professorship which was offered through Dr. Edwin Walker, president of the Presbyterian girls' school. He will move his family to Charlotte before September 1.

The son of the late Dr. Thomas W. Currie who was president of Austin Theological Seminary, Austin, Tex., Mr. Currie has two brothers who are Presbyterian ministers, and a sister who is associate in Youth Work in the Board of Christian Education. These are Dr. Tom Currie, Jr., of Bellaire, Texas, the Rev. David M. Currie of Texas City, Texas, and Miss Bettie Currie of Richmond, Va.

Mr. Currie is a graduate of the University of Texas and Austin Seminary, and has done graduate work at Union Seminary, New York, in addition to the doctoral studies at Emory. Mr. Currie served as pastor of First Church, Haskell, Texas, and at First Church, Taylor, Texas, before going to Fulton, Missouri, in 1949. He has been a member of the Board of Trustees of Louisville Seminary, and stated clerk of the Presbytery of Missouri.

Decatur — Announcement was made some months ago by Columbia Theological Seminary that Dr. Cecil A. Thompson had been granted sabbatic leave for special study during the coming year, and that he would not be on the campus to serve as Director of Field Work. Because suitable assistance in that department has not yet been found, Dr. Thompson has consented to postpone his leave of absence and to serve throughout the fall in supervising the field work of students. It is hoped that he will be able to go forward with his projected program of study later in the year. In the meanwhile, and until further notice, communications concerning field work by Columbia Seminary Students should be addressed to Dr. Thompson as in the past.

Saving The Christian Sabbath

New York — The Lord's Day Alliance of the United States has launched a campaign to give an effective Christian witness to the individual members of the 48 state legislatures and to the members of the Congress of the United States.

According to the general secretary of the Lord's Day Alliance, the Rev. Melvin M. Forney, this is the first time that a concerted drive has been made to give the legislators of our nation the Christian position on moral legislation. Mr. Forney said that "the liquor interests, the gambling promoters, the publishers of lewd magazines and books and those who would destroy the Lord's Day are constantly bombarding the legislators with propaganda advancing their particular cause."

The plan of the Alliance calls for the publication of a paper, entitled, "The Other Side of the News," which will present the facts as they exist in our country today and will urge the adoption of good, strong moral and Sunday legislation.

Letters have been sent to outstanding Christian leaders in each of the 48 states requesting them to serve as representatives of the Lord's Day Alliance of the United States in their respective commonwealths. Early acceptances to the invitations have come from fifteen of these, including North Carolina, represented by Rev. C. Grier Davis, D.D., of Asheville First.

The general secretary of the Lord's Day Alliance said that "the time has come for the Christian Church to express itself in the legislative programs of the various states so that the high moral and spiritual tone, which was at the foundation of America's success, may be maintained throughout our nation."

BOOKS

EXPOSITORY OUTLINES ON THE WHOLE BIBLE. Charles Simeon. Zondervan Publishing House. $3.95 per volume.

Vol. I—Genesis - Leviticus
Vol. II—Numbers - Joshua
Vol. III—Judges - II Kings
Vol. IV—I Chronicles - Job
Vol. V—Psalms 1 - 72
Vol. VI—Psalms 72 - 150
Vol. XXI—Revelation

Charles Simeon had a passion to state in the most simple and edifying language the divine truth of the Scriptures. He prepared these expositions as a service to the Church of Christ and especially to lead the minds of younger ministers into the riches of expository preaching. Describing his own method, Simeon said, "As far as was in my power I have endeavored to unfold the most important and instructive parts of Holy Writ, such references to Scripture as should leave no reasonable doubt of its accordance with the mind of the Spirit of God.

In every one of the Discourses also I have so clearly marked the method that the entire scope of the passage may be seen with the glance of an eye; and the young minister may be able to prosecute his work with ease according to his own judgment making no other use of what is contained within the brackets than to enlarge or confirm his own views of the subject." Young ministers are shown how to introduce, divide, discuss, and apply all Biblical subjects. More experienced ministers will also profit by the methodology of these expositions.

All of these expositions have been subjected to three tests. The author has consistently kept in mind these questions for testing the validity of his own work. Does this interpretation tend to humble the sinner? Does this interpretation tend to exalt the Saviour? Does this interpretation tend to promote holiness? These questions have been applied to the general scope and tendency of the expositions.

The author is exceptionally talented in vindicating the great doctrines of salvation by grace through faith in Christ. He has studied the Bible objectively to ascertain the way of salvation and then to express it in clear and simple language for the benefit of those who read his writings. In preparing the first volume, he writes, "The author feels it impossible to repeat too often or avow too distinctly that it is an invariable rule with him to endeavor to give to every portion of the Word of God its full and proper force without considering one moment what scheme it favors or whose system it is likely to advance. Where the Inspired Writers speak in unqualified terms he thinks himself at liberty to do the same; judging, that they needed no instruction from him how to propagate the truth. He is content to sit as a learner at the feet of the holy Apostles, and has not an ambition to teach them how they ought to have spoken. . . . He wishes much that the practice of expounding the Scriptures which obtained so generally and with such beneficial effects at the time of the Reformation were revived. He has in his present work introduced many Discourses constructed upon this model; and he cannot but earnestly recommend to his Younger Brethren in the Ministry, especially those who preach three times in the week to reserve at least one of these seasons for exposition."

Zondervan Publishing Company is to be commended for the fine work it has done in making this work available in large, readable type and also for the attractive format. Here is Biblical scholarship at its best. The preacher as well as the Bible school teacher will find here an exhaustless wealth of material to help in presenting the teachings of Scripture in a fresh and interesting manner. Dr. Harold J. Ockenga, one of the finest of present-day expositors of Scriptures, does not exaggerate when he writes concerning the **Expository Outlines of the Whole Bible** by Simeon: "Simeon is the finest example of expository preaching I have yet discovered. . . . The perfect illustration of expository preaching at its best."

HELP US GET NEW SUBSCRIBERS

Any Book listed on Page 20 will be sent you free and postpaid as an award for one New Subscription sent us before September 1st. Earn as many books as you will send in new subscriptions.

Send for Sample Copies. Free and Postpaid.

WHAT THEY BELIEVE. G. Edwin Covington. Philosophical Library. $4.50.

In this volume the author writes his analysis of the replies to a questionnaire setting forth the religious and ethical concepts of more than 800 young people between 16 and 23 years of age. These young people represent a cross-section of various cultural and economic levels.

The study reveals a correlation of faith to the traditional Judaeo-Christian theological dogma under the impact of modern thought. According to the author, the trend of faith among modern youth moves toward enlightened humanism. The author's findings are the opposite of the reviewer's experiences. This book might be of some value for workers among groups of college students, but it should be read with discrimination. J.R.R.

CURRENT PROBLEMS IN RELIGION. Hermon F. Bell. Philosophical Library. $10.00.

The author discusses in this volume such basic problems as, "Shall man live again?" "Beliefs and Disbeliefs," "How Can The Old and New Theology Live Together?" The valuable part of the book is the supplement that consists of an extensive anthology of selective religious readings.

The author's personal theological position is that of humanism. He holds to the view that dogmas and creeds are road blocks to progress. He affirms that "no fixed, no final, creed is accepted; and tests or examinations as to agreement with official church decisions are completely out of order, both as respects members or communicants, and especially ministers or clergy. The writer counts himself happy to be free, absolutely free, of such entanglements. This in the writer's opinion puts him in a unique and much preferred position."

In a day when the soul of man is seeking a solid foundation on which to rest, the author's views are void of help. The main value in this volume is to be found in the selections quoted from literary and religious classics.

THE WORLD'S GREATEST NAME. Charles J. Rolls. Zondervan. $2.50.

Continuing the monumental task he began in "The Indescribable Christ" Dr. Rolls here presents the stirring series of messages on the titles of Christ which reflect His greatness. This series of messages reflects the glory of Christ as the "Head of the Church" as the great "I AM" presented throughout the Old and New Testaments. The author discusses the wonderful name of Jesus in the depths of meaning which lie behind the glorious word. These studies will appeal not only to mature Christians but to those who are young in Christ as well.

THE VALLEY OF SILENCE. Compiled by Jack Shuler. Zondervan Publishing Co. $2.50.

In this volume Jack Shuler has selected 94 poems which he considers to be his favorites culled from Christian literature. Each poem conveys messages on faith, hope, and love. They speak to the home, the church, and the individual. Some of them are beautifully expressed prayers. The Christian will find here poems for every occasion, every need, and every mood. They can be used effectively in sermons or addresses. Each of these poems will entertain and inspire.

LUKE THE PHYSICIAN. William M. Ramsey. 3aker Book House. $4.50.

This book consists of a series of studies in the iistory of religion by the noted archeologist, Sir Villiam M. Ramsey. The volume takes its title rom the first of these studies. There are twelve tudies in all. The author discusses such subjects .s "The Oldest Written Gospel," "The Morning ;tar and the Chronology of Christ," "St. Paul's Jse of Metaphors Drawn from Greek and Roman .ife," and "The Date and Authorship of the Epistle o the Hebrews." Ramsey's studies are always hallenging and instructive. Those included in this ook are no exception.

THE SECRET OF THE UNIVERSE, MAN AND 1ATTER, by Nathan R. Wood. Tenth Edition. V. B. Eerdmans. Price $2.50.

This is a reprint of a book first issued over twenty years ago. The fact that it has gone through so many editions is itself a strong proof of the unusual quality of the book.

It is unique in the simple way it deals with a profound subject.

The secret in the universe is God Himself in His Triune nature. The author shows in a truly marvelous way how everything in the universe is stamped with the seal of God's Triunity. It is the best treatise on the Trinity that I have ever read.

The only way to appreciate this book is to get it and read it over and over again. It gives one a new conception of God and His universe.

Martin A. Hopkins

THE SOUTHERN PRESBYTERIAN JOURNAL

A Presbyterian weekly magazine devoted to the statement, defense and propagation of the Gospel, the faith which was once for all delivered unto the saints.

VOL. XV NO. 19 SEPTEMBER 5, 1956 $2.50 A YEAR

. EDITORIAL .

A Homeward Call to Realistic Preaching

One Lord, One Faith, One Baptism:
One God and Father of All of Christ's People

++++

Our Lord's Attitude to The Old Testament
By John R. W. Stott, M.A.

The Reformed Doctrine of the Means of Grace
By Rev. G. Aiken Taylor, Ph.D.

Should We Change Our Confession of Faith?
By Rev. Robert Strong, S.T.D.

The Person of Christ
By Rev. Floyd E. Hamilton

++++

Anglers — Helps To Understanding Scripture Readings

Sabbath School Lesson for September 16, 1956

Young People's Department

Women's Work — Church News

THE SOUTHERN PRESBYTERIAN JOURNAL
The Journal has no official connection with the Presbyterian Church in the United States
Rev. Henry B. Dendy, D.D., Editor..Weaverville, N. C.
Dr. L. Nelson Bell, Associate Editor..Asheville, N. C.
Rev. Wade C. Smith, Associate Editor..Weaverville, N. C.

EDITORIAL

A Homeward Call to Realistic Preaching

Without a shadow of doubt the greatest need within the Church is that Christians should live as Christians. Because the overwhelming majority of Church members are engaged in a tremendous variety of secular pursuits ranging from the home to every type of laboring and business activity it rests with us, usually spoken of as the "laity," to make our witness, either for or against our profession as Christians.

Because a Christian's impact for righteousness on his environment depends directly on his own personal commitment to Christ, in all of the implications of that word, how important is that matter of total surrender!

Certainly one of the most vital factors in both the winning of men to Christ and in the development of their lives in the art of Christian living centers in the minister under whom they sit Sunday after Sunday. Along with this, and even more important, is the nurture of the spirit which comes through Bible study and a definite and ordered prayer life.

Obviously the Christian minister faces two tasks: winning men to a saving faith in Jesus Christ and then leading them on to a positive and consistent life for Him.

In a rather wide experience, talking with and living with and working with men whose names are on the rolls of various Protestant churches the writer is convinced that a great proportion of these men have but the remotest idea of what it means to be a Christian, either as to the Person and work of the One Whose name they bear, or, of living in a way consistent with the name "Christian."

Because of this demonstrable fact — and it can be confirmed by any one living out in the world of business today — the obvious conclusion is that somewhere along the line something vital has been missed, that a superstructure has been built without an adequate foundation.

Unless we are committed to a non-biblical concept of Christianity we must admit that there are certain steps which form a part of the emergence from death to life, from darkness to light, from unbelief to faith.

These steps may develop as a blinding personal encounter with the Lord Jesus Christ, after which all things are changed and from which time we know that we are His.

Or, they may come quietly and unnoticed over a period of years until some day we realize that we belong to Him and have no recollection of when the transition took place.

Unfortunately, there are many today who have accepted the invitation to "join the church" who have never had a corresponding experience of receiving Christ as Saviour from sin and surrendering to Him as Lord of life.

The apostle Paul, writing to the Romans, lays down a principle which has been valid in each succeeding generation and is valid today: *"How shall they call on him in whom they have not believed? and how shall they believe in him of whom they have not heard? and how shall they hear without a preacher?"*

He further pin-points both the message and the method in I Cor. 1:17-31. In the 21st verse he writes: *"For after that in the wisdom of God the world by wisdom knew not God, it pleased God by the foolishness of preaching to save them that believe."*

The Scriptures make it plain what preaching really is — it is proclaiming the whole counsel of God and this has its root and its flower in the redemptive work of Christ, the eternal Son of God.

But what has often happened? Some illustrations may help answer the question, even though they seem extreme: An honest surgeon does not operate on a man for a hare-lip when he has a cancer which needs immediate attention. One does not stand on the bank of a river and expatiate on the beauties of a sunset to a drowning man. Few people would knowingly sit in a burning house while they finish reading an interesting story.

All around us, and sitting in every congregation, men are living and dying in sin, while they hear sermons on social, moral, political, racial, ecclesiastical and a thousand and one other issues which may be important but which are *secondary* to the great central message of the gospel itself.

There are evidences that this crying lack in past and contemporary preaching is now being recognized. From many sources one hears a call back to biblical preaching. One of America's leading ministers has recently said that three-fourths of today's preaching is beside the mark.

The centrality of the gospel message—of sin and judgment, of love and redemption, of Heaven and Hell, of the living Christ and His Holy Spirit, of the authority and integrity of the Scriptures—these and hundreds of other Bible-centered messages and doctrines are crying out to be preached *and men are hungry to hear them.*

Preaching finds its greatest justification and outlet when God and His Christ are exalted; when the Cross becomes central; when men are told *how* to become Christians. Plant the gospel in all of its fullness in the human heart and by the transforming power of the Holy Spirit God's salvation and His living presence will be manifested in daily lives.

The Chinese have a proverb which translated says: "One cannot carve rotten wood." Have not many of our efforts been directed to the "carving rotten wood," — trying to make non-Christians act like Christians?

Let us never forget that Christ did not come into this world so much to preach the gospel but that there might be a gospel to preach.

It is the preaching of that gospel which God honors to redeem souls and transform lives.

L.N.B.

One Lord, One Faith, One Baptism: One God and Father of All of Christ's People

On a non-political visit to Western North Carolina, the Vice President of the United States recently asked the representatives of the three leading evangelical bodies for the Churches to exercise their influence in softening the tensions between the races in our land.

Such a request is appropriate. The Church has the task of proclaiming the message of the prophet: What doth the Lord require of thee, O man, but to deal justly and love mercy and to walk humbly with thy God. The Church lays upon her members the golden rule enunciated by the Master: All things whatsoever ye would that men should do unto you, do ye even so unto them. Before the story of the Good Samaritan, Jesus tells us, Go thou and do likewise. And these simple everyday truths applied in sundry circumstances will lessen the tensions in society, both racially and economically and politically.

We have never permitted racial differences to keep us from attending the Church of the other race when there was a funeral of one close to us, or a wedding, or at times a "christening." It has been usual for the white neighbors to help in the building of Negro Churches.

The pillars of the ancient Church gave to Paul and Barnabus the right hand of fellowship that they should go to the Gentiles and Peter to the Jews, only they asked Paul to remember the poor. This he was zealous to do, bringing a considerable offering from the Gentile Churches to the poor disciples in Jerusalem. If we were to take a leaf from this example, we might today *bring* our gifts to our nearby Negro congregation when they have a building program. And some of them are now strong enough likewise to give and bring a gift when the white congregation has a similar task. And such visits to bring a helpful needed contribution toward a building or an expansion program in a congregation, might well be made the occasion for expressing our unity in the faith of Jesus Christ.

Of course, such an expression ought to be carefully arranged by representatives of the two congregations and graciously carried out. All those of every race and nation and denomina-

The Southern Presbyterian Journal, *a Presbyterian Weekly magazine devoted to the statement, defense, and propagation of the Gospel, the faith which was once for all delivered unto the saints,* published every Wednesday by The Southern Presbyterian Journal, Inc., in Weaverville, N. C.

Entered as second-class matter May 15, 1942, at the Postoffice at Weaverville, N. C., under the Act of March 3, 1879. Vol. XV, No. 19, September 5, 1956. Editorial and Business Offices: Weaverville, N. C. Printed in the U.S.A. by Biltmore Press, Asheville, N. C.

ADDRESS CHANGE: When changing address, please let us have both old and new address as far in advance as possible. Allow three weeks after change if not sent in advance. When possible, send an address label giving your old address.

tion who believe in Jesus Christ are brethren in Him. And concrete expressions of this oneness in Christ by a white and a Negro congregation located near each other could well soften our tensions and help our two races (in Henry W. Grady's words) "to walk together in peace and contentment." W.C.R.

Our Lord's Attitude to The Old Testament

By John R. W. Stott, M. A.

One church in London which will be found filled both Sunday morning and night is All Soul's, Langham Place. The Rector, Rev. John Stott, is a relatively young man but he is already considered one of the greatest preachers in the Anglican Church. This article is taken from his small book, "Fundamentalism and Evangelism" and copies of this book may be secured from the Journal office on request. It should be noted that the word "Fundamentalism" has a slightly different connotation in England than here in America. L.N.B.

The evidence is abundant that Jesus wholeheartedly and unquestioningly accepted the authority of the Old Testament. In many ways this for Christians should be the final issue. The authority of Christ and the authority of the Bible stand or fall together. Let us examine the facts.

To begin with, *He accepted the testimony of Scripture.* The first recorded word of His public ministry, in the Greek of St. Mark's Gospel, is "fulfilled . . ." (Mark 1. 15). He believed and taught that through His ministry and mission centuries of Old Testament anticipation were being fulfilled. Soon afterwards, He visited Nazareth, where He had been brought up, and attended the synagogue on the sabbath day according to His custom. He was given the scroll of Isaiah. He found what is our chapter 61 and read: "The Spirit of the Lord is upon me, because He has anointed me to preach good news to the poor. He has sent me to proclaim release to the captives and recovering of sight to the blind, to set at liberty those who are oppressed, to proclaim the acceptable year of the Lord."

He then closed the scroll, returned it to the synagogue attendant and sat down. And, as the eyes of the congregation were fixed on Him, He said "Today this Scripture has been fulfilled in your hearing" (Luke 4. 16-21, R.S.V.). In other words, Isaiah was writing about Him. He said that Abraham had rejoiced to see His day, that Moses wrote of Him and that the Scriptures bore witness to Him (John 8. 56; 5. 46 and 39). And after His resurrection He insisted that everything written about Him "in the law of Moses and the prophets and the psalms must be fulfilled," and "beginning with Moses and all the prophets He interpreted to them in all the Scriptures the things concerning Himself" (Luke 24. 44 and 27, R.S.V.).

Next, *He believed the statements of Scripture.* For instance, He said to the disciples on Maundy Thursday "You will all fall away; for it is written, 'I will strike the shepherd, and the sheep will be scattered'" (Mark 14. 27, R.S.V.). However loyal they might seem, whatever protest they might make, He knew that He would be smitten and that they would be scattered because the Scriptures said so. So He predicted His passion and resurrection, because the prophets had foretold the sufferings and the glory of the Christ. The progress of events did not take Him by surprise because He believed that what had been prophesied of Him would take place.

Thirdly, *He obeyed the commands of Scripture.* He voluntarily accepted a position of subordination to the Word of God. He followed its moral teaching in His own life. So deeply had He absorbed the spiritual lessons which God was teaching Israel in the wilderness of Sinai, that when in the wilderness of Judea the tempter came to Him, He was prepared. Three times He quoted the Word of God not just to the devil but to Himself in the devil's presence. He was resolved not to fail where Israel had failed. He would give to God the obedience, the trust and the worship which in His Word He demands (cf. Deuteronomy 8. 3; 6. 16 and 13). The same holy zeal for God's law is revealed throughout His ministry. He boldly cleansed the temple of its mercenary traffickers because it was written that God's house should be called a house of prayer (Mark 11. 15-17); and when the lawyer asked Him about the great commandment He was ready with His penetrating combination of Leviticus 19. 18 and Deuteronomy 6. 5, giving to the Church of all ages the duty to love both God and man.

Fourthly, *He applied the principles of Scripture.* When drawn into controversy with Pharisees and Sadducees, His court of appeal was the Scriptures. "Is not this why you are wrong," He asked, "that you know neither the Scriptures nor the power of God?" (Mark 12. 24, R.S.V.). The Scribes tended to be blindly and coldly literalist in their applications of the law, and Jesus rebuked them for rejecting the commandment of God in order to keep their own tradition (Mark 7. 7-9). It was not their adherence to the law which He rebuked, but their interpretations and traditions which had the effect of obscuring the essence of the law. They would lift a sheep out of a pit on the Sabbath day but would not allow Christ to heal a man. They would take their cattle to water on the Sabbath day but would not allow His disciples to eat in a cornfield. They would rather a man kept his vow to dedicate his money to God, and neglect his parents, than that he should break his vow and use his money to support his parents in their need. The whole perspective of the Scribes and Pharisees was awry. Jesus urged them to see that a person is of more value than a cow or a vow, and a spiritual principle than a literal code. "Go and learn what this means," He told them, "I desire mercy, and not sacrifice" (Matthew 9. 13, R.S.V.; cf. Hosea 6. 6).

Lastly, *He felt the compulsion of Scripture.* The word "must" was often on His lips. He knew Himself to be a child of destiny. True, He set Himself voluntarily to obey the law's teaching; but He also felt Himself involuntarily constrained by its prophecy. His will consented to it, but a certain constraint was there. "Everything that is written of the Son of man by the prophets will be accomplished." He declared (Luke 18. 31, R.S.V.). Again, "I tell you that this Scripture must be fulfilled in me, 'And he was reckoned with transgressors'; for what is written about me has its fulfilment" (Luke 22. 27, R.S.V.). So He allowed Himself to be arrested in the garden, although He knew that the Father would at His appeal immediately send more than twelve legions of angels to His aid. "But how then should the Scriptures be fulfilled" He asked, "that it must be so?" (Matthew 26. 53-54, R.S.V.).

His reverent acceptance of the Old Testament Scriptures is beyond question. He fed His own soul on them and specially loved Deuteronomy, the Psalms and Isaiah. He interpreted His mission in the light of them. He declared that they were fulfilled in Himself. He referred to them in controversy as the final arbiter. He rebuked His contemporaries for their ignorance of them. He had come, He said, not "to abolish the law and the prophets . . . but to fulfil them. For truly, I say to you, till heaven and earth pass away, not an iota, not a dot, will pass from the law until all is accomplished" (Matthew 5. 17, 18, R.S.V.). Again He affirmed, "Scripture cannot be broken" (John 10:35 R.S.V.).

All this is the more remarkable when it is remembered that Jesus possessed supernatural wisdom and authority. Both were clear characteristics of His teaching and invited comment from His hearers. "Where did this man get all this?" they asked. "What is the wisdom given to Him?" . . . "Is not this the carpenter . . . ?" (Mark 6. 2-3, R.S.V.). "They were astonished at His teaching, for He taught them as one who had authority, and not as the Scribes" (Mark 1. 22, R.S.V.). Yet His wisdom did not contradict the wisdom of the Old Testament, and His authority did not overthrow the authority of the Old Testament. It seems to us a serious matter to think lightly of the Scriptures of which He thought so highly, and to reject what He accepted.

Some would reply that Jesus deliberately accommodated Himself to the opinions of His own day and that He spoke to His contemporaries in the categories they could understand and accept, while not holding them Himself. But surely He who called Himself the Truth would not thus have compromised the truth? And He who fearlessly rebuked sin and hypocrisy, human pride and human traditions, would not have been slow to expose so great an error if He had regarded it as such? But, someone else will say, surely Jesus the eternal Son of God "emptied Himself" when He took the form of a servant and was made in the likeness of men (Philippians 2. 7, R.S.V.)? And, our critic will continue, did not this emptying of Himself involve the adoption of the limited outlook and mentality of an ignorant (though remarkable) first-century Jew? The suggestion is not now that He deliberately accommodated Himself to false teaching but that the Incarnation involved Him in the same error. If so, we cannot rely on His teaching as authoritative.

Now this application of the doctrine of "kenosis," or self-emptying, is popular in certain circles today and is too big a problem to attempt to solve briefly here. Suffice it to say that it seems to many of us dreadfully derogatory to the unique glory of our blessed Lord. It is very dangerous to begin with such a presupposition as "to err is human," and then to add "therefore to be human Jesus must have erred." Could we not equally well argue that "so sin is human and therefore Jesus must have sinned"? But the unanimous testimony of the Scriptures, which the Church has always accepted, is that our Lord was sinless. Of course sin and error are part of our fallen human nature, but they are no necessary part of the perfect human nature which God made and Christ assumed. The evidence of Scripture is that the man Christ Jesus, through the perfect surrender of His mind to the revelation of God, was inerrant, and through the perfect surrender of His will to the will of God, was sinless (see John 7. 16; 12. 49; 5. 30; 8. 29).

The Reformed Doctrine of The Means of Grace

By Rev. G. Aiken Taylor, Ph.D.

One of the strongest planks in the platform of the Roman Catholic Church is its doctrine of the means of grace, although it doesn't call it that. But this church recognizes that the important question in religion is how contact is made between the Divine and the human. And it has a ready answer.

With the grace of God available in a sort of spiritual reservoir, as it were, and with the needs of men below in a sort of thirsty land, there must be some point of contact, some channel, some way or means of transmitting or of delivering this grace in order that man be "filled with all the fullness of God."

The Roman Church meets this very real problem with its doctrine of the "Keys." Because it believes itself to be "official" in every sense of the word; because it is the agent which is properly authorized; because it is the point of contact between God and man, the church is the main dispensary of grace. And with its ordinances and sacraments it dispenses grace and the blessings of God to those who come to receive them. When a believer comes to the Mass and takes the wafer on his tongue, he receives Jesus Christ. When a penitent does the twelve stations of the cross he confidently expects to receive a due measure of good.

A worshiper entering a cathedral drops to his or her knees before the Host and makes the sign of the Cross. That act of faith is ordinarily worth one hundred indulgences. If the worshiper dips his or her fingers into holy water before he or she makes that sign of the Cross, the value of the act is doubled.

With such a system of barter and trade, the Roman Church carries on its business. It offers a clearly defined program of spiritual communication whereby the faithful receive the benefits they seek through real and particular means.

As everyone knows, the Reformation made sweeping and revolutionary changes in the practice of religion. But many moderns do not realize that John Calvin, the great systematizer of Reformed Doctrine, thought and wrote in terms with which new converts from Rome were familiar. When Calvin broke with Rome he did not discard the doctrine of a real and particular church dispensing grace through real and particular means.

It shocks some people to hear that John Calvin very firmly believed that "outside the church, there is no salvation." Of course, he did not have the Roman idea of the Church when he said this, but he did have in mind a very real doctrine of the Means of Grace. He believed that God works through His Church, the Body of Christ on earth. And he believed that the Church has in its hands an effective channel or means whereby one can receive the benefits of salvation through Jesus Christ. Taking the place of holy relics, of miraculous water, of blessed oil, of transubstantiated bread, John Calvin believed in the efficacy of the one thing which we know to be from God: the one thing which is of divine origin and which is vibrant with potential spiritual power, namely the Word of God. For Calvin, the Word of God was the true and primary means of grace.

The Reformer believed that when a minister of God stands in the pulpit and proclaims the Word of God something happened to those who hear it. Salvation comes through hearing the Word. This is because the Word is the means of grace. There is nothing magical or mechanical about the Word. It is simply the channel through which grace flows. When one hears the inspired words of John 3:16, for instance, he feels his heart strangely warmed, because the Holy Spirit uses the Word to accomplish His saving work.

Calvin's idea, of course, is altogether Scriptural. He remembered that the New Testament declares that "the Word of God is sharper than a two-edged sword, piercing to the dividing asunder of the joints and the marrow."

And he was mindful that "through the foolishness of preaching, God is pleased to save those who believe." Not just any word, of course, has this potent effect. It must be the Word of God. But Calvin was supremely confident that he had in his hands the Word of God. This is why he held to the high view of the Bible which has characterized followers of the Reformed faith ever since. He did not worship a book. He reverenced the *effect* which the contents of this Book had on people, not because the words in themselves were magic, but because they were the means through which the Holy Spirit did His work of salvation.

We can understand exactly what the Reformer had in mind when we consider his doctrine of

This Reformed idea has many practical applications. The Sunday School teacher, for instance, who gathers her children about her and gives them the truth of God is providing the occasion for the Holy Spirit to work in their lives. Anyone who opens the Word of God to another is doing what the priest of Rome thinks he is doing when he places the wafer on the tongue of a worshiper.

It should now be perfectly evident why the Reformed faith has traditionally placed so high an emphasis upon the Bible as a primary source book. We are jealous for the authority of Scripture. We reverence the Word of God. We don't want to see it mutilated or relegated to a position of secondary importance. We feel that a preacher's job is to preach it, and a teacher's job is to teach it. Nothing else will do. Other things may be true, other things may be valuable in human experience. But nothing else has the same spiritual value, for the Word of God is the divinely appointed Means of Grace unto Salvation.

Should We Change Our Confession of Faith?

By Rev. Robert Strong, S.T.D.

What a tremendous amount of business the General Assembly has to give attention to in a period of time that does not exceed four full working days. It should not be wondered at that some matters receive only the most cursory treatment.

From accounts in the church press this was the case with the report of the Ad Interim Committee on Marriage, Divorce and Remarriage (for the full text of the report see General Assembly Minutes, p. 132 ff.). There are splendid sentiments embodied in this report, and it is obvious that the committee was thoroughly diligent. The report contains material, however, that is highly debatable, so that one regrets the practice of adopting such reports as a whole. When time pressure is so great, it would seem advisable to receive this kind of report and take action only on its recommendations.

An illustration of debatable items is paragraph 4 (Minutes, p. 133). Arguing from the principle of the separation of Church and State the report decries the participation of ministers in the marriage ceremony as being tantamount to constituting them officers of the State. Is this not faulty thinking? Separation of Church and State does not mean that a wall is raised between the two, that cooperation between them is not possible nor desirable. On the reasoning of the report we ought not to consent to our ministers serving as chaplains in the armed forces or in legislative bodies or offering prayer at inaugural ceremonies.

Again, it is offered in paragraph 2 (Minutes, p. 137) that Jesus in the Sermon on the Mount is intent to show that the law of His Kingdom transcends the law of Moses. Any disparaging of Moses would be most difficult to urge in the light of Matthew 5:17-19. And the fact that nowhere in the Old Testament is it said, "Thou shalt love thy neighbor, and hate thine enemy" (quoted by Jesus as current Jewish thinking, Matthew 5:43) is one of numerous indications that should help us to see that Jesus is not at odds with Moses but is engaging in extensive correction of faulty scribal or traditional interpretation of Moses.

The really serious misgivings about the committee's report arise when it is alleged (Minutes, p. 135) that there is no valid biblical basis for the teaching in the Confession of Faith, Chapter XXVI, Paragraphs V and VI, that a marriage may be dissolved on the ground of adultery or of irremediable desertion.

In support of the recommendation to delete these two paragraphs from the Confession of Faith the report asserts in an Addendum that our Lord never spoke the exceptive clauses ("except for unchastity") recorded in Matthew 5:32 and 19:9. The exceptive clauses, it is suggested, crept into the text of Matthew through "some scribe seeking to soften the rigorous teaching of Jesus."

In spite of the fact that a majority of New Testament scholars are appealed to as "strongly convinced that these words form no part of Jesus' teaching," many of us will be troubled, I feel sure. Majority vote does not settle an issue of fact. The real point would appear to be, What is the manuscript evidence? Do the ancient copies of the Greek New Testament hint that the text of Matthew has undergone editing at these two points? There is no evidence to show that the text of Matthew 5:32 is corrupt, and the best manuscript evidence upholds also Matthew 19:9 in its familiar form.

The doctrine of the inspiration of the Scriptures requires us, does it not?, to expect to find the Scriptures in agreement, to compare Scripture with Scripture, not to pit Scripture against Scripture. Should we not seek some other answer to the difference in reporting as found in Mark 10 and in Luke 16 than to import the unsupportable hypothesis of scribal tampering with the text of Matthew?

Excellent assistance in dealing with the issues confronting us in the whole discussion may be received from Prof. John Murray's little book DIVORCE (order, if interested, from *The Southern Presbyterian Journal,* Weaverville, N. C. Price $2.00.) On the point immediately before us he works through the problem and concludes "that Mark and Luke are not envisaging the situation created in the event of adultery and are not reflecting on the rights of the innocent spouse in such a case. They are concentrating rather upon the abrogation of certain Mosaic provisions anent divorce and upon prevalent customs in both Jewish and Gentile circles. They report our Lord's teaching as it was directed to these specific evils. Matthew does likewise. But the latter conveys to us additional information regarding our Lord's teaching on this question, namely, his teaching upon the contingency of adultery. Matthew informs us of two things: (a) a man may put away his wife for adultery; (b) he may marry another when such divorce is consummated" (DIVORCE, p. 52).

At a time when it is proposed that our presbyteries strike two paragraphs from the Confession of Faith, paragraphs that have the solid support of Scripture, it would be unfortunate, I think, if careful preparation were not made for the discussion in which we shall be asked to engage. I do not attempt here to do more than touch briefly on some of the questions involved. But I do recommend that the admirable, up-to-the-minute, exegetical study written by Professor Murray be widely consulted. Dealing as it does with all the pertinent passages (Deuteronomy 24:1-4; Matthew 5:31,32; Matthew 19:3-9; Mark 10:2-12; Luke 16:18; I Corinthians 7:10-15; Romans 7:1-3) it should prove a most useful tool in the hands of our presbyters. One is confident that they will not wish to see our Confession of Faith changed in the way now proposed.

The Person of Christ

By Rev. Floyd E. Hamilton

Centreville, Alabama

"And we know that the Son of God is come, and hath given us an understanding, that we know him that is true, and we are in him that is true, even in his Son Jesus Christ. This is the true God and eternal life." I John 5:20.

This week we take up our fourth discussion of the issue of Modernism. After showing that Evangelicalism and Modernism are opposed to each other on at least thirteen major points of Christian doctrine, we discussed first the inspiration of the Bible. Evangelicalism teaches that the Holy Spirit so guided and controlled the writers of the Old and New Testaments that what they wrote was true and the truth God wanted His people to have. Modernists deny this. Then we discussed the doctrine of man.

Evangelicals hold that God created man a living soul, holy and perfect, but that man fell into sin and spiritual death. Only the new birth can change man to an obedient believer in Christ. Modernists regard man as not needing any new birth, but as the highest product of evolution. Then we showed that the Bible way of salvation is through belief in the atoning life and death of Jesus Christ, while Modernists deny man's need of salvation or at least claim that man is perfectly able to save himself if he needs any saving.

In this article we take up the very important point of doctrine regarding the Person of Christ. The Bible teaches that Jesus Christ is the eternal Son of God, the Second Person of the Triune God, who came to earth and took upon Himself a true body and reasonable soul, so that he was and continues to be both God and man, one person and two natures. We do not pretend to understand how this can be, and yet we know from the testimony of the Word of God that it is true.

The Modernist on the other hand almost always *denies* the true deity of our Lord and Saviour. He pays little attention to the teaching of the Bible on this point, in a verse such as our text: "This is the true God and eternal life," and simply asserts that Jesus was only a man. The Modernist claims to have great reverence for Jesus the man, and most Modernists would claim that he was the pinnacle of the evolution of the human race, the highest moral product of human ascent from savagery. They would say that Jesus is our highest moral ideal and example; that he is head and shoulders above the rest of struggling humanity, but that he is in no way different in quality from the rest of mankind. He is said to have lived a life of sacrifice, and finally to have given his life as a martyr for the high cause which he believed in.

The beautiful word tributes which Modernists pay to Jesus the man, deceive many Evangelicals into thinking that there cannot possibly be anything wrong with men who hold such high views of Jesus Christ. You see Jesus *was* truly man as well as truly God. He was a sinless man; and all the high tributes which the Modernists pay him are true. That is why the tributes of such men are so deceptive in their effects on evangelicals. A single example will show what I mean. Let us examine the beautiful hymn which we find in almost all hymnals,

"O Master, let me walk with thee,
In lowly paths of service free;
Tell me Thy secret; help me bear
The strain of toil, the fret of care.

Help me the slow of heart to move
By some clear, winning word of love;
Teach me the wayward feet to stay,
And guide them in the homeward way.

Teach me Thy patience; still with Thee
  In closer, dearer company,
In work that keeps faith sweet and strong,
  In trust that triumphs over wrong.

In hope that sends a shining ray
  Far down the future's broadening way
In peace that only Thou canst give,-
  With Thee, O Master, let me live."

Beautiful words, are they not? Words which strike a responsive chord in the heart of every Christian who sings them, for they are true, since Jesus Christ is our Master and can and will give us all the help and comfort that the verses sing about. But let us not forget that these words do not give the whole picture of Jesus Christ, for there is nothing of the deity of Christ in the words, and in fact they were written by Dr. Washington Gladden, a minister who *definitely denied the true deity of Jesus Christ!*

How many of us know that the beautiful hymn in which we all take such delight, "In the Cross of Christ I Glory, Towering o'er the wrecks of Time," was written by Sir John Bowring, a Unitarian who denied the deity of Christ?

You see that is why Modernists are able to lead countless thousands of true Christians astray. The words which they usually write or speak are not in themselves untrue. As far as they go they are true, but they are only half the truth. Usually it is not what the Modernist says on these subjects that is wrong; it is what he leaves unsaid, the part of the picture that is left out that is the trouble. When a true Christian reads or hears such words as those quoted, he interprets them in the light of his own beliefs and unconsciously adds the Scripture teaching about Christ's Deity to the words of the Modernist, and then holds that the Modernist is orthodox!

This situation if further complicated by the fact that many times the Modernist even declares that he believes in the divinity of Christ, meaning that since we are all children of God we all partake of the divine nature of God, and that Jesus who was the very highest point of the evolution of the race, partook more fully of the divine nature than the rest of us.

Thus the Modernist who holds this view can assert that he believes in the deity of Christ but does not add the fact that he thinks we too are divine. The mere assertion that he believes in the deity of Christ, therefore, does not mean that the Modernist holds the view that Christ was co-equal with God the Father. In order to be sure that such a man holds to the orthodox belief in the deity of Christ, we need to know more about what he means when he asserts his belief in the deity of Christ.

You see the Bible teaches that Jesus Christ in his divine nature was different in quality from every man that ever has lived. It was not merely that God dwelt in him as God dwells in the soul of every true Christian. Jesus was not merely a God-in-dwelt man: he *was* God, in the same sense that God the Father is God, and in a sense in which no other man that ever lived was. He not only towers head and shoulders above the rest of humanity, He was on the Godward side of an impassable gulf between man and God, for He was God in a sense that never was or is or will be possible for man.

Some Modernists are willing to say that Jesus was the Son of God, but they are unwilling to say that He was God in the very sense in which God the Father is God. In other words these Modernists of whom I am now speaking hold that Jesus was subordinate to God the Father, so that when they say Jesus was the Son of God they mean that he was on a lower level of being than God the Father. Somewhat as did the Arians of the fourth century, they might go even so far as to say that Jesus was created before the rest of the universe came into existence, and therefore is a rank higher than humanity, but still below the rank of God the Father. They therefore do not hesitate to speak of Jesus as the Son of God in a unique sense, while they really mean that he was a being higher than men but still not "very God of very God" as the Athanasian creed asserts. All this is very confusing to the ordinary Christian, so many orthodox Christians are deceived into thinking that these men are orthodox because they give such high honor to Jesus.

Now do not get the idea that it makes no difference what we think of Jesus Christ. Only if we have a Saviour who could redeem an infinite number of souls because He was the infinite God the Son, can we have a Saviour who can really save us. Only if it is really true that "All power hath been given unto" Him in heaven and on earth, can we have a Saviour who could really redeem sinful humanity by taking our place on the cross.

Praise God we have such a Saviour, the one who was and is and will always be "the same yesterday, today and forever" our Lord and Saviour and our God. Is He your Saviour? Is He your Lord? Do you trust Him alone for salvation?

ANGLERS

By WADE C. SMITH

Lesson No. 155

STUDY CLASSES IN PERSONAL EVANGELISM

For Study Classes, larger groups may be formed by combining those groups whose personnel may find the same hour for meeting practicable. In these Study Classes the thing to be learned is how to approach people and how to tell them the Gospel story and invite them to accept Jesus Christ as Saviour. The first step is to become familiar with the Bible statements about sin and salvation, and of course that places first in importance as a text book the Bible itself. The Pastor is the trained leader for this sort of study, and usually it is most desirable that he be the teacher; but any good Bible student whose heart is burning with evangelistic zeal would make a good leader for the class in the Pastor's absence. The Scripture plan of salvation should be learned so that it may be stated in the Bible's own language. The many passages in Scripture which answer objections and excuses should be learned. Methods of approach and getting the point of contact should be studied. Remember, there is no universal method which will apply in each specific case, for there is an infinite variety in circumstances, conditions and personalities to deal with; but there are certain basic principles which are useful and necessary; these, supplemented by the Spirit's guidance, can be effectively employed in each individual (or peculiar) case.

It will increase interest and helpfulness in the class for the members to give their experiences in trying to do personal work, telling of apparent failures as well as successes, letting the leader, or other members, comment upon the report and make suggestions. All of it, of course, is to be done in the spirit of humility which is so necessary in every phase of this work.

One method the writer tried proved to be very interesting and instructive. The class was divided into two groups and separated to each side of the room. One side took the part of the "sinner sought" and the other side "the personal worker." The "sinner" offered the usual stock of objections and excuses. They had the easier part to perform. The "personal worker's" part was to practice meeting the objections and excuses with the Scripture answers. Theirs was the more difficult; yet the Bible answers were right there, only requiring the ability and diligence to use them. After a few minutes the "sides" were exchanged, and it was interesting to note that the "objections and excuses" were not the same (for the devil has his hopper full of them), nor were the Scripture answers the same, but varied to meet the need. This was called a "Sword Drill" by which soul winners may learn how to "parry and thrust" with the invincible Sword of the Spirit. "For the Word of God is quick and powerful, and sharper than any two-edged sword, piercing even to the dividing asunder of soul and spirit, and of the joints and marrow, and is a discerner of the thoughts and intents of the heart." (Heb.4:12.)

The objection will certainly be made to this "strenuous" program that in this busy and complex life of ours, crowded to the limit with engagements of various kinds (and worthy engagements!) it is not possible for a group to meet, say five nights in the week, or two nights in the week - or *even once a week* for study in Personal Evangelism. Is that really true? I notice that the department stores are advertising and conducting study classes in the use of cosmetics and how to beautify the skin, or in some cases a cooking class. An expert from a distant city has been employed at great expense to lead the morning and evening sessions. All the elevators are crowded "going up" and there is much enthusiasm, for this is "a wonderful opportunity." How do they find time for it?

The Y. M. C. A. or the Club is putting on a physical training course, followed by a shower and a rub down, and even the busy executive is *making it possible* to get around there each morning for an hour and avail himself of this opportunity to conserve his physique. How do they find time for it? This is the answer: you will somehow manage to find time to do the thing you *want* to do. You will make a place in your day's schedule for the thing you regard as of most importance. This leads to the question: which is the more important, those things which are of only transient value, of only a few years use at the most; or those things which are of eternal value?

(More of this study in the next lesson).

Helps To Understanding Scripture Readings in *Day by Day*

By Rev. C. C. Baker

Sunday, September 16, *Psalm* 103. Choice passages of Scripture are like choice morsels of food; though partaken of frequently, they never lose their appeal and never cease to satisfy. Consider vv.1-5 of Psalm 103 in terms of what the Lord has done for your soul in Christ. How many of the blessings of vv.3-5 can you say have been true in your life? Study each of the conjunctives and connectives in vv.9-18 to see how the Psalmist's thoughts are developed. What thoughts do the words "for" and "as" connect (vv.10-15)? How do the clauses of vv.10-12, 13-15 introduced by "so" and "nor," add to clauses they follow? What thoughts does the word "but" of v.17 connect? With the fruit of this study in mind, again praise God with the Psalmist for all His benefits (vv.1-2).

Monday, September 17, *II Kings* 5:1-14. The lessons Naaman learned before he could be cured of his leprosy are the same lessons we must learn if God is to meet our spiritual needs. Naaman first learned that the resources of the world could avail little (vv. 1-7). Notice that while the mistress instructed him to go to the prophet of God (v.3), Naaman first looked to the King of Israel (v.6). He next learned that God's ways are often foolish in the sight of the world (vv.8-12). He finally realized that God could not meet his needs unless he, himself, met the conditions God laid down (vv.13-14). Do you have spiritual hungers you try to satisfy through secular resources? God meets our spiritual needs as we embrace the foolishness of the cross (I Cor. 1:18) and humbly allow the Person of Christ to live His life in us (Matt. 11:28; John 6:35,51).

Tuesday, September 18, *Luke* 4:1-13. There was divine purpose in God's allowing His Son to be tempted (v.1). Consider the appeal of the first temptation (v.3) in the light of Jesus' obvious physical hunger (v.2). Think about the temptation of vv.5-7 in the light of the agony of the cross. How did the cross accomplish the mission of Christ in a way that yielding to the temptation of vv.5-7 could not? In what way was the temptation of vv.9-11 contrary to the whole manner in which Jesus carried out His mission (note Acts 10:38-40)? Would the methods of vv.9-11 engender faith in the observer? Because Christ was tempted He understands what we endure and is able to succor us in times of temptation (Hebrews 4:15). Do you look beyond the temptations that beset you to the divine purpose God would accomplish in your life through your conquering of

Saturday, September 22, Romans 12:1-21. Paul gives the Christian a two-fold commission - to turn to God (v.1) and away from the world (v.2). For many Christians non-conformity to the ways of the world (v.2) is a negative matter, a list of things they must not do. Make a list of all the commands given in vv.3-21, which, if kept by the Christian, would make him distinctively different from the non-Christian. Are these commands primarily negative or positive? See if you can find any negative exhortation that does not have a positive counterpart. If someone were to judge your position before God by what he saw of obedience to the commands of vv.3-21 in your life, what would his verdict be? Are you willing to be transformed (v.2) in any area of your life (vv.3-21) in which you are still conforming to the standards of the world?

LESSON FOR SEPTEMBER 16

Christ Among The Churches

Background Scripture: Matthew 18:20; John 21:1-14; Revelation 1 - 3
Devotional Reading: Revelation 3:7-13

The Golden Text, "Behold I stand at the door and knock," etc., is an invitation, or exhortation, to the church. It is also a blessed invitation to the outsider, the unsaved man, and is often used in evangelistic meetings. If we examine the context, however, we see plainly that it is written to a lukewarm, self-satisfied church, urging them to let the Head of the church come into their midst. Is it possible for a church to become no more than a club, or social gathering? Paul speaks of "having a form of godliness, but denying the power thereof." The church has no power apart from her Head, the Lord Jesus Christ: "Apart from me ye can do nothing," said Christ to His disciples in John 15. The church, apart from Him, becomes as helpless and as worthless as a dead branch, or one separated from the vine. With Christ the church can be victorious. Jesus calls the church, "My Church"; Upon this rock I will build my church, and the gates of hell shall not prevail against it.

I wish to use the first two selections, (Matt. 18:20, and John 21:1-14), to emphasize this thought. In Matthew 18:20 Jesus said, "For where two or three are gathered together in my name, there am I in the midst of them." Here we see a real church. There is no special building, no organization, no large congregation; just two or three people gathered "in my name," and the Head of the church in their midst.

In contrast to this, you might have a million dollar cathedral, a hundred thousand dollar organ with most beautiful music, an organization with all its numerous officers and work, and a congregation of thousands of worshippers, but if Christ, the Head of the Church is not present, then there is no true church. The essential Person is missing. In John 21:1-14 we see the disciples — part of them — discouraged and uncertain and helpless. The best thing they can think of doing is to go fishing; to return to their old occupation. Sometimes we feel that way, too. As they fished, however, they had the transforming experience described in these verses. Christ comes back in all His miraculous power and stands in their midst. He, the risen Saviour, brings to them all they need in order that they may go forth as heroes and conquerors. Let us now turn to the main selection for our study, Rev. 1-3.

I. *The Vision:* Revelation 1.

The Book of Revelation has many mysterious figures in it and many types and symbols. It also has some of the plainest and most practical lessons for us. I believe that the neglect of this book has weakened and hurt the church and that a study of it will recall the church to her allegiance to her Head, and will encourage Christian people to live and work for the advancement of the Kingdom. The book is written to warn and encourage the church. It tells the story of the Trials and Triumphs of the Church and her future glory.

The author is John, the beloved disciple; the place, the isle of Patmos, the time of writing 95 to 96 A. D. A special blessing is pronounced upon those who read and study it; "Blessed is he that readeth, and they that hear the words of this prophecy, and keep those things which are written therein." It is full of "Doxologies." We have one of these in verse six, after the description of Jesus Christ in verse five; "Unto him that loved us, and washed, (loosed) us from our sins in his own blood," etc. John was "in the Spirit on the Lord's Day, and heard behind me a great voice, as of a trumpet, saying, I am Alpha and Omega, the first and the last: and what thou seest write in a book and send it to the seven churches which are in Asia." This is Asia Minor, the scene of much of Paul's missionary work, where he established many churches.

The vision follows, and it is an overwhelming experience for John. "And when I saw him, I fell at his feet as one dead." I think that we would have done the same thing. I believe that it would do the church good to stop looking at the many man-made, and man-imagined pictures which we see, and think more about this God-given portrait of our Risen and Glorified Lord. I feel embarrassed and ashamed when I see some of these pictures of Christ. I saw one the other day on the back of one of the church publications which was particularly obnoxious and repulsive. I cannot imagine my Saviour looking anything like this ugly counterfeit. Some are not ugly or repulsive, but the

1. Ephesus. The Church that left her first love, or as one of our modern translations put it, "You do not love me as you did at first." This church is commended for certain good points; its works and labor, and patience, and faithful adherence to the truth. It is censured for this one fault, its loss of love. The one vital thing, which Jesus looks for above all others, is LOVE. "Simon, son of Jonas, lovest thou me," is the question above all others. If the bride does not love the bridegroom, marriage is a mockery.

2. Smyrna. This is a rather weak and poor and persecuted church, but it is commended, and promised a crown because of her faithfulness. It is one of the two churches with which no fault is found. It is a type of many poor, persecuted bodies of Christians which have been, and are found in the world.

3. Pergamos. This church stands approved for much in its life: it had been holding fast His name and witnessing for Him in the place "where Satan's seat is." It is warned against false teaching, even the doctrine of Balaam, and the Nicolaitanes, both of which were extremely hateful to Christ. We can turn to our Old Testament and see how Balaam, the strange prophet, managed to corrupt Israel, by telling the king of Moab how he could lead them astray, and bring punishment upon them. No one seems to be sure just what was the doctrine of the Nicolaitanes. The lesson for us and the church is very obvious: Beware of false teaching. Jesus warned against the leaven, or doctrine, of the Scribes, Pharisees, and Herodians, and spoke often of false prophets which were wolves in sheep's clothing. False teaching has been, and is, one of the worst plagues of the church.

4. Thyatira. Much in this church is also commended, but some very gross evils must be corrected. Its reference to Jezebel would indicate immorality, especially in connection with worship, for it was Jezebel who introduced Baal-worship into Israel. Jeroboam was bad enough, but Jezebel was worse. Full and speedy repentance is commanded, or a terrible punishment will come.

5. Sardis. It has a name to live, but is dead. Even in Sardis there are a few who are alive.

6. Philadelphia, the Faithful church.

7. Laodicea. Lukewarm, the rich, but poor, self-satisfied church. The great invitation is given to it, 3:20.

YOUTH PROGRAM FOR SEPTEMBER 16

Taking Time For God

Suggested Devotional Outline:

Hymn: 'Fairest Lord Jesus, Ruler Of All Nature"

Prayer

Scripture: Psalm 46

Hymn: "Dear Lord and Father of Mankind"

Offering

Hymn: "I Love To Steal Awhile Away"

Leader's Introduction:

"Be Still, and know that I am God!" Those eight short words hold a wealth of true advice for us and for all people who live as we do. So frequently we regard activity as being all important. Unless we are forever on the go, most people are apt to think we are lazy, and no one wants to be considered lazy. We certainly do not want to give the impression that God favors laziness, but being still is not being lazy, and God tells us that we ought to be still.

Many accusations were brought against Jesus during His earthly life, but they never accused Him of being lazy. Even His bitterest enemies did not criticize Him for His times of quiet solitude. From reading the record we know that on numerous occasions Jesus went apart to pray and to commune with His Father. If the Son of God found it necessary to take out time to be alone with God, certainly we cannot afford to do without such times. "Be still, and know that I am God!" That is no mere suggestion. It is a command from God. Let us take care that we obey it.

First Speaker:

Why is it necessary to take out time for God? Why is this commandment given to us? We have it for the same reason that we take time to become well acquainted with any person. Our best friends are not the persons to whom we have just been introduced. Our best friends, our closest friends are the persons we have been learning to know for a long time. It has been suggested that one reason so many marriages are failing is that those who enter into them do not know each other well enough. Love at first sight is an insufficient basis for a lifetime of living together. Lasting friendship and love takes time to develop. We must not expect to know God in a fully satisfactory way unless we are willing to take time to know Him better.

How many times in our lives have we said that we would like to do some particular thing but that we just did not have time for it. An elderly minister asked his young friend if he liked to fish. The young man said he liked to fish all right, but that he could not find time for it. "If you really liked to fish," said the older man, "you would make time to do it." There is truth in what he said. We usually find time to do the things that we consider most important. There is really no such thing as spare time. There are just so many hours in a day, and there are usually more demands on our time than there are hours to meet them. The only time we have is the time we take. Do we think God is important enough that we take time to be alone with Him?

Second Speaker:

The church is usually asking us to take time for God by doing things - attending meetings, working on projects, planning programs, singing in the choir, etc. Just now we are suggesting that a more important thing than activity is to be still in the presence of God. As has already been mentioned, you can never know a person well until you spend some time alone with him. In all seriousness, that is why boys and girls who are learning to love each other want to spend some time alone. It is unnatural to be always doing something in a big crowd. It is unnatural to be always by oneself. God expects us to live for Him in the crowd, but He also expects us to spend some time with Him alone.

"Know that I am God!" It is possible to be so busy about so many things that we forget that He is God, but if we spend some time alone with Him each day, it will be impossible to forget Him. We can be sure that every person who is well acquainted with God is one who is faithful in spending quiet times alone with Him. There are sixteen hours in a waking day. In those sixteen hours there are 192 five minute periods. Surely it is not asking too much of us to give the Lord 1/192 of the day in private, but how many of us are there who actually do it? One thing is certain, if we do give the Lord five minutes of every day, it will be the best five minutes of our day.

Third Speaker:

Being still does not ordinarily agree with the American people. We would rather do something than keep still. We would rather talk than be quiet. Meditation does not come easy

:or us, and we may feel ill at ease when we try :o be still before God. Quiet meditation is ;omething that has to be learned and practiced ɔefore we can do it satisfactorily. Here are ;ome simple suggestions which have been help- :ul to many.

1. Spend some time each day just thinking ıbout God . . . what He is like, what He has lone, and what He has promised to do. It is :omforting and inspiring simply to think about ;od.

2. Spend some time each day with the Bible. ?erhaps you will read only a verse and think ıbout it. Single verses have brought rich bless- ngs to many people. The Bible is God's Book vritten to make Him known to us. The knowl- :dge received from it can be trusted to inspire, :o strengthen, and to acquaint you with God.

3. Spend some time each day in private prayer to God. You expect to converse with your closest friends in private, and you do it as frequently as you can. Why should it be any different with God? He is the best friend of all. Just as we feel closer to earthly friends after a heart-to-heart talk with them, so will we be drawn closer to God after times of private prayer.

We first heard about God like some great and famous person. Then we became personally acquainted with Him through faith in His Son. That is salvation. We become His close personal friends by working with Him in His church, and by spending this time with Him alone. We can be sure that the activities of the church will not suffer because we take some time to be alone with God. Whatever we do with our time, this time for God should be set aside first.

Women's Work

Woman and the Tithe

Your Responsibility. Statistics reveal that vomen control practically one-half of the indi- 'idual wealth of the country. Husbands and vives should be real partners in the administra- ion of the family income. It is up to the vomen in many cases to see to it that the family :nters into partnership with God. The woman ıy virtue of her position in the home can see nore deeply into the truth that "man does ıot live by bread alone," and she realizes that he income must be used in providing for piritual as well as physical needs.

Your Guidance. The question, "How much hould I give to God?" is one that can be de- ided only by the individual. Giving to God ; an act of worship, therefore our giving should e acceptable and pleasing to Him. In His Vord we find the principles to guide us in eciding how much to give. Lev. 27:30, Deut. 4:22, Mal. 3:7-10. The tithe is the minimum.

Your Example. When Christ came into the 'orld He set for us the supreme example and ıotive in giving: "God so *loved* . . . that He *ave* . . . " Jesus had much to say about earn- ıg, keeping, spending, and giving. We can be ıre that Jesus tithed, for if He had failed, ıe Pharisees would have been quick to accuse Iim. To be sure that our giving comes up to ıat standard, the tithe will have to be the :arting point in our giving; and love will lead s beyond.

Your Testimonies. To those who have never adopted the principle of the tithe as a method of giving, we would say, "Ask the person who tithes." When you get tithers to talking, here are some of the things they say:

"One of the most glorious Christian experiences that I have known has been to accept the challenge of the tithe."

"The first and greatest value we have received from tithing is joy."

"For years I have practiced tithing, for the practice of tithing gives recognition to God as Owner and Giver of all things."

"When I tithe the supply never runs out. God's providing hand never fails."

Let us bring our tithes "into the store-house" that we may have an abundant spiritual, as well as financial blessing.

I Am The Church

I am the heaven-sent Agent through which the Divine Christ sends His Saving Gospel to sinning, suffering, sordid, selfish souls.

I am a necessity to all who prize peace, progress, and purity.

I am hung about with sweetest memories — memories of beautiful brides, memories of saintly mothers, memories of grandfathers who slowly groped their way down the long, long trail.

I am decked with loving tears, crowned by happy hands, and aided by heroic hearts.

I lift up the fallen, relieve the burdened, strengthen the weak, help the distressed. I show mercy to the man in purple and fine linen, and bestow kindness on the man in homespun and cotton.

I restore to defeated hearts the freshness, the eagerness and the spirit of conquering courage.

I am calling you!

I Am The Church

—From TIDINGS

A Moment With the Master When Guilty of Gossip

Finally, brethren, whatsoever things are true, whatsover things are honest, whatsoever things are just, whatsoever things are pure, whatsoever things are lovely, whatsoever things are of good report; if there be any virtue, and if there be any praise, think on these things.—Phil. 4:8.

O Lord, I am so ashamed. This noon I sat at luncheon with a group of friends, and I am so miserable over what was done - and not done - around that table. We talked so gayly about so many things and the conversation went so easily into a discussion about an absent friend of ours. It began, I'm sure, Lord, with interest and concern. But remarks piled up - you know how women are, Lord, - one thing led to another, ugly things were said and unnecessary things told. We broke up later, still gay and happy over our good time together, but as I walked home I began to feel so guilty. Even if I didn't say any of the ugly things myself - I listened - and yes, Lord, I guess now I must have even nodded my head several times. I know now I could have changed that conversation. I could have said something kind about that person. She is a fine woman in many ways, and I could have said I thought so. Oh God, why was I so weak? Will I never learn to:

Keep my tongue from evil
and my lips from guile?

Dear God, if ever I needed to feel clean again, it is now. Help me, I pray Thee. Tell me what I can do to make amends for that thoughtless, hurtful hour I spent today. I know that words spoken are like "arrows shot into the air," and cannot be recalled. I am so ashamed and sorry.

Please give me another day, dear Lord - another chance to be more kind, another opportunity to speak up - with Thy love in my heart and on my lips. Thou hast said:

"I have blotted out, as a thick cloud, thy transgressions, and as a cloud, thy sins."

Father, give me more faith to believe this wonderful promise. I know too:

"If we confess our sins, He is faithful and just to forgive us our sins and to cleanse us from all unrighteousness."

I do believe these promises, and dear Lord, I am so thankful for them! Help me to rest upon them in simple trust and faith. I realize anew now, just what they mean — what they have always meant — and with thankful heart, I pray now for strength, strength, dear Lord, to face another day! To talk with friends, to live more joyously, to see in every contact an opportunity, and to use every opportunity that Thou dost send, for Thee alone.

This I recall to my mind, therefore have I hope:
It is of the Lord's mercies that we are not consumed . . .
His mercies are new every morning.

O, I thank Thee, Lord, for the new days ahead, and for this peace and conviction in my heart. Amen.

"Pray! Christians, Pray!"

This was the urgent plea of a man of God in an hour of great decision. Every hour now is an hour of decision and of destiny. God seems to call from His Word, "Pray, Christians, pray" - as He invites, entreats, urges His people to pray, and expresses grief that so few do pray. He still holds out promises of power which, across more than two thousand years, challenge us to prayer.

Pray! Christians, Pray! — God has all Power

"Behold, I am the Lord, the God of all flesh: is there anything too hard for me?"

"All power is given unto me in heaven and in earth. With God all things are possible."

Pray! Christians, Pray! — This is an Hour of Need

Men's lives are in danger.

The number of grief-stricken people is mounting hourly.

Our nation's leaders need to make humble acknowledgment of their weakness and seek the help of Almighty God.

Church members engage in practices that deny they are followers of Jesus.

Acknowledged Christians are jealous, self-seeking, censorious, holding grudges, engaging in harmful practices.

Many sincere Christians show no concern for those who are strangers to Jesus Christ.

There are signs of hope. More people are praying. Now is the Church's great hour for advance.

Pray! Christians, Pray! — Your Asking Cannot Outdistance God.

God is able to do exceeding abundantly above all that we ask or think, according to the power that worketh in us.

Church News

WORLD MISSIONS RECEIPTS

Budget for 1956	$3,300,000.00
Receipts to date	1,767,019.34
Percentage of annual budget received for 1956	58.90%
Balance needed for 1956	1,532,980.66

GEORGIA

Rabun Gap - Nacoochee School

Dr. Karl K. Anderson became the new president of the Rabun Gap-Nacoochee School, Rabun Gap, Georgia, on August 1, 1956, succeeding Mr. C. C. Skinner. Mr. Skinner, who has been the president of the school for the past seven and one half years, has retired from school work for reasons of health, age, and family responsibilities.

Dr. Anderson, a native of Wisconsin, received his college training at Whitewater State College, Whitewater, Wisconsin. After three years service in the Army Air Force during World War II, he completed his masters and doctoral work at Teachers College, Columbia University. He has been teaching in Georgia for the past ten years. The Rabun Gap-Nacoochee School, controlled and partially supported by the Synod of Georgia, is beginning its 54th year of service. Its unique program includes a Christian High School with dormitories for 50 boys and 50 girls. The school is also a service to the community with about 120 local students attending as Day Students at the High School. There is an adult education project carried on at the school called the Farm Family Program. Fourteen school farms are available to families who want to learn better farming methods and send their children to the school. These farms are available for a family to live in for a ten year period.

SOUTH CAROLINA

Edisto Island—At the congregational meeting of the Presbyterian Church of Edisto Island, S. C., on August 12, 1956 the following resolution was passed:

Resolved that our Heavenly Father in his infinite wisdom has seen fit to call higher our former pastor, Rev. W. H. Goodman. We with sorrowing hearts bow in submission to his will, yet we deeply feel his loss and do most sincerely sympathize with his beloved family.

Be it further resolved that a copy of these resolutions be sent to the family of our dear departed friend and brother. And also that a copy be placed in the minutes of the Session and a copy be sent to "The Christian Observer", and "The Southern Presbyterian Journal."

William P. McKinnon
J. G. Murray

"Ten Seconds To Live"

Two years ago Raymond M. Eastman, young Des Moines advertising man, wrote a widely quoted article, "Ten Seconds to Live." It was an imaginary portrayal of the thoughts of a motorist about to be killed in a traffic accident.

Eastman, age 29, and another young man died recently of car crash injuries. The sheriff said Eastman's car "clipped" another automobile while passing it and careened into a bridge. He said it was not known who was driving.

One wonders if Raymond Eastman was conscious ten seconds before he was killed; and if so, what he thought in those ten seconds.

He, of all persons, after having written such an article for automobile drivers, should have been prepared for a sudden and violent death. We trust he was—but how about you?

Are you ready to meet your Maker? If not, take the time right now to settle the most important matter in life, by definitely placing your faith in the Lord Jesus Christ as your personal Saviour. Any of us may have only "ten seconds to live."—Evangel.

Miracles Plausible to Scientists

Scientists now admit the possibility that Christ raised the dead and that Moses parted the waters of the Red Sea. So said Dr. John R. Brobeck, professor of physiology at the Medical School of the University of Philadelphia, addressing a convention of medical doctors in Toronto.

"Science is changing," he said. "One of the results is that a scientist is no longer able to say honestly that something is impossible. He can only say it is improbable."

He told the doctors that the one factor that can account for the miracles is a source of energy unknown to the scientific system. "In the Bible," he said, "it is known as the power of God."

Questioned by reporters afterward, Dr. Brobeck said: "A miracle has happened to me which makes me accept these miracles. This miracle is the New Birth, which every one of us who is a Christian has experienced. It is the application of God's power which brings about this change which is a miracle. It cannot be accomplished by any biological or psychological force. It creates within us the will to believe."—Exchange.

THE SOUTHERN
PRESBYTERIAN
JOURNAL

A Presbyterian weekly magazine devoted to the statement, defense and propagation of the Gospel, the faith which was once for all delivered unto the saints.

VOL. XV NO. 20 SEPTEMBER 12, 1956 $2.50 A YEAR

THE SOUTHERN PRESBYTERIAN JOURNAL
The Journal has no official connection with the Presbyterian Church in the United States
Rev. Henry B. Dendy, D.D., Editor....Weaverville, N. C.
Dr. L. Nelson Bell, Associate Editor....Asheville, N. C.
Rev. Wade C. Smith, Associate Editor....Weaverville, N. C.

EDITORIAL

The Source of Paul's Confidence

In every generation there arises the unending urge to compromise, dilute, alter or deny the vital content of the Christian message. Whether this is more prevalent in our time than in the past is difficult to ascertain for Satan has never ceased his efforts to eliminate the gospel from a place of transcendant importance in every age. Satan's methods change but his objective is always the same — to turn men to *anything*, provided that on which they center their attention and faith is something which does not redeem from sin.

The apostle Paul, writing a letter of affectionate greeting to the Christians in Rome and reiterating his desire and intention to visit them, makes this simple assertion:

"For I am not ashamed of the gospel of Christ: for it is the power of God unto salvation to everyone that believeth; to the Jew first, and also to the Greek."

In our own time, when there is such a confusion in the minds of men as to what constitutes the Christian message it is incumbent on all who hear the name Christian to ask themselves this question: "What is the gospel"?

From a study of Paul's epistles, it is crystal clear that the gospel which Paul preached was supernatural in its content and also supernatural in the method in which it was revealed. For that reason we owe it to ourselves to search out the answer in terms of one to whom so much was committed and who so faithfully discharged his trust.

First of all, it is clear that the gospel has its roots sunk deep *in the Old Testament revelation*. It is popular today in some circles to brush aside the Old Testament as irrelevant, as "sub-Christian," and "woefully unscientific," as "inaccurate and untrustworthy," and by any number of other phrases which would detract from its truthfulness and its authority.

What does Paul say? From beginning to end of his letters there are constant references to the Old Testament. *Not once* does he question either its relevancy, its integrity or its authority. Listen: *"Paul . . . separated unto the gospel of God, which he had promised afore by his prophets in the holy scriptures."*

As one reads the messages from this man to whom God committed the content, meaning and full implications of the gospel one is inexorably confronted with that which is the central theme of Christianity — God's redemption of individual sinners through faith in the person and work of His Son.

What is the gospel? What is it that Paul believed and which he preached? Was it a system of ethics? Was it primarily a program for a better world? Was it aimed at the political, social and moral problems of his day?

Paul was not ashamed of the gospel, even should he preach it amid the glamour and sophistication of Rome. He faced his task with supreme confidence because it was not a man-made message which he had to proclaim. His assurance stemmed from the knowledge that the gospel is God's power unto salvation to everyone who believeth.

How desperately important it is for Christians of each succeeding generation to stick close to the gospel which had power then and which has the same power today! How urgently should we examine our own hearts to see that the diversions and changes of time do not becloud our thinking thereby making us look for something new which is *not* God's power unto salvation but a humanly contrived system of ethics, *a form of godliness which denies the power of the gospel.*

To answer the questions asked above would require a volume. Let the reader answer them by reading Paul's letters, seeing there portrayed God's only plan whereby men may be saved. The gospel which Paul preached and in which he had so much confidence is the gospel which is completely supernatural in origin and action. It is the gospel which once and for all deflates human egotism and brings man to his knees in confession of sin and to his absolute dependence on God for mercy and forgiveness.

Furthermore, it is the gospel which magnifies both the person and the work of the Son of God, the Lord Jesus Christ. Paul's gospel does not consist of a schizophrenic theology which speaks in terms of words divorced from their rightful meaning, nor does it lend itself to the vague existentialism of today which is concerned with unreal concepts. All of which make the searching sinner cry out: "They have taken away my Lord and I know not where they have laid Him."

The apostle Paul had a transforming experience with the living Christ; he was the recipient of a direct revelation of the content of the gospel itself, (Galatians 1:11,12); and he preached and wrote of a marvelous and transforming fact of history which, when believed by men, brought to their souls and lives the power of God unto salvation.

Does it not behoove us to search the Scriptures and find out what Paul believed and preached? While some seem to think that revelation and spiritual perception have progressed since his day there is little in the fruits of such a belief to commend it to the wary.

Paul had every reason to have supreme confidence in the gospel which he preached. He knew from whence he had received it. He had experienced its transforming power in his own life. He knew it was the power of God unto salvation to all who would believe it.

It is just that today. L.N.B.

One Christian's Concept of Government

The writer was recently riding in the elevator of a hotel in the nation's capital. Three other passengers were coming from the top-floor banquet room where one of our most prominent Senators had just spoken to a convention to which they were delegates. These men were jubilant because in his address the illustrious Senator had promised his hearers to work for certain additional financial benefits from the federal government for the organization of which they were members.

This incident set in motion a train of thoughts, scme of which we feel constrained to set down in this editorial. During the coming weeks all Americans will be confronted with the pleas of eager candidates, from the local to the national level, all competing for votes and support.

In such a situation and in such an atmosphere Christians have a peculiar responsibility. Above all others the Christian should be a good citizen. To be such one must have an intelligent understanding of the implications of government, of sound economics, and of the principles which must obtain if our nation is to fulfill its obligations on a high plane.

For twenty-five years we have seen much and heard more of a philosophy of government which has within it the seeds of national destruction. We say this advisedly because we believe the economic advisers of the thirties and forties were men whose counsel, if followed to its logical conclusion, will lead to national ruin.

There are basic laws of economics which can be violated only at terrible cost. There is no such thing as honestly "spending our way out of a depression." "Government spending" is essentially a dishonest phrase. The only money the government has is that which comes from tax payers, unless it resorts to the ultimate in government financing — opening the flood-gates of printing-press money for which there is no adequate reserve.

Not only has a generation been wilfully raised up which only too often feels that the government owes it a living but with this philosophy there has come its inevitable corrolary — get everything you can from the government.

Such a philosophy breeds a political climate where office is *bought* by men who offer most to the largest number of individual and organized pressure groups. National policies, instead of being studied on the plane of national interest, tend to descend to "planks" which promise the most to selfish interests.

These are harsh words but they need to be spoken. We all want representatives who will do the most for their respective constituencies, for there are many legitimate ways in which a member of Congress can rightly serve those who elected him to office. But, when public interest runs counter to purely local and often selfish advantage, it rarely has a chance because of anticipated political repercussions.

The Southern Presbyterian Journal, *a Presbyterian Weekly magazine devoted to the statement, defense, and propagation of the Gospel, the faith which was once for all delivered unto the saints,* published every Wednesday by The Southern Presbyterian Journal, Inc., in Weaverville, N. C.

Entered as second-class matter May 15, 1942, at the Postoffice at Weaverville, N. C., under the Act of March 3, 1879. Vol. XV, No. 20, September 12, 1956. Editorial and Business Offices: Weaverville, N. C. Printed in the U.S.A. by Biltmore Press, Asheville, N. C.

ADDRESS CHANGE: When changing address, please let us have both old and new address as far in advance as possible. Allow three weeks after change if not sent in advance. When possible, send an address label giving your old address.

Another matter to which the Christian should give serious thought is the role of government in national life. No system is perfect but with all of its imperfections the system of government established by our founding fathers has brought the greatest good to the greatest proportion of its citizens of any government in the world. The basic concept of such government is that government is the referee, not the participant in business. This concept has been increasingly violated in recent decades until we now see the government *competing* at times with private enterprise and using the tax payers money for that purpose.

How much better if government makes honest and fair rules and then sees that these rules are observed. None should be penalized and all should be given an equal chance. Good government makes good rules and honestly administers them. Poor government arrogates to itself the right to make the rules, play the game and penalize the individual all in one.

Those who advocate more and more intrusion of government into business and private affairs cite the Post Office Department as an illustration of successful socialism, or state ownership. We would venture this answer: Turn the Post Office Department over to private enterprise and we believe it would be run more efficiently and pay its way, *which it is not doing now.*

The economic policies of the last quarter of a century have decreased the value of the American dollar by half. At the same time our national debt has become so great that there is no foreseeable way for it ever to be paid off. To put it bluntly, we have countenanced governmental fiscal policies which would have landed the leaders of private industry into jail.

Should not a Christian demand of his government those basic policies of fiscal honesty which are a part of the Christian code for personal living? When we hear politicians promising more governmental control and more governmental spending should not that be a warning to turn elsewhere? Such promises, if kept, can but lead our nation further and further down the road to bankruptcy, both moral and financial.

When all of this is said and done we are not for one minute intimating that our industrialized society does not present social and economic problems which did not exist one hundred years ago. What we are saying though is that such problems must be met by sound fiscal policies, not by politically expedient subterfuges which violate the very foundation principles of honest business practice.

The writer has visited many foreign countries during the past ten years. Again and again we have been told that our foreign aid is, *without exception,* being funneled through economic programs which are governmental and socialistic. We who have prided ourselves on our "free enterprise" are bolstering *in every case* the socialistic concept and practice abroad. That some of this spending abroad has been *fantastically profligate* has not commended our vaunted American intelligence in those areas. "Made work" is a poor substitute for honest endeavor.

All of which leads us to this final thought: America cannot indefinitely continue on her present course without the gravest consequences for all concerned. Christians owe it to themselves and to their country to state clearly for all to hear that above all we want honesty in government, not only in its administration but also in its program, both at home and abroad.

Politicians have keen ears. They are sensitive to public opinion and to personal appeals. Let us pray for a new era when more than anything else those who guide the destiny of our nation shall put the national welfare first.

This is asking a lot, but it is not asking too much. L.N.B.

You Are Either a Missionary or Need One!

By George S. Lauderdale

Every person in the world has an interest in Christian missions: We either are missionaries or we need to have them minister to us! A church should have a vital part in sending evangelists to the nations, and if they do not, *missionaries must come to them.* Are you winning souls to Christ or does your soul need to be won to Him? According to one source, one hundred thousand persons die daily who have not heard the gospel, making it imperative that all who profess to know Christ be fishers of men.

Multitudes of church-goers have heard sermons from the Word of God since childhood regularly, but have never witnessed to their friends for Christ. God's plan is that those who are taught instruct others in the things of the Spirit: it is wrong for redeemed men not to say so. In rebuke of silent hearers of eternal truths, God says, "For when for the time ye ought to be teachers, ye have need that one teach you again which be the first principles of the oracles of God." Hebrews 5:12.

Your Honor

Being a missionary of the Lord is a high privilege, 2 Corinthians 5:20 asserting that our status is that of ambassadors to the world from the court of the King of kings. The soul winner is the personal representative of the

Creator and Ruler of the universe! Rise to this rank which God freely offers you by His grace: "All things are of God, who hath reconciled us to himself by Jesus Christ, and hath given to us the ministry of reconciliation." 2 Corinthians 5:19.

To be loved by God so much that He sends to us a man with a message for our good, is also an honor. Those countries are wonderfully favored which contain Christian churches, and the witness of consecrated men, contrasting with the sad conditions of heathen areas. There is no shame in serving as a missionary and no shame to have an evangelist visit and invite us to know Jesus Christ; only if we hear the good news and do not respond are we guilty. If we say that we believe on the Saviour and are doing nothing to tell the world His story, then our shame is very great.

Hate Spectator Christianity

It is good to be on the sending rather than the receiving end of missionary endeavor, for then we are like Christ Who came not to be ministered unto but to minister. It is better to be an evangelist than to need one! Let us not take the valuable time of God's servants who could be telling men in darkness how to be saved. Unless a preacher is leading his hearers to be witnesses, he should go to those who have not heard the gospel the first time.

Workers are needed to train and encourage professing Christians to witness for Christ. Such workers are missionaries for their efforts result in the spread of the truth in all parts of the earth. Bible conferences are not an end in themselves, but those attending should learn how they can carry on the equivalent of a Bible conference in their own neighborhood.

The Truth About Missions

How easy it is to think that missionaries are only those who sail for foreign places! The deceiver Satan wants us to think that way, and he wants us to be so intent on the applause of men that we refuse to witness for Christ unless many are present, unless we are paid for so doing, or hold an ecclesiastical title, "Study to show thyself approved *unto God.*" 2 Timothy 2:15.

What is needed to carry on for Christ in the world? Physical equipment and many followers by no means head the list, but rather love for Christ and lost souls, a desire to keep humble and mindful of heaven. At every church service, the persons present should go seeking salvation for themselves or for others; all Christians are co-laborers with the preacher. Get busy for the Lord today among the people who surround you; do not be embarrassed by having God send a missionary to you when you could be a missionary to others.

Verbal Inspiration: Yesterday and Today

By Gordon H. Clark, Ph.D.

Search the Scriptures

1. *The Biblical Claims*

The inspiration of the Scriptures, bearing as it does on the truth and authority of the Word of God, is of such obvious importance to Christianity that no elaborate justification is needed for discussing the subject. Indeed, it is even pardonable to begin with some very elementary material. Not only pardonable, but in fact indispensable. No discussion of inspiration can contribute much of value without taking into account the elementary Scriptural data. These data must be kept in mind. Yet, unfortunately, a number of these details may have faded from our aging memories. More unfortunately the younger generation, owing to the low standards of many seminaries, may never have learned the Scriptural data. Therefore I wish first of all to make some simple statements about the doctrine of inspiration as it was commonly explained a hundred years ago.

It was in 1840 that Louis Gaussen published his famous little book ***Theopneustia.*** Gaussen was a Swiss theologian who, like J. Gresham Machen in this century, was deposed from the ministry and driven out of the church because of his adherence to the truth of the Scriptures. And his book ***Theopneustia*** is a defense of inspiration. In it Gaussen amasses the astounding amount of material that the Scriptures have to say about themselves. And although that was a century ago, no one should approach the question of inspiration without a good knowledge of Gaussen's work, or at least without a good knowledge of what the Bible has to say about itself.

The effect is cumulative; and it is most unfortunate that instead of examining and determining the significance of a hundred references, we must this morning select only a few.

For example, Gaussen notices the three times that Isaiah says, "The mouth of the Lord hath spoken it," as well as other similar expressions in Isaiah. Gaussen calls attention to II Sam. 23-1-2, "The Spirit of the Lord spake by me and his word was in my tongue." Again, "In the second year of Darius came the word of the Lord by Haggai." To Moses, God said, "I will be with thy mouth." And Acts 4:25 asserts, "Thou, Lord, hast said by the mouth of thy servant David."

The cumulative effect of several dozens of such verses is the conclusion that the prophets do not claim to speak on their own authority but that they testify that the Spirit gives them their message and makes them speak.

One should note well that the Spirit-given message is not merely the general idea of the passage, but rather the very words.

Deut. 18:18 "I will raise them up a prophet . . . and I will put *my words* in his mouth . . . and whosoever will not hearken unto *my words* which he shall speak in my name, I will require it of him."

Jer. 1:9 "Then Jehovah put forth his hand and touched my mouth; and Jehovah said unto me, Behold, I have put *my words* in thy mouth."

There is time for only one more reference to show that the prophets claim to speak God's words. Hear therefore the statement of our Lord himself: "If ye believed Moses, ye would believe me; for he wrote of me. But if ye believe not his writings, how shall ye believe *my words.*" (John 5:46-47).

Once again I say, the effect is cumulative. One ought to read all of Gaussen's references and to note carefully the significance of each. Only so will one have an adequate basis for the doctrine of inspiration.

The last reference takes us one step further into this elementary material. Someone in ignorance might object that even though God gave the prophets his words and made them speak, the speaking has ceased these thousands of years, and we have only reports of the speeches. This question, concerning the relation of the spoken word to the written word, was answered by Christ in the last reference. Note carefully, our Lord says, "Moses . . . *wrote* of me (and) if ye believe not his *writings,* how shall ye believe my words?"

When the words that God gave his prophets are written, they become *The Writings,* i.e., the Scriptures. And it is the Scriptures, the Writings, that Jesus tells us to search for eternal life. In his temptation, Jesus repels Satan by saying, "It is written." Also in John 6:45, 8:17, 12:14, 15:25, the phrase, "It is written" settles the points at issue.

Permit me finally to refer to one more exceptionally important passage. In John 10:34-35 Jesus is defending his claim to Deity. He quotes Psalm 82. Does he quote this Psalm because Psalm 82 is more inspired and more authoritative than any other passage in the Old Testament? Not at all. He says, "Is it not written in your law . . . and the Scripture cannot be broken." Christ here has appealed to Psalm 82 because it is a part of the Scripture, and since all Scripture is given by inspiration of God, this passage also is inspired, for the Scripture cannot be broken.

Let me now repeat for the third time that the effect is cumulative. One should have in mind the hundreds of instances in which the Bible claims verbal inspiration. Now, to conclude this first section, this survey of elementary detail, I would like to ask a pointed question. If the prophets who spoke, if the authors who wrote, and if our Lord himself, are mistaken about verbal inspiration, if they are mistaken these hundreds of times, what assurance may anyone have with respect to the other things they said and wrote? Is there any reason to suppose that men who were so uniformly deceived as to the source of their message could have had any superior insight and accurate knowledge of man's relation to God? Still more pointedly: Can anyone profess a personal attachment to Jesus Christ and consistently contradict his assertion that the Scriptures cannot be broken?

II. *The Dictation Objection.*

Since this elementary and abbreviated account of verbal inspiration has been based on a volume of a century ago, the next step, before bringing matters completely up to date, will be the examination of a century old objection.

The idea that God gave his words to the prophets seems to many liberals a mechanical and artificial theory of revelation. God, they tell us, is not to be pictured as a boss dictating words to his stenographer. And further, the writings of the prophets show clearly the freedom and spontaneity of personal individuality. Jeremiah's style is not that of Isaiah, nor does John write like Paul. The words are obviously the words of John and Jeremiah, not of a boss dictating to several stenographers. The stenographers of one boss will turn out letters of the same literary style; they do not or should not correct his English. Now, therefore, if God dictated the words of the Bible, the personal differences could not be accounted for. From which it follows that the doctrine of verbal inspiration is untrue.

In answer to this objection, and to many other objections against various phases of Christianity, it is useful to note that the antagonists rather uniformly misrepresent the doctrines they attack. Accordingly, the first and indispensable step in making a reply is to show clearly what does and what does not belong to the doctrine of verbal inspiration.

Now, let us keep certain facts clearly in mind. In the first place, the differences in style — and they are so obvious that even a translation cannot obscure them — show decisively that the Bible was not dictated as a boss dictates to a stenographer. There have been indeed a few theologians who have used the idea of dictation. Whether they all meant dictation in the sense in which it occurs in a modern business office, or whether some of them meant it in the more general sense of a command and authoritative imposition, we need not discuss. What is chiefly to the point is that the great majority of theologians who hold and have held to verbal inspiration never accepted the dictation theory. One could easily suppose that unbelievers found it easier to ridicule dictation than to understand and discuss verbal inspiration as it is actually taught by evangelical theologians.

How, then, are the differences of style to be accounted for, and what does verbal inspiration mean? The answer to these questions, involving the relation between God and the prophets, takes us quickly away from the picture of a boss and a stenographer.

When God wished to make a revelation, at the time of the exodus or of the captivity, he did not suddenly look around, as if caught unprepared, and wonder what man he could use for the purpose. We cannot suppose that he advertized for help, and when Moses and Jeremiah applied, God constrained them to speak his words. And yet this derogatory view underlies the objection to verbal inspiration. The relation between God and the prophet is totally unlike that between a boss and a stenographer.

If we consider the omnipotence and wisdom of God, a very different representation emerges. The boss must take what he can get; he depends on the high school or business college to have taught her shorthand and typing. But God does not depend on any external agency. God is the Creator. He made Moses. And when God wanted Moses to speak for him, he said, "Who hast made man's mouth? Have not I, the Lord?"

Verbal inspiration therefore must be understood in connection with the complete system of Christian doctrine. It may not be detached therefrom, and *a fortiori* it may not be framed in an alien view of God. Verbal inspiration is integral with the doctrines of providence and predestination. When the liberals surreptitiously deny predestination in picturing God as dictating to stenographers, they so misrepresent verbal inspiration that their objections do not apply to the Calvinistic viewpoint. The trouble is not, as the liberals think, that the boss controls the stenographer too completely; on the contrary, the analogy misses the mark because the boss hardly controls the stenographer at all.

Put it this way. God from all eternity decreed to lead the Jews out of slavery by the hand of Moses. To this end he so controlled events that Moses was born at a given date, placed in the water to save him from an early death, found and adopted by Pharaoh's daughter, given the best education possible, driven into the wilderness to learn patience, and in every way so prepared by heredity and environment that when the time came, Moses' mentality and literary style were the instruments precisely fitted to speak God's words.

It is quite otherwise with dictation. A boss has little control over a stenographer except as to the words she types for him. He did not control her education. She may be totally uninterested in his business. They may have extremely little in common. But between Moses and God there was an inner union, an identity of purpose, a cooperation of will, such that the words Moses wrote were God's own words and Moses' own words at the same time.

Thus when we see God's pervading presence and providence in history and in the life of his servants, we recognize that business office dictation does not do justice to the Scriptures. The Holy Spirit dwelt within these men and taught them what to write. God determined what the personality and style of each author was to be, and he determined it for the purpose of expressing his message, his words. The words of Scripture, therefore, are the very words of God.

III. *Contemporary Theories*

Inadequate though this elementary exposition and defense of verbal inspiration has been, a little time must be reserved for a third and last section on the contemporary state of affairs. With the decline of Ritschlian liberalism and the rise of existentialism, neo-orthodoxy, and logical positivism, the point of attack has shifted. It is no longer a question whether the words of the Bible are the words of God or merely the fallible words of a man; today a more sweeping objection is made on the basis of a theory of language. Philosophers have become interested in semantics, and some of their views would so alter the significance of words that with all the verbal inspiration imaginable, the Bible would be emptied of its Christian meaning. According to various writers either all language is metaphorical and symbolic or at least all religious language is. No religious statement should ever be taken literally. For example, John Mackintosh Shaw, professor of the Systematic Theology in Queen's College, Ontario, refers to the terms ransom, justification, propitiation, expiation, and reconciliation as metaphors or figures of speech (Christian Doctrine, p. 207). From this sort of view it may and has been concluded that divine revelation cannot be a communication of truth.

That religious language cannot be true literally has been supported by the following arguments. One author gives the illustration of a very ordinary preacher preaching a very ordinary sermon. But though trite and dull this sermon or a sentence in this sermon becomes a vital message to someone in the congregation. The person's life is changed. Yet the changed life could not be the result of the literal meaning of an undistinguished sentence. The words must have conveyed a religious content quite beyond any literal meaning. This religious content, so the argument concludes, is the meaning, the metaphorical, symbolic, or religious meaning of the words; and if perchance the words had any literal meaning at all, it would be quite beside the point.

Although this argument is found in a scholarly journal published by the National Council of Churches, its faulty analysis and its failure to prove that religious language cannot be literal are so obvious that no time will be wasted explaining it.

Another author who holds that all religious terms are metaphorical or symbolic, sketches a religious epistemology that is based on images. God, he says, always—and note the *always*—God always speaks to man through images; and "religious experience is a process of being hit by such images." This process, which may be called a sort of mental idolatry, is then assimilated to art and mythology. The specification of myth as the form of religious writing is of course a prominent contemporary theme.

But if religious content cannot be literally spoken, and must be expressed in the pictorial language of myth, some explanation is required as the choice of myths. One group of people choose Greek mythology and another group choose Christian mythology. Doubtless such choices are often made unreflectively under the influence of society. But there comes a time for thought; there comes a time of conflict between two religions; and a person is asked to choose deliberately. Does it then make no difference? If neither myth is true literally, if both are equally symbolic, is not the one as satisfactory as the other?

Now, Greek mythology is such an unlikely choice today that the author last referred to, convinced as he probably is that modern times are superior to ancient, asserts the possibility of making a rational choice among myths on the basis of their adequacy to explain the facts of existence as we confront them in daily life and action.

It seems to me, however, that neither this nor any other attempt to justify a choice among myths can be successful. If myths were literal truths, one might be more adequate than another. The Greek myth of Zeus' method of producing rain might be considered more adequate or less adequate, than the myth about the windows of heaven, attributed to the Hebrews. But if these stories are both mythological and symbolic, simply symbolic of the literal fact that it rains, it is hard to judge what adequacy might require. A literal statement from Aristophanes' *Clouds* might explain, but a myth explains nothing. Furthermore, if the language is symbolic, it seems clear that one symbol, before historic events have fixed its meaning, is as good as another. Today the swastika symbolizes National Socialism, and the hammer and sickle, Communism; but at the start there was no reason why the communists could not have chosen the swastika and Hitler the hammer and sickle. To push this preliminary criticism one step further, we might ask the question, What is a religious symbol the symbol of? The cross no doubt is the symbol of Christ's crucifixion; but can the crucifixion itself be a symbol or metaphor of anything? The prima facie meaning of statements about the crucifixion is literal. And if someone says that religious language cannot be literal, there appears to be no rational method of determining what the crucifixion is symbolic of. Is it pessimistically symbolic of an inherently unjust universe or is it symbolic of the love of God? On what grounds could one decide, if nothing in the account can be taken literally? But suppose now that someone decides without rational grounds.

Suppose that the crucifixion, although it never occurred literally, were said to be symbolic of God's love. Then we must ask, is it a literal truth that God loves men, or is this symbolic too. Obviously this must be symbolic too, if all language is symbolic. And what is God's love symbolic of? No doubt it is symbolic of another symbol— that is symbolic of another — ad infinitum.

Although doubtless we are chiefly interested in the effect of modern semantics on the literal meaning of the Bible, it would be a mistake to suppose that the Christian ministry should not concern itself with the several secular theories from which the religious implications derive. Although a detailed analysis of these philosophies cannot possibly be undertaken here, one fundamental aspect of them ought not to be passed by in silence. I refer to the status of logic in these philosophies, and in particular to the law of contradiction. Although academic logic may seem somewhat distant from mythology and religious metaphor, the main matter of verbal inspiration and its immediate effect on Christian work is only thinly veiled by the professorial terminology.

Just this spring I received a letter from the mission field in which my correspondent lamented the fact that so many of his associates who were engaged in translating the Bible had accepted or were deeply influenced by contemporary linguistic relativism. Now, it seems to me that the best way to handle this philosophy is to show what it does with the law of contradiction.

This philosophy of analysis, as it is sometimes called, not only repudiates divine revelation, but all metaphysics as well. In particular it denies any innate or *a priori* forms of the mind, traditionally regarded as necessarily true. Logic and mathematics are explained as linguistic conventions that have been arbitrarily selected. Past history exemplifies different selections. The logic of Whitehead and Russell is one and the logic of Aristotle is another. And to quote A. J. Ayer, "It is perfectly conceivable that we should have employed different linguistic conventions from those which we actually do employ."

Positivistic, humanistic, or atheistic as this philosophy is, it apparently attracts Biblical translators and even teachers in American Bible schools. Last September an instructor in one of the well respected Bible Colleges published an article in which, along with what seemed to be a mechanistic theory of sensation, he rejected Aristotelian logic as an unwarranted, unnatural verbalization and accepted at least some of Dewey's instrumentalism. This sort of thing is seen also, though perhaps in a less conscious form and to varying degrees, in the pietistic deprecation of a so-called human logic as opposed to some unknowable divine logic.

In defense of so-called human logic, in defense of the literal meaning of words, and therefore in defense of verbal inspiration, I wish to challenge the opposing viewpoint to face the argument and answer unambiguously. I wish to challenge them to state their own theory without making use of the law of contradiction.

If logical principles are arbitrary, and if it is conceivable to employ different linguistic conventions, these writers should be able to invent and to abide by some different convention. Now, the Aristotelian logic and in particular the law of contradiction requires that a given word must not only mean something, it must also not mean something. The term dog must mean dog, but it must not mean mountain; and mountain must not mean metaphor. Each term must refer to something definite and at the same time there must be some objects to which it does not refer. The term metaphorical cannot mean literal, nor can it mean canine or mountainous. Suppose the word mountain meant metaphor, and dog, and Bible, and the United States. Clearly, if a word meant everything, it would mean nothing. If, now, the law of contradiction is an arbitrary convention, and if our linguistic theorists choose some other convention, I challenge them to write a book in conformity with their principles. As a matter of fact it will not be hard for them to do so. Nothing more is necessary than to write the word metaphor sixty thousand times. Metaphor metaphor metaphor metaphor.

This means the dog ran up the mountain, for the word metaphor means dog, ran and mountain. Unfortunately the sentence "metaphor metaphor metaphor' also means, Next Christmas is Thanksgiving, for the word metaphor has these meanings as well.

The point should be clear. One cannot write a book or speak a sentence without using the law of contradiction. Logic therefore is not an arbitrary convention that may be discarded at will. And all pious talk about our fallible human logic, as well as all modern metaphorical theories of religious language make verbal revelation impossible. But, fortunately, these theories make themselves impossible as well.

Therefore the orthodox Christian may well conclude, in my opinion that verbal inspiration has no objections to fear. The older objections were successfully met a century ago. The more recent objections are still easier to dispose of. But though from an intellectual or academic standpoint we have no objections to fear, so one-sided is the propaganda imposed on students in universities and seminaries that there is a great need to make the Calvinistic position universally known and widely understood.

Born of the Virgin Mary

By Floyd E. Hamilton
Centreville, Ala.

"And Mary said, Behold the handmaid of the Lord; be it unto me according to thy word." Luke 1:37.

In our previous discussions of the issue of Modernism and Evangelicalism it was pointed out that there is, first a difference regarding the inspiration of the Bible. The Holy Spirit so guided and controlled the writers of the Old and New Testaments that what they wrote was true and was the truth God wanted his people to have. Modernists do not accept this teaching. The Bible teaches that man was created in the image of God in knowledge and holiness. Most Modernists think that man was evolved from the higher animals. The Bible teaches that man fell and is dead in trespasses and sins until the Holy Spirit regenerates him. Modernists regard man as needing no new birth or radical change. The Bible teaches that belief in Christ is the only way of salvation. Modernists hold that there are many ways to God and that man can save himself if he needs any saving. The Bible teaches that Jesus Christ is both God and man different in quality from any man that ever lived. The Modernist regards Christ as the best man that ever lived but not as the very God of very God as the Bible teaches.

Dr. J. Gresham Machen the great champion of orthodoxy told of meeting a leading layman on the train and having a discussion with him about these issues of Modernism and Evangelicalism. The layman said in effect, "You will have difficulty making all the other points of difference between Modernism and Evangelicalism plain to the average layman, but when you are talking about the Virgin Birth of Christ, any one can understand the difference between the two points of view."

You see the issue on this point is clearly drawn. So clearly drawn that there can be no possible way of covering up the issue. Either Christ was born of the Virgin Mary or he must have been born of two human parents. There is no middle ground and no way of glossing over the differences on this point.

The Bible is perfectly plain on this point. It was clearly prophesied in Isaiah 7:14, "A virgin shall conceive, and bear a son, and shall call his name Immanuel" (God with us). The word Almah translated "virgin" is translated "young woman" by the new Standard Revised Version, in spite of the fact that the word almost universally means "virgin," though of course every virgin was a young woman. The fact that the New Testament translates this word by "parthenos," "virgin" should be conclusive as to the correct rendering of the word. A virgin is a young woman who has never been married and who is assumed to be morally pure. When the Bible uses the term of Mary, it is an assertion that she had never been guilty of immorality.

The Modernists almost universally reject the doctrine of the Virgin Birth of Christ, and of course hold that Jesus was only a man, not the God-Man that the Bible declares him to have been. Now it is important to understand that the reason for the denial of the Virgin Birth is not because the textual evidence for it is weak or inconclusive. Sometimes Modernists try to discount the doctrine by saying that it is mentioned in only two Gospels, and not in Mark or John or Paul. In reply let us note that Mark begins his Gospel with the story of John the Baptist at the beginning of the public ministry of Jesus Christ, and makes no pretense of telling about either the birth or the childhood of Jesus. The fact that he does not men-we could not accept it as true, but it did not concern an ordinary person. It concerned the supernatural person Jesus Christ, who healed the sick, who raised the dead, who fed the five thousand men, who walked on the water, and commanded the wind and the waves to be still and they obeyed him.

It concerned the one who cleansed the lepers, made the blind to see and the lame to walk. It concerned the person who healed the man with the withered arm, and raised the daughter of Jairus. It concerned the person who raised Lazurus from the dead and who Himself rose from the dead on the third day and who forty days later ascended into heaven. When we are told that such a person was born of a Virgin, the account becomes believable, when it would not be believable regarding an ordinary man.

Some people say that we do not need the doctrine of the Virgin Birth in order to believe in the incarnation of our Lord. Possibly that might be true had we no account of his birth. But we do have an honest, reliable account which bears all the marks of genuineness. In the setting of the accounts of the life of Christ found in the Gospels, the doctrine of the Virgin Birth of Christ becomes natural and believable.

It is not by accident then that the only ones who deny the Virgin Birth of Christ are those who deny His Deity. If Jesus Christ had been only a man, then of course he could not have had a supernatural birth, no matter how convincing the evidence for such a birth might be. Denial of the true Deity of Christ then of necessity carries with it the denial of the Virgin Birth, for he could not be just a man if he was born of a Virgin, conceived by the Holy Spirit. The Modernists who regard Jesus as only a man, therefore, to a man deny the doctrine of the Virgin Birth, not because the evidence is weak for the Virgin Birth, but because, were it true, they would be forced to recognize that Jesus was more than a man.

That is why this doctrine of the Virgin Birth of Christ becomes such an excellent touchstone about theological beliefs. If a person believes the Bible accounts of his birth, he will probably be found to accept all the other doctrines of Evangelical Christianity. On the other hand, if a person rejects this doctrine, it is a safe assumption that he is a Modernist regarding other doctrines as well.

Praise God, our salvation is sure because we have a supernatural Saviour, able to save to the uttermost those who put their trust in Him. Is he your Saviour?

ANGLERS

By WADE C. SMITH

Lesson No. 156

EVERY CHURCH MEMBER A SOUL WINNER!

That may sound like spiritual "Utopia," but as a matter of fact it is a perfectly reasonable statement. It denotes *normal* Christianity. Anything less is sub-normal. It is an inspiring goal to work for, and in striving for it spiritual growth and power will result.

For the actual beginning of the *"Every Member Evangelistic Effort"* several ways have been suggested. One is the beginning by groups, as described in lessons 152 to 154. Another is to call the congregation together, after the way has been prepared by prayer on the part of Pastor and Session, and appropriate sermons have been preached, for the purpose of enlisting those who are willing to join in the study of Personal Evangelism and to practice it as the way is made clear.

In making the call, let it be understood that coming to the meeting will not be regarded as a pledge, but a willingness "to be exposed" to an idea, and with a prayer that God's will may prevail. Even a very timid church member can take this first step.

It would be well to begin with a week or ten days' intensive study. That is, meet daily for a certain period.

The plan which has proved most practicable for both men and women in a downtown church is to have a noon luncheon — a very brief lunch, just sufficient to tide over to the evening meal — where the Pastor will lead in a forty minute discussion of how to do Personal Work. Fifteen minutes should be sufficient time for eating. Let the clearing away of the dishes be delayed until the meeting is over. Where the lunch is served by the women, as is so often the case, it is desirable that those women also may have the benefit of the discussion.

The whole meeting lasting only 55 minutes gives time afterwards for the care of the dishes, etc. The strictly observed time for beginning and stopping will also be additional inducement for business men and women to attend. Rotary, Kiwanis and other civic club luncheons have been popularized by this strict adherence to the one-hour limit. Business members know they will not be kept longer than the allotted lunch hour. It is surprising how much can be accomplished in that short time when preparation is made so that the program may move off with promptness and proceed with no waste of time.

If the women's circles are handling the daily luncheons, each unit should be ambitious to have lunch ready on the minute for beginning, the table all set and everything placed, even the pie if a dessert is had, and nothing to add but pouring the coffee. Service like this will make 15 minutes ample time for eating, including the start with an inspiring verse of song and a none too hurried grace.

If the church is in a residential district, and far from business, the hour for meeting may be better fixed at a supper-lunch time, or for an evening hour.

Note the term "lunch" is used here advisedly. It is no time for a social feast or an elaborate meal.. The object for the meeting is for business — big business, and the eating is an expedient. It is the means and not the end. No one is harmed by letting one of the three daily meals be a "light repast." Doubtless it will be beneficial, for as a rule, we eat too much.

This is the proven best way to make it possible for all members to meet at one time and place. And I believe it will be discovered that a church can by this means institute an all-year-round revival which will be far more fruitful than the "annual series of meetings" requiring the services of a visiting evangelist — be he ever so good. But it will take prayer and personal sacrifice.

(Next lesson will show the A.B.C. institution of the plan.)

Helps To Understanding Scripture Readings in *Day by Day*

By Rev. C. C. Baker

Sunday, September 23, *Hebrews* 12:1-7. The "cloud of witnesses" of verse one consists of the Old Testament men of faith mentioned in chapter eleven. What advantage does the Christian have over these Old Testament heroes (Cf. 11:39, 12:2)? In the race he is to run (v.1), where are the eyes of the Christian to be centered (vv.2-3)? What is his attitude to be toward sin (vv.1,4)? What is the purpose of chastening in his experience (vv.5-11)? How has Christ been the forerunner in this chastening experience (vv.2-3)? How can the witness of the saints of 11:32-38 be an encouragement in time of adversity? Do you find that you spend most of your Christian life standing still, or do you think of your Christian experience as a course to be run? In times of discouragement do you focus your eyes upon Christ and the lives of men of faith who have gone before?

Monday, September 24, *Hebrews* 2:9-18. In this passage you can see again something of the wonder and glory of your salvation. Do your best to comprehend the facts about Christ mentioned in 2:10 and 1:2-4. Where else in the Bible are similar statements made about Jesus? Now read vv.9-18 and list the things Christ has done and is doing for you. If Christ has tasted Death for you (v.9) and broken the power of him who controls death (v.14), what attitude can you have toward the grave? How is Christ able to help you in times of temptation (v.18)? Even though Jesus is now crowned with honors (v.9), He still intercedes before the throne of God in your behalf (v.17). Give praise to God the Son for who He is and what He has done for you.

Tuesday, September 25, *Psalm* 107:17-22. The children of Israel, scattered by exile, have now been gathered together by God (vv.2-3). Read vv.4-32 and list the afflictions they had experienced. What was the cause of their condition (vv.11,17)? What did they do in their predicament (vv.6a,13a,19a,28a)? Observe how readily the Lord responded to their cries (vv.6b,13b, 19b,28b). Study each answer to prayer and notice how completely God met the need of each cry (vv.4-9,10-16,17-22,23-32). What should be the response of the petitioner to such answers to prayer (vv.1,8,15,21,31-32)? Do you believe God can thus meet the needs of your heart? Do you know what it is to have specific answers to prayer?

Wednesday, September 26, *Philippians* 4:8-13. It is possible that Paul learned the lessons of vv.11-13 in Acts 23-24. For years he had yearned to preach the Gospel in Rome and in the mission fields beyond Rome (Romans 15:23-24). After a brief visit to Jerusalem, Paul expected to continue on to Rome (Romans 15:25-28; Acts 19:21; 23:11), but instead he was forced to spend two years in jail (Acts 24:27). What was Paul's crime (Acts 24:24-27)? With the compulsion to move on to other mission fields, how must Paul have been tempted to feel while in jail? What lessons must he have learned? What verses in Philippians 4:8-13 particularly speak to you when you face delay or closed doors in the performing of a task close to your heart?

Thursday, September 27, *II Timothy* 1:1-10. Paul writes to Timothy, his son in the Spirit, much as he would a son in the flesh (vv.1-2). Paul prays constantly for Timothy (v.3). He expresses his love for him (v.4). He expresses appreciation for what Timothy is (v.5). He admonishes him in regard to his weaknesses (vv.6-7). He exhorts him to a bold witness (v.8). Paul sets an example for Timothy to follow (vv. 11-12). He reminds Timothy of what he has taught him (v.13). Is Paul out of order in any of the advice he gives Timothy? Does he give it in a Christian spirit? Would Paul make a good father? What do you find in this passage that should make you a better parent? Are you a spiritual as well as a physical parent to your child?

Friday, September 28, *John* 11:20-27. Mary and Martha have just experienced the death of their only brother (vv.11-14). What is the answer to the Jews' question of v.37? Were Mary and Martha right in their feeling on this subject (vv.21,32)? Did Jesus know about Lazarus' sickness before he died (v.3)? Have you ever gone through a time when you really needed the Lord and He did not respond to your cries for help? Study vv.5-6. Notice especially the "therefore" of v.6 ("so" - R.S.V.). Why did not Jesus respond to their plea according to these verses? Can you find comfort from this truth in time of need? What lessons do you think Jesus was trying to teach Mary and Martha (vv.17-27,38-44)? Are you willing to let God direct the events of your life in whatever way He will, that others may profit (vv.14,45), and He may be glorified (v.4)?

Saturday, September 29, *Psalm* 71:17-24. Many folk who are approaching old age are faced with the fear that they will be forsaken by family and friends and left alone. What is the Psalmist's concern in v.9? To whom is he talking in this verse? Observe what this Psalm tells us about the author that would lead us to believe that his prayer of verse 9 for the reality of God's fellowship will be answered. Does he expect to spend his old age in idleness (v.18)? Is he waiting until he is old before he puts his trust in the Lord (vv.5-6,17)? What is the one desire of his life (vv.14-16)? How real have his experiences with the Lord been (vv.1-4,19-24)? Can you find a message for your life in one of the following verses (Ecl. 12:1; Isaiah 46:4; Proverbs 16:31; Titus 2:2)?

LESSON FOR SEPTEMBER 23

The Kingdom Triumphant

Background Scripture: Matthew 6:4-13; Revelation 7:9-17; 11:15-19a
Devotional Reading: Psalm 91:1-9

When we think of "the secret place of the Most High" and "The shadow of the Almighty," we realize that the Kingdom of God is a Triumphant Kingdom. To dwell and abide there is to feel safe and secure, no matter how troubled the world is, or how strongly we are tempted to be afraid. Psalm 91 has been a comfort to many of the people of God in dangerous days. I talked to a soldier once who said that it had sustained him on the battlefield amid all the dangers and horrors which surrounded him. It does our souls good to meditate upon the Almighty God Who can hide us from all the enemies that may threaten us. We are the children of the King, the Most High, and citizens of a Kingdom which can never be shaken, an Eternal and Triumphant Kingdom. In the throne room, the secret place, we can quietly rest even when the world is in convulsions and shaking like a leaf in a fearful storm. A man was relating his experience while going through a great manufacturing plant with its deafening roar of machinery. He was finally taken to the "Quiet Room," the place where all the power to run the plant was generated.

Amid all the noise and confusion of our world today we can "be still and know that I am God." It is a wonderful experience to visit the "Quiet Room" of this universe, the secret place of the Most High, and the shadow of the Almighty.

I wish to divide our Lesson very simply into (1) The Prayer, and (2) The Answer; the Prayer in Matthew, and the Answer in Revelation.

I. *The Prayer: "Thy Kingdom Come":* Matthew 6:4-13.

Jesus had been speaking of prayer, and that His Father, seeing in secret, would reward us openly. He then gives The Lord's Prayer as a sample of how we should pray. In this prayer we have the petition, Thy Kingdom Come. Our Shorter Catechism sums up the meaning of this petition as follows: "In the second petition, which is, Thy Kingdom Come, we pray that Satan's kingdom may be destroyed, and that the kingdom of grace may be advanced, ourselves and others brought into it, and kept in it, and that the kingdom of glory may be hastened."

There is a battle to fight. Satan's kingdom is strong. He is the god of this world, and he exercises a great deal of power. The "strong man" has been bound, however. Christ came to destroy the works of the devil. Satan did his worst while Christ was here, but he has been defeated. He knows that his time is short. The Church is now a "Militant Church." We sing, Onward, Christian Soldiers, and the Son of God goes forth to war, A kingly crown to gain. The weapons of our warfare are not carnal, but mighty to the pulling down of strongholds. We are fighting, not against flesh and blood, but against mighty spiritual enemies. We must put on the whole armor of God.

The kingdom of grace is to be advanced. We are to go into all the world heralding the good tidings, beseeching men to be reconciled to God, saying, Today is the accepted time, Today is the day of salvation. It is our duty and privilege to invite all to come; to go out into the highways and hedges and compel them to come in.

The Kingdom of Glory will arrive when all the kingdoms of this world become the Kingdom of our Lord and of His Christ. The Crowning Day is coming By and By, when we shall Bring forth the royal diadem and Crown Him Lord of all. On His head shall be many crowns, or Diadems. It is most fitting that our Confession of Faith should close with these words from Revelation: "Come, Lord Jesus, come quickly. Amen."

II. *The Answer: Revelation* 7:9-17; 11:15-19a.

The first part of chapter seven, verses 1-8, give the Sealing of the 144,000 of God's servants. I wish to state briefly the most satisfying (to my own mind) interpretation of this rather mysterious and highly symbolic passage. It is given by Dr. Lenski in his splendid Interpretation of Revelation. According to this view this 144,000 represents the whole Old and New Testament Church — All of God's redeemed people. They belong to Him. They are sealed; therefore safe. Not one is lost. The second part of the chapter, which is our lesson, reveals to us the fact that the 144,000 is in reality a vast

the mark of "Great Saints." We are not carried to the skies on flowery beds of ease. Jesus spoke of a "cross." Must Jesus bear the cross alone, and all the world go free? In the second place, these saints have washed their robes and made them white in the blood of the Lamb. There are some who stumble over, and even sneer at the precious blood of Christ. They would reach heaven by their good works, or good character. I, for one, expect to go home by the way of the cross and the precious blood of the Lamb. I know of no other way. It is His robe of righteousness that I shall wear, for it will be washed in His blood. He has loosed us from our sins in His blood. Therefore are they before the throne. No one can stand there except those who have been cleansed in His blood.

7. There are some lessons about the condition of these saved ones as we see them in these verses. (1) Heaven will be a place of glorious Service. They will be serving Him day and night in His temple. We will have blessed work to do. No one is happy who has nothing to do. They are supremely happy who have something to do that they love to do. This will be the case in heaven. (2) It will be a place of Perfect Fellowship. God will spread His tabernacle over them. There will be fellowship with God, with Christ, with our loved ones, with all the great saints of all time. (3) A place of Utmost Satisfaction : hunger no more, thirst no more. The Good Shepherd shall lead them. This is a picture of Ideal conditions. It will be eternal satisfaction, for the eternal water of life will be ours. In Pilgrim's Progress when Christian read of the glories of the Celestial City his heart was "ravished" with delight and longing. So with us! "There is a land of pure delight, Where saints immortal reign; Infinite day excludes the night, And pleasures banish pain. There everlasting spring abides, And never-with'ring flowers; Death, like a narrow sea, divides This heav'nly land from ours. I want to go there; don't you?

8. The picture in 11:15-19 emphasizes the truth of the Triumphant Kingdom.

YOUTH PROGRAM FOR SEPTEMBER 23

What Can I Do?

Suggested Devotional Outline:
Hymn: "The Church's One Foundation"
Prayer
Scripture: John 15:1-8.
Hymn: "I Love Thy Kingdom, Lord"
Offering
Hymn: "Lead On, O King Eternal"

Suggestions for Program Leader:
The purpose of this program is to help your group of young people to see exactly what their opportunity and their responsibility is in the life and work of the church. The best way to do this is to set before them the specific plans which have been made for your group for the fall months. It should not be a matter of your ordering the other young people to do certain things, but rather of showing them opportunities for service and of asking their cooperation and advice. If you follow this suggestion, it will mean that the officers of your organization must do some careful planning beforehand. You will need to have definite ideas and plans for programs, projects, and activities which you hope to carry out before the end of the year. It would be best not to make these plans so hard and fast that the suggestions of other members could not be incorporated into them.

Leader's Introduction: (It would be most appropriate for the President of your group to lead this program.)

What can I do in the church? In answering this question some young people may think no farther than the organization for young people. It is a serious mistake to think that our responsibility to the church begins and ends in the young people's group. This is merely the place where we have fellowship with those of our own age group and where we learn how to participate in the total life of the church. We must not think of the church as a combination of separate departments for men, women, children, and young people. It is a fellowship of all the believers in Christ . . . of all those who have been "called out" to be children of God through faith in Christ.

Those of us who have been chosen as your officers and leaders have been working on some plans for the next three months. We have tried to bear in mind opportunities for service in the total program of the church as well as in our own particular organization. We do not claim to have found all the answers, and as we share these plans with you, we want your suggestions for improvements and additions to them. Working together under the guidance of the Holy Spirit we believe we can find out what there is for us to do in the church.

(If your group is organized according to the commission plan, you will already be familiar with the five following areas of Christian growth and service. If you are not organized in this way, you will do well to consider these areas in your planning.)

1. The aim of CHRISTIAN FAITH is "to lead the young people of the church and congregation to grow in effective Christian living by knowing Jesus, accepting Him as Lord and Saviour, following His principles in daily living . . . "

2. The aim of CHRISTIAN WITNESS is to follow His principles in daily living, and lead others to know and follow Him.

3. The purpose of CHRISTIAN OUTREACH is to find "opportunities for Christian service both at home and abroad."

4. CHRISTIAN CITIZENSHIP seeks "to bring the way of Christ to bear on the needs of society."

5. The aim of CHRISTIAN FELLOWSHIP is "to develop Christian fellowship among the members in their relationship to each other and to the community."

Above quotations are from the *Handbook of the Senior High Fellowship.*

Closing Comment by Program Leader:
It is likely that some of us never realized how many answers there could be to the question "What can I do?" as it is applied to the church. Now that we are aware of all these opportunities, the next thing for us to do is to dedicate ourselves to meeting them. All the work will not be done, and the church will not be as strong as it ought to be, until every Christian young person undertakes very seriously to do his part.

Women's Work

A Moment With the Master When Misunderstood

"The thorns in my path are not sharper than composed His crown for me . . ."

What brought back to my memory just then hose words I heard so long ago? One whom truly love had just used sharp, accusing words howing she completely misunderstood me, and ow refused to accept my sincere explanation nd plea to be forgiven for whatever had so ffended her. That simple hymn comforts my ounded heart.

I thought: Jesus' "thorns" must have been hat He was often misunderstood by His own amily, even though they loved Him. Believing Iim "beside Himself" they tried to silence His ivine ministry. But His love held them and laimed them at last to be His devoted folowers.

His chosen disciples rebuked Him sharply hen He foretold His own suffering and death. "Be it far from thee, Lord!" cried Peter — little understanding the central place of suffering in His Messiahship. When they forsook Him and fled from His Cross He loved on, till He met them and reclaimed their undying loyalty in the new light of His resurrection.

Bitterest of all must have been the willful, fierce misunderstanding of the leaders of His religion, who accused Him of blasphemy and did their worst to turn His own people against Him. "Hatred without a cause" finally accomplished His crucifixion. But love like His finally conquers, so "a great company of the priests" themselves came at last to believe on Him.

When I then, through no conscious fault of my own, am so misunderstood, can I, like my loving Lord, love on, even when my sincere efforts to clear the trouble fail? Some one who knows Him well says, "Every bit of human nature is transfigured in Christ . . . " in the constant "contemplation of His life."

If "I would be like Jesus," I must meet misunderstanding, as He did. I cannot be blameless as He ever was, so I must *pray* for new light to reveal my possible fault that I may try a new way to mend this break. (Prayer was His unfailing resource of strength.) I must *open my Bible,* as He used His (my Old Testament) so constantly and read again Psalm 37, and find there:

Commit thy way unto Jehovah; trust also in him, and he will bring it to pass. And he will make thy righteousness to go forth as the light, And thy justice as the noonday.

So I quiet my troubled heart before Him, praying that the thorn of misunderstanding may be removed by my renewed "delight in the Lord," asking Him who was so cruelly misunderstood to enable me to "roll my way upon the Lord" — and "wait patiently for Him" to clear away this cloud of misunderstanding.

Church News

Christianity and Health

In accordance with the directive of the General Assembly a copy of the report of the Ad Interim Committee on Christianity and Health has been mailed to every Clerk of Session in the Assembly. It is intended that this report shall be used throughout our Church as a basis for study and individuals and churches may obtain copies from the undersigned. Prices are as follows: Single copy 5c; 50 copies $2.00; 100 copies $3.00; 500 copies $12.50; 1,000 copies $20.00. All orders should be received not later than November 1 and remittance accompany orders.

Rev. E. C. Scott, Stated Clerk
341 - A, Ponce de Leon Avenue, N.E.
Atlanta 8, Georgia

Dr. "Bill" McCorkle Takes a Pastorate

After three and a quarter fruitful years as the General Assembly's Secretary of Evangelism Rev. Wm. H. McCorkle, D.D., has accepted a call to become pastor of the First Presbyterian Church, of Bristol, Tennessee.

Owing to the pressure of a very busy schedule in the Board of Church Extension, of which the Division of Evangelism is a part, Dr. McCorkle will not enter upon his new duties at Bristol until the last of October. His home address will then be Foxcroft Road, Spring Garden, Bristol, Virginia.

ALABAMA

Montgomery — Dr. Henry Edward Russell, pastor of Trinity Presbyterian Church, Montgomery, Ala., is one of six Protestant clergymen to conduct preaching missions this fall at American air bases throughout the Far East. Dr. Russell leaves for his assignment by plane from McGuire Air Force Base, New Jersey, October 3. He will be away approximately thirty-five days.

Dr. Russell's schedule carries him to Newfoundland, Labrador, and Greenland, with the Alabama minister speaking to a number of Air Force bases and to one Naval station.

NORTH CAROLINA

Montreat — About 300 teachers, representing more than 100 colleges and universities attended the third Southeastern States Faculty Conference at Montreat, August 27 - 31.

The conference, sponsored jointly by the boards of education of the Presbyterian Church, U.S., and the Methodist Church, brought together many outstanding Christian leaders from America and abroad to discuss the theme "Freedom, Responsibility and the Christian Faith."

TENNESSEE

Nashville — Mr. and Mrs. Ira Moore and family of our Congo Mission arrived in this country Aug. 20 for a furlough. Upon their arrival they proceeded to Nashville, Tenn.

Miss Gussie Fraser of our Taiwan Mission is scheduled to arrive in the United States in early September for her regular furlough.

years. In the course of the first three of these years he earned his Ph.D. at Edinburgh, the subject of his thesis being "The Doctrine of Man in the Qur'an'."

Dr. Thomson has contributed articles to the **Expository Times**, to the **Scottish Journal of Theology**, and to **Vetus Testamentum**, and has been invited to serve as a contributing editor of the new publication, **Christianity Today**. He is a member of The Society of Old Testament Study in Great Britain and of the Glasgow Oriental Society and has read papers before those societies.

Dr. Thomson is an ordained minister of the Church of Scotland. For eight years he and his wife were missionaries in Algeria, French North Africa, where they worked among the Arabic Speaking Muslims.

It is expected that Dr. and Mrs. Thomson with their thirteen year old daughter will come to the United States late in October. He will begin his teaching duties at Columbia Seminary with the opening of the Winter Quarter, January 3, 1957.

Dr. Whale To Come as Guest Professor

The Reverend Doctor John Selden Whale, distinguished British clergyman, educator and author, has accepted an invitation to serve as Guest Professor at Columbia Seminary during the Winter Quarter.

Dr. Whale holds the degree of M.A. from Oxford University and was made a Doctor of Divinity by the University of Glasgow. He is a minister of the Congregational Church and was at one time pastor of the Bowdon Downs Church at Manchester. He was for some years the McKennal Professor of Ecclesiastical History at Mansfield College, Oxford, and later served as President of Cheshunt College, Cambridge University. He is at present retired and makes his home at Widecombe in the Moor, New Abbot, Devon, but finds time for an extensive program of writing and lecturing.

Among the numerous works published by Dr. Whale are "The Christian Answer to the Problem of Evil," "What is a Living Church?" "This Christian Faith," "Christian Doctrine," "The Right to Believe," and "The Protestant Tradition."

Dr. Whale is to be at Columbia Seminary for a period of six weeks, beginning January 3, 1957. He will offer two elective courses in Theology, the exact titles of which will be announced later.

Other News Concerning Faculty Members

Dr. Wm. C. Robinson returned to Decatur in mid-July after spending a year of Sabbatic Leave in Europe. Dr. Robinson devoted most of the year to study at Cambridge University and at the University of Basel, but also traveled extensively in Britain, Italy and other parts of Europe. He will resume his usual teaching duties in September.

Prof. Thomas H. McDill, Jr., has spent the summer in graduate study at the University of Chicago. He has been granted leave of absence during the Fall Quarter in order that he may continue that program of study but will return to teach during the Winter and Spring Quarters.

Prof. Hubert Vance Taylor has studied throughout the summer at Northwestern University, but will carry on his courses without interruption during the school year.

Prof. Cecil Thompson had been granted Sabbatic Leave for graduate study during the coming year and it has been announced that he would not be here to serve as Director of Field Work. Because suitable assistance in that Department has not yet been found, he has consented to postpone his leave of absence and to serve throughout the fall in supervising the field work of students. It is hoped that he will be able to go forward with his projected program of study later in the year.

Dr. Manford Geo. Gutzke will be granted leave of absence during the Winter Quarter in order that he may be free to engage in writing a book for future publication.

Plans for the Ministers' Institute

An unusually full and rewarding program has been arranged for the seminary's annual Ministers' Week which will be held October 29 - November 3.

The Smyth Lectures are to be delivered by Dr. Joseph Haroutunian of McCormick Seminary, whose subject will be "The Christian Use of the Mind." Dr. Halford Luccock, formerly of Yale University, will deliver a series of lectures in the field of Homiletics and Dr. John Leith of Auburn, Ala., will lecture on some of the ethical implications of Calvinism. Dr. Louis Evans of Los Angeles, Cal., will preach each morning during the week. The Alumni of the seminary will hold their annual meeting at lunch on Tuesday, October 30.

Further announcement concerning this program will be made later. In the meanwhile ministers of the area are asked to circle these dates on their calendars and to plan to be present.

In Memoriam to Charles N. Kell

Decatur, Ga.

WHEREAS, God, in His infinite wisdom, has taken from our midst in this earthly life, Charles N. Kell, who was one of Decatur's best loved citizens, and

WHEREAS, Charles N. Kell was a member of the Session of the Decatur Presbyterian Church, and,

WHEREAS, Charles N. Kell served the church in many capacities; As Superintendent of the Sunday School; as a very active member of the Board of Deacons; as Chairman of the Building Fund Committee, which successfully raised funds for the construction of the present sanctuary, chapel and church offices, and,

WHEREAS, he served unselfishly and earnestly in these places of importance, he also served his Lord with humility in doing many great and small deeds of kindness and devotion, which will be long remembered, and,

WHEREAS, Charles N. Kell contributed, by his life and example, and by service to the welfare of this church and to this community, and,

WHEREAS, he was a man of great faith and willingness to work constructively, he accomplished much for his Lord and for his fellow man, and,

WHEREAS, he was ever faithful in the evangelistic visitation work of his church, inviting the newcomer, the stranger and those without church homes to find their Lord in the fellowship of this church, therefore,

BE IT RESOLVED that the Session of the Decatur Presbyterian Church extend to his beloved wife and family its deepest sympathy in the great loss that they have suffered and that a copy of this Resolution, signed by the Pastor and the Clerk, be sent to his widow; that a copy be placed in the minutes of the Session and be published in the Decatur Presbyterian Church Bulletin and the church papers.

— LETTERS —

What Do You Think?

In the July 13th issue we asked our readers to share with us their views as to whether the Church, as such, should use her influence in social, moral, and other issues, or whether this influence should be exerted in society by individual Christians.

Some of our readers were unwilling to confine their views to the requested 100 words; others were unwilling to have their names signed to their views.

The following are typical of the replies and we appreciate the interest shown in this request.

The Editors

The Church should enter the lists on social, ethical, moral and spiritual issues.

The limits should be as broad as Christ's command to preach the gospel to every creature - declaring God's judgment upon every man and God's covenant promise to regenerate any repentant sinner.

The sound basic policy guiding such activity should be the great commandment: love God (i.e. worship only Him privately and publicly) and love your neighbor as yourself (i.e. in all governmental, social, economic and civic relations).

Any Church seeking by legislation in a democracy to coerce non-believers to follow particular Christian practices (i.e. observance of the Lord's Day) is "political bludgeoning."

Since the Holy Spirit is promised by Jesus to gatherings of His disciples no less than to them individually, it is proper for the "constituted authorities" of the Church (her elected officers in meeting assembled) to speak authoritatively for the Church on any matter.

David M. Currie
First Presbyterian Church
Texas City, Texas

I believe that the Church should concentrate her efforts in the winning of the individual to Christ and his development in the Christian fold, for three main reasons:

1. Political, economic, social and legal questions are the affair of the State. We believe in the separation of Church and State. We demand that the State keep free from the affairs of the Church. We should equally follow the same rule.

I believe the church has a definite mission. That mission is with individuals as Christians. If the individual is truly Christian he will so deal with individuals of other races. Only to the extent of personal conduct as Christians can the church take any rightful stand dealing with social, ethical or moral issues. If it acts otherwise it will only resort to politics and thus lower its influence in the world.

Mrs. Delos W. Thayer
Washington, D. C.

BOOKS

EDUCATION OR INDOCTRINATION. Mary L. Allen. The Caxton Printers, Ltd. $4.00.

Something has happened in our public schools. This book is written to present an analysis of what has happened. The concern over the content of modern education is spreading throughout America. "Our schools," observes the author, "once the proud heritage of all children in America, have become the center of confusion, emotional wrangling, and extreme differences of opinion.

All over the country boards of education have met resistance from the people they represent and the teachers they employ." What has happened in our public schools to thrust them in the forefront of the battle of ideas? This is the question wide-awake and intelligent citizens are forced to consider. A careful examination of a large number of currently used text books on American government, says the author, reveals some startling facts. Little or no attempt is made in these books, she holds, to present the point of view of those large segments of our citizenry who oppose and recognize the dangers of too much centralized authority, and too wide ramifications of government interventions in the affairs of private citizens. On the other hand she discovered that the vital and significant part played in daily life by free enterprise or by voluntary organizations is either completely overlooked, or, at best, sparingly mentioned.

The blame for this situation, avers Mrs. Allen, should not be put upon the teachers because with few exceptions the teachers are not specialists in political science and they must teach from the textbooks given them and in accordance with instruction and directives received from their supervisors and administrators. The responsibility for the current situation, the author maintains, must be placed upon school administrators, curriculum makers, teacher trainers, and textbook writers. Frequently top administrators would have citizens to limit their concern to school buildings, school equipment, and taxes, but **not** what is taught or how it is taught.

Mrs. Allen is a mother who has devoted a great deal of time, effort, and ability to understanding both the substance and method of public school education today. She has given us the first full and complete report of the Pasadena school crisis of 1950-51. The aim of her book is to stir parents into action at the local level. She stresses the fact that we need a shift of emphasis in the school policy to the end that more time will be devoted to education and less to indoctrination.

Surveying the past Mrs. Allen writes, "Yesterday, a high school graduate was instructed in moral values, proper behavior, English grammar, American history, civics, citizenship, geography, arithmetic, and various other courses. He was a literate citizen. America was proud of the product of her public schools."

Today the author informs us we hear a different story: "People are wondering why children with equal intelligence are failing to respond with equal literacy. They are disturbed with the lack of discipline and the discourtesy permitted in the classroom. There is so much pressure for conformance to the group that parents wonder how long the individual child can maintain his individual identity."

Seeking to throw light upon our educational muddle, the author asks, "Is it possible that the general citizenry have one set of goals for education and the educators have another? Can it be that the American people think they are going down a road toward knowledge, the American way of life and literacy, and the educators are knowingly or unknowingly leading them down a path toward a new way of life?" If so, she says the confusion in education is easily explained.

Intelligent Americans are asking: Where is present day American education leading us? Will it destroy us or will it strengthen us? The author answers these questions. It is the duty of the American people to examine the facts she presents and then determine where the educational program of today is leading.

Since the public schools belong to the people of America and since public school administrators and teachers are employed by the people, the writer insists that the people's wishes should be considered. She reminds parents and citizens that it is their duty to take a livelier interest in the public schools. She concludes with this sober thought. "In the next decade America will probably make a choice between education or indoctrination. Let us solemnly hope that education will be the victor."

This volume contains an excellent bibliography, an index of both authors and subjects, and is well documented throughout. Because of the prominence of education in American thought, this book should make a wide appeal to educators, school administrators, and parents. J.R.R.

AN ADVENTURE IN LOVE. W. Taliaferro Thompson. John Knox Press. $2.50.

For over 30 years the author taught courses in Understanding Children and in Understanding Youth at Union Theological Seminary and at the General Assembly's Training School for Lay Workers in Richmond. Hundreds of thoughtful men and women have taken questionnaires to parents and to boys and girls and given to the author their wisdom in papers and classroom discussions. Most of all he has benefited from his own home in observing his six children grow into manhood and womanhood. This volume was written to show that family life can be richer and more meaningful than is usually experienced in most homes.

One of the most worthwhile chapters in this enlightening volume is on "Love and Adolescence." Intelligent parents know that this is a critical time in a growing young person. Dr. Thompson tells us that these adolescents should have sex education. He writes, "It is when we get to this place in our thinking that we realize that our boys and girls must be given an understanding of the meaning of sex in their lives. They are very conscious of the physical changes they are experiencing of the primary and secondary sex characteristics which are so evident and of the accompanying emotions which are so upsetting." He refers to a recent volume in which this question was asked, "What, according to high school students, is the most important personal problem facing them today?" And their answer was, "What should we do about sex?"

Dr. Thompson states that the answer to that question requires knowledge. The author advises, "We should enable teenagers to know that this urge is a natural part of life at this period, as natural as the desire for food and drink and as natural for the girl as for the boy. We would have them understand that it is a strong urge, more pervasive in the girl, involving her whole body, and more localized in the boy; that it is more easily and quickly excited in the boy, especially by physical contact; and that when it is aroused it may become overwhelming. It is stronger in some persons than in others, and in the same person more uncontrollable at certain times than at others. For both boy and girl to know this may help them to be on their guard against going, in their physical intimacies, beyond a point of no return."

In dealing with teenagers, Dr. Thompson insists that important as knowledge is, it is not enough. Ideals must be built into our boys and girls — ideals not only about sex but about life as a whole, which are determined by their conception of God and persons. He remarks, "If we could get our boys and girls to see the sacredness of personality because of its relationship to God, it would be difficult for them to engage in the kind of prolonged petting which majors in bodily intimacies and measures a date by the physical thrills experienced." Help, says the author, should come from the home. Teenagers need the freedom to talk with someone, preferably someone at home.

Dr. Thompson closes this inspiring volume with this high note: What our sons and daughters need as their problems multiply, what our nation needs as it faces these strange and terrifying days, and what the church needs as it girds itself for a better witness, are parents who love each other and their children with an understanding and growing devotion; and who love God whom they have come to know in Jesus Christ, through whom alone true love is born and matures. It is the love of Christ, revealed in the Cross, that constrains us to love Him and others."

This volume is packed full of wholesome counsel and it is designed to be beneficial to parents and counselors of young people. J.R.R.

MARK'S SKETCHBOOK OF CHRIST. Helen J. Tenney. William B. Eerdman's. $2.00.

The author has written this volume to present an example of personal Bible study. It was used first to meet the needs of teenage young people who wanted answers to certain questions.

This is a Bible study book and it combines the best features of the inductive method with an integrated outline. The method of Bible study provided in this workbook will prove useful in Bible courses in Christian high schools, weekday church programs, summer camps, vacation Bible school curricula, and on the foreign mission field.

THE SOUTHERN
PRESBYTERIAN
JOURNAL

A Presbyterian weekly magazine devoted to the statement, defense and propagation of the Gospel, the faith which was once for all delivered unto the saints.

VOL. XV NO. 21 SEPTEMBER 19, 1956 $2.50 A YEAR

. EDITORIAL .

THE SOUTHERN PRESBYTERIAN JOURNAL
The Journal has no official connection with the Presbyterian Church in the United States
Rev. Henry B. Dendy, D.D., Editor..........**Weaverville, N. C.**
Dr. L. Nelson Bell, Associate Editor..........**Asheville, N. C.**
Rev. Wade C. Smith, Associate Editor..........**Weaverville, N. C.**

EDITORIAL

Needed, One Message

One of Methodism's outstanding leaders has recently made an impassioned plea for "unity." The basis for this plea was that a "divided world will not heed a divided church."

This statement sounds clever and it also seems reasonable. The only trouble is that it fails to properly diagnose the real problem.

Nowhere in Scripture have we any intimation that the willingness of men to hear is based on the nature of an ecclesiastical organization.

Furthermore, the scandal of our generation is not a divided church. The tragedy is found in a *divided message.* Within the church itself there is no unanimity even as to *what* the message is.

This is a bald statement of fact and one which needs to be repeated until Christians everywhere take note. We are not talking about varying interpretations of minor doctrines which have been and will obtain wherever men of differing backgrounds are to be found. Uniformity in such matters is impossible to attain, nor is such uniformity of great importance.

But, anyone at all conversant with the situation in the Church today knows that from different sources every cardinal and vital doctrine of the Christian faith is under attack. There seems to be one point on which most agree; that Christ is "God and Saviour" and this would be heartening but for the fact that many who so affirm are not talking about the Christ of the New Testament but a synthetic person, the figment of human speculation and unbelief.

The message is a divided one because of a fundamental disagreement about both the person and the work of the Lord Jesus Christ. To some he was virgin born; to others the product of a human father and mother. To some He performed miracles; to others these acts are denied or explained away as natural phenomena. To some He died on the cross in atonement for our sins; to others He died as a supreme example of unselfishness. To some He arose again from the dead and showed Himself in bodily form by many infallible proofs; to others the post-crucifixion appearances were imaginative or of spiritual implication only. To some He will come in person again, bringing this age to a cataclysmic conclusion; to others His personal return is mere nonsense.

Yes, there is a divided Church but the denominational divisions are of minor importance. The *great divide,* a distinction which runs straight through all denominational lines, centers on what men are to believe, to preach and to do — on what the Christian message actually is.

Every ecclesiastical division in Christendom could be eliminated by one giant plan of unification and there would still be a divided Church.

A divided world will continue until all men come to know, believe in, worship and serve the Lord Jesus Christ and there is but one such Reality — the Christ of the Scriptures. L.N.B.

Does Paul Describe the Spiritual Body as Non-Physical?

This question is raised by conflicting statements by Christian brethren in current books. In HEAVEN AND HELL, a prominent New York Pastor writes that Paul "emphasizes the difference between the physical body and the new spiritual body" received at the resurrection. On the other hand, Dr. J. A. T. Robinson in a 1952 SCM book, THE BODY, A STUDY IN PAULINE THEOLOGY, says: "For the fact that it is a spiritual body does not mean that it is not physical." Which statement is correct?

The first statement may appeal to at least two American translations for support, namely that by Dr. E. J. Goodspeed and the Revised Standard Version, which in the case before us follows Goodspeed. The statement by J. A. T. Robinson has in its support most of the English and all of the German translations I have seen.

Did Paul say that the present body is sown a physical body as Goodspeed and the RSV render I Cor. 15.44-46? The Greek adjective which the Apostle here contrasts with Spiritual is not physical, but psychical. The same two adjectives, psychical and Spiritual, are contrasted earlier in the same epistle, I Cor. 2.14-15. Goodspeed there renders psychical as "material" and as "unspiritual." Logically Goodspeed's rendering would mean that at conversion one becomes an immaterial man. But most of the converted or Spiritual men, have as much material as they had prior to their conversion —and some are heavier. Accordingly, in following Goodspeed, the RSV omits his word "material" and uses his other word "unspiritual."

Goodspeed's rendering ought to have made us suspicious of the meaning he gets from the contrasting adjectives. Since psychical may not mean material or physical in I Cor. 2.14-15 lest the converted man be described as non-physical or immaterial, neither can it have that sense in I Cor. 15: 44-46. In neither case does the adjective describe the matter or the composition of the body which dies, or of that which is raised. Instead the two adjectives point to the principle of life in the two bodies.

The principle of life in the present body is psychical, that is, soul, *nephesh, psyche.* The principle of life in the resurrection body is Spirit, *ruach, pneuma.* Accordingly, the Spiritual body of I Cor. 15:44-49 is a body raised by the life-giving Spirit of the heavenly Adam, cf. Rom.8.11: Jas.2.26, a body of which the Holy Spirit is the life principle, a body motivated by true spirituality, that is, by Christ-likeness, Phil. 3.21: I Jn. 3.2; I Cor. 15.49.

This spiritual body is to be a real body and dwell in the New Jerusalem, in the new heaven *and the new earth.* The converted or spiritual man in I Cor. 3.15 is still a physical, or if you wish, a material man. The spiritual food and spiritual water of I Cor. 10.3-4 were physical, or if you please, material. There is nothing in I Cor. 15.44-46 to keep the resurrection body from being likewise physical.

The book, HEAVEN AND HELL, also asserts that Paul differs from the Pharisees on the nature of the resurrection. Of course, Paul finds the ground and cause of the believers' resurrection in Christ while the Pharisee found it in good works. But Professor W. D. Davies, PAUL AND RABBINICAL JUDAISM, pp. 303-310, concludes that Paul is thoroughly pharisaic in the presentation of the nature of the resurrection in First Corinthians fifteen, using sundry analogies that were common among the rabbis. Moreover, Paul describes himself as a Pharisee as touching the law, Phil. 3.5; and Luke cites him as repeatedly testifying his accord with the Pharisees on the resurrection: "I am a Pharisee, the son of a Pharisee, touching the hope and resurrection of the dead I am called in question." Acts 23.6; 24:15,21;26.5-8. The Platonists rejected Paul's preaching of the resurrection at Mars Hill, Acts 17.18,31-32; but the Pharisees defended him in the matter. Possibly, Paul, as cited by Luke, is a good exegete of the Apostle's views, and possibly both the Platonists and the Pharisees understood him.

It is assumed, however, that I Cor. 15.50 teaches that the resurrection body will not be physical. May we ask a little deeper study of that verse. The phrase, flesh and blood, is used in the Bible, e.g., Isaiah 31.3; Mt.16.17; Gal. 1.16; Hebr. 2.14, not to describe the physical side of man as against his mental or spiritual side. Rather it describes fallen human nature in its distinction from or opposition to God or His Spirit. Paul is not talking Greek dualism here, but Christian salvation. He does not say that our future body will be soul and spirit, not flesh and blood. Rather, he says that our fallen human nature cannot inherit the kingdom of God by any virtue or merit or work of its own, Cf. John 3.3-6. It must be changed by the Holy Spirit from its enmity against God, Rom. 8.7, and from its corruption. "If the Spirit of Him Who raised up Jesus from the dead dwell in you, He Who raised from the dead Christ Jesus will make alive also your mortal bodies by His Spirit Who dwells in you." Rom. 8.11.

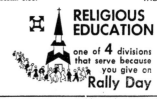

W.C.R.

The Southern Presbyterian Journal, *a Presbyterian Weekly magazine devoted to the statement, defense, and propagation of the Gospel, the faith which was once for all delivered unto the saints,* published every Wednesday by The Southern Presbyterian Journal, Inc., in Weaverville, N. C.

Entered as second-class matter May 15, 1942, at the Postoffice at Weaverville, N. C., under the Act of March 3, 1879. Vol. XV, No. 21, September 19, 1956. Editorial and Business Offices: Weaverville, N. C. Printed in the U.S.A. by Biltmore Press, Asheville, N. C.

ADDRESS CHANGE: When changing address, please let us have both old and new address as far in advance as possible. Allow three weeks after change if not sent in advance. When possible, send an address label giving your old address.

The Old by the New

There is nothing the liberal theologian fears and opposes more than the time-honored acceptance of the New Testament's estimate of the Old. Despite the fact that our Lord, the writers of the four gospels, the apostles in the Acts and the writers of the epistles *all* unite in accepting both the integrity and the authority of the Old Testament record, modern liberal scholarship stands firmly against their method of approach, and their conclusions.

To get around the obvious position of the New Testament in this matter we are told the following: Our Lord and those associated with Him and with the early Christian movement were either ignorant, confused, deliberately deceptive or so circumscribed by their own current traditions that they were unable to give either a true or accurate interpretation of the Old Testament meaning.

To put it buntly: Christians today have their choice between the New Testament and modern higher critics, between the record of our Lord's acceptance of the reliability and authority of the Old Testament and the modern qualification of both.

As one reads the New Testament and its repeated references to the Old, particularly in the realm of fulfilled prophecy, one is forced to the conclusion that here we find the recognition of a *depth and degree of inspiration we would not otherwise dare to assume.*

As we have said in these columns many times, liberals are not so much concerned with the inspiration of *words,* against which they inveigh; rather they are opposing the *doctrines* some of these words so clearly affirm, — the virgin birth, the bodily resurrection, the reality of Heaven and Hell, the substitutionary atonement, etc., etc.

The New Testament is a God-given commentary on the Old. The Old Testament is a God-given basis for the New. We all would be wise to search the Scriptures daily for here God speaks through the ages. L.N.B.

America's Mission for Christ

By George S. Lauderdale

Like Israel in Canaan, Americans live in a land which flows with milk and honey; we learn from this that God loves us and that He has important work for us to do in His Name. In the fruitful Promised Land, God's people did not have to worry about what they should eat or wear: their minds were free to seek ways to glorify God before other nations; they had time to assemble for seasons of glad thanksgiving and the study of God from His Word. The Lord did not will that they be driven to exhaustion eking a hard existence from barren soil! Their enemies could then have mocked them and little time given to the worship of His Name.

Because America is so rich, her farms, mines and factories supporting many others in addition to the millions dwelling in her borders, from this land must ascend to heaven the praises of hearts united in gratitude. Her Christian churches should be filled at the stated hours of worship on the first day of every week, as well as at special services of revival; the fires of expressed devotion should burn brightly in every home as families worship daily in Spirit and truth.

America at the Front

God's Word is a greater blessing than fertile fields and big harvests. "Remember the word which Moses the servant of the Lord commanded you . . . ", was Joshua's exhortation to Israel as they entered Canaan. Americans are to remember this Word of faith, "That if thou shalt confess with thy mouth the Lord Jesus, and shalt believe in thine heart that God hath raised him from the dead, thou shalt be saved." Romans 10:9. As milk and honey, nourishing to the body, flows from the land on which Americans live, so the Bible abounds in delightful, strengthening spiritual food. This is the Book which made America great.

Plainly, God intends that the United States bring glory to Him. How earnestly should American Christians pray and work to make the nation a fit instrument in God's hand to bless all other peoples! Without fear of want we can seek first God's kingdom and His righteousness; our resources are to be dedicated to the evangelization of the world. We are as a city set on a hill which cannot be hid; God's blessings have thrust us to a place of leadership; other nations are watching.

America at the Crossroads

Israel failed God in the land of promise, forsaking Him for idols and provoking His anger. "Your country is desolate, your cities are burned with fire: your land, strangers devour it in your presence, and it is desolate." Isaiah 1:7. If America continues living after her own lusts, God will likewise punish her! God will not be mocked, nor will He be hurt by our sins: if we love Christ and preach the gospel to every creature, He will be honored; if we refuse and rebel, He will remove us from our land in such a way as to advance His glorious holiness.

This is America's day of decision. In spite of marvelous mercies shown us, unequalled in human history, this nation has strayed far from God and like the prodigal, wastes much of her substance in riotous living. To the multitudes eating, drinking and making merry God is saying, "Come now, let us reason together . . . though your sins be as scarlet, they shall be as white as snow." He can cite ancient Israel and many other nations to prove His argument: "If ye be willing and obedient, ye shall eat the good of the land: but if ye refuse and rebel, ye shall be devoured with the sword." Isaiah 1:18-20.

Before it is too late, let Americans turn to God by faith in Jesus Christ! God's only begotten Son is Judge of the nations. Since He at a future time will bring righteousness and peace to every land ("they shall beat their swords into plowshares, and their spears into pruning hooks: nation shall not lift up sword against nation, neither shall they learn war any more." Isaiah 2:4), Jesus Christ can *now* heal America of her backslidings, surround her with invincible protection, and use the Christians in her to show many other states the right way.

America Must Choose Christ?

Many countries are becoming independent as we became in the eighteenth century. These peoples are flexing their mental muscles, and Satan, alert to their new awakening, is making Communism attractive. May God grant that the races now hungry for learning and general betterment of their welfare, not be lured into hell by the worship of earthly power! God could use the United States to show all others that to know Christ is the life, that obedience to Him rather than abundance of things gives joy, but before God can do so, America must repent.

Should global war come again, American civilians will probably find themselves in the long lines of refugees walking miles away from home. Instead of reading in the newspapers about box cars filled with men being deported *en masse* to new lands, Americans will be on the trains and others will be reading about us! God can thus cause foreign mission work to be one, for American Christians would tell others of the Saviour in the places where they were evacuated. How much better, however, to witness for Christ in peace; let us *now* serve the Lord!

The Reformed Faith as Related to the Virgin Birth According to Isaiah 7:14

By Rev. Robert F. Gribble, D.D.
Austin, Texas

The Reformed Doctrine is articulated in the authority and integrity of the Bible. It presupposes the reality of the supernatural. It maintains the full Scriptural view of the person of the Saviour. The Virgin Birth of our Lord is directly involved in each of these areas. For the manner of His entrance into this world requires the supernatural, even as it is inevitably bound up with the authority of Scripture; and is necessary for a complete and true view of Himself. There comes to mind Dr. Machen's appropriate reference, at the end of his classic volume on this subject: . . . we receive and rest upon Him alone for salvation *as* He is freely offered to us *in the Gospel.*"

Our present interest is the bearing of the notable verse, Isaiah 7:14, on our Faith. It should be said that whereas this point in that Faith does not depend upon whatever contribution the verse affords, yet it is with sound reason that we believe it to be a cogent factor in establishing the Biblical doctrine of the Virgin Birth.

The general background is quite necessary in approaching this matter. It is the eighth century B. C. Assyria is the great aggressor nation, advancing in seven-league boots to the West and threatening to engulf lesser peoples of the Mediterranean area. Damascus (Syria) and Ephraim (Northern Israel) combine to oppose the Assyrian, determining to force Judah into alliance, thus making the hearts of Ahaz, Judah's king, and of his people, tremble like trees before the wind. The city and dynasty of David are in peril.

In this crisis God makes move through His prophet Isaiah, speaking to the king as he inspects the water-supply against the threatened siege. Supremely confident in Jehovah and in His promise of inviolability to Zion, the prophet belittles the combine, calling its leaders two tails of smoking firebrands, and urging trust in God upon the faltering king. Here Isaiah utters one of his notable expressions, which has been rendered: "If you will not believe you shall be left." And then, as a guarantee of the truth of God's promise, we read that there is offered to Ahaz any sign he might desire, whether as high as Heaven or as deep as Hell. (For those who seek reason for the Church's historic belief in inspiration, it may be noted that two times here the words of the prophet are the words of God!) The faithless king refuses to exercise his option, apparently posing as a very pious person, whereat Isaiah condemns him for trifling with both man and God. And then comes verse 14: (literally) "Therefore the Lord Himself shall give to you a sign. Behold, the virgin (young woman) pregnant and bearing a son, and shall call his name Immanuel."

In defense of the Messianic character of this verse, note the following data, which, taken together, give strong presumption, if not definite assurance, that the passage is indeed referable to the Messiah, and, according to the New Testament revelation (Matt. 1:21ff), is fulfilled only and truly in the Virgin-born Lord Jesus Christ.

1. The expression "to you" is plural. Ahaz has just refused any sign. Isaiah states that this word is to "the house of David." Of course, in general, the king is included; but now, the word is no longer to be of *hope* to *him*: it is, so far as he is concerned, a message of condemnation, though also of hope to the faithful of Israel. And since the previous offer to Ahaz seems plainly to imply something extraordinary, the sign now, logically, may be thought of as beyond the common. Especially significant in such connection is the word "therefore," as also "the Lord *Himself*."

2. Next, look at the word "behold." Along with its shorter form, it is employed a minimum of fifty times in Isaiah. But the longer form, · here used — when preceding a participle, as here, regularly refers to the future. This rather rules out any idea of a present or an immediate, or life-cycle birth. (Parallels, say as in the case of Hagar, are not prophetic, and are therefore impertinent). And the climactic solemnity of the prophet's message, in the light of its superior context, seems to excite the messenger's astonishment, as though Isaiah speaks beyond himself.

3. Next, look at the word translated "sign." According to the Hebrew usage, a sign may have a very peculiar character. It may be a coming fact, or even an aspect of such fact, and lying far in the future. Thus, the promise to Moses at the burning bush (Ex.3), was a sign; but that promise was that Israel would worship God "on this mountain, an event certainly more than one, and perhaps several years, in prospect.

Yet it was a sign to Moses that Jehovah's people would be delivered from Pharaoh's power, involving the whole revolutionary transaction at Sinai, in the far future. The sign here, then, is not a promise but a threat, so far as the faithless are concerned: neither Ahaz, nor his line, nor the generally hardened house of David, would be used of God in the deliverance of His people. And conversely, it was not a censure but a promise, as relates to the faithful in Judah, in that by means of the nameless *almah,* God would produce a Divine Deliverer, (and in the light of the subsequent context) even while tribulation was the lot of His own. This should be very clear. The perpetuity of the House of David is guaranteed, as according to II Sam 7, but in a supernatural manner. Let the unfaithful Ahaz, the "Judas of the Old Testament" fail: God's purpose cannot be thwarted. And the sign of such a wondrous fact contemplates an unknown and indeterminable future, so far as the revelation to the human spokesman goes.

4. Now we come to the word which is translated in all save late "versions" by the word "virgin," a subject of much dispute. The unquestioned textual reading is a noun, feminine, singular, with the article: "The young woman," "the maid," "the virgin." But what is the correct translation? It seems to vary with the translator! Those who favor "young woman" as the proper translation, quite correctly point to the technical Hebrew word for virginity, viz., "bethulah." But that it must necessarily have been employed in a case where virginity is contemplated, is not so easy to prove. Anyone who cares to make a study will find that these words are not consistently used in the sense which they are supposed to convey. For, "almah" on occasion is found in the Old Testament in reference to one who seems unquestionably to have been a virgin (say the cases of Rebekah and Miriam), while "bethulah" occurs relative to one who was not such! In Joel 1:8, a "bethulah" laments for the *husband* of her youth. While we must admit that theoretically, and in harmony with the Hebrew usage, "almah" commonly designates "a young woman of marriageable age," we must also insist that in all ages there have been plenty of maidens who unquestionably qualify as virgins under that clause. And be it further insisted that whatever the translation of this word, it does certainly signify an actual female *person.* "Bethulah" on the other hand, in one-third of its occurrences, is used not of a real woman, but figuratively, of a city, and

that, with particular reference to the city Jerusalem which had broken her vows, gone into spiritual harlotry, and could not be looked upon as a virgin, save in the ideal sense. On the other hand one could hardly misunderstand "almah": it consistently refers to an individual.

Surely it is not without deep significance that the weight of the various versions of the Bible is wholly on the side of "virgin" as the proper translation, in this verse. (It has remained for quite modern translations to correct the error of the ages!) Take, for example, the earliest version of them all, the LXX, the Septuagint, the Greek equivalent of the Hebrew. Its translators who were Jews employed the word "parthenos" with the article, exactly parallel to the Hebrew, which means that they understood that a virgin is here contemplated. For although "parthenos" is sometimes found contrary to its teachnical sense, it is none the less the Greek word for "virgin."

There is no extant evidence that any change in word occurred before the time when our present copies of the LXX were made, - by Christian hands, even though Professor Orlinsky of the R. S. V. Committee hints at such a theory. To Justin Martyr, who lived two hundred years before our LXX copies came into being, and would most likely have known of any variations, is attributed the story that it was a Jewish scheme to make alterations, in order to silence Christians. Aquilla, Symmachus, and Theodotion, each made revisions of the LXX, in the second century A.D., and supplanted the word "parthenos" with the word "neanis," in Isaiah 7:14, so as to make the prophet say "young woman," thus depriving Christians of argument for the Virgin Birth of the Lord based on "almah-parthenos" in this famous verse. (History seems to be repeating itself!)

Other interesting data may yet be cited: No father is mentioned: the mother names the child (though not unique in the O.T.). But indeed, why is any parent mentioned at all? It is not done in chapter 9. And why a woman, a mother? Why not the father, which is more common Hebrew custom? And why "THE maiden"? The generic use of the article is hardly the way out of the difficulty presented. It seems quite far-fetched that a then present "young woman," enciente, (as some), or a number of such, (as others), or the general fact of motherhood, could, any of these, be the sign in this instance. The force of Isaiah 7:14 is hardly exhausted in the commonplace (though none the less remarkable) fact of reproduction. Nor does the passage admit of the view that a then present maid's condition corresponds to a future duplicate thereof. We are rather compelled to find here the extraordinary. In passing it may be noted that "almah" is a most appropriate word, if in retrospect from the N.T. viewpoint, we think of the virgin *wife* of Joseph, as according to the record.

But there is more: The boy of chapter 9, with the four-fold name which falls nothing short of Deity, and the branch from Jesse of chapter 11, with the remarkable factors attending, gear in admirably with our verse here, the key all along being the recurring expression "Immanuel." As we ponder the verse, we cannot but think of Genesis 3:15, the "seed of the *woman,*" and on the other hand, there is the baffling word of Jeremiah (cp.31), "a *woman* shall encompass a man," with its peculiar nouns. And Isaiah's contemporary Micah (5:2), makes his contribution: ". . . she who travaileth hath brought forth," touching the promise of one "whose goings forth have been from of old, from everlasting." Now these expressions comport fittingly with Isaiah 7:14; they may the rather be said to create expectation of something extraordinary in nature here, though of course not necessarily virginity.

It remains of course for Matthew (1:21ff) to clinch the argument, and to settle the matter once and for all in the eyes of those who hold the Bible supernatural. We are left in no doubt that "virgin" is the correct translation. Even the R.S.V. does not alter the N.T. translation! Regarding the word "almah" then, we conclude that language gives naught to forbid understanding *virgin* here. In view of the versions and of tradition, there is strong argument for *virgin.* And when we make examination by analogy of Scripture, proof seems conclusive in favor of *virgin.*

Of the three standard arguments against a Messianic interpretation of this verse under discussion, viz., that it would violate context and exegesis, that it would be no benefit to Ahaz, and that it would show Isaiah mistaken, only the last is of significance. For Ahaz forfeited his sign; and it depends on how one interprets the subsequent context, - it can mean opposites. Regarding the third objection, it seems plain that Isaiah's word is not invalidated even if Messiah came half a millenium later and more. The prophet seems never to have been disappointed. On the other hand, as others have pointed out, chapter 8:16 (the binding up of the testimony), contemplates extended delay. And verses following evidence long night, - moral and spiritual, before the promise is fulfilled. The child of 9:7 and the sprout of Jesse in chapter 11, coinciding each with Immanuel, are to come after the destruction of Assyria.

Micah 5:1ff, inseparable from Isa. 7:14, indicates that the King is still not at hand, a quarter of a century later. And in 701 (Isa. 32-35), the Messiah is still in the future. But nowhere is there expressed any disappointment due to failure of prophesy. And as the years passed, and as the prophet's other predictions were fulfilled and his counsels vindicated, he gained in favor and influence with king and people, - an impossibility, had this great word of 7:14 proved false.

Calvin's limitation of Messiahism to verse 14 seems the easy way out. To hold that the following verses are Messianic and true, creates difficulty; but there we stand, insoluble though the problem may be. Most students think that Isaiah pictures the child's boyhood, - we hold Him to be Messiah - as co-incident with the Assyrian invasion. Read it again, and see that surely there is nothing in the prophesy to mark the date of its fulfilment. Far or near, the point is the preservation of the kingdom, in connection with the coming Immanuel. If indeed there appears confusion in the time element, this text is not greatly different in such respect from a number of others.

Matthew 24 affords quite a bit of difficulty: who can draw the lines? Prophesy is rather moral and spiritual than temporal. Both Old and New Testaments leave much uncertainty touching the time of the Lord's coming. We may say with propriety that more than one of the prophets spoke better than he knew. For the spirit of Christ which was in them, did not always reveal a complete or a clear picture. Certain limitations are of the nature of prophecy: but its great principles are plain. Isaiah's light increases; but the germ of all is in 7:14. And in fact, a lack of clarity in this matter, as elsewhere, rather indicates a Divine, as over against a human, word.

If there be objection on the score that the prophet seems to describe certain events as taking place under the Assyrian domination, whereas the Saviour lived under Roman rule, let it be recalled that here again the Scripture is peculiar. For in its pages, Assyria seems to be the name for all succeeding world powers, taking rise from it. Ezra, for instance (6:22) speaks of the Persian king as the "king of Assyria." And in II Kings 23:29, the expression "king of Assyria" is employed as though a customary designation for Babylon's sovereign. In Isaiah's vision, Assyria is *the* world power. Our Lord in truth was born under a universal empire whose name at that time was Rome, conditions being similar to those of Ahaz' time. Prophecy may thus be "foreshortened." But whatever the explanation, or lack of valid explanation, the important matter in this is that God will never allow His purposes to fail. Ahaz is without faith: but the covenant Jehovah will raise up in miraculous manner a supernatural seed to David. This is Isaiah 7:14.

In the light of all this detail, we must conclude that whereas the people were thinking about their present situation, God was contemplating the future; the crowd had in mind a physical leader, but God envisioned a spiritual deliverer; they were expecting a human champion, but God would send a Divine Sovereign; they had hopes for deliverance from Syria and Ephraim and Assyria, but God was looking to the deliverance of His people from sin! We hold then that Isaiah was speaking prophetically, that his great word of this verse related to the far future, and that, however limited and mysterious the general nature of the words were to him, - and still are to us, the Spirit of God, speaking through him, contemplated the Virgin-born Messiah, Whom the writer Matthew confirms, and Whom without question we accept, (a vital component of our Faith): The Lord Jesus Christ of Bethlehem, Judea, Son of Man, Son of Mary, Son of God. R.F.G.

The Resurrection of Christ

By Rev. Floyd E. Hamilton
Centreville, Ala.

"If Christ hath not been raised, your faith is vain; ye are yet in your sins." I Cor. 15:17.

Perhaps it might seem that the subject of the Resurrection of Christ should only be discussed at Easter time, but every Sunday we really celebrate the resurrection of Christ, and this theme is so important to our eternal welfare that it is never out of place. None of the points of difference between Evangelicals and Modernists can be considered unimportant, but as we see from the verse quoted from Paul, this doctrine is at the very basis of our faith. Our attitude toward the inspiration of the Bible is of course basic, for it will determine whether we believe the Bible or trust our own feelings about what the Bible says. The view we take of man will determine whether we think man needs saving or not. It is vitally important for us to know that there is only one way of salvation, belief in Christ.

We can have no living faith in Christ that is worth while unless we believe in His true deity, and our belief in the Virgin Birth of Christ is really the touchstone of our belief in His deity. But Paul tells us that if Christ has not risen from the dead, we are still in our sins and resting under the eternal condemnation of those sins.

Now the reason for this stress on the doctrine of the bodily resurrection of Christ is because it carries with it God's stamp of approval on all that Jesus Christ said and did. Imagine, for a moment, that Christ never rose from the dead. Humanly speaking the Christian Church would not have gotten started. The attitude of the disciples was that of the two disciples on the road to Emmaus: "We had hoped that it was he who would redeem Israel," but He is dead. The other disciples were hiding in the upper room in Jerusalem. Their hearts were filled with sorrow and discouragement. Thomas had gone away from them in complete disillusionment. A few days later Peter and others went back to their nets on Lake Galilee. A few of his disciples would doubtless have stuck around Jerusalem for a time, but without the belief in his resurrection they would never have become enthusiastic preachers of salvation through belief in Jesus Christ alone. Like so many other historical movements, the Christian movement would have died a-borning if Christ had not risen from the dead, and their leader had stayed dead like other great men. Christianity did not rest primarily on the truth or falsity of certain ideas; it rested on the occurrence or non-occurrence of the events surrounding the life of Jesus of Nazareth, and all the other events in his life would have been relatively unimportant if he had not proved that his message of redemption was true by rising from the dead.

The Modernists, therefore, in attacking the doctrine of the bodily resurrection of Christ are really attacking the main trunk of the tree of the Christian religion. Perhaps the most subtle of the Modernist attacks on the resurrection of Christ is to say that they believe in the spiritual resurrection of Christ rather than his physical resurrection. They like to say that what is important about Christ's resurrection is not the question of whether or not Christ's body is or is not in some Palestinian tomb, but whether he is alive today, and in one sense of course they are right. Every true Christian thrills at the song,

"I serve a risen Saviour,
He's in the world today;
I know that He is living,
Whatever men may say;
I see His hand of mercy,
I hear His voice of cheer,
And just the time I need Him
He's always near.

He lives, He lives, Christ Jesus lives today!
He walks with me, and talks with me
along life's narrow way.
He lives, He lives, salvation to impart!
You ask me how I know He lives?
He lives within my heart."

It *is* true that He lives within our hearts! It *is* true that we know He is living today! All that is perfectly true and inspiring to every Christian. But that truth rests ultimately on the conviction that Jesus came out of the tomb alive, so that the tomb was empty after his resurrection.

When the Modernist says that he believes in the spiritual resurrection of Jesus Christ, he means that while the body of Jesus did not rise from the dead, his spirit was alive and lives today. If that were all that there was to the resurrection of Christ, it would be no different from what happens to souls of all believers when they die. Their souls are spiritually alive. That is, they are living today with Christ in glory. To say that they believe in the spiritual resurrection of Christ when at the same time they say that the body of Jesus remained in the tomb or was carried elsewhere, is just to deny that Jesus really rose from the dead and to assert that he was just like other dead people, whose bodies are still in the grave while their souls are with their Maker.

Now it is perfectly true that Jesus Christ rose in a spiritual body. That is, Christ's body *became* a spiritual body, so that there was nothing left in the tomb after he arose. He arose in the self-same body from the tomb, but in the rising that body was changed to a spiritual body which could pass through doors that were shut, could rise into the clouds and which could appear and disappear at will. Yet that same body had flesh and bones. It could eat with the disciples. They could handle Him and put their fingers into the print of the nails in His hands and could put their hands into the spear hole in His side. It was the same body that suffered on the cross, and yet it was a changed body, a glorified body. That body does not need food and drink in order to stay alive. We are told that we shall all be changed at the last trump and receive bodies that are like the glorious body of our Lord. But when we so assert that Christ had and has a spiritual body, we do not at all mean that the physical material body of Jesus still remains in Palestine. Yet that is what the Modernists claim when they say they believe in the spiritual resurrection of Jesus but deny his bodily resurrection.

It is easy to see why they deny the bodily resurrection of Jesus. The bodily resurrection would imply that Jesus Christ was truly what he claimed to be, the Son of God and our Substitutionary Saviour. Only a supernatural Jesus could come out of the tomb after he was dead for three days, and the Modernist asserts that Jesus was only a man, even if he was the best man that ever lived. They must, therefore, deny the true bodily resurrection of Jesus, not because the evidence for the resurrection is weak, but because their premises will not allow the supernatural to be genuine.

The evidence for the resurrection of Jesus is stronger than the evidence for any other event in history. The Jews were afraid he would rise from the dead, so they arranged to prevent deception by sending guards to watch the tomb. The disciples all disbelieved in his resurrection at first and were only convinced by his repeated appearances to them. They did not even believe the testimony of one another at first. Peter and John doubted the testimony of the women. Thomas doubted the testimony of the other ten disciples that they had seen the risen Lord. The disciples on the road to Emmaus did not believe that the story of the resurrection told by the women was true. There was no attitude of expectancy on the part of the disciples which might make it easy for them to be deceived about the reality of the resurrection. Moreover there was no doubt in any one's mind that the tomb of Jesus was empty. The disciples knew that none of them had stolen the body and of course they had no motive for stealing it even if they had had an opportunity. The enemies of Jesus not only had no motive for causing the body of Jesus to disappear, but they would have moved heaven and earth to have been able to produce the dead body of Jesus and so refute the story of his resurrection. The body was simply not in the tomb or elsewhere. Then we must remember that from that time on, one after another of the disciples gave his life in attestation of the truth of his assertion that Jesus Christ had risen from the dead. People do not give their lives for what they know to be false. It was the belief in the resurrection that turned them from cowards into lions of bravery, and started the Christian Church. Praise God our faith in Jesus Christ rests on the warm facts of history and experience. He does live in our hearts today. Does he live in your heart?

Women As Elders

By Rev. Thomas L. Casey

Ours is a Presbyterian Church. That means that we believe that church government in all its fundamentals must be strictly in accord with the Word of God. Episcopalians know that their form of church government is not so much derived from Scripture as from expediency. Roman Catholics realize that you cannot find sanction for their church government from the Scriptures alone, but you must go to "tradition" also. Most Independents believe they derive their church polity from Scripture, but in reality they deny it by "getting together" in conventions, associations and the like.

We alone, of all other historical forms of rule in the church, actually have a polity which conforms to Scripture in all its several basic principles. Now this is our glory. Certainly we rejoice in the possession of the Reformed Faith so ably set forth in our confession and catechisms. We exult in the Calvinistic convictions which we have come by through the Grace of God. Yet, these great affirmations of

compare with standard versions. "I will, therefore, that men be praying in every place, lifting up holy hands without wrath and disputings; likewise also (I will that) women in modest adornment with shamefacedness and sound judgment be adorning themselves, not with plaitings and gold or pearls or expensive garments, but rather (with that which is proper for women professing godliness) by means of good works. Let a woman be learning in quietness in all subjection. But for a woman to be teaching, I do not permit, neither to be exercising authority over the man, but rather to be in quietness. For Adam was first formed, then Eve; and Adam was not deceived, but the woman having been deceived, was in transgression; but she shall be saved through childbearing if she abide in faith and love and holiness with sound judgment."

1. The "therefore" of verse 8 refers to the redemption purchased by Christ. Because of Christ's redeeming work, men are to pray everywhere, women to adorn themselves soberly.

2. Notice that the entire passage is concerned with a contrast dealing with the respective duties of men as over against women, and vice versa. V.8 "I will that the men (Greek *Tous Andras*) pray everywhere;" V.9 "Likewise also the women." Duties proper to each sex are being considered, the relationship of the sexes in these duties, the relative stations of the sexes in relation to each other. The man is to pray in the official assemblies of the churches (lifting up holy hands) he is to take the leadership in the conduct of Divine Worship. His prayers are to be characterized by the absence of worldly lusts.

As for the woman, she also, as well as the man, while not leading the worship services of the church, is to imitate the godly men in her own peculiar way—in the way of outward adornment and good works. Now as for her being able to "lift up holy hands," or to lead the worship services of the church in the ministry of the Preached Word, the woman is not to do so. Neither is she to exercise authority or "lord it over" the man. It is *his* place to exercise authority. For the woman to try to do so would be, as the King James Version translates it, to "usurp authority" over the man. Rather, as has been stated, she should be "in silence."

Now, so far as this relation of the one sex to the other is concerned with respect to teaching and ruling, the reason for maintaining that the man must rule and the woman be "in silence" is two-fold. First, because of the order of creation, "Adam was created first, then Eve." Secondly, because Eve was the first to be in the transgression - fell prey to the tempter's allurements.

Does this mean, however, that the woman is "inferior" to the man? That she is less likely to be saved than he? Not at all. By serving God in her own peculiar way (here childbearing) as man is to serve in his, she shall be saved. Now this serves merely as a directive to our thoughts. It simply indicates the line of the apostle's thought by pointing up the way in which he compares and contrasts throughout the passage the man's duties and those of the woman. Paul recognizes an inherent difference between the sexes which reflects itself in the sphere of religious duty and authority. Just as the woman is to practice godliness through the way she dresses, so she is not to teach or exercise authority in the church. Just as the man is to pray in public without unholy affections so he is to bear the rule in the church. However, the interesting thing is that Paul gives man the authority here negatively - i.e., by *restricting* the woman from such rule. Thus it would appear that if the man is to properly bear the authority in the church, the woman must not be allowed to do so. That would conflict with his prerogatives.

3. Now to vv.11-12.

"But for a woman to be teaching, I do not permit, neither to be exercising authority over the man, but to be in quietness. For Adam was first formed, then Eve; and Adam was not deceived, but the woman having been deceived was in transgression."

(a) "for a woman to be teaching I do not permit." Now just what is meant by "teaching" here? Is Paul saying that the woman may not even teach her own children, or that she may not teach a group of children in a Sunday School or in other ways admonish and edify the church? No, of course not. Paul commends Lois and Eunice for their instruction of Timothy, and who would dare to say the apostle would condemn Priscilla for teaching Apollos the way in Christ more perfectly?

Of course the "teaching" must not be an all inclusive thing. To what then does the teaching prohibition refer? Why,. the only reference could be to *official* ministration of the Word in the official assemblies of the saints, where the Word was preached, the Sacraments served, and discipline administered. If the prohibition is at all meaningful, is to make any sense at all and is not to be conceived of as countering Scripture elsewhere where women exercise the prophetic gifts and teach privately, then it must refer to the formal preaching or teaching of the Word in the solemn assemblies.

This interpretation is obviously agreeable to I Cor. 11:3 "Let your women keep silence *in the churches* . . . for it is not permitted to them to speak; . . . " The same Greek word is read here (*epitrepo*) as in I Tim. 2:11 for "permit."

how strongly put the alternative to teaching and exercising authority is! "To be in silence." Could anything the apostle might have said be any more eloquent of the woman's position with respect to the preaching of the Word and the exercise of ecclesiastical power than this?

The Reasons for this restriction.

What reasons does Paul give for such a prohibition? As serious as it is, there must be a very good reason for it. There is. Not upon circumstances prevailing at the time of writing does Paul base his directive to Timothy. Not upon a temporary situation existing because of the attitude of men towards women. Not at all. Now we come to the very *crux* of the matter. Why this prohibition? Could anything be plainer than the fact that this commandment is based upon a timeless principle? That it is intended to remain in effect for all time because it finds its basis in a past reality which can never be altered or set aside? "For Adam was first formed then Eve; and Adam was not deceived, but the woman, being deceived, was in the transgression." This injunction has its explanation in *Creation* and the *Fall;* the priority of Adam's *creation,* and the priority of the woman's *defection.*

Now whether or not we believe the Bible to be the infallible word of God cannot change the plain and obvious meaning of the passage. We may not wish to submit to it as the ultimate authority. We may insist inanely that it has been misinterpreted. But the plain and obvious meaning of the passage stands. Paul is insisting that the woman cannot hold ecclesiastical offices not because of some temporary social situation, but because of Adam's prior creation and of her prior defection.

Now if that does not make the rule laid down by Paul here relevant and authoritative for all time it would be impossible for him to so make it. The passage teaches that women are not to be ordained in the church. We must remark briefly that no matter how we may insist upon the restriction of I Cor. 14:34-35 being temporary and occasioned by the attitude of men towards women, it is not so conditioned. Why is a woman according to that passage to be silent, under obedience? Because of the *law!* "As also saith the law." An obvious reference to the creation order of I Tim. 2:11.

Let me state also that the use of Galatians 3:28 "There is neither Jew nor Greek, there is neither bond nor free, there is neither male nor female: for ye are all one in Christ Jesus" in support of women Elders and Deacons is quite pointless. Let us be careful that we do not *prove too much* with this passage. Does Paul mean that Christians are not men or women? A sort of neuter sex? That the distinction between Jew and Greek Christians is completely obliterated? They no longer are members of their respective races? There is no such thing as a Hebrew Christian or a Gentile Christian? Does it mean that we who are believers are no longer distinct individuals? "Ye are all one in Christ Jesus." That would be ridiculous. Yet, that is the only logical conclusion to be derived from the use of this Scripture to permit women Elers and Deacons.

This passage deals with salvation. Redemption through Christ here is shown to place all believers on an equal footing so far as their relation to God by faith in Christ is concerned. Paul is not here dealing with the subject of church authority or the particular order in the church. He is refuting the Judaistic heresy of salvation by works — the necessity of becoming a Jew to be saved. He deals with church order in I Timothy and I Corinthians where the passages already treated are found. It is the genius of Barthianism and liberalism to ignore distinctions: to mix their theology all up so that passages actually bearing no direct relevance to a question are cited and those being relevant are overlooked. A deception is thus foisted upon the unwary soul, and confusion results to the detriment of God's Church.

We are faced with these questions.

Shall we obey God's Word and retain our integrity in the matter of Elders and Deacons, or shall we ignore God's voice calling to us in the words of Holy Scripture and thus forfeit the right to be called Presbyterian? Which shall it be? Remember, that if we ordain women Elders and Deacons there will be sitting in authority in our church courts those who have no right to sit there. No sense in arguing that we don't have to ordain women in our local congregations — they will sit in Presbytery, Synod, and General Assembly. Listen to our Book of Church Order, Par. 19: "The exercise of ecclesiastical power, whether joint or several, has the divine sanction, when in conformity with the statutes enacted by Christ, the Lawgiver, and when put forth by courts or by officers appointed thereunto in His Word."

According to this statement, a decision rendered or an action taken by a church court although valid in itself, would be *"Without Divine Sanction"* if anyone debated or voted in that court "not appointed thereunto in His Word."

An action of Session is out of order if a Deacon votes with the Elders. An action of the Diaconate would be out of order if an ordinary member voted on the board. Such individuals are not "appointed thereunto in His Word." They do not have the *right* to exercise ecclesiastical authority. They have not been ordained and installed after the Scriptural pattern.

A woman according to Scripture cannot be ordained. Therefore if she is ordained and sits in the courts of the church, she sits as one not "appointed thereunto in His Word." The action of the court would be, therefore, out of order according to Par. 19, Book of Church Order and "Without Divine Sanction." No amount of amending the constitution by assemblies and Presbyteries could alter that fact.

Therefore any action of any court throughout our denomination would be out of order if a woman sat as an Elder in that Court. No longer could proper ecclesiastical authority be exercised. Our entire system of ecclesiastical polity would be thrown out of gear. Can you imagine what such a catastrophe as this would mean? To say the least, every Presbyter and Deacon who believes that woman should not be ordained would be grievously compromised. Every Presbyter believing in Presbyterian form of Church government as set forth in the Holy Scriptures and in our confession and Book of Church Order would be pitifully embarrassed. I would plead with those who take an opposite viewpoint to consider what the adoption of this amendment would mean to those of us who hold the Book of Church Order as it now stands in this matter to be truly Scriptural. If this amendment is voted through, then I testify to you all, my brethren, with all the earnestness at my command, that *"Icabod,"* "the glory hath departed," will be inscribed over the door of every church in our denomination. We may still be a true church: but we certainly are no longer Presbyterian.

ANGLERS

By WADE C. SMITH

Lesson No. 157

Three Grades of Personal Work

In order to encourage timid members to volunteer, the term "Personal Work" may be classified in three grades which would be called A, B and C. Beginning at the lowest, grade C, to show that any one can do at least this form of Personal Work, it is described as simply going to see a prospect and *personally* inducing him to come to the church service — or at least *endeavoring* to induce him. That does not mean merely a casual invitation, but a genuine effort to get him there.

It may involve the offer to call by in one's automobile, or to get someone else to call. It is a bona fide personal effort to get one under the preaching of the gospel. Anybody who is in earnest can do this. Yet it is a very important service, and the kind that is sorely needed to be done. But wait a minute: the most important thing you will do is to Pray before you go. Ask the Holy Spirit to enable you to persuade your prospect to come to the service; and when he comes, that something in the service will serve to bring him under conviction, causing him to confess sin and accept Jesus Christ as his Saviour. Any Christian can make that prayer; at once the effort is lifted into the supernatural, and supernatural results can be expected. When the prospect appears at the service, make sure that he is recognized and made welcome — but don't overdo it. Make it more or less casual, but definitely sincere. Now this is grade C, the lowest of the three, and on the level of the most unskilled and untrained worker, but fraught with limitless possibilities. One thing is almost certain: if undertaken as above directed, it will lead right up to grade A. Nothing less will satisfy.

Now grade B. This is concerned with detached church members living in your community. It is a ripe field for reaping. People moving in are so much absorbed with new adjustments, in business, school, housekeeping, new social environment and everything except their church affiliation that they grow spiritually indifferent. They may have been active members of the church in the community they left, but they are slow to connect in the new situation. They may have various reasons for this, but it is the business of the B personal worker to "rope them in." This of course requires tact, but above all things, Prayer. Pray before you go to see them. Ask the Holy Spirit to make your visit so attractive that when you leave they will be saying, "Well I believe I would enjoy being in a church where that person is a member." Some of these movers-in church members may never have been born again; have only been nominal Christians up to this time. Your prayer will include the petition to make their coming into this new church relationship the occasion for saving their souls. That lifts the effort into the supernatural; supernatural results can be expected. Some people, good church members (?) moving into a new home wait to be invited to transfer their membership. It would be too bad to allow them to grow cold.

If the newcomers, for sentimental reasons, dislike to write a request to their former pastor for their church letter (and there are some like this) ask them for authority for your pastor to write for it. Many letters of transfer have been secured in this way. It is really better to get it in writing. That prevents any misunderstanding and makes sure about the spelling of the names. Typewritten slips with these words would serve the purpose for such cases:

Desiring to transfer my membership from the Blank church of Blank, to the Blank church at Blank, I hereby authorize application for a letter of dismissal.

(Signed) ______________________

Date ______________

Reclaiming a "lapsing church-member" may be just as important as bringing in a new member.

(Grade A — the highest type of Personal Work will be treated in next lesson.)

Helps To Understanding Scripture Readings in *Day by Day*

By Rev. C. C. Baker

Sunday, September 30, *I Corinthians* 15:53-58. The hope of the resurrection should occupy a very important spot in the Christian's heart (Philippians 3:20,21). How does the illustration Paul uses in vv.36-37 help explain the relation of the resurrected body to our present bodies? The resurrected body will have much the same form - so we will be able to recognize each other - but it will differ in substance. List the various ways mentioned in vv.42-50,51-53 in which our new bodies will differ from our present bodies. Will there be any pain or decay connected with our new bodies? Will we have any need for hospitals or old age homes? The hope of the resurrection is certain because Christ has risen (v.20) and therefore victory over death is already ours (vv.54-56). What specifically does the hope of the resurrection mean to you? What effect should this hope have upon your daily activity (v.58)?

Monday, October 1, *I Corinthians* 11:23-36. Observe the debauchery that characterized the communion services of the Corinthian Christians (vv.20-21). In vv.23-26, how does Paul bring out the importance of the Lord's Supper? Who instituted it? What is its purpose? How central is the Christian message in the event the Lord's Supper brings to mind? What happens to the force of the Christian message if the cross is omitted? What warning does Paul give his readers in vv.27-28? What should a person look for in examining himself in preparation for Communion (v.28)? How should the message of the cross guide one's self-examination? Do you honestly search yourself in the light of the cross before partaking of the Lord's Supper?

Tuesday, October 2, *Isaiah* 53:7-11. Isaiah 53 describes the suffering and death of Christ in considerable detail. Can you find new insights into the ways in which we are to be like Christ in His death (Mark 8:34) from this passage? Are you willing to give yourself for others (vv.5-6) if, in so doing, you must become distasteful or repulsive to those you are trying to serve (vv.2-3)? Are you willing to give yourself for others (vv.5-6) if they have no appreciation of your efforts or intentions (v.4)? Are you willing to give yourself for others (vv.5-6) if, in so doing, you must suffer quietly for wrongs that are not yours (vv.7-9)? Are you willing to give yourself for others (vv.5-6) if, in so doing, you must endure physical pain or death (vv.9-10)? What motivation for a life and death of self-sacrifice did Christ have according to vv.11-12? Do you have the satisfaction of knowing that your life is producing eternal results (vv.11-12)?

Wednesday, October 3, *John* 16:25-33. Jesus has been speaking to his disciples about His departure from earth (vv.20-23), but the disciples have not been able to understand His meaning (13:36; 16:17-18). Acknowledging that He had been speaking in figures because the disciples have not been ready for a fuller revelation (vv.12-13), Jesus says they will understand later on (v.25). What new insight did the disciples receive (vv.29-30) through Jesus' plain statement of v.28? With this new insight, how must the statement of v.32 have puzzled them? How would v.33 be an encouragement? Though the disciples received new insights, did they, at this point, understand all Jesus was talking about? Though you cannot as yet understand everything about the Christian faith, are you willing to accept those doctrines that are beyond your comprehension if they are taught in Scripture?

Thursday, October 4, *II Corinthians* 5:14-19. The Gospel message produces certain definite effects in the lives of those who receive it. What is it in the message of our Gospel that especially reveals the love of God (v.21)? What effect does the message have in the hearts of those who receive it (v.17)? How should it affect the new Christian's outlook on the world (vv.18b,19b)? It is the love of Christ within him (v.4) that compels the Christian to share the Gospel with other men (v.20). Do you have the compelling urge to share with others the faith you have? How does this message affect the Christian's view of his purpose in life (vv.9,15)? his attitude toward the afflictions of this life (4:16-18)? his attitude toward the future life (vv.1-8)? Has the Christian message altered your basic attitudes toward life?

Friday, October 5, *Romans* 6:8-11. When a person accepts Christ as His Saviour, he identifies himself with the death and resurrection of Christ. In the cross the death grip of the old self upon the soul has been completely broken (vv.6,7); the Christian now has the power to rise in newness of life in the living, resurrected Christ (vv.4,5). Paul, therefore, exhorts the Roman Christians to yield no longer to temptation and the lusts of the flesh (vv.12-13), but to reckon themselves as dead to sin (v.11). He encourages them to yield themselves to the Lord (v.13) as those to whom God has given a brand new life in Christ (vv.11,13). Do you persist in dabbling in sin even though the Lord Jesus has implanted a new life in your soul? Are you willing to consider yourself as dead to the old nature and your life as completely wrapped up in Jesus Christ?

Saturday, October 6, *Romans* 8:9-11. The Old Testament Law was not adequate to save (v.3) but simply made a person aware of his sin and of the consequences of his sin (v.2). What is the status before God of a person who is in Christ (v.1)? What did Christ do that the Law could not do (vv.3-4)? If a person is in Christ, God has imparted to him His Holy Spirit (v.9). The Christian, though he may stumble many times, has as his deepest aim the desire to do right (v.10) and to please the Spirit of God (v.5). What are the consequences in the life of the person who sets his mind to live for Christ (vv.6b,10b,11b)? in the life of the person who determines to live in sin (vv.6a, 7-8)? Does the Spirit give witness in your life that you are a child of God? Is it your deepest desire to live your life after the Spirit?

SABBATH SCHOOL LESSONS — REV. J. KENTON PARKER

LESSON FOR SEPTEMBER 30.

The Great Invitation

Background Scripture: Mark 10:13-16; Revelation 3:20; 21:1 - 22:21
Devotional Reading: Isaiah 55

Isaiah 55 is a great Invitation Chapter. The Old Testament prophet is urgently and lovingly inviting us to the Banqueting House of Jehovah. It is an invitation to a Feast of good things which will make the soul delight itself in fatness. It is an invitation to a Fellowship which is guaranteed by an everlasting covenant, even the sure mercies of David. It is an invitation and command to forsake sin and seek by real repentance, and obtain full and abundant pardon for all our sins. It is an invitation to a Refreshing from on high which will fill our hearts with peace and joy.

The Bible is full of these invitations, many of them beginning with the word "Come." His invitation — the invitation of the King — is also a command. He has the right to issue these commands and invitations, for He created us, cares for us, and has redeemed us. Our Topic for today, "The Great Invitation," is summed up in this word, "come," so often repeated in Revelation 22:17.

I. *An Invitation to the Children:* Mark 10:13-16.

"Suffer the little children to come unto me." These beautiful words from the lips of our Saviour have brought a blessing into the hearts of parents and children all down through the centuries. The attitude of the disciples greatly displeased Jesus; He was "moved with indigna-

Remember this entire "family" of educational divisions with a generous Rally Day Gift.

on." He warned them that, Whosoever shall ot receive the kingdom of God as a little child, e shall not enter therein.

Most grown folk seem to have an idea that ıey can save themselves. A little child will t you do all the saving. Are we willing to :st upon Him alone for salvation as He is of- :red to us in the gospels, or are we trying to ıve ourselves? so that, perchance, we can have ımething to boast about? When we are ready ı come as a little child, then we will be welcomed, even as Jesus received the children who came to Him

II. *An Invitation to a Church:* Revelation 3:20.

This is a part of the letter to the church at Laodicea, a lukewarm, self-satisfied church which thought it had need of nothing, but in reality was poor and wretched and blind. After commanding it to repent, Jesus gives them this well-known invitation. It is often used as an invitation to the sinner to repent and let Jesus come into his heart, but we must not forget that it was, when first given, as we see the context, an invitation to a lukewarm church to let the Head of the church come in. It is entirely possible for the church as a whole, or some particular church, to find itself in this sad condition. This could be true of a poor church as well as a rich one, but we can easily see that the temptation would be stronger in a church like the one at Laodicea, rich and prosperous.

"I will sup with him and he with me." He is willing to "sup with us"; even as He came into the homes of people like Mary and Martha. He will eat and drink what we set before Him. If we will sit at His feet, as Mary did, we will partake of all that He has for us; far better food than we can prepare for Him. This is a beautiful picture of the sweet fellowship we enjoy when we invite Him into our midst, or answer His invitation to us.

This invitation can be applied also to the unsaved man; the man outside the church. He is keeping Christ out, and should open the door and let Him come in. For the unsaved, and for the lukewarm church member the vital question is, as the boy said to his father when they were looking at the famous picture of Christ knocking at the door; "Father, did He get in?" Let us be sure that we are not keeping Him standing outside the fast-closed door. Let Him in!

III. *Invitation to ALL:* Revelation 21:1 - 22:21.

"The Great Invitation" is verse 17 of chapter 22, our Golden Text. Before we take up this, let us look at some of the glorious things revealed in these two last chapters of the Bible. Revelation relates "The Trials and Triumphs of the Kingdom of God." In these two chapters we have the Consummation, or final glorious Triumph of God's Kingdom. Paradise was lost in Genesis; it is regained in Revelation.

"A new heaven and a new earth." God had made everything good and beautiful when He created the heavens and the earth "in the beginning." Satan and sin came to spoil the picture. The Bible gives us the inspired account of God's Plan of Salvation for a lost and ruined world. The plan required the making of all things new; new people, and a new place for them to dwell. In these chapters we have a very striking symbolic picture of this "new place."

It is described as a holy city, new Jerusalem, coming down from God out of heaven, prepared as a bride adorned for her husband. We have all felt the thrill of seeing a lovely bride, dressed in her bridal attire, as she slowly walks down the aisle of the church. All eyes turn to watch her. The time for the marriage of Christ and His Bride, the Church, has now come. God is going to live with His people and wipe away all tears from their eyes. All sin will be excluded from that city; the only city to have no sin. He now proceeds to describe the "City Foursquare" in terms of the most beautiful and most precious things in the world, gold, and silver, and many precious stones. The city will need no light of sun or moon, for the Lamb is the light thereof. The saved people of all nations shall be in that city, while all abominations will be shut out. Again, the symbolism is changed into that of a great river - the river of life - a vision similar to that seen by Ezekiel in chapter 47.

The "River of Salvation," or "River of Life," is for the healing of the nations. Sin has made the world sick, sick unto death, but now His "Saving Health" has overflowed the world, and healed its diseases. Blessed are they who have washed their robes, and have a right to the tree of life and can enter in through the gates into the city. At last God's redeemed people shall enter into that state described in our Catechism as "the full enjoying of God to all eternity."

In reading this marvelous description of our future Home let us remember that no symbol can be as wonderful as the thing symbolized. Eye hath not seen nor ear heard, neither hath it entered the heart of man, but God has revealed some of it to us. Then the "Welcome Home" sign is hung up for all to see and read and hear, "The Great Invitation"; one of the most glorious and comprehensive verses in the Bible: "And the Spirit and the bride say, Come. And let him that heareth say, Come. And let him that is athirst come. And whosoever will, let him take the water of life freely."

As I read these words and the context, especially verses 12 and 20, I am convinced that this is a two-fold, or two-sided, invitation. The Church, the Bride, is crying out to the Head of the Church to come back quickly and bring about the blessed state described here. Then there is the invitation on the part of the Spirit and the bride, and all who hear, and all who are thirsty, and all who will, to come.

I believe that the Church has forgotten at times that her King is coming back. Certainly there has been little said about His return. We rest satisfied to live without Him. We have no longing for the Wedding Day. I wonder sometimes if the church would welcome Him. This is a pitiful and perilous condition, described by Jesus in one of His parables; They will say, My lord delayeth his coming, and begin to mistreat their fellow servants, and live carelessly. We should all be longing for His return. I am glad our Confession of Faith closes as the Bible does, Even so, come Lord Jesus, come quickly. Amen.

I read of a wife whose husband had to go to a distant land on business. He sent her beautiful presents from different places. One day, while she was looking at his gifts, she raised her eyes, and her husband stood in the door. She brushed the gifts aside and with a glad cry rushed to clasp him in her arms. Will we feel that way? His gifts are wonderful; It is He himself we long to see!

Now let us come to the usual interpretation of this verse, and it cannot be stressed too much. We are living in the time of the Spirit's manifestation; and the Spirit is saying, COME. The Holy Spirit is wooing and welcoming sinners to Come and be saved. The Holy Spirit says, TODAY; if ye will hear His voice, harden not your hearts. The Bride, the Church, is saying, Come. If the Church is true to her mission she is going out into the highways and hedges and compelling them to come in. She is beseeching men to be reconciled to God. Those who hear the word are commissioned to invite others to Come. Whoever is thirsty, whether they have heard or not, are invited to the feast. It is the same invitation which Isaiah gave. Then, Whosoever will, let him take the water of life freely. Could there be a more inclusive or more loving invitation than this. Only a man inspired with the Spirit could write such an invitation.

I cannot close without pressing this invitation. Perhaps one unsaved person may read this. If so, I urge you to say YES to "The Great Invitation." Read it again. No one is left out. The door to heaven is open wide, and the words, Come, Welcome Home, are written above the door. Come, Sinner, Come!

YOUNG PEOPLE'S DEPARTMENT — REV. B. HOYT EVANS

YOUTH PROGRAM FOR SEPTEMBER 30.

Time In - For Fun

Suggested Devotional Outline:
Hymn: "Jesus, Thou Joy Of Loving Hearts"
Prayer
Scripture: I Corinthians 13
Hymn: "All The Way My Saviour Leads Me"
Offering
Hymn: "For The Beauty Of The Earth"

Suggestions for Program Leader:

(For the month of August the Men of the Church and the Women of the Church were scheduled to have a joint meeting. The recommended theme for the joint program was"Family Use Of Leisure Time." You might contact some of the men and women of your church, asking them to come to your meeting to share with you their findings and to lead you in a discussion of family fun. Since this is a program of family life, it would seem very appropriate to have representatives of your church families to have a part in presenting it. If you do invite guests to lead your meeting, their discussion will naturally take the place of what is printed below.)

When we say "Time in - for fun," we are referring to fun as a family. In this age of independence and specialization, when every person is expected to live his own life, many people are coming to the conclusion that family life is suffering. All of us are interested in having fun, but are we independent in this respect too? Do we ever think of having fun as a family? A great many young people have indicated that they wish their families would do more things together than they do. What do you think about it?

That there are some very important values to be received from having fun in the family circle is not hard to demonstrate. It is possible to carry our ideas of independence too far. There are times when we need very desperately the security, love, and shelter of our families, and family recreation is a great help in binding the members of the family closer together. It is not too much to say that the happiest and most wholesome people are those who have had a closely knit family life.

We need to recognize that family fun is something which does not "just happen." If we are to have it and enjoy it, we must work for it. It is quite possible that there are several people even in our group who would like to do more about having fun with their families, if they just knew how to go about it. The purpose of this program is to make some practical suggestions about planning for fun with the family.

First Speaker:

One of the most perplexing problems about having family fun is finding time for it. The larger the family, the more things there are for each member to do, and the less time there is to spend together as a family. There is no such thing as spare time. If we intend to have a time for fun as a family, we shall have to take the time . . . take it from something else that is not so important.

Surely the best way for a family to decide on a time for their recreation is for all the members to come together with suggestions of the best probable times. Let them choose the time which is most convenient for all concerned, and then let all agree to cooperate by keeping this time free of other engagements. Even if it is only a short time each week, let it be dedicated wholly to the family.

Second Speaker:

Another problem with regard to family fun is the matter of what to do. The average family is made up of people of widely varying ages and interests. Are there any activities that all can truly enjoy doing together? Many families have found that there are. One way of facing this problem is to ask each member of the family to suggest activities interesting to him which he believes would also be interesting to the others. When these lists are pooled, they are bound to bring up at least some likely possibilities for family fun.

As families consider this question of what they shall do together, they ought to bear in mind the value of learning to do and to enjoy new activities. In this respect, having fun as a family presents an opportunity to overcome selfishness and to broaden our own interests and to enrich our lives. (Ask your young people to suggest activities in which families can engage together, and list their suggestions on a blackboard or a large sheet of paper.)

Third Speaker:

Probably the most pressing question on the whole subject is that of how to begin. If your family is not doing much about having fun together, the first thing for you to do is to make up your mind to make a beginning today. Go home this very day and propose to your parents and the other members of your family that you talk together about this matter of taking time for fun. If it is not satisfactory to have the discussion today, then set a time when all members of the family can be present. When that time comes, you can follow the suggestions which the other speakers have made concerning the choosing of a family hour and the activities which are most likely to appeal to your family.

Program Leader:

As important as it is for a family to have fun together, there is something which is still more important. The most essential practice for your families is that they join together to worship God. Members of Christian families are bound together by two kinds of ties. We must recognize them both. We are bound by ties of blood kinship. We recognize those ties when we have fun together. We are also bound together in our mutual relation to God through faith in Christ. When we worship as a family, both at home and in the church, we are recognizing our physical relation and our spiritual relation.

Women's Work

A Moment With the Master

When the Day is Dark and Uncertain

The little dog was very brave as he ran hither and yon ahead of his mistress, deaf to any appeal from her to come back to her protective side. With canine defiance of authority, he rounded the corner out of sight where he met the "big dog." Face to face with real trouble he returned in perfect trust to obey his mistress.

Each one of us at some time is sure to meet the "big dog" trouble. And, so whether my trouble is physical or mental, real or imaginary, due to circumstance or persons, concerning myself or another; like the little dog, I seek my Master's presence where I find protection and guidance.

I go to my room — a quiet place alone, yet not alone, for Jesus is there. With my Bible and a favorite devotional book, I consciously and deliberately relax and read, partly from memory, verses from the Bible which bring quietness and peace to my soul:

"Fear thou not for I am with thee . . . "
"Be still and know that I am God . . . "
"In nothing be anxious; but in everything by prayer and supplication, with thanksgiving let your requests be made known unto God . . . "

I confess my sins saying with Job, *Cause me to know wherein I have erred.* Believing that God will not hear my prayer if I regard iniquity in my heart, I try to make a complete confession, praying for God's help in remembering.

I count my blessings, making a list of everything I can think of. Time and again peace and calm have come before this list is finished.

I lay the problem before the Lord, often writing out every detail of it, affirming that He *is able to do exceeding abundantly above all that we ask or think,* and with God *all things are possible.* I talk this over with God and ask Him to solve it for me, that is, tell me what to do and help me to trust His decision without fear.

This is the place where I so often miss His guidance and power, and therefore, fail to achieve the victory, for not until I am ready to obey His will can He answer my prayer. But, when I am willing and tell Him so, the solution is made plain and I leave the burden at His feet. And though His decision may not be the

Askings for 1957 from medical missionaries in the 15 stations listed above have been received, screened according to a Master List of White Cross Supplies, accepted by the Board of World Missions and the Board of Women's Work. From those listed, quotas have been proposed to the sixteen synodical chairmen of White Cross and to the three chairmen in Central Alabama, Georgia-Carolina, and Louisiana-Mississippi Presbyterials. The three latter quotas were accepted by the respective executive boards meeting during the Women's Training School, Snedecor Region, August 1-8, 1956. In 1957 the chairman of White Cross in Central Alabama will receive gifts from those three presbyterials, pack and ship same to the Lapsley Memorial Hospital, Bulape, Congo Belge. The 1956 gifts were packed and shipped by the chairman in Birmingham Presbyterial, who was shipping to the same hospital.

In sending in lists of supplies needed in 1957 three of the medical missionaries added words of appreciation as follows:

"We are grateful to the Women of the Church for their interest in the work and for what the White Cross means to us. I just wish more of them could see just what a big work it does and helps us in a tremendous way. We have worked here at Moma in the medical work before we ever got White Cross here, and then I have been here after we began getting White Cross and it is really wonderful what a help it was. Often I laugh when I think of the bandages we rolled from men's underwear and worn out dresses of ours, and bedspreads and everything we could find to use for bandages when our work began down here, and before we were getting White Cross. So I know what it is like to get it and what it is like not to get it, and it makes a whole lot of difference. We appreciate their help more than we can express."
—Miss Lucile McElroy, R.N., Moma, Africa

"Let us express again our appreciation for and dependence on White Cross. As we use the sheets, towels, gowns, . . . it is a very evident tie between the individuals in the Church in the States and the individual patients here in Japan. Sometimes a patient's remark like, 'My, this is a soft warm gown' is a good opportunity to tell him of the concern of Christians in America for those in Japan who do not know Christ, and the reason why we have this beautiful hospital. We are thankful for all that the ladies are doing to help bring others into God's Kingdom."

—Miss Nell Swenson, R.N., Yodogawa Christian Hospital, Osaka, Japan

"Please convey to the ladies our deepest appreciation and gratitude for this work they are doing, without which we would have an almost impossible task of keeping our medical work going."

—Dr. Tinsley Smith, Mutoto, Congo Belge

"Many thanks for your wonderful help."

—Rev. E. T. Boyer, Soonchun, Korea

"The White Cross gifts for 1955 were a wonderful 'gold mine' for this poor little hospital. Much of the goods is in use, but I saved some against the day when we get our new operating room."

—Miss Charlotte Dunlap, R.N., Changhua Christian Hospital, Changhua, Taiwan, writing February 25, 1956. (Supplies to Taiwan this year were delayed in shipping several weeks due to difficulties in making satisfactory arrangements.)

Church News

SOUTHEASTERN STATES FACULTY CONFERENCE

Montreat, N. C.—

College and university teachers from more than 100 Southern church, private, and state institutions were challenged to resist the secularization of American thought and life at the third Southeastern States Faculty Conference here, August 27-31.

The conference, sponsored by the boards of education of the Presbyterian Church, U.S., and the Methodist Church, brought more than 250 teachers together to re-examine their vocations in the light of the Christian faith. Program chairmen of the meeting were Dr. Hunter Blakely, Richmond, Va., secretary of the Division of Higher Education of the Presbyterian Church, U.S., and Dr. Richard N. Bender, director of religion in higher education of the Methodist Church. Dr. F. Heisse Johnson, dean of Tennessee Wesleyan College, Athens, Tenn., and Dr. Joseph Lee Vaughan, professor of English, College of Engineering, University of Virginia, Charlottesville, were deans of the assembly.

Theme of the conference was "Freedom, Responsibility, and the Christian Faith." Ten seminars, made up of professors from the fields of Bible and religion, the natural and social sciences, the arts, and other disciplines, gave major attention to studies of the Christian doctrine of man.

Delivering four lectures on the conference theme was Dr. Peter A. Bertocci, professor of philosophy at Boston University, Boston, Mass. The scholar, he said, has no right to an opinion unless he is willing to accept the obligation to find the evidence. He called upon teachers to "reaffirm the freedom to think with full respect for all available facts." He warned that human freedom means responsibility. "The search for security is self-defeating. Happiness can never be man's lot if it is defined as absence of frustration and insecurity. To live completely is to do the best one knows—to live creatively amidst insecurity. It is often to stand firmly against the lashes of social disapproval. But when a man does what he believes to be his duty, there comes that peace which goes beyond security. No wonder Jesus promised his disciples not happiness, not peace of mind, but blessedness."

Dr. Eric Baker, secretary of the Methodist Conference in Great Britain, declared that "theology must again become the Mother of the Sciences," if modern thought and life are to be rescued from complete secularization.

Scientific answers, Dr. Baker said, are "true as far as they go," but Christian teachers are responsible under God for concern with the "ultimate truth" underlying all the truths of religion, philosophy, and science. Christian teachers must stand forth in the freedom that boldly exposes the limitations of natural science to save men from despair and destruction. Jesus Christ, he said, has revealed the fundamental truth about man, his nature, and his destiny.

Dr. John W. Dixon, Jr., executive director of the Faculty Christian Fellowship, led worship services each day. "The community of learning," he said, "ought not to be primarily the community of master and disciple but the community of the forgiving and the forgiven."

A call to an intellectual rebirth that will lead to a new Reformation of the Church was voiced by Dr. Eugene Carson Blake, president of the National Council of Churches of Christ in the U.S.A., in an address entitled, "Wanted: Christian Scholars." He said: "What is wanted is such a renaissance of Christian scholarship that professors, ecclesiastics, and Christian people can lead our churches to such a revitalization that when men look back from the vantage point of centuries they will call our time too a reformation."

He sharply criticized American Protestantism for "anti-intellectualism." This attitude has hurt scholarship and weakened the Christian witness in the modern world.

Other speakers and leaders included Dr. Hendrik Kraemer, visiting professor at Union Theological Seminary in New York City; Dr. Samuel E. Stumpf, chairman of the department of philosophy at Vanderbilt University, Nashville, Tenn.; Dr. John Oliver Nelson, director of religious field work and professor of Christian vocation at Yale University, New Haven, Conn.;

GEORGIA

Revival Meeting at Smyrna

Rev. John H. Knight, pastor of Smyrna Presbyterian Church, Smyrna, Georgia, reports that that Church has just closed a very successful revival meeting under the evangelistic preaching of Rev. Carroll Stegall, pastor of Pryor Street Presbyterian Church, Atlanta.

Mr. Stegall is a chalk-talk artist and singer, as well as an effective evangelistic preacher. Mr. and Mrs. Elden Allain of the East Lake Christian Alliance Church of Atlanta directed the gospel singing. There were six additions to the Church. The meetings continued for one week, closing on Sunday night, August 26.

Mr. Knight reports that the church is greatly strengthened, and the Smyrna people desire to thank Pryor Street for the use of their preacher in this evangelistic ministry.

TEXAS

Talpa — Mrs. Floyd Thompson, president of Mid-Texas Presbytery's Women of the Church, and member of Talpa Presbyterian Church, was honored recently by the presentation of an Honorary Life Membership in the Women of the Church.

Dr. W. Bristow Gray of Brownwood was in charge of the service, and the presentation was made by Mrs. Joe Dobson of Talpa. Mr| Raymond Rush, clerk of the Session, Mrs. Maggie Beaver, president of the local Women of the Church, and others paid tribute to Mrs. Thompson's work with the young people, the Sunday School, the Women, and the community.

Following the service, a large number of friends were guests at the ranch home of Mr. and Mrs. Joe Dobson at a dinner honoring Mrs. Thompson.

THE SOUTHERN PRESBYTERIAN JOURNAL

A Presbyterian weekly magazine devoted to the statement, defense and propagation of the Gospel, the faith which was once for all delivered unto the saints.

VOL. XV NO. 22 SEPTEMBER 26, 1956 $2.50 A YEAR

THE SOUTHERN PRESBYTERIAN JOURNAL
The Journal has no official connection with the Presbyterian Church in the United States
Rev. Henry B. Dendy, D.D., Editor....................Weaverville, N. C.
Dr. L. Nelson Bell, Associate Editor....................Asheville, N. C.
Rev. Wade C. Smith, Associate Editor....................Weaverville, N. C.

EDITORIAL

Education: Child-Centered or Christ-Centered?

This is the issue in education today according to Principal J. Chr. Coetzee of Potchefstroom University for Christian Higher Education. According to this veteran scholar:

> "Jesus Christ's claim on modern education is a total claim: a renewal of the aim of education, a return to the Christian view of man, a restoration of the teacher as the responsible partner, a new program of studies in Nature and in Scripture, a rebirth of the Christian idea of freedom and obedience, a complete surrender of man to God."

In a current number of the Evangelical Quarterly, Coetzee writes: "Modern education is more than a mere negation of Christian education; it is a systematic non-Christian, sometimes even an anti-Christian education. In the American John Dewey and in the Englishman T. Percy Nunn, modern education has found its two great exponents: both reject creation and a Creator . . . Although there may be divergent modern philosophies of education, they all have the same fundamental ideas, viz., humanism, evolutionism, and pragmatism or instrumentalism or experimentalism." Conversely Christian Education also has "just three fundamental ideas, viz., theism, creationism and revelationism."

The child-centered education has six "new" articles of faith, namely: (1) freedom, (2) child initiative, (3) the active school, (4) child interest as the orienting centre of the school, (5) creative self-expression, (6) co-operative living. The Christian school likewise has some six articles of faith: (1) the foundation is the Word of God, the guiding principle the life and world view deduced from that Word, (2) the biblical doctrine of man as created by God in His image, fallen into sin, saved by Christ, called to know, love and serve God, (3) the teacher acts in the place of the parent as the responsible partner co-operating with the ones taught, (4) the syllabus covers both Scripture and nature, (5) the medium is love, love towards God and towards man, love in freedom and in obedience, (6) the Christian school lives and thrives by the covenant of God with man. W.C.R.

Living!!

The validity of the Christian faith rests squarely on the fact that Christ is living today. We do not worship a dead Christ. Such an one would be unworthy of worship.

We praise God for the fact that He died on the cross and we know that our salvation depends on that which He did for us at Calvary.

But this redemption was made valid through His overcoming the power of death and the grave, and the resurrection becomes the capstone of the gospel message. It was the theme, the final convincing proof of God's power, to which the early apostles appealed and was a basic factor in the spread of the church across the world.

The resurrection of Christ — a physical, bodily fact — is attested by the record. He was seen by one, by two, by eleven and one time by about five hundred individuals.

These separated appearances, to many types of individuals and under differing circumstances, were accompanied, we are told, by many infallible proofs.

These men *saw* Him; they *touched* Him; they *ate with* Him; they *heard Him speak;* they saw Him taken up from their presence and heard the clear statement of His certain return.

We center our love, our faith and our hope in a living Christ:

He lives, He lives, Christ Jesus lives today,
He walks with me and talks with me,
Along life's narrow way,

He lives, He lives, salvation to impart,
You ask me how I know He lives?
He lives within my heart.

—Alfred H. Ackley

Soon after his conversion Stuart Hamblen was sitting in an airport reading his New Testament. A man stopped and struck up a conversation, then remarked: "You don't believe what you are reading, do you?" Hamblen replied: "I sure do." The inquisitive one sneered: "Why the man they are talking about in that book has been dead nearly 2000 years." As quick as a flash Hamblen said: "Listen, brother, I have news for you; I was talking with Him just ten minutes ago."

The risen and living Christ is the very center of our faith and hope. He is also the center of the message which brings eternal life within the scope of human attainment. L.N.B.

Christian Marriage

"Whom God has joined together, let not man put asunder."

The whole matter of marriage, divorce, and the re-marriage of divorced persons is before our presbyteries for action. The 1956 Assembly adopted an Ad Interim Report of a Committee, for whose members we hold the highest respect. The fact that this has been sent down to the presbyteries invites discussion that the lamp of truth being shaken the light may shine the brighter.

First, we note that the committee acknowledges that they have no clear guidance as to the will of the Holy Spirit on the matter. Since that is the case, why not wait on the Lord until His will becomes clear? Why change our Confession when there is no clear leading as to the way in which we ought to go.

Secondly, is the reason that the Church ought not to share through her ministers in establishing marriage likely to increase the sanctions thrown around this event, or to decrease them? Most people think of marriage in the church by the minister, the ambassador of God, as the sign of God's blessing and action in establishing marriage. A church marriage has been a tower of strength in maintaining the tie unbroken. Because there are civil matters for the state to decide, it does not follow that there are not divine sanctions involved. The act of the Church of God is the assurance that God has joined the two in Christian marriage.

Thirdly, let us get the main drive of Moses in Genesis 1 and 2 as in Deuteronomy, of our Lord Jesus in Mark, Luke and Matthew, of Paul in Romans 7 and in I Cor. 7 before focusing on detailed variations. Each was intent on maintaining the sanctity and permanence of marriage. Will the total effect of suggested changes further that intent, or will the divergence from the teaching of our Lord, in its fundamental intent, be greater as a result of the change than now?

Fourthly, as to the detailed variations between Matthew on the one hand and Mark-Luke on the other, certain considerations are here offered. If objection be taken to "the Matthew exception" on the ground that it is the view of the Shammai school of scribes; may not objection be made to the Markan form on the ground that in its statement and in the reason annexed it is almost identical with that of the Damascus Sect? In both cases, however, the motive of our Lord was different, namely the desire to do the pure will of God.

May the case of the exception, given twice in Matthew, be the result of a question or objection made by a hearer, accepted by the Teacher and combined by Matthew? May not the Risen Lord have guided Mark and Luke to give the condemnation of divorce in a single, ringing testimony against the free and easy customs of the pagan world? And may He not likewise have guided Matthew to write the exception for the Jews in view of the way that the issue then stood among them? W.C.R.

The Gospel Solves the Puzzle of Philosophy

The Saviour tells us that the scribe in the Kingdom should be like a good householder, bringing out of his storehouse things new and old. After a considerable study of much of the current thought on the resurrection it is interesting to return to the DISCOURSES ON REDEMPTION by Stuart Robinson of Kentucky for he has a good distinction between the Apostolic doctrine of immortality and everlasting life and that of the philosophical schools.

The reasoning of Socrates, Plato and Cicero for immortality was not very conclusive. Socrates replied to his judges: "To die is one of two things: either the soul is annihilated or it passes into some other state." Nor is their doctrine very comforting. For leaving out of account the grace of God and the mission of Christ, this reasoning, if valid, lands one in "an immortal hell." Nor thirdly, is it very logical, since the being that re-

The Southern Presbyterian Journal, *a Presbyterian Weekly magazine devoted to the statement, defense, and propagation of the Gospel, the faith which was once for all delivered unto the saints,* published every Wednesday by The Southern Presbyterian Journal, Inc., in Weaverville, N. C.

Entered as second-class matter May 15, 1942, at the Postoffice at Weaverville, N. C., under the Act of March 3, 1879. Vol. XV, No. 22, September 26, 1956. Editorial and Business Offices: Weaverville, N. C. Printed in the U.S.A. by Biltmore Press, Asheville, N. C.

ADDRESS CHANGE: When changing address, please let us have both old and new address as far in advance as possible. Allow three weeks after change if not sent in advance. When possible, send an address label giving your old address.

ceives the reward or the punishment is only a soul and so is not the same order of being as did the good or the bad acts.

"As a matter of fact, moreover, the utmost extent of the argument of the classic philosophy is to prove that the soul *may* exist, because it has a capacity for endless existence. But this is very far from proving that it shall exist. Socrates argued that the soul is uncompounded, and therefore, dissolves not as the body, and may continue to exist. But while the soul is an uncompounded existence, it is yet a ***dependent*** existence, and therefore, if God please, may cease to exist. God need only stop the outgoing of life from Himself, and in a moment He would be alone in the universe."

* * * * *

"The Apostolic argument finds the basis of an immortality, not in the inherent nature of the soul itself, which is a dependent existence, and therefore if God please may terminate, but in the connection of the race with the Redeemer who has secured the immortality not only of the soul but of the whole compounded nature—physical as well as spiritual."

* * * * *

"Any and every attempt to subvert the great truth of the resurrection (of Christ) as an historic fact—no matter under what pious disguise, or from what intention—is nothing else than simple infidelity, and leads us back to mere heathenism. For, as the Apostle declares, If Christ be not risen, then is our preaching vain, and your faith is also vain. Yea and we are found false witnesses of God, and those which are fallen asleep in Christ are perished." W.C.R.

"This I Believe"

Many of us have heard Edward R. Murrow's program under the above title. Some have read the two books already published in which will be found about one hundred of these "affirmations."

That these statements of faith come from many prominent people has greatly increased the interest with which they have been received. For that reason, the tragic lack of any true Christian faith in most of them is all the more to be regretted.

On the one hand they indicate man's innate desire to believe something. On the other they reflect the futility of setting up one's own religion.

Humanism is a welcome substitute to some for the Christian faith because it magnifies man and caters to the ego of those who espouse it.

On the other hand the Christian faith demands an humbling of mind and heart and a bending of the will to God and His Christ. As a result the Christian magnifies Christ and not his own beliefs.
The Christian believes in Christ.

The Humanist believes in himself and in man round about him. L.N.B.

Man Is Responsible!

Calvin on Job. 34.27

One of the interesting features of the recent meeting of the Board of World Missions was the presentation of a first edition of Calvin's Sermons on Job, a gift from the Theological Seminary at Montpelier, France. Rev. Paul Vreeland, to whom the valuable book was given in the first place, announced that it was to be placed in the Library of Union Theological Seminary, Richmond. This was a most appropriate designation since Union has given generously to help the Seminary at Montpelier.

The late Professor Auguste Lecerf of Paris used Job 34.27 to show that Calvin did not let his doctrine of Predestination destroy man's will or responsibility. In *Etudes Calvinistes,* p. 27, he writes: "If they will repent and believe the Gospel they will be saved. And one cannot object that the loss of free will, that the original inability puts them in the position that willing it is impossible. If it be true that they are not able of themselves, it is also true that in the call of God there is given the physical and psychological ability to respond:

"Because," says Calvin, "when your God teaches you, when He accords you the privilege of the revelation of His will, it is as if He puts life in your hands; but you reject it and you seek for nothing else but death! . . . If anyone turns himself away . . . he cannot say that he has erred because he could not do better; but on the contrary, he is the cause of all the evil and that ought to be imputed to him entirely."
Sermon on Job, 34.27

In the Institutes, III.ii.35 Calvin agrees with Augustine that it was in order to teach us that the act of believing is owing to the divine gift, not to human merit that our Saviour declared, "No man can come to Me, except the Father which hath sent Me draw him; except it were given unto him of My Father." "It is wonderful, that two persons hear: one despises, the other ascends. Let him who despises, impute it to himself; let him who ascends not arrogate it to himself. . . . Christ, when He illuminates us with faith by the power of His Spirit, at the same time ingrafts us into His body, that we may become partakers of all His benefits."
W.C.R.

From Another Age

By Gordon H. Clark, Ph.D.

John Donne was born in London in 1571 or 1572. He was reared a Roman Catholic and lived a dissolute life. After a time his studies led him to abandon the Roman church, and still later he became an Anglican. This change was undoubtedly based on a true conversion, for he broke off his evil ways, became a vicar, and preached with evident sincerity to his former companions in vice.

Donne was not favorably impressed with Calvinism. He considered reprobation a harsh doctrine. The diffidence, the gloomy tinge of Puritan character, the morbidity of the Reformed people repelled him. In one of his sermons he says that he met with seven diffident and dejected souls for every presumptuous one.

Well, times have changed. Today we no longer meet so many diffident souls nor so few presumptuous ones. Evangelists sometimes teach that assurance is of the essence of salvation; they even doubt the salvation of any individual who has not full assurance. This, of course, is not Reformation doctrine.

It is rather strange, at any rate, that Calvinism should be pictured as a gloomy religion. If Donne accepted the Arminian view, if he denied predestination and irresistible grace, we may wonder how he could be so happy about it? Those who believe that one may fall from grace, those who believe that salvation once possessed can later be lost, have no good reason for confidence. Their perseverance depends on their own power, not on God. How can they be sure that they will attain heaven? It is Calvinistic theology alone that can give solid comfort to the diffident heart.

Now, it may be true that the sixteenth century and early seventeenth had too much of a tendency toward timidity and doubt. John Bunyan, for all of his Pilgrim's Progress, was not a happy soul. But it is also probable that the twentieth century is too light-hearted, too insincere, too careless, too indifferent to the things of God, too comfortable in the sinful world. The times have indeed changed, but not necessarily for the better.

With an acknowledgement of great variety among personalities, each of us should seriously measure his life by the Scriptural standard. Let us then lay aside every weight and run the race with patience and circumspection.

The Reformed Doctrine of The Bodily Resurrection of Christ

By William Childs Robinson, Th.D., D.D.

This address by Dr. Wm. C. Robinson on the Bodily Resurrection of Christ, was a popular presentation based on a carefully prepared and fully documented paper. The full thesis was written for use in his course in Apologetics and possibly for publication in a theological periodical at a later date. If so used, it is hoped that the full text will be circulated in our Church. Meanwhile the Southern Presbyterian Journal is presenting from its tape recording that part of the work which was set forth in the address at Weaverville on August 15th. H.B.D.

Forty years ago an old professor, Dr. L. A. Fox of Roanoke College, took the time and trouble to show to the students from the Scriptures that Jesus Christ really rose from the dead, and by His cross the living Christ, the risen Christ, called some of us into his ministry.

The incarnation, crucifixion and resurrection of Jesus Christ are the events which distinguish Christianity from Mohammedanism and Judaism. Whatever similarities there may be between the teacher of righteousness of the Qumran sect and Jesus, the Resurrection marks out the vast difference between the two.

A renewed emphasis upon the resurrection is, however, relevant at this time. In Latin Christianity the profusion of crucifixes focuses the eye upon the crucified, dead Jesus, leaving to the evangelical church a special responsibility for proclaiming the risen living Lord. In American Protestantism the weight of old liberalism still swings many away from the bodily "physical" resurrection of Christ witnessed in the New Testament to a so-called "spiritual resurrection" at death befitting Plato's society of souls in an idealistic universe. European scholarship is disentangling the Hellenistic man from the Biblical man, recognizing that the body is God's handiwork and accepting the unity of the whole inner and outer man both in this life and in the age to come. Yet the influence of existentialism leads some of these scholars to present the death of Christ as the sole factual event in the Gospel with the resurrection as merely an expression of the eschatological significance of His death, a myth whose meaning is real only in faith. The pessimism resulting from inadequate presentations can be lifted only by the proclamation of the bodily resurrection of Jesus Christ as a factual occurrence, an act of God's self-disclosure in truly divine dimensions.

THE GOSPEL OF THE RESURRECTION

By the resurrection of the Lord Jesus as the summation of his whole ministry, God brought the blessings which Israel looked for only in the future into the present. Since Christ died for our sins and rose for our justification, in Him we have today the forgiveness of sins and the peace which passes human understanding. Since the risen Christ breathed upon his disciples and poured upon them at Pentecost His Holy Spirit, therefore, God's Spirit bears witness with our spirits that we are the children of God. Since God raised up Jesus our Lord from the dead, He has raised us from the death of sin to the newness of life with Christ, and His resurrection is the measure of the exceeding greatness of God's power to work in believers. As our faith receives the mighty work of God in the resurrection of Christ, we share in the Christian hope of the new Heaven and a new earth. We believe in the Almighty who makes the dead alive and creates the things that are from nothing. The God who raised Jesus the Lord from the dead is able to save and keep and raise those who are Christ's. Each of these blessings comes from the nail-pierced hands of the risen Redeemer. The whole New Testament Gospel is inseparably one in the proclamation of the Risen One as the crucified. The present exalted one is expressly the crucified, the sympathizing High Priest, the Lamb in the midst of the throne.

The gospel not only includes the fact of the death of Christ, but also the fact of the resurrection of Christ, and in I Corinthians 15 the fact of the witnesses to that resurrection. On their eyewitnessing the gospel of the Church was built, and to that ocular testimony the Church must constantly return if She would fully safeguard the self-communication of God which came to us in Jesus. The resurrection of Jesus is not a mere product or precipitate from our present meeting with Christ. It is the other way around.

The event of the resurrection is prior to faith in the risen Christ. It is the resurrection which creates, makes possible, calls forth and directs faith to the Risen One. The fact of the resurrection proclaimed in the gospel calls us to a meeting with Christ in faith. The Church proclaims the forgiveness of sins and the hope of glory on that ground. The resurrection of Jesus as the deed of God is the presupposition of the preaching of the Cross, of the Church of God in Christ Jesus, of the Christian faith in the triune God. The resurrection is the center that holds the whole gospel together.

THE LORD OF THE RESURRECTION

In revealing Himself to men today, the Risen Christ is sovereign as truly as He was sovereign in the various encounters He had with His disciples recorded in the New Testament. The Lord is free to deal graciously with us in our presuppositions and in our places as, and when, and how he will. He may use the whole gospel with one man on one occasion, a particular part on another occasion. We remember that one disciple was led to faith by the empty tomb, namely John; Peter by the appearing of Christ to him; Thomas by the appearing *plus* the command to put his hand in the nail prints; some disciples after such a command only when the Lord had table fellowship with them. And so the Holy Spirit continues to bring people to faith in Christ in His own way, and we may not direct Him how.

While Christ is the Lord, we are not the Lord. It is our duty as His servants to proclaim the whole counsel of God.

Jesus was Lord in the New Testament appear ances, Lord in the early appearances of the forty days as truly as He was in the later one to Paul. His activity has the ruling place in the accounts of the resurrection appearances. The disciples didn't seek out and find the Risen Lord. Each appearance was initiated and carried out by Him. He came, He drew near, He went with them, He appeared to Peter, He met the women, He stood in the midst, He vanished from their sight. Even when He was seen and heard, He was only perceived as He willed it. He appeared not to all, but to chosen witnesses.

In these primary appearances the purpose seems not to be to magnify His glorious state. There is not one word in the appearances during "the forty days" about a light shining from the Risen Jesus Himself. I know there is at the transfiguration. I know there is later to Paul and to John on the Isle of Patmos and to Stephen, but not in the forty days. In fact, in that period He was even mistaken for a gardener. Each story, however, reaches its climax in a recognition scene. In the Old Testament Theophany stories proof is usually offered of the supernatural or the divine character of the Visitant. In the gospel stories the proofs tend to show His real humanity. He has flesh and blood. He bears wounds in His body. He even eats human food.

Moreover, these several appearances recall the earlier meetings with the disciples. He Who fed the thousands and sat as housefather at the Lord's Table is again made known as He blesses and breaks the bread. The Risen One finds the fishermen at their old haunts, and the second miraculous draft of fishes reminds us of the first. Peter's leaving the boat to go to Jesus on the land reminds us of his earlier leaving the boat to walk upon the waters. The Great Commission in Matthew reminds us of His instruction to the disciples earlier in the 10th chapter of Matthew, and the Church Order in that Great Commission reminds us of the Church Order in Matthew 18: 15-20. Mary recognizes her Master when He calls her by name.

Three times Jesus is reported as directing to His hands, His feet, or His side the eyes of His disciples. Moreover, when He raised up His hands to bless the bread, the wounds would have been made visible there. Thus, our Risen Lord identified Himself to His disciples as Jesus of Nazareth and His body as the one that had been crucified for us.

THE COMPLETENESS OF THE RESURRECTION

The Bible sets forth the unity of the whole inner and outer man as God's handiwork. The Bible idea of personality is an animated body, not an incarnated soul. The Bible does not teach a Platonic, an Orphic, or a Gnostic dualism which places the soul, or spirit, over against the body as different in source, origin, and ultimate destinies. According to the Bible our bodies are not prisons of the soul; they are temples of the Holy Ghost. They are members of Christ and are not to be made the members of a harlot. Death is not the great friend of the soul, but the last enemy of Christ. It is death not the body which is conquered in the resurrection of Christ, for his resurrection is a bodily resurrection.

It is not that a part only of Jesus lived again, or was resurrected. The whole man Jesus died and rose, emptying the grave. The Risen One had a body. He could draw near, walk with the disciples, recline with them at the table, break the bread, eat and drink, and thus, had a real body. The Risen Jesus had his own real body, the body which had been crucified.

While the resurrection was a corporeal or a physical event, it was, of course, not merely a bodily event. The wisdom of the Risen One opened the minds of the apostles to interpret the Old Testament Messianically. His Lordship challenged their wills with the Great Commission. His love made their hearts burn with a new devotion. His spiritual blessings endued them with peace, repentance, pardon, restoration. His fellowship with them established the Church of God in Christ Jesus. And each of these impacts of the Risen Saviour upon His disciples was an added confirmation of His resurrection. Each of the several modes of manifestation buttressed the others, making a cumulative effect upon the apostles' perception. They established the objective character of the resurrection as a thing of God's doing, not of the disciples' making.

THE WITNESS OF SENSE PERCEPTION

Our Lord showed the fullness of His victory over death and the grave and the completeness of the Creator's control over earth as well as heaven by the bodily nature of His resurrection, and by its attestation to the physical senses of the disciples.

In revealing His risen presence, Christ appears to them that their eyes may identify Him as their Master of Galilee and Saviour of Calvary. He directs them to handle Him that their hands may attest that He is no apparition, but Himself in the body. Since the ultimate purpose of the resurrection is the unveiling of God to men, every appearance is bound to a revelation in words. Even on the road to Damascus Paul not only saw the Lord, he also heard the voice of His mouth.

The several appearings and the meeting with a number of persons (above 500 at one time) removed the possibility that these phenomena could be merely one individual's hallucination. In accord with Jewish prejudice the eleven dismissed the testimony of the women, but when they made their testimony to Thomas, he also doubted.

Indeed some even doubted on the Mount, and unbelief is repeated over and over again in the longer ending of Mark. The Holy Spirit used their physical as well as their social, intellectual, and spiritual contacts with the resurrected Christ to draw the company of disciples around the corner from unbelief to faith in the victory of their Lord and Saviour. In the light of His resurrection, the corporate witness of the apostolic body is: God has reconciled us to Himself by the death of His Son.

THE TESTIMONY OF EYE-WITNESSES

The New Testament accounts do not present the appearances of Jesus as the imaginings of false witnesses, but as facts outside the witnesses which on that account called them to faith. Luke 24:34-43 is a kind of comprehensive gospel of the resurrection in which Jesus stands in the midst of the disciples. In reciprocal conversation He meets the doubts and dialectics of their troubled hearts.

He directs them, "Behold my hands and my feet and convince yourselves that it is I myself. Handle me and see, because a spirit has not flesh and bones as ye behold me having," or as Dr. Dodd renders it, "Feel me and look. A ghost has not flesh and blood as ye see that I have." The Holy Spirit brings the Church back to these eye-witnesses again and again that She may be sure of the reality of the revelation which God made of Himself in Jesus Christ.

THE TESTIMONY OF HEARING THE RISEN CHRIST

In the gospels the Risen Jesus speaks to His disciples as one weeps in the garden, as two walk by the way, to some at the table, to others by the sea, to an appointed gathering on the mountain. He engages in conversations with them, meeting their questions with His assurance, "It is I myself." At times he calls one sheep by name "Miriam,

Thomas, Simon, Saul." At other times the address is to a group, "All hail!" "Peace be unto you." He uses the familiar words of blessing at the table. He reminds them of the words He has spoken before His crucifixion. He teaches them again of repentance and forgiveness. He asks for food. He promises the Spirit. He gives solemn commandments, charges, commissions.

Matthew gives the Great Commission in a stupendous sweep that is worthy only of the Lord Jesus, the conqueror of death. Luke records His showing the disciples in the Old Testament that the Messiah must suffer, rise from the dead, enter into His glory, and that repentance and forgiveness be preached in His name unto all nations. Thus were the disciples made apostles that they might bear witness of the things which they had seen and heard, supporting their testimony by the word of prophecy and looking to the Spirit to use it to bring their hearers to faith in Christ, crucified and risen.

THE TESTIMONY OF HANDLING THE WORD OF LIFE

When the Risen Jesus met the women returning from the tomb, they laid hold of his feet and worshipped Him. The account of Jesus' meeting with Mary Magdelene (John 20) is variously interpreted. The King James' rendering may be understood thus: "Touch me not, for I have not yet ascended, but I am about to ascend to my Father, and thereafter I can be touched and handled." When the Risen One did appear later that day to the apostles and breathed upon them the Spirit, presumably He had already ascended to the Father, had already been glorified, for He bids them handle Him.

Since the present imperative with "Me" (the Greek is Me Mou Hoptu) means to "make an end of an existing situation," several translations and commentaries render Jesus' words to Mary: "Stop touching me. Do not hold me. Do not keep clinging to me." The same is then interpreted: "Cease holding me. It is true that I have not yet ascended to my Father and your Father, but I am about to do so. This is what you are to tell my brothers." According to Dr. Barrett, the most recent English commentator on the Gospel of John, John was of the opinion that the resurrected body was physically real.

Luke 24 records the command of the Lord to the disciples to handle Him that they may know He is not a spectre, but flesh and bones. In his epistle to the Smyrnian Ignatius of Antioch who wrote about 110 is the following: "And when the Risen Jesus came to those with Peter, He said to them, 'Take hold, handle me and see that I am not a bodiless demon.'" The Johannine record refers to the same appearance. Here the Lord bids the disciples to see His hands and side and probably lays His hands on them as He breathes on them the spirit and ordains them apostles.

Thomas could find some ground for his insistence that he put his finger in the nail holes and his hand into the pierced side in the word of the Lord to the other disciples to handle Him and see that He had flesh and bones and in their reports of doing what their Lord commanded them to do. The natural longing of the human heart is to grasp again a loved one. Moreover, only by an assurance of the reality of the resurrection could Thomas give his testimony with full conviction. The Risen Lord met his request in every detail that the apostolic faith might be distinguished from an illusion and the apostles' witness to the resurrection of the Lord Jesus might sound forth with power and great grace be upon the people.

On this appearing to the apostles, the risen Lord again bared the wounds of the cross in His hands and in His side and bade Thomas, "Reach hither thy finger and see my hand. Reach hither thy hand and put it into my side and be not faithless, but believing." Thomas answered and said unto him, "My Lord and my God!" Amid various interpretations of this meeting the following is offered from Professor Markus Barth now of Chicago. "While John 20:29 only mentions the seeing, there is scarcely any room for assuming that the touching which Thomas had requested and which Jesus now commanded was not carried out." Thomas' "My Lord!" was no abstract affirmation. As the disciple obeyed his risen Lord, it was true of Thomas as of the other apostles "that which we have seen with our eyes and our hands have handled declare we unto you."

The risen Lord appeared and spoke to his apostles that they might accept and proclaim the revelation in Him. He offered them His body to be handled that by the grace of God their bodies might bear witness to Him. He bared to them the precious wounds that they might stand when they were called to be martyrs for Him Who died for them and for us.

On two occasions when the disciples were gathered within, the doors having been closed for fear of the Jews, Jesus came and stood in their midst. In these cases we have something which is an absolute miracle. Our acceptance of these unexplained miracles does not in itself contradict other elements in the account, such as the Lord's bidding Thomas handle His wounds. Neither does it reverse the doctrine in John's Gospel that the resurrection of the dead means their coming forth out of the tomb and the rebuilding of the temple of the body. Most of all this acceptance accords with what is evident in all the appearances, namely that He Who has all authority in heaven and earth is Lord.

If, however, instead of starting with the miraculous fact THAT our Lord came and stood in the midst of the disciples one begins with rationalistic inferences as to *how* He entered, sundry hypotheses are possible. Yet it is not evident that the writer of the Gospel favored any of them. One view is that He passed through the closed doors. The Bible doesn't say that. It is only a hypothesis. From this some assume that he must have been or have become a ghost in order to accomplish the feat. This thinking often ends in a Doketic resurrection and a Christ over whom man's inferences and the mere doors of the house were lord. The angel of the Lord twice brought Peter out of prison, the doors of which had been closed and locked. Yet the disciples' inference that the one knocking at their door was only Peter's angel was in error as you will find if you read Acts 12:10-15.

Many of the first century houses were built around an open court. Their two massive doors, one following the other, were on the side adjoining the street while the dining room was regularly on the opposite side of the court. If the disciples were in such a triclinicum or dining room absorbed in discussing the reports of their Lord's appearances they would not have known if these outer doors had opened before and closed behind the entering Lord, as the iron gate opened of its own accord before Peter and the angel. Our older reformed exegetes such as John Calvin and Matthew Henry understood that the doors were opened to admit the Lord. Indeed, by His death and resurrection the Lord opened for His Church even the gates of death and the doors of the Kingdom. (Matthew 16).

A third hypothesis (or, if you want to call it that, a third guess. These are all guesses) is that our Lord descended into the open court (if he ascended at all he had no trouble descending into the open court), leaving the great doors still closed. As we do not know how the Lord saw fit to accomplish the miracle of His coming and standing in their midst, we may not say that He had to be a bodiless spirit in order to enter.

THE TESTIMONY OF TABLE FELLOWSHIP WITH CHRIST

At the Last Supper the Lord spoke of eating and drinking again with the disciples in the Kingdom of God. After the resurrection there are accounts of our Lord's having table fellowship with the disciples, twice in Luke, once certainly and twice probably in Acts, once in John, once in the longer ending of Mark, once in Ignatius to the Smyrnians, once in the Gospel to the Hebrews. These occasions are reflected in Revelation 3:20 "If any man hear my voice and open the door, I will come in to him and sup with him and he with Me."

The risen Jesus came close enough to the disciples to eat with them, to touch and be touched by them, to breathe upon them. Until the resurrection they had been concerned with fragrant ointments for His burial. Yet so tremendous was the actuality of the resurrection that many days after His death there was no suggestion of that which Martha feared at the tomb of Lazarus. On the contrary, the oral gospel in Acts uses the phraseology of the Psalmist "His flesh did not see corruption" to set forth the reality of the resurrection as God's victory over sin and death, the enthronement of Christ in His heavenly reign.

There is an interesting testimony, if we have time to mention it, that has recently been discovered from the middle of the second century that shows the disciples using their five senses. This comes from the sermon called *The Gospel of Truth:*

> After the resurrection of Christ, He gave them the possibility of knowing, for as they *saw* and *heard* Him - He granted them to *taste* and *smell* and *touch* Him — the Beloved Son. He came in the flesh without anything hindering His path.

(Chairman calls time).

May I say this in closing? I have here before me a full discussion of Paul's treatment in I Corinthians fifteen, but there is not time to present it. Paul does not teach that our resurrection will not be physical. There is a translation to that effect in the RSV, but it is an erroneous rendering of the Greek. Paul says that our present body is psychical, not physical as the RSV gives. The future body will be Spiritual, but not in the sense that it is non-physical. This body is psychical, that is, its life-principle is soul or psychology. The resurrection body will be Spiritual in the sense that it will be raised by the Holy Spirit and of it the Spirit will be the life principle.

Neither does Paul say that the future body will not be flesh and blood as a hasty reading of I Cor. 15.50 may signify. "Flesh and blood" is the subject of that sentence, not the predicate. And "flesh and blood" does not mean the physical or material side of man as against his intellectual or spiritual side. In the Bible it means the whole man, human nature, as against God and His Spirit. This fallen human nature cannot inherit eternal life. It must be changed by the Spirit from its enmity against God and its corruption. Paul is talking Christian salvation in I Cor. 16; not Hellenistic dualism. When by God's grace through Jesus Christ the Spirit changes our corrupt human nature and takes away our opposition to God, we shall live with God in our Spiritual bodies in a new heaven and a new earth. Paul believed in the bodily resurrection of Christ and of His people. He said, "He shall come and change our vile bodies and make them like unto His glorious body."

The resurrection is God's "Yes" to life, God's declaration that not death but life is the last word. The resurrection of Christ's body is God's "Yes" to the body. Jesus Christ was crucified publicly as a malefactor. That is not God's last public word about Christ. He shall come in His glory - publicly. As the resurrection reveals God's "Yes" to the body and "Yes" to life, so the resurrection reveals God. Only God can raise the dead. Those that believe in the resurrection of the body have a God-centered faith and a God-centered hope. Thank you.

A Biblical Study of the Position of Women in the Church

By JAMES E BEAR
Union Theological Seminary
Richmond, Va.

In this issue we are carrying two articles on the above subject, one by Dr. James E. Bear of Union Theological Seminary, Richmond, Va., the other by the Rev. Gabriel Abdullah.

This Journal will carry further articles on this subject. We believe our church would make a serious mistake to vote for the ordination of women elders. Among these reasons is the inescapable fact that such ordination would place women in a position of ecclesiastical authority over men, a position we believe contravenes the clear teachings of both the Old and New Testament. It is interesting to note that the Canadian Presbyterian Church has voted down the suggested plan to ordain women elders and deacons. The Editor.

This is the title of the Ad Interim Report on the subject presented to the 1956 Assembly, which report, with its recommendations, was adopted by that Assembly. The Committee that prepared this report believes that it presented a *Biblical* argument which justifies its recommendations that women be allowed to speak in the courts of the church, and that women may be ordained as deacons and elders.

As the General Assembly has sent the question of amending the *Book of Church Order* so as to permit the ordination of women as deacons and elders down to the Presbyteries for their consideration and vote, it seems wise that the Biblical argument which moved the Assembly to this action should be discussed fully.

Since this Ad Interim Committee Report is rather long, the writer is undertaking to restate and condense the line of Biblical argument presented by the report. We believe the argument given below is in essential harmony with the thought of the report, but the writer takes full responsibility for this statement as it is here printed. We realize that no summary of a report can do it full justice. We only hope that this summary may lead many to secure and study the full report, so that they may be able to arrive at a balanced conclusion on the Biblical teaching on this subject.

THREE BASIC TRUTHS.

In discussing the Biblical teaching about the position of women in the Church, three fundamental truths must be taken into account.

First, *The Church.* The "church" in which the women are to take their proper position cannot be limited to the local, organized church with its deacons and elders. The church consists of all those who profess the true religion. (*Confession of Faith,* Ch. XXV, Sec. 2). Thus the church is found wherever God's people meet

sidered man's prerogative to lead and teach and direct. There is no New Testament authorization for *female* missionaries, and yet today out of our total missionary force of 464, there are 278 *women,* who have the duty of leading and instructing the converts, and who have an equal voice with the 180 *male* missionaries in running the work of the mission. Is this development, unauthorized by the example or teaching of the New Testament, the work of the devil, exalting women where they do not belong? Or is it the work of the Holy Spirit? Your Committee believed that the Spirit of God called these women into this service, and that the Spirit led the church to send them forth to "teach" and "act" along with the male missionaries.

TEXTS THAT SEEM TO SUBORDINATE WOMEN IN THE CHURCH

Among these texts, the Ad Interim Committee selected two passages for special consideration. This does not mean that the Committee was unacquainted with the other texts that might be added to them. But these two were selected because they set forth in clear, concrete terms what women should not do in the church. Let us look at them. I Cor. 14:33b-35. "As in all the churches of the saints, let the women keep silence in the churches: for it is not permitted unto them to speak; but let them be in subjection, as also saith the law. And if they would learn anything, let them ask their own husbands at home; for it is shameful for a woman to speak in the church." I Tim. 2:11-12. "Let a woman learn in quietness with all subjection. But I permit not a woman to teach, nor to have dominion over a man, but to be in quietness." (A.S.V.) The subordination of women is seen in three things: women are to *be silent* in church, they are *not to teach,* they are not to *"have dominion over a man,* (A.V. "usurp authority"; R.S.V., "have authority".)

It has been the fixed tradition in our church that these and like verses laid down an absolute and permanent rule which prohibited women from being elected to the office of deacon or elder. But the prohibitions in the above verses are far more sweeping. They cover the whole area of women in the church, not just the matter of women deacons and elders.

If these verses are to be taken as an absolute and permanent rule, then it would mean that in any meeting of God's people, only *men* could talk, *men only* would teach, *men only* would make decisions. The women would be silent, be in subjection. If any one on the basis of these verses opposes women deacons and elders, on the same basis, if he is consistent, he should oppose much in the present life and activity of our church. He should advocate the silencing of women in the congregational meetings, on the committees of the local church, in the Church School. He should advocate the withdrawal of women from the Boards of our Church and from the Mission Fields. He would silence all women teachers in our church colleges. These verses speak of women being *silent in the church,* and the question of women deacons and elders is but a small part of the problem for which consistentcy would demand the same solution.

We will look forward with interest to seeing articles from those who oppose opening the diaconate and eldership to women in which they will set forth what our church should do with our women if we are to consistently apply the prohibitions to the women in church, forbidding them to speak, to teach, or to rule.

Your Committee is not faced by this dilemma. We do not believe that these and like verses give a *rule* which is *without exception* and *permanent.* Perhaps these verses lay down the *principle* that normally the responsibility for speaking, teaching and ruling rests on the men. A principle may have exceptions. If God, who created men and women, equips and calls some women to positions of leadership, then they are God's exceptions, and they should not be barred from serving God by any man-made church rule.

GOD HAS CALLED WOMEN
TO LEADERSHIP

Normally, in Bible times, men took the leadership. They spoke, and instructed and ruled. And yet, even then, the Bible shows us that God raised up some women to positions of leadership among his people. In the Old Testament we have women like Deborah the Judge of Israel (Judges 4:4), and Huldah the Prophetess (II Kings 22:14ff.) In the New Testament we have Phoebe the deaconess (Rom. 16:1) (The term applied to her, *diakonon,* may be translated "servant" and the word often is. Our word "deacon" is a transliteration of this same word, so we might just as well translate Phil. 1:1, "bishops and servants," and I Tim. 3:12, "Let servants be the husband of one wife." The question of whether the word should be translated "servant" or "deacon" depends on whether the translator thinks it is used as an official title. Phoebe seems to have had a position of special responsibility in the Church of Cenchrea, and many feel that the word here should be translated "deacon." cp. Abbott-Smith, *Manual Greek Lexicon of the New Testament.*

The New Testament also tells us of Priscilla who helped to instruct the learned Apollos about Jesus (Acts 18:26), and about the four daughters of Phillip who prophesied (Acts 21:9). These exceptions may be few, but they are there in the early days of the church. In

qualify women for these offices. God calls whom he wills, when he wills, and who are we to say to what offices he may call them?

For this reason the Committee favored a change in *The Book of Church Order.* It felt that our church would be wise if it rescinded the church-made restriction against women being ordained as deacons and elders. If the Spirit of God should call women to those offices, who are we, by our rules, to prevent them from serving?

"On The Position of Women in The Church"

By The Reverend Gabriel Abdullah
Westminster Presbyterian Church
Jacksonville 6, Florida

This report of the Committee on the position of women in the Church indicates much thought and careful study of the issues involved. The Standing Committee on Bills and Overtures recommends the Moderator of the last assembly to make a thorough Biblical study of the issues involved. One request of Suwannee Presbytery on the question of women speaking in Church courts, and the other request of the Presbytery of Granville for the General Assembly to take the proper and necessary steps to amend "The Book of Church Order" to provide for the eligibility of women to hold the offices of Ruling Elder and Deacon in the congregations of the Presbyterian Churches in the United States on a permissive basis. As good as this study may be it is not in my opinion thorough —it is only the continuation of a study begun in the organization of the Old Testament Church, and which continued in the first century New Testament Church and has come to the forefront in our own Presbyterian Church periodically since 1880.

To this study I should like to add my observations. I seek only in this study to assist this capable committee to formulate a right answer to the mentioned overtures. But there is one infallible rule of faith and practice - the Scriptures, and one "infallible rule of interpretation of Scripture - the Scripture itself; and therefore, when there is a question about the true and full sense of any Scripture, (which is not manifold, but one) it may be searched and known by other places that speak more clearly." This statement is in the Confession of Faith, (Ch. 1, Sec. 9).

The Scripture begins with the statement "In the beginning God . . . " We have come to know this God to be God the Father, Son and Holy Ghost. One God, three persons, three male persons. And this masculine Triune God said, "Let us make man in our image . . . "

" . . . then the Lord God formed man of dust from the ground, and breathed into his nostrils the breath of life; and man became a living being." It came to pass, in the course of time, to alleviate man's loneliness, that "the Lord God caused a deep sleep to fall upon the man, and while he slept took one of his ribs and closed up its place with flesh; and the rib which the Lord God had taken from the man he made into a woman. . . . "

"A woman is of man - a rib of a man, never forget this, my son," my mother would often say to me as a youngster. "She is not as strong as a man so be gentle with her" she would remind me when sister and I would get in a strong and heated argument and sometimes as children we would fight.

The report speaks of few women who occupied positions of leadership among God's people. In the Old Testament "Deborah" Judges 4:4 and Huldah the prophetess, II Kings 22:14ff. And in the New Testament of Phoebe a deaconess Rom. 16:1, of Priscilla and her husband, Acts 18:26, and the four daughters of Phillip who prophesied, Acts 21:9. Such women who have prayed and prophesied in public worship have always been in the Church. There have been and I pray there will always be exceptional and gifted women in the Church, but nowhere is there in the Scripture where there ever was a woman Elder. The office and work of the Elder today dates back to Genesis where the term referred for the most part to age and progressively connoted leadership and authority among the people. They were recognized as respected leaders and emissaries of the Israelites.

The references in Exodus 3:16-18; 4:29; 17: 5-6; 19:7; 24:1,9; Leviticus 4:15 and 9:1; Numbers 11:16-17, 24, 25 are convincing that the office and work of an Elder are ordained by God. And in the New Testament Church we find confirmation that the time-honored and God-given office was being continued and recognized.

God was clear during the period of organization of His Church in specifying to Moses in Exodus 22:29 " . . . The firstborn of your sons you shall give to me." Let us take notice that God asked specifically for "the first-born of your sons"; He did *not* ask for the first-born of the daughters.

Our Lord Jesus exalted womanhood when He, as God incarnate, was born of a woman. He chose twelve *male* Apostles to serve with Him in the ministry of instruction and the leadership of the believers.

As concerning Paul's writings we may point to the fact that the Church through the Ages has found that God has spoken and continues to speak through all of Paul's letters. We have the testimony of God's Spirit in our hearts telling us so. Let us not fear to trust the Scriptures, for we follow the saints who through the ages have proved them in life and found them true.

Paul did much to lift the status of women in various cultures. His statement that "there is neither male nor female in Christ" classifies him as a radical in his time. He gave a much larger place to women than they ever had before. Women in his view, a view partly Jewish and partly liberated by his understanding of the mind of Christ, were to be considered as human beings whose personalities were of supreme worth before God. This was a revolutionary idea then, and across the centuries it has done much, both directly and indirectly, to lift the status of women in the world. Yet Paul wrote in I Cor. 11. "But I would have you know, that the head of every man is Christ, the head of a woman is her husband, and the head of Christ is God. . . . . a man . . . is the image and glory of God; but woman is the glory of man. (For man was not made from woman, but woman from man. Neither was man created for woman, but woman for man.) "—I Cor. 11:3, 7, 8, & 9.

While Paul, who wrote the inspired passage of Galatians 3:28 which reads ". . . there is neither male nor female; for you are all one in Christ Jesus," also wrote the inspired passages of I Corinthians 14:33-35 which reads "The women should keep silence in the churches. For they are not permitted to speak, but should be subordinate, as even the law says . . . For it is shameful for a woman to speak in church."

Why does Paul not permit women to speak in the church at Corinth? His reasons are given in verses 34 and 35. It is apparent that Paul forbade women to speak for two reasons. The first was that it was against the law. Did he mean the law of Moses, the law of the land, or the law of nature? The second reason was that it was shameful for a woman to speak in church. Did he mean that it did not become her, that she would be out of character, out of place to speak in the church? It is a shame to take a beautiful race horse, a horse born for racing, trained for racing, and make him plow corn. It is also a shame to invest a lot of money, time, and patience in training a horse to race which was made to plow. It is a shame to waste talent which may be used profitably in other pursuits. It is manifest in how many ways that woman is better adapted than man for much work which needs doing today at home and abroad. There is much work for women —"rescue work" for example—which women do best.

The woman's heart and sympathetic nature has often given her a power over degraded men which men can never wield. A woman is man's helpmate, man's companion, man's wife, the mother of his and her children. A helper fit for man. A woman is of man, taken from his side. A woman is made to be loved.

It is a shame for a woman to teach or have authority over man, and to allow this is to do violence to the plain teachings of God's word.

Let us not dodge the fundamental order of importance suggested by Paul that"God is head of Christ, Christ is head of man, and man is head of woman." "Let a woman learn in silence with all submissiveness. I permit no woman to teach or to have authority over man; she is to keep silent." Thus writes the Apostle Paul in I Timothy 2:11-12, inspired of God, and recorded for us in our only infallible rule for faith and practice. This is a directive of God, and like all His directives, it is a directive of love for the good of His church and her members. And this directive of God, as always, has the woman's interest at heart. It is for her sex's sake.

A wise woman told me in Montreat: "As for myself, I insist I should keep silence in the church."

A minister attending the meeting of the General Assembly in Montreat, told of seeing a picture of a "Bobby-sox Elder," she was elected an elder in a denomination that permits the ordination of women.

A girl student at Montreat College agrees she would far rather be the wife of an elder than to be an elder.

Eight girls agreed that men ought to be elders—"It makes them feel better."

Women have never publicly given the bread and wine of the Supper. There is no masculine "priestism," in this however, or in the restraining of the woman from the office of the public teacher. "But they are often better qualified to teach, than the man who stands up to teach them." Perhaps, but such hard cases make bad law. The salutary, seemly, general binding rule gives the man the conduct of the worship in

he felt that he was too old now to begin it; but as Grade C meant only to invite someone to church he would do that - and, too, he would pray before starting out, as suggested. Prayer had been made that the Holy Spirit would direct the "drawing." The elder drew a card bearing the name of his competitor in business, one who had by clever business methods captured many of his customers. Although acquainted, he had not spoken to the man in several years, because there was ill feeling. It was a hard assignment, but true to his pledge (before drawing) upon returning from the luncheon he bowed his head at his desk and asked the Lord to bless the visit. Going to his competitor's store, he learned that the man had not come down to business that day, but was confined to his home with a severe cold. The elder decided to call at the man's house that evening on his way home. He was met at the door by the man's wife, who looked surprised, but directed him to her husband's bedroom door.

Now listen to the elder's story as he told it next day at the noon luncheon.

"When I came to his door and saw him sitting there, just looking out the window, something said to me, 'You've got something for this man better than merely inviting him to church.' It scared me and thrilled me, too. The Something that spoke to me seemed to take possession of me. The man looked up, surprised of course to see me, but greeted me kindly and asked me to take a seat. I said, 'Neighbor, I am ashamed of myself for I am a coward, and came here intending only to invite you to come to the special services going on at our church; but I have a far more important invitation for you than that. I'm inviting you to accept the Lord Jesus Christ as your Saviour!' "

The elder paused here to say, "Folks I could hardly believe it was I saying it, and yet I felt very happy in it, and strangely calm. The sick man looked away for an instant; then he turned to me and said, 'I believe the Lord sent you. When you came in I was just sitting here thinking. Today I have had more time than usual to think about something else besides business. And I've been wondering what is next? for me. This illness has reminded me that I can't live on and on. I have succeeded in business, have educated my children at the best universities and they are married and in their own homes; I have a luxurious home here, but only my wife and the servants to occupy this big house. It is all coming to an end sooner or later - and I've been wondering, What then?'

"He had an appealing look in his eyes as he turned to me and said, almost in a whisper, 'Won't you pray for me?' Folks, I just dropped right down on my knees by that man's chair and I poured out my heart to God for him, as I never prayed before in my life. If you had told me yesterday morning I would be doing such a thing as that - and for that man, my competitor - I would have thought you were crazy. I could hardly believe it was my voice praying; seemed like it was Something praying through me; I never heard myself sound like that before. When I said 'Amen' I saw tear drops on the arm of his chair, as his head was bowed. He looked up and stuck out his hand and grasped mine - and, Folks! can you believe it? he accepted Jesus Christ as his Saviour right then and there! Don't you know I'm happy; I just wish you could hold my heart in your hand and see it beat!"

As he told his story, I noticed people all around the lunch table lifting their handkerchiefs to their eyes; and the pastor, whose seat was next to mine, bowed his head on the table and was audibly thanking God. He told me afterward that this one incident was worth more to his people than all the expense and work getting up the meeting.

This of course is outstanding, but is just one of many cases where I have seen a nominal church member advance from C. to A.

(*Next lesson: Assimilating new converts into church life.*)

Helps To Understanding Scripture Readings in *Day by Day*

By Rev. C. C. Baker

Sunday, October 7, *Jeremiah* 31:31-34. As total destruction comes upon the land, God holds out hope for the future. Jeremiah buys a field at Anathoth (c.32). The people will return from exile (30:1-3). But more than this, there is a promise of a New Covenant (31:31-34). What will the New Covenant mean in terms of the peoples' relationship with God (vv.31-34)? How will God look upon their sins (vv.34b,37)? What will the New Covenant mean in their personal lives (vv.12-14,25)? How will it affect their conduct (vv.9,33)? The people will be ruled by a prince (30:21) like unto David (30:9). How does this picture of the New Covenant compare with what we have in Christ? How many of the spiritual blessings mentioned in today's passage have you found in your Christian faith (vv.9,12-14,25,31-34)?

Monday, October 8, *Psalm* 1. Observe that the "blessed" man of v.1 does not refuse to associate with sinners, but he does refuse: (a) to heed their advice, (b) to do the evil things they do, (c) to entertain the attitudes and language they employ. When Jesus associated with publicans and sinners, did He ever compromise His own integrity in doing so? What is the end of the man who "goes along with the crowd" (vv.5-6)? What is he like (v.4)? In what does the "blessed" man delight (v.2)? What is his relation to God (v.6)? How does he fare as he lives his life in this

ies. Now study the Psalm on your own to discover how thoroughly God met his need for physical protection as well as how intimately He met the nnermost longings of his soul. The Lord is strength (v.1b), but He is also light (v.1a). The Lord is mighty in battle (vv.2-3), but he is also full of beauty (v.4) and loving, tender care (vv.5,10). Notice the confidence (vv.2-3), the faith (v.13) and courage (v.14) that the Psalmist finds in the Lord. Do you find in this Psalm any prayers or desires that you would like to express to the Lord on your behalf today (notice vv.4,8-9, 11)?

Saturday, October 13, *Psalm* 119:41-48. This Psalmist was utterly dedicated to the Word of the Lord. What thought does v.44 emphasize concerning the way in which he kept God's law? Was this unwavering obedience to the will of God a difficult, burdensome thing for the Psalmist (v.45)? Why was it not difficult (vv.47-48)? Was he ashamed to speak of his God to others (v.46)? Why was he not ashamed (vv.47-48)? How did the Psalmist's reliance on God's Word in time of trouble reveal the depths of his confidence in the Word (vv.42-43)? Think through all the verbs in vv.41-48 that reveal the Psalmist's devotion to God's Law: "trust" in thy word, "hope" in thy ordinances, "keep" thy law, "sought" thy precepts, etc. What do these words reveal to you of your own personal dedication to the Word of God?

SABBATH SCHOOL LESSONS — REV. J. KENTON PARKER

LESSON FOR OCTOBER 7

The Creation Story

Background Scripture: Genesis 1:1 - 2:3
Devotional Reading: Psalm 104:24-33

In verse 34 of Psalm 104 we have these words: "My meditation of him shall be sweet." There are many of these "Nature Psalms." Eastern people, especially the Hebrews, saw God in Nature. As they gazed up into the heavens at night, or looked on the wonders they saw all about them every day, they thought of God as both Creator and Preserver and Ruler of the Universe. These thoughts were very sweet to them. They saw His Power, Wisdom, and Goodness, (Love expressing itself) in the beauties and glory of sun, moon, and stars, and earth. To see God in nature and to meditate upon Him was real worship. To the heathen, these objects of nature became gods. To the Jews they were His handiwork, and the evidence of the True and Living God Who created them : the heavens declared the glory of God and the earth showed His handiwork, "Forever singing as they shine, The hand that made us is divine."

"The earth is full of thy riches." These words meant much to the writer of the 104th Psalm. How much more do they mean to us today! We are beginning to see how rich the world is. It is only in recent years that men have discovered some of the hidden resources of the world. The tremendous deposits of coal, iron, and oil; the power of steam and electricity; the power of the A-bomb and the H-bomb. Even waste and desert lands sometimes hide most valuable minerals. The earth is full of *Thy riches*. I wish to emphasize these last two words. Man often behaves as though all this wealth belonged to him. He forgets the Creator and Owner. Man has not only forgotten God and His ownership, but he has abused these "riches untold." These things became the object of his covetousness and greed, and have been often used to curse the earth by destroying or oppressing mankind.

Just to take the latest discovery, Atomic Power. So far it is being developed almost exclusively as a weapon to be used in the "next war." Is it possible, or even probable, that the human race will be destroyed by the misuse of this great power? Just yesterday thousands of men and women were evacuated from most of our large cities as imaginary bombs were dropped from the skies. Sometimes, also, the riches of the earth incite men to commit terrible crimes. Men will not only steal, but kill, in their lust for riches.

Our lesson, "The Creation Story," may be divided into three parts as we notice the three times the word, "create" is used: First, in a general way, when it speaks of the creation of the universe; "In the beginning God created the heavens and the earth"; second, in connection with the bringing forth of life, or living creatures, in verse 21; "And God created great whales, and every living creature that moveth"; third, when man was created: "So God created man in his own image." To "create" is to make out of nothing. The other words used signify making, ordering, or apportioning.

Before taking up these divisions in more detail, I wish to use very freely the material found on Genesis in the New Analytical Bible published by John A. Dickson, an edition which I find most helpful. "In some respects this is the most remarkable book in the Bible. The first announcement is the greatest that can be uttered - the fact of the being and creative power of God. The Bible begins with the truth of God, that God is, that there is one God, and that he is the Creator of the universe, that the latter is not self-existent.

"The same is true of man. He was not only made by God, but in the image of God, the supreme creative act of God.

"Thus we have the three great basic facts — the fact of God, man created by God, the genesis of the moral history of man. The fourth great fact gives us the foundation of the whole Biblical system — the first promise of a Redeemer for the salvation of a fallen race. (3:15). Thus does the book of Genesis in the first three chapters furnish the groundwork for all that is to follow. "This brief statement makes clear two things: That the design of the Bible is to reveal the Divine plan of redemption in Jesus Christ. The other fact is that the understanding of the Bible requires a knowledge of the book of Genesis."

This account in Genesis does away with both Pantheism, which declares that all is God, and also with Materialism. "From every consideration, Biblical and scientific alike, the theories of Pantheism and Materialism break down."

When we note the plural form of the name of God with a singular verb, the idea of trinity and unity is suggested. When we combine this with what John says about the creative work of the Word, (Christ), and the fact stated in Genesis that "the Spirit of God moved upon the face of the waters," we see the doctrine of the Triune God revealed.

There is a progressive development in creation. This is the truth of Genesis and the truth of science as well. This development is from the lower to the higher. It begins at the bottom of the scale and proceeds upwards. "It is impossible to read this marvelous sketch, the account of creation condensed into a single brief chapter, without realizing that God alone by the Holy Spirit could have communicated this outline of the creative work the truth of which is supported in the twentieth century, and that no human being in that early day could have framed."

This first chapter of Genesis and the first chapter of the Gospel of John should be read together:

In the beginning God -
In the beginning was the Word.
Created the heavens and the earth.
All things were created by him.
And God said, Let there be light.
That was the true Light.
Let us make man in our image.
And the Word was made flesh.

Let me call your attention to the word translated "firmament" in our King James Version, which should be translated "the expanse above the earth." The word in the Hebrew does not mean something firm and solid, but "something that is very thin, extended, spread out; just the best word that could be chosen to signify the atmosphere."

We will now take up the three divisions of this chapter as indicated by the use of the word "create."

I. *The Beginning of all existence:* the Creation of the Universe; verse one: "In the beginning God created the heavens and the earth."

This general statement would include the whole universe, the magnitude of which exceeds all imagination. With our naked eyes we can see enough to make us marvel at its grandeur and beauty. With our greatest telescopes we can penetrate further into its mysteries and glory. The old saying that "the undevout astronomer is mad" is certainly true. Even the "star-gazers" without the aid of instruments stand amazed at the glory and beauty and vastness of the sky above them. How must we feel when we behold all of this magnified a thousand times! No wonder the Psalmist exclaims, The heavens declare the glory of God and the firmament showeth his handiwork.

From verse one to verse twenty we see God making a beautiful world fit to be inhabited by the animal creation. This is sometimes called "mediate creation," and let us note that all is done by the word, or command of God. "And God said, Let there be light; and there was light." "And God said, Let there be an expanse above the earth," and God made that expanse. Even in this "mediate creation," the making, or reforming, or placing of things out of existing materials, it is God Who does the "making," Our Catechism puts it thus: The work of creation is, God's making all things of nothing, by the word of his power, in the space of six days, and all very good. The psalmist says, (33:6), By the word of the Lord were the heavens made.

II. *The Beginning of all animate existence:* 21-25: The Animal Kingdom.

In the preceding verses we had the beginning of all existence. Now we come to the animal kingdom: the great whales and living creatures which live in the waters of the earth; the fowl that fly in the sky; the cattle and creeping things ınd every beast after his kind which live upon the earth. When we think of the extent and wonders of this vast animal kingdom we begin to see something of the magnitude of this creative work. Here is a "new" development in His work of creation, and the distinctive word "create" is again used.

II. *The Beginning of all Spiritual Existence:* Creation of Man : 26-31.

When we come to the creation of man there is a distinct change: "And God said, Let us make man in our image, after our likeness. As Psalm 8 says, "For thou hast made him a little lower than the angels," (God), "and has crowned him with glory and honor." Man was to be a "king"; to have dominion over the earth. So God created man in his own image, male and female, and God blessed them and said to them, Be fruitful and multiply and replenish the earth . . . and have dominion. The image of God was spiritual likeness; knowledge, righteousness, and holiness. And God saw all that He had created, and it was very good.

Chapter 2:1-3 tells us that God rested the seventh day from all His work. This is one of the reasons behind the keeping of the Sabbath Day.

YOUNG PEOPLE'S DEPARTMENT — **REV. B. HOYT EVANS**

YOUTH PROGRAM FOR OCTOBER 7

"Live Wires For Christ"

Suggested Devotional Outline

Hymn: "We Have A Story To Tell To The Nations"

Prayer

Scripture: Romans 10:10-15

Hymn: "Ye Christian Heralds, Go Proclaim"

Program Leader:

When we speak of "Live Wires for Christ," we are using that term in a literal sense, because we have reference to the live wires which send out the message of radio and television. In this program we want to discover how these media of modern communication can be used in the service of Christ. It is being claimed that radio and television can be used to fulfill the great commission to "go into all the world and preach the gospel to every creature." We want to find out whether or not this is an accurate claim, and if so, what we can do to have a share in preaching the gospel by these means.

It is evident that Assembly's Youth Council considered radio and television important to the work of the church, because they have chosen a phase of that work to be one of our financial objectives for a second year. The aspect of radio and television work which has been selected to receive our support as Presbyterian young people is the providing of a mobile radio and television studio. Before the program is over you will be hearing more of this mobile studio and of the purposes which it will serve.

First Speaker:

One question which we shall do well to consider is the kind of audience which can be reached through a Christian radio and television ministry. If the church tries to proclaim the gospel by means of radio and television, who will hear it? In answer to this question there comes immediately to mind a great host of people who are truly unable to attend church services. In this group we find the sick, the aged, and those who are practically isolated from organized Christianity. These people need the hope, encouragement, and instruction of the gospel, and one way of providing them these blessings is for the church to send out its message over the live wires of radio and television.

Another group we can hope to reach is made up of those who are not interested in Christianity and who never go to church at all. This is the evangelistic opportunity for the church to use radio and television. There are many more people in the United States who listen to radio programs and watch television than who attend church. If the church can send out a clear and appealing gospel message over the air ways, some of the indifferent and hostile multitude will be bound to hear it. If for no other reason, some will hear the message of Christ out of curiosity, and some of those who hear will believe and be saved. If even one lost soul can be reclaimed for Christ through our radio and television work, then it will be worth our while to carry it on and support it with our gifts.

Second Speaker:

Another matter which deserves our consideration is the program of radio and television work which is now being carried on by our church. In other words, what are we doing already? In the first place, our church is one of four denominations sharing in the work of the Protestant Radio and Television Center in Atlanta, Georgia. One of our own ministers,

Dr. John M. Alexander, is director of the Center. The Center is equipped to prepare and produce religious programs for the large networks. These have included series of sermons, Bible studies, Sunday school lessons, and religious dramas.

Churches which are awake to their opportunities can also have a helpful ministry through local radio and television programs. Nearly every local station is willing to sell, and often to give, time to the churches of the community for religious programs, provided that the programs are of creditable quality. This local ministry accounts for daily devotional services and the broadcast of Sunday church services in many communities. (This would be a good place to have a discussion about the number and quality of Christian radio and television programs which are available in your area.)

Third Speaker:

As was pointed out by our program leader, one of the primary aims of this program is to give information about the Mobile Radio and Television Studio which is our fourth financial objective for 1956. Just what is it? It will consist of an automobile, a trailer, and all the basic equipment found in a radio and television studio, such as television cameras, lights, recording equipment, microphones, etc. Who will use it? It will be used by the staff of the Protestant Radio and Television Center. What purposes will the mobile studio serve? For one thing, it will enable the staff of the center to conduct training programs among religious leaders in local communities. The previous speaker indicated that it is important that Christian programs originating in local stations be of high quality. The mobile studio will be used as a class room to teach ministers and others how to produce better religious programs.

Another purpose which the studio will serve is to enable the staff to make on the spot recordings of sermons, services, and programs. At present, practically all of the program production must be carried on in the Atlanta studios. The mobile studio will make possible a wider variety of programs, and should lead to greater interest.

Program Leader:

We have heard a brief description of our church's venture into the field of radio and television. We have seen something of the opportunities which are awaiting this kind of ministry, and we have been told of the part which we can have in this work through our gifts. As we hear the voice of our church proclaiming the good news of Jesus Christ over the live wires of radio and television, we can be glad that we have had a share in it.

(Receive the offering at this time, or explain that a share of your benevolent budget has been set aside for this objective.)

Prayer of Dedication
Hymn: "I Love To Tell The Story"

with God through our Lord Jesus Christ . . .
He is our peace . . .

In the presence of such a Saviour, I confess my sins and pray:

Create in me a clean heart, O God, and renew a right spirit within me.

And declare my faith as did Job:

I know that Thou canst do everything, and that no thought can be withholden from Thee.

Again I hear Jesus' reassuring words:

With God all things are possible. I will make you to become fishers of men. Go tell my brethren. Ye shall be witnesses unto me.

And I offer unto Him my prayer of re-dedication:

To tell the story of God's great, redeeming love is my desire, Oh, Lord. I come anew to Thee asking that Thou wilt make me become a faithful intercessor, a witness with power, a worker filled with Thy Spirit. Teach me, O God, the disciplines of patience that the fruit of love may ever be patience, and kindness in word and in thought. May my strength not be dissipated by discourtesies or un-Christian thinking or any disobedience to Thee. In newness of spirit may my love to Thee and to all people abound yet more and more that my life may be filled with the fruits of His righteousness, which are by Jesus Christ, unto the glory and praise of God. In His Name, Amen.

A Thank You

Five of us from the Lakeside Presbyterian Church have just finished the Area Laboratory School held at Ginter Park Presbyterian Church here in Richmond. We wish to express our appreciation to the Board of Women's Work and the Women of the Church for giving part of your 1956 Birthday Offering for this work in training teachers in our church.

It is a wonderful experience to see outstanding teachers teach a group of boys and girls. There are many lay teachers who never see the correct way of teaching except through such opportunities as a Lab School. I feel that the quality of teaching in our churches over the Assembly will improve because of those who attended these Lab Sschools and have been challenged to do a much better job as they returned to their local churches.

Mildred Wilson

Faith in Five Tongues

Two missionaries, a Taiwanese pastor, and their assistants, learned recently on Taiwan that five languages are sometimes better than one. Visiting a little bamboo church in a mountain village of the aborigines, they conveyed the gospel message piecemeal. One of the missionaries could speak English and Taiwanese, the other English and Mandarin. The pastor could speak Taiwanese, a little Mandarin, and Japanese. Their assistants could speak Taiyal, understood by all of the tribespeople, and each of them had some knowledge of at least one of the other languages. By considerable word juggling, the message passed from lip to lip and reached listeners.

More than a hundred churches have been erected in the mountains by the people of five tribes. The gospel spreads like a prairie fire, carried from village to village, by laymen and laywomen.

Stewardship

A good church member works for and through the church, even as he works outside for the church, to redeem his pledge of faith and love. He offers the skill of his hands, his professional talents, the gifts of his spirit and, not least, the superb grace of his faithfulness. He seeks with others a division of labor in the enterprises of the church so that laymen may assume such burdens as otherwise overtake the minister and distract him from his irreplaceable task. Working for God in His church does not substitute for living with God, but follows from it.

—David H. Sandstrom

Church News

Opening of General Assembly's Training School

Dr. S. J. Patterson, Jr., Secretary of the Division of Men's Work in the Board of Christian Education spoke at the opening exercises of the General Assembly's Training School on Thursday, September 13th. An enrollment of eleven men and eighty-seven women was reported, with thirty-nine in the senior class and fifty-nine in the junior class. The five states having the largest numbers enrolled are: Virginia 20, Florida 11; North Carolina 10; South Carolina 8; and West Virginia 8. In addition 15 other states are represented in the enrollment. There are three students who are daughters of missionaries, one from the Philippines and two from Formosa; and young women natives of Brazil, Ceylon and Japan.

Although Presbyterians predominate in the student body, it also contains members of Baptist, Methodist, Moravian, Episcopal and Congregational Christian churches.

For the first time two couples are enrolled as students. They are Mr. and Mrs. Dick R. Kinser of Baton Rouge, La., and Mr. and Mrs. Merle I. Kelly of Huntington, W. Va., and Apopka, Florida.

GEORGIA

Atlanta—Dr. E. C. Scott, Stated Clerk of the General Assembly, on Thursday, Sept. 6, took a 24-hour cruise on the aircraft carrier USS Saipan as guest of the Secretary of the Navy. Dr. Scott was one of twenty nationally known churchmen and the only member of Presbyterian Church, U.S., invited to take the cruise.

the campaign for funds and the plans for the establishment of the college at Laurinburg.

The report of the Church Extension Committee showed most gratifying progress being made in this field. Most of the churches are supplied either with regular pastors or regular services; the salary scale is being increased; church properties are being improved. The Dellabrook Negro Mission in Winston-Salem presented a petition signed by 18 persons asking to be organized into a church; a commission was appointed to handle this matter. The Rev. P. J. Garrison, Jr. is the Executive Secretary of Church Extension.

The Board of Trustees of Glade Valley School presented a report showing that this School has been making most satisfactory progress during the past year; it has a full enrollment of students for this year. The Presbytery authorized the Board to purchase an additional piece of property adjacent to the campus to be used for a camp site.

The Stewardship Committee of Presbytery's Council again recommended that all churches conduct a "Prebudget Canvass", and are making plans to have teams visit the churches to discuss this matter with the officers.

The Rev. R. F. Brown, who has been without a regular charge for several years, was honorably retired. The Rev. J. Harry Whitmore offered his resignation as Pastor of the First Presbyterian Church of Thomasville and asked that the pastoral relationship be dissolved; the Church concurring in this the request was granted and he was honorably retired.

Presbytery adjourned to meet in Adjourned Session January 15, 1957 at a place to be selected by the Moderator and Stated Clerk.

J. Harry Whitmore,
Stated Clerk

SOUTH CAROLINA

Clinton—Presbyterian College in Clinton has resumed campaigning on its Diamond Jubilee Development program which produced more than $600,000 in cash and pledges during the first nine months.

According to President Marshall W. Brown, drives in six regions in South Caolina and Georgia will be conducted simultaneously during September and October, as Presbyterians of these two states who own and control the college seek to raise at least $750,000 for the institution during 1956.

Just over one-half of the two-state area was covered during the first nine months of the campaigning before activity was suspended during the vacation months of July and August.

Preparations are well underway for campaigns in these four South Carolina regions: Columbia, including most of Congaree Presbytery; Rock Hill, encompassing all of Bethel Presbytery; Sumter, one-half of Harmony Presbytery; and Kingstree, the other half of Harmony Presbytery.

Simultaneously, the program is underway in the Athens Presbytery region and in the Macon region, including approximately one-half of Augusta-Macon Presbytery.

Official records show that a total of $604,716.33 has been subscribed by 3,925 contributors during the first nine months, and this subscription averages $154.00 per contributor.

Presbyterian College, through the development program, will add a new chapel-auditorium and new student center to its campus facilities, and will increase its endowment.

TEXAS

Death of Rev. Raymond A. Partlow

Commerce — The Rev. Raymond A. Partlow, pastor of the First Church of Ferriday, Louisiana, Red River Presbytery, died in Temple, Texas on September 2. Mr. Partlow was born in Bartlett, Texas January 4, 1885. He was graduated from Austin College and Austin Presbyterian Theological Seminary and was ordained by Dallas Presbytery July 5, 1929. Mr. Partlow, a veteran of World War I, served pastorates in Happy, Texas, Grand Avenue Church in Sherman, Texas, Brownsville, Texas, Paris, Texas, Honey Grove, Texas, and Ferriday, Louisiana. He was for a time director of religious education and home mission superintendent in El Paso Presbytery. For a period he was a member of the Austin College board of trustees and instructor in the Bible department there. He is survived by Mrs. Partlow and two children, Lou Ray and Ralph Gray. Funeral services were held from the Grand Avenue Church in Sherman, conducted by the Rev. John A. Mintner and the Rev. Walter Lazenby, Jr., of Commerce, pastor and former pastor of the church, and the Rev. Hudson A. McNair of Temple.

BOOKS

THE BOOK OF EZEKIEL. Charles R. Erdman. Fleming H. Revell. $2.00.

Ezekiel is one of the most difficult books of the Bible to interpret. Dr. Erdman offers sane guidance in the interpretation of this book. He tells us that the figures of speech of Ezekiel were designed not to conceal but to reveal the truth. The author compares Ezekiel with the Revelation of St. John who frequently borrowed from the language of Ezekiel. Ezekiel is praised as the prophet of comfort and cheer to the Hebrew exiles in Babylonia.

Dr. Erdman observes, "By such a vision of Messianic blessing the hearts of the exiles were comforted, their faith was renewed and a repentant and purified remnant became the nucleus of the people, through whom finally were fulfilled the promises of redemption for the world." This volume carries an inspiring message for a nation's darkest hours.

CLIMBING THE HEIGHTS. Compiled by Al Bryant. Zondervan. $2.50.

The Editor-in-Chief of Zondervan Publishing House prepared this volume to encourage Christians to spend sufficient time in prayer and meditation upon the Word of God to equip them for the daily battle of life. The meditations here are designed to build a strong and healthy Christian life. There is a page for each day of the year. The selections are well chosen.

VICTORIOUS CHRISTIAN LIVING. Alan Redpath. Fleming H. Revell Co. $3.00.

The author is serving at present as pastor of the Moody Memorial Church of Chicago. He has been favorably known both in England and America as an expository preacher.

The author has high regard for the Old Testament. He realizes that the Old Testament is preparatory to the New. The New cannot be understood apart from the Old. He said we begin to discover that God's way of dealing with man in the Old Testament is but a picture of the dealing with man in the New.

He remarks that once we grasp the truth that the Old Testament is a record of God's dealing with His people in the same way in which He deals with us today, it is transformed from a Book of dry history into a Book of divine revelation.

In this volume the author gives an exposition of the Book of Joshua, which he holds to be the pattern of God's redemption in personal life. The author's views concerning victorious living are sound and Biblical and free from many extreme interpretations sometimes presented on this subject. The emphasis in this book is on the going onward in Canaan, the land of promise, which awaits us here and now.

PHILIPPIANS. Merrill C. Tenney. William B. Eerdman's. $2.00.

Dr. Tenney's treatment of the Epistle to the Philippians is illuminating. He brings to his subject a mind well disciplined by the Scriptures and the abilty to set forth the meaning of the Word in a simple and highly readable style. In Philippians, he says Paul gives us information concerning the Beginning, the Fellowship, the Pattern, the Experience, and the Effects of the Gospel. This book equips the reader to understand the Gospel better and to live more fully in terms of it.

Dr. Tenney observes that the Gospel was to Paul a term that included much more than a formulated theology. It represented an entire dynamic and sphere of life which embraced all other relationships. If one wants to see the Gospel at work, this exposition of Dr. Tenney's will be helpful to this end.

SPURGEON'S SERMONS ON THE SERMON ON THE MOUNT. Charles Haddon Spurgeon. Zondervan. $2.00.

The ministry of Spurgeon has lasted well over a century. More of his sermons are printed today than of any of his contemporaries. His messages are still timely and moving.

The messages in this volume have been selected from Spurgeon's **Treasury of the New Testament.** Every one is based on Matthew Chapters 5, 6, and 7. Portions of the messages which had only a purely local interest have been deleted. The fourteen messages here will bless the heart of any reader.

ELISHA. F. W. Krummacher. Zondervan. $2.95.

Dr. Krummacher was a famous German Lutheran preacher in Berlin. He was a man of deep spiritual insight and is rated as one of the greatest of all preachers in Germany in the middle of the Nineteenth Century. This volume gives us an analytical work of the character of Elisha. It is a moving biography of one who proved God and was himself faithful to the mission God gave him.

THE SOUTHERN PRESBYTERIAN JOURNAL

A Presbyterian weekly magazine devoted to the statement, defense and propagation of the Gospel, the faith which was once for all delivered unto the saints.

VOL. XV NO. 23 — OCTOBER 3, 1956 — $2.50 A YEAR

. EDITORIAL .

THE SOUTHERN PRESBYTERIAN JOURNAL
The Journal has no official connection with the Presbyterian Church in the United States
Rev. Henry B. Dendy, D.D., Editor..........Weaverville, N. C.
Dr. L. Nelson Bell, Associate Editor..........Asheville, N. C.
Rev. Wade C. Smith, Associate Editor..........Weaverville, N. C.

EDITORIAL

We Oppose Errors . . . We Do Not Judge Individuals

A young defender of the faith was talking with a grand old Scottish stalwart about a certain minister who was teaching rationalistic views. The older man remarked, "We must be careful to remember that we are opposing errors in doctrine. We are not here to judge an individual. He has One Who does judge him, the Same One Who judges us." Since stumbling upon this incident, I have been turning over in mind the great word of our Saviour:

> For neither doth the Father judge any man, but He hath given all judgment unto the Son . . . He gave Him authority to execute judgment, because He is the Son of Man.

Does this mean that as the Father has resigned judgment to the Son, so ought we, at least as private individuals, likewise leave judgment in His holy, gracious, nail-pierced hands?

No doubt there has to be judgment to keep order in the civil community and in the Church. But God has ordained the State to administer the one and the Church the other. We have responsibilities, from time to time, in the one and in the other; but then we act as responsible accusers before or as agents of these governments, not as private persons. No one can properly contend that either of these governments gives perfection, but they provide at least a measure of order under which we live and in which we proclaim the Gospel.

One of the current Scottish theologians has sought to draw a line between what a man holds in the top of his head and what holds him in the bottom of his heart. In trying to maintain the faith, we often have to differ with what comes from the top of a man's head and through his pen. It does not become us to sit in private judgment upon what is in the bottom of his heart. There his Lord is his Judge. W.C.R.

Seeing the Glory of God

To a sorrowful and doubting Martha our Lord exclaimed: *"Said I not unto thee, that, if thou wouldest believe, thou shouldest see the glory of God?"*

This promise has not been altered. It remains valid today in all of its marvellous implications.

There are many words which stand out like beacons in the Scriptures. "Faith" is one of them. It is, in fact, the cornerstone of the attitude with which man must approach God. It was the recapturing of the Biblical concept of faith which brought about the Reformation. Hence its meaning is vitally important to Christians of every generation.

One of the serious problems of contemporary thinking is the substitution of human speculation for faith. To the unregenerate it is unreasonable to believe in something which is to them intangible; this despite the fact that everyday we live by faith: faith in things we do not understand and for which there is no adequate proof other than that results justify such faith. Food is consumed without an understanding of the process of digestion and metabolism. Almost every act of daily life involves some kind of an act of faith.

But when we come to the spiritual we may hang back, demanding proof before we believe. To the unbelieving the Christian faith is utterly unreasonable and the gap between the non-Christian and the Christian is crossed by an act of faith in which a decision of the will in some mysterious way makes unreality become reality.

A few months ago the writer was characterized by a brilliant Christian scholar as being "anti-intellectual." This hurt, but we believe the fault is our own because that which we have written has not been clear. God does expect us to use our reasoning powers and He gives us all ample evidence on which to use reason and from that to proceed to faith.

We have probably at times unwittingly con-
:used the word "reason" with "speculation." \ statement we have made on several occasions nay also have been misunderstood. The tatement is : "There is much unbelief abroad oday which is masking under the guise of cholarship."

We do not retract this for one minute be- :ause it is true. However, it should be clarified ınd amplified. Much scholarship is character- zed by genuine faith and we all owe an in- :alculable debt to those reverent scholars who ıave searched the Scriptures and related sub- ects and who in so doing have brought glory o God and honored His Word.

But, is the glory of God real to those who efuse to believe? Is the Bible to be approached ,s one would dissect a cadaver, or, with the :are a surgeon would use in operating on a iving person? If it is a human book, the former ıpproach is justified. If it is God-breathed, then t stands to judge men, not to be judged of hem.

The findings of scholars depend on the ›hilosophical presuppositions with which they ,pproach their task. If biased for and commit- ed to a concept antagonistic to divine revela- ion and the supernatural, their findings will eflect that bias. If reality is thought to be ınattainable; if it is assumed that there are ıo absolutes; the outcome will be devoid of ertainty or finality.

On the other hand if one's bias is *for* divine evelation and the supernatural as a *logical* oncept of God and His dealings with His reation, the resulting findings will reflect that ıith.

That the faith of all men is not alike is bvious. Some of the early disciples had little ifficulty accepting the fact of the resurrection. 'homas had to be shown our Lord's scarred *ody* to believe. But Christ said to him: *Blessed are they that have not seen, and yet ave believed."*

With the eyes of faith we behold the glory : God; earth-bound though we be, God has ,ven to them who believe to *see* that which ıe world does not see, to *have* that which the orld does not have.

Moses illustrates this spiritual insight, this :avenly vision. Egypt offered him everything the world could possibly hope to afford, but he forsook it all: *"for he endured, as seeing Him who is invisible."*

Abraham had a similar faith: *"For he looked for a city which hath foundations, whose builder and maker is God."*

Such faith is not easy in the sophisticated Twentieth Century. Man has progressed far in the road of discovery and of scientific achievements which even in one generation have transformed the world in which we live. Is the faith of Abraham and Moses any less needed today? Has the heart of man changed? Have his needs been altered one whit?

The validity of the gospel of the Lord Jesus Christ is proven by the fact that man and his basic needs are identical with those of men in every generation. This gospel is received in but one way — by faith. To the world it is foolishness; to those who are saved, the power of God.

The age of reason in which we live is also the age of decision — of individual decision, and insofar as the Christian faith is concerned that decision requires an act of faith.

The faith of Martha was probably very small but it was real faith. And she saw a stupendous miracle — a man who had been dead walked forth alive.

Did this miracle convince all present? It did not. We are told that some believed; others were so confirmed in their unbelief that they went about to destroy the One Who had performed the miracle.

God still honors even a little faith and with that faith we who were spiritually dead walk forth in newness of life—born again. He performs this miracle for us and for all who will believe.

Can we do less than cry out: *"Lord, I believe, help thou mine unbelief!"* L.N.B.

News Distortion

Christian people should realize that news dispatches in the secular press are often distorted and, so far as other Christians are concerned, give them the benefit of the doubt.

On Monday, September 17th the Rev. Billy Graham spoke to 1200 people in New York. The

The Southern Presbyterian Journal, *a Presbyterian Weekly magazine devoted to the statement, defense, and propagation of the Gospel, the faith which was once for all delivered unto the saints,* published every Wednesday by The Southern Presbyterian Journal, Inc., in Weaverville, N. C.

Entered as second-class matter May 15, 1942, at the Postoffice at Weaverville, N. C., under the Act of March 3, 1879. Vol. XV, No. 23, October 3, 1956. Editorial and Business Offices: Weaverville, N. C. Printed in the U.S.A. by Biltmore Press, Asheville, N. C.

ADDRESS CHANGE: When changing address, please let us have both old and new address as far in advance as possible. Allow three weeks after change if not sent in advance. When possible, send an address label giving your old address.

occasion was a banquet given in his honor by the New York Crusade Committee.

The writer heard this address and it was one of the most impassioned pleas for the necessity of the new birth we have ever heard. In addition four people gave their testimonies; a former vice racketeer; a former Communist; a politician and the head of a modelling agency.

These testimonies showed what God had done in the hearts and lives of four people who have been born again and many in the audience literally were moved to tears. In its number were some of the world's most prominent people.

The press reports quoted Mr. Graham as saying:

"We're not coming here to clean up New York. We're coming to get the people to dedicate themselves to God and then send them to their own Church—Catholic, Protestant or Jewish."

He said nothing of the kind. What he did say in substance was: "We are not coming to New York with the grandiose idea that we can clean up New York. We are coming in all humility to work for and with the churches of this area. Those who make their decisions for Christ will be channeled into the churches of their choice."

"All are invited to attend the meetings: Protestants, Catholics and Jews."

The confusion of these statements and merging them into one by the news agency may have been unintentional, or it may have been done deliberately. In any case they were *not* merged in the address and Christians would be wise to withhold judgment when such obvious misquotes are read. L.N.B.

A Meditation

One day at noon I was walking home from the University. It had been raining off and on during the morning, and it was my first day back at teaching after a mild case of flu. Since I had neither umbrella nor auto, I had wondered an hour before about walking home. I did not want to get wet, and I did not want another case of flu.

But now at noon, although the sidewalks were still wet, the rain had stopped and the sun had come out. As I crossed the campus in the smile of early spring, I thought how God was good to stop the rain so that I could get home comfortably.

Being a professor, however, I was also aware of what unbelievers might say if they had known my thoughts. Do you suppose, they would have said with scorn, that God turns off the rain just for you? Don't you know anything about meteorology? Don't you have any conception of natural law? It is ridiculous to think that God, if there is a God, adjusts the universe for the benefit of one person, or even for the human race as a whole.

Then I went on a few steps as a last cloud passed across the sun. Yes, it is true, I admitted to myself, that God does not turn on and off the rain just for my benefit, and possibly not just for the benefit of the human race as a whole. But, at the same time, though God may not have made the universe only for man, he made it entirely for man. His purposes may very well be wider than the affairs of the human race, but so intricate are his plans and so perfect that the whole conspires to let me walk home comfortably that particular day.

"The Lord . . . maintainest my lot. The lines are fallen unto me in pleasant places; yet, I have a goodly heritage." (Psalm 16:5-6)

G.H.C.

To The Far Corners

By George Burnham

Dr. Billy Graham, in recent months, carried the simple message of Jesus Christ to the far corners of the earth—making a 40,000-mile tour of India, Thailand, the Philippines, Japan, Formosa, Hong Kong, Korea and Hawaii.

I would like to tell you some of the things God did with the message, delivered by His dedicated messenger. And Billy would be the first to tell you that it was the message that contained the power. His attitude throughout the tour was "To God be the glory, great things He hath done."

It was my privilege to go along, stand on the sidelines, and put some of the wonderful happenings on paper for 600 newspapers throughout the United States, Canada and Great Britain. God performed a miracle to make this possible. Two weeks before the scheduled departure, I underwent major stomach surgery and the doctor said there was no hope of my going. But this doctor, Doyle Currey, was a man of God first and doctor of medicine second. He held a Gideon prayer meeting in my room the day after the operation and these Chattanooga businessmen prayed that God would raise me up if it were His will for me to make the trip. Less than two weeks later I flew to Atlanta for a yellow fever shot and was in New York on time to leave with Billy.

On the long plane trip from New York to Bombay, India, Billy spent much time reading his Bible and praying that God would do big things for the people of the Far East.

Shortly after the craft left Cairo, Egypt, we crossed the Red Sea and then in a few minutes came alongside Mt. Sinai. As a gesture to Billy, the pilot slowed the engines. A little white cloud hovered over the mountain. Billy said with just a little imagination he could see Moses and God talking together. As we continued to fly over the Sinai Desert and looked at mile after mile of nothing but nothingness, Billy remarked:

"No wonder God had to feed the children of Israel with manna from Heaven. No wonder he had to furnish them with water from a rock."

In Bombay, a city of filth, intrigue and hate, we ran into a series of riots. The riots were not because of Billy, but had been started by the people over the redivision of Indian states to ease the tangled language situation. In India, people who live 20 miles apart can't understand the other's language. Over 50 people were killed during the week we were there and the big rally had to be cancelled after two people were killed outside the stadium where it was to be held. Big meetings were held, however, for the press and Christian workers. A reporter made a decision for Christ at the press conference and a number of decisions were noted at the meeting for Christians. Some of those who raised hands were in clerical attire.

It was in the southern part of India where God moved in a mighty way. Crowds of 30,000 to 40,000 turned out each night in Madras. Billy had to speak through two interpreters, one in Tamil and the other in Telegu. But God was not bound by such handicaps. The results were greater than when he spoke, uninterrupted, at Fort Worth, Chattanooga, St. Louis or Los Angeles. When the invitation was given, people rushed to the front. Some of them fell in the dust at the foot of the platform and called out to the wonderful Jesus they had just heard about.

Occasionally, during his talk, Billy would use a bit of humor. There would be three outbursts of laughter, once when he told it and once each when it was translated.

Thousands of students made their decisions for Christ at special morning meetings. A missionary, with tears in his eyes, remarked:

"This is the first time the students have been reached with the message of Christ."

At Kottayam, Billy had the largest crowds of the tour. The meetings were held in a huge open-air area literally carved out of the mountainside by hard-working women, who transported thousands of baskets of earth on their shoulders. A crowd of 100,000 gathered for one of the services. The people had walked 15 to 20 miles through the dense jungles in order to get there. Many of them thanked God for a full moon, so they could see the deadly cobras along the jungle trail. It's extremely doubtful if people in America would walk five miles along a paved thoroughfare in broad daylight to attend a religious service.

As in Madras, the response was immediate. Thousands poured toward the platform. They had heard an inspiring solution to the drabness of their temporary lives on earth.

During the preliminary remarks at the service, Billy remarked about all the bugs flying around the lights on the platform. The interpreter didn't have a word for bugs, but did the next best thing. He inserted the word "bed-bugs." Another speaker, who once addressed a rally in India, began by saying "I'm tickled to death to be here." His interpreter thought for a few seconds and did the best he could, by translating it like this: "Our speaker is so happy to be here that he's caught the itch and scratched himself to death."

At Palamcottah, farther south, Billy witnessed an even greater hunger for the message. Several thousand responded each night. Many wore the mark of Hindu holy men on their forehead. One was noted as he knelt in the dust and cried, "Jesus, save me; Jesus, save me." The message presented had been a far cry from that of Hinduism, a pagan religion with over 30,000 gods.

The same enthusiastic response was noted everywhere—Delhi, Calcutta, Benares and other points. In Delhi, Billy had an audience with Prime Minister Nehru and told him about how God had changed his life at the age of 17. The testimony made a great impression on Nehru.

When the message was preached at Manila, over 5,000 surged from the crowd of 40,000 to make decisions for Christ. It was the greatest response on the tour.

The hand of God was seen at every stop. People were born again and a new life came to the churches as Christians rededicated themselves. Over 1,000,000 came out to listen on the tour and more than 40,000 responded to the invitation to accept a new way of life.

Why did these things happen? One of the great reasons was that Christians around the world were praying. Billy Graham is probably the most prayed for man in history. God heard the prayers.

Another reason was the message was presented in language the people could understand. Billy has often remarked that too many preachers preach to other preachers instead of to the people.

What was the message? In effect, it was this:

The people were told that the cause of all their problems was sin — . "All have sinned and come short of the glory of God." They were told the story of Jesus Christ in plain terms, but with all His glory and power. They were told that Christ died and rose again and would forgive their sins if they turned to Him in simple, childlike faith.

The people were told they would have to obey Christ if they wanted to live victorious lives. They were told they would have to be faithful in reading the Bible, spending time in prayer, witnessing for Christ and worshipping in church.

Billy was tired at the conclusion of the tour. He had filled a schedule that would have been impossible to a man using only his own strength. But he wasn't too tired to repeat once again:

"To God be the glory, great things He hath done;!"

The Attack on Presbyterianism in Brazil

By Langdon M. Henderlite

Some of you are asking for information about the articles the Rev. Mr. Carl McIntire is publishing in the U. S. about conditions in Brazil. We have read the circular letter some of you received from Mr. McIntire soliciting funds and which you forwarded on to us. It is a shame the work that Mr. McIntire is attempting to do here on the pretext of modernism and liberalism. If there is today a church in the world that is free of modernism it is the Presbyterian Church of Brazil.

I do not know of one minister, and there are about 335 of them, who is even tainted with liberalism. Mr. McIntire, as he has done so often, uses the pretext of a non-existent modernism to sow the seeds of discord, hatred, suspicion and disruption in churches with the apparent sole purpose of building up his own schismatic group.

His own church, the Bible Presbyterian Church, that he helped to organize by separating from the Orthodox Presbyterian Church which had separated from the U. S. A. Presbyterian Church, seems to be awakening to the real spirit and motives that appear to control Mr. McIntire, and that church has now pulled out of his American Council and his International Council, repudiating him and his policies.

We have studied carefully his movement here in Brazil, and we do not know of one positive contribution that his movement has made to build up the Kingdom of our Lord. The National Church evangelizes and builds, and so do the missionaries of the Presbyterian missions of the U. S. and U. S. A. churches. When the churches are prospering, the people in them worshipping and serving in real fellowship, then McIntire and his agents try to step in with an issue that is unknown and non-existent in an attempt to break the fellowship of these new Christians and new churches. We are still to find one instance in which one of his missionaries has gone out into a new field and preached the Gospel to the unsaved. Their only interest seems to be to break up the work that others have done, bringing charges against National ministers and missionaries that are based on falsehoods, misrepresentations and bad faith.

Here in Brazil we have one Presbyterian, Dr. Israel Gueiros, who follows Mr. McIntire in his purposes and methods. There is one more, Mr. Roderick Carneiro, who long before the issue of McIntire had arrived in these parts, had signified his intention of leaving the Presbyterian ministry because of doubts as to his calling. This man, who has left the Presbyterian Church of Brazil is now with Dr. Gueiros and teaching in his seminary. Note that there is really only one. This man claimed and so did Mr. McIntire that he had the overwhelming majority of the Presbyterian ministers with him when he was attempting to raise funds in the United States to establish a seminary here in Recife to fight modernism in the Presbyterian Church of Brazil. Last month, his Presbytery, the Presbytery of Pernambuco, deposed Dr. Gueiros from the Presbyterian ministry and excluded him from its communion. Of the full Presbytery with 18 ministers and elders present, they voted 16 to 2 to depose him and exclude him from the communion of the church. Of the two votes cast for Dr. Gueiros, that is not to depose him, one was cast by his brother who chose to remain faithful to the Presbyterian Church of Brazil, and the other was cast by the Moderator of the Presbytery who had been assigned by the Presbytery to be the pastor of the faithful element of Dr. Gueiros' church, and although he opposed Dr. Gueiros he did not wish his vote to be recorded against Dr. Gueiros under the supposition that it might prejudice his opportunities to win over the dissident part of the church. Dr. Gueiros' own church is divided. Of the estimated 400 members of his church, a little over a hundred have repudiated his leadership and are worshipping today in the continuing Presbyterian Church of Recife. This faithful element is bringing through the Presbytery and the General Assembly a civil action to repossess their property from Dr. Gueiros and the dissidents.

The Synod is solidly against Dr. Gueiros, against this separatist movement and so is the General Assembly. To our knowledge there is not one minister in the church who is with Dr. Gueiros in his movement to divide the Presbyterian Church of Brazil on an issue that does not exist here — that of modernism within the church. It is a shame that good Christians in the States, for lack of adequate information and mis-placed confidence in the testimony of Mr. McIntire and Miss Margaret Harden, are sending money to support a movement whose sole purpose is to divide a strong young church and sow the seeds of suspicion, discord, and hatred among brethren.

Let us say here that the Presbyterian Church of Brazil is one of the fastest growing Presbyterian churches in the world. It is autonomous, independent and self-supporting. The missions and the missionaries have no voice whatever in the forming of the policies of this church. The missions are also autonomous and independent and they cooperate closely with the National Church. As soon as our mission churches become self-supporting we turn the church and its members over to the jurisdiction of the Presbytery and no longer do we have jurisdiction over them.

It might be said that the Presbyterian Church U. S. A. is the father and the Presbyterian Church U. S. is the mother of the Presbyterian Church of Brazil. However this daughter has attained her majority, runs her own establishment, and the parents have no jurisdiction of any kind over her affairs. The missions are helping this church to carry on its immense program of evangelization and education that the church itself has set up, and we cooperate under the general policies that the church has established.

The Presbyterian Church of Brazil is not a member of the World Council of Churches because she does not want to be. The church is not a member of the International Council of Mr. McIntire for the same reason that it does not want to be. The official position of the church is that of equidistance of the two councils. The charge that the Brazilian Church is in favor of the World Council is a plain falsehood based on the assumption that since the church is not in the International Council of Mr. McIntire it is necessarily in favor of the World Council.

The same statement is made in regard to the Presbyterian missionaries. All Presbyterian missionaries working in Brazil are modernists on the assumption that since we did not join this movement, repudiate our Southern Presbyterian Church and accept the leadership of Mr. McIntire we are therefore modernists. We personally don't like everything about the World Council of Churches, and we suspect that very few Southern Presbyterians do like everything about it. But we like much less the International Council of Mr. McIntire. In fact, we do like some things about the world Council. They are few, we do admit, but we have still to find one thing to like about the International Council of Mr. McIntire.

The Raising of Lazarus

By The Rev. Floyd E. Hamilton
Centreville, Ala.

"Lazarus, come forth. He that was dead came forth, bound hand and foot with grave clothes; and his face was bound about with a napkin."

—John 11:43-44.

Sometimes men say, "Why does not God perform miracles today so that all men would believe?" One of the greatest miracles that Christ ever performed was the raising of Lazurus, but instead of winning the rulers of the Jews, we are told later in John 11:47-48, "What do we? for this man doeth many signs. If we let him alone, all men will believe on him; and the Romans will come and take away both our place and our nation!" Instead of winning the rulers to belief in Christ, it turned them against him and determined them in their plan to crucify Jesus. In that fact we find the principle that unless a man be born again he cannot see the kingdom of heaven. When I was in Annisquam, Mass., a woman told me that the miracles of the Bible had no more effect on her than the reputed miracles of the great Roman Catholic shrines, and that neither led her to believe in the Bible as the Word of God.

Now of course there is all the difference in the world between the so-called Roman Catholic miracles and the miracles of the Bible such as the raising of Lazarus. I wouldn't for a moment deny that there have been notable healings connected with the Roman Catholic shrines, though it is equally unquestionable that the vast majority of such reputed miracles are either self-deceptions or instances of pious frauds. Genuine instances of healings at such shrines seem to be almost certain effects of mental therapy, and show the tremendous effect which the mind of man has over the disease in one's body. But even were there instances of genuine miracles it would not mean that the world would therefore believe in Christ. Unless God's Spirit changes the heart of man, no amount of miraculous proof will make men believe unto salvation.

But to put such instances of healings and cures in the same class as the miracles Christ wrought in Judea and Galilee is to fail completely to understand just what happened in the miracles of Jesus. Where in history is there an instance of someone touching the eyes of one born blind and causing him to see? Where in history is there another case of healing a man with a withered hand and making it like the other at a word from a person like the Son of God? Where in history has there been another instance of feeding a crowd of 5,000 men with five loaves and two fishes? Where in history has there been an instance of commanding a leper to be cleansed and the flesh becoming clean like that of a little child? Where has there been another instance of commanding the waves and the winds to obey him and a great calm occurring? Where has anyone walked on water that was not frozen?

Above all, where else in history has there been an instance like that of raising a dead man to life again at a word from the Lord of life? The miracles of Jesus are different from any instances of healing that have taken place from the time of the apostles to the present, for they were examples of supernatural power intervening in the natural order of events here in this world. They were instances of a change in the way God ordinarily acts, purposed changes from all eternity, to attest the validity of Jesus' claims to be the Son of God and our Saviour.

But it is not at all surprising that the miracles of the Bible leave many a person cold and unbelieving. Even such a miracle as the raising of Lazarus did not make the Sadducees believe in Jesus, and if that miracle did not make everyone believe in Christ in his day, how can we expect that miracles would make everyone believe in Him today? That is not because the evidence for the raising of Lazarus from the dead was not conclusive. It is just as conclusive today as it was in the time of Christ. Inconclusiveness is not the difficulty. The difficulty lies in the fact that the Holy Spirit *must first change the heart of the doubter before he can believe in Christ and his miracles.* All the evidence in the world would not, alone, make a person believe that the Son of God is our Saviour because he raised Lazarus.

Remember that the chief priests and Pharisees had no doubts about the fact of the raising of Lazarus. That wasn't their trouble. They *would* not yield their wills to Christ and become his followers. They were essentially self-centered and they thought only of what would happen to their position and their nation if all men accepted Jesus as their king, thus causing a rebellion against Rome. They had no doubt that Rome would win in such a rebellion, and they knew that they personally would be held responsible for it by Rome when the inevitable defeat occurred. They were not concerned with the truth about Christ; they were only concerned with their own privileges. They realized too well that they would lose their wealth and position if they followed Christ, and *they put those things first in their lives!*

But let us consider the evidence about the raising of Lazarus. In the Gospel of John we have an account of an eye witness of what happened. Any fair minded person who reads the Gospel of John carefully with no prejudice in his mind, cannot help but feel the sincerity of the writer. The author was not writing fiction; he was telling the intimate experience he had had with the Saviour whom he loved and who loved him. He was not writing this biography of Jesus to make money. He even sealed his testimony with imprisonment on the island of Patmos and later with his death as a martyr for his faith. He had nothing to gain by attempting to falsify the account. He believed with his whole heart that the Jesus about whom he was writing was the Son of God. He believed with all his heart that the only way of having eternal life was through trusting in him alone for salvation. Listen to him at the end of his book, (20:21), "These things are written that ye may believe that Jesus is the Christ, the Son of God, and that believing ye may have life in his name."

Now notice the straightforward account of the events. A friend of Jesus, the brother of Mary and Martha, was taken sick. Jesus had stayed repeatedly in his home. He loved Lazarus as a brother. When Lazarus became sick the first thing that Mary and Martha thought of was to let Jesus know. "Lord, behold, he whom thou lovest is sick." Probably at first Lazarus thought it was nothing that would not pass off in a day or two. But then he began to get worse hour by hour. The sisters became really alarmed and decided to send for Jesus. Just as we send for the best doctor we can get when a loved one is ill, so Mary and Martha sent for the great physician whom they had seen perform so many miracles of healing. They thought they had an extra claim on him because they knew that Jesus loved their brother. They felt certain that Jesus would come, out of love if for no other reason.

But notice what Jesus said when the messenger brought the news to him. "This sickness is not unto death, but for the glory of God that the Son of God may be glorified thereby." (11:4). So Jesus stayed two whole days where he was instead of going to Bethany at once. Then when he knew that Lazarus was dead, though no one had told him, he started back to Judea. His disciples remonstrated with him over it. They knew that the Jews were trying to kill him and they did not want Jesus to go into danger. Jesus' reply to them was in the terms of a great spiritual principle, though Jesus put it in the form of a parable. "Are there not twelve hours in the day? If a man walk in the day, he stumbleth not, because he sees the light of this world." The principle was this: there is no danger to a child of God while he is doing the will of God. A child of God cannot be killed and cannot die until his work on earth is accomplished. Until that time comes, "A thousand shall fall at thy side and 10,000 at thy right hand, but it shall not come nigh thee."

Jews, fell at the feet of Jesus, with the same words that Martha had spoken, "Lord, if thou hadst been here, my brother had not died!"

When Jesus saw her weeping and saw the hypocritical weeping of the Jews who were with her, "he was moved with indignation in his spirit." This indignation was at the hypocritical sympathy of the Jews who were with Mary. But at the same time he was moved with love and sympathy for Mary and Martha, and we are told that Jesus wept.

Let us never for a moment suppose that Jesus does not care when our sorrows are more than we can bear, and when all that we hold dear on earth is taken from us! He grieves with us sincerely, and longs to lighten the burden of our grief, if we come to him believing and trusting him to do that which is for the best.

In this case, however, the glory of God the Father and his own honor demanded that he do something then and there about it. He told them to take away the stone from the mouth of the cave. Then follows a touch in the story that proves the reality of the death of Lazarus. Martha said, "Lord, by this time the body stinketh, for he hath been dead four days!" Apparently it had taken four days for Jesus to reach Bethany after he knew that Lazarus was dead. Jesus rebuked her gently, "Said I not unto thee, that if thou believest, thou shouldst see the glory of God?" Martha kept silent and trusted Jesus.

Then Jesus uttered the strange prayer: "Father I thank thee that thou heardest me. And I know that thou hearest me always, but because of the multitude that standeth around I said it, that they may believe that thou didst send me." Then came the miracle. Jesus cried loudly, "Lazarus, come forth!"

Someone has rightly said that if Jesus had said, merely, "Come forth," all the people in the tombs would have come forth! Lazarus obeyed him. Life again flowed in the veins of Lazarus. The rotten flesh was made clean. Strength came into his body and in spite of being bound hand and foot, he came out of the tomb with the napkin still around his head. After loosing him from the bandages, what a reunion that was for the happy family! And the effect? Many believed, but some went to tell the Pharisees, and stir them up against Jesus.

The Pharisees realized that unless there was something done about Jesus at once, all the people would believe in him and the Romans would come and take away their place and their nation. Then the wicked high priest uttered the great prophecy about the meaning of the death of Christ, "It is expedient for you that one man should die for the people and that the whole nation perish not." Then John uttered the words, "and not for the nation only, but that he might also gather together into one the children of God that are scattered abroad." The meaning of Christ's death is set forth as substitutionary. He bore the sins of his people on the cross.

Notice that even the enemies of Jesus did not doubt the reality of the miracle of the raising of Lazarus. When the 70 men in the Sanhedrin gathered to condemn Jesus, not one of them disbelieved the miracle, yet only Nicodemus was willing to follow Jesus. What is our attitude toward this mighty miracle? Has the Holy Spirit enabled you to believe to be saved?

If we believe in an omnipotent God the question of miracles becomes one of evidence. Evidence supports belief in the miracles of the Bible.

— BOOKS —

THE APOSTOLIC FATHERS. J. B. Lightfoot. Baker Book House. $3.95.

This volume represents an attempt to give the writings of the Apostolic Fathers the wide distribution which they deserve. A complete unabridged edition of the best translation of the Apostolic Fathers is here made available in one convenient reasonably priced volume. This volume should be of great interest especially to ministers who are interested in the field of Church History.

AMERICAN PROTESTANTISM. T. Valentine Parker. Philosophical Library, New York, New York. $3.75.

The purpose of this book is to appraise American Protestantism. It shows us both the excellencies and the defects of the Protestant Church in our Day.

The first chapter is concerned with the history and origin of Protestant churches. The author believes that there must be a consideration of logical backgrounds to see the logical implications.

While recognizing that some divisions of Protestantism are unreal, the author is sensible enough to concede that Sectarianism, contrary to what many affirm, is not the great sin of Protestantism. He comments, "A few moments thought should convince anyone that other sins, like unbrotherliness, are far greater. Diversity is both the penalty and the reward of freedom. While it cripples effectiveness, it enriches experience. In our religion there are many contributions."

The fundamental weakness of this book is that it does not recognize the significance of the Christian creeds. The author holds to an ecumenicity that is based simply upon the idea of cooperation. He says, "Any plan for a united church must erase absolutely any rule for conformity beyond the simple requirements for working together. We try to agree upon a creed. We can't. Why should we try? Any statement of belief that would be generally accepted would be so emasculated as to have little meaning or would be subject to such a variety of interpretations as to nullify its apparent affirmations."

There are certain observations in this appraisal for which we should thank the author. There are also certain slants in this volume that lead in the wrong direction. The student of contemporary Protestantism who reads this book with discernment, will find some sections helpful, but other sections must be read with caution. J.R.R.

ANGLERS

By WADE C. SMITH

Lesson No. 159

Assimilating New Converts Into Church Life

It would be difficult to name a more important phase of church life than this—putting a new member happily to work in the church's program. Stomach trouble is a common complaint the world around; but people do not suffer more from indigestion than the Church suffers from an unassimilated membership. It is not enough to secure one's profession of faith in Christ and get his name on the church roll. Yet in many cases, perhaps in the majority of cases, he is left right there. But he does not remain there. He drifts back to the old life, and the last estate of that man is worse than the first.

Also, the church is worse off. To leave a new convert "at the church roll" is like placing a new-born baby out there on the grass to shift for himself. He needs nourishment and nursing, and protection from the many ills which threaten infant life. He does not know how to get for himself what he needs, and could not if he knew. He does not even understand his needs.

A new convert who knows practically nothing of God's Word, very little about prayer, and absolutely nothing about Christian service, is under a heavy handicap and needs a lot of sympathy, a lot of help, and a lot of encouragement to get rooted and growing in his new-found relationship. Unless he does get rooted and growing he becomes at once a distinct liability to the church instead of an asset.

To get the new member interested in the church's mission and taking an intelligent part in its work is perhaps one of the church's greatest problems today. Yet, surely there is a way to solve it. Some new converts are eager for service and will begin giving testimony (sometimes "zeal without knowledge") wherever opportunity offers. These need to be directed in the study of the Word and to be shown how to develop a program of regular devotional life, - to stabilize their experiences. Every new convert needs such assistance.

Every church should have some definite plan for engaging new members in Christian service. It requires careful discrimination to employ them happily and avoid misfits. Why should there not be a Personnel Committee, or at least one capable officer to make it his business to ascertain what gifts or talents or training the new member has, and on the basis of this, make recommendations to the Session, or the Sunday School Superintendent or other department leader, with the object of enlisting these capacities in the church's many activities?

The writer knows of one young man who came into the church and for awhile was forgotten "at the roll." He drifted away. He was a mechanic. One day a church officer discovered him down in the city at his work, doing some electrical wiring. It was the first time any church member knew of the young man's trade. There was some wiring to be done at the church for Christmas festivities. He was engaged to do it, and when asked for his bill refused to accept pay. He said he had been wishing there was something he might do in the church; he felt so useless there - so absolutely unnecessary. Now he was happy "to put an oar in and do some pulling, even in this small way."

To shorten a long story, this man became "the church's electrician." He found a number of ways to make his skill serve the church. Among other devices he installed was a very original illuminated sign, out front. The congregation wondered how they had gotten along without him and he was very happy in a new-found fellowship. He was doing something worthwhile for his church and it helped him to gear in on the real blessing. There are folks with musical talent, artistic talent, clerical training, capacity for leadership, for learning to teach - everybody is good for *something*. It might be said to the glory of the Church's program, if we were alert to discover usefulness, that here is one place where nobody is good for nothing! There is something for every member to do. But it takes intelligent thought on the part of somebody to help the new member to find his place.

Of course the main object is to eventually enlist every member in some real spiritual service. Soul winning is valuable here. It is a simple thing to do, yet most vital. If the new convert is living in a manner consistent with his new-found faith he can begin this service at once . See that he gets into one of the Personal Workers' groups.

(Next lesson: Some By-Products of Personal Evangelism)

Helps To Understanding Scripture Readings in *Day by Day*

By Rev. C. C. Baker

Sunday, October 14, *Psalm* 95. An invitation to praise the Lord is repeated in vv.1-2,6. We are to praise Him for the fact that He alone is the true God (v.3), the Creator and Owner of all that is upon the earth (vv.4-5). Do you honor the Lord in the stewardship of all He has entrusted to your possession? What other reason (v.7) does the Psalmist mention for our praise of God? Because the Lord is not only our Creator (vv.4-6), but also our Shepherd, the Psalmist exhorts us to love and honor Him with our hearts (vv.7b-8). In the past Israel had hardened her heart against God (vv.8-10; Numbers 14:20-23; 20:1-13) with grevious results (v.10). Does your heart respond to God as you behold His shepherd's care over you?

Monday, October 15, *Psalm* 73. What was the sin into which the Psalmist slipped (vv.2-3)? Is this a besetting temptation for you? In vv. 4-14 what does the Psalmist say concerning the prosperous wicked as to: their general welfare (vv.4-5,12), their relation to others (v.10), their personal lives (vv.6-8), their attitude toward God (v. 9)? How did coming into God's presence change the Psalmist's attitude toward the wicked rich (vv.17-20)? What had his attitude toward God been before this experience (vv.21-22)? Into what new relationship with the Lord did he enter (vv.1,21-26,28)? Where did he find the contentment that replaced his former bitterness (vv.25-26)? Does a heart of bitterness rob you of fellowship with God (vv.2-3)? Do you look at the world through the eyes of God or the eyes of men?

Tuesday, October 16, *Psalm* 51:1-17. Read through the Psalm and allow it to speak for you to God concerning sins you have committed. The Psalmist is deeply aware of the fact of his sin (notice the personal pronouns in vv. 1-5). Observe his sorrow over his sin (vv. 1-5), his earnest desire for cleansing (vv.2,7-9), his longing for a pure heart (v.10). Do you long for a heart of purity as you confess your sins? The whole desire and aim of the Psalmist is to be purified from sin in order to serve God (vv.10-15). When you have found forgiveness of sin, is there a sense of praise in your heart (vv.14-15) and a renewed desire to live for God (v.13)? Do you desire the fellowship of the Lord more than the pleasures of sin (vv.9-12)?

Wednesday, October 17, *Psalm* 32. This Psalm is a natural sequel to Psalm 51. The Psalmist had acted in the stubbornness of v.9 and refused to confess his sin (v.3). Mark the phrases in vv.3-4 that picture the Psalmist's consequent inner feelings. He then confessed his sins (v.5) and in vv.1-2,11 describes the change that took place in his heart. Through meditating on the expressive phrases of vv.1-4,11 try to sense the release, the new life that came to the Psalmist with the confession of his sin. Are there known sins in your life that you have not confessed? The Psalmist will continue to be tempted but God will hold him fast (v.6). Notice how complete and all-sufficient becomes God's strength and guidance to him (vv.7-8).

Thursday, October 18, *Psalm* 121. The Psalmist casts his eyes upon the hills around him (v.1a). A question comes to his mind as to the source of his protection and strength (v.1b). His answer is that it is the Lord, who made the hills (v.2b), who watches over him and keeps him (v.2a). In vv.3-8 the Psalmist tells us in what ways God watches over us. What phrases mark the idea of God's being over His people at all times? Even while we sleep by night (v.6b) God watches on (vv.3-4). What is said about how close God is to His own (v.5)? How all-sufficient is God's presence (vv.3a,6-7)? Wherever we go, wherever we are, God's watchful eyes and protecting hands are always close to the believer (v.8). Think about these things when you behold the hills.

Friday, October 19, *Psalm* 45:1-9. Here is a combination of a tribute to an earthly king and a foreshadowing of the Messiah. Historically it may refer to a marriage of David or Solomon. Notice in Hebrews 1:8-9 the use the New Testament makes of vv.6-7 in reference to Christ. Of what hymn do the words of vv.7-8 remind you? At what points could vv.2-8 have reference to the Second Coming of Jesus Christ. Some think that vv.10-17 speak of the Church, the whole Psalm referring to the marriage of the Lamb and the Bride (see Revelation 19). If this is true, what does v.11 indicate of the Church's relation to her Lord and how she should regard His coming (vv.10,14-15)? Do you recognize Jesus Christ as the one true head of the Church? Is your devotion to Him like unto the pure, joyous devotion of a bride to her husband (vv.12b-15)?

Saturday, October 20, *Psalm* 72:1-14. The kingly reign for which prayer is offered in this Psalm is that of Solomon. However, as magnificent as the reign of Solomon was, the reign pictured in this Psalm was never realized in Solomon's time. Hence it looks forward to the Messiah who would establish a kingdom that would be righteous (vv.1-4), continuous (vv. 5-7), universal (vv.8-11), humane (vv.12-15), happy (vv.16-17). With the above division in mind read through the Psalm, remembering the petition of the Lord's Prayer, "Thy Kingdom come." Is the royal reign pictured in this Psalm one that befits the Kingdom of God? Is the king pictured here like unto Jesus Christ? Which aspect of the coming Kingdom means most to you?

SABBATH SCHOOL LESSONS

REV. J. KENTON PARKER

LESSON FOR OCTOBER 14

The Ten Commandments

Background Scripture: Exodus 20:1 - 21
Devotional Reading: Psalm 19:7-14

In our study of "The Great Passages of the Bible," only a few of these "Great Passages" can be selected, and they will often be separated by many years, and even centuries. I would like to mention some of the momentous events which took place in the long period of time between our last lesson and the one for today.

The Creation Story, which left everything beautiful and "very good," is quickly followed by the sad and tragic story of the Fall of man and the rapid spread of sin in the world until mankind became so corrupt that God had to send the Flood which destroyed all flesh except Noah and his family. God made a Covenant with Noah and promised that the world would never be swept by another flood. It was not long before men in their pride sought to build a tower which should reach so far into the sky that no flood could drown them again. The Tower of Babel was built, or started, and the confusion of tongues came upon them as a punishment, and their plan came to an end.

Men began to congregate in cities, and two of these, Sodom and Gomorrah became notorious for their wickedness and were destroyed by fire and brimstone from heaven. God called Abram to leave his country and kindred and go

psalm ends with a plea for cleansing and keeping from sin and acceptance in the sight of God.

I. *The Ten Commandments:* Exodus 20:1-17.

In the Preface to these commandments we are assured that "God spake all these words." This is Verbal Inspiration. Moses wrote what God inspired him to write, and right words are as vital as right thoughts. Then there follows another reason for their keeping these commandments: He is the Lord Who brought them out of the land of Egypt and out of the house of bondage. He therefore, has the right to issue these commands.

All of them except the Fourth and Fifth are put in the form, "Thou shalt not," but a reasonable interpretation of their far-reaching implications is given to us in our Catechism, and in other parts of the Scriptures. Then, when we read the summary of these Ten as given in the Old Testament, and by Jesus in reply to the question as to which is the greatest, we see that there is a positive side which undergirds the negative: "Thou shall love the Lord thy God . . . and thy neighbor as thyself."

They are usually divided into two tables: the first telling us of our duty to God, the second, our duty to our fellowmen. The Fifth, the only one with a promise, has been called a "connecting link" between the two parts, for it deals with our duty to our parents. The Roman Catholic Church has a different division. They combine the first and second commandment and divide the tenth into two. Their reason for this unnatural division is to avoid the plain teaching of the Second Commandment, which forbids worshipping God through images or likenesses. The First command forbids the worship of any god except the Living and True God; the Second, the worship of God through some image. This was the command that was broken by the Israelites when they made the golden calf, for they exclaimed, "These be thy gods, O Israel, which brought thee up out of the land of Egypt."

With our use in these days of many "Visual Aids" to worship, I am afraid that we are in danger of breaking this command.

The First Commandment says, Thou shalt have no other gods before me. This forbids polytheism, a plurality of gods. The Second says, Thou shalt not make unto thee any graven image, or likeness, and bow down and serve them. This forbids idolatry. Idolatry may take two forms. An idol may be an image of some false god, or it may be an attempt to make an image of the true God. The sin of Jeroboam when he made the calves for the Northern Tribes to worship, was the latter. Later on, under Ahab and Jezebel, idolatry of the worst form was instituted; the worship of

Baal. Jeroboam, however, was rebuked and punished for causing Israel to sin. Those who use pictures of Christ explain that they are not worshipping the picture. I am not at all sure that people in heathen lands make this distinction. All attempts to paint a picture of our Blessed Master are but vain efforts, for the Gospels give us no description of Him. Let us remember that God is a Spirit, and we are to worship in spirit and truth. The Body of our Lord is not the important thing to remember.

The Third Commandment can be broken, and is broken, in a variety of ways. We cannot be too careful about His Name, or anything by which He makes Himself known, for His Name stands for His character. Reverence is a fine plant to keep growing in the garden of life. We have a good many slang expressions which border on profanity, and some at least, have a profane origin. I feel that we should be extremely careful about using some verse in the Bible as the basis of a "joke," or some amusing "play on words."

The Fourth Commandment is a double one; a command to work, and a command to rest, and keep the Sabbath as a Holy Day. Six days shalt thou labor. God expects us to do our work. Paul says, If a man will not work, let him not eat. Jesus sets us an example in this as in all other matters. Idleness is a terrible sin. We have a great many people who are parasites. They eat the bread of idleness and are a burden upon society. Then, on the other hand, there are people who want to steal the Lord's Day, either for work, or for play. Many are turning the Lord's Day into a holiday. Monday is usually a bad day in places where workers are used. Many of them are so worn out with "having a good time" that they are in no condition to do an honest day's work. If we rest and worship and confine our labors to works of necessity and mercy, we will be in fine shape to take up our duties on Monday. The Sabbath was ordained "for man"; to be a blessing to him. One of our outstanding national sins today is the breaking of this commandment, in both of its parts.

The Fifth Commandment concerns the home, and especially the duty of children to their parents. Paul, in Ephesians 5:22-6:9 gives more details on the Christian Home. Study what he says.

"Thou shalt not kill." How this command convicts and shames America! God says that blood defiles the land. This is one of the worst of our sins. Think of the many ways in which we are killing men and women and children. On the radio, a few hours ago, we were told that it would be a miracle if the deaths on our highways did not soar above last year. The newspapers are full of murders. Then turn to the Sermon on the Mount and read what Jesus says about this command.

"Thou shalt not commit adultery." See what Jesus says about this, too. Our land is full of impurity of every description. Our book stalls are full of obscene literature; our "Best-Sellers" are often stories about adultery, or uncleanness.

Take the rest of these commands and measure our country by them and then pray that God will have mercy upon us! How we need a Revival!

YOUNG PEOPLE'S DEPARTMENT — REV. B. HOYT EVANS

YOUTH PROGRAM FOR OCTOBER 14

"But We Are A Christian Nation"

Suggested Devotional Outline:

Hymn: "Come, Thou Almighty King"
Prayer
Scripture: Matthew 23
Hymn: "Am I A Soldier Of The Cross?"
Offering
Hymn: "Who Is On The Lord's Side?"

Program Leader's Introduction:

There are many facts to indicate that the United States *IS* a Christian nation. Just last month an announcement appeared in the newspapers stating that American church membership now exceeds the hundred million mark. In recent years there has been a revival of interest in religion. Religious books and movies are more poular than ever before. There seems to be a new appreciation for spiritual things among our government officials. The words "In God We Trust" still appears on our money, and we have added the words "under God" to the pledge of allegiance to the flag. All of these are hopeful signs. Our nation is probably more religious than it has ever been before, but there is still reason for raising the question of how "Christian" we are. There is a great deal of difference between being religious and being Christian.

Our first speaker will describe some of the symptoms which indicate that our nation is not as spiritually healthy as we would like to think. The second speaker will attempt to diagnose the case . . . to explain the real

P.S.

Many friends at church ask to be remembered to you. Never forget how much the church is interested in you while you're in college.

ɔEAR PRESBYTERIAN STUDENT:

Yes, your church is keenly interested in your velfare.

You'll find that many fellow students are nore active in Christian work at college than hey were at home. Under experienced leader-hip, there is a thrill in sharing experiences with ther young Christians.

Westminster Fellowships have a challenging rogram in which you should take part. You'll ind, in the Campus Christian Life worker, a riend and counselor you will admire and trust. Jse the opportunities open for Christian wit-.ess.

Don't take a vacation from spiritual matters. 'his is a time when they can mean the most to ou and to the development of your whole per-onality.

Presbyterian Educational Association of the South

Box 1176, Richmond 9, Virginia

And here's GOOD NEWS for students, too.

In many synods, our Presbyterian Church is going forward with financial campaigns to undergird educational institutions.

This means we shall have more classrooms, more dormitories, better libraries, more student centers, and stronger colleges and seminaries.

They will help our Church provide *quality education*—the only kind with w h i c h our Church should be concerned.

These campaigns are vital if our Church is to meet the needs of our increasing college population.

nature of the spiritual sickness which produces the symptoms.

First Speaker:

Of the reported hundred million church members in America only about sixty million are in the Protestant churches. This means that more than a hundred million of our people are outside the pale of evangelical Christianity. Of the sixty million Protestants, it has been estimated that only one out of six is truly active in the support of the church. This is borne out by the facts that average church attendance is about a third of the membership and that Americans spend eight times more money for alchohol than they give for the support of all the churches.

Another symptom of spiritual sickness which is related to the faltering support of the church is the philosophy of materialism which is so rife in America. Our advertisements, our attitudes, and our actions reveal that we all put a very high premium on our material possessions. We are nearly all victims of the feeling that the "abundant life" consists of the possession of all the latest gadgets, conveniences, and luxuries. Even those of us who are Christians find that we are often more concerned about material trappings than we are about the welfare of our souls.

Still other serious symptoms are crime, divorce, and alcoholism which are increasing as rapidly, if not more so, than our church membership. We have the feeling that if church membership is on the increase these things ought to be decreasing. These things are certainly not compatible with Christianity. Can it be that there is a lack of vital Christianity in our churches? A growing church ought to mean a growing Christianity. In the light of these facts, perhaps we ought to change our statement to a question. Instead of saying "But we *ARE a* Christian nation" we should ask "But ARE we a Christian nation?"

Second Speaker:

Our first speaker has described some spiritual symptoms to be found in America. Let us now try to make a spiritual diagnosis to determine what is the nature of the sickness which produces these symptoms.

It seems quite clear that the ailment is the disease called sin. It is always sin which keeps people from supporting and attending their churches faithfully. It is sin that makes people more concerned about their bodily comforts than their souls. It is sin that produces divorce, crime, hatred, strife, alcoholism, and every other moral and spiritual ill which troubles us. Christ came into the world to conquer sin. As long as our nation gives indication of granting sin so large a place in its life we must be hesitant about referring to it as a Christian nation.

Sin makes itself evident in two classes of people. It appears first in those who are still dead in their sins. These are the people whose natures have not been changed by Christ. It is perfectly natural for them to produce all the symptoms of sin because it is deeply rooted in their natures. The power of sin in the lives of these people and the effects of sin in the life of the nation will not be overcome until sin itself is radically removed from their natures by the power of God in Christ.

Sin also expresses itself in the lives of people whose natures have been changed by Christ. This is unnatural because they are the children of God, and God's Spirit dwells in them. It is abnormal for the Spirit of God and sin to be in the same life, but that is the struggle which goes on in the life of Christians. We have been made new creatures in Christ, but we allow the lost world, the world of sin, to set the pattern of our living.

The citizens of the British Commonwealth expect exemplary conduct from their royal family, and the members of that family expect to live in a way that will do honor to their high position. We Christians are children of a King. We too are members of the royal family. Our nation will not be truly Christian until its Christian citizens begin to live in a way that is consistent with their heavenly citizenship.

Program Leader:

Having heard the symptoms and the diagnosis, let us do some serious thinking about the cure. What can we do to help as individuals and as a group? We shall be looking for a remedy in our program next week.

brought to all who have entered into this reading program.

The book named for Bible Mastery reading this year is I Corinthians. Since the book is longer, it is suggested that we read four chapters a day thereby reading the Epistle eight times during the month.

October is also a time to remember the work and workers in Church Extension. A bookmark with a guide for reading I Corinthians on one side and on the other side topics for special prayer related to the Church Extension program of our denomination is available from the Board of Women's Work, price 50c per 100.

Week of Prayer and Self Denial for Church Extension

October 14-21, 1956

This final week of the Church Extension season will be observed by the whole Church as a time for special prayer and the denial of self in order that the people of the Church invest themselves in this great program for Christ in our Southland. Every church is urged to make it a church-wide observance united in intercession for the work and workers in our Assembly's Church Extension program.

A Guide to group prayer for this week has been prepared by Mrs. T. D. Connell under the significant theme, "Let Us Walk As Children of Light." The local president and local chairman of Spiritual Growth will work with the chairman of Church Extension and others responsible to enlist all of the members of the church in this service by prayer and sacrifice that Christ's work through our Church may have added power. All women are called to enter into this observance.

To Lead Others, Follow Christ

By George S. Lauderdale

Missionaries do many things which men in other professions do. They write letters, make talks, take trips; they attempt to lead people. Nearly every person, at some time in life, has to be a leader. Parents know this responsibility, as do soldiers, business men, farmers.

The missionary has in God a Helper which every leader needs. The devil is a driver, Jesus Christ a leader; Pharoah was a driver, Moses a leader; Saul was a driver, Samuel and David leaders; before his conversion, Paul was a driver, but as an apostle, he was a leader. Drivers always fail, leaders succeed, and for this reason the missionary enterprise of the Lord Jesus Christ's church will be completed.

Christian missionaries are leaders, not drivers!

Leadership does not mean compromise, or that rules are abandoned for the sake of harmony. There are schools where the pupils rule over the teachers; there are homes in which the children rather than the parents have the last word, and the divine order of the headship of husband to wife is reversed. There are mission activities which result in the preacher's being won to the heathen way of life rather than their conversion to Christ. May God pity such weakness.

Humility Essential

True leadership is characterized by strength, wisdom, and patience, but none of these traits is needed by the driver. The use of one's faculties and consequent cheerfulness is in the lot of those who are led; loss of individuality, complaining, contempt for the master, are the tendencies of those who are driven.

The leader encourages his followers to use their minds due to his love for them, whereas the driver, lacking love, has no interest in the individuals under him and has a suspicious attitude. It is better to walk and work with people than to put them behind and beneath us.

God says, "In many things we offend all." "In lowliness of mind let each esteem other better than themselves." James 3:2; Philippians 2:3. Jesus Christ has set the example for His followers: He came not to be ministered unto but to minister and to give His life a ransom for many. Those who are put in authority in the world exercise lordship, but to His disciples, Christ has said, "So shall it not be among you: but whosoever will be great among you, shall be your minister: and whosoever of you will be the chiefest, shall be servant of all." Mark 10:43,44.

Stubborn Problems Solved

The great difference between driver and leader is in their dealing with the rebellious. (Balkers cannot be ignored, for they will influence others to make trouble.) It never occurs to the driver that he may be the cause of stubbornness in the ranks, and instead of profiting from the experience and laying aside his gruffness, he thinks he must prove who is boss and beat and threaten the wayward into line. The driver is ever fearful of loss of face.

Leaders are challenged by contrariness to become better. Christian missionaries search their hearts, lest some wickedness of their own is turning others away from God. We do not get harsh but humble when we are vexed! We give more attention to the sheep who are doing right and encourage them so as to provoke to emulation and repentance the trouble maker. Thus the apostle Paul by winning Gentiles stirred a profitable jealousy in the hearts of some of his own countrymen, the Jews, and led them to know Christ.

Christ Teaches How

If wise leadership fails to hold the loyalty of certain men, the missionary is not discouraged. God comforted Samuel when the people insisted, against his advice, that they have a king like other nations. "They have not rejected thee, but they have rejected me, that I should not reign over them." I Samuel 8:7. Men of God are bound to succeed! Satan will get no credit that multitudes have followed his directions to hell, because he has driven them by deception and has appealed to their wickedness; Jesus Christ cannot fail even though a handful follow Him all the way. If all should turn back, the fault would not be His.

Suggesting is better than commanding, praising than scolding, promising than threatening. God can show you how to catch men as others catch fish. Let Him lead you by the Holy Spirit and *make you a leader* by the same Spirit. What must you do to receive the Spirit? Repent of your sins and believe on the Lord Jesus Christ. How joyful is the work of leading others out of darkness into light! You can have power with God and men. Right now join Jesus Christ.

Church News

ALABAMA

Birmingham—Avondale Presbyterian Church in Birmingham, Aug. 26 held its last service in the sanctuary built in 1892. After the services, the members began moving pews, pulpit, railing and other furniture to the first unit of its new home, a structure that eventually will be an adult fellowship building.

On five acres of property, the Avondale Presbyterian Church also plans an education building, a youth building and a sanctuary. The 83-year-old minister of the church, the Rev. David Park, has been the leader in bringing about the new home for the church. He retired 18 years ago, but was brought back into the ministry, first to build up the Ensley Presbyterian Church, and then to inject new life into the Avondale Church.

With 50 years in the ministry, the Rev. Mr. Park was a missionary to Siam, now Thailand, in 1899. His wife, who died four years ago, worked with him through his ministry. He has been in Birmingham since 1912.

In the new church home, the Rev. Park hopes that members will be drawn from new communities near the church.

Mr. Park said the cost of the new church development, including four buildings, landscaping and private driveways will be approximately $130,000.

Birmingham—Dr. J. H. McCain, pastor of the Shades Valley Presbyterian Church, Birmingham, observed the 10th anniversary of his ministry at the church at the worship service September 1.

His sermon, "After 10 Years," was based on Psalm 103.

Membership of the church totaled 102 when Dr. McCain preached his first sermon on September 1, 1946. Present membership is approximately 900. Average school attendance is 500. Since January 1 this year 110 new members have been received.

From a small structure on Cahaba Road, the church moved in March, 1953, to the new sanctuary on Montevallo Road that seats 600. The new Sunday School building was completed in July. It will take care of 700 students, Dr. McCain said. Total value of the property is $500,000. The buildings are of colonial design. A lighted cross at the top of the steeple can be seen throughout Shades Valley.

NORTH CAROLINA

Davidson — Charles F. Myers, of Greensboro, N. C., has been elected president of the Davidson College Alumni Association succeeding Charlotte attorney Howard B. Arbuckle, Jr.

He will be installed during the Davidson Homecoming festivities Oct. 27, and will serve for one year, Alumni Secretary John L. Payne said.

Elected vice-presidents this year were Alexander S. Moffett, Tampa, Fla., business executive, and the Rev. Alfred G. Taylor, Greenville, S. C., minister.

Mr. Myers is treasurer and a director of Burlington Industries, and a civic leader. Mr. Moffett is executive vice-president and general manager of the Tampa Coal Co. and several allied industries, and also active in church and civic work. The Rev. Mr. Taylor is pastor of the Fourth Presbyterian Church of Greenville, and was formerly Minister to students at the University of Florida.

The annual alumni fund totaled $117,000 during the past year while Mr. Arbuckle was president. This was an increase of more than $30,000 over the previous year. The fund has a goal of $125,000 for this coming year.

TENNESSEE

Missionary News

Nashville—The Rev. and Mrs. John Wood of our Mexico Mission announce the arrival of a son, Daniel Edward, born on June 29 in Morelia.

Mr. and Mrs. John Pritchard of our Congo Mission announce the arrival of a son, David Hunter, in the Congo on July 7.

Mr. Pritchard, a layman, is a native of Lothair, Ky., but now considers Hazard, Ky., to be his home. He is a member of First Presbyterian Church in Hazard. He is a graduate of Davidson College, and took a year of special training at Louisville, Ky., Seminary.

Mrs. Pritchard, the former Miss Helen Norwood, was born in Bay Minette, Ala. She received her education at Columbia Bible College, and Presbyterian College. Prior to going to the Congo, she taught Bible in the public schools of Chicamauga, Ga. She is a member of Royal Oak Presbyterian Church of Marion, Va. The Pritchards were married in the Congo. They have one other child, a daughter, age 2 years.

The Rev. and Mrs. William P. Boyle of our Japan Mission announce the arrival of a son, Donald Banks, in Japan on August 20.

Miss Louise Miller of our Korea Mission is now in Atlanta, Ga. for her regular furlough. She arrived in late August.

Miss Miller was born in Martin, Ga., but considers Hartwell, Ga., home. She received her education at Chicora College in Columbia, S. C., Peabody College, in Nashville, Assembly's Training School and Columbia Seminary. She is a member of Druid Hills Presbyterian Church in Atlanta. Miss Miller first went to Korea in 1920, and has been serving there since that time in evangelistic work.

Miss Marge Rice of our Congo Mission arrived in the United States September 6.

She has just completed her second three year term in the Congo. She was born in Clarkton, Mo., but considrs Memphis., Tenn. home. She is a member of Ildewild Presbyterian Church in Memphis.

The Rev. and Mrs. George A. Hudson of our Taiwan Mission arrived in the United States in early September for their regular furlough.

Mr. Hudson is the son of former missionaries of our Church in China. He received his education at the University of South Carolina, Davidson College, and Columbia Seminary. He is a member of Enoree Presbytery.

Mrs. Hudson is the former Miss Katherine Hodgson of Spring Green, Wis. The Hudsons will make their home at Mission Haven in Decatur, Ga., during this furlough year.

Miss Doris Moore of our Congo Mission arrived in the United States in August for her regular furlough.

Miss Moore is from West End, N. C. She received her education at the Woman's College of the University of N. C. and the Assembly's Training School. She is a member of the Culdee Presbyterian Church of West End.

Rev. and Mrs. L. A. McMurray of our Congo Mission arrived in this country in late August for their furlough.

Mr. McMurray was born in Lynchburg, Va., but considers Hedgesville, W. V., home. He is a graduate of Washington & Lee and of Union Seminary. He is a member of Winchester Presbytery.

Mrs. McMurray is the former Miss Jean Frances Harlan of Martinsburg, W. V. She received her education at Shepherd College and State Normal. She is a member of Falling Waters Presbyterian Church of Hedgesville, W. Va. The McMurrays have three children ranging in age from 18 to 23. They will make their home at Mission Court in Richmond, Va., during this furlough year.

Dr. and Mrs. Henry S. Nelson and family of our Congo Mission are scheduled to arrive in the United States in early September for their regular furlough in this country.

Dr. Nelson was born in China where his parents were missionaries. He considers Nashville, Tenn., home. His parents, Dr. and Mrs. Oscar G. Nelson, live in Nashville. He received his BS degree from Vanderbilt University, where he also received his M.D. degree. He is a member of the Second Presbyterian Church of Nashville.

Nashville—The appointment of two new missionaries and the approval of the employment of a new editorial assistant for the Educational Department were among the important actions taken by the Board of World Missions in its annual September meeting here.

Appointed an evangelistic missionary to Mexico, to go out in 1957, is Miss Ann B. Baron, of Gastonia, N. C. Miss Baron is a director of Christian education for the Associate Reformed Presbyterian Church at Gastonia. Appointed as teacher of missionary children, to go out to the field immediately, is Miss Rebecca Glenn of Clover, S. C. Miss Glenn, who has been teaching in Glade Valley, N. C., will be on a three-year appointment to the West Brazil Mission.

Named new editorial assistant to Dr. D. J. Cumming, is Mrs. Ethel Wharton, long-time missionary to Africa and author of the widely popular history of African mission work, "Led in Triumph". Mrs. Wharton, widow of the late Dr. Conway Wharton, missionary and pastor, will aid in editing manuscripts for publication.

A study, of an evaluative nature, is to be made of the medical work being done in Korea by the Church, so as to guide future development. Dr. L. Nelson Bell, member of the Board from Montreat, N. C., was asked to supervise the study.

Medical work in Korea by the Church has suffered a set-back, the Board was told, by the loss to the Army of Dr. Paul Crane, surgeon and head of the Chungju Presbyterian Hospital. Dr. Crane, now Major Crane, will serve for two years and then return to the hospital. During his service, he will serve the Army as liaison between Army medical units and Korean doctors.

An appropriation of $1200.00 was approved for the Presbyterian Church, U.S. portion of the support of the just-organizing Presbyterian Committee on Cooperation in Latin America. It is jointly supported by Latin American synods and assemblies, the U. S. Board of World Missions, and the Presbyterian, U.S.A., Boards of National (with work in Puerto Rico and Cuba) and Foreign Missions.

Another appropriation, of $1500, was made to pay this Church's portion of the All-Africa Curriculum Conferences which have been held, and are to be held, in connection with the development of a new curriculum for mission areas in Africa.

At the recommendation of the Home Base Committee, the Board approved a three state conference presbytery and synod world mission committee chairmen, and the U. S. A. Churches. Chairmen of the Women of the Church Missions Committees on presbytery and synod levels are also being invited to the October meeting in Louisville, Ky. Synods involved will be Missouri, Kentucky and West Virginia. Purpose of the conference will be discussion and coordination of missions presentation in these areas in which all three denominations are at work. This is the first conference of its kind.

Dr. C. Darby Fulton, executive secretary of the Board, reported that an offer of copies of the Martin Luther film, for showing in mission races, has been taken up by five missions. Mr. C. A. Rowland, Athens, Ga., businessman and long a member of the Board, in July presented a copy of the film to be used in North Brazil Mission and said that any other mission wanting a copy would be given one. Requests have been received from the Taiwan, West Brazil, Portugal, Japan, and African fields, Dr. Fulton reports. East Brazil Mission already has a copy, in addition to that given to North Brazil.

THE SOUTHERN PRESBYTERIAN JOURNAL

A Presbyterian weekly magazine devoted to the statement, defense and propagation of the Gospel, the faith which was once for all delivered unto the saints.

VOL. XV NO. 24 OCTOBER 10, 1956 $2.50 A YEAR

"To take the condemnation of sin and the wrath of God against sin out of the Gospel message is to cut its very nerve.

When men speak today of redeeming the old order of society or transforming life from sordidness into sainthood, without the Cross, they follow a forlorn hope. When John came preaching repentance, the fullness of time was also at hand. Revolutionary changes were taking place in the whole Roman Empire and in the Jewish Church. There had been much preparation. There was great expectancy. There was deep despair of the old order. But John ushered in the new epoch by proclaiming a new Redemption: 'Behold the Lamb of God that taketh away the sin of the world.'

It is a redemption of the old order that we desire, but it must be redemption by the Blood. The Cross of Christ is the only hope of the world."

Quoted from: EVANGELISM TODAY: Message Not Method
By Samuel M. Zwemer — Fleming H. Revell Co.

THE SOUTHERN PRESBYTERIAN JOURNAL
The Journal has no official connection with the Presbyterian Church in the United States
Rev. Henry B. Dendy, D.D., Editor..........Weaverville, N. C.
Dr. L. Nelson Bell, Associate Editor..........Asheville, N. C.
Rev. Wade C. Smith, Associate Editor..........Weaverville, N. C.

EDITORIAL

Security

There are two kinds of security, the one material the other spiritual.

In the Bible the classic example of a man who had a full measure of material security earned God's condemnation in these words: *"Thou fool, this night thy soul shall be required of thee."*

In marked contrast Paul's eternal security is affirmed in these words: *"Henceforth there is laid up for me a crown of righteousness, which the Lord, the righteous judge, shall give me at that day."*

No where does the Bible inveigh against prudent provision for the necessities of life, both immediate and for old age. But it makes it very plain that material possessions are temporary and that they can become a snare. Also we take none of them with us when we die.

The whole thrust of the gospel is the necessity of man coming into a saving relationship with Jesus Christ, which brings with it the assurance of eternal life, and after this redeeming and transforming event has taken place the Bible makes it clear that such a fact shall be translated into right attitudes and actions towards our fellow men.

It is our impression that too little emphasis is placed on eternal security today. In fact there are circles where man's hope of Heaven is played down or belittled as "pie in the sky."

Where a Christian accepts God's redeeming love and then sits down to wait for Heaven one can but wonder how genuine is his understanding of the meaning of faith. But, where a sense of eternal security expresses itself in an abiding love for the One Who has made that security possible and a constant urge to make the good news known to others it is such a faith which the world needs and to which many will respond.

A nationally known surgeon recently remarked to the writer: "My specialty brings me an unduly high percentage of cancer cases of a type which offer little hope of cure; I want to help these people; something which offers a hope for the future."

Faith in Christ is the only hope for eternity; the only assurance of happiness beyond the grave. This hope and assurance is a valid reason for stressing the importance of faith in Him here and now.

Death is a certainty.

Eternity is a certainty.

That which we do about Christ now determines whether we have eternal security or not.

If a sure cure for cancer should be discovered it would be in banner headlines across the front pages of every newspaper and made available to all who have the disease.

There *is* a sure cure for sin. This is the world's greatest news.

L.N.B.

Calvinism and Confusion

An evangelist, several members of a city mission board, and various people in various places have said to me that faith in Christ must precede regeneration. The evangelist in his sermon told the audience that first they must put their faith in Christ, then they must repent, and then they must be born again.

But this is so confusing. And if the people who hear this type of preaching are not confused, it must be because they do not think about what they hear.

The Bible teaches that man is dead in sin. Before he can do anything spiritual he must be raised from the dead, or, to use another figure of speech, he must be born again. A dead man cannot do anything. Now, since faith is a spiritual activity, pleasing to God, a man must be spiritually alive before he can show the evidences of a spiritual life. That is to say, a sinner must be regenerated and given a new heart before he can believe in Christ. The carnal mind is enmity against God.

This Calvinistic message is not confusing. It makes sense and can be understood. But to put the matter in still clearer terms, consider the confusion into which the evangelist throws the doctrine of justification.

Faith is the sole means of justification. This theme was a major part of the Reformation doctrine. Justification by faith was the message that swept away Romish superstition, idolatry and dependence on works. But if faith precedes regeneration, it would be possible for a man to be justified, to be clothed upon with the righteousness of Christ, and therefore to be saved, without being born again. Yet the Scripture very definitely says, Ye must be born again. But of what use would regeneration be, if one is already justified, accepted as guiltless before the throne of God, pronounced righteous — all without being born again? This just does not make sense. It is confusion.

And it is a shame when evangelistic sermons are full of confusion. The message of redemption should be made clear and plain. That is why evangelistic sermons should be strongly Calvinistic. G.H.C.

A Basket of Fruit:
The Fruit of the Spirit (Galatians 5:22, 23)

The fruit of the Spirit is LOVE.

This is the most beautiful basket of fruit that was ever seen. Christian love is something to covet; to pray for; to be wrought in our hearts by the Spirit.

I. *The Holy Spirit enables us to LOVE GOD AS WE SHOULD.*

This is the First Commandment; Thou shalt love the Lord Thy God.

1. All Nature should teach us to love God. He has made everything beautiful; He has also thrown in a lot of "Extras."

2. Our own wonderfully made Body and Mind and Spirit — made in the image of God — should teach us to love our Maker.

3. His Providential Care over us, as He protects and provides and satisfies every desire of our hearts, ought to make us love Him.

4. His Sacrifice on Calvary, as He bore our sins in His own body on the tree, ought to compel us to love Him.

5. But it takes *more than these;* these things help, but the only way we will ever love Him as we ought, is for the Holy Spirit to take our hearts, and minds, and souls, and strength. This is *the Fruit of the Spirit.* He alone can write upon our hearts His Name of LOVE.

II. *The Holy Spirit enables us to LOVE OUR NEIGHBORS AS OURSELVES.*

1. All mankind should be bound together by the tie of Love. We know this, but we also know that instead of love there is hatred and jealousy and strife and bloodshed and war. Look in any direction today and we see that this is true.

2. All Christians should love one another. This is one of the marks of a true Christian; we know that we have passed from death to life because we love the brethren; This is my commandment, that ye love one another. All who read Church History are shamed by the quarrels and persecutions which have marked the Church.

4. We should love the unfortunate people of the world; the sick, the poor, the ignorant, the oppressed, and we do where the Spirit of Christ is in us.

5. We should love the unsaved and have them upon our hearts.

6. We should love our enemies and do good to them.

The LAW says, LOVE. Only the Spirit can make us LOVE; LOVE is the fruit of the Spirit.

J.K.P.

The Southern Presbyterian Journal, *a Presbyterian Weekly magazine devoted to the statement, defense, and propagation of the Gospel, the faith which was once for all delivered unto the saints,* published every Wednesday by The Southern Presbyterian Journal, Inc., in Weaverville, N. C.

Entered as second-class matter May 15, 1942, at the Postoffice at Weaverville, N. C., under the Act of March 3, 1879. Vol. XV, No. 24, October 10, 1956. Editorial and Business Offices: Weaverville, N. C. Printed in the U.S.A. by Biltmore Press, Asheville, N. C.

ADDRESS CHANGE: When changing address, please let us have both old and new address as far in advance as possible. Allow three weeks after change if not sent in advance. When possible, send an address label giving your old address.

Back To The Bible

All Scripture is given by inspiration of God . . . and is profitable . . .—II Tim. 3:16-17.

Sermon delivered by Rev. G. T. Gillespie, D.D., Litt.D., as Retiring Moderator of Central Mississippi Presbytery.

Published at request of the Presbytery.

Christianity goes forward by going back. This may seem to be a paradox but it is true. Every real advance in the history of the Christian Church has been marked by a turning *back to the Bible* on the part of the people of God.

John Wycliffe heralded the dawn of a new day, after the long night of the "Dark Ages," by translating the Bible into the common speech of the English people; Martin Luther, Father of the Reformation, performed no greater service than by giving the Bible to the German people in their own language, and thus breaking the shackles of superstition and ecclesiastical despotism, and undergirding the whole Reformation Movement throughout Europe, with the Word of God.

John Wesley, in the Great Revival Movement of the 18th century, led the people back to a systematic study of the Bible, and a fresh emphasis upon its simple Gospel truths. Likewise the great Evangelists of the past generation, Moody, Chapman, Billy Sunday, Gypsy Smith, and many others, all accepted the Bible with unquestioning faith, and preached it with demonstration of the Spirit, and with soul-saving power.

In our own day, Billy Graham, in his unprecedented world-wide ministry to countless multitudes, speaking to vast audiences in the great centers of both the Christian and the non-Christian world, and by radio and television, punctuates his sermons constantly with the expression, "The Bible says." Without quibbling or apology, he has held up the Bible as the inspired and infallible Word of God in the chief intellectual centers of the world, and the mouths of the critics and the skeptics have been stopped by the manifest blessing of God which has attended his preaching.

This is but one of many indications that Christianity is moving forward to meet the challenge of a new age, while a genuine *Back to the Bible* movement is definitely under way. The latest report of the American Bible Society indicates that the Bible has now been translated into 1,084 different languages and dialects, and that it is being circulated and read throughout the world more widely than ever before. The total Bible volumes to be published by that Society alone, for the year 1956, is estimated to exceed 14,500,000. This does not take into account the publications of British and foreign Bible societies nor of private publishers. And it is a matter of common knowledge that every year the Bible tops the list of the world's "Best Sellers."

A New Appraisal of the Bible Needed

Sir Walter Scott, the great British novelist, as he lay dying, said, "Bring me the Book." Someone asked, "Which book?" He replied, "There is but one book—the Bible." William E. Gladstone, great British statesman and scholar of the Victorian Era, in a remarkable volume in defense of the integrity of the Bible, described it as "The Impregnable Rock of Holy Scripture." Dr. Walter W. Moore, the late distinguished president of Union Theological Seminary in Virginia, one of the ablest Hebrew scholars of his generation, and a staunch defender of the Conservative position, indicates his own high estimate of the nature and function of the Bible in the title of his remarkable little book, "The Indispensable Book."

In contrast with this high appraisal, which has generally prevailed among reverent scholars and leaders throughout the English-speaking world for the past several centuries, modern Biblical scholarship has so largely concerned itself with critical questions concerning the authorship, the authenticity, and the integrity of the Biblical text, and such effective propaganda has been used to publicize these views through religious publications, church literature, and other channels of communication, that there has come to be a widespread feeling of confusion and uncertainty today, among many of the younger ministers and the lay membership of the churches as to what we can believe concerning the origin, the nature, and the authority of the Scriptures.

All of this emphasizes the importance of a new and fresh appraisal of the Bible for this generation, not in the technical terms or the complicated hypotheses of so-called "Modern Biblical Scholarship," but in the non-technical language of the man in the street, and in accordance with a common-sense evaluation of the testimony which the Bible gives concerning itself, for the Bible is its own best witness.

The Bible Claims To Be the Inspired Word of God

The statement of the Apostle Paul to the young minister, Timothy, that "All Scripture is given by inspiration of God," II Tim. 3:16, is matched by the statement of the Apostle Peter, that "Holy men of God spake as they were moved by the Holy Ghost," II Pet 1:21. These are not isolated statements. Generally, throughout both the Old and New Testaments, it is clearly assumed, and often distinctly stated by the servants of God, that they wrote or spoke with divine authority. "Thus Saith the Lord," was the favorite introduction used by many of the prophets, but the absence of such an expression does not imply that other passages or books may not be equally inspired.

Our Lord constantly appealed to the Scriptures of the Old Testament as the word of God, stating emphatically that, "the Scripture cannot be broken," John 10:35; and also that "Till heaven and earth pass, one jot or one tittle shall in no wise pass from the law till all be fulfilled. Whosoever therefore shall break one of these least commandments, and shall teach men so, he shall be called least in the kingdom of heaven; but whosoever shall do and teach them, the same shall be called great in the kingdom of heaven," Matt. 5:18-19.

Our Lord did not raise any critical questions concerning the authorship of the books of Moses, or Isaiah, or Jonah, or Daniel, nor did he question the historicity of the stories of the creation, the flood, the exodus, or even the story of Jonah and the whale. To assume, as modern scholarship seems to do, that these records are not authentic, but only reflect the legendary beliefs of a primitive people, and that Jesus did not know that they were fictitious, is virtually a denial of His deity; while to assume that Jesus did know that they were fictitious, but dealt with them as true, and allowed his followers to go on believing that they were true, because he was concerned with them only as he used the parables, for their teaching value, is, to say the least, a serious reflection upon His sincerity and trustworthiness as a teacher. In either case, the "scholars" would seem to be impaled upon the horns of a dilemma; and as events have shown, the practical effect of their hypotheses is a tendency to weaken the faith of many in the authority of the Scriptures, and in the ability of Christ to deal with the problems of the modern mind.

To be fair, we must recognize that Modern Biblical research, and the development of sound critical techniques, have added greatly to our store of accurate knowledge concerning the Bible and Bible times; for which we should be ready to give credit where credit is due. At the same time, it is to be feared that many of our most prominent preachers, teachers, and writers, by their pre-occupation with critical questions, and by their excessive emphasis upon the so called "assured results of modern scholarship," have been propagators of doubt rather than of faith, and have, on the whole, rendered a distinct disservice to vital Evangelical Christianity.

The fact that, "All Scripture is given by inspiration of God," is the basis of our assurance that the Scriptures are without essential error. We are not called upon to explain how this is possible, or to formulate and defend any precise theory that will answer all the questions which may be raised, but to all of those who question and doubt, we may well answer as the Master did the skeptics of his day, "Ye do err, not knowing the Scriptures, nor the power of God," Matt. 22:29.

Obviously, no intelligent student of the Bible can afford to adopt an ostrich attitude, and close his eyes to the questions arising concerning authorship, source materials, textual variations, and other such problems; but it is gratifying that these problems have been honestly faced by many competent scholars, whose findings are entirely consistent with full confidence in the authenticity and credibility of the Biblical records.

The Bible Is in the Language of Men

The Bible is essentially a *human* book; it is unthinkable that it should have been otherwise. If God was to make his thought and will known to men, he must of necessity put it into words that men could understand. Even though, "Holy men spake as they were moved by the Holy Ghost," they spoke the language of their time and their cultural group, which like all human language is subject to the limitations and the imperfections of human nature. For, as the Apostle Paul says, "We bear this treasure in earthen vessels."

It is this inescapable fact which gives rise to the dilemma which has baffled the wisdom of men: How can the infallible wisdom of the infinite and eternal God be preserved in the imperfect and constantly changing language of fallible men? In other words, the problem is: How can the Bible be an authoritative and infallible revelation of God, and how has it been preserved without essential error, when there is no doubt that many of those who wrote it were "ignorant and unlearned men," and we know from reason and actual observation that hundreds of minor errors occurred in laborious transcriptions by hand over many centuries, and in the numerous translations which have been made, in spite of the extreme care which was taken by the Hebrew copyists, and the diligence and fidelity with which the translators have usually done their work.

When all the facts which bear upon this question have been gathered and studied, there still remains a mystery which reason has not been able to fathom. It is the same profound mystery which confronts us as we try to grasp the truth that the Eternal Son of God took upon himself the nature of man, so that he was, and continues to be, "truly God and truly man," in two distinct natures and one person forever. Surely the analogy between the Eternal Word, which "became flesh," and the written Word in the language of men, is not accidental or incidental. Our faith rests upon the *Incarnation* or the dual nature of the Living Word. it also rests upon the *Inspiration*, or the dual nature of the Written Word. Neither of these truths can be fully comprehended or explained, they can only be apprehended by faith, but taken together, they support and confirm each other, and enable us to sing with glad hearts:

"How firm a foundation, ye saints of the Lord,
Is laid for your faith, in his excellent Word."

The Bible Is One Book

One of the most convincing proofs of the divine authorship of the Bible, is its essential unity. Though consisting of sixty-six different books, written by two score or more individuals, over a period of fifteen centuries, it carries within itself unmistakable evidence of being *One Book*, which points conclusively to one divine author, whom the Apostle identifies as the Holy Spirit.

This unity is not that of a didactic treatise, or a static revelation. It is the unity of an organism, representing a gradual and progressive unfolding of a great central theme and a dynamic purpose, like that of a growing plant, "first the blade, then the ear, then the full corn in the ear," or like a rosebud opening its petals day by day until the full-blown rose appears in all its fragrance and beauty.

For example: we have in Genesis the story of the beginning of all things, including the heavens and the earth; in Revelation we have the final consummation of all things, and the vision of The New Heavens and The New Earth; in Genesis, we have the story of the earthly paradise, and how it was lost through the wiles of Satan and the sin of man; in Revelation we have the story of "Paradise Regained," through the triumph of the "Seed of the Woman" over Satan and Sin and their final banishment from the Paradise of God; in Genesis, we have the story of the First Adam and his bride, being given dominion over the whole earthly creation; in Revelation, we have the story of the Second Adam and his bride, The Church, being given dominion over a redeemed and transformed world.

In the prophecy, recorded in Genesis, concerning the "seed of the woman," who should "bruise the serpent's head," there is the first faint promise of a redeemer, but it was a star of hope in the black night of gloom in which the destiny of the race was enshrouded at that tragic hour. To Abraham the promise was renewed in more explicit terms, and confirmed by an oath; and then to Isaac, to Jacob, to David and the Psalmists, to Isaiah and the other prophets, the star grew brighter and brighter, until it appeared to the Wise Men and led them until it stood at last above the manger in Bethlehem where after all those centuries, was born the promised "seed of the woman," who was to save His people from their sins, and destroy the Devil and all his works.

If time permitted, it would be interesting to trace the history of all the great doctrines of our Christian faith, such as the doctrines of God, man, sin, salvation by faith, the atonement, back to their roots in the first deposit of divine truth contained in the books of Moses, and then to trace the working out and growth of these doctrines in the experience of God's people, as shown by each of the books of the Old and New Testaments.

The cumulative weight of this evidence of the unity of the Bible, in spite of its obvious diversity, leads to the conclusion, which has been so clearly stated by the writer of the Epistle to the Hebrews, chapter 1:1-2,2:1: "God who at sundry times and in divers manners spake in time past to the fathers by the prophets, hath in these last days spoken to us by his Son . . . Therefore we ought to give the more earnest heed to the things which we have heard, lest at any time we should let them slip."

This leads also to the practical aspect of Paul's Doctrine of the Inspiration of The Scriptures—for all of Paul's doctrines had a practical application.

fidence upon the promise of our Lord: "Heaven and earth shall pass away, but my words shall not pass away," Matt. 24:55.

A homely, but impressive illustration of the eternal and indestructible character of the Word of God, is found in the following poem by an unknown author:

THE ANVIL

Last eve I paused beside a blacksmith shop,
And heard the anvil ring the vesper chime,
Then looking in, I saw upon the floor,
Old hammers, worn with beating years of time.

"How many anvils have you had," said I,
"To wear and batter these hammers so?"
"Just one," said he, and then with twinkling eye,
"The anvil wears the hammers out, you know."

And so, thought I, the Anvil of God's Word,
For ages, skeptic blows have beat upon;
Yet though the noise of falling blows were heard,
The anvil is unharmed, the hammers gone.

More About Extraordinary Oscillations

By J. V. N. Talmadge, D.D.

In 1953 the writer wrote several articles for the *Journal* regarding the extraordinary oscillations of climate and sea-level during the antediluvian age. He suggested that the cause of these mysterious oscillations was to be found in a counterclockwise spiral movement of the North Pole called polar precession. After spending 1954 and 1955 in Korea doing a special form of missionary work, he returned to America and spent the first part of the present year in the library at Rice Institute in Houston checking the effect of the latest scientific discoveries upon these theories. He was delighted to find that the latest science fully confirmed the general principles, but caused several corrections in details. Below we give some of the more important points as corrected and enlarged.

1. The Creation, which is definitely assigned to a glacial age by Biblical description of the Pishon River, cannot be confidently dated as having taken place during the Warthe glaciation in Germany and the Lowestoft glaciation which reached London. This can be shown to have been contemporaneous with what American geologists call the Warim Bradyan Interval in the plains. It was much warmer then than now, and the date, though still disputed by geologists, cannot be more than 15,000 years ago. In spite of vociferous claims to the contrary, no human tool or bone has ever been found by non-Christian archeologists that is older than that date. All older dates are purely philosophical speculation.

2. Radiocarbon dating has proved exceedingly useful, but by itself it cannot be trusted. For instance, geologists admit that "dead" carbon from limestone deposits often causes exaggeration in dating. Readers are warned against accepting radiocarbon dates of material in limestone caves where there has been evidence of very moist conditions. All the early dates are worthless, even though non-Christians accept them. These false dates are some of the few remaining arguments for evolution.

3. The silt found on the site of Ur, the native city of Abraham, is dated about 11,000 years ago by radio carbon, and is shown to be contemporary with the last advance of the ice sheet half way down Lake Michigan. This silt was deposited long before the Flood of Noah. This date was also the time of strong volcanic action especially in Africa, and of the upper deposit of volcanic ash on the bottom of the Atlantic ocean, and of great ethnic movements.

4. The date of the Flood of Noah has had to be advanced to nearly 7,000 years ago because of many forms of evidence. It had to be placed before the Jemdet Nasr painted pottery culture rather than afterward as the writer originally thought.

5. Postdiluvian chronology has now been clarified by recent evidence. The Tower of Babel and Nimrod's Kingdom can now be accurately described.

6. There has been a marked tendency to shorten these extravagant dates of stone age men even among those who reject the Bible. Drs. Ewing and Dunn of Columbia this summer published a paper advocating a theory of polar movement, but this was merely the beginning of a trend in the right direction.

7. Strange to say, while non-Christians were shortening their chronology, many self-styled conservatives have declared they could accept the long dating; and in our seminaries some boldly proclaim the early chapters of Genesis as myths. These men are completely out of step with science.

8. The writer attended in August a scientific convention of Christian scholars. It was very satisfying to hear Bible questions discussed by Christian men who recognized the Bible stories as true instead of calling them myths. The writer had one great disappointment, he could not find any one who was doing research in the same field as himself. Science has become so specialized that college professors in one field relied on the conclusions of men in other fields without regard to whether they were Christians or not. A Christian, reborn by God's Spirit, looks on scientific data with a wider horizon than the non-Christian, and we must take that into consideration when accepting scientific "findings."

ANGLERS

By WADE C. MITH

Lesson No. 160

By-Products of Personal Evangelism

"This work of soul-winning carries with it the greatest possibility of elevation of character. Not asceticism, but activity is the secret of growth in Christ and the knowledge of Christ. Not the monastery, but the manufactory may be the place of greatest advance in the Christian life. Not in the convent, but in the church is the greatest opportunity for spiritual culture. We are in the world to save others and by that very service we are bringing the best into our own lives. He helps himself most who helps another most. In spiritual exercise is the secret of strength. When one is actually engaged in personal work to rescue others, doubts vanish, sensitiveness disappears, self-consciousness is banished, envy is lost, jealousy takes to itself wings, and anxiety and dissatisfaction and unrest change into peace and quiet and calm. The noble elements of character rush into life along this pathway of personal work."

—Cortland Myers.

A good thing begets good things. It is a good thing to win a soul to Jesus—a great and priceless privilege. This is the high objective of Personal Evangelism. But in the process there are many other "peaceable fruits of righteousness" falling to the worker, and to the church, perhaps as a gracious surprise.

In Bible reading. One of the first of these by-products is new light and new inspiration coming to the soul-winner out of his Bible. You get right into the heart of God's Word when you go into personal work, for you are inevitably thrown back upon the authoritative statements, to make sure of God's plan, God's proposition and God's promises. There is no doubt but that one must study the Word more carefully in order to answer questions than in order to preach. It is a rare thing for people to interrupt the pulpit preacher with a question. His thoughts may flow on in the way he has planned; but when one speaks to another alone on the subject of salvation he will meet with many questions he should be prepared for. You are driven to your Bible for this preparation like nothing else drives you. No other theme in religion draws such disconcerting questions — if unprepared. The devil sees to that. A forceful preacher told the writer that although he had been preaching for years before he seriously began to do personal work he never knew his Bible until he had to search it for the answers to questions that were flashed back at him in private interviews. Studied in

and brings forth sin's consequences — spiritual death (6:23). In Christ we are set completely free from the penalty of God's laws (8:1-2). This penalty was paid by Christ Himself (v.3). Observe what vv.7-8 say about a person who refuses to repent of his sin and accept Christ. What basic change must take place in a person's life when he becomes a Christian (vv.4-6)? Do you understand the basic difference between the life that is lived under the law and the new life that is lived in Christ?

Tuesday, October 23, *Psalm* 119:81-105. Observe in verses 81-88 the predicament of the Psalmist. To what does he say he will cling (vv.81-88)? Each verse of this Psalm is addressed to God and has something to say about the Word of God. In these verses the Psalmist uses the words "precept," "judgment," "law," "word," etc., in speaking of the Scriptures. The Word of God holds true and is valid for all times (vv.89-91). In his difficulties what does God's Word mean to the Psalmist (vv.92-93, 103-105)? How is it more than adequate for the circumstances of his life (vv.98-100)? The Psalmist's deep love for the Word (v.97) is accompanied by obedience to it (v.101). Have you found God's Word adequate for your needs? Do you read it regularly with the determination to obey it consistently?

Wednesday, October 24, *Ephesians* 2:1-10. We do not always realize how dependent we are upon God for our salvation. Observe in vv.1-3 how helplessly we were lost before we came to know Christ. What phrases in vv.2-3 picture the non-Christian's walk as being diametrically away from God? What do the phrases "children of wrath" (v.3) and "dead in sin" (vv.1,5) indicate of our former relation with God? Upon what basis does God save us (vv.4,8)? What is the purpose of His saving us (v.10)? Who is going to be glorified through our salvation (vv.6-7)? Is your Christian experience a genuine testimony to what God can do in a life? Praise God once more for the depth of the mercy in which He saved you.

Thursday, October 25, *Romans* 5:1-10. The Christian faith is one that brings the individual into direct contact with God (v.1) and enables him to share in the very life of God (vv.2,5). What do vv.6-8 reveal about the love God pours into the heart of the Christian (v.5)? Upon what does the Christian base his hope of sharing God's glory (vv.9-10)? How is this hope different from hopes that do not have their basis in God (v.5a)? The Christian is able to share in God's glory and love (vv.2,5), because the barrier that separates him from God has been removed (vv.9-10) and he is at peace with God (v.1). How does man find peace with God (4:24-5:1)? How are you seeking peace with God?

Friday, October 26, Hebrews 10:9-25. What differences exist between the sacrifices of the Old Testament and the sacrifice of Christ (vv.9-18) as to the frequency of the sacrifice (vv.10-14) and the effect of the sacrifice (vv.10, 11,14-18)? What confidence ought the truth of vv.14,17,18 give to the Christian? Do you have this confidence (vv.19-22)? Notice again that it is Christ's faithfulness and not the faithfulness of the Christian that makes the Christian acceptable before God (vv.23,10-11,17-18). Notice also, however, that the salvation that Christ offers involves not only the pardon of our sins, but also an inner change in our attitude toward sin (vv.14-15). What two practical exhortations are given in vv.24-25? As a Christian, are you concerned primarily for your own spiritual welfare, or are you quick to encourage the spiritual growth of others (vv.24-25)?

Saturday, October 27, Col. 1:9-18. List the things Paul tells the Colossian Christians he has been asking of the Lord for them (vv.9-14). Notice particularly the superlatives in this passage: "all," "every," "filled," and "fully" (vv.9-14). Paul says in the first part of v.9 that there is a reason for his praying for such a full spiritual life for these Christians. Look in vv.3-8 for this reason. Because Paul knows that the Colossians have experienced the reality of the Holy Spirit (v.8), have known a real Christian love (v.4) and a fruit-producing faith (vv.4,6) — because their Christian lives have shown such wonderful growth — Paul sees the opportunity for them to grow yet more and more into full maturity (vv.9-14). Do you look upon your spiritual achievements as a basis for pride or complacency, or as an indication that you can now press on to a closer, fuller walk with God?

SABBATH SCHOOL LESSONS — REV. J. KENTON PARKER

LESSON FOR OCTOBER 21

Hear, O Israel

Background Scripture: Deuteronomy 6
Devotional Reading: Psalm 78:1-7

The writer of Psalm 78, Asaph, is thinking about "the generation to come." He desires that the children should be better than their fathers; "And might not be as their fathers, a stubborn and rebellious generation." We are under a deep obligation, not only to our children, but to God, to instruct and teach them the commandments of the Lord. "We will not hide them from their children, showing to the generation to come the praises of the Lord, and his strength, and his wonderful works that he hath done."

Moses, the great leader and statesman and lawgiver, knew the vital importance of this sort of instruction. The key-words of the book of Deuteronomy are "remember," "forget not." Moses in these matchless orations spoken in the plains of Moab just before he left his people, is reviewing the history of Israel and impressing upon them the importance of keeping God's commandments. He expected them to remember and keep and teach these precious truths to their children. The chapter we study today is one of the great chapters of the Bible, and is a part—a most thrilling part—of one of these speeches.

"Hear, O Israel." These are most important words which he is about to utter. To hear, to listen, to hearken to the message of God; this is what the messengers sent from God insist upon: "Hear, O heavens, and give ear, O earth: for the Lord hath spoken," cried Isaiah; "O, earth, earth, earth, hear the word of the Lord," cried Jeremiah; "Hear, and your soul shall live"; "He that hath ears to hear, let him hear," said our Saviour over and over again. The Bible is full of exhortations and warnings in regard to the importance of listening when God speaks. Moses wants his people to hear that it may be well with them and that they might increase mightily in the land to which they were going. What is the message? First, "The Lord our God is one Lord." They were going into a land where there were many gods. It was vital for them to know that there is but One Living and True God; Monotheism, in contrast with polytheism. Second, their relationship to God was to be that of LOVE.

In the first two verses he had told them that they must fear the Lord and keep His commandments. This verse goes deeper. There must be a closer relationship than "fear." When Jesus was asked which was the first commandment He quoted these words. (see Matthew 22:37,38). Love is the fulfilling of the Law.

much do we talk about "these things"? Yet, these are the most important things in the world. I am writing this with a deep sense of shame that I have not done more of this. I have had visiting ministers in my home who seemed to have the "knack" of steering the conversation into these channels. It would be a great blessing if more of us had this ability. May the Lord be merciful and forgiving! When thou liest down and when thou risest up. The best way to go to sleep at night is with a verse of Scripture; and it is the finest way to begin the day. Thy Word is a lamp to my feet, and a light to my path. We will work better and travel safer if we begin the day with "this Book."

3. Upon our hands: Bind them for a sign upon thine hand. We work with our hands. Will our work today be worthwhile? Will we do with our might what our hands find to do? Will our labor be honest and faithful. The hand of the Christian should have a "sign" upon it; it must be guided by the Word. We also help people with our hands. Our hands should be kind hands, ministering to all who need us. Think of Jesus' Hands! He used them in the carpenter shop; He used them to touch and heal and bless all who needed Him. Bind the Bible around our hands and remember that "inasmuch as ye did it unto the least of these my brethren, ye did it unto me."

4. Write them upon the posts of thy house. Many American Homes are tumbling down. (Not the houses, but the Homes). This is the number one problem of our country. How can we save our Homes? Many suggestions are being made. I believe this command of Moses is the best one. When we build our homes on the Bible, we build on the rock. The wise man built his house upon a rock!

5. And on thy gates. A gate is for protection. It keeps dogs out; it keeps the children in. There are enemies that prowl about, like the wild beasts and the Indians used to prowl. Our homes today need the protection of the Word of God. If rightly used it safeguards these precious homes of ours.

II. *"Beware lest thou forget."*

It is so easy to forget. Israel was about to enter the Promised Land, a land full of good things. In their days of hardship and travel and danger they did not always remember God; they often forgot. It would be much easier for them to forget when they were in a land of plenty. Moses is earnestly and solemnly warning them of this danger, the danger of forgetting the One Who had brought them out of Egypt, and the One Who had given them this goodly land.

They were to fear the Lord and serve Him, and "shalt swear by His name." This last expression does not mean, of course, the taking of His name in vain, but the sacred use of His Name in oaths. They are warned not to go after the gods of the nations around about them. It is very strange that people who know the True God will turn from Him to the gods of heathen people, and the revolting worship of Baal and Ashteroth. Why will they leave the living fountain to drink from broken cisterns, filled with impure water? Ye shall not tempt the Lord your God, as ye tempted him in Massah. (see Exodus 17:7) It was at Massah that the Israelites had no water to drink and strove with Moses, almost ready to stone him.

"When thy son asketh thee in time to come, saying, What mean these testimonies and judgments?" they were to tell them about what God had done in delivering them from Egypt, and in bringing them to their good land. One of the best ways to keep from forgetting is to tell someone. In telling their children they would keep from forgetting, and also their children, the generation to come.

I believe that there is a very practical and timely lesson for us in this country in our lesson for today, both as to putting the Bible in its proper place in our homes, and also in this matter of "forgetting"? America is enjoying a season of prosperity at present. Have we forgotten God and what He has done for us? O Lord God of Hosts, Be with us yet: Lest we forget;. lest we forget.

YOUNG PEOPLE'S DEPARTMENT — REV. B. HOYT EVANS

YOUTH PROGRAM FOR OCTOBER 21

Wanted: A Nation Under God

Suggested Devotional Outline:

Hymn: "Wonderful Words Of Life"
Prayer
Scripture: Matthew 25
Hymn: "I Love To Tell The Story"
Offering
Hymn: "My Hope Is Built On Nothing Less"

Program Leader's Introduction:

We observed last week that the words "under God" have recently been added to the Pledge of Allegiance to the Flag. We also discovered many factors indicating that we are a nation "under God" only in a partial sense. There are and have been many genuine Christians among the citizens of our nation, and these have had a profound influence in moulding the character of the national life. Christian principles pervade our laws and our traditions. These benefits came from Christian people who conscientiously practiced their faith. We must be deeply grateful for the blessings of Christianity which we enjoy in this land, but we must not be satisfied with anything short of the best. What we seek is a nation which is thoroughly Christian. It is our purpose in this program to discover how a nation may become genuinely Christian, and to discover what we can do to secure this blessing for our nation.

First Speaker:

In the program last week it was pointed out that the basic cause of the spiritual weakness and sickness in America is the presence of sin. If the sickness is to be cured, we must quite obviously do something to remove sin. We immediately recognize that the removal of sin is quite beyond our very best powers. We are helpless in the face of this problem, but we are not hopeless. There is a way of escape. There is a way of overcoming sin completely and finally. Christ the Son of God conquered sin and the death which results from it. Those who believe in Him as their Saviour share in His victory. Their lives are transformed and they are no longer subject to sin and death. There is no other way of transforming sinful human nature than through faith in Jesus Christ. The only way to free a nation from sin and its power is for its citizens, one by one, to be transformed through faith in Christ.

Second Speaker:

It is only natural to suppose that every person who is transformed by Christ will show by his life that this wonderful change has been wrought in him. Unfortunately, this is not always the case. There are many who claim to believe in Christ whose way of living is unchanged, from all outward appearances. We shall not have a genuinely Christian nation until all the people who claim to be Christians begin to live like Christians ought to live. It is certain that we are not saved by keeping commandments, but we surely ought to keep the commandments of

Women's Work

The Companion

Here in my workshop where I toil
  Till head and hands are well-night spent;
Out on the road where the dust and soil
  Fall thick on garments worn and rent;
Or in the kitchen where I bake
  The bread the little children eat—
He comes, His hand of strength I take,
  And every lonely task grows sweet.

—Author Unknown

World Day of Prayer and Your Community

We share with you the thrilling story of the outgrowth and lasting result of a World Day of Prayer committee in Amarillo, Texas. We will be glad to receive other answers to the question, "What have been some of the results of World Day of Prayer in your community?"

The women of Amarillo had been observing the World Day of Prayer together since 1930. Then in 1935, women of nine churches met to consider a project in which they could unite their efforts. With a consecrated awareness of the need for Christian social service, they decided to use their combined efforts for character-building work among underprivileged girls. To establish their project, the women purchased an old two-story frame house, remodeled it, and the first home of the Social Center for Girls came into being. Within a year the institution was serving from three to five hundred girls each month.

In 1939, the old frame building was wrecked and a new $25,000 building was built. The center had become a community-chest supported agency, though sponsored and partially supported by United Church Women. In 1943, the time seemed right and evidence seemed conclusive that a Y. W. C. A. would better serve the community; two years later the UCW approved transferring the funds and the deed to the social center building to the Amarillo Y. W. C. A.

The council of church women had long observed the three special days. They were providing milk for Mexican children, sponsoring a vacation Bible school for Negro children, and helping to underwrite a Bible Chair in the Amarillo High School. They had built and equipped a library for the Negro school, and were recognized as a powerful organization in the city.

In 1952, when plans were being made to build a $600,000 Y. W. C. A., the UCW pledged $25,000 for a chapel. Within *four* years the $25,000 was raised. On April 8, 1956 our state president, Mrs. L. C. Curlin, came to dedicate the little jewel of a chapel. It was built through faith and co-operation and "Dedicated to All Who Come Seeking Peace of Mind and Heart."

—Mrs. Sam W. Johnson, president United Church Women, Amarillo, Texas.

Spiritual Growth, Whose Job?

Every two years we elect a Spiritual Growth chairman and give her certain duties. She is to order any literature she thinks helpful in this area, bring special emphases before the group from time to time, be responsible for arranging for circle the Bible study and the special Bible study that comes once a year, co-operate with other chairmen in joint programs, and in general prepare and serve spiritual food that we need for spiritual growth.

But, it is not her duty either to spoon feed us, or to be the sole partaker of this spiritual food. She cannot cram it down our throats. She cannot grow for us. Each of us has a responsibility to grow in the Christian graces and ever closer to God.

Too many of us neglect to grow. Thinking in the realm of the spiritual is a task; we don't believe in some of the emphases and we have heard others so many times that actually we fail to hear them again. We have become indifferent.

But, when we allow our ears to become dull and our senses lulled into a stupor, we have robbed ourselves of all the joy of close communion with God. True, we have escaped some crosses we were meant to bear, but we have also missed the still small Voice of love, the warmth of His Presence, and the joy of growing in the Faith.

Don't expect your Spiritual Growth Chairman to do your growing. We are our own Spiritual Growth chairmen.

Sabina Wheeler Hayes

Church News

ALABAMA

Birmingham — Dr. R. D. Bedinger was named moderator of the Birmingham Presbytery at a meeting Sept. 11, at Wylam Presbyterian Church of Birmingham.

He replaced Dr. Alexander Henry, who retired. Dr. Bedinger has been executive secretary of the group for more than two years.

Three new ministers were received into the Presbytery. They were the Rev. James M. Gregory, new pastor of the Woodlawn Presbyterian Church, former pastor of Napoleon Ave. Church in New Orleans; Rev. Eugene P. Poe, new assistant pastor of South Highland Church, former pastor of First Presbyterian Church of Brewton, Ala.; and the Rev. Donald A. McInnis, who will serve as regional director of Christian Education for the Synod.

Birmingham—The Men of the Church of the Birmingham Presbytery held their annual barbecue Sept. 15, at the newly acquired conference area near Springville.

The conference ground is three miles south of Springville, and is a 50-acre site with a lake covering 18 acres.

The speaker following the barbecue was the Rev. John L. Hottel, pastor of the First Presbyterian Church of Fort Payne, Ala. He is a veteran of World War II with more than four years service with the Army, also having spent two of these years in India, where he was assigned to a Japanese intelligence group.

Before the dinner, the men toured the site of the conference ground.

Birmingham—Between 50 and 75 Birmingham Presbyterian laymen and ministers went to Talladega, Ala., for the annual Men's Day of the Synod of Alabama, held at the Presbyterian home for children, in early September.

The men along with others from the Alabama Synod, visited the campus of the children's home and were treated to a barbecue. The home is supported by all of the churches of the Alabama Synod. They care for 95 to 110 children. The home is under the direction of the Rev. Allen Jacobs.

FLORIDA

Miami—A Presbyterian minister and his wife will receive an all-expense, roundtrip to Athens, Greece, as winners of a contest on the National Broadcasting Company's TV "Home" show, NBC has announced.

The Rev. Dale H. Ratliff of Alta Vista Presbyterian Church in Miami wrote the letter considered best on the subject, "Why I Would Like To Visit Athens".

In his letter Mr. Ratliff explained that he became the sponsor of a Greek child three years ago and that he would like very much to see the baby in whose welfare he has such a strong interest. Mr. Ratliff appeared on the TV program Sept. 24.

LOUISIANA

New Orleans—The 43rd annual meeting of the 'omen of the Church of the Synod of Louisiana ıs held in the First Presbyterian Church of ɜw Orleans, Setember 25-26.

Mrs. Walter Truluck, Jr., of Pine Bluff, Ark., :e-chairman of the Board of Women's Work, dressed the meeting on the first day. Dr. Edırd D. Grant, state director of institutions spoke . the closing day.

Also included in the program was a worship rvice led by Mrs. Guy J. Belt. Officers were ɜcted during the sessions.

New Orleans—Mr. W. P. Whitesides will serve rst Presbyterian Church of New Orleans as inrim choir director for this year. Mr. Whitesides a graduate of Davidson College and did gradu- ɜ work at the University of North Carolina.

Last year, he was a member of the Robert Shaw ıorale.

Red River Presbytery — Trinity Presbyterian Church Jonesville, La. — Sept. 11, 1956

ʋODERATOR'S SERMON by Rev. Wm. E. Giddens, . "The Sign of our Times" from Matt. 16:1-4; 12:40-41.

:ORD'S SUPPER OBSERVED: Rev. Robert Shepperı, Rev. Paul Currie & Elders, Twenty nine Ministers; ɾenty four Elders and guest present.

MODERATOR & TEMPORARY CLERK: Rev. Leonard Swinney & Rev. Arthur Strickland were elected.

SALARY RAISE: Rev. R. McNair Smith $1020 yearly, Call change approved.

REPORTS FROM GENERAL ASSEMBLY COMMISSIONERS HEARD (1956 Assembly) Commissioners commended and discharged.

MINISTERS RECEIVED AND DISMISSED: Rev. Frank O. Brown from Asheville Presbytery received commission set to install him September 23, 1956, 7:30 P. M., for Bossier City, First Church.

Rev. H. H. Thompson requested dismissal to Presbytery of Granville, N. C., to serve as Director of Evangelism Synod of N. C. Pastoral Relation at Ruston dissolved October 1, 1956.

Candidate James Walter White received at Called Meeting of Synod in Ruston Church July 17.

Rev. Cyrus S. Mallard, Jr., received from Presbytery of Tuscaloosa at Called Meeting of Synod in Ruston Church July 17 to serve as assistant in First Presbyterian Church, Shreveport.

Rev. Wade H. Boggs requested dismissal at Called Meeting of Synod July 17 to Presbytery of Atlanta. This was done.

Candidate Ray U. Tanner dropped from rolls as Candidate at his request. Rev. O. M. Anderson, Rev. S. E. McFadden reach retirement age. Anderson to serve at Bastrop until January 1, 1957. McFadden to continue at Alabama on yearly basis. Rev. E. D. Holloway requested retirement status and his Stated Supply Relation with Alto, Archibald Union terminates December 1. Special resolutions and prayers were offered for these.

Pastoral Relation of J. Watt Jeffries and Rayville Church terminated July 1, 1956, due to illness.

Memorial read and suitable prayers for family and service rendered the Church by Rev. Raymond A. Partlow of Ferriday, La. (deceased September 2, 1956.)

LAKE PROVIDENCE CHURCH TO BE ORGANIZED, Commission set to organize this Church October 14, 1956. *SALARY SCALE FOR PRESBYTERY RAISED:* Single man $3300; Married $3600; dependent children $150 each; car allowance $300, and manse. Request each Home Mission Church accept one-half of this increase.

SYNOD EVANGELISTIC EXCHANGE March - April, 1957; South to North, March 10-17; North to South April 7-14.

NEW NEGRO CHURCH SHREVEPORT BEGUN as project of Div. of Negro Work & First Presbyterian Church, Shreveport. Minister called, work begun.

CAPITAL GIFTS COMMITTEE: Trustees of Presbytery requested to transfer $3,000 to Capital Gifts Committee from rental property for current projects, Winnsboro manse, Sterlington manse, John Knox Church B. City. $5500 already raised by Committee. Commended for fine work.

Presbytery's Council: Per capita tax 31 cents for 1957; Benevolent Budget for 1957 $137,000; General Assembly $80,000, 58.4%; Synod $30,000, 21.8%; Presbytery $27,000, 19.8%. Also $10,000 Campus Christian Life campaign apportioned to Churches. Slides available G. A., Synod, Presbytery work.

VOTE ON WOMEN ELDERS & DEACONS, Winter Meeting Presbytery.

CAMPS & CONFERENCES DATES SET: 1 Senior, 3 Pioneer, 2 Junior Camps '57.

NOMINATIONS: John A. Richardson, Moderator Designate; Everett H. Phillips preach Doctrinal Sermon Winter Meeting "Pres. Doctrine Last Things"; L. R. Swinney, Higher Education; John Humble, Chairman Home Missions, John Wilson on H. M. Committee; J. W. Head, Evangelism.

NEXT MEETING Memorial Presbyterian Church, West Monroe, La., Feb. 11, 1957 at 9:30 A. M. — Called Meeting September 25, 10 A. M. 1st Shreveport.

GEORGIA

Atlanta—Mr. John Wellford, Memphis business man and leading Presbyterian layman of that city was the key-note speaker at the Fall meeting of the Atlanta Presbyterian Officers' Association which was held on Tuesday, September 25, at 6:30 p.m. in the Gordon Street Presbyterian Church of Atlanta.

According to Mr. Ed Hammond, president of the sponsoring organization, approximately 1000 elders and deacons, office-bearers in the Atlanta Presbyterian Churches, are members of the Association whose aim is to promote the Christian growth of the Atlanta area through the medium of the church. Many of these were expected to attend Tuesday's meeting.

Mr. Wellford has the distinction of being the originator of a new and most effective plan now being widely used throughout the Presbyterian Church to encourage giving to the world-wide benevolence causes of the denomination. The plan is known as the "Every Church Canvass".

A feature of the Presbyterian Officers' meeting was the presentation of $12,500 to three newly-formed Atlanta churches in the form of a gift. The three checks presented at this time go to:

Raleigh — The 44th annual meeting of the Women of the Church of the Synod of North Carolina was held in the First Presbyterian Church of Raleigh Sept. 25-26.

Mrs. R. A. Willis, Jr., of Monroe, president of the Synodical, presided over the two day session.

The following Presbyterial presidents made their annual reports: Mrs. George B. Moore for Albemarle Presbytery; Mrs. E. Johnston Irvin of Concord Presbytery; Mrs. George V. McLeod of Fayetteville Presbytery; Mrs. Raleigh Griffin for Granville; Mrs. R. L. Ellis for Kings Mountain; Mrs. Lloyd E. Ardey of Mecklenburg Presbytery; Mrs. J. Victor King of Orange Presbytery; Mrs. E. N. Pittman for Wilmington, and Mrs. Charles M. Sprinkle for Winston-Salem.

Raleigh—The new sanctuary of the First Presbyterian Church in Fairmont is nearing completion.

The congregation expects to begin using the new building around the first of November. An educational building at the rear of the sanctuary, and a manse were completed in the spring of 1955 and have been in use since that time. Cost of the entire building program will be in the neighborhood of $100,000. The Rev. James F. Dickenson is pastor of the Church.

SOUTH CAROLINA

Columbia — Congaree Presbytery is scheduling four stewardship conferences Sept. 24-27, with the Rev. J. S. Patton, D.D., Secretary of the General Council invited to lead the meeting.

Meetings will be conducted at the Eastminster Church, Columbia; Lebanon Church, Winnsboro; Bethesda Church, Camden; and Fairview Church, North Augusta.

Congaree Presbytery has adopted the 1957 benevolent budget and will try to get contributions totaling $150,188 for 1957. This is an increase over the previous budget of $148,789. The 1957 budget will apportion $66,284 for the General Assembly's causes; $41,569 for the Synod's causes; and $42,355 for the Presbytery's causes.

The stewardship committee of the Congaree Presbytery, under which the four conferences are authorized were composed of the following: the Rev. Claude McIntosh, chairman; the Rev. Joe Beale; secretary, Mr. J. W. McLaurin; Mr. Frank G. Vance; Mr. Joel A. Smith; Mr. L. C. Newton; Robert Lee Scarvarough; the Rev. Cecil Brearly, Jr.; and the Rev. Fred C. Debele.

Clinton—A former president of Davis Elkins College is the new professor of chemistry at Presbyterian College, President Marshall W. Brown announced.

He is Dr. Raymond B. Purdum, who served as president of Davis Elkins for 10 years after heading its chemistry department for 18 years.

Kingstree—A $44,000 contract for renovations to the Williamsburg Presbyterian Church of Kingstree has been awarded.

Work is to be completed by February. The sanctuary is to be enlarged by revising the chancel area. Plans call for the addition of air conditioning, insulation, rewiring, and repainting.

The Rev. Donald B. Bailey is pastor of the church. Mr. David S. Epps is chairman of the building committee. Plans were approved at a congregational meeting September 9.

TENNESSEE

Bristol—King College started classes on Saturday, September 15th, after a registration of approximately 250 students. This represents an increase of 25 over the year 1955-56 and crowds housing facilities on the campus to the limit. The early days of the week before the opening of classes on Saturday were largely devoted to general receptions and orientation of new students. There are about 100 Freshmen in this year's enrollment.

Two new members of the faculty were presented to the students: Dr. James C. Morecock as head of the Mathematics Department; and Miss Margaret Baumgardner as instructor in the English Department. Dr. Morecock comes to King College from Auburn Institute in Alabama; and Miss Baumgardner ended a long tenure of office with the Bristol, Tennessee, public schools system last June.

Nashville—Two unusual honors have been paid missionaries of the Presbyterian Church, U.S., who are at work in Brazil, the Board of World Missions has been informed.

Miss Edith Foster, working in the East Brazil Mission field of Varginha, was honored by the whole city, and had the title of citizenship in the city conferred upon her. Miss Foster is a native of Spartanburg, S. C., and her church membership is in the First Presbyterian Church there. She is a graduate of Converse College in Spartanburg. She first went to the field in 1924.

The other honor was the "resolution adopted spontaneously and sincerely by the members of the congregation" of Encruzilhada Presbyterian Church, Recife, expressing "profound appreciation and gratitude for the work accomplished by the Donald Williams family. A letter signed by the pastor, the Rev. Abelardo Paes Barreto, praises Rev. Mr. Williams' work, and emphasizes "the intelligent and dedicated work of his attractive and lovable wife, Dona Laura, in the organizing and developing of the Beginners Department of the Sunday School."

Mr. Williams is a native of Black Mountain, N. C. He is a graduate of Columbia Bible College and Columbia Theological Seminary. He is a member of Asheville Presbytery. He has been in the North Brazil mission field since 1946. Mrs. Williams is the former Laura Gordon of Spray, N. C. She received her education at Columbia Bible College, and Wheaton College. The Williams have two sons and two daughters.

Miss Foster was honored by a special session of the municipal government of Varginha, which presented her a diploma conferring citizenship. The honor took recognition of "the many years of faithful and efficient service which she has rendered the youth of the city." Speeches by city government and business leaders, men who had been her pupils, cited the important role she has played in the education and character building of the youth of the city.

In the evening a special dinner and program of the Rotary Club, with invited guests, added to the honor paid Miss Foster. Eleven of the Presbyterian Missionaries in the East Brazil Mission were present. Here again testimony was given to the faithful service of Miss Foster to the people of Varginha. At the close of this program, everyone was invited to accompany the officials and Miss Foster to the school, where there was unveiled a bronze plaque reading: "Emerita Educadora, Miss Edith Foster, Varginha Agradecida."

Nashville—Mr. and Mrs. William L. Brandt of our North Brazil Mission announce the arrival of a son, Robert Rice, in Brazil on September 9.

The Brandts are just completing their first term of service in Brazil, having gone there in 1952. They are scheduled to arrive in this country for furlough in December. Mr. Brandt is engaged in radio and educational work in Brazil. The Brandts have two other children.

VIRGINIA

Salem — At a Called Meeting of Montgomery Presbytery, held in the Salem Presbyterian Church of Salem, Va., on Tuesday, September 18, 1956, Rev. James M. Ammons of the High Bridge Church of Buchanan, Va., was dismissed to Potomac Presbytery that he may become pastor of the Greenwich Church of Nokesville, Virginia.

Rev. Fred S. McCorkle of the Churches of Bouldin Memorial and Stuart of Stuart, Va., was dismissed to Potomac Presbytery that he may become pastor of the Poolesville Church of Poolesville, Md.

Rev. J. Wilson Rowe, Jr., of the Bedford Church of Bedford, Va., was dismissed to Greenbrier Presbytery that he may become pastor of the Churches of Salem and Unity.

Rev. Marion L. Simmons was received from Lexington Presbytery that he may become pastor of the Green Ridge Church of Roanoke, Va.

The next Stated Meeting of Montgomery Presbytery will be held in the Blue Ridge Church of Ararat, Va., on Tuesday, October 30, 1956, at 10:30 A.M.

To arrive at the Blue Ridge Church take state route No. 8 to route No. 103, take route No. 103 to route No. 104, take route No. 104 to the Church.

E. W. Smith
Stated Clerk

BOOKS

IMMORTALITY. Loraine Boettner. Wm. B. Eerdman's Publishing Co. $2.50.
$2.50.

Dr. Boettner is the well-known author of "The Reformed Doctrine of Predestination", "Studies In Theology", "The Christian Attitude Toward War", and "A Summary of the Gospels". The author is a lucid exponent of the Reformed Faith. He writes with a fine background of scholarship, yet in understandable language.

The first portion of this volume discusses the nature of physical death. Death is interpreted as the penalty of sin. The author distinguishes between 3 kinds of death: spiritual, physical, and eternal. He states that the Christian is subject to physical death but not spiritual death. The futility of prayers for the dead is discussed in this section. The author remarks, "Prayers for the dead imply that their state has not yet been fixed and that it can be improved at our request. . . . We find an abundance of Scripture teaching to the effect that this world only is the place of opportunity for salvation, and when this probation or testing period is past only the assignment of awards and punishments remain. Consequently we hold that all prayers, baptisms, masses, or other rituals of whatever kind for the dead are superfluous, vain and unscriptural."

His discussion of the burial or the cremation of the body is most helpful. The author realizes that there is a great difference between burial and cremation. He observes, "Certainly under normal conditions we show much more respect for the bodies of our loved ones if they are tenderly laid away in the earth under the coverlet of green in the posture of rest or sleep and in as good a state of preservation as possible. The body is as really and eternally a part of man as is his spirit and the resurrection of the body is an indispensable part of his salvation. We cannot bring ourselves deliberately to take the body of a dear one only less precious than the soul that it enshrined and give it to the flames for violent destruction, even though we know that the spirit has departed. If we attach sentimental value to a Bible or an article of clothing or other keepsake, how much more should we treat reverently the body that has been so much more intimately associated with the person. No matter with what refinements cremation is carried out, it still carries with it the idea of violence and destruction. . . . In the New Testament the same teaching is continued as in the Old. We have particularly the example of Jesus whose body was reverently embalmed with precious spices, wrapped in a clean linen cloth and tenderly laid in a tomb. Surely the Divine precedent in the burial, not the burning, of His body should be the authoritative example for all Christians. Christians need no other reason for burial than that. . . . Cremation was thus not the practice of the saints of God in either the Old Testament or the New. Rather it was of heathen origin. The early Christians followed the Jewish custom of burying the dead and repudiated cremation which was customary in the time of the early Roman empire." In this connection Dr. Boettner quotes the eminent church historian, Philip Schaff to this effect, "The primitive Christians always showed tender care for the dead under a vivid impression of the unbroken communion of the saints and of the future resurrection of the body in glory. For Christianity redeems the body as well as the soul and consecrates it as the temple of the Holy Spirit. Hence, the Greek and Roman custom of burning the corpse was repugnant to Christian feeling and sacredness of the body."

The author defines immortality as the eternal, continuous, conscious, existence of the soul after the death of the body. The only reliable information concerning the state of the soul after death, says the author, is to be found in the Bible. He notes, "That which the philosophers cannot fathom, nor the scientists explain, God has revealed in His Word. Much is presented by direct statement; much is also assumed as an undeniable postulate. It takes for granted that the characteristics of our nature are permanent, that we shall continue to possess intelligence, affection, conscience and will. Every facet dealing with the future life assumes that we shall be then as we are now reverential and social beings, loving God and one another."

An excellent discussion of the intermediate state is found in Section 3. The author discusses in this phase of the subject second probation, soul sleep, annihilation, purgatory, and spiritualism.

There are volumes in existence that are more exhaustive than the present one under review, but it is doubtful if any monograph on this subject has ever been published that treats it in a more convincing and challenging manner. Dr. Boettner has rendered a valuable service to the Christian faith in the production of this volume. The intelligent layman as well as the experienced theologian will profit by its message.

John R. Richardson

INDEBTED TO CHRIST'S RESURRECTION. C. W. Gault. Pageant Press, Inc. $3.00.

This book is a moving anthology which recreates the drama and wisdom of Christ's words and actions after His resurrection. The author considers each appearance of Christ against the actual historical and psychological background and the result is a dramatic account of the greatest spiritual force in history. It will be a source of inspiration to all who read it. Each chapter begins with a paragraph from the New Testament which has been chosen according to the proper chronological order of events. The preaching of the resurrection gave the early church the greatest religious power in the Roman Empire. The author not only explores the historical impetus of this great spiritual event but also discusses the beginnings of the church, with Christ shown to be the Author of the Apostolic preaching. This volume is inspirational, deeply reverent, dramatic and historically accurate. It will appeal to layman as well as the Christian scholar.

THE WESTMINSTER HISTORICAL ATLAS TO THE BIBLE. G. Ernest Wright and Floyd V. Filson. Westminster Press. $7.50.

The original edition of this work was published in 1945. This volume is the 1956 revised edition. This new work now contains 130 pages and 33 maps in full color. Many new photographs and drawings are added. The maps are all in half tone engravings which present graphically the relief and topography with new states and excavations clearly identified. All the new discoveries have been incorporated making these maps and articles up-to-date.

An interesting introduction to this volume has been written by Professor William Foxwell Albright. A new index of modern place names contains a complete tabulation of Biblical sites. Any place mentioned in the Bible can be located readily.

While this work, in many respects, is superb, it should be pointed out that the authors' interpretations are sometimes influenced by their liberal presuppositions. The minister and the Bible teacher will find this volume an interesting guide in the study of the historical geography of Biblical lands.

John R. Richardson

SPURGEON'S MORNING AND EVENING. Zondervan. $3.95.

This is the complete and unabridged text of Spurgeon's classic of daily readings—available for the first time in large readable type. These pungent paragraphs of devotional meditation, one for the morning and one for the evening of every day in the year, 732 in all, are perfect guides for family devotions as well as individual private devotions.

THE SOUTHERN PRESBYTERIAN JOURNAL

A Presbyterian weekly magazine devoted to the statement, defense and propagation of the Gospel, the faith which was once for all delivered unto the saints.

VOL. XV NO. 25 | OCTOBER 17, 1956 | $2.50 A YEAR

Dr. A. B. Rhodes (left front) and the Entering Class at Louisville Seminary School Year 1956-57.

(See page 21 for news item)

THE SOUTHERN PRESBYTERIAN JOURNAL

Rev. Henry B. Dendy, D.D., Editor....Weaverville, N. C.
Dr. L. Nelson Bell, Associate Editor....Asheville, N. C.
Rev. Wade C. Smith, Associate Editor....Weaverville, N. C.

EDITORIAL

Welcome and Congratulations to

CHRISTIANITY TODAY

The *Southern Presbyterian Journal* extends a hearty welcome and congratulations to the new magazine, CHRISTIANITY TODAY, which has gone out to subscribers this week.

This is the most ambitious venture in Christian journalism in the history of Protestantism and we wish it every success.

Designed to fill a need not now met, it has drawn to itself over one hundred outstanding scholars and Christian leaders from America and abroad and these contributors argue well for the quality and tone of the publication.

We have seen an advance copy of the first issue and not only are the contents of the highest order but the technical production of the magazine places it in a class by itself.

One department of CHRISTIANITY TODAY, written in a lighter vein, is *"Preacher in the Red,"* an embarrassing or otherwise unwelcome experience of a minister. The first issue quotes one from our own Dr. C. Darby Fulton. With the permission of the Editor we quote Dr. Fulton. It is titled "Publicans and Republicans":

> The Synod of Georgia convened in Decatur in mid-September, 1948. Eloquent Republicans and Dixiecrats were inspiring the political conventions that feverish election year. Having been named Moderator of the General Assembly three months before, I felt a sort of keynote speech was expected of me to set the tone of our denomination.
>
> The front pews were occupied by 150 theological students. In the congregation were ex-moderators of our denomination, college presidents, prominent pastors, leaders of our Church women. I wanted to do well, to lift the congregation above the throbbing political issues of the day and to uphold the dignity of the Church.
>
> It happened during the Scripture lesson. With chosen emphasis I was reading the verses leading to my text, "Be ye therefore perfect, even as your Father which is in heaven is perfect" (Matt. 5:48).
>
> Suddenly, near the end, I made an unscheduled intrusion into politics: "For if ye love them which love you, what reward have ye? Do not even the republicans the same?"
>
> There was an astonished silence. Then a seminary student snickered, like a fuse setting off the blast. The whole congregation was in uproar. Never have I seen a public assembly so completely demoralized. I stood, red and speechless. It seemed the violent and unbridled laughter would never subside. When I managed to finish with my text, I knew that it was an empty performance. The Synod of Georgia had hopelessly reverted to the political psychology of the day.

* * * * *

One of the most heart-warming articles in the October 15th issue has to do with the place of the Bible in evangelistic preaching by Dr. Billy Graham. Again, with permission, we quote:

> In 1949 I had been having a great many doubts concerning the Bible.
>
> I thought I saw apparent contradictions in Scripture. Some things I could not reconcile with my restricted concept of God. When I stood up to preach, the authoritative note so characteristic of all great preachers of the past was lacking.
>
> Like hundreds of other young seminary students, I was waging the intellectual battle of my life. The outcome could certainly affect my entire future ministry.
>
> In August of that year I had been invited to Forest Home, Presbyterian conference cen-

ter high in the mountains outside Los Angeles. I remember walking down a trail, tramping into the woods, and almost wrestling with God.

I dueled with my doubts, and my soul seemed to be caught in a crossfire. Finally, in desperation, I surrendered my will to the living God revealed in Scripture. I knelt before the open Bible and said: "Lord, many things in this Book I do not understand. But thou hast said, 'The just shall live by faith.' All I have received from thee, I have taken by faith. Here and now, by faith, I accept the Bible as Thy word. I take it all. I take it without reservations. Where there are things I cannot understand, I will reserve judgment until I receive more light. If this pleases Thee, give me authority as I proclaim the truths of Thy word, and through that authority convict me of sin and turn sinners to the Saviour.

Within six weeks we started our Los Angeles crusade, which is now history. During that crusade I discovered the secret that changed my ministry. I stopped trying to prove that the Bible was true. I had settled it in my own mind that it was, and this faith was conveyed to the audience. Over and over again I found myself saying, "The Bible says." I felt as though I were merely a voice through which the Holy Spirit was speaking.

Authority created faith. Faith generated response, and hundreds of people were impelled to come to Christ. A crusade scheduled for three weeks lengthened into eight weeks, with hundreds of thousands of people in attendance. The people were not coming to hear great oratory, nor were they interested merely in my ideas. I found they were desperately hungry to hear what God had to say through His Holy Word.

I am not advocating bibliolatry. I am not suggesting that we should worship the Bible, any more than a soldier worships his sword or a surgeon worships his scalpel. I am, however, fervently urging a return to Bible-centered preaching, a Gospel presentation that says without apology and without ambiguity, "Thus saith the Lord."

* * * * *

Those who may wish further information bout CHRISTIANITY TODAY are referred ɔ their advertisement on Page 24.

H.B.D.

In the New Testament We Find Female Missionaries, but Not Women Elders

It is argued that "there is no New Testament authorization for *female* missionaries," and that since our Church is using many without such authorization, therefore we do not need explicit Scriptural warrant for women elders.

With the highest esteem for our distinguished brother and his associates on the Ad-Interim Committee, we reply: *First,* there is New Testament example for use of women in missionary work. The precursor of mission boards was composed of women who, having been healed of evil spirits and infirmities, ministered of their substance to support Jesus and the Twelve in their missionary work of preaching the Gospel through cities and villages, Lk. 8:1-3. Using the word in its general sense of ones sent, the first missionaries entrusted with the good news of Jesus' resurrection were women, Mat. 28:7-8; Mark 16:7; Luke 24:9, 22-23; John 20:17. The four virgin daughters of that redoubtable missionary to Samaria, to the Ethiopian Eunuch, to the cities from Azotus to Caesarea, Acts 8:5, 29, 40, supported and continued the missionary work of their father Philip by prophesying, Acts 20:9.

There were two major mission movements in the primitive Church. Peter led the one to the Jews and looked to James and Jerusalem for direction. In their missionary work, Cephas, the brethren of the Lord and the other apostles took their *wives* with them, I Cor. 9:5.

The second movement stemmed from Antioch, sought to reach the Gentiles, and was led by Paul. In Corinth, Paul worked with Aquila and Priscilla, took them with him on his missionary journey to Ephesus, left them there to nurture the infant mission and to expound to Apollos the way of the Lord more accurately, Acts 18:2, 18, 26. So effective was the work of this couple that the Apostle commends them in three epistles, declaring:: Salute Prisca and Aquila, my fellow-workers in Christ Jesus, who for my life laid down their own necks; unto whom not only I give thanks, but also all the churches of the Gentiles, and salute the Church that is in their house," Rom. 16:3-5. This is full and explicit approval of a *female* missionary.

Secondly, it is a matter of grave concern that in this and in other matters there seems to be

The Southern Presbyterian Journal, *a Presbyterian Weekly magazine devoted to the statement, defense, and propagation of the Gospel, the faith which was once for all delivered unto the saints,* published every Wednesday by The Southern Presbyterian Journal, Inc., in Weaverville, N. C.

Entered as second-class matter May 15, 1942, at the Postoffice at Weaverville, N. C., under the Act of March 3, 1879. Vol. XV, No. 25, October 17, 1956. Editorial and Business Offices: Weaverville, N. C. Printed in the U.S.A. by Biltmore Press, Asheville, N. C.

ADDRESS CHANGE: When changing address, please let us have both old and new address as far in advance as possible. Allow three weeks after change if not sent in advance. When possible, send an address label giving your old address.

a tendency to treat church practice as of more authority than the Bible. Historically and confessionally we stand for the sufficiency and the authority of Holy Scripture. How far will the other point of view lead our church? It was church practice and popular piety which brought in the dogma of the Assumption into heaven of the body of the Virgin and which is today leading Rome toward an additional dogma, namely Mary as co-redemptrix.

Thirdly, it is not Presbyterian for the the proponents of this change to shift the burden of proof onto those who hold the present positions. According to Lutheran tradition, the Church may introduce or continue anything that is not forbidden in Scripture. But the Reformed and Presbyterian tradition is that one ought to have a positive divine warrant from Scripture for anything introduced into the government or the worship of the Church. This is the position of our Confession of Faith, chapter 1, paragraph 6, and of our Book of Church Order, paragraph 10. The burden of proof rests on the affirmative. It is up to the proponents of the innovation to offer "*clear* Bible evidence" to the effect that God has authorized a woman to be an elder in the Church.

It is our conviction, moreover, that we have offered evidence from the New Testament which is clear on this matter. We repeat: "The head of every man is Christ, and the head of the woman is the man, and the head of the Christ is God." "Subject yourselves one to another in the fear of Christ. Wives be in subjection to your own husbands as unto the Lord. . . . Let the wife see that she reverence her husband." "The bishop must be the husband of one wife . . . one that ruleth well his own house, having his children in subjection with all gravity." "But I permit not a woman to teach, nor to have dominion (usurp authority, take authority for oneself) over a man."

W. C. R.

Negative Preaching

In religious periodicals today there are frequent recommendations of the power of positive preaching. It is even suggested that our daily ills and annoyances can be cured if we only think positively. Negativism is bad and leads to mental disorders.

Undoubtedly positive preaching and thinking are necessary. For example, when a little boy is fussy because he does not know how to occupy his time, the wise mother will make a positive admonition to go skating or to play with finger paints. The little boy needs some definite direction because he does not know what to do.

But we are not all little children, and many of our daily situations do not correspond to this example. If to avoid strain on the heart a man decides to reduce, his physician will tell him not to eat butter and other fats. Or, in cases of allergy, the physician will direct him not to eat tomatoes, or not to get in contact with chicken feathers, or not to do something else. The patient may do pretty much as he pleases, except that he must not do this one thing.

The same thing is true in religious matters, whether preaching from the pulpit, or conversing with friends, or private meditation. Of course, positive statements must be made. Sinners must be told positively that Christ died for their sins. But it is unwise to avoid negative statements. Sinners also need to be told negatively that they cannot earn heaven by their own merits. To be sure, we should positively require the worship of God in spirit and in truth. But we should also negatively prohibit bowing before images and praying to the Virgin.

Negative preaching and thinking is necessary because it is exemplified in the Bible. It is God's method, at least a part of God's method of dealing with us. Thou shalt not make unto thee any graven image. Thou shalt not commit adultery. Thou shalt not covet. Nor does it take much brilliance to see the wisdom of this method. Suppose a young man asks himself who he should marry. Well, there are a lot of girls, and he is free to marry any of them—except a certain few. He must not commit adultery or incest. A positive command could apply to one person only. God might tell Hosea precisely whom to marry; but such a command applies to no one else. A general command for such practical problems must usually be a negative command. Raise sheep, buy real estate, sell cloth, make money in nearly any way you wish; but, says the Lord, Thou shalt not steal.

Now, why is the wisdom of negative thinking recognized in medicine, in child training, in all secular matters, but so vehemently condemned in religious affairs? Why—unless our popular religious leaders have discarded the Bible and are blind to God's example? G.H.C.

By Comparison

Ask the average Church leader what is the most important issue facing America and the Christian Church today and the overwhelming majority will reply that it is the race issue.*

Admitting that intolerance and bigotry are in some measure abroad in the land, and that this intolerance and bigotry is found in some on *both* sides of this problem, the writer would say that the race issue is NOT the one which deserves major consideration.

**Dr. Bell's own clear and unequivocal position on this is found in the October 1st issue of LIFE magazine.* Ed.

Christ shall rise, *therefore* certain things should follow in the life of those possessed of this hope.

"My beloved brethren" indicates the addressees of this admonition—those who have been initiated into the fraternity of the redeemed through their acceptance of the Lord Jesus Christ as personal Saviour. In this faith we are to be "steadfast" and "unmoveable." There must be a Gibraltar-like quality to our Christian profession in keeping with Paul's exhortation elsewhere. " . . . continue in the faith grounded and settled and be not moved away from the hope of the Gospel" (Col. 1:23); " . . . henceforth, be no more children, tossed to and fro, and carried about with every wind of doctrine, by the sleight of men and cunning craftiness whereby they lie in wait to deceive." (Eph. 4:14). We are informed, "he that *abideth* in the doctrine of Christ hath both the Father and the Son." (II John 9).

However, steadfast and unmoveable faith is not a static thing. On the contrary, it is productive of action. A giant ocean liner is a very sturdy and stable object. It cannot easily be tossed about by the wind and waves. But this does not mean that it does not move. Under proper direction it is capable of movement which is both powerful and serviceable. So also the steady and sturdy Christian unmoved by alien winds and waves is capable of vigorous and productive movement when the Captain of his salvation is at the helm. "Always abounding in the work of the Lord" is our vocation. It is not enough to be always abounding in work. The language is most lucid. It must be the work of the Lord.

The Bible makes it very plain that Christians build their fortunes in heaven by their fidelity on earth. One is saved by faith in Christ's finished work, but is rewarded for faithfulness in Christian works. In the third chapter of his first letter to the Corinthians, Paul speaks of these two principles as the foundation and the building. The Lord Jesus Christ is the foundation upon which we must build. But upon that foundation it is possible to build either a superstructure of "wood, hay and stubble" or of "gold, silver and precious stones." The former represent activities and interests which are legitimate, but not Christ-honoring—hence have no abiding value. The latter symbolize works done for Christ in the power of the Holy Spirit—hence, will stand the test of time and eternity.

As the redeemed of the Lord, we are to be constantly about the Lord's business. This is right and proper inasmuch as He has both created us, "loved us and loosed us from our sins in His own blood." (Revelation 2:5). But additionally, He holds out an added incentive, the certainty of a reward—"Forasmuch as ye know that your labour is not in vain in the Lord."

As objects of so glorious a redemption and the subjects of the King of Kings, can we do less than labor lovingly in His service? As Jonathan Goforth, that valiant missionary to China, used to say: "There is all eternity to speak of victories won for Christ, but only a few short hours before sunset to win them."—G.S.

How a Roman Catholic Priest Was Converted

The following very unusual incident is related by Dr. W. C. Taylor, a Southern Baptist missionary in Brazil, reported to be loved and honored personally and for his work's sake both at home and abroad. The priest made an embarrassing mistake, but it resulted in a disillusionment which enabled him to walk out of darkness into light. W.C.S.

One of the fifty or more converted Catholic priests who have joined Baptist churches in Brazil is one of the pastors of the great old First Baptist Church in Sao Paulo city. I was preaching in his church and, as we left the pulpit one day, I said to him: "How did you happen to be a Baptist? I never heard." His reply was: "I went to the wrong funeral." There is a ceremony in Latin, said over the corpse at prominent funerals, which commits the body to the sacred soil and the soul to the flames of Purgatory. This priest was called over the phone a few years ago, to go to a certain street, address given, but not noted by him. He went to that street, saw a hearse and cars waiting and went in and said his Latin over the corpse mechanically and said to the undertaker and the family: "You may take the corpse." Nobody moved. He said it three times. As if paralyzed with surprise, they then came to life. A little Methodist preacher, who was waiting to conduct that funeral, arose and said: "Mister priest, you have come to the wrong funeral. Your funeral is on up the street. This man was a believer in the Saviour. He needs no ceremony. His soul is in heaven with Jesus. While he was alive, by faith 'he committed his soul to the faithful Creator', as the apostle Peter said do, in his First Epistle. He stands in no need of your services." Very ashamed and confused, the priest backed out and away; but he remembered the quiet calm of that bereaved home, where believers sorrow not as those who have no hope. What HOPE is Purgatory—half a hell for half an eternity? He went on to his own funeral, in mental anarchy. He read First Peter 4:19 in his office, meditated a lot on that great commitment of the soul to God. Now it happens that *O Estado de Sao Paulo*, his daily paper, the greatest daily south of the *New York Times*, carries notices of evangelical church services. They have published my sermon notices on various occasions. He read the notice of a meeting in the Braz Baptist Church and decided he must go. Sunday, at the hour appointed, he slipped his pistol in his robe and appeared at the door of the Braz Church. The usher welcomed him. "Come right in, sit anywhere you like. You are welcome." He went in, in his long black robe, before the amazed congregation. Missionary Paul Porter, great educator who became a marvelous evangelistic leader of that mighty State, was the preacher and he was preaching that day on "The Church" and went right ahead. "I was amazed," the priest told me, "to discover that that was a subject on which I was absolutely ignorant." The light broke. When the great national Eucharistic Congress met in Sao Paulo he had trained and led the choir of a thousand voices that sang before the Cathedral. In the Baptist Jubilee celebrations, a few years later, he led the magnificent Baptist choir, and is a good minister of Jesus Christ. He made the commitment which is saving faith and does away with Latin follies said over the deaf ears of dead bodies.

A Basket of Fruit

The Fruit of the Spirit (Galatians 5:22,23)

The Fruit of the Spirit is . . . JOY.

This note of Joy is very prominent in the Bible. The Psalms are full of it; the Gospels begin with "Good tidings of great joy"; Paul tells us to "Rejoice in the Lord alway"; and the book of Revelation rings with shouts of joy and praise and thanksgiving.

Everybody wants to be happy; everybody ought to be happy; everybody is not happy; even all Christians are not happy, and very few of us are happy all the time. How can I have a Joy that stays with me even when sick or suffering or persecuted? The source of Joy must be beyond this world: The fruit of the Spirit. What sort of Joy does the Spirit give us?

I. *The Joy of Salvation*; The Joy of thy salvation.

1. Salvation is a big word, and a very inclusive word. We speak of a person being "saved", and sometimes limit it to one big experience. Salvation is the joy of being alive instead of dead. My son was dead, and is alive again, said the father of the returned prodigal. That meant great Joy.

2. The Joy of salvation is the Joy of forgiveness. Oh the happiness of the man whose transgression is forgiven, whose sin is covered.

3. The Joy of salvation is the Joy of Growth. We are cleansed and healed, and now we can grow in grace and in the knowledge of Him.

How Smart Can We Get?

By Carl W. McMurray, Ph.D.
Marion, N. C.

The main streams of the Christian Church for more than 1900 years have acknowledged and accepted the plain statements of the Bible that the ordained officers of the Church should be masculine. However, the wise men of our day have become smart enough to read the Bible aright. Indeed, we are being told that the Bible really teaches that we should ordain women as Elders and Deacons. Perhaps no one should be surprised for we are capable of very smart arguments today.

This "new discovery" of what the Bible teaches will certainly change the complexion of things. For one thing, it will require a whole flood of new guidance pamphlets on such subjects as "The Proper Behaviour of an Elder's Husband". This will be difficult but essential since the Bible offers guidance only to the wife of an Elder and neglects to give even the least word of counsel to the husband of an Elder. We will need another pamphlet or perhaps a book for the guidance of the feminine Elders around such biblical snags as "wives be. in subjection to your own husbands," but I suppose we are smart enough to quickly provide the necessary literature.

Beyond this, our gentlemen Elders and Deacons may find themselves on the horns of a dilemma when the upholding of their convictions concerning the work of the Church comes into conflict with their high respect and deference toward a woman. It is no secret that men are not averse to arguing questions with other men, but most men prefer not to argue with the feminine viewpoint, even about a hat. In this embarrassment, men may find it difficult to take a stand against a woman's viewpoint on crucial matters in the Diaconate or Session or Presbytery. Of course, it might be possible for the men to argue themselves out of their old fashioned sense of politeness and deference toward the wives and mothers of other men, but that would hardly be to the credit of our noble Presbyterian gentlemen.

Therefore, it may come to pass that the men will find themselves too "tongue-tied" to serve effectively as Elders and Deacons. Truly, then the complexion of things will be changed, and we will need some mighty smart women to figure how to get the men back into the responsibilities of the Church. Immediately, there will be needed another flood of new pamphlets on such subjects as "How to Organize and Build Up the Men's Auxiliary."

It is altogether possible that the women will not be happy over their new official titles. Unfortunately, the etymology of the word "elder" seems to smack of advancing age. What if someone in an unguarded moment should speak openly of some charming lady of the congregation as an "elder" woman? Then the Church will forget that it ever had any trouble before. If we use the full title "Ruling Elder", it will be much more embarrassing, for it is one of the unwritten laws of nature that when a woman exercises her ruling powers, she always does so without letting it be known, and she might count it as slander of her feminine traits to speak of her as a ruling anything. So we may as well get set to revise further the Book of Church Order and to change the time honored and scriptural title of "Ruling Elders" to something else, but frankly it may be necessary to revise the English language to find suitable terminology.

Perhaps some other generation of wise men will become smart enough to revise biblical titles and even to devise arguments to convince themselves that the Bible ought to be interpreted in reverse so that it would really mean that women only should be Elders and Deacons. However, it would be better for us to awake to the blessed simplicity of the Bible and find ourselves on the way back to an acknowledgement that all plain statements of the Holy Scriptures are valid and also best for the prosperity of the Church after all.

The End—not to be continued.

JARMO

By J. V. N. Talmadge, D.D.

I doubt whether the readers of the *Journal* remember reading about Jarmo in current periodicals a few years ago but I hope to show them that it is well worth remembering.

Among archeologists who have been hunting in the Near East for sites of the earliest men, few have been more enthusiastic than Dr. R. J. Braidwood of the University of Chicago. He is really an expert and his wife, Linda, has been an able helper during his trips to Syria and the Zagros Mountains on the Iran-Iraq border. The discovery which seems to have pleased them the most, and which has received widest publication is Jarmo.

Jarmo is a relatively small mound in a plain nestled in the Zagros Mountains. During the last ice age the valley was covered with a thick layer of silt, thus making it very fertile. After the time that silt was deposited at Ur, erosion set in and now there are deep canyons leading outside the valley. Jarmo is situated on the side of one of these canyons and is not now occupied. As Dr. Braidwood read the story from the mound, some stone age people who knew a little about farming settled at Jarmo when it was hot and arid down in the Mesopotamian valley. They used partly Mesalithic (middle stone age) tools with a few Neolithic (new stone age) ground tools. During their sojourn for a century or more, a mound was formed from the debris of old houses. In the lower layers there were stone tools only, but in the upper layers pottery sherds and signs of other more advanced cultures were found. Dr. Braidwood claimed that these were the first people to advance from the stone age to primitive civilization, that other people learned civilization from their neighbors, but these Jarmo people evolved of themselves. In other words Jarmo appeared to Dr. Braidwood as the most important milestone in the long ascent of man from the naked half ape-like savage of 500,000 years ago to modern man of the atomic age. At the request of Dr. Braidwood, Dr. Limmy tested some charcoal and shells, and found they dated about 6600 years ago.

The writer feels that the Chicago expert has made a very interesting discovery, but he seriously doubts whether his chronological sequence is warranted by the facts. The writer therefore was long puzzled as to just what was the meaning of Jarmo, and it was only recently that the whole story became clear. The wonderful facts discovered by the expert are capable of an entirely different interpretation.

A word is necessary regarding the mounds of the Near East. There are hundreds of mounds of all sizes in arid parts of the country that were inhabited by ancient peoples who lived when the climate was much better than today. The mounds are divided into layers depending upon how many times the town was rebuilt, for each time a place was rebuilt, debris of former houses was leveled off and the new town was built on a higher level. The layers are dated by cultural objects found in them. In general there are two divisions of culture in the ancient mounds of Mesopotamia, the oldest culture was the Chalcolithic (copper stone) when bronze was unknown. The later cultures were first bronze, then iron and pottery. In some of the mounds farther from the center of civilization there were layers with a Neolithic culture (new stone) with ground tools and sometimes pottery but no metal. We can forget the Neolithic culture for the present as it is very complicated.

According to Dr. Braidwood's system of chronology, the Bronze Age started about 5000 years ago, or 3000 B.C. Thus we have about 1500 years to account for them between Jarmo and the Bronze Age. How are we going to fill up that gap? Here is where we must differ from the learned scholar.

Since Dr. Braidwood believes in the gradual evolution of culture he has decided that the

Chalcolithic belongs to that gap, purely on philosophical grounds. There was considerable difficulty in doing this, because, before he discovered Jarmo, he thought the Chalcolithic Age must have lasted about 3000 years. It was really a tight squeeze to get the Chalcolithic with its many divisions into that 1500 years, but Dr. Braidwood strongly believes in his philosophy and he squeezed it in anyway.

Now we will look at Jarmo from the standpoint of the Bible. The FLOOD, we noted in the first article, seems now with fair certainty dated at about 7000 years ago or a little less. Jarmo then began about 200 years after the FLOOD. Then the question arises how much time do we need to allow for Noah's family to multiply? With this multiplying, there is no room for all the Chalcolithic after Jarmo, so it will be necessary to place it before Jarmo and the FLOOD, and date it during the last glacial age. Careful examination of all the Chalcolithic mounds betrays many signs of all those extraordinary oscillations known to the old stone age man of Europe. Civilized man and stone age man were therefore contemporary. There was no evolution.

Does Jarmo fit in with this changed order of events? Perfectly! When Noah came out of the ark after the FLOOD, he was in the mountains, and he journeyed to the East. He did not go down into the lowlands for geology tells us it was hot and arid there. Dr. Wright of University of Minnesota agrees with this. When they first settled at Jarmo the family was few in number, so had a very simple economy and used only stone tools, and gourds, etc. But as the family grew in number, they branched out in various trades, and some built kilns, and some hunted for copper. If the old patriarch was still alive, he must have told them of the antediluvian civilization, and since they were worshippers of God, progress was fast. This is just what Jarmo shows.

The writer feels that he voices the sentiments of the readers when he adds a word of great appreciation of Dr. Braidwood's fine work in discovering our ancestral home of 6600 years ago at Jarmo.

I hope when you see the 66 in the yellow and black sign at the service station you will remember that it was 66 hundred years ago when our ancestors lived at Jarmo.

The Religion of the Bible

By Rev. Floyd E. Hamilton
Centreville, Ala.

Pure religion and undefiled before our God and Father is this, to visit the fatherless and widows in their affliction, and to keep oneself unspotted from the world." James 1:27.

It is a trite saying that man is a religious creature. He cannot get along without religion, no matter what his religious views may happen to be. Even those who pride themselves in their irreligion are in reality religious, and prove it by making a cult of their irreligion. One of the reasons back of the recent revolt in the province of Georgia in Russia was that the youth had made for themselves a god out of Stalin and refused to give him up.

It is a familiar teaching of the Modernists that all religion started with fetish worship and animism, that is the worshipping of nature objects such as trees and rocks and plants and sticks and stones. These natural objects were endowed by the worshippers with souls and then worshipped as gods. Then it is claimed that the next step was upward to the worship of animals and the powers of nature such as the wind, the sun and the moon and the stars. Then it is claimed that people began to distinguish between the objects worshipped themselves and the spirit which manifested itself in the form worshipped, and so polytheism, or the worship of many gods is thought to have arisen with pantheism not far behind.

The next step upward according to these scholars is the religion of henotheism, the worship of one tribal god, while at the same time believing that other tribes had their own separate gods.

Then last it is thought that as religion gradually evolved monotheism or the belief in one universal god arose late in the history of Israel. This teaching of the evolution of religion is accepted as an axiom by many of these students of religions and as a matter of course, then applied to the religion of the Old Testament.

But here a difficulty arose for these religious evolutionists. The Bible apparently did not conform to their preconceived ideas of what religion ought to be like. Instead of starting with animism and working gradually upward to Monotheism of the later prophets, what purported to be the first books of the Bible, Genesis, Exodus, etc., apparently taught Monotheism, one universal God.

On their presuppositions this was impossible, so they set out to discover the traces of the lower religions in the books of the Bible, claiming that a later author had covered them up and largely eliminated them from the text of the Old Testament. They thought they discovered traces of this assumed original animism at various places in the Old Testament, and in such parts were assumed to have belonged to the primitive religion and to have been a part of the earliest documents, while the places where monotheism seemed to be inescapably taught were assumed to belong to later documents, while the whole was assumed to be the product of the latest author, who was assumed to have combined the earlier documents into the Old Testament as it now stands.

The next step assumed to have occurred in the history of religion was the development of a religion of a God of love found, it is asserted, in the religion of the New Testament. This God of the New Testament, is asserted to be entirely different from the Jehovah of the Old Testament, for that God is assumed to be a god of cruelty, while the God of the New Testament is assumed to be just a God of love.

All this raises the very pertinent question: Just what is the religion of the Bible? It is to answer that question that we will speak this morning. In the first place, let us disabuse our minds of the idea there is any real difference between the God of the New Testament and the God of the Old Testament. It is true that the doctrine of the Trinity was not explicitly developed in the times of the Old Testament, but even in the Old Testament we have references to the "Spirit of the Lord" referring undoubtedly to the Holy Spirit. The appearances of Jehovah to Abraham, for example, show that the Son of God manifested God to men in human form at various times in the Old Testament period, for Jesus himself said, "No man hath seen God (the Father) at any time; the only begotten Son who is in the bosom of the Father, He hath declared (or manifested) him."

Nor is it true that the Jehovah of the Old Testament is not a God of love. Where in the New Testament will one find the love of God more clearly taught than in God's dealings with Israel when God forgave them in love repeatedly for their backslidings? God was indeed a God of justice then, when he ordered the extermination of the Amorites, but where in the whole Bible will one find God's justice more clearly set forth than in the Book of the Revelation, where great sections of the unbelieving world are wiped out at a single stroke? If there is any truth at all to the claim that the God of the New Testament is different from the God of the Old Testament, it is in the fact that

the Jews was that they refused to believe that the Son of God was really the God-man he claimed to be. Now make no mistake about it. From that time onward the god the Jews worshipped after their rejection of Jesus Christ as their Messiah, was not the true God but an imaginary god of their own manufacture, an idol. Neither the Jews nor the Mohammedans today worship the true God, for the true God is the Triune God, Father, Son and Holy Spirit. The Jews do not worship merely the first person of the Holy Trinity: because they reject the deity of Christ they worship an idol, not it is true of gold or silver, but an idol of their mind. The god worshipped by the Jews after the coming of Christ never did exist. Nor does the god of the Unitarians or the Mohammedans exist. All those who refuse to worship the Triune God of the Bible, are worshipping idols, not the true God.

The religion of the Bible is the religion revealed by God in the Bible. But it is *more* than the theology of the Trinity. We may understand fully the theology of the Bible, but if we accept the religion of the Bible we must apply our belief in that theology to our everyday life. That I take it, is what James meant when he said, "Pure religion and undefiled before our God and Father is this, to visit the fatherless and widows, and to keep oneself unspotted from the world."

He is advocating the work-a-day religion of the Bible, putting into daily practice the theology of the Bible. Yes, it is necessary for salvation to believe in the Triune God of the Bible and in the atoning work of Jesus Christ the Second Person of the Trinity, but true religion then manifests itself in charity to those in need, and in a holy life in a sinful world. Are you practising this pure religion?

Helps To Understanding Scripture Readings in *Day by Day*

By Rev. C. C. Baker

Sunday, October 28, *Acts* 5:27-29. Following Pentecost the apostles preached everywhere—against the express wishes of the Jewish hierarchy (4:1-3,17;5:17-18). Each time the religious leaders tried to suppress the disciples, their attempts were thwarted (4:17-21;5:18-21). Notice the great boldness of the apostles in 4:18-20 and 5:29-32. As we observe in these same verses the bluntness of the apostles as they replied to the accusations of the Jewish leaders, we must remember that they were speaking to the very men who had crucified Christ (4:5-6). How was the advice of Gamaliel in 5:33-39 wise? What was his criterion for judging the validity of the apostles' faith (5:38-39)? Do you try to disparage or discourage Christian groups who show more enthusiasm than you in preaching the Gospel or perhaps use different methods? What message does 5:39 have for you?

Monday, October 29, *Luke* 2:41-52. Verses 40 and 52 summarize the period of our Lord's life between His infancy and the beginning of His ministry. Make a mental list of the characteristics of Jesus mentioned in these two verses and see how each of these characteristics is illustrated in the story. What does the very fact of the long journey from Nazareth to Jerusalem each year indicate as to the boy Jesus' physical health? Does v.44 give the impression that he was a normal boy in his social relationships? What does the mention of obedience (v.51) reveal about his home life? What in vv.46-47 reveals extraordinary traits for a boy of twelve? The Christian young person should be a normal, all-round person with a healthy interest in spiritual things. Do you stress the importance of the spiritual life with your children?

Tuesday, October 30, *Luke* 4:1-15. Jesus faced temptations more severe than any we will ever face. Think of the intensity of each temptation in the light of Jesus' circumstances, the first (v.3) in the light of His hunger (v.2), the second (vv.5-7) and third (vv.9-12) in the light of His coming trials and final crucifixion. How might the suggestions of vv.5-12 have tempted Christ to accomplish his mission other than according to the will of the Father? Observe how Satan challenged Jesus to prove His Deity by submitting to his suggestions (vv.3,9). Notice, again, in v,13 that Satan struck at Jesus at times when He was most vulnerable, i.e., when He was tired, hungry, or at a major turning point in His life. When Satan attacks us at our most vulnerable points in our weakest moments, we can be assured that we have One who "can sympathize with us in our weakness . . . who has been tempted in every point like as we have been tempted, yet without sin."

Wednesday, October 31, *Matthew* 9:27-38. Verse 35 summarizes the chapter. Begin reading with verse one and observe the reception the crowds gave Jesus (vv.8,10,26,31,33). List all the various circumstances under which people responded to Him (vv.2,10,18,20,27,32). What varieties of background are mentioned in vv.9-10,18? What attitude did Jesus have toward those who came to Him (vv.36-38)? Would so many people under so varied circumstances have responded to Him if this attitude had not been in His bearing? Do people in trouble come to you because they know you love them? Notice the religious leaders (vv.3,11,34). Are you jealous of those in your church to whom others go with their troubles, or those who, in some other way, are more successful in their work for the Lord than you?

Thursday, November 1, *Luke* 11:37-54. Jesus did not refuse to associate with the Pharisees (v.37) and in His denunciation of them He never said anything about them that He did not say to their faces (vv.39ff). What did Jesus feel was basically wrong with the Pharisees (vv.39-41)? What was the nature of the sins for which He condemned the Pharisees and the lawyers (vv.42-44)? In what did they fail (vv.41-42,46)? How did they feel about spiritual truth and those that proclaimed it (vv.47-52)? Is the reaction of vv.53-54 a natural one? What would you have done if Jesus had spoken to you in this manner? Is there anything mentioned about the Pharisees and lawyers in these verses that Jesus might say to you?

Friday, November 2, *Matthew* 8:18-20. List the different miracles Jesus performed (vv.1-4,5-13,14-15,16-17) just prior to today's interviews (vv.18-20). How did the people respond to these wonders (v.18a)? Two members of the crowd came to Jesus individually and expressed their desire to be His followers (vv.19,22; Luke 9:57,61), but Jesus discouraged rather than welcomed them (vv.20,22). Why? Perhaps they had been so impressed by His power and popularity, they failed to realize how He had cut Himself off from the comforts of material possessions and normal associations with family and loved ones. Jesus does not want for His disciples those who are anxious to share only in the benefits and glory of His ministry, but those who have considered the cost of discipleship and are willing to share His suffering and sacrifice (Mark 8:34).

Saturday, November 3, *John* 6:24-40. What all-important question do the crowds ask Jesus in v.28, and what answer does Jesus give in v.29? Believing in Christ (v.29) is like eating living bread and drinking living water (vv.53-55). It is appropriating the very life of Christ for ourselves (v.56). What results from thus believing in Christ (vv.33,35,40,50,51,54,56,57,58)? What results from refusing to believe in Him (v.53)? The Jews could not believe in Christ because they were interested only in the physical benefits He could give (v.26). Which do you esteem more highly—physical or spiritual life (v.63)?

ANGLERS

By WADE C. SMITH

Lesson No. 161

By-Products of Personal Evangelism (Continued)

In individual Christian growth. Personal evangelism expands one's horizon and then helps him to grow out to it. Many a church officer, though an assumed leader in God's great expansive program, has lived for years cramped up in the little shell of a limited vision and limited service—self-devised. He has long ago made up his mind that he will serve to a certain extent and no further. He will pay his dues to the church regularly and promptly as he has obligated; he will attend the regular board meetings (not promising anything about the extra ones called); he will be on hand at regular services; and he will conduct himself discreetly in the business and social world so as to bring no reproach upon the church, realizing he is an officer; but there it ends. No getting caught in any special church "rousements," either financial or spiritual, for him! He is a man of his own and knows his own mind, and rather prides himself that he is as immovable as Gibraltar.

That man lives a cramped life. He becomes spiritually stunted. He is no inspiration to the young people when the tide of fine youthful impulse runs high. He pours cold water on any progressive move started in the church, by attitude if not outspoken disapproval. He is preparing himself for a funeral that will make the preacher and the people wince when the words, "Blessed are the dead who die in the Lord" are read.

. . . But suppose one day the Holy Spirit cracks that crust of many years thickening and hardening, with which he has been enclosed, and he gets a vision of himself lifting some poor groping soul out of the darkness into the light of a Saviour's love! That man comes out of his shell and begins to live. He looks back upon his boasted morality and regularity as only a counterfeit. His Bible becomes a new book—a veritable love letter from God; his prayers now have some meaning, and when he rises from them he is refreshed in spirit as he never knew before. His church is a living enterprise and not something to "get by" with—not an insurance agency; it engages his best capacities—those he had devoted solely to business and pleasure. His pastor's approach is no longer to be dreaded for fear he is going to want to start something. Rather, he is actually calling the

pastor for interviews about plans for expansion. Verily this is a new man in Christ Jesus. The Spirit did it for him through a vision of soul-winning.

In Christian fellowship. It is a question if we are getting all the blessing available to us as Christian workers through Christian fellowship. No man holding aloof from other servants of Christ can be at his best. There is something heartening and stimulating about the friendly mutual interchanges in service. God blesses His people in a pecurlar way through each other. Personal work promotes Christian fellowship in a way that nothing else does. There is always something new to be learned on each side when real soul-winners get together. That is partly because the work itself is so full of variety and ever producing new and interesting experiences. No two cases exactly alike. In Hebrews it is written, "And—let us consider one another to provoke unto love and good works; not forsaking the assembling ourselves together, as the manner of some is; but exhorting one another and so much the more, as ye see the day approaching." (10:24, 25)

In church morale. It is a matter of commoı knowledge that in military warfare the moral of the army, so important, is not difficult t maintain when the forces are attacking th enemy, even though in the face of great odds It is in retreat, and while waiting in the trenche that fighting efficiency is sapped by loss o morale. That was why "Y" huts used by th A.E.F. in France were made places of amuse ment and diversion; it was a backfire to preven the discouragement which comes from long wait ing and delayed results.

The church that is not continuously winnin souls can hardly, at best, be said to be standin still. It is in retreat. And men grow sick at hear in retreat. But let the word go down the lin that an advance has been ordered and a bette spirit gets hold, morale is restored. A churcl may have a grand preacher, a grand choir, a grand membership and a grand "sanctuary" anc yet its spiritual power at a low ebb. The soul winning program for a church, so arranged tha all may take part yields a by-product in im proved morale. And that's an understatement.

(*More By-Products in next lesson*)

SABBATH SCHOOL LESSONS — REV. J. KENTON PARKER

LESSON FOR OCTOBER 28

The Shepherd Psalm

Background Scripture: Psalm 23
Devotional Reading: Ezekiel 34:11-16

Certainly no list of "Great Passages from the Bible" would omit the Twenty Third Psalm, The Shepherd Psalm. It has been the delight and comfort and strength of God's people all through the ages. Like other beautiful passages, it needs no interpretation or exposition. The snow-white lily, or the sparkling diamond, are not meant to be analyzed, but to be gazed upon with wonder.

There are two kinds of shepherds. In Ezekiel 34, (our Devotional Reading), we have a striking picture of the "shepherds of Israel" who fed themselves, and neglected the flock. The prophet reproves and warns these false shepherds who were allowing the flock to be scattered upon all the face of the earth. Jesus also tells us of the "hireling" who cares not for the sheep, and flees when danger approaches.

In verses 11-16 of this chapter from Ezekiel we have the portrait of the Good Shepherd Who seeks out and finds and cares for the flock. "I will feed my flock, and I will cause them to lie down, saith the Lord. I will seek that which was lost, and bring again that which was driven away, and will bind up that which is broken, and will strengthen that which was sick." In the balance of the chapter He gives a further description of His loving care for the flock, and closes with these words: "And ye my flock, the flock of my pasture, are men, and I am your God, saith the Lord God." David had good reasons for saying, The Lord is My Shepherd.

It would be well, I believe, to read and study the Tenth Chapter of the Gospel of John along with this psalm. In this familiar chapter Jesus describes Himself as the Good Shepherd and speaks of the hireling who flees when the wolf comes. The Good Shepherd lays down his life for the sheep. He knows his sheep, and they follow Him. He gives them life, even abundant life. He came to the lost sheep of the house of Israel, but "other sheep I have which are not of this fold: them also I must bring, and they shall hear my voice: and there shall be one fold and one shepherd". He is looking forward to the Gentiles who will come into the fold. Paul tells us that the middle wall of partition is broken down between Jew and Gentile and we are one in Christ. He is the Great Shepherd of the sheep Who has been raised from the dead, and will raise us up also.

In the study of this matchless psalm the best way, perhaps, is to just look at each verse as we would look at the pearls on a string of pearls.

"The Lord is my shepherd: I shall not want". This tremendous thought undergirds the whole psalm. All the other parts follow. It was natural for David, the shepherd boy, to think of God in this way. We can imagine him out in the field at night, alone, as far as men are concerned, with the stars shining brightly in the sky. He sees and marvels at all these beautiful wonders above him, and his mind goes back of them to the God Who made them and him, and this thought comes to him, given by the Spirit of God. Just as he, David, is looking after the little flock entrusted to his care, so the Creator and Preserver of the universe is caring for His own. If the Lord is his Shepherd—the Lord of the universe—then the natural sequence is: "I shall not want". David might not be able to give his sheep all they wanted, but this is not true of God; He is able, and His sheep shall not want.

"He maketh me to lie down in green pastures; He leadeth me beside the still waters". Sheep need food and water and a quiet place to rest; so do we. Give us this day our daily bread, Jesus taught us to pray. The Shepherd will lead his sheep to the places where they can find grass and water and shade. In like manner the Great Shepherd feeds His sheep. In His discourse after the feeding of the five thousand, our Lord called himself the Bread of Life. Another time He cried out, "If any man thirst, let him come unto me and drink". To the woman at the well he said, "If thou knewest the gift of God, and who it is that saith to thee, Give me to drink; thou wouldst have asked of him, and he would have given thee living water". "Whosoever drinketh of this water shall thirst again, but whosoever drinketh of the water that I shall give him shall never thirst; but the water that I shall give him shall be in him a well of water springing up into everlasting life". The gospel invitation is to a feast of good things: "Ho, everyone that thirsteth, come ye to the waters, and he that hath no money, come ye buy wine and milk without money and without price."

"He restoreth my soul: he leadeth me in the paths of righteousness for his name's sake". Just as food and water and rest restores the body, so our Good Shepherd restores our spiritual strength. "Come ye apart, and rest awhile," He said to His disciples. Our souls get tired as well as our bodies. Then he leads in the paths of righteousness: His ways are ways of pleasantness, and all his paths are peace. He understands every need both of body and of soul.

"The valley of the shadow of death". When darkness and gloom and danger come, our Shepherd is always near. "I do not believe I could have stood it", said a young missionary who had just buried his wife and infant, "unless the Saviour had stood by my side". He is always "by our side" when we pass through the "valley of the shadow", whether it is our time to die, or whether it is the death of one dear to us. The Saviour Who wept at the grave of Lazarus will weep with His heartbroken children. The rod and staff guided, protected, and sometimes chastened, the sheep, so, He will guide and comfort us. Fear not, He says, I will be with thee. When we go through the deep waters they shall not overflow. We can "touch bottom", as Bunyan describes it in speaking of the crossing over of one of the pilgrims.

"When thro' the deep waters I call thee to go,
The rivers of sorrow shall not overflow:
For I will be with thee, thy troubles to bless,
And sanctify to thee thy deepest distress".

I will not leave you comfortless: I will come unto you. Then, too, He promised to send the Holy Spirit, the Comforter, The "One-called-alongside-to-help". Our Great Shepherd has made abundant provision for us when our time comes to go through the "valley of the shadow".

"Thou preparest a table before me in the presence of mine enemies". Sheep have many enemies; so do Christians. David protected his sheep from the lion and the bear, and later on God protected him from the Philistines. Jesus is our Shepherd-King. As our King He restrains and conquers all His and our enemies. We are "More than conquerors" through Him that loved us. We not only gain the victory but we feast on the good things of God, even while our enemies look on. So many early Christians went to the stake singing. They were given supernatural strength. Today the church stands surrounded by bitter enemies. True Christians are feasting, however, while the world is starving, for God is able to spread a table for us even in the presence of these enemies.

"Thou anointest my head with oil". Anointing with oil was a sign of high position and privilege. Kings were anointed and priests. We are made kings and priests unto God, honored by Him.

"My cup runneth over". A little child said, "When God fills the cup, He fills the saucer too". Children love to sing the chorus, "My cup is full, and running over". These "overflowing mercies and gifts" have been called "God's Extras". There are many of these all about us in the world: the beautiful flowers, blossoming in desert and waste places; the singing of the birds as we wake in the morning; the colors of the rainbow, and the glories of the sunrise, or sunset; all the manifold blessings which are over and above what we have a right to expect.

"Surely goodness and mercy shall follow me all the days of my life". The psalmist, in Psalm 71:18 prays, "Now also when I am old and greyheaded, O God, forsake me not". The people of the world sometimes forget and neglect and even mistreat us when we are "old and greyheaded". God never does. One of the marks of a Christian land is the care we take of the old and helpless. Where we find homes for the aged, and for incurables, and feebleminded, we know that the influence of Christianity has been felt. E'en down to old age our Shepherd will care tenderly for us.

"I will dwell in the house of the Lord forever". The shepherd gathered his sheep in the fold at night. He himself would lie down sometimes and literally become the "door to the sheep-fold." I am the Door, said Jesus. In some of our cemeteries there is a sign, "Perpetual Care". This is a guarantee that the graves in that cemetery will be cared for always; never neglected, so that the weeds and briars never take possession. "I go to prepare a place for you," said Jesus; I will come again and receive you unto myself. The souls of believers are at their death made perfect in holiness, and do immediately pass into glory, and their bodies, being still united to Christ to rest in their graves until the resurrection. The Christian is "safe in the arms of Jesus," both in this life, and forever. No one can pluck us out of His hands.

YOUNG PEOPLE'S DEPARTMENT — REV. B. HOYT EVANS

YOUTH PROGRAM FOR OCTOBER 28

"The Family Coffers"

Suggested Devotional Outline:

Hymn: "I Gave My Life For Thee"
Prayer
Scripture: Luke 12:16-21; 18:23; 21:1-4
Hymn: "We Give Thee But Thine Own"
Hymn: "Take My Life, And Let It Be Consecrated"

Suggestions for Program Leader:

(It is intended that this program be a joint effort of the men, women, and young people of the church. If it is possible to arrange such a joint meeting, it will surely prove a helpful way to consider this question. If it is not possible to plan a meeting of this kind, it will be most helpful to invite adults to have a part in the program given for the young people. If you follow the outline given below, you could ask adults to discuss the first and second topic. We are offering some suggestions for those who lead these discussions. For the second topic it will be better to use a parent who does not have a son or daughter in the youth organization at the present time.)

Program Leader's Introduction:

This is another program recognizing the emphasis on Christian family life in the Forward With Christ Program this year. It should be obvious to us by now that the home is one of the very best places to practice Christian living and to promote Christian growth. We spend more time in our homes than we do anywhere else (or, at least, we ought to). We act more normally, more sincerely, in our homes than we do elsewhere. There is less temptation to "put on airs" at home, or to "make an impression." If we are really moving forward with Christ, it will be proved on the testing ground of our homes and families.

If our homes are the best places for practicing our Christian faith, then the realm of money matters is one of the most important areas in our homes. It has been demonstrated that money matters can prove a sore spot even in the lives of Christians, even among the members of families who love each other very much. It is quite in order, then, that we who are interested in Christian family living should give some serious thought to the ways a Christian family manages its money. The family coffers are very important to family Christian life.

First Speaker: (Suggestions for presentation)

What is the Christian way of conducting family finances? Your own personal experiences and observations will mean more to the young people than any printed speech. You will undoubtedly want to indicate that a plan for the family coffers is essential. The plan, of course, must recognize responsibility to the church (the tithe) and also our responsibility to God in the use we make of all our money. Stewardship involves all our money and all our life, not merely what we give to the church. A plan for Christian family finances surely ought to be a real family affair, one that recognizes all the members of the family. Young people are generally more considerate of the family coffers when they have a share in the financial planning.

Second Speaker: (Suggestions for presentation)

What are the financial aspects of having a senior age young person in the home? There are many young people who seem to think their drain on the family coffers begins and ends with their allowance or their spending money. It will be helpful if you can make them realize that they represent a very considerable financial investment on the part of their parents. A recent magazine article indicated that the average cost of bringing young people from birth through high school is $11,300 for girls and $11,600 for boys. Specific information from your own experience will be most interesting and helpful. In dealing with this matter you want to be especially careful to avoid the impression that young people are an unwanted financial burden. The investment in their lives is gladly made because of their parents' great love and high hopes for them.

Third Speaker: (This part can be taken either by a young person or an adult.)

What are the advantages of an allowance for a young person? In answering this question use as many personal observations and experiences as possible. We are suggesting three advantages which you may wish to include with your own: (1) An allowance gives a young person his own money to give to the church. (2) An allowance teaches a sense of values in that he must manage his own money and learn by experience how far it will go. (3) The management of one's own money is excellent preparation for the future when larger sums must be wisely used.

Program Leader:

Give an opportunity for questions and discussion about any of these matters. You could also discuss the advantages and disadvantages of having mothers and young people working to augment the family income.

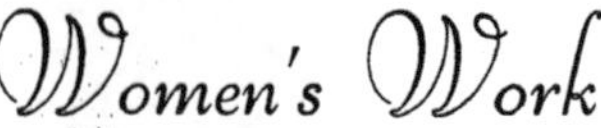

A Prayer for the United Nations and World Peace

Almighty and ever-living God, our eternal Father, in whose will is our peace and strength: Teach Thy warring children, we beseech Thee, the way of understanding and peace.

Forgive us the national sin that so often besets us: the pride of wealth and power that leads us to take international action by ourselves alone, the selfishness that blinds us to the needs of other people, the suspicion and fear of the stranger within and outside our gates. In Thy deep mercy, eternal God, grant that our beloved country may join with other nations in acts of compassion for a suffering humanity, in working together to reconcile differences between peoples, in seeking to establish a foundation of trust on which to build a more peaceful world.

Bless the United Nations, we pray Thee, and all those international servants who work through it to save this and succeeding generations from the scourge of war. Do Thou cause its work to prosper in many lands and among many peoples, that all Thy children may be helped to find a finer and more abundant way of life.

Lead the entire world, our Father, to have a new birth of freedom and justice, of mercy and truth—to the glory of Thy Holy Name. Amen.

Annual Meeting of Women of Synod of Georgia

Decatur—Mrs. J. Swanton Ivy of Athens, has been named president of the Women of the Church, Synod of Georgia, at the women's forty-seventh annual meeting at Columbia Theological Seminary, in September. Mrs. Ivy is a member of Friendship Church in Athens.

Mrs. L. R. Wooten, also of Athens and member of Friendship Church, was elected corresponding secretary; Mrs. E. S. Brannon, Rome, and member of First Church there, was named chairman of spiritual growth; Mrs. D. R. Nimocks, First Church, Gainesville, was elected chairman of annuities and relief; and Mrs. J. O. Cobb, Smyrna and a member of Smyrna Presbyterian Church, was appointed World Missions chairman to fill the unexpired term of Mrs. Wallace Martin. The new officers were installed by Dr. J. McDowell Richards, president of Columbia Seminary and former moderator of the General Assembly.

About 100 women from Georgia's six presbyterys heard Dr. Henry Edward Russell, pastor of Trinity Church, Montgomery, Ala., speaking on "Christian Citizenship", call the "production of Christian citizens" the primary function of the Church.

Others on the program were Dr. Manford G. Gutzke, professor at Columbia Seminary, who led a Bible Study on the Minor Prophets, and Mrs. S. H. Askew, Decatur, who gave a preview of the 1957 Circle Bible Study on Jesus and Christian Citizenship. Mrs. James Boyce, missionary to Mexico, and Petrie Mitchell, who is serving in Korea, presented messages about the 1957 Birthday Objectives, student work in Mexico and medical aid in Korea.

Other speakers were Miss Elizabeth Sheffelton of the Belgian Congo, who told about her work in that area; the Rev. Robert B. McNeil, pastor of First Church, Columbus, who introduced a panel on Christian Higher Education; James Baird, student at Columbia Seminary and Mrs. Harry Phillips, wife of a student at the seminary, who led devotional services; and Mrs. E. L. Secrest of Savannah, who previewed 1957 literature the women will use.

The Total Church Program was topic for a panel, moderated by Dr. J. G. Patton, Executive Secretary of the General Council, and including four other executive secretaries of boards and the Assembly's Stated Clerk. Dr. C. Darby Fulton, Board of World Missions, Nashville, Tenn.; Dr.

since I always look forward to the information and inspiration it brings, it would please me for you to send a small gift to the Journal for its work."

The Board voted unanimously to send you the enclosed check in honor of their friend and yours, Mr. A. E. Harman.

Emma Wysor Dunlap

Church News

World Missions Receipts

Budget for 1956	$3,300,000.00
Receipts to date	2,067,061.85
Percentage of annual budget received for 1956	62.63%
Balance needed for 1956	1,232,938.15

Thanksgiving for the Vacation Fund!

For more than forty years the Vacation Fund of our Church has been a benediction to an ever increasing number of our ministers. During the summer of 1956, 116 of our ministers were enabled to have a restful and spiritually enriching experience in one of the great conference centers of our church. A few of them attended one of the preaching clinics at a seminary.

The Board of Managers wishes to thank each contributor to this fund. These contributions were the means of making the recipients better prepared to do their work in an even more effective way. They have requested us to thank the contributors for them. We, therefore, include here some quotations from their letters of gratitude for this assistance from the Vacation Fund.

One minister wrote as follows:

"Through the Vacation Fund, my family and I were able to have a very enjoyable week at Montreat this summer. I think that it is the most profitable week that we have ever had there and thank you and those who make the fund possible, for this very delightful vacation."

Another says, "Thanks to you for this generosity which we assure you we needed. This was the first Church Extension Conference we ever attended. It was good, and it gave me a new perspective of the work of our great church on the home front. I can apply myself with a new appreciation to the tasks of the months to come in a country parish. It was generous of you and the Committee to extend to us this helpful favor this summer. We were at Montreat nine days which included some of the Bible Conference. We enjoyed that too."

A third wrote, "We wish to acknowledge with THANKS the check for $75, from you, and the Vacation Fund, for our vacation at Montreat this summer. You have done us a great favor, which is very much appreciated. It has been two years now since we have had a vacation, not having been absent from my pulpit a single Sunday and only two Wednesday nights."

Still another wrote: "It was my privilege to share in the Vacation Fund this year and I am writing to express my unbounded appreciation and gratitude to you and all the generous people who make this Fund possible.

"My wife and I attended the Bible Conference and I don't think we have ever enjoyed and been helped as much in a conference at Montreat, or at any place, as we were this year. It just seemed that every speaker and teacher who appeared on the program 'was a man sent from God' to refresh and inspire our dry and thirsty souls. I have been able to preach with more zeal and assurance that Christ can and does change men's lives since returning from Montreat and the mountain top experience which it offered.

"For us both, let me say THANK YOU, AND GOD BLESS YOU!"

The above are typical of scores of others.

On behalf of the Board of Managers of the Vacation Fund.

Wade H. Boggs, Manager

The Miami Presbyterian Men's Convention

Atlanta — The Miami convention committee raised its sights in planning the greatest Protestant men's convention in American history at a recent meeting here. The committee, with John Matthews, Fayetteville, Tenn., attorney, as chairman, voted to increase its budget for the Oct. 10-13, 1957, convention in Florida from $48,000 to $58,000.

Dr. Andrew R. Bird, Jr., Huntington, W. Va., chairman, submitted the report of the program and speakers committee, indicating that its work was nearing a successful conclusion more than a year ahead of the convention dates.

Mr. Matthews announced the names of two of the principals on the program. Dr. Louis H. Evans of Hollywood will deliver the keynote address and Dr. Ernest J. Sommerville, of Birmingham, Ala., will conduct the four devotionals.

Registration for the convention, the committee was told, is ahead of the total on the same date prior to the New Orleans convention. The goal is 12,000 men and as this will be a "bring-your-wife" convention, upwards of 5,000 wives also are expected.

Progress in preparations at Miami was reported by William C. Swain, of Miami, chairman of the local arrangements committee. There will be sufficient accommodations for all in any price range you desire. Summer rates will apply and local prices were declared to be comparable to New Orleans.

John J. Deifell, Greensboro, N. C., president of the Assembly Men's Council, and chairman of the attendance committee, submitted a report on the work of one of his sub-committees, publicity. Radio scripts, TV shorts and a color movie with sound for churches and church clubs were recommended. The cost of this promotion, not included in the original budget estimates, resulted in a four hour discussion. The recommendations were adopted, the budget increased and the cost of this phase of the publicity was set at $2,600.

Mr. Deifell introduced chairmen of his subcommittee, Bruce Whitfield, transportation, Huntsville, Ala.; Blue Book, Carl Marcelius, Andalusia, Ala., and Ralph Brewer, publicity, Alexandria, La.

Other reports were submitted by W. Legare McIntosh, Columbia, S. C., follow up, Walter Humphrey, Fort Worth, fraternal delegates, and T. Marshall Gordon, Richmond, Va., treasurer.

The next day the A.M.C. executive committee met with John Deifell, president, presiding. Most of its time likewise was focused on convention plans.

Minister." Retreat is a basic part of orientation and inspiration for the school year. It is entirely sponsored and financed by the student body organization.

LOUISIANA

The Presbytery of Louisiana met in Stated Session in the Jackson Street Church in Alexandria, September 18, 1956, with all resident ministers present and all but three Churches represented.

Mr. William S. Smith was examined for ordiination and a Commission appointed to ordain and install him as pastor of the Zachary and Jackson Churches.

The Rev. Wm. D. O'Neal was received into the Presbytery and a Commission appointed to install him as pastor of the Broadmoor Church in Baton Rouge.

The Committee on Bills and Overtures recommended that two interim committees study the proposed amendments sent down to the Presbyteries and make recommendation to the meeting of Presbytery on January 15th, at which time the vote will be taken.

The report of the Committee on Church Extension showed that the two Churches organized during the past year are doing well and that one already has a building and is on a self supporting basis.

The Presbytery also is contributing $15,000 toward the construction of a new Church building with Student Center for the Negro Church in Scotlandville, where Southern University is located. The budget for Church Extension was set at $34,000.

The Presbytery's Council presented the benevolence budget for 1957, which is $126,000. This was adopted and the askings are to be considered by the Churches as the Council visits them in an Every Church canvass.

The World Missions report emphasized the need for the local Churches to make a special effort in education of the people, and plans are being made for missionary speakers to visit the Presbytery.

The next meeting will be in the Second Church, Baton Rouge, on January 15, 1957.

R. D. Earnest, Stated Clerk

Baton Rouge—The Rev. William C. Sistar, who until the first of August was president of Palmer Orphanage in Columbus, Miss., has become Director of Child Care Program in Louisiana, it has been announced by Coyne M. Talmage of New Orleans, chairman of the Board of Trustees of Child Care, and an elder at Napoleon Avenue Presbyterian Church, New Orleans.

Mr. Sistar has already taken up his new duties and is located in Baton Rouge.

He is now guest minister of the First Presbyterian Church in that city.

Mr. Sistar's duties involve the setting up of a Child Care Service, and duties of a promotional nature, aim of which is to stress Child Care Service activities, and to promote that field of effort, especially from now through the Thanksgiving season.

The Rev. Robert Earnes of Baton Rouge is treasurer of the Child Care Fund.

NORTH CAROLINA

Albemarle—Dedication Services were held September 23 at the Second Presbyterian Church at Albemarle, in recognition of the removal of all indebtedness from the church property.

Dr. Charles D. Whiteley, pastor of the church, chose as his sermon topic "Great Things for Us."

Newell Blalock, chairman of the Board of Deacons, made the presentation during the ceremonies, and S. T. Marbry, chairman of the Board of Trustees, made the acceptance.

Second Presbyterian Church was organized by Mecklenburg Presbytery in 1940. The present church building was completed in 1945, with the first service in the building held the fourth Sunday in September of 1946.

Mooresville—An entire worship service at Prospect Presbyterian Church near Mooresville, will be heard around the world. The service at historic Prospect Church was recorded by James C. Moore, Director of Religious Programming for the Voice of America. The material, gathered from this service in September, will be the first in a series of recorded regular church services to be used by Voice of America on its international broadcasts—which are heard even in Behind-the-Iron-Curtain countries. The recording will be rebroadcast in forty-two other languages.

Mr. Moore included in the broadcast, interviews with sixteen members of the congregation.

The Rev. Carlyle A. McDonald, pastor of Prospect Church, Rural Church Award winner for the South in 1954, delivered the sermon that the world will hear. Mr. McDonald brought a message on the sermon topic, "The Life We Now Live," from the text in Galatians 2:20—"the life I now live in flesh, I live by the faith of the Son of God, who loved me and gave Himself for me".

Wade—U. S. Senator Kerr Scott was the principal speaker at the 198th anniversary Reunion of the Bluff Presbyterian Church near Wade, N. C., September 23.

On the fourth Sunday in September, several hundred descendants of the Scotch Highlanders who settled in the Cape Fear area, annually gather at the historic old church.

The Rev. Robert E. Merrell is the present pastor of the Bluff, Godwin, and McMillan Presbyterian Churches, all of which owe their beginnings to the early Scotsmen who settled in the area, and built their churches shortly after they built their homes.

The Old Church, located high on a bluff over looking the Cape Fear River was given its name because of its picturesque setting.

Senator Scott is a Ruling Elder of the Hawfields Presbyterian Church, another of the old churches of the state, and is a past moderator of Orange Presbytery.

SOUTH CAROLINA

Clinton—Groundbreaking ceremonies for Presbyterian College's new Memorial Student Center will be held as a part of the homecoming program on October 6, as announced by Marshall W. Brown, president of the College.

The proposed building will be erected as a memorial to the 65 alumni of the college who lost their lives in World War II, and the five who gave their lives in action in Korea.

The Memorial Center is a major objective of the Diamond Jubilee Development program now in progress.

Georgetown—Miss Yvonne Reftelis was approved as a candidate for lay service by Harmony Presbytery during its adjourned summer meeting of Sept. 18 at Indiantown Church near Hemmingway.

Miss Reftelis, who left here on Sept. 11 to enter the General Assembly's Training School in Richmond, was examined before her departure by Presbytery's Christian Education Committee meeting at the Andrews Church the evening of September 4. Upon the basis of the examination the committee recommended her approval by Presbytery.

A member of the Friendfield Church just outside of Georgetown, Miss Reftelis is taking the two year course at the General Assembly's Training School to prepare herself for work as a director of Christian education.

TENNESSEE

Nashville—The Rev. and Mrs. David V. Miller of our Congo Mission announce the arrival of a daughter, Nancy Lorraine, in Congo, on September 12.

Mr. Miller is a native of Johnson City, Tenn. He studied at East Tennessee State College, Davidson College, and Union Seminary, in Richmond. He is a member of Holston Presbytery.

Mrs. Miller is the former Miss Polly Jean Yandell of Charlotte, N. C. She is a member of the North Charlotte Presbyterian Church. She received her education at Mars Hill Junior College and the Assembly's Training School.

The Millers sailed in August 1954 going to Belgium for language study for a year. Following that they proceeded to Congo where they have been in evangelistic work since that time. The Millers have one other child, a son.

Texas

The Presbytery of Paris—Meeting at Camp Gilmont, Presbytery's beautiful pine-covered campsite six miles north of Gilmer, the fall meeting of the Presbytery of Paris was held September 25. The retiring moderator, Rev. W. Cooper Cumming of Texarkana, preached the opening sermon on "Rally Day and Christian Education."

L. Harold Dial, elder in First Church, Kilgore, was elected moderator. Rev. David Pittinger was received from the Presbytery of Dallas to become pastor of the Sulphur Springs church and Rev. John C. Ramsey from the Presbytery of Mangum to become pastor of the Waskom church.

Dick Poteet of Paris and Dick Carey of Tyler were taken under care of Presbytery as candidates for the ministry. Rev. W. Henry Benchoff of the Marshall church was named moderator-in-nomination for the winter meeting of Presbytery to convene in the Gladewater church January 15 at 9:30 a. m.

The meeting of Presbytery was preceded on Monday evening by the fall rally of the Paris Presbytery Men of the Church, attended by about 315 men, largest in the history of the organization, for which Dr. William M. Elliott, Jr., minister of the Highland Park Church of Dallas, was guest speaker, addressing the men of the subject, "Every Man In His Place."

Austin—Dr. David L. Stitt, president of the Austin Presbyterian Theological Seminary in Austin, Tex., announced today the first winners of the Sam B. Hicks Scholarship of $1000.00 won by James B. Brown, senior student from Shreveport, La., and second year student Marvin Williams of Dallas, Tex.

These scholarships will be awarded annually to second and third year students on the basis of academic achievement, Christian character, and promise of effectiveness in the ministry.

Austin—Members of the Westlake Hills Presbyterian Church in Austin, Tex., have voted unanimously to accept the preliminary plans recommended to them by their building committee.

Mr. Wallace H. Flatt, chairman of the committee, presented the elevated drawings and floor plans for their consideration. The cost of the new building has been estimated at approximately $41,000. It will be rock or brick veneer, centrally heated, and air-conditioned.

Laredo Church Celebrates 75th Anniversary

The First Presbyterian Church of Laredo, Texas was organized August 7, 1881, by the Reverend W. E. Caldwell and the Reverend J. R. Jacobs. There were ten Charter Members and eight of them were ladies. The first pastor, Reverend Franklin P. Ramsey, arrived two months later. He came by special appointment and appropriation of Missionary Funds by the General Assembly of that year.

The celebration of this church's birthday was postponed until September 23, when special services were held both morning and evening with the Reverend Jan A. McMurray of Georgetown, Texas, preaching. Mr. McMurray was born in Laredo and his father, the Reverend Stonewall Jackson McMurray was pastor here when the present church sanctuary and old manse were erected.

Texarkana—Paris Presbytery had its regular Fall meeting at its Camp Gilmont on Sept. 25th. Rev. Mr. Cooper Cumming of Texarkana, retiring Moderator, preached the opening sermon on "Rally Day and Religious Education" and Mr. L. H. Dial, an elder of the Kilgore Church, was elected to succeed him.

Rev. R. B. Brannon Jr., was dismissed from Hallsville to Dallas Presbytery (the Ennie Church) and Rev. Harry L. Johnson was dismissed from Overton to the Bonham Church. Rev. David V. Pittenger and Dr. J. C. Ramsey were received from Dallas and Mangum Presbyteries to be installed at Sulphur Springs and Waskom, respectively. Richard B. Poteat of Paris and Richard Carey of Tyler were received as candiates for the ministry. A minimum salary rate for ministers was set at $4200. Presbytery's Council was authorized to confer with the Council of Dallas Presbytery to make plans for the new Dallas- Paris Presbytery.

A Committee on an Old Folks Home was appointed to meet with a similar Committee of Dallas Presbytery. The invitation of the Gladewater church was accepted for the January 15th Winter Meeting of Presbytery.

A Special Committee was appointed to study the proposed changes in the Church Standards and report to the next meeting.

BOOKS

OUR REASONABLE FAITH. Herman Bavinck. Eerdman's. $6.95.

All who are familiar with Reformed Theology hold in the highest esteem the name of Herman Bavinck. He was one of the theological giants of the past generation. He was appreciated in his native Holland for his clear-headedness and his ability to express his fecund ideas in vigorous language. The centennial of his birth was widely celebrated in Holland in 1954. A hundred years after his birth the finest of European theologians are recognizing afresh his solid theological scholarship. Bavinck became Abraham Kuypur's successor at the Free University when Kuypur became prime minister of the government at the Hague.

Our Reasonable Faith was first published in 1909 under the title **Magnalia Dei** or **The Wonderful Works of God.** It is a compendium of his original four volume **Reformed Dogmatics.** This volume is a work of basic Christian dogma. It presents clearly and in fine perspective the fundamental doctrines of Biblical teaching.

Bavinck is known primarily as a Scriptural theologian. As Landwehr has put it, "Just as Calvin gathered his thoughts out of Scripture, so Bavinck was always dipping into the Bible for his ideas and was being guided by Scripture in his systematization of them." Bavinck entertained a high conception of the mission of a theologian in the church of Christ. In his inaugural address at Amsterdam he declared, "A theologian is a person who makes bold to speak about God because he speaks out of God and through God. To profess theology is to do holy work. It is priestly ministration in the house of the Lord. It is itself a service of worship, a consecration of mind and heart to the honor of His name."

The motif that runs through Bavinck's work is the philosophy of revelation and this revelation is the answer to the problems of life and the world and this answer satisfies both the heart and the mind.

This volume contains 24 delightful chapters. They deal with various aspects of God's revelation; the being, nature, and works of God; and the great salvation wrought by Jesus Christ.

One of the finest chapters in this volume has to do with the two natures of Christ. He points out that if Christ is to be the object of our worship, He must possess a divine nature as well as a human nature. He writes, "The basis for the religious worship of Christ can only be His divine nature, so that whoever denies this and yet maintains the worship becomes guilty of deifying the creature and of idolatry. The deity of Christ is not an abstract doctrine but something which is of the highest importance for the life of the church."

One who reviews books should be careful not to use unwarranted superlatives. If, however, there is ever a book that would justify the use of superlatives, this is such a book. It is the finest presentation of Biblical truth that we have seen in many years. It is rich, stimulating, moving, and satisfying. All who are looking for the best in theological literature would do well to invest in **Our Reasonable Faith.**

John R. Richardson

THE JEWS FROM CYRUS TO HEROD. Norman H. Snaith. Abingdon. $2.50.

This volume is a study of the political history and religious development of the Jewish people during the 5 centuries preceding the birth of Christ. The author holds that the message of Christ cannot be fully understood unless the reader knows something of the hopes and expectations of the Jewish people. The first part of the book surveys the historical background of the period tracing the rise and fall of the great empires—Persian, Greek, Egyptian, Syrian, Roman, and their direct influence upon the history of the Jews. The second part of the book deals with the religious development of the Jews during the same period. There is also a section that deals with the intertestamentary period. The volume also provides a background for an understanding of the Dead Sea Scrolls.

There is a real need for a new history of the Jews. Dr. Snaith gives us this book covering 5 centuries of Jewish history from the liberal point of view. We hope that someone will give us a complete history from the conservative point of view.

John R. Richardson

FAMOUS STORIES OF INSPIRING HYMNS. Ernest K. Emurian. W. A. Wilde Company. $2.50.

Here is a collection of 50 true and inspiring stories back of the words and music of many of our noblest hymns and most appealing gospel songs. The stories are interestingly written and thus ideal for youth programs, Sunday evening services and anecdotes for all occasions. They provide the busy minister with 50 true illustrations that are adaptable to almost every circumstance. Many are sermons in themselves, all the more effective because they are historically true. The well-indexed compilation maintains a fine balance between old and new hymns as well as between hymns and gospel songs. The author is an authority on this subject and his work is designed to instruct as well as to inspire the reader.

SIMPLE SERMONS ON TEN COMMANDMENTS. W. Herschel Ford. Zondervan. $2.00.

In ten sermons, one covering each commandment, Dr. Ford shows the inter-relation of each commandment, how the first four laws concern man's relationship to God and the latter six his relationship to his fellow man. He convincingly concludes that love is the key to keeping the law. The application of love, he says, to the individual life would channel man's actions so that he would live according to the Ten Commandments in relation to both God and man.

THE SOUTHERN PRESBYTERIAN JOURNAL

A Presbyterian weekly magazine devoted to the statement, defense and propagation of the Gospel, the faith which was once for all delivered unto the saints.

VOL. XV NO. 26 OCTOBER 24, 1956 $2.50 A YEAR

NEW SUBSCRIPTIONS

Hundreds of New Subscriptions have been added to our rapidly growing list in the past two weeks.

Many of our old Subscriber Friends have sent in from one to dozens of New Subscriptions.

One Youth organization in a Presbyterian Church in Alabama has just sent 47 New Subscriptions and asked that we send them for their new Church Library the 42 Free Award Books listed on page 20 of this issue. These have gone forward to them along with 5 Additional Books of our choosing to complete the Awards for these New Subscriptions. Would *YOU* like to help *YOUR CHURCH LIBRARY?*

See Back Cover of this Journal. Get your Free Sample copies of The Journal and go to work at once. Soon you will have many New Books for your Sunday School or Church Library, and the Journal for many to read every week!

THE SOUTHERN PRESBYTERIAN JOURNAL

Rev. Henry B. Dendy, D.D., Editor....Weaverville, N. C.
Dr. L. Nelson Bell, Associate Editor....Asheville, N. C.
Rev. Wade C. Smith, Associate Editor....Weaverville, N. C.

EDITORIAL

Faint Praise

Damning with faint praise is a well known rhetorical device, examples of which can be found in current campaign oratory. There is another twist of logic, not so well known, that could be called praising with faint damns. It could, and probably does, occur in criminal cases at law. The defendant's lawyer may admit that the accused did indeed once make a minor mistake and that of course he cannot claim to be absolutely perfect; and by this admission the lawyer hopes to direct the jury's attention away from the very serious crime of which he is accused.

This device also occurs in instances in which the gospel is diluted. Man, instead of being portrayed as thoroughly guilty and dead in sin, is partly exonerated by softening the charge. Plain language, like miserable sinners, is avoided.

Take for example the familiar hymn, Beneath the Cross of Jesus. At the ending of the second stanza, the author wrote:

And from my stricken heart with tears
Two wonders I confess:
The wonders of redeeming love
And my own worthlessness.

It may not be too surprising that some cheap gospel songbooks, edited by persons of Arminian tendencies, have altered this beautiful hymn so that the last line reads:

And my unworthiness.

But it is more unfortunate when this dilution of the gospel finds a place in hymn books that are supposed to be Calvinistic. In 1955 there was published *The Hymnbook,* with the approval of the northern Presbyterian church, the southern Presbyterian church, the United Presbyterian church, the Reformed Church of America, and with one editor from the Associate Reformed Presbyterian church. Beneath the Cross of Jesus is number 190 in that hymnbook. Now it is hard to believe that the editors were unaware of what the author had written. In the excellent hymnal, revised in 1911, and used for years in the U.S.A. church, the hymn, number 470, is correctly printed. Therefore the change must have been deliberate. It is certainly deleterious.

First of all, it dilutes the gospel. Instead of recognizing man's complete lack of merit before God, the change softens worthlessness to unworthiness. Man is no longer pictured as a miserable sinner, guilty of the wrath and curse of God; but rather man is said merely to be unworthy. What pride is concealed in this admission of unworthiness! Of course I am not perfect, the hymn now says, but still I am not completely evil.

The change not only dilutes the gospel, but it also makes nonsense of the hymn. The author knew what she was writing. One may doubt that the modern editors had a clear idea of how their change changed the hymn into nonsense. The author confesses two wonders. One wonder is the utter sinfulness of man. The contrast is sharp. But the new version says that it is a wonder that man is unworthy before God. Such praise with faint damns hardly indicates a wonder. There is no longer any reason for the tears of a stricken heart. The hymn has here been reduced to nonsense. But Calvinism is not nonsense —

And from my stricken heart with tears
Two wonders I confess:
The wonders of redeeming love
And my own worthlessness.

G.H.C.

The New Universalism

It should be a matter of deep concern to all Protestants that in respected and influential circles universalism is being accorded a hearing.

The Universalist Church is, along with the Unitarian, still outside the pale of recognized evangelical denominations, but neo-unitarianism and a frank universalism are now to be found *within* Protestantism.

Unquestionably the entering wedge has been the unscriptural doctrine of the *universal* Fatherhood of God and brotherhood of man, so popular and so fraught with danger. While God is the Father of all mankind by creation the Bible teaches that the Father-son relationship has been broken by sin and can only be reestablished by the new birth.

Once deny the integrity and authority of the Scriptures or any basic doctrine and a whole Pandora's box of heresies will begin to unfold. Universalism is one of them.

The article in this issue, "Calvanism or Universalism," describes a situation abroad in the land today, one which calls for spiritual and theological giants such as have blessed Presbyterianism in past generations.

Universalism must be challenged wherever it is met. It strikes at the very heart of the Gospel itself. L.N.B.

By His Grace — Our Fellowship Is With the Father and With His Son Jesus Christ

Irenaeus insists that God did not form Adam because He stood in need of man, but that He might have someone upon whom to confer His benefits. Nor did Christ stand in need of our service when He ordered us to follow Him, but He thus bestowed salvation upon us. "For as much as God is in want of nothing, so much does man stand in need of fellowship with God."

"God Himself, indeed, having need of nothing, but granting communion with Himself to those who stood in need of it." *Against Heresies* IV.xiv.1-2. Indeed the same writer goes further back and insists that God did not need even the angels to help Him form man. For He always had His own hands. "For with Him were always present the Word and Wisdom, the Son and the Spirit, by Whom and in Whom, freely and spontaneously He made all things." By these *hands* of God was Adam formed and by the same blessed hands shall we be made anew. "Our bodies are raised not from their own substance but by the power of God." God shall be glorified in His handiwork. For by the hands of the Father, that is, by the Son and the Holy Spirit man was made in the likeness of God. Ibid, Iv.xx.1; V.i.3; V.vi.1.

Scripture does not limit the description of the Son and the Spirit to the hands of God, but the general thought is that each is God in action. Blessed be His Name the Father of grace freely opened the counsels of His peace, the fellowship of His bosom, to us in the Incarnation of His Son and through the outpouring of the Holy Spirit.

All that God did in and through our Lord Jesus Christ makes the new and living way open to sinners. And in and by the Holy Spirit God works faith in our hearts so that we may come unto the Father by this door which is the Good Shepherd Himself. In mercy and grace, God has opened His heart and brought us in. Truly our fellowship is with the Father and with his Son Jesus Christ. W.C.R.

The Third Alternative

Fifty years ago, convinced that science had disproved much of the Bible, modernism felt itself entrenched and invulnerable.

With a theology and a view of Scripture which stemmed from underlying philosophical biases which minimized both divine revelation and the supernatural, the modernist of former years went on to magnify the inherent goodness in man and set out to bring in the Kingdom of God by human means.

This does not mean that all modernists were alike. There were supernaturalists of the Hegelian type, virtually pantheistic in outlook; and there were the naturalists following in the train of Dewey.

But both had one thing in common; they repudiated a *special,* unique divine revelation.

With World War I and its subsequent events there came a sober revaluation. Unregenerate man, capable still of sin at its blackest, rudely refuted man's optimistic view of himself. Much heart searching resulted.

Into this era of uncertainty there came an entirely new approach which with vigor de-

The Southern Presbyterian Journal, *a Presbyterian Weekly magazine devoted to the statement, defense, and propagation of the Gospel, the faith which was once for all delivered unto the saints,* published every Wednesday by The Southern Presbyterian Journal, Inc., in Weaverville, N. C.

Entered as second-class matter May 15, 1942, at the Postoffice at Weaverville, N. C., under the Act of March 3, 1879. Vol. XV, No. 26, October 24, 1956. Editorial and Business Offices: Weaverville, N. C. Printed in the U.S.A. by Biltmore Press, Asheville, N. C.

ADDRESS CHANGE: When changing address, please let us have both old and new address as far in advance as possible. Allow three weeks after change if not sent in advance. When possible, send an address label giving your old address.

clared man's sinfulness and God's intervention. The resulting crisis experience of the sinner was stressed.

This discrediting of the old modernism by the reaffirmation of a more sober view was a welcome change which all should admit. Theology was revitalized and the uniqueness of Christian experience again became a subject of lengthy discussions.

But as time has gone on even some of the most ardent devotees of this new approach have begun to raise searching questions about their own concepts. Some have frankly admitted that the schizophrenic theology they have espoused confuses both the teacher and the one who is taught. Most important of all, it tends to develop a generation of theological theorists, not practical Christian leaders.

The basic difficulty is the same as that of the older modernism; a denial of the plenary inspiration and authority of the Bible. The modernist of former generations eliminated great portions of the Scripture by higher criticism. This new approach denies that the Bible is the Word of God, affirming only that God speaks through the Bible and when this occurs as a work of the Holy Spirit that particular message is the Word of God for the particular individual receiving it. This predicates revelation on the perceptive ability of the individual and not on the fact of revelation itself.

But this viewpoint is neither logically consistent, nor is it coherent. It limps when proclaimed from the pulpit and halts when brought to bear on human lives in time of need. This unrealistic concept is taught in the stratified atmosphere of the class room, preached from many pulpits and is found in countless weighty books and articles today. In much of this there is endless repetition of what others have thought and written. And the man in the street and the man in the pew are left in confusion and in need.

To the two dimensions—frank denial by the old modernism and confused denial by others—there is a new dimension which is again receiving belated but searching attention. This third dimension is a return to faith in the Bible as God's fully inspired revelation, man's authoritative chart for personal faith and daily practice.

In the course of reverent textual criticism not one thing has been discovered to affect any basic doctrine of Christianity. Furthermore, as time has progressed, seeming discrepancies have themselves been resolved.

During these controversies the lay Christian has only too often been forgotten. Some who would have taken from him the Book in which he has trusted and which he had found to work, now find the necessity of belatedly handing it

The Fruit of the Spirit Is Peace

This is our third bit of fruit from the basket. The Bible has much to say about Peace. There is a universal longing for peace, and yet we always seem to be on the brink of war. Harold E. Stassen, after traveling all over the world, said that everywhere he went there was a deep yearning for peace. He suggested several things that we might do. The last was: "You can pray for peace." The best thing that comes over our radio each day is at twelve o'clock when we are invited to pray for righteousness and peace. Gideon's prayer is a good one: "The Lord send peace."

I. *Peace in relation to some other fruit in the basket.*

1. Peace is the foundation for Joy. No one can be happy without peace.

2. Peace is the companion of Righteousness, or Goodness. There is no peace, saith my God, to the wicked.

3. Peace, in its turn, is founded upon Faith. We must trust God, if we are to have peace. We must also trust our fellow-men, as far as we are able.

II. *Peace in relation to Ourselves;* our great Need of peace.

1. We have *Troubled Hearts.* There are different kinds of heart trouble. The worst is not physical, but sorrow, or fear, or worry; some spiritual burden.

2. We have *Troubled Homes.* This is the number one trouble of our country. We have lots of beautiful houses, but our Homes are tumbling down.

3. The *Church is Troubled.* Unbelief has a strangle-hold upon part of the church; another part is suffering persecution; indifference and worldliness are present in many places; the leaven of Pharisees, Sadducees, and Herod is at work.

4. *Nations are Troubled;* our own nation has problems to face which it never had before. We need all the Heavenly Wisdom God can give, to let us live.

5. We live in a *Troubled World,* groping in the darkness of sin. Everywhere we look there are "Trouble-Spots." It is like living on top of a volcano.

III. *Peace in Relation to God.* What has God done to bring peace?

1. He is the God of Peace; Christ is the Prince of Peace; the Gospel is a Gospel of

Peace; "Glory to God in the highest; on earth, peace and goodwill to men."

2. He makes peace. Sin is the great disturber. It is at the bottom of all the hatred and strife and wars of the world. God has made peace by taking away sin by the sacrifice of Himself; He bore our sins in His own body on the tree; He is our peace. He has broken down every wall which separates us from God and from our fellow-men. He purchases peace with His own precious blood shed on Calvary.

3. He promises peace to all who will come to Him. Our ministry is a ministry of reconciliation; we say to men, Be ye reconciled to God.

4. He Gives Peace; My peace I give unto you. This is His legacy to us.

5. He Keeps us in peace; Thou will keep him in perfect peace whose mind is stayed on Thee. He Guards our hearts and minds in Christ Jesus.

6. He gives us this peace through the Holy Spirit, Who cleanses from sin, Who dwells within us, Who guides into all truth, Who is called alongside of us; In other words; "The fruit of the Spirit is . . . PEACE" : Sweet Peace, the gift of God's love. J.G.P.

— LETTERS —

THE PRESBYTERIAN CHURCH
Meadville, Mississippi
October 12, 1956

Sir:

I am compelled to cancel my subscription to the *Journal.* After reading those two articles by Dr. Bell covering that trip to South America I came to the conclusion that I could no longer subscribe to the *Journal.*

Doctor McIntire is a personal friend of mine, but that is not the primary reason for my cancelling my subscription. My main reason is that I feel that Doctor Bell has made a PERSONAL issue out of a matter that so far as the general public is concerned, they have heard but little.

Dr. McIntire, Dr. Gueiros and the *Christian Beacon* have seen fit to attack our missionaries in Brazil and the Brazilian Presbyterian Church. Dr. Bell has taken the time, the effort and the money to visit the scene and report at first hand. If his able defense of the work in Brazil constitutes an attack on its detractors, one wonders just how the original unfounded charges are to be characterized. Ed.

Recommend The Journal To Friends

Universalism

W. Brown*

What is universalism? There are different shades of this doctrine. Some theologians would call themselves "conservative universalists" as opposed to "liberal universalists." The "conservative" is grounded in a view of "the Fatherhood of God and the brotherhood of man" to the point of stating that God is a loving Father of all and all men are united in and through the one Father. At first glance, this appears to be doctrinally sound. But when we contend, as does the "conservative universalist," that God, the Father, is aware that He has children who will die and leave this earth without ever having heard of Jesus Christ, and that He , the Father, makes allowances for such ignorance of the Savior, and, consequently, must make separate provision for the salvation of such men, we are teaching extra-biblical doctrine. This is a direct refutation of the autonomy of Christ and the doctrine of adoption. *"God sent forth His Son . . . so that we might receive adoption as sons."* (Gal.4:4,5)

The "liberal universalist" goes a little farther afield. His claim is that God realizes that He has created imperfect children and must make allowances for His shortcomings in having done so. The allowance He makes is that, if men will accept the Saviour He has provided, they will be made perfect. But, if we are disobedient and reject this Saviour (due to our imperfection, for which God is to blame), He cannot honestly condemn us, for, after all, our faults are not of our own doing, then, being the all-loving Father that He is, God, at the time of Judgment, will "feel sorry" for us and take us into His bosom. Here we might quote Christ Himself: *"I am the way, and the truth, and the life; no one comes to the Father but by me,"* but the "liberal universalists" will usually discount such quotations with the flimsy remark, "Oh, that doesn't mean what it says," or, "The writer of that gospel misquoted Jesus." And, believe it or not, some people swallow it!

"Salvation for the man in west China" is a hypothetical case much discussed by theological students — future ministers in the Presbyterian Church. The problem it poses is this: A man in west China has never been able to find peace and security in his native religion, or anything else. For twenty years he strives to know the truth, seeking it in numerous philosophies and beliefs, but without satisfaction of soul.

Eventually, he is reached by a missionary, who unfolds for him the "Good News" of Christ.

The citizen of west China is elated at hearing of Jesus and the salvation He offers, and immediately knows that his search for truth is ended. Now the question is this: had this man died ten years prior to the arrival of the missionary, would he have been saved?

He hadn't known the identity of Christ. He had not the remotest idea that such a one even existed. Were his good intentions, his desire for truth and his search for same, sufficient unto salvation? The universalist says "yes." And the grounds for his affirmative answer lie in the fact that he cannot comprehend a God who would be cruel enough to condemn a man who had never heard.

It is characteristic of man to forget that he is limited by time and space and that God is not so bound. We all know — or, at least, we say we know — that though the results of a divine decree may seem to be harsh and cruel to us today, the end result, as God intended all along, is something great, wonderful, a definite blessing. Had we lived at the outset of the Exodus, our sympathetic hearts would have ached for Pharaoh and his doomed army. Yet, since we are privileged to look back on the "slaughter at the Red Sea," we view it as a providential act of God through which He chose to reveal His might and power. When we preach it, never do we picture it as a severe cruelty on the part of God.

There are many more similar historical events. "The cruelty at Jericho," "the cruelty of Joseph's brothers," "the damnation of Israel." Yet, we never view them as such, for we know as we look back upon such events that each had a constructive end in God's Plan. Just because we cannot put our finger on the reason for God's damnation of the man in west China doesn't mean that something equally constructive might not come of it in the future.

Dale Evans Rogers, in her little book, "Angel Unaware," tells of how she and her husband found Christ through an invalid child. They had yearned for a baby and eventually one was born to them. But from its birth, the child was a hopeless case. It did live for three years and in that time, by loving the child, caring for it patiently, and losing self for its sake, the parents were transformed. The experience had led them to Jesus Christ. And then the child died.

For some reason, God allowed such a hopeless little child to come into this world. Could it have been for the sake of the parents' salvation, or does that appear to make God cruel, heartless?

Let's look at these things honestly. We are rejecting too much of the truth simply because our finite minds cannot fathom it. Universal-

Christ Die?

oyd E. Hamilton,

ille, Ala.

spiritual unity that would sweep away national boundaries, and under the fatherhood of the one God, unite all men in one great kingdom of righteousness on earth, where all men would be brothers.

This great social vision of Jesus, they say, was too far advanced for His day, and the religious leaders in Jerusalem turned jealously upon Him, and eventually ended His career ignominiously on Calvary. Thus Jesus died gloriously fighting for a cause that will eventually triumph, the unity of mankind, under the banner of the fatherhood of God and the brotherhood of all mankind. He failed, say these men, but His cause will eventually be successful.

The only trouble with this view is that it *just is not so!* Jesus never taught the fatherhood of God and the brotherhood of man in the sense mentioned, and instead of being a failure, an unfortunate accident in the social struggles of mankind, Jesus accomplished *just what He came to earth to do!*

But what was it that the Son of God came to earth to do? There are those who tell us Christ came to earth to teach mankind how much God hates sin. Mankind was regarding sin as something unimportant, they say, as a mere idiosyncracy of his nature, as something that was somewhat unpleasant to others, but of no relative importance in the upward struggle of mankind from bestiality. God, therefore, say these folk, determined to give a spectacular illustration of what sin really was, something heinous and revolting, so He sent Christ to earth to teach men how much God hated sin, but loves the sinner, and then to die on the cross to drive home the lesson of God's hatred for sin.

Mankind is supposed to look upon the Saviour hanging on the cross, and to say, to himself, "if God hates sin *so* much, and loves me so much, I will turn away from sin" This is all well and good, for sin *is* heinous and revolting. God does hate sin. The cross does reveal both God's love for men and His hatred of sin. If mankind were simply in a weakened condition because of sin, and if he were open to persuasion, then possibly the spectacle of the cross might lead him to decide that it would be better not to sin, and so turn him to a good moral life. But, alas, that is not man's natural condition. Not only is he not merely weakened by sin, he is *dead* in sin. but far worse than that (if anything could be worse than being dead in sin), man has sinned against Almighty God and must suffer the penalty for his sin, for the wages of sin is death.

Even were he to be so impressed with the hatred of God for sin that he determined to stop sinning, that would not better his condition one bit, for he would still be under the sentence of death, the wages of sin. That penalty must be paid before there can be any talk of turning from sin.

Moreover the fact that he is dead in sin renders him incapable of turning from sin to God and a new moral life. Something must happen to bring his dead soul to life before he can turn to Christ and live a new life.

The Bible is very definite as to the purpose for which Christ died. When he instituted the Lord's Supper, he said, "This is my blood of the covenant, which is poured out for many unto the remission of sins." Matt. 26:28. He declared that "The Son of Man came not to be ministered unto, but to minister, and to give His life a ransom for many," Mark 10:45. On another occasion He declared, "I lay down My life for the sheep," John 10:15, and a moment later, "Therefore doth the Father love Me, because I lay down My life, that I may take it again," John 17,18.

It is true that Christ was a great teacher, but to recognize Him as a great teacher while at the same time rejecting Him as an atoning Saviour is an affront to His whole being. That was what Nicodemus tried to do, you will remember. He told Jesus, "We know that Thou art a teacher come from God," and Jesus immediately told him that he could not see the kingdom of God nor enter it unless he was born again. While a secondary purpose of Christ's coming was to teach men truth, Christ came to earth as Paul said, to redeem "us from the curse of the law, having become a curse for us," Gal. 3:13.

God sent Him forth "to be a propitiation, through faith, in His blood," Rom. 3:25. John tells us, "He is the propitiation for our sins," I John 2:2, while the author of the Epistle to the Hebrews tells us, "Now at the end of the ages hath He been manifested to put away sin by the sacrifice of Himself," Heb. 9:26.

The prophet Isaiah dealt with this with exceptional clarity, "He was wounded for our transgressions, He was bruised for our iniquities; the chastisement of our peace was upon Him; and with His stripes we are healed. All we like sheep have gone astray; we have turned every one to his own way; and Jehovah hath laid on Him the iniquity of us all. He was cut off out of the land of the living for the transgression of my people to whom the stroke was due. . . . When thou shalt make His soul an offering for sin. . . . He shall justify many; and He shall bear their iniquities. . . . He bore the sin of many, and made intercession for the transgressors." Isaiah 53:5-12.

When John the Baptist saw Him coming toward him after His baptism, as a prophet he said, "Behold the Lamb of God that taketh away the sin of the world," John 1:29. And Peter tells us, in addition to the eloquent words of our text, "We have been redeemed, not with corruptible things, with silver or gold . . . but with precious blood, as of a lamb without blemish and without spot, even the blood of Christ," I Peter 1:18-19.

All this means that Christ died as a sacrifice, in our place on the cross, and his death opened the way to God when the veil of the temple was rent from the top to the bottom, signifying that the way into the holy of holies was open to all. Christ has "made peace through the blood of His cross," Col. 1:20. His death, then, was not the death of a martyr for a great cause. He came, He said, "for this cause," that is, He came to make propitiation for the sins of His people. He came definitely for the purpose of dying on the cross for our sins.

A recent writer said that it was not the will of God that Christ should die on the cross, but Jesus Himself said that he came for that very purpose unto that hour when He would die in our place on Calvary. He had power to lay down His life and had power to take it up again, so His death was not an accident, an unfortunate incident in the history of the world. His death was the climax of the ages, the supreme purpose of eternity, the very focal point in all history, for it was the very point planned by God from all eternity when man would again be reconciled to God and brought back into union and fellowship with God through the Redeemer.

In the debtors' prisons of England a few centuries ago, there was no escape for those who were thrown into the prison, until someone came and paid the debt owed in full. The debtors could not be set free to earn the money to pay their own debts. The only way they could be set free was for someone else to pay the debt for them. No one but the eternal Son of God could pay our debt and set us free. *That* was why Christ died. God sends His Holy Spirit with power into our hearts to make us alive and enable us to believe in this atoning sacrifice of Christ. Have you put your faith in Christ alone for salvation?

which ponded up behind them wide, cold fresh water lakes. When the North Pole moved studdenly to Alaska, the level of the north Atlantic Ocean rose to an unknown height and floated the two glaciers and changed those basins and the ponded lakes into arms of the sea.

Dr. R. F. Flint of Yale University in a paper published this year, said that all the evidence indicates the marine invasion of the St. Lawrence River occurred about 7000 years ago. In the Eastern Hemisphere the latest known radiocarbon date for the antediluvian people is 7000 years ago (Caspian in Africa). The latest European date is slightly earlier.

The postdiluvian period then started 7000 years ago with a warm climate and high sea level in Europe and Near East. This is the time of Jarmo, and explains why the Jarmoites stayed up in the mountain valleys.

But by 5000 years later the whole situation had changed; America was hot but ice had come down to Stockholm and Helsinki. With a sinking sea level the Baltic was once more a lake. Mesopotamia had become a second Eden while cold winds swept through Jarmo. Even in Lower Egypt there was abundant rain.

One cannot be surprised to find that those Jarmoites had left, and that cities had sprung up in the lowlands. This is the time of Nimrod and the Tower of Babel (described in a later paper). But back in Europe on the fertile valleys of Egypt, there was not a human being to hunt the abundant game, nor plow the fertile valleys. This is the HIATUS. Archeologists search in vain for stone tools or ruins of villages. The FLOOD was not a myth, but a terrible fact.

When 1000 years of the 1500 had passed, things had changed once more, the pole was nearer America and warm climate with little rain but high sea level had routed the would-be builders of Babel and other cities. Ponded rivers left silt on the mounds left by these people. Some might imagine the people going back to Jarmo, the ancestral home; but that was impossible, for in the 1000 years the people had multiplied and had been divided into tribes with different languages. They scattered in every direction, and all archeologists attest to a mysterious diffusion of culture. Of course, it is not mysterious to us; but we believe there was a FLOOD while the archeologists do not. Some of the tribes traveled far, for a great heap of discarded shells on the Tagus River in Portugal must be dated at this time because of the signs of a contemporaneous high sea.

(We will take up the remainder of that 1500 *years in next issue.)*

Helps To Understanding Scripture Readings in *Day by Day*

By Rev. C. C. Baker

Sunday, November 4, *John* 10:11-18. Read 9:1-7,13-17,28-38 for the occasion that prompted today's passage. List the benefits mentioned in 10:9-15,27-29 that come to the believer because the Lord Jesus is his Shepherd. What has the Lord done for us as our Shepherd (vv.11,15) that other religious leaders have not done (vv.8, 12)? How is the picture of c.10 of Christ as the Good Shepherd in contrast to the picture of the religious leaders of c.9 (notice 9:22,34)? What motivates Christ to watch over His sheep (v.13)? How thoroughly do you think the Lord Jesus knows you (vv.14,27)? Does He know your name? your character? your problems? your dreams? How adequate is Christ's Shepherd care against the forces of evil (vv.28-29)? How does Jesus' healing of the blind man illustrate His Loving Shepherd's care for His own? Is Christ your Shepherd this real to you (9:25b; 10:14,27)?

Monday, November 5, *Deuteronomy* 26:1-11. When the people of Israel came into the Promised Land they were to bring an offering to the Lord (vv.1-4). What facts were they to recite about God's past dealings with them when they brought this offering (vv.5-9)? What part of the harvest were they to bring (vv.2a,10a)? How might the Israelites' offering of the first portion of their material goods have revealed the attitude of their hearts toward God? God has worked a mightier deliverance for the Christian than He did for the Israelite, rescuing the Christian from his sins through the cross and giving him a new life in Christ. What attitude toward God do your offerings reveal?

Tuesday, November 6, *Genesis* 4:1-15. God accepted Abel's sacrifice rather than Cain's (vv.3-5) because of the heart attitude of each. What part of his possessions did Abel bring to the Lord (v.4)? What sin did Cain commit when the Lord did not accept his offering (v.5)? What warning did God give Cain (v.7)? Observe in v.8 that Cain's murder of his brother was premeditated. What attitude toward God did Cain display in v.9 when questioned about his brother? From what you see of Cain in vv.5-9 what attitude toward God must he have had when he brought his offering to God in v.3? Do you present your tithes and offerings in a manner acceptable to the Lord?

Wednesday, November 7, *I John* 1:4-10. What truth about God does John present in v.5? This truth of v.5 underlies the statements of vv.6-10. What does v.6 say about the person who professes to be religious but who lacks the reality of God in his life? According to v.7 what is necessary in order to have fellowship with God? Suppose sin blocks that fellowship (v.9)? What do we do to our relation to God if we deny that sin is in our lives (v.10)? What do we do to ourselves (v.8)? What does an unclouded relation with God do for our relation with fellow-Christians (v.7)? Is there conscious sin in your life that keeps you from close fellowship with God? with others?

Thursday, November 8, *Romans* 12:1-21. Think of two or three words that summarize the qualities Paul seeks in each aspect of the lives of these Christians. What words would be appropriate for their relation with God (vv. 1-2,11)? their relations with each other (vv.3, 9-10,13-20)? their relation to the Church (vv. 4-8)? for their own minds and hearts (vv.2,9, 11-12)? Why does Paul mention their relation with God first (vv.1-2)? Which of the above four relationships is basic to the others? What is the connection between a person's relationship with God and the presence of Christian qualities in his soul (vv.1-2)? What is the relation between a person's social conduct and what is in his heart? Is your daily conduct the fruit of a good relationship with God?

Friday, November 9, *Psalm* 103:15-22. Observe how all-powerful is the Lord (vv.19-22). He created the universe (v.22). He rules over His creation (v.19). His creatures obey Him (vv. 20-21). Yet see how concerned He is for the individual sinner (vv.8-14). In vv.8-14 notice especially the depth of God's patience and graciousness. How does the picture of the heavenly Father (vv.13-14) contrast to the picture of the all-powerful God (vv.19-22)? How do the dimensions of God's forgiveness (vv.11-12) compare to the dimensions of His creation (v.22)? God's Kingdom rules over all (v.19); yet observe the extent of His grace (vv.8-10). Remember that vv.8-14 apply to the *repentant* sinner (vv. 15-17). In the light of vv.8-14, do you come boldly to your Creator asking forgiveness of sin?

Saturday, November 10, *I John* 4:7-12. Make a list of everything that is said about God in this passage. What definition of God do you find in v.8? How has God demonstrated His love for us (vv.9-10)? Is it possible to see God (v.12)? Is it possible to know Him (vv.7-8)? Is it possible for Him to dwell in our hearts (vv.7,12)? Does v.9 indicate that God desires fellowship with us? Does man, without Christ, desire fellowship with God (v.10)? Have you realized how deeply God longs for your fellowship? He sent His Son to die for your sins. To what depths, then, should you love your fellow-Christians (v.11)?

ANGLERS

By WADE C. SMITH

Lesson No. 162

More of the By-Products of Personal Evangelism

Say what you will there is something stimulating about a "Revival." There is an atmosphere of expectancy in the revival meeting which is not found in the average church service. People may attend revivals simply out of idle curiosity, but it is with the thought that they may get some kind of a thrill. We do not want to encourage sensationalism and certainly not for producing thrills; but are we not overcareful to preserve the orderly uneventful routine in our church services? In a letter to the writer from a layman, commenting on the monotonous sameness of the average church service, he says: "It seems to me that here rests a great responsibility on the ministers. So many of them are not evangelistic and rarely give the gospel invitation. I do not intend it as unkindly criticism of my own pastor, but in all the years he has been pastor here I have never heard him give the invitation, and I do not think he is an exception. I sometimes wonder how a minister can preach year in and year out and never 'draw the net' or seek to get definite decisions from his hearers. It is like a salesman going out and talking his goods and showing them, but never trying to get any buyer to sign on the dotted line. Another thing that discourages personal evangelism is that our services are so formal. It seems to me there should be more opportunity given for questions and expressions, and for testimonies. I remember Dr. Broughton once telling of an experience he had in a church he served. A young woman, member of his choir, had gone astray and had been obliged to leave the church. A few months later she entered during the 11 o'clock service, taking a back seat. When the invitation was given she came forward and broke down in bitter weeping before the whole congregation and was received back. The congregation was shocked, but Dr. Broughton said it was one of the most helpful incidents that had ever happened in the church, closing his story with the remark that *it was such an unusual thing to see a person saved in the* 11 *o'clock service!*

It may not be practicable to throw the morning service open "for expressions and testimonies" but this layman is certainly justified in his insistence on less formality and more soul-saving effort in the regular church services. One of the by-products of an every member soul-winning program in a church would be the quickening of life in the church services, the quickening of interest, and the lifting of the whole enterprise to a level of *practical religion.*

(One more lesson on the By-Products of Personal Evangelism; and "School is out!")

SABBATH SCHOOL LESSONS — REV. J. KENTON PARKER

LESSON FOR NOVEMBER 4

The Suffering Servant

Background Scripture: Isaiah 52:13 - 53:12; Matthew 1:18-21
Devotional Reading: I Peter 3:14-22

The Suffering Servant is Christ: "For Christ hath once suffered for sins, the just for the unjust, that he might bring us to God, being put to death in the flesh, but quickened by the Spirit . . . Who is gone into heaven, and is on the right hand of God; angels and authorities and powers being made subject unto him." So Peter tells us in our Devotional Reading. In Philippians 2:5-11 Paul says, "And let this mind be in you which was also in Christ Jesus: Who, being in the form of God, thought it not robbery to be equal with God, But made himself of no reputation (emptied himself), and took upon him the form of a servant, and was made in the likeness of men: And being found in fashion as a man, he humbled himself, and became obedient unto death, even the death of the cross. Wherefore God also hath highly exalted him, and given him a name which is above every name: That at the name of Jesus every knee should bow, of things in heaven, and things in earth, and things under the earth: and every tongue should confess that Jesus Christ is Lord, to the glory of God the Father."

In Matthew 1:1-21, which is part of our Background Scripture, we have the very simple and clear account of the Virgin Birth of our Lord. Luke, the physician, goes into more detail. In many other places, especially John's Gospel, chapter 1:1-5,14, and Hebrews, chapters one and two, we have further explanation of this most vital and glorious truth. It is summarized thus in our Shorter Catechism: "Christ, the Son of God, became man, by taking to himself a true body and a reasonable soul, being conceived by the power of the Holy Ghost, in the womb of the Virgin Mary, and born of her, yet without sin." Our Catechism also speaks of "Christ's Humiliation," and "Christ's Exaltation," both of which are very prominent in today's Scripture. I wish to treat the lesson under these three words: Humiliation; Substitution; Exaltation. These three thoughts are interwoven in this beautiful prophecy.

I. *Humiliation:* 52:14; 53:1-3; 7,8,9,10.

In these verses we have many expressions describing the humiliation of our Saviour. None of us can, I am sure, fully understand the degree and extent of the agony of the Suffering Servant. The best we can do is to look at some of these words and try to realize what it meant to Him, the Son of God, to go through all He endured. Suppose we take the Catechism as a guide in trying to see just what this humiliation meant to Him.

The first step in that humiliation is His "being born": the Incarnation, the Word becoming flesh, is an amazing thing. One of our professors in the Seminary used to put it this way: If one of the tremendous stars in the sky should suddenly become a speck of dust flying in the air, it would be nothing compared to Christ, the Son of God, leaving all the glory which He had with His Father, and being born of a Virgin here on earth.

He was born "in a low condition"; not in a palace as befitted a King, but in a stable; not as the son of some rich person, but the son of an ordinary Jewish maiden. He was laid in a manger, and the first visitors He had were the lowly shepherds from the hills around Bethlehem. The wise men came later to bring their gifts and worship the newborn King. He had to be taken hastily and carried into Egypt to escape the cruel edict of King Herod.

He was "made under the law." He was reared as a Jewish child and was subject to the law of Moses. In His circumcision, His presentation at the temple, His baptism in the river Jordan, and in all the ordinances of the Law He subjected Himself to the Law. When John the Baptist objected to baptising Him, Jesus said, Suffer it to be so now, for so it becometh us to fulfill all righteousness.

He had His share, and more, of "all the miseries of this life." He had to work as a Carpenter. When He started out on His public ministry of preaching, teaching, and healing, He was supported by those who followed and loved Him. "He came unto his own, and His own received him not," says John. He had his year of popularity when the multitudes flocked to hear Him and be healed and fed, and at one time, they wished to take Him by force and make Him a King. The bitter opposition of the leaders of the Jews increased. He was criticized, called every bad name they could think of, and plotted against by those who should have received Him gladly.

He was betrayed with a kiss by one of His own disciples, Judas Iscariot, and after a mock trial was shamefully treated and sent to Pilate, the Roman governor who, although convinced of His innocence, gave way to the demands of the Jews to crucify Him, and He was led to Calvary where they crucified Him. Then He was buried and continued under the power of death for a season. In this way our Catechism gives the different steps in His Humiliation.

Now, let us look at some of the terms used by Isaiah in telling about the Suffering Servant: "His visage was more marred than any man, and his form more than the sons of men." Think of how He was beaten and crowned with thorns and spit upon by the inhuman mob. "He was despised and rejected of men." The religious leaders of His nation rejected and despised Him. "A Man of Sorrows." This is a most appropriate name for Him. Jeremiah was called "The Weeping Prophet"; Jesus might be called "The Weeping Saviour." The shortest verse in the Bible is one of the sweetest: "Jesus wept."

As we see Him at the grave of Lazarus, weeping over the city of Jerusalem, or in the Garden, where with strong crying and tears, He prayed His prayer, we can begin to realize how appropriate this name was. He was stricken, wounded, bruised, chastised, oppressed, afflicted, led as a lamb to the slaughter, and His soul travailed in agony. No one else stooped as low as Jesus did. This Amazing Humiliation is truly a symbol of Amazing Grace, which has been the subject of our greatest hymns.

II. *Substitution:* Verses 4-6,8,10,11.

No thinking man can read Isaiah 53, and the accounts of the crucifixion as given in the Gospels, and not ask the question, WHY? Why did Jesus die? Why this death so different from every other death? Paul answers that question when he says, Christ died for our sins, died for us, died for the ungodly, was made sin for us, and in many other verses. Let us look at the uniqueness of His death. Death is the result of sin, Death hath passed upon all men, for that all have sinned. But Jesus had not sinned; In Him was no sin. Here we have the death of the only innocent man since the Fall of man. We can easily understand why other people die. God said to our first parents, Ye shall not eat of it . . . lest ye die. Men died spiritually when Eve and Adam ate of the forbidden fruit, and their bodies began to die. In the second place, the death of Jesus was a Voluntary death: "I have power to lay it down, and I have power to take it again." "No man taketh it from me." All the power of the Jewish leaders and of the Roman Empire would have been as nought if He had not chosen to die. Again, the death of Jesus was a Lonely death. He was surrounded by a mob, it is true, and His mother and John and some others were nearby, but the cry which came from His lips, My God, My God, Why hast thou forsaken me, was the cry of a lonely soul. He was being "made sin" for us, and even His Father turned His face for a moment. It was not the mere physical pain; He died of a broken heart; He poured out His soul unto death. It was indeed the painful and shameful death of the cross.

The question, Why, is answered by Isaiah, the Evangelical prophet. "Surely he hath borne our griefs and carried our sorrows." Sin had filled the world with sorrow; every heartbreak and every tear was caused by somebody's sin. He came to take away sin and wipe away tears. "He was wounded for our transgressions," "bruised for our iniquities; the chastisement of our peace was upon Him, and by His stripes we are healed."

This account in Isaiah prepares us for what Jesus said, This is my body, broken for you; this is the blood of the new covenant, shed for the remission of sins. It prepares us also for the logical answers of the apostle Paul in Romans 5, and in I Corinthians 15. We do not have a "theory of the Atonement"; we have the simple and sublime statement that Christ died for us; He was our Substitute : He bore our sins in His own body on the tree.

III. *Exaltation:* Isaiah 52:13; 53:11-12.

I wish to turn again to our Shorter Catechism. Question 28 reads, Wherein consisteth Christ's exaltation? And the answer is, Christ's exaltation consisteth in his rising again from the dead on the third day, in ascending up into heaven, in sitting at the right hand of God the Father, and in coming to judge the world at the last day. In this definition we have many Scripture passages combined. One of these is in Philippians 2:9, "Wherefore God hath highly exalted him and given him a name that is above every name, that at the name of Jesus every knee should bow," etc. Jesus spoke of it when He said in answer to the question, Art thou the Christ? "I am: and ye shall see the Son of Man sitting at the right hand of power, and coming in the clouds of heaven." Here, at the lowest point in His Humiliation, we find Him proclaiming His Exaltation.

Isaiah pictures it in the passage we are studying. He begins with this thought of exaltation, and ends with it. He shall be exalted and extolled and be very high. He shall see of the travail of his soul and be satisfied. In the book of Revelation we see the consummation of this exaltation and hear the many beautiful "Doxologies" which are sung to His praise.

YOUNG PEOPLE'S DEPARTMENT — REV. B. HOYT EVANS

YOUTH PROGRAM FOR NOVEMBER 4

"*Where The Church's Dollars Go*"

Suggested Devotional Outline:

Hymn: "He Leadeth Me"
Prayer
Scripture: Matthew 6:1-4, 19-21
Hymn: "A Charge To Keep I Have"
Offering
Hymn: "More Love To Thee, O Christ"

Suggested Procedure:

(Invite two qualified adults to come to your meeting to discuss the subject "Where The Church's Dollars Go." One should speak of the budget, how it is made, how pledges and money are secured, and what are the expenses of operating the local church program. An appropriate person for this task would be the church treasurer or one of the deacons. The other person should speak about the total benevolent program of the church. If your church has a separate treasurer for benevolent funds, he would be ideal for this assignment. One of the deacons, one of the elders, the treasurer of the Women of the Church, or the minister would also be likely prospects. Whoever you secure, ask them to consider the points suggested below in their discussion of the subject.)

Leader's Introduction:

On one occasion Jesus said "Where your treasure is, there will your heart be also." Matthew 6:21. This means that our true devotion and our money go together. If we are really concerned about a thing, we will give our money to it, and if we give our money generously, it is strong evidence of genuine concern. According to this idea, we can make an accurate measure of our interest in Christ and His church by the gifts that we make.

There is another factor that strongly influences both our interest and our gifts, and that thing is knowledge. There was a church member who had always given to the church, but whose gifts were small in proportion to his ability. One day he decided to make a small contribution to one of the institutions of his church, and he sent the gift to the denominational treasurer. In a few days he received a receipt. The receipt astounded him. On this small slip of paper were listed all the agencies and activities of the church with a space after each one to acknowledge a gift to that particular cause. The thing that amazed the man was the large number of services his church was rendering of which he was totally unaware. He was appalled at his own ignorance. From that time onward his offerings to the church were greatly increased. Because he had not known what the Church was doing, he was not very interested or impressed, and because he was not interested, he had not given generously of his means.

We have invited some of the leaders of our church to our meeting to inform us about the activities, services, and needs of our church . . . to tell us "Where The Church's Dollars Go."

Suggestions for First Speaker:
Explain how the budget of the church is made up. Tell the young people how pledges are secured and how the money is received. Explain to them how the money is used in the local program of the church for salaries, various supplies, services (heat, lights, etc.), upkeep on buildings and equipment, provision for new building, and special benevolent projects such as scholarship funds and the support of a particular missionary or mission project. Show the young people what they can do to be of greatest help in the support of the Lord's work in the church.

Suggestions for Second Speaker:
You are expected to describe the benevolent program of the church. Begin with the activities of your presbytery (home missions, education programs, camps, homes, schools, etc.) Next is synod with its home mission program, schools, colleges, homes. Last of all is the General Assembly with its boards, agencies, and institutions. Be sure to indicate the various activities of the Assembly's agencies such as the many divisions and departments of the Board of Church Extension. It will be most helpful and inspiring to the young people to learn how thorough-going is the program of their church. The better they are acquainted with the service the church renders, the more they will appreciate its worthiness of their material support.

Women's Work

From Strength to Strength

Not merely in the words you say,
  Not only in your deeds confessed,
But in the most unconscious way
  Is Christ expressed.

And from your eyes He beckons me,
  And from your heart His love is shed,
Till I lose sight of you—and see
  The Christ instead.

—Author Unknown

Young People Won't Behave When Elders Set Bad Example

The time has come for a national awakening to the seriousness of the danger. Too often juvenile crime is regarded as something minor. A 15-year-old bank robber, a 12-year-old burglar—these are hard for many Americans to believe. Yet day after day these youngsters are wreaking great damage to society.

Of over 1,000,000 arrests reported by 232 cities over 25,000 in population last year, 7.8 per cent were of persons who had not yet reached their 18th birthday. Moreover this group accounted for 19.4 per cent of all arrests for robbery, 36.9 for larceny, 47.8 for burglary and 52.6 for auto theft.

This is indeed a story of misery, unhappiness and corrupted lives.

Juvenile delinquency is a reflection of the moral tone of the nation. Young people can't be expected to behave if their elders don't. A society which produces a high incidence of divorces, broken homes, illegitimate births and adult crime creates juvenile misbehavior. Remedial action can only come from a renewal of civic responsibility. This responsibility must start in the home. There is no alternative.

Time after time, in studying juvenile offenders, I have noted the utter lack of interest of some parents in their youngsters. They have been too busy, too concerned with other activities, or simply didn't care. The children were deprived of that love, loyalty and companionship which can only come from a father and mother. All too often they were forced to seek values in life outside the home and drifted into crime.

The home must be returned to its rightful place as the center of family life. Far too many American homes have become substitute hotels,

cellent results were obtained in at least 91 per cent of the cases, he said, with some securing dramatic relief from nervous tension, pain or mental agitation within a few minutes. One woman who was frightened badly whenever her husband drove from 55 to 60 miles an hour, lost her apprehension after a few days treatment. Another one returned for more vitamin injections because her husband said she was "easier to get along with," after she had received them. And, above all, the treatment was found to be an important method of improving family harmony and thus reducing juvenile delinquency.

It is interesting to compare this medical finding with an important parallel the Christian has long found to be true in his everyday life: our spiritual efficiency and growth depend upon daily nutrition. When we take time to read and meditate daily upon a portion of God's Word, our whole life seems to run along more smoothly and we are enabled to take a stronger stand for what we believe.

The apostle admonishes us to take our vitamins in I Peter 2:2 and 3: "Desire the sincere milk of the word, that ye may grow thereby: if so be ye have tasted that the Lord is gracious."

Have you had your spiritual vitamins today?

Church News

RESOLUTIONS ADOPTED BY THE MONTREAT COTTAGE OWNERS ASSOCIATION IN THEIR REGULAR MEETING JULY 26, 1956

Many of us who love Montreat have seen its growth and development for many years. This has been largely because some few have devoted themselves to its service. To all who contributed in any way to make Montreat what it now is in its beauty, its convenience and usefulness and delight to those of us who may live but for a week or a year, we are greatly indebted. Dr. R. C. Anderson who builded so well was able to get the support of a few that enabled him to render a fine service. We recorded our gratitude to him and Mrs. Anderson while he was living and directing the development of Montreat, and we shall continue to be grateful for what they have done.

During the past nine and one-half years Montreat has continued to develop in a remarkable way under the leadership of Dr. J. Rupert McGregor.

Let us review a few of the things that have been accomplished.

A comfortable annex has been constructed for our Negro employees. Howerton Hall, with its cafeteria, after remaining unfinished for two years, has been completed and approximately a half million dollars paid on its construction. It will be completely paid for by appropriations made by the General Assembly.

The Assembly Inn kitchen has been modernized at a cost of $32,000.00, and other repairs and improvements have been made that mean better service to the thousands that come.

A water reservoir has been built and adequate water supply made available for the future growth of Montreat. Electric power equipment has been provided, so that any who wish it may have full use of electric equipment.

Think of the thirteen streets that have been hard surfaced, which makes such a great difference to all of us. New areas have been opened and new homes are being built. There have been built here in these years 61 new homes and 76 homes have been purchased, most of which have been remodeled and made more attractive.

The young people's and children's program—a joy and pride to all of us—has outgrown all of its equipment. The number in these programs has increased from a little more than 500 to probably 2,000 this summer.

The new social recreation hall is something that we have wanted for years. Some of us recall that we appointed a strong committee after World War II to erect a memorial building for the young of Montreat Clubs who had given their lives for us. This effort raised less than $1,200.00. Now we are seeing the completion of a $175,000.00 building for the use of our children, our grandchildren and the thousands of others who will come to Montreat for generations. Dr. McGregor will find gifts so that it may be finished. How many of us have helped on it?

We have also watched interest in our Conference Program increase as the Boards of our Church are encouraged and helped in making the summer mean more to our whole Church. In 1955 the Association spent on the summer's program $29,950.00.

In 1955 the Mountain Retreat Association received in gifts $125,376.96. Perhaps the most significant thing Dr. McGregor has done for Montreat, as related to its finances, is that the Church has been led to accept a responsibility for its maintenance and development.

Montreat College in 1955 received in gifts for current operations $88,988.50. The assets of the College at the end of the year were $741,376.76. In this year of 1956—up until now—gifts to the College have been made which amount to more than $500,000.00.

NOW THEREFORE

We do not believe that Dr. McGregor should relinquish his services to Montreat. That which has been done indicates that he has yet greater things to lead in getting done for our Assembly Grounds, our Church Home.

Therefore we earnestly petition the Trustees and Board of Directors of the Mountain Retreat Association that both by re-election and insistence they urge Dr. McGregor to continue to serve as president longer than it is rumored here that he plans to.

That we express our gratitude to Dr. McGregor for all these accomplishments,

AND to Mrs. McGregor for the beautiful manner in which she has equally served.

Dr. Kim Hyun Mo, who holds a doctorate from Austin College, and Mr. Kim Qui Dong, who has his master's degree from Columbia Seminary, came to the United States to act as secretaries to Dr. Crane while he finished his literary work in Gulfport. This has been a crowning experience in the life of this missionary. The volume, now in its second edition is used by several denominations.

The first volume of the text on Theology sold out practically in six months. The text sold 3,400 to 5,000 volumes in two years to students of all Protestant seminaries in Korea. Dr. Crane hopes to complete the English edition in Gulfport, Miss., where he and Mrs. Crane will make their home when they arrive in the States.

Dr. Crane has done much translation work with other writings. He held membership on the Committee for revision of the Korean edition of the New Testament, a work that was accomplished in 1936-37. He has translated a number of Korean textbooks and is the author of "The Sacerdotal Prayer of Our Lord," published in 1940.

Dr. and Mrs. Crane went to Korea in 1913 and served stations at Soonchun and Pyeng Yang. He was at the seminary at Pyeng Yang from 1937-41, returning there in 1954 to take the chair of theology and to introduce his book on theology. The seminary was closed by the Communists but missionaries were squeezed out in 1939 by the Japanese.

Mrs. Crane, formerly Miss Florence Hedleston of Oxford, Miss., is widely known as an artist and author, with flowers and the folklore of Korea being her favorite subjects.

Dr. Crane is a native of Yazoo City, Miss. He studied at the University of Mississippi, received the B. A. degree from Colorado College, Colorado Springs, Colorado, and the B. D. degree from Union Theological Seminary in Richmond, Va. For a time he was professor at Chamberlain Hunt Academy, Port Gibson, Miss. He was ordained by Central Mississippi Presbytery in 1913. For a number of years in Korea Dr. Crane was principal at Watts Academy.

From 1942-46 he served as stated supply minister at Pascagoula, Miss.

The Cranes have four children: Dr. Paul Crane, missionary doctor to Korea and head of Chunju Hospital; Mrs. Thompson B. Southall, wife of the Rev. Mr. Southall of Statesville, N. C., former missionaries to Korea; and Mrs. William Hefelfinger, wife of a St. Louis, Mo., engineer.

TEXAS

The First Presbyterian Church of Freeport, Texas, has just completed a $116,000.00 sanctuary, equipped with cushioned pews, acoustical aids including a public address system and ear phones, and air conditioning in the sanctuary and throughout the building. Most of the cost has been raised in cash during the past three years.

The service formally opening and consecrating the sanctuary was held at 4:00 p. m. on Sunday, October 7, 1956. Rev. David M. Currie, pastor of the First Presbyterian Church of Texas City and former pastor of this Church, brought the message. He was assisted in the service by Rev. P. P. Dawson of Angleton, Rev. S. G. Stewart of Lake Jackson, Rev. C. M. Boyd of Brazoria, Rev. J. H. Freeland of the Gulf Prairie Church of Freeport, and Chaplain L. E. Gilbert of the Texas Prison System.

Rev. Lawrence M. Malloy is pastor.

THE SOUTHERN PRESBYTERIAN JOURNAL

A Presbyterian weekly magazine devoted to the statement, defense and propagation of the Gospel, the faith which was once for all delivered unto the saints.

VOL. XV NO. 27 OCTOBER 31, 1956 $2.50 A YEAR

DEGRADING RELIGION, YOU DEGRADE ALL

When theology occupies the professor's chair in the midst of Christian flocks, its relations with them, constantly keeping before its eyes the realities of the Christian life, constantly recall to it also the realities of science: man's misery, the counsels of the Father, the Redeemer's cross, the consolations of the Holy Ghost, holiness, eternity . . . theology renders in its turn, to Christian flocks, services with which they cannot long dispense without damage.

But on the contrary, when theology and the people have become indifferent to each other, and drowsy flocks have lived only for this world, then theology herself has given evident proofs of sloth, frivolty, ignorance, or perhaps of a love of novelties; seeking a profane popularity at any cost; affecting to have made discoveries that are only whispered to the ear, that are taught in academies, and never mentioned in the churches; keeping her gates shut amid the people, and at the same time throwing out to them from the windows doubts and impieties, with the view of ascertaining the present measure of their indifference; until at last she breaks out into open scandals, in attacking doctrines, or in denying the integrity or the inspiration of certain books, or in giving audacious denials to the facts which they relate.

—The Inspiration of the Holy Scriptures
By L. Gaussen.

THE SOUTHERN PRESBYTERIAN JOURNAL

Rev. Henry B. Dendy, D.D., Editor........Weaverville, N. C.
Dr. L. Nelson Bell, Associate Editor........Asheville, N. C.
Rev. Wade C. Smith, Associate Editor........Weaverville, N. C.

EDITORIAL

All Three Must Go Together

The unregenerate human heart has three desperate needs; to be emptied; to be cleansed; to be filled.

But owing to the imperfections in the best Christians, and the constant warfare in which we all find ourselves engaged, we all have the same lack in some measure.

There is the need to be emptied of self because self is ever-present and demanding. The "old man" with his deeds, about which Paul writes, is a lively ghost ever present.

But to be emptied is not enough. A cleansing is necessary and this is through a supernatural agency available in Christ alone. Strange and mysterious as it is, that agency is the blood of Christ, accepted by faith in His atoning work.

The third necessity is an infilling with a supernatural Person — the Holy Spirit. We Christians have the witness in our spirits that we are Christ's and that He is ours but so often we deliberately push the Holy Spirit over to one side to make room for the flesh and the works of evil.

In this marvelous work which God is willing to do for us the place played by His sovereign grace is of paramount importance. But for this grace none of us is ever saved. But there is obviously an operation of the human will, either for or against God's loving mercy, which must be brought into the picture. Man is not an automaton, a puppet; God has endued him with the power of decision, the right to make for himself a choice.

It is not wise to place God's part and man's part in separate compartments and say they are incompatible. Are not we looking at two aspects of the same work of grace? Some have let predestination become a stumbling block and in so doing have failed to take into account God's omnipotence as well as His omniscience. Or, confusion is caused by failing to realize that our power to accept or reject is but a part of God's grace manifested in His foreknowledge and power.

In any case we all need a work in our hearts which God alone can do and for which He has made full provision.

If our hearts are emptied of self and the sin which so easily besets us; if they are purified by the One Who makes all things new; if they are filled with the Spirit of the Living Christ, then there are certain inescapable corrolaries:

Where now we are weak we will become strong. Where there is now no real power in prayer the very opposite will be the case. Where we bungle, despite good intentions, we will be given the wisdom which comes from the God of all true wisdom. Finally, when the Holy Spirit takes up residence in our hearts we begin to look at this world, its people and its tasks with true spiritual perception. Instead of the near-sightedness of earth-bound perspective we find that clear 20/20 vision which sees the seeable in the light of eternity.

Yes, our hearts need these three things and they are ours for the asking and the receiving. Sinless perfection? Nonsense. For the first time we will truly recognize our own sinfulness and hate our sins for we will see ourselves with something of the viewpoint of His holiness. And, we will know and love the One Who has freed us from the guilt and penalty of sin as we have never loved Him before.

Emptied; cleansed; filled! ! !

A simple prayer could be: "Lord, You will have to do *all* of this for me, *but I am willing.*"

L.N.B.

Two Steps in Solving Juvenile Delinquency

The increasing incidence of juvenile delinquency shows it to be a social problem of the greatest significance and importance.

That the primary cause rests with parents seems too evident to cause argument. Adult delinquency does not necessarily show itself in the same way as in children but pagans living with the veneer of Christian culture while denying the validity and personal responsibilities of commitment to Christ have no right to expect higher principles in the children which they beget.

Some pagan cultures have higher and more effective philosophies of life than is to be found where Christianity is a word but not a faith. Shall we be forced to turn to the older Chinese culture which has produced a measure of filial piety and social responsibility which seems lacking in America today?

In America we are seeing directly fulfilled the fruitage of cultured paganism on the one hand and a form of godliness on the other which denies the dynamic of redemption itself.

There are two drastic steps which need to be taken immediately. If they require special laws then those laws should be passed.

a. Parents should be held responsible for all property damage caused by their children, either through acts of vandalism or wilful carelessness.

b. Juveniles guilty of vandalism and hoodlumism should be publicly thrashed, not with brutality but with authority.

These two things could go far to correct the present situation. When parents have to pay for property losses caused by their children there may be a more sober evaluation of things at home. When juveniles find themselves on the receiving end of corporal punishment it takes all the glamour and dare out of acting like hoodlums.

Of course the basic solution is one of Christ in individual hearts, not only for the transformation of human lives, but also for Christians to join in every legitimate effort to remove the *contributing* causes of delinquency.

But, along with the law of the love of Christ there is needed also the stern restraints of the law of the land which are exercised without fear or favor.

These two steps will not cure our problem but they would lessen it. L.N.B.

A Basket of Fruit

The Fruit of the Spirit (Galatians 5:22,23)

The Fruit of the Spirit is . . .
Longsuffering (Patience)

Christian, in the House of the Interpreter, saw many strange things. One of the most interesting was a room in which there were two children; one was calm and happy, the other was bitterly crying. Name of the one was Patience, and the other, Passion. Passion wanted everything NOW; Patience was willing to WAIT. Bunyan, as usual, has caught one of the great truths of the Bible. Many of the heartaches, and troubles, and tragedies of the world have been caused through lack of patience.

I. *Our God is a Longsuffering God, the God of Patience.*

1. He was patient with a wicked world before the Flood and waited for one hundred and twenty years before Judgment fell, while Noah built the ark and preached to the people.

2. God was very patient with Israel during their Wilderness wandering, in the time of the Judges, and all through their history, sending prophet after prophet after prophet to plead with them to return to Him.

3. How patient Jesus was with the disciples! They were so "slow of heart to believe," so full of faults and weaknesses.

4. God was very patient with individual men; with Jacob; with Peter.

5. Jesus wept over Jerusalem while He cried, How often would I — ye would not. God has been waiting for nearly 2,000 years for our world to repent.

II. *We Have Need of Patience.*

1. We need it in our lives; it is a necessary part of character. We need the patience to wait; wait to understand; wait for God to carry out His purposes; wait for our prayers to be answered. There are many promises to those who "wait on the Lord"; They shall mount up . . . run . . . walk.

We need patience to "run the race set before us," to persevere, to endure to the end, to face the trials of life. This was the "patience of Job."

The Southern Presbyterian Journal, *a Presbyterian Weekly magazine devoted to the statement, defense, and propagation of the Gospel, the faith which was once for all delivered unto the saints,* published every Wednesday by The Southern Presbyterian Journal, Inc., in Weaverville, N. C.

Entered as second-class matter May 15, 1942, at the Postoffice at Weaverville, N. C., under the Act of March 3, 1879. Vol. XV, No. 27, October 31, 1956. Editorial and Business Offices: Weaverville, N. C. Printed in the U.S.A. by Biltmore Press, Asheville, N. C.

ADDRESS CHANGE: When changing address, please let us have both old and new address as far in advance as possible. Allow three weeks after change if not sent in advance. When possible, send an address label giving your old address.

2. We need patience in our homes. Its lack has ruined many a happy home.

3. We need patience in dealing with neighbors and friends.

4. We need patience in the Church; forbearing one another in love.

5. We need patience in dealing with the problems that confront us in the United States. A little patience would have saved us from the terrible "war between the States." We have a great problem now which will call for patience of the highest and best sort, if we are to be saved from dreadful consequences.

6. We need patience in dealing with the other nations of the world. A hasty, false move will start another World War.

We realize the NEED. How can it be met?

III. *Patience is a Fruit of the Spirit.*

It is a BIG Grace, a combination of many graces:

It takes Faith to be patient; we must Trust in the Lord.

It takes Courage to be patient; courage to face ridicule and evil talk.

It takes Humility to be patient; we realize that we do not "know it all."

It takes Understanding, and Sympathy, and LOVE.

May the Holy Spirit make this fruit abound in our lives!

— LETTERS —

Women Elders

Mr. Editor:

I attended the Fall meeting of our Presbytery where they had this question up for reply to the General Assembly. There was quite a spirited debate and it was very interesting for a while. However, the monotony was relieved by an explosion of laughter when an elder from one of the country churches arose and solemnly addressed the Moderator, as well as I can recall, as follows:

"Mr. Moderator: I represent a little church of 37 members. It used to be a U.S.A. church, but afterwards came into the Southern Assembly. In the U.S.A. days we had a woman elder. She was a fine lady, a good Bible scholar and a most proficient teacher of the Adult class — men and women. She was highly esteemed in the community and I have no word except praise for her as a Christian woman; BUT, Mr. Moderator, WE DON'T WANT ANY MORE WOMEN ELDERS ! ! ! "

That was all. He sat down. The question was called for, and the vote was 29 to 14 AGAINST.

Helps To Understanding Scripture Readings in *Day by Day*

By Rev. C. C. Baker

Sunday, November 11, *Genesis* 2:7. Read 1:26-2:24 and observe God's provisions for man's needs. What special relation did God give man to Himself (1:26)? What was the nature of the environment in which God placed man (2:9)? In the tree of life (v.9) the very presence and life of God was with man. Read Revelation 21:1-4 for something of what God's actual presence must have meant. How did God care for man's physical needs (1:29;2:9, 16)? his social needs (2:18-24)? What purpose in life did God give man (1:27;2:15)? In the Garden of Eden man had every opportunity to develop a rich and wonderful life under the joyous care and fellowship of his Maker. Notice, therefore, the utter folly of sin (2:16,17;3:16-24). Are you aware of the terrible power of sin to destroy all that is good and worthwhile in your life?

Monday, November 12, *Psalm* 130. The Psalmist is deeply aware of sin he has committed (v.3) and cries to the Lord in his distress (v.1). Notice the two declarations of v.5. Trusting in what God says in His Word (v.5b), the Psalmist knows that God will forgive him (v.4; Exodus 34:6-7). The Psalmist also waits anxiously in the presence of the Lord until God cleanses his soul from the stains of sin (vv.5a,6). After confessing your sin, learn to wait upon God in prayer until the Holy Spirit heals the wounds left by sin. Out of his own experience the Psalmist encourages others to find mercy in the Lord (vv.7-8). Does your experience witness to the forgiving and cleansing power of God?

Tuesday, November 13, *Psalm* 30. The Psalmist entertained a spirit of self-sufficiency (v.6) and as a result God withdrew His presence from him (v.7b) and he fell away from God (vv.3,9). Notice, however, the contrite spirit of the Psalmist that followed (vv.2,10). When humbled and aware of his need for the Lord, God quickly answered the Psalmist's pleas and helped him (vv.2-3,11). Observe the happiness of the Psalmist (vv.1,4-5,11-12) and his praise to God for the experience he has been through (vv.4-5,11-12) as he abides in the

(vv.7ff). What words in vv.7-10 characterize the Word of God? List the things mentioned in vv.7-8 that the Word of the Lord will do in the human heart. Is what the Psalmist testifies to in v.10 concerning the Scriptures your experience? What effect does God's Word have upon the author in regard to obedience to God and His Law (vv.11-14)? As you behold the glory of God in creation and hear Him speak to you in His Word, allow v.14 to be your prayer.

ANGLERS

By WADE C. SMITH

Lesson No. 163

BY-PRODUCTS OF PERSONAL EVANGELISM (Concluded)

In the Church Attendance.

If a church has an average of 50% of its members in attendance upon both services on the Lord's Day and 25% at mid-week prayer service, it is well above the average. Some churches have abandoned the mid-week prayer meeting. This writer, stopping over one Wednesday night in one of our largest Southern cities, after supper at the hotel, wended his way to the First Presbyterian Church for prayermeeting. Arriving a minute or two ahead of time he found the sexton, patiently at his post, and was kindly greeted. Ten minutes later the pastor came in and also kindly greeted the visitor. The pastor said the radio had announced the weather might be inclement. So far, however, it was quite clement. That was all. We chatted pleasantly for fifteen or twenty minutes and then dispersed —in three directions.

Actually there are many church buildings which cannot seat more than half the membership at one time, so fully accepted is the matter of wholesale absenteeism from worship. It is almost embarrassing at weddings and Easter, the lack of seating space for the membership. Yet, it should not be so. If a church with a membership, say, of 300 could enlist 20 of its members in a definite, permanent program of soul-winning it would increase attendance upon services 25 to 50% within a surprisingly short time. If each one of the 20 personal workers should *see* and invite *only one person a week* to the services, that would total 260 for the quarter, and if *one-fourth* of them accepted there would be 65 additional people coming to church. That is allowing only for grade "C" personal work, as has been described in the foregoing lessons. Think of the enlarged service and increased interest resulting from "A" and "B" personal work on the part of those twenty!

Everything that is wholesome for the church and promotive of its progress may result from a thorough-going personal evangelism program.

In the Preaching.

Perhaps one of the best By-Products would appear in the improved quality of the Pastor's preaching. Think what it would mean to a pastor coming into his pulpit on a Sunday morning to know that, sitting out there in the congregation are, say, twenty men, women and young people whom he has good reason to believe have each made an honest effort during the previous week to win a soul to Jesus Christ. Accompanying some of these would very likely be some of the "prospects." And it would also mean that during the service and while the sermon was being preached there are earnest prayers going up from his workers, asking God to bless their pastor's message, to open the hearts of his hearers and beseeching the Holy Spirit to bring conviction to lost souls, that some may be saved in that very service.

If that would not put life and spirit into a preacher and cause him to throw everything he had into the effort, what would? Yes, that quickening of the preacher would have begun back in the week during the preparation of his sermons, for he would have had many evidences over the telephone and in interviews and inquiries that his forces were working and that great things might be expected on the next Lord's Day.

Evidently the Lord intended that the spirit of Personal Evangelism should be at the center of all activities in His Church.

* * * * *

This closes the Anglers series of "lessons." The suggestion has come from several readers that they should be compiled in a study book with questions for classes at the end of each lesson. But it costs more money than ever now to publish a book, and it is a venture that requires very careful consideration. Much would depend upon how general would seem to be the demand. If you heartily approve the idea of making a study book of Anglers, write a postcard to the Editors, and the number of such received will have considerable bearing upon the decision in the matter.

Traveling back to the Near East, we find that the warm Climatic Optimum had brought very warm climate to Egypt, but along with the approach of the equator came abundant equatorial rains, and Egypt was extremely prosperous.

If one notices the full dress styles of those prosperous days he will understand what I mean when I say the climate was warm. Even the kings on the throne were naked to the waist.

But outside of Egypt the warm arid climate was a handicap. In Mesopotamia there was a high sea level which left silt on some of the city sites. We must not get this second silt deposit confused with that of Yoldia days when the inhabitants of Babel were scattered. This second so-called "flood" left silt at higher levels. This occurred during the first Dynasty of Ur, just after the time of the famous Royal Cemeteries. In Kish they found two deposits, one several feet above the other.

In Mesopotamia the time between the Yoldia high sea level and the Littorina high sea level of about 1000 years more or less is known in archeological circles as the Early Dynastic Period, or the Early Bronze Age. *It was the time of the beginning of nations.* During the middle part of the period, the climate was good and man was prosperous. In Egypt it rained during the time of the Predynastic Gerzians and during the reign of the first king Menes. Actually this Early Bronze age began several centuries before 3000 B. C. We have shown the strange history of the 1500 years of the Jarmo.

There is sure to be among the readers some one who has studied archeology. He is sure to say "the writer does not know the ABC's of archeology, for every learned archeologist dates the climatic oscillations in the Baltic and the contemporaneous Mesolithic men before Jarmo, not after, and there were no climatic oscillations after Jarmo. These experts do not recognize a FLOOD or a HIATUS or a TOWER of BABEL or a DISPERSION." The learned archeologists who reject the Bible cannot find the cause of the ice ages because of their topsy turvy chronology.

Women In The Church Today

By Rev. Edward C. Thornburg
Greenville, N. C.

It is being widely maintained at the present time that the position of women in the church today is not in harmony with the spirit of the times. The increased influence of women since the passage of the Nineteenth Amendment is said to be at variance with the principle of the church which restricts the actual government of the church to men.

Granted that this may be the case, that women do occupy a place in the total picture of modern society far different from that which they knew in New Testament times, does this mean that we are not only antiquated, but also unscriptural, in practice if not in intent, in defining the relation of women to the church?

This question is not one that may be dismissed with a hasty "yes" or "no," but demands a careful examination, both of the teachings of Scripture and of modern society. It will, however, be readily seen that the spirit of the age is not a valid (or stable) criterion by which to judge the matter. The increased presence and influence of women in government, medicine, industry, education and other fields has not been an unmixed blessing, as we can see from the rising tide of marital difficulties and delinquency due directly or indirectly to the absence of the wife and mother from the home.

Women have definitely proved to be at least the equal of men in most occupations, but they have failed to prove in a great number of cases that they could be both homemaker and breadwinner. Certainly we cannot ignore the times in which we live, and so lose all practical contact with modern man (and thus all ability to reach him with the Gospel), but we generally are in much more danger of allowing our ways of thinking to be moulded by the spirit of the age (and so lose the vital force of the Gospel).

Therefore we must follow the Confession, and maintain the Scriptures as the rule of faith and practice. The principle which is to regulate the life of the Church in every sphere of its activity is that all things not expressly given in Scripture, or good and necessary inferences from it, are forbidden, whether it be in faith, worship, or church order. So we must then show the order which Scripture establishes for the proper administration of the work of the Church.

1. There are in each church elders (Titus 1:5) who are almost, if not exactly, the same as bishops. (compare Acts 20:17,28; Titus 1:5,7) They are called bishops because of their function as overseers of the church, and elders due to their age and/or their respected position in the church.

From I Timothy 5:17 we would also get the impression that while all of the elders had the duty of ruling, some were especially honored because they taught as well as ruled. From this and other passages (Romans 12:7,8; I Corinthians 12:28) we see the traditional Presbyterian distinction between the ruling elder and the teaching elder (or pastor). There are thus given here the offices which fill two functions of the church, ruling and teaching.

2. The office of the deacon is the third of these offices in the church, discharging the function of showing mercy. This office is first instituted in Acts 6 (if there is a place where it is instituted in the New Testament), and is found in the church at Philippi, where in Philippians 1:1 Paul addresses both the elders and deacons of the church.

Thus there has been given in the Church three separate offices, each for the accomplishment of a special function. The question is, may any or all of these be filled by women? That there was an office to which a woman might be called is seen in I Timothy 3:8-13, where Paul shows the perpetuity of the office of the deacon in the Church. In verse 11 it is not only the wives of deacons, but were themselves deaconesses. (See E. K. Simpson: *The Pastoral Epistles,* Grand Rapids, 1954; page 56)

That women were called to such an office is seen also in that in Romans 16:1 Paul refers to Phebe as the servant (margin - deaconess) of a particular church. In the case of this verse we would not ignore the fact that often it is held that Phebe was simply a servant of the church, and not an officer, but this is often done in the interests of excluding women from any office in the church.

Certainly there are acts of mercy done in the name of Christ and His Church which necessitates the ministry which a lady alone could render, today as well as in the early church.

In Europe the deaconess hospitals exist as a testimony to this fact. There does, then, on the basis of these Scriptures exist an office of the church which both by divine institution and by its nature may be filled by men or women, and if we hold that the men ordained in Acts 6 were ordained to the office of deacon, then women are to be set aside for the office by the laying on of hands.

However, in distinction from this office, which by Scripture may be freely held by women, there is no Scriptural prerogative for the admission of women to the tasks of teaching and ruling in the churches. Such passages as may seem to give Scriptural warrant for such do not really do so. Deborah is said to be such an example of the place of leadership which women enjoyed in the Old Testament.

However, the whole tone of the story implies that this was a highly exceptional case, because there was no man who would lead Israel. This is especially seen in the rebuke by her of Barak. (Judges 4:9) The instance of Priscilla and Aquila in Acts 18:26 proves only that it is not necessary for one to be a minister of the church to do private teaching, in distinction from the teaching and preaching of the Word in the churches. Timothy is an example of one who profited from the teaching he received in the home.

There is an argument from silence against having lady elders, in that while we are told that there were lady deacons in the Church, and we are given the standard for their behaviour, we find no such examples in Scripture of lady elders, nor any hint that in the future development of the Church there will be such.

Is the matter of lady eldership one which developed through a progressive understanding of the Word of God? Is it not rather in basic disagreement with a general statement and principle of Scripture, that the woman is to be in subjection to her husband in all things?

In I Corinthians 14:34 we are told that the woman is to have this relation to her husband in the church, and in Ephesians 5:22-24 this principle is applied also to their relationship in the whole family experience. This subjection, of course, is not to be abused by the husband, as Paul continues in Ephesians 5:25-33, that this rule is to be exercised in love. It is not a relationship of a superior who rules and an inferior who is ruled, but a subordination for the sake of an economy of operation.

It is perhaps significant that as far as this writer was able to ascertain, the question never came up in Presbyterian churches until 1920, in an age of doctrinal indifference. Are we to assume that Augustin, Calvin, Knox, Thornwell, Dabney, and a whole host of other theological giants, with their insights into the truths of Scripture, were not sufficiently aware of the issues involved in this matter? Our primary and basic reference is to the Word of God, but we cannot wisely ignore the testimony of history.

There is, however, another mistake which we must not make, to have such a conception of the judicatories of the Church that women are prevented from ever being heard. The presbyteries, synods and general assemblies of the church are not gatherings for worship as such, but church courts. As such they have full right to call upon any person to appear before that court to testify, whether it be for a matter of discipline, or to deliver a report. The previously mentioned command for women to keep silence in the churches in its context clearly refers to the worship services of particular congregations, and not to the church court as conceived under the Presbyterian system.

Let us be careful, then, in our desire to see that the Gospel of the grace of God is effectively preached, that we fail to go far enough, or attempt to go further than we may in fulfilling the demands of Scripture in this matter as in every other with which the church is faced.

My Responsibilities As A Pastor

By The Rev. Archie Davis

Union, S. C.

The purpose of this message is to give my conception of the doctrine of the Ministry and my responsibilities in relation to my high calling in Christ Jesus.

Paul exhorted young Timothy with these words, "Preach the Word; be instant in season, out of season; reprove, rebuke, exhort with all longsuffering and doctrine." (2 Tim. 4:2) I think the preacher's primary interest should be preaching the gospel of good news. But, I think it extends further than the pulpit or exhortations. To be "instant in season and out of season," means to be able to give sound and helpful advice to those who are in great need at the time the opportunity may arise.

I get my method and theology from the Apostle Paul. I think Paul sets forth qualifications of a true minister in Romans 1:14-17. Paul begins by saying, "I am debtor." A debtor is one who owes another something. Paul is indebted in a two-fold way. First of all he is indebted to God, who called him. I remember most vividly that it was God who chose me. "You have not chosen me but I have chosen you." (John 15:16) I am sure it was brought to Paul's mind very forcefully that it was a power outside himself that brought him face to face with Jesus Christ on the Damascus Road. The Lord spoke to Ananias and told him to go lay his hands on Saul of Tarsus. Ananias was hesitant and "the Lord said unto him, Go thy way: for he is a chosen vessel unto me, to bear my name before the Gentiles and Kings and the children of Israel." (Acts 9:15).

In my own experience; I rebelled against the call of God to full time service. One night after hearing a message on yielding one's self completely to the Lord, I went to bed, but I could not go to sleep. After a lengthy argument or wrestling with the Lord, I got up and began to read the Bible. Through the leading of the Holy Spirit, I began to read I Corinthians and these words stood out, "For ye see your calling, brethren, how that not many wise men after the flesh, not many mighty, not many noble, are called: But God hath chosen the foolish things of the world to confound the things which are mighty." (I Cor. 1:26-27) That night I surrendered my all to the Lord and promised Him that I would follow His leading and preach His Word.

Secondly, Paul was a debtor because of the people around him. He realized what God did for him he could do for others. The God that Paul was serving was no respecter of persons; why should he be? He was a debtor "both to the Greeks and to the Barbarians; both to the wise and to the unwise." (Romans 1:14)

This teaches me that I have a responsibility to all men regardless of race or status in life. I have a message of God's love to get across to the learned and to the ignorant. Whether a man lives in a stately mansion or in a shack across the tracks, he is my individual responsibility. I am indebted to all men of all races and all classes; because I firmly believe what God did for me, he can do for them.

Paul then declares "I am ready to preach the gospel to you at Rome also." (Rom. 1:15) Whether it be a public place or perilous place, Paul was ready to serve his Lord. I have asked myself the question many times: Am I ready or willing to serve my Lord in every circumstance regardless of how difficult or insignificant?

The first step in being ready to serve Christ is to realize that one has a debt to Christ, the Church and his community. Next is to search out his motives for entering the ministry. Paul had a pure motive, "For the love of Christ constraineth us." His heart's desire was that souls might be saved. "Brethren, my heart's desire and prayer to God for Israel is, that they might be saved." (Rom. 10:1) I believe it takes motives like that to make a powerful servant of God. Love makes a man a servant of his Lord, and to his people. I realize that the Christian minister should be a servant to his people and a bondslave of Jesus Christ.

Thirdly, Paul was ready because he had a message burning in his heart. The message was this: "For I determined not to know anything among you save Jesus Christ, and Him crucified." (I Cor. 2:2) I am convinced that we as ministers have the greatest message in the world to give to people who are starving for something to fill the longings of their souls. I am sure that if I lift up Christ and Him crucified He will draw all men to Himself. This does not mean only in my preaching, but also in my activities in the community. I must lift Christ up not only on Sundays, but daily as I minister in the homes.

Paul knew how to meet men. His methods of reaching men proved that he was prepared to serve Christ. Whatever the situation that had arisen, Paul knew how to face it. "For I have learned, in whatsoever state I am, therewith to be content. I know both how to be abased, and I know how to abound: everywhere and in all things I am instructed both to be full and to be hungry, both to abound and to suffer need." (Phil. 4:11-12) The real secret of a minister is learning to fit into every social situation.

Paul knew that if he was going to be an effective minister he was going to have to meet men on their own grounds and terms. To the Jews, he became as a Jew. To those under the law he became as under the law. To the weak he became as the weak. Paul makes it even more emphatic in his own words, "I am made all things to all men, that I might by all means save some." (I Cor. 9:22) A good minister should be able to talk the language of the people to whom he is ministering. I realize I must meet the people on common grounds if I am to win them first to myself and then to Christ.

Paul's method of preaching was a very simple one. Although he was a very learned man, he did not use it in his preaching. To the Church at Corinth, he wrote, "and brethren, when I came to you, I came not with excellency of speech or wisdom, declaring unto you the testimony of God . . . and my speech and my preaching was not with enticing words of man's wisdom, but in demonstration of the Spirit and of Power." (I Cor. 2:1,4) Jesus Christ taught in parables because he wanted the people to understand what he was saying. The parable usually related to something very familiar to the hearers.

Finally, Paul makes this affirmation "I am not ashamed of the Gospel of Christ." (Rom. 1:16) A man would make a poor salesman if he were ashamed of his product. A minister would be a very poor preacher if he was ashamed of the gospel or message he was preaching.

I am convinced beyond a shadow of doubt that Christ is the answer to all the world's needs. The gospel which we preach is the power of God unto salvation to everyone that believeth. It is our job to make the gospel plain, so that people can understand and believe. The love of God as presented in preaching the gospel reaches down to the vilest sinner and lifts him up and places his feet on the solid rock and establishes his goings. The gospel gives to men new aims and directions in life.

To those who have burdened hearts and troubled minds we must point them to Jesus Christ who cares infinitely for them. Many are suffering from mental disorders or undue anxiety. As ministers of the gospel of Our Lord and Saviour Jesus Christ, we should present Christ in such a manner that the troubled mind

the foot soldiers, much less executed. System eps men occupied, and lets them know what expected of them. Jesus Christ, King and ead of the Church, has work for every mem- r on every roll in order that His will be rried out, and every creature hear His gospel.

Keeping records and making plans avoids iste of time and material. How often things e lost because they were not properly filed ray; facts about people are important, but ie to carelessness God's people forget their ighbors' needs and they are lost.

Difficulties and Dangers

Church leaders are tempted to seek the praise men and show off their authority rather than use their office to serve others and lay up avenly treasures. People are prone to fill in ports as an end in itself instead of actually penting of the sins and giving God the praise r good things done. The fact that lies are metimes told to make ugly situations appear l right on paper shows the desperate need of rtain systematic men for Christ.

Leaves can atone for fruitlessness no better ow than on the day our Lord cursed the barren g tree! God is not mocked by statistics which und successful although no souls have been ved. True achievement comes as a result of hristian love supplied to our hearts by the irit of God. We may function as smoothly a well-trained team of professsional ball indlers, but if we lack love, we are as useless God as if we were playing games.

What Is Your Goal?

To make Jesus Christ known is the duty of every group in the local congregation: the choir sends out truth of His saving power in such a way as to tug at the hearts of sinners. Sunday School classes learn of Him to teach others. By acts of kindness, deacons recommend Him to the needy. Elders give themselves to the ministry of the Word and prayer, instructing and catechising publicly and from house to house, showing all the way to heaven. Christ is the way.

Let Christian choirs welcome opportunities to sing at mission stations and evangelistic services. Sunday School classes should ever seek to form new groups for Bible study. Deacons are to channel money to missions and elders intercede for all who proclaim the gospel to pagans.

To Your Work

Guided by men who have a burden for the salvation of multitudes without hope, youth groups can be powerful forces for missions through concerted prayer, sacrifice and study. They should be challenged to lay down their lives for Christ's sake and the gospel's.

Be sure to have right aims in your Christian fellowship. Ask yourself on each report blank how much you are doing in making Jesus Christ known to the world. Labor with others to send out missionaries and support them in prayer and with money.

After Death, What?

By The Rev. Floyd E. Hamilton

"Have ye not read in the Book of Moses, how the bush God spake unto him saying, I am e God of Abraham, and the God of Isaac, and e God of Jacob? He is not the God of the ad, but the God of the living."

As might be expected, we find that there is vital difference in the answer given by Mod- nists and Evangelicals, to the question, After ath, What? The Modernists question the ility of eternal punishment for unrepentant n and women, saying that God is too good inflict that kind of punishment on human ngs. Most Modernists would probably be- ve in some kind of future life of bliss for men, but they would recoil from any dis- mination about who will enter such a state bliss.

However, no matter how much men may tend to ignore it, they have an insatiable interest in the future life. The reason spiritualism is so popular is that it pretends to secure information about life after death and give it to people living in this world. The only reason that the case of Bridey Murphy has captured the imagination of millions of Americans is that it has what is claimed to be proof of life after death in what is called reincarnation, that is, the coming back of the soul of one who had died, to live again in the body of someone alive today. A popular comic strip today has as its theme pretended reincarnation. I have recently received a book entitled, "Immortality," by Loraine Boettner, and on the cover is the following statement: "There is scarcely any other subject of religious thought that commands such universal interest as that of the future life. In the heart of every man is the longing to enter into a larger life and destiny after death. To the question, What next? Dr. Boettner gives a clear and unmistakable answer."

All this emphasizes the point that people have almost a morbid curiosity about what comes after death.

Now while the non-Christian is completely at sea in this matter, and consequently falls an easy prey to such things as the Bridey Murphy hoax and spiritualism, there is no reason for the Christian to be ignorant on the subject. The Word of God gives us very definite information on the matter and all we need to do is to assimilate the information it gives us.

In the first place we should understand clearly that the Bible does not teach what is called "soul sleep," contrary to the claims of the Jehovah's Witnesses, Seventh Day Adventists and others. While I was in Korea before World War II, I was listening one Sunday afternoon to a broadcast sermon over our short wave radio. I never found out whether the speaker was a Seventh Day Adventist, a Jehovah's Witness or what, but the sermon was an attack on the Christian teaching about life after death.

It gave one of the most warped interpretations of the precious words of Jesus to the dying thief on the cross I have ever heard. The words of the text are, "Lord, remember me when thou comest into thy kingdom. And Jesus said unto him, 'Verily I say unto you, Today thou shalt be with me in Paradise.' "

The speaker said that Jesus was not teaching that the thief's soul would that very day be with Jesus in Paradise but that the common punctuation was wrong, and that the text should read, "I say unto you today, thou shalt be with me in Paradise (in my future kingdom)." Not only would such an interpretation be contrary to the rest of Scripture, it would make nonsense of the verse itself. Why in the world would Jesus use an expression that would tell the thief he was speaking to him that very day when he (the thief) could hear him speak? The only sensible interpretation is that which the Greek text demands, namely, that Jesus was promising to the dying thief entrance into heaven on that very day.

The idea of reincarnation, that is the coming back of the soul of a person who has previously died, to indwell the body of a person who has just been born, is an oriental idea growing out of Hinduism and Buddhism which teach that our future life depends on our conduct in this life, and that if we are bad we will be reborn as animals or insects. Hindu holy men (who are usually anything but holy) have someone walk in front of them along a path with a broom to sweep all the insects out of the path, lest they accidentally step on their reincarnated ancestors!

A new twist has been given to the old idea of reincarnation recently by the case of Bridey

But this same story of the rich man and the beggar Lazarus is one of the strongest passages proving the conscious existence of the souls both of believers and unbelievers after death. Some regard this story as a parable, rather than actual history, but whether it was true or a parable, the teaching is the same. It teaches that the unbelievers are in conscious torment, that they can see and understand what they have lost by unbelief. It teaches that there is a great gulf between the souls of the righteous and the souls of the wicked, and that that gulf is impassable. More important to us is the fact that this teaches the conscious and joyous existence of the souls of the righteous after death, and other passages tell us that that existence is in communion with Christ and the redeemed.

In II Samuel 12:23, King David, as a prophet, testified to his belief in the salvation of elect infants, and also in the conscious existence of the souls of believers, after death, with God.

In Revelation 14:13 we are told, "Blessed are the dead who die in the Lord, while in Rev. 7:15-17 the apostle John saw them before the throne of God, and again in Rev. 20 he saw the souls of the martyrs reigning with Christ in glory at the present time. In Philippians 1:23-24 Paul tells us that to depart and be with Christ is far better than to continue alive here on earth, and in Eccles. 12:7 we are told that the spirit returns to God who made it, while in Eccles. 3:11 we are told that God has put eternity in our hearts, and of course that implies conscious existence after death.

Not only were Moses and Elijah having conscious existence on the mount of transfiguration, but Jesus himself said in the words of our text, that Abraham, Isaac and Jacob were alive with God, and if they were with God, of course all other Christians are also alive and conscious after death.

But the most terrible feature of this immortality, however, is that the souls of unbelievers are in conscious torment after death. The Day of Judgment simply declares official the judgment under which they already rest, for unbelief. It is indeed a terrible thing to fall into the hands of the living God.

When Christ comes again the bodies of all men are to be resurrected, united to their souls and then throughout eternity there will be either joy with Christ and the redeemed or anguish in separation from him. There is no second chance or purgatory where we may be purified and then brought back to God. Death ends our last chance for eternal life with Christ. Repent and believe in Christ and thou shalt have eternal life.

SABBATH SCHOOL LESSONS — REV. J. KENTON PARKER

LESSON FOR NOVEMBER 11

The Lord's Requirements

Background Scripture: Micah 4 and 6
Devotional Reading: Isaiah 1:11-17

As a general background for this lesson let me use, (and often quote), the fine material in the Analytical Bible. "The prophet Micah was a native of the little town of Moresheth in the western part of Judah." "Unlike Isaiah and Jeremiah he did not belong to the capital, but lived in the country. He was, however, on the international highway and in a position to observe the political movements of Western Asia. He was the contemporary of Isaiah, whose labors began a bit earlier in the reign of Uzziah. He witnessed the moral and religious corruption in Judah which began in the reign of Joram and reached its climax in the reign of Ahaz. Then came the reformation under Hezekiah, but his son, Manasseh, returned to the sins of Ahaz. Judgment was coming and was only stayed for a time because of the good reign of Josiah. "The general moral corruption of society, sin rampant in official and family life, will bring the state to ruin. The foundations are rotting, being eaten away . . . and the whole structure will fall apart. No prophet presented this truth in more diversified way than did Micah. It is the truth, not only for Israel and Judah, but for the nations of every age." Would that the nations today, as they assemble in the United Nations would see this truth! Would that our own beloved land would see and heed the warning before it is too late!

"All the prophets went to the heart of the matter in condemning the empty formality, and the useless perfunctory performance of rites and ceremonies, but none of them stated it more clearly and forcefully than did Micah (see 6:8).

"Some writers have very mistakenly gone to the extreme of saying that the priestly sacrificial system has no place with the prophets and by them was abandoned. Nothing could be more mistaken than such an interpretation of the prophets. The sacrificial system was divinely appointed to be continued and fulfilled in Jesus Christ. One of the last acts of our Lord was to celebrate the Passover. What the prophets condemned was the empty and meaningless observance of these ordinances."

This is what Isaiah is speaking of in our Devotional Reading. In the second verse of the first chapter he cries out: "Hear, O heavens, and give ear, O earth: for the Lord hath spoken. I have nourished and brought up children, and they have rebelled against me."

In verse 10 he compares them to the people of Sodom and Gomorrah, and asks the heart-searching question, To what purpose is the multitude of your sacrifices unto me? saith the Lord: I am full of the burnt offerings of rams, and the fat of fed beasts; and I delight not in the blood of bullocks, or of lambs, or of he goats. All of their sacrifices and ceremonies were an abomination to the Lord, because their lives were full of sin. Their sacrifices were meant to be the expression of repentant people who were forsaking sin and seeking forgiveness. Instead of this, these worshippers were using them as a would-be covering. They seemed to think that these offerings and sacrifices would act as a sort of bribe, and that God would excuse and overlook their sins because of the multitude of their offerings. Is not the same idea in the minds of some today who give much money to the church, but keep their sins? The prophet, in the name of his God, scorns them and their gifts. Their hands are full of blood; their hearts full of sin. "Wash you, make you clean; put away the evil of your doings from before mine eyes; cease to do evil; learn to do well" . . . "Come now, and let us reason together, saith the Lord: though your sins be as scarlet, they shall be as white as snow: though they be red like crimson, they shall be as wool." This is one of the most beautiful and meaningful and amazing promises in the Bible, but let us remember the preceding verses. *Genuine repentance must precede this gracious and full forgiveness.* It is the same message that John the Baptist brought to the people of his time. It is the message we need in our day. When we turn from sin with grief and hatred, then there is no limit to the pardon and forgiveness of God. His full and free forgiveness is not to be bought with money while we keep our sins and love them. A broken and contrite heart is essential when we seek the face of God.

Now, after this long introduction, let us turn to our Scripture for today. There are two subjects suggested: (1) The Glory of the Coming Kingdom, and (2) The Requirements for true worship.

I. *The Glory of the Coming Kingdom:* Chapter 4.

This is one of several beautiful passages describing the condition of the earth when Jesus comes back to reign and rule. They stand out like refreshing oases in a desert land. All of us realize that our earth is far removed from such a blessed state at the present time. As I write these words I remember the editorial I saw in the morning paper about the powder keg at the Suez Canal and the lit fuse which may cause an explosion at any time.

All the nations are busy "learning war," and trying to outstrip each other in making instruments of destruction. There seems to be no way of stopping what all agree is the most foolish of all the follies of mankind. All the nations — even Russia and Red China — claim that they want peace. The Bible vividly describes this condition when it says, The nations have drunk of the wine of Babylon; therefore the nations are mad, (insane).

This "Babylon"; this confusion of nations, will be completely demolished. (For a complete and dramatic description of this "Fall of Babylon" see the 17th and 18th chapters of Revelation). Micah is describing the Glory of the Kingdom. It will be a time when many nations shall say, Come, and let us go up to the mountain of the Lord, and to the house of the God of Jacob; and he will teach us of His ways, and we will walk in his paths: for the Lord shall go forth of Zion, and the word of the Lord from Jerusalem."

Verses three and four tell of a time and condition which we all yearn to see; a time of peace and prosperity, and absence of all fear. It is the dream of poet and philosopher and statesman. It will come when the King comes and reigns in justice and righteousness. We should continually pray the prayer of John, Even so, Come, Lord Jesus.

We should keep this picture before us at all times. There will be many struggles and trials for God's people, for the Church Militant, while we continue to fight the good fight of faith and witness for our Lord on earth. The final triumph of Christ's Kingdom is assured, and this glorious prophecy, together with many others, will be fulfilled. The meek shall inherit the earth and shall delight themselves in the abundance of peace. May we do all in our power to hasten the "Kingdom of Glory" of which our Confession of Faith speaks!

II. *Requirements for True Worship*: Chapter 6.

"The Lord hath a controversy with His people." What is this controversy? It concerns the requirements for true worship. God has a right to be worshipped. He redeemed them out of

Egypt. This failure to worship him in the right way was a very grave and heinous sin. It began with Cain, and was very prevalent all along in their history as a nation.

Verses 6 and 7 state the question; Wherewith shall I come before the Lord, and bow myself before the high God? Several answers are put in the form of questions: Shall I come with burnt offerings? Thousands of rams, rivers of oil, my own children? (This was common among heathen; to offer their children.) Can the "fruit of my body atone for the sin of my soul? The implied answer to all these questions is, NO! No material sacrifice or gift is sufficient. If the heart is not right then all is wrong.

Verse eight gives the threefold requirement: To do justly, love mercy, and walk humbly with thy God. In other words, Justice, mercy (kindness), and humble faith. In order to be acceptable as a worshipper we must have these three things. In Psalm 15 we have a more detailed picture of a "Citizen of Zion": He that walketh uprightly, worketh righteousness, and speaketh the truth in his heart, etc.

In Psalm 24:3 and 4, we read, Who shall ascend into the hill of the Lord? or who shall stand in his holy place? He that hath clean hands and a pure heart, etc. Micah puts them in a three-fold statement. Back of all our material gifts there must be an inner righteousness, even the righteousness of the Lord. We are to worship in the "beauty of holiness."

Where can we obtain this "beauty"? Where can we get this justice, mercy and faith? Only as God gives us a new heart. Only as the righteousness of Christ is first "imputed" and then "imparted," to us. We are justified and sanctified through Christ. In Hebrews 4:4-16 this way is described: Seeing then that we have a high priest that is passed into the heavens, Jesus the Son of God, let us hold fast our profession . . . Let us therefore come boldly (with confidence) unto the throne of grace that we may obtain mercy and find grace to help in time of need. In our great hymn, Rock of Ages, it is expressed in a beautiful way: Rock of Ages, cleft for me, Let me hide myself in Thee. Nothing in my hand I bring: Simply to Thy cross I cling, etc.

As we read these "Requirements," let us cling to our Saviour Who alone can give us the cleansing which we need.

YOUNG PEOPLE'S DEPARTMENT — REV. B. HOYT EVANS

YOUTH PROGRAM FOR NOVEMBER 11

"Where My Dollars Go There Is My Heart"

Suggested Hymns: "I Am Thine, O Lord"
"I Gave My Life For Thee"
"We Give Thee But Thine Own"

Program Leader's Introduction:

Last week we learned what happens to the money which is given to the church and what it accomplishes. The way the church's money is spent indicates the main interests of the church. In the program for today we want to think about the use we make of our dollars and what it indicates about our interests. We shall try to find answers to the following questions: How much of what we call "our possessions" belongs to the Lord, and why? How does our practice of stewardship indicate our spiritual attitude and condition? What are the practical ways of honoring God in our stewardship?

First Speaker:

In much of the talk we hear about stewardship we get the idea that all that is involved is the gifts made to the church. A great many Christians feel that they are doing all that stewardship demands if they are giving a tenth of their income to the church. Certainly the tenth, or the tithe, is the minimum a Christian can give to the Lord's work, but this is only a small part of true Christian stewardship. In one of the Scripture passages read to us we heard that "the earth is the Lord's, and the fullness thereof; the world, and they that dwell therein." It is not, then, just the tenth that belongs to God, but all that we are and all we have. Real Christian stewardship involves honoring the Lord with all we have: time, talents, and possessions.

We usually think of ourselves as being masters of our own lives. Why is it that we must consider ourselves as belonging to God? There is a story which illustrates this question and answers it. There was once a boy who worked very carefully over a long period of time to fashion a very fine model sail boat. It was as nearly perfect as he could make it in every detail. One of the nicest features of it was that it would really sail, and he frequently took it for cruises on a large lake near his home. One day tragedy struck. The string by which he held the boat became unfastened, and the boat sailed away out of reach and out of sight. So far as the boy was concerned, his boat was lost. Some time later he saw in a shop window a sail boat which looked very familiar. A closer examination revealed that it was truly his own boat, so he went inside and claimed it.

The shopkeeper, however, said that he had paid for it, and that it was his boat. The only condition under which he would part with it was for the lad to pay the price. It was such a fine boat that the price was high, and it took the boy many weeks to earn the required sum. Finally he had the amount agreed on, and he bought the boat and carried it home. As he left the shop he said to the boat lovingly held in his arms, "Now you are twice mine, because I made you and I bought you." Those of us who are Christians are twice the Lord's. First, He created us, and then, when we were lost in sin, He redeemed us. We belong to God by a double claim, and we ought to glorify Him accordingly. This is the real meaning of stewardship.

Second Speaker:

There are always those who are ready to criticize the church when anything is said about money. Those who raise objection are often inclined to contend that the church ought to concern itself with spiritual matters. Jesus said, "Where your treasure is, there will your heart be also." Our attitude toward our money indicates our attitude toward spiritual matters. The use we make of our material possessions reveals our estimate of God, and our spiritual condition. Our possessions represent us. The money you have is what you receive in exchange for your time, talent, and effort. When you spend money, you are spending yourself. When you use your money for the glory of God, it is the same as using yourself for the glory of God. When you use your money to buy pleasure, for instance, you are spending yourself for pleasure.

Sometimes we deceive ourselves about our spiritual condition, about what we believe to be most important, about the allegiance of our hearts. If you really want to know what we consider to be the most important, then let us examine how we spend your money. "Where my dollars go — there is my heart."

Discussion. (to be conducted by program leader)

Ask the young people these questions, and make a list of the answers they give. Discuss any other questions that arise.

1. What are some of the ways we can glorify God with our money besides giving it to the work of the church?

2. How may we serve God with our time and talents over and above the work we do and the time we spend in connection with the program of the church?

3. Make up a good definition of stewardship.

4. What are some of the vocations which lend themselves to good stewardship besides church-related vocations (ministry, missionaries, etc.)?

Women's Work

From Strength to Strength

Your loneliness is a cathedral.
You are the priest.
You are the congregation.
You are the choir and the organ.
You are the music.
You are the altar and
The white burning candles
And their yellow light.
Your solitude is multitude;
A cloud of witnesses surrounds you.
The Lord of Hosts encompasses you.
Your solitude is multitude.
Your solitude is a cathedral.

Author Unknown—

Irreverent Greeting Cards on Way Out

This year's output of Christmas greeting cards will return to a religious theme. Americans will be exchanging two billion greeting cards this season according to word from the greeting card manufacturers, and among the significant changes you will note when making your own selections this year, is the return of the religious theme to the Yule greeting cards.

In recent times, due to the cynicism brought about by World War II and the Korean conflict, religious cards have accounted for about five per cent of the total sold. This year the proportion of religious Christmas cards will be about 25 per cent.

What has brought about this dramatic change? Milton K. Harrington, president of the Chapel Art Studios, St. Louis, Mo., the industry's sole exclusive manufacturer of reverent Christmas cards, attributes the change to the general rise in religious thought and church membership, and to the determination to "put Christ back into Christmas," expressed from many pulpits in recent times.

Although Chapel is the first company in the field to devote its entire line to Christmas cards

Each institute has been planned by a special committee representing the area. Invitations are being sent to pastors nominated by their Presbytery Executive Secretary, or Chairman of Church Extension. However, all pastors are invited to attend, and you are urged to write and ask for a program for the institute in your area.

Our Adult Bible Classes provide scholarships through our Scholarship Fund. Each Adult Class is urged to make a donation to this fund which is used toward the expenses of our pastors in attending these institutes. Checks for this cause should be made to "SCHOLARSHIP FUND", and sent to me.

James M. Carr, Secretary
Town and Country Church Department
341-B Ponce de Leon Avenue, N. E.
Atlanta 8, Georgia

Billy Graham at the Louisville Presbyterian Theological Seminary

The new Coliseum at the Kentucky State Fairgrounds is the largest indoor auditorium in our country. But the Greater Louisville Crusade led by Billy Graham has been filling it to capacity and sometimes to overflowing. So last Sunday afternoon (October 14) the meeting was held in the outdoor Fairgrounds stadium which seats 26,000. Even this was overflowed so that about 2,000 additional attenders, including my wife and I, were standing in the football field through the service. We rejoice in this good work among us.

Our seminarians have been attending the meetings and the ministers' breakfasts with the Crusade team. On October 10 Dr. Graham spoke in an extended chapel service at the Seminary. In the enclosed photo Dr. Caldwell and Dr. Graham are preparing for the chapel service.

L. C. Rudolph
Assistant to the President

Special Montreat Committee

At the recent meeting of the Board of Trustees of the Mountain Retreat Association the following action was taken:

"That a committee be appointed to consist of three members of the Board of Directors, two members of the Board of Trustees, and four from the Church at large, to be appointed by the Chairman of the Board of Trustees: To make a full survey and study of Montreat's administrative organization, operation and services to the Church, and that this Committee be authorized to co-opt others selected by them, not necessarily members of the Board of Trustees to serve with them, and report the recommendations of this committee at the 1957 meeting of the Board of Trustees, if the way be clear."

In seeking to carry out the will of the Board of Trustees, I have appointed the following members of this committee and each has accepted:

From the Board of Directors: Dr. John Richards, Macon, Georgia, Convenor; Dr. Frank Jackson, Davidson, North Carolina; Mr. Albert Noe, Jackson, Tennessee.

From the Board of Trustees: Mr. Adrian Williamson, Monticello, Arkansas; Dr. John Wilson, La Grange, Georgia.

From the Church at large: Dr. Charles King, Houston, Texas; Mr. Ed Grant, Baton Rouge, Louisiana; Mr. Ashton Phelps, New Orleans, Louisiana; Dr. Charles Gibboney, Augusta, Georgia.

John C. Frist, Chmn.

ALABAMA

Birmingham—Groundbreaking ceremonies were held by the congregation of Ensley Presbyterian Church here, on Sunday, October 14, beginning construction for a new $100,000 educational building which will connect to the existing church building.

Guest of honor at the groundbreaking was Dr. Frank Cross, pastor of Central Presbyterian Church, Meridian, Miss., who was formerly pastor of the Ensley Church, having served the congregation for 22 years. A week of revival services followed the groundbreaking and the Homecoming, which marked the 55th anniversary of the church's founding.

Birmingham—The Birmingham Presbytery has authorized the purchase of property in Huffman, Ala., for organization and building of a new Presbyterian, U.S., church.

The authority was granted October 2 during an adjourned session of the Presbytery, meeting at First Presbyterian Church, Birmingham. A petition from 26 Presbyterians living in the Huffman area was presented, and the strategy committee of the Presbytery then asked the authority to purchase a site at the cost of $28,000.

The Presbytery voted to allow the strategy committee authority to borrow not more than $20,000 to add to the amount on hand to purchase the property.

Dr. E. V. Ramage, as chairman of the stewardship committee presented the budget for benevolent causes. The budget as adopted by the Presbytery is $139,850. This budget includes $55,350 for General Assembly's causes; $45,050 for Synod

The collection includes an 1850 edition of the complete work of John Calvin, and 54 complete volumes of the Parker Society Publications containing the writings, prayers, and sermons of early church reformers in England. Also among these books are several containing experiences and activities of early missionaries in North America. Several volumes of the collection are thought to be in the rare book class, although the final classification of the books has not been completed.

LOUISIANA

Lake Providence — Sunday, October 14, a commission of Red River Presbytery met to organize a Presbyterian Church in Lake Providence, adding the 46th Presbyterian church to the roll of Red River Presbytery.

Mr. Dan Lott, a student in Columbia Presbyterian Seminary, has served in Lake Providence for the past two summers. The Presbyterians have been meeting for worship for over 18 months, using the Episcopal Church for some of the time, and later meeting in the city hall. Nineteen names were affixed to the petition which was submitted to Presbytery requesting organization.

Bossier City—Construction has begun on the first unit of the John Knox Presbyterian Church of Bossier City. Only the exterior "shell" of the building will be completed by the contractor, as the members plan to do the work on the interior of the brick building themselves.

The design of the new church building is contemporary. The site is a four acre tract on airline drive in the eastern section of the city. The present construction will provide a central assembly area to be used for worship until the sanctuary is built at a later date. Also included in the plans for present building construction are nine classrooms, pastor's study, storage space and restrooms. The building will be air-conditioned, and the location of the building on the lot provides sufficient off-street parking to the front and side of the building. The Rev. John M. Williamson is pastor of the church.

Jonesville—The Trinity Presbyterian Church of Jonesville observed its centennial in September.

The church was organized in the community of Trinity, La., on April 20, 1856 with 13 members, several years before Jonesville became a town.

The first full-time pastor, the Rev. Kenneth Seawright, came to the church in 1935, 79 years after its organization. The present manse was built the first year of his ministry. The church had before this time been served by various visiting ministers, and stated supply ministers. The church had moved to the town of Jonesville in 1920. The Rev. Carl Lazenby was ordained and installed as pastor in 1953, and served the church until 1955. The Rev. Paul Currie, a graduate of Southwestern College, and Louisville Seminary, was ordained and installed as pastor of the church February 19, 1956.

Shreveport—The First Presbyterian Church in Shreveport for Negro Presbyterians is now under construction in Hollywood Heights, and will be completed in about two months.

The new building, a one-story masonry structure, will have an auditorium to seat 150 persons. The First Presbyterian Church of Shreveport is cooperating in the planning and financing of the Hollywood Church, which will be situated on a two and one half acre tract.

New Orleans—The Presbytery of New Orleans has adopted two resolutions calling for the more than 10,000 Presbyterians in the Presbytery, to "use every influence at their command to stamp out gambling" in that area. The presbytery thus joined the Greater New Orleans Federation of Churches and other groups in their stand against gambling and for stronger law enforcements.

The presbytery's stand was taken at a meeting in Slidell, October 9, and the resolutions were unanimously adopted by the 65 ministers and elders attending presbytery.

The Rev. Walter D. Langtry, pastor of Prytania Street Presbyterian Church, presented the resolutions, which were proposed in the form of amendments to a report of the committee on Christian Relations.

The following is the text of the Presbytery's first resolution:

"The Presbytery has observed with deep concern the increase in gambling and other forms of evil and lawlessness within our borders. We commend the activities of our law enforcement agencies in their excellent fight against some areas of criminal activity, as in the enforcement of the anti-narcotic law. However, we are distressed at the apparent unwillingness to enforce statutes against gambling and evils which are related to it.

"Therefore, we call upon the members of our churches to speak out boldly against the return of commercialized gambling, to use every influence at their command to stamp out gambling in any form.

"We call upon the enforcement agencies of the parishes to enforce the laws without favor or discrimination.

"We call upon the governor, Earl K. Long, and the superintendent of state police to take steps to restore adequate law enforcement where local officials are unwilling or unable to enforce the law."

Following is the text of the second resolution aligning the presbytery with the church federation:

"The Presbytery appreciates the importance of an efficient and incorruptible police department to maintain order and to uphold the laws which are the protection of our people against disorder and vice.

"Therefore, the Presbytery concurs with the statements of the Greater New Orleans Federation of Churches in endeavoring to secure the high reputation of the police department in that city."

MISSISSIPPI

Laurel—A young adult rally of the Meridian Presbytery was held Sunday, Oct. 7, at Shelby State Park, south of Hattiesburg. The theme for the rally was "The Christian Home."

Speakers for the program included: Frank Montague, Jr., Hattiesburg; Scott Kelso, Hattiesburg; Mrs. W. C. Brown, Ellisville; Mrs. James McDaniels, Sandersville; Bob Newton, Wiggins, and Walter P. Green, Laurel.

Jackson—Building for the church home of the new Pearl Presbyterian Church near Jackson, Miss., is complete. Dedication is planned soon.

---

served as deacon, and at the time of his death was serving the church as an elder.

Mr. Paxton willed $10,000 to the church with the proviso that the "Executors shall not be required to pay such sum immediately but may make payment of this bequest in such installments and at such time as in their judgment will be consistent with the efficient administration of my estate. In any event, the payment shall be made within a period of five years from and after the date of my death."

Mr. Paxton further stated in his will: "that this bequest shall be used by the Trustees of this church in the promotion and furtherance in the Town of Wilson of the general religious and educational program of said church. It is my thought at this time that this bequest can be used most effectively if applied to a fund, which, with other contributions, may or will be used in the erection of the Fellowship Hall.

SOUTH CAROLINA

Marion—The Men of Pee Dee Presbytery held their Fall Rally, Sunday afternoon, October 14, at Camp Harmony. Families attended. The president of the Men's Council for the Presbytery, Mr. B. Pratt Gasque of Marion presided.

Columbia — Congaree Presbytery launched its drive to raise $70,000, its part of Presbyterian College's $750,000 long-range program of improvement, at a dinner for the fund raisers at Laurel Hill on October 8.

The fund will go toward construction of a chapel-auditorium, student center, modernizing existing buildings, and scholarship aid endowment. The campaign commemorates the 75th anniversary of Presbyterian College.

The Diamond Jubilee fund campaign has already raised $605,000, according to Mr. Lawrence B. Avison, campaign director.

Dr. F. V. Poag, pastor of Shandon Presbyterian Church, Columbia, S. C., gave a brief conviction talk at the dinner meeting. Mr. Avison then presented a motion picture and explained the emphasis in carrying out the drive in the area. First reports of the results of the Presbytery's drive will be announced at a meeting on October 15.

Clinton—Mr. J. Edward Means, Jr., of Greenville, S. C., has been selected the new president of the Presbyterian College Alumni Association, succeeding Mr. J. Marion Kirven of Columbia. Mr. Means will serve two years.

Mr. A. B. Poe, Rock Hill, S. C., was named new Secretary-treasurer, succeeding Mr. Harry Hicklin, also of Rock Hill.

Selected as one of the three alumni representatives to the Presbyterian College Board of Trustees, was Mr. Joseph L. Barnet of Gastonia, N. C. Mr. Barnett succeeds Mr. Hugh F. Dick of Charlotte, N. C., who retired after serving the limit of two terms of three years each.

TENNESSEE

Memphis—Chelsea Avenue Presbyterian Church observed its 100th anniversary this month with special Sunday services starting October 14.

The church has the oldest building still standing of any congregation in Memphis, according to Mr. Clyde Zink, church publicity chairman. The church was organized 100 years ago with 13 members, Mr. Zink said, and the congregation built the present house of worship in 1858.

TEXAS

Austin — Austin Seminary will celebrate the founding of the first presbytery in America with a series of special lectures to be held October 28, 29 and 30. This Presbytery was organized in March of 1706 in Philadelphia.

Joining other branches of Presbyterianism in celebrating this beginning, the Seminary has chosen the last Sunday of October, usually set aside for special services as Reformation Sunday. Both occasions will be commemorated in the Sunday night lecture.

Dr. Henry P. Van Dusen of New York will give the opening address, to be held at University Presbyterian Church. Dr. Van Dusen is a member of the Presbyterian Church, U.S.A., and is president of the Union Theological Seminary, New York.

The Rev. Marion A. Boggs, pastor of the Second Presbyterian Church, Little Rock, Ark., and a member of the board of trustees of the seminary, will lecture on the "Thrill of Presbyterian Beginnings in Arkansas." The Rev. Horace Craig Casey, pastor of First Presbyterian Church in Enid, Oklahoma, one of the strongest Presbyterian, U.S.A., churches in the Southwest, will lecture on the beginnings of Presbyterianism in Oklahoma, and the Rev. Malcolm L. Purcell will lecture on the beginnings of Presbyterianism in Texas. Mr. Purcell is executive secretary of the Committee of Church Extension for Brazos Presbytery, and edited "History of Texas Presbyterianism," from a manuscript left by his uncle, Dr. W. S. Red.

The Rev. Leonard R. Swinney, the editor of the Louisiana **Red River Presbyterian** will lecture on the beginnings of Presbyterianism in his state. At the present time, Mr. Swinney is pastor of the First Presbyterian Church, Homer, La.

Plans are underway for either a reception for Dr. Van Dusen, or a dinner to include all Austin Presbyterian ministers. On both Monday and Tuesday evenings coffee chats are planned to be held in faculty members' homes where students and par-

BOOKS

1500 THEMES FOR SERIES PREACHING. William Goulooze. Baker Book House. $2.50.

This book presents suggestions for no less than 300 series of 3 to 10 suggested texts and themes for each series. Each theme seeks to focus the attention on the central truth expressed in the text or passage of Scripture.

DEVOTIONS FOR ADULT GROUPS. Wallace Fridy. Abingdon Press. $1.50.

This book contains 25 devotions bringing guidance for more successful Christian living. The material is simple, direct, and easy to understand. Included for each devotion are two hymns, a Scripture lesson and a prayer.

THE VITALITY OF FAITH. Murdo E. MacDonald. Abingdon Press. $2.50.

The author is pastor of St. George's West Church, Edinburgh. He has given in this volume 24 vigorous messages to show how Christ is the only answer to the problems which confront the world today. The author states, "I believe that the gospel we have preached was not sufficiently bold and demanding, that the Christ we have proclaimed was not big enough."

These messages are largely topical in nature, and the main theme seems to be that the Christian should not come to easy terms with the world but is commissioned to proclaim the terms of God's decisive deliverance to the world. Each message is brief, and the style is characterized by excellent readability. J.R.R.

EFFECTIVE BIBLE STUDY. Howard S. Vos. Zondervan Publishing House. $3.50.

Sixteen different methods of Bible study are set forth in this volume plus chapters studying the Bible as literature and teaching the Bible. The author defines the method under discussion and then develops an example making further suggestions for studying the subject. In addition, the author includes helpful appendices on the subject of Homiletics and Filing. The study of this volume will lead to a new appreciation and understanding of the Bible.

THE SOUTHERN PRESBYTERIAN JOURNAL

A Presbyterian weekly magazine devoted to the statement, defense and propagation of the Gospel, the faith which was once for all delivered unto the saints.

VOL. XV NO. 28 NOVEMBER 7, 1956 $2.50 A YEAR

EXAMPLE OF JESUS CHRIST

How Does He Quote The Scriptures?

Follow Jesus in the days of his flesh. With what serious and tender respect does he constantly hold in his hands "the volume of the Book," to quote every part of it, and note its shortest verses. See how one word, one single word, whether of a psalm or of an historical book, has for him the authority of a law. Mark with what confident submission he receives the whole Scriptures, without ever contesting its sacred canon; for he knows that "salvation cometh of the Jews," and that, under the infallible providence of God, "to them were committed the oracles of God." Did I say, he receives them? From his childhood to the grave, and from his rising again from the grave to his disappearance in the clouds, what does he bear always about with him, in the desert, in the temple, in the synagogue? What does he continue to quote with his resuscitated voice, just as the heavens are about to exclaim, "Lift up your heads, ye everlasting doors, and the king of glory shall come in?" It is the Bible, ever the Bible; it is Moses, the Psalms, and the prophets: he quotes them, he explains them, but how? Why verse by verse, and word by word.

—L. GAUSSEN

THE SOUTHERN PRESBYTERIAN JOURNAL

Rev. Henry B. Dendy, D.D., Editor....Weaverville, N. C.
Dr. L. Nelson Bell, Associate Editor....Asheville, N. C.
Rev. Wade C. Smith, Associate Editor....Weaverville, N. C.

CONTRIBUTING EDITORS

Mr. Chalmers W. Alexander
Rev. W. W. Arrowood, D.D.
Rev. C. T. Caldwell, D.D.
Dr. Gordon H. Clark
Rev. R. Wilbur Cousar, D.D.
Rev. B. Hoyt Evans
Rev. W. G. Foster, D.D.
Rev. Samuel McP. Glasgow, D.D
Rev. Robert F. Gribble, D.D.
Rev. Chas. G. McClure, D.D.
Dr. J. Park McCallie
Rev John Reed Miller, D.D.
Rev. J. Kenton Parker
Rev. John R. Richardson, D.D.
Rev. Wm. Childs Robinson, D.D.
Rev. George Scotchmer
Rev. Robert Strong, S.T.D.
Rev. Cary N. Weisiger, III, D.D.
Rev. W. Twyman Williams, D.D.

EDITORIAL

Not — "Lord, Lord" "But He That Doeth . . ."

There is a movement today to which has been given the ambitious title, "The 20th Century Reformation." In another area are to be found the vigorous exponents of a "new orthodoxy." One wonders if there is not needed yet another emphasis, one which recognizes the vital importance of Christian doctrine and couples with this emphasis on revealed truth a warm and personal Christian life translated into love in everyday contacts with others.

It is unhappily true that one can be rigorously orthodox and utterly obnoxious at the same time. It is equally true that one may exude something like a Satanic sweetness and be completely pagan.

Neither of these characterizations should be true of Christians. If we have been born again we are new creatures in Christ and as such should honor the Name we profess.

There is needed a new emphasis on Christian faith on the one hand and Christian living on the other. Faith centered in the person and work of the Lord Jesus Christ as He is revealed in the Scriptures is of vital importance. But that faith shows its validity only as it is translated into Christ-like lives.

Let those who pride themselves in their social consciousness be sure that it is a Christ-centered and Christ-directed concern, not a mere humanitarianism in which an enlightened pagan might gladly share.

Let those who take pride in their orthodoxy be sure that it goes farther than the orthodoxy of the Pharisees.

Shall we insist on Christian doctrine? Of course, for without it there is no Christianity. Shall we demand truly Christian living? Most assuredly, for without it our profession of faith is as a sounding brass or a tinkling cymbal.

If Christianity is to be a vital personal experience on the one hand and an effective testimony for our Lord on the other, then sound doctrine and changed lives must become synonymous. L.N.B.

Pulling Up Wheat

"The servants said unto him, Wilt thou then that we go gather them (the tares) up? But he said, Nay; lest while ye gather up the tares, ye root up also the wheat with them." Matt. 13:28,29.

Impetuosity is a characteristic of zeal without knowledge; of action without thought; of human limitations being intruded into areas where the divine perspective alone serves God's purposes. Impetuous action only too often stems from man's concern without a corresponding recognition that God is even more concerned and that He is competent to act.

While the impetuous servant is always a trial to his Master the indifferent servant is even more a cause of sorrow. The church members at Laodicea were indifferent; their tepidness demanded their rejection by the Lord.

The true Christian must be concerned but his impetuous desire to do something about the problems which he sees inside and outside the Church must be controlled by a stronger impulse — to find out God's will and then do it.

Tare (and wheat) pulling is not a new activity. The tendency to usurp God's prerogatives has been a failing of man in every generation.

The temptation to call down the fires of God's wrath on those who seem to fail to meet His standards confronts many Christians. That such is the case shows our own blindness and need of Christ's wisdom and love in our hearts.

There are grave dangers in the present separatist movement. Among these dangers are to be found spiritual pride, confusing interpretations of minor matters with basic doctrines, personality clashes, an utter lack of love and courtesy which makes a mockery of the name Christian, and a wilful disregard for the command of our Lord to "let both grow together."

Does this mean there should be no concern over error, no opposition to heresy? Just the opposite is the case. The Church has always thrived on Spirit-directed controversy. Such controversy makes for pure doctrine. But such concern must be based on truth, motivated by love, undergirded with prayer and translated into action in true humility.

Are there Scriptural grounds for separation? We believe there are probably only three. First, when so-called Christians live in open sin from which they will not turn away the Christian should separate himself from them. Second, when heresy with reference to the person and work of our Lord is tolerated or espoused and propagated such heresy must be repudiated or a true Christian must separate himself from it. Finally, if the right to give one's own testimony for Christ is refused or limited by ecclesiastical or other pressures then there is no recourse other than that of the early disciples who affirmed that they could "but speak the things which we have seen and heard."

To lay impatient hands on the tares is a pressing temptation. But, our chief concern is not the tares but the wheat. It is the Church of the living Christ, composed of true believers, about which we must think. In God's own time the tares will be taken care of.

The ultimate end of the unbeliever is a tragically certain one. At the time of harvest the Lord of the harvest will say: "Gather ye together first the tares, and bind them into bundles to burn them."

The Christian's objective must be the conservation of and the multiplication of the wheat. It is this harvest of regenerated souls which will be gathered into the barn of God's eternity.

Because Christ commands it: *keep your hands off of those tares ! ! !* L.N.B

A Basket of Fruit

The Fruit of the Spirit (Galatians 5:22,23)

The Fruit of the Spirit . . .
Gentleness (Kindness)

The kindness of God our Saviour; With everlasting kindness; His marvelous kindness; Be ye kind one to another. How the Bible is filled with the Loving-kindness of God! I like this definition of courtesy; "Courtesy is to do and say, the kindest thing in the kindest way."

I. *The Kindness of God our Saviour:* Titus 3:4.

We have a beautiful hymn, "Awake, My Soul, In Joyful Lays." I wish to use the chorus of this hymn to guide in our thinking about His Loving Kindness:

1. His Loving Kindness, O how free! Think of the "Alls," the "Everyones"; the "Whosoevers": Come unto Me all ye that labor; Ho, everyone that thirsteth; Whosoever will, let him take the water of life freely, etc.

2. His Loving Kindness, O how great! Out of the pit; out of the depths; From sinking sand He lifted me; With loving hands, He lifted me.

3. His Loving Kindness, O how Strong! The forces of evil are strong; He can save us, if we lean upon Him; My strength is made perfect in weakness.

4. His Loving Kindness, O how good! When trouble, like a gloomy cloud, has gathered thick and thundered loud; Cast thy burden upon the Lord.

5. His Loving Kindness changes not! O Thou, Who changest not, Abide with me. He is the same yesterday, today, and forever. He was kind to Elijah; He will be kind to me. Think of how kind Jesus was to all who needed Him! He went about doing good. His eyes saw those in need; His ears were open to their cry; His feet led Him all over the hills of Galilee; His hands touched, lifted, healed; His heart was moved with compassion. The Loving Kindness of God, our Saviour!

II. *Be ye kind one to another:* Ephesians 4:32. What sort of kindness?

Kind Feelings, which spring from loving hearts.

Kind Thoughts: "Think on these things," said Paul, in Philippians 4:8.

The Southern Presbyterian Journal, *a Presbyterian Weekly magazine devoted to the statement, defense, and propagation of the Gospel, the faith which was once for all delivered unto the saints,* published every Wednesday by The Southern Presbyterian Journal, Inc., in Weaverville, N. C.

Entered as second-class matter May 15, 1942, at the Postoffice at Weaverville, N. C., under the Act of March 3, 1879. Vol. XV, No. 28, November 7, 1956. Editorial and Business Offices: Weaverville, N. C. Printed in the U.S.A. by Biltmore Press, Asheville, N. C.

ADDRESS CHANGE: When changing address, please let us have both old and new address as far in advance as possible. Allow three weeks after change if not sent in advance. When possible, send an address label giving your old address.

Kind Words: The law of kindness was on her tongue; A word fitly spoken is like apples of gold in a network of silver; words spoken in the right place and in the right kind of voice; words of Comfort, of Encouragement, of Exhortation, of wise counsel, of warning; spoken humbly and lovingly.

Kind Deeds; Every time we read the Bible, or hear a sermon, we ought to do something for somebody. (I read this somewhere). Look all around you, find someone in need; Help somebody today! That somebody may be a little child, or an aged man or woman, or a helpless cripple, or someone with a burdened soul, or a "down and out" man in the ditch, or somebody who has erred and we can restore him. O the good we may all do while the days are going by!

Where can we find such a brand of "Gentleness," or "Kindness"? It is a fruit of the Spirit.
—J.K.P.

Our Children Need the Grace of the Covenant-Keeping God

Over the last week-end it was the writer's privilege to preside at the Table of the Lord in a retreat for the local Westminster Fellowship. By choice I used, as I usually do, an order of service found in the *Book of Common Worship*. There are many other useful forms and aids in this book.

May I suggest, however, that we do not put entirely aside the *Directory of Worship* of our own *Book of Church Order*. Particularly, in the questions asked of parents presenting their children for baptism, our Book is much richer and clearer than the questions in the Book of Common Worship. Use the introductory or closing statements from the Book of Common Worship, and recognize the congregation in some way. I like to have the whole congregation stand and repeat the Apostles' Creed, as I am told, the Scottish Church does. But compare the questions of the two books and you will be impressed by the superiority of our own in the fullness of its statement of Gospel truth, in the greater clarity of its Augustinian and Calvinistic doctrine. Don't merely drift into an exclusive use of the Book of Common Worship. Take the time and trouble to think through the matter. Put the two together and draw up your own service.

Zwingli considered the sacraments as exercises in which the believer thinks of Christ, remembers His past work for us, meditates on Him. For this line of doctrine, Christ is not objectively present, but is only the object of man's thought. When Calvin realized the emptiness of this conception it held him back for a time from Protestantism. Calvin's own views were closer to Luther than to Zwingli. In the early work, *Instruction in Faith*, par. 27, Calvin defines a sacrament exclusively as something the Lord does. In the final edition of the *Institutes* he defines a sacrament primarily as what the Lord does; but, with his usual balance, he also defines it secondarily as what we do. The two questions in the Book of Common Worship seem to be entirely devoted to what man does, that is, with what is Zwinglian and is only secondary to Calvin. And even here the Book of Common Worship questions are not nearly so ample as are those of our Directory of Worship. Most of all, notice how full of Gospel truth is the appeal in our questions to the action of God for the child of the covenant. Our questions are those of a real covenanting in which we appeal to God to do what He alone can do, and we, on our part as parents, promise to do what we can.

We look to God for four things for our covenant child.

According to the questions of our Directory we acknowledge our child's need: (1) of the cleansing blood of Jesus Christ; and (2) of the renewing grace of the Holy Spirit. We claim for him (3) God's covenant promises in his behalf, and we look in faith (4) to the Lord Jesus Christ for his salvation as we do for our own.

Then, secondarily, we on our part, in addition to confessing our child's need and looking in faith to Christ for his salvation promise some four things. As we dedicate or give our child to God, we promise (1) to set an example before him, (2) to pray with and for him, (3) to teach him our holy religion, and (4) to strive to bring him up in the nurture and admonition of the Lord.

Compared with this rich and full form of covenanting the Book of Common Worship has an impoverished set of questions, namely:

"In presenting your child for baptism, do you confess your faith in Jesus Christ as your Lord and Saviour; and do you promise, in dependence on the grace of God, to bring up your child in the nurture and admonition of the Lord?"

"What is the Christian name of this child?"

In these two questions the parent makes no appeal to God, the Father and author of the covenant, to the Son and Saviour of sinners, or to the Holy Spirit, the giver of faith, to do anything for the child.

In quite Zwinglian fashion the parents reprofess their own faith and they promise to bring up their child in the nurture and admonition of the Lord. My Father's son needed something more than my godly parents were able to do for me. I needed what only the Triune God of the covenant can do. W.C.R.

Women Should Not Be Ordained Leaders of the Church

The recent General Assembly approved by a majority of *eight* votes an Ad Interim Committee report to allow women to serve as elders and deacons in our church. Each presbytery will now vote on it, and a *majority* of the presbyteries will have to vote in favor of it before it will be allowed in our church.

Some of the reasons why *we should defeat this report in the presbyteries* are:

1. This proposal will *undermine the Scriptures as our authority* for the standards of our church. When it comes to the qualifications of those who are to stand officially in a position of leadership in the church of Jesus Christ, we are not left in doubt; these qualifications *clearly emphasize and assume that it is to be a man.*

In I Timothy 3, Paul states, under the guiding of the Holy Spirit: "If a man desire the office of a bishop (elder), he desireth a good work. A bishop then must be blameless, the husband of one wife, vigilant, sober, of good behavior, given to hospitality, apt to teach." It is quite obvious from the Scripture that the position is *masculine*—among other things the husband is to rule his own house, having in subjection his own children. It seems quite clear as you study the qualifications that they do not in any sense leave an open door for the ordination of women. We have the same truth set forth in Titus 1:5-9.

2. From the very beginning, and throughout the entire Old Testament, there can be no question as to the authority of man to be the head of the wife, the family, and when commissioned thereto the head of the church.

3. This headship of man was not changed in the New Testament. In Ephesians where the relationship of the wife to the husband is likened to the church, we read, "Wives, submit yourselves unto your own husbands, as unto the Lord. For the husband is the head of the wife, even as Christ is the head of the church; and He is the saviour of the body. Therefore, as the church is subject unto Christ, so let the wives be to their own husbands in everything." (5:22-24)

4. All recognize the fact that subjection or subordination *does not necessarily mean inferiority.* We have that lesson set forth in the Holy Trinity where the Son and the Holy Spirit, though not inferior to the Father, yet are in subjection to the Father. This is illustrated all about us. The private in the army may be the physical and mental superior of his officer but he is nevertheless in subjection to him. Remember therefore, *subordination does not mean inferiority.*

5. *Nowhere in Scriptures are women given places of authority over men in the church.* I Cor. 11:3 states the *divine order* clearly. "But I would have you know that the head of every man is Christ, and the head of the woman is the man, and the head of Christ is God."

6. This does not mean that women cannot serve in the church nor have a vital part in the work of the Church. It merely means that they *are not to be elevated to the office of ordained leaders.* Where ordination of women has been permitted, it has often resulted in disintegration. We are all quite aware that men certainly have made their share of blunders and mistakes and history records clearly how some have contributed to heresy and error. Generally speaking, where are the women today who are ordained to the ministry? For the most part in the liberal churches, in the emotional groups and in the cults and isms, such as Mary Baker Eddy and Christian Science. One would conclude, therefore, that where women are permitted to take the leadership *contrary to the Word of God,* you are opening wide the door for trouble.

7. There is little indication that the women in our church desire the office of elder and deacon, or such a change in our Book of Church Order.

8. If the ordination of women as elders and deacons is approved by our church, it will be the *first step toward ordaining women as ministers.* The Northern Presbyterian Church this past year approved the ordination of women as ministers after having previously allowed them to be ordained as elders and deacons.

We should not let those in favor of this report confuse the issue by pointing out the wonderful work the women are now doing in the Church, that other denominations allow this, etc. We should stand on *the authority of the Scriptures, as we bel*ieve all of our standards are, *that women are not to be ordained and placed in authority over men in the government of the church.*

We should do everything possible to enlighten our brethren as to all that is involved in this issue and make every effort to defeat this report when it is voted upon in our Presbytery.

How I Learned To Pray For The Lost

(An Echo from Anglers)

We know that believers everywhere are burdened for unsaved or backsliding loved ones. However, many are praying in a spirit of fear and worry instead of in faith.

This has caused the writer to seek for definite light on how to pray, feeling the need of praying the right prayer, also the need for a definite promise or word from God upon which to base our faith when praying for the unsaved. Praise God, He never fails to give such needed help.

Perhaps because the salvation of some looked to us to be an impossibility, the first Scripture that was given us was Mark 10:27, "With God all things are possible."

The next Scripture had occupied our attention sometime before but with new emphasis now: "For the weapons of our warfare are not carnal, but mighty through God to the pulling down of strongholds; casting down imaginations (margin—"reasonings"), and every high thing that exalteth itself against the knowledge of God, and bringing into captivity every thought to the obedience of Christ" (2 Cor. 10:4, 5). This shows the mighty power of our spiritual weapons. And we must pray that all this be accomplished in the ones for whom we pray; that is, that the works of the enemy be torn down.

Finally we were given the solid basis for our prayers—the ground of redemption. In reality, redemption purchased all mankind, so that we may say that each one is, actually, God's purchased possession although still held by the enemy. We must, through the prayer of faith, claim and take for God in the name of the Lord Jesus that which is rightfully His. This can be done only on the ground of redemption. We do not mean to imply that because all persons have been purchased by God through redemption they are thus automatically saved. They must believe and accept the gospel for themselves; this our intercession enables them to do.

To pray in the name of the Lord Jesus is to ask for or to claim the things which the blood of Christ has secured. Therefore each individual for whom prayer is made should be claimed by name, as God's purchased possession, in the name of the Lord Jesus on the ground of His shed blood.

We should claim the tearing down of all of the works of Satan, such as false doctrine, unbelief, Communistic teaching, hatred, etc., which the enemy may have built up in their thinking, and that their very thoughts shall be brought into captivity to the obedience of Christ.

— LETTERS —

Men—, Never Women, Were Called To Be Elders

Sir:

The current issue, Shall women be elders?, disturbs me very much.

I am a 73 year old woman, the daughter of an elder.

I am the wife of an elder, the sister of an elder; also I am the mother of an elder, as well as the mother-in-law of elders. But *never* have I wished to *be* an elder.

Since I was eighteen I have taught in the Sunday School, till ill health has prevented that service.

In women's work I have held every office in that organization; some, even President, more than once. Also the Presbyterial offices were mine, as long as I could accept them. Still, never have I wished to be an elder.

Why?

First, - I never even *thought* of such presumption. The Bible says an elder shall be husband of one wife", (Titus 1:6), so, obviously, *I* do not qualify.

Second—As I began to consider the question, I wondered how *any* one could even *think* of electing a *woman* to that office. I searched the Scriptures for an answer. I did not find it, but I *did* find a number of admonitions to women *not* to hold any authority over a man. He is called the "head" of a woman, as Christ is "Head" of the church. She is to "be in subjection," not to in any way "have authority over man." To place a woman in such an office in the church, is entirely *un*scriptural, if one believes, and accepts, the Bible as God's Word.

Third—I question *why* men wish to share their God-given authority in the church to women? Is it because they are ashamed of the complications, not to say mess, they have led us into? Or, are they *tired* of carrying the responsibility, the burden of authority, and seek help from us women?

Why is it? Perhaps ministers think they can control women better than they can handle men.

As I consider this danger, I pray God, I may never be in a church so far misguided, as to have women pass me the elements in the Lord's Supper. (Mrs.) D. L. Norris

There's So Much Beauty in Little Things

By R. Ross Parkhill

There's so much beauty in little things
I often wonder why
We do not pause to look at it
Instead of passing by.

What mystery lies in spaniels' eyes
Of almandines' brown hue,
Or charm in wild, blue violet blooms
All jeweled with the dew.

What lovelier sight than candle light,
And shadows on a wall,
Or a flickering flame from fat pine wood
Like a midget fireball.

And green wood moss flecked with fairy floss
Deep in a shaded nook
Where nimbly flows, in playful mood,
A merry little brook.

Have you ever heard a hummingbird
Greet the nectared flower,
Or listened to a cardinal
Singing in a shower?

Have you ever seen a nectarine
Picked, fresh, from off its twig,
Or felt the damson, satin skin
Of a tree-ripened fig?

Did you ever hold a bit of gold,
A tiny buttercup—
A gilded chalice elfins use
When they are wont to sup?

Some beach birds swing, when on the wing,
Into the ocean breeze,
Then scatter far like thistle down
Upon the plunging seas.

All these are lovely; and many more
Are found in Beauty's face.
Oh, how could anyone be blind
To such delightful grace?

The Journal has a poetic friend
Who sends us gems like this.
His poems are lofty from start to end
And filled with loveliness.

We asked him if, instead of "it"
On third line of first verse
He'd consider changing "it" to "them",
Or would that make it worse?

Now see how well he answered us
And how stupid we must feel!
He knew full well his syllabus—
And we were off our keel.

"Beauty" is "it"
And "little things" are strong
And we admit
That "spaniels' eyes" and "almandines" belong.

This is the poet's response to our ill conceived attempt to edit. W.C.S.

In cogitating what I've writ
I'm glad it seems a gem.
Though Beauty singular is "it"
And never, never "them".

This is what I had in mind,
Yet if you want to change
I'll not be one to wholly bind
An editor's free range.

The "little things" in Beauty's face,
'T is true are numberless,
But still 't is Beauty sets the pace
Or I shall miss my guess.

It seems a pronoun might confuse
Unless strict rules apply,
And in this instance proper clues
Must certainly comply.

We speak of blossoms in a bowl,
"It is a lovely sight."
And they so gathered as a whole
Is "it" though recondite.

And so the "little things" we see
Are not, themselves, the prize,
But rather what each ought to be—
Pure beauty to our eyes. R.R.P.

10,000 years ago, radiocarbon time. The Warka mound is well known because of its long succession of ruins of great temples, the last of which before the FLOOD are in Layer IV. One of these was especially magnificent, both in size and finish. It was built on a great platform which is a mute witness to the labors of thousands of oppressed peoples of those wicked days. In Layer IV the oldest known writing has been found. (Note this was before the FLOOD).

Nimrod's temple, the ruins of which are found in Layer III (just above Layer IV) was much smaller in every way than the antediluvian temples, as one might expect. The FLOOD had destroyed a thickly populated land, and as yet Noah's posterity had not multiplied greatly. The most interesting feature of this temple of Nimrod was a ditch, which some archeologists claim was used for the burial of burnt offerings. If the interpretation is correct, it is very valuable information, for burnt offerings, where the entire animal is burnt have never been popular among heathen, who much prefer "sacrifices" where most of the animal is eaten. This is in harmony with the Bible, which records that Noah offered burnt offerings after the FLOOD, and it seems to confirm that there were many worshippers of God yet in Nimrod's day.

Layer III has three subdivisions which indicates that the Jemdet Nasr culture lasted several centuries. Frankfort's estimate of nearly a millenium cannot be accepted.

It seems probable that Babel, the first in the list of Nimrod's cities, refers to Jemdet Nasr, which was not occupied in later times, and so would not be mentioned in Babylonian literature. Which of the Jemdet Nasr sites of Accadia (northern Mesopotamia) is meant by the Biblical Accad is not known, though several sites with Jemdet Nasr culture have been excavated. Notice how accurate the contemporary account is, for no great cities founded later are mentioned.

PART II

The Culture of Nimrod's Times

Let us try to visualize the people of Nimrod's (Jemdet Nasr) times in the light of archeology. These times were very different from those before the flood in every way. They began perhaps about 500 years after the FLOOD, and probably some of the passengers of the ark were still living. The lessons of the FLOOD were fresh in the minds of all, it was no *myth* to them even though they could not give a scientific explanation of it. Here was a society in which God was known and consequently there was a rapid advance in culture. We have space for only a few glimpses at an early happy people.

It was a prosperous society, for the climate was cool and moist, and farming was without irrigation. There were no enemies without. There were many varieties of food, but we would call the tools crude.

One gets the impression of an equal economy. There was as yet no great gulf between rich and poor as in antediluvian days. More houses were built of unbaked brick instead of being mere huts. They had floors of baked brick with tile drains.

The great distinctive feature from an archeological point of view is the pottery. (Its broken pieces are preserved by nature) Pottery of Nimrod's days was better made and more artistically decorated than that of antediluvian days which was plain. One has to go back in history much nearer the time of Adam to find such pretty pottery. Much was decorated in many colors.

Art was not restricted to pottery alone, for the people were expert in carving various kinds of stone. Vases of alabaster and other materials have been found. A fine example is a basalt carving of two hunters slaying three lions. The women had finely spun clothes, and pretty ornaments. They wore their hair down their backs. The men enjoyed their fishing, and had a game similar to checkers. Noah had not forgotten to take his pet dogs into the ark, and everywhere in postdiluvian days dogs accompanied their masters.

It would be helpful if we could find more information about the religion of Nimrod's time, but spiritual religion leaves little material traces behind. At Asmar to the north there is a small temple with an altar by the northwestern wall. There is a similar temple at Khafaje, not far distant. So far nothing that can be called an idol has been found. Langdon thinks there was as yet monothesism. God was called "An." But sad to say before the Jemdet Nasr period was over, idolatry seems to have begun to infiltrate.

Helps To Understanding Scripture Readings in *Day by Day*

By Rev. C. C. Baker

Sunday, November 18, *I Peter* 3:8-12. The Christian Church is made up of people who love one another. Think about the various exhortations in vv.8-10 and consider how each would contribute to harmony of a local church. How would failure to heed these exhortations stir up strife in a church? Which exhortation hits at a need in your life? Are you guilty of the sin forbidden in v.10? What desirable fruits are mentioned in vv.10-12 that come to the person who is truly loving? How does God regard the contentious (v.12b)? Verse 15a provides the answer to an unloving spirit. If we love Christ supremely we will also love others. How real is your love for Christ (1:8)?

Monday, Nov. 19, *Psalm* 46. The theme of the Psalm is set forth in vv.1,7,11 and the first line of verse 2. The Lord of Hosts achieves His purposes among the nations (vv.8-10). He can speak a word and dissolve the earth (v.6). Surely, then, the Psalmist's statement of v.2a should be true for anyone who trusts in God, even in the face of the catastrophies of verses 2-3. God lives within the tabernacle (v.5) that is in the midst of His people (v.4). How do the personal pronouns in vv.1-2,7,11 also reveal God's closeness to the Psalmist? What do the phrases "a very present help" (v.1) and "that right early" (v.5) add to the theme of vv.1,7,11? Does the close presence of the Lord of Hosts in your life keep you from fear?

Tuesday, November 20, *II Corinthians* 9. Paul was traveling among the early churches receiving offerings for the relief of the hungry Christians in Jerusalem (Romans 15:25-26). The Corinthian church had made certain pledges (8:10-11), but had delayed in paying them (v.5). Observe the Christian love and tact Paul used in dealing with them. How did he express confidence in them (v.2)? What effects did he hope his boasting would have on them (vv.2-4)? Notice the motivation Paul presented for their giving (vv.6-14). What effect would it have on them as givers (vv.6,8,11)? What good would it do to those who received (vv.12-14)?

Iow would it glorify God (v.13)? Notice that 'aul did not go to the Corinthians at once (v.5). How must this have avoided embarrassnent? Have you learned to deal tactfully and ovingly with those who procrastinate or, in ome other way, neglect their Christian duty?

Wednesday, November 21, *Acts* 2:43-47. The vents of these verses occurred on the day of 'entecost, the day on which the Holy Spirit vas poured out upon the Church (vv.1-4). Observe the response of the crowd to Peter's sernon (vv.37-41). See how quickly these new Christians were drawn together in love for one mother (vv.42,44-45). Notice their faithfulness n worship and communion (vv.46-47), their concern for the physical well-being of the group (v.45), their rejoicing in their faith (vv.46-47), heir growing in faith (v.42), their witnessing for the Lord (v.47). Notice, again, the spontaneity of the behavior of these Christians (vv.42-47). Here is the primitive Church in ll her power, with few physical resources but with a wealth of spiritual treasure. Pray for mother outpouring of God's Spirit upon the Church.

Thursday, November 22, *Psalm* 96. Praise is often missing in the Christian's prayer life. Notice from this Psalm that praise results from a realization of who God is. What discovery has the Psalmist made about the Lord in relation to other gods (vv.4-6)? What other facts does he know about the Lord (vv.10,13)? What results in the heart of the Psalmist from his knowledge of what God is like (vv.1-3,7,8)? Meditate on the imagery of vv.11-12. Observe the place of dedication and worship in the Psalmist's praise (vv. (vv.8b-9). How is missionary interest developed (vv.1,3,7,9,10)? The author virtually "bubbles over" with joy. Can you think of any way in which praise has deepened your Christian life?

Friday, November 23, *Hebrews* 11:32-38. People in the Old Testament were saved by faith (v.2) as they looked forward to a better world prepared by God for them (vv.13,16). Observe what faith accomplished in Noah (v.7), Abraham and Sarah (vv.8-12), Moses (vv.23-28), the Israelite nation (vv.29-31), others (vv.32-34). How was obedience related to faith in each of these cases? Can a person have true faith in God without obedience to God? Each forward movement of God's program in the Old Testament was accomplished as men committed their lives to God by faith. Notice what faith cost these Old Testament saints (vv.35-38)? Yet, they did not know the revelation of Christ, having only promises of something better to come (vv.39-40). Does your faith in Christ include obedience to Him?

Saturday, November 24, *Matthew* 6:24-34. The Christian is continually making choices that involve his first allegiance. What is the advantage in the next life of making right choices now (vv.19-21)? What advantages result in this life from seeking first the Kingdom of God (vv.26,30,33)? What is characteristic of the inner life of the person who seeks God's kingdom first (v.22)? What is his basic attitude toward God (v.24)? What often motivates a person to make wrong choices (vv.31-32)? What is true of that person's inner life (v.23)? of his attitude toward God (v.24)? of his future reward (vv.19-20)? What do the choices you make concerning the things of God reveal of your inner life? of your attitude toward God? of the nature of your eternal reward?

SABBATH SCHOOL LESSONS — REV. J. KENTON PARKER

LESSON FOR NOVEMBER 18

The Beatitudes

Background Scripture: Matthew 4:23 - 5:20
Devotional Reading: Psalm 15:1-5; 24:3-6

Our lesson with its Background Scripture includes more than the Beatitudes, and a better title might be the Young People - Adult Topic; Qualities of a Christian, but even that does not cover all, for we begin with a Summary of Jesus' ministry. We would call it, The Character of the Citizens of the Kingdom.

Our Devotional Reading gives us a picture of a Citizen of Zion as seen through the eyes of the Psalmist. I mentioned some of these characteristics in our last lesson. Let us look at some more. The question is asked, Lord, who shall abide in thy tabernacle? Who shall dwell in thy holy hill? The answer is, He that walketh uprightly, and worketh righteousness, and speaketh the truth in his heart. He that backbiteth not with his tongue, nor doeth evil to his neighbor, nor taketh up a reproach against his neighbor. There is more to this description. Compare it with the verses we have in our lesson from the Sermon on the Mount. In Psalm 24 a similar question is asked and the answer is, He that hath clean hands and a pure heart; who hath not lifted up his soul unto vanity, nor sworn deceitfully. Both of these descriptions fit what Dr. Shearer calls the Text for the Sermon on the Mount; For I say unto you, that except your righteousness shall exceed the righteousness of the scribes and Pharisees, ye shall in no case enter into the Kingdom of heaven. In other words, God looks at the "hidden man of the heart," and insists upon sincerity.

I. *A Short Summary of Jesus' Ministry*: Matthew 4:23-25.

The public ministry of Jesus has a three-fold nature; Teaching, Preaching, and Healing. In His Preaching Jesus proclaims the Kingdom of God as at hand, and calls upon men to repent and believe the Gospel. In His Teaching, which is closely related to His Preaching, of course, we find Him instructing His disciples and all who would hear, in the principles and practices of those who would enter the Kingdom. We have a sample of that teaching and preaching in the Sermon on the Mount, a part of which forms our lesson. In His healing He cured all manner of sickness and disease and cast out demons. He thus proved that He had the right to heal the sin-sick souls of men and deliver those who were in bondage to Satan. Great multitudes followed Him, both to be healed and to hear Him, for "never man spake like this man."

II. *The Beatitudes: Character of the Citizens of the Kingdom:* Matt. 5:1-12.

Who is the "blessed," or "happy" man? The first Psalm tells us about him and we find his portrait in these first twelve verses of the Sermon on the Mount. If you were to ask the average man of the world, or man on the street, this question, you would probably get a variety of answers: wealth, pleasure, position, home and friends, would no doubt be mentioned. As we read and ponder these words of Jesus let us ask ourselves if we measure up to His specifications.

"Blessed are the poor in spirit." Luke says only, Blessed are ye poor. (Luke 6:20). The Jews regarded wealth as a special mark of God's favor, and were inclined to despise poor people. A great many of God's finest people have been poor as far as worldly possessions were concerned, and many of these have been very happy. The thought goes much deeper than this, however, and refers to the condition of the soul.

A good example, as Dr. Broadus says, is found in the parable of the Pharisee and the publican. The Pharisee had a haughty spirit, very proud of its righteousness, while the publican cried out, God be merciful to me a sinner. We must recognize our spiritual poverty before God can make us rich, and happy, or blessed.

"Blessed are they that mourn." This, in the eyes of the world, seems almost a contradiction. Tears are not usually associated with joy. If our sorrow leads us to the Source of all comfort, then the result of our experience is to have the "joy in the morning," of which the Psalmist speaks: "They that sow in tears shall reap in joy. He that goeth forth and weepeth, bearing precious seed, shall doubtless come again with rejoicing, bringing his sheaves with him"; "weeping may endure for a night but joy cometh in the morning." If it is sorrow for sin, a mark of genuine repentance, then we can say with David, "Blessed is the man whose transgression is forgiven, whose sin is covered." A godly sorrow, which worketh repentance, leads to joy.

"Blessed are the meek, for they shall inherit the earth." (see Psalm 7:11) It looks sometimes as though the proud would inherit the earth, when we see the so-called world-conquerors parade across the pages of history. These proud men will go down to the pit, for God resisteth the proud, but gives grace to the lowly. Not only grace, but the "inheritance" will be to the meek.

"Blessed are they which do hunger and thirst after righteousness : for they shall be filled." The man who has a strong desire after personal righteousness will be filled; the man who desires holiness will be made increasingly holy. The trouble with most of us, I am afraid, is that we are satisfied to be half-fed; we do not yearn after full satisfaction. Few of us can really say with David, "As the hart panteth after the water brooks, so panteth my soul after Thee, O God." Would it not be very fitting for us to stop right here and ask God to make us really hungry and thirsty for Him; for righteousness?

"Blessed are the merciful: for they shall obtain mercy." The world is full of "hard-boiled," cold-blooded people who show no mercy on their fellowmen. The horrors of two World Wars have shown us how hard and cruel men can be. We read not long ago of one notorious woman in Germany who had slain thousands upon thousands of helpless men and women. Jesus' parable of the Unmerciful servant should be read and heeded by all of us.

"Blessed are the pure in heart: for they shall see God." Our God is Holy, which is the same as pure. Without holiness no man shall see Him. The end and purpose of sanctification is holiness, as we more and more die unto sin and live unto righteousness, being renewed in the whole man after the image of Christ. "More holiness give me," is not merely a beautiful hymn to sing, but a prayer that we should utter every day.

"Blessed are the peacemakers." There are plenty of "war-mongers" in the world whose delight is to stir up strife between nations and races and classes. It is a blessing when we have rulers who do all they can to "keep the peace." There are those who are "bent on mischief" and seek to break up homes and stir up trouble in communities. The children of God are peacemakers, both in large and in small affairs. The devil and his followers stir up strife.

We come now to the two most surprising of the Beatitudes. How can a man be blessed or happy when he is reviled and persecuted? and when men speak all manner of evil against him? Notice the three qualifying phrases; "persecuted for righteousness' sake"; "falsely"; "for my sake". If we are reproached for the name of Christ, happy are we. He, our Saviour, was reviled and persecuted, and called every mean name. If we suffer for His sake then happy are we.

III. *The Usefulness of such Citizens:* 5:13-16.

"Ye are the salt of the earth." Salt is a very useful thing. The world is awfully corrupt, even as meat which is unsalted. Citizens of the Kingdom help to preserve the world from complete corruption; from moral and spiritual decay. Directly, or indirectly, their influence is felt in society. Someone has said, "Sodom and Gomorrah have come down to earth again"; the whole social and economic and political world is "rotten with sin." Why has not judgment come? God is waiting for men to repent. Millions of true Christians are acting as "salt" in a world of sin. Ten righteous people could have saved Sodom from destruction.

Salt has another use. It gives flavor to food. We season things with salt to make them taste good. Life is very tasteless and meaningless to me without God, without Christ, without Salvation in all its rich flavor. Is life worth living? is a question which some answer in the negative. To live for Christ; to make our one aim in life the glory of God, is to make life worthwhile and meaningful. Only Christians can have the abundant life. Are we adding "flavor" to the world? Notice the word of warning; the salt that has lost its savor is good for nothing. To be a real Christian is to be "good for something."

"Ye are the light of the world." In John 8:12 Jesus says, "I am the light of the world," and later on, As thou has sent me into the world even so send I them into the world. He came as the LIGHT, to reveal the Father, and to show us the way back home. We are to let our light shine so that men may see and glorify God and Christ. There used to be a church somewhere in Europe which had no lights. When the people came to church at night each one brought his own light. Are we lighting up the world for Jesus? There is a word of warning here, too. We must not hide our light, but let it shine. We are His witnesses; His torch-bearers.

IV. *Our Rules; The Commandments:*
Jesus came to fulfil the Law.

YOUNG PEOPLE'S DEPARTMENT — **REV. B. HOYT EVANS**

YOUTH PROGRAM FOR NOVEMBER 18

Thanksgiving

Scripture: Psalm 95:1-7a; I Cor. 15:54-57; II Cor. 9:15; Phil. 4:4-7

Suggested Hymns: "Now Thank We All Our God"
"Come, Ye Thankful People, Come"
"Rejoice, Ye Pure In Heart"

Suggestions for Program Committee:

(For the Thanksgiving season you may want to undertake something more elaborate than your regular youth meeting. You might plan a special Thanksgiving service for the young people, or a youth sponsored service for the entire congregation, if you do not already have one in your church. There is also the possibility of working with young people in the other churches of the community in an interdenominational service. Possible times for a Thanksgiving service would be the Sunday before Thanksgiving Day, the Wednesday evening before Thanksgiving, and Thanksgiving Day itself. If you do decide to conduct such a service, you ought to recognize that it will require careful planning and faithful work if it is to be a success.)

Leader's Introduction:

We have many reasons for being proud of our country, and one of the best justifications for our pride is the fact that we have a day of thanksgiving. Thanksgiving is strictly American. There is nothing like it anywhere else.

There are other nations that have more national holidays than we do, but there is none that has a day set apart for the giving of thanks to God for what He has done for us. It is not at all difficult to point out spiritual shortcomings in America, but we ought to be very grateful that we still observe Thanksgiving Day as a nation, and we ought to work and pray to the end that it will be observed properly.

Our speakers will remind us of some of the many blessings we have for which to be thankful, and they will suggest some practical ways of expressing our thanks to God.

First Speaker:

The story is told of a man who came as a visitor to the United States from one of the poverty-stricken, war-ravaged countries of Europe. The American friend who met him as he came from the ship in New York harbor decided to show him the whole country. Together they made a swing down the east coast, across the nation to the Pacific coast, and then back to New York. The visitor reserved all comment until the journey was over. Quite naturally the host wondered what his guest thought of what he had seen, so he asked him. The visitor said very simply, "You Americans need nothing, because you have everything, and you can do everything."

It is very likely that few of us realize how much we do have in the way of material blessings compared to the rest of the world. We think it strange that people of other nations have the idea that all Americans are rich, but measuring by the standards of most countries we ARE all rich. Perhaps we would appreciate our material blessings more, if we were better acquainted with conditions in most other places throughout the world. If we would only take some time each day to count our blessings, we would begin to see how wonderfully God has provided for us, and it would change our whole outlook on life.

Assuming that we are aware of our blessings, how can we best express our thanks to God? The most obvious way is to thank Him by our words and in our thoughts. Too often we think of prayer as a synonym for requests made to God. The Lord wants us to address our requests to Him, but He also wants us to thank Him for what He has done for us. How often do we think thoughts of thanksgiving to God? How much of our praying is devoted to the giving of thanks? Our spoken prayers and our thoughts afford two very practical and important avenues of thanking God. Let us see that we use them.

The words we speak are not very convincing unless our deeds back them up. This is true

gift ideas *for Children*

SING-A-BIBLE STORY. A grand new gift for the "small fry." Twelve Bible pictures and twelve action songs . . . full color throughout. Shiny Kromekote cover . . . inexpensive, too. Ideal for parents and teachers to give.

No. 3161 . . . . 50c.

ACTION STORIES TO MAKE. A fascinating new project activity! Bible pictures and companion present-day pictures to color and assemble. Two-way action story as tab is pulled out from picture. Children love them. . . . . . . **10 for $3.00**

No. 2461, Book 1 . . . . Early Life of Jesus
No. 2462, Book 2 . . . Jesus' Ministry and Resurrection

FOLD-UP STORYBOOKS. Two delightful books with brightly colored pictures and flaps that lift up to show what's going on "inside." Each has brief stories and prayer.

No. 2922. House Full of Prayers . . $1.00
No. 2707. Ark Full of Animals . . . $1.00

FOUR NEW GIFT BOOKS FOR CHILDREN. Colorful! Illustrated! Inexpensive! Ideal for home or class giving. Size, 5 x 7 inches, 16 pages . . . . **Each, 15c.**

For smaller children

No. 2003 . . . . God's Gifts to Me
No. 2004 . . . . . . My First Story of Jesus

For older children

No. 2007 . . . . Prayers for Children
No. 2008 . . . . Loving God

De Luxe BIBLE STORY BOOKS

Here are two books of Bible stories children will read over and over again. Each has 44 stories and full-page Bible pictures in bright color. . . . . . . **Each $1.95**

No. 2735. Bible Stories About Jesus
No. 2736. Bible Stories for Little Folk

BIBLE STORIES READERS. De luxe books for every child's library. Best-loved Bible stories, Biblical art and modern full-color drawings. **Book One (under 6 yrs.), Book Two (6 yrs.), Book Three (7 yrs.), Book Four (8 yrs.), Book Five (9 yrs.).**

Price, each $1.50

At Your Bookstore or
STANDARD PUBLISHING Cincinnati 31, Ohio

Women's Work

This Is PRESBYTERIAN SURVEY Week

If you are a subscriber, now is the time to check your subscription and make sure it is good for the year.

If you are not a subscriber, enter your subscription now - that your home may have the influence of this your Church magazine - full of Christian inspiration.

If your Church does not have the magazine going to every home that the whole Church family may have the SURVEY this is a good time to see if this can be arranged in order that your people may have information and inspiration.

YOURS CAN BE AN INFORMED FAMILY!

YOURS CAN BE AN INFORMED CHURCH FAMILY!

Subscription price for year - $2.00. Order from Presbyterian Survey, Presbyterian Building, Box 1176, Richmond 9, Virginia.

East Mississippi Presbyterial

The forty-ninth annual meeting of the Women of the Church of East Mississippi Presbytery was held in the First Presbyterian Church, Pontotoc, Miss., on October 16 and 17.

"Forward with Christ by prayer, thanksgiving, in Christian Citizenship" was the theme used for the meeting, which was presided over by Mrs. Richard Penney, Presbyterial President, of Corinth.

Included among the featured speakers were the Rev. Mac N. Turnage, pastor of the host church, and chairman of Women's Work; Mrs. John Eakes, Synodical President, of Jackson; Mrs. Patsy Turner, home mission worker, Canoe, Ky.; the Rev. Spencer Murray, pastor of First Presbyterian Church, Amory; the Rev. Oscar Landry, Indian Village, Texas; Mrs. Arch McKinnon, Bible leader - and retired missionary, Greenwood; Miss Sara Wright, Bible Instructor of the Pontotoc, Miss., High School.

Mrs. Eakes, Synodical President, conducted the installation service for the newly elected officers. They are: Mrs. T. E. Veitch, President, Starkville; Mrs. Chesley Hines, Corresponding Secretary, Starkville; Mrs. Enoch Stephenson, Chairman of Spiritual Growth, Columbus; Mrs. E. T. George, Chairman of Church Extension, Macon; Mrs. W. L. Holland, Chairman of Annuities and Relief, Amory; Mrs. T. B. Thrower,

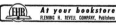

the radiant figure of Him who makes God's companionship real and authentic across the miles and years. . . . These verses will rest like a benediction upon many hearts."

Rev. Albert G. Butzer, D.D. — Pastor Westminster Church, Buffalo, N. Y.

"These poems of Mrs. Wheeler's . . . have obviously sung themselves first in her own soul, and then, one suspects, her heart impatiently called to her hand to put them on paper."

President Dean G. McKee — President Biblical Seminary, New York City.

"Ruth Winant Wheeler, from 1916 to 1931 Field Representative of the Seminary in her most recent volume of poems is a close observer of the little, personal but revealing things of everyday life . . . Dominic Cocco, the Samaritan Woman, and her water pot; Christmas Wrappings, A Young Girl Prays reveal a warm, sensitive spirit who combines a wholesome grasp of Scripture with a love of people . . . Such writings may help to keep the scholar human, the preacher alive in his imagination and all of us, in the common round, aglow with new insights and deeper faith."

Order from the Presbyterian Book Stores.

Church News

Missionary News

Colin Benson Cain, first child of the Rev. and Mrs. Benson Cain, was born in Yodogawa Christian Hospital, Osaka, Japan, at 12:20 p.m., October 7th. The baby's mother is the former Coline Gunn of Micanopy, Fla.

Mrs. Cain attended Florida State University, the University of Florida, Rhode Island State College, and is a graduate of the Assembly's Training School. She went out as an evangelist-educational missionary in 1950.

Mr. Cain, of Montgomery, Ala., is a graduate of Presbyterian College and Columbia Theological Seminary. He went to Japan in 1953 as an evangelistic missionary. The couple are working in Tajime.

Young Benny arrived on the first anniversary of the Cains' marriage.

Two of our missionaries to Japan have been named to offices of the Japanese Missionary Quarterly.

The Rev. Arch B. Taylor, Jr., of Winston-Salem, N. C., has been named editor of the publication. Mr. Taylor is currently serving on the staff of Shikoku Christian College in Zentsuji, Japan. The Rev. William P. Boyle, evangelistic missionary in Tokushima, Japan, has been named by the Fellowship of Christian Missionaries, sponsoring organization of the publication, to the magazine's board of directors.

The magazine which Mr. Taylor has been elected to edit is the publication which serves Protestant missionaries in Japan as an avenue for exchanging information and comment on the missionary enterprise in that country. Both missionaries and Japanese Christians write for the publication.

Washington, D. C.—Rev. John Randolph Taylor, Ph.D., was installed pastor of the Church of the Pilgrims on Sunday, October 7, at 7:30 p.m., with a large congregation present. Rev. D. C. Crawford of Leesburg, Va., moderator of Potomac Presbytery, presided and propounded the constitutional questions. The sermon was preached by Dr. H. Kerr Taylor of Dallas, Texas, father of the minister-elect. He remarked at the beginning that this was the third time he was preaching this sermon, the other occasions being when his other two sons were being installed in their respective pastorates. Dr. A. R. Bird, pastor emeritus, led the congregation in prayer. A charge to the pastor was delivered by Rev. Kenneth G. Phifer of the Old Meeting House Church in Alexandria, Va., and to the congregation by Dr. Carl R. Pritchett of the Presbyterian Church in Bethesda Maryland. The prayer of installation was led by Rev. William D. Varker of the Presbyterian Church in Culpepper, Va. Elders Robert B. Foster of Munson Hill church, and Colin M. Hudson of Chesterbrook church were also members of the Presbytery's Commission.

Dr. Taylor is an honor graduate of Davidson College and of Union Seminary in Virginia. The Seminary awarded him a fellowship on the basis of which he has spent the last two years at the University of Aberdeen in Scotland. He was called to this pastorate on August 19 and led his first services on Sunday, September 30.

The EVERY CHURCH CANVASS is conducted by the Stewardship Committee which has co-opted the laymen to be their representatives. These laymen were prepared for the Canvass by a briefing session in Little Joe's Presbyterian Church, Barium Springs, October 7. Members of the Committee in Charge are: Fred H. Brown, Lenoir, Chairman; Rev. J. T. Barham, Hickory; Rev. J. Malcolm Murchison, Concord; Rev. J. H. Armfield, Woodleaf; and Mrs. E. Johnston Irvin, Concord.

Davidson—Davidson College ranks with the top eight colleges and universities in the United States in the number of graduates who have won fellowships from the Danforth Foundation.

An annoncement received from the Foundation by the college states that only seven other institutions have graduated as many Danforth Fellows as the six Davidson alumni who have been named.

The six are Denison University in Ohio, Duke, Harvard, Pomona, Williams, Wooster and Yale. Pomona and Duke have seven, the others six.

Danforth Graduate Fellowships were established in 1951 "to bring into higher education a larger number of young men, thoroughly trained according to highest scholastic standards, who are aware of the place for moral and religious values in teaching and counseling."

Blowing Rock—The Rev. Walter K. Keys, graduate of King College and Union Theological Seminary, was installed as pastor of the Rumple Memorial Presbyterian Church of Blowing Rock, N. C., on September 30th by a Commission appointed by Holston Presbytery. The Rev. J. Kenton Parker of Boone, N. C., presided; Dr. L. T. Newland of Black Mountain, N. C., preached the sermon; Ruling Elder J. E. Holshouser of Boone charged the pastor, and the Rev. Dan Thomas of Banner Elk, N. C., charged the congregation; while Ruling Elder Ivan Stafford of Crossnore, N, C., read the Scripture lesson. Dr. Keys served this church as pastor from 1940 to 1948. For the past several years he has been directing the Young People's work for the Town of Blowing Rock. He and Mrs. Keys will continue to live, for the winter, in their Blowing Rock home, "Keyhole Kabin". Dr. Leroy T. Newland, who served this church as pastor for the past three years, resigned recently and he and Mrs. Newland are now living in Black Mountain, N. C.

MISSISSIPPI

Meridian Presbytery—The regular fall meeting of the Presbytery of Meridian was held in the Magee Presbyterian Church, Oct. 16, 1956. Dr. G. Thomas Preer, the Moderator, presided.

The opening sermon, being the doctrinal sermon, was preached by Dr. Raymond W. Rien, pastor of Oakland Heights Church, Meridian. His subject was: "The Doctrine of Love."

There were thirty-two Ministers and forty Ruling Elders present. Also a number of visitors.

Rev. Fred W. Hoffman, for the past several years pastor of the Mt. Olive group of churches, at his request, was Honorably Retired from the active ministry. This becomes effective, with the pastoral dissolution, on Nov. 1.

Presbytery received and approved a petition, signed by twenty-one people, requesting the organization of a church in Lucedale, Miss. This work has been promoted by the Superintendent of Home Missions. Presbytery appointed a Commission to perfect the organization.

Presbytery unanimously disapproved the amendment to the Book of Church Order and the amendment to the Confession of Faith, on the grounds that they are unscriptural.

The Presbytery was delighted to meet on this occasion in the new house of worship of the Magee congregation. Greatly enjoyed was the noon-day meal served by the Ladies of the host church. Rev. William B. Hooker is the pastor.

The next regular meeting will be held on Jan. 15, 1957, in the First Church, Pascagoula, Miss.

L. A. Beckman, Jr., S. C.

TEXAS

Dallas—The Rev. Charles S. Sydnor, Jr., pastor of the Leatherwood Presbyterian Church of Leatherwood, Ky., began two weeks of speaking engagements at Presbyterian churches in the Dallas area October 15.

His visit is sponsored by the Board of Church Extension, and the Church Extension Committee of the Presbytery of Dallas and the Women of the Dallas Presbytery. His message covers the church extension program and deals particularly with his own work in the coal-mining area of Kentucky.

His engagements call for him to speak in Presbyterian Churches in Dallas and Dallas County, and Denton, Wichita and Grayson Counties.

Dallas—Historic First Presbyterian Church in downtown Charlotte, N. C., is to be the site of the 1958 General Assembly after formal acceptance of that church's invitation, presented to the Committee on the Office of the General Assembly, meeting in Dallas, October 16.

Dr. Felix B. Gear, professor at Columbia Theological Seminary in Decatur, is chairman of the 18-man permanent committee.

Dr. Ernest Lee Stoffel, pastor of the First Church in Charlotte where the Assembly will be held, Jones Y. Pharr, and Philip F. Howerton, appeared before the committee to extend the invitation from Charlotte's First Church and Mecklenburg Presbytery. Mr. Pharr and Mr. Howerton, laymen, are co-chairmen of the church's committee on arrangements.

Plans call for the 1958 Assembly to convene in Charlotte sometime in April of that year.

The 1957 General Assembly will meet in the South Highland Presbyterian Church, Birmingham, Alabama, on April 25th.

THE SOUTHERN PRESBYTERIAN JOURNAL

A Presbyterian weekly magazine devoted to the statement, defense and propagation of the Gospel, the faith which was once for all delivered unto the saints.

VOL. XV NO. 29 | NOVEMBER 14, 1956 | $2.50 A YEAR

THE SOUTHERN PRESBYTERIAN JOURNAL

Rev. Henry B. Dendy, D.D., Editor........Weaverville, N. C.
Dr. L. Nelson Bell, Associate Editor........Asheville, N. C.
Rev. Wade C. Smith, Associate Editor........Weaverville, N. C.

EDITORIAL

A World in Agony and Some Things We Forget

As this is written the exploding situation in Central Europe and the Middle East is so heart-breaking and so fraught with danger for the entire world that one is driven to cry out to God for those who find themselves involved in the maelstrom. Suffering, death and destruction are spreading like a horrible nightmare.

Many are showering abuse on Israel, England and France. That their action was a blow to allied unity, as well as to the North Atlantic treaty concept, none will deny. That it may prove a terrible blunder may also eventuate. But there are historical facts which need to be remembered.

Furthermore, it is both unfair and unrealistic to place the actions in the Middle East in the same category as Russia's ruthless suppression of a people's desire for freedom as seen in Hungary.

The little nation of Israel is not only hated by her Arab neighbors but the writer has talked to many Christians who express total sympathy for the Arabs and none for Israel.

Here are some facts which need to be remembered:

Twenty years ago the number of Jews in the world was about sixteen million. Six million were killed by the Hitler regime in Germany. An additional two and a half million are estimated to have lost their lives in Russia. In other words over half of the Jews in the world have been done to death by evil men and nations in the last two decades.

At the termination of World War II it became imperative to resettle the hundreds of thousands of refugee Jews scattered around the world. Also, tens of thousands were clamoring to leave those areas in Central Europe where life had become intolerable.

The logical place for them to settle was in Palestine, their historic home. That an ultimate compromise was worked out which resulted in the displacement of some nine hundred thousand Arabs was tragic for these people. The writer, with many other Christians, has seen some of these camps of displaced Arabs in Lebanon and elsewhere and they are truly pitiful. What is not known is that many feel this refugee problem could have been solved years ago but for the intransigent attitude of some of the Arab leaders. These camps have been used as testimony to the ruthlessness of Israel and as a propaganda weapon against that nation.

There is another aspect which is open for all to see for themselves. The Israeli are inspired with an indomitable will to work, and to fight for their country. These people through initiative and hard work have truly made the desert to blossom like a rose. Industry of every kind is flourishing. And, these people are willing to fight for home and country. Without disparagement of others it is safe to say that the Israeli army is, for its size, the best army in the world. Largely anti-religious? Yes. But the nation of Israel is a political entity which has brought undying fear into the heart of the Arab world.

The Arab nations which immediately surround Israel are, in large measure, the very antithesis of that little nation. Only too often lacking in initiative and industry; content to live with a minimum of effort; an economy often dependent on fabulous oil reserves rather than work; inspired by a fanatical adherence to the Moslem faith, these descendants of Ishmael are no match for their cousins from the line of Isaac, and they know it. This inferiority complex has begotten an insatiable hatred of Israel whom they consider an intruder into that part of the world they have dominated for hundreds of years.

The Arab world has been electrified by the bold actions of Nasser and they have turned to him as their inspired leader. That he took illegal and unilateral possession of the Sue

Canal thrilled them even more. That Egypt had for two years maintained a strict boycott of Israeli ships, not permitting them to pass through the Canal, is little known. One wonders why the United Nations let this sore continue to fester?

England and France have found themselves hamstrung by the United Nations: Faced with confiscation of their rights and a continued outlook of a Canal open only by the whim of a man obviously greedy for power and prestige, they have gambled on recovering the Canal and maintaining it as an international waterway, open and guaranteed to all.

Whether this gamble will pay off is doubtful. Action which might have been effective weeks ago is now so late that not only the Canal itself but the oil pipe lines may be indefinitely lost. The lack of unified support in England and France is in itself a sad commentary.

Before condemning the action of England and France it may be well to consider whether they themselves have not been the victims of a Pollyanna policy of fecklessness on the part of nations who a generation ago would have put international honesty above international politics.

The writer is no prophet but he believes that just as World War II resulted from *inaction* when Hitler marched into Sudetenland and Japan marched into Manchuria, so we face the possibility of another world conflagration because of wishful thinking in the face of international robbery.

As for the tragedy of Hungary and Poland. For all of our vaunted morality America has stood by through the years and watched regretfully but inactively while the nations of Central Europe have been enslaved by a godless tyranny. Many young people in America have never even heard of the independent nations of Latvia, Lithuania and Esthonia. Polite expressions of regret have not saved these nations from slavery, nor have they helped Poland, Hungary, or Czecho-Slovakia.

Now we see these peoples making a desperate struggle against their Communist masters and our hearts bleed for them. Are they not like the wounded man on the road to Jericho? Have we forgotten moral and spiritual principles? Are we so naive as to think that governments such as the Kremlin understand any kind of restraints other than force or temporary expediency? For years we have temporized with Communism. We gave diplomatic recognition to Russia and ever since that day this recognition has been a snare and a sorrow. We sit in the same United Nations with the world's greatest enemy and hope that by conciliation and compromise and conference we can change the leopard's spots.

What should we do? With all of these brave words the writer might be expected to have an answer. We have none. We believe the opportunities for containment and a new day in international morality are so compromised by our international commitments that until the slate is cleared and we start anew there is little we can do.

The high hopes of Hungary of a few days ago seem shattered at this writing. Blood, suffering and death has come to thousands who had the courage to stand for freedom, even more than death.

Peace? Where is peace to be found? Certainly not in a man-made organization of either men or nations. Man does not will to have peace and then have it. Peace is conferred by God and comes on His terms. Here in America too many want peace so that they may continue to serve the Devil in luxury and quiet.

The answer seems axiomatic: There is no peace to the wicked. In Christ only will mankind find peace; For He is The Prince of Peace. L.N.B.

A Basket of Fruit

The Fruit of the Spirit (Galatians 5:22,23)

The Fruit of the Spirit is . . .
Goodness

Two Old English words, "good," and "bad." To be really good, a thing has to be "good all the way through," as the boy said about the apples he was peddling. We don't like a man like Pecksniff, or a Pharisee, who is only good on the outside, but within is full of corruption.

God made man good, but he lost his goodness. He has to be made into a New Man in Christ Jesus; There is a green hill far away . . . He died to make us good. What constitutes a good man? He has two parts; Inner and Outer.

The Southern Presbyterian Journal, *a Presbyterian Weekly magazine devoted to the statement, defense, and propagation of the Gospel, the faith which was once for all delivered unto the saints,* published every Wednesday by The Southern Presbyterian Journal, Inc., in Weaverville, N. C.

Entered as second-class matter May 15, 1942, at the Postoffice at Weaverville, N. C., under the Act of March 3, 1879. Vol. XV, No. 29, November 14, 1956. Editorial and Business Offices: Weaverville, N. C. Printed in the U.S.A. by Biltmore Press, Asheville, N. C.

ADDRESS CHANGE: When changing address, please let us have both old and new address as far in advance as possible. Allow three weeks after change if not sent in advance. When possible, send an address label giving your old address.

I. The Inner Man; the hidden man of the heart; good on the inside.

1. He has a Good Heart. The old heart of stone has been removed. His heart has been made clean, tender, loving; "A copy, Lord, of Thine."

2. He has a Good Mind. His foolish, darkened mind has given place to a mind enlightened in the knowledge of Christ, one that is humble and that catches a vision of what God wants it to be.

3. He has a Good Conscience; taught of God; one that is alive and responsive to the God Who made it.

4. He has a Good Will. The will is the strong house, the citadel. We were left to the freedom of our wills, and fell into sin. Some wills are weak; some are stubborn. A good will is one that is submissive to the will of God, completely yielded to Him; one that can say, Not my will, but Thine, O Lord.

II. The Outer Man: Good on the outside.

We live in Bodies, and they should be consecrated to God.

1. Good Eyes; the Eye-Gate is very important. We realize that today. Good eyes are eyes that have been opened so that we can see the things of God.

2. Good Ears. O earth, earth, earth, hear the Word of the Lord. There are many distracting noises in our world. May we listen, so that our souls may live!

3. Good Feet. Feet that never lead into sin; feet like the feet of Jesus, as He went about doing good. We can see His footprints everywhere.

4. Good Hands, like the Hands of Jesus.

Only the Holy Spirit can make us good all the way through; the fruit of the Spirit is . . Goodness.

Are There People Actually in Financial Need?

The above question, on the face of it, appears to be facetious. Strangely, there is a feeling today that there is not too much financial need in any group.

We have become used to reading about endowment insurance, company retirement plans, social security, community welfare assistance, etc. Quite naturally, we assume that some one of these plans, and maybe several of them, will certainly care for the aged. And yet, within our own Presbyterian Church family there are those who will never be the beneficiaries of any of the above forms of assistance. Through no fault of their own, they are without adequate means of subsistence. These are our aged, retired ministers and their dependents. In many cases, they do not come under our Ministers' Annuity Fund (retirement annuity plan for ministers.)

The Fund went into effect in 1940, and even those who are under it had very little time to build up a reserve before they, too, were retired. Furthermore, Social Security for ministers did not become effective until 1955, and so many will get no aid in old age from that.

It is unlikely that they were able to save any money from salaries which at best only barely met living necessities while they were active, for it is a notable fact that clergymen throughout the country are always at the lower end of the pay scale.

Even if a minister retired last year, with 15 years in the Fund, his annuity very likely is small, because pay raises for the minister in the past 15 years have by no means kept pace with rising price of living, and what we paid him 15 years ago barely kept him going. His annuity is, of course small, yet he is probably getting the maximum. Quite naturally, this annuity must be supplemented, and the Joy Gift every Christmas season makes a big difference.

Now, what about the minister, or his dependents, who have no income from the Annuity Fund? Ministerial Relief is the only answer. Members of the Board of Annuities and Relief have pondered from time to time the use of the word, "Relief." It certainly is not a pleasant word to apply to the recipients, and in a very large sense the word is inaccurate. Technically, these wonderful people may be on "relief." Morally, and certainly from a Christian standpoint, any money they receive is deferred salary . . . money they should have been paid while they were active. Our Joy Gifts are really tributes to them. This does not point the finger at any particular local church, it simply means that our Church, as a whole, has had its part in underpaying ministers. We can't go back to the original setting, but as a group of people with comparatively large incomes we can now provide the gifts that will enable these fine servants of this Church to live out their days in some reasonable kind of security.

Strangely, too, often facts about the circumstances of those aided must be solicited, since these ministers do not ordinarily promote their own welfare. In the thick file of thank you notes received each year in the office of the Board there are many sentences, the gist of

But in all this process, primary responsibility rests upon local people. The Board renders certain valuable services but most of the work is done and most of the money is raised at the community level. This de-centralized plan of procedure may work more slowly than the one referred to in a sister denomination, but it goes further and gets more done, for the very reason that it enlists more persons. This means for every $1,000.00 of Assembly funds invested in new churches there has been many times that amount raised locally. It is very important that this first $1,000.00 be available at the right time, but it alone would never even begin the job.

The Board of Church Extension takes pardonable pride in what it has been able to do in this field of new church planning and building. But the large credit belongs to those strong congregations which have been willing to send out colonies and put real money behind them; it belongs to groups of laymen in many cities who have put money and business brains behind this expansion program; and, most of all, it belongs to Presbytery Committees and Executives who have seen the opportunities and have worked ceaselessly to capitalize upon them. A very valuable service has been rendered by the religious press in publicizing both the needs and the achievements in this field. It would require a lot of orchids to go around.

Our denomination depends largely upon local initiative in its expansion program and the results would appear to commend the plan for continued use. There is yet much land to be possessed. Indeed, the years just ahead may amaze us. Therefore, it is urgent that the people nearest to these opportunities take advantage of them with large vision, hard work and earnest prayer. Paul may plant and Apollos water but only God is able to give the increase of spiritual fruit. The Board of Church Extension salutes all those who are in this partnership with us. We have developed a working formula whose most important ingredient is local initiative.

An American Thanksgiving

By Wayne H. Davis

English Instructor and Dean of Boys,
Glade Valley School, Inc.

Scene: Dining room of an American family home.

Props: Table covered with white table cloth; dishes, cutlery, drinking glasses; milk pitcher, turkey, mashed potatoes (turkey can be constructed by art class and milk can be made by mixing white powder in water; mashed potatoes can be dough or white colored clay); microphone.

Casts Announcer-interviewer; family consisting of father, mother, son, daughter; guests consisting of one man and one woman.

Announcer-interviewer:

Hello, fellow Americans, and a Happy Thanksgiving Day to all of you! Today, as millions of Americans throughout the length and breadth of our beloved land are observing a Day of Thanksgiving to Almighty God for the many blessings which are ours, this radio-television station, in cooperation with the Glade Valley School is bringing you an "on-the-spot" Thanksgiving Day observance in the home of a typical American family.

We have brought you to the dinig room of the home of Mr. and Mrs. John Q. Public. Seated around the table, which you see is loaded with good things to eat, are the members of the Public family and their two guests.

In addition to Mr. and Mrs. Public, the family consists of John Jr. and Sandra. Johnny and Sandra are twins, fourteen years of age, and in the ninth grade at Glade Valley School.

The guests are the Rev. Mr. Brown, pastor of the church which the Public family attends, and Miss Smith, a member of the Glade Valley faculty and a teacher of the twins.

As I am speaking to you now you will notice that the family and their guests are having Grace. This is a regular practice in the Public home, for they are a devoted family. Today, being Thanksgiving Day, they are especially conscious of their many blessings.

As soon as Grace has been completed I shall interview each member of the Public family and their two guests, for we want to hear the thoughts each is thinking at this moment.

(PAUSE) (Announcer-interviewer turns to glance at people seated at table.)

Announcer-interviewer:

I see Grace has been completed and dinner is now in progress; so, with their kind permission, we will ask each one to leave the table and come to the microphone.

Mr. Public, sir, will you please tell us the thoughts that were going through your mind as Grace was being asked?

Mr. Public:

I will be most happy to do so. I was listening closely to the words of Rev. Brown as he prayed the Grace just now, and I whispered several silent "Amens" as he spoke.

You want to know my thoughts at this time? Well, I have many thoughts about the many wonderful things for which I have to be thankful, but I'll name some of them for you.

First of all, I'm very thankful for the wonderful family I have! My wife—and my two fine twins! I'm thankful for the love we have for each other, and which we share together. I'm thankful for our health, and I'm thankful for our *faith in God.*

I'm thankful that I've got a job and am able to provide for my family. Oh, we're not rich, of course, when you think of being rich in terms of money, but I make a pretty decent wage, we own our home, and I'm able to give Johnny and Sandra at least a *few* little extras.

We are rich, though, in the things that really count: health, love and respect, happiness! When I think today how I sometimes complain,—well, I feel ashamed, and I say a little silent prayer that from now on I'll be more content and recognize, daily, the blessings God has seen fit to give to me and to my wonderful family!

Announcer-interviewer:

Thank you, sir, and I am sure we all agree with you that you *do* have much for which to

Announcer-interviewer:

Now, Johnny?

Johnny:

We—ll, I dunno, I guess I'm just thankful for the same things most young kids in America are thankful for.

I'm glad we can all be here together and have a *swell* dinner like this, and, ——well, I'm *sure glad* I've got the Mom and Pop I've got! They're swell parents, really! Oh, sometimes I guess I think they're kinda tough on me—you know, like makin' me stay in and study sometimes when I'd rather be out runnin' around—or to a movie with some of my pals, but, I guess they *know best*. And, they let me do a lot of things—when I get right down to thinking about the privileges I have.

Sandy said she was even thankful for me, so I guess I'll have to say I'm glad she's my sister. I am, too, when I see *some* of the sisters some of my buddies are stuck with! Sandy's real keen compared to some girls I know!

I'm glad Mr. Brown and Miss Smith can be here with us today, too. Mr. Brown, he's our preacher and sometimes his sermons are kinda boring to a kid—guess we don't always understand just what he's sayin', but he's a regular guy. I remember once at a Sunday School picnic—he caught a high fly that I thought for sure was goin' to be a home run and lose the game for our side!

And Miss Smith—she makes you study, and sometimes she piles on lots of home work, but, I dunno, she's fair—all the kids *know* that—and she seems to be really interested in us; — so, I'm just glad they can be with us today. I just hope Sandy don't blab it all over school we had Miss Smith to dinner, though!

Announcer-interviewer:

God bless you, Johnny and Sandra. No wonder your mother and daddy are so proud of you! I just hope every boy and girl in America—and every boy and girl in the whole world—have the same thankfulness in their hearts today!

Miss Smith, you're Johnny and Sandra's teacher, aren't you? You must also be a pretty good friend of the Public family, since you're eating Thanksgiving Dinner with them. Will you tell us what is on your heart today?

Miss Smith:

I have so many things for which to thank God! Love and loyalty, health, memories, happy days and even unhappy times—because you know, sometimes our unhappy experiences make us stronger in Faith.

I'm thankful for a job to do. Sometimes I think I have the most difficult job in the whole world, but, oh! it's an *important* job—and it's a rewarding job! When I see some boy and some girl whom I've scolded, whom I've taught sometimes with impatience but *always* with *love;* when I see them succeed—graduate from junior high school and go on to high school, — well, it is then I realize I'm a *rich* woman! Money couldn't buy the satisfaction which is mine then!

And, I keep track of my boys and girls—I follow them through high school, and on to college or out into life. They don't know this, I suppose, but when I hear that some little boy I knew has become a business man, or a fellow teacher, or a doctor—or has a good job in a factory, — well, I say a little prayer of thanks to God that I have had the *privilege* to touch his life—even in a small way. When I hear that some little giggly girl I once had in class has gone on to greater things I feel a tear or two of happiness trickle down my face.

I'm thankful to God that He has given me the privilege to work with boys and girls—for they are of *His* making, and they are wonderful—in spite of their nervous energy and their mischievousness! They are so *terribly* important, for they so soon become tomorrow's citizens, and our country—our world—depends upon them! They are *OUR FUTURE.*

Announcer-interviewer:

Thank you, Miss Smith. You could not have put it in plainer words! Lastly, but certainly not least, Rev. Mr. Brown, you asked the Blessing a few minutes ago. Will you tell us, sir, why this *particular* Thanksgiving Day has meaning for you?

The Rev. Mr. Brown:

This particular Thanksgiving Day has meaning for me because it is just *that*—A Day of Thanksgiving. Of course, to the believer, *every* day is a day of *thanksgiving* to Almighty God for His Bountiful Blessings to us, His children. We must *never* cease thanking God for all His Goodness.

But, today, as we look around the world and see it more in peace than it has yet been in the lifetime of these children here, we cannot *help* but be thankful. Things *could* be better, of course—and we hope and pray that conditions will get better, but, oh! they *could* be *so very much worse* than they are!

This particular Thanksgiving Day has special meaning in that I have the privilege to be a loved guest in the home of one of my church families. I, as a minister, am *truly* grateful to have such wonderful people in my church!

I am thankful for our beloved America and *all* that it means to all of its people. I am

repentant, self-sufficient person who is unwilling to have Christ's yoke placed upon him (vv.20-24)? Could the hand of God be in your hardships and toils to bring you to Christ? Thanks be to God who allows us to feel our own weakness that we may find our sufficiency in Him.

Tuesday, November 27, *Mark* 1:16-22. Mark pictures Jesus as a person of decision and action. Observe how readily men become His disciples (vv.16-20), leaving behind position (v.18) and family (v.20). What does the word "immediately" in vv.18,20,21,29 suggest? Notice how quickly Jesus establishes His authority (vv.21-22,27) and gains attention (v.28). Though He is the Son of God (vv.11,24), there are a number of human factors which help account for all this: the presence of the Holy Spirit in His life (v.10), His own personal victory over temptation (vv.12-13), His personal prayer life (v.35). Could a lack of the power of the Spirit, defeat in temptation, or absence of prayer be factors keeping you from serving Christ boldly and decisively?

Wednesday, November 28, *John* 14:25-31. As Jesus is about to leave His disciples (13:33) He prepares them for the future (vv.16ff). Whom does Jesus promise to send in His place (vv.16-17,26)? What functions will this Person perform as a teacher (v.26)? Why does the Spirit's presence dwell in the lives of some and not in others (v.17)? Can the Spirit, who is called "holy" (v.26) and the "Spirit of Truth" (v.17a) live in any but the heart of the Christian? As the Holy Spirit dwells within, what relation will Christ have with the believer (vv.18,20)? What other ministry will the Holy Spirit perform (vv.16,26b)? What will this mean in the believer's heart (v.27)? What functions have you been aware of that the Holy Spirit has performed in your heart?

Thursday, November 29, *Mark* 10:28-31. Read the incident that precedes this passage (vv.17-22). Observe Jesus' attitude toward the young man (v.21a). Is this stumbling block the possession of riches or the love of riches (vv.21-22)? What is your reaction to Jesus' statements of vv.23-25? Is it similar to that of the disciples (v.26)? What does Jesus' reply in v.27 reveal about the doctrine of election? How does it tie in with Matthew 11:27 and John 6:44? The ties of this world are often a grave stumbling block to following Christ, but observe the reward to those that do put these things secondary (vv.29-30). What ties of material wealth or human companionship keep you from fully following Christ?

Friday, November 30, *John* 16:7-15. Deep ties of loyalty have bound the hearts of the disciples to their Master (13:36-37), but now He says it is to their advantage that He leave them (16:7). In His prayer to the Father (v.17) what does Jesus say He has accomplished in the lives of the disciples (17:6-8)? Has He done all that the Father has given Him to do with them (17:8,14)? For what does He pray in their behalf for the future (17:11,15,17)? How will the Holy Spirit finish the work in their hearts that Christ has started while in the flesh (16:13-15)? Are you willing to leave the future of some work that you have begun for the Lord in His hands, should He call you to some other task?

Saturday, December 1, *Matthew* 28:16-20. The Book of Revelation reveals Christ in His Kingship while the gospels, on the whole, portray Him as the Lamb of God. In giving the Great Commission, however, the risen Christ manifests Himself in His royal power (vv.18,20). His disciples give Him worship (v.17). He has all authority (v.18). He equates Himself with the other two members of the Trinity (v.19). He holds the future in His hands (v.20b). Compare this picture of Christ with that given in Revelation 1:5-7,17-19. Revelation 1:12-16,20 tells us that this Kingly Christ is standing in the midst of His churches. Meditate upon what Christ says about Himself in the Great Commission together with the portrayal given of Him in Revelation 1. Do you have a new sense of the authority and presence of the One who has given you the Great Commission?

The Bible: Worth Living By and Dying For!

By George S. Lauderdale

In the whole world there are but these basic factors: God's Word, that which needs God's Word, evil forces which would prevent the Word from getting into men's hearts, and good powers which put the Word into hearts. All sin is opposition to God's gospel; righteousness is faith in and obedience to the heaven-sent message.

God is interested in man's response to His Word, being sad when it is ignored or called a lie by unbelief. He rewards those who receive His Spirit-inspired truth. "Keep all his statutes and his commandments . . . that thy days may be prolonged . . . that it may be well with thee." Deuteronomy 6:2,3.

The severest wrath falls upon men who handle God's Word deceitfully. Some preach in order to gain fame but the true reason for carrying God's holy Word to others is love. Missionaries need the Holy Spirit Who gives love, for without it we are false witnesses of Jesus Christ and liable to His condemnation.

Centering Your Interest in the Scriptures

Jesus Christ commanded men to lose their lives for His sake and the gospel's. He refused to turn stones into bread when He was hungry with the Scripture text that man shall not live by bread alone but by every word which proceeds from God's mouth. He would not be made king by the multitude who cared little about food for their souls.

You should trust the Lord Jesus Christ because He is honest: in love He will give you what you should have rather than what you want. Best of all, He can convert our minds so that we want the truth of God. He can help you want what you ought to have! The gospel is the power of God unto salvation!

The Bible For Maturing Minds

Children need God's Word. In the home and classes at church let them learn the Bible. In heathen lands, men are childish, being fascinated with beads, colorful dress; in civilized pagan nations, men are attracted to machines as children to toys. All these minds should be instructed in the Word of God.

God's Word causes men's minds to mature, but most important it shows them the way to heaven. Fellowship with God now and eternally is promised in the gospel: Christ died to remove our guilt enabling God to accept us as His children when we believe on His Son.

Build Your Life On Solid Rock!

What joy awaits all who trust God's Word! We should be willing to go any place in order to put the gospel into the hearts of men. The apostle John "was in the isle that is called Patmos, *for the word of God, and for the testimony of Jesus Christ.*" Revelation 1:9. Let your whole life be directed by God's Word; let no power keep His truth from you or prevent you from putting it into the hands and hearts of others.

Since God loves His Word, He will help you be a missionary to all men, whom He also loves. He will open doors and ways wonderful to you that His message of salvation will reach many ears. Will you not begin today being a missionary for Jesus Christ?

SABBATH SCHOOL LESSONS — REV. J. KENTON PARKER

LESSON FOR NOVEMBER 25

The Prodigal Son

Background Scripture: Luke 15:11-32
Devotional Reading: Psalm 103:1-13

To understand the three parables of Luke 15 we must read the first two verses of that chapter. Many publicans and sinners had drawn near to Jesus, to hear Him. The Pharisees and scribes murmured, saying, This man receiveth sinners and eateth with them. He spoke the three parables which follow as an answer and rebuke to these critics, and to explain why he welcomed these outcasts of society. The point of the three parables is the same; the Love which He has for the Lost. He relates the parable of the Lost Sheep, the Lost Coin, and the Lost Boy. The first two illustrate His "Seeking Love," and the third, which is our lesson, His Welcoming, or Forgiving Love. He compares His love for men with the love that a father has for a wayward and lost son. We usually take this last parable as a picture of our Heavenly Father's love. We know that God so loved the world that He gave His only begotten son, etc., and the father in this story is like our Heavenly Father. Jesus, however, spoke this parable to illustrate His own love for the Lost. Since Jesus and the Father are one, the story fits them both, for the Son and the Father have the same love for lost sinners.

In Psalm 103:1-13 we have a beautiful picture of the God we worship. When you read these verses how can you imagine anyone saying that the God of the Old Testament is different from the God of the New? There are those who try to picture the God of the Old Testament as harsh and cruel and unforgiving. Where even in the New Testament, can you find a description of a more Loving and Forgiving God than we find in these verses? Just take a few: Who forgiveth all thine iniquities; Who healeth all thy diseases; Who redeemeth thy life from destruction; Who crowneth thee with lovingkindness and tender mercies . . .

"And when he came to himself." David came to himself when Nathan told him a simple story, and then said, Thou art the man. No prophet or preacher is mentioned as speaking to the prodigal. The Spirit of God was working with him. He works when and where He will. The boy remembered his home and his father. Memory is often used by the Spirit in calling sinners home. The prodigal saw clearly and vividly the contrast between his position in his father's house and his present plight.

He did not stop with these memories. He said, I will arise and go. Here is genuine repentance. He could have easily died in the hog pen if he had not made this resolve, and then *acted upon it.* Judas went out and hanged himself; Simon Peter went out and wept bitterly. The prodigal went back home with grief and hatred for his sins; And he arose and came to his father.

II. *The Father:* 20 - 24.

We find here a beautiful portrait of Jesus and of God the Father.

"When he was yet a great way off his father saw him." Someone has said that the father's heart followed his boy all the way to the hog pen. "Like as a father pitieth his children." How his father must have pitied him as he saw him go further and further away and deeper and deeper into sin and misery! How the loving heart of Jesus went out to publicans and sinners! How the heart of God yearns over a wicked world! "It grieved Him at His heart," is the expression used about God just before the Flood, and when He was dealing with Israel in the wilderness.

In the following verses we have a beautiful picture of "Welcoming Love." The father had compassion and ran and fell on his neck and kissed him. He did not wait until he had taken a bath and put on clean clothes. "Just as I am, poor, wretched, blind, O Lamb of God, I come"! The boy began his confession but was interrupted before he finished. The best robe, the ring, the shoes, are brought, for he is again a member of the family. He was not to be a servant, but a son.

This is not all, however, for a feast is to follow. It is a time of joy. Go back and read all these parables, and note how they end. Rejoice with me, said the shepherd; Rejoice with me, said the woman; Let us eat and be merry, said the father. It is indeed a time of rejoicing when a sinner is saved.

This has been called "The most beautiful story ever spoken or written," and it well deserves this high praise. Nowhere do we find the Redeeming and Forgiving Grace of God more beautifully described.

III. *The Elder Son (and Brother)*: 25-32.

We hate to bring him in; he is like the fly in the ointment. He, however, illustrates the point of all three parables. The chapter begins and ends with "the elder son," for the elder son represents the scribes and Pharisees. They were the ones who "murmured" in the second verse of the chapter. He is the one person who is angry and will not go in and take a part in the festivities of the occasion.

The Pharisees and scribes despised the publicans and sinners even as the elder son despised his brother. Instead of rejoicing when they saw these classes being saved, they were jealous and angry and called Jesus all sorts of names because He associated with them. Now there is no doubt that these scribes and Pharisees were better men in many respects than these outcasts. They were respectable, and honest, and moral, as far as outward observances of the Law was concerned. They kept themselves aloof from all low and evil associates, and would never be caught eating with them.

They forgot that these publicans and sinners were their "brothers." They would have been insulted if you even suggested such a relationship. The elder son called the prodigal, "thy son," not "my brother," you will notice, and no doubt you could have felt the "scorn" in the tone of his voice.

Is this "elder brother attitude" still seen? Do we look with a bit of contempt upon those who live on the wrong side of the railroad track? or in the slums, or in cabins in the mountains? Do we despise the foreigner and call him by names he hates? Do we neglect and look down upon those of another color or race? Especially do we scorn those who have sunk very deeply into sin; the drunkards, the alcoholics, the criminals, the outcasts of society?

It is good to be an elder son, and an elder brother, *if we keep our hearts warm and tender,* and are ready to welcome a lost brother home. What a help he could have been if his heart had been like his father's heart; To stay at home, to obey our father and keep ourselves strong and clean, are all commendable, but we need to *watch our hearts.*

I want to suggest that you read Dr. Boreham's book on The Prodigal Son. He indeed has a "sanctified imagination" when writing.

YOUNG PEOPLE'S DEPARTMENT — REV. B. HOYT EVANS

YOUTH PROGRAM FOR NOVEMBER 25

"*What The Bible Says About Prayer*"

Scripture: Matthew 6:5-15
Suggested Hymns: "Take Time To Be Holy"
"Sweet Hour Of Prayer"
"I Need Thee Every Hour"

Note to Program Leader:

(We are beginning a unit of three programs on prayer. The purpose of the programs is to deepen and enrich the devotional life of your young people. If these services are to be most effective, those of you who plan the programs and present them will need to be especially faithful in prayer and diligent in your preparation.)

Leader's Introduction:

The Bible instructs us in all matters which pertain to our spiritual growth and development, and prayer is no exception. The Bible has a very high view of prayer and of its importance to the child of God. For this reason we may expect to find in Scripture a full explanation of what prayer is, what it accomplishes, and how it should be done. Some of the very richest teaching of the Bible concerning prayer is found in the words of Christ Himself which have been read to us as our Scripture for this program.

First Speaker:

First of all, the Bible tells us that prayer should be made to God our Father. Jesus said, ". . . pray to thy Father . . ." and in the prayer of instruction, called the Lord's Prayer, He tells us to say, "Our Father, which art in heaven." The Bible also tells us that we are to make our prayers in the name of Christ. (Read John 14:13,14;16:23; and Col 3:17.) We make our prayers in the name of Christ because He is the only one who can mediate between us and God. Christ is our high priest. (Read Hebrews 7:25-27.) Scripture also teaches that in our praying the Holy Spirit helps us to pray acceptably. (Read Romans 8:26.)

Second Speaker:

The Bible gives us instruction as to the content of prayer. Almost the entire Book of Psalms is an admonition to praise God. One of the great themes of the Bible is "Hallelujah"

Women's Work

An Act of Thanskgiving for Our Unity in Christ

We give thanks to Almighty God, Father, Son and Holy Spirit, that we are one in our Lord Jesus Christ; not by the agreement of our minds or the consent of our wills, but by that which He, in His infinite Grace, has done for us in His incarnation, death and resurrection, and by the gift of the Holy Spirit.

We Thank Thee, O God.

We give thanks for the knowledge that though we are divided in outward form we all are the objects of the love and grace of God.

We Thank Thee, O God.

We give thanks for the joy that we have found in sharing the treasures of worship and devotion that we even now hold in common.

We Thank Thee, O God.

We acknowledge that our understanding of the truth as it is in Jesus has been limited by our pride, wilfulness and narrowness of mind, and that our witness to the world is weakened by our divisions.

Lord, Have Mercy Upon Us.

We pray that all men everywhere, in a world distracted and divided, may turn to Christ, who makes us one in spite of our divisions; that He may bind in one those whom many worldly claims set at variance; and that the world may at last find peace and unity in Him; to Whom be glory for ever.

Lord, Hear Our Prayer.

Gifts of Mercy

Have you seen the picture on the cover of the leaflet, "Gifts of Mercy," published by the Board of World Missions to give information to the Church about the continuing need for overseas relief and inter-church aid? The picture, "Kind" (Child in German) is one of fifteen art works given in 1955 to the Presbyterian Church U.S. in appreciation for food and clothing given through the Department of Overseas Relief and Inter-Church Aid, as a "Thanksgift of the German People." One cannot look into the eyes of that child and fail to feel the tragedy of war, to have compassion for such little ones, and to give more generously to their relief.

"Thirty million refugees, homeless, hopeless, living in misery. Four out of five people in the world are *hungry*. In many countries of Europe *Protestant churches* have to struggle for existence. Victims of natural disasters need emergency help . . . Privation knows no age . . . the child and the grandparent, the infant and the aged, as well as the youth and the adult—all kinds and conditions of PEOPLE are suffering." They are cold, they are hungry, they are despairing, awaiting your GIFTS OF MERCY.

Do you need to be reminded that $1.00 will distribute over 100 pounds of food worth approximately $28.00 through Christian pastors and workers abroad? US government surplus is available free of charge in almost unlimited amounts: milk, cheese, butter, vegetable fats, wheat, rice, dried beans, corn . . . Church World Service is sending millions of pounds annually to over thirty countries in Asia, Africa, Europe and the Near East.

You can help this "Share Our Surplus" S.O.S. project by sending your "Gifts of Mercy" to the Department of Overseas Relief, Box 330, Nashville, Tennessee. CROP (Christian Rural Overseas Program) is also a fine way to help. Sponsored by Church World Service it is a part of our own relief efforts. Support such a program, if there is a CROP drive in your area.

Keep clothing collections moving, at least twice a year, spring and fall, but send material relief goods at any time to Church World Service. Gifts made on November 2nd by United Church Women, will go through Church World Service for such needy people.

"The importance of doing relief work through Church channels cannot be over-emphasized. Funds received by the official agency of our Church and handled by Church World Service are carefully accounted for, wisely administered and overhead expense is kept to a minimum." Such gifts are a witness to the compassionate love of Christ flowing through Christians. Further information will be given by Rev. Paul B. Freeland, Secretary, Department of Overseas Relief, Board of World Missions, Box 330, Nashville, Tennessee.

To stimulate further interest and support of this relief program two films are recommended: "I Saw the Need"; how CROP distributes food gifts among hungry people in the world. Free to church, farm and youth groups. Address request to CROP Headquarters, Elkhart, Indiana. Include first and second choice of dates wanted, your name and address, name of your church or organization for which you plan to show the movie. "The Waiting Ones": World Service, 215 Fourth Avenue, New York 3, New York. A story of refugees and how you can help.

These films will be a stimulus to the support of Relief Work. 1956 is the year when the destiny of thousands of refugees will be decided, for the present Refugee Relief Act closes the door of the USA at the end of this year, unless something radical is done quickly.

Is Yours a House or a Home?

The mother, father, and five children all under the age of 12 were riding toward the city when the third child said, "Daddy, what's the difference between a house and a home?" The father explained, "A house is just any house in which people may live, but a home is where there is love — where everybody loves everybody else and cares." The definition satisfied, and no more questions were asked.

That night the children all were asleep on the sleeping porch when an electrical storm came up. At 1:30 the mother and father were moving in their arms one by one the children to inside bedrooms. The little lad who had asked the question the day before opened his eyes enough to look into his mother's face and say, "Mama, we live in a home, don't we?"

—From "Sterling as Silver"

Miss Alice Laura Eastwood

Miss Alice Laura Eastwood, daughter of Samuel and Alice Stone Eastwood, born November 11, 1880, died October 20, 1956, after a protracted illness. She attended Smith College in Northampton, Mass., where she graduated in 1902.

Immediately on her return to Louisville, Kentucky, where she lived throughout her entire life, she became active in Presbyterian Youth work, and was instrumental in the very beginning of Young People's work in the Synod of Kentucky.

She was one of the first twelve women elected by the General Assembly of the Presbyterian Church, U.S., to membership on its Executive Committees. She was one of the three women of our Church who served from the very first on the Committee on Christian Higher Education, first when it was allied with the Committee on Christian Education and Ministerial Relief.

She served in various capacities for a number of years on the Board of Women's Work in the General Assembly, and has served in virtually every position in Presbyterial and Synodical Boards through the years.

Miss Eastwood was the author of a number of articles and pamphlets, and co-author of several books concerning the Higher Educational work of our Church.

738 automobiles are stolen, somewhere in America.

Commenting on the abrupt rise in crime this year, Mr. Hoover said that unless the present trend is reversed, 1956 will set a new record for lawlessness. It will be the first year in which the total crimes have reached the 2,500,000 mark. There were 1,291,120 crimes in the first six months of this year, as compared with 1,128,350 in the same period of 1955. Every 12.2 seconds a major crime was committed. Every 4.1 minutes there was a murder, manslaughter, rape, or assault with intent to kill.

It is a sordid situation. Well might our souls be shocked and our hearts tremble within us as we think what these statistics mean. Think of the lives that are snuffed out, the hearts that are broken, the homes that are shattered by these awful deeds. Worst of all, think of the many never-dying souls that are at stake. Hell must enlarge itself to receive all who are responsible for these sins against God and man. —Evangel.

Barber Shop Provides Organ Music for Customers

A haircut while joining in an impromptu hymn recital? A shave while listening to "Rock of Ages" played on an organ? Either or both of these can happen when you visit Ken's barber shop in Wilkinsburg, a Pittsburgh suburb.

Kenneth Mack, a Korean War veteran who took to barbering, is ready to provide his customers with almost any service. He keeps a supply of umbrellas for folks caught in rainstorms. On hand, too, is a typewriter and a ham radio set for anyone desiring to use them. In a corner Ken keeps a compact, Army-surplus organ he bought for the hymn recitals. Although he doesn't play himself, Ken is willing to let anyone with the ability to sit down and give it a try.

Even strangers waiting for streetcars on a nearby corner are invited to play. With so many players coming in and out of the shop, one is likely to hear a hymn recital at any time of the day.

Ken, a friendly, deeply religious man, is always ready to help the church or anyone in need. He is a member of the local Youth for Christ. While in Korea, he drove a jeep for evangelist Billy Graham when he toured the battlefields.

Wilkinsburg is known as the "town of churches" and most of the district's ministers come to Ken's shop. Ken is flattered but he says he's not sure whether it's because of the music; because no swearing is allowed, or because they like the original oil paintings by his father-in-law which decorate the walls.

Worldwide Bible Reading Thanksgiving to Christmas, 1956

Theme: THE BIBLE SPEAKS TODAY

November

22 Thanksgiving	Deuteronomy	5:1-21
23	Psalms	19:1-14
24	Psalms	27:1-14
25 Sunday	Psalms	46:1-11
26	Psalms	103:1-22
27	Psalms	121:1-8; 130:1-8
28	Psalms	145:1-21
29	Proverbs	3:1-20
30	Isaiah	40:1-11, 28-31

December

1	Isaiah	55:1-13
2 Advent	Luke	6:20-49
3	John	1:1-28
4	John	1:29-51
5	John	3:1-36
6	John	4:1-38
7	John	15:1-27
8	John	17:1-26
9 Universal Bible Sunday	Luke	8:1-21
10	Acts	17:16-34
11	Romans	8:1-39
12	Romans	12:1-21
13	I Corinthians	13:1-13
14	Philippians	4:1-23
15	Hebrews	11:1-40
16 Sunday	Luke	10:23-42
17	Luke	11:1-17
18	Luke	12:22-34
19	Luke	15:1-10
20	Luke	15:11-32
21	Luke	1:1-23
22	Luke	1:24-38
23 Sunday	Luke	1:39-56
24	Luke	1:57-80
25 Christmas	Luke	2:1-20

Christians around the world will be reading the above passages on the days between Thanksgiving and Christmas. The women of our Church are invited to join in this reading, and to enlist their families in this worship experience with the Christians of many lands. Bookmarks listing these are available from the American Bible Society, 450 Park Avenue, New York City.

Church News

ALABAMA

Phenix City — The Rev. J. M. McKnight, formerly of Crestview, Florida, began work in Phenix City, Alabama, on October the first. The Presbytery of East Alabama is sponsoring a church in this industrial city, across the Chattahoochee River from Columbus, Georgia. There was once a small Presbyterian Church in Phenix City but it was dissolved about twenty-five years ago. Plans are being made to erect a suitable building and put on a full time program.

Missionary News

Nashville — Miss Katherine Gray of our Mexico Mission arrived in the United States about October 9 for her regular furlough.

Miss Gray first went to Mexico in 1923 and has served there since that time in the educational work of the Mission. She has been connected with the Central Bible School in San Luis Potosi.

Mr. and Mrs. L. G. DeLand of our Congo Mission are arriving in the United States about October 26 to begin their furlough.

Mr. and Mrs. Eric S. Bolton of our Congo Mission, now on furlough in the U.S.A., announce the arrival of a son, William Theodore, born September 15, in Wooster, Ohio.

Bluford B. Hestir of Atlanta, Director of Publicity for the General Council, and the Rev. Eugene Daniel, Nashville, Candidate Secretary for the Board of World Missions, returned October 29 after a seven-weeks trip to the Orient.

The men made their trip by plane, via San Francisco and Honolulu, and visted Korea, Japan, and Taiwan, to witness "on the spot" work of Presbyterian missions in those areas. They talked with numerous American missionaries and natives, observed the work of the churches in the Orient, and visited church-related schools and hospitals.

GEORGIA

The annual Home-coming of the Summerville Presbyterian Church was held on October the 14th.

It was the same sweet occasion with old members coming back and home folks bringing wonderful food; the singing of merry old hymns and reminiscing of the long ago days.

We had one disappointment, Dr. William Glass was unable to come on account of two deaths in his congregation.

Mr. Pooley preached in Dr. Glass' place a wonderful sermon on Stewardship. Will Joe Abbott from Acworth gave a message in the afternoon.

The visitors and old members present felt as if it was a very happy day with the Spirit of Christian Fellowship prevailing.

service presenting the themes for the year. Theme will be "Who is my brother?"; theme hymn will be "God of Grace and God of Glory"; theme picture will be "The Church's One Foundation.

The first workshop was a skit, "Unto Us Much Is Given," led by Miss Emmah Leah Young, of Synod's Youth Council, who gave her explanation of how God has seen fit to place the splitting of the atom in the United States. Miss Young based her skit on her talk presented in the national science contest at the recent Louisiana division of the National Chemical Society in New Orleans.

A second workshop consisted of panel discussions on "Youth Wants to Know," presented by Bill Burge, of the Gentilly Church, president of the Presbytery Fellowship. This panel dealt with problems confronting adult advisors in the various churches, and answered from the youth's point of view.

New Orleans — The Presbytery of New Orleans voted at a recent meeting to merge four congregations into two churches. Napoleon Avenue and Prytania Street churches will merge to form the Church of the Covenant. The consolidated congregation will occupy the present site of the Napoleon Avenue Church. A commission of the presbytery will meet November 18 to merge the churches officially.

Bethel Presbyterian Church USA will be dissolved and will merge with Claiborne Avenue Presbyterian Church US.

Also at the meeting of the presbytery, the group voted for the honorable retirement of the Rev. A. L. Ash, minister of Kenner Presbyterian Church, from the active ministry, on December 31.

New Orleans — Miss Alice Lewis, the new director of Christian education at Canal Street Presbyterian Church, will remain in this position until the beginning of school next year when she will join her future husband at Austin Seminary. She will be married in late November.

He will finish his term in the United States Navy next summer, and after completing his seminary study plans to go to the Belgian Congo as a missionary.

Miss Lewis was educated at Columbia, Miss., High School, Belhaven College, and Louisiana State University. She had previously served as D.C.E. at First Presbyterian Church, Natchez, Miss., and First Presbyterian Church, Savannah, Ga.

NORTH CAROLINA

Charlotte — Sharon Presbyterian Church observed the 125th anniversary of its organization on October 7 with many former members and visitors present. After morning service dinner was served on the grounds (picnic style) and at 2:15 P. M. the anniversary service was held with the principal address given by Dr. William Childs Robinson of Columbia Theological Seminary on the subject "Our Presbyterian Heritage."

Sharon Presbyterian Church held its Second Missionary Conference October 10 - 14. Speakers at the Conference were the Rev. Donald E. Williams who is supported by the church and is missionary in North Brazil; the Rev. Alex McCutchan, of Belgian Congo; the Rev. John G. Viser, of West Brazil, and the Rev. and Mrs. Frank Lemmon, missionary-appointees to Mexico. The conference came to a conclusion Sunday with two fine sermons by Dr. C. Darby Fulton, Executive Secretary of our Board.

The first step in an expansion program is fast drawing to completion, as the new $60,000 Educational Building now under construction will soon be finished. This building will house the Children's and Young People's Departments of the Sunday School. It should be ready for occupancy in December. Other steps include renovation of the present Educational Building, and the erection of a Fellowship Building.

Dunn — Members of the First Presbyterian Church of Dunn, N. C., have dedicated 4.1 acres of land as the site of the erection of a new church plant to cost approximately $350,000 in a long range building program.

The Rev. Leslie C. Tucker, Jr., pastor of the church, presided over the dedication service which was held in October.

Plans now call for an educational building to be the first erected on the site. It will be used for worship services until the sanctuary is completed.

Mount Mourne — Meeting here Tuesday, Concord Presbytery voted disapproval of the proposed amendment to the Book of Church Order of the Presbyterian Church, U. S., admitting women to the eldership and diaconate. It approved sending a youth caravan to Mexico next summer.

The meeting was held in the historic Centre Church of which Rev. J. K. Parker is the pastor. The church has just completed its beautiful new fellowship hall in which the Presbytery was entertained at luncheon.

Dr. Frank McCutchan, a ruling elder of the First Presbyterian Church of Salisbury, presided as the moderator. Rev. L. T. Edgerton, minister of the Poplar Tent Church, Concord, was chosen as moderator-nominee for the next meeting of Presbytery.

Rev. Alan B. Wells was received from the Presbytery of South Carolina in order that he may become the pastor of the Back Creek Church, Mt. Ulla. His installation by a commission of Presbytery took place November 4, 7:30 p. m.

Rev. Robert J. Blumer was received from the Presbytery of Potomac in order that he may become the minister of the First Presbyterian Church, Newton, where a commission of Presbytery installed him as pastor, November 4, 7:30 p. m.

Mr. Woodrow McKay will be ordained by a commission of Presbytery in the First Presbyterian Church, Salisbury, November 11, 11:00 a. m. He will serve as assistant pastor in this church.

It was announced that the pastoral relations had been dissolved between Rev. James E. Porter and the New Salem and Shiloh Churches. Mr. Porter is no longer serving as a Presbyterian minister since he has recently become a member of the Stony Point Baptist Church. At his own request to the church and Presbytery, the pastoral relations were dissolved between Rev. Lewis B. Metts and the Franklin Presbyterian Church, Salisbury, on account of his ill health. Rev. Ralph S. Carson, minister of the Second Presbyterian Church, Mooresville, having reached the age of retirement, announced that he would leave the service of this church December 31.

Rev. John W. Foster, minister of the Calvary Presbyterian Church, Davidson, having reached the

Date for the formal organization of the church will be decided upon later by a commission, appointed by the presbytery and consisting of the Rev. Harry F. Petersen, executive secretary of the presbytery; the Rev. Arthur M. Martin and Mr. Johnson, pastors of the Columbia area and one elder from each Presbyterian church in that area.

Clinton — Presbyterian College has launched its 76th session with its largest enrollment in history, despite increasingly stringent academic requirements for entrance.

A total of 541 students registered for the start of the 1956-57 school year after admittance had been refused almost one out of every two new students who applied.

Among the new faculty additions at Presbyterian College this year are a former Davis-Elkins president, a past dean of Clemson and an outstanding religious writer.

These three men are: Dr. Raymond B. Purdom, who served as president of Davis-Elkins College for ten years after heading its chemistry department for 18 years—professor of chemistry; Col. Albert J. Thackston, Jr., recently retired Army officer who was dean of men at Clemson College for three years—dean of students; and Dr. Joseph M. Gettys, author of numerous religious books and pamphlets—professor of Bible.

Other appointments to the 40-member faculty include: Dr. Karl A. Scheele, assistant professor of economics; George W. Clark, assistant professor of history; and William H. Jones, instructor in mathematics.

Of the 541 total who enrolled at Presbyterian College, approximately 200 are listed as new students. The number of women students also runs higher this session, with 39 co-eds registered.

TENNESSEE

Memphis — The First Presbyterian and First Methodist Churches, neighbors in downtown Memphis, Tenn., have combined their efforts to produce a bi-annual "Saturday Round-up" for the benefit of neighborhood children who are extremely underprivileged.

Every fall, and again in the spring, the two churches have the "Round-up" each Saturday for a period of six weeks. The program is similar to that of a vacation Bible school. First the children are met at the local playground for an hour of supervised recreation. Following this period, the children and their leaders return to the two churches where they divide into groups for Bible lessons, song sessions, and lessons in handcrafts. The children, ages 5 - 11, are given a free lunch at noon, and in the afternoon a movie is shown, usually a cowboy show. Attendance is usually over 100 each Saturday.

Memphis — Presbyterian Churches of the Memphis area are sponsoring a leadership school, to be held at Idlewild Presbyterian Church in Memphis October 29, through November 2.

The 1956 session is the 33rd in the history of the annual Memphis area school. Five courses will be offered to teachers, workers, and members of Presbyterian churches in the greater Memphis area. Dean of the school this year is the Rev. William David Brown, associate minister of Evergreen Presbyterian Church. Faculty Chairman is Dr. Paul Tudor Jones, minister of Idlewild Church. Faculty Committee, the Rev. Paul Corbett, of Frayser Presbyterian Church, and Miss Tempe Claxton, of Whitehaven Presbyterian Church.

Memphis — Southwestern College in Memphis has begun a new program of teaching "Christian Service Projects" to students interested in becoming better workers in their own churches.

Class and discussion groups meet one night each week over a two-month period, in the Adult Education Center of the College library. The first three sessions are general lectures given by members of Southwestern's Bible faculty. These concern aims of Christian Education, understanding people, interesting children in the Church, and similar subjects. The other sessions are specialized classes so that each student may choose the field of most interest to him. At the end of the training sessions the students will go to many of the bigger churches, and to Wesley house, where they will observe work done, and work under supervision and guidance. Mrs. W. M. Cone of Memphis is in charge of this new project.

TEXAS

Commerce—Interdenominational Laymen's Sunday was observed in the First Church with laymen of the congregation having complete leadership of morning worship. Paul F. Street, associate professor of biology in the local East Texas State Teachers College and deacon in the church, gave the laymen's message on the subject "The Scientist Knows God." Sgt. Malcolm D. Calhoun, member of the teaching force of the Sunday School and of the ROTC staff at the local college, led the worship service.

Others participating in the leadership of the worship were Grover Sims, local area Boy Scout executive, one of the most recent additions to the membership of the church, and George W. Bartlett, Elder emeritus, a member of the local session for thirty-four years. Leading Sunday evening worship on the Sunday evening before Laymen's Sunday was Joe Fred Cox, diaconate chairman and product of the student work and Sunday School of the local congregation. Earlier in the fall, at a morning worship, charter presentation ceremonies were held for the church's Boy Scout Troop 26. Participating were Grover Sims, executive, Kenneth Michels, troop committee chairman, and scout leaders Sgt. Murray D. Parham and Tommie Morris.

VIRGINIA

The Presbytery of West Hanover met in its last session as at present constituted, October 23, 1956, in the Charlottesville Church, its first and last meeting in this beautiful new building. Effective January 1, 1957, most of the territory of West Hanover north of the James River, including Charlottesville and Orange, will be in Lexington Presbytery, while the City of Lynchburg and all of Roanoke Presbytery except Henry County (which will go to Montgomery Presbytery) will be included in West Hanover, the number of churches in which will thus be increased from 37 to 80. A good deal of the business at this fall meeting had to do with this change.

Rev. C. Lloyd Arehart was received from Winchester Presbytery, and arrangements made for his installation as pastor of the Farmville Church on November 4.

Presbytery voted 22 to 12 against the proposed amendment authorizing ordination of women as elders and deacons, and 19 to 13 against the proposed amendment concerning marriage and divorce.

W. Twyman Williams, Stated Clerk

Change of Address — Rev. Fernando Gutierrez, from Palacios, Texas, to 607 South Guadalupe Street, San Marcos, Texas, as pastor of the Mexican Presbyterian Church.

Change of Address: Rev. Plumer Smith, from Mutoto, Luluaburg, Congo Belge, to 1206 Rennie Avenue, Richmond, Va.

BOOKS

EARLY WILL I SEEK THEE. Eugenia Price. Fleming H. Revell Co. $2.50.

Many of our readers have benefited by the former writings of Miss Price. This last volume maintains the high quality set in her former works. The aim of the author in this new book is to stand aside and let Christ speak through her to those whose hearts long to follow Christ as the Lord of their lives. This work is largely autobiographical. It is a record of a heart that longed and found Christ who is more than life itself. She insists that Christ is the end of every man's search. She emphasizes the inexhaustibility of Christ. She writes, "Even if you are already one with Him there is more for you. There is more for me. This is a book for all longing hearts everywhere."

Mrs. Ruth Bell Graham has written the introduction. In it she says, "This book is primarily for the wistful, eager heart—weary, as it were, of the copies, longing for the Original. Once more Genie Price brings to us our Saviour, removing the confusion of thought that so often enshrouds Him, so that we see Him as He is—right beside us, invisible to our mortal eyes but infinitely more real than we are, the source of our longing and its satisfaction."

Miss Price makes an eloquent plea for objectivity in our lives. She states that she longed for objectivity in her life before she met Christ. This objectivity she has now found in Christ. To put it in her own language, "Christ lives in me and I can be off my own hands and into His hands, looking and living and writing and loving from His point of view and no longer my own. This is a great, great relief. Jesus Christ . . . the only person outside of ourselves who is attractive enough to pull us out of our subjective boxes and set us free to live—objectively!"

It is obvious that this book was written primarily to appeal to the lay mind. It should be pointed out, however, that any Christian minister would be benefited from the reading of this stimulating bit of autobiography. J.R.R.

THE SOUTHERN PRESBYTERIAN JOURNAL

A Presbyterian weekly magazine devoted to the statement, defense and propagation of the Gospel, the faith which was once for all delivered unto the saints.

VOL. XV NO. 30 NOVEMBER 21, 1956 $2.50 A YEAR

Remember

Your **Church Orphanage**

With A **Generous Donation**

At The **Thanksgiving Season**

"Inasmuch as ye have done it unto one of the least of these my brethren, ye have done it unto me." Matt. 25:40.

THE SOUTHERN PRESBYTERIAN JOURNAL

Rev. Henry B. Dendy, D.D., Editor....Weaverville, N. C.
Dr. L. Nelson Bell, Associate Editor....Asheville, N. C.
Rev. Wade C. Smith, Associate Editor....Weaverville, N. C.

EDITORIAL

"Architecture for Presbyterian Worship"

This is the title of a timely article in the September 15th issue of *Presbyterian Life* written by the Reverend Professor James Hastings Nichols of the University of Chicago. This follows an earlier REPORT ON THE ARCHITECTURAL SETTING OF PRESBYTERIAN WORSHIP prepared for and presented to the Presbytery of Chicago by a committee consisting of the best historians in that Presbytery, such as Professor Nichols and Professor Trinterude. This report is used in the class work at McCormick Theological Seminary, and has been used in a smaller degree by the writer at Columbia Theological Seminary. A copy was mailed to our Secretary of Church Architecture in the Board of Church Extension.

In these and other matters we have no desire to be lords over other men's faith. We emphatically disapprove of heteronomy. But in the Church of the living God, autonomy is not less to be rejected. One is our Master, even Christ. Slavery to Christ alone is the true and only freedom of the human soul. We do stand for Theonomy, and seek to bear our testimony to the truth of God. If so far as any and everything we mention in these matters is our own, let it fall to the ground and be forgotten. In so far as we bear witness to the truth of God as He has revealed it in the Word of which Jesus Christ is the theme, in so far as the history of the Church and particularly our Presbyterian heritage has clarified that truth we beg our brethren to heed NOT BECAUSE IT IS OUR TESTIMONY BUT BECAUSE IT IS GOD'S TRUTH.

Dr. Hasting's article calls attention to some three features of architecture befitting Presbyterian Worship. A complete editorial should be devoted to each of these items. Briefly, they are: first, that we gather around the Table of the Lord to celebrate a sacrificial meal, to enjoy the holy communion God has established with His people by the one sacrifice of Christ offered once for all. We do not come to an altar to offer a sacrifice to propitiate an unreconciled God.

Secondly, the ground around the Table of the Lord is level. The pastor who presides is not a mediating priest and he ought not to be forced to symbolize that he is by ministering in a long chancel in which he alone comes to the altar or Table at its head. God's people have a right to the Table of their heavenly Father and ought to come to that Table either by gathering directly about the Table — as was done at the World Council in Amsterdam — or else by having their representatives the elders (and for the offering plate the deacons) come all the way to that Table.

Thirdly, it is un-Presbyterian to attach God's presence and power to a particular place or object such as an altar or an icon. The popular "pictures" of Christ are described by Dr. Jenkins of Chicago as "icons of the liberal Jesus."

God has forbidden us to make any representation of Himself and bow down ourselves to it. We understand this to forbid the use of a so-called picture of Jesus as a worship center, as a wallet card for devotional purposes, or as a picture thrown upon a screen in connection with a dedication service. Instead it has pleased God to reveal Himself in that He the Word became flesh. God the Word reveals Himself in the incarnation, crucifixion and resurrection of Jesus Christ. Neither by bowing down to pictures of Jesus as a mere human hero, nor by philosophizing about Christ as a mere phantom or idea, but by the preaching of the Word of the Cross it pleases God to save. We are ambassadors of God proclaiming His message: we are reconciled to God by the death of His Son.

Christ reveals His salvation to us by the preaching of this Word, by sealing the Gospel with the sacraments, as the Holy Spirit accompanies and uses the God ordained means of grace. The gracious Lord Jesus has issued a varning against those who disregard even the east of God's commandments — or who teach nen so. How about the Second Commandnent? "If ye love ME, ye will keep MY comnandments." W.C.R.

Joy vs. Sorrow

The Gospel is preached to bring both sorrow ınd joy—sorrow for sin and joy for forgiveness.

Paul told the Corinthian Christians: *"For ;odly sorrow worketh repentance to salvation, ıot to be repented of: but the sorrow of the vorld worketh death."*

The paradox that sorrow can eventuate in oy while a world-inspired joy ends in sorrow s but one of many such truths to be found in he Bible.

One of the results of Bible study is the seeing ıf one's self as God sees us. This brings con·iction of sin with accompanying sorrow for in, and if this is followed by turning to Christ or forgiveness, joy is the end result.

Woe to the man who finds his joy in that vhich this world alone has to offer for such oy turns to ashes and to a sorrow which ends ınly in death.

The Gospel is rightly called the "Good News" or in it man finds the right perspective between his life and the next; between himself and his ;od; between joy and sorrow.

Introspection can become morbid, but a selfudgment which is the work of God's Holy pirit, is a healthy exercise. David was convicted f sin and cried out for forgiveness and that here might be restored to him the joy of God's alvation.

God wants us to be happy, but that happiness ıust be in and from Him. L.N.B.

Justification and the Children of The Covenant

Justification by God's sovereign grace received y faith in Jesus Christ alone is the cardinal octrine and the touchstone of the Reformation. Vhenever the salvation of the children of the ovenant is presented in such a way as seems ɔ upset this great reality, uncertainty and confusion ensue. Some modify their Reformation heritage, others become Baptists. The Reformation sees salvation as a very personal relation with the gracious God, Who stooped for our salvation all the way to the Cross on Calvary and awakened faith in our hearts by the power of the Holy Spirit. It sees this faith as a personal conscious response of trust in God Who has come to us in Christ and Who forgives our sins for Christ's sake. Saving grace and responding faith are both personal and conscious. How are we to relate thereto the baptism of the infant children of the covenant?

In baptism God is the primary doer. He acts in sealing upon the baptized an assurance that he is heir to the promises of the covenant of grace. In the case of believers, baptism is a confirmation of all the promises of the covenant, but it is especially a seal of the righteousness of the faith they already have. In the case of the children of the covenant, God thereby seals upon these His covenant promises, included in which is the assurance that He will bring these children, whose adoption into His family the Father declares in baptism, to future faith, repentance and forgiveness.

Calvin does not present the baptism of believers and of their infant seed as in every respect the same. He says that the circumcision of Abraham did not mean exactly the same thing to the believing father as it did to Isaac his infant son, Commentary on Romans 4.11. As was true in circumcision, so these children of the covenant are baptized INTO FUTURE REPENTANCE AND FAITH. For though these graces have not yet been formed in them, the seeds of both are nevertheless implanted in their hearts by the secret operation of the Spirit, Institutes IV.xvi.20. In the Geneva Catechism, 333, distinction is made between the faith and repentance required of us for baptism in that this must go before the sacrament in the case of those of age and discretion, but for little children it is sufficient that they show forth these fruits of baptism when they come to age.

Again, while for Calvin the children of the covenant are acknowledged by God as His children as soon as they are born and are assured of their adoption as the people and family of God by baptism, yet he asserts that our children "are born sinners as both David and Paul affirm," IV.xvi.17, and "even infants themselves bring their own condemnation into the world with them, who, though they have not yet pro-

The Southern Presbyterian Journal, *a Presbyterian Weekly magazine devoted to the statement, defense, and propagation of the Gospel, the faith which was once for all delivered unto the saints,* published every Wednesday by The Southern Presbyterian Journal, Inc., in Weaverville, N. C.

Entered as second-class matter May 15, 1942, at the Postoffice at Weaverville, N. C., under the Act of March 3, 1879. Vol. XV, No. 30, November 21, 1956. Editorial and Business Offices: Weaverville, N. C. Printed in the U.S.A. by Biltmore Press, Asheville, N. C.

ADDRESS CHANGE: When changing address, please let us have both old and new address as far in advance as possible. Allow three weeks after change if not sent in advance. When possible, send an address label giving your old address.

duced the fruits of their iniquity, yet have the seed of it within them," IV.xv.10.

Further, for Calvin the promise sealed in baptism both for adult and for infant is the forgiveness of sins and the imputation of Christ's righteousness, IV.xv.1,10; IV.xvi.3, 4. The promise is the same in both, including the paternal favour of God, the remission of sins and eternal life. The infants of believing parents "also receive righteousness, such as the people of God may obtain in this life, that is ONLY BY IMPUTATION, because the Lord in His mercy accepts them as righteous, IV.xv.10. In line with Calvin, Professor E. Boehl writes:

"The growing young Christian was righteous by imputation but original sin remained." "This is in accordance with sound pedagogical principles to behold the full and perfect guarantee, the unrestrained and gracious privilege of being received into the covenant, of being made an heir of God and joint-heir with Christ . . . and on the other hand to regard the same child as *impius*, and permit his justification to come in the course of his life." . . . "From the earliest times of the Reformation no one thought of impairing the doctrine of justification by a baptism operating *opus operatum*. With them, baptism was much rather an act coming within the life of the individual, and the regeneration promised in baptism was a sincere promise on God's part. But this was in no way prejudicial to the other truth that the subject of baptism lives within the Church as an *impius* (ungodly person) until God actually justifies him, that is, gives him the Spirit, and the man learns to understand by faith that God is reconciled through Christ." *The Reformed Doctrine of Justification*, pp.219-220,225-226.

Similarly, Principal John Macleod sets forth the *Scottish Theology*, p. 304, as teaching that in the case of the children of the covenant "their baptism can be regarded as in the full sense a seal of their oneness with Christ only when they indeed take His yoke upon them. Then and not until then have they the righteousness of faith of which their baptism is a seal."

The covenant of grace holds all these blessed facts in itself. We and our children are fallen, sinful, guilty. Our righteousness before God in this life is never that of our own works nor our infused goodness. It is always the righteousness of Christ imputed to us and received by faith alone. We are brought to this faith in Christ by the work of the Holy Spirit. Accordingly, we and our children need the cleansing blood of Jesus Christ and the renewing grace of the Holy Spirit. As children of the covenant, we and our children need faith and repentance or conversion. And as Calvin said, this faith and repentance generally come after the baptism of the child of the covenant. "Whom He called, them He also justified." W.C.R.

5. It will, if passed, deprive evangelicals of evangelizing by usage of the radio. We must remember that New Testament evangelism was not based upon the allocation of privilege to the largest religious body, but upon the fact that men were lost in sin and the message of salvation was to be made known to all mankind.

Our freedom is at stake in the U.S.A. We have rallied to protect the principles of democracy of peoples in other parts of the world, now we must protect our own religious freedom. The NAE is attempting to do this for all evangelical broadcasts and telecasts whether members of NAE or not. . . .

This is not a time for wishful thinking, hoping that everything will turn out all right! We must arise in the strength of the evangelical witness and recognize that Freedom is Everybody's Business, especially among evangelicals.

We are praying that this national appeal to all NAE members and friends will have a large enough response to fight this battle of liberty and freedom to a successful conclusion. . . . "Keep the Channels Open for Evangelicals."

—Paul P. Petticord, President NAE

THE TOWER OF BABEL

By J. V. N. Talmage, D.D.

Although the writer has always recognized the historicity of the story of the Tower of Babel, it was not until this spring that he could find anything in the archeological field which answered the Biblical description. The reason for this was that until the chronological place of the FLOOD was firmly established in archeological sequence there was no clue as to where to hunt for the Tower of Babel.

When geological and archeological data proved without the slightest doubt that the FLOOD of Noah must have occurred about 7000 years ago, not long before the Jemdet Nasr cultural era, the time had come to keep an eye open for the Tower. In reading Dr. V. G. Childe's valuable book, "New light on the Most Ancient East, a reference was found to a platform which Dr. Langdon discovered in the mound at Jemdet Nasr, that was 200 by 300 meters in size. Upon it were the foundations of a building 92 by 48 meters, which was dubbed a palace at first; but later that explanation was rejected when the name of God was found written in it.

Its purpose remains a mystery to the archeologists, but to us it strongly suggests the long lost Tower of Babel. Miss Ann Perkins of Yale University, an archeological expert, notes that in the construction burnt and unburnt brick were used.

As far as he knows the writer is the first to make this identification, though of course he has no positive proof as yet that this was the real Tower of Babel, described in the Bible. But in every way it answers to the need. The writer has not seen Dr. Langdon's original report, which is in German, but he is sure that a careful study of this report by one who reads German will be helpful.

Here are some of the relevant facts in identifying the Tower:—

1. The timing is right. It was long enough after the FLOOD for men to have multiplied, and was just before the great dispersion.

2. The location is good. The place seems to be centrally located amid Jemdet Nasr settlements. Some were 150 miles to the south and others as far to the north.

3. What we know about the construction fits the Biblical description, but more details are needed.

4. Unlike other identifications for the tower the foundations though large do not support a high building. This suggests something happened, leaving it incomplete.

5. The place was never occupied again and the name forgotten.

6. So far there is no other brickwork that can compete for the dishonor. If any one of the readers knows of a competing location, the *Journal* would like to know about it.

In conclusion we may state that until this mysterious brickwork is explained, any one is foolhardy to call the story of the Tower of Babel a myth.

Unless one has worked in foreign lands he cannot realize the great importance of the Biblical record of the Tower of Babel and the ensuing confusion of tongues. The Bible thus impresses upon us two important facts which enable us to appraise correctly race relationships. On the one hand it contradicts an impulse of the human heart to think his own race is superior, by showing that all races have come from one family, in spite of differences of language, culture and physical features. On the other hand it disapproves the ideas that some men have of a one-world government under the control of a few, by showing that racial and language barriers were set up by Divine intervention in order to preserve local freedom.

This does not mean that all the present languages and races were suddenly differentiated at Babel, but that the divisions and dispersion begun there have led to the diversified world we know today. God has seen fit to preserve in a marvelous way this vital story for us.

Several years ago, during a young people's conference, the writer attended a class taught by a young preacher from the southwest. Although the preacher himself had no faith in the historicity of the early part of the Bible, he taught the young people the story of the Tower of Babel, explaining everything in a naturalistic way, drawing mostly on his own vivid imagination. After the class he told the writer he thought that the story of the Tower of Babel and preceding chapters of Genesis were "myths."

Sir Leonard Woolley, the great archeologist, in his fine little book, "Ur of the Chaldees," claims that the eight feet of silt found on the lower part of the mound of Ur were left by the FLOOD of Noah, and that the great Ziggurat at Babylon "in Hebrew tradition became the Tower of Babel." These two events were perhaps four thousand years apart, at least, and Woolley's identifications, though absolutely false, are given as examples of loose statements made by otherwise great men. Such errors are often quoted by the unwary and uninformed, as in the October 29th issue of *Time* (page 50).

One cannot condemn the preacher from the southwest for not knowing much about the archeological background of the Tower of Babel, but was he justified in classifying the story to young people as a myth merely because of his own complete ignorance?

A Prophetic Ministry

I Kings 22:1-40

By Rev. Everett K. Brown
Mount Vernon Presbyterian Church
Alexandria, Va.

Why did you come to church this morning? Did you come automatically? Is going to church on Sunday morning just a habit with you? Did you come because the children wanted to come and you had to bring them, so in order to save trips you decided to come to church? Did you come just to get away from home and some of your home chores? Did you come to meet some friendly people and to see your friends? Or, did you come to worship God? I am told that:

> Some people go to church for the walk,
> Others go to gossip and talk.
> Some go to church to sleep and nod,
> And others go to worship God.

I think that you will agree with me that the purpose of this service, and the reason why we are here is to worship God. True worship involves a revelation of God to man and a response on the part of man to that revelation. True worship is a divine-human encounter with man making a response to the encounter. This is vividly illustrated in the sixth chapter of Isaiah. In this chapter the Prophet Isaiah describes his conversion. In the year that King Uzziah died Isaiah saw the Lord sitting upon a throne, high and lifted up. The seraphim cried, "Holy, holy, holy is the Lord of hosts: the whole earth is full of his glory." Isaiah saw God exalted and holy. Then he looked at himself and recognized his own unholiness, and confessed, "Woe is me! for I am undone; because I am a man of unclean lips, and I dwell in the midst of a people of unclean lips:". After confessing his sin Isaiah was forgiven and his sin purged away. Then he heard the voice of the Lord saying, "Whom shall I send,"? and Isaiah responded, "Here am I; send me." In this conversion experience of Isaiah, we have the pattern for worship. True worship is an experience in which we are confronted by God, and in which we respond to that confrontation.

I come to church to worship. I come to church hoping for and expecting some new knowledge or some new insight, or some new understanding of God and His will. I come expecting a revelation of God which will enable me to see myself as I am, and will enable me to accept His gracious gifts and be transformed into the likeness of His Son, Jesus Christ. My coming here may be habit. It may be automatic, like eating and drinking. Nevertheless, I come here for that spiritual nourishment without which I cannot live. I come here not just because my children want to come. I come because I want my children to know and love

Jesus Christ. I do not come here because it makes me feel good. I come because it offers the only way I know to make me good.

If the church is truly the church, and if it is truly the body of Jesus Christ, it will be a fellowship of believers in which people worship God. If we are to worship God, it is imperative that the church enable us to see God and to know Him. Therefore, I want and I expect the church to offer a prophetic ministry. In I Kings 22, we have recorded for us an incident which underscores the nature of a prophet's ministry and the temptation which the prophet faces.

What Is a Prophetic Ministry?

What do we mean when we speak of a prophetic ministry? In I Kings 22, we have an account of the events which took place near the end of Ahab's reign as the king of Israel. The account also underscores for us the function of the prophets and the nature of their ministry.

The Assyrian menace had passed with the Battle of Karkar. King Ahab of Israel was free to make war on Benhadad, the king of Syria. Benhadad had taken Ramoth-gilead from Omri, Ahab's father. So Ahab summoned his vassal Jehoshaphat, the king of Judah, to Samaria and proposed that they retake Ramoth-gilead. Jehoshaphat was agreeable to the proposition, but he insisted that Ahab enquire at the word of the Lord. Jehoshaphat wanted to know if this alliance and venture was God's will. Ahab summoned the prophets. There were about four hundred of them, and he asked, "Shall I go against Ramoth-gilead to battle, or shall I forbear?" And the four hundred prophets with one voice said: "Go up; for the Lord shall deliver it into the hand of the king." Zedekiah, one of the prophets made horns of iron and said, "Thus saith the Lord, With these shalt thou push the Syrians, until thou have consumed them." And again the prophets said, "Go up to Ramoth-gilead, and prosper: for the Lord shall deliver it into the king's hand."

The primary task of the prophets was not to predict future events. The prophets did foretell things that would come to pass, because they could see that to follow a certain course would lead inevitably to certain results. When Jehoshaphat asked Ahab to enquire of the Lord, his question was, "Is this God's will?"

The Hebrew word which is translated "prophet" literally means "one who speaks for God." The prophet therefore was the person through whom God spoke to the people. Through the prophets God made known his will to men. Therefore, the prophet began his message with "Thus saith the Lord."

A prophetic ministry is one that declares the Word of God. A prophetic ministry is one which makes God and His will known. A prophetic ministry proclaims the Word made flesh. I would not be so presumptuous as to stand before you, or any other congregation, and preface my own words with "Thus saith the Lord." Nevertheless, there is need today for prophetic ministry. There is a need for a message which can be prefaced with "Thus saith the Lord." Everett Brown has no word of wisdom or advice which would be of any value to you. I have no right to occupy this holy place and talk about what I think is true or right. For at best it would be trivial. We need a prophetic ministry. Therefore, we need to hear a word which is rooted and grounded in God's Word. We need to hear, not trivial human words, but the Word of God. So as a minister of the Gospel, it is my duty and privilege to proclaim the message of the Bible which is the Word of God, the only infallible rule of faith and practice.

A prophetic ministry is one which enables people to see God, to know God, and to love God. It is a ministry which reveals God, what God has done, and what God is doing. A prophetic ministry is one which heralds the "Good News" that God was in Christ reconciling the world to himself.

Ian Maclaren in his book, *Beside the Bonnie Briar Bush*, tells of a young minister who had been graduated with honors from a School of Theology. He returned to his home church to preach his first sermon. The sermon he had prepared for the occasion was a scholarly discussion of higher criticism and intricate theological propositions. His mother was dead, so he was staying in the home of his aunt. On the eve of the Sunday before he was to preach his first sermon, his aunt said, "Laddie, I hope you have remembered your mother's wish." He then remembered the words which his mother had spoken to him from her death bed. She had said, "Laddie, say a good word for Jesus Christ." The lamp light shone from the window of his room for many hours that Saturday night. The manuscript of the sermon he had prepared was burned in the fireplace one page at a time. A new sermon was prepared, and on the Lord's Day in the village church the worshippers heard the young minister proclaim the Word of God, the Word made flesh, even Jesus Christ our Saviour. This is prophetic preaching.

The Danger of Losing a Prophetic Ministry

Next, our Scripture underscores the fact that not everyone who says "Thus saith the Lord" is a true prophet. Jehoshaphat was not con- [illegible] the word which Zedekiah and the other prophets had spoken was the true Word of God. Jehoshaphat knew that the prophetic office was being prostituted by false prophets who gathered in the court of the king and spoke words pleasing to the ears of the king, instead of the Word of God. So he asked Ahab if there was not another prophet of the Lord of whom he might enquire. Ahab replied, "There is one more, Micaiah Ben Imlah, but I hate him; for he doth not prophesy good concerning me, but evil." An officer of the king was dispatched to get Micaiah Ben Imlah. The messenger advised Micaiah to join the chorus of the four hundred prophets and say what the king wanted to hear.

Apparently the messenger was more interested in pleasing the king than he was in the Word of God. The messenger wanted the prophet to give divine sanction to what the king wanted to do, instead of proclaiming what God wanted the king to do. Likewise, we may not like the Word of God. In fact, we do not like it because it cuts directly across the grain of our human nature. The Word of God is not popular. The Word of God and the Gospel do not make people feel good. The Word of God measures our lives and our thinking and what we are by God's standards. It is a message which is not intended to make you feel good. It is a message which can make you good. It is not intended to salve your conscience. It is designed to bring your life into conformity with God's will and enable you to accept the forgiveness that God freely gives those who confess their sins. It is not a message which is designed to give divine sanction to what you want to do or think. It is a message which can transform your life and enable you to say, "Not my will, but thine be done."

The Christian church has always faced the danger of losing her prophetic ministry. There is the danger that her voice will speak for the State or for some dominant class or group. There is always the danger that the church will accommodate her message to human standards and conform to this world instead of proclaiming the Word of God which alone can transform the world. People expect it. They want to dictate the terms of their surrender to God. But we don't come to God on any terms other than God's terms. We have heard "He who pays the fiddler, calls the tune." And we use department store thinking in the church and say "the customer is always right." These sayings cannot hold true in the church if the church is to have a prophetic ministry. The temptation to win approval and be accepted puts the church in constant danger of losing her prophetic ministry. The temptation to win approval prompts the voice in the pulpit to say what people want to hear, instead of proclaiming the Word of God. We know that not everyone is receptive to the Word of God and the Gospel. The Apostle Paul found that to some it was foolishness, to others a stumbling block, to still others it was nonsense, but to those who had ears to hear and eyes to see, it was "the power of God unto salvation." So when the church is tempted to water down her message and accommodate it to human standards, she must remember that the only approval worthwhile is the approval of God.

Our Lord warned his disciples to beware of false prophets. They may come in sheep's clothes, but inwardly they are ravening wolves. You will know them by their fruit.

SOME FAITHFUL PROPHETS

The temptation to ignore God and bend to the wishes of man is real, but there are many faithful and true prophets who fearlessly proclaim the Word of God without fear of consequences.

When the messenger asked Micaiah to speak a good word to the king and join with the voices of the four hundred prophets and say what Ahab the king wanted to hear, Micaiah replied: "As the Lord liveth, what the Lord saith unto me, that will I speak." Micaiah came before King Ahab of Israel and King Jehoshaphat of Judah. They were arrayed in their royal splendor, surrounded by their horsemen and chariots ready to march off to battle. Ahab asked Micaiah if they should go against Ramoth-gilead to battle or if they should forbear. Micaiah answered, "Go ahead and do what you will, for the Lord shall deliver it into the hand of the king." But it was evident from the way Micaiah spoke that this was not the Word of God. Ahab rebuked him. Then Micaiah said, "I saw all Israel scattered upon the hills, as sheep that have not a shepherd: and the Lord said, These have no master: let them return every man to his house in peace." And Micaiah accused the four hundred prophets of being filled with a lying spirit. The faithful prophet Micaiah was bound and imprisoned. Ahab and Jehoshaphat went off to battle. Ahab tried to escape the fate foretold in the prophecy of Micaiah by disguising himself. However, he was killed by the arrow of an archer who shot without aiming. And the battle was lost.

The Scriptures abound with examples of faithful prophets who have fearlessly proclaimed the unpopular Word of God. Amos, the shepherd from Tekoa, was called by God to go up to Bethel and speak the Word of God. Amaziah, the priest at Bethel, tried to silence Amos. The Word of God which came from the lips of Amos made both priest and people uncomfortable. Amos said that God had judged Israel and found her wanting. He had measured her with a plumb line and found her out of line. Therefore, the land would be destroyed and laid

you, and learn of me; for I am meek and lowly in heart: and ye shall find rest unto your souls."

Thus saith the Lord: "I am the way, the truth and the light."

Thus saith the Lord: "This is my commandment, that ye love one another, as I have loved you."

Helps To Understanding Scripture Readings in *Day by Day*

By Rev. C. C. Baker

Sunday, December 2, John 12:35-46. Jesus has spoken of Himself as the Light of the World (8:12). He now warns His listeners to respond to Him while the opportunity remains (12:35-36). What results in the lives of those who do turn to Him (8:12; 12:36,46)? What will happen to those who do not respond (v.48)? What has been the reaction of most of the Jews who have heard Christ (vv.37-40)? What basis have they had for judging whether or not He was the Messiah (v.37)? What was true even of many of those who believed in Christ (vv.42-43)? Whenever the Gospel is preached the listener is forced to make a decision concerning Jesus Christ. Has Christ, who is the Light of the World, brought light into your life?

Monday, December 3, John 1:1-14. List three facts mentioned about the Word in vv.1-2. According to v.14, who is the Word? Have you realized that Jesus lived before He was born into the world (8:57-58)? What statements of Christ can you recall in which He claims to be God? Notice John 10:30;14:9. How do the statements about Christ in v.1 tie in with the doctrine of the Trinity? Glance through Genesis 1:1-27 and then meditate on the fact mentioned about Christ in John 1:3. How does the truth of v.3 heighten the great tragedy of vv.9-11? Here is the marvelous wonder of our salvation — the Creator becoming flesh to be crucified for our sins.

Tuesday, December 4, John 1:35-46. Observe how each person mentioned in this passage begins to follow Christ as he discovers something of Who Jesus is. What insight of John the Baptist prompts two of his disciples to follow Christ (vv.35-37)? What conclusion does Andrew come to after spending the day with Jesus (v.41)? What effect does this discovery have upon Andrew's brother, Simon Peter (vv.40-42)? What conviction does following Jesus fix in Philip's heart (vv.43-45)? How is Nathaniel's skepticism turned to faith (vv.45-49)? Would Nathaniel have believed if Philip had not [illegible] Christ (vv.45,49)? Would

Andrew have believed without Peter's witness (vv.40-41)? Would John's two disciples (vv.35-37) have been attracted to Jesus without v.36? Do you share with others what you personally have discovered about Jesus Christ?

Wednesday, December 5, John 3:8-21. Verse 16 contains the heart of this passage, but other verses help explain its meaning. What facts should a person accept if he is to believe in Christ (vv.16-18)? What point does Jesus make with Nicodemus concerning the way to become a Christian (vv.1-7)? Was Nicodemus a professingly religious man (v.1)? If a "religious" person has not been born of the Holy Spirit, can he have true faith in Christ (vv.3,5,7)? What must a person's attitude be toward sin (vv.19-20)? What does v.36 say about personal commitment to Christ? True faith in Christ involves both a turning from sin and a personal commitment of obedience to Christ.

Thursday, December 6, John 4:27-38. Jesus is constantly trying to focus the eyes of the disciples upon spiritual realities. How does Jesus do this in terms of the food the disciples have brought (vv.8,31-34)? With what are the disciples primarily concerned (vv.31,33)? Jesus, like His disciples, has physical needs (vv.6-7), but His primary concern is for the spiritual needs of others. One example of His spiritual emphasis is found in His interview with the Samaritan woman (vv.7-26). So Jesus gives the testimony of v.34 and throws out the challenge of vv.35-38. Though you must spend much time and effort in providing the physical necessities of life, do you keep your eyes centered primarily on spiritual needs — both your ow[n] and those of others?

Friday, December 7, John 15:18-27. Jesu[s] speaks to His disciples as though the norma[l] experience of the Christian will be oppositio[n] from the world. What facts would He hav[e] His disciples remember as they face oppositio[n] (vv.18-21)? If you do not encounter some op[-]position to your Christian testimony, could [it] be that your life is too much of this worl[d] (v.19)? What reason does Jesus point out fo[r] the coming of opposition (vv.19,21)? Observ[e] that opposition to Jesus was not due to an[y] faulty or unattractive presentation of the trut[h] but simply to the holiness of His life and test[i]mony (vv.24-25). What does Christ provide t[o] hold and strengthen the Christian in time o[f] opposition (vv.26-27;16:7-11)? Does your Chri[s]tian life have the cutting edge that causes othe[rs] to think about their sins?

Saturday, December 8, John 17:17-26. Verse[s] 25-26 point up the striking difference betwee[n] the disciples of Christ and the rest of the worl[d]. It is in behalf of His disciples that Jesus give[s] Himself utterly and completely (v.19). No[w] Jesus prays for them (v.9) that: (a) they ma[y] be kept faithful (v.15), (b) they may be on[e] (vv.22-23), (c) others may believe throug[h] their witness (vv.18,23a). The disciples ca[n] be faithful, unified and able to win others onl[y] as Christ's nature and love abides in the[m] (vv.13b,21b,23a,26b). Can a person know Go[d] except as He abides in Christ (vv.1-3,26)? D[o] you try to accomplish any phase of God's wor[k] apart from the presence of Christ?

SABBATH SCHOOL LESSONS — REV. J. KENTON PARKE[R]

LESSON FOR DECEMBER 2

"Let Not Your Hearts Be Troubled"

Background Scripture: John 14
Devotional Reading: II Corinthians 4:7-15

These are among the best-known and best loved words of Jesus. They are read at almost eve[ry] funeral, and often when the pastor sits beside the sick, or is visiting in a home where there h[as] been some sorrow or bereavement.

We live in a world full of trouble; "troubled on every side." Trouble, like a gloomy clo[ud] has gathered thick and thundered loud. How can we keep our hearts from quaking with fe[ar]? How can we keep these troubles from getting within? Our frail bark is being tossed to and fro by the winds and waves. How can we keep afloat? How can these angry waves be quieted? There is only one answer to these and other disturbing questions. It is the one given by Jesus when His disciples awakened [Him] when He was asleep in the storm. "Peace, be still," said, and the winds and the waves obeyed Hi[m]. Whether it be a storm on the sea, or the sto[rm] in the breast of the man of Gadara, He c[an] calm the storm.

Paul knew something about storms: "Thrice I suffered shipwreck." The worst storms which he had to face, however, were those caused by his persecutors. He says that they "are persecuted, but not forsaken; cast down, but not destroyed" (see Devotional Reading). The Lord always stood by him, giving him grace to bear his troubles, and a peace which passed all understanding.

The disciples were troubled as they gathered in the upper room to keep the Passover. It may have been a somewhat vague feeling of some coming disaster. The storm swept down so suddenly after the Supper, that it seemed to take them by surprise in spite of the warnings which He had given them. In this great chapter we have the cure for troubled hearts: *It is faith:* Faith in God; Faith in God the Father, Faith in God the Son, Faith in God, the Holy Spirit.

I. *Faith in the Father:* "Ye believe in God"; Verses 1,2,6-13,16,28.

Jesus came to reveal the Father; the only begotten Son, Who dwelt in the bosom of the Father, came to live and die in order that men "might know Thee, the only True God, and Jesus Christ, Whom Thou hast sent."

Jesus loved to talk about "My Father," "your Father," "our Father," "The Father." He sought to glorify His Father and finish the work which His Father had given Him to do. Wist ye not that I must be about My Father's business, He said to His mother when she found Him as a boy in the temple, (or, "In My Father's house"). "Father, into thy hands I commend my spirit," He said on the cross, as He died.

Faith in the Father; faith in the God Who has revealed Himself in the Bible, and in the face of Jesus Christ, will cure troubled hearts. Our Father is not like the God of the Deist, Who is cold and distant, taking no interest in His children. He is the God described by the psalmist when he says, Like as a father pitieth his children so the Lord pitieth them that fear Him, and in many other passages in the Old as well as the New Testament. Our Father knows that we have need of the many "things" about which we are sometimes anxious. Fear not, little flock, for it is the Father's good pleasure to give you the kingdom. He is with us in our times of trouble and trials, when we pass through the fire or the water. The picture which we have of our Father in the Bible comforts our hearts.

In this chapter Jesus tells us many things about the Father: In my Father's house are many mansions; If ye had known me ye should have known my Father also; He that hath seen me hath seen the Father; I am in the Father, and the Father in me; I go unto my Father; that the Father may be glorified in the Son; I will pray the Father and He shall give you another Comforter: etc. Sixteen times in these thirty-one verses He says something about His Father. We need never be worried or anxious when we have such a loving Heavenly Father Who cares for us.

II. *Faith in the Son:* "Believe also in me."

Faith in Jesus Christ, God's Son, is a cure for troubled hearts. He is the express image of the Father. He not only reveals His Father, but He reveals Himself as a loving compassionate Saviour of men.

Jesus was always curing troubled hearts. From the time of His first miracle, when He cured the worried heart of His mother — troubled over a somewhat trivial matter, that of the wine giving out — to the last word He spoke to her from the cross, as the sword was piercing her soul, He was constantly healing somebody's broken heart. To heal the broken-hearted was part of His mission. He was the Great Physician Who had the power to heal all manner of sickness and all manner of disease, bringing health and peace. To all sorts of men and women He spoke words of comfort and encouragement in their times of need.

His works, His words, His life, were all parts of the proof that He was the Son of God. In this chapter He claims to be one with God, the only way by which men can come to the Father. "I am the way, the truth, and the life; no man cometh unto the Father but by me." Now, faith in Christ, the Son of God, is a wonderful cure for troubled hearts. His life, as He bore our sicknesses and carried our sorrows; His ministry, as He stretched out a loving hand to all who needed Him; His words of peace and comfort; all contributed to the healing of broken hearts. He never turned away anyone who came with their burdens or sorrows; instead, He invited them to come to Him, saying, "Come unto me all ye that labor and are heavy-laden, and I will give you rest." He is the same, yesterday, today, and forever. He still invites us to come and bring our burdens to Him. He is a faithful and merciful High Priest, able to succor and sustain us and give peace to our troubled hearts. Peace I leave with you; my peace I give unto you. One of the most popular and loved hymns is, What a Friend we have in Jesus, All our sins and griefs to bear. Many of our hymns are saturated with this thought. He is an All-sufficient Saviour.

III. *Faith in the Holy Spirit:* "Another Comforter."

Not only does Jesus tell us much about His Heavenly Father, and about Himself in this chapter, but He promises them another Comforter Whom they will send to be with them so that they will not be comfortless. He speaks of the Holy Spirit as One Whom He will send, and the Father will send. He tells them that it is expedient for them that He go away. This is a most precious and important promise. It is one that we can rejoice in today.

The Holy Spirit does many things. He comes to convict the world of sin and of righteousness and of judgment. It was the work of the Holy Spirit in the hearts of the people at Pentecost that caused them to cry out, Men and brethren, what shall we do? It is the work of the Spirit today to so move the conscience and heart that men will turn from sin unto Christ. The Holy Spirit regenerates. Nicodemus came to Jesus and was told that he must be born again, and when this ruler asked, How? Jesus told him about the work of the Spirit. The Holy Spirit guides into all truth. He enlightened the mind of Peter so that he understood the meaning of Old Testament prophesies, and could preach Christ to them. He guided the men of the Old Testament and New as they wrote. He guided the Church in all its activity. The Acts of the Apostles might well be called, "The Acts of the Holy Spirit." It was He Who led Paul in his missionary journeys.

The Holy Spirit is here called "The Comforter," or The One called alongside to help. He helps in every time of need, but especially when our hearts are sad and sorrowful.

There are many things which trouble our hearts in these days. Some are what people call the "Big Problems," or the "World Problems," and we certainly have plenty of these. Every way we turn our eyes there is a "Trouble-spot," it seems. To read the papers or listen to the news is enough to make us jittery and fearful. How can we keep calm and have peace? The answer is found in this chapter. Have Faith in God, not in men, except as they represent and follow Him. The Psalmist says that we cannot trust men of "high degree," or of "low degree"; we must put our trust in God. Over and over again we are exhorted to trust only in Him. Let us trust the Triune God; He is our Father, our Saviour, our Comforter. The Father, the Son, and the Holy Spirit, all unite to calm our hearts.

Then, we have our "Little Problems," our Personal Problems. They are not small to us. Where can we go for comfort? The Fourteenth Chapter of John has been the unfailing source of strength and comfort for God's people. It has been wet with the tears of suffering saints, tears which came from distressed and then relieved, hearts, as they found the comfort they needed. Let not your heart be troubled; Believe in God; Believe in me; We will send "Another Comforter"; Let not your heart be troubled, neither let it be afraid. Peace I leave with you; My peace I give unto you.

Let us praise God for this beautiful part of His Word; the Words of Jesus as He sought to cure the aching hearts of His disciples.

YOUNG PEOPLE'S DEPARTMENT — REV. B. HOYT EVANS

YOUTH PROGRAM FOR DECEMBER 2

What's The Answer?

Scripture: II Chronicles 7:14; John 14:13,14; and I John 5:14,15.

Hymns: "Abide With Me"
"Take Time To Be Holy"
"What A Friend We Have In Jesus"

Program Leader:

A lady medical missionary told of a very interesting thing that took place in 1948 as the Chinese Communists were over-running the country and driving out the missionaries before them. This particular missionary was left alone on her station with all her medical and hospital equipment. Word came that she would have to move her hospital to a new location hundreds of miles away. Things were in such a state of confusion that any kind of transportation was impossible to arrange. There seemed to be no solution at all to her problem. Finally the day came when it was absolutely necessary to leave, and with that day came a way of escape. Just at the right time, and without any previous planning or knowledge on her part, space on a naval vessel was made available for her and her equipment. To make the story even more amazing, the vessel was bound for the very place which had been chosen as the new location for her hospital.

It is thrilling to hear of that remarkable experience, and it must have been even more thrilling to have actually experienced that modern miracle. According to the missionary, though, there was a good reason for God's gracious intervention at that particular time. That eventful day was the same day that her name appeared for prayer in the *Day By Day* devotional booklet. On that particular day thousands of people all over our church were offering special prayers for that lady and her work for the Lord.

in time she lived to see her son yield himself to Christ and become one of the most useful servants in the history of the Christian church.

John Bunyan spent twelve years in Bedford jail. It has been suggested that he surely must have prayed many times to be released, but God said, "Not yet," and God used the time Bunyan spent there to bring forth *Pilgrim's Progress* which has been a blessing to millions of people. We must all learn that God has good and sufficient reasons for delaying to answer our requests. (Ask for personal experiences with postponed answers to prayer.)

Fourth Speaker:

The most difficult answers to prayer for us to accept and understand are the times when God says, "No," to our requests. We must recognize that those times do come. Paul prayed that his thorn in the flesh might be taken away, but God did not grant his request. Jesus prayed that, if possible, He might not have to drink the cup of sorrow and suffering, but it was not possible for it to be passed by. As for us, the Bible says that we know not what we should pray for as we ought, so we are certain to ask for things which God, in His wisdom and love, cannot give us. When we do receive an answer of "No" to our prayers, we must remember that God deals with us according to His wisdom, love and mercy. (Read Matthew 7:9-11.) Ask the young people to tell of some of their prayers which have received "No" answers.)

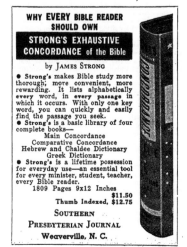

Women's Work

Alcohol and God's Temple

The Eighteenth Amendment has been repealed, but there has been no repeal of the liquor problem, for fifty million Americans drink alcohol in wine, beer, and distilled spirits. The alchohol goes into the person's stomach, which cannot change or digest alcohol, so very soon it gets into the upper intestine and from there gets into the blood stream. The blood makes a round trip throughout the body in about a half-minute. Alcohol goes everywhere the blood goes and all the time it is exerting its power as a poison to that person's brain, which is affected first.

Alcohol begins by dulling the powers of attention, judgment, and discrimination. Some other harmful things of alcohol are: it fails to provide vitamins, minerals and proteins, and may lead to nutritional diseases; it cannot be stored in the body and so does not build a reserve of calories; it is not used to build or repair ills; it slows reactions, reduces endurance, and causes the loss of co-ordination; it depresses the higher brain centers which control voluntary behaviour; it is a depressant, not a stimulant; it develops chronic inflammation of the stomach, deficiency diseases, and reduces the resistance of the individual to numerous other diseases such as pneumonia and heart disease; it is habit -forming, thus weakening the person's will-power and lessening the power of judgment.

Alcohol makes a person slow and dull in mind and body, makes him do poorer work and less work, makes a driver take risks, lessens his hearing, vision and judgment, hinders the co-ordination of his nerves and muscles, makes him slower in deciding what to do, and it hinders the judgment, thinking, co-ordination, spirit of sportsmanship and endurance of an athlete.

We know that smoking and alcohol are injurious to the health and efficiency of the body, so we must keep our bodies strong and efficient, not only for our own sakes but for the sake of God, who gave us our bodies. The Christian's body is a temple of the Holy Spirit — "Know ye not that ye are the temple of God, and that the Spirit of God dwelleth in you? If any man defile the temple of God, him will God destroy; for the temple of God is holy, which temple ye are."

Here is our final challenge — "I beseech you therefore, brethren, by the mercies of God, that ye present your bodies a living sacrifice, holy, acceptable unto God, which is your reasonable

Slow Me Down, Lord

Slow me down, Lord! Ease the pounding of my heart by the quieting of my mind. Steady my hurried pace with a vision of the eternal reach of time. Give me, amid the confusion of the day, the calmness of the everlasting hills. Break the tensions of my nerves and muscles with the soothing music of the singing streams that live in my memory. Help me to know the magical, restoring power of sleep. Teach me the art of taking minute vacations—of slowing down to look at a flower, to chat with a friend, to pat a dog, to read a few lines from a good book.

Remind me each day of the fable of the hare and the tortoise, that I may know that the race is not always to the swift; that there is more to life than increasing its speed. Let me look upward into the branches of the towering oak and know that it grew great and strong because it grew slowly and well.

Slow me down, Lord, and inspire me to send my roots deep into the soil of life's enduring values that I may grow toward the stars of my greater destiny. In Jesus' name, Amen.

—The Notwen Club

Huge Cross Planned for Illinois

Governor William G. Stratton of Illinois pledged support of a nation-wide campaign to raise three million dollars for erection of a huge cross in his state, described as the largest cross in the world.

The General Federation of Women's Clubs, sponsor of the project, plans to erect a 500-foot cross and chapel atop Bald Knob, a hill in Shawnee National Forest near Carbondale, Illinois. It will be dedicated to greater unity of thought and effort among the major Christian faiths.

Leaders of the project said they will seek to have Bald Knob's name officially changed to Mount Calvary, and to have the section of Illinois State Highway 127 bordering its base redesignated as "The Way of the Cross." Easter sunrise services have been held on Bald Knob since 1937. —Exchange

Church News

THE GENERAL FUND AND INTERCHURCH AGENCIES

Statement of Receipts

Jan. 15 - October 31, 1956

THE GENERAL FUND AGENCIES	
Budget for 1956	$846,581.00
Received from Jan. 15th through October 31, 1956	371,477.94
Percentage of annual budget received to date	43.88
Balance needed for the year	475,103.06

INTERCHURCH AGENCIES	
Budget for 1956	$21,495.00
Received from Jan. 15th through October 31, 1956	11,732.60
Percentage of annual budget received to date	55.00
Balance needed for the year	9,762.40

World Mission Receipts

Budget for 1956	$3,300,000.00
Receipts to date	2,331,351.08
Percentage of annual budget received for 1956	70.64
Balance needed for 1956	968,648.92

Board of Church Extension

Report of October 1956

Budget 1956	$1,400,000.00
Receipts to date	597,722.65
Percentage of annual budget received to date	42.69
Balance needed for the year	802,277.35

GEORGIA

Atlanta—The General Council of the Presbyterian Church, U.S. in its annual fall meeting here Oct. 30-31, re-elected as its chairman for a third year Dr. J. Fara Van Meter, physician from Lexington, Ky. At the same time it named Dr. Emmett B. McGukin, pastor of First Presbyterian Church, Lynchburg, Va., to succeed Mr. Everett Repass of Salem, Va., as vice-chairman. Mr. Repass' term on the Council expired in the spring of 1956.

The Council devoted much of its meeting to hearing reports of special committees, including two created as the result of General Assembly actions.

Important among these is the committee named to study the effectiveness and efficiency of the present organizational structure of the Church, as

12, 1956, at synod's meeting in Macon, Ga., by a standing, unanimous vote the consolidation of Rabun Gap Industrial School and the Nacoochee Institute into one school was approved. Friends of Rabun Gap Industrial School promised to raise $150,000 to build a new school at Rabun Gap and to pay off accumulated debts.

Today the Rabun Gap - Nacoochee school includes a Christian High School with dormitories for 50 boys and 50 girls. The main building has been extended to include a beautiful chapel and a library and auditorium. The chapel of the school is also used for services by the local Presbyterian Church. Recently a new shop building has been completed. The school is a service to the community with 120 local students attending as day students at the High School along with the 100 dormitory students.

There is an adult education project carried on at the school called the Farm Family Program. Fourteen school farms are available to families who want to learn better farming methods and send their children to the school. These farms are available for a family to live in for a ten year period.

LOUISIANA

Alexandria—Dr. S. J. Patterson, Jr., secretary of men's work, spent a busy week in the Louisiana Synod, Oct. 21-28. He attended training sessions and rallies and spoke in Lake Charles, New Orleans, Opelousas, Alexandria, Shreveport and Camp Alabama, climaxing his visit with a Sunday night address at the Alabama Church, one of the outstanding rural churches in the South.

On the itinerary were a leadership school, Synod and three Presbytery men's council training sessions, two district rallies and one civic club address. He was accompanied by Rev. George Ricks, Baton Rouge, regional director. Ralph Brewer, Alexandria, president of the Synod council, presided at the Alexandria meeting and attended the Louisiana Presbytery rally at Crowley, the Presbytery training sessions at Opelousas and the two district rallies at Shreveport and Camp Alabama and the Red River Presbytery council training session.

MISSISSIPPI

Canton — A $55,000 educational building was dedicated at the First Presbyterian Church, Canton, recently, with Dr. Charles R. McCain, for seven years pastor of the church, preaching the dedicatory sermon, and Mrs. Peter Marshall of Washington, D. C., speaking later in the day to one of the largest congregations in the history of the church.

Mrs. Marshall spent ten years of her childhood in Canton when her father, the Rev. John A. Wood was pastor of First Church here. The widow of the distinguished minister of New York Avenue Presbyterian Church in Washington told her audience that present-day people seem to be afraid to ask God for the big things in life. She urged that people use three yardsticks with which to measure their dreams: first "what we want must be in accord with our own being; second, we have to abide by God's rules; and third, we have to want our dream with our whole heart and know ahead of time whether what we want is God's will".

At the morning service, Dr. McCain reviewed the progress and growth of the church during the past seven years.

Following the afternoon address a reception in honor of Mrs. Marshall was held in the new educational building.

Hollandale—The Presbytery of Central Mississippi held its quarterly State Meeting on October 18th in the First Presbyterian Church of Lexington, Rev. Hayes Clark, Minister, and a brief adjourned meeting in the Canton First Church, Dr. Chas. R. McCain, Minister, on October 24th.

The Retiring Moderator, Ruling Elder Leroy B. Allen of the Leland Church, brought the opening message. Rev. E. C. Brasington, Minister of the Leland Church, was elected Moderator, and Dr. John Reed Miller of the Jackson First Church was elected Vice Moderator.

Evangelistic powers, and permission to labor outside the bounds of the Presbytery, were granted to Rev. David L. Parks, who has been appointed to World Mission service in Korea.

The Presbytery voted disapproval of both of the proposed amendments sent down by the General Assembly: that to the Book of Church Order on the ordination of women, and that to the Confession of Faith on Marriage and Divorce.

Presbytery approved as a Candidate for the Ministry, Mr. James Albert Turner, of the Louisville First Church, a student at Belhaven College in Jackson.

At the lunch hour, members of Presbytery visited the site, three hundred acres, about four miles from Lexington, which Presbytery has voted to purchase for development as a camp and conference site.

Rev. George F. Johnson, of the Ackerman group, was dismissed to Ouachita Presbytery, in order that he may serve the Star City and Mt. Zion churches. Rev. E. L. Gage, of the Mt. Salus church at Clinton, was dismissed to New Orleans Presbytery, in order that he may serve the First Street Church in New Orleans.

The January Stated Meeting will be held in the Canton First Church on January 17, 1957.

W. A. Gamble, Stated Clerk

TENNESSEE

Jackson—A very significant action in the Tennessee Men's Council when they met Oct. 26-27, in Jackson, Tenn., was launching of a concentrated effort to present the total program of the Church to all local Men's groups.

Action taken at the Council urged that the Council undertake to present the total program of the Church to the men of every local church in the Synod, either through Round Tables or by personal visits on the part of Council members. We will especially explain the Men's Work Calendar and present the manual, "The Work of The Church—Whose Responsibility?" and seek to diligently explain the Men's Work.

A full attendance at the meeting heard encouraging reports concerning the Men's Work in the Synod of Tennessee, and made plans for their work during 1957.

Mr. E. A. "Andy" Andrews, Jr., director of Program and Plans of the Division of Men's Work in Richmond, Va., was in charge of the training session held the first afternoon of the meeting. At the Friday evening session the council heard the report of the regional director, the reports from the presbytery presidents, and from ministers, representing the synod and the presbyteries. A social hour followed the business meeting.

The council heard plans for the Men's Convention to be held in Miami, Fla., October, 1957 from Mr. Quinton Edmunds of Jackson. Mr. Cliff Milton, of Memphis, program chairman, reported detailed plans for the Men's Conference to be held at NaCoMe, May 31 through June 2, 1957. Dr. Reuben Crawford, Fayetteville, presented the financial report, and the 1958 budget was adopted.

One action of the council taken at this meeting was to agree to have as continuing projects: the full support and betterment of the Men's Conference at NaCoMe each summer; and full support of the Miami Convention in 1957, with real effort being put forward to reach the Tennessee Synod's quota of 400 men attending the convention; and support of the school for leaders. They further pledged their continuing efforts to call to the attention the men the necessity to volunteer as teachers in the Sunday School, especially in the Children's department; and to recognize and show the need, and the importance of having men to counsel for the Youth Conferences and the Pioneer Camps.

VIRGINIA

Montgomery Presbytery met in its 242nd Stated Meeting in the Blue Ridge Church of Ararat, Va., on Tuesday, October 30, 1956, at 10:00 A.M. There were present 38 ministers and 46 Ruling Elders.

Ruling Elder A. B. Richardson was elected Moderator and Rev. John A. Ricks was nominated to be Moderator for 243rd Stated Meeting which is to be held on January 22, 1957, in the Presbyterian Church of Buchanan, Va.

Plans were made to install Rev. Marion L. Church of Roanoke, Va.

Rev. Homer C. Holt was received into Presbytery and arrangements made to install him as pastor of the Campbell Memorial Presbyterian Church of Vinton, Va.

Rev. R. P. Hayes was dismissed to Lexington Presbytery in order that he may become pastor of the Craigsville Church.

Rev. B. F. Sperow was dismissed to Holston Presbytery that he may accept work there.

Presbytery voted to have an inter-Presbytery exchange of ministers with Lexington Presbytery in conducting evangelistic services in the spring of 1957.

Presbytery approved the proposed Amendment I to the Book of Church Order concerning election of women to the office of Ruling Elder and Deacon. This was passed by a vote of 41-23.

Presbytery disapproved proposed Amendment II concerning Chapter XXVI of the Confession of Faith by a vote of 63 to 4.

Presbytery overtured the General Assembly as follows:

Whereas, the studies of marriage and divorce by our church courts during the past several

large bibliography indicates another rich source of information. This is a book for pastors and all who have any responsibility for the support of religious work and institutions. It is a powerful stimulus to Christian stewardship upon the part of all who read it. The treatment is comprehensive and fair. The book shows how far we have come in Christian stewardship and creates an incentive to go the rest of the way.

THE PRESBYTERIAN ENTERPRISE. M. W. Armstrong, L. A. Loetscher, and C. A. Anderson. Westminster Press. $4.50.

This book records from American Presbyterian sources the lives of men and women who were the Presbyterian Church from Colonial times to the present. From the stories told here, it is a striking and unescapable conclusion that the Presbyterians have exerted a far wider influence on American life than their comparatively small numbers would suggest.

The book is divided into three parts. The first deals with Colonial Presbyterianism presenting minutes of the first Presbytery in 1706 and the organization of the church down to the adoption of the Standards. Part 2 deals with the development of the church from the close of the Revolution down to the end of the Civil War. The third part of the book covers Presbyterianism from 1870 to the present. The last chapter relates the work of the Presbyterian Church, U. S. A., from 1937 to 1956.

"UNDERSTANDING AND COUNSELING THE ALCOHOLIC." Howard J. Clinebell, Jr. Abingdon Press. $3.75.

One of the most pressing and perplexing problems of our day is alcoholism. This book is written for those who want to help in contributing something to the solution of this problem. It offers practical suggestions as to how to handle the alcoholic who comes seeking counsel. Specifically it is designed to be an aid to the person who wishes to apply religious resources more effectively to the problem of alcoholism. The author shows that adequate understanding of the problem is a first essential in dealing with this widespread and persistent evil. He holds that without the solid foundation of understanding, counseling tends to be misdirected and ineffective.

The second part of this volume is written to help the reader profit by the experience of those religious groups which have been especially concerned with helping alcoholics. It presents three varied types of religious approaches to alcoholism with an evaluation of the strength and weakness of each, together with a psychological analysis of how each operates. It also describes the dynamics of the process by which religion can provide a psychological and spiritual substitute for alcohol and thus become a solution to the problem of alcoholism.

It should be pointed out that this work is not primarily a study of either the ethics of social drinking or the problems that arise from immoderate use of alcoholic beverages in our country. The book limits itself to one problem area, namely the sickness called alcoholism.

The author believes that in all the dark history of the handling of the problem of alcoholism the brightest ray of hope and help is Alcoholics Anonymous. He states that this organization has to its credit 130,000 individuals who have been won to sobriety and lives of usefulness.

He is fair enough, however, in his appraisal to state that the Alcoholics Anonymous is not the complete answer to the problem of alcoholism. It is helpful to many, but has its inadequacies. This reviewer has been dealing with alcoholics and alcoholism for 30 years. He has found Alcoholics Anonymous to contribute a great deal to this baffling problem. In our judgment, however, we believe that the method employed by the Hebron Fellowship at Boone, North Carolina, is an improvement over Alcoholics Anonymous.

After all is said and done on the subject, the author is stating an undeniable fact when he writes that the church's most important task in relation to the problem of alcoholism is prevention. To put it in his words, "Prevention is the only real solution to the problem. As things are now we are like Alice in Wonderland running as hard as we can to stay at the same place.

"Alcoholics are being created wholesale while all the therapeutic agencies together are able only to treat them retail. . . . Too many are falling over the cliff into the morass of the sickness of alcoholism each year. Somehow we must build a fence that will reduce the number of new alcoholics."

This work can help the pastor in making his counseling more effective. It is not necessary for one to agree with all the thinking of the author to profit from the materials he offers the pastor in this volume. J.R.R.

EXPOSITORY OUTLINES ON THE WHOLE BIBLE. Charles Simeon. Volume VII Proverbs - Isaiah 26. Volume VIII Isaiah 27 - End. Volume IX Jeremiah - Daniel. Volume X Hosea - Malachi. Zondervan. $3.95.

One of the best known figures of the later years of the evangelical revival in England was Charles Simeon of Cambridge University. He was converted and brought into a deep knowledge of God when a student and was for 50 years Vicar of Holy Trinity Church, Cambridge, England. He died in 1836. His power and influence have left an ineradicable mark upon the whole evangelical movement.

Many of Simeon's expository works were published at the beginning of the 19th century. They had a tremendous influence upon the preaching of that day. Zondervan has republished this set and the four volumes here under review represent some of Simeon's finest work and expository preaching in the Old Testament. The best of brain and the finest of the Christian heart have gone into the composition of these expositions. Any minister who turns to them will find them a great stimulus to engage in this kind of preaching. Simeon still speaks to us out of these pages with freshness and vigor.

EVANGELISTIC SERMONS BY GREAT EVANGELISTS. Russell V. DeLong. Zondervan. $2.50.

Within the covers of this book are gathered some of the best messages of leading contemporary evangelists. Many of them have a world-wide ministry. Some of the evangelists represented are Billy Graham, Mervin E. Rosell, Hyman J. Appelman, Jack Shuler, J. Edwin Orr, and Eddie Martin. Bishop Arthur J. Moore has written an excellent foreword in which he says that these messages have come out of the keen minds and warm hearts of Godly men.

THE SOUTHERN PRESBYTERIAN JOURNAL

A Presbyterian weekly magazine devoted to the statement, defense and propagation of the Gospel, the faith which was once for all delivered unto the saints.

VOL. XV NO. 31 | NOVEMBER 28, 1956 | $2.50 A YEAR

Ground Breaking Services Bethpage Presbyterian Church, Near Kannapolis

Left to right: Mr. J. W. Cook, Chairman Finance Committee; Mr. John Vanpelt, Chairman Planning Committee; Rev. John A. Cannon, Jr., Pastor; Mr. R. D. Grier, Moderator Synod of N. C.; Dr. Frank McCutchan, Moderator Concord Presbytery; Mr. Gip Rumple, Chairman Building Committee. (See article on page 17.)

THE SOUTHERN PRESBYTERIAN JOURNAL

Rev. Henry B. Dendy, D.D., Editor........Weaverville, N. C.
Dr. L. Nelson Bell, Associate Editor........Asheville, N. C.
Rev. Wade C. Smith, Associate Editor........Weaverville, N. C.

EDITORIAL

The Christian Paradox

A paradox may be defined as a seemingly contradictory statement or position, one opposed to common sense, and yet true in fact.

The Bible is full of paradoxes and it is inevitable that such should be the case, for the wisdom of God and that of unregenerate man are at opposite poles.

The viewpoint, the reactions, the values, the perspectives of God and the world are completely different. There is no clearer evidence of this than in the truths encompassed by the Beatitudes. Here we have statements which are the very antitheses of world-accepted values.

The Apostle Paul expresses the same thought when he glories in his thorn in the flesh, and the buffeting of the world, and says: ". . . *for when I am weak, then am I strong.*"

The Lord revealed the same truth to Samuel in these words: *"For the Lord seeth not as man seeth; for man looketh on the outward appearance, but the Lord looketh on the heart."*

The paradoxes of Christianity stem from the fact that when we are born again we see life and this world in an entirely new perspective, that of eternity. For the first time we realize that this world and everything in it is going to pass away, that only those who know and do God's will shall abide forever.

This new concept is based on redemption, not reformation; on regeneration, not a natural transformation. Out of such an experience the kingdom of heaven is for the poor in spirit; there is comfort for the mourner; the earth becomes the heritage of the meek; spiritual hungering and thirsting is provided for; mercy is the reward of the merciful; spiritual perception is given the pure in heart and they see God; and adoption into the household of God a part of the peacemaker's end.

This paradox, arrant foolishness to the world, means joy and great reward for persecution, reviling and false accusation. That such experiences should be the cause for "great gladness" is something the unregenerate cannot possibly understand.

The paradox of peace in the midst of danger; comfort in spite of sorrow; rejoicing in the face of adversity; all are confusing to the world but they make wonderful sense to the Christian.

Little wonder that the Gospel brings division; that Christians are misunderstood; that the closer we live to Christ the more the world turns from us. In all of this there is no room for a martyr complex; rather there is joy in knowing that, "so persecuted they the prophets which were before you."

The great paradox of Christianity centers in the fact that the Son of God Himself came into this world to die for sinners. *"He was in the world, and the world was made by him, and the world knew him not. He came unto his own, and his own received him not. But as many as received him, to them gave he power to become the sons of God; even to them that believe on his name."* L.N.B.

Shall Culture Dominate Christian Faith?

This is a question that comes to the front as one reads the current issue of *Theology Today*. Sometimes this effort undertakes to strip the Bible of its supernatural miracles because they are declared impossible for the man of modern culture. At other times the attack is much further out on the circumference where we are told that current culture requires women preachers. Is human reason to go its own way thinking God according to its own lights, or is it bound to think God's thoughts after Him? When we come to the heart of Christian faith are we to start with the Christ of God set forth in His Word as did the primitive Christology, or are we to start with our own powers of judgment ("value judgments") as to what we would have Christ to be?

Professor Herzog finds here the distinction between Karl Barth and Reinhold Niebuhr as set forth in the former's *Church Dogmatics* and in the latter's *Literalism, Individualism and Billy Graham.* Barth does not go as far as does Berkouwer, our leading Calvinist theologian, in accepting *en bloc* the Bible witness. He has, however, "made it quite clear that he could not accept as an implication of theological honesty the relevance of 'the standards of the whole world of culture' (Niebuhr) for theology. He flatly denied that the reality ascertainable by culture encompasses the reality of faith." "He saw no reason why culture should necessarily own *the* yardstick by which the truths of the Biblical witness should be measured." God reveals Himself in the preaching of the Word of the Cross. That which the world calls foolishness is the power of God unto salvation for the people of God. In the risen Christ who died for our sins are hidden all the treasures of wisdom and knowledge. W.C.R.

The Word and the Sacrament

In the preliminary draft presented to the Section of the World Council on Faith and Order at Evanston it was twice asserted that the Holy Spirit was bestowed in baptism. As to the Word, that draft asserted that "the Word of God through preaching makes known and offers to men the forgiveness and reconciliation by God."

As a result of protest against this apparent discrimination against the Word as a means of grace, the final draft reads, "He has given the Scriptures, the preaching of the Word, Baptism and Eucharist by which the Church proclaims the forgiveness of sins and by which, in the power of the Holy Spirit, faith is quickened and nourished."

The objection to giving the Word a subordinate place to baptism is in accord with Calvin's *Antidote to the Council of Trent.* Treating of the sixth session which presents baptism as the instrumental cause of justification, Calvin objects to the omission of the Gospel and to the high place assigned to baptism. He says: "It is a great absurdity to make baptism alone the instrumental cause. If this be so what becomes of the Gospel? Will it not even get into the lowest corner? But, they say, baptism is the sacrament of faith. True; but when it all is said, I will still maintain that it is nothing but an appendage of the Gospel. They act preposterously in giving it the first place; and this is just as if one should say that the instrumental cause of a house is the handle in the workman's trowel. He who putting the Gospel in the background, numbers baptism among the causes of salvation, shows thereby that he does not know what baptism is or means, or what is its function and use." In the Institutes, Calvin compares the Word to the foundation on which a building rests and the sacraments to supporting stays. The sacrament is so connected with the Word that it is not to be separated from it, yet it is to be distinguished from and held subservient to the Word, IV.16.5.

The New Testament teaches that the Holy Spirit uses and accompanies the faithful proclamation of the Word. This is conspicuous in the case of Peter's preaching to Cornelius and is set forth by Peter in his first epistle, 1.10-11. It was likewise true of the preaching of Paul as he indicates in First Corinthians, First Thessalonians and Galatians. Indeed the sword of the Spirit is the preached Word of God. W.C.R.

Who Said That?

The significance of a statement very often depends on *who* made the observation.

When one runs down through the third chapter of Hebrews he can well be in for a shock, or more truly he will feel a thrill in his heart: *"Wherefore (as the Holy Ghost saith . . . "),* and there follows a long quotation from the 95th Psalm.

But, when one turns to the 95th Psalm and begins to read, there is no difference in the impact which it makes when compared with other Psalms. Why? Because in each one God the Holy Spirit is speaking.

In the first chapter of the book of Acts Peter stands up to speak and here are his words: *"Men and brethren, this scripture must needs have been fulfilled, which the Holy Ghost by the mouth of David spake before concerning Judas . . . "*

This reference to the 41st Psalm brings a meaning to the words of David which the Holy

The Southern Presbyterian Journal, *a Presbyterian Weekly magazine devoted to the statement, defense, and propagation of the Gospel, the faith which was once for all delivered unto the saints,* published every Wednesday by The Southern Presbyterian Journal, Inc., in Weaverville, N. C.

Entered as second-class matter May 15, 1942, at the Postoffice at Weaverville, N. C., under the Act of March 3, 1879. Vol. XV, No. 31, November 28, 1956. Editorial and Business Offices: Weaverville, N. C. Printed in the U.S.A. by Biltmore Press, Asheville, N. C.

ADDRESS CHANGE: When changing address, please let us have both old and new address as far in advance as possible. Allow three weeks after change if not sent in advance. When possible, send an address label giving your old address.

Spirit inspired on the one hand and the significance of which the same Holy Spirit made plain to Peter centuries later.

In the last words of David, recorded in II Samuel, 23:2 we read: *"The Spirit of the Lord spake by me, and his word was in my tongue."*

Our Confession of Faith affirms the right of the Scripture to speak for itself and when we approach the Book with the assurance that God's Holy Spirit is speaking through those to whom He entrusted its writing it becomes a living and inspired document and we find encouragement to search its pages for truths which are spiritually discerned and *which can be apprehended in no other way.* L.N.B.

A Basket of Fruit

The Fruit of the Spirit (Galatians 5:22,23)

G. The Fruit of the Spirit is . . .
Faith, (or Faithfulness)

May I state it this way: A Faith that leads to Faithfulness; a Living Faith, that works by love. Only the Holy Spirit can give such a Faith.

Faith; the Foundation Grace; It is a great thing to be able to say, "I Believe." I wish somebody would say over the radio, on "This I believe," some of the great facts that really count, and not "beat around the bush," so to speak. There are some Great Truths which we should believe. The world is divided into two classes; He that believeth; and he that believeth not. It makes a lot of difference as to which class we belong: he that believes is saved: he that believes not is lost.

I. *Some Great Facts to Believe.*

"I believe" that "This Book," the Bible, is the Word of God; that "holy men," moved by the Holy Spirit, wrote it.

,"I believe" that in This Book we have a Revelation of the True and Living God. He is One, but He exists in Three Persons, The Father, the Son, and the Holy Spirit.

"I believe" that I have a Saviour, a Redeemer, born of a virgin, Who lived and died and rose again. He died for my sins. He is my all-sufficient High Priest. He is coming back in glory to judge and rule.

'I believe" that the Holy Spirit convicts of sin, regenerates us, and sanctifies us, renewing us in the image of Christ, and enabling us to more and more die unto sin and live unto righteousness. He is our Guide and Comforter.

"I believe" in the Forgiveness of sins through Christ; in salvation by grace through faith; in the Church which is the Body of Christ; in the resurrection of the body and in Life Everlasting; and in *much more.*

This sort of Faith is Saving Faith; it is Serving Faith, working by love; it is Victorious Faith, overcoming the world. Only the Holy Spirit can give it. It is a Fruit of the Spirit.

II. *Such a Faith Leads to Faithfulness.*

Faithfulness in Personal Growth in grace. We will build out of the best materials a character that will stand the test.

Faithfulness to Home Duties and Responsibilities. We will have our Family Altar and we will seek to make our Home as much like heaven as we can.

Faithfulness in the Church, whether we are leaders or just ordinary members. We will do all we can to be fellow-helpers to the truth, and build up the Church.

Faithfulness as Citizens of a great country. We will use our influence to make and keep our nation a Christian nation.

If we are Faithful unto the end our reward will be great; Well done, good and faithful servant, enter into the joy of thy Lord.

The Fruit of the Spirit is . . . Faith, (Faithfulness).

A Desert Prowler

By Wade C. Smith

I have a brother who has been a missionary to the Navajo Indians in Arizona the past 35 years. His name is Rev. Hugh D. ("Shine") Smith, the "Shine" having been given to him by the Navajos and they do not know him by any other name. He lives alone in a trailer, in which he cruises from place to place among the hogans and trading posts. The trailer also serves for a study and reception room where the Indians come for counsel and advice concerning their problems, domestic and otherwise. He has made several trips to Washington to plead with the Interior Department for their rights and needs. For the past ten years he has held an annual Christmas party for the Indians, beginning with an attendance of several hundred and growing each year, until last Christmas when something over 6,000 were in attendance.

He is expecting 7,000 this year. There is a big feast on butchered and barbecued sheep and beef, and a present for every child; also a wool blanket for every family. The blankets are contributed by manufacturers in Chicago and elsewhere whose interest has been enlisted.

During the years this information has gotten around to many Indian lovers in the United States. Packages of all kinds of goods (and money) begin arriving at Flagstaff in the Fall and it requires several warehouses to store them until time for the Christmas Party distribution.

His ministry is both wholesale and personal. One night in zero temperature on the mountain he stripped off all the burnable parts of his Ford car to make a fire that saved a little Indian girl from freezing, then made use of the engine and chassis to get her to the hospital where she was nursed to health. Once or twice he has performed the marriage ceremony in a plane soaring over the Grand Canyon. His Indians wanted it that way. All this is in keeping with Paul's plan of being "all things to all men, that I might win some."

But his latest episode is what prompts me to write this little sketch about "Shine." A letter received from him this morning reads as follows:

"Well, yesterday an Indian baby was born in my car while I was going sixty miles an hour. I heard a baby's cry back there, and knowing there was no baby in the car when I left, I slowed down to a stop. At the same time I discovered I had a flat tire. Troubles never come singly; if it isn't twins, something else comes with it. There was a lady traveling in a car behind and when she drew up and saw the situation she went back and brought out some of her own baby's clothes, saying she had had a baby once in an elevator and knew how bad these things were needed under the circumstances. As soon as I got the tire mended I thought of course the parents of the new baby would want to go right on to the hospital — but I don't know Indians YET; they said, 'NO! Let's go back to our hogan.'

"So I turned round and took them back 15 miles to their hogan. They even twitted me on the way back, saying the baby just didn't want to be born in a white man's hospital, and when they began planning a name for the baby I suggested they name her 'Highway 89.' Then I learned something else. The Navajos believe that the after birth should be carried away to the East, and they told me that on a former occasion when this detail was being attended to, the old grandfather called out, 'No! more to the left, more to the left' — of course in Navajo.

"One lesson I got as I looked at that tiny infant, swaddled in a stranger's wrappings, was: Wouldn't it be wonderful if all that life could be devoted only to the Great Spirit, forsaking all the many foolish detours — just looking to Him for every thought and movement!"

The Book Of Jonah And Its Critics

By Rev. Oswald T. Allis, Ph.D., D.D.

"Jonah and the Whale" has been the stumbling block and laughing stock of sceptics for centuries. The higher critic solves the problem by calling it myth, legend, romance, and now especially a missionary tract of very signal importance. For the Christian the great obstacle to all such unrealistic treatments of this little book is the way in which it is treated in the New Testament. For in this case as in many others the use made of the passage in the New Testament is the greatest objection to the "conclusions" reached by the critic of the Old Testament.

Jonah is referred to twice in Matthew and once in Luke. In all three passages the reference to Jonah is in response to the demand for a "sign," that is, for a signal and probably supernatural attestation of Jesus' unique claims. In Matt. 12:39f both the "fish story" and the repentance of the Ninevites are referred to by Jesus. In 16:4 Jesus refers to the "sign of the prophet Jonah," but does not define it; the same is true also of Luke 11:29f. Consequently, it has been claimed that Matt. 12:40 is a gloss and that the N.T. knows nothing of the "fish story." But there is no evidence to support the claim that this verse is not an integral part of the text of Matt. 12. And the demand for a sign favors the view that the miracle of the swallowing by the great fish was expressly referred to by Jesus.

Scholars who regard Matt. 12:40 as genuine, but deny the historicity of the book of Jonah are accustomed to explain it as myth or legend. But the question then arises, Is it conceivable that Jesus used a popular legend which had no basis in fact as the sign of what He knew was to become the great central fact of Christianity, His own death and resurrection? We believe that it is not. It seems perfectly clear that Jesus appealed to it as historical fact. To hold that He did not know that it was unhistorical, or that knowing it to be such, He used it because He knew that His hearers believed it, carries implications which no one whose beliefs regarding Him are founded on the New Testament will entertain for a moment. The greatest reason for accepting the historicity of Jonah is the testimony of Jesus Himself.

Various attempts have been made to eliminate the "fish story" from the book of Jonah or to give a "reasonable" explanation of it. J. H. Moulton claimed that it was an editorial addition to the prayer in Chapter 2, that some unknown copyist failed to understand that the words "out of the belly of sheol" were figurative and added a marginal note explaining them as referring to a fish which swallowed Jonah, and that this prosaic note somehow got into the text itself.

A. S. Peake, likewise denying the historicity of the narrative regarding the fish, sought to explain it in terms of allegory and myth. Allegorizing Jonah as representing Israel, he appealed to Jer. 51:34,44 where Babylon and her king Nebuchadnezzar and her god Bel are likened to a great dragon which has swallowed Israel and must yield her up; and he found there the explanation of the story of Jonah. He supported it with the claim that Jonah's prayer says nothing about the great fish and is quite out of harmony with it. He claimed further that the fish story is a "trivial issue" and that the book is to be regarded as a protest against the narrow exclusivism of the Jews and a call on Israel "to accept the mission appointed to it and save the Gentiles by the proclamation of the truth." In short, according to this view, which is rather widely held today, the book of Jonah is not historical; it is a missionary tract and it is a matter of indifference whether it has any real basis in fact.

Let us turn now to the Book of Jonah and consider some of the most important issues connected with its interpretation. The first is the fish incident. We shall not pause to discuss the possibility of the miracle. Those who are abreast of the discoveries which have been made by the bathyscope will hesitate to deny that there may be monsters in the great deep today which would qualify for the role assigned to the fish. And the Christian will not forget that we are told that "the Lord prepared a great fish to swallow Jonah."

For him the more important question is this, Is the story of the fish out of harmony with the narrative as a whole? We are told that Jonah's prayer makes no mention of the great fish, but merely describes feelingly and poignantly the sensations of a man who all but drowned in the sea. This is the claim; and we do not hesitate to say that it is perfectly justified. Most or all of us have seen in illustrated Bibles or Bible story books, pictures of Jonah being cast — into the sea? Not at all. He is thrown overboard, is perhaps in midair and the fish is waiting with yawning mouth to receive him. Jonah passes directly from the ship into the "belly" of the fish; and the sailors are witnesses of the amazing outcome of their

who asked Jesus to accredit Himself to them by an act of superhuman power.

We turn now to the second marvel which is recorded in this little book, the preaching to the Ninevites and its result. After his amazing experience when he sought to flee to Tarshish, "the word of the Lord came unto Jonah the second time." Again he was commanded to declare the judgment of God upon the wicked city. This time he obeyed and went to Nineveh. We cannot date this mission at all definitely. The name of the Assyrian king is not given. The statement in 2 Kings 14:25 only defines the period in a general way. It tells us that Jonah foretold the recovery of the Northern Kingdom under Jeroboam II. But it does not tell us how long in advance Jonah uttered his prophecy nor whether it preceded or followed the incident described in the Book of Jonah.

Between the reigns of Adad-nirari III (810-783 B.C.), who apparently died several years after Jeroboam II became king of Israel, and Tiglathpileser III (744-727 B.C.) there is an interval of forty years during which so far as we know no Assyrian king campaigned in the West. It may be that the probably quite brief "repentance" of the Ninevites belongs within this period.

Nineveh was an ancient city when Jonah went there. How large it was, we do not know from secular sources. The Biblical narrative tells us that it was "exceeding great," that it was a city of "three days' journey" and that there were in it "six score thousand persons" unable to distinguish between their two hands. Such figures are by no means impossible when we compare them with the figures which appear from time to time in ancient records. Nineveh was the center or a center of the vast Assyrian war-machine. The building of its great temples and palaces must have brought to it at times a vast corvee. The huts and fragile tenements of such slave-labor would leave little behind them for the archaeologist to uncover. It is also possible that in speaking of Nineveh as a city of "three days journey" the writer included the extensive suburbs of the city lying in the triangle between the Tigris and the Upper Zab, even as far south perhaps as the ancient capital Calah, 20 miles to the south. The mention of "much cattle" (4:11) would certainly favor a somewhat expansive use of the word. Nineveh might be as ambiguous a term as London is today. London has more than three million inhabitants, Greater London more than eight million, the City of London only some ten thousand, although probably more than half a million do business in "the city" every week day. The phrase "three days' journey" may also mean, not that it required three days to walk through Nineveh, but that it required three days to go up and down the principal streets of the city as a town crier would be expected to do in order to make his tidings known to the whole city.

The message of Jonah was a very simple one, "Yet forty days and Nineveh shall be destroyed." But it had back of it the accrediting story of the messenger's unique experience. It is important to bear this in mind. For it accounts for the amazing effect of Jonah's preaching. We know that the Assyrians were an intensely superstitious people. A large proportion of their religious texts consisted of omens. All sorts of unusual, grotesque, or fantastic happenings were recorded and studied by their priests and augurs. The appearance in the streets of Nineveh of a man like Jonah, coming from a distant land, impelled to deliver a message of doom because of an amazing personal experience was calculated to produce exactly the effect which we are told it did produce, both on king and on people. The story may sound absurd. But the careful student of history will not be the one to pronounce it so.

We come now to a point which requires careful and discriminating study: the repentance of the Ninevites. We have seen that it is customary with those who reject the historicity of the Book of Jonah to make much of the book as a missionary tract. We are told that "the lesson of the Book of Jonah is analogous to the foreign mission idea of developed Christianity."

Indeed, we have even been told that "a tribute of the highest admiration" must be paid to the Book of Jonah "when we recall Matt. 10:5-6 and 15:24-26," a statement which may imply that the author of Jonah was more missionary-minded than our Lord Himself. That there is no warrant in the Bible for such exaggerated claims as these should be clear to anyone who studies the Biblical account carefully. Jonah's message was one of judgment, "Yet forty days and Nineveh shall be destroyed." It struck terror to the hearts of king and people. The king and his nobles exhorted the people: "Let them turn every one from his evil way, and from the violence that is in their hands." They obeyed; and the Lord spared the city. They repented of their violent acts under the threat of the imminent destruction of their city. But that was all. They did not become worshippers of the God of Israel, as we are told took place under somewhat similar circumstances in the days of Esther (Esth. 8:17). There is not the slightest evidence in history of the "conversion" of the Ninevites to serve the God of Israel. And we have only to read the Book of Nahum to realize that their repentance was but temporary, inspired by terror. The hand of vengeance was stayed only for a time; and then the sword fell upon the bloody city and it became a ruinous heap.

The last chapter of this little book is in some respects the most remarkable of all. It gives us the reason for Jonah's attempted flight to Tarshish, a reason which few readers of the first three chapters would even dream of: Jonah was sure that the Lord who was sending him to Nineveh to foretell its destruction, would not, being a God of Mercy and grace, carry out his sentence of destruction, if the people repented. He had felt sure they would repent and had attempted to flee to Tarshish; and now he was "displeased exceedingly" and "very angry" when the people did repent and were spared as he had confidently expected would follow. Why he was so angry we are not told. Perhaps he foresaw something of the havoc which Assyria would wreak in Israel in the coming days and hoped against hope that this great enemy of his people might be removed from her path forever. Perhaps he feared that he would lose face as a prophet of the Lord, if his woe-ladened prophecy were not fulfilled within the time appointed. Whatever may be said for Jonah, his "hard-boiled" attitude stands in tragic contrast with the revelation which is given us of the love and compassion of God; His patience with wicked Nineveh; His gracious dealing with His rebellious and hard-hearted servant. We have here a wonderful illustration of the truth of the words: "For my thoughts are not your thoughts, neither are your ways my ways, saith the Lord."

The Book of Jonah ends abruptly. It may seem to leave Jonah still in his state of angry disappointment. For we are not told how he reacted to the rebuke of the Lord! What became of him we do not know. We read elsewhere that he uttered a prophecy of comfort and hope for Israel. But whether this was before or after his preaching against the Ninevites we have no way of knowing. The only light which is given us on the meaning of the Book of Jonah comes to us from the Lord Himself. He treats it as history. He sees in Jonah's encounter with the great fish the type of His coming triumph over death and in the repentance of the Ninevites, when Jonah preached to them destruction. He sees a solemn rebuke and warning for those who fail to repent at the preaching of a greater than Jonah, who comes to bring them glad tidings of great joy. He does not use the Book of Jonah to rebuke them for their failure to preach salvation to the heathen. He uses it to denounce them for their refusal to accept Him as their promised Messiah. It is only if true that Jonah's unique experience makes him a sign to the Ninevites. It is only if true that their repentance makes them a rebuke to Jesus' hearers. It is only if true that the Lord's rebuke of Jonah is a rebuke to the narrow nationalism of the Jews. The critics of the Book of Jonah cannot excuse their rejection of it as history, by fulsome praise of it as an unhistorical missionary romance.

— LETTERS —

1622 North Augusta St.,
Staunton, Va.,
Nov. 12, 1956.

Gentlemen:

It was good to see in the November 7th issue of the *Southern Presbyterian Journal,* a letter written by my friend and one-time school mate, Mrs. D. L. Norris, in regard to women as elders in our Southern Presbyterian Church.

Even if it were not so plainly stated in the Bible that God chose men to be elders (Titus 1:5), with the requirements listed in 6,7,8,9, one of which does not apply to women, I do not believe that the women of our church want to push the men aside, or even share in their God-given "tasks"; and those men who are in favor of women as elders, must consider it a "task," or just something more to be turned over to the women of the church.

We women can, and have found all the work we can possibly do without changing God' law and plan for the men of the church; and we certainly cannot meet one of the requirements, as Mrs. Norris points out, that of being "the husband of one wife," but we can help the men (those of us who have men in the family) to live up to the other requirements in verses 6,7,8,9, without actually shouldering their responsibilities and "taking over" the duties that God in His Word delegated to the men as elders.

Women and Men of the Church, please read in the King James Version of God's Holy Word; Titus 1:5,6,7,8,9, regarding the qualifications of elders and see how you fit into the picture, as God planned it!

Sincerely yours,
(Mrs.) J. H. Bell

Helps To Understanding Scripture Readings in *Day by Day*

By Rev. C. C. Baker

Sunday, December 9, *Luke* 8:16-21. A great responsibility rests upon all those who hear the Good News of salvation (vv.8,18,21). A person's eternal status depends upon how he hears the Word of God (vv.12,18). List the different things mentioned in vv.11-14 that keep a person from receiving the Word sincerely. Have any of these factors hindered your genuine interest in spiritual things? Observe that while there were many who received the Word (vv.13-14,15), only a few persisted in their faithfulness and were found approved of God (v.15). Continual obedience to the Word is a must (v.21). The light that has been established in one life must continue to shine and bring forth fruit in the lives of others (v.16).

Monday, December 10, *Matthew* 25:31-46. Jesus teaches that good deeds done in this life have great consequences in the life to come (vv.34-36). Failure to perform these deeds now brings grievous results in the next world (vv.41-43). Observe that those who did or failed to do the tasks mentioned did not realize that their actions were of great concern to Christ (vv.37-39,44). Notice how simple and everyday were the tasks mentioned by Jesus (vv.35-36ff). Are you aware of the spiritual implications of the little deeds you do or fail to do? Observe that it is Christ who will do the judging (vv.31-33). Are the good deeds you do done as unto Him?

Tuesday, December 11, *I Kings* 17:8-16. A drought had come upon the land (v.1). God, however, watched over and provided for the needs of His servant, Elijah (vv.2-6). Observe God's faithfulness in leading Elijah from one place to another as supplies became exhausted (vv.7-9). God also provided for those who were hospitable to His servant (vv.10-16). Elijah was utterly dependent upon God as he was fed in supernatural ways (vv.6,14-16). Would God have supplied his needs if Elijah had not obeyed Him (vv.5,9-10)? Often we have dire spiritual hungers which can only be met in a supernatural way by God in Christ (John 6:35,51). This is done as we yield our lives to Him in obedience (John 15:4-7,11).

Wednesday, December 12, *Luke* 10:30-37. When men came to Jesus with insincere motives (vv.25,29), He had a way of turning their questions and making them face a decision about their own spiritual welfare (vv.28,37). What methods did Jesus use to do this (vv.26,30-37)? Is it obvious from vv.26-27 that the lawyer already knew the answer to his question of v.25? In the story of the Good Samaritan, remember that the priests and Levites (v.v.31-32) were in the same religious category as the lawyer (11:42-46), and that the very word "Samaritan" (v.33) was an unspeakable curse word for the Jews. How, then, was Jesus' question of v.36 particularly pointed? Are you ever guilty of raising questions that are designed more to cover up your obvious responsibilities than to discover new truth?

Thursday, December 13, *Luke* 24:13-35. Sense the despondency of these two disciples as they walked along the Emmaus road following the crucifixion (vv.13-21). What facts did they know about Christ (vv.19-20)? What "rumors" had they heard (vv.22-24)? Observe how the risen Christ revealed Himself to them — first the questions (vv.17, 19), then the teaching (vv.25-27), finally the revelation (vv.28-31). The questions (vv.17,19) won their confidence (vv.18,19-24,29). The teaching (vv.25-27) reached their hearts (v.32). The revelation (vv.28-31) sent them out proclaiming the good news (vv.33-35). How would Christ's teaching (vv.25-27) preserve the certainty of the discovery of vv.30-31)? Observe their change of mood (vv.33-35). The certainty of the presence of the risen Christ in the Christian's life should turn despondency into hope.

Friday, December 14, *John* 11:32-44. "All things work together for good." Sometimes this is a difficult truth to accept. If Jesus had not delayed in coming (vv.3-7) Lazarus would not have died (vv.21,32). It was not due to neglect or indifference to the family that Jesus deliberately delayed in coming (vv.5,34-36) but in accord with divine purpose (vv.15,40). Mary and Martha believed Jesus was the Messiah (v.27); they believed in His power to heal dead (v.39)! How would the incident of vv.38-44 increase the faith of Jesus' followers? How would it give them hope as they saw Jesus, Himself, put to death (vv.49-53)? When circumstances are bewildering and uncertain, can you trust God that somehow all things will eventually work together for good?

Saturday, December 15, *Psalm* 71:17-24. The Psalmist is old (vv.9,18) and trouble is on every hand (vv.4.10-11,13). He knows God as his refuge (vv.1,3,7) and meditates upon Him continually (vv.8,15,24). The Lord has been with him and watched over him from his youth (vv.5-6,17). It is to this God that he looks in his present situation (vv.2-3,12). As the Lord has been with him in the past (vv.5-6-17), he now prays with confidence (vv.20-21) that God has already heard his prayer and answered it (vv.14,16,22-24). Hence praise and testimony to the Lord's goodness is already in his mouth (vv.14-16,22-24). Does your walk with God in the past enable you to look to Him with confidence for the future?

SABBATH SCHOOL LESSONS — REV. J. KENTON PARKER

LESSON FOR DECEMBER 9

More Than Conquerors

Background Scripture: Romans 8
Devotional Reading: Psalm 27:1-10

The Psalmist, in Psalm 27, is telling us how we may conquer our fears. Fear is one of the earliest and most persistent of our troubles while on earth. As children, we are afraid of the dark, or of a dog, or a thunderstorm, or even of people. As we grow older we may lose our childish fears to some extent, but new fears take the place of the old. We are afraid of men in a different way; we fear their opposition, or ridicule, or persecution. We no longer fear the dark night; we now fear the "dark future." We begin to have aches and pains and we wonder if we are going to have cancer, or heart trouble. We think of growing old and helpless, of being in need, and we take out insurance, or social security, or try to lay aside something for the "rainy day" which we fear is just around the corner. We worry about the dangers of the highway. We think of approaching death, our last great enemy.

For all of these, and other fears, the Psalmist has a simple remedy. It is put in the form of a question: The Lord is my light and my salvation; whom shall I fear? The Lord is the strength of my life; of whom shall I be afraid? David had many enemies. They threatened his life constantly. He is confident that the Lord will hide him in the day of trouble; that the Lord will lift up his head above his enemies. He can sing and rejoice because God's face is turned toward him. In other words, David, like Paul, knew the secret of being "More than Conquerors." Do you know that secret? May the Spirit of God enable us to find and rejoice in it as we meditate upon this marvelous chapter, Romans 8.

In the seventh chapter of Romans Paul has been discussing the struggle that goes on in the human soul between good and evil. He says, When I would do good, evil is present with me, etc. This fight is so fierce that he cries out in verse 24, "O wretched man that I am! Who shall deliver me from the body of this death?" He is like a man chained to a dead body, which was sometimes done by the cruel Romans. In verse 25 he gives a shout of victory, "I thank God through Jesus Christ our Lord." In chapter eight he explains at length what he means and tells us of the "Great Deliverance"; tells us how we can be "More than Conquerors." It is a wonderful thing to be a conqueror; it is still better to be a rejoicing victor; to have a crown of rejoicing and a crown of glory awaiting us.

When I read and study a chapter like the one we have today I feel so helpless; so overwhelmed. What can a mere man say when faced by such glorious facts? May the Holy Spirit Who inspired Paul to write these verses open our eyes, our minds, our hearts. There are three things which make us "More than Conquerors": (1) The Spirit of God, (2) The Purpose of God, and (3) The Love of God.

I. *The Spirit of God:* 1-27: "Walk not after the flesh, but after the Spirit.

The Holy Spirit, as we saw in our last lesson, is One Who is called alongside to help, and He helps us in our struggle against sin. When a sinner is saved he is regenerated by the Holy Spirit. This is the New Birth of which Jesus spoke to Nicodemus: except a man be born again he cannot see the kingdom of God. The Holy Spirit comes to dwell in his heart. The old nature, the "old man," or "the flesh," is to be "put off," put to death. The old man is to be crucified with Christ, and the new man is to live. If any man be in Christ he is a new creature, (a new creation), old things are passed away, and all things have become new.

We are solemnly warned about grieving, or quenching, the Spirit. We are led by the Spirit; we are to walk after the Spirit. We can be "more than conquerors" when we yield ourselves completely to the Holy Spirit; when we are "filled with the Spirit," as the disciples were at Pentecost. We cannot please God if we continue to live in the flesh, and follow our old sinful nature. When we thus yield to the Spirit, then the Spirit bears witness with our spirit that we are the children of God. Why do Christians have so little assurance? Is it not because we fail to yield ourselves to His power?

Then if we are children of God, we are heirs of God and joint-heirs with Christ. If we suffer, we suffer together with Him, and we will be glorified with Him. We know that we shall be delivered from the bondage of corruption into the glorious liberty of the children of God. The whole creation groans together, waiting for the Redemption of our bodies. We look for that time to come and wait with hope.

The Spirit also makes intercession for us with groanings which cannot be uttered. Jesus said to Simon Peter, Satan hath desired to have you that he might sift you as wheat, but I have prayed for thee that thy faith fail not. He ever lives to make intercession for us, as our Great High Priest. Now we are told that the Spirit also is interceding for us. With these Two praying for us, we can be "more than conquerors." We are not alone in our battle with our enemies. We have the mercy-seat, and all the hosts of hell cannot defeat us if we come to the throne of grace where we find grace to help in time of need. Some of our most beautiful hymns have this for their theme: Holy Spirit, faithful guide, Ever near the Christian's side; Gently lead us by the hand, Pilgrims in a desert land.

The soul that yields to the Spirit and walks after the Spirit will be able to be "more than conqueror." That soul will be sealed and safe, victorious and rejoicing, as it faces the trials and hardships and battles of life. We have a fine example of such a victorious life in the apostle who wrote these words. The Spirit had such complete possession of Paul that he could rejoice in tribulations.

II. *The Purpose of God:*
"According to His purpose" : 28-34.

This section starts out with one of the most amazing promises in the Bible: "For we know that all things work together for good to those that love God, to them who are the called according to His purpose." If we belong to those that love God, then this promise is ours, and this, in itself, is enough to make us "more than conquerors." Our constant prayer should be, More love to Thee, O God; More love to Thee, O Christ. May the Lord fill our hearts with such a love! Then we can claim this glorious promise.

God has a purpose, a Plan, for us. That Plan is for us to be conformed to the image of His Son. He has foreordained us; He knows all about us. He has called us and we have answered His call. He justifies us; He sanctifies us; He adopts us into His family; He will glorify us. We are not to go down in defeat. He Who has begun a good work in us will finish that work.

He may have to chasten us. Whom the Lord loveth, He chasteneth. He deals with us as with sons. No chastening for the present seems pleasant, but grievous, but afterwards it yields fruit. The purpose of God is to have the image of Christ in us. Our Saviour was "more than conqueror" as He faced the temptations, trials, and sufferings of life. We conquer in His name and through His power. The purpose of God is not defeat, but victory. If God be for us, who can be against us? We know He is on our side. He Who spared not His own Son, but delivered Him up for us all, how shall He not with Him freely give us all things?

III. *The Love of God:* "The love of God, which is in Christ Jesus our Lord."

In verses 35 to 39 we have the glorious climax to this wonderful chapter. When we begin to examine *our love* for God we are ashamed that we do not love Him more, and we pray that our love should be made greater. In these concluding verses Paul tells us of God's love, Christ's love *for us.* Jesus loved His disciples, and He loved them unto the end, even when they all forsook Him and fled. Herein is love, John tells us, Not that we loved God, but that He loved us and sent His Son to be the propitiation for our sins, and not for ours only, but for the sins of the whole world. John 3:16 tells us of the love of God for us. We love, because He first loved us. These verses are full of questions and answers.

Who shall separate us from the love of Christ? shall tribulation, or distress, or persecution, or famine, or nakedness, or peril, or sword? The Christians of Paul's day had to face all of these things. Paul faced them. They were like "sheep for the slaughter"; death stared them in the face all the time. They were thrown to wild beasts or burned at the stake. In these things they were given grace to be "more than conquerors." They met death and suffering with songs of praise. They were thoroughly convinced that nothing could separate them from the love of their Saviour. I sometimes wonder how well we in our day would stand up under such fiery trials. If we are as sure as they were of the love of Christ, we could be as heroic and rejoicing as they were.

He closes with a list of things which might seem to separate us from the love of God: For I am persuaded that neither death, nor life, nor angels, nor principalities, nor powers, nor things to come, nor height, nor depth, nor any other creature shall be able to separate us from God's love.

YOUNG PEOPLE'S DEPARTMENT — REV. B. HOYT EVANS

YOUTH PROGRAM FOR DECEMBER 9

How To Approach The Bible

Scripture: Psalm 119: 17-24.
Suggested Hymns:
"Wonderful Words of Life"
"How Precious Is the Book Divine"
"Lamp of Our Feet, Whereby We Trace"

Program Leader's Introduction:

On this day, the second Sunday in December, people throughout the world observe Universal Bible Sunday. We are reminded especially of the work of the Bible societies in the Christian nations of the world. The aim of these fine organizations is to translate, publish, and to distribute the Bible to all who need it. In the United States it is the American Bible Society which does this work. Our own denomination contributes directly to the American Bible Society through its benevolent budget. (You may want to have a special share in the work of the Society by receiving an offering at your meeting.)

While it is very important to know the advances which are being made in providing the Scriptures for people all over the world, it is necessary that we know how to use the Bible for ourselves. It is even more necessary that we actually do use the Bible in our own lives. In our program for today we want to discover how to approach the Bible. Our speakers will offer some suggestions.

First Speaker:

A wealthy man once sent a parcel to his friend, a poor but hard-working bricklayer. Included along with some small items in the package was a very fine mason's trowel with a mahogany handle. Some years later the giver of the trowel had occasion to visit the bricklayer, and much to his surprise, he found the trowel displayed over the chimney-piece as a curiosity. The gift had never served its intended purpose because its owner thought it too good to use.

Most of us have a high opinion of the Bible, God's gift to us, but the Bible is a book to be used and not merely as an ornament to be displayed with great respect. We must approach the Bible with a determination to use it. God intends that we should study the Bible in order that we may know Him and His will for our lives. Only those who make proper use of the Bible find the gems of wisdom, the riches of truth, and the priceless gift of salvation which it has in store. The diligent students of the Bible are the people who really enjoy its blessings.

A nobleman once gave a celebrated actress a Bible, telling her at the same time that there was a treasure in it. She, thinking he meant religion, laid the Bible aside. She died, and all she had was sold. The person who bought the Bible, on turning over its leaves, found a note for $2500 in it. Had the actress read her Bible, she might not only have found the money, but also the "pearl of great price."

Second Speaker:

A young lady laid down the book she had been reading, exclaiming in disgust that it was the dullest, most uninteresting story she

CHRISTMAS GIFT SUGGESTION

Wade Smith's Books For The Young People

The Little Jetts Bible $2.50

The Little Jetts New Testament $2.50

The Little Jetts Pilgrim's Progress $2.50

The Little Jetts Youth Talks $2.00

Any One Of These For two New One-Year Subscriptions

THE TESTAMENT FOR FISHERS OF MEN

Price $3.25 Leather Binding — This vest pocket Testament has attained world-wide popularity as a personal worker's handbook. Over 450,000 have been sold.
The Journal offers it as a premium for two new one-year subscriptions.

Any of the above five Wade Smith titles will be etched and autographed on the flyleaf by the Author, if requested.

Send Orders For These—**Or Any Other Books Published**—To

The Southern Presbyterian Journal
Weaverville, N. C.

ETCHING FOR FLY-LEAF IN F. O. M. TESTAMENT

Women's Work

Annual Meeting Board of Women's Work

Atlanta — The Board of Women's Work, meeting here in its annual fall session, approved: (1) Reorganization of the Board's office into four departments, (2) the appointment of a new head for one of the departments, (3) a visit to the Belgian Congo by two staff members, (4) preliminary plans for a Women's Work building in Montreat, N. C., and (5) a caravan to Mexico in March, 1957.

The four departments through which the Board will now do its work in the Atlanta offices are the Program Department, Leadership Education Department, Editorial Department, and Business and Finance Department. Miss Mary Quidor, treasurer of the Board since 1938, heads the latter.

Miss Evelyn Green, program secretary since 1951, heads that department.

Miss Louise Farrior, associate editor of the Division of Religious Education, Board of Christian Education, has accepted a call to become the director of the new Editorial Department, effective January 1. Miss Farrior, now serving as editor of *Day by Day* and of *Presbyterian Action,* is a graduate of East Carolina College, Greenville, N. C., and of Assembly's Training School.

No appointment has been made to the position of director of the new Leadership Education Department. The reorganization replaces two divisions and four departments with the four departments that embrace all the functions of the six former units.

Mrs. L. M. McCutchen, executive secretary of the Board, and Mrs. Arena L. Devarieste, field representative for the Board, will visit the Congo during the month of March. Approval of the visit was given by the Board, following an invitation from the Congo Mission. The representatives of the Board will take part in a General Conference of Congolese women and missionaries, and will visit most of the mission stations.

The proposed new building for Montreat is still in the planning stage, but the Board gave its approval to preliminary drawings for a structure that will cost about $25,000. It will replace the old Winnsborough Pavilion, with an open-air pavilion of the same type, but with concrete floor and new roof, and will attach the new Winnsborough Pavilion to a small office building that will have a literature room, two offices, and a small outdoor, unroofed but concrete floored, social area.

The fifth item of important action, concerning a caravan to Mexico, is designed to encourage interest in the Birthday offering for 1957. One half of the offering will go to Student Work in Mexico, the other half to work among the tubercular sufferers of Korea. One representative from each Synod and the Snedecor Region will be selected for the caravan, and the 17 women will be led by a tour director. It is expected to be an eight to ten day tour. One qualification for selection will be a willingness to aid Women of the Church groups with their educational work for the Birthday Offering. Cost of the Caravan will be borne in part by the Board of Women's Work and the Board of World Missions, but each woman going on the caravan will be asked to carry a part of her own expenses.

The Board also approved contributions, both for the first time in Board history, to the support and work of United Church Women and the Joint Commission of Missionary Education. The contributions were made in recognition that the work "of these inter-denominational agencies is in each case an integral part of the total work of the women of our Church, and through the UCW and JCME, it is possible to do work that the Women of the Church could not otherwise do. The Board has always had close cooperation on the Assembly level with United Church Women, but the new action is the first to give direct support, and it is taken with the hope of encouraging participation and support by more of the synod, presbytery, and local women's groups in the work.

Our Home Made Christmas

"Why do bells at Christmas ring? Why do little children sing?
Once a lovely shining star, seen by Wise Men from afar,
Gently moved until its light made a manger-cradle bright:
There a darling Baby lay, pillowed soft upon the hay,
While His mother sang and smiled, 'This is *Christ, The Holy Child,*'
That's why bells at Christmas ring! That's why little children sing!"

We, too, the older ones, begin to sing happily as *the* day of the year draws near, and evergreens for remembrance, gay with berries, reach us from our friend in the mountains, filling our rooms with the pungent fragrance of God's winter world.

Greeting cards remind us, mail by mail, of friends far and near, new and old; adding their loving words to the songs in our hearts, while our hands are busy making Christmas stars for our Christmas tree — only a little one now on a table, since there is no longer a child with us to delight in its wonders. Our stars, of vari-

So we "keep Christmas," year by year, never old, ever old, ever new, our old-fashioned home-made Christmas, with hearts made light and "merry," like little children's, with "great joy" in the sins forgiven by Him who was born, "in Bethlehem of Judea, *the Saviour, who is Christ the Lord.*"

Last of all there comes a moment of wordless worship, outdoors, under the silent Christmas stars, when we lift up our eyes to the glory of that night-sky, and our hearts to Him who has "set his glory upon the heavens," whose birth-star guided those worshippers from the East—ah, then we think we can hear His angels singing to us as to the watching shepherds, and the "Watchmen" calls to us.

"Traveler, Lo, the Prince of Peace! Lo, the Son of God is come!"

—Mrs. S. H. Askew

The Alcoholism Problem

Evanston, Ill. — The President of the National Woman's Christian Temperance Union said recently that God remains the best physician and the Bible the best prescription for the prevention and cure of alcoholism.

Mrs. Glenn G. Hays said in a statement on "The Current Problem of 4½ Million Alcoholics" that drink has always been the first step away from the church and return to religion the one most necessary to rehabilitation.

She declared that the theory that alcoholism is due to a disease existing before the victim starts drinking has "become an 'out' for the alcoholic beverage industry."

"Some 43 state commissions," Mrs. Hays said, "are now studying the rising problem of alcoholism, but without too much if any consultation with their ministers of church organizations.

"To the drinker, alcohol is a temporary crutch for whatever weakness, but the Christian religion has over the centuries been proven the most permanent support.

"Various so-called scientific methods, including those of mental institutions, have produced only a 35 to 50 per cent permanent rehabilitation, while for Christianity the ratio has always been much higher."

Mrs. Hays said that the success of Alcoholics Anonymous is largely due to that part of its formula in which the alcoholic is advised to go to church. She added:

"Men or women who follow God and the Bible rarely if ever become or remain drinkers, and alcoholism is impossible if one does not drink alcohol."

Church News

Church Officer Training School in 1957

Sponsored by the Kentuckiana Presbyterian Men's Council, the fourth Church Officer Training School will be held in January and February 1957. The exact dates are January 20th and 27th, and February 3rd and 10th. The meetings will be held in different churches in the area, the first one to be in the Bardstown Road Presbyterian Church, Louisville. There will be two one-hour sessions each Sunday night, from 7:30 to 9:30 o'clock, with a break in between and a coffee hour afterwards.

Dr. Julian Price Love, professor of Biblical Theology in Louisville Presbyterian Seminary, will lead the study the two nights in January on the theme "How We Got Our Bible." On the two Sunday nights in February, Dr. Andrew K. Rule, professor of Church History and Apologetics in Louisville Presbyterian Seminary, will lead in the study of the theme "How We Are Saved" or "The Christian Doctrine of Salvation."

There will be a registration fee of $1.00. Men and women are invited to attend these meetings.

Board of World Missions

The Board of World Missions engaged in the ceremony of the laying of the cornerstone of the new Board of World Missions building, situated at Hillsboro Road and Linden Avenue-Nashville, Tennessee, at 2 p. m. on November 13, 1956. The building under construction was sufficiently advanced for the cornerstone to be in place with the copper box set in it to receive the documents selected for preservation.

Rev. William M. Elliott, Jr., Ph.D., D.D., Chairman of the Board, presided at the ceremony. The Rev. Walter L. Caldwell, D.D., Chairman of the Board, 1948-1950, offered an appropriate prayer. Selections of scripture were read responsively by the leader and the people present. This was followed by the placing of the documents in the cornerstone deposit by members of the Staff: the Minutes of the General Assembly for 1955 by Dr. D. J. Cumming; copies of the Annual Report of the Board of World Missions, 1955, and of the Manual in the revised edition of 1951 by Dr. S. Hugh Bradley; a brief outline of the history of the Board and two photographs of the present building by Mr. Curry B. Hearn; a list of the Board members, 1861-1956, by the Rev. Paul B. Freeland, and a copy of the cornerstone laying

The couple first went to Brazil in 1948 and have been engaged in evangelistic work. They have two other children, a daughter age six, and a son, age four.

ALABAMA

Birmingham—David P. Anderson, elder of the South Highland Presbyterian Church, Birmingham, and a member of that church since 1904, has been saluted by fellow members as "Mr. South Highland of 1956".

Mr. Anderson, who is in the mortgage loan business in Birmingham, was cited as "the man most typical of the ideal church member and one contributing most to the spiritual life of the church."

One of Mr. Anderson's sons is the Rev. Tom B. Anderson, pastor of the First Presbyterian Church in Lubbock, Texas. Another son is Dr. David P. Anderson, Jr., surgeon at Austin Clinic, Austin, Minnesota.

Birmingham—A four-day workshop and conference on evangelism was held in Birmingham, Oct. 28-31, under the cooperative sponsorship of the Presbyterian Church, U. S. A., the Presbyterian Church, U. S., and Cumberland Presbyterian Church.

The workshop session was held at Sixth Avenue Presbyterian Church. Following a young people's supper on the opening evening, a message was brought by Dr. Gary Demarest of the Riverside Park Church, Jacksonville, Fla. Other speakers included the Rev. Robert Beach Cunningham, secretary of the eastern area of the Presbyterian Division of Evangelism, Presbyterian Church, U. S. A., and the Rev. Albert Dimmock, associate secretary of the Division of Evangelism, Board of Church Extension, Atlanta. Part of the program included a meeting of local church evangelism committees to discuss local program and plans for evangelism.

NORTH CAROLINA

Ground Breaking Ceremonies

Ground Breaking Services were observed on Nov. 4th for the new Church Sanctuary of the historic old Bethpage Presbyterian Church of Rt. 4, Kannapolis, North Carolina.

The Bethpage Church was organized in 1795 and is among the oldest Presbyterian Churches in the Kannapolis-Concord Area. The Church was originally established sometime prior to 1795 about three miles northeast of the present location in Rowan County. The original site is now occupied by the Bethpage Methodist Church. The present Sanctuary which is to be replaced by the new Church was erected in 1840. It is of frame construction, and it is said that the logs were hewn out in the woods nearby and numbered and assembled at the building site with as little noise as possible, following the scriptural example of building the first Temple. The structure stands now, with a very few minor changes, as it did when originally constructed. The old Church has been a landmark in Cabarrus County for 116 years, having been erected 21 years before the beginning of the Civil War.

The New Sanctuary is to be of Colonial Design with a Spire Steeple and is to cost about $85,000.00 when completed. The seating capacity is to be 475.

The contract calls for the building to be "substantially completed" by June of 1957.

One of the most inspiring features of the projected building program has been the financial program. On January 16, 1955 the Finance Committee of the Church made a special report to the Congregation at the Morning Worship Services. At that time it had taken five years to raise $7,600.00 toward the new Church. At the present time there is in hand $36,350.00. This represents an average monthly collection of $1,400.00 for the building fund, and in addition Current Expense and Benevolent Collections have increased. The Church is careful in giving God the praise and Glory.

Ground Breaking Ceremonies were held as a part of an all day program. The Rev. Robert Turner, Associate Pastor of the Covenant Presbyterian Church of Charlotte, and a former Pastor of the Church, was the guest speaker at the morning Service. Dinner was had on the Church Grounds at 12:30 P.M. and at 2:00 P.M. the Afternoon Service was held. The Rev. T. B. Southall, Ex. Secty. of Concord Presbytery, brought the Afternoon Sermon and Mr. R. D. Grier, Moderator of the Synod of North Carolina, brought greetings from the Synod. Dr. Frank McCutchan, Moderator of Concord Presbytery, brought greetings from the Presbytery. Fraternal Delegates from six neighboring Presbyterian Churches were present and brought greetings from their Congregations.

At the Building Site after the Afternoon Service Elder H. A. Eudy, an Elder of the Bethpage Church led in the invocation, and Mr. R. D. Grier, Elder of the First Presbyterian Church of Statesville, N. C., and Moderator of the Synod of North Carolina, turned the first Shovel Full. He was followed by the Moderator of Concord Presbytery, the Pastor, Chairman of the Building Committee, Distinguished Guests present, and representatives from every organization in the Church.

At the conclusion of the ground breaking, the Congregation sang the Doxology, and the Pastor, the Rev. John A. Cannon, Jr., pronounced the Benediction.

SOUTH CAROLINA

Greenville—The Rev. C. Edward Davis, pastor of Third Presbyterian Church, Greenville, S. C., has been named new chairman of the Home Missions Committee of Enoree Presbytery.

Mr. Davis follows the Rev. Clyde Foushee, who has accepted a call to be pastor to the First Presbyterian Church, North Little Rock, Ark.

Conestee—The Reedy River Presbyterian Church near Conestee, S. C., has dedicated a new Sunday School building.

This project denotes an outlay of approximately $15,000. Dr. E. D. Patton is the stated supply pastor who has helped to direct the work of the Reedy River Church.

Pacolet—The Presbyterian Church of Pacolet, S. C., has completed an addition to the church plant which gives additional class room space, and a new fellowship hall.

With other new equipment which has been added to the facilities, the expenditure for the church has reached approximately $4000.00. The Pacolet Church has an average enrollment in the Church School of 45, while membership in the Church is about 31.

The Rev. R. F. Coon, who has helped to direct the work of this church, as pastor of the Fairforest-Pacolet group, accepted a call to the First Presbyterian Church, Avoca, New York, in mid-July.

TEXAS

Commerce—Officers of the Westminster Fellowship, serving students and faculty of East Texas State Teachers College, for the current academic year are O. Gay Janes, II, of Cooper, president; Jo Anne Gray, Commerce, vice-president and program chairman; Bill Wilson of Leonard, enlistment chairman; and Texanna Latimer of Leonard, stewardship chairman. Mr. and Mrs. V. L. Lieb and Dr. and Mrs. Carey T. Southall, Jr., are co-directors of Westminster Fellowship. Mr. Lieb and Dr. Southall are members of the education faculty of the local college. Officers for the Men of the Church, to be installed in December, for 1957 are Sgt. Malcolm D. Calhoun, president; Grover Sims, vice-president; Tom R. Young, secretary; and Paul F. Street, treasurer. He succeeds Robert E. Baker, also past president of the Men of the Church of Paris Presbytery, as head of the local men's organizations.

WEST VIRGINIA

McKinnon Memorial Church, near Charleston, W. Va., enjoyed a gracious revival October 18 through 28. The evangelist was Rev. Roger P. Melon, pastor of the Montgomery Church and former moderator of the Synod of West Virginia. Certainly the day of mass evangelism it not over. The church was filled each night, with an average attendance of 157. A total of 20 came forward when the invitation was given, including 15 first-time decisions for Christ. Following the meeting the pastor, Rev. C. W. McNutt, received 14 new members into the church, 11 on profession of faith and 3 by letter and reaffirmation. Of the 14 thus received, 11 were adults. The whole work of the church has been greatly strengthened by the meeting.

BOOKS

BILLY GRAHAM. Stanley High. McGraw-Hill. $3.95.

Concisely stated, this book is the personal story of Billy Graham with an evaluation of the man, his message, and his mission. It is an intriguing story of the dynamic evangelist who has been called "The phenomenon of the mid-twentieth century."

The reader is orientated in the field of evangelism through an introduction to this volume. The author analyzes the meaning and history of evangelistic movements since the beginning of the Christian era. The net conclusion is that there is substantial evidence that Billy Graham stands in the succession of great evangelists. He says, "I do not believe that any observer whose prejudices were not insurmountable could make a close-up protracted study of the man and his ministry and fail to find such substantial evidence."

The Church of Scotland magazine **Life and Work** commented during the crusade in Scotland, "Billy Graham is not remarkable for his gifts. He is remarkable for what he is making of God's gift."

Graham proves to be the human instrument of revival in our time, one thing I think is certain: such a revival will come from the preaching of no other or no lesser Gospel."

This volume is valuable viewed from many angles. It is chock full of human interest. It is a case history account of the meetings Billy Graham has conducted in recent years. It is a confirmation of the power of Biblical preaching, and is a real contribution to the cause of Christian evangelism. J.R.R.

HEAVENLY SUNSHINE. Mrs. Charles E. Fuller. Fleming H. Revell. $2.00.

Mrs. Fuller has selected some representative letters that have come in to the Old Fashioned Revival Hour and they are published in this volume. These testimonies come from all over the world. Some ask for prayer. Others tell about the blessings of the ministry of Dr. Fuller.

THE PRAYERS OF SUSANNA WESLEY. W. L. Doughty. Philosophical Library. $2.50.

Susanna Wesley is largely known because of her two famous sons, John and Charles. She is, however, worthy of appreciation on her own account as a woman of keen intellectual sympathies and profound Christian convictions.

These prayers found in this volume which are adapted from her meditations shed a great deal of light upon her inner life and Christian character. These prayers show that Susanna Wesley in forming her Christian creed dug deep and laid her foundation upon a rock and the storms and adversities of life never shook it. Her faith sustained her through life and it was unimpaired in her death.

My Joy Gift

THE SOUTHERN PRESBYTERIAN JOURNAL

A Presbyterian weekly magazine devoted to the statement, defense and propagation of the Gospel, the faith which was once for all delivered unto the saints.

VOL. XV NO. 32 DECEMBER 1956 $2.50 A YEAR

The Vote On Ordination Of Women Elders

Twenty-five Presbyteries have reported on their vote on Women Elders.

Twelve Presbyteries have voted *Yes.* These are Montgomery, Westminster, Brazos, East Hanover, Greenbrier, Lafayette, Louisville, Muhlenberg, New Orleans, Potomac, Potosi and Roanoke.

Thirteen Presbyteries have voted *No.* These are Central Mississippi, Concord, Winchester, West Hanover, Memphis, Birmingham, Kanawha, Knoxville, Meridian, North Mississippi, South Carolina, Asheville and Everglades.

THE SOUTHERN PRESBYTERIAN JOURNAL

Rev. Henry B. Dendy, D.D., Editor........Weaverville, N. C.
Dr. L. Nelson Bell, Associate Editor........Asheville, N. C.
Rev. Wade C. Smith, Associate Editor........Weaverville, N. C.

EDITORIAL

Doctor and Mrs. Bell on Trip to Korea and Japan

Our Associate Editor, Dr. L. Nelson Bell and Mrs. Bell left Asheville Wednesday afternoon November 21st for a flying trip to Korea and Japan. They are going on behalf of the Board of World Missions of the Presbyterian Church, U.S. They will visit their son-in-law and daughter, the Rev. and Mrs. John Somerville, missionaries in Korea, and inspect missions of our Church in Japan with particular reference to the Medical and Hospital work. We ask that all our readers remember them in prayer for a safe and profitable journey. They expect to return home about the middle of January 1957. We also ask for prayer for the other members of our staff. H.B.D.

The Churches and Hungarian Relief

The tragic news from Hungary has brought forth a deep feeling of compassion for the human beings who are suffering, and a quick response on the part of the churches. "The world-shaking events of the past few weeks have enforced anew the importance and value of having readily available the proper channels of relief for the victims of war and oppression," states the Secretary of Overseas Relief and Inter-Church Aid, Rev. Paul B. Freeland.

In regard to the present situations in the Near East and Hungary, Mr. Freeland reports that all possible help is being sent, including $1,000 for Hungarian relief from Easter Offering receipts, and calls on church groups and individuals to make collections of clothing, blankets, etc., and send them to Church World Service warehouses, 4165 Duncan Avenue, St. Louis 10, Missouri, or New Windsor, Maryland.

Into Hungary, immediately after the outbreak of the freedom revolt, Church World Service and the World Council of Churches rushed all stocks of clothing, food and vitamins in Austria to Budapest. A vivid eye-witness account of this hazardous operation is given by Dr. Edgar H. Chandler, W.C.C. Director of Service to Refugees.

"We decided to go as far as we could into Hungary. We bore Red Cross identity cards and made slow progress with our convoy through a heavy snow storm. When we were stopped by a military officer one kilometer from Gyor, we suddenly saw that we were surrounded by huge Russian tanks. We were signaled on and made contact with Reformed and Lutheran Church officers in the region.

"Gyor was made a central depot for a proposed convoy service of the World Council of Churches and Lutheran World Federation. We planned to send food daily using this mid-way point and making trips by vehicles either way in daylight to or from Budapest or Vienna. The tension was so high that we had then to return to Vienna, but our neutral Austrian drivers were allowed to go through to Budapest.

"After delivery of their load to the churches they left at the last moment on the morning of Saturday, November 4. Though they were stopped nine times on their way back by Russian tanks blocking the road, they rejoined us safely in Vienna."

Churches in many parts of the world have swiftly responded to urgent pleas sent out by Dr. Leslie E. Cooke, Director of the Division of Inter-Church Aid and Service to Refugees of the World Council of Churches. Many gifts and promises have already streamed in: Church World Service $10,000; churches in Sweden $4,000; Lutheran World Federation $7,500; World Council of Churches $5,000; Lutheran Church of Canada $1,000.

The British Council of Churches has appealed for funds and materials and promised aid. Twenty tons of C.W.S. "Share Our Surplus" commodities in France have been made available. Eight and one-half tons of food came from Austrian church relief 115,000 DM worth of blankets (5,000) were sent by German church relief.

One million vitamin tablets, 10,000 doses of penicillin, 2 cartons of sutures, 2 shipments of clothing and one of blankets were shipped through Church World Service, New York City. Seven hundred pounds of tea, coffee, and chocolate from the World Council of Churches were delivered personally. The French Protestant Church Federation has launched a major appeal for funds and materials. Special action is being taken in all parishes by Swiss church relief.

Latest reports from Austria tell of effective material help and spiritual guidance for the refugees in two improvised reception centers on the outskirts of Vienna. Two Hungarian-speaking Austrian pastors have been moving among the refugees. In addition to the delivering of cheese, milk, butter, butter oil, rice, and blankets, the churches have volunteered in Austria to provide emergency housing in homes and hostels for quotas of refugees.

Something Different

In some respects the saying is true: "Variety is the spice of life." Sometimes in the dreariness of dull routine there comes a surprise and the pulse quickens with a new and unexpected interest. Driving across the mountains on the highway last week I came upon some halted cars, facing both directions. Three or four "road cops" were stopping them to examine drivers' licenses. The patrolman who came asking to see my license was a splendid looking young fellow, a picture of perfect physical manhood. As he copied the details of my license on his notebook I noticed he held a slip of paper in his left hand. Just as a matter of routine I asked him if he was a Christian. His face brightened with a smile as he replied, "Oh yes, Sir, I'm glad to tell you that I am, and here's a ticket I was going to give you." With that, he handed me the slip while he reached in his other hand and shook mine with a hearty grasp.

Thus read the slip:

A MOTORIST'S PRAYER

Our Heavenly Father, we ask this day a particular blessing as we take the wheel of our car. Grant us safe passage through all the perils of travel; shelter those who accompany us and protect us from harm by thy mercy; steady our hands and quicken our eye that we may never take another's life; guide us to our destination safely, confident in the knowledge that Thy blessings go with us through darkness and light . . . sunshine and shower . . . forever and ever, Amen.

Contacts with "road cops" are not all like this. From some, we may drive away with a heavy heart — possibly as much our fault as because of the officer's brusqueness. But this time the "motorist" proceeded along his way with a buoyancy of spirit that lasted not only to the end of the trip, but lingers yet in memory, made possible by a patrolman who was brightening his own drab duties with a bit of personal work and a different kind of a "ticket."

I thought that prayer, with a few additions, would be very good for the Life Journey as well. Surely it would reduce highway hazards. W.C.S.

From Slavery to Freedom

By Lowell Saunders
Moody Bible Institute, Chicago

Tiny radios placed in the brain may make possible someday the control and enslavement of an entire nation!

Curtiss Schafer, project engineer for the Norden-Ketay Corporation of Milford, Connecticut, speaking recently at the National Electronics conference in Chicago, said that such "bio-control" may become a reality within 50 years.

Surgeons could equip each child a few months after birth with a socket placed under the scalp and electrodes reaching selected areas of the brain tissue. Later a miniature radio receiver and antenna could be plugged in.

"From that time on," said Schafer, "the child's sensory perceptions and muscular activity could be either modified or completely controlled by bio-electric signals radiated from state-controlled transmitters."

Such enslavement is almost too horrible to contemplate. Yet in another form, perhaps less dramatic but no less real, it exists already.

The apostle Paul wrote concerning his life prior to conversion, "I am the slave of sin.

The Southern Presbyterian Journal, *a Presbyterian Weekly magazine devoted to the statement, defense, and propagation of the Gospel, the faith which was once for all delivered unto the saints,* published every Wednesday by The Southern Presbyterian Journal, Inc., in Weaverville, N. C.

Entered as second-class matter May 15, 1942, at the Postoffice at Weaverville, N. C., under the Act of March 3, 1879. Vol. XV, No. 32, December 5, 1956. Editorial and Business Offices: Weaverville, N. C. Printed in the U.S.A. by Biltmore Press, Asheville, N. C.

ADDRESS CHANGE: When changing address, please let us have both old and new address as far in advance as possible. Allow three weeks after change if not sent in advance. When possible, send an address label giving your old address.

For what I do, I do not recognize as my own action. What I desire to do is not what I do, but what I am averse to is what I do. The will to do right is present with me but the power to carry it out is not. For what I do is not the good thing that I desire to do; but the evil thing that I desire not to do, is what I constantly do" (Romans 7:14, 15, 18, 19).

Millions of people today find themselves unable to perform the right and resist the wrong.

Escape from bio-control enslavement, should it ever come about, may be impossible. Escape from sin is provided already. "God sending his own Son condemned sin." "Christ Jesus has made me free from the law of sin" (Romans 8:2,3). "Sin shall not have dominion over you" (Romans 6:14).

Here is perfect freedom that cannot be lost. "If the Son therefore shall make you free, ye shall be free indeed" (John 8:36).

Getting at the Big Job

By George S. Lauderdale

Jesus Christ has commanded His church, "Go ye . . . teach ALL NATIONS." Matthew 28:19. This is a tremendous assignment! A person is not taught all the things Christ wants him to learn in one brief contact. Our missionary task is as extensive as the wide world, and it must be very intensive with each creature under heaven whom God loves earnestly.

As with all big labors, the work must be divided into parts in order to get the whole accomplished. So large is our duty that we might become discouraged before we start, saying that it is useless for us to attempt world evangelization. However there are ways for Christians to have unbelievably great shares in the missionary program and in the heavenly rewards, which are fabulous, according to the Scriptures. "And they that be wise shall shine as the brightness of the firmament; and they that turn many to righteousness as the stars for ever and ever." Daniel 12:3. God says that it is possible for us to turn many to Christ!

Starting Points

After a person gives his own life unreservedly to Christ, he is in a position to be of service to God in the highest, most difficult, and challenging work of soul winning. Let the Christian carefully study God's Word, seeking the guidance of the Holy Spirit. Let him candidly take stock of his abilities. God will show each Christian how to help with the harvest right away: the Christian should pray first for the unsaved members *of his own family,* including aunts, uncles and cousins.

Christmas Gift Subscription

ORDER BLANK

The Southern Presbyterian Journal

Weaverville . . . North Carolina

RATES—$2.50 a year each subscription. $2.00 a year each subscription in groups of five or more.

Please send **The Southern Presbyterian Journal** to the following names, and send notice on Gift Cards, as indicated.

I enclose $__________for________subscriptions.

Name______________________________

Address____________________________

____

Name______________________________

Address____________________________

____

Name______________________________

Address____________________________

____

Name______________________________

Address____________________________

____

Name______________________________

Address____________________________

____

Order sent by_______________________

Address____________________________

PLEASE PRINT ALL NAMES

miah God promised that following Judah's destruction and exile there would be a day when the country would prosper again (vv.27-28). Jeremiah also prophesied that there would be a time when God would have an entirely new relation to His people, above and beyond the Old Testament covenant (vv.31-32). Though God's people utterly fail Him (v.32b), His mercy and love toward them cannot be destroyed (vv.28b,31-34). How is the new covenant superior to the old (vv.32-33)? What hope do God's people in this age have for a better time to come (v.34)?

Thursday, December 20, *Micah* 4:1-5. Sin polluted the land in Micah's day (3:9-11) and God's judgment was imminent (3:12). Yet, Micah points to a future day (4:1) when God will reign and righteousness will predominate (4:1-8). Observe that in that day people everywhere will come to the Lord seeking His ways (vv.1-2). The law of God will be taught to all (v.2b) and He will judge between the nations (v.3a). Notice that universal peace will result (v.3b) and every man will dwell in security (v.4). Observe the care taken for the unfortunate (vv.6-7). In that day all the hopes and dreams of mankind will be fulfilled because God will rule (v.7b). Pray for that day to come soon (Matthew 6:10).

Friday, December 21, *Isaiah* 11:1-5. Jesse (v.1) was the father of David to whom God had promised that there would never fail to be a person sitting upon His throne (II Samuel 7:12-16). Jesus, to whom this passage refers, was the son of David (Luke 1:31-32). Notice the absolute fairness with which Christ will judge when He reigns (vv.2-5). Upon what basis will He judge (vv.3-4)? What will be the nature of His Kingdom (vv.6-9)? What will be the relation of His subjects to Him (v.10)? Is the day spoken of in vv.3-10 similar to the day Micah speaks of in yesterday's study? The day of Christ's return is as certain as was the day when Christ came the first time. Do you look forward to the day when He will reign?

Saturday, December 22, *Isaiah* 9:2-7. Isaiah has predicted the fall of Israel (chapters 7-8). The regions of Zebulun and Naphtali (v.1) would be the first to fall to the Assyrian onslaught (II Kings 15:29) but would also be the scene of much of the coming Messiah's labors (compare vv.1-2 with Matthew 4:12-16). How does v.2 vividly describe what the Messiah's coming will mean? The two comings of Christ into the world are wonderfully blended in vv.6-7. He will be born as a child (v.6a) and yet some day hold the office of an eternal King (vv.6-7). What does each of the descriptive words ascribed to Christ and His Kingdom in vv.6-7 suggest about Him? Which titles contribute to the establishment of everlasting peace? We look back to the manger at Christmas time in order that we may look forward to what God has planned for His people in the future.

Good Advice or Good News

By Rev. Frank A. Brown, D.D.

The Proverbs of Solomon and the Analects of Confucius have much in common. A Chinese missionary after a comparative study of these two classics published his conclusions in parallel columns. It was astonishing to see how the two great sages, separated by four centuries and eight thousand miles, agreed. Their code of morals, their appeals to keep these standards, their warnings against those who broke them, were in hearty agreement. On two points they differed. The Chinese philosopher taught that music appreciation was necessary for the culture of "the princely man," while the Hebrew king is silent on that subject. Solomon emphasizes man's relation to his Maker, while Confucius taught his five relations of man to his fellow man, but ignores his relation to God.

Five centuries before Solomon, the priests and Pharaohs of Egypt drew up strict moral codes to govern their conduct. The sins warned against were hypocrisy, falsehood, idleness, cheating and adultery. A philosopher gives his son sound advice, on honesty, self control and friendliness. Hear a worshipper protesting his innocence before his god. "O Cracker of Bones, I come to you without sin. I gave bread to the hungry, water to the thirsty, clothing to the naked and a ferry to him without a boat."

In the wisdom literature of Egypt it is possible to trace "the dawn of conscience." Breasted, the great Egyptologist, in referring to the reformer Akhnaton — most pathetic figure of all the Pharaohs — says, "so lofty were the ideals he cherished that he became the first individual in history." Finnegan believes that "the Book of the Dead teaches that happiness after death is dependent upon the ethical quality of earthly life."

Where can you find a philosophy more spiritual yet practical than the meditations of the emperor Marcus Aurelius (161 A.D.)

ten they shall see to whom no tidings of Him came, and they who have not heard shall understand." I have never forgotten the awakening that came to me when I read in 1902 for the first time this marginal new translation of the A.R.V.

You realize this sense of the newness of the message when you drive up to a new village in China, throw back the top of the car, throw down the windshield for a pulpit, spread your tracts, posters, and Bibles, and make your proclamation. "I know this village is centuries old, and during that long time many important events have happened, but never before has any one brought you as important news as we bring you today for it concerns the welfare of every man, woman and child standing here." By this time you are surrounded by from one hundred to three hundred human faces, lifted to you and "hearing their one hope with an empty wonder."

When you put yourself in their shoes and think of the ties that pull them backward, you wonder why any should fling away their idols and believe in an unseen God. But then when you picture the happiness, the glory that would surely be theirs if they only accepted your Saviour, you wonder why the whole crowd does not surge forward and come.

But those of us who have not the inestimable privilege of preaching to those who have never heard; how shall we tell the old, old story as a new story? (a news story). We cannot lift ourselves by our boot straps nor manufacture a new emotion. Yet surely the preacher's own experience of daily renewing grace makes the glorious message new every morning, repeated every moment. The experience of Dr. James Chalmers of Scotland is well known. He had been preaching ethics and philosophy for years; exhorting his people to live on a higher plane, but seeing little change in their lives. Then there came an awakening in his own soul and he emphasized the great doctrines of grace, the good news. Among these subjects was his famous sermon on, "The Expulsive Power of a New Affection." He soon saw marvelous changes in the lives of his parishoners.

John Masefield referring to his own conversion sings:

"Oh, glory of the lighted mind
How dead I'd been, how dumb, how blind,
The station brook, to my new eyes,
Was babbling out of Paradise.
The waters rushing from the rain
Were singing Christ has risen again."

Another way to preach as news, the good news, is to preach to youth. To each generation the experience of salvation must come with the same freshness as it did to the first generation, who heard the message. This is why every preacher feels inspired by his audience when he faces youth. Also preaching to strange people in strange places keeps the message from growing stale to the messenger. A vacant store on Saturday nights; a factory at the noon hour; the jail or reformatory; a tent; a migrant trailer camp are exactly what the Master meant by "highways and byways." A new vocabulary is also a great help in making the old proclamation. Books by C. S. Lewis and J. B. Phillips (New Testament Christianity) are a help here.

Of course there is no antithesis between good advice and the good news. Ethics is assuredly a part of the message, but it is not THE message. The sermon on the mount, the practical advice given in the thirteenth of Romans, and the exhortations to holy living scattered through the doctrinal portions of the Epistle to the Hebrews, all show that the Gospel has an important place for codes of conduct. I have found Dr. Henry McLaughlin's advice true. He told his students that often the best book for distribution to children in public schools is Proverbs.

Dr. E. G. Tewksbury of China set forth a little parable to show the difference between good advice and the message of salvation. "A certain man visited a friend, a criminal condemned to die. He found him in the death house, and proceeded to cheer him up with small talk. He brought him gifts, toilet articles, including a tooth brush, a manual on hygiene, how to keep fit, with setting-up exercises; and as he was leaving advised his friend to keep a stiff upper lip. Then just as he was closing the cell door, he suddenly turned, and taking from his pocket a big envelope with the seal of the state upon it, said, "Oh I forgot, the governor is giving you a full pardon, and here it is."

In contrast to this fanciful story here is the experience of my former colleague Rev. E. H. Hamilton, who preached the Gospel as news to the people of China, Japan, Korea and to the tribesmen of Taiwan.

"In Deember 1937 I was invited by the Salvation Army to visit the Ward Road Jail in Shanghai which holds 6,000 prisoners, perhaps the largest in the world. In the death cells we talked with those condemned to die, about twenty-five in number. The Salvation Army had given a Bible to each, and many had found the Saviour. I asked one prisoner, as I pointed to his Chinese Bible, Have you read any of it? Yes, every bit of it, was his reply. I then asked what chapter had meant most to him. He opened his Bible to the fifty-third chapter of Isaiah and turned it around for me to read between the bars.

"He was wounded for our transgressions, he was bruised for our iniquities, the chastisement of our peace was upon him, and with his stripes we are healed. All we like sheep have gone astray; we have turned every one to his own way, and the Lord hath laid on him the iniquity of us all."

SABBATH SCHOOL LESSONS — REV. J. KENTON PARKER

LESSON FOR DECEMBER 16

The Way Of Christian Love

Background Scripture: I Corinthians 12:27 - 13:13
Devotional Reading: I John 4:7-21

The First Epistle of John is saturated with this thought of LOVE. In our Devotional Reading from chapter 4 we are told of God's great love for us, and the love we ought to have for each other. Here are a few of these beautiful verses: Beloved, let us love one another : for love is of God; and every one that loveth is born of God, and knoweth God. He that loveth not knoweth not God; for God is love. Herein is love, not that we loved God, but that he loved us, and sent his Son to be the propitiation for our sins. Beloved, if God so loved us, we ought also to love one another. If any man say, I love God, and hateth his brother, he is a liar : for he that loveth not his brother whom he hath seen, how can he love God whom he hath not seen? And this commandment have we from him, That he who loveth God love his brother also.

In Chapter 12 of First Corinthians Paul has been discussing very fully the subject of "spiritual gifts." The members of the church at Corinth were blessed with an abundance of these "gifts," and there appeared to be a little jealousy among them, some of them feeling that one gift was greater than another; the man who could "speak with tongues" would be tempted to "look down" upon someone who did not possess this gift, or someone who had the gift of healing feeling superior to someone who did not have this power.

He reminds them that all these "gifts" are bestowed by the same Spirit; that we are all members of one body, and just as all members of the body do not have the same office or functions, so we do not all have the same kind of work to do. He closes the chapter with these words; Are all apostles? are all prophets? are all teachers? are all workers of miracles? Have all the gifts of healing? do all speak with tongues? do all interpret? But covet earnestly the best gifts : and yet shew I unto you a more excellent way. It is this "More excellent Way," the "Way of Christian Love," that he explains and eulogizes in Chapter Thirteen. This Poem on Love has always been considered one of the most beautiful chapters in the Bible.

To try to write about this chapter is like trying to describe a lovely string of pearls. About all you can do is to say, as you hold it up, *Look at it,* and then, as you hand it to the one looking, *Wear It; Take it and wear it!*

Let us look at it; Let us see how beautiful it is.

1. *Love is a Necessary Gift; it is Indispensable.* 1-3.

Paul takes up several spiritual gifts and shows that Love is essential to them all:

Eloquence without love is empty and valueless. A man may be able to speak with the tongue of a great orator, or even as an angel, and if there is no love in his heart for those to whom he speaks, it is like sounding brass or a tinkling cymbal. An empty wagon makes lots of noise as it rattles down the road. So it is with our speech if it comes from a heart empty of love. An old farmer heard a long speech like that one day, and said as he turned away, An hour's rain would have done lots more good.

Knowledge without Love is nothing. In another place Paul says that "knowledge puffs up, but love builds up," (edifies). A balloon is pretty big sometimes but the prick of a pin lets out all the air. There is a tremendous difference between a skyscraper and a balloon; one is "built up" from a deep foundation, with steel and stone; the other is inflated with gas or air. The world has far greater need for "Heart-giants" than for "Head-giants." Knowledge is a wonderful possession but is worthless without LOVE.

"All Faith" : we think of Faith as the foundation grace, but it makes all the difference in the world what sort of faith it is. Faith may be dead. It is faith that *"works by love"* that is able to really "move mountains." It is this kind that grows like a mustard seed. Saving faith is filled with love. Simon, son of Jonas, Lovest thou me, said Jesus three times to Peter.

Generosity; Charity; Benevolence; "Though I bestow all my goods to feed the poor." I wonder if we always remember this when we stress the "Benevolent Gifts" in our church work. "The gift without the giver is bare," is not only an old saying; it is true. Are all our gifts to God and to men "Love Gifts"? Is not any other sort of giving but mockery?

Sacrifice; even a martyr's death; "Though I give my body to be burned." We think of martyrs as having a kind of "priority in heaven." Read a book like Fox's Book of Martyrs and our hearts burn within us as we see their heroism. But even a martyr may have a wrong motive. Is his sacrifice motivated by Love? Is

other deeds done by men and women : Love to God and Jesus Christ; Love to men.

Is not easily provoked. It will do more to keep tempers from flaring than any amount of will power.

Thinketh no evil. It will put the best, and not the worst construction on the deeds and lives of others; it covers a multitude of sins, like a blanket of snow covers the ugly spots on the ground.

Rejoiceth not in iniquity, but rejoiceth in the truth. Some people are rather glad when others do wrong for it makes them seem better.

Christian Love is a tremendous gift.

3. *Love Is Strong* : verse 7.

Some people have an idea that love is weak. Some kinds of love may be, but Christian love is STRONG. Strong to *bear*. Love will not only carry its share of the load; it will "bear one another's burdens." Strong to *believe.* If we love a person we will trust him; if we love God, we will trust Him. Hopeth all things. Love makes us believe, and faith issues in hope. Strong to *endure*. True love does not wear out.

4. *Love is Permanent:* it lasts forever.

Some gifts are of use only in this life. Prophecies are fulfilled; tongues cease; knowledge vanishes. Some gifts are for us while we are children. Love is for grown men and women.

II. *Let us Wear it!* It is meant to be worn.

I said at the beginning of this study that this chapter might well be compared to a string of pearls.

It is good to look at such a beautiful piece of jewelry and marvel at its beauty. Now, if we could just *buy it*, make it our own! This is one priceless thing which we cannot buy. It is a GIFT from our Father in heaven, a Gift which He is ready and willing to bestow upon all His children who desire it and ask for it. Each one of us can have it without money and without price.

The next, and best thing, is to WEAR IT. Not merely on Sunday, or on some special occasion, but *wear it all the time,* every day in the week : wear it in the home, as we travel, in the office, or mill, or classroom, or on the farm. The more we wear it the more beautiful it becomes.

The great crying need of the world is Christian Love; the Love of God and of Christ, constraining us to love our fellowmen and bring them to the Christ Who can save them from their sins!

YOUTH PROGRAM FOR DECEMBER 16

The Christmas Star

Scripture: Matthew 2:1-12

Suggested Hymns:
"Joy To The World, The Lord Is Come"
"We Three Kings Of Orient Are"
"O Little Town Of Bethlehem"

Program Leader:
The Christmas star has come to have a very important place in our Christmas decorations. It is pictured on our Christmas cards. We use it as an ornament on our Christmas trees. We make use of it in our Christmas decorations about the home. It is often very prominent in the lighting displays employed by cities, businesses, and industries at the Christmas season. All of this is very fitting, because the star occupies an important place in the Scriptural account of the first Christmas. It is always a good thing when our observance of Christmas makes use of symbols and ideas which relate to the real significance of the season, namely, the birth of Christ. This is certainly true of the Christmas star.

There have been, and continue to be, many explanations of the star. These explanations are both natural and supernatural. Some have sought to minimize the miraculous nature and the spiritual significance of the star's appearance. Some of the great astronomers have endeavored to prove that its appearance was both scientifically possible and spiritually meaningful. Many of these discussions and theories are apt to be over our unscientific heads. We may not be able to give or even to understand a scientific explanation of the star, but the Bible makes clear the service which it rendered to certain men who were spiritually inclined. God used the star to guide the Wise Men of the East to the birth place of Christ. These men were undoubtedly familiar with the prophecies concerning the birth of the Saviour. They were watching for His coming (as we should be watching for His coming again), and the star served them as a sign and a guide.

First Speaker:
We will do well to adopt the star as the symbol of the Christian church. It is the purpose of the church to guide people to Christ. Even as God used the star to guide the Wise Men to the manger in Bethlehem, He has told the church of its responsibility to point the way to Christ. We have all been commissioned to perform this service. We are fully aware that the world needs Christ. Apart from Him there is no salvation for the sin-wrecked human race. Apart from Him there is to be found no deliverance from the eternal death which is sin's wage. Christ is indeed the hope of the world, and it is our business in the church to point out to the world the way of hope.

Second Speaker:
Not only does Christ afford the only hope of salvation for the people of the world, but He is due worship and homage from the world. The Wise Men were seeking Christ in order to worship Him and to present Him their rich gifts. Undoubtedly they received a far more valuable blessing than they bestowed. Men can never come to Christ in humility and sincerity without receiving infinitely more than they give. Nevertheless, the world does owe Christ honor and worship, and the church is to show men the way to worship and service. The star led the Wise Men to Christ so they could bless and be blessed. The duty of the church is to lead men to Christ that they may be saved and that they may serve. It is not difficult to see the similarity. How bright is the star of our church?

Third Speaker:
How bright is the star of our church? In answer to this question, it is well to note that the light of a church is no brighter than the light given out from the lives of those who are its members. The effectiveness of our church as a guiding star depends on the light which shines from our lives. Last summer the young people at one of our presbytery conferences met for vespers in the darkness of a mountain valley. At a given point in the service all artificial lights were turned out, and for a moment everyone sat there in black darkness. Then, the leader of the group lit a match, making a mere pin-point of light in the blackness. He then asked all the young people present to strike the matches which had been given to them and to hold them up. Suddenly the whole vesper area was aglow with the warm light of more than a hundred tiny flames. The light of the church is like that. Its brightness depends on the collective effort of individuals who are willing to shine for Christ.

Fourth Speaker:
In our unscientific way of speaking we make no distinction between stars and planets. We refer to them all as stars. We cannot tell whether the Star of Bethlehem was a star proper or a planet. The difference, of course, between the

Checklist for Christmas, 1956

Please send me copies of books as marked below:

Name ____________________

Address ____________________

____

City ____________________ State

☐ CASH ☐ CHARGE

........*Walks of Jesus*

These meditations by B. Lewis help readers walk their own daily ways with a renewed sense of His companionship. **$1.50**

........*Moments of Eternity*

Betty W. Stoffel writes with her heart simple and moving poems about the really important moments of life. **$1.25**

........*Heaven in My Hand*

........*Angels in Pinafores*

More than 100,000 owners of these two books have been charmed by Alice Lee Humphrey's vivid stories about first graders. Each, **$2.00**

........*Prayers for All Occasions*

This selection of prayers by Stuart R. Oglesby will provide inspiration for general use and special occasions. **$1.25**

GIFT BOOKLETS

These short stories, true to the Christmas ideal, make distinctive gifts. Each in mailing envelope. Each, **50c**

........*The Pullers of the Star*

........*The Empty Cup*

........*Mr. Jones Goes to Bethlehem*

........*My Son*

........*The Man Who Owned the Stable*

........*A Star Is Born*

Clip this and mail to:

PRESBYTERIAN BOOK STORES
Box 6127, Atlanta 8, Georgia
Box 1020, Dallas 21, Texas
Box 1176, Richmond 9, Virginia

CHRIST, THE ANSWER

If we can understand this deep spiritual truth, things will begin to happen in our lives:

We will be stirred as we have never been stirred before.
We will have power we have never known before.
We will have poise that we have never known before.
We will have peace that we have never known before.
Good men will realize we have something they want.
Evil men will fear us because they will see God in us.

The victory of Christ in our lives is first evident in our mind. Where anxiety and worry once dwelt, trust and peace now abide.

CHRIST, THE ANSWER

The victory of Christ is also evident in the Body. The religiously inclined of all peoples and all faiths have recognized the flesh as a barrier to spiritual attainment. The follower of Christ who can keep the body under, has discovered the secrets of the victorious life.

CHRIST, THE ANSWER

The victory of Christ is supremely evident in the Spiritual Nature. Its hallmark is love. If the Christian can truly say in the language of the popular chorus, "I have the love of Jesus down in my heart," he has the power to conquer and overcome all evil.

CHRIST, THE ANSWER

In love, Christ died for us.
In love of Christ, we die of self.
In love of Christ, we live unto Him.
In love of Christ we win others.

Pass it on to the ends of the earth!
CHRIST is the answer — OURS! YOURS!

—Mrs. W. L. Baine

Bright Colors Please Koreans

"The constant inflow of White Cross goods from the home church is indeed wonderful. I might interject a somewhat humorous situation which arises from the difference in Korean and American customs. First let me say the bright new pajamas that are sent are fine and the bright reds and other colors are good for the morale, I think. However, Korean patients usually wear the pajama over say a skirt or underclothes, so that it is not infrequent to see patients strolling about the hospital grounds in these very bright and gaudy pajamas and no one considers it a bit unusual. In fact some of the women patients' night gowns are used as we would use any ordinary dress due to the nice material (better than they would generally wear) of which they are made. And I have seen almost well patients who have a permit to go into the city on some matter stroll through the streets in flowing night gowns exciting no curiosity at all."

—Excerpt from letter written by Dr. Herbert

Step by Step

He does not lead me year by year,
Nor even day by day,
But step by step my path unfolds;
My Lord directs the way.

Tomorrow's plans I do not know,
I only know this minute;
But He will say, "This is the way,
By faith now walk ye in it."

And I am glad that it is so,
Today's enough to bear;
And when tomorrow comes, His grace
Shall far exceed its care.

What need to worry then, or fret?
The God who gave His Son
Holds all my moments in His hand
And gives them, one by one.

—Selected

Appreciations for Ministerial Relief

"It has been rather hard trying to manage and always thinking of what would happen . . . if you could have seen me when your letter arrived you might have seen tears, but they were tears of joy."

"I appreciate very much the increase you have made which will be a great help in meeting the medical needs, and increase in the high cost of living—also, I appreciate your saying 'this is done with pleasure.' "

"The medical profession seems to have increased the life span of elderly people, but you wonder sometimes if it is worth the struggle—with drugs, expenses, etc. This will help and ease my mind."

"If the time ever comes when you know of sickness among retired ministers, and they are in need of more help, don't hesitate to give them part of mine."

"The doctors say nothing can be done to relieve my mother because of her years, but she has what she needs to make her as comfortable as possible because of the great kindness of the Church."

"Just a word to thank you for the extra money. You can never know what it means to me and how much I appreciate the Church making it possible."

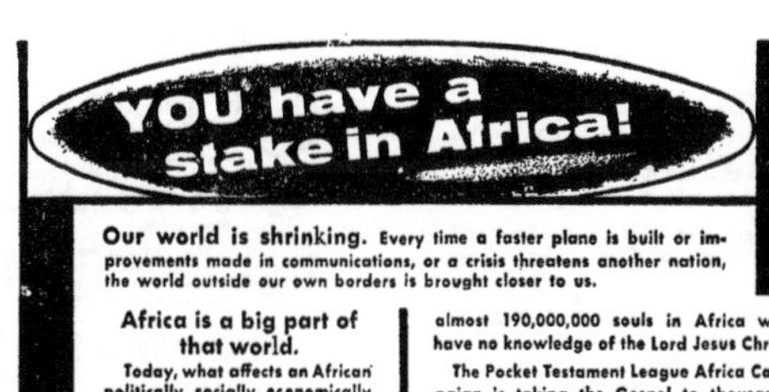

"Thank you very much for the needed extra ten dollars you sent me. It will go a long way in this rising cost of living."

"I have recently had eye treatment, and due to condition, I had to have new glasses. So, when your check came I immediately thanked our Father in heaven for such a gift."

"On my way home from work I was asking God if it would be right for me to have something I wanted very much. Then I came in and found your letter (with check). Would you say this is a 'yes' to my question?"

"I am so very grateful to God for the monthly check that means the difference between security and no hope at all."

"You could not have sent a check at a better time. . . . after looking after my tithes, I paid the taxes on my home—what a relief to know this has been done."

"God always sends things when you need them most. The Church is generous to the old ministers and widows, and we feel very grateful."

"I appreciate more than I can tell you the peace of mind and security this generosity brings me."

Formula for Escaping Responsibility

1. Don't think.
2. If you have to think, don't talk.
3. If you have to talk, don't write it down.
4. If you have to write it, don't publish it.
5. If you have to publish it, don't sign it.
6. If you have to sign it, write a denial.
7. But most important, don't think.

—From *Stewardship Facts*

Passing of Mrs. Wm. F. Junkin, Missionary to the Chinese

Mrs. William F. Junkin, Sr. died in Tazewell, Va., at 2:30 a.m., November 3rd. Funeral services were held in the Tazewell Presbyterian Church at 2 p.m. on November 3rd, with Dr. A. B. Montgomery and Dr. Houston Patterson officiating. Interment was in the Maplewood Cemetery in Tazewell.

Nettie Lambuth DuBose Junkin was born April 28, 1878. She was the daughter of Rev. Hampden C. DuBose, D.D. and Pauline McAlpine DuBose, pioneer missionaries to China. She was the wife of Rev. Wm. F. Junkin, D.D., who died in 1947. She is survived by two brothers, Rev. Warner DuBose, D.D., of Johnson City, Tenn., and Rev. Pierre DuBose, D.D., of Zellwood, Florida; two daughters, Miss Nettie DuBose Junkin of Formosa and Mrs. Albert G. Peery of Tazewell; one son, Rev. Wm. F. Junkin, Jr., of Formosa and seven grandchildren.

Mrs. Junkin received her education in China and at Augusta Female Seminary (now Mary Baldwin College). After graduation with highest honors, she returned to China as a missionary of the Presbyterian Church, U.S. It was there that she married Dr. Junkin in 1900. As their marriage took place just before the Boxer Rebellion, they fled to Japan for their wedding trip. Returning soon after, they went immediately to Dr. Junkin's place of service, Sutsien in North Kiangsu Province. Here they served for over forty years.

Dr. and Mrs. Junkin were leaders in the building of an indigenous Chinese church and had the joy, with their co-workers, of seeing the birth and growth of over a hundred congregations in the Sutsien area and a self-supporting, self-governing synod. (During her long illness, Mrs. Junkin prayed daily, by name, for leaders in these churches now behind the bamboo curtain.) Mrs. Junkin was a pioneer in the teaching of a phonetic script to the women of the area who otherwise would have remained illiterate and unable to read the Bible. She led in the establishment of training schools for lay women and shared the work of establishing Christian primary and high schools. Her chief work was the taking of the good news of salvation through Jesus Christ to women and children in countless homes.

Her Chinese friends loved her dearly. She was their friend in war and peace, in birth and death, in trouble and gladness. Her missionary co-workers found her wise and tactful, and one whose every thought, word and deed was love.

When Japan attacked Pearl Harbor, Dr. and Mrs. Junkin were interned in China until their exchange for Japanese prisoners on the "Gripsholm" in 1942. Retired from missionary service, the Junkins took up work in Jewell Valley, Va., where Dr. Junkin served as pastor of the Jewell Valley Presbyterian Church. Ill health forced them to give up this work in 1946. It was then that they moved to Tazewell where Mrs. Junkin was, until recently, active in the Presbyterian Church. For the past three years she has lived with her daughter, Mrs. Albert G. Peery.

—Clinch Valley News

The Advent Tryst — 1956

This is the second year that Presbyterian women of the United Presbyterian Church, Associate Reformed Presbyterian Church, the Presbyterian Church U.S.A., and the Presbyterian Church U.S. unite in an Advent Tryst. This tryst in which the women of these four Presbyterian Churches unite is designed —

"To prepare, as individual women, for the great privileges of witnessing to our love of the Master in home and in community during the Christmas season," and to lead us —

To pray together, as a fellowship of women in the church, in order to hasten the coming of good tidings of great joy to every person throughout the whole wide world."

There is a booklet to guide the women in this united fellowship. The introduction to the booklet "Let Your Light Shine" was written by Mrs. A. R. Craig, the Chairman of the Board of Women's Work of our Church. The meditations and Scripture readings for the four weeks leading up to Christmas, December 2 through 29, develop the theme "The people have seen a great light" as follows:

In the Individual Heart

In the Home and Family

In the Church

God's Miracle of Light in the World.

The meditation for the second week is written by Mrs. T. Smith Brewer of our Church, a former chairman of our Board of Women's Work. The other meditations have been written by women leaders in the United Presbyterian Church, the U.S.A. Presbyterian Church, and the Presbyterian Church in Canada. The folder contains on the back cover a complete list of the "Family of Reformed and Presbyterian Churches" around the world which we are called to remember especially at the Advent season which has come to be celebrated largely by families.

The guide to this united worship of Presbyterian women entitled "The People Have Seen a Great Light" is available from the Board of Women's Work, price 5 cents. Every Presbyterian woman will want to be a part of this fellowship. The booklet is most attractive and appropriate to enclose as "an extra" in early Christmas greetings at this glad season.

SOUTH CAROLINA

Bennetsville

Mrs. Robert R. Glenn of Hamer, S. C., was elected president of the Women of the Church of Pee Dee Presbytery, succeeding Mrs. F. D. Rogers, Jr., at the 52nd annual meeting held in Cheraw.

Other officers elected to serve with Mrs. Glenn are: Mrs. A. E. Carmichael of Lake View, recording secretary; Mrs. D. D. McDonald, Hamer, corresponding secretary.

Committee chairmen are: Mrs. J. W. Dunlap, Spiritual Growth, Darlington; Mrs. J. R. Woods, World Missions, Timmonsville; Mrs. L. M. Rogers, Annuities and Relief, Dillon County; Mrs. W. M. Timberlake, Christian Education, Hartsville.

Two district chairmen were chosen: Miss Nancy Busbee of Jefferson, for district 1; and Mrs. Henry L. Reaves of Florence, district 4.

The Rev. C. P. Coble of Florence, chairman of Pee Dee Presbytery's Women's Work, installed the newly elected officers.

Recommend The Journal To Friends

Church News

Presbyterian Youth Convention

Registrations are now being received in the eight Presbyteries of the Synod of Virginia for a Presbyterian Youth Convention to be held at Natural Bridge, December 27-29.

Following the theme "Young Christian Citizens", four hundred senior-high young people from all parts of the Virginia Synod will hear addresses by Dr. E. G. Homrighausen of Princeton Theological Seminary, Dr. George M. Docherty of New York Avenue Presbyterian Church, Washington, D. C., and Dr. James A. Jones, President of Union Theological Seminary in Richmond.

Dr. Howard T. Kuist of Princeton Theological Seminary will direct a Bible study on "Jesus and Christian Discipleship". The young people will also participate in Seminar groups on "Christian Race Relations", "Choosing My Vocation", "My Place in My Home", and "My Place in Christ's Church". Among the Seminar leaders are the Rev. David Burr, Dr. Harold Dudley, The Rev. Wm. H. Foster, Jr., Dr. Edward H. Jones, Miss Lillian Pennell, Dr. Carl R. Pritchett, Miss Alla H. Rogers, Mr. Dallas H. Smith, The Rev. Richard F. Taylor, The Rev. John R. Winter, The Rev. James A. Allison, The Rev. Philip A. Roberts.

With music under the leadership of Dr. and Mrs. Walter Eddowes, Ministers of Music at First Presbyterian Church in Huntington, West Virginia, and Recreation led by Dr. Harold Dudley, Executive Secretary of the Synod of North Carolina, the two-day program will provide a balanced offering of inspiration, study, discussion, and fellowship. Dr. George D. Jackson of Winchester is the Convention Chairman.

GEORGIA

Atlanta—At a recent meeting of Atlanta Presbyterial, in Atlanta, the presbyterial was reorganized into three area groups. Because of the large size of the original group the division took place, with each of the three new areas now having only about 22 - 25 churches. The new groups, to be known as the East, Central and West area, each has four districts.

Mrs. Van P. Enloe of Atlanta is president of the Atlanta Presbyterial which was meeting at Central Presbyterian Church and which was observing its 50th anniversary during its November 6 and 7 sessions.

A vice president will be in charge of each area in the new organizational setup. Newly elected vice presidents are: Mrs. Jack Murrah, Oakhurst Presbyterian Church in Atlanta, executive vice president; Mrs. D. A. Carson, Peachtree Road Church, Atlanta, East area; Mrs. Ben Carmichael, McDonough, Ga., Central area; and Mrs. Lamar Potts, Newnan, Ga., West area. Mrs. J. P. Wood, Ingleside Church, Avondale Estates, Ga., is the new secretary.

Returning for a second term are Mrs. J. G. Stephenson, Peachtree Road Church, Atlanta, as treasurer, and Mrs. T. T. Stubbs, Emory Church, Atlanta, as corresponding secretary. Mrs. Enloe is to continue for two more years as presbyterial president.

At the Atlanta meeting, two charter members of the presbyterial were honored: Mrs. Samuel H. Askew of Decatur who has been active in the work of the presbyterial for 43 years and who installed the new officers, and Mrs. Henry M. Sharp of Macon.

Taking parts on the program at the anniversary session were Mrs. Cecil Lawrence, Atlanta, who gave the Bible Meditation on the Prophets, Mrs. J. Swanton Ivy, synodical president, who spoke on Georgia Women at Work, Dr. James Ross McCain, Decatur, who spoke on the topic, Looking Up at Jesus, a message which included a brief history of the Women of the Church in Atlanta Presbytery, the Rev. Robert B. McNeil, pastor of First Church, Columbus, Ga., who spoke on Christian Citizenship; and Mrs. James R. Boyce, missionary to Mexico, now on furlough in Decatur, Ga., who talked about Presbyterian work in Mexico.

Dr. Stuart Oglesby, pastor of the host church, conducted the communion service for the presbyterial meeting.

New district chairmen, elected for a three-year term, were Mrs. H. P. Williamson of Atlanta; Mrs. Charles E. Riley, McDonough; Mrs. F. A. Straub, Jr., Atlanta; and Mrs. W. H. Park of Lithonia.

Other district chairmen, already in office and who are to continue their position for sometime longer, are: Mrs. Walter J. Thomas, Atlanta; Mrs. M. M. McLeod, La Grange; Mrs. John L. Wilson, Griffin; Mrs. Hugh King, Covington; Mrs. Charles E. Burnham, East Point; Mrs. E. L. Jaillet, Tallapoosa; Mrs. Joe E. Patrick, Decatur, and Mrs. J. O. Morgan, Atlanta.

Atlanta—The Board of Church Extension announced November 16, following its fall meeting, that the Rev. Lawrence W. Bottoms will become the head of its Negro Work Department on January 1, 1957. Dr. P. D. Miller, executive secretary of the Board, made the formal announcement from the Atlanta offices.

Mr. Bottoms is a native of Selma, Ala., and was educated at Tuskegee Institute and the Reformed Presbyterian Theological Seminary. From the position of Director of Religious Education in

Snedecor Memorial Synod, he came to the Board of Church Extension in 1952 as assistant to the late, beloved Dr. Alex R. Batchelor. Since Dr. Batchelor's death, the Negro Work of the Southern Presbyterians has been jointly administered by Mr. Bottoms and the Rev. James J. Alexander, who had also served with Dr. Batchelor.

On January 1, Mr. Alexander will become Assistant Secretary, Division of Home Missions and Negro Work, continuing to give his major attention to Negro Work. The Board hopes, Dr. Miller explained, that Mr. Alexander may carry most of the office responsibility for Negro Work so that Mr. Bottoms can spend more time in the field helping to open new work and strengthening the large program already under way.

The Presbyterian Church, U.S., has 71 Negro churches, 20 of which have been organized since 1945. The Board of Church Extension has spent $600,000.00 on property and buildings for Negro churches in the past three years, as a result of a Churchwide campaign for funds to strengthen Negro work in the denomination.

Dr. Miller concluded his announcement with the statement: "We have complete confidence in Mr. Bottoms and believe that the announcement of his appointment to head this work will meet with unanimous approval throughout the Presbyterian Church."

Atlanta—Stillman College now seems certain to be able to claim the last $40,000 of a provisional grant given by an anonymous foundation. This report was given to the Board of Church Extension, meeting here in its annual fall meeting, by Dr. P. D. Miller, executive secretary of the Board.

The Negro Work Campaign, from which Stillman is receiving half of all contributions has now received over $1,797,000, and disbursements to the Presbyterian Church, U.S. Negro colleges have received $898,595, Dr. Miller reported. The provisional grant of $100,000 was to be paid when the Church had contributed $900,000. In recognition of the need of the college, and in trust that the Church would reach the agreed figure, the foundation earlier this year contributed $60,000 of the grant, and gave the Church until the end of 1956 to reach the $900,000 figure. This one year extension in the terms of the grant has made it certain, Dr. Miller stated, that the whole $900,000 will be in hand to claim the full amount. The amount received however, is still several hundred thousand dollars short of the amount pledged in the campaign.

The Board was also told, by its treasurer, Mr. G. B. Strickler, that receipts for Church Extension work are running well ahead of a similar period in 1955. Receipts through the first three quarters of 1956 represent 36% of the approved budget, as compared with 33% of the approved budget for 1955 received in the same period. Although receipts are running ahead of previous years, the Board is operating in the red, Mr. Strickler said, hoping that year-end receipts from the Church will cover the earlier deficits, as usually happens.

The reports on financial matters also stressed that the Board has an all-time high record amount on loans to churches and expanding old facilities. As a result, almost all funds available to the Board for building loans are committed. The total now on loans is $1,083,467, and an additional $186,000 in loans have been approved but not yet closed. Well under $100,000 remains in the Board's revolving loan fund.

This record total of loans and unusual low ebb of funds available for loans was explained as the result of the "tight money" market throughout the nation, which is making it increasingly difficult for churches to get financing through normal loan channels for building programs.

An unusual feature of the Board loans, which make possible many church building programs that would not begin otherwise, was reported by Finance Committee Chairman Ralph Huie, who said that the record of the Churches for security of loans was unequalled:

"Of the $1,083,000 on loans, payments on interest and principal are current on every loan save one, and the church involved in that one case has asked extension for one pay period on its payment of $315 for a very excellent reason."

The pressing need for additional funds for loans to keep up the building program of the Church was underlined in Board discussions. An additional $4,000,000 in loan funds would not more than cover the need by churches which cannot easily get loans through normal channels, Board members stated.

In other action, concerning finances, the Board approved a near-record budget for Home Missionary support in 1957. A total of $531,713, only $66 short of the 1956 record high, will go next year to the support of workers in sixty presbyteries. The total approved is some $50,000 short of the amount requested by the presbyteries, but represented all the Board could expect to have for applying to the support of home administration.

LOUISIANA

New Orleans—The organization service of the Church of the Covenant in New Orleans was held November 18, merging the Napoleon Avenue Presbyterian Church and Prytania Presbyterian Church. The Napoleon Avenue sanctuary will be used by the united congregation.

The sermon at the organization service was preached by the Rev. John S. Land, pastor of St. Charles Avenue Presbyterian Church of New Orleans. Chairman of the organizing commission of the Presbytery of New Orleans is the Rev. David Shepperson, Jr., of Morgan City, La. Other members of the commission are the Rex. Max Ecke, Jr., the Rev. Albert B. Link, and Ruling Elders J. J. Manson, Jr., of First Church, and David Remont of the Carrollton Church.

First Worship service of the Church of the Covenant will be conducted November 25. Full services are planned for Sundays at the new church, with morning and evening worship services, and supper meetings for the Pioneer, Senior, and Older Young People's fellowships.

Last worship services held in the merging churches were conducted November 18.

New Orleans—Officers for the Women of the Church of the Covenant, newly organized in New Orleans, were elected and installed November 5.

Mrs. Morgan Shaw as president will assume her new duties in January 1957, when the two Women of the Church groups complete consolidation of their organizations. Other officers for the new organization are as follows: Mrs. Jules Laine, vice president; Mrs. Walter Stone, recording secretary; Mrs. D. W. Huff, corresponding secretary; Mrs. T. J. McMahon, treasurer; Mrs. George Dicks, historian.

Committee chairmen elected are: Mrs. Elliott Cowand, spiritual growth; Mrs. W. D. Newport, world missions; Mrs. W. E. Wakefield, church extension; Mrs. A. H. Siebert, Christian education; Mrs. William Maier, stewardship; Miss Emma Tebo, flowers; Mrs. E. J. Kearney, general fund agencies; Mrs. Ashton Phelps, Annuities and Relief.

New Circle chairmen include: Mrs. John Douglass, Mrs. Kent Carruth, Mrs. Emile Jordy, Mrs. F. J. Simon, Mrs. H. Jackson, Mrs. Chester Cook, Mrs. Ritchie Holbrook, Mrs. Frank Teufer, and Miss Mary Coughlin.

New Orleans—Mrs. J. O. McKinnon is newly elected president of the Women of the Church, New Orleans Presbytery. Mrs. McKinnon and the other new officers were elected at the annual meeting held November 9 at St. Charles Ave. Presbyterian Church.

Other officers are: Mrs. P. A. Gaudet, appointed vice president to fill an unexpired term; Mrs. C. B. Thomas, treasurer; Mrs. H. G. Rose, recording secretary; Mrs. John Marquez, historian; Mrs. S. M. Otis, corresponding secretary.

Committee chairmen to work with new officers are: Mrs. Guy Belt, Mrs. L. Johnson, Mrs. Russell Burton, Mrs. J. J. Munson, and Mrs. R. M. Means.

Mrs. Warren A. Griffith, retiring president of the Women of the Church of the Presbytery presided at the meeting. Mrs. William K. Dunn of Lake Charles, La., synodical president, also took part in the program.

MISSISSIPPI

Madison—Just completed is the new building for 103 year old Mt. Hermon Presbyterian Church, located at Madison, Mississippi.

The completed building is the educational building which is planned to serve the congregation until a sanctuary is built according to plans for future development of the church.

Groundbreaking services were held in September, and on November 11, the building was dedicated. The Rev. Sam Patterson of French Gap preached the sermon at the consecration service, and Dr. G. T. Gillespie officially received the keys to the church. Dr. Gillespie, president-emeritus of Belhaven College, has been the supply minister of the Mt. Hermon Church for 35 years.

Cost of the new building was $25,000. Members of the Building Committee included: Mr. Murray Cox, Sr., Mrs. Carl Newson, Mrs. Julius Harris, Mr. George Culley, and Mr. A. E. Gatlin.

Lucedale—The First Presbyterian Church, Lucedale, Miss., was organized on Sunday, Nov. 11, with a charter membership of twenty three.

The Commission appointed by Presbytery at the October meeting, in response to a petition, was composed as follows: Revs. L. A. Beckman, Jr., Chairman; R. D. Littleton, Walter L. Bader, and W. Harvell Jackson; Ruling Elders, G. C. McLeod of Leaksville, and N. C. McLeod, Sr., of Wiggins.

The following officers were elected: Ruling Elders, E. E. Pipkins, C. O. Gilbert, and Frank Pearce; and Deacons, N. W. Blackledge, C. M. Greene, F. L. McLeod, Jr., and Richmend McInnis. Messrs. Pipkins and Gilbert, having been previously ordained as Elders in other churches, were then installed by the Commission. Mr. G. C. McLeod led the installation prayer.

This church began with services being held in the home of Mr. Gilbert, by Mr. Beckman, Superintendent of Home Missions. Services were held two Sundays a month. During the past summer one of our Candidates, Mr. Malcolm Bonner, a student in Columbia Seminary, supplied the mission, holding services every Sunday. The Superintendent of Home Missions will continue to provide the church with services until a pastor can be secured.

TENNESSEE

Knoxville—Sequoyah Hills Presbyterian Church of Knoxville has completed the new $100,000 Children's Building. It was occupied in its entirety for the first time Sunday, November 11.

The building is designed especially for children, according to the Rev. Julian Spitzer, primarily for children from infancy through 11 years. Furniture in the rooms is sized for children of those ages. Windows in the building are a foot and a half from the ground. Special lavatory facilities are available for each room in the nursery and kindergarten departments. Interior colors are pastel shades of cream, green, pink, and blue.

The architectural design follows that of the rest of the church plant. The red brick veneer building is trimmed in white stone, and has a slate roof.

In the 10,500 square-foot building are four nursery rooms, two kindergarten rooms, three primary rooms, and three junior department rooms.

Knoxville—A special offering for Home Missions was taken by the churches in Knoxville Presbytery on November 11. According to Dr. Joseph B. Mack, Presbytery Home Missions superintendent, the Knoxville Presbytery's Home Missions Committee has a budget of $81,644.

Half of the money will go to work within the presbytery and the other half to the Church Extension program of the General Assembly.

The most immediate project for the presbytery's committee is the organization of a Presbyterian church in Oak Ridge, Tenn. The Rev. Arthur M. Field, Jr., is chairman of the committee to organize the church. He is pastor of Eastminster Presbyterian Church, and the moderator of Knoxville Presbytery.

Also to be aided by this fund is a Sunday School already organized in Clinton, which Mr. Field said is expected to develop into a new church, and a Presbyterian Church in Gatlinburg is part of the projected program. Some of the fund will help John Sevier Church, organized in 1948, to complete its building.

Zion Church, Columbia, was the scene of a unique service on the night of November 11, 1956, at which honor was paid to Dr. Samuel Percy Hawes, D.D. Many whom he had baptized, or received into the church, or united in marriage were present paying him honor. Dr. Hawes was ordained and installed as a minister of the gospel at Zion Church on November 11, 1893, exactly 63 years ago. Scenes from his life were presented in pageant form by members of Zion Church. The service was given in connection with the Joy Gift and was held on this date, rather than in December, because it was the anniversary of his ordination and because he is one who had served and retired before the Ministers' Annuity Fund went into effect, an example in our midst of one who benefits from the Joy Gift.

After ministering at Zion Church from 1893 to 1911, Dr. Hawes went to the Maxwell Street Church in Lexington, Kentucky, and from there he went to Spring Hill, Tennessee. He then went to Charleston, Miss., from which church he retired in 1940. He and Mrs. Christine Watkins Hawes now live in Columbia, Tennessee, he again a member of Columbia Presbytery and she again a member of Zion Church, where they regularly attend services.

Under Rev. W. M. Ford, minister at Zion Church, plans for the sesquicentennial celebration of Zion are being worked out. The date has been set for June 15-16, 1957.

Board of World Missions

Nashville—The appointment of five new missionaries and the formal approval of the first budget for the Presbyterian Church, U.S., participation in missionary work in the Near East were among highlights of the Board of World Missions meeting here in November. The Board also took part in the laying of the cornerstone for the new Board of World Missions Building.

Newly appointed missionaries are Dr. and Mrs. George L. Landolt of Sherman, Tex.; Dr. and Mrs. Robert Phillips of Charleston, S. C.; and the Rev. Kenneth E. Boyer of Fort Gaines, Ga. It is planned that all will go to their mission fields in the late summer or fall of 1957.

Dr. and Mrs. Landolt were given three year appointments as educational missionaries of Taiwan, where Dr. Landolt will be in charge of setting up the chemistry department of the new Tunghai University in Taichung. He is head of the Chemistry Department of Austin College in Sherman, and has served both as business manager and vice-president of that institution in the past. Dr. and Mrs. Landolt have also served earlier for a short-

Approved the proposed Women's Caravan to Mexico, for one representative from each of the Synods. It is to be sponsored jointly by the Board of World Missions and the Board of Women's Work, in connection with the Mexican mission's effort to present to the Church the needs that will be met by a part of the 1957 Birthday offering.

Heard a report on plans to prepare regulations to govern registration of young people attending the Young People's Section of the World Mission Conference at Montreat. Last year more than 500 attended this section and shortage of accommodations created a problem that regulations of registrations will attempt to avoid in the future.

The Board also noted with pleasure that over-all receipts for the Board's work are running slightly ahead of receipts for 1956, and that contributions in the Easter Offering for Overseas Relief and Interchurch Aid have already exceeded by $8,250 the total for 1955. The total now stands at $97,094, and experience has shown that additional contributions from the Easter Offering will continue to come in through December.

TEXAS

Dallas Presbytery—The members of the Presbytery of Dallas in its regular fall meeting held on November 13, 1956, at the First Church, Irving, marked an unusual spiritual experience.

The Committee on Examinations, prepared beforehand, conducted an unusually complete though concise examination of five ministers being received into the Presbytery.

The Committee on Candidates conducted a very satisfactory examination of two mature young men, applying for reception as candidates.

Rev. J. Sherard Rice of the First Church of Tyler, at the request of the retiring moderator Elder C. R. Cole, preached a challenging sermon on The Theology of Stewardship. Following this the moderator, Rev. Richmond McKinney, using an order of service prepared by the Committee on Worship inducted the two candidates into their position as candidates with due constitutional questions, a brief charge, and a prayer of consecration.

The five men who were being received then stood before the altar, answered the obligations contained in the "ex animo" statement and one by one affixed his signature to that statement. These then knelt as the moderator led the whole Presbytery in a prayer of consecration and rededication concluding with the Lord's Prayer and benediction.

This significant service set a seldom-experienced high spiritual tone upon all the proceedings of the day.

New members received were: Robt. B. Brannon, Jr., Ralph D. Bucy, Jr., B. J. Danhof, Quentin Payne, and John B. Spragens.

Candidates admitted were Robert E. Key, son of Mrs. Ethel Key, and member of the Oak Cliff Church, and Wilbur H. Willard, member of First Church of Denton and son of Elder and Mrs. Claude Willard of the Wynnewood Church, Dallas.

Rev. Edward A. Jussely was dismissed to the Presbyterv of Meridian to acept the call of the church at Waynesboro, Miss.

VIRGINIA

Richmond—Mrs. Alice G. McKelway has succeeded Mrs. L. C. Majors as special representative for the Division of Field Service of the Board of Christian Education.

Rev. W. Norman Cook, division secretary, announced that Mrs. McKelway would continue with the duties performed by Mrs. Majors, who retired in September after 35 years on the board staff.

THE MORNING ALTAR. Harold Lindsell. Fleming H. Revell. $2.00.

This is a splendid volume of daily devotions for this year. In each there is a short Scripture text with an exposition applying the topic to each individual's daily life. In addition to constant reference to the teaching of the Word, there are illustrations and quotations from great Christian leaders. This volume will help to deepen the experiences of young or new Christians and to reassure the faith of those more mature.

PERSONAL EVANGELISM. J. C. Macaulay and Robert H. Belton. Moody Press. $3.25.

Here is a fresh approach to personal evangelism by two writers who speak out of their experience in witnessing and in teaching principles of evangelism in the classroom. The work of the Holy Spirit is emphasized. Practicality and tact are two words which may be said to characterize this text. This is a book for Bible schools, evangelists, pastors, and individuals looking toward a more effective Christian witness.

300 SERMON OUTLINES. W. Robertson Nicoll. Baker Book House. $2.50.

Here are 300 outlines for sermons on the New Testament by preachers of great ability in Biblical preaching. There is a refreshing variety in these sermon outlines. This is a book of inspiration, guidance and Scripture illumination.

THE GOSPEL MYSTERY OF SANCTIFICATION. Walter Marshall. Zondervan. $3.95.

This work was originally published in 1692 It is a classic that has been rescued from a regrettable obscurity. The best preachers of the 18th and 19th centuries found gold mines of spiritual truth in this work.

In addition to Marshall's masterpiece on sanctification, there is included in this volume his famous sermon on the doctrine of justification and also a biographical sketch and appreciations of eminent contemporaries.

Despite the fact that the structure of this volume is somewhat archaic and some sentences obscure, it is the considered judgment of this reviewer that this is the finest single volume in existence on sanctification. To Christians who will be willing to devote thought and study to this work we have no hesitation in saying it will prove highly rewarding. We are grateful to Zondervan Publishing House for another reprint classic.

J.R.R.

SERMONS ON THE LORD'S PRAYER. Compiled and edited by H. J. Kuiper. Zondervan. $2.00.

The Lord's Prayer is discussed in this volume by an outstanding group of active pastors and Christian educators. Here is superlative sermonic treatment of a text familiar to all Christians—inspired messages that will help Christians to further realize their riches in Christ and their responsibilities to be witnesses for Him in all walks of life.

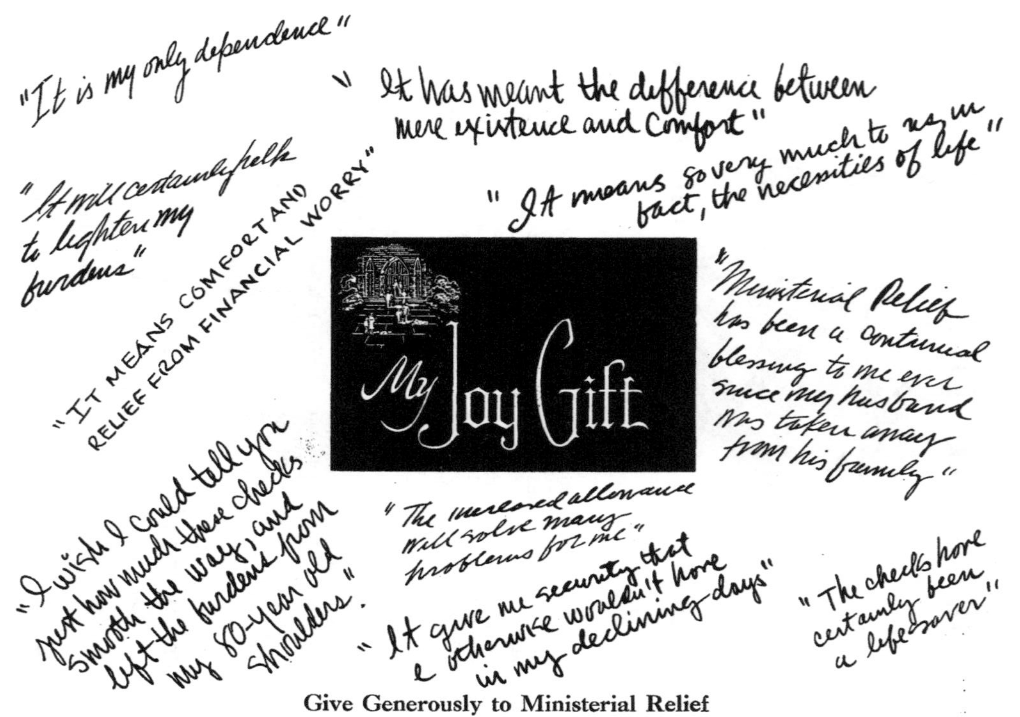
"It is my only dependence"
"It has meant the difference between mere existence and comfort"
"It will certainly help to lighten my burdens"
"It means so very much to us in fact, the necessities of life"
"IT MEANS COMFORT AND RELIEF FROM FINANCIAL WORRY"
My Joy Gift
"Ministerial Relief has been a continual blessing to me ever since my husband was taken away from his family"
"I wish I could tell you just how much these checks smooth the way, and lift the burdens from my 80-year old shoulders".
"The increased allowance will solve many problems for me"
"It gives me security that I otherwise wouldn't have in my declining days"
"The checks have certainly been a lifesaver"

Give Generously to Ministerial Relief

THE SOUTHERN PRESBYTERIAN JOURNAL

A Presbyterian weekly magazine devoted to the statement, defense and propagation of the Gospel, the faith which was once for all delivered unto the saints.

VOL. XV NO. 33 DECEMBER 12, 1956 $2.50 A YEAR

.EDITORIAL.

Icons

What To Preach: An Objective Guide

A Basis of Judgment

The Finality of the Christian Faith (Hebrews I)

NCC's Radio "Purge"

A Basket of Fruit

The Fruit of the Spirit Is Meekness, Humility

"Missions Now and Always" Declares the Bible

By George S. Lauderdale

Helps To Understanding Scripture Readings

Sabbath School Lesson for December 23, 1956

Young People's Department

Women's Work — Church News — Book Reviews

THE SOUTHERN PRESBYTERIAN JOURNAL

Rev. Henry B. Dendy, D.D., Editor........Weaverville, N. C.
Dr. L. Nelson Bell, Associate Editor........Asheville, N. C.
Rev. Wade C. Smith, Associate Editor........Weaverville, N. C.

EDITORIAL

Icons

During my recent travels I stayed one night in a seminary building used for classroom and dormitory purposes. The seminary is one that prides itself on its evangelical standing. No modernism is evident. The Bible from cover to cover is its standard.

On the first floor of the building was a small room, about six by ten. Against one of the longer walls was a sort of altar. Above this shelf, hanging on the wall, was a large picture of Christ. And in front of it was a prie-dieu or kneeling cushion.

Dr. William Childs Robinson, in a recent editorial here, was entirely right when he said, "It is un-Presbyterian to attach God's presence and power to a particular place or object such as an altar or icon. The popular pictures of Christ are . . . icons."

Not only is this un-Presbyterian. It is un-Baptist, un-Protestant, un-Scriptural, and ungodly.

There were also some other visitors at that seminary, every one a good evangelical, a Bible-believer, and one might even say, a fundamentalist. Yet two of these staunch conservatives openly denied the verbal inspiration of the Scriptures. One of them said that the thought was inspired but not the words.

From a number of such experiences, occurring in widely separated localities, one may conclude that some of the leaders of theological conservatism are not so conservative after all. They claim to defend the faith against modernism, higher criticism, and unbelief. But apparently they do not know what the faith is. They have read the second commandment, but they do not obey it; they can see what the Bible says about itself, but they do not believe it.

However, without further berating these lame leaders of evangelicals, we ought to observe the significance of all this for ourselves. Could it be that we too do not know what the Bible teaches? Have they alone succumbed, while we have escaped the secular and un-Christian influences of our educational system and materialistic society?

If anyone will take my most urgent advice and read some of the fine Puritan and Presbyterian literature of the seventeenth century, he will, I am sure, conclude that we too know all too little of God's revelation. G.H.C.

What To Preach: An Objective Guide

The first summer out of Seminary I floundered around until about Friday of every week trying to decide what to preach. That only left about forty-eight hours to prepare the message. A few years ago, Dr. W. M. Anderson of Dallas suggested a through the Bible course of preaching. This plan caught on like wildfire . . . perhaps because too many of our ministers were in the same boat I was in as a theological student.

These two illustrations bring out the need for some objective guide for each minister to find for himself as to what to preach. Each one of us has his hobbies and eccentricities. If the guide is purely subjective we shall run into our own ruts . . . or if you like the figure better, on our own pet rails.

There are a number of objective suggestions that have been used and may be used. To some extent most of our Pastors use the Church year, that is, Christmas, Easter, Pentecost. Some denominations have the Church Year arranged with selected pericopes from the Gospels and the Epistles for each Sunday in the year. I have no wish to see such a plan made mandatory, but many of our ministers might find such a suggested objective program a way of presenting a richer and more varied program in their preaching. Under this scheme half of the year is called the semester of the Lord (from Advent through Trinity), and the other half the semester of the Church.

Zwingli began the Reformation in Zurich by preaching straight through a book of the Bible, and Calvin followed in Geneva. There are many advantages of such a plan. It gives cumulative force and holds interest. It turns the attention away from the opinions of the pastor to the Word of God. It brings in touchy questions naturally. For example, if one preaches through Matthew he comes at a regular place to the matter of divorce and touches on it without preaching against a particular divorce in the congregation.

The Larger Catechism of the Westminster Divines was prepared for use in preaching. I have found the regularly used exposition of the Shorter Catechism a fine way of stimulating attendance at the evening service. In this way the congregation is taken through our understanding of the faith and duty laid down in God's word. In effect this is a study of the Apostles' Creed, the Ten Commandments and the Lord's Prayer. Of course, each of the above can be and often is used for a series. I understand that in the Christian Reformed Church, each pastor is required to preach once a week on the Heidelberg Catechism. There is no purpose in this article to make a law, but to invite the brethren each to find for himself a wise objective guide for preaching.

Some find the several incidents in Acts a good series. Others like to go through the miracles or the parables in the Gospels. A series on selected psalms is most helpful to the problems of the soul. Paul has a series of prayers. The words to the seven churches in Asia Minor would search any congregation. In every program — or lack of program — may our preaching be true to God's way of revealing Himself to sinners, namely, His coming to us in the Incarnation and Crucifixion and Resurrection and Intercession of Christ brought home to our hearts by the Holy Spirit. W.C.R.

A Basis of Judgment

After the regular evening service three ministers stood at the back of the church talking about an evangelist who had been advertized as about to come to town. This evangelist made a specialty of divine healing, and one of the three ministers wondered whether there was anything to it. On a previous occasion he had attended such a service and had come away perplexed.

The second minister, a serious man of sober judgment, replied that although he was not a Pentecostal like this evangelist, his more formal denomination also included a man who thought well of divine healing. Therefore he could not condemn divine healing merely on the basis that the Pentecostals were noisy and disorderly. Yet, after some consideration, he had come to condemn it.

The basis of his condemnation was that the preaching and practice of divine healing tends to divide the church. Some people are instantly repelled, and others are attracted. Thus the church is split into two factions, and therefore divine healing should be frowned upon.

The purpose in recounting this conversation is not to open a discussion on divine healing. There is a much more fundamental point at issue. It is this: on what basis can we properly judge something to be good or bad for the church? In this age of the disintegrating atom there is a great tendency toward collectivism. Governments are becoming more socialistic, and churches are becoming ecumenical. Anything divisive, anything that impedes unity, any individualism attracts the frowns and suspicions of the multitudes.

For this reason there is an urge not only to unite churches of similar polity, but to unite all Protestantism, to unite with the Greek Catholics, to unite all Christendom, and in fact to unite all religions. Therefore doctrinal unity, a different type of unity, the kind of unity the Bible stresses, is disowned. The teaching of Christ that in the world the tares and the wheat must grow together until the angels harvest them is transferred from its worldly reference and inserted into the sphere of the church, from which it is concluded that the church has no authority to maintain standards of sound doctrine. Thus bad exegesis serves un-

The Southern Presbyterian Journal, *a Presbyterian Weekly magazine devoted to the statement, defense, and propagation of the Gospel, the faith which was once for all delivered unto the saints*, published every Wednesday by The Southern Presbyterian Journal, Inc., in Weaverville, N. C.

Entered as second-class matter May 15, 1942, at the Postoffice at Weaverville, N. C., under the Act of March 3, 1879. Vol. XV, No. 33, December 12, 1956. Editorial and Business Offices: Weaverville, N. C. Printed in the U.S.A. by Biltmore Press, Asheville, N. C.

ADDRESS CHANGE: When changing address, please let us have both old and new address as far in advance as possible. Allow three weeks after change if not sent in advance. When possible, send an address label giving your old address.

scriptural principles and the divine commands concerning ecclesiastical discipline are ignored.

But why should we choose organizational unity as the basis for judging divine healing or anything else. God has given us very clear principles for judging all things. For the Scripture is inspired throughout, and it is profitable for doctrine and correction; and by attending to the words of the Lord the man of God may be furnished completely unto every good work.

The erring church needs to be recalled to the position of testing all things by God's revelation. G.H.C.

The Finality of the Christian Faith

Hebrews 1

Is the Christian faith final? This is a practical and timely question in the light of modern liberalism, and the tendency of many to place Christianity alongside other religions, asserting that each is good in its place, and for its followers.

This tendency to me is sin, and disloyalty to our Saviour and Lord, who claimed, "I am the way, the truth, and the life: no man cometh unto the Father, but by me." Modernists, who claim that Christianity is one among many, forget to their peril that Jesus was crucified not because He claimed to be God, but because He claimed to be the only God, and claimed exclusive worship. Had He been willing to assume a place of equality among other religious leaders, and for Christianity to take its place among the comparative religions of the world, there would have been no cross.

True Christians must believe in the "Finality of the Christian Faith" for at least four reasons. First, because Christ is God's last word to man. The Bible, our only infallible rule of faith and practice, teaches that God, "who at sundry times and in divers manners, spake in time past unto the fathers by the prophets, hath in these last days spoken unto us by His Son." (Hebrews 1:1&2.)

In the parable of the Wicked Husbandmen in Mark 12, we are reminded of the fact that after the people had beaten, and stoned, and killed God's messengers, He sent His one Son, His wellbeloved saying, "They will reverence My Son." Jesus, is indeed, God's last appeal.

We must ever remember that Christianity is Christ, not some moral code, and set of laws, as good as these may be in their place. What think ye of Christ is, and always will be, man's supreme question. The greatest drag on Christianity today is a diluted message, which is "unsound, unscientific, and a juggling of the facts."

We believe in the finality of the Christian Faith in the second place, because in Christ we have One who identifies Himself with man at the level of his most crucial needs. These needs evolve around the fear of death, the fear of suffering, and the fear of the consequences of sin. But Christ tastes death for every believer, gives new meaning to suffering in His vicarious death, promises the forgiveness of sin under His conditions, and promises eternal life.

A Scotchman put it this way. I need light, forgiveness, and humility. Christ as my prophet sheds light upon my way, as priest He brings forgiveness to my burdened heart, and as King He rules and reigns in my heart in such a way that humility replaces pride. What a Saviour?

In the third place we believe in the finality of the Christian Faith because it offers free and unrestricted access to God. The invitation in Hebrews 10:19 is, "Come boldly into the holiest by the blood of Jesus Christ." At the death of Jesus the veil in the Temple was rent in twain. What a contrast to the teachings of pagan religions? What progress from the days of Moses when only the High Priest could enter the holy of holies, and that only once each year.

It is from passages such as this that the great Protestant Doctrine of the "priesthood of believers" comes. No intermediary is needed. The believer has the privilege, and responsibility, of direct access to God in prayer. No law, or fiat of a court, or threat of a dictator, can block the channel.

And, finally, we believe in the finality of the Christian Faith because it works, it effects that which it promises. Men and women who surrender to Him are made into the stature of the fullness of Christ. "Therefore, if any man be in Christ, he is a new creature: old things are passed away: behold, all things are become new." The immoral has clean hands and a pure heart. The proud become humble. The dishonest speaketh the truth in his heart. The sinner becomes the saint.

In Hebrews 11 we have the "Hall of Fame" of those who were changed by the message. The list is only partial, and if it had been written later, or today, it could have been lengthened greatly. Yes, the supreme accomplishment of the Christian Faith is that it takes the man who has lost the image of God through sin, and restores that image. Paradise lost is regained through this faith.

With the saints of all ages let us hold to the "Finality of the Christian Faith." C.G.M.

Christmas Gift Subscription

ORDER BLANK

The Southern Presbyterian Journal

Weaverville . . . North Carolina

**RATES—$2.50 a year each subscription.
$2.00 a year each subscription in
groups of five or more.**

Please send **The Southern Presbyterian Journal** to the following names, and send notice on Gift Cards, as indicated.

I enclose $____________for__________subscriptions.

Name________________________________

Address______________________________

Name________________________________

Address______________________________

Name________________________________

Address______________________________

Name________________________________

Address______________________________

Name________________________________

Address______________________________

Order sent by__________________________

Address______________________________

PLEASE PRINT ALL NAMES

A great responsibility rests upon the National Religious Broadcasters, Inc., (the radio arm of the National Association of Evangelicals) to counter this NCC propaganda and keep the airwaves free for the broadcasting of the "faith once for all delivered to the saints." Furthermore, it behooves all evangelical radio-television broadcasters to join the NRB and help plan and finance an effective strategy.

The millions of evangelicals who want to hear the Gospel over the air should pray and write and talk to this end. The ever-faithful God will honor every worthy endeavor in His name.—United Evangelical Action.

"Missions Now and Always," Declares the Bible

By George S. Lauderdale

Proof abounds in every passage that the Bible is a missionary book. God has not given His Word to a select group, but to all men. For example, the lengthy sections forbidding image-worship give the missionary to pagan peoples many texts to expound. If idolators do not see these truths and repent, they will perish forever in the fires of hell!

There are biographies of great men in the Bible. What relation have they to our task of preaching Christ to every creature? Missionaries must be mighty men, faithful, calm under attack, unmoved by tension and stress to do or say rash things. Let the lives of David, Moses, Paul, and others be carefully studied; the Holy Spirit would use such to show us how to get things done for God the way He wants.

What is the message of the whole Bible? God's love for lost mankind, told only in the Bible, is the basis of missions; the duty of man to love God with all his heart and his neighbor as himself obligates us to obey Christ and send forth His gospel. This love of God is poured into our hearts by the Holy Ghost, given to all who believe on the Lord Jesus Christ.

LEARNING TO LOVE

Books of the Bible such as Genesis and Ruth, and passages such as Malachi 2:11-16 and Ephesians 5:22-6:9, describe God's ideal for home life and must be practiced by Christian parents to raise up missionaries for the future. If we do not love one another at home, we will not love those away from home.

The numerous promises of the Bible are given to encourage us in these last days to evangelize the nations before the return of our Lord Jesus Christ. The fearful warnings show Christians

passion; the crown of Vicarious Suffering; the crown of Universal Dominion.

Read Paul's description of the mind which was in Christ, in Philippians: 2:5-11.

Look at Him as He takes the towel and washes the feet of the disciples.

Listen to His words: Come to me . . . I am meek and lowly.

II. *Our Meekness, or Humility.*

1. In our attitude toward God; do we have humble and contrite hearts?

   When we see our frailty and His Majesty and Power.

   Our Sinfulness and His Holiness.

2. In our attitude toward other men.
   Let each esteem other better than themselves.

   In our willingness to serve; Gird yourselves with humility, to serve one another, says Peter. Was he thinking of that night in the upper room?

3. In our attitude toward ourselves; not to think more highly.

   In our attainments and Christian graces.

   In our work for Him.

God has a great promise for the meek; the meek will He guide in judgment, and the meek will He teach His way.

Only one way to have such Humility; The fruit of the Spirit is meekness.

Helps To Understanding Scripture Readings in *Day by Day*

By Rev. C. C. Baker

Sunday, December 23, *Isaiah* 7:10-14. The combined forces of Syria and Ephraim, the Northern Kingdom of Israel, made an attack on Judah, the Southern Kingdom of Israel (vv.1,4-6). Notice the figure in v.2 that describes the terror that resulted in Jerusalem. God, however, instructed Isaiah to tell Ahaz, the King of Judah, that Jerusalem would not fall (vv.3-5,7-8). Isaiah challenged Ahaz to look to God in faith and ask for a miraculous evidence of God's protection (v.10). Ahaz disdainfully refused (v.12). A sign was given, but not concerning Ahaz (vv.13-14) — a prophecy was made of the miraculous birth of the coming Messiah (v.14). Sometimes when the Christian is in real trouble and refuses to look to God for help, he misses the opportunity to see God's miraculous hand at work in His life.

Monday, December 24, *Luke* 2:1-20. If possible use a modern translation in reading today's passage to capture the drama of what occurred. Picture the commonplace circumstances of the birth of Jesus (vv.1-7). Picture the glory of the revelation of the angels to the shepherds (vv.8-14). What would be your reaction to such a manifestation (vv.9-10)? The sight of vv.13-14 is something no mortal will again see this side of the grave. Imagine what the announcement of the Messiah's coming must have meant to these Jewish shepherds (vv.11,16-20). What would His coming mean to the world (vv.10,14)? Thus the greatest news in the world was of an event that occurred in a stable. Can you imagine God's doing something great through the little circumstances of your life?

Tuesday, December 25, *Matthew* 2:1-12. Notice the methods Herod used to attempt to destroy the new king at his birth. How did he use the worship of sincere men for his own purposes (vv.7-8)? How did he pervert the Word of God to his own use (vv.3-6)? Observe how clearly and plainly God directed those who were sincerely seeking His Son (vv.2,9). Notice how easily God thwarted Herod's efforts (vv.12-13). Herod, for all his cunning, reacted with cruel, immature judgment when he was thwarted (v.16). Satan often uses these same methods to try to destroy the Christian: pretending to be an angel of light (vv.7-8); twisting Scripture to evil ends (vv.3-6); outright opposition (v.16). However, in the power of God the Christian can be victorious (Ephesians 6:11-16).

Wednesday, December 26, *Philippians* 2:1-11. The deep humility of Christ sets the example

(vv.31-32), a thought quite repugnant to most Jews. How must Simeon have differed from most of the people in this concept of a Messiah? The Scribes and Pharisees made no effort to go to Bethlehem when the wise men came (Matthew 2:1-6). Do you think God would have revealed to you the coming of His Messiah if you had lived when Jesus was born?

SABBATH SCHOOL LESSONS — REV. J. KENTON PARKER

LESSON FOR DECEMBER 23

The Word Became Flesh

Background Scripture: John 1:1-18; Luke 2:1-20
Devotional Reading: Isaiah 9:2-7

In our Devotional Reading we have a series of "Great Things."

First, there is a "Great Light": The people that walked in darkness have seen a great light. The whole world was lost in the darkness of sin; the Light of the world is Jesus. Jesus said, I am the light of the world; also, Ye are the light of the world. This "Great Light" has been spreading and shining ever since Jesus came into the world.

Second, there is "Great Joy" : the joy of harvest; the joy of those who divide the spoil. The Psalmist said, (Psalm 126:5), He that goeth forth and weepeth, bearing precious seed (seed for sowing), shall doubtless come again with rejoicing, bringing his sheaves with him. Jesus came sowing precious seed as He taught and preached; sowing still more precious seed, as He laid down His life for men; Except a corn of wheat fall into the ground and die it abideth alone : but if it die, it bringeth forth much fruit. (John 12:24). The joy of harvest, and the joy of victory.

Third, there is a "Great Victory." Jesus came to set men free. He came to destroy the works of the devil. The Jews were often in bondage, in spite of their boastful words, "We have never been in bondage to any man." The worst form of slavery is slavery to sin; Whosoever commits sin is a servant, (slave) of sin. If the Son shall make you free, ye shall be free indeed. Jesus breaks the yoke of the oppressor, Satan, and sets men free.

Fourth, there is a "Great Child." His Name is Great. A whole series of sermons can be preached on the names of Jesus as given here. His Name, or Names, reveal His character. His Name shall be called Wonderful. Everything about Him is wonderful; the wonder of His Cradle; the wonder of His Cross; the wonder of His Crown. He is the Wonderful Counsellor, the Mighty God, the Everlasting Father; the Prince of Peace. His Government is Great. His kingdom will be universal and everlasting. It will be marked by Peace, Justice, and Righteousness.

This beautiful prophecy of Isaiah forms a most fitting and splendid introduction to our lesson on "The Word Becomes Flesh."

I. *The Record of John:* John 1:1-18.

1. *As to the Deity of Christ:* 1-5.

It is interesting to note that in Matthew's Gospel, written especially for the Jews, the ancestry of our Lord is traced back to Abraham, the founder of the Jewish nation; in Luke, written with the Greek in mind probably, His ancestry is traced back to Adam; while in John, written with the view of Jesus as the Son of God, it is traced back to "In the beginning." (He is the Son of God, of course, in all the gospels). John wrote, as he tells us in 20:31, that ye may believe that Jesus Christ is the Son of God, and that believing, ye might have life through His name. He is the Son of Abraham, the Son of Adam, the Son of God.

The very first verse of John's Gospel settles the whole question of the deity of Christ. It is a simple clear statement of a great fact; The Word was God. In our Confession of Faith it is stated thus: The Son of God, the second Person in the Trinity, being very and eternal God, of one substance, and equal with the Father. He was very God of very God. The same was in the beginning with God.

He is Creator. In Genesis we read that in the beginning God created the heavens and the earth. We also read that the Spirit moved upon the face of the waters. All three Persons of the Godhead had a part in Creation. What One does, all do. We see this especially in the creation of man, God said, Let *us* make man in our image.

In Him was life : and the life was the light of men. His life revealed to men the truths they needed to know. In Him they saw God. In Him they also saw the Ideal Man. He was indeed a burning and a shining Light; the Light that Isaiah spoke of in his prophecy. The darkness apprehended it not. Very few came to the light. Jesus explained it in John 3:19 : And this is the condemnation, that light is come into the world, and men loved darkness rather than light, because their deeds were evil. Turn up a stone in a field and all the ugly bugs and worms will run for cover : they love darkness. So it is with men.

2. *As to the Witness of John the Baptist:* 6-8; 15; 19-36.

John the Baptist came to prepare the way. He was a great preacher. He pointed men to Christ. His mission was to get men to repent and turn from their sins. When questioned by the priests and Levites from Jerusalem, asking, Who art thou? He confessed and denied not; but confessed, I am not the Christ. When further questioned, he said, I am the voice of one crying in the wilderness, etc. His special witnessing to Christ, as we see later on in the chapter, is in these repeated words; Behold the Lamb of God. His testimony caused Andrew and John and others to follow Christ.

3. *As to His Reception in the World:* 9-14.

The world which He created did not know Him when He came to visit it. This is still the case after all these years of Gospel preaching. The world is busy with its own affairs; politics and business and pleasure and crime and war, It has no place or time for Him. Great false religions hold sway over the minds and souls of the majority of mankind.

Far worse than the coldness and indifference and hostility of the world, was the attitude of His own people, the Jews, the nation that had the Revelation and the Promises and the Prophets. The Jews as a whole rejected Him and put Him to death. They even went further in their hatred than the heathen world. Pilate would have released Him but for the cries of the Jewish leaders, Crucify Him. Dr. Gordon paraphrases this scene by saying, He came to His own home. It was warm and comfortable inside, but they shut the door and left Him out in the cold dark night. (This is not a direct quotation, but something like it, as I remember.)

There is a silver lining to the dark cloud. There were some who did receive Him. To them He gave the power (the right) to become the sons of God. These are the "Twice-Born Men," born not of blood, nor of the will of the flesh, nor of the will of men, but of God. They saw Him, the Word made flesh, and beheld His glory, the glory of the only begotten of the Father, full of grace and truth.

4. *As to His Revelation, or Mission;* A Revelation of God, of grace and truth.

The Law was given by Moses. It was holy, and just, and good. There is something greater than Law, however; it is Grace. Jesus was full of Grace and Truth. Truth and Grace form a marvelous combination. Jesus spoke the truth. Because I tell you the truth, ye believe me not, He told the Jews. Is not this the sad experience of many of God's messengers? Men will believe a lie quicker than the truth. The final victory, however, will be the victory of truth and grace. Jesus came also to reveal God to me: the only begotten Son reveals Him. He that hath seen me hath seen the Father, said Jesus, to Philip, in the upper room. We have two reasons for Jesus' coming; to reveal God, and to reveal grace and truth.

In the balance of the chapter we have another reason. John the Baptist gives that reason when he cries out, Behold the Lamb of God which taketh away the sin of the world. The angel gave the same reason to Mary; Thou shalt call His name Jesus for he shall save his people from their sins. He came to take away sin by the sacrifice of himself. His Mission was two-fold; Revelation and Redemption.

5. *The Record of Luke*: Luke 2:1-20.

This is the account of the birth of Jesus which we nearly always read in our Christmas Programs. It is simple, beautiful, familiar to all.

Notice how earthly rulers carry out the plan of God without being aware of what they do. When Caesar Augustus sent out the decree that all the world should be enrolled (with the idea of taxation in mind), he was getting the stage set for a minute fulfillment of prophecy. The prophet had said, (see Matthew 2:6, and Micah 5:2) "And thou Bethlehem, in the land of Judah," etc. So Mary and Joseph went up from Nazareth to enroll, because he was of the house and lineage of David. While there, Jesus was born and the prophecy fulfilled. The rulers of this world are but the servants of the Ruler of the universe: He does as He will with them.

A crowded inn; a stable; a manger; a Baby. This is the scene which has captured the hearts of all men. Artists, poets, and musicians have vied with each other as they have tried to tell in their own way the Bethlehem story. What would we do without our Christmas Carols, or such hymns as Holy Night, and O Little Town of Bethlehem. God uses the little things to shout His praises.

Then, the shepherds keeping watch over their flock by night. What could be more fitting or more beautiful? The Babe in Bethlehem is to be the Shepherd of Israel, the Good Shepherd, the Great Shepherd of the sheep. It is natural that His birth should be announced to the lowly shepherds. They were ready to listen to the message from the skies. If it had been announced to Herod on his throne, we know what he would have done. If it had been given to the rulers of the Jews, we can easily imagine their coldness and envy. The shepherds were simple folk, ready to hear and see and go and tell what they had seen.

"Glory to God in the highest." There are many things which bring glory to God, but this will be the most amazing of all.

"On earth peace." Will peace ever come to this war-torn world? The answer is found in these words.

YOUNG PEOPLE'S DEPARTMENT — REV. B. HOYT EVANS

YOUTH PROGRAM FOR DECEMBER 23

"*Peace On Earth*"

Hymns: "It Came Upon The Midnight Clear"
"Angels From The Realms Of Glory"
"O Come, Let Us Adore Him"
"Silent Night, Holy Night"

Scripture: Luke 2:8-20.

Program Leader's Introduction:

A skeptical person might question the promise of peace which the angels made when Christ was born. He might ask, "Where is the peace which they promised?" There was a kind of peace over the world at the time of Christ's birth, but it was not very acceptable. It was a peace which was endured by enslaved people who were not able to throw off the yoke of their Roman masters. It was not a real peace.

There was no peace in the life of our Lord after He entered upon His public ministry, except the peace in His own heart. His enemies never relaxed their efforts until He was hanging on the cross. His ministry was a time of conflict and not of peace. Is it possible that the angels were mistaken?

The history of the whole world from that time until this has been a succession of wars. Even at times when there is no major display of armed hostility, such as the present, the peace is so uneasy that it hardly deserves the name. We can be thankful any time that people are not actually killing each other, but we are always wishing and hoping for a real peace on earth. We cannot believe that the angels were wrong in announcing peace when Jesus was born, but what did they mean in the light of all the conflict which has prevailed since that time?

First Speaker:

To understand this problem we must know its real nature. What is the cause of all the conflict which we know, and what is the nature of true peace? The basic conflict in all the world is the conflict of evil against God. Real peace comes when this basic conflict is settled. Any satisfactory peace on earth must be based on peace with God. This applies on the personal, the social, and the international plane.

Since sin is opposed to God, people who are sinners are themselves the enemies of God. They can have no peace in their lives until the enmity against God is overcome. Sin must be conquered and sinners must be changed before there can be any real peace. Sin is the enemy of God and the enemy of peace. Do something about sin, and peace is possible.

Second Speaker:

The angels' promise of peace was not a vain one, because God did do something about sin when His Son Jesus Christ was born into the world. The coming of Christ, therefore, established a basis for real peace. When Christ was born, God came into the life of the world in a very real way. People no longer had to wonder what God was like. They could look at Jesus and see God. Christ said, "He that hath seen me hath seen the Father." It is only when we behold God in all His righteousness and love that we see ourselves as we really are. We have to know God before we can know ourselves and our sinfulness. We need to have a vision of God in order to appreciate the conflict of our sinfulness with His righteousness. Seeing God in Christ enables us to view the whole scene of peace and conflict from a true perspective.

Third Speaker:

Christ not only reveals our sin, He destroys it. Christ is rightly called the Prince of Peace and the giver of peace, because He brought the enemy of peace out into the open and then conquered him. How did Christ conquer sin? He took on Himself the nature of humanity, He made Himself subject to the law, and kept it perfectly. As a sinless human being He voluntarily became our representative as sinners, and as our substitute, He received in His own body and soul the punishment due for our sins. Still acting as our representative, He rose from the dead to newness of life. He becomes our representative both in death and in life when we put our faith in Him. When we believe in Christ we have forgiveness of sins and newness of life. This is the only ground of real and lasting peace.

Program Leader:

The angels were not wrong. When Christ came, peace came. If we do not have peace in our lives and in our world, it is because we have not sought it or because we have not sought it from Him Who is alone able to give it to us. Peace is a gift. We cannot make it in our own strength. We must accept it with thanksgiving from the Prince of Peace.

During this Christmas season let us ask our Lord and Saviour to give us His peace in increasing measure, and let us be seeking new ways of pointing a tension-tormented world to the One Who can give perfect peace.

Women's Work

December Is "My Family" Month!

It began with the "Sugar Plum Tree." I wanted to start a family tradition in addition to those our son and daughter grew up knowing, one which the grandchildren would associate with me in memory all their lives, one they might want to continue with their own children.

So — the annual family gathering which I call "The Sugar Plum Tree" began when two grandchildren were three and four; two were one year old. It is held five to seven days before Christmas to relieve some of the week-before-Christmas tension.

An evergreen tree five feet tall is selected. It may remain green or be sprayed white or pink. It has lights, "snowflakes" — but no Christmas ornaments. Confections in tiny, gaily wrapped boxes hang from the branches on narrow pastel ribbons, individual pieces of candy and other sweetmeats are wrapped in sparkling cellophane of all colors and hang by bright ribbons laid across tree twigs for easy removal by small fingers. At the base of the tree is a favor for each child. The finished tree sparkles and twinkles, a delectable fairyland sugar plum tree.

The families come to a simple buffet supper; no dessert — the sweets are on the Sugar Plum Tree. After supper, each child is given a basket and starts picking sugar plums. Unnoticed by them, our son takes color transparencies which we treasure — and so will they.

When each child has filled his basket, examined and sampled everything, we find ourselves around the piano. Our daughter plays, the grandchildren gather round, the rest stand behind them and we sing. Hymns, carols — we call for more and more.

The parents go home, the grandchildren stay overnight, an important part of the event. (The fourth year there were five boys, and one girl; — two three-year-olds, two four-year-olds, one seven, one eight. What an adventure that was!) After the children are in bed, stories are read; some for the older — some for the younger — and we enjoy them all.

Next morning there is breakfast together, then games, and often each one makes something simple and useful to take to his mother. Before noon they are back in their own homes with enough sugar plums left in their baskets for several days and they know the Sugar Plum Tree will miraculously grow more for them to pluck during Christmas week.

The Sugar Plum Tree led me into "My Family" Month. No fanfare, no proclamation, just my own designation of a special month for setting aside all commitments to allow maximum time for family companionship, for appreciating my family, its togetherness; a month whose days should be fitting in the month of joyous climax, the celebration of the birth of our Saviour.

—(Mrs. Morrell) Lucille DeReign
Caruthersville, Missouri

The Strangest Thing

Somehow God weaves the strangest things
Into a pattern fair.
He took an angel song, a star,
A Hebrew peasant pair,
Some shepherds on Judean hills,
And unknown Wise Men three;
A stable cold and dark and damp,
A manger 'neath an inn—
And now—
A weary world kneels hopefully
Before the Babe of Bethlehem

—Author Unknown

Women as Torchbearers

"*You* are the *light* of the world. A city set on a hill cannot be hid. Nor do men light a lamp and put it under a bushel, but on a stand, and it gives *light* to all in the house. Let your *light* so shine before men, that they may see your good works and give glory to your Father who is in heaven. Think not that I have come to abolish the law and the prophets; I have come not to abolish them but to fulfill them. For truly I say to you, till heaven and earth pass away, not an iota, not a dot, will pass from the law until all is accomplished. Whoever then relaxes one of the least of these commandments and teaches men so, shall be called least in the kingdom of heaven; but he who does them and teaches them shall be called great in the kingdom of heaven. For I tell you (unless your righteousness exceeds that of the scribes and Pharisees, you will never enter the kingdom of heaven."

FIRST VOICE: "LIGHT, the first creation of God!"

SECOND VOICE: "Before the sun, before the heavens, thou wert . . ."

THIRD VOICE: "LIGHT! Nature's resplendent robe . . ."

FOURTH VOICE: "LIGHT is the symbol of truth."

ALL VOICES: "You are the LIGHT of the world."

Leader: Walk boldly and wisely in the LIGHT thou hast; there is a hand above will help thee on. Walk in the LIGHT and thou shalt see thy path, though thorny — bright; for God, by Grace, shall dwell in thee, and God himself is LIGHT."

RESPONSIVE READING

LEADER: "LIGHT is the shadow of God."

AUDIENCE: "Moral LIGHT is the radiation of the diviner glory."

LEADER & AUDIENCE: "The LIGHT of nature, the LIGHT of science, and the LIGHT of reason, are but as darkness, compared with the divine LIGHT which shines from the word of God."

LEADER & AUDIENCE: "We should render thanks to God for having produced this temporal LIGHT, which is the smile of heaven and the joy of the world, spreading it like a cloth of gold over the face of the air and earth, and LIGHTING it as a TORCH, by which we may behold his works."

LET US PRAY!

—By Mrs. W. L. Baine

Church News

Missionary News

Nashville—Miss Florence Nickles of our Mexico Mission is scheduled to leave there November 19 for a short furlough in the United States.

Miss Nickles considers Due West, S. C., home. She received her education at the College for Women in Columbia, S. C., and at the Bible Teachers' Training School in New York.

Miss Nickles was first appointed to China where she served from 1915 to 1948. When she was unable to return to China, she was appointed to serve in the Mexico Mission. She went to Mexico in 1950.

Upon her arrival in the United States, Miss Nickles will proceed to Greenville, S. C., via Miami, Florida.

The Rev. and Mrs. Ernest Pettis, Jr., of our Korea Mission have announced the arrival of a daughter, Ada Ruth, in Chunju on October 26.

Mr. and Mrs. Pettis and family are scheduled to arrive in San Francisco on Jan. 3 for furlough in the United States.

Miss Louise Miller of our Korea Mission is scheduled to return to Korea on December 6, following a six months furlough in this country.

Miss Miller was born in Martin, Ga., but considers Hartwell, Ga., her home. She received her education at Chicora College, Peabody College, and Assembly's Training School. She studied one fall at Columbia Seminary.

Miss Sara Dixon of our Mexico Mission returned to Mexico on October 26 following her regular furlough in the United States.

A native of Hendersonville, N. C., Miss Dixon attended Montreat College, Southeastern State College in Durant, Okla., and the General Assembly's Training School. She is a member of the Presbyterian Church in North Wilkesboro, N. C.

Miss Elizabeth Templeton of our Congo Mission is scheduled to sail on December 12, returning to Belgium following her furlough in the United States.

When serving in the field, Miss Templeton is medical technician, teacher of laboratory techniques, is station secretary, and short wave radio operator.

Dr. and Mrs. William Rule of our Congo Mission announce the arrival of their son, John Heddon. born in Knoxville, Tenn., on October 30.

The Rules have five other children, William, 14, Charlotte, 12, Elizabeth 10, Paul, 8, and Barbara, 3.

Miss Nancy Boyd of our North Brazil Mission is scheduled to arrive in the United States on December 13 for her regular furlough.

Miss Gertrude Mason of our North Brazil Mission is scheduled to arrive in the United States on December 13 for her regular furlough.

Miss Margaret Sells of our Taiwan Mission was scheduled to arrive in the United States about November 28. She left the field on October 9, going via Hong Kong, Jerusalem, Cairo, etc., before coming on to this country.

KWANGJU, Korea—Celebration of the 50th anniversary of the organization of the First Presbyterian Church in the city of Kwangju was held October 23 in the sanctuary of Central Church, which afforded the largest seating capacity available.

The program was planned and carried out by a committee of Presbytery representing the thirteen Korean churches in the city and environs. The Moderator of Cholla Namdo Presbytery presided, and was assisted by other pastors. Guests of honor were missionaries resident in Kwangju, and the early Christians, included retired pastors, elders, Bible Women, deacons, and school teachers. Each guest was presented with a flower badge and a gift from the Women of the Church. The gifts were decorated, individually marked, and distributed by church kindergarteners.

The music was presented by the combined choirs of the city churches. This service, which lasted three hours, was followed by a luncheon for the honor guests and the representatives of the Presbytery.

Mrs. Jas. I. Paisley, of our Mission in Kwangju, reports that the evening was the high point of the day of celebration for the average Korean Christian. All Christians in the city met at dusk on the ball field of Sung Il Boys' High School for a worship service, thanksgiving, and dedication. After the worship service, they marched in procession behind the Sung Il band, which played "Onward Christian Soldiers". Each church group followed a lighted cross which bore the name of their church. Mrs. Paisley says there were 3,000 people in the march by count. "This city of 230,000 had never seen such a sight," Mrs. Paisley said. Kwanjgu is the fifth largest city in the nation.

On October 24, a city-wide athletic meet was held with teams from each church and Christian institution participating. The athletic meets are attended by all the families and friends of participants, so that the whole community was involved.

According to Mrs. Paisley, when she and her husband, the late Rev. James I. Paisley first went out to Kwangju, the only organized church in the city of Kwangju, and the Central Church was an outpost, outside the North Gate of the city wall.

ALABAMA

Tuscaloosa Presbytery—The 24th, 25th, and 26th of October were days in Tuscaloosa Presbytery when the majority of the Churches were well represented in attendance upon three highly important Conferences which the Executive Secretary had scheduled in three strategic centers of the Presbytery.

These Conferences were designed to set forth a challenge to the leaders of the channels in the Fields of Stewardship, Christian Education, and Evangelism. Dr. James M. Carr, the Secretary of our Town and Country Division of Church Extension in our Assembly was with us for the three days, and brought addresses and Sound Movie Films to show how the total Program of the Church is co-ordinated in the life and work of the Church with special emphasis upon the Rural Churches and the Larger Parish Program. Dr. Sam B. Hay, President of Stillman College, brought such stirring messages upon Stewardship of life and possessions as to leave an indelible impression upon the minds of all who attended. The Reverend Don O. McInnis, Regional Director of Christian Education for the Synod of Alabama, gave a panoramic view of the Services and Material available for the Program of Christian Education in the local church, and the challenge to the churches to develop such a Program of Christian Education as will use these Materials and Services. Mr. Frank Cochran, Jr., of the First Presbyterian Church, Selma, gave stirring addresses on the Primary Function of Christ's Church, and that is "Evangelism". We were shown how Stewardship and Evangelism work in the closest type of union in the church, and we were also shown our failures, in both of these divisions in Tuscaloosa Presbytery.

The Conference of October 24th was in the Hadden Church, the 25th in the Pisgah Church, and the one on the 26th in the Bethel No. 2 Church. We were served delicious suppers by the Host Churches and the Fellowship was indeed most enjoyable. The Program lasted in each church from 3:30 P.M. until 8:15 P.M. with supper served during the break between the Afternoon and Evening Programs. We all look forward to similar Conferences to be held in our Presbytery next year with arrangements and details to be worked out through the Office of the Executive Secretary, The Reverend J. David Simpson of Tuscaloosa, Alabama.

Birmingham—Vine Street Presbyterian Church dedicated the new $90,000 educational building here November 18. The Rev. Archie C. Smith, assistant to the Stated Clerk of the General Assembly, and former pastor of the Vine Street Church; the Rev. Glenn M. Willard, present minister of the Church; and Wilmot C. Douglas, architect, assisted in setting the cornerstone of the building in place.

FLORIDA

Sarasota—The Whitfield Estates Presbyterian Church, thought to be the first in America planned and designed as a "drive-in" church, recently acquired 10 additional lots adjacent to its present property, and a corporation composed of certain members of the Church took title to 32 additional lots.

It is the purpose of the corporation to hold their lots until the needs of the church for additional property can be determined.

The 10 lots immediately acquired by the church brings the total present property up to 42. When the new lots are cleared, a number of additional speakers will be added for worshippers who prefer to worship while seated in their cars. It is planned to provide a total capacity of 400 cars with individual speakers, according to Dr. B. L. Bowman, pastor. There will be inside seating for 500 worshippers.

The additional electronic equipment that will be used for the extra speakers and for the new church use has been purchased and is awaiting installation.

GEORGIA

Scottdale—Fifty five of the one hundred six wage earners of the Ingleside Presbyterian Church of this textile community, have pledged to tithe their income for 1957. In all ninety five wage earners made pledges representing sacrificial giving, in this industrial congregation of two hundred and five members.

Ingleside follows the plan of the pre-budget canvass, and is at present exceeding its budget schedule 1956, when, with forty two tithers, a budget for $19,600 was adopted. Over $1,000 per month has been put into the building program during 1956.

In June of this year the congregation moved into its beautiful new church, including a sanctuary and educational plant, built at a cost of over $100,000. Such construction has been possible only because of the blessing of God and the sacrifices of the congregation. And although the congregation would be considered a poor one, her "poverty has abounded unto the riches of her liberality."

The testimony of Ingleside seems unique, and she would like to hear from other small churches who have similar blessings to report. The people of Ingleside are justifiably proud of their new church and their record of giving, wondering how many, if any, congregations record over half the wage earners as tithers. This is a real testimony of what the small church can do if all the people have "a mind to work." That the congregation is proud does not mean that it takes credit for this wonderful blessing. All credit, it feels, and all glory, is to Him who promised to "open you the windows of heaven, and pour you out a blessing that there shall not be room enough to receive it." This congregation merely took God at His Word, and God has proven Himself abundantly faithful.

"To God be the glory—great things he hath done,
And great our rejoicing through Jesus the Son;"

Atlanta—Miss Marietta Yarnell, for the past six years the Assistant Secretary of Promotion for the Board of Church Extension here, has accepted a call to become Church Worker for the Brown Memorial and Tilford Presbyterian Churches in Leatherwood and Tilford, Ky. Her resignation from the Atlanta position will become effective Jan. 15.

LOUISIANA

New Orleans—The Rev. Walter D. Langtry was named pastor of the newly organized Church of the Covenant here Sunday, November 18, when two Presbyterian churches merged. Merger was completed by a commission of the Presbytery of New Orleans.

The joining of Prytania Street Presbyterian Church, and Napoleon Avenue Church, created a new church with a charter membership of 685, according to the clerks of the two merging churches.

Officers of the new church elected and installed at the organization meeting were: Mr. C. S. Potter, chairman of the board of deacons; Mr. George S. Dinwiddie, vice-chairman; William Maier, secretary; and Mr. Emile F. Jordy, treasurer. Elders and deacons of the merging churches were elected to similar offices in the new church during the meeting conducted by the commission with the Rev. David Shepperson, Jr., of Morgan City, la., as chairman.

New Orleans—Westminster House, the new Presbyterian student center at Tulane-Newcomb was formally dedicated November 18.

Assisting in the dedicatory services were: The Rev. Alex W. Hunter, minister of First Presbyterian Church, chairman of the Louisiana Synod's campus Christian life committee; Myron Turfitt, finance chairman, local committee on student work; Dr. John S. Land, minister of St. Charles Avenue Presbyterian Church, litanist; Dr. Ray Fortna, minister Carrollton Ave. Presbyterian Church; the Rev. Henry Moore, minister of Westminster Presbyterian Church, (U.S.A.), invocator; Linda Smith, student president; Mrs. Vernon Applewhite, interim student worker; and Gladys S. Rogers, representing all Presbyterian, U.S.A., students.

The student center was purchased from the Episcopal Diocese of Louisiana in July by the Synod of Louisiana. Recently the Presbyterian Church, U.S.A., joined the synod in the student center effort. According to Mrs. Applewhite, there are about 400 Presbyterian students attending the two university schools.

NORTH CAROLINA

Salisbury—The women of the church of Concord Presbytery, meeting in the First Presbyterian Church, Salisbury, November 15-16, celebrated their Fiftieth Anniversary. Mrs. E. Johnston Irvin, Concord, presided. The first meeting of the organization was held fifty years ago in the same church.

A highlight of the two-day meeting was the historical pageant, "A Story To Tell." Mrs. J. S. Evans, Jr., Statesville, is author of the pageant and directed it.

Special addresses on Christian citizenship were given by Mrs. Lacy Godwin, of Fayetteville, Rev. Charles S. Sides, Jr., Harrisburg, and Mrs. R. A. Willis, Jr., Monroe, President of the Women of the Church of the Synod of North Carolina.

A Life Membership pin was presented to Mrs. C. A. McGirt, Salisbury; for outstanding service to the church. The presentation was made by Mrs. H. Reid Newland, Salisbury.

Mrs. Thompson B. Southall, Statesville, reported on the Presbytery's project to send a Youth Caravan from Concord Presbytery to visit Mexico Mission stations of the Presbyterian Church, U.S., this coming summer. She stated that the Executive Board had approved sharing in the support of this venture. Offerings were received during the meeting for this purpose.

A group of new officers was elected and installed by Mrs. A. R. Craig, Rutherfordton, Chairwoman of the Board of Women's Work of the General Assembly, Presbyterian Church, U.S. General officers of the Women of Concord Presbytery now are: Mrs. E. Johnston Irvin, Concord, President; Mrs. J. S. Evans, Jr., Statesville, Vice President; Mrs. George Willard, Salisbury, Treasurer; Miss

SOUTH CAROLINA

Columbia—Two additional persons have joined the staff of Shandon Presbyterian Church. Miss Sara McNeill, coming from Reidsville, N. C., has joined the staff as director of Christian Education and Frank D. Needham, Columbia, becomes the church's business manager. Mr. Needham retired last summer after 31 years as manager of the J. C. Penney Company department store in Columbia. The new business administrator will serve without compensation. He has already served the church as director of its recent Every Member Canvass. Mr. Needham has been a member of Shandon Church since 1925 and served as chairman of the building committee for the recently completed educational building of the church. Shandon now has plans to enlarge its sanctuary.

Union—Members and friends of the McCutchen Memorial Presbyterian Church have hearts full of Thanksgiving to God for the Spiritual Blessings poured out upon them. Special Revival and Evangelistic Services were held beginning on Wednesday, October 31 with Evangelist Charles W. Solomon bringing an inspirational message to the 75 or 80 gathered for the mid-week prayer meeting. Thursday and Friday nights following supper served by the Women of the Church, a visitation program was held conducted by the pastor, The Rev. Robert G. Balnicky and Mr. Solomon. More than 30 people came out each evening to go visiting, many of these for the first time ever to try this type of Evangelism. Each of these teams returned with glowing reports of first time decisions and many encouraging promises from others to attend the services and to give serious consideration to the matter of making a decision for Christ.

A special emphasis for the children and youth was the use of visual aids. The peak attendance of youth under 21 was 114.

A special reconsecration service was held on Thursday night, at which time many came forward to reconsecrate their lives to the Lord and to pray for someone who was lost. Nineteen came on profession of their faith in Christ and twenty one came forward to rededicate their lives to the Lord and renew their vows to Him.

TEXAS

Houston—Construction on the Westminster Presbyterian Church is expected to be completed here by February 1. The church was originally at a different location where it was established before 1900.

The new structure, first of a planned church plant, contains a fellowship hall, five classrooms, two offices and a kitchen. It will be of brick exterior, and is expected to be valued at about $68,000, according to the Rev. Robert M. McLaren, pastor of the church.

Resolutions Regarding Katherine Christine Recknagel

WHEREAS, on the 10th day day of October, 1956, God, in His infinite wisdom and love, called to her eternal home, our beloved member and co-worker, Miss Katherine Christine Recknagel; and

WHEREAS, the Women of the Church of the First Presbyterian Church, Marshall, Texas, feel deeply the loss of a loyal and devoted member, whose memory they cherish and whose life shall ever be an inpsiration; and

WHEREAS, her gracious personality endeared her to all with whom she was associated, while her fidelity to her Lord and to her church, was the outstanding quality of a rich and beautiful character;

THEREFORE, BE IT RESOLVED that we, the Women of the Church, express sincere gratitude to God for the years she lived and worked so faithfully among us; that we bow in humble submission to His Will, remembering, that we "sorrow not, even as others which have no hope."

BE IT FURTHER RESOLVED that a copy of these resolutions be placed upon the minutes of the Women of the Church and a copy be presented to the members of her family, and copies be sent to "The Christian Observer" and to "The Southern Presbyterian Journal."

Signed:
Mrs. C. B. Scheer, Chairman
Mrs. Raymond Blalock
Resolutions Committee,
The Women of the Church,
First Presbyterian Church,
Marshall, Texas

Sandlick Chapel

The first Presbyterian place of worship in Dickenson County of Southwest Virginia was Sandlick Chapel. The past and present story of this chapel should be inspiring to all who are interested in the spread of the Gospel "in the regions beyond."

When, in 1930, the Rev. T. K. Mowbray, Presbyterial Evangelist, organized a church in this hitherto unevangelized section of Dickenson County, the Great Depression was at its worst. With no financial backing, the building of a church on a field where most of the citizens were either indifferent or hostile toward any "furrin" religious denomination, seemed an impossible task. However, the Rev. Mr. Mowbray and his summer helper, Mr. H. Hoover Bear, a Union Seminary student, pooled their own slender resources and purchased an old office building in the deserted mining town of Drill, which was some forty miles from Sandlick where the new church was to be located.

With local help they tore the building down, transported it to Sandlick, and by means of a community "church raising" reconstructed it in

It will be of interest to our readers to find that the author intelligently defends such disputed passages of the New Testament as John 7:53 - 8:11, Matthew 6:13, and the last 12 verses of Mark. He tells us that the modern critical attack upon the last 12 verses of Mark must be judged as unconvincing for 3 reasons:

1. No satisfactory theory has been advanced as to how Mark's gospel could have ended at 16:8.

2. No objection has been raised against Mark 16:9-20 which cannot be readily answered.

3. Thus there is no counter-consideration which can avail to set aside the tremendously weighty evidence in favor of this concluding section of Mark. The evidence of almost all the Greek manuscripts and of 4 church fathers of the 2nd century.

Although this book is dedicated to the defense of the King James version, only a few pages are specifically devoted to this old English translation. The endeavor, however, has been to defend the text of the King James version, not its literary quality which needs no defense, or the accuracy of its English renderings.

The author shows how this version ought to occupy the paramount place in a consistently Christian system of thought. The author prefers the King James version to its modern rivals, not primarily because of its marvelous literary quality, but mainly because it is a faithful translation into English of this same text. Thus the Christian who rejects the King James version and adopts one of its modern rivals, by this very action, the author says, places himself on the high road to liberalism. For along with the King James version he has rejected the only concept of Providential preservation of Scripture which gives him any assurance that a pure New Testament text has been preserved down through the ages and is obtainable today.

The author would not hold that minor improvements cannot be made in the venerable translation. He concedes that certain obsolete expressions may be modernized but these changes must be kept down to a minimum and introduced with great care in order that the matchless beauty of this great piece of classic English prose may in no wise be impaired.

This book is of exceptional merit. It contains the very finest of New Testament scholarship and yet each of the six chapters are lucid and easy to understand. We strongly recommend this volume to our readers and feel sure that no one will be disappointed. It should be of priceless value to theological students and young ministers. J.R.R.

PELOUBET'S SELECT NOTES FOR 1957. Wilbur M. Smith. W. A. Wilde. $2.75.

This is the 83rd annual volume of this popular commentary. It is the 23rd time that Dr. Wilbur M. Smith has edited it. The same high standards of the past are maintained in this current volume. Teachers who use the International Bible lessons will continue to find this commentary for Christian teaching one of the very best. This work is true to the supernatural elements of the Bible and is suggestive to the teacher who desires to make the class interesting and profitable.

THE SOUTHERN PRESBYTERIAN JOURNAL

Rev. Henry B. Dendy, D.D., Editor..........Weaverville, N. C.
Dr. L. Nelson Bell, Associate Editor..........Asheville, N. C.
Rev. Wade C. Smith, Associate Editor..........Weaverville, N. C.

EDITORIAL

Was Bethlehem's Babe Truly God?

Could Bethlehem's beautiful yet tiny Babe have been truly the Mighty God of the rolling spheres? The sweet cadences of the angel's songs echoed that He was. The three earthly "Kings of Orient are", opened their lovely treasures and produced gold, frankincense and myrrh fit only for a heavenly King. They bowed in humble heartfelt adoration as they worshipped Him for Whom they had searched so long. The bright star which they followed for so many nights and lost awhile, told of a divine Messenger and Saviour. No ordinary mortal was He. The star's silvery beams formed a fitting diadem for a monarch so divinely supreme and its rare beauty silently told of Him who is both transcendent and eternal.

Jesus, the Son of the Heavenly Father, became man, but at no time did He, "become God". He was God from the beginning. One vainly searches the whole gamut of Scriptural testimony for a "part-time" God or a "half-way" Diety. Such would be a blasphemous absurdity. Let all critics get in a huddle and explain such a preposterous idea.

In some way beyond the ken of dim human reason and by the sure light of a perfect revelation the wee feeble babe in Bethlehem's lowly manger was the Mighty Son of God, King of Kings and Lord of Lords. But someone hastens to add,—this places an imponderable tax upon the credulity of man. It is psychologically impossible. On the surface, so it may seem, but let no one become confused. "With God all things are possible."

God has a way more rare and exquisite than man can imagine. The Son of God, Jesus our Lord, was a miracle from beginning to end. You can't explain anything which He did or was, apart from that fact. The wisest of earth cannot fathom the simplest word that He said and the deeds which He performed every day of His earthly life. Can the most penetrating intellect, unaided by the sure word of Scripture, explain how God could wash the dirty feet of his faithless friends with a crude basin of water, girded with a pl coarse towel? How rare and distilled was genuine love portrayed when He prepared a sav breakfast for a group of hungry disciples on shores of Tiberius? Think of cleaning fish frying them along with some battercakes when had just gone through the throes of Calvary the triumph of the Resurrection. This was ra peculiar conduct to say the least. Was it (or not who called those weary men to break and served them as a common cook that ordin hunger might be satisfied? A rather menial t you say, for Him who fashioned Arcturus Orion in company with all the gigantic host the Milky Way. You may attempt the fe reply that it was for the magnificent purpose restoring old wayward Peter back to the apost fold again. So it was, yet a rather homely t in spite of the exalted purpose which He had mind.

How could God waste His time on a han of Palestine beggars or a few thousand sick f scattered along its dusty paths and rocky bywa How could He argue, as surely He did, with pitifully narrow-minded Scribes and Pharis listening to their raucous jargon and feeling t hateful venom day after day?

Before the golden beams of the sun began brighten and enliven the day or the silver ray the moon adorned silent night, Jesus was C Yes, the Babe of Bethlehem, pitifully weak as other infant is, none the less was the mighty of God. He was and is, Immanuel, Saviour, K and Friend for all who trust Him today.

We Protestants have gone too far, at ti in emphasizing the humanity of Christ. is true that He was born a babe in Bethleh and a fact that He was truly human as as truly divine. But with all the emphasis the humanity of the Christ child, we fo that this one who was born unto us CHRIST THE LORD.

The babe whom we worship at the ma is the same one of whom John heard the ıerable host of heaven singing, "Worthy is Lamb that was slain to receive power, and es, and wisdom, and strength, and honor, glory, and blessing."

ur Saviour is Lord, He is the King, glorious triumphant, who reigns over His creation, causes even the wrath of man to serve Him. :re is deep and abiding joy in the assurance He controls all things in His providence, even deeper joy in knowing that I have endered the course of my life to His Lord-
ı.

"I've found a friend, O such a friend!
All power to Him is given,
To guard me on my onward course,
And bring me safe to heaven.

From Him, who loves me now so well,
What power my soul can sever?
Shall life or death, or earth or hell?
No; I am His forever."
—J. G. Small

Rejoice in the Lord always!" ". . . . old, I bring you good tidings of great joy, . For unto you is born . . . a Saviour ı is Christ the Lord." —R.W.C.

The Table of the Lord

is a pleasure to note that historical scholar- ı in Chicago is calling for a return to the byterian architecture as the proper setting Reformed worship. Reference has been made ı pamphlet prepared by a Committee of :ago Presbytery, headed by Professor L. J. ıterud of McCormick; and to the good article *'resbyterian Life* for September 15, 1956, by 'essor James H. Nichols of the University Chicago. It is also reported that Professor 'ard Dowey, McCormick's authority on Cal- has accumulated a set of pictures illustrat- church interiors in the Reformed tradition.

he center of this historical testimony is the children of God gather for the Lord's per around the Table of the Lord. At this le a minister serves the supper or meal ıined by the Lord. We do not come to altar where a mediating priest offers the y of Jesus to propitiate an unreconciled y for the sins of the living and the dead. Reformed faith has a sacrificial meal based the one sacrifice offered once for all at Calvary. It has not a sacrifice repeating or continuing the one sacrifice of Christ, as though that were insufficient or incomplete.

At the Table the preacher is a member of the priesthood of all believers serving the supper to the others who are equally with him priests of the Most High God. He is not a hierarchal priest mediating between the people and an altar at the head of a long chancel which is reserved exclusively for the clergy. He serves from a Table not from an altar modeled after the old flat tombstones and supposed to contain in it the bones of saints and martyrs.

According to the Gospels the Last Supper was celebrated by Jesus and the Twelve not before an altar, but around a Table. Further, the Apostle Paul expressly refers in the First Corinthians 10 to THE TABLE OF THE LORD. In the Epistle to the Hebrews and in the Book of Revelation, the altar is seen with the eye of faith in the heavenly tabernacle which God pitched, not man. The focal center of New Testament worship is the Lamb standing in the midst of the Throne as He had been sacrificed, the High Priest ever living to intercede for us with the Majesty on High. The more successfully any congregation focuses the physical eye of the worshipper on a chancel altar or a worship center picture, the more it detracts the attention of the eye of faith from that center which God has given, namely, the Interceding Christ.

While in Rome I was taken through the Catacombs of St. Callistus by a Roman Catholic priest. There one sees a picture dating from about 200 A.D. of a primitive Christian standing behind a modest wooden table on which there is a round loaf. Our guide told us that he had investigated this matter in the Papal Archives which were opened to the Congress of Historians in the summer of 1955, and found that the picture was true to the early Christian worship until Bishop Felix of Rome decreed that henceforth the Eucharist be celebrated exclusively on the tombs of the martyrs.

That is, in Rome the tombstone altars come from this decree of 272.

Archaeologists are agreed that a simple wooden table was used in the Church of Dura-Europas which antedates the Victory of the Church, and historians posit the same light structure for the "altar" which Athanasius' presbyter was accused of overturning in 332. Dr. Walter Lowrie

'he Southern Presbyterian Journal, *a Presbyterian Weekly magazine devoted to the statement, defense, and propagation of the 'pel, the faith which was once for all delivered unto the saints,* published every Wednesday by The Southern Presbyterian Journal, , in Weaverville, N. C.

:ntered as second-class matter May 15, 1942, at the Postoffice at Weaverville, N. C., under the Act of March 3, 1879. Vol. XV, 34, December 19, 1956. Editorial and Business Offices: Weaverville, N. C. Printed in the U.S.A. by Biltmore Press, Asheville, N. C.

ıDDRESS CHANGE: When changing address, please let us have both old and new address as far in advance as possible. Allow three ks after change if not sent in advance. When possible, send an address label giving your old address.

concludes that in the early Church the Lord's Supper was partaken at a table, the substitution of an altar for a table came later, *The Church and Its Organization in Primitive and Catholic Times,* pp. 268,281-288.

At the time of Constantine the modest house churches were replaced with magnificent buildings built according to the plan of the imperial Basilicas. These state buildings had an apse at the front of the auditorium in which was the seat of the Judge and his associates and before which was an altar for libations to the pagan deities. The apse became the cathedral of the bishop with the presbyters on either side of him.

The pagan altar plus the fact that Bishop Felix had ordered the substitution of tombstone altars for the Tables of the Lord brought the altar into the Christian Church. One finds such an old basilica in the house of the Caesars in Rome. This Church, dedicated to Mary, has the apse for the presbyters and a stone table or altar before it, behind which the presbyters stood as they administered the Lord's Supper. The old custom of the minister of the Eucharist standing behind the Table or Altar is still found in St. Peters and in the other large churches in Rome and in cathedrals elsewhere, such as Chartres. In these great structures the high altar is in the transept and the minister officiating there faces the nave and the congregation as he celebrates the mass.

In the liturgical revival now going on in the Anglican Church, this custom of facing the congregation is coming back, e.g., in the Cathedral of St. John, the Divine.

In England the altars were taken out of the churches three times, namely, under Edward the sixth, under Elizabeth the first, and on petition of the Westminster Assembly of Divines.

In the Reformed Churches in the Netherlands, the communicants in turn gather about a large table. In Switzerland, the ministers and several elders stand behind the Table and serve the communicants as they come in turn to stand before the Table.

In the English Presbyterian Church the minister and elders sit around the Table and from it take the bread and the cup to the people in the pews. As the people of God gather about the Table of the Lord, either directly or through their chosen representatives, they are assured of a share in the bounty of their Father's hand and the love of His heart. Through the sole mediation and the constant intercession of the Lord Jesus Christ they have direct access to God without any propitiatory sacrifice of a mass, offered on a tombstone altar by a priest who mediates in a chancel between altar and people.

We need to have our Feelings controlled; they are God-given.

II. *Control of our Thoughts,* our Minds.

"Think on these things," says Paul, and if we follow his list we do well. Thoughts are Basic; "As a man thinketh in his heart, so is he."

Communists try to "brain-wash" their victims. Here is the height of Satanic shrewdness.

Suppose our brains are washed by the Spirit of God! Think of some men who have been thus inspired, with Spirit-controlled minds. Our Bible was written by such men, inspired in the highest degree. Others have been inspired in a different way and have gone out to be a blessing to the world.

III. *Control of our Wills.*

There are three kinds of wills: the weak will, unable to resist any temptation; the stubborn will, which makes men obstinate and rebellious; the will that is yielded to God and controlled by Him; the Consecrated Will.

IV. *Control of our Words.*

The tongue is a fire. Is it set on fire from Heaven, or Hell?

Our words today can be heard thousands of miles. Our age might be called, The Battle of the Tongues. The power of speech for good or evil is almost unlimited today.

The tongues of the disciples were set on fire by the Holy Spirit at Pentecost. Oh, that our tongues might be so filled with power!

V. *Control of our Acts.*

People say they want to "do as I please." The Christian says, "I want to do what pleases God."

God is not mocked; if we sow to the flesh, we shall reap corruption; if we sow to the Spirit, we shall reap life everlasting.

The Fruit of the Spirit is Temperance, or Self-control.

Recommend The Journal To Friends

Zentsuji, Kawaga Ken, Japan
Shikoku Christian College
29 November 1956

The Editor
Southern Presbyterian Journal
Weaverville, N. C.

Dear sir:

Thank you very much for the article on universalism in the issue of October 24, which we received a few days ago. Mr. Brown deals with a matter of importance in a clear manner. Mr. Wade C. Smith's contributions are always helpful and inspiring. You would do well to give more space to such articles as these.

To many of us, however, it seems that too often your efforts are wasted on a totally negative type of criticism. A very good example is the editorial by G.H.C. (Dr. Clark, we presume), in the same issue. Under the guise of exalting "Calvinism" the writer takes occasion to criticize the editors of **The Hymnbook** for an alleged "dilution of the gospel" by means of the version of "Beneath the Cross of Jesus" which is used in that book. The writer points out that the original version of the second stanza ends: "And from my stricken heart with tears two wonders I confess: The wonders of redeeming love and my own worthlessness.", According to your editorialist, Calvinism teaches man's worthlessness, whereas the **Hymnbook** editors have admitted an "Arminian" tendency at this point, thus giving place to human pride.

We seriously question, however, that true Calvinism—at least that of Calvin himself—teaches the worthlessness of man. In his **Institutes** (seventh American edition, 1936, Vol. I page 208), the great reformer admits that the image of God in man has been corrupted and horribly deformed by sin, yet, he says, "we will allow that the Divine image was not utterly annihilated and effaced in him . . ." That man, even in his unredeemed state, is created by Almighty God and still retains some trace of the Divine image, is enough to convince most Calvinists that he is something more than worthless. Unworthy he undoubtedly is; that he is worthless few would dare to affirm. To go so far as to insist upon the worthlessness of redeemed man, and to do so on the grounds of "Calvinism," is not only to misrepresent the reformer but also to offer a serious affront to the majesty of our Lord and Saviour, who said, "You are of more value than many sparrows."

We have no sympathy for any tendencies which would exalt man over against God, but we believe that nothing but harm can ultimately come from debasing man beyond what is warranted in Scripture. To confess oneself unworthy before God is something which any redeemed sinner can honestly and humbly do; to insist that he is worthless smacks of dishonest humility which masks pride behind an exaggerated self-abasement.

Instead of being so consistently negative in your criticisms, why do you not from time to time adopt a more positive attitude? Why do you not take the time and effort to commend those whom you have attacked when they do or say something worthy of commendation? Some time ago your paper advanced a very legitimate criticism against a phrase in the hymn by James Russell Lowell entitled "Once in Every Man and Nation." In the original version of the hymn, mention is made of "some great cause, God's new Messiah/offering each the bloom or blight . . ." It is certainly proper to raise a voice in question of that phrase about the "new Messiah." However, so far as I have been able to note, you have not called attention to the fact the **The Hymnbook** has altered that phrase to read "some new decision," and has further omitted one stanza which spoke of Christ "toiling up new Calvaries." In these points **The Hymnbook** has made a real advance in an area where you have been critical, yet you have not seen fit to recognize the fact.

Another case in point is the rather severe criticism you leveled against the editors of **Christianity and Crisis** for an article derogating Billy Graham. It turned out that the original article had been written by Dr. Reinhold Niebuhr, but his co-editor, Dr. H. P. Van Deusen, took occasion to point out that it did not express his own views of Billy Graham and went so far as to offer his sympathies for the evangelist's work and hope for success in his New York campaign. Notice of Dr. Van Deusen's repudiation of the Niebuhr view was taken even in the secular press (TIME magazine, e.g.), but I have looked in vain for any recognition of it on your part. Dr. Van Deusen has, I seem to recall, been the object of critical remarks from you on several occasions in the past; why can you not be gracious enough to give him due recognition on this particular point?

Such a lack of balance and charity on your part, together with such bitingly sarcastic articles as that of Dr. McMurray ("How Smart Can We Get?"—Oct. 17) can ultimately do nothing but harm to the very faith which you claim to defend. "The faith which was once for all delivered unto the saints" is **our** faith as well as yours. We should all be allies in its propagation as well as in its defense; but sometimes you make us wish you were not on "our side." A little more grace, a little more charity, a little more sympathy in giving praise and credit where they are due, will make your part far more effective and less divisive than it is often inclined to be.

Very cordially yours,
Arch B. Taylor, Jr.

Helps To Understanding Scripture Readings in *Day by Day*

By Rev. C. C. Baker

Sunday, December 30, Ephesians 2:1-10. We do not always realize how dependent we are upon God's grace for our salvation. Notice how

Thursday, January 3, Job 1:13-22. Satan contracted with God to test Job's faith through suffering (1:7-12; 2:3-6). List the calamities that came upon Job (1:13-19; 2:7-9). What was Job's philosophy concerning these things (1:20-21; 2:10)? Though prosperous, what place did Job's wealth evidently have in his scale of values? If your physical world collapsed, would your relation with God hold you steadfast? Observe that Job's wife was spared by Satan to "encourage" him (2:9) and his "friends" were spared to exhort him to repent (2:11-31:40). Does your relation with God hold you firm when those who misunderstand and misrepresent your motives bear false witness against you? In what difficult circumstances have you found Christ's presence sufficient to keep you steady?

Friday, January 4, Ephesians 5:15-20; *I Peter* 4:1-3. Take Paul's command of v.15a literally for your life, and examine carefully your plans for the day. Do you look upon the hours that are before you as full of opportunity to do things for the Lord (v.16a)? Why does Paul say you must be careful to make the most of your time (v.16b)? Will you spend the day according to your own human plans, or will you seek to know God's will for it (v.17)? Will your living be motivated by your own desires for physical pleasures, or will it be directed and empowered by the Holy Spirit (v.18)? What will you do specifically in the service of the cause of Christ (v.19a)? How much of your time do you think ought to be devoted to personal communion with God (vv.19b-20)? What does I Peter 4:1-3 add to these thoughts on the seriousness and singleness of purpose with which God would have you face the day?

Saturday, January 5, Ephesians 5:21-6:4. In ancient times the wife was regarded as the property of her husband. Notice the beauty of the Christian husband-wife relationship as it is depicted in Christ's relationship to the Church (vv.23-25,29). What was the purpose, as far as the Church was concerned, of Christ's giving Himself for her (vv.26-27)? How, then, is the Christian husband to treat his wife (vv.25, 28-29,33)? How intimately is the Church tied to Christ (vv.23-30)? How is the Church to regard Him who gave Himself for her (v.24)? What do you find in this picture of Christ and His Church to aid your home life? Do divine realities have a place in your home?

His Memorial Name

—Unto us a CHILD is born
Unto us a SON is given—

By Rev. Samuel McPh. Glasgow, D.D.

Who is the Babe, upon the straw, in the stable, behind the inn in Bethlehem?

Whose are those tiny ears that hear, but do not note, the echoes of the Angels' song over the Judean hills that holy night?

There was a hush upon those hills as the Heaven-born carol broke the silence of the centuries:—

"Glory to God in the highest,
and on earth peace,
good will toward men."

Isaiah, with prophetic eye, sees the dim distant glory and cries out:—

"For unto us a child is born,
unto us a Son is given: and
the government shall be upon His shoulder:
and His name shall be called Wonderful
Counsellor,
the mighty God, the everlasting Father,
The Prince of Peace.
Of the increase of His government and peace
there shall be no end, upon the throne of David,
and upon his kingdom, to order it, and to
establish it with judgment and with justice
from henceforth even forever. The zeal of
the LORD of hosts will perform this." Is.9:6,7

Heaven's supreme gift to men, rests in a manger, in the city of David. The recurring generations have cried; "Oh Lord how long?" And now, O what a "NOW"; He has come:-He is here: "a Child,—a Son"! No longer the slow, dragging, centuries test the faith of the faithful. The climaxing of the coming of the Christ has emerged in Bethlehem.

What marvel then that a broken, tired, lost world again at Christmas turns its heart's hope to the Babe born in Bethlehem centuries ago?

Here is HIS MEMORIAL NAME, a prophetic, pen portrait of His character. The picture fits into man's life at four focal points of universal, critical need.

WONDERFUL COUNSELOR — Wisdom — HE KNOWS: for man's ignorance, his misty shadows, unsolved problems, baffled mind, and his unanswered quests.

MIGHTY GOD — Power — HE CAN: for man's weakness, his conscious limitations, his impotence to secure and hold life's greater values.

EVERLASTING FATHER — Love — HE CARES: for man's inarticulate cry, his hidden heart-appeal, his yearning, homesick soul.

PRINCE OF PEACE — Peace — HE WILL: for man's restlessness, his life's friction, its failure and frustration.

WONDERFUL COUNSELOR — WISDOM — HE KNOWS

Life is marked and marred by a recurring sense of incompletion. Our vaunted knowledge is so limited and fragmentary and in constant change even about essentials. We find it silent on life's supreme essential — GOD. Man, by searching, cannot find out God. Scholarship fails to unveil the Saviour men need.

All that science can do is to find some of the facts that God has created and hidden away in His universe. The WONDERFUL COUNSELOR tells us what they mean and what to do with them that they may really serve and bless us. He can properly arrange them according to their purpose, their value and their potentiality. How ignorant we are of ourselves, our origin, our present life, and our destiny! What confused and twisted ideas we have about sin and its tragedy, about God and His nature! The greater our circle of knowledge, the vaster the unknown beyond! But Jesus, the WONDERFUL COUNSELOR, knew God, His Father; He knew man and what was in man. He can speak a word of light and life to every generation, to every listening, humble, obedient spirit.

To us a child of hope is born,
To us a Son is given,
Him shall the tribes of earth obey,
Him all the hosts of Heav'n.

THE MIGHTY GOD — POWER — HE CAN

All man's efforts reach their limits so soon. We can do so little about so many things with which our lives are involved. Man dreams but he cannot execute, man feels but he cannot satisfy the soul's deepest eagerness. There's a sense of frustration after all human striving. Man finds that he cannot control the forces he has discovered and liberated.

What strength and hope is spoken to our hearts when we see the Mighty God, the Creator, sustaining and harmonizing as Sovereign the physical, mental and moral universe. "Unto

poor human efforts to find peace. This old world is out of joint, tension is the tyrant today. All the oiling of the ages has failed to make it run smoothly. It jolts and creaks and groans its weary way through the centuries.

One of the finest testimonies that a Christian can give today is his serenity, exposing the fact that the peace of God which passeth understanding is keeping his heart and mind through Christ Jesus, who was born in a Manger while the angels sang.

We should be Christians of the conscious fellowship as we catch and keep step with the PRINCE who is at our side.

Our Lord Christ completely fulfills "The Name" Saying "I Know, I Can, I Care," then fronting the cross He cries - "I Will."

And, what underscores and underwrites our confidence that all this shall come to pass? What signature did the old prophet find for so glorious a promise as this? How can we be sure? "THE ZEAL OF THE LORD OF HOSTS WILL PERFORM THIS."

And I heard as it were the voice of a
great multitude,
And as the voice of many waters,
And as the voice of mighty thunderings,
Saying——
ALLELUIA: FOR THE LORD GOD
OMNIPOTENT REIGNETH.

God's Unspeakable Gift

By Rev. J. Russell Woods, Th.M.

"Thanks be unto God, for His unspeakable Gift."
—2 Cor. 9:15.

Christmas is the time for giving and receiving gifts, because this season of the year commemorates the Gift of God's Son at Christmas.

Paul spoke of the Gift in our text.

The Gift that was precious and valuable, because of the Gift itself: God's Son, Jesus Christ, Who had been the Lord of Glory from all eternity; Who was born as a baby in Bethlehem; Who came to be the Saviour of the world. A gift, of course, is free, and all we need to do is to believe to receive the Gift of God.

And, yet, so many people think they must pay for Salvation, they must do things, they must be a certain kind of people to receive God's Gift. And some gifts are so valuable we can use and enjoy them for years. Along with God's Gift, we receive the blessings of salvation: the forgiveness of sins and joy and peace; we receive Eternal Life: the Life that begins now, the Christian Life, and the Life that, in Christ will never end; we become the Children of God and the Friends of Jesus.

The Gift was "gift-wrapped," with the beautiful Christmas stories: There were Angels, who delivered God's Message, of a Saviour born, and who sang the first Christmas Carol; there was "the Glory of the Lord that shone round about them"; there were shepherds who came to Bethlehem, found the Babe, told of the Child, and returned glorifying God"; there was a Star in the Western sky; and there were Wise Men, who followed the Star, who worshipped the young Child, and presented their gifts: gold and frankincense and myrrh."

Our gifts at Christmas-time are gift-wrapped, and we enjoy the bright paper, the ribbons and the decorations; but we open them that we may also enjoy the gifts. Too often we linger with the "wrappings" of God's Gift and fail to find God's Son as our Saviour and Lord.

And Paul called it an "Unspeakable Gift."

With us today, "unspeakable" means something that is bad, that ought not to be mentioned. But Paul was referring to the Gift of God's Son, his Saviour and Lord, it must have a good meaning, and it is used here the only time in the whole Bible. "Unspeakable" because we cannot tell all about it, so important that words fail us. We cannot say too much about it, we cannot speak of it too often. We cannot understand nor fully explain it, but we can receive and enjoy the Gift. Many of us do not understand all about a gasoline engine, but we drive and enjoy our cars; we do not understand all about electricity, but we use and enjoy electrical appliances.

Paul also spoke of the Giver in our text:

"HIS unspeakable Gift," it was from God, it was God's Gift.

God is the Lord of Heaven and earth, Who possesses all things, He is perfectly able to give "good gifts." His "Checks" are good for any amount. God is our Father in heaven, and so is willing to give. He knows what things we have need of; and Jesus said "If ye being evil know how to give good gifts unto your children, how much more will your Heavenly Father give good things to them that ask Him."

God has given the greatest Gift of all, His Son, His Only Son. It shows that God really does love us, and, in Romans, Paul referred to it as the guarantee of other blessings to follow, "He that spared not His own Son, but delivered Him up for us all, how shall He not also with Him, freely give us all things?" If God started off with the Greatest Gift of all, surely He would give other gifts we might need.
Then Paul spoke of our response to God's Gift.

"Thanks be unto God," there will be appreciation and gratitude in our hearts for the gift and for His "thought" of us; and there will be the expression of our appreciation in the words that we speak to Him, and in the lives we live.

Before the expression of thanks, we have usually received a gift. We have already received the Lord Jesus as our Saviour and Lord. We have already received this gift from God and so we say "Thank You" to God.

After we say "Thank you," we use the gift and say, "We will think of you as we enjoy it." We will use God's Gift and we will think of Him as we enjoy it. We will love God and His Son; we will follow Him and have fellowship with Him; we will live with Him and for Him, as we witness of Him to all men.

And we will offer gifts to Him: gifts of our love and heart's adoration; the service and loyalty of our lives; gifts of money for the service of His Church; and gifts to others in His Name, for Jesus said, "Inasmuch as ye did it unto one of the least of these my brethren, ye did it unto Me."

A young missionary landed in Shanghai, China, where she was met and welcomed by an older missionary, a friend of the family. She

(Continued to bottom of page 13)

The Ladder From Heaven

By The Rev. M. A. Hopkins, D.D.

Gen. 28:10-22; John 1:43-51; Isa. 9:6.

A man named Jacob had a dream, "and, ehold, a ladder set up on the earth, and ıe top of it reached to heaven; and behold, ıe angels of God ascending and descending n it. And, behold, Jehovah stood above it."

This was no ordinary dream, but one in- ›ired by the Spirit of God, and in which the ternal God revealed Himself to Jacob. The ıdder with the angels ascending and descending n it symbolized communion between God and ıan, intercourse between heaven and earth. For ne end of the ladder rested on the earth, and ıe top reached to heaven. At the bottom was ıe man Jacob; at the top was the Lord God limself. Between the two were the ascend- ıg and descending angels, carrying up man's esires to God and bringing down God's bless- ıgs to man. The ascending is put first, because hile Jacob was unaware of their presence the ngels of God had already descended and were y his side. For he said, "Surely Jehovah is ı this place and I knew it not." Before he as aware of it the angels were there, and when e beheld them they were first ascending, and ıen descending. What a comfort to know that ᵣen when we are not aware of His presence, od is with us?

Jacob's dream was not only an inspired dream, ut it was prophetic of the far distant future. or some eighteen hundred years later a man ımed Jesus said: "Verily, verily, I say unto ›u, ye shall see the heaven opened, and the ıgels of God ascending and descending upon ıe Son of man."

From the order of the words "ascending and ›scending" it is very evident that Jesus was ferring to Jacob's dream and the ladder he w. The ladder that Jacob dreamed of, and l that it symbolized of communion with God as fully realized in the Lord Jesus Christ. sus Himself is the LADDER set up on the rth, the top of which reaches to heaven, and ı Him the angels of God are ascending and ›scending. He is the sole and perfect medium communication between God and man. "For ere is one God, and one mediator between od and men, the man Christ Jesus, I Tim. 2:5.

Now ladders are built to reach heights that uld not be reached without them. They are metimes disappointing when they are set up ıd it is found that they do not reach far ıough. Or they may be worse than disap- ›inting if they break down under the load ıt upon them.

A ladder that is not long enough, or that not strong enough, or that has broken rungs, is worse than useless. Such are all man's efforts to reach God — all man-made religions. Men have set up ladders on the earth, but the tops of them do not reach heaven. They are not long enough. They are not strong enough. They have many broken rungs in them.

But God has let down a LADDER from heaven. It is long enough to reach all the way down to earth, to the lowest depths of sin and misery into which men have sunken. It is strong enough to bear all the weight that men can put upon it. It will never break down. There are no broken rungs in this ladder. A ladder is a simple homely affair, but it is absolutely indispensable if one wants to climb out of a hole.

In the carpenter shop at Nazareth there were doubtless ladders. Jesus Himself had used them, and probably had made them. He knew what they were for; and it is significant that the Son of God and Saviour of men, likened Himself to a ladder: "Verily, verily, I say unto you, ye shall see heaven opened, and the angels of God ascending and descending upon the Son of man."

The prophet Isaiah prophesied: "Unto us a child is born, unto us a son is given." The angels announced to the shepherds: "There is born to you this day in the city of David a Saviour, who is Christ the Lord." Unto us a child was born in His humanity, and unto us a Son was given in His deity. The ladder that Jacob saw has truly been set up on the earth in the person of the Son of man, resting on the earth in His humanity, and reaching to heaven in His deity. "And no man hath ascended into heaven, but he that descended out of heaven, even the Son of man, who is in heaven," John 3:13. He is the only LADDER without broken rungs, and which, unlike all human ladders, does not come short of heaven's gate, nor break down under the weight imposed upon it.

"No one knoweth the Son save the Father; neither doth any know the Father save the Son, and he to whomsoever the Son willeth to reveal Him," Matt. 11:27. "I am the way, and the truth, and the life: no one cometh unto the Father, but by me," John 14:6.

The great German commentator Delitzsch has the following illuminating comment: "The Old Testament in relation to the New Testament is night. In this night there rise in opposite directions two stars of promise. The one describes its path from above downwards;

it is Jehovah who is about to come. The other describes its path from below upwards; it is the hope which rests on the seed of David, the prophecy of the Son of David, uttered at first in tones wholly human, and only earthly. These two stars meet at last. They mingle so as to form but one. The night vanishes, and it is day. This one star is Jesus Christ, Jehovah and David's Son in One Person, the King of Israel, and at the same time the Redeemer of the world; in a word, the God-man; blessed be He!"

To return to the figure of the ladder, our LADDER is composed of two parts, the human nature and the divine nature of Christ, "who was born of the seed of David according to the spirit of holiness, by the resurrection from the dead," Rom. 1:3-4. "The only Redeemer of God's elect is the Lord Jesus Christ, who being the eternal Son of God, became man, and so was and continueth to be, God and man in two distinct natures and one person forever." There are many strong and unbreakable rungs in our wonderful LADDER, some of which are as follows:

Rung I. *The virgin birth.*

It was by means of the virgin birth that this LADDER came down to earth. "The Son of God became man by taking unto himself a true body and a reasonable soul, being conceived by the Holy Spirit in the womb of the virgin Mary, and born of her, yet without sin."

Without a true human nature our LADDER could not reach down to earth where we sinful men live, and struggle, and die. God promised to Adam and Eve that the "Seed of the woman" should overcome the serpent. This promise was fulfilled literally in the virgin birth of our Lord, who was born without a human father.

This great event was prophesied by Isaiah: "Behold a virgin shall conceive, and bear a son, and thou shalt call his name Immanuel," Isa. 7:14. And Micah prophesied of this event: "But thou, Bethlehem Ephrathah, which are little to be among the thousands of Judah, out of thee shall One come forth unto me that is to be a ruler in Israel; whose goings forth are from of old, from everlasting. Therefore will he give them up, until the time when she who travaileth hath brought forth. Then the residue of his brethren shall return unto the children of Israel. And he shall stand and feed his flock in the strength of Jehovah; in the majesty of Jehovah his God, and they shall abide; for now shall He be great unto the ends of the earth. And this Man shall be our peace," Micah 5:2-5. "And Mary said unto the angel, How shall this be, seeing I know not a man? And the angel answered and said unto her, The Holy Spirit shall come upon thee, and the power of the Most High shall overshadow thee; wherefore also the holy thing which is begotten shall be called the Son of God," Luke 1:34,35.

Rung II. *His holy life.*

The virgin birth of Christ was the basis of His sinless life. The heathen myths contain stories of virgin births, but in none of them is virgin birth made the basis of a holy and sinless life. Herein the Bible record of Christ's virgin birth is utterly unique and different. A sinless life in a sinful world is as great a moral miracle as a virgin birth is in the physical world. And our Lord claimed to be holy and sinless. To the Jews He threw down this challenge, "Which of you convicteth me of sin?" John 8:46. "The prince of this world cometh, and hath nothing in me," John 14:30. Pilate went out again unto the Jews, and saith unto them, I find no crime in him," John 18:38. The Apostle John who knew Him most intimately said, "And ye know that He was manifested to take away sins; and in Him was no sin," I John 2:3-5. "For such a high priest became us, holy, guileless, undefiled, separate from sinners, and made higher than the heavens," Heb. 7:25.

Rung III. *His wonderful teachings.*

At the end of the Sermon on the Mount we have this record: "And it came to pass, that when Jesus had finished these words, the multitudes were astonished at His teaching: for He taught them as one having authority, and not as their scribes, Matt. 7:28,29. Those who went to arrest Jesus, when asked why they did not bring Him, answered, "Never man so spake," John 7:46. Even when a lad of only twelve years He astounded the learned men in the temple, who "were amazed at His understanding and His answers," Luke 2:47. Of His own words He said, "The words that I have spoken unto you are spirit and are life," John 6:63. All fulfilled the prophecy of Isaiah who said that He would be called "Wonderful Counsellor," Isa. 9:6.

Rung IV. *His miracles.*

On the day of Pentecost Peter said, "Ye men of Israel, hear these words: Jesus of Nazareth, a man approved of God unto you by mighty works and wonders and signs which God did by Him in the midst of you, as ye yourselves know," Acts 2:22. The purpose of these miracles was twofold: (1) To convince the people that He was the Son of God. "The works which the Father hath given me to accomplish, the very works that I do, bear witness of me that the Father hath sent me, John 5:36. "Believe me that I am in the Father and the Father in me: or else believe me for the very works' sake," John 14:11. (2) The second purpose of the miracles was to convince people that He had authority to forgive sin. After healing the paralytic, He said: "Which is easier, to

are "Looking for the blessed hope and appearing of our great God and Saviour Jesus Christ," Titus 2:13. See also Acts 1:11; Heb. 9:24-27.

Such is God's wonderful LADDER, let down out of heaven for us sinful men, so that we can climb on it out of the miry pit of sin and wickedness and woes in which we live, Psalm 40:1-3. Let us lay hold of it by faith. It is a perfect LADDER, reaching all the way to heaven to the throne of God. It cannot be improved on. All the rungs are absolutely necessary from the first to the last. Some would omit one or the other, but what is left is a poor broken thing that will not avail for the salvation of sinful men. Let us take the LADDER just as God has given it to us. "I am the WAY, and the TRUTH, and the LIFE. No man cometh unto the Father but by ME." Christ is

"The only LADDER that faith will trust.

Faith wants no earthly stepping-stones,
Nor ladders men devise,
The only LADDER faith will trust
Was lowered from the skies.

This LADDER Jacob first beheld
In that eventful night
When angels hovered round his bed,
And God spoke from the height.

Christ is the LADDER long enough
To bridge the awful span
Between earth and Paradise,
Once lost by sinful man.

Christ is the LADDER strong enough
All contrite souls to bear
Up to the height of Gloryland,
And lead them safely there."

—W. M. Czamanske.

GOD'S UNSPEAKABLE GIFT

(Continued from page 10)

will never forget the kindness and a remark of the older missionary, for when she expressed her appreciation and asked, How can I ever thank you enough? Her friend replied, "Do the same for someone else."

We say to God, We certainly appreciate your Gift, how can we ever thank you enough? And God replies, "Do the same for someone else, freely ye have received, freely give."

Sometimes Christmas packages are unclaimed in the Post Office. And some people do not receive their gifts. Have you claimed and received your Gift from God? Because we have received God's Gift, we will appreciate the Gift, and we will use and enjoy it; we will love the Giver; we will tell others of the Lord Jesus; and, with Paul, we will say,

"Thanks be unto God, for His unspeakable Gift"

LESSON FOR DECEMBER 30

By THE REV. J. KENTON PARKER

The New Heavens And The New Earth

Background Scripture: Revelation 21

Devotional Reading: Revelation: 7:9-17

There are no chapters in the Bible which surpass these last two in beauty. They give us a picture, in symbols, and types, of the Eternal Home of God's people, and form a most fitting climax and consummation to the Plan of Salvation, the Plan which God has for this world in which we live. There are three very simple, but very meaningful symbols used: (1) The Holy City, (2) The River of Life, (3) The Tree of Life. Our lesson takes up only the first of these but we should finish the fascinating story by reading and meditating upon chapter 22. Where could we find more expressive symbols than a through the Bible to picture spiritual things.

The New Heavens and the New Earth are described as the Holy City, New Jerusalem. One of the first things which men undertook, after the Flood, was to build a city. They said, Go to, let us build us a city and a tower. Men have been city-builders ever since, and the history of the world is centered around many of these cities.

Dr. F. W. Boreham, in his book, The Drums of Dawn, has one chapter on the Tower of Babel. Let me quote some of his concluding words: "The Tower of Babel, therefore, was a Tower of Blunders. Every brick was a blunder. These early builders were wrong in their *motive*, wrong in their *method*, wrong in their *materials* — wrong in everything." "Their motive was wrong," he says earlier. What was their motive? "To make us a name." Their method was wrong: their method was like the Battle of the Waters, a battle between the geyser and the cloud. The best things do not spring up, like the geyser, only to fall back again on the earth; *they come down*. The "bread from heaven," of which Jesus spoke, comes down; is rained down. The divine fire, which Elijah witnessed on Carmel, came down from heaven. The New Jerusalem, the Holy City, comes down from heaven. Then, their materials were wrong. They had brick for stone and slime for mortar. You cannot build a road to heaven with bricks and slime. Benjamin Franklin tried it; Martin Luther tried it before he discovered that "the just shall live by faith." (Most of this quoted from Boreham.)

The history of the cities of the world discloses the same earthly pattern for them that the men tried in Genesis eleven. They speak of the vanity and egotism of "earth-dwellers." They are built up from a foundation of sand; they are constructed of earthy materials. Abraham, in contrast to these, was seeking a city that hath foundations, whose builder and maker is God.

Since we recently studied the passage selected for our Devotional Readings, I wish to limit our study to this most beautiful chapter (chap. 21) Remember that this is a symbolic picture. But also remember that the spiritual realities so symbolized are far more precious than the symbols, however lovely they are.

I. *The Holy City Comes Down From God Out of Heaven:* 1:3.

We talk a great deal these days about "building up" the kingdom of God, and there is a sense in which we do build it up, but I cannot help but feel that some of the mistakes we have made are similar to those made so long ago by the builders of Babel. What is our motive, for instance, when we spend a million dollars for a new church? Is it to make us a name? to have the biggest church in our city? In our methods, do we not sometimes use the "geyser method" rather than the "cloud method." After Moses built the Tabernacle, and Solomon the Temple, it was only when "The glory of the Lord filled the house of the Lord," that they became real dwelling places for God. The real glory of a church *must come down from heaven.* Do we ever try to build up the kingdom of God out of "bricks and slime"?

Let us see clearly that the Holy City that John saw "came down from heaven."

II. *The Holy City has no Ugly Spots or Blemishes:* 4-8.

1. What are these "ugly spots"?

Every earthly city has been marred and scarred by SIN. Indeed, the word "City" and the word

ous things He hath prepared for those that love Him." He reveals them to us through His Spirit, and this is what John is doing here. In Proverbs we are told that Wisdom is far better than silver and gold and precious stones. So, the realities of heaven are far better than these symbols, however wonderful they are. What is it that makes a city beautiful? Is it not beautiful people whose hearts are filled with Purity and Peace and Love? Just as the Lamb, the Saviour, is far better than a jasper stone, so are these spiritual realities far better than gold and precious stones. We shall be "like Him," and He is the brighest Jewel of heaven.

The City "had a wall great and high." This may represent our Safety. No Eastern city was considered safe unless it had a "wall"; a wall that excludes all its foes, and includes all who have a right to be there. In the Holy City we shall be safe from all that could harm us.

The City "had twelve gates." Like the "cities of refuge" in the Old Testament, this city had its "gates." It can be entered from every direction. Jesus said that they should come from the East and West and North and South.

The City "lieth foursquare." It is a perfect cube. There is plenty of room; there are "many mansions."

It has a beautiful Foundation. Abraham was seeking a city that had foundations; this is the City. Its foundation is as precious as the character and promises of God.

No Temple is needed, for God is now dwelling with His people. No need for sun or moon, for the glory of God enlightens it, and the Lamb is the light thereof.

Such a Place; such a Home; such a City, the Saviour has gone to prepare for us! Will it be this earth of ours, purified by fire, filled with righteousness; all the "ugly spots" removed? Will the final Home of God's people be a New Heaven and a New Earth? The meek shall inherit the earth and shall delight themselves in the abundance of peace. Of one thing we are sure, wherever that Place, that Home, that City is, it will be what John is trying to describe for us in these beautiful and precious symbols. No wonder that the hearts of the Pilgrims were "ravished" as they talked together by the way. Read and study chapter 22.

Tithe

It's not what I'd do with a million
If riches e'er be my lot,
It's what I'm doing at present
With the dollar and a quarter I've got!

YOUNG PEOPLES Department

YOUTH PROGRAM FOR DECEMBER 30

By THE REV. B. HOYT EVANS

Watch Night

Scripture: Matthew 24:42-51

Suggested Hymns:

"Who Is On The Lord's Side?"

"Take Time To Be Holy"

"A Charge To Keep I Have"

"Take My Life And Let It Be Consecrated"

(This program can be used for the regular Sunday program for the young people, or it can be adapted for use as a Watch Night program on New Year's Eve. If you do plan to use this material for a real Watch Night service, you will need to do some careful planning to make sure that your program will be concluded just at the midnight hour. Discussion periods and hymn singings are flexible, so you can use them and adjust your timing. It is most appropriate and effective to be actually in prayer when the midnight hour strikes.)

Program Leader:

The term "Watch Night" is usually associated with the coming of a new year. The idea, of course, is that people come together in a Christian service of worship and see the New Year in with prayer and praise to God. This is a very worthy kind of watching . . . this watching for the New Year . . . but as Christians, there are other things for which we should be watching all through the year. While we are thinking about seeing in this year of 1957, let us give thought to some of the matters which deserve our earnest consideration on each of this year's 365 days.

First Speaker:

On the ships of the Navy watches are posted to protect the ships and their crews from harm and to warn when the enemy approaches. Christians have a spiritual enemy who is ever on the lookout for ways to lead them astray and to cause them harm. On the night of His agony in the garden Jesus charged His disciples, "Watch and pray, that ye enter not into temptation." The Scriptures warn us that Satan is a wily foe and that we should take every precaution to arm ourselves against him. In Ephesians 6:10-18 we find a description of the spiritual armor which is available for our warfare against the Devil. (Read these verses.) The armor will not be worth very much unless we are able to recognize our enemy when he comes to attack us. If we would ward off his temptations, we must ask God for wisdom and strength, and we must be willing to watch faithfully. The new year should be a year of watching for the Devil and for his temptations. (Discuss with the young people how to watch for and avoid temptations.)

Second Speaker:

Every newspaper, every magazine, and every publishing company has its proof readers. These proof readers are trained to observe very carefully, and it is their responsibility to find all the errors and mistakes in the written material before it goes to the presses to be printed in its final form. They are watchers for errors. We who are Christians need to be watching for spiritual error. The Bible warns us about believing everything we see and hear. Jesus said, "Take heed that ye be not deceived: for many shall come in my name, saying, I am Christ; and the time draweth near: go ye not therefore after them."

In I Corinthians 16:13 we read, "Watch ye, stand fast in the faith." This does not mean that we are to be suspicious of everything and everyone, but that our knowledge of the Scriptures should increase so that we may measure what we read and hear by the standard of God's revealed truth. (Ask for suggestions of ways in which young people can be on watch for spiritual error.)

Third Speaker:

In order to be a good quarterback on a football team a young man must be able to see opportunities for gaining yardage. A quarterback, among other things, is a watcher for opportunities. Christians ought to be watching for spiritual opportunities constantly. Before there can be any worthwhile service rendered to the Lord, the opportunities for service must be seen and seized. (Read Matthew 25:1-30.) A truly successful Christian is one who takes seriously the responsibility of watching for opportunities. (Make a list of opportunities which young people normally have for serving the Lord. Ask for suggestions from your group.)

Fourth Speaker:

When Jesus was on earth in the days of His flesh, He said that He would go away, but that He would also come again to receive His own. There are many passages in the Bible which indicate that Christians should be watching for His return. "For our conversation is in heaven; from whence we also look for the Saviour, the Lord Jesus Christ." Phil. 3:20.

"Looking for that blessed hope, and the glorious appearing of the great God and our Saviour Jesus Christ." Titus 2:13. "So Christ was once offered to bear the sins of many; and unto them that look for him shall he appear the second time without sin unto salvation." Heb. 9:28. "Watch therefore: for ye know not what hour your Lord doth come." Matthew 24:42. As Christians we ought always to be watching for and keeping in readiness for the return of our Saviour, because the Bible makes it very clear that none can predict when that time will be. (Ask the young people to suggest ways of preparing for the coming of Christ.)

The Changeless Christ

By Vernon W. Patterson

O changeless Christ within a changing world,
Unshaken Thou through all the shocks of time!
Though 'gainst Thee Satan's darts are ever hurled,
Thou art the same in every age and clime.

Unchanged the love that brought Thee down to earth,
Unchanged the grace that bought and keeps the soul,
Unchanged the matchless wonders of Thy worth,
Though earth remove and heaven roll up as scroll.

Eternal pow'r, unbounded love Thou art,
And grace beyond the ken of sinful man;
Though sense deceive and sin defile the heart,
Thou failest not through all life's fitful span.

Man's glory fades, all earthly things decay;
But Thou remainest, risen Lord above.
Amid earth's raging storms and darkening day,
Thou art eternal Light, and Life, and Love.

Dear loving Jesus, tender, pure, and fair,
As Thou didst call the children to Thy breast,
Enfold us in Thine arms and let us there
Forget our cares and find in Thee our rest.

Christmas in the Congo

By Gertrude Hillegist Cousar

Here at Bibanga, as in every place where the Birthday of our Lord Jesus is remembered, there is a glow in the Christians' hearts as this beautiful season approaches.

Weeks before the Birthday of Jesus groups of young people are gathering together to practice the old familiar carols, or learning some new hymns which they will sing in the choir or pageant. The Hallelujah Chorus is always a favorite with the young men and they really make the air ring with its majesty. It is a time of great rejoicing and thanksgiving, and one hears humming, or whistling, or harmonizing of these favorites.

Congolese Christians love being in or seeing the pageant each year. All ages come—from the eldest to the tiniest babies sleeping in their mothers' arms. Passages are read from the Old Testament foretelling of the Saviour's coming and from the Gospels, telling of His miraculous birth and the visit of the Shepherds to the Infant Jesus in the Manger, with Mary His mother and Joseph tenderly watching over the Child. A light in the manger represents the Christ Child's presents. And always the coming of the Wise Men with their gifts of gold, frankincense and myrrh—each part enacted with quiet reverence and dignity.

Pageants are given on the mission stations but out in the villages farther away Christians will decorate their chapels with palm fronds and whatever kind of flowers they can find—from the bright yellow Japanese sunflowers to purple bougainvillea, and worship Him with their evangelists, pastors, or elders.

On the morning of Jesus' Birthday every Christian who can navigate goes to the nearest church or chapel to worship—others come just for this special occasion. The choir of young people and the congregation sing with the spirit and the uplifted voice. How our people love to sing!

At the Leper Camp their chapel will be decorated with garlands of palm fronds and flowers. These greatly afflicted people will be all dressed in their best clothes and they will sing with a fervor that outrivals all others. To them Jesus' Birthday means hope. They genuinely appreciate His coming the first time to deliver them from their sins and look forward with a lively hope to His return when He will give them new and glorified bodies. Their love is evidenced in their unusual and generous sharing—their gifts exceed all offerings elsewhere.

This is a time of rededication of life and loyalty to Him. This season and day center around Jesus. It is a privilege to sing praises and bring gifts to Him, to tell the world that Jesus belongs to us and we belong to Him and—that He offers to whomsoever will come to Him the same rich blessings and promises of Life Eternal. All praise to His Name—JESUS! Can you think of a more wonderful way to remember Jesus' Birthday?

A Christmas Message

As we approach the glad Christmas season I am wondering if we are giving thought for the peoples of the world for whom Christmas has no meaning.

There are people waiting,
Over all the earth,
To hear the Christmas story
That tells of Jesus' birth.

We have this story still. The matchless story told by the angels on a Judean hillside to the shepherds nearly two thousand years ago: "Fear not for behold I bring you good tidings of great joy—unto you is born this day in the city of David, a Saviour which is Christ, the Lord." Is that the *exact* message? No, I left out an important part: "I bring you good tidings of great joy which shall be to all people." The good news was not for the chosen few—but for all people. We are among the fortunate who know the story. It is our responsibility to those who are still waiting.

There are people listening
They have waited, oh, so long.
To hear the glorious echo
Of the angels song.

The song sung by the angels, "Glory to God in the highest and on earth peace good will to men." This song has echoed and re-echoed through the ages by those who know Him who said: "My peace I give unto you."—"In the world ye shall have tribulation, but be of good cheer I have overcome the world." Because we know this blessed truth and comfort we have a song in our hearts and on our lips. A song of glory to God and a message of peace to men. This song can not be stilled by wars, plagues or tribulations. It is a song of God's redeeming love to be sung to all nations.

There are people waiting
To hear from you and me
About our precious Saviour
And His death on Calvary.

A Saviour to share! "You know the grace of the Lord Jesus that though He was rich yet for your sakes He became poor that ye through His poverty might be rich." So wrote the Apostle Paul, and spent his life in telling others of Christ. Many hundreds of years before Isaiah had written: "For unto us a Child is born, unto us a Son is given, and the government shall be upon His shoulder, and His name shall be called Wonderful, Counselor, the mighty God, the everlasting Father, the Prince of Peace." This Child whose birth was heralded by the song of angels, and the brightness of a shining star, that first Christmas night, was to be called Jesus for He was to save His people from their sins—"There is no other name given under heaven whereby we must be saved." No other but Jesus.

If we did not have this story to tell, this song to sing and this Saviour to show there would be no Christmas. May we keep this in mind that we will know the happiness of keeping His day as He would have us.

Help us keep Thy day, Lord,
  So all people will see
And follow our example
  To serve and honor Thee."

—Alice Barbour Bennett

Story of Silent Night

On Christmas Eve in 1818, Franz Gruber, church organist in the little town of Oberndorf, Bavaria, made an alarming discovery. The organ would not play!

For several days previous to Christmas Eve, Oberndorf had been snowbound. Gruber, knowing there was no one in Oberndorf capable of repairing the organ, was afraid there would be no music for Christmas. He could hardly imagine Christmas without music.

Quickly he went to the vicar, Joseph Mohr, and told him his story. He asked Mohr to write a new Christmas song which could be easily sung without the use of the organ.

Later as Mohr sat reading Christmas stories from his Bible . . . "Unto you is born this day in the city of David a Saviour . . . ," the words welled up in his soul like a heavenly anthem. Long into the night he sat meditating on them. As the full meaning gripped his soul, he wrote a poem about the wondrous story.

Early the next day, Gruber took the newly written words and composed a melody. Now the people were gathering at the church. There was one man who could pick out tunes on a guitar. He was asked to accompany the new carol.

The people of Oberndorf loved the song immediately . . . and thus Joseph Mohr and Franz Gruber gave the world one of the most beautiful and best loved of the Christmas carols. It was not long before the Tyrolean Singers took the song to America. For years it went under the title, "Song from Heaven." It was more quickly and better known in America than in Europe and today, "Silent Night" is sung in nearly every language of the world.

A Time for Remembering

From Chile to Ceylon, from Paris to the Philippines, American Foundation for Overseas Blind, Inc., is making steady headway in its continuous crusade in behalf of the world's blind persons.

The accomplishments attained thus far were made possible only through the generosity and devotion of the American public. But even as we review and rejoice at the advances which have taken place, our thoughts turn to the needs still to be met; the goals still to be fulfilled.

The poignant picture of 14 million sightless persons striving desperately for a chance at life—a life of usefulness and independence—is not readily forgotten.

In this season, the traditional time for remembering, we know that our friends throughout the nation will give special thought to the plight of the world's sightless.

In the same spirit of dedication, we pledge ourselves to the continuance and expansion of our relief, rehabilitation and education services to the visually handicapped the world over.

—Bulletin—American Foundation for Overseas Blind, Inc.

CHILDRENS Page

A Brave Fighter

David kept his father's . One day a came and attacked the and carried a little away. David after the beast and it, and set the free.

David played on a very sweetly and he could a sling extra well. One day he was invited to the palace to before the who liked it so much that he invited David to come and stay. Another day the prophet Samuel visited David's home and under God's direction anointed him to be the king of Israel.

(more about David next week) E.

CHILDREN: Please write and tell us how you like our new page written just for you.

Editor

NEWS of CHURCHES around the World

THE GENERAL FUND AGENCIES AND INTERCHURCH AGENCIES

Statement of Receipts

Jan. 15 - Nov. 30, 1956

THE GENERAL FUND AGENCIES

Budget for 1956	$846,581.00
Received from Jan. 15th through November 30, 1956	420,826.41
Percentage of annual budget received to date	49.71
Balance needed for the year	425,754.59

INTERCHURCH AGENCIES

Budget for 1956	$ 21,495.00
Received from Jan. 15th through November 30, 1956	13,011.32
Percentage of annual budget received to date	60.1
Balance needed for the year	8,483.68

World Missions Receipts

Budget for 1956	$3,300,000.00
Receipts to Date	2,543,584.24
Percentage of Annual Budget Received for 1956	77.07%
Balance Needed for 1956	756,415.76

ALABAMA

Birmingham—First Presbyterian Church, here, celebrated 50 years of the progress of the church with a loyalty dinner December 1.

Most of the more than 700 member congregation attended the meeting to discuss plans for future growth of the church, including the new education building which is now being completed.

Mr. William J. Rushton presented a five-year plan for paying the $100,000 due on the new addition. Dr. Marion Dick discussed projected plans for the growth of the church and Dr. Richard T. Eastwood presented plans whereby the church can grow in service to the community. Mrs. Allen P. Brinson, president-elect of the Women of the Church, drew an analogy between the growth of the church and the building of the temple in Jerusalem by King Solomon.

Music was presented by the church choir and visiting musicians under the direction of Vernon Skooge. The dinner was given by two of the deacons, Henry McClellan, and Wilbern Wengel. Dr. Edward V. Ramage is pastor of the church.

GEORGIA

Decatur—Dr. Richard T. Gillespie, professor of homiletics at Columbia Theological Seminary in Decatur, has accepted a call to become pastor of the First Presbyterian Church, Anderson, S. C., effective January 1st.

Dr. Gillespie has been serving as professor of homiletics at Columbia for the past six years.

He is a native of Florence, S. C., and a graduate of Presbyterian College, Columbia Seminary, Emory University, and Union Theological Seminary in Richmond. He has served as pastor of Rock Spring Church, Atlanta, and the First Presbyterian Church in Thomasville, Ga.

For six years Dr. Gillespie was Candidate Secretary of the Board of World Missions before coming to Decatur in 1950.

Recently he has assisted in the organizing and developing of Memorial Drive Presbyterian Church near Atlanta.

Passing of Mrs. Vernon S. Broyles

Mrs. Vernon S. Broyles, Jr., wife of the pastor of North Avenue Presbyterian Church in Atlanta and former executive secretary of the Board of Church Extension, died December 2 at Emory University hospital in Atlanta. Mrs. Broyles had been ill for several months.

Funeral services were held December 4 at North Avenue Presbyterian Church, with Dr. J. Cecil Lawrence and the Rev. Kirk N. Nesbit officiating. Dr. Lawrence is associate pastor, and Mr. Nesbit is Minister to Students at North Avenue Church. Members of the Session and the Board of Deacons served as honorary escort.

Mrs. Broyles was a graduate of Mississippi State College for Women and taught at that college for five years after graduation. She was the daughter of the late Percy Virden and Mrs. Bena Maxwell Virden.

Dr. and Mrs. Broyles were married in 1935. They lived in Canton, Miss., until 1941 when Dr. Broyles came to Atlanta to be pastor at North Avenue Church. He was executive secretary of the Board of Church Extension from 1950-54, and after that returned to his former pastorate at the Atlanta church.

Besides her husband, Mrs. Broyles is survived by two daughters, Bena and Betsy Broyles of Atlanta, a son, Vernon S. Broyles III, a student at Davidson College, and a brother, Wilson Virden of Rolling Folk, Miss.

NORTH CAROLINA

Kinston — About 250 members of the First Presbyterian Church, Kinston, gathered recently for the groundbreaking of their new church. A description of the proposed structure was given at the ceremonies by F. E. Wallace, chairman of the executive committee of the building program. A message of congratulations and greetings was presented to the congregation by executive secretary Tom Davis of Albemarle Presbytery.

The proposed $314,000 church is expected to be completed in about one year. Four major units will make up the church: a fellowship hall, which will be used temporarily for church services; and at a later date, a sanctuary, an educational unit, and an administrative unit. Included in the educational unit will be a parlor, a music room and a chapel which will seat 134 people.

Wilmington—Dedication services for the newly completed Cape Fear Presbyterian Church here were held December 2.

Dr. E. D. Witherspoon, pastor of the St. Andrews-Covenant Presbyterian Church was speaker at the services. The Rev. J. A. Marrow, Jr., is pastor of the church which has a membership of 220.

The new building is a modern edifice valued at $75,000. It contains a sanctuary with a seating capacity of 300, 10 class rooms, a church office, pastor's study, kitchen and storage rooms.

SOUTH CAROLINA

Clinton—Two new regions launched their Presbyterian College Diamond Jubilee development program during the first week in December with dinner meetings.

Dr. W. Taliaferro Thompson, moderator of the General Assembly, delivered the main address at the dinners held in Charleston, S. C. on Dec. 3, and in Savannah, Ga., on December 4.

Savannah Presbytery has set a goal of $60,000 to be raised for Presbyterian College in the weeks ahead, while lower Charleston Presbytery has established a goal of $40,000. Upper Charleston Presbytery has reported $5,095 toward its $12,000 goal after the first report meeting.

In the upper Charleston area, centered around Orangeburg, thirty subscriptions were turned in as two churches in the area exceeded their established quotas. The Bamberg, S. C., Presbyterian Church reported $750.00 from four gifts to hit 171% of its quota, and the Allendale Presbyterian Church brought in $1,500 from five subscriptions to achieve 163% of its goal. The First Presbyterian Church of Orangeburg reported $2,395 from 19 gifts.

TENNESSEE

Nashville—Miss Helen Pemberton of our Mexico Mission arrived in the United States in November for her regular furlough.

Nashville — Miss Vivian Hodges of our West Brazil Mission is scheduled to return to the United States sometime in December for her furlough.

Miss Hodges is just completing her first term of service in Brazil where she has been serving in the evangelistic work of the mission. She first went to the field in 1951.

TEXAS

Dallas—Dr. Edward D. Grant, Director of Louisiana Institutions and former Executive Secretary of the Board of Christian Education in Richmond, was "Ladies Night" speaker at the Men's Club of the First Presbyterian Church, Dallas, at the last meeting of the club for 1956, held recently.

Dr. Grant, a native of Scotland, went to Louisiana in 1952 at the invitation of the newly organized Board of Institutions for the State of Louisiana. That Board had just assumed the functions of 22 separate state boards and agencies, including the supervision of 6 charity hospitals, 3 tuberculosis hospitals, 3 mental hospitals, 3 juvenile correctional schools, the state colony and training school for mental defectives, and the state prison system.

Dr. Grant's work has received national attention.

Kerrville — Groundbreaking ceremonies for the first unit of the Gus Schreiner Student Center have been held at Schreiner Institute, Presbyterian junior college here. Construction of the Center began immediately after a brief groundbreaking service, led by Dr. Andrew Edington, president of the school.

Board members present included Mr. W. Scott Schreiner, Mr. Charles Johnston, Mr. Louis Schreiner, the Rev. R. G. Ryan, and Mr. Gus Schreiner who took part in the actual groundbreaking.

The swimming pool for the center is expected to be ready for use in the spring of 1957. Detailed plans for the remainder of the building will be submitted to the Board of Trustees in January.

Besides the swimming pool, the student center will have offices, a post office, student snack bar, a game room with a three-lane bowling alley, ping-pong tables, a reading room, and a lounge. A large trophy case will be placed in the center to house the trophies that have been won by the students.

The center will be completely air conditioned.

Dallas—Billy Graham, world-known evangelist, spoke here recently at the First Presbyterian Church's Sundown Vespers. His message marked the sixth service in a two-month series emphasizing the theme, "Our Common Faith for These Uncommon Times."

Graham has preached face-to-face to more people than any minister in all of Christian history, having addressed more than 20,000,000 persons. Another 20,000,000 listen to his weekly "Hour of Decision" radio program. Over 1,000,000 persons have been converted under Dr. Graham's ministry.

Corpus Christi — Laymen of Presbyterian churches of the Corpus Christi area already are well along in their plans for a second intensive evangelistic effort, featuring a nationally known speaker, and held in the city auditorium.

Building on experience gained in the December, 1955, evangelistic crusade, the Presbyterian Committee on Evangelism for Corpus Christi has begun preparations for the March 17 - March 24, 1957 series that will feature Dr. Louis Evans, minister-at-large for the Presbyterian Church, U.S.A. The planners have already booked Del Mar Auditorium and held preliminary planning sessions with the ministers of the Corpus Christi Presbyterian churches, and with the presidents of all the Women of the Church groups in the city.

The Sessions of each church are being asked to approve plans, and to provide financial and programming help. Mr. Franklin Flato, a leading elder in the city, has been suggested as General Chairman, and already approved by votes of Sessions of five of the Presbyterian churches.

The 1955 series, for which Dr. William M. Elliott, pastor of the largest Presbyterian Church, U.S., congregation, at Highland Park Church,

Dallas, was the speaker, brought out record crowds and resulted in important additions to all churches. Designed as a revival, the series put hundreds of lay persons to work for the period, in cottage prayer groups, in visitation, in providing counseling for interested people, and in caring for a great number of children for whom baby-sitting services were provided in one of the churches while the series was being held in the auditorium.

THE RISE OF THE CULTS. Walter R. Martin. Zondervan. $2.00.

Mr. Martin possesses one of the most complete libraries on non-Christian cults in existence. It consists of over a thousand volumes. He has spent 10 years in research in the primary sources of cult history and theology. He has studied particularly the activities of non-Christian religions and cults where evangelical Christianity and its missionary efforts were involved.

In the introduction to this volume by Wilbur M. Smith he correctly observes, "Apart from sheer unbelief and the deep paganism of our modern civilization, the greatest hindrance to an acceptance of the saving gospel of Jesus Christ is the teaching of those false cults which, on the periphery of Christianity, deceivingly and inaccurately use many of the sacred terms of the true Christian faith. These cults are spreading with phenomenal speed, and by them millions are being led astray. . . . The danger is that too many in the Church, unacquainted with, and really uninterested in the history and actual teachings of these groups are lulled into a state of indifference toward them, or, even worse, into believing that these false religions are also a true way to God, whereas they lead to nothing else but eternal death." In this statement Dr. Smith sets forth succinctly what is involved in the church's concern as to the rise of the cults.

This volume presents a survey of the cult problem and then discusses Jehovah's Witnesses, Theosophy, Mormonism, Christian Science, Unity, and "Father Divine." The author closes with this appeal, "Let us therefore cease the petty squabbles that split the camp of true Israel today; rather let us join our forces to resist the onslaught of corrupt doctrines so evident in cultism."

It is difficult to write a book on this subject without becoming too technical for the layman or not thorough enough for the theologian. The author has succeeded in a remarkable way in presenting a volume that can be appreciated by both layman and theologian. He has rendered a signal service in presenting facts that will help readers to understand the differences between major cult deviations and the truths of the changeless gospel.

J.R.R.

TOOLS FOR BIBLE STUDY. Balmer H. Kelley and Donald G. Miller. John Knox Press. $2.00.

The eleven chapters in this volume appeared in successive issues of Interpretation. This work discusses such tools as concordances, New Testament lexicons, Bible dictionaries and encyclopedias, grammars of the Greek New Testament, archeology, Hebrew grammars and lexicons, Biblical geographies and atlases, commentaries and the Rabbinic writings.

Since there are 11 different authors we naturally expect different points of view and this is exactly what we find in this volume. Some of the chapters encourage the use of tools prepared by the liberals while others recommend tools developed by conservatives.

The tools recommended here can be used by ministers but most of them are beyond the skill of laymen.

J.R.R.

VOL. XV NO. 35 DECEMBER 26, 1956 $3.00 A YEAR

THE SOUTHERN PRESBYTERIAN JOURNAL

Rev. Henry B. Dendy, D.D., Editor....Weaverville, N. C.
Dr. L. Nelson Bell, Associate Editor....Asheville, N. C.
Rev. Wade C. Smith, Associate Editor....Weaverville, N. C.

EDITORIAL

Forty Years Later

We have just flown from Seattle to Tokyo in 21 hours. Exactly forty years ago we made the same trip by steamer in 19 days, having been buffeted by a fierce Pacific storm all the way. This time we flew above the storm.

On arriving at our Tokyo hotel we told the clerk we wished to place a phone call and his immediate and matter of fact question was, "To America?" Had we replied in the affirmative, New York or Miami or Montreat would soon have been on the line. Forty years ago the streets of Yokohama and Tokyo were filled with rickshaws. Not one of these man-drawn vehicles was now to be seen while motor traffic was just as dense and considerably more chaotic than Chicago.

These four decades have brought many other changes: a formerly able and imitative people developed into an aggressive and dangerous foe, only to be conquered and then, in some measure, won over as friend and ally.

During all of this time a Christian witness in Japan has been maintained. Despite this the Christian Church of Japan is woefully weak and a genuine Spirit-sent revival is imperative if Japan is to be adequately evangelized.

The obstacles; the problems; the difficulties; the divergencies of opinions among Christian leaders: all combine to call the Church of America to pray for the Japanese Church and for the missionary witness in that land.

What we all must remember is that none of these problems are as great as the mercy and love and power of God. He is able to overcome and resolve these difficulties and to work them out for His Own glory. To that end we would urge our readers to pray for our own missionaries and for the entire Christian witness in Japan today, that for all concerned there may be a mighty outpouring of the power and presence of God's Holy Spirit.

—L.N.B.

Hugh Franklin Dickson

Hugh Franklin Dickson, a native of South Carolina, died in his sleep during the morning hours of Thursday, November 29th, at his home in Atlanta, Ga. He was in his 63rd year. His passing came as a surprise as he had been active during the day at his office and visited in the home of his daughter, Mrs. Harry Phillips, the evening before.

Mr. Dickson was a prominent figure in the business world. He was an investment banker and was active in business enterprises from New York to Texas.

Early in life Mr. Dickson began his business career with the United Drug Co. and later became an executive with Liggett and Myers Drug Co. He helped organize the Lane Drug Stores in 1929 and served as its first president. Later Mr. Dickson helped organize the Wade Hampton Hotel of Columbia, S. C., and was part owner.

During World War I Mr. Dickson served as Sergeant Major with President Dwight Eisenhower. At the time of his death Mr. Dickson was serving on the Board of Directors of Mading Drug Stores, Houston, Texas, Sommers Drug Stores, San Antonio and Beaumont, Texas, the Griggs Equipment Co., Temple, Texas and The Southern Presbyterian Journal.

Mr. Dickson was a ruling elder in the Westminster Presbyterian Church of Atlanta, Ga. He served as an elder in many capacities. He rendered valuable service as a member of the Executive Committee of Camp Westminster. He was devoted to the work of young people and had a vision of Camp Westminster becoming the finest Christian camp in the nation.

Funeral services were held at the Westminster Presbyterian Church, Dr. John R. Richardson, the pastor, officiated. The burial was in Westview Cemetery.

Surviving are his wife; daughters, Mrs. John Druery of Hicksville, Long Island, New York, and Mrs. Henry Watson Philips of Decatur, Ga.; sisters, Mrs. Howard Paddock of Cullman, Ala.; Miss Mary Dickson, Miss Sula Dickson both of Anderson, S. C., Miss Sarah Dickson of New York City, Mrs. Prue Clinkscales of Anderson, S. C.; brothers, Norman Dickson of Atlanta, Ga., W. M. Dickson of Wilmington, N. C., Harvey R. Dickson of Anderson, S. C., and three grandchildren.

Mr. Dickson will be greatly missed by a wide circle of friends. His example of fidelity to his dynamic Christian convictions will be a potent influence in the lives of all who were privileged to enjoy his friendship.

The Southern Presbyterian Journal acknowledges with gratitude the fine service rendered by Hugh Dickson as a valuable member of our Board of Directors. We extend to the members of the family our profoundest sympathy and commend each one to the God whose consolations are not too small for our deepest needs.

"And I heard a great voice from heaven saying unto me, Write, Blessed are the dead who die in the Lord from henceforth: Yea, saith the Spirit, that they may rest from their labors; and their works do follow them."

Ecumenical Regimentation

Word comes from Saint Joseph County, Indiana, that a "liberal"-controlled program of church extension is about to be imposed on Protestant churches in this area. The plan seems to be part and parcel of the super-church, ecumenical program of the National Council of Churches.

Dr. Merlin Clark, professor of research and urban church planning of the Federated Theological Faculties of the University of Chicago, has been authorized by the Council of Churches of Saint Joseph County, through its Department of Comity and Church Planning, to set up a survey and allocate sites for future church construction and expansion. The Council will assume authority to represent Protestants in dealing with city and county planning groups, public utilities, real estate developers and suburban municipal officials.

Already some twenty denominations have bound themselves by agreement with the Council not to purchase building sites or lay plans for new congregations without consulting the Council of Churches. Evangelical bodies not cooperating with the Council feel that they have inalienable rights as Christians and as Americans to plant churches wherever the Lord leads, but they are already beginning to feel the pinch of ecclesiastical regimentation.

The National Association of Evangelicals is alert to this situation throughout the country and has representation in the American Institute of Planners which held its annual meeting in Providence, R. I., last month. Evangelical groups can look to the NAE to safeguard their rights.—United Evangelical Action.

The Three Wise Men

By Wade C. Smith

Some years ago, in the Little Jetts column in the *Sunday School Times* illustrating the Christmas lesson, Matthew's account of the quest of the Magi, I presented the Followers of the Star in the generally accepted number of three men riding on camels. A sincere critic wrote me a six-word letter, asking "By what authority *three* wise men"?

It may be of interest to *Journal* readers at this Christmas season to read the answer given to an interesting query, as follows:

My first general answer is, By no authority, but with a reason — several reasons. First: Presenting the wise men (or the Magi) three in number, without any compromise of principle or truth, makes my own path easier. If I had presented them as two wise men, or four wise men, I would have had scores of inquiries like yours, challenging "By what authority?" As it is, I receive only one — yours; and that affords me the real pleasure of writing you a letter.

Really, I have no authority even to put the wise men on camels. I have just been looking at an illustration of this scene in one of the most noted works, entitled "The Life of Christ," and there are several imposing looking potentates on camels, surrounded and followed by a large retinue of men on foot and on horseback, some leading asses with treasure boxes and camp equipment, men with bows and arrows and spears — quite an army; and the big men on the camels are pointing across the

The Southern Presbyterian Journal, *a Presbyterian Weekly magazine devoted to the statement, defense, and propagation of the Gospel, the faith which was once for all delivered unto the saints,* published every Wednesday by The Southern Presbyterian Journal, Inc., in Weaverville, N. C.

Entered as second-class matter May 15, 1942, at the Postoffice at Weaverville, N. C., under the Act of March 3, 1879. Vol. XV, No. 35, December 26, 1956. Editorial and Business Offices: Weaverville, N. C. Printed in the U.S.A. by Biltmore Press, Asheville, N. C.

ADDRESS CHANGE: When changing address, please let us have both old and new address as far in advance as possible. Allow three weeks after change if not sent in advance. When possible, send an address label giving your old address.

wilderness to a star. If I had imitated that picture I am sure I would have received a great number of "By what authoritys?"

Another reason: the most commonly and universally accepted thought of the Christ-child-seekers is in three persons of high degree (as philosophers, astrologers or kings) coming upon camels. On camels because the camel was the long distance carrier of that country, and most likely to be used. Well accepted tradition, you know, names these three as Melchior, Caspar and Balthasar, three kings; the first an old man with white hair and long beard; the second a ruddy and beardless youth; the third swarthy and in the prime of life; thus being representative of three periods of life. Moreover, that Melchior was a descendant of Shem, Caspar of Ham, and Balthasar of Japheth — three racial divisions. It is even claimed that the skulls of these three were gathered up by Bishop Reinald in the twelfth century and are now exhibited among the relics in the Cathedral of Cologne. You are also aware of how this visualization of the Magi has influenced the great artists of the past nineteen centuries, as witness the masterpieces of Paul Veronese, Giovanni Bellini, et al.

So it is the generally accepted conception of the personnel of the Magi who came westward following the star. These traditions, not being sufficiently authenticated, have little real value, of course. But since the Bible is silent on this feature, and since the presentation does no violence to the great central truth of the story in the Bible, rather giving it fitting and appropriate ornamentation, arousing a profitable interest, it seems good to portray it in the manner named.

Your inquiry suggesting the necessity for authenticated accuracy of details in a Bible illustration, raises the question whether Bible scenes should be picturized at all. To do this, an illustrator, in the absence of minor and unimportant details in the text, must sometimes draw upon the imagination — aided by such knowledge as may be had of the customs of the time and the place. If no damage is done to the text or the context, I believe such illustrations are very helpful and have certainly been used to kindle fresh interest in the vital truth.

One thing the Little Jetts try to guard with great care: it is right along the line of your question about the Magi. That is, to get the right number of persons in a scene *when the Bible states that number,* and also to put the right equipment in, when the equipment is named. I learned my lesson in that particular soon after the Little Jetts got into action about 40 years ago. I sent Naaman to Elisha in a *palanquin,* not having read the text carefully enough.

Of course, as a general in the Syrian army he would ordinarily ride a horse or drive a chariot; but he was a sick man and I considerately put him in a palanquin. I got a come-back on that all right, which sent me again to the text; I had overlooked the plain statement that Naaman "came with his horses and with his chariot, and stood at the door of the house of Elisha."

Again, bringing Eliezer back from Nahor, where he had gone on his thrilling quest for a bride for Isaac, I portrayed only one woman in the returning caravan, but on the check up I discovered there were at least two women in the party; for Rebekah's nurse accompanied her. And by the way, the nurse's name was Deborah — did you know that? (Gen. 35:8.)

Also, in Peter's party going to the home of Cornelius, I pictured four men — Peter and the three messengers sent by Cornelius. On the check up I discovered that "certain brethren accompanied them," so I added a minimum two to the party, making six, and was about to let the strip go to the *Sunday School Times* for publication. But fortunately a little further check in Acts 11:12 where Peter was telling the brethren at Jerusalem about it, revealed that "six brethren" accompanied him, making ten in the party.

So you see, even so crude a vehicle as The Little Jetts must "watch their step" lest a more serious matter than the speculative number of the "Three Wise Men" and the beasts they rode should overtake them. Doubtless they have made other mistakes, but they have had a good time these 40 years trying.

Sincerely yours

Christmas in the Far East

By E. H. Hamilton

Probably the only country in the Far East where Christmas is entirely ignored is Red China, and even there no doubt many of the Churches put on Christmas plays of the manger scene, the shepherds and the wise men. And there even in Red China Christmas is in the hearts of hundreds of thousands of Christians, who thank God for the coming of His Son into the world.

In Japan more outward ado is made over Christmas than in any other Oriental country. This is because of the up-to-date business methods employed in their department stores. In Tokyo, Kobe, Osaka, and other large cities, great banners of "Merry Christmas" in English and in Japanese are displayed, and heroic sized effigies of Santa Claus exhibited in the windows, to stimulate trade. And of course the Churches in Japan make much of the birth of Christ.

In Formosa thousands of Christmas cards are sold in the shops along with new year cards, and they are being bought and used, especially by Christians. And the Churches are all decorated with elaborately made scenes of the Shepherds and the Wise Men, and even Christmas trees are adorned. And Christmas carols are sung by the hospital nurses and other young people, often at an unearthly hour of the morning.

There are twenty-six Christian Churches in the city of Taipei, eleven of them Presbyterian. Frequently at Christmas their choirs all unite at a great mass meeting held either in the stadium or in the city auditorium, and there Christmas is celebrated by Christians from all over the city, through carols and hymns, and messages given by Christian Pastors, and occasionally by a missionary, in Mandarin (the official Chinese dialect) and in Formosan. This meeting is a great time of witnessing for Christ.

It is to be regretted that the Chinese National Government, many of whose leaders, including the President and Madame Chiang Kai-shek, are Christians, declares a holiday on the birthday of Confucius, but takes no official recognition of the birthday of Christ. And so the students of all schools from the primary grades through the university attend classes as on any other day.

Nevertheless the students in our Christian Student Center ("Friendship Corner"), near the National Taiwan University in Taipei, celebrate Christmas in a big way.

Last year on Christmas eve about sixty of the University students who love Friendship Corner gathered at the Center and filled two chartered buses, and we went all over the city singing Christmas carols (in English — they love to sing in English!) at the homes of Christian university professors and others.

At midnight, after we had "sung out" and were finishing the tour, Sophia Hsu, a very dear university student who was in the group who were to be baptized at our Friendship Corner Church the next morning, said to me, "Oh, Mr. Hamilton, this has been the happiest day of my life." "Yes, Sophia," I answered, "And tomorrow will be happier still." "Yes," she answered wistfully, *"It will be my birthday!"*

And the next morning at our English Worship Service there at Friendship Corner, in Taipei, Formosa, the joy of her own birth into the Church was to be forever associated with the joy of the birth of the Son of God into the world.

Joy To The World

By Rev. Kennedy Smartt

"No Christmas! No Christmas!" were the words of the town criers in England during the time of the Puritan's control of the Parliament in the days of Oliver Cromwell. The Puritans, under the influence of their Calvinistic teachings, deplored Christmas, both as a pagan practice and as a human invention. Christ would never have approved of it, they felt, it merely leading to excessive revellings and wrong doings. And so the observing of Christmas was outlawed, and everyone was ordered to go to work as usual. Anyone found to be celebrating was given a heavy fine. Even here in America in 1659, the Puritans of Massachusetts passed a law forbidding Christmas observance and set a fine of five shillings for all offenders.

How the times have changed! There is certainly no danger of Christmas celebration being outlawed in our land today. But in one sense, at least, times have not changed. There are the same excessive abuses of the holiday as there were in the days of old. Under the guise of celebration of our Lord's birthday the revellings and banquetings are equally disturbing. We are a people who call ourselves Christian and who lead respectable, moral lives, by and large, but on the one day when we should be keenest for worship are completely overcome by commercialistic idolatry, gluttony, and all too often drunkenness.

"No Christmas! No Christmas!" we are tempted to cry, when we see what is happening to Christmas. The selfishness, the covetousness, the impatience with the traffic and the crowds; the dread of forgetting someone who will not have forgotten us; the physical demand of getting everything done and going every place we are expected to go; the rivalry in buying, decorating, and entertaining. And there is also the burden of getting back to normal after it is over. So this is Christmas, so this is our Lord's birthday, or at least the day we have chosen to observe as such. Can the Christmas carols, blared out over loud speakers to milling, pushing throngs, sanctify this commercial idolatry? Can pretty lights and multi-colored decorations cheer our distracted souls?

But the theme of the angel's announcement of the birth of Christ was joy. "Fear not: for, behold, I bring you good tidings of GREAT JOY, which shall be to all people. For unto you is born this day in the city of David a Saviour, which is Christ the Lord."

The message of Christmas is joy. The message of Christ's birth is joy. The message of the angels is true, joy has come to the world. But alas, we are missing it. We have sought our joy at the flesh pots of Egypt rather than in the manger of Bethlehem. We have drunk a bitter cup in search for joy, seeking in the world that which comes only to those who listen to heaven for this blessed evangel of which first the angels sang. Those who do not seek their pleasure in Christ shall never discover the joy He has brought to the world.

There is a legend that on one occasion St. Augustine dreamed that he had died and that when he came to the gates of heaven, and the keeper of the gates said to him, "Who are you?" he replied, "I am a Christian." But the porter replied to him, "No, you are not a Christian, you are a Ciceronian, for you have thought and studied more about Cicero than about Christ."

Well, if the legend be true, St. Augustine mended his ways and sought only the things of Christ. But what of us? Do not our Christmas antics indicate that we are worldlings and not Christians by the way we seek our joy which is promised us in connection with the birth of Christ?

The true joy of Christmas is to be found in the angels song. Its message fairly bursts with joy. In the first place this joy is found in the announcement of a Saviour who has come into this world submitting Himself to all the negative and positive requirements of the law, and who was yet without sin. A Saviour who is God incarnate in the flesh, who is willing to take upon Himself our sins and go to the Cross of Calvary and there suffer the wrath and rejection of God in our stead: that we might have the forgiveness of sin and assurance of salvation through Him.

It is the message of a Saviour who was manifest to destroy the works of the devil, and to deliver those, who, because of the fear of death, were all their life time subject to bondage. It is the joy of knowing that our Saviour who walks with us through the valley of the shadow of death has broken the bands of death by becoming the trailblazer of our resurrection. It is the joy of knowing that He who is acquainted with our griefs and who carried our sorrows, is now at the right hand of God making intercession for us. It is the joy of knowing that there is no depth of ruin beyond His ability to redeem and restore. Hear again then the message of the angels.

'Behold, I bring you good tidings of GREAT JOY . . . For unto you is born a SAVIOUR."

The second great note of joy in this announcement is found in the words, "UNTO YOU is born . . . " UNTO YOU, whether you are rich or poor, whether you are learned or untutored: What you are or who you are makes no difference, for UNTO YOU a Saviour is born. If you are abiding under the shadow of death, or if you are yoked to some grievous circumstance or affliction, this all sufficient Saviour has come unto you. If you are languishing under a heavy burden of sin, or enduring a trial of your faith, just listen to what the angels are singing, *"UNTO YOU"* this Saviour has come.

The great joy of this announcement is determined not merely by the fact that the Saviour has been born unto you, but even more by the event that you are born again unto the Saviour, as you open the door of your heart in order that through faith the Saviour might be born within you. It is not enough to know just that a Saviour has come, for the joy is in the assurance that through faith I have let Him come into my heart. To hear not only the angels say, but to hear the internal testimony of the Holy Spirit in my heart also, say, "UNTO ME" has been born a Saviour. This is the joy of the new life in Christ.

"Joy to the world, the Lord is come;
Let earth receive her King;
Let every heart prepare Him room."

The third great note of joy in this announcement is in the word that this Saviour who is born unto us is CHRIST THE LORD.

Your Tax Tithe

By The Rev. Donald C. Graham

Christians everywhere should be reminded at the year's end that they should be "doers of the Word and not hearers only" in the matter of their income tax. Many will not have to give final reckoning of their benevolences to Uncle Sam for another few months but the tax year closes December 31 and this happens to be when the Lord closes His books on their benevolence accounts.

How much will you, professing Christian, claim as your benevolence deduction on your income tax report — 10% - 13% - 18% — just how much? Now, how much will you *actually* give in your total benevolences?

Cheating here is dangerous business. It may net you an immediate monetary advantage but it may bring upon you untold spiritual losses. God keeps books on your finances and He is an infinitely perfect Accountant. He knows if you report 10% but actually gave only 7%. It is a common enough sin but it dare not be common to you as a Christian for you know "the righteous judgment of God" that is re-free and generous spirit and at the same time for a test period, to keep careful record of these contributions. To my amazement, sir, I have proved myself one of the least generous Christians in your church by falling far short of the tithe."

God is keeping books! Why should not we?

Helps To Understanding Scripture Readings in *Day by Day*

By Rev. C. C. Baker

Sunday, January 6, *Matthew* 3:13-17; 4:1-4. There is a direct connection between the affirmation from heaven that Jesus was the Son of God (3:17) and the temptations He endured (4:1-11). Observe that Satan tempted Jesus by calling into question His Sonship (4:3,6). Satan challenged Jesus to prove that He was the Son of God by performing miracles at his bidding (4:3,6). If Jesus had yielded to Satan and doubted that He was the Son of God, how would His ministry have been affected? What was the purpose of Jesus' miracles (John 14:11)? Did Satan need to have miracles performed to prove to him that Jesus was the Son of God (James 2:19)? Be careful that Satan does not try to rob you of your conviction that through Christ you have become a son of God. How does this conviction strengthen you as you work for the Lord?

Monday, January 7, *Matthew* 4:5-7. Jesus had to be tried before He could be used by God. Observe that the first mission of the Spirit after He had come upon Jesus (3:16) was to lead Him into the wilderness to be tempted (4:1). Evidently it was the Holy Spirit that constrained Jesus to fast for forty days (4:2). It was from the successful endurance of temptation (vv.3-11) that great power and fruit came in Jesus' ministry. At His simple bidding, men dropped everything to become His disciples (vv.18-22). Great crowds followed Him (vv.23-25). (Locate on a map all the places from which people came in, vv.22-25.) He possessed power to heal (vv.22-24). He uttered His greatest teachings (the Sermon on the Mount, chapters 5-7). God will be able to use you if you learn to overcome temptation.

Tuesday, January 8, *Matthew* 4:8-11. Jesus overcame Satan by remembering the words of His Father (3:17) when His Sonship was questioned (vv.3,6) and by quoting Scripture (vv.4, 7,10) when He was directly tempted. Did Satan appear to be in outright opposition to Jesus in any of the temptations? Imagine how hungry and weary Jesus must have been (v.2). How easy it would have been for Him to satisfy His hunger this easy way (vv.3-4). How much easier it would have been for Him to make a spectacular entrance than to plod daily with slow disciples and unbelieving crowds (vv.5-6) or to listen to the whisper of Satan than to face the agony of the cross (vv.8-9). Are you guilty of the sin of self-indulgence by engaging in "harmless" pastimes when you should be doing things that require serious and perhaps sacrificial effort? Keeping your thoughts on the Lord and passages from the Scriptures can keep you from sin even when you are tired and weary.

Wednesday, January 9, *Matthew* 16:13-26. After the disciples had discovered who Jesus was (v.16), Jesus began to teach them why He had come (v.21). What was the source of Peter's conviction that Jesus was the Messiah (v.17)? This was a truth that had probably been crystalizing in Peter's mind for a long time as he has witnessed Jesus' miracles and listened to His teachings. Was there any divine revelation in Peter's remark of v.22? Do you think he had been meditating on it for very long? Notice the greatness of Christ's praise in vv.17-19 for Peter's remark of v.16 and the depth of the condemnation in v.23 for the remark of v.22. Are the statements you make about spiritual truths snap judgments of your own wisdom or convictions that have crystalized in your mind as you have been taught of God?

Thursday, January 10, *Matthew* 22:15-22. Attempts were made to ask Jesus questions that would cause His downfall (v.15). What was the purpose of the statement made to Jesus in v.16? Was it a true statement? If Jesus had answered the question of v.17 in the affirmative, what charges could have been made against Him before the Jewish people? If He had answered in the negative, what charges could have been made against Him before the Roman government? How did Jesus circumvent the problem (vv.18-21)? Was His answer evasive (v.22)? What was the final outcome of these questions that were designed to trap Him (v.46)? When people ask you about your belief in the doctrines of the Christian Church, are you able to answer them intelligently (I Peter 3:15)?

Friday, January 11, *Matthew* 26:36-46. Glance through the rest of chapters 26 and 27 to see all that Jesus faced as He knelt in Gethsemane (26:36-46). Notice especially 26:48-49,66-68; 27: 22-23,26b-31,35,46. How would you feel if you were facing these events? Notice the abhorence

LESSON FOR JANUARY 6

By THE REV. J. KENTON PARKER

Wise Men Seek Jesus

Scripture: Matthew 1 and 2
Devotional Reading: Micah 4:1-5

Wise men still seek Jesus, for "In Him are hid all the treasures of wisdom and knowledge." These wise men were from the East. Micah had prophesied that, "many nations shall come, and say, 'Come, and let us go up to the mountain of the Lord." We might look upon these wise men as the first of a host of people from all nations who have sought and found the Christ.

The gospel of Matthew, a Jew, is written especially for the Jews. It is full of references to the Old Testament Scriptures. It seeks to prove that Jesus is the long-expected, promised Messiah. If, today, we are trying to convince a Jew that his Messiah is indeed come, then this gospel of Matthew is the very place to begin, for it links up the Old Testament with Jesus.

Let me quote from the New Analytical Bible: "There is no question as to the design of this Gospel. It is suggested by the opening statement — 'the book of the generation of Jesus Christ, the son of David, the son of Abraham.' The lineal descent of our Lord is carried to Abraham, and this is the Gospel for the Jew. It sets forth Christ, not only as the greatest Prophet and Lawgiver, but as fulfilling the Law and the prophets, that He is the Messiah of Old Testament predictions, the fulfilment of the promise of the Abrahamic Covenant, and the King of the true Israel in the Davidic line.

"Matthew constantly keeps before his people the Old Testament Scriptures and by quotations and allusions refers to them nearly one hundred times, and to the prophets about fifty times. It abounds in statements to show that Jesus fulfilled the prophetical Scriptures. The Jew would require such a procedure and in this manner only could the Messianic claims of our Lord be established. Thus in His person, His words and works is furnished the proof that Jesus of Nazareth is the Messiah. It is the Gospel of the Kingdom. In the training of the Twelve, by His earlier discourses, Jesus presented the Law of the Kingdom, and by parables the progress of the Kingdom, and by many details peculiar to this Gospel is the fact that our Lord is the promised King."

There are in these first two chapters several interesting facts about Him.

I. *The Genealogy of Jesus:* 1:1-17.

Genealogical records were very important to the Jews. Only in this way could the successors to the throne, to the priesthood, and to tribal headship be safeguarded. The first thing that a Jew would ask about the Messiah would be, Does he have the right genealogy? Is he descended from Abraham, and from David? The Promised Messiah was to be a descendant of both, and rightful heir to the throne of David. It is natural for Matthew, writing especially for Jews, to begin as he does with a long list of the ancestors of Jesus Christ. He must belong to the right family if he claimed to be the rightful Messiah.

It is always most helpful, inspiring and refreshing to turn to Bishop Ryle's Expository Thoughts. You are never disappointed. Let me quote a few words of his on this Genealogy: "The Gospel of St. Matthew begins with a long list of names. Let no one think that these verses are useless. Nothing is useless in the Bible. Every word of it is inspired." Then he gives some very practical lessons.

"Learn from this list of names that God always keeps His word. He had promised that in Abraham's seed all the nations of the earth should be blessed. He had promised to raise up a Saviour of the family of David. These sixteen verses prove that Jesus was the son of David, and the son of Abraham, and that God's promise was fulfilled." (It will repay you to read the balance of this, see Ryle on Luke).

II. *The Virgin Birth of Jesus:* 18-25.

In these verses we have a simple, clear statement regarding the Virgin birth of Jesus. Compare this with the account in Luke, and you get the full picture. This basic fact of our faith is confirmed by many other passages such as the Incarnation as given by John, and the description of Christ in Hebrews, chapter one. If we believe in a supernatural religion — and what other kind is worth anything — then the Virgin birth of our Lord is very easy to believe, for it presents no difficulties. If you are determined to do away with the supernatural, then, of course, you will try to explain away this clear statement.

III. *Visit of the Wise Men:* 2:1-12.

This is our printed lesson and the theme for our study today. The men of the East were noted as "Star-gazers." The sun, moon, and stars were objects of interest, and often of worship. I have always felt that worship of the heavenly bodies was the easiest explained, and the highest form of idolatry, for all of us feel a certain kind of awe when we gaze at the heavens by day or night. There is something so silent, mysterious, and marvelous about it that it inspires a feeling of reverence, and unless we know the true explanation, would easily lead to worship. To worship an earthly object is degrading; to worship a heavenly body, is elevating to a certain degree. When we see the Creator behind His Creation then we get a very glorious concept of God, such as the psalmist had when he said, The heavens declare the glory of God. There is no indication in Scripture that there were just three of these men. We do not know how many there were.

"His star." This was a special star. Those who like to explain away all miracles, or make them conform to Nature's laws, have tried to put their finger on some star, or conjunction of stars, which appeared just at this time. Notice the different things said about it and I believe you will agree that only a miracle can explain this particular star. Why not? This is the most tremendous event since creation and miracles are to be expected in connection with it.

These wise men were wiser than some of their comrades. They do not worship the star, but the King to Whom the star leads them. All the phenomena of Nature should lead us to Worship the God of nature.

The reaction in Jerusalem is most interesting: Herod and "all Jerusalem" is troubled. We can understand the jealousy and uneasiness of Herod, but that of the scribes and chief priests is different. I wonder what would be the reaction among political leaders, and even among some who occupy high positions in the Church, if a similar event should take place? Would our politicians and churchmen be "troubled"? The leaders of the Jews could answer Herod's question as to where Christ was to be born, but they were in no mood to accept Him.

Herod gives his instructions to the wise men, shrewdly hiding his real feelings and purpose, and they go on their way to follow the star to Bethlehem. They find the Child, worship Him, presenting their gifts, and being warned of God, go home another way. Joseph takes the Child and his mother and flees to Egypt.

IV. *The Cruel Edict of Herod:* 16-18.

In the book of Revelation we have the picture of the dragon waiting to devour the Child as soon as He is born. (see Rev. 12:4). In symbolic language we are told of the rescue of the Child. Satan tried to destroy Jesus and used Herod as a willing tool. The devil has a way of doing this. I think we can see his hand in many of the events which have taken place in recent years. Pharoah in the Old Testament, is a distinct type of Satan, and many world rulers have been agents of his in persecuting Christians, or in the words of Revelation, And the dragon was wroth with the woman, and went to make war with the remnant of her seed. So Herod sends out his fiendish order that all the children in Bethlehem and her borders, from two years old and under should be slain. Again we find Old Testament prophecy fulfilled.

Our hearts are sad as we read this story. Let us remember, however, that these children escaped much of the troubles of this world and went immediately into the presence of God, where, around the throne of God thousands of children stand singing. There is much comfort for weeping mothers in this thought, just as there is for us when some darling child is taken from our home.

V. *"He Shall be Called a Nazarene":* 19-23.

When Herod died the angel appeared to Joseph again and told him to take the young child and his mother and go into the land of Israel. When he heard that Archelaus reigned in the room of his father Herod, he was afraid to go on, and being warned, turned aside into the parts of Galilee and came and dwelt in a city called Nazareth, that it might be fulfilled which was spoken by the prophets, He shall be called a Nazarene. To be called a "Nazarene" was a reproach, for a common question of that day was, Can there any good thing come out of Nazareth? Have you not seen a beautiful white lily coming up from a slimy mudhole? Our Saviour chose to be born in a stable, and to grow up as a Boy in the wicked town of Nazareth. Environment is considered very important in the rearing of children. We like for our children to be brought up in a good neighborhood. This is part of the deepest humiliation of Christ, and His willingness to be made in all points like as we are.

YOUNG PEOPLES Department

)UTH PROGRAM FOR JANUARY 6

By THE REV. B. HOYT EVANS

What Is A Leader?

ogram Leader:

We are living in a time when Christian lead-s are very much needed all over the world. ll Christian young people who are ambitious the right sense aspire to be used as leaders. here is nothing wrong with such an ambition, it is real Christian leadership which we have mind.

It is obvious that not all people have the me opportunities for leadership, and some-nes those who have the opportunities do ɔt make very good leaders. It is not often that ≥ can do very much about our opportunities r leadership, but there are things we can do improve our capabilities as leaders. What a leader? What are the qualities a Christian ader needs, and what can be done to develop em? If, in this program, we can find answers these questions, and if we will make applica-ɔns to our own lives, we shall be making ogress toward becoming Christian leaders for e present time and for years to come.

rst Speaker:

A Christian leader is one who has the right titudes toward God, toward other people, and ward his task as a leader. This means that must be a Christian himself. He must be a rson whose sins are forgiven and whose nature is been changed by faith in Jesus Christ. No rson can have the right attitude toward God toward other people until he has come to ɔd through Christ. A Christian leader is one 1o looks on his place of leadership as an portunity for service and not as an occasion exalt himself in the eyes of others. Christ ade this very clear when He said, "Whosoever ll be great among you, shall be your minister: d whosoever will be the chiefest, shall be :vant of all. For even the Son of man came t to be ministered unto, but to minister, and give his life a ransom for many."

A Christian leader is one who recognizes that owes his all to the Lord and who uses his dership for the glory of God and the good of ıer people. This is vastly different from the ɔre common idea that a place of leadership to be used to force others to conform to the ider's will and to compel them to give him their honor. The greatest leader who ever walked the earth, Jesus Christ, looked on His leadership as an occasion for service. Our attitude toward leadership should be like His.

Second Speaker:

Another requirement for leadership is ability. We can readily see that some people are born with more ability than others. Those who are endowed with the greatest gifts of mind and personality are potentially the best leaders, but it does not always work out that way. Sometimes those who have been most generously blessed do not make the best use of their gifts, while others, who have less native ability, put it to far better use. It is quite true that there are definite limits to our native abilities, but few of us ever come near to exploring the limits. In His parable of the talents Jesus made it plain that we are only held responsible for making the best use of what we have. Rather than sitting around envying others who have received greater endowments than ours, and rather than gloating over others who are less blessed than we, let us ask God to show us the gifts that are ours, and let us work diligently and patiently to develop them into qualities of Christian leadership.

Third Speaker:

In speaking of the need for diligence in developing our talents for leadership, we need to be reminded of the importance of faithfulness as a quality of leadership. In a recent meeting of youth workers one adult adviser asked what could be done in cases where able young people accepted places of leadership but could not be depended on to fulfill their duties.

Do you think a person who is not faithful to his duties is really qualified as a Christian leader? There are few things that can eat away at the life and health of an organization like having undependable leaders. Those of us who aspire to be leaders in the name of Christ can do an important thing by resolving here and now to be faithful in all our duties. If we say we will take a part on the youth program, let us be sure that we can be depended upon to do it. If we offer to plan games for a social, let there be no doubt about its being done.

(Continue to Top of Page 16)

David goes on a Mission

David's father called him from the flock to go and find his three brothers in King Saul's army to see how they fared and bring back word. He told David to take them some good home cooking. When David found the army the soldiers were all trembling with fright because the army of the heathen had a giant who came out and dared any man to come and fight him. David was surprised and said, Why should God's soldiers be afraid of any man, even tho he be a giant? The men said somebody should run and tell King Saul about this lad, for he talks like he might be willing to go out and fight with this giant. (to be continued) E.

CHILDREN: Please write and tell us how you like our new page written just for you.

Editor

A Call to Prayer New Year's Day 1957

Thirty-three years ago on January first, nineteen ndred and fifty-seven, will be the anniversary of e World-Wide Revival Prayer Movement which ne into existence in the great port city of Shang-i, China, when a devoted group of God-fearing ristians, representatives of the different denomi-tional Mission Boards, met to pray for revival, rld-wide and there was brought to birth "A vement that knows neither plan nor pledge, but ly the Spirit's breathing through the living Word, o the hearts of believers." Since that year, the y has been observed in prayer and fasting by nultitude of God's people. One of our Presidents ued a National proclamation for prayer on three ccessive occasions, beginning January 1940, when e War clouds of World War II were threatening d imminent. Will each reader of this appeal ite a personal note to our President, Dwight D. senhower, with assurance of prayer. No Presi-nt of these United States has ever borne a eater burden, not even George Washington or raham Lincoln. This notice is being sent to a ge number of denominational weeklies which ll reach many thousands of readers, who it is ped will respond to this appeal.

"When we depend upon organization, we get what organization can do,
When we depend upon education, we get what education can do,
When we depend upon man, we get what man can do.
When we depend upon prayer, we get what God can do."

—Selected.

'Prove me now herewith, saith the Lord of hosts."
Malachi 3:10.

World-Wide Revival Prayer Movement
5 S. Oxford Avenue, Ventnor, N. J.

The Universal Week of Prayer

The first full week in each year has been for ne years designated "The Universal Week of ayer." The intention of this Universal Week Prayer is that Christians enter such decisive eting with God that we may hear His word t the fashion and purpose of our lives may be ered and redeemed by Him. This is a week nsored by the Evangelism Department of the tional Council of Churches. Annually, a devo-nal guide is made available to those who would re this spiritual fellowship. The guide for use the week of January 6 to 12, 1957 has as its me "God's Word Through Prayer."

To His disciples' question "Why could we not t out the dumb spirit?" Jesus answered: "This d cannot be driven out by anything but prayer." e are all like the shepherd boy of Mark's gospel needing one or another of God's indispensable gifts that cannot come to us by anything but prayer. The meditations of this week suggested by chapters 2 through 7 of the gospel of Luke will direct us toward hearing God's Word through the encounter of prayer. For copies of the guide to use this first four weeks in January, 1957, you may address your order to the Joint Department of Evangelism, National Council of Churches in the U. S. A., 297 Fourth Avenue, New York 10, N. Y. The price of the leaflet is 15c per copy. You are requested to send money when ordering the leaflet.

To many Christians these are days of storm and stress, confusion and deep concern, of uncertainty and insecurity, prayer can make a difference in the lives of us all. Intercessory prayer is needed. You are invited to enter with countless Christians of many denominations in the observance of the Universal Week of Prayer, praying together one for another and for ourselves that we may know permanent growth in a continuing prayer life in this new year.

The Advent in Poetry

"It is by no breath,
Turn of the eye, wave of the hand, that salvation joins issue with death!
As thy love is discovered almighty, almighty be proved
Thy power, that exists with and for it, of being Beloved!
He who did most shall bear most; the strongest shall stand the most weak.
'Tis the weakness in strength, that I cry for! my flesh, that I seek
In the Godhead! I seek it and I find it. O Saul, it shall be
A Face like my face that receives thee, a Man like to me,
Thou shalt love and be loved by, forever: a Hand like this hand
Shall throw open the gates of new life to thee! See the Christ stand!"

—Browning in SAUL.

A Christmas Chant

"At last earth's hope was granted,
And God was a child of earth:
And a thousand angels chanted
The lowly midnight birth.

Ah! Bethlehem was grander
That hour than paradise;
And the light of earth that night eclipsed
The splendors of the skies."

—Ryan in A Christmas Chant.

NEWS of CHURCHES Around the World

Church Extension

Report of November 1956

Budget 1956	$1,400,000.00
Receipts to Date	725,039.70
Percentage of Annual Budget Received to Date	51.79%
Balance Needed for the year	674,960.30

G. B. Strickler
Treasurer

The William Black Home

Miss Jeanette McQueen, Raeford, N. C., will on and after January 1, 1957 receive applications for reservations in the William Black Home at Montreat, according to an announcement by Dr. E. E. Gillespie, of Greensboro, who is president of the controlling Board of Trustees.

Miss Sara Lytch, of Raeford, who has been manager in the past will be assisted next season by Miss Mary Frances Luke, of Glendale Springs, N. C. and currently of the Glade Valley School faculty. The Home will be opened on June 15th and will receive guests until the last of August.

Missionary News

Mr. and Mrs. Rob Roy Robertson of our Congo Mission announce the arrival of a son, Richard Blackwell, in Luebo on November 12.

Miss Elisa Gonzales of our East Brazil Mission is scheduled to arrive in the United States about the middle of December for her regular furlough. Miss Gonzales is just completing her first term on the field, having gone to Brazil in 1951 where she has been engaged in evangelistic-educational work.

Rev. and Mrs. Lawrence G. Calhoun of our East Brazil Mission are scheduled to arrive in this country for regular furlough on December 20. The Calhouns have three children ranging in age from thirteen to twenty-four. Upon their arrival in the United States, they will proceed to Barium Springs, N. C.

Nashville—Mr. Guy S. Mitchell, missionary for the Presbyterian Church, U.S., to Zentsuji, Japan, has been honored by the Japanese National Government for his work among boys in Skikoku Reformatory. A gift and an official scroll were presented by the Honorable Ryozo Makino, Minister of Justice for the government.

The Mitchells, whose home is in El Dorado, Arkansas, are now in the United States on furlough, so the citation was accepted for Mr. Mitchell by Professor N. Naitch, a member of the faculty of Shikoku Christian College in Zentsuji.

Although Mr. Mitchell's missionary assignment is as educational and business missionary working in Shikoku Christian College, the Presbyterian College for the island of Shikoku, he has had charge of Christian work among boys in Shikoku Shonenin since shortly after going out to Japan in 1953 He supervises the weekly visits to the reformatory by students from the college, and occasionally speaks to approximately 200 inmates himself through an interpreter. He has also frequently shown slides of the United States and religious film-strips and moving pictures.

Presentation of the gift and scroll was made in Takamatsu, near Zentsuji. A translation of the wording of the scroll follows:

"You have been contributing to the reform work of the reformatory for a long time. We appreciate very much your genuine feeling and greatest support which have been given to this work. At the time of putting into operation the movement of making society brighter, we present you a remembrance to express our deep appreciation."

Minister of Justice
(Japan National Government)
(signed) Ryozo Makino

ALABAMA

Birmingham—Mrs. J. J. Baird has been chosen to lead the Women of the Church, Birmingham Presbytery, at their November meeting.

Elected to serve with Mrs. Baird are: Mrs. J. L. Thweatt, first vice-president; Mrs. A. J. Roddy, chairman of general fund agencies; Mrs. F. A. Shelton, treasurer; Mrs. Alva M. Gregg, chairman of church extension; Mrs. E. L. Portis, recording secretary; Mrs. Stratton Daniel, chairman of district four; and Mrs. Elbert Johnson, chairman of district two.

Birmingham—Formal organizational services for the Huffman Presbyterian Church near here were held December 2. The young church, which has been holding worship services since October 1, has a charter membership of 60.

A pulpit committee of five has been selected to provide the church with a pastor. In the meantime the Rev. R. D. Bedinger, executive secretary and moderator of the presbytery, who has been serving and advising the church, will continue to supply the pulpit. A commission of the presbytery to organize the church was made up of Dr. T. S. Daniel Mr. Glenn Willard, the Rev. B. A. Sykes, the Rev James Cantrell, Mr. A. C. Hazen, Mr. G. E. Burgen Mr. C. F. Davis, and Mr. C. R. Culverhouse. The Rev. George Bacon headed the commission for acquiring the three-acre lot and housing where the church was established.

GEORGIA

Atlanta—Receipts for the General Fund and Interchurch Agencies continue to run ahead, both in totals, and in percentages of the year's budget of contributions received during the same period in 1955. In the latest report issued by the office of the Stated Clerk of the General Assembly, the General Fund Agencies are reported as receiving $420,826.41 through Nov. 30.

tures will probably put the total close to $140,-000,000 for the decade.

Each of the past ten years has seen a new record set in amount spent for building, Mr. Caudill stated. This year's total is expected to pass $20,-000,000, far above the $18.3 million for 1955.

In the nine years for which figures were complete, the Synod of North Carolina has led in the grand total, with an expenditure of $20,308,000, and the Synod of Texas has been close behind, at $18,880,000. The Synod of Virginia ranks third among the 16 Synods, with a total of $11,764,000. The Synod of Georgia is fourth, with $9,026,000, Florida fifth, at $8,360,000; and South Carolina is sixth at $7,913,000.

Mr. Caudill's figures on church building showed the council that totals spent in building have progressed from $5.2 million in 1947, by one to two millions each year. No synod spent as much as a million for building in 1947, but both North Carolina and Texas have put in that much and more every year since, with Texas leading the North Carolina Synod in four of the nine years. The North Carolina total of $3,000,546 in 1952 has not been surpassed by any other synod, although Texas' 1955 total of $2,065,832 barely trailed.

The totals spent, 1947-1955, for building, by synods are as follows:

Alabama	$5,585,768	N. Carolina	20,308,769
Appalachia	5,824,858	Oklahoma	701,921
Arkansas	3,383,927	S. Carolina	7,913,695
Florida	8,360,040	Tennessee	5,531,450
Georgia	9,026,108	Texas	18,880,746
Kentucky	3,622,474	Virginia	11,764,218
Louisiana	4,672,644	W. Virginia	3,665,674
Mississippi	5,106,394	Snedecor Region	30,435
Missouri	2,701,474		
			$117,908,595

KENTUCKY

Louisville—A three-day consultation on world missions, between representatives from three Presbyterian branches, closed here on Nov. 28. The first affair of its kind ever attempted the consultation brought together more than 60 leaders of United, U.S., and U.S.A. Presbyterian missionary work from ten states.

Chairmen of presbytery and local committees on world missions, as well as synod and assembly leaders in the field, took part in the conference. "How to" information was exchanged among the representatives as they met in Warren Memorial Presbyterian Church.

Preliminary methods for mutual cooperation were worked out, so as to facilitate promotion and education on missions. Missionaries of any one of the three churches, visiting the areas involved, will be made available to speak in churches of the other Presbyterian branches. Missionary literature and audio-visual materials will be shared among the three denominations.

Among missionary leaders who attended were Dr. D. J. Cumming, educational secretary of the Board of the Presbyterian Church, U.S.; Dr. E. E. Grice, personnel secretary of the United Presbyterian Board; and Dr. Phillip O. Evaul, of Chicago, east-central area secretary of the Presbyterian, U.S.A. Board. States from which representatives came to the consultation were Pennsylvania, Ohio, Michigan, Indiana, West Virginia, Kentucky, Missouri, Tennessee, Alabama, and North Carolina.

Much of the conference time was spent in workshop discussions which brought out need for appointment in every church of a world missions chairman, the suggestion that all Presbyterian Seminaries "give greater emphasis to missionary education"; and the recommendation that more men be drawn into supporting the foreign mission cause in the local church, perhaps as chairmen of local committees.

LOUISIANA

New Orleans—Miss Florence Bennett of Paducah, Ky., has been named field assistant to the regional director of Christian Education, Louisiana Synod.

Miss Bennett will assume major responsibility in the area of children's work, but will also assist in all of the Christian education programs in the Synod, Presbytery, and in local churches by invitation.

SOUTH CAROLINA

Abbeville—A diamond Jubilee dinner, launching the Presbyterian College Development program for the Abbeville-Greenwood region was held here Dec. 6.

An estimated 160 Presbyterians from the area heard addresses by the Rev. Fred V. Poag, pastor of Shandon Presbyterian Church, Columbia, and Mr. Joseph Walker, Jr., also of Columbia, a member of the firm Joseph Walker and Company. Mr. Poag and Mr. Walker are chairmen of the P C development program for the Synod of South Carolina.

These speakers were introduced by Dr. Marshall W. Brown, president of the college. Prominent parts of the program were taken by the regional co-chairmen, the Rev. B. Herman Dillard, Pastor of Abbeville Presbyterian Church, and Mr. Joel Morse, also of Abbeville.

TENNESSEE

Zion Church near Columbia, Tennesee, was again filled with Presbyterians and others for Thanksgiving services on November 22, 1956. For the past several years Zion Church and the First Church in Columbia with the Garden Street Presbyterian Church (U.S.A.) and the Cumberland Church in Columbia have held thanksgiving services together, rotating from church to church. This year Zion Church was the host and the offering was for the benefit of the Monroe Harding Children's Home. Rev. Edmund W. Tratebas of the Garden Street Church preached the Thanksgiving sermon. The sacrament of the Lord's Supper was administered by Rev. W. M. Ford of Zion and Rev. Burns Drake of the Cumberland Church.

Zion Church continues preparation for its sesquicentennial celebration to be held in June, 1957. The church will be open during that month with guides on hand to show visitors through the church and churchyard. Planned for June 15 and 16 are outstanding speakers, a diorama and pageant.

Bristol—

The Rev. Claude Allen Calcote, 60, died recently at his home, 900 Pennsylvania Avenue, Bristol.

The Rev. Calcote has been the stated clerk of the Holston Presbytery since 1949. He was serving Meadowview, King Memorial, Paperville, and Lippencott churches at the time of his death.

The funeral services were held Wednesday afternoon in the First Presbyterian Church, Bristol, Tenn., with Dr. William McCorkle in charge. He was assisted by Dr. John Yelton and Dr. Ralph A. Brown. Dr. Goodridge Wilson was not able to be present to represent Abingdon Presbytery. Ministers of both presbyteries served as pallbearers. Mr. Calcote served two churches in each presbytery as supply: Paperville and Meadowview in Holston; King Memorial and Lippencott in Abingdon.

YOUNG PEOPLE'S DEPARTMENT

(Continued from Page 11)

Practicing faithfulness in small things from day to day will make us more dependable when the larger opportunities come to us. Let our faithfulness be used to the glory of God and for the good of others.

Fourth Speaker:

It has been said that a person cannot become a good leader until he has first proved that he can be a good follower. Our opportunities to lead may be limited, but our opportunities to follow are many. After all, following is just as necessary as is leading. A person may possess all the things we have described, right attitude, ability, and faithfulness, and still be a failure as a leader, if people refuse to follow him.

No leader can succeed, no matter how able he may be, without faithful and loyal followers. Our world is so complex that almost every leader is also under the authority of someone else. Every Christian is under the authority of Christ. We cannot become worthy leaders in any area until we learn to follow faithfully those who are in authority over us. We can be Christian leaders only when we are loyal servants of Christ.

This issue and the next issue are cut in size in order to give our force and the printers a breathing spell for the Christmas Holidays. **H.B.D.**

The Southern
PRESBYTERIAN
Journal

VOL. XV NO. 36 JANUARY 2, 1957 $3.00 A YEAR

For The New Year

We wish for all our readers much Joy and Happiness and a year of real Christian Growth and Service. We covet your prayers for our Journal Staff and Office Force for the days ahead.

"Blessed be the Lord, who daily loadeth us with benefits, even the God of our salvation."

SOMETHING NEW—

With this issue we have something new in the Women of the Church Department . . .

Special Treatment on the General Bible Study
of
The Minor Prophets
and
Help on the Circle Material for Bible Study

THE SOUTHERN PRESBYTERIAN JOURNAL

Rev. Henry B. Dendy, D.D., Editor..........Weaverville, N. C.
Dr. L. Nelson Bell, Associate Editor..........Asheville, N. C.
Rev. Wade C. Smith, Associate Editor..........Weaverville, N. C.

EDITORIAL

Ebenezer and Immanuel 1956 - 1957

Here, at the close of 1956, we raise our Ebenezer. Hither by God's help, we've come. Samuel erected a stone between Mizpah and Shen to celebrate the HAND of the Lord in overcoming the Philistines. I Samuel 7.12. They had been terrified at the approach of the doughty lords of Philistia. But the Almighty was entreated for Israel and saved His sore-tried people by speaking with a great thunder that discomfited their conquerors. Once again the Lord of the Covenant owned Israel as His Son, His servant, and His witness among the nations.

God has given us this same assurance in bringing us despite many dangers, trials, failings and defeats to the opening of a New Year. With the old hymn, we too have been prone to wander, prone to leave the God we love. In I Samuel four, Ebenezer is the place where the Philistines defeated the Israelites, slaying some four thousand in the first battle. The same chapter records the second battle of Ebenezer when the Philistines again smote Israel, killing some thirty thousand footmen, two of the priests of Israel, and capturing the Ark of the Lord.

Indeed, so great was that disaster that old Eli fell and broke his neck at the news thereof and his daughter-in-law gave birth to a babe whom she named Ichabod, "The glory is departed from Israel."

The victory, then, was the third battle of Ebenezer. It was wrought by God's grace, God's power, for God's glory. In our own strength, in our own fancied moral sufficiency or spiritual loveliness we build only Ichabods, not Ebenezers.

In the wonder of His Grace which chose us in the Beloved, in the all-sufficiency of Christ Jesus our Saviour, God has received us and kept us unto this hour, in the might of His Spirit He has been pleased to lift the testimony of the *Southern Presbyterian Journal* to truth as it is in Christ Jesus.

"And we hope by His good pleasure
Safely to arrive at home."

After Ebenezer what? By the mercy of th Lord, IMMANUEL. The fellowship of th Most High is the blessing of the people of Go through the Old and New Testaments. Th promise of His Presence runs thus:

"The Lord, thy God He will *go over befor thee*" across the Jordan and across the line tha divides between 1956 and 1957. "Be strong an of good courage . . . for the LORD th God, He it is that doth *go with thee.*" "Lo, I ar with you alway."

"He *will not fail thee nor forsake thee.*" Fea thou not, for I am with thee; be not dismaye for I am thy God: I will strengthen thee; yea, will help thee, yea I will uphold thee with th right hand of my righteousness."

God's blessed Presence with His people er tered our human life at the advent of Chris In the full sense of the word the Lord Jesu is our IMMANUEL. "And Jesus Christ is th same yesterday, today, and forever."

In Him the LORD is my helper, and I wi not fear what man can do unto me. Whateve the future hath of wonder or surprise, it b longs to the Redeemer Who has overcome an is set down at the right hand of the Majest on High.

—W.C.R.

Know Your Bible

Making full allowance for the advances i every field of learning today it is still a fa that the Christian worker's greatest single nee is a knowledge of the Bible.

This truth should be axiomatic but becau of the pressures from so many other worthwhi sources it is very easy to let other things crow in on our lives until the Bible becomes se ondary and our witness and ministry is ce tered in material and intellectual interests which are not of primary spiritual importance.

The Apostle Paul, nearing the end of his active missionary life, in speaking to the elders from the Ephesian church said: *"For I have not shunned to declare unto you all the counsel of God."*

The record of Paul's ministry and his letters to the churches and individuals show his burning passion to preach Christ in His fullness. A study of his messages will show the depth and breadth of that witness — centered in a supernatural revelation and burning with a conviction that this message was the one thing which men must have for eternal life and also as the way of practical daily living.

It is interesting to note Paul's confidence in and dependence on the Old Testament revelation. This, coupled with the special revelation which he had himself received, was that Christ was the One foretold by the prophets, and the Son of God come to redeem sinners by His Own shed blood, and that those who accepted Him became members of His body, the Church, a glorious fellowship of believers.

With Paul's obvious concentration on making Christ known, he has set an example for Christians of every generation, an example we all would be wise to follow.

What is the "counsel of god"? What is the Gospel message in its entirety? What is the content of Christian truth? As important and helpful as many books about the Bible may be there can never be a substitute for the Scriptures themselves. Christians need to be steeped in the Bible, not only in the facts of the Bible but the truths these facts proclaim. We need to memorize the Bible, to have its passages at our command, for when appropriately used they verily prove to be the Sword of the Spirit.

Erudition is good. Eloquence attractive. A social consciousness is tremendously important. Intellectual competence and academic learning are of the greatest value. But all of these amount to nothing unless they are captivated by and inspired by a thorough knowledge of the Scriptures.

In the various emphases in modern religious education we must not lose sight of the one thing which alone can make other learning effective—a knowledge of the Bible itself.

—L.N.B.

Abib

"The Beginning of months"
Ex. 12; 1&2 *Ex.* 13; 3&4

A new Calendar for the sacred year of the Hebrew nation. The first month of the year, commemorating Israel's Release from Egyptian Bondage. — The EXODUS. — THE WAY OUT.

This is not The Real Exodus.

This is not the REAL Way Out as we have always thought. It was a real event, it was an Exodus, it was a great Deliverance of God's people; but in Reality it was a Picture, a Moving Picture, A Pageant.

In reality their journey out of Egypt, the land of bitter bondage, across the Red Sea, through the desert wilderness, following the pillar of cloud and fire, with manifold, varied experiences of God's warnings, punishments, instructions, encouragements, and ever present providential care—is a demonstration of the NEW LIFE God has for His people, in that day, that dim day; and in the coming Noon Day Brightness for all the ages ahead.

OUT OF BONDAGE — THROUGH THE WILDERNESS — INTO THE LAND OF PROMISE.

Nevertheless this is not the REAL EXODUS, but only a vivid foreshadowing of the Climax coming, EVENT - The EXODUS for all races of men, for all time. The Deliverance not only from physical bondage, and sordid slavery, but from Spiritual death and hopeless degradation and defeat.

THE REAL EXODUS,
THE COMPLETE DELIVERANCE

The First, the Picture — EXODUS — The Passover Lamb. Ex. 12:3-17; the Second, the REAL EXODUS — THE LAMB OF GOD. Lu. 9:28-36.

Moses is central in both the Picture-Exodus and the Real-Exodus. The same Greek word is behind them both, and it means "The Way Out." One is physical, the other is spiritual. One is a single event in history, the other is an endless experience blending into eternity.

On the mount of transfiguration Moses, with Elijah, is present with Jesus and "They spake of His decease which He should accomplish at

The Southern Presbyterian Journal, *a Presbyterian Weekly magazine devoted to the statement, defense, and propagation of the Gospel, the faith which was once for all delivered unto the saints,* published every Wednesday by The Southern Presbyterian Journal, Inc., in Weaverville, N. C.

Entered as second-class matter May 15, 1942, at the Postoffice at Weaverville, N. C., under the Act of March 3, 1879. Vol. XV, No. 36, January 2, 1957. Editorial and Business Offices: Weaverville, N. C. Printed in the U.S.A. by Biltmore Press, Asheville, N. C.

ADDRESS CHANGE: When changing address, please let us have both old and new address as far in advance as possible. Allow three weeks after change if not sent in advance. When possible, send an address label giving your old address.

Jerusalem." The word for "Decease" in the Greek is "EXODON," meaning as in the Egyptian experience, the WAY OUT, the DELIVERANCE. So here is central, His "Decease, His Death, His CROSS, appearing on a lonely hill.

He is the SIN-BEARER
He is the SCAPE-GOAT
He is the SACRIFICE FOR SIN

His 'Way Out" is Our Way In, Our Deliverance; His Death is Our LIFE, Our ETERNAL LIFE. Because He could not be holden of death, because He Arose from the dead, because He LIVETH; we SHALL LIVE ALSO, Live with Him FOREVER.

As He CRIES, "It is finished," an invisible hand from above reaches down to the veil in the temple protecting "The Holy of Holies," the VERY PRESENCE OF GOD; and it is rent *from the top* to the bottom. So now a new and living way is open to God through Christ and His all sufficient sacrifice for sin.

So God set ABIB, the beginning of months, a new year for Israel's journey from the land of bondage to the promised homeland of GOD'S FELLOWSHIP — their EXODUS. And now, with the dawning of 1957, a new year for us. Let us quicken our pace on our EXODUS, our way out, our deliverance; walking with Him on His way here, and dwelling with Him in His Homeland there, forever.

—S.McPh.G

Infants In Calvinism

Certain aspects of Presbyterian doctrine seem to be very difficult of comprehension. Even among Presbyterians, some give impression of wandering vaguely as though in a theological labyrinth. It is not surprising then that many non-Calvinists hold woefully mistaken notions about Presbyterian beliefs. Notable among such, whether due to ignorance or calumny, is the matter of infant salvation. From early ministerial years comes the memory of attempted sport at the expense of the young Calvinist. And associated with the accusation that Calvin believed there are infants in Hell a span long, are the lines from a rhyme put in the mouth of his spirit made perfect: ". . . My name was Calvin, but I see things different now." As in other instances, so in this, many folk who should have been taught better, fall in with the hue and cry, saying that Presbyterians believe in infant damnation.

It is more than passing interest to note that the Westminster Standards (our creed), above all other formulations of belief ever framed, give the "fullest and clearest" statement on this matter. In the Confession of Faith, Ch. 10, we have this: "Elect infants, dying in infancy, are re-what they really are — only the shell, and underneath there is the problem of sin and its only cure.

The greatest blessing the home Church could receive would be to get a new vision of man's lost estate without Christ. Confusing the advantages and content of Western civilization and culture with Christianity itself we look at the cultured pagans all around us and because of their personal attractiveness we forget that they need Christ just as much as any one else.

This confusion of values makes it hard to realize that the mink coated matron driving her own Cadillac convertible is as lost without Christ as the unlettered woman beating clean the family wash by a Korean stream.

How easy it is to forget that the sophisticated student at Davidson or Southwestern needs Christ exactly as does his counterpart in the Japan International Christian University, or Seoul National University.

In God's sight there is no difference between the night club habitue of Broadway and the witch doctor of the Congo; between the business man in Atlanta and the scientist in Tokyo — all need Christ because He is the *only* way.

The doctrine of man's depravity, of God's condemnation of sin, of man's sole hope resting in the atoning work of Jesus Christ is easier to believe when we think of world missions. We need to be shocked into a realization that Americans and Japanese and Koreans and Brazilians and all others stand in equal need of forgiveness of sins and Christ's redeeming blood.

In the midst of the blessings of our God-favored land we need to face the reality of a coming judgment and of our stewardship of the Gospel which we have heard and the propagation of which is our greatest responsibility. Church extension? Yes. Evangelism of every kind? Yes. World Missions? Yes. Personal witnessing? Yes. Why? Because *all* have sinned and come short of the glory of God.

He that believeth on the Son hath everlasting life: and he that believeth not the Son shall not see life; but the wrath of God abideth on him.—John 3:36.

—L.N.B.

The Minor Prophets

By The Rev. R. Wilbur Cousar, D.D.

The "Book of the Twelve" is the title given in the Hebrew Bible to those writings mistakenly called "Minor Prophets," in our English version. This description "Minor," of doubtful value comes from the fact that they were shorter than the other prophets who wrote more extensively, such as Isaiah, Jeremiah, Daniel, Ezekiel, etc.

Explanation of Prophecy

George Adam Smith has partially described the names and functions of a prophet. This is how he puts it: "In vulgar (common) use the name 'prophet' has degenerated to the meaning of 'one who foretells the future.' Of this meaning it is perhaps the first duty of every student of prophecy earnestly and stubbornly to rid himself. In its native Greek tongue, 'prophet' means not 'one who speaks before,' but, 'one who speaks for, or, on behalf of another.' ". We agree with most of this, but reserve for ourselves the clear opinion that there are multiplied cases where the prophets told of the darkness of coming woes and of the unutterable brightness of the coming of the Son of God and His Kingdom.

What We Will Study

Our women this year will not study the entire "Book of the Twelve," but six authors picked as worthy samples or representatives of the rest, namely Amos, Hosea, Micah, Habakkuk, Zechariah and Malachi. Interestingly enough these will furnish sketches, so to speak, of the Assyrian, the Babylonian and the Persian periods. Assyria conquered the Northern Kingdom of Israel; Babylon conquered the Southern Kingdom of Judah and Persia allowed and assisted the Return from Exile.

In this article we want to make a few brief observations on the first three writers. We will tag them with three words, which may seem like over-simplication at first, but may help as pegs to hang our thoughts upon and perhaps help to remember them by at a later time. Here goes — Amos, JUDGMENT; Hosea, LOVE; Micah, HOPE. We hope you will literally rivet these broad terms to each prophet.

Historical Background

Both Northern and Southern Kingdoms greatly expanded their borders in the earlier days. In Amos' and Hosea's time Assyria and Egypt, the two great world powers, were at peace. Move down, if you will, a few decades, and the dread armies of Assyria began to march. They conquered the smaller nations between Assyria and the Mediterranean. Israel the Northern Kingdom was no match for such a power. The dreaded year 721 B. C. marked the conquest of this proud people and the end of their national existence. Thousands were carried into captivity while the poorest and the least promising of the nation were left behind to till the wasted soil and look after the olive groves that remained. There was much anguish and loss. The climate of their life had changed. The old luxury and plenty was gone. Judgment clouded the whole sky. Men, women and children were in trouble. Truly, this was it. Against this, Amos and Hosea warned the people.

In the case of Micah, we have a prophet of the Southern Kingdom, who witnessed the armies of Assyria as they came up to the very walls of Jerusalem the capital, but never conquered little Judah. Another power, Babylon, approximately a century later, was to accomplish this sad mission. During Micah's day, however, there was the signal reformation, or revival, in Judah led by good King Hezekiah, in which no doubt Micah had a definite part. In spite of this splendid awakening the seeds of decay were still germinating in Judah's life which finally led to its complete overthrow, long after Hezekiah was dead.

I. AMOS

God uses all sorts of people. Do not worry too much if He is using some people that you may think of as queer. Amos was peculiar, or shall we say odd, to say the least. He was a crude sheep herdsman of Tekoah who became a powerful preacher of righteousness. The messages he delivered were both plain and at times terrible. His preaching probably made a lot of people uncomfortable.

Professor George L. Robinson in his book, "The Twelve Minor Prophets," says this about Amos, "By many Amos is supposed to be the earliest prophet whose writings have come to us. If so, then his book is the oldest volume of 'sermons' extant! Be that as it may, he is one of the most forceful preachers of repentance and judgment of all the prophets of the Old Testament."

His Warnings

While he pronounced God's judgments upon the surrounding nations of Damascus, Gaza,

space forbids us from discussing the various theories as to what this means. Let us say, we can't help but believe that this is far greater than the Returns under Ezra and Nehemiah, - and much grander in import and accomplishment than the movements of modern Zionism. We believe we see, in fact, a wee, tiny, key-hole picture of the great everlasting Kingdom of our Lord and Saviour. "So then all Israel shall be saved." "The Kingdoms of this world are become the Kingdoms of our Lord, and of His Christ; and He shall reign forever and ever."

II. HOSEA

This is the first great prophet of LOVE. Think of telling this wonderful story before anyone else. It is magnificent. His marriage to an immoral woman named Gomer, by God's command, is strange indeed. Yet, it is a clear picture of God's love for His unfaithful rebellious people. Professor George Robinson outlines seven processes which he discovers in Hosea as the successive steps in Israel's downfall (1) Lack of knowledge, "My people are destroyed for lack of knowledge" (4:6) i.e., for lack of head! The nation is ignorant of God's law. (2) Pride, "and the pride of Israel doth testify to his face" (5:5) i.e., Israel has a diseased heart! They were not only patriotic but arrogant. (3) Instability, "For your goodness is as a morning cloud, or as the dew that goeth early away." (6:4) ; i.e., life is stifled by hypocrisy and ritual. (4) Worldliness - "Ephraim he mixeth himself among the peoples. Ephraim is a cake not turned" - 7:8) ; i.e., the nation's politics were bad! (5) Corruption - "They have deeply corrupted themselves as in the days of Gibeah" (9:9) ; i.e., their religion was rotten. (6) Backsliding - "My people are bent on backsliding from me" (11:7) ; i.e., backsliding had become a habit! (7) Idolatry - "And now they sin more and more, and have made them molten images of their silver, even idols according to their own understanding" (13:2) ; i.e., they had become guilty of complete abandon! Remember, God loved Israel in spite of all their backsliding.

James Russell Lowell spoke important words on the occasion of the 25th anniversary of Harvard University: "I am saddened when I see our success as a nation measured by the number of acres under tillage, or of bushels of wheat exported, for the real value of a country must be weighed in scales more delicate than the balance of trade. — The measure of a nation's true success is the amount it has contributed to the thought, the moral energy, the intellectual happiness, the spiritual hope and consolation of mankind."

III. MICAH

Micah was a prophet to the Southern Kingdom of Judah. He appears to have been a young contemporary of Hosea, as Hosea was of Amos. The writer opens with a trembling note at the destruction of Northern Israel and Judah, as either quite imminent or actually in process at that time. In fact, the verb he uses makes possible that Samaria, or the Northern Kingdom, had already been destroyed. One can imagine the news that Washington has fallen to the Communist invasion and that all government officials are in jail or have been hanged as traitors. Jerusalem looks as if it will be next on the agenda of destruction.

May we make briefly five comments about the contents of Micah's message.

(1) He was a champion of the poor. The rich were absorbing their lands. The lot of the poor was impossible. Social injustice was crying to heaven for redress. The invasion of the enemy was the judgment of Jehovah.

(2) He told of the establishment of God's final Kingdom. In chapter four, he says, "the mountain (or Kingdom) of the house of the Lord shall be established in the top of the mountains (or Kingdoms.) — and many nations shall come and say, Come and let us go up to the house of the God of Jacob" etc. A benevolent and beautiful picture follows of universal peace, security and righteousness. "The Lord shall reign — in Mt. Zion — forever."

(3) The coming King. Bethlehem shall be his birthplace. "For now shall He be great unto the ends of the earth."

(4) The exponent of true righteousness. He calls for the hills in chapter six, as a witness of the truth of Jehovah's message. In the face of "wicked balances," "deceitful weights," "violence," "lies" and the like he utters a sublime word that has echoed across the centuries, "What is good and what doth the Lord require of thee, but to do justly, and to love mercy and to walk humbly with Thy God." Wrapped up in this are all the tenets of faith, salvation and obedience. It is a picture of the good life.

(5) A believer in a God of mercy, forgiveness and love. Chapter seven, the final part of his message, presents a back drop of even greater measures of deceit and intrigue, "A man's enemies are the men of his own house." Yet as he draws his message to a close he reverently and joyously declares, "Who is a God like unto thee that pardoneth iniquity and passeth by the transgression of the remnant of his heritage? — because He delighteth in mercy. He will turn again. He will have compassion upon us."

---

a little segment of our planet, but the entire "world." "Ye are the light of the *world.*" The Master could see the witness, the example, the influence of His followers penetrating the darkness, the doubt, and the corruption of humanity. Yes, let's keep the idea of *penetrating* or *permeating* as imperative in our thinking. Where shall it be? Well, the places are numerous,—the home, the circle, the club, the P.T.A., the church, the Sunday School, the shopping center, the neighborhood, the world. How blessed, how uplifting is the force of one loving, courageous, tactful, unselfish Christ-like person in a group. Such a one may be popular, usually they are, but not always. Jesus our Lord never guaranteed popularity. "In the world you shall have tribulation, but be of good cheer, I have overcome the world."

The Salt

What is salt like? Dr. Thompson says, "Salt has two functions, to season and to preserve." Christians should always be the ones to make life more wholesome, more attractive, more joyous. We have to watch out for this "seasoning" function, lest we become so prejudiced, so bitter, so narrow we repel rather than attract others to our Lord. This quiet "seasoning" influence with its "tangy" flavor should affect all races regardless of their color, social standing, or economic condition. It should stretch out kind hands to those across the seas, for we are the salt of the "earth." Our missionary impulses should be stronger, our support more generous for the spread of the gospel.

Salt, as the writer points out, not only seasons, but it also preserves. In Palestine they had no ice, then, and they have very little now. Salt keeps decay from acting and destroys a great many dangerous germs. He points out the fact that there are destructive forces at work today that would annihilate the individual as well as the home. They would destroy our economic life, our political independence, and our social well-being. Our international understanding is constantly being undermined by the termites of Communism and a super-nationalism. A Christian influence, nevertheless, through our churches and our government should be a potent influence for fair-dealing for righteousness. Christian statesmen backed up by an awakened Christian constituency can wield an influence that is both wholesome and world wide in its effects.

The Light of the World

Dr. Thompson develops the likeness of our Christianity and its influence to light. Jesus would light not only the shining torches of brilliant minds but also the flickering candle lights of homely hearts. The Author quotes the appropriate words of Dr. Merrill, "Christianity has spread through the shining lights, Brooks, Drummond, Moody, Wesley, Luther, Wycliffe, Saint Francis, and a host of others, who shine like great beacons that cannot be hid. But it has spread at least as much, probably far more, through the simple candlelight in innumerable homes." Whether a candle or a beacon, the light of the Christian must shine out across the world until the road is clear for men to walk along and the path of duty is made plain.

We are reminded of Laura Copenhaver's earnest and beautiful words:

"Through desert ways, dark fen and deep morass,
Through jungles, sluggish seas, and mountain pass,
Build ye the road, and falter not nor stay;
Prepare across the earth the King's highway.

Lord give us faith and strength the road to build,
To see the promise of the day fulfilled,
When war shall be no more and strife shall cease
Upon the highway of the Prince of Peace."

LESSON FOR JANUARY 13

By THE REV. J. KENTON PARKER

Jesus Baptised and Tempted

Background Scripture: Matthew 3 and 4
Devotional Reading: Hebrews 3:1-14

In the Epistle to the Hebrews we are taught that Christ became one of us in order that He might be a faithful and merciful High Priest. He was faithful to Him that appointed Him. Moses was faithful as a servant; Jesus Christ was faithful as a Son over His own house. He was baptized, not that He had any sins to be confessed and put away, but to fulfill all righteousness. He was tempted in all points like as we are, yet without sin, in order that He might succor those that are tempted. In today's lesson we are considering both of these events, His Baptism and His Temptation; both for us.

I. *His Baptism:* Chapter 3.

John the Baptist begins his ministry, preaching, and saying, Repent ye : for the kingdom of heaven is at hand. Great multitudes came to hear him, and to be baptized in the river Jordan, confessing their sins. He warned the scribes and Pharisees who came that they must bring forth fruits worthy of repentance. True repentance, like saving faith, must show itself in works. Our definition of Repentance unto life is a good one for it combines the teaching of the Bible upon that subject. It is needed in our generation, both to be taught and preached, and also to be put into practice. Our idea of repentance, like so many other ideas, has become somewhat vague and meaningless. Real revival must start with genuine repentance.

Besides preaching repentance, and baptizing, John bore witness to the One who was to come after him, the One Who would thoroughly purge His floor, gathering the wheat into the garner, but burning up the chaff. Turning now to the gospel according to John, and comparing it with this account in Matthew, we see that John also bore testimony to Christ as the Lamb of God Who should take away the sin of the world. Matthew tells the people that, "He that cometh after me shall baptize with the Holy Ghost and with fire." Combining all these statements we see that John the Baptist had a clear conception both of the person and work of the Messiah. Let me summarize briefly: Jesus was to be "mightier than I"; He was to baptize with the Holy Spirit; He was to be the Lamb of God; He was to be the Judge, separating wheat from chaff.

Knowing all this about Jesus, it is not surprising that, when Jesus came to be baptized, John hesitated and objected, saying, I have need to be baptized of Thee, and comest thou to me? Jesus' answer explains the reason; Suffer it to be so now, for so it becometh us to fulfill all righteousness. Jesus was "made under the Law," and subjected Himself to all its requirements and regulations. He was taking the place of sinners. He had no sin, and therefore needed no repentance, or water baptism, which was a sign of cleansing, but He subjected Himself to this ordinance because He was made like unto His brethren.

I would like to give my own personal conviction as to the mode of baptism used by John. To me the picture is very clear. Both John and Jesus were wearing sandals, which could be easily slipped off. John, I believe, stood in the edge of the river Jordan, and as Jesus stood before him, took a hyssop branch and dipping it in the running water, (which was clean water) sprinkled Jesus with this water. This fully satisfies the reading in the Greek, and was the natural way for John to baptize. I can see no immersion in this picture, and I believe I follow My Lord in baptism when I pour or sprinkle water on the one being baptized.

Notice, too, the vast difference between Jesus' baptism and that of the others. The Holy Spirit descends in the form of a dove and rests upon Him, and a voice is heard saying, This is My beloved Son, in whom I am well pleased. The water came down, and so did the Spirit. Water, after all, is but a symbol. Water can never wash away sin. The real baptism is that of the Spirit. A cup full of water is just as much a symbol of cleansing as a river full. We have in this picture another confirmation of our belief in the Trinity. All three persons of the Godhead are present.

From this chapter we learn some most important and practical lessons. We are taught that true repentance is more than words and form; it must bear fruit in a changed life. There must be "full purpose of, and endeavor after, new obedience." If a man says, I repent, and still continues to live a life of sin, we know that his repentance is not genuine. I am afraid that there is a great deal of merely professed repentance without any change in direction or purpose or practice. We see also how much greater Jesus is than John the Baptist. John was a great man; Jesus was a Great Saviour. We see, too, that the baptism that counts is the baptism of the Holy Spirit. We learn also that Jesus was willing to become in all points like as we are, except for sin. His Baptism and Temptation both show this.

II. *His Temptation:* 4:1-11.

This passage has been studied so often that it is very familiar and its truths and lessons are known to us all. It will do us good, however, to go over it again, for we never read or study the Bible without seeing new things, if the Holy Spirit guides us. As we go over these familiar verses let us keep in mind this verse from Hebrews: Tempted in all points like as we are, yet without sin. These are but samples of the many temptations which came to Him while in the flesh.

This whole picture should make us sure of the reality and personality of our great adversary, the devil. There is a great deal of shallow thinking and speaking and writing about Satan and his work. I believe that when we try to speak or write about our "adversary" that he tries to hinder all he can. We do not hear many sermons about the devil or about sin. It has become "old-fashioned" to mention such disagreeable subjects. In this chapter we get a glimpse of Satan; his cunning and his power and his boldness. If we read our Bibles we will see "the trail of the serpent" as it stretches from Eden to the bottomless pit, and to the lake of fire. It is a crooked, slimy trail, winding its way into every home, every community, and every nation. When we treat lightly his power, his activity and his influence, we are playing into his hand. The most foolish mistake a general can make, said Robert E. Lee, is to underestimate the strength of the enemy. It was no minor foe that Jesus met in "The Battle of the Wilderness," but the head of all the forces of evil, the prince of the power of the air.

1. The first temptation is to doubt; not doubt that He is the Son of God, but doubt as to His Father's care. The word, "If" seems to be more like "Since"; since thou art the Son of God, command that these stones be made bread; use your prerogative as the Son to create bread as you used that power to create the world.

Now, remember that Jesus took upon Himself the form of man, and that He is here as a Man. We, as ordinary men and women, have our temptations to sometimes doubt God's care over us. Will the Father let His Son starve to death out there in the wilderness? He has fasted forty days and is hungry. Will He trust His Father? Jesus answers from the Scripture: "It is written, Man shall not live by bread alone, but by every word that proceedeth out of the mouth of God." Man is more than body; he is a spiritual being, and the spirit is more important than the body.

In these days when so much stress is laid upon proper food for our bodies, this lesson comes home with added meaning. We are anxious and worried for fear that we will starve to death, or be undernourished. I wonder if the old custom of fasting would not be good for many of us? Do not many of us stuff our bodies and starve our souls? The most important food is still, "every word that proceedeth out of the mouth of God." Let us trust our Father.

2. The second temptation seems to be a temptation to Presumption. It is the opposite of the first. The devil quotes a promise in support of his suggestion: "If thou be the Son of God, cast thyself down, for it is written, He shall give his angels charge concerning thee; and in their hands they shall bear thee up, lest at any time thou dash thy foot against a stone." We can presume upon a promise of God. For instance, Jesus said that "They shall take up serpents: and if they drink any deadly thing, it shall not hurt them." (Mark 16:17,18). Does this promise mean that we Christians are to "show off" by going around handling deadly snakes? Are we that foolish? This promise was fulfilled in the case of Paul when a viper came out of the heat and fastened upon him and he shook it off and felt no harm. But Paul had more sense than to go around hunting vipers and letting them bite him, to prove that God would take care of him.

Surely no one would claim this promise as insurance against drinking carbolic acid. Even in this matter of healing the sick we have to guard against the temptation to "show off." I was listening to one of the best known "Faith Healers" recently. He preached a good gospel sermon, and he made no claim to heal by his own power. However, when several people presented themselves for healing, I could not help but feel that he was making a spectacular show out of it. I do not wish to misjudge. I know God heals the sick in answer to prayer, and the disciples were given power to so heal, and I am sure that there is a place for such healing today. Let us be careful not to presume. Jesus rejected Satan's suggestion.

(Continued on Page 17)

YOUNG PEOPLES Department

YOUTH PROGRAM FOR JANUARY 13

By THE REV. B. HOYT EVANS

"That Ye May Know"

Scripture: I John 5:1-13

Suggested Hymns: "I Love To Tell The Story"
"More About Jesus"
"Fling Out The Banner! Let It Float"

(This program presents one of the five financial objectives selected by Presbyterian young people for 1957. Some groups will receive a special offering for each of these objectives, and others will designate a definite part of the benevolent budget. In either case, be sure to have a prayer of dedication for your gifts. Our prayers and our sincere interest are fully as important as our material gifts.)

Program Leader:

In writing his letter to the early Christians John gave a definite statement of his purpose. He said that he wrote those words in order that the readers might know that they had eternal life. The Scriptures are superior to all other Christian literature in that the Holy Spirit inspired the writing of the Bible in a special way, but all Christian literature shares in the purpose of the Scriptures: that those who read it may come to know certain things.

The first purpose of Christian literature is to help us know and understand the Bible. Knowing the Bible, we come to know Christ. If we know Christ as Saviour and Lord, we know that we have eternal life. It is only when we know all these things that we can really know how to live in a way that is pleasing to God and helpful to others.

In this program we are considering one of our financial objectives for 1957. A portion of our money is being used again this year to provide a three month supply of free literature for new Sunday Schools. We are providing these teaching and learning materials in order that others may have the knowledge necessary to Christian life and growth. We are giving that they may know.

Our gift of literature to these newly established Sunday Schools should benefit them in at least three ways. Our speakers will tell us what they are.

First Speaker:

The most obvious advantage to a new Sunday School in receiving a supply of free literature for the first quarter of its life is a financial one. Many of us belong to Sunday Schools in which the purchase of literature presents no problem. The secretary and superintendent may complain from time to time about the rising cost of all printed materials, but there always seems to be enough money to buy whatever is needed. Suppose your Sunday School is just beginning. There has been no previous quarter to save up offerings to purchase supplies needed for this quarter. All your families are in the lower income brackets, and most of those interested in the Sunday School are children and young people who have no incomes of their own. You can readily see that in such a situation the purchase of supplies would be a real problem. Many new Sunday Schools find it necessary to begin their work with an inadequate supply of inferior literature. The gift we are making through our financial objective will enable these new schools to make a strong start.

Second Speaker:

Another advantage of the free literature being provided through our gifts lies in the experience of those who prepare and apportion the materials. The supply of literature sent to each new school is carefully selected according to the numbers and ages of the students. This is a service which is most valuable to many inexperienced administrators of young Sunday Schools. It takes considerable experience and training to know what kind and what amount of literature to order for a Sunday School. Many of our newly organized Sunday Schools are lacking in leadership with such experience and training. The service we are providing through our financial objective will bring experience to where it is needed.

Third Speaker:

There are inevitable discouragements and disappointments to be encountered in the organization of new Sunday Schools. Many times those who are engaged in this important work are tempted to think that the rest of the church is unmindful of their problems and not interested

(Continued on Page 17)

Helps To Understanding Scripture Readings in *Day by Day*

By Rev. C. C. Baker

Sunday, January 13, *John* 20:26-31. When Jesus called His disciples to go where there was real danger of death (John 11:7-8), it was Thomas who expressed a willingness to die with Him (11:16). What do you suppose the state of Thomas' mind was when he made the statement of 20:25? How must the sight of Christ's crucifixion have affected one as loyal as Thomas? The other disciples had not believed that Christ had risen when they first heard the news (Luke 24:9-11). Observe Thomas' action when the risen Christ revealed Himself to him (vv.27-28). Was there any lack of loyalty to Christ on Thomas' part when he expressed his doubts (v.25)? Christ is more than willing to help sincere Christians who are confused in their personal faith.

Monday, January 14, *Exodus* 19:3-6. The children of Israel had left Egypt and come to the foot of Mount Sinai (19:1-2). In chapter 19 preparations were made for God's coming down upon the mountain to deliver the Ten Commandments (c.20). Why do you suppose the death penalty was imposed upon anyone who entered God's presence (vv.11-13,20-21)? Try to picture the scene of God coming down upon the mountain (vv.16-19). How did the people react (20:18-19)? Here is God in all His holiness meeting face to face with His people. Sometimes we, who have Christ to mediate for us, are not aware of the holiness of our God, but a holy walk is required of us, as well as of the Children of Israel (vv.5-6), if we are to walk with Him. Read Hebrews 12:18-25.

Tuesday, January 15, *I Samuel* 1:21-28. For years the Word of the Lord had been little heard in Israel (3:1). God began to move by allowing disappointment and frustration to come into the life of an obscure woman named Hannah (1:2-8). She became the object of scorn (1:2,6) and even her prayers were misunderstood (1:12-14). Notice the depth of Hannah's distress in her desire for a child (v.10). Do you think she would have reached the dedication of v.11 if she had not experienced adversity? How do vv.24-28 reveal the sincerity of the vow that she made in v.11? Thus the purposes of God were accomplished through the birth (1:20) and consequent ministry of Samuel (3:19-20). Notice Hannah's deep joy (2:1ff). Will you give all the disappointments and adversities of your life to God, asking Him to work out His own purposes through them?

Wednesday, January 16, *Proverbs* 3:1-4. The teachings and commandments of the Lord are the ways of blessing for men. List the blessings mentioned in vv.1-10 that come to the person who heeds the ways of the Lord. Notice what is involved in heeding His ways: (a) a trusting of Him to lead and guide in perplexing and difficult problems (vv.5-6); (b) a willingness to learn new truth from Him (vv.5,7); (c) a willingness to apply His ways to our lives (vv.1-3) and turn from sin (v.7; (d) an acceptance of the circumstances of our lives as from Him (vv.11-12); (3) the honoring of God with the first fruits of our income (v.9). Which of the above requirements reveals a lack in your life in your relation with God?

Thursday, January 17, *Ruth* 1:14-18. In a foreign land Naomi's two sons married foreign wives, Orpah and Ruth (vv.1-4). Both sons died (v.5) and as Naomi returned to Bethlehem, she encouraged her daughters-in-law to return to their own homes (vv.7-18). What was Naomi's reason for urging them to go (vv.9,11-13)? Notice the strong bonds of affection that bound them together (vv.8-9,14). Orpah, however, did return to her home (vv.14-15), but Ruth remained (vv.15-18). Be sure to notice that Orpah returned to her people *and to her gods* (v.15) while Ruth remained with Naomi *and followed the Lord* (vv.16-17). Ruth subsequently became the great grandmother of David (4:13,17) and an ancestor of the Messiah (Matthew 1:5-16). Are you willing to put all those things that are precious to you secondary to following Christ? Unexpected blessings await you if you do.

Friday, January 18, *Ephesians* 6:10-18. Because the Christian in his own strength is helpless against the power of Satan (vv.11-13) Paul instructs the believer to put on the armor of God (vv.10,11,13). The believer finds all the equipment mentioned in vv.14-15,17a in Christ. Notice that the Christian's armor covers the body from head to toe; his protection in Christ is complete. In taking the shield of faith (v.16) the believer turns the temptations that are hurled at him over to Christ and trusts Him to overcome them. Daily Bible study (v.17b) and prayer (v.18) also fortify the believer against temptation. Do you try to overcome temptations in your own strength or do you turn them over to Christ to conquer for you?

Saturday, January 19, *Daniel* 6:1-10. Read the entire story of Daniel and the Lion's Den (vv.1-28). What facts about God stand out in this story (vv.22,26-27)? Contrast the edict Darius made about himself before Daniel was put in the den of lions (vv.7b,12) and the edict he made about God after the incident (vv.25-27). What truth about himself did Darius discover? about God? Observe the craftiness of Daniel's adversaries (vv.4-13) and yet the outcome of their lives (v.24). What facts about God account for their thwarted efforts (vv.22,26-27)? No man's scheme, no king's law can impair the hand of God (cf. vv.12,27). It was this view of God that gave Daniel courage (v.10) and faith (v.23). Fix your eyes upon this same God who watches over you.

CHILDRENS Page

David Tells The King

David's brothers scornfully told him to go back home to his little sheep this was no place for a kid like him. But when men told King Saul that David was not frightened by the giant, the King said Bring him to me. So David came to the royal tent, and the King said, What is this I hear about you, young man? Then David said, O my lord the King, thy servant will go out and fight this big bluffer. What! said the King, Why look at him, he is a giant, clothed in steel, trained to war. Boy, he would kill you in a jiffy! Then David answered, Thy servant kept his father's sheep, and there came out a lion and took a lamb from the flock, but thy servant caught him by the beard and slew him and delivered the lamb from the lion's mouth. The Lord God did it, and He will deliver me from the giant, seeing he hath defied the army of the Living God. (TO BE CONTINUED) Y.

NEWS of CHURCHES Around the World

A.T.S. News

A professor and a former faculty member of he General Assembly's Training School were .warded honorary degrees early in December by)ueens College, Charlotte, N. C. Dr. Rachel Henlerlite, professor of Applied Christianity and Christian Nurture, and Miss Myrtle Williamson, a raduate of the Training School and former diector of Field Work, each received the degree, loctor of humanities.

Miss Henderlite has been on the faculty of he Training School since 1944. Miss Williamson, who served the School from 1946 to 1948, is now)irector of Christian Activities and member of he faculty of the department of Religion at Stillnan College, Tuscaloosa, Alabama.

Plans are in process for opening the Demonstraion Kindergarten on January 28, 1957, under the irection of Miss Josephine Newbury. The specially esigned building is nearing completion and will ccomodate 25 children. The observation booth, quipped for 20 persons, has one-way vision glass, nd also has an electronics system by which obervers can hear conversations in the play room; nd with the use of ear phones and a dial, can ollow an individual child or group for any period f time desired. Observation will be a part of the raining for the students who take the kindergaren course. Parents of children enrolled in the indergarten will be encouraged to avail themelves of observation opportunities, and to attend eriodic parent conferences. To a lesser extent ther parents and interested persons may be exended observation privileges.

SOUTH CAROLINA

Clinton — Presbyterian College's Diamond Jubiee Development Program moved close to the $800,-00 mark early in December, as Upper Charleston 'resbytery almost reached its goal, and the Macon egion turned in its first report on December 9.

A total of $11,320 from 81 subscriptions was eported by the little Upper Charleston area which ad set its sights on $12,000. And although the rive there has officially closed, the Rev. Hubert . Wardlaw of Orangeburg, and Mr. Alex Mc'rackin of Bamberg, co-chairmen of the region, xpressed confidence that the goal would be comleted in that area within a short time.

Macon area Presbyterians brought in $18,773 rom 71 subscriptions at their first report meeting. The goal set for the campaign in this area is $40,240. Leading in this area are co-chairmen Mr. Henry K. Burns, and the Rev. John E. Richards, both of Macon.

The latest returns from these two regions pushed the development program total to date to $795,378. The campaign has already exceeded its minimum goal of $750,000. The campaign is being conducted within the Synods of South Carolina and Georgia.

NORTH CAROLINA

Charlotte — Baptist, Presbyterian, Lutheran, and Methodist churches — seven separate congregations — paid honor to Queens College recently, as part of the centennial celebration of the Presbyterian institution.

These seven groups joined in the school's celebration, as each of the seven churches had at an earlier time been sheltered on Queens' campus.

The convocation, beginning with an academic procession, was held in Myers Park Baptist Church, one of the churches that had had its beginnings on the campus.

Charlotte — Baptist, Presbyterian, Lutheran, and Methodist churches — seven separate congregations — paid honor to Queens College recently, as part of the centennial celebration of the Presbyterian institution.

These seven groups joined in the school's celebration, as each of the seven churches had at an earlier time been sheltered on Queens' campus.

The convocation, beginning with an academic procession, was held in Myers Park Baptist Church, one of the churches that had had its beginnings on the campus.

TEXAS

Dallas — An organizational meeting for a new Presbyterian church in Dallas was held here December 9th. The new church is the ninth new one to be sponsored by the Presbyterian Extension Committee of Dallas in the last eight years.

Members of the commission of the Presbytery of Dallas in charge of the organization were: The Rev. Robert P. Douglass, chairman; Dr. William M. Elliott, Jr., Dr. Walter A. Bennett, Mr. B. T. Erwin, Mr. Austin B. Watson, Mr. George R. Allen, and Mr. James P. Williams, Jr.

Dr. Elliot, pastor of the Highland Park Presbyterian Church of Dallas, preached the sermon. His topic was "Every Man in His Place."

Minister for the new congregation is the Rev. W. A. Dealey, Jr., a graduate of the University of Texas, Austin Theological Seminary, and the Andover-Newton Theological Seminary of Boston, Mass.

Charter membership of the new church is nearly 100, Mr. Dealy said.

Dallas — On Sunday, December 9, at special services held at 3:00 P. M. a commission of the Presbytery of Dallas organized the Churchill Way Presbyterian Church.

Members of the Commission were Rev. Messrs. Robt. P. Douglass, Preston Hollow pastor; Walter A. Bennett, Westminster pastor; Wm. M. Elliott, Jr., Highland Park pastor; and elders B. T. Erwin, James P. Williams, Jr., George R. Allen, Chairman of Presbytery's Committee on Church Extension, and Austin P. Watson, President of the Presbyterian Extension Committee of Dallas.

A total of 82 people presented themselves for membership at this service of organization, with an additional 26 who had signed the organization petition but were unable to be present at this first service. Of the 104 petitioners, 45 came from membership in the Preston Hollow Church, 17 from Highland Park, and 10 from Westminster. Seven people were received on re-affirmation and 4 adults on profession. There were three adult baptisms and at the same service the baptism of infant children of two of the new families.

Officers installed were - Elders: B. T. Erwin, Henry W. DuBois, O. H. Grubbs, and James P. Williams, Jr.; deacons W. H. Wilson, Jr., James R. Young, Frank H. Pillsbury, E. A. Olson, Scott DeLee, and Gene Mundy. This is the ninth church organization, effected as a result of the work of the Presbyterian Extension Committee of Dallas in the past eight years.

Dallas — Lloyd S. Kreidler, a student at Southern Methodist University, has become part-time worker in the Christian Education Department at Highland Presbyterian Church. His main service will be to the Youth Work of the church.

Mrs. Joseph M. Wilson and three children, members of Highland Park Church, have presented a set of Rex Brasher's "Trees and Birds of North America" to the Rare Book Collection of the University of Texas.

Dallas — The "50 Plus Club," an organization in Highland Park Presbyterian Church, Dallas, has been written up in STAMPS, a magazine for those interested in philately.

The "50 Plus Club," organized two years ago, meets once a month for fellowship among those persons over fifty years of age. Those who attend, for the most part, are retired persons or free from much responsibility, and who enjoy a place of recreation and fellowship.

One of the first members, Mrs. Annie Jenkins, collected used stamps. The American Bible Society benefited from the collection, which was expanded after Mrs. Jenkins' death. Today the project brings in thousands of stamps from around the world and establishes a person-to-person friendship between members of the "50 Plus Club" and citizens of other countries.

BOOKS

THE BIBLE AS HISTORY. Werner Keller. Wm. Morrow & Co. $5.95.

This book has achieved considerable circulation here in Houston, and some one lent me a copy. The book has some very fine points but also some very weak ones. It was reviewed in "Time" of Oct. 29th by a very liberal editor, which unfortunately gives one the wrong impression of its merits. On the cover it is labelled a "Confirmation of the Book of Books," but the confirmation is limited mainly to political conditions and material facts, while often discrediting the Bible in the more important spiritual matters. The book represents a current trend among scholars of the liberal school to acknowledge more and more the material side of the Old Testament as factual in a rather loose degree of accuracy, while rejecting it as the trustworthy Word of God. While we who trust the Bible welcome this swing in the right direction, we cannot relax our guard against unbelief still present. We must learn to take advantage of the wealth of information which makes the Bible stories more vivid and realign facts used to discredit the Bible in their true place so that they will credit it. It is extremely unfortunate that most books which deal with Old Testament setting are from the hand of those who do not trust it.

It is impossible to point out the many mistakes in the book but the Christian who knows his Bible will recognize most of them. These should not deter us from enjoying the wealth of information on the political conditions of the various periods of Biblical History. Outside the one described below, the only important difference which the reviewer has with the chronology of the book is that he feels the Exodus occurred in the reign of Thothmes, not Rameses.

It is highly unfortunate that Dr. Keller begins his book with the biggest chronological and scientific mistake, and as it is a common mistake among conservative writers, attention must be called to it. He describes a silt deposit which Sir Leonard Woolley found between two layers of painted pottery at the mound of Ur where Abraham lived when young. He thinks it is a confirmation of the FLOOD of Noah, but actually it was deposited many many centuries before the Biblical FLOOD. The identification has persisted since Sir Leonard sent the famous telegram "We have found the FLOOD" and thereby was able to raise more funds for his excavations. Dr. Keller has an excellent description and from it one can easily see that Dr. Keller and Noah have written about two very different events.

According to the book, Woolley found this ten foot layer of silt between two layers of (Obeid) painted pottery. The lower pottery was hand-made, and there were no signs of metal among the sherds. The upper layer was wheel-made accompanied by signs of metal. He has a map showing the extent of the FLOOD as covering the low-lying land between the two rivers, Tigris and Ephrates. He also notes the Persian Gulf as reaching to Ur. The increase in culture indicates that the inundation lasted many decades at least. (He has one small error in that he mentions Kish which was not founded till long long afterward.) Such an account, factual though it is, does not confirm the Biblical story of the FLOOD, but declares it false, unless redated.

However, the description Dr. Keller gives does confirm the Bible in another way. That silt indicates a period of high sea-level in antediluvian times, showing that both the Bible and archeology teach that men lived in the glacial ages. But the importance of that silt deposit between pottery layers shows that early civilizations of the Near East existed in the glacial ages which picture-drawing cave-dwellers hunted reindeer in France. That lower Obeid pottery was much later than the beginning of civilization, and it was a mere accident that Sir Leonard found no traces of metal in the lower layers, for archeologists have found copper and even traces of iron in the mound left from the earliest painted pottery culture, called Hassunah, long before the ancestors of those reindeer hunters left Mesopotamia.

After the Obeid painted pottery times, economic and social conditions deteriorated because of the wickedness mentioned in the Bible and painted pottery vanished for a long time before the FLOOD. After the FLOOD during the regenerated social condition of Noah's posterity in Babel (Jemdet Nas) times painted pottery reappeared. The Biblical FLOOD was not recorded by silt, but by a HIATUS in human culture, noted by archeologists from many parts of the world. **IT WAS NOT LOCAL.**

That silt at Ur which Dr. Keller describes is very important in the history of antediluvian times and is one of the conclusive proofs that civilized man reaches back in the Near East into the glacial ages as far back as the stone age men in Europe. All were the children of Adam and Eve.

Dr. Keller merely followed non-Christian scientists and made a great mistake. How can we who are not informed, as Dr. Keller evidently was not, detect these scientific mistakes? It is very easy. That is just why God gave us the Bible to guide us. If one trusts the Bible it will be exceedingly instructive to read this interesting book discarding the relatively few things that contradict the Scriptures and enjoying the great part which confirms the Bible.

—J. V. N. Talmage

PUT YOUR CHURCH IN THE NEWS. Robert Walker. Scripture Press. 60 cents.

This booklet is to show one how to write news articles about the church's activities that will be published in local newspapers. The author is experienced in journalism.

HOW TO SUCCEED WITH YOUR HOME DEPARTMENT. Henry Jacobsen. Scripture Press. 60 cents.

This booklet has been prepared for those who want to launch a home department in their Sunday School and for those who want to improve the home department they now have. This work should be helpful to the Sunday School superintendent and home department officers and workers.

THE WHITE NIGHTS. Boris Sokoloff. Devin-Adair Company. $3.75.

Dr. Sokoloff, author of many books on medical and scientific subjects, proves himself a fine story teller in these pages. He was an army physician in pre-Communist Russia. He was in the midst

ability to forcefully express what we now know. The net result of the reading of this volume leads us to the inescapable conclusion that there is nothing to be said in favor of alcoholic beverages and by every honest consideration it should be condemned and removed from the social order.

J.R.R.

ENCYCLOPEDIA OF MORALS. Vergilius Ferm. Philosophical Library. $10.00.

Some 50 scholars have contributed to the preparation of this encyclopedia. It is a reference work and we find here substantial articles as well as brief notations on various topics related to moral behavior. There are cross-references so that the reader, if he chooses, may handily find multitudinous ideas associated with morals as these have been treated however much or little in the context of the larger topics. Thus the topic contents are indexed. Major ideas and their proponents are presented as well as interesting examples of social behavior among societies quite unfamiliar to most readers.

Moral relationships are described here from many points of view. Some emphasize the ethical aspects. Others discuss their views from a standpoint of the sociologist and anthropologist. The reader will find here samples of the moral behavior and codes of indigenous and non-historical people from remote corners of the globe. In the religious areas some but not all of the major religions are included.

The factual data presented here are interesting and stimulating. Christian readers will accept some interpretations in the volume and reject others. The discussions as a whole are written more from the secular point of view rather than from the Christian perspective.

Spirit-Imbibers Are Sober Christian Soldiers

By Rev. George S. Lauderdale

To say, "Either you are a Christian missionary or you need one," is to say, "Either you have been baptized with the Holy Spirit or you need to be." Missions is the work of the Holy Spirit: "We are laborers together with God." I Corinthians 3:9.

Jesus promised, "Ye shall receive power *after that the Holy Ghost is come upon you:* And ye shall be witnesses unto me both in Jerusalem, and in all Judea, and in Samaria, and unto the uttermost part of the earth." Acts 1:8. Without God's Spirit, we cannot win men to Christ; with God's Spirit, we cannot fail to do so!

Overflowing Joy

The Holy Spirit brings such joy (Galatians 5:21) to the Christian that he wishes everybody else could share the new life he is experiencing. Being Spirit-filled has some resemblance to intoxication with strong drink; actually, beverage alcohol is the best substitute Satan can offer men and women for the genuine pleasures of baptism with the Holy Ghost? Satan's best is as hogwash.

"These men are full of new wine," said mockers on the day of Pentecost, when the Spirit came upon Christ's waiting, believing disciples. Acts 2:13. Showing that He has something better than Satan to offer every man, drunkards too, God pleads, "Be not drunk with wine, wherein is excess; but be filled with the Spirit." Ephesians 5:18.

Be Blessed To Be a Blessing!

Proof that God does not give Christians His Spirit merely for their exhilaration, (no more than He instituted holy wedlock for this reason only), or that they might make a big impression on men, is given in Acts, chapter 2. Why were the disciples given utterance by the Spirit to speak in foreign languages at Pentecost? Was it that they might preach a better sermon than a nearby rabbi, to have a larger congregation? No! They were given the Spirit "because there were dwelling at Jerusalem Jews, devout men, out of every nation under heaven." Acts 2:5.

Missions the Purpose of Spirit-Fulness

The Holy Spirit benefits the person who receives Him in order that others of all nations might hear the wonderful works of God! Simon Peter, when he was anointed with the Third Person of the Trinity, preached with the hope that others might also be baptized from above. "Repent, and be baptized every one of you in the name of Jesus Christ for the remission of sins, and ye shall receive the gift of the Holy Ghost." Acts 2:38.

Peter was not seeking men's praise or "showing off": he longed to share this blessed Gift of the Spirit with Israel. Later, at the home of Cornelius, he was led to see that the Spirit is for Gentiles too. Acts 10:44-47. Thus today, Christ's church on earth is the witnessing, united group of born again men now living, our boldness to witness for Christ and our unifying love being supplied by the Spirit of God!

Both Jew and Gentile believers in Christ have access by one Spirit unto the Father "and are built upon the foundation of the apostles and prophets, Jesus Christ himself being the chief corner stone; in whom all the building fitly framed together GROWETH unto a holy temple in the Lord." Ephesians 2:20, 21. Do you want to win others to Christ? Do you want your church to grow? *With the Spirit* you will have good success!

Our Jewish Mission in Baltimore

The Emmanuel Center, an agency of our Presbyterian Church, is seeking to reach the more than 90,000 Jews in the City of Baltimore. It is conducted by the Rev. Ludwig R. DeWitz under a committee composed of the Potomac Presbytery of the Presbyterian Church U.S. and Members of the Presbytery of Baltimore of the Presbyterian Church U.S.A. Mr. DeWitz is assisted by two full time lady workers, Miss Penman and Miss Dunkerton, and by a number of volunteer workers.

The activities of the Center are housed in a commodious building which is situated in the heart of the Jewish center. There are many Synagogues close by and a school for the training of Rabbis is within walking distance. Thus we have a golden opportunity at the very door of the center and the Lord has graciously blessed us in the more than 40 years of our continuous ministry.

The activities of the Center include a Day Nursery for preschool age children, a Parents' meeting, a Bible study and discussion group, some children's classes, and regular visitation in the homes of the neighborhood. Some of the Jewish mothers of the children are now assisting in the Nursery School, and thus are hearing—most of them for the first time—that the Lord Jesus Christ is the Messiah, for Whom Israel still waits.

Through the stories in both the Old and New Testaments we teach the children that the Christ whom they have often been taught to hate, is indeed the Son of God and the Saviour of the world. This creates some opposition as it did in the days of the Apostle Paul; but on the whole we have been kindly received and our message heard with a reasonable degree of patience and interest. As a result some have been found of the Church Shepherd. We always encourage the converts to unite with and to be faithful to our churches near which they live; and as a pastor who has received many of them into our church, I can testify that they make excellent witnesses for our Lord.

The work is very different from that in our churches. The Jew is fearfully afraid of becoming a Christian. First, because if he does he will become a Gentile (an erroneous idea which most Jews hold) and second, because of the opposition which he knows he must face from his family. Within my own experience we have had Jews confess our Lord in baptism, and immediately be ostracized by their own. But in spite of the difficulties there are encouraging results. Interest is maintained and new faces constantly appear. Recently, in one of our monthly "Parents' Nights" a doctor who was present became so interested that he asked Mr. DeWitz to come to his home and explain to him what Presbyterians believe. On the day of the meeting the doctor had invited some of his Jewish friends and from 9 P.M. until 1:30 A.M. Mr. DeWitz had the privilege of presenting the claims of the Lord Jesus Christ to this group.

The great need of the work is for the prayerful cooperation of the redeemed people of God. Every Christian ought to be concerned to see that "the lost sheep of the house of Israel" hear the Gospel and thus have an opportunity to know Him Whom to know is Life eternal. Jerusalem, nor any other portion of the earth, can never know peace, until they know and yield to the Saviour; and so it is only as the Holy Spirit opens blinded eyes, and persuades stony hearts to believe and receive the truth "which is in Jesus"—only so can peace be found. Brethren, pray for us as we seek to bring Christ to these people.

T. Roland Philips
Arlington Presbyterian Church
Baltimore, Md.

A One-Minute Message on Stewardship

A new year offers fresh opportunities - new adventures for Christ. He gives each one of us a new day - do we return it to Him empty or full - full because the Time - Abilities - and Money that He has entrusted to us were used in His service? He has promised that we may come to Him in prayer for re-dedication of ourselves to HIS will and for the encouragement and power needed.

He loved us so much that He gave His Son for our redemption.

"If any man is in Christ, he is a new creature, the old things are passed away: behold they are become new."

God's love overflows to us. He was in Christ reconciling the world to Himself.

"You shall love your neighbor as yourself."

This is the month set aside to consider especially "Christian Relations." Our love must overflow to those of other races, other groups, the unlovely, peoples we have not seen.

Let us pray that His overflowing love will be the foundation upon which our Christian Citizenship and Christian Stewardship is built in 1957 and the years to follow.

Mrs. Mary Butler Green
Homer, La.

The Southern PRESBYTERIAN Journal

VOL. XV NO. 37 JANUARY 9, 1957 $3.00 A YEAR

SOUTHWOOD PRESBYTERIAN CHURCH
TALLADEGA, ALABAMA

Developed from an outpost Sunday School started by the First Presbyterian Church a few years ago. Building erected in 1954, and church organized shortly thereafter. Rev. William Hammond is the pastor. Mr. Herbert Carson, Atlanta architect, provided the plan and specifications.

The interior of the sanctuary is of Middle English construction, and much admired. The building is beautiful for situation, occupying a two acre plot on a high elevation. There is a spacious Sunday School of two stories including a recreation room. Entirely free from debt.

THE SOUTHERN PRESBYTERIAN JOURNAL

Rev. Henry B. Dendy, D.D., Editor..............Weaverville, N. C.
Dr. L. Nelson Bell, Associate Editor..............Asheville, N. C.
Rev. Wade C. Smith, Associate Editor..............Weaverville, N. C.

EDITORIAL

Christ or Culture? Who Is Lord?

Is Jesus of Nazareth the Christ of God, the Lord of each life and the King of the Church, or is "some great cause God's New Messiah"? This is the issue that the Church has had to face down through the ages in a thousand varied forms. Shall we start where God has graciously placed us — in Christ Jesus — and move from Him as the Lord, the Absolute, to sundry forces and factors in life? Or shall some popular appeal be treated as the Absolute and from that point Jesus be reckoned a relative aid to be used and corrected as this Absolute may demand.

In the decade of the 350's the Arianizing leaders accepted Emperor Constantius as the voice of the living Logos, with Jesus of Nazareth as only a past expression of that same Logos and thus less authoritative. Against this imperialism, Athanasius and the Nicaeans insisted that God, the eternal Word, became man in Jesus of Nazareth Who is consequently the absolute Lord.

In the 1930's "the German Christians" insisted that the great issue was theism against atheism, that the Nazis were believers in God and revivers of national religion; consequently that religious fealty should be given to Hitler as the Leader against atheistic Communism.

The Confessing Church countered this effort to bypass Christ Jesus in the Barmen declaration that the one word we have to hear in life and in death and obey is the Lord Jesus Christ.

So in our common experiences there is the question. Shall we start with the Lord Jesus as the Absolute and from Him, the Living Word of God, meet the issues that confront us, whether they be war, alcoholism, racism, sex, equalitarianism, et al.? Or shall one begin with whichever of these issues happens to be in the popular eye and from that assumed absolute treat the Lord Jesus and His Word as a relative?

For example, in their intense opposition all use of force, some pacifists went so far to say that, if Jesus really struck anyone wi the whip of cords He used to cleanse the Ten ple, said pacifist was done with Jesus.

In the interest of collectivism many have d nounced the profit motive, but without givir up their own sundry salaries based thereoı Another man starts with the evils of alcoholisı as set forth in recent American studies an concludes that therefore Jesus was wrong i making wine at Cana in Galilee. From th assumption he proceeds to reason that Jesı must have been ignorant of the evils of alcoho ism and consequently must have emptied Hin self of His Divine wisdom.

This reasoning ignores the fact that even t day in many Mediterranean countries one mu either drink bottled water (which the ear centuries did not have) or the wine of tl country or go down with intestinal disorder More fundamentally, it overlooks the questio of who is Lord.

In First Corinthians twelve three, the Apost says that no man is speaking by the Spirit God when he says, Let Jesus be anathema. Paul were writing today would he say th a man is speaking by the Spirit of God whe he proclaims some cultural demand as absolu and bypasses or relativizes or corrects Jesus? The the Apostle adds, "And no man can say th Jesus is Lord, except by the Holy Spirit."

As we face the sundry issues which confroı us, may God the Holy Spirit give us grace say that Jesus is the Lord, the Absolute, tl Foundation beside which no other can be la (I Cor. 3.11), the Beginning from Whom v start as we consider all issues. W.C.I

From One Generation to Anothe

We are writing of a personal matter for bı one reason — to witness to the faithfulne of God.

As this is written it has been exactly forty 'ears to the day since we spent our first Sunday n an interior mission station in China. These our decades are filled with multiplied experinces of God's loving care, His guiding hand and he faithfulness of His promises.

We have spent this fortieth anniversary in a nission station in Korea and have had brought o mind afresh the goodness of God for we have een our third daughter stand with her husband nd dedicate their second son to Him as he eceived the sacrament of baptism. What is here of special significance in this event?

We must go back eighteen years . . .

Isolated in an interior station in China . . . var is raging . . . already the Japanese have ombed our city many times . . . strong ressure from American consular and embassy fficials for us to leave . . . strong pressure rom missionary friends to the South . . . a etter: "You have no right to stay there and ubject your two small children to the dangers, orror and shock of war and the capture of our city."

As these words were read there came imnediately to mind, as though a flash from eaven: "The promise is to you and to your hildren."

The decision was made. . . . months of ncertainty . . . more bombings . . . aily work in crowded hospital wards where S NEVER BEFORE there was the sense of od's presence and help . . . Chinese docors and nurses and staff members all united vith us in a joyous bond of Christian love and n a task we knew God was blessing.

Months passed . . . more fighting . . . nceasing work and a sense of God's presence at ll times . . . several days of intensive warare close . . . a night of numerous exploions in the city (public utilities being blown p by retreating Nationalist forces — but we id not know the cause that night) . . . then, he next morning the Japanese flag flying over he city and Japanese patrols all about.

What of the two children, a boy and a girl? hey did not see one thing to shock them. They vere keenly aware that God had been very near o us all of these months. Furthermore, their resence in the hospital compound proved a rotection and a blessing for the Japanese were mazed and *pleased* to find them there with us.

As a result we worked on for two and a half years more in that hospital, the only one in all of Japanese-occupied China where the entire Chinese hospital staff of over a hundred was able to continue its work without interruption. Furlough just before Pearl Harbor.

The years passed . . . the hospital destroyed in the Communist-Nationalist fighting and ultimately the entire area taken over by the bloody hand of Communism.

The Children? Years in college, teaching, nurses' training, seminary, etc. The boy now almost ready to enter his work as a minister of our church. The girl, married, two sons, a missionary in Korea.

Today, as we saw her stand with her husband and her baby boy in a mission station in Korea and take the vows to train that little one for God there was thankfulness in our hearts as her mother and I watched, and there was a renewed understanding of these words:

"But the mercy of the Lord is from everlasting to everlasting upon them that fear him, and his righteousness unto children's children."

Psalm 103:17.

—L.N.B.

They Shall Bring Forth Fruit in Old Age

The two brightest gems which the Christmas season brought to the desk were pamphlets by two of our distinguished senior ministers. If any young brother wants Scriptural meditations expressed in elegant English adorned with poetry and rich in the Word let him beg of Dr. Joseph Dunglinson, Box 612, Black Mountain, N. C., a copy of GLIMPSES OF HIGHER THINGS. These sermons and sermonettes will surely prime one's pump and cause the streams of refreshment to flow more copiously from his preaching.

Some years ago our Church was credited with two pulpit orators, Dr. James I. Vance and Dr. William Crowe. The latter after teaching a short time in Kentucky followed his father into the ministry and served notable congregations in Memphis, St. Louis and other places. Then he took a smaller church in Talladega. On a visit there, Dr. Crowe said: "William, I am preaching better sermons here than I did in Memphis or in St. Louis. I have more time to study."

The Southern Presbyterian Journal, *a Presbyterian Weekly magazine devoted to the statement, defense, and propagation of the Gospel, the faith which was once for all delivered unto the saints,* published every Wednesday by The Southern Presbyterian Journal, Inc., in Weaverville, N. C.

Entered as second-class matter May 15, 1942, at the Postoffice at Weaverville, N. C., under the Act of March 3, 1879. Vol. XV, No. 37, January 9, 1957. Editorial and Business Offices: Weaverville, N. C. Printed in the U.S.A. by Biltmore Press, Asheville, N. C.

ADDRESS CHANGE: When changing address, please let us have both old and new address as far in advance as possible. Allow three weeks after change if not sent in advance. When possible, send an address label giving your old address.

The Talladega News requested Dr. Crowe to contribute a weekly comment on a Bible verse of his own choosing. The Alabama State Bureau of Publicity and Information mimeographed these leaflets and distributed copies to all the newspapers in that State. A recent survey showed that 34 newspapers in Alabama alone are publishing these leaflets regularly and thus reaching some 276,000 Alabamians. At the Christmas season, Mr. Cecil Hornady, editor of the Talladega News, gathered a Melange of these Meditations and distributed them with the title, UNDER THE STUDY LAMP.

The preacher who is afraid to use Dr. Dunglinson's sermons lest he use them so fully as to be guilty of plagiarism may turn instead to these briefer meditations by Dr. Crowe and with one of these as a start go on to great preaching.

The ministers of the Synod of Alabama are striving to follow Dr. Crowe as he follows Christ. We invite our brethren of other synods to do likewise. —W.C.R.

Modernism Is Not Dead Yet

Religious modernism is by no means dead yet. Witness a recent article by Roy A. Burkhart, pastor of one of the twelve churches selected in a 1950 poll as America's most outstanding.

Burkhart wants to see us live "creatively and dynamically with others" and to that end he urges certain emphases in our teaching and preaching. The first is that we hold that the baby at birth is good. He would emphasize the nature of God in terms of an indwelling spirit which is God seeking to be revealed in one's everyday living: "God is the universal sun of which you are a ray." Jesus is to be presented as the elder brother we must imitate: "He became one with God. If you follow Him with all your heart you will share his insight, tap his power, reveal God as he did." Albert Schweitzer is quoted approvingly as he minimizes Jesus as historically known and asserts that contact with the spirit of Jesus is all that counts.

For all the true things Burkhart has to say about the power of love, the necessity of understanding people's problems, the duty of becoming growing persons, his is the voice of modern unbelief.

The inspirationalist has captured all too many pulpits. The psychologist has become the prophet of multitudes. An easy optimism about human nature, an essentially pantheistic notion of God, a Master who saves us by love not by death in our place on the cross, a vague mysticism that would set us to seeking the spirit of Jesus instead of the supernatural Christ of

Religious Freedom on Television Suffers

Religious freedom on television was again threatened by a recent action of WGN-TV, Chicago. Originally scheduled for its world TV premiere on December 21, the film, MARTIN LUTHER, was cancelled as a result of pressure by a minority religious group. The film's sponsor was Community Builders, Inc., which carries a regular film show on this television station.

In a statement released to the press, the station stated its reason for cancelling the film was their wish not to antagonize any segment of Christian opinion, and that there had been an "emotional reaction" expressed to the showing. Officials said further that the decision was on the level of station policy and that they assumed full responsibility for it.

In a letter of protest to WGN officials, Dr. George Ford, Executive Director of the National Association of Evangelicals, said:

"Your action would . . . seem to greatly restrict the programming of W. G. N. if you indicate you have taken this action because you do not want to antagonize any section of Christian opinion. We would strongly feel that this would mean, first of all, the discontinuance of the Christopher Program such as the one shown on Saturday, December 8. It would also mean that all films to be shown would have to be previewed to ascertain if there is any content that extols, lauds, or in any way benefits one particular segment of the Christian movement."

He also added that he did not feel WGN-TV would desire to be so limited, that the NAE did not feel it fair to the television audience to thus restrict programming, but that if such a policy were to be followed the NAE would feel compelled to strongly protest.

The letter was released to the press for publication.

Korea . . .

Our Medical

By L. Nelson

Editor's Note: This is the first of three articles by Dr. Bell dealing with our Korea Mission's medical work in Korea. The second article will appear in an early issue.—H.B.D.

FOREWORD

In writing of our medical work in Korea today a basic observation should be made. Due to the increase in medical schools in Korea and the increasing number of doctors graduating, medical mission work has advanced to embrace a new concept of its responsibility. No longer is a small general hospital located in each mission station. This is due in part to lack of personnel and money. It is also due to the fact that many feel the greatest contribution which can now be made to the Christian witness in Korea medically speaking is through the efficiency and example of institutions and work not otherwise available. This does not mean that present-day medical graduates in Korea are adequate in number, nor does it mean that they are fully competent according to Western standards. But these men have been trained according to the Western concept of medicine and they can recognize a first-rate medical work when they see it. Our church through its medical personnel in Korea is setting a standard to which these young doctors may look and at the same time bearing a Christian testimony which is a credit to the Church of Jesus Christ.

This program of specialization embraces four fields: The Presbyterian Medical Center at Chunju, an institution dedicated to the finest in the surgical field; the Graham Memorial Tuberculosis Hospital at Kwangju, the only tuberculosis sanatorium in an area with a population greater than the state of North Carolina, and the object of half of the 1957 gift from the Women of the Church (along with smaller grants for tubercular work in our other stations); the long-established R. M. Wilson Leprosy Colony at Soonchun and a Public Health Center to be established at Mokpo.

The Chungu Presbyterian Medical Center

A Medical Center is a teaching institution, a hospital where there is a program for training and teaching internes, residents, technicians and nurses is being carried out. Never before in the annals of our medical mission work has such a program been undertaken. This is a unique institution and one worthy of a visit

The Laboratory, under the direction of Miss Ocie Respess, would be a credit to any similar hospital in America. All types of laboratory determinations are made in the various departments, including excellent histo-pathological sections. Eleven technicians working from morning to night account for a quality and quantity of work which is the background of scientific medicine at its best. This Laboratory is a part of the teaching program of the Center with a recognized school for medical technicians as its objective.

In 1955 Dr. Frank Keller, well known pediatrician of Mobile, Ala., offered his services to the Board of World Missions. Although past the age when new missionaries are usually sent to the field the Board accepted Dr. Keller's offer and he came to Chunju to take over the department of Internal Medicine and Pediatrics. Dr. Keller not only has added to the professional quality of the Center's work but his Christian character, gentleness and concern for Koreans and missionaries alike has endeared him to all. A bachelor, this deficiency was soon remedied by his marriage to Miss Janet Talmage, R.N., of the nursing department.

Mr. and Mrs. Thomas Taylor came to the Center in 1954 and he is an indefatigable worker, having assumed the post of Business Manager. An institution of this size demands a tremendous volume of business and financial transactions and Mr. Taylor's efficiency in this department has grown with his knowledge of the language and people. In recent months graphs have been set up to show the income and outgo of each department of the hospital and a detailed system of cost accounting has been set up.

A year ago Miss Betty Boyer, R.N., daughter of our Korea Mission, came out on a short-term appointment and has ably taken over supervision of nursing care in the hospital and also supervision of the drug supplies.

There are three outstanding Korean physicians on the staff — Drs. Pak and Song, surgeons, and Dr. Im, head of the Eye, Ear, Nose and Throat Department, trained in Korea and America. These men are outstanding in Christian character and ability and share in the teaching program for the nine internes and three residents now working in the hospital.

From the foregoing the reader can know something of the staff personnel of the Medical Center. What of the quality of the work? As a professional man of many years experience both in China and America the writer would express the wish that Christian doctors in America might have the privilege of visiting and seeing for themselves.

One day we saw gastrectomies (removal of the stomach), being carried out simultaneously in two different operating rooms. Ulcers of the stomach are so common in Korea and gastrectomies are so routine that even hospital residents perform this operation. We saw various types of bone grafts including one case where an entire fibula was grafted from elbow to shoulder to establish function for an arm where all of the bone had been destroyed by osteomyletis. We saw skin grafts, tube grafts, a corneal transplant and many other procedures. Also we saw four cases where patients had had the oesophagus destroyed by drinking lye.

All of these would have died of starvation but for a series of ingenious operations whereby nutrition was first restored by an opening for feeding directly into the stomach (a gastrotomy), after which a loop of intestine was separated and one end sewed into the stomach and the other then carried up under the skin of the chest wall and sutured to the upper and unscarred portion of the oesophagus. The result — normal eating and a normal way of life. This too is a common operation in this Center.

We could write at great length about the quantity and quality of the work but space does not permit. Sufficient to say that the Chunju Presbyterian Medical Center is an institution unique in all of our medical work and it is at the same time a Christian witness for which our church should be profoundly proud and thankful.

What is the serious crisis which has arisen to jeopardize this work? Two elements are involved, personnel and financial.

Dr. Crane: Despite the fact that Dr. Crane was doing a work of the greatest value to the rehabilitation of Korea, a work of real international significance, last year he was classified 1-A by his draft board and notified he would be called to active service with the United States Army. Knowing such a call was being processed, Dr. Crane applied for appointment to the U. S. Army in Korea and in July he was assigned for duty. Recognizing his outstanding ability as a surgeon he was made acting chief surgeon at a 400 bed Army hospital near Seoul, the U. S. Army's largest base hospital in Korea.

All familiar with the situation feel that our government has been exceedingly short-sighted in calling up for service a man who already was making a contribution to Korean life and rehabilitation far in excess of any service he can render the Army, particularly as his place at Chunju could not be filled.

Dr. Seel: Two years ago Dr. Seel developed a lesion in his lung. Refusing to be invalided home he was put on complete bed rest in his home near the Medical Center. There he con-ability to manage a library. Nevertheless, if a math major or a French or science major felt led to apply the present faculty members will handle the high school English and Library work.

The third opening is for a Music Teacher to conduct a regular, scheduled program of music instruction. The most important single qualification would be the ability to teach piano, but it is hoped that the teacher could work with choral groups and individuals in voice. She would also be expected to teach a class in music appreciation and perhaps even one or two academic subjects which appeal to her, should the need arise. This teacher should also arrive on the field in August 1957 in time for the opening of school.

Only two more Board meetings remain before the Matron should be on her way to Congo, so time is of the essence. Won't you help us by checking your congregation for likely prospects? If you know of a person or persons who would like to use their life in a fuller way for Christ as a matron or teacher of missionaries' children please get in touch with me immediately.

The needs are *urgent* — Please Help Us!

Helps To Understanding Scripture Readings in *Day by Day*

By Rev. C. C. Baker

Sunday, January 20, *Matthew* 25:14-30. Two whole chapters (24-25) are devoted to teachings on Christ's Second Coming. The parables in 25:14-46 illustrate how the Christian can be ready when Christ comes. What were each of the servants to do with their talents while their master was gone (vv.15-17)? Each was given according to his ability (v.15). Of what sin was the unworthy servant guilty (vv.18,25-26)? What things are listed in vv.31-44 that an ordinary Christian can do to use his talents for God? Are there things in this list within your ability to do that you are failing to do? Would you be ashamed if Christ should return in your lifetime because you are not using your talents for Him?

Monday, January 21, *Matthew* 7:13-14. The Christian life is difficult (v.14) and many false paths tempt the Christian to go astray (vv.13, 15-23). Observe that those who lead others astray are false religious teachers (vv.15-20). How can we recognize them (vv.16-17)? Verses 21-23 warn of the danger of substituting activities in the name of Christ for genuine obedience to Christ Himself. Do you find a tendency in your religious life to be swept along in church activities without ever really bearing fruit for Christ? The true disciple stays on the road to life (v.14) by listening to and heeding the words of Christ (vv.26-27).

Tuesday, January 22, *Hebrews* 11:17-28. Think about each of the stories that the writer of the Book of Hebrews gives as an example of faith (notice especially vv.7-9,17-31). In which instances did the person of faith find it necessary to turn his back on the world (cf. vv.7, 24-26,31)? What incidents give illustrations of people who believed God and, in the face of the impossible, acted upon what God said (vv.8,17-19,22,28-29,30)? What was accomplished in each case? How was God's program pushed forward? Would His program have moved forward without the faith of these men? What motivated them to faith (vv.14,16,26,27b)? Does the hope for things eternal move you to place the things of this world secondary and live by faith for God and His Kingdom?

Wednesday, January 23, *Luke* 10:38-42. To sit at Jesus' feet and listen to Him is better than to serve Him (vv.38-42). Is Mary or Martha more typical of the average American Christian? What basic weakness exists in the church that stresses organization and activities but places little importance upon prayer and Bible study? Though you are an active Christian, do you neglect these latter disciplines? Jesus stressed the need for service (the story of the Good Samaritan is found in vv.30-37), but prayer always pervaded all His activities (11:1). The disciples watched many good deeds that Jesus performed, but they felt their deepest need was to learn to pray (11:1). Notice in Jesus' teaching on prayer (11:2-4) that concern for the things of the Father precedes prayer for physical needs.

Thursday, January 24, *Genesis* 12:1-3. Notice how old Abraham was (v.4) when God gave His call to Abraham, and what He asked Him to leave (12:1). List the promises God gave to Abraham (vv.2-3,7). How was the Promise of v.2a fulfilled when Abraham's descendants went down into the land of Egypt (Exodus 1:5-7)? When was the promise of v.7 fulfilled (Joshua 1:1-2,10-11)? How is God making it possible for all the families of the earth to be blessed through Abraham's descendants (Galatians 3:7-8; Matthew 28:19-20)? Thus the rest of the redemptive story of the Old and New Testaments can be traced back to God's promises to Abraham. This reveals God's faithfulness in standing behind all the promises He has made in Scripture. Does your heart respond in faith to the promises God has made to you (12:4; 15:5-6)?

Friday, January 25, *Mark* 7:24-30. At this point the disciples were almost as blind as the Pharisees in understanding spiritual truths (Matt.15:12-16,23). The Syrophoenician woman

LESSON FOR JANUARY 20

By THE REV. J. KENTON PARKER

Gospel Righteousness

Background Scripture: Matthew 5 - 7
Devotional Reading: Matthew 6:25-33.

We have for our lesson the Sermon on the Mount. Our Golden Text: For I say unto you, That except your righteousness shall exceed the righteousness of the scribes and Pharisees, ye shall in no case enter into the kingdom of heaven. Dr. Shearer considered this verse the Text for the Sermon. What was the fatal defect in the righteousness of the scribes and Pharisees? It did not go deep enough: it did not reach the "hidden man of the heart," but only the external. Jesus describes it later by saying that it is like a whited sepulchre, or an unclean platter. The sepulchre was white on the outside, but full of dead men's bones; the platter had been washed on the outside, but not within. The lives of the scribes and Pharisees were outwardly clean, but unbelief and indifference, and lack of love marked their conduct in relation to their fellow men.

Those who say rather blithely today that the only Creed they have is the Sermon on the Mount, are ignorant and foolish. No man can have the righteousness described in this Sermon until he has been regenerated by the Spirit of God. Jesus put it plainly, and rather bluntly, to one of the Pharisees when He said to him: Except a man be born again he cannot see the kingdom of God. In the words of Paul we must have the righteousness of Christ, imputed to us, and imparted to us; we must be justified and sanctified. We are justified by the death of Christ, and sanctified by the work of His Spirit in our hearts. It will take grace — all the grace God can give — to live the righteous life pictured for us in these chapters. As I read and ponder its demands, I, for one, cry out for a Saviour from sin, and a Saviour Who can make and keep me pure within. The Sermon on the Mount, like the Law, is our schoolmaster to bring us to Christ in order that we may be saved by grace.

I am not quite sure where I got the Outline I am using. I believe it is Dr. Shearer's. It is a well known outline, and I believe, a good one.

I. *Citizens of the Kingdom;* their Character, Rewards, and Influence: 5:1-16.

1. The Beatitudes: the Character and Rewards of Citizens; each of these Beatitudes gives a distinguishing trait of character and the resulting reward.

The poor in spirit possess the kingdom, pride shuts the door to spiritual possession, for God resists the proud, but gives grace to the humble. Those that mourn are comforted, especially those that mourn over their sins. Tears of true repentance bring comfort to the heart. The meek shall inherit the earth. This promise will be fulfilled some day. Those that hunger and thirst after righteousness shall be filled. These words should lead us to pray, Lord, make us hungry; make us thirsty! Do we have an appetite for spiritual blessings? The merciful obtain mercy. How do we feel when we see others in need, or trouble? The pure in heart see God. It is sin that keeps us from seeing God. The peacemakers are called the children of God. God is the Great Peacemaker. The persecuted for righteousness' sake own the kingdom. Those who are treated shamefully "for my sake" will receive a great reward.

The people described by Jesus are the "Blessed," or "Happy," people. His teaching is contrary to the world's idea of happiness. Jesus is taking the "Long View" and the "Sound View" of life. He knows the end from the beginning. Those who try His way find that it works and that His is the only Philosophy of life that brings lasting joy to the souls of men.

2. The Influence of these Citizens of the kingdom: 13-16.

Jesus uses two very simple illustrations. The first is that of salt. Salt is very common and very necessary in our lives. It seasons, or gives flavor, to our food; it preserves our food; it is most important. The true follower of Christ does for the world what salt does for our food. If it were not for the true Christians in the world it would become as corrupt as the world before the Flood.

Only the Christian can give real meaning, real "flavor" to life, and make it worthwhile.

Notice that Jesus stresses the thought that the salt must be good salt, must not lose its savor. Are we "salty Christians," or are we living so much like the world that men can see no difference? The second illustration is equally simple. Light was the first thing that God made after He created the world. A world without light would be a terrible place in which to live. The devil has succeeded in "shutting out the sunshine" from much of the world. Jesus is the Light of the world — the Great Light — but to us He gives the keeping of the "lights along the shore." May we keep our lights burning!

II. *The Law of the Kingdom:* 5:17-48.

Jesus did not come to destroy, but to fulfill the Law. The Law is holy, just, and good. He fulfilled it in two ways: (1) He kept it perfectly in spirit as well as letter, and (2) He taught the full and rich and deep meaning of the Law, as we shall see. Righteousness is keeping the Law in its full meaning. We are measured by the Law: to break one of the least of the commandments is to be least in the kingdom; to do and teach them is to be great. Jesus proceeds to give some samples of what He means.

"Thou shalt not kill." This does not look so difficult. Few of us have actually murdered somebody. There are more ways to kill than this, however. To be angry with our brother, or hate him, is to break the spirit of this command, and sometimes leads to murder itself. I saw an impressive picture the other night on TV. It was the "Trial" of the janitor of the school for the death of a boy who had fallen, or been pushed, through a faulty railing. Before the "Trial" was over almost a third of the spectators were involved in some way. The janitor failed to tell the building inspector; the inspector made a superficial inspection; the doctor who was called did not come promptly, but laughed at the message; the teacher had forgotten; even the boy's father, some eight years before, had neglected to finish his job by putting the proper brace on the railing. We are killing thousands of people on our highways. If the full truth were known many of us would be guilty. How about the man who sells the whiskey or beer to the driver of a car? Do all of us observe the traffic laws at all times?

"Thou shalt not commit adultery." We might say at once, I have never broken that law. Wait and see what Jesus says. The look, the desire, the impure thought; have none of these ever been in our minds?

"Swear not at all." Watch our words. We may refrain from actually taking the name of God in vain, and yet be guilty of breaking this command.

Do we never feel like "paying him back," getting even with somebody who has said or done something which we did not like. "Love your enemies." Does it not take supernatural power and grace to do this? The whole Law is fulfilled in one word, LOVE. As I read what Jesus said I am glad I have a Saviour who has kept the Law perfectly and is my Advocate at the throne of grace.

III. *Life in the Kingdom:* 6:1 - 7:12.

Christians are to Give. The scribes and Pharisees gave alms, but they gave to be seen of men. Our giving is to be different; in secret; without display.

Christians are to Pray. The hypocrites prayed on street corners to be seen and heard of men. The praying that counts is secret praying, "Enter into thy closet." Beware of "vain repetitions"! He then gives them a prayer for the guidance, which we call The Lord's Prayer. Fasting and prayer usually went together. Real fasting must not be a mere form, as we sometimes see during Lent.

The Christian is to lay up treasure in heaven. This is the only safe place to keep treasure. Such treasure must be of a spiritual nature.

The Christian is to serve one Master. When he accepts Christ as Lord and Master there must be no divided allegiance. "When I came to America, I came all," said an immigrant. When we come to Christ, let us "come all."

The Christian is not to be anxious and worried about "things." Our Father knows that we need food and clothing. If we seek first the kingdom of God and His righteousness, all these "things" will be added.

The Christian is not to judge others. He has enough to do to judge himself. When we have succeeded in getting the beam out of our own eyes, then we can, in meekness, help our brother get the mote out of his eye.

He is to ask and seek and knock, thus entering into all the riches of the kingdom which belong to him as a "child of the King."

This section closes with the Golden Rule, a fit summary of Life in the Kingdom. Only those who have "Golden Hearts" can keep the Golden Rule, and a Golden Heart — a renewed heart — is the gift of God in Christ Jesus.

IV. *How to Enter the Kingdom:* 7:13-29.

We can never enter the Kingdom by "following the crowd," for the crowd is headed in the other direction. The entrance to the Kingdom is a narrow one; there is room for body and soul, but not for body and soul and sin, as someone well said.

Beware of false prophets. There have always been plenty of these, and they are trying to lead

(Continued on Page 23)

YOUNG PEOPLES Department

YOUTH PROGRAM FOR JANUARY 20

By THE REV. B. HOYT EVANS

The Theme For 1957

Scripture: Luke 10:25-37.

Suggested Hymns:

"God of Grace and God of Glory"

"In Christ There Is No East Nor West"

"I Sought the Lord, and Afterwards I Knew"

Note to Program Leader: (If you plan to observe Youth Sunday in your church with a program for the entire congregation, be sure to save this information about the theme for use at that time.)

Leader's Introduction:

The people who really accomplish important things in life are those who know where they are going before they start and who have some particular ideas and ideals to guide them as they live and work. It is most important that we have a spiritual destination and some guiding ideas and ideals for our work as the young people of the Lord's church. The Assembly's Youth Council has suggested a theme, a picture, and a hymn to serve as guides for our thinking and our service this year. For our program today we shall have an explanation of the picture and the hymn and a discussion about the theme.

First Speaker:

(Try to have at least one copy of the theme picture for display. The pictures may be ordered from the Board of Christian Education, Box 1176, Richmond, Va. The picture also appears on the front cover of the January-March *Presbyterian Youth.*)

Our theme picture for this year is entitled "The Church's One Foundation," and it was painted by Mr. Ralph Coleman of Jenkintown, Pennsylvania. In this picture Mr. Coleman has depicted a great multitude of people . . . of all races and classes, stations and occupations of life. Looking through the faces of the people is a shadowy face of Christ. This represents the truth that when people believe in Christ they are a part of Him and He of them.

Jesus expressed this idea Himself when He said, "At that day ye shall know that I am in my Father, and ye in me, and I in you." John 14:20. As we look to this picture all through the year, let us be reminded that Christ is in us to make us strong, and that we are safe in Him. Let us also be reminded of the strong tie that binds us together with those who believe in our Saviour and Lord.

Second Speaker:

"God of Grace and God of Glory" is the title of our theme hymn. The words were composed by Dr. Harry Emerson Fosdick, who, before his retirement, was pastor of the Riverside Church in New York City. Dr. Fosdick has long been a leader of the so-called liberal movement in American Christianity (those who question or deny much of the supernatural content of the Christian faith).

This hymn is one of the writer's better expressions. We find here many noble sentiments and desires to which we can ascribe and which we can make our prayers. In the fifth stanza as we sing "Let us search for Thy salvation," we are not to think that God's salvation is something we have to find and create for ourselves. It is God who finds us and saves us for Himself. Jesus said, "No man can come unto me, except the Father which hath sent me draw him." John 6:44. Another hymn states the truth correctly when it says, "He moved my soul to seek Him, seeking me."

The tune to which we sing the words is a Welsh hymn called Cym Rhondda (pronounced coom roantha). This particular tune is celebrating its golden anniversary, having been composed in 1907. The music lends itself to powerful congregational singing and has been a favorite among the Welsh people ever since its composition.

Third Speaker:

Who is my brother? this question is our theme idea for 1957. The Scriptures use the word "brother" in three main senses: (1) the ordinary understanding—those who are the children (sons) of the same parents, (2) those who were descendants of Abraham were considered brothers to each other, and (3) those who have come to God the Father through faith in Christ are said to be brothers. Our concern is with this third usage. Who is my brother? According to the New Testament every Christian is my brother.

There is a doctrine which has gained wide acceptance called the universal Fatherhood of

(Continued on Page 23)

CHILDRENS Page

David Defies Goliath

King Saul was amazed by David's "nerve", offering to fight the giant. But he said David must wear the King's own armor and the King's sword. David said No, my lord, the King, let me take my sling, and the Lord will go with me. So he ran down to the brook and picked up five smooth stones and placed them in his shepherd's bag - then went forth to meet the giant. When Goliath, the giant, saw David coming he was enraged and he roared, Are you, kid, coming to fight with me? and with that little sling? He cursed David and said Come on, and I will kill you and feed your dead body to the wild beasts. But David came right on and stood before Goliath saying, You come to me with sword and spear and shield, but I come to you in the name of the God of Israel whose army you have defied, and I will take your head off your shoulders, that all the earth may know there is a God in Israel. -(To be continued) E.

FIRST PRESBYTERIAN CHURCH

Oak Hill, West Virginia

December 21, 1956

Dear Dr. Robbie:

Excuse a hurried note, but your recent article in the *Journal* on "What to Preach: An Objective Guide," struck home in my ministry so that I could not resist the temptation of writing to thank you for same. I do not think you would be presumptuous at all in suggesting an even more detailed guide. In fact if you have such a suggested guide in mind or written it I would deeply appreciate same for my own use.

I have completed a series on the Ten Commandments and have been through John for my evening sermons and am now in Acts. I have found this way most helpful and the response has been good.

Suggested plans for one, three and even five year periods could certainly help a minister in his pulpit work. The Larger Catechism, I have found indeed rich and helpful, and for Sunday School we use selections of your comments on the Shorter Catechism. Again many thanks for helping a preacher apply, in a practical way, the great statements of our faith found in the Westminster Standards. Truly our people need to learn Christianity "full orbed" as our church has always believed it.

Sincerely in Christ,

Dick Robertson

December 22, 1956

Dr. Henry B. Dendy,
Weaverville, N. C.

Dear Henry:

I am seated at my desk at home, and have just completed work on my Sunday School Lesson for tomorrow.

I am enclosing, for I thought it might interest you, one of our church cards* mailed out for tomorrow. This one was mailed to one of my daughters.

The 2nd paragraph of the card refers to me, and while thinking of how long I have been teaching this class, the thought came to me that I had been using with great profit and enjoyment for many years the Sabbath School Lessons in the *Journal* by Rev. J. Kenton Parker, without expressing my thanks to either the *Journal* or to Rev. Parker.

If you can, will you express my thanks to Rev. Parker and tell him his lessons have been a great help to me. Also please keep a large measure for the *Journal* for furnishing such excellent material.

Wishing you and yours all the compliments of the season, I am

Sincerely yours,

Randolph B. Lee

*Sunday morning Mr. R. B. Lee will be teaching his 1000th lesson to the Men's Bible Class. Let's show our appreciation by all of The Men being present.

South Frankfort Presbyterian Church

December 22, 1956.

The Editors
The Southern Presbyterian Journal
Weaverville, N. C.

Sirs,

I want to express my appreciation for your having published the letter from Arch B. Taylor, Jr. Mr. Taylor suggests the spirit and attitude which would make the Southern Presbyterian Journal an outstanding periodical. Along with Mr. Taylor I have been disturbed by the spirit of acrimony and unmitigated criticism constantly evident in your otherwise excellent publication. I was glad that Mr. Taylor called your attention to the un-Calvin Calvinism frequently expressed by your contributors and in the editorials.

I would suggest that prior to setting up a defense of Calvinism that the writers spend a period of intensive study of Calvin's Institutes and sample liberally his other writings. Unfortunately, the original Calvinism of the Reformation has gotten tangled up with later interpretations, enlargements and applications so that we sometimes think that certain positions are Calvinist that really are a far cry from Calvinism.

Another suggestion. Let your writers and editors spend a few days reading I Cor. 13 within its context. We would hardly dare argue with the inspired Apostle in his exaltation of "love." Even when it is compared, contrasted and evaluated with "faith" and "hope." It is extremely to the detriment of our Christian life to see and know individuals of great faith and possessors of the blessed hope who are very disagreeable folks to live with. It is little wonder that the child prayed, "O God, make all the bad people good, and all the good people nice."

Yours sincerely,

H. Glen Stephens

"With Christ Into 1957"

Seldom is Time spoken of as a blessing; often it is labeled as a tyrant. Time rules us, yet we possess it. When we use it, it expands; when we waste it, it shrinks; when we kill it, we lose it!

Time is eternity; for our reference we package it as a second - a day - a year. We extol each year as it arrives, we celebrate its coming as the end of disappointment and evil; as the rebirth of our opportunities, of our resolve, of our endeavor.

How significant that one week after the day celebrated as the birthday of our Saviour a new year comes, symbol of the end of darkness and death and the rebirth of man after the coming of the Redeemer! Truly, since that time, Christ goes with us into each new year.

"With Christ into 1957" — in that light how meaningful our sense of new opportunity, new resolve and new endeavor! Our Church gives us a field for new endeavor by asking that we learn more of our responsibility as citizens of the Kingdom of God and carry into our citizenship of our community, state, nation and the world the attitudes and actions of Christian Citizens. For the Women of the Church and the members as individuals there have been prepared thought - and action-provoking studies and discussions in this field or related to it.

This can be a real adventure in thinking and living! Look at the Circle Bible Study, and picture a small group, all allowed to give voice to an idea or an experience. They talk about what responsibility they have, whether they want responsibility or not; what they feel about their own country and other countries; what they must decide if there seems to be a conflict between what belongs to worldly governments and what belongs to the Kingdom of God; they will talk about how to bring to pass the things which they think should be. One of them will have special help in bringing up the matter to be discussed and in guiding discussion so that it stays on the subject and within the time allotted.

The programs for the general meetings can be explosive! Does that word startle you? We use it here in its meaning of being capable of sending into sudden action. An explosion releases energy, enormous energy — and it need not always be destructive. We may release energy where there was no evidence any existed! If local program leaders sense the excitement packed into each topic-of-the-month for general meetings and use it with imagination and appreciation of the interest-potential of their local groups, we shall have more and more women coming to hear: What *is* an adult delinquent, and what can the Church do with or about the adult delinquent? What are the barriers in *our* community — barriers to what, to whom? We don't want the thorny, poisonous weed of Communism to grow — but are we tending the roots of democracy?

To the question, "Would you prefer to select your own special Bible study and not have it prepared and sent out by the Board of Women's Work" the presidents of local Women of the Church meeting in Montreat cried, "No! No! Send it to us, imperfectly though we may accomplish it!" The Special Bible Study in 1957 is *very* special indeed. We meet some Prophets of the Old Testament who amaze us because they speak so definitely *to us,* although they were speaking to their own people at the time.

How can people in 1957 be so like people 2,000 years ago - and more? Our houses are different, our clothing, our transportation; our occupations have other names - but we act and react alike. If one of these prophets came today, he could point a finger at us and say the same things in modern terms! Let us look first at what he is saying about the other fellow and notice how we approve and credit this voice from the past. Maybe then we can bring ourselves to peek cautiously from our closed-in self satisfaction and catch a few words that blast *us* - not only us as women, but us as people. We may duck back into ourselves when the bombardment gets pretty hot, but we'll find courage to listen some more for we don't want to miss any of this. Why didn't some one tell us before that these speakers, whom we pigeonholed as "Minor Prophets" were so interesting and up-to-date? Wouldn't it really be *fun* to be able to observe what some of these audiences did when suddenly these word-bombs fell among them? Our interest is caught also by the speakers themselves. One of these prophets faced a domestic crisis and tragedy that is completely modern — how could he have dealt with it so completely illustrating the love of God and not the revenge of man at a time when the love of God had not been shown by the Saviour? These men stand facing us and through them comes the voice of God which did not become silent within the first walls which heard it but is borne to us and through us continuing through the ages.

As we contemplate what the year holds for us we know that our feet are set on a path of learning, understanding and exemplifying the love of Christ through the many facets of what we call "Christian Citizenship."

—Mrs. Morrell DeReign
Caruthersville, Mo.

Plan Used in 1956

Special Bible Study in the McDonough Presbyterian Church

After a study of the overall plan of work of the Women of the Church, it was decided to have the Special Bible Study from Deuteronomy (*Messages to Homemakers,* prepared by Dr. James Sprunt) early in the year.

It was desired to include the entire family in this study, since it dealt with the home and family life. With enthusiastic co-operation from the pastor and the youth groups, a program was worked out for member participation in family groups. The programs were held at a six o'clock vesper service on the second and fourth Sunday nights during the months of February, March and April. This time seemed the most appropriate one to include all members, from the little ones on up.

There was a total of six programs, with the pastor selecting one of the six lessons from Deuteronomy as his text. The choir was composed of the Pioneer and Senior Youth Groups, with special numbers also being given by the Cherub Choir.

The last Sunday in January of each year is Assembly's Youth Sunday. On this day, the young people are in charge of one of the church services, and at this time give a resume of the preceding year's work. But this year our youth groups decided to have this service on the first Sunday night in February, as an introductory program to the special services that would follow, beginning the second Sunday evening. Cards were written to all members encouraging them to come in family groups to this service, and to the six following special programs. Refreshments were served by the young people. The result of this program was a great interest and wholehearted co-operation from all, many of whom had rarely ever attended evening services in the church.

During the three month Bible Study period (February, March, April), Deuteronomy was stressed at the women's meetings also, which culminated in a special Friday afternoon service before Easter Sunday. This was held as a Bible Study group in the form of a quiz. At this meeting one person was in charge of each of the six lessons in Deuteronomy. The women were questioned on these lessons, and if they failed to give the answers, the women in charge would answer for them.

These women's meetings plus the six special vesper services were regarded as very successful in presenting the theme of Home and Family Life to all members of our Church. But, perhaps, the most gratifying thing of all was that the special vesper services have developed into a permanent thing. They are held on the second and fourth Sundays of each month at six p.m. The young people all co-operate by holding their meetings after the service, in order that every one may attend and worship in family groups.

Because of these services, the Church is now enjoying one of the largest increases in evening attendance that has ever been obtained.

—Reported by Atlanta Presbyterial Chairman of Spiritual Growth.

My Community for Christ

My community for Christ is the dream of every Christian. Surely that would solve many terrible problems. How could such a thing come to pass? Only as individual men and women accept Christ as their Lord and Saviour.

To become a Christian who would really count means to realize you are not your own. You are bought by the price of God's only Son giving His life for you and your sins. It means loving Him so that you feel His presence and want Him to direct and guide you the remainder of your life. It means you will let Christ's love decide every future act. You will see *all men* through *His* eyes. You will endeavor to know and treat all men as brothers. You will feel that every cent you have comes from Him and will ask His direction in spending it all.

Love for Christ will keep you praying without ceasing. Love for Him will make you radiant whenever you are doing His will. Such love will glorify His church and any service that you can give through the church will be your most burning desire.

The transformed life that a surrender to Christ brings makes you see all men through His eyes. If you see a brother sin you love him with Jesus' compassion and pray for him whether you know him or not.

A Christ surrendered life keeps you praying constantly for eternal peace, you pray for all religious and national and international leaders. Every week end when ministers are preparing their messages for different churches you agonize in prayer that the Holy Spirit will so fill their hearts and minds with His love and power that all who hear will be changed.

In this *new* life, you get the greatest thrill out of studying the Bible. It is your life. Daily you search the Scriptures to learn His will. You know well you cannot reach the heights of a true Christian without His power and wisdom. You plead for Him to hold your hand and lead you every hour. So you learn the truth of the Bible, of how God always keeps His promises. Your faith is strengthened and you feel certain that He is able to do exceeding abundantly above all you ask or think.

You give Him your life, your love, your all —thus going forward with joy and hope. You know that He will keep you safe until you meet Him face to face in Heaven with all those you've loved and have lost a while.

A Christian realizes that her Saviour loves the entire community. She will give the very best she has to assist in all the uplifting, Christ-revealing projects of her city.

This obedience to God will keep a Christian's head high and her heart singing until all she meets will know that she has walked and talked with Jesus, her Redeemer, her Lord and her King whom she loves passionately with all her heart and mind and soul.

—Mrs. Verner Moore Lewis

Spotlighting Christian Relations

THE BIBLE SAYS:

There is ONE BODY
ONE SPIRIT
ONE LORD
ONE FAITH
ONE BAPTISM
ONE GOD AND
FATHER OF ALL!

God who made the world and everything in it . . . giving to all men life, and breath, and everything. And He made from ONE every nation of men to live on all the face of the earth, having determined allotted periods and the boundaries of their habitation, that they should seek God, in the hope that they might feel after Him and find Him.

Truly, I perceive that God shows no partiality, but in every nation anyone who fears Him and does what is right is acceptable to Him. For there is no difference between Jew and Greek, for the same Lord over all is rich unto all that call upon Him. God so loved the world that He gave His only begotten Son that whosoever believeth in Him should not perish, but have everlasting life.

Can any man forbid water that these should not be baptized which have received the Holy Ghost as well as we? Making the Word of God of none effect through your tradition which ye have delivered: and many such like things ye do. As many as received Him, to them gave He power to become sons of God. But now in Christ Jesus ye who sometimes were far off are made nigh by the blood of Christ. He is our Peace, who hath made both one, and hath broken down the middle wall of partition between us . . . for through Him we both have access by one Spirit unto the Father.

Now, therefore, ye are no more strangers, and foreigners, but fellow citizens with the saints, and of the household of God; and are built upon the foundation of the apostles and prophets, Jesus Christ Himself being the chief corner stone in whom all the building fitly framed together groweth unto an holy temple in the Lord. Follow peace with all men, and holiness, without which no man shall see the Lord.

Behold, how good and pleasant it is for brethren to dwell together in unity! It is like the precious ointment upon the head, that ran down upon the beard, even Aaron's beard; that went down to the skirts of his garments.

Many shall come from the east and west and sit down with Abraham, Isaac, and Jacob in the kingdom.

Acts 17:24-27; 10:34-35; Rom. 10:12; John 3:16; Acts 10:47; Mark 7:13; John 1:12; Eph. 2:13,14,18-21; Heb. 12:14; Psalm 133:1-2; Matt. 8:11.

—(Mrs. C. J.) Mary Knapp

"And the King of Glory Shall Come In"

Read Psalms 24 (Slowly and Distinctly)

As we think this year of "Forward with Christ in Christian Citizenship," let us remember that we are citizens, not only of our community and our land and our world, but we are citizens of His Kingdom, — *if* we will open the gates of our hearts, so that "The King of Glory Shall Come in."

This is the phrase upon which our interest centers as we read this Psalm, written by King David so many centuries ago, and it applies so well to our lives today. That was, and is, the absolutely important fact which can make all the difference in the world, — without Him, life can be lukewarm and lack lustre, but *with* Him rich and rare. "And the King of Glory Shall Come in," helping us to look upon the problems of our world, our community, our families, as He would have us to do.

Ann Morrow Lindberg has said, "Bible stories are so simple that they are like empty cups for people to fill with their own experiences over and over again through the years." . . .

Surely *she* must have heard with joy, the friendly footfalls of the Son of God coming down His secret stairs into her life. Let us pray — (pause) that we too may hear His footfalls coming into our lives — (pause a moment) — Amen.

Because "the earth is the Lord's, and the fullness thereof" — we should have a deep concern over "they that dwell therein." And we have Home and Foreign Missionaries, whose privilege and duty it is to help others to "open the gates of their hearts so that The King of Glory Shall Come in!"

We know that the great purposes cannot be achieved without women's participation, — we are humbly proud and thankful for the gifts which the Women of the Church have made to the mission fields through their Birthday Offerings each year.

There are so many worthy causes sponsored by our church — and none of this work can be done alone. It is all a matter of opening the gates of our hearts so that "The King of Glory Shall Come in." Let us pray — (pause) for all of our missionaries who are giving of themselves so unselfishly — (pause) and for all the other committees of our church, who are endeavoring to enlarge and enrich the work of His Kingdom. (Pause a moment) Amen.

King David asks, "Who shall ascend into the hill of the Lord? and who shall stand in His holy place?" Today we would ask: We wonder what kind of people have an absolute yearning in their hearts for worship? And we might venture to say everyone has a desire to worship God, but there are so many in our community who seem restless, and unsatisfied and unconscious of this need in their lives. We do not need to keep on being only half-a-person, — His gentleness can make us great.

Have you ever noticed how almost everybody drags through drab days? doing this or that dusty duty? maneuvering this or that monotonous meal, from market place to dinner table, — or I might say from Super market to TV tray? All this listless, loveless living is hunger, — a hunger deeper than the meal can satisfy! It would be a thrilling thing to invite to your table, Him "who made the earth and the fullness thereof." All it would take would be a few moments to read some Scripture verses, and a sentence of sheer gratitude, — thus inviting the King of Glory to Come in. Let us pray (pause)

"Lord Jesus be our Holy Guest
Our morning joy, our evening rest,
And by Thy grace, Thy love impart
The joy and peace to every heart." Amen

King David answers his question concerning worshipers — "He that hath clean hands and a pure heart, who hath not lifted up his soul unto vanity, nor sworn deceitfully" — of all the worshipers none could be purer or cleaner or more exciting than Helen Keller. She is keenly aware of God and of the needs of all mankind. She has made a wonderful statement about her life's work. She says "I long to accomplish a great and noble task; but it is my chief duty and joy to accomplish humble tasks as though they were great and noble . . . and the world is moved along, not by the mighty shoves of its heroes, but also by many tiny pushes of each honest worker." And *I* would say, if each Woman of the Church could be inspired to realize that, *just* by regularly attending the circle meetings and the general meetings, she will, by these tiny pushes be opening the gates so that "the King of Glory Shall Come In." Let us pray (pause) that each woman will realize that as a Christian citizen she must take part in the activities of her own church, putting Him and His work first in her life. (pause) Amen.

This is the generation of them that seek the face of the King of Glory — all sorts of people have learned to open wide their doors for the "Imperishable Presence" to enter. We join with an unknown Christian of the 2nd Century who wrote these lovely lines:

"Whenever the sun shines brightly,
I arise and say:
'Surely, it is the shining of His Face.'
And when a shadow falls across the window of my room
Where I am working at my appointed task,
I lift my head to watch the door, and ask if He is come."

Open the gates so that "The King of Glory Shall Come in," — to touch with divine tenderness each daily duty, — to mend by His everlasting mercy each broken relationship, — to give us wisdom so that we may put Him and His work first in our home, our community, our world.

He is standing waiting!

As we bow our heads let us pledge anew our allegiance to the King of Glory. (Silence for a moment closing with:)

"Now unto Him that is able to do exceeding abundantly above all that we ask or think, according to the power that worketh in us, Unto Him be glory in the church by Christ Jesus throughout all ages, world without end. Amen." (Eph. 3:20-21).

—Mrs. J. L. Shweatt,
Birmingham, Ala.

NEWS of CHURCHES Around the World

Protestant Preachers Protest Persecution

New York — Thirty-four Protestant ministers, including Dr. W. Taliaferro Thompson, moderator of the Presbyterian Church, U. S., have urged that the United States government call on the United Nations to condemn Egypt's "new racist policy" and her "persecution of Jews."

In an open letter to President Eisenhower, the group of clergymen urged the United States to exert "as much pressure for this action" as it had in seeking compliance with the United Nations' resolution against Soviet deportation of Hungarians.

The letter pictured present anti-Jewish activities in Egypt as "clearly imitative of the Hitler pattern and the present Communist pattern in Hungary," and warned that the world may again see open war unless these activities are ceased.

"In canceling citizenship, in ordering deportation of citizens, or stateless persons and nationals of other lands, in taking away property, in confiscating bank accounts, in the establishment of concentration camps, and in holding men and women as hostages, we find an awful and terrible imitation and refinement of the Hitler program and practices which ultimately plunged the world into war," the letter said.

"Unless the United States opposes firmly and immediately the reappearance of racism in Egypt, in whatever guise, this pernicious evil will endanger the spiritual foundations of morality and freedom in all the world," it said.

The ministers urged President Eisenhower, as a leader of the "highest prestige and influence," to "appeal to the public opinion of mankind, to the conscience of Christendom, and to all who believe in human brotherhood to save not only those who are persecuted today, but to save civilization from the violation of those human ideals of freedom which are the symbol and hope of mankind."

The message declared that what is happening to the Jews in Egypt today "can neither be excused nor explained by the military conflict between the governments of these two nations. . . . Nor should one's view of this evil be affected by whatever view one may hold as to the Arab-Israeli conflict in the Middle East."

Rev. P. D. Miller Succeeds Dr. Wade H. Boggs as Manager of the Vacation Fund

The Vacation Fund of the Southern Presbyterian Church has made it possible for many sacrificing preachers in small churches to spend a most profitable vacation at one of the great conference centers of our church. This splendid work has been a joy to supervise during the past thirteen years while I was serving the Board of Annuities and Relief, and its predecessor, Committee of Christian Education and Ministerial Relief.

Now that I am no longer in such service, I have resigned that position, and Rev. Patrick D. Miller, D.D., Executive Secretary of the Board of Church Extension, 341-B Ponce de Leon Ave., N.E., Atlanta 8, Ga., has been elected to serve as manager of that fund and also Geneva Hall at Montreat, N. C.

I sincerely hope that those who have so generously supported this noble work in the past will continue to do so under the leadership of Dr. P. D. Miller. All contributions to this fund should be sent to Mrs. Ira D. Holt, Treasurer, Montreat, N.C.

—Wade H. Boggs

PASSING OF REV. H. R. BORTHWICK

Rev. Henry R. Borthwick, H.R., member of the Presbytery of Lexington, died at his home, Route 1, Staunton, Virginia, Tuesday, December 11, 1956. He was 87 years of age, born Dumfries, Scotland, January 25, 1869; buried Pulaski, Virginia, December 13, 1956.

Hungarian and East European Refugees

The Protestant Churches have been in this program since the beginning of the emergency. We will continue to serve through Church World Service and the World Council of Churches.

THE NEED: The churches have agreed that their primary responsibility at present is for refugees in Austria rather than to attempt to enter Hungary with church supplies.

Over 145,000 refugees have fled across the border of Hungary to Austria. Most have brought nothing along except the clothes on their backs. Refugees are met at the border by representatives of our churches, given hot soup and dry socks and sent to reception camps where they are fed, changes of clothing provided and transportation given to camps. Here interviewing, security clearances, and medical examinations take place for those desiring to go to the U. S. or other countries.

One-third of the refugees coming across the border are Protestant. Of this third, one-third are Reformed. Other Protestant denominations are included in the remainder.

The World Council of Churches has a staff of over 50 workers on the scene. A Church World Service team of three persons has been sent to Salzburg to interview possible entrants to the United States. Of the first 5,000 visas granted by the U. S. Government, 1,000 were CWS-WCC cases. Of the 21,500 to be admitted to the U.S., some 4,000 will be our responsibility for resettlement help. Enough assurances have already been received to care for all of these, no more are needed.

THE PROGRAM: CWS immediately made available 465 tons of food and clothing when the emergency began. Subsequently shipments were made of penicillin, sutures, blankets (5,687), multivitamins (1 million tablets), sulfa drugs, and antibiotics. $10,000 was sent for emergency purchase of medical supplies, sugar and cocoa. In addition, CROP sent $5,000 for local purchase of foods overseas plus $11,000 for canned meat and cottonseed oil. More material relief is being sent to meet the emergency needs.

The spiritual needs of the refugees are being cared for by Hungarian speaking pastors. Three chaplains are being sent overseas to come back on the Navy transports. Spiritual ministries are being coordinated at Camp Kilmer in New Jersey.

THOUSANDS OF REFUGEES ARE DEPENDENT UPON OUR FUTURE GIFTS FOR EMERGENCY SHELTER, FOOD, AND CLOTHING.

The total value of C.W.S. shipments for Hungarian refugees to date is $673,600.

"GIVE THROUGH YOUR CHURCH"

Through

The Department of Overseas Relief and
Inter-Church Aid
Box 330
Nashville, Tennessee

ALABAMA

Tuscaloosa Presbytery — The 24th, 25th, and 26th of October were days in Tuscaloosa Presbytery when the majority of the churches were well represented in attendance upon three highly important conferences which the Executive Secretary had scheduled in three strategic centers of the Presbytery.

These conferences were designed to set forth a challenge to the leaders of the churches in the fields of Stewardship, Christian Education, and Evangelism. Dr. James M. Carr, the Secretary of our Town and Country Division of Church Extension in our Assembly was with us for the three days, and brought addresses and sound movie film to show how the total program of the Church is co-ordinated in the life and work of the Church with special emphasis upon the Rural Churches and the Larger Parish Program.

Dr. Samuel B. Hay, President of Stillman College, brought such stirring messages upon Stewardship of life and possessions as to leave an indelible impression upon the minds of all who attended.

The Rev. Don O. McInnis, Regional Director of Christian Education for the Synod of Alabama, gave a panoramic view of the services and material available for the Program of Christian Education in the local Church, and the challenge to the churches to develop such a Program of Christian Education as will use these materials and services.

Mr. Frank Cochran, Jr., of the First Presbyterian Church, Selma, gave stirring addresses on the Primary Function of Christ's Church, and that is "Evangelism." We were shown how Stewardship and Evangelism work in the closest type of union in the church, and we were also shown our failures, in both of these divisions in Tuscaloosa Presbytery.

GEORGIA

Atlanta — Miss Eva Lou Miller has closed 37 years of service to the Presbyterian Church, U. S. With her resignation from the Board of Annuities and Relief in December, she has ended a record of service to the Church that has few equals among employes of boards and agencies of the Church.

Miss Miller, whose home is Louisville, Ky., joined the staff of the Executive Committee on Christian Education and Ministerial Relief in the early fall of 1919.

LOUISIANA

New Orleans — An organizational service for the Parkway Presbyterian Church, Jefferson parish, was held here Sunday, December 9, with the Presbytery's commission in charge.

The Rev. Ray Riddle, minister of the Lakeview Presbyterian Church, is chairman of the commission which included Dr. John S. Land, the Rev. William Crosland, the Rev. Fred Reeves, Mr. Myron Turfitt, Mr. Goyn Talmage, Mr. Henry Shepherd, and Mr. Thomas Quarterman, all of whom participated in the service.

New Iberia — On November 11th, construction began on the First Presbyterian Church in New Iberia, with groundbreaking ceremonies that will lead to the building of a new $75,000 building.

The building will be at a new location. Building Committee members include W. G. Weeks, chairman; Ralph Brownlee, co-chairman; Walter Klentzman, J. R. Wood, Mrs. Leslie H. Riley, Lloyd Broaddus, and Mrs. A. H. Romain. Mrs. Romain is secretary of the group.

MISSISSIPPI

Jackson — Over three hundred Mississippi ministers of all denominations gathered at Whitfield December 13 to discuss and study mental illness.

The ministers met with psychiatrists from the Mississippi State Hospital and the University Hospital who gave presentations of medical data on mental illness and the problems it presents.

Mrs. Louise West, chief social worker for the State Hospital, says "This meeting will be significant for us because the minister is frequently the only one the patient goes to for professional help when he returns home from the hospital. If our Mississippi pastors can get a better understanding of the problems that the mentally ill face, that will help us do a better job of rehabilitating the patient back home, and of directing others to get help when the early signs occur."

Two Presbyterian, U. S., ministers were among those who led the group during the discussion. Dr. G. T. Gillespie, president emeritus of Belhaven College, and Dr. J. Moody McDill, pastor of Fondren Presbyterian Church, participated in the program. Dr. Gillespie led in a panel discussion of Mental Illness and Community Life, while Dr. McDill was the leader of one of the afternoon seminars.

NORTH CAROLINA

Brevard — The first services in the new $165,000 Brevard-Davidson River Presbyterian Church were held here December 9. Former pastors of the church held thanksgiving and consecration services each evening for the week following the first service.

Attendance at the first service was in excess of 500. Membership of the church is 375.

The sanctuary seats 400, and the plant includes educational, recreational, and social facilities. The Rev. Benjamin F. Ormand is pastor of the church.

SOUTH CAROLINA

Georgetown — The Rev. Mr. Robert G. Balnicky has just completed a successful evangelistic and revival service in Friendfield and Pawley's Island churches, G. Fenton Miller, pastor of the churches said recently.

Services at Friendfield Presbyterian Church, located one mile west of here, ran from November 25 through November 30. Four persons accepted Jesus Christ as Lord and Saviour and many others were drawn closer to Him.

At Pawley's Island Presbyterian Church, 13 miles north of here, five were led to Christ in services running from December 9 through December 14.

At both churches preaching at night was supplemented by Bible studies in the mornings and by morning devotions over radio station WGTN.

Mr. Balnicky, currently chaplain of the Department of South Carolina of the American Legion, was converted from Roman Catholicism on his 21st birthday. He served seven years in the U. S. Navy as flight engineer, and was acting chaplain on Peleliu Island, and did missionary work among the natives while in the South Pacific.

TEXAS

Austin — Will Wilson, a member of First Presbyterian Church in Dallas, former judge of the Texas Supreme Court, was recently elected Attorney General for the State of Texas.

The Wilsons — Will, his wife Marjorie, and two children, a daughter, Lou, 12, and son, Will, 6, attend the University Presbyterian Church in Austin where Mrs. Wilson teaches a Sunday School class.

The newly elected attorney general was in his sixth year on the State Supreme Court bench when he resigned to enter the attorney general's race.

The Presbyterian lawyer is strong in his belief that the leadership of men with Christian principles is the hope of the nation for better government. He too, believes that childhood religious training is the strongest hope of future good government.

"People can always change, but the man with a foundation of good childhood training is usually more likely to retain and draw on these resources as an adult," says Wilson. His wife, teacher of a primary class, agrees with her husband that the teaching of Christian principles is most important in preparing a child for his later life.

VIRGINIA

Richmond — Rev. Robert Turner, associate pastor of Covenant Presbyterian Church, Charlotte, N. C., became regional director of Christian Education for the Synod of North Carolina on January 1, 1957.

He succeeds Rev. J. O. Mann, D. D., who retires at the end of this year after 23 years in the field of Christian Education, all of them in North Carolina. For 18 of those years Dr. Mann has been a staff member of the Board of Christian Education.

The retiring regional director was honored by his fellow workers in the Board's Division of Field Service at a dinner here last week. Gifts were presented to Dr. Mann from the division by Rev. W. B. Sullivan, D. D., regional director for Virginia, and by Rev. Marshall C. Dendy, D. D., executive secretary of the Board.

The incoming regional director is now chairman of Christian Education for the Synod of North Carolina and chairman of Home Missions for Mecklenburg Presbytery. Before coming to the Charlotte church, Mr. Turner was executive secretary of Concord Presbytery in North Carolina.

Richmond — The 1957 Town and Country Pastors' Institute, held annually at Union Theological Seminary in Richmond, will be January 22 - 25, and for the fourth year is being sponsored by the Methodist and Presbyterian Churches.

Since its beginning, the Town and Country Pastors' Institute at Union has taken place annually except for a period of three years when the seminary's Rural Church Department had no director.

Presbyterian and Methodist ministers from the Synods of Appalachia, North Carolina, Virginia, and West Virginia have received invitations to attend. The Institute is under the direction of Dr. James Appleby of Union Seminary, the Rev. James Scott of Richmond, of the Methodist Church, and Dr. James M. Carr, Atlanta, Ga., Secretary of the Town and Country Church Department of the Presbyterian Church, U. S.

SUNDAY SCHOOL LESSON

(Continued from Page 12)

men astray. Think of the False Religions of the world, and the many "Isms" which swarm in our own land.

To enter the kingdom we must not merely say some nice things, and make some promises; we must *do the will of our Father in heaven!*

To enter the Kingdom we must build on the Rock. Paul tells us that other foundation can no man lay than that is laid, which is Christ Jesus. On Christ the solid Rock I stand; All other ground is sinking sand.

I believe that you will agree with me that he who keeps the spirit of the Sermon on the Mount must have a new heart; he must be a new man in Christ, born of the Spirit.

YOUNG PEOPLE'S DEPARTMENT

(Continued from Page 13)

God and brotherhood of man. The idea of this doctrine is that all men are children of God and brothers to one another simply by virtue of being the creatures of God. This teaching does not take into account the separation caused by sin. Some Christians have mistakenly thought that these were Biblical teachings, but they most definitely are not. The Bible says that the sons of God are those who believe in the name of Christ. (Read John 1:11-13). We must be born again spiritually before we can be the children of God. (Read John 3:3-5.) We cannot know God as Father, and we cannot come to Him, until we come by way of faith in Christ. (Read Matthew 11:27 and John 14:6.) If we are the children of God through faith in Christ, then all the other children of God are our brothers and sisters. This is the consistent teaching of the New Testament.

One very practical truth which we need to understand and apply in our lives is that we have far more in common with those who are outwardly different from us but who are Christians, than we do with those who are very similar to us outwardly but who are not Christians. The Korean Christian on the other side of the world is our spiritual brother, but the unbeliever with whom we rub elbows at school is not. This will be a surprising revelation to some of us.

Fourth Speaker:

In the Scripture which was read in our devotional service another question appeared which deserves an answer and an application. The lawyer who tempted Jesus knew that the law required him to love his neighbor, but he asked, "Who is my neighbor?" Who is our neighbor today? Our neighbor is not quite the same as our brother. According to our Lord's parable, all people are our neighbors. We have a responsibility to them even though they are not our brothers and sisters in Christ. We are responsible for showing them kindness, even as the Samaritan showed kindness to the Jew who probably hated him. If God loved the lost world, then His children ought to love it too. If Christ came to seek and to save those who were lost, then His children ought to be engaged in that work too. The best service we can render our neighbor is to work by every possible means to lead him to believe in Christ. If we can do that, our neighbor will become a child of God and our brother.

STEWARDSHIP OF POSSESSIONS

SPECIAL EMPHASIS

The 1956 General Assembly designated the year 1957 as a year of *Special Stewardship Emphasis* in the "Forward with Christ " program. It urged that particular stress be laid upon increasing the benevolence giving in each church in accordance with the "Forward with Christ" goals, and that Synods, Presbyteries, and local churches be urged to make a united effort to meet in full the needs of the benevolence agencies of the General Assembly, Synods, and Presbyteries.

This action of the Assembly takes into consideration the fact that for the last ten years the amount of money given to benevolences in proportion to that given to current expenses has been continually decreasing. Not including amounts given to building expense, the churches of the General Assembly of 1945 contributed 37% of their local budgets to benevolences while in 1955 this percentage had dropped to 32%. In amounts contributed, the increase to current expenses during the ten years amounted to 203% while the increase to benevolences amounted to 141%.

There are two things that every church can do in increasing its benevolences: First, it can study its own record and adopt a policy for increasing its benevolence giving each year. Every church can do this. Some churches which have recently finished paying for building projects can make tremendous strides in turning the generosity of their people to the benevolence work of the Church. One large church thus increased its benevolence giving last year by 300%.

The second thing which every church can do is to see to it that the members of the congregation are educated in the benevolence work of the Church. There are numerous ways in which this can be done. It can be done by stressing the messages printed in the Presbyterian church bulletin. Some churches use three minutes of every Sunday morning service in telling the story of some benevolence cause. One church of which we know is planning an entire series, covering all the winter months, to tell about the benevolence program of the Church at its midweek church night meetings.

The "Forward with Christ" goal is that the Assembly may continue to incrase its benevolence giving until the denomination gives as much to benevolences as to current expenses. We trust and pray that each church may strive this year to help reach that goal and to change the trend of the past few years in regard to benevolenve giving.

—Forward With Christ
Plan Book for 1957

THE SOUTHERN PRESBYTERIAN JOURNAL

Rev. Henry B. Dendy, D.D., Editor..Weaverville, N. C.
Dr. L. Nelson Bell, Associate Editor..Asheville, N. C.
Rev. Wade C. Smith, Associate Editor..Weaverville, N. C.

EDITORIAL

That I May Dwell in the House of the Lord

The one thing the Psalmist desired was to dwell in the house of the Lord all the days of his life. He would rather be a doorkeeper in the house of God than to dwell in the tents of wickedness. The final assurance of the Shepherd Psalm is that I will dwell in the house of the Lord forever. In His house one beholds the beauty of the Lord, and one, bereft of this privilege, yearns to see "Thy power and glory as I have seen them in the sanctuary."

The First Epistle to the Corinthians is written to a Church torn with schism and strife. Here the Apostle undertakes to bind the torn fragments together upon the one foundation which God has laid, namely, JESUS CHRIST. And he solemnly warns the readers that if anyone destroys this temple of God him shall God destroy — for the Temple of God is holy.

When William Farel and John Calvin were expelled from Geneva, the life of the Church deteriorated. The preaching was not as good, discipline declined, the deacons let the care of the poor and the sick lag. Accordingly, the friends of the exiled Calvin wrote him that they were leaving the Church which had expelled him. Calvin wrote them that to desert the Church was to become a traitor to God. He said that those who would have God for their Father must have the Church for their mother, since God willed to generated children by the Church, to nurture them in the Church, to discipline and guide them through the Church until they divested themselves of this mortal flesh.

The Church exists where the Word is preached from its fundamental message CHRIST CRUCIFIED AND RISEN, and where the sacraments are properly administered. As did our Scottish forebears, we must learn to distinguish between the true and the pure Church. The true Church is shown by these marks of the Word and the sacraments with discipline in the third (not in the first) place. The pure Church is in heaven.

In our own denomination we have sought to keep the Church on its God-given foundation — JESUS CHRIST — by a General Assembly declaration that our ordination vows involve accepting Christ as the Holy Scriptures present Him: true and Eternal God Who became also truly man by being born of a Virgin, Who offered up Himself a sacrifice to satisfy Divine justice and reconcile us to God, Who rose again from the dead with the same body with which He suffered, and Who will come again to judge the world.

Moreover, as Calvin well says, the Church's stay is Jesus Christ at the right hand of God. The Church rests upon the everlasting throne of Christ. We have received, in His exaltation to the right hand of the Majesty on High, a Kingdom that cannot be shaken.

And this note of the Kingship of Christ is magnificently set forth in the second chapter and in other paragraphs of our Southern Presbyterian Book of Church Order.

We sympathize with those who seek a truer and purer Church. We pray God to begin His purifying work in us. But we beg those who yearn for more holiness in the house of God, not to forsake the assembling of themselves together as the custom of some is.

God has kept His Church through many decadent periods — the pornography of the tenth century — the three competing popes of the early fifteenth century — the Borgia Pope, Alexander VI, who condemned Savonarola.

God is in the midst of His Zion today. God will help her and that right early. And God will do it not through those who desert their banners, but through the faithful watchmen upon the battlements of Zion. Those in whose hearts are the highways of Zion shall go from strength to strength in the Lord. Those who wait upon the Lord shall renew their strength, and, it may well be, behold the Lord reviving His work in the midst of the years.

—W.C.R.

Receiving Correction

A Reply to Rev. Arch B. Taylor, Jr.

In the Christian fellowship we are to receive admonition and correction from the brethren. That was the purpose of the Venerable Company's meetings in Geneva. And so, we editors ought each to hear the word from our missionary brother calling us to more grace, more charity and more sympathy. It is, however, a bit difficult to reply to his letter in detail since different writers have contributed the various articles to which he takes exception.

The one for which I am directly responsible is the objection to the line, "Some great Cause, God's Messiah" in Lowell's poem or hymn. It is a pleasure to have Mr. Taylor's backing in voicing this objection; and proper that we offer our belated thanks to the Committee for revising this line for the *Hymnbook*. In this case the current Committee was more receptive of this criticism than was the Richmond Committee of Publication which put out the *Hymnbook for Christian Worship*. One of the members of that Committee replied to my objection by defending the use of the line. So we are grateful for the improvement in the *Hymnbook*, but one still wonders why a poem written by a Unitarian contained such contra-evangelical thoughts as "God's new Messiah" and "new Calvaries" ever found a place in any Presbyterian hymnal.

We trust that Mr. Taylor's condemnation of the notion that some great cause is God's Messiah means that he and those of his general position are standing against every effort to make ecumenism, or interracism, or pacifism, or equalitarianism or any other "ism" the Alpha, the Subject, the Lord beside which even Jesus Christ becomes a secondary concern, a relative predicate.

John Calvin was careful to set forth that God's grace toward us in Christ is ultimately determined neither by our moral merit nor by our personal worth, as one may find by reading his commentary on the first chapter of Ephesians, and that on I Peter 1.1-2, thus: "In adopting us, therefore, God does not inquire what we are, and is not reconciled to us by any personal worth." "The foreknowledge of God excludes every worthiness on the part of man."

The translation of Calvin's Catechism used by the Kirk of Scotland, answer 11, reads, "There is no worthiness in us why God should either show His power to help us, or use His merciful goodness to save us." A. Mitchell Hunter cites with approval this translation of one of Calvin's hymns:

"I greet Thee Who my sure Redeemer art
My only trust, and Saviour of my heart!
Who so much toil and woe
And pain didst undergo
For my poor worthless sake; . . . "

Of course, Calvin's fundamental thought is that God's love is freely and graciously bestowed upon us only in and for Christ's sake, and we are happy to note that Mr. Taylor is at one with him and us in this faith. "The name of Christ excludes all merit."

It is a distinct pleasure to emphasize the following words from Mr. Taylor's letter: "THE FAITH WHICH WAS ONCE FOR ALL DELIVERED UNTO THE SAINTS" IS *OUR* FAITH AS WELL AS YOURS. WE SHOULD ALL BE ALLIES IN ITS PROPAGATION AS WELL AS IN ITS DEFENSE." We accept this as meaning that if another world theologian comes to the International Japanese Christian University who denies both the Virgin Birth and the empty tomb, Mr. Taylor will stand up against him and defend the Virgin Birth and the bodily Resurrection of our Lord.

"For other foundation can no man lay than that which is laid, which is Jesus Christ."
—W.C.R.

Our Greatest Weakness

By Ralph Brewer

We are proud of our church and we have great strength, but we also have a critical weakness and there is no reason we should close our eyes to it. Do you know that we are slipping backward in our efforts to fill vacant pulpits? What can we do about it?

We have 3,800 churches and 3,200 ministers, and that doesn't tell the story. Some ministers are college presidents and professors, missionaries, regional directors and stated clerks. Some large churches hesitate in calling associates and assistants because of the shortage.

The minister alone cannot solve this problem, nor the Sunday School teacher, nor the vocational guidance program, nor the parents

The Southern Presbyterian Journal, *a Presbyterian Weekly magazine devoted to the statement, defense, and propagation of the Gospel, the faith which was once for all delivered unto the saints*, published every Wednesday by The Southern Presbyterian Journal, Inc., in Weaverville, N. C.

Entered as second-class matter May 15, 1942, at the Postoffice at Weaverville, N. C., under the Act of March 3, 1879. Vol. XV, No. 38, January 16, 1957. Editorial and Business Offices: Weaverville, N. C. Printed in the U.S.A. by Biltmore Press, Asheville, N. C.

ADDRESS CHANGE: When changing address, please let us have both old and new address as far in advance as possible. Allow three weeks after change if not sent in advance. When possible, send an address label giving your old address.

in the home. We cannot "lead" men into the ministry; God calls them. But we can pray more about it. We can talk more about it.

Recently a young man said to me: "I believe I would have gone into the ministry with a bit of encouragement. No one ever opened the door for me." We can and should encourage those that feel the call. We should stress its importance and its rewards, the satisfaction that comes to a man serving God. So the responsibility rests on the parents, the Sunday School teachers, the elders and deacons and on the ministers themselves. They should not hesitate to talk about it in the pulpit, to young people's groups and to John and Mary privately. In our strength, progress and growth, this is our greatest weakness, and a church problem we must solve.

Let us make this a church-wide project: To pray that God will call more young men and women for fulltime service, not forgetting that the place to begin is at mother's knee.

The Gospel Is Bittersweet

By Rev. Kennedy Smartt

"And I took the little book out of the angel's hand, and ate it up; and it was in my mouth sweet as honey: and as soon as I had eaten it, my belly was bitter." Revelation 10:10.

The Word of God is sweet as honey in our mouth, but often times when we have received it it becomes bitter in our belly. In God's Revelation to John he is shown much that shall come to pass in the history of the world. He beholds as Christ, the only one found to be worthy, removes the seven seals unlocking the story of the future and thus learns of certain conditions which must come to pass before the final judgment. But midway in the revelation he sees an angel holding a little book and hears a voice telling him to take the book and to eat it. He is also told that the book will taste as sweet as honey in his mouth but shall be bitter in his belly.

I believe this little book held out to John by the angel represents John's own personal future which Christ asks him to accept. His future is represented as participating in the ministry of the Gospel, which shall always be sweet as honey in his mouth, to his soul, but which shall result in his belly being made bitter, which shall result in difficult assignments, tasks hard to fulfill, tribulation, conflicts, trials, hardships, etc., which would make life unattractive at times. For a long time I have been reading about this in God's Word, not only here in Revelation, but also in the Psalms, in Jeremiah, and in Ezekiel. But I have avoided preaching on it because my first response to it was that it didn't make much sense, that it had no message. The idea of taking a book and eating it always seemed revolting to me; in fact I considered it absurd. But my attitude has changed completely now that I have studied the matter to see what God is saying to me in it.

Ezekiel was commanded to take the roll of God's Word, God's message to the House of Israel, to eat and fill his bowels with it. Ezekiel did as God commanded him and said that it was sweet as honey in his mouth for sweetness. But when the Spirit lifted him up and took him away to proclaim the message he had received, he reports that he went in bitterness. (Ezekiel 3: 3 and 14). There is no question in my mind that this experience of John and Ezekiel in eating the Word and finding it sweet to their mouths and bitter to their bellies is an experience which every true child of God must expect and should accept and prepare himself for as he walks in the Way. Every child of God will have the experience of coming to God's Word and finding it sweet as honey to his soul, and also he must expect that there will be experiences of grief, heartache, tribulation, and conflict which he never had to face as a non-Christian; experiences which will be bitter to endure.

When we are grieving and find comfort in God's Word, it is sweet as honey in our mouth. When we search for assurance that God will answer our prayers and find the promise so boldly stated in God's Word, it is sweet as honey in our mouth.

When we wonder if our soul shall escape death, or when we are troubled about whether our sins can be forgiven, and we find God's promises to be yea and amen in Christ, the Word is sweet as honey in our mouths.

When we are in trouble, or alone, or feel that people do not understand, or when we are falsely accused and ridiculed, and read the Psalms and understand that God knows just what we are going through and that He has promised to defend us, then the Word is sweet as honey in our mouths. The message of Grace is always honey in our mouths.

Why then is the message given us through John and Ezekiel that the Word when received will be bitter in our belly? Does such a message encourage us to take the Gospel, to embrace the promises in faith? Will the warning attract people to feast their souls on that which is sweet as honey to the mouths if it is going to be bitter to their bellies? Did you realize when you came to the Lord that the Christian life would not be all sweetness? Did you contemplate the responsibility and the consequence of siding with Christ in a world that is alien to Him? Do you remember what followed your conversion, the stand you took for Christ, if in truth you took such a stand? Was it all sweetness? Do you remember bitter experiences? Responsibilities hard to accept? Did you expect them? Were you warned to expect them?

The rich young ruler came to Christ, the Gospel message sweet as honey in his mouth. The promise was of eternal life and an everlasting Kingdom. But Christ warned him in effect that the message would be bitter to his belly. To follow Him he must first go and sell all that he had and give it to the poor, and then he would be free to follow Him.

At this the rich young ruler went sorrowfully away, unwilling to accept the bitter with the sweet, even though it was not worthy to be compared with the glory that would have been revealed in him. The mistake I have made as a preacher, and we have made as a church, I believe, is that we have given people the impression that the Gospel message will be nothing but sweet in our mouths, never bitter in our bellies. We have told them, in effect, to expect to be "carried to the skies on flowery beds of ease while others fought to win the prize and sailed through bloody seas."

We have not prepared our converts, nor our people, to expect opposition from all the demon hosts of hell which will rage against their walk of obedience to Christ. We have led them to expect a life free of all conflict, discouragement, accusation, and unfriendliness. We have advertised the way of the cross as a cure for some of the actual bitter experiences that result from accepting it, and from participating in the fellowship of Him whom the world has crucified and whose truth is opposed not only by typical America today, but also by all the devil himself.

To accept Christ is not to take a seat at an armistice table, but rather to take a front line position in a battle that shall know no peace until our Saviour returns to subdue forever all opposition to His Kingdom. Victory? Yes. Confidence? Yes. Freedom from conflict? No.

Is it any wonder that many have turned back discouraged? Is it any wonder that so many lack assurance? They haven't been taught to expect such as this in the Christian life. But true it is, that a bitter experience of some sort has followed every genuine conversion if life has continued long enough to permit it.

Can any one of us say that since the day we received Christ we have known nothing but ease, a soft sort of existence typified by a bed of roses? Is it not true of every Christian life that there have been temptations, trials, testings, accusations, hardships, griefs, difficult responsibilities, tasks hard to fulfil and continual opposition to a walk in victory and obedience. If any confessing Christian were to claim freedom from these, I would be forced to wonder in my mind about the genuineness of his testimony of faith.

One thing we must remember, and should preach, is that when this message of the Gospel has come "sweet as honey" it is followed by the words of our Lord Jesus Christ, "If any man will come after me, let him deny himself, and take up his cross daily and follow me."

The cross is an altar of sacrifice. Upon it our Saviour was offered, and upon it we are called to offer our bodies a living sacrifice, to reckon ourselves to be there crucified with Christ. Self-denial and reckoning ourselves to be dead are bitter herbs for our flesh to take.

Our flesh can glory in such promises as eternal life and the victory of Christ's coming Kingdom. But not so with the humbling challenge of our Lord that we deny ourselves of ourselves, that we "sell all" and follow him, that we turn the control of all that we have and are over to Him, that we love Him above consideration for our families or even for ourselves. This message turns to bitterness the sweet and easy promise of the Gospel that was sweet as honey in our mouths. Did you expect this when you first came to Christ? I don't believe I did. I believe it would have been easier for me along the way if I had. Don't you think so too?

And I see the application of our text in another way too. Christ asks us to take the message of salvation, which is sweet as honey in our mouths, to take and eat it. To let it work its purifying, purging grace within us, though it be as wormwood to our flesh. To accept along with the sweetness of "blessed assurance" the responsibility to take this message to a stiff hearted, gainsaying people, and to live it in a world which is hostile to the way of our Lord. It means the bitter reward of being reviled, misunderstood, laughed at, and rejected by those whose friendship we may have counted dearest. It often means the sacrifice of our standing in a group considered by us to be important.

Nathan the prophet knew the meaning of this when he denounced David for his sin with Bathsheba. John the Baptist understood as he denounced Herod for living with his brother's wife, Stephen as he preached Christ to those who stoned him to death knew, too, and so also many others. Bordalou, the court preacher of Louis XIV, tried to bring conviction to that Sovereign by talking about sin in terms of abstract people. Finally he realized that it was useless and he turned to the king and said in the words of Nathan, "Thou art the man," knowing that in so doing he was risking his very life. These accepted the bitter with the sweet in embracing the promises of God.

When God, through the suffrage of the people, chooses officers for our church, the honor that comes is a high one, to share in the ministry as undershepherds of the Chief Shepherd. It is an honor that is sweet to our souls, but every officer so chosen must accept the bitter aspects of his responsibility also. The responsibility of giving himself and his time unselfishly when it would be within his rights to claim the time for himself or his family. He has a responsibility to learn to do things he has never done before, perhaps. He must do difficult, humbling things. He must be able to ask any member of his congregation to "follow my example and walk as a good citizen of the Kingdom of our Lord."

He must either do or be willing to do if possible, all that he would ask any other member of the church to do as a good soldier of Jesus Christ. In fact it should be true of all of us who name the name of Christ, that we are willing to accept the bitter with the sweet.

There is an angel of God standing before each of us, holding a little book. It is the book of our future, of our participation in the fellowship and ministry of Christ. It is God's plan for us. It will be sweet as honey in our mouth, but there will be bitterness too. God asks us as good disciples to take and eat it. To accept it all. "If any man will come after me, let him deny himself, and take up his cross daily, and follow me."

"When I survey the wondrous cross
On which the Prince of Glory died,
My richest gain I count but loss,
And pour contempt on all my pride."

Conquest By Association

By Dr. Harold E. Kershner

"Vice is a monster of so frightful mien,
As to be hated needs but to be seen;
Yet seen too oft, familiar with her face,
We first endure, then pity, then embrace."
—Pope's Essay on Man.

The secret and deadly weapon of the Communists is the uncanny ability to influence and re-mold Western ideology in its own image so that we become more and more like that which we abhor and fight against.

The American people loathe Communism, yet we are rapidly adopting its major tenets and shaping our social, political and economic institutions in a way that will inevitably bring it upon us.

Run through the objectives of the Communist Manifesto and note the extent to which they have triumphed in revolutionizing our institutions. Our income and inheritance taxes have probably exceeded Marx's wildest dreams. The control of our banking system by government is surely as complete as he hoped for. The same is true of education. The state rigidly controls transportation and communication. Its control over agriculture is already very extensive and is rapidly increasing. Government owns over a third of our land, operates vast business enterprises, and steadily increases its control over economic activities.

As we look at these facts it is perfectly obvious that, dislike Communism as we do, we are still being remade in its image.

It has invaded the Christian church and has many defenders within the ranks of the clergy. It has its spokesmen in our public schools and colleges, and the Communist line is defended and promoted by many of the textbooks used in our educational institutions. It flourished in the White House and in many departments of our government. It had its appeasers under the Capitol dome and its apologists in the religious and secular press of our country. The combined influence of those who defended it in all these quarters was sufficient to force us into the Second World War, the result of which was to vastly advance Communism throughout the world.

There is much evidence to indicate that Hitler could and would have been overthrown as early as 1938, and by his own generals and the army, had we not played into the hands of the Communists by the Peace of Munich. Emergency peace campaigners, unwittingly furthering Communist policy, helped to bring about this tragedy. The opponents of Hitler in Germany were discouraged and were forced to conclude that no outside help could be expected. After the beginning of the war all overtures on the part of responsible Germans to end it by over-

and then find it easier to stop as one's speed continues to accelerate.

Our danger is not from Communist bombs and armies but rather from our continued absorption of Communist ideology, involving us in more government control of the activities of the people with continual expansion of the bureaucratic instrumentalities of such control. We have tolerated Communism and associated with Communists so long that we are not only enduring it but beginning to embrace it.

Four Presidents and their Secretaries of State refused to recognize the Communist government of Russia, but in 1933 this wrong step was taken. For twenty-three years it has been followed by increasingly close collaboration with the Communist government of Russia and during latter years with other Communist governments. We send and receive missions of businessmen, churchmen, and government officials. We accept decorations and laudations from these mortal enemies of everything which we believe to be right and good. We entertain them and are entertained by them with rivers of vodka and other Bacchanalia. Our leaders are pictured with theirs and chummy, back-slapping posters are used as propaganda to prove to the world that the materialistic, atheistic, Communistic officials are accepted socially by our leaders.

Such action on our part discourages opposition within the Communist countries and has taught our own people to endure and finally to embrace much Communist ideology. The progressive trend downward began with recognition and has continued with association, camaraderie, cooperation in many fields, with an increasing degree of embracement.

How can we save ourselves? The first move is to come wide awake, to realize what is happening, and to stop all association with Communists and their governments. Had it not been for recognition, co-operation, loans, technical assistance, mountains of goods, and the great respect accorded them by the Western world, it is highly probable that the U.S.S.R. would long since have crumbled from the internal pressure upon it. We have relieved this pressure by proving to the Russian people that we will not help them in their aspirations to overthrow their gangster leaders but choose rather to be hail-fellows-well-met with them.

Secondly, we must stop expanding government and begin demobilizing it — reducing its functions and lessening its power. This should be accompanied by increasing the area of freedom wherein our citizens determine their own destinies. It would mean setting up a free market economy, including sound money of intrinsic value, and a government limited to the few simple functions set forth by the Constitution.

We must sweep away the pragmatic philosophy that right and wrong are a matter of custom and usage and return to the belief and practice that the absolute standards established by the Ten Commandments and embodied in the Christian religion must govern the conduct of mankind. We must honor the First and Great Commandment by putting God first and allowing nothing to interfere with our supreme loyalty to Him and our willingness to live and work as He directs.

The right of life, to freedom, to earn and to own comes from God and not from the state. The place of the state is to insure these rights to all men against the predators who would violate them. If the state is allowed to exceed those powers and begin the process of taking wealth from some and giving it to others (which is the objective of all forms of state intervention in the economic activities of the people) we shall find no limit to state expansion until we approach the Communist ideals of a supreme state which is not the servant of the people but rather their master—a state which controls their lives and their liberties; determines what property they may possess, what work they shall do, how they shall be educated, the wages they may receive, the kinds and amounts of clothing they shall wear, the food they may eat, and the houses they may live in.

Why should we arm ourselves and our friends against Communism while steadily adopting its ideology in our own country? Only a return to God-directed living will save us from being remolded in the image of that which we most abhor.

Helps To Understanding Scripture Readings in *Day by Day*

By Rev. C. C. Baker

Sunday, January 27, Rev. 7:9-17. Try to catch the drama of vv.1-8 as God halts the winds of persecution and calamity to seal with His seal those who belong to Him (vv.1-3). The entire Church is sealed; everyone from every tribe and tongue that belongs to Christ is known to God (vv.4-8). Verses 9-17 reveal God's own as having gone through their ordeal on earth, standing in heaven before God (vv.13-14). How are words of vv.15-17 especially appropriate for them? Listen to the joy that is in their hearts as they sing the praises of God (vv.9-12). This passage assures every Christian that God knows him, has His hand upon him, and will see him through to happier days, even in the most adverse of circumstances.

Monday, January 28, Acts 1:1-8. After the resurrection Jesus rounded out the disciples' understanding of the things they needed to know about the Kingdom of God before He left them (vv.3,9). The disciples were also full of "enthusiasm" (Luke 24:52-53). However, they were not ready to preach the Gospel. What was lacking (vv.4,5,8)? If they had not tarried in Jerusalem (vv.4-5) before going out to preach (v.8), would their work have been a success? Even if a minister is well-educated and zealous for the Gospel, if His zeal is of the flesh his ministry will not prosper under God. How would the power of the Holy Spirit keep the disciples from placing their primary emphasis on outward organization and programming? Is your zeal for God primarily of the flesh, or have you learned to wait upon God in prayer until He gives you His power in your life?

Tuesday, January 29, Mark 12:28-34. Observe Jesus' keen knowledge of Scripture as He dealt with people who came to Him. The Sadducees were familiar with the Scriptures, but twisted their teachings to their own prejudices (vv.18-23). [They didn't really believe in the resurrection (v.23).] How did Jesus thwart their trickery and perversion (vv.24-27)? The Scribe who came to Jesus (v.28) also was familiar with the Old Testament. Jesus chose two isolated passages (Deuteronomy 6:4; Lev. 19:18) to summarize the teachings of the whole Old Testament (vv.30,31). Observe the scribe's reaction to Christ's answer (vv.32-33). From that time no one dared try to refute Him (v.34b) as He taught from the temple itself (vv.35-37). People will almost always respond to the teacher who knows the Bible thoroughly and explains it clearly and sanely (v.37b).

Wednesday, January 30, Rev. 2:8-11. The Church in Smyrna was poor in physical resources and slandered by "Jews" (v.9). The Christians there faced the prospects of persecution, imprisonment and death for their faith (v.10). An observer might have concluded that their adversary had been completely victorious over them (v.10a), but faithfulness unto death produces victory for the Christian (v.10b). Though physically poor, these Christians were spiritually rich (v.9a). It is not physical death that is to be dreaded, but the "second death" (v.11b), that is, spiritual death (20:14-15). What must it have meant to this Church for Christ to be revealed to it as the "first and the last, who was dead and is alive" (v.8b)? How must it have lent authority to the message of (vv.9-11)? Thus Christ reveals Himself to us, giving us hope that is adequate for the worst of situations.

Thursday, January 31, Luke 17:7-10. The purpose of Jesus' parables was to teach one central truth. Today's parable is not intended

(Continued on Page 17)

SUNDAY SCHOOL Lessons

LESSON FOR JANUARY 27

By THE REV. J. KENTON PARKER

Needs That Jesus Meets

Background Scripture: Matthew 8:1 — 9:34
Devotional Reading: James 5:13-20

In these two chapters we find Jesus meeting the needs of the men and women of His day. A great many things have changed since that day, but human nature and human needs remain the same. We have a hymn which begins, "I need Jesus," and it beautifully expresses that personal need which calls for the help of Jesus. As we read these verses we can classify some of these needs.

I. *We need Jesus in Sickness:* 8:1-17.

There were a great many sick people in Jesus' day, sick with divers diseases. The first one mentioned is the leper. Leprosy was an outstanding type of sin and uncleanliness. The leper was an outcast from society, with his cry, Unclean, unclean. He was an "untouchable." We get an insight into the love and compassion of Jesus as He reached out His hand and touched him, and said, I will, be thou clean. He could have easily healed without the touch, and in that touch we see the tenderness of our Saviour. He is careful to tell the healed man to report to the priest and observe the law of the land in regard to healed lepers.

The second is the servant of the centurion. These Roman centurions seem to be especially responsive to Jesus. This one was very humble and had great faith. That makes a splendid combination. We find Jesus marveling at the unbelief of His own race. He marvels now at the faith of this man; "I have not found so great faith, no, not in Israel." Today we marvel at the stubborn unbelief of the Jew, and sometimes at the unbelief in civilized countries, while heathen people respond to the gospel.

Jesus comes to Simon Peter's house and finds his wife's mother sick of the fever. He touched her hand and the fever left her.

In verses 16 and 17 there is a summary of His work. He healed all who were sick. This was a fulfillment of the prophecy of Isaiah, Himself took our infirmities and bear our sicknesses.

There are several other miracles of healing mentioned in these chapters: the man with the palsy, 9:1-8; the woman with an issue of blood, 9:20-22; and the blind and dumb man in 9:27-34.

We need the Great Physician in our times of sickness. God often heals in answer to prayer, and we should bring our loved ones to Him. I have had personal knowledge of His healing power. I have known Christian doctors who believed in prayer and relied upon it. A clear picture comes to me of a trip I took to see a sick child. In the car were the father of the child, a deacon, the grandfather of the child, an elder, the doctor, also an elder, and myself. The doctor stopped just before we got to the home and asked that we have prayer, and we did.

There is danger that we overemphasize the importance of the healing of the body. Even those whom Jesus healed died later of some disease. It is a blessed experience when our children are healed, or our loved ones, but after all the most important part is the healing of the soul. It is better for the sick to be saved than to be healed, and it is not always God's will to heal the body.

II. *We need Jesus in time of storm:* 8:23-27.

This is a most remarkable scene. There arose a great tempest. I have seen it suggested that Satan stirred up this storm with the purpose of drowning Jesus. Jesus was asleep in the midst of the storm. The disciples awoke Him, saying, Lord, save us: we perish. This indicates the severity of the storm. He rebuked the winds and the sea and there was a great calm. This miracle naturally made a deep impression on the men in the boat. We have seen men face a storm with courage; we have seen others terrified, trying to hide from it; but none of us have ever seen a man rebuke the wind and the sea. What manner of Man is this? None other than the Son of God, the Creator of wind and sea.

I think we ought to get a very simple and very comforting lesson from this incident. We are living in a stormy world. Our little boat is tossed hither and yon on the waves. Is it not a comforting thought to know that the Master of the winds and waves is our Saviour, our Companion, our Friend? He is indeed a shelter in the time of storm, but He is more than a Shelter; He has the power to turn the storm into a "great calm."

III. *We need Jesus when demons assail us:* 8:28-34.

There were many of these demon-possessed men in Jesus' day. Satan was using all his helpers to try and hinder the work of Christ. The storm on the sea was bad enough, but here was a tempest in a man's soul. These two men were miserable and dangerous. There is a strange ending to this story. The whole city came out to meet Jesus, and when they saw all that had been done, and the loss of the hogs, they besought Him to depart out of their coasts. The men had been healed, but some of their property had been destroyed, and so they asked Him to leave.

We talk and write a great deal about cleaning up our slums and bettering the condition of our poor people. If someone came and really cast out the demons of lust and strong drink and debauchery, would not some of our devilish business be ruined? Would not many of our respectable citizens who own stock in saloons and gambling dens and night clubs, cry out that the reformers had gone too far, and ask that they get out of town? The trouble is that people love sin, and make money out of sin. We do not want the demons cast out if it interferes with making money. I am afraid that the average city or town would do like these people did; ask Jesus to leave. The only hope of demon-possessed men and women is Jesus. I believe that we have men and women today who are literally "possessed with demons," and there are many other things which we call "demons," like the appetite for drink. Jesus has the power to cast out all kinds of demons.

IV. *We need Jesus when sin is in the heart:* 9:1-13.

The man sick of the palsy was sick in body, but the first thing that Jesus said to him was: "Son, be of good cheer; thy sins be forgiven thee." The scribes said within themselves, This man blasphemeth, who can forgive sins but God only? Jesus knew what they were thinking and proved that He had the authority to forgive sins by healing the man's body. The worst trouble this man had was not a palsied body, but a paralyzed soul. In our dealing with sick people let us, too, put first things first. It is far more important to be saved than healed; to be healed within rather than healed without.

Right after this Jesus called Matthew the publican to be His disciple, and as He sat at meat in his house a great many publicans and sinners were there. This aroused the Pharisees, and they said, Why eateth your Master with publicans and sinners? Their idea of holiness was to keep away from all who were in the despised class of sinners. Jesus replied, They that be whole need not a physician, but they that are sick. These very Pharisees were sick with sin, but they did not realize their condition.

We are living in a world filled with sinsick people. We are doing a lot for sick bodies, but many do not realize that the number one problem of the world is not sick bodies, but sick souls. We need Jesus. These sinsick men and women need Jesus. If, in answer to prayer, He heals our bodies, let us be very grateful, but the main business of preaching the gospel is to heal sick souls, to have our sins forgiven by the Great Physician.

V. *We need Jesus in time of death:* 9:18-26.

Jairus had a daughter who was "even now dead." She was at the point of death when he came to Jesus, and died while Jesus was on His way, delayed as He was by the woman who came and touched Him.

Death is an enemy which must be faced by all, and is feared by most people. There is a deep desire in the hearts of men to live. I have known two or three old people who were not only prepared to die, but seemed to wish to depart and be with Christ. We can understand how they feel. Paul said, To depart and be with Christ is far better. Where one is a great sufferer it is natural to want relief.

For the believer in Christ the sting of death has been removed, for the sting of death is sin, and he knows that he has gained the victory over sin. The words of Jesus to Martha when her brother died are a great comfort to us; I am the resurrection and the life: he that believeth in Me, though he were dead, yet shall he live: And whosoever liveth and believeth in Me shall never die. Believest thou this? If we really believe this glorious statement of Jesus, then death has lost its terror for us.

We need Jesus while we live. We need Him when our loved ones leave us. We need Him when we feel that death is knocking at our own door. "I need Jesus" : you need Jesus : every sinner, every sufferer, every dying mortal, needs Jesus. Someone has said : Jesus is absolutely necessary; He is absolutely sufficient : He is absolutely accessible. He will meet your need. Have you come to Him?

YOUNG PEOPLES Department

YOUTH PROGRAM FOR JANUARY 27

By THE REV. B. HOYT EVANS

Youth Sunday Program

(This is a program to be presented to the entire congregation of your local church. Its main purpose is to acquaint the adult members of the congregation with the total program of youth work being carried on by their church. In the material printed below we are not offering a collection of ready-made talks. It will be far more helpful and the people of your church will find it far more interesting, if you prepare your own speeches with specific information about the work of your local youth organizations. We are offering some suggestions which we believe will help you in preparing your own talks and your program.)

THINGS TO BE DONE IN PREPARATION FOR THE PROGRAM

1. Pray for God's guidance in the planning and presentation of the program.

2. Secure permission from the Session to present the program and to receive an offering for youth work.

3. Call together for a planning meeting the adult leaders and representatives of all the youth groups in the church. (We are repeating the procedure of last year in which all the young peoples' organizations share in the Youth Sunday instead of the seniors only, as in former years.)

4. Decide on a definite time and place for the program. (This should be cleared through the Session.)

5. Let the planning committee outline the program.

6. Choose the personnel to take part in the program. (Those to lead the worship, speakers from each group, choir members, ushers, etc.)

7. Designate adult advisors to help the youth speakers prepare their talks.

8. Appoint a publicity committee to make use of posters, pulpit announcements, bulletin announcements, etc.

9. Decide how the offering is to be divided and used.

10. Set definite times for practice sessions after all the parts of the program are planned.

(A program which is good in all its parts may be very ineffective if it is not properly put together. Practice will make it smooth.)

A SUGGESTED ORDER OF SERVICE

Prelude

Call to Worship (spoken by leader or sung by choir)

Invocation

Hymn

Responsive or Unison Reading—Psalm 119:9-16.

Prayer

Leader's Introduction

Talks by Representatives from Organizations other than Senior High Fellowship

Hymn

Presentation of the Senior High Theme for 1957

The Theme Hymn "God of Grace and God of Glory" (To be sung either by the congregation or a youth choir.)

Talk on the Work of the Local Senior Organization

Talk on the Denominational Work of Seniors

Explanation of the Offering

Offering and Offertory

Prayer of Dedication

Hymn

Benediction (Prononunced by the minister)

SUGGESTIONS FOR THE TALKS

Leader's Introduction:

Express your appreciation for an opportunity to come before the congregation to describe for them their own church's program of youth work. Point out that the young people are not only preparing for the future but that they are endeavoring to serve Christ in the present. The speakers who follow will show how the young people are preparing for future

(Continued on Page 17)

CHILDRENS Page

David Slays Goliath

As the giant, waving his great spear advanced upon David, the boy did not flinch, but ran toward the giant, having placed a stone in his sling. Then he whirled the stone from the sling and it went straight into the opening in the giant's helmet, crashed thro his skull and sank into his brain. The giant dropped his spear, threw up his hands and fell to the ground on his face and rolled over — dead! David ran up and drew the giant's sword from its scabbard and cut his head off. When the heathen army saw their champion fall, they turned and fled for their lives, and King Saul's army ran after them and chopped them to pieces. King Saul sent Abner, his general, out to bring David to the royal tent, and David came dragging the giant's head by the hair. "Who are you, young man"? asked the King. "My lord, the King," answered David, "I am the son of thy servant, Jesse".

WOMENS work

Helps for Circle Bible Study for February

CITIZENSHIP GOALS

By Rev. Carl W. McMurray, Ph.D.
Marion, N. C.

What should be our objectives as citizens of the United States and of the particular state and community in which we live? This vital question deserves prayerful consideration. The Christian cannot afford to evade the sphere of citizenship responsibility.

Two Scripture portions have been assigned for this lesson, and it is to be noted that these passages were not designed by our Lord as lessons on citizenship. In Luke 4:14-24, we find Jesus in the Nazareth synagogue where He read that wonderful Messianic prophecy of Isaiah (Isa. 61:1-2), and then declared Himself to be the fulfillment of the prophecy. The focus of the passage is not upon His citizenship but upon His Messiahship and His redemptive mission as the Messiah. In harmony with the redemptive mission of Jesus, set forth in this passage, Christians are commissioned "to preach the Gospel" to all the needy of the earth, but this is a task that transcends our citizenship obligations.

The other assigned passage in Matthew 6:9-13 is the Lord's Prayer. Our Lord's high purpose in this prayer is to guide His followers in the blessed experience of prayer and worship. It is the prayer heritage of those who have "received the Spirit of adoption whereby we cry: Abba, Father," but its light is not focused on the civic task. Since the assigned Scripture passages were not intended by our Lord as lessons on citizenship, it seems much better for us to seek light on our theme from other portions of Scripture which were specially designed to give us clear guidance in the sphere of our responsibilities as citizens.

In Romans 13:9 we find that the Christian citizen should make it the aim of his daily life to live according to the moral law and to be an example of moral integrity in the community. This is according to the example and teaching of Jesus.

In His words and actions and in the spirit of His life there is no moral fault (see John 8:46; Matt. 26:23). Likewise the apostles exhort us to have "a good conscience," that "they may be put to shame who falsely accuse your good manner of life" (see I Peter 3:16; Acts 24:16).

The moral law is the fundamental basis of a good society. The legal code of our land demands moral uprightness and provides severe penalties for crime against the moral law. Widespread crime has become a major threat to our national life. What can a Christian as a citizen do? He can set an example by "denying ungodliness and worldly lusts, to live soberly, righteously, and godly, in this present world" (Titus 2:12). He can witness against commerce in crime such as the traffic in strong drink, and against destructive literature and propaganda which is so often designed with devious cleverness to seduce the minds of both young and old with vain philosophies and perverse ideologies by which many are led to make their own gods, become profane, desecrate the Sabbath, dishonor parents, nurture hate, despise decency, embrace dishonesty, practice perfidious deceptions, and covet that which belongs to others (see Exodus 20:1-17)

In I Peter 2:13-16 it is emphasized that in the sphere of citizenship the Christian should dedicate himself to the Scriptural principle of law and order in society (see Acts 25:8-11). In the Scriptures we are exhorted to be blameless and harmless, without rebuke, in the midst of a crooked and perverse nation (Phil. 2:15). As law abiding citizens we should give our support to the enforcement of law according to constitutional authority (Rom. 13:4). We should always recognize that the privileges and responsibilities of citizenship are both sacred and limited. The field and function of the state is limited by our Constitution in accordance with Scriptural principles (Matt. 22:21; Romans 13:7).

There are realms in which the state has no right to enter as for example the home, the church, and the thoughts of men. The powers of both state and nation as well as the Legislative, Judicial, and Executive branches of government are restricted in sphere by the Constitution. Likewise our citizenship is under restraint. The citizen has no right to ask for special privileges or exemptions, nor to use bribery, commit treason, nor to join pressure groups to practice blackmail in the political arena, etc. No people can remain free if they depart from the moral law or constitutional principles, for tyranny is the inevitable fruit of sin and lawlessness (John 8:33-34).

Far reaching principles are involved in the classic statement of Jesus: "Render unto Caesar the things that are Caesar's and unto God the things that are God's" (Matt. 22:17-21). In this Jesus makes it very clear that under God we have solemn obligations to the state as distinct from our religious obligations. It should be the aim of Christians to fulfill our citizenship duties which include paying of taxes, honor to rulers, respect for lawful authority, intelligent faithfulness in voting, patriotic services, constructive spirit, etc.

In making a distinction between the things that belong unto Caesar and the things which belong unto God, we recall that our Confession of Faith, in harmony with the teachings of Jesus and the apostles, recognizes that the Church and State were ordained of God for different purposes with different spheres of action (Matt. 22:21; Rom. 13:6; I Peter 2:14; I Tim. 3:15.) Therefore, the Church must not "intermeddle in civil affairs," nor should the State interfere in the sacred functions of the Church. Let the Christian citizens perform his citizenship duties as a citizen and not seek to involve the Church in civil affairs.

In Paul's classic passage on citizenship (Rom. 13), civil government is declared to be a divine institution ordained of God and armed with the power of the sword, given of God to punish evil, and therefore, we must be in subjection to civil authority "not only for wrath but also for conscience sake" (Rom. 13:5).

However, it is to be remembered that the lawful powers of State are limited of God. The State has no right to command what God forbids. If the State assumes prerogatives contrary to the laws of God, then it is legitimate for citizens to disobey such commands of the State on the apostolic grounds that "we ought to obey God rather than men" (Acts 5:28-29). (See Daniel 3:16-18; 6:12-13).

In making such decisions Christian citizens must prepare to suffer the vengeance of the tyrannical power as did the apostles and the Christian martyrs. Christians must ever remember that they have a mission beyond the realm of citizenship. We are ambassadors of Christ to a lost world, and like the apostles we must be faithful to Christ even if it involves the loss of our freedom as citizens (Acts 28:20).

As citizens, Christians should render a faithful and constructive service in the community and State. We may learn an important lesson by watching Jesus in the carpenter shop at Nazareth. There He rendered a vital service in the community, and beyond that He earned a living from honest toil. This is a first principle of good citizenship (Eph. 4:28); and a second one is like unto it, namely, that we should live and act and speak and think so that we will count for good in every realm of influence (Matt. 12:35.)

Let us not be problems in the community, but rather let us seek to give strength and light and healing in all the relationships of life. (James 3:16-18). To be a trustworthy and constructive spirit in the community is to fulfill one of the chief phases of citizenship.

Jesus, in the days of His ministry, "went about doing good." He had compassion on the distressed and the needy. He healed the sick and fed the hungry. In the parable of the Good Samaritan Jesus interpreted this as the neighborly spirit (Luke 10:36-37), which reaches beyond the Christian brotherhood, even unto all men. As we have opportunity, let us do good to all men even though we have a special obligation to our Christian brothers in the household of faith (Gal. 6:10). As Christians we are to do this for Christ's sake and to the glory of God (Col. 3:17; Matt. 25:40; Mark 9:41).

As citizens of the state and nation, Christians should ever be mindful of our heavenly citizenship, "for our citizenship is in heaven" (Phil. 3:20 A.R.V.). We are children of the kingdom of God. We are not of this world, but we have a mission in the world (see John 17:16-18), and promised glory in the day when Christ shall be triumphant in the earth (Rev. 3:21). Therefore we have a secret to live by, and our citizenship should be better than that of pagans.

As citizens, Christians should not become party to ideological schemes and Utopian fancies contrary to the light of Scripture, or the light of nature. It is incumbent upon us to be prayerful and faithful in the study of God's Word that we may be able to discern the fallacies of the many deceptive slogans and philosophies current in our time.

One of the most urgent obligations of Christian citizenship today is to prepare ourselves in the light of God's Word so that we may not be swept into the orbit of clever, false philosophies which would result in tyranny and destroy the freedom for which our fathers died. Surely it is time for godly vigilance in this day when the mission of the church is being confused with political and social ideologies, and the dream of world socialism is being proclaimed as the kingdom of God, and the world missionary objective is being interpreted as Scriptural authority for the promotion of some scheme of world government whereby we would be "unequally yoked" with myriad multitudes who know not, nor do they appreciate the treasures of freedom, and also with the anti-God forces of the world which hate the truth and despise the moral law and forbid the preaching of the Gospel.

In conclusion, let us as Christians be faithful in that which transcends our citizenship duties. Let us put on the whole armor of God

The film — a 16 mm, sound, black and white production — runs for 15 minutes. It was produced by Richard Carver Wood, director of the 1955 Academy Award-winning feature length documentary. The Foundation is now making "Assignment Overseas" available for showing to interested groups throughout the country for a nominal charge of $2.50 to cover cost of handling and mailing. Anyone interested in obtaining the film for group showings is urged to write to AFOB's Public Information Office, 22 West 17th St., New York 11, N. Y.

Appreciation

To the Women of the General Assembly of the Presbyterian Church U.S.:—

The Tampa Union of Presbyterian Church Women wish to express their thanks to all who so generously gave to the 1956 Birthday Offering.

For the past thirty-five years the Presbyterian women of Tampa, Florida, have worked with and for the Ybor City Presbyterian Church; and can now look forward to the expansion of this church in the West Tampa area.

You, the women of the General Assembly, have made this expansion possible. Soon a new building will rise on the West Tampa property and our Ybor Church will have a sister church to help meet the needs of this growing, ever expanding Latin-American population.

Rev. and Mrs. Walter Passiglia join with us in this appreciation of your interest, your prayers and your gifts.

Gratefully yours,
(Mrs. L. M.) Bertha G. Anderson
Tampa Union of Presbyterian Women

The Christian Viewpoint

Prepared by Department of Bible
Presbyterian Junior College
Maxton, North Carolina

"The Son of Man has come lowly" are the words under a picture of a stable scene on the front of a Christmas card sent out by the John Knox Press of Richmond, Virginia.

Sometime when you are in Rock Hill, South Carolina, drive out to the campus of Winthrop College and ask to be directed to a stable and carriage house which was moved brick by brick from the old campus of Columbia Theological Seminary in Columbia and re-erected as a memorial in Winthrop. It had been built by Ansley Hall, a captain of industry in the first year of the nineteenth century, as the stable for his mansion, which was designed by Robert Mills, a famous architect. The mansion was purchased from the widow and donated and used for the campus for ninety-seven years by the theological seminary. Plans were to build a chapel, but because of a scarcity of workmen due to the erection of the state capitol building in Columbia, the stable was converted into a temporary chapel.

Dr. George Howe wrote: "We were comforted by remembering that our Saviour was said to have been born in a stable and cradled in a manger; and so sweet have been our seasons of religious instruction and enjoyment in that place often since, that we have forgotten that it ever was a stable at all."

In a young people's meeting in that chapel in the winter of 1873-74, Frank J. Brooke asked all who would accept Jesus Christ as Saviour and Lord to come to the front seat. Thomas Woodrow Wilson, a son of a member of the faculty, came forward to make his first public profession of faith. Years after, while president of the United States, Woodrow Wilson said in this table-chapel stable, "I have heard much eloquent speaking, but on the whole the best speaking I ever heard in my life was in this little chapel."

On November 15, 1886, David Bancroft Johnson enrolled nineteen students in that little chapel to begin what is now Winthrop College. "Who hath despised the day of small things?" (Zechariah 4:10)

The King came hidden as a servant.
The Deliverer drew no sword.
The Son of man has come lowly.

Tither's Surprises

The Christian who begins to tithe will have at least six surprises. He will be surprised:

1. At the amount of money he has for the Lord's work.

2. At the deepening of his spiritual life in paying the tithe.

3. At the ease of meeting his own obligations with the nine-tenths.

4. At the ease in going from one-tenth to larger giving.

5. At the preparation this gives to be a faithful and wise steward over the nine-tenths that remains.

6. At himself in not adopting the plan sooner . . .

NEWS of CHURCHES around the World

FLORIDA

Orlando — One of the most unusual Sunday School classes in the South, the Newton P. Yowell Class of First Presbyterian Church, Orlando, went far toward proving its unique quality when it celebrated its 50th anniversary in December.

The class that started out as a bunch of 12 rowdy boys in their early teens and has stuck together through fifty years, was recognized during its golden anniversary celebration as an "organization that has had more to do with establishing the spirit of the community" than any other aside from the Church. The anniversary was celebrated with three big days of fun, feasting and reminiscing.

Most unusual feature of the anniversary was the presence of the class founder, Mr. Yowell, now 85, and nine of the 12 charter members of the class. Further emphasizing the continuity of the class that grew up in more ways than one, was the participation of more than two dozen of its past presidents in the services which honored the founder and the charter members.

Of the nine charter members who attended, only four still call Orlando home. Present to receive special citations and gifts from the founder were George Dolive, Tom G. Lee, Ches G. Magruder, and James B. King of Orlando; Bert Walker of Daisytown, Pa.; E. Kirby Douglas, Houston, Texas; E. P. Hyner, Cave Springs, Ga.; James Post, Glenridge, N. J.; and Walter Post, Green Cove Springs, Fla. The other three of the original 12 are now deceased, one of them killed in the First World War.

The class, first called the "Young Presbyters," changed its name in 1924 in honor of the founder and teacher, to "Yowell's Young Presbyters." Mr. Yowell, merchant and civic leader, owner of a leading department store until he sold out and retired 12 years ago, taught the class for 47 years, and is still active in its leadership. He has given his teaching duties into the hands of lawyer Addison Williams.

NORTH CAROLINA

Davidson — Five hundred books will be provided annually for the Davidson College Library through a new endowment fund that will total $50,000.00 when in full operation.

Edward Dwelle, Jr., of Jacksonville, Florida, formerly of Charlotte, has established the Fay Ross Memorial Fund in memory of his mother, the late Mrs. Edward C. Dwelle of Charlotte. It is the first and only Davidson fund specifically designated for the purchase of library books.

Billy Graham at Old Sharon

On December 9 Billy Graham preached at the morning worship service to a congregation estimated at 2000 people. Billy was brought up in Sharon Community and attended Sharon School, and knows many members and officers of the church. His uncle, Tom F. Black and his first cousin, W. Frank Black are elders.

He held a week of meetings here in 1939 and spoke several times since then, but this is the first time he has spoken in the church since he has gained international prominence. The church was packed with between 700-800, and a public address system carried his message to 300 more in the Educational Building, to more than 500 in cars outside in the parking area and to several hundred standing around two microphones outside the church. It was a great day for Sharon as Billy spoke on John 3:16 and gave the invitation many stood to indicate their decision for Christ.

As of January 1, Sharon Church is taking on the support of two new missionary families, the Rev. and Mrs. Frank Lemmon, of Mexico, and the Rev. and Mrs. Hugh Linton of Korea. This gives the church representation in four fields—North Brazil, Belgian Congo, Mexico, and Korea. This is a result of the Missionary Conference held in October.

YOUNG PEOPLE'S DEPARTMENT

(Continued from Page 11)

service and engaging in present service. Explain that all the youth organizations of the church are being represented on the program, and introduce each speaker by name, telling which organization he represents.

You will also be responsible for explaining the offering at the conclusion of the program. Tell very briefly how it will be divided and used.

Representatives from Organizations other than Senior High Fellowship (Pioneers, Junior groups, Boy Scouts, Girls Scouts, etc.)

Give the name of your organization, the number of members, and the names of your officers and leaders. Tell when you meet and what takes place at a normal meeting. Describe briefly your programs and activities.

Presentation of the Senior High Theme:

Read Luke 10:25-37. Present the theme idea, "Who is my brother?" Describe the theme picture, displaying it, if possible. Tell something about the theme hymn, "God of Grace and God of Glory." The hymn will be sung immediately after your explanation is finished. For information on the idea, the picture, and the hymn you should consult the material for the January 20 program.

Talk on the Work of the Local Senior Organization:

Give the name of your organization and the names of its officers and leaders. Give a brief description of your programs, activities, and projects. Tell of any outstanding accomplishments during the past year. Outline your plans for the coming year. Add any items which you believe will give the congregation a better picture of the work and service of your local organization.

Talk on the Denominational Work of Seniors:

Explain that Presbyterian young people of the senior age group are organized on presbytery, synod, and General Assembly levels as well as locally. Tell of presbytery camps, conferences, and rallies. Describe the activities and services of Presbytery, Synod, and General Assembly youth councils. Be sure to mention the financial objectives to which all Presbyterian young people contribute: (1) Reconstruction of Seoul Seminary (2) Supply Christian Education Literature for New Sunday Schools (3) Purchasing of Permanent Playground Equipment for West Tampa Center (4) Building Conference Centers through the Ecumenical Fellowship Fund in East Germany (5) Building new churches in Leopoldville.

THE EARLY CHURCH. Oscar Cullmann. Westminster Press. $4.50.

Dr. Cullman is well known in America by his two major works — "Christ And Time" and "Peter: Disciple - Apostle - Martyr." His writings have been received by American theologians with high appreciation.

This volume is a collection of some of Cullmann's shorter writings and articles. They present outstanding examples of Professor Cullmann's contributions to varied aspects of early church history and theology. Conservatives will agree with the author when he tells us "Critical study ought to have in common with the Christian faith above all the obedient willingness simply to listen to what the authors of the New Testament have to say to us, without too quickly, from the very beginning, confusing the issue by introducing the other question whether we can reconcile their faith with modern philosophical theories. Such a mixture of two different questions can only obscure correct exegesis of the texts." The author holds that the real center of early Christian faith and thought is redemptive history, especially in its consistent application to the post-resurrection age in which we live — to the time of the Church and of the already now realized, though invisible, kingship of Christ who reigns at the right hand of God.

Dr. Cullmann has a fine chapter on "The Return of Christ." It tells us that the return of Christ is the real hope of the New Testament. He warns us that to eliminate this hope is to do great violence to the gospel message because it is a gospel of hope.

He agrees with Paul that the whole creation, including man, is now waiting for a return of Christ. The Christian's expectation is in the final consummation fulfilled in the return of the Lord and the creation of a new heaven and a new earth. The author says, "This is why Christ will return to earth. The decisive event, like the first decisive event which took place under Pontius Pilate, will take place on earth because matter itself has to be re-created."

It is only after the return of Christ and everything has been subjected to Him and He will make all things subject to the Father, will His role of mediator come to an end.

Cullmann puts it, "Christ must therefore return as the glorious Saviour this time surrounded by His own to inaugurate the new age. . . . At the beginning of this new period when time will yield to eternity, He will still play the part of fulfiller and judge."

Dr. Cullmann urges the contemporary church to follow the example of the church of the New Testament and preach the Christ who was crucified in the past and who now reigns hidden from our eyes at the present and pray in truth for His return.

Another excellent chapter in this volume is called "The Proleptic Deliverance of the Body according to the New Testament." The author insists that the resurrection of Christ has consequences for our bodies. This being so, the human body, far from being despised in New Testament thought, to which dualism is foreign, receives special honour in the light of Christ's resurrection.

He further observes, "Because the body in the Church is already united with Christ's resurrection-body, it must be watched carefully so that it preserves its dignity as a temple of the Holy Spirit. That is why Paul introduces the ethical part of the epistle to the Romans with the exhortation that they present their bodies to God as an acceptable sacrifice." Moreover he shows that the New Testament doctrine of the resurrection of the body differs greatly from the Greek belief in the immortality of the soul.

Theological students who have welcomed Dr. Cullmann's former writings will surely appreciate this recent work. It is informative and reverent in approach. While we do not subscribe to all of Dr. Cullmann's interpretation, we appreciate his conservative approach and believe that this volume will strengthen Christian faith.

—J.R.R.

FAITH HEALING AND THE CHRISTIAN FAITH. Wade H. Boggs, Jr. John Knox Press, Richmond, Va. $3.50.

Is divine healing Scriptural or un-Scriptural? Are the claims made by the faith healers true or false? These questions are being asked with increased frequency in recent years. The answers must be based upon the careful examination of the Scriptures and also upon the claims of the faith healers. Ministers of the Gospel must not ignore these questions. The people in the pew must be informed or they will become victims of modern religious fads.

There are many books on faith healing which are being widely read today and they should be judged in the light of Scriptural truth. Dr. Boggs believes that some of them mislead their readers by trying to arouse hopes which are unjustifiable in the light of the Bible's teaching and therefore there is a need for someone to carefully sift the wheat from the chaff. This volume is designed especially for laymen, but also carries a message for pastors who must give a Christian interpretation of sickness and health.

In this volume the author gives a Biblical appraisal of the claims, teachings and practices of the faith healers. He states the positions of the faith healers with reference to various questions under discussion and then makes an appeal to the Bible to discover whether or not their position is in harmony with the Christian revelation.

One of the most incisive chapters deal with the question "May We Believe Their Claims?" The question presses upon all who have considered this subject as to whether we may believe the claims of the faith healers or not. The author says that his study of authentic investigations leads him to believe that a small number of the faith healing cures are genuine and permanent. There is, however, a difference of opinion about how these cures are wrought. It is pointed out that the theories behind these healing movements vary widely and in fact are often radically opposed to one another. The Christian Science sect denies every doctrine of apostolic Christianity—the personality of God, the creation of man, the Trinity, the atonement, the reality of sin, sickness and pain and yet it claims the power to heal. Dr. Boggs says, "All of them alike can point to certain successful cures and all of them alike have a high percentage of failures."

Chapter 6 discusses the question, "May sickness be attributed to the Devil?" and in our judgment is unsatisfactory. In this chapter the author affirms, "The story of the fall in Genesis 3 bears traces of early origin, perhaps as early as the 8th Century B.C. Satan, however, does not appear in this story, although on the basis of an apparent identification of the serpent with Satan in Revelation 12:9 and 20:2, we are furnished with some ground for making the identification ourselves, provided we realize that such an idea was not in the mind of the original author. It was not until the Babylonian exile that the Jews came into contact with people who seem to have influenced their beliefs about Satan. During the Exile, they were in close contact with the Babylonians, Assyrians, and Persians, and Langton believes that all of these may have made some contribution to the Jewish belief in demonic powers." This reviewer dissents from such a notion. We believe that this idea is without foundation and exhibits a low concept of Scripture.

The conclusion that the author reaches is that every benefit to health which the faith healers have discovered can be retained by the Christian who refuses to accept their partial truths and share their illusions. This conclusion we have embraced for over 30 years. We therefore concur with the author when he writes, "The will of God for mankind is Christlikeness in character and everything else, including sickness and health, derives its significance and value in relation to that divine goal."

From some standpoints this volume is a helpful one. It deals realistically with the claims of faith healers and evaluates their pretentions. We regret, however, that helpful as this book is in portions, it is marred by certain inferior theological and Biblical presuppositions.

John R. Richardson

THE CHAOS OF CULTS. J. K. van Baalen. Eerdman's. $3.95.

The Chaos of the Cults has been published before. It is recognized as one of the very best books on the major cults in America. It is authoritative, readable and comprehensive. In the last few years the cults have succeeded in capturing the loyalties of an alarmingly large number of people.

This book is a weapon well-suited for the fight against the common enemy: the cults. This second revised and enlarged edition gives the latest facts about the growth and development of every major cult. It gives new material on Mormonism and Jehovah's Witnesses. A new chapter not found in previous editions is devoted to Swedenborgianism. This book is a valuable aid to all defenders of the Gospel, to all seekers after the truth and all who will want to know how to intelligently meet the religious challenges of our day.

Recommend The Journal To Friends

Waco, Texas, Dec. 15, 1956.

Dear Dr. Dendy:

Enclosed you will find my check for $25.00 which I hope you can use in help with the work of the *Journal.*

This is sent as a Memorial to my beloved wife, Louise M. Smith, who died Nov. 28, 1956.

Sincerely,

Norman H. Smith

The *Journal* profoundly appreciates this Memorial Contribution. It embraces the thought that a departed loved one may "be yet speaking" through a printed page which carries messages of grace and salvation through our Lord Jesus Christ. The *Journal* is dedicated to do just that.

An invitation comes to the *Journal* requesting our presence at the 25th anniversary of the Rev. and Mrs. John H. McKnight, December 23rd, at Smyrna, Ga. Congratulations!

The Editors.

SHARON PRESBYTERIAN CHURCH

Sharon Road, Route 2

Charlotte, North Carolina

December 27, 1956

Dear Dr. Dendy:

Let me congratulate you on the first issue of the new improved **Journal.** When it came in the mail the cover was so beautiful that I did not recognize the magazine until I had opened it and saw the editorial page. The captions over the various headings and the illustrations also improved it a great deal I believe.

I am sure that with these features and others that the paper will enjoy an even greater popularity and present an increasingly effective ministry in the proclamation of the Gospel.

I trust that you have had a happy Christmas season, and may the Lord's blessings rest upon you during the coming year.

Sincerely yours,

Edward B. Cooper

In your will, remember Him!

Many Christian men and women have found satisfaction in leaving part of their earthly goods to advance the work of God's kingdom.

Your Board of World Missions is one favorite medium for thus aiding the cause of Christianity after one's earthly activities have ended. You simply name the Board in your will, for whatever you wish to give.

All you have to do is consult your lawyer regarding your bequest. The suggested wording is contained in our pamphlet "Have you, too, forgotten . . . in your will?" which we will be glad to send you on request. Just write

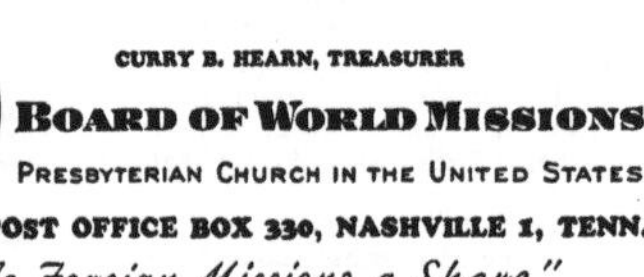

CURRY B. HEARN, TREASURER

BOARD OF WORLD MISSIONS

PRESBYTERIAN CHURCH IN THE UNITED STATES

POST OFFICE BOX 330, NASHVILLE 1, TENN.

"To Foreign Missions a Share"

Journal

JAN 28 1957

VOL. XV NO. 39 JANUARY 23. 1957 $3.00 A YE

Men from our church studying at New College of the University of Edinburg this year: (front, left t right) Rev. Richard Bass, Rev. Holmes Ralston III, Rev. George Webb, Principal Burleigh of New Colleg Lawrence Cater, Rev. Henry L. Smith, Mrs. Horace Holden; (back row, left to right) Rev. Henry McKenni Goodpasture, Rev. John B. Evans, Rev. Thomas Young, Rev. David Maxwell, Rev. Thomas Cook, Re Clarence Durham, Horace Holden, Rev. Joseph Walker.

THE SOUTHERN PRESBYTERIAN JOURNAL

Rev. Henry B. Dendy, D.D., Editor........Weaverville, N. C.
Dr. L. Nelson Bell, Associate Editor........Asheville, N. C.
Rev. Wade C. Smith, Associate Editor........Weaverville, N. C.

EDITORIAL

Justification by Faith Is Justification Through Christ

This is the emphatic testimony of Professor Gustaf Wingren in the current issue of the Journal of Scottish Theology. Luther shows that the human reason has the law for its object and busies itself about what I have done and have not done. But "faith in its proper function has absolutely no other object than Jesus Christ, God's Son, delivered up for the sins of the world. Faith does not look upon love (that is, not on *man's* love) it does not say, What have I done? Which sins have I committed? Which merits have I achieved? But rather it says: What has *Christ done?* What has He merited? Then the Gospel truth answers: He has redeemed you from sin, the devil and eternal death. Faith therefore sees that in this person, Jesus Christ, it has the forgiveness of sins and eternal life."

"Faith lays hold upon Christ and has Him present, enclosing Him as the ring encloses the precious stone which is set in it. And he who is found to have laid hold upon Christ with such a faith and have Him in his heart, God counts for righteous." "Because you believe in Me, says God, and because your faith lays hold upon Christ, Whom I have given you to be your Justifier and Saviour, therefore be thou righteous."

But an evil Satanic power is continually tempting each of us to offer his own religiosity or legalistic moralism to deck out or supplement that which Christ has done. And by so doing man denies the completeness and sufficiency of God's work for us in Christ, deprives Christ of the praise which is due to Him alone, and at the same time, turns into selfishness the works of service that one ought to do for his neighbor. For one who does works for his neighbor under the veiled purpose of adorning himself before God is acting selfishly. Justification by faith alone gives God in Christ all the glory of saving the sinner and gives to the neighbor truly good works — that is, works done out of genuine love to the neighbor. Justification through Christ alone glorifies the grace of God and preserves the purity of works. Only when one knows that he is already saved in Christ, does he engage in works for the good of his neighbor with no selfish interest for himself.

—W.C.R.

Interesting Experience

By Rev. Wade C. Smith

Some years ago Mrs. Smith and I were entertained in a home in Coatesville, Pa., in connection with an evangelistic meeting. Our hosts were Mr. and Mrs. Charles Huston. Mr. Huston, now gone to his rich reward, was president of the Lukens Steel Company, engaged at that time in producing armor plate for Uncle Sam's battleships. He conducted us through the great plant, and we were much impressed by the giant machines rolling out huge steel ingots into ribbons ten inches thick, and cutting them into slabs weighing a ton or more apiece. But the most interesting thing we saw was out in the area where freight cars of scrap steel and pig iron were being unloaded for the melting furnaces. A magnetized metal disc, itself weighing a half ton, was being manipulated with a crane to unload this heavy material from the cars. The disc, powered by electricity, would be lowered above the heap and a ton or more of the scrap, or pig iron, would leap upward and adhere to the disc; then the crane would shift it over the side of the car to a truck which carried it into the plant.

Mr. Huston told the men to shift the disc to the point where we stood, watching with bated breath. Littering the ground about us were various fragments of steel and iron, from very small bits to pieces several inches in size. Mr.

Huston took from his pocket a handful of silver coins, dimes, quarters and half-dollars, and tossed them on the ground among the littered scraps. Then he told the men to lower the disc to a point about four feet above the ground. Instantly the litter — every bit within a radius of several feet, leaped up to the magnet and clung to it, while the crane shifted it away. And to our great surprise, the silver coins remained on the ground! "That," said Mr. Huston, "is a fair illustration of what will take place (not "happen"!) when the Lord Jesus comes to claim His own. Some very unimportant people, in the world's eye, will be lifted up and carried to eternal bliss, while some others whom the world regards as very important will remain, amazed and stunned by what has taken place."

The Hustons proved to be charming hosts. On the morning of our leaving, at family devotions Mr. Huston prayed, "Lord keep our guests safe on the road. Enable Brother Smith to drive carefully — and Lord, that man who meets him, make him drive carefully, too"! I liked that prayer. As he shook hands, saying goodbye, I felt something like a small wad of paper in mine, and when I drove away I opened it to see a fifty dollar bill — the only fifty dollar bill I ever saw — before or since. The church had given me a check for my services, the night before. It was a very interesting and happy visit.

The Vote On Ordination Of Women Elders

Twenty-eight Presbyteries have reported on their vote on Women Elders.

Thirteen Presbyteries have voted *Yes*. These are Montgomery, Westminster, Brazos, East Hanover, Greenbrier, Lafayette, Louisville, Muhlenberg, New Orleans, Potomac, Potosi, Roanoke, and Indian.

Fifteen Presbyteries have voted *No*. These are Central Mississippi, Concord, Winchester, West Hanover, Memphis, Birmingham, Kanawha, Knoxville, Meridian, North Mississippi, South Carolina, Asheville, Everglades, Atlanta, and Paris.

Why Build a Chancel?

The word chancel seems to come from the lattice work or cross pieces which separate the section of the Church reserved for the clergy from the nave in which the body of believers gathered. Perhaps the beginning of this distinction is to be found in the old Roman basilicas at the front of which was a semi-circular apse for the judge and his associates.

With the victory of the Church, basilica shaped Churches were built with the bishop's chair, cathedra, taking the place of the exalted judge's seat and with the presbyters seated around him in the apse.

With the coming of the cruciform architecture the short end of the crucifix became the section set apart for the seven orders of the clergy. During the Dark Ages young boys were inducted into the lower orders, lived with the bishop and were educated by him in the chancels. The bishop's cathedra was perhaps the first and often the only academic chair in the community.

These sections of the churches, partly shut off from the larger body of the building by a screen, lattice, or (in the East) iconostasis could be given a little heat. In them, the clergy gathered several times a day for worship and for instruction in singing, reading the Latin of the service, and figuring the date of Easter. From these chancel schools came the only persons who could read and write, the clerks of the middle ages.

Lay people completed their weekly duty by attending the parish mass at nine o'clock. In Collegiate churches and cathedrals this would be said AT THE PARISH ALTAR AT THE HEAD OF THE NAVE; matins and vespers would be said by the canons beyond the screen in the chancel.—DEANESLY, *History of the Mediaeval Church,* p. 205.

When the old cathedrals and abbeys became Protestant the chancels were an embarrassment. In some of the old church buildings in Switzerland the Protestants have sealed off the chancel and made it a separate room. Those who are conscious of their New Testament heritage accept the priesthood of all believers, not a mediating priest caste known as clergy. A choir arranged in two rows facing each other is a fine setting for a service sung by said choir

The Southern Presbyterian Journal, *a Presbyterian Weekly magazine devoted to the statement, defense, and propagation of the Gospel, the faith which was once for all delivered unto the saints,* published every Wednesday by The Southern Presbyterian Journal, Inc., in Weaverville, N. C.

Entered as second-class matter May 15, 1942, at the Postoffice at Weaverville, N. C., under the Act of March 3, 1879. Vol. XV, No. 39, January 23, 1957. Editorial and Business Offices: Weaverville, N. C. Printed in the U.S.A. by Biltmore Press, Asheville, N. C.

ADDRESS CHANGE: When changing address, please let us have both old and new address as far in advance as possible. Allow three weeks after change if not sent in advance. When possible, send an address label giving your old address.

as one can testify from the magnificent singing in King's Chapel, Cambridge. But such an arrangement is not the best for leading a congregation of believers in the praise of God.

We have other places for Christian education, and for general education today. We do not accept the lattice, or rails, or steps elevating one group of believers as clergy above another group as laity.

All of the people (laity) of God are a royal priesthood, I Peter 2.9, yes God's heritage (clergy) I Peter 5.3.

Why symbolize that which we no longer believe? Why perpetuate an anachronism? Why suggest that we are thirsting for the flesh pots of Romanism? Architecture that is appropriate for Reformed Worship can be beautiful, as may be seen in the sanctuaries of the First Presbyterian Church of Charlotte, the Independent Presbyterian Church of Savannah, the Shenandoah Presbyterian Church of Miami, the First Presbyterian Church of Marietta, Georgia, and the one in Fincastle, Virginia.

—W.C.R.

Christianity Diluted

An excellent way of weakening the force of Christianity is to attach the name to ideas and practices which slightly resemble but considerably distort the real thing. In the Medieval period the mendacious monks, the superstitious mass, the veneration of relics, and the sale of indulgences virtually extinguished Christianity because they were called Christianity.

Today the stress on the universal brotherhood of man, the socialistic reconstruction of society, along with bingo and fish-fries, obscure the teaching of the Bible. And on a more academic level the merging of secular philosophies with a few Scriptural terms accomplishes the same thing.

For example, Professor Richard Kroner, lately of Union Seminary, N. Y., now of Temple University, has just published the first of three volumes in which he hopes to explain the entire history of philosophy on the basis of an antithesis between human speculation and divine revelation. As one might expect there are many statements in the book, *Speculation in Pre-Christian Philosophy,* to which no exception can be taken. In particular, he has written a very fine chapter on Aristotle. But along the way he has also made some assertions that give us pause.

There seems to be, at least in my opinion, no good reason for saying that Thales, the first Greek philosopher, practiced a form of speculation or enjoyed an insight that is the "analogue to the revealed truth on which Christian thinkers later relied." Nor can I believe that Heraclitus, who held that the universe develops out of an original fire, should be said to have "a strong affinity with Biblical revelation." Nor can Parmenides be justly pictured as "paving the way for the Christian age."

Of course, the pantheism of these thinkers helped to undermine the polytheism of the popular Greek religion, and in this sense they might be said to prepare the way for the Gospel. But to suppose that their theories had any affinity with Biblical theology is to press beyond the truth.

Subordinate only to the conception of God transcendent, the Biblical conception of man sharply differentiates Greek paganism from Christianity. In some respects Kroner notices this. He acknowledges that the Greek thinkers were autonomous, that they recognized no other authority than empirical observation and the demands of their own minds. This acknowledgment is commendable and important. Nonetheless, although he had an excellent opportunity to point out another and even more obvious difference, Kroner neglects to mention the Christian teaching of man as a sinner.

On page 140 Kroner says, "Socrates discovered a new dimension of the human soul . . . the dimension of the Biblical conceptions of man and God." Now, in the first place, Socrates had the haziest conception of God; it is uncertain that he even believed in a life after death. In the second place, his idea of man is alien to the Biblical picture.

Granted that he was sincere and conscientious to a greater degree than his contemporaries, still it does not follow that "Socrates discovered the dimension of the moral conscience, a dimension unknown to the Greeks." Still less does it follow that his morality was Christian. His attendance at drinking bouts (even if he stayed sober) and his tolerance of pederasty contrast with Christian views. And underlying this is the absence of the concept of sin. This is not to say that he did not in some fashion distinguish between right and wrong; but most emphatically it means that he shows no consciousness of the need of a Saviour.

One should not condemn a man, even a minister in the pulpit, for noting superficial similarities between Christian principles and pagan culture. But when there is a persistent attempt to present these similarities as profound, Christianity is *ipso facto* diluted. Rather it is to be desired that the Gospel should be stated with accuracy, clarity, and definiteness. Superficial impressionism tends toward mystical vacuity. Precision, exactitude, and the fullness the situation permits are not supererogatory ideals in proclaiming salvation.

—G.H.C.

Our Wonderful Heritage

By The Rev. Leonard T. Van Horn
Covington, Ga.

Many times as the believer is marching heav-nward, he should find himself chanting the .nes written by Isaac Watts many, many years go:

> The hill of Zion yields
> A thousand sacred sweets
> Before we reach the heavenly fields,
> Or walk the golden streets.

The very same thought is brought out in a ıore theological way in the phrasing of the horter Catechism's Question and Answer Num-er 36:

Q. What are the benefits which in this life do ccompany or flow from justification, adoption, nd sanctification?

"A. The benefits which in this life do ac-ompany or flow from justification, adoption nd sanctification, are assurance of God's love, eace of conscience, joy in the Holy Ghost, ıcrease of grace, and perseverance therein to ıe end."

What a wonderful heritage for the Christian. t is so hard to understand how we as Christians are to murmur, complain, gripe against our ,ord, in the midst of our circumstances, with ıch a grand heritage. Whenever I read this articular part of the Catechism I am reminded f hearing the Superintendent of an Orphanage ell of the reaction of a child when he told the hild of what awaited him at adoption. As e explained the wonders of having a home, f gifts to come, of the love of parents with o one else waiting in line, of the many won-erous blessings of being in a family — the child 'as in a family — the child was simply amazed. rom time to time the child would speak up, Really and truly Sir? All for me?" And he ıid that the child's eyes lit up like a Christmas 'ee when he finished. When he uttered his last 'ords the child said, "Oh, Sir. I just can't wait!"

And so we believers should have the same ttitude, day by day, in regard to this wonder-ıl heritage of ours. We should start out each ay with our eyes lit up like a Christmas tree ır these wonderful benefits are flowing toward s by the grace of God. Each day we should start ith the words of praise flowing from our lips: Great is Thy Faithfulness!" Do we have the ght attitude toward these benefits? Let us ote them, one by one, with an open heart and ıind, all to His glory.

First of all, "The Assurance of God's Love." : is right and proper that it should begin with this one for if we can be sure of this then we know that indeed "all things work together for good . . ." If we will but read Romans 5:6-8 we will note that in it the Apostle Paul gives to us the rock-bottom reason that makes us sure that God loves those who believe on His Son.

As we look about us we can see the love of God flowing through His witness of general revelation, or of good will, in the gifts of nature. But it is only the special gift of His saving grace in Christ that convinces us that He really loves us. It is only by this special Gift that we can be convinced and can be the receiver of His saving love.

Secondly, "Peace of Conscience." Conscience is an inner consciousness that judges one's con-duct, whether it be good or evil. The phrase "Peace of Conscience" is not a Bible phrase but the idea is certainly Scriptural for much is said in The Word about "peace in the soul" and about a "good conscience."

We can see that peace of conscience flows from justification, for this is what brings to the believer forgiveness of sin and acceptance as righteous in the sight of God. It flows from adoption, for this is what gives the soul quiet-ness and rest in God's family of the redeemed. It is closely associated with sanctification, for here God's spirit leads the soul to love of holi-ness and leads it in the performance of works that are pleasing to God.

Thirdly, "Joy in the Holy Ghost." Here we have an expression right from Scripture, from Romans 14:17. It is a truth that the soul's true joy comes not from material possessions or the exciting stimulants of the day and age but from the presence of God's Holy Spirit who brings the joy of salvation.

Even though the spirit of the age offers to the people of today excitement in all forms, things that will guarantee, (if you would believe them), to stimulate them into the state of happi-ness — the people of this world soon find that the handbills of enticement are not true. They can only find true joy in the Holy Ghost as He comes through salvation.

No matter what sad situation we might find ourselves in, no matter what the world might do to us, no matter how much sorrow might be our lot, we can be the possessors of the joy of the Holy Ghost. All these worldly troubles that come upon us are overbalanced by the fact that Christ is ours, by the fact that He is, the "believer's inner portion."

Fourthly, "Increase of Grace." Really this means the increase of God's grace that helps the believer to show forth Christian graces, the fruits of the Spirit. The Calvinistic divines of the past made much of what they called "prevenient Grace," meaning the grace that goes before or precedes and excites all our efforts after the things of the Spirit. Peter tells us in II Peter 3:18, "But grow in grace, and in the knowledge of our Lord and Saviour Jesus Christ. To him be glory both now and forever. Amen."

It is true that in the ways in which we increase in grace there is much variety. Some will increase in prayer; some in the study of The Word; some in love toward their fellow-Christians. But since we are His, we can be sure that we shall have His help and that we shall be the receivers of an increasing amount of grace from Him in order that we might please Him in our walk.

Lastly, "Perseverance therein to the End." The Bible teaches it directly. Note John 10:28, 29; Roman 11:29; Philippians 1:6. This perseverance follows from the doctrine of election, which is election to a perfect salvation. It can be inferred from the efficacious sacrifice of Christ for His own. For as God, His sacrifice would have the power to produce the intended effect. What a wonderful blessing this is. This one alone should be enough to cause us to "resist unto blood, striving against sin."

What should be our response to these benefits flowing toward us from the Throne of God? We should appreciate them by studying them, by meditating on them. We should make sure they are being made manifest in our lives. We should witness of them to the world and show them by so doing the contrast to their false hopes and joys.

What a wonderful Saviour we have! What a wonderful heritage he left us! What a serious responsibility is ours!

Our Medical Program Today

By L. Nelson Bell, M.D., F.A.C.S

Editor's Note: This is the second in a series of articles by Dr. Bell telling of our medical work in Korea. The first, on the Chunju Presbyterian Medical Center, appeared in our issue of January 9th. The third article will be printed in an early issue.—H.B.D.

The Graham Memorial Tuberculosis Hospital

Kwangju, Korea

Tuberculosis is the No. 1 public health problem in Korea. One out of every twenty people has the disease. Of the 22,000,000 living in South Korea it is estimated that 2,000,000 have tuberculosis. Of this number 1,000,000 are estimated to be active, a constant menace to those with whom they come in contact.

That the reader may compare this situation with that obtaining here in America: last year 2,000 new cases were discovered in the state of North Carolina, 1 to 2,200, and all of these patients can secure adequate hospitalization and treatment. How different the situation in Korea!

Our Korea Mission has caught the vision of establishing an institution where tubercular patients may be properly cared for; where there can be a public demonstration of modern techniques for adequate treatment and care; where nationals may be trained in this all-important public health program; and, where at the same time an intelligent and effective program of home treatment for tubercular patients for whom no hospital facilities are available may also be carried out.

Coupled with this modern scientific program this hospital has a Christian atmosphere and message which brings hope and comfort to all.

The director of this institution is Dr. Herbert Codington, Jr., and he is ably assisted by his wife, Page. Lancaster Codington, a graduate nurse, and by Miss Astrid Kraakaness, a nurse who is one of those rare finds—a consecrated Christian and a "wheel-horse" whose indefatigable and efficient ministry in this hospital is of value beyond estimation. Sharing in this work is a staff of consecrated Korean doctors and nurses.

The Tuberculosis Hospital at Kwangju is not just "another institution," treating patients with a pill in one hand and a gospel tract in the other. It is carrying out the very latest and best in scientific treatment of tuberculosis while at the same time it is giving a daily living witness for the Healer of the soul, the Lord Jesus Christ.

interval of time is cut down as indicated for individual patients.

Another important link in the chain of adequate care is the laboratory and its necessary addition to the composite picture of the patient's condition. Here again we found a laboratory manned by a staff capable of all the necessary procedures and the patient's charts showed that a close record was being kept of those aspects of the disease referable to such tests.

The records themselves are adequately kept and one can find the treatment, daily care, progress, laboratory, X-ray and other findings which give a complete picture of the condition of any given case.

Space forbids a detailed report on the kitchen, laundry and nursing service but we were impressed with the care with which dishes are boiled after using and with the common-sense techniques which make such a work effective.

The atmosphere. Here we are not speaking of the air the patients breathe but the surroundings which make for a sense of peace and hope. As indicated, soft Christmas music could be heard throughout the hospital while we were making rounds. There were Christmas decorations in each room and the expression on the faces of the patients was one of absolute contentment. Little wonder, when one compares their surroundings in the hospital with those from which most of them had come.

Care. The modern treatment of tuberculosis requires a judicious use of the newer drugs, knowing how much to use and when to change from one to another. The quantity of the three recognized drugs used in the treatment of tuberculosis at this hospital is impressive. Much of this is furnished by the Korean Government, and, as is the case here in America, they are proving of tremendous worth. While there is yet no known specific cure for tuberculosis these drugs greatly hasten the arresting of the disease in the majority of cases and the prognosis for a restoration to a useful life is greatly enhanced.

But drugs are not enough in themselves. Lungs with cavities need collapsing and the pneumoperitoneum is proving an invaluable aid in treatment. However, there are cases which require radical surgery: pneumonectomy, thorocaplasty, etc., etc., and these are sent to the Medical Center at Chunju by ambulance.

Proper nursing has both its physical and psychological effect and here we saw patients receiving the maximum of "T.L.C." (tender loving care), under the constant supervision of Miss Kraakaness and her nursing staff.

Finances. Because the treatment of tuberculosis is both expensive and long drawn-out the economic factor looms large, both with patients and also with the hospital. For this work the Mission appropriates $14,000 (seven thousand from regular appropriations and seven from relief funds). In addition the Korean Government gave $4,000 last year, some drugs and enough rice for fifty patients for part of the year. Of the 180 beds 140 are free, although some of these in the free wards bring in enough rice for a part of their stay. That a hospital of this size, and doing the *quality* of work which is found there, should carry on on a budget like that is a marvel of good management and hard Christian common-sense.

Rehabilitation. The average stay of patients in the hospital is only 4 months and many of these cannot return to the active lives they lived before contracting the disease. First of all they learn the techniques of personal care and of the protection of those with whom they will come in contact. Then, according to their background and skills they are being taught useful occupations: sewing, weaving, chicken-raising, etc., etc. Not only does this open up a new hope for self-support but it also proves a great morale builder.

Home Care. There is no governmental Public Health Department to which may be reported either new or arrested cases. With the large incidence of the disease hospital facilities for all is an impossibility in the foreseeable future. To in some measure cope with the problem a program of home care has been started. When cases are discovered and there is no room for them in the hospital this home care department of the hospital sets up a regime for the patient in the home. Visits to the patients and their relatives, showing them the rudiments of hygiene and protection of others, are started. Medication, rest and diet are also prescribed. This is followed by regular visits to these patients in their homes. While far from ideal it is a practical approach to a most difficult problem and one which is getting results.

Christian Witness: Last year about 12% of the patients admitted were Christians. Of the remainder about 25% made a profession of faith in Christ during their stay in the hospital. But, *all* heard the Gospel message daily and they *saw* a practical testimony to the love of Christ about them all the time. Eternity alone will give the true picture of such a ministry.

The writer has before him many pages of statistical facts about the hospital and its work. For the purposes of this article let is be said that the Presbyterian Tuberculosis Hospital at Kwangju is being richly used of God; that it is a credit to our church; that its staff consists of a group of dedicated Christians, Korean and

SUNDAY SCHOOL Lessons

LESSON FOR FEBRUARY 3

By THE REV. J. KENTON PARKER

Mission Of The Twelve

Background Scripture: Matthew 9:35 - 10:42
Devotional Reading: Matthew 10:34-42

Up to this point the Mission of Christ had been personal; He had been doing all the preaching, healing, and teaching. The disciples had been following Him, marveling at His wonderful words and works, but taking no part with Him in these things. It had been a period of training for them; they had been with Him and had been learning from Him. The time is now ripe for them to take an active part in the work. Here is a distinct turning-point in the ministry of Christ.

I. *The Need and the Prayer:* 9:35-38.

Verse 35 gives another summary of the work that our Saviour was doing; teaching, preaching, healing. Great multitudes followed Him, and He was moved with compassion. How do we feel when we see the multitudes today? Do we ignore or despise them, or grow weary of the sight? I am ashamed of myself when I think of these multitudes. I fear that oftentimes my greatest desire is to get away from them. Brother Bryan of Birmingham when on his death bed was heard repeating, "So many people; so many people." Someone asked him if they were worrying him, thinking of the many visitors he had, and he said, "Oh, No," but "So many people without Christ." So, today, the multitudes are all around us; so many people without Christ. Do we feel like Jesus felt when He saw the multitudes, and had compassion on them?

These multitudes are like ripe fields of grain. In the Spring we see such fields, ripe and bending low, waiting for the reapers. Sometimes the harvest is lost because the reapers do not come in time; the combines may be few. In the work of saving men this need calls for prayer; we are to ask the Lord of the harvest to send forth laborers into the harvest. These multitudes at home and abroad are in themselves a call to prayer. Can we not hear the voice saying, Whom shall I send, and who shall go for me? May we answer, Here am I; send me.

II. *The Selection of the Twelve:* 10:1-4.

Laborers in this harvest field are chosen by the Lord of the harvest. It is work that requires selected workmen. Later on we find Jesus sending out the Seventy, and when He leaves them to return to the Father, He gives the command to all, Go ye into all the world and preach the gospel to every creature. He still needs selected leaders, but there is some work for all. Paul gives us a description of the various kinds of work to be done in building up the Body of Christ, (see Ephesians 4:10-16). He tells us that we are God's fellow-workers, or workers together with God. It is a great honor and privilege to help God in His work of saving men. In the harvest-field there is work to do; work for all; To every man his work. Remember that these men — the Apostles — were just ordinary men. They were not selected because of their extraordinary ability, or their social standing, or their place as leaders in the Jewish Church, or their education. They were trained by the Greatest Teacher the world has ever known, and thus fitted for their task.

III. *Instructed:* 5-15.

Their mission at this time was limited; they were to go to the lost sheep of the house of Israel. In God's plan the Jew was to be given the first opportunity to hear and accept the Gospel. The Jew had been the custodian of the true religion all these centuries. To them had been entrusted the Law and the Revelation of God with all the advantages of the Covenant which God made with Abraham. They constituted the Church in the Old Testament. They should have been ready and eager to accept the Good News of the coming of their Messiah. A few of them were, even from the birth of Jesus, but the majority of the chosen people hardened their hearts, closed their eyes, and stopped their ears. He came unto His own, and His own received Him not. These are sad words, but true words.

The Twelve were to preach a simple, but urgent, message: The kingdom of heaven is at hand. The King Himself had been proclaiming this truth, and the disciples were to continue to proclaim it. They were given credentials: they were to heal the sick, cleanse the lepers, cast out devils, raise the dead. Surely with such "signs" the people would believe them!

They were to take no provisions with them; the workman was worthy of his food. They were giving much more than they would receive in the way of food. It is still true that those who labor in spiritual things should be supported by the ones who receive spiritual food at their hands. Let us who are shepherds be sure that we "feed the flock," and not simply feed ourselves! They were to seek a place to stay where the house was "worthy." If it was worthy, then peace would come to that house; if not, then this peace would be withheld. Where people would not receive them, they were to "shake off the dust of their feet." Such a house or city would be severely condemned. It is no small sin to reject a messenger of the Gospel.

IV. *Warned:* 16-39.

Messengers from God are often treated shamefully. This was true of the Old Testament prophets; it was true of the disciples in the early days of the church; it has been true of missionaries in all ages. Christ warns His followers that their task will be a disagreeable, and often, dangerous one. Let me call your attention to some of the expressions which so vividly tell the story.

"As sheep in the midst of wolves." Sheep are about as helpless as any animal, for they have no means of protection; no way to fight back. Wolves are among the fiercest of wild beasts. The Christian faces his foes as a sheep faces a wolf. "Wise as serpents, and harmless as doves."

Now the serpent was more subtle than any beast of the field. We are to receive from above, and exercise, all the wisdom we have as children of the Father, and disciples of the Master of all wisdom, but we are not to resort to force or violence. As Jesus said, those that take the sword shall perish with the sword.

The church has at times sought to use the sword of the State and has become entangled in the web of politics and brought disaster upon herself.

The weapons we need are not carnal. They are mentioned by Paul in his well-known passage in Ephesians. Our Sword is the Sword of the Spirit, which is the Word of God "But beware of men." Our mission is to men; we are to reach and save men; but these men will often prove to be our enemies and persecutors. They will treat us as they treated Christ. This persecution, however, will give us an opportunity to testify in behalf of Christ. A fine illustration of this is seen in the life of Paul. He was brought before the governors and kings, and as he told the story of his conversion, some trembled and others were "almost persuaded."

Verse 19 has been strangely misinterpreted: "Take no thought how or what ye shall speak." Some have said that this means that a preacher should make no preparation for his sermons, but trust the Spirit to tell him what to say. This has nothing to do with the ordinary preaching of the gospel. Paul says, Study to show thyself approved unto God, a workman that needeth not to be ashamed, rightly dividing the word of truth. This verse applies to our defense before our persecutors. God will tell us how best to defend ourselves, and His guidance will be better than the advice of the best lawyer, or any words of our own.

In verse 21 and also in verses 34-39 we see a sad and strange situation. Brother shall deliver a brother to death, and a man's foes shall be they of his own household. This has often been true in big and tragic ways, and also in small ways. If a Jew becomes a Christian today the family considers him dead. All of us have seen the small ways in which a man's foes are in his own home; not to kill, but to discourage and hinder and oppose, and be indifferent. Sometimes the husband is the stumbling block; sometimes the wife, as in the case of John Wesley. The family is often divided and unhappy. Even Jesus was not treated too well in His own home, for His brethren did not believe until after His resurrection.

They, and we, are warned that Christ must come first; that not even love of father or mother, or life, can have the first place. He that loves even these best things more than Christ, is not worthy of Christ. The only way we can find our lives is to lose them for the sake of Christ. We must be ready to take up our cross and follow Him. These are solemn, heart-searching words! They touch bottom. To many, in these "soft times" the Christian life is just an easy-going way without any hardships or severe tests. Jesus is warning His followers that the way of the cross is not an easy way. It calls for surrender and sacrifice. Not all of us, or even many of us, are called upon to face the problems touched on here. Let us be grateful for this, for there is no virtue in persecution and privation in themselves, and we ought to be thankful that we do not have to suffer as some have suffered. The question which keeps coming up in my own mind is, How would I stand such a test, if it came?

V. *Encouraged:* 40-42, (also 26,28-31)

In the midst of these warnings He says, "Fear not." We may have a hard time, but our Father cares for us. If we confess Christ, He will confess us; we are His.

YOUNG PEOPLES Department

YOUTH PROGRAM FOR FEBRUARY 3

By THE REV. B. HOYT EVANS

Consider Your Call

Scripture: Luke 19:1-10; Isaiah 6:1-8; Acts 9:1-6
Hymns: "I Sought the Lord" "Where He Leads Me, I Will Follow" "Jesus Calls Us: O'er The Tumult" "Jesus Is Tenderly Calling"

(The week of January 27 - February 3 is known as Community Youth Week. In some communities the occasion is recognized by letting the youth groups of the various churches undertake a cooperative project such as a clothing collection for Hungary. Another way of observing the week would be to have a party or social including the young people of several churches. Others may want to have a union service on this last Sunday of Youth Week. If this is done, you may want to invite an inspirational speaker to lead you in thought and worship. If you plan a youth participation program, the material below can be adapted for such a purpose.)

Program Leader:

When a soldier travels under orders, he has no doubt about what he is supposed to do. He may not understand the reason behind his orders, but that is not his responsibility. The person who issued the order is responsible for the rightness or wrongness of it. The soldier is only responsible for carrying it out. There is a kind of security and comfort about working under orders. It is a kind of life that is similar in some respects to the life of a Christian. A Christian is a person who works under orders. He has submitted himself to Christ as his commander. A Christian is one who has agreed to surrender his own independence in order to become a follower of Christ. Every Christian has received a call to obedience and a call to duty from his leader. When the call of Christ comes, he is living, working, and traveling under spiritual orders just as really as any soldier of the army.

First Speaker:

The first phase of our call as Christians is the call to salvation. The New Testament word for "church" is one which means "called out." It refers to those who are called out from sin unto salvation in Christ. Peter said the promise of salvation is "unto you, and to your children, and to all that are afar off, even as many as the Lord our God shall call." Acts 2:39. The Bible teaches that those who are justified before God are those whom God calls. (Read Romans 8:29,30) We know that there is no salvation apart from Christ, and He said, "No man can come to me, except the Father which hath sent me draw him." John 6:44. Our salvation, then, does not depend on us, but on God. It is not a matter of our goodness, but of God's goodness applied to our account. It is not a matter of seeking out God to be saved, but of His calling us to believe in His Son.

Second Speaker:

The second part of our Christian call is the call to service. When a young man is called into a special, personal relation to the armed forces of our government, we say that he has gone into the service. We have already discovered that the Christian is one who is called into a special relationship to God . . . he is one of the redeemed and a child of God. He is also called to give his life in service to the One who has saved him. "I beseech you therefore, brethren, by the mercies of God, that ye present your bodies a living sacrifice, holy, acceptable unto God, which is your reasonable service." Romans 12:1. Our Saviour has set the example for us in this respect, because he came not to be served but to serve. "For even the Son of man came not to be ministered unto, but to minister, and to give His life a ransom for many." Mark 10:45.

We are truly under orders to serve Christ, but how are we to do it? There are numerous ways of serving, but there are certain avenues of service that none of us can overlook. Every Christian must serve his Lord through prayer and the faithful reading of the Scriptures. Every Christian ought to serve through joining in the assemblies of worship in the church. Every Christian is obligated to honor Christ with a holy life. Just as every soldier in the army has certain general duties regardless of his specialty, so every Christian is expected to serve the Saviour in these general ways.

Third Speaker:

The third part of the Christian's call is that which we call vocation. It is the particular kind of work or service which God ordains that he should do. Every soldier in the army has a particular specialty as well as his general duties. We believe the Bible teaches very clearly that God has a plan for every life. If God has a plan for us, it is certainly reasonable that we cannot be happy until we are living according to His plan. Also, if God has a plan for us,

(Continued on Page 20)

CHILDRENS Page

The First Two Brothers

Adam was the first man. He had no father or mother, for God created him out of dust. Then God created Eve to be his wife, and their first two children were boys, named Cain and Abel. These were the first two brothers in the world. Cain was a farmer and Abel was a Shepherd. They both worshiped God. Each one offered a sacrifice to God. Abel offered a lamb on his altar, and Cain offered some produce from his farm. God was pleased with Abel's sacrifice, because it was a blood offering; but He was displeased with Cain's because it had no blood in it. Cain didn't like that. He grew very angry and quarreled with Abel. He became so angry that he rose up and killed his brother. Then God called him to account: "Where is thy brother"? and Cain said "I know not; am I my brother's keeper"? That was a lie, and he talked back to God. Then God drove Cain out of His Presence into the wilderness where he could never be happy again.

A Statement on Christian Tithing

Two Kinds

He could recognize only two tunes, Mark Twain liked to insist; one was America, and the other wasn't.

Tithing is much like that, too. There are two kinds of tithing. One kind is Christian. The other isn't.

The Other Kind

The other kind of tithing begins with Old Testament laws, and usually stops there. It is the fact that it stops at that point that compels many Christians to reject tithing. For all too often the tither comes to feel that he has now obeyed God's law and therefore has fulfilled his total obligation as a Christian. And, of course, he hasn't. He can't. One never fulfills his obligations to God. All he can do is to pour forth his gratitude in every way possible for God's abundant love. The tithe is one way of my saying my thanks to God — only one way — a reasonable way.

Christian Tithing

Christian tithing begins with Christ. Its whole emphasis is upon Him. The central fact in the life of the Christian is the coming of Jesus Christ into the world to give Himself upon the cross for man. Through Him man comes to God; through Him man finds forgiveness and reconciliation. Here is giving and love that is beyond human understanding. It is grace — God's love given freely without our having deserved or merited any part of it.

And right here is where Christian tithing begins — in man's understanding of that central fact of Christian faith, and in his response to it. For, he asks himself, if God has been so good to me, how can I help but give my thanks to Him in every act of my life? And in my giving, how can I do less for His work than set aside at least one-tenth of my income as a first step? Christian tithing begins with Christ!

Only a Beginning

The simplest definition, therefore of Christian tithing is that it is a Christian person, tithing. This is not just a play on words. For the point that such a definition emphasizes is that it is not tithing that makes a person a Christian. He is a Christian *first,* through faith in Jesus Christ, and *then* a tither. Let no one believe that tithing and the tithe are tests of one's Christianity. They are but the evidence of one's faith.

It is all of us that God wants, all of our life. The tithe, therefore, is never the final expression of our love. It's only a beginning. Some, in their abundance, undoubtedly can and must go far beyond the tithe. For others, a God-satisfying portion may be "two small coins." But for most of us, the tithe is a reasonable first step. For most of us it is the least we can do in our gratitude to Him for all His goodness to us.

—By Clarence C. Stoughton in CHRISTIAN FACTS

Devotional on Stewardship

We mature Church Women are familiar with our accepted teaching on Stewardship. We recognize our Lord's just claim upon a tenth of our money, a seventh of our time, and of such of our admitted talents as can be used for His service. Theoretically, we subscribe to that service program.

Because it is definite and easy to figure, I assume we all give at least a tenth of our money. Or, do we? Many give time generously. Do you?

False modesty suggests excuses on talents. Are napkins for wrapping and hiding purposes in unnecessarily generous supply? Let's explore that field a bit. Please practice approved self-service methods and select your shoe according to fit.

David said: "I will not give to the Lord, my God, that which cost me nothing." Sam. 24:24-RSV.

Malachi said: "Bring the *whole* tithe into the storehouse, saith Jehovah of hosts."—Mal. 3:10 RSV.

Paul, writing the Corinthians of the generosity of the Christians at Antioch, which had greatly exceeded his fond hopes, explained it this way: "In accordance with the will of God they first gave *themselves* to the Lord and then to us, as I can testify, beyond their means, begging us earnestly for the favor of a part in the relief of the saints."—II Cor. 8:3-5 RSV.

Dr. Luke, describing the ministry of the apostles in Acts wrote: "The people gathered from towns around Jerusalem. They even carried the sick out into the streets and laid them on pallets that, as Peter came by, at least his shadow might fall upon them and they were all healed." —Acts 5:15,16.

Robert Louis Stevenson, in his charming *Child's Garden of Verse,* writes:

"I have a little shadow that goes in and out with me,
And what can be the use of him is more than I can see."

What *is a shadow?* The dictionary says a shadow is a shelter from the direct rays of the sun in the shape of the interposed body, as the shadow of a tree or a man.

Ah, the welcome coolness of the tree whose outspread branches protect us from the burning sun! Isaiah knew the desert's pitiless glare when he wrote, "A man shall be as a shadow of a great rock in a weary land."

Instead of the poet's "shadow" today we say "personality," that overworked carry-all word. The other day my niece wrote me about her newly acquired dog. "Aunt Jess, you should see him. That pup has personality plus." And I knew what she meant. Personality is the unique combination of qualities which produces individual character. Personality is the you-ness of you. Personality is the "little shadow that goes in and out with me." What use is your shadow, or mine?

Are we spiritual "typhoid Marys," spreading germs of evil as we go, or does Christ shine through us, so people are blessed by our shadows as we walk by?

We all know both sorts. I'm not the only coward who dodges into a doorway or turns a corner to avoid meeting some people.

But, thanks be to God, there are many others —many in our church, many in this room, who radiate the sunshine of faith and good cheer. To meet them is to hear the Amen of our great benediction, to walk on our way straighter and stronger, to see the sun shine through our clouds.

You — I — all of us, have a little shadow who goes in and out with us — the question of Christian Stewardship is this: What are *we,* as individuals, doing with our own selves?

Sick people were healed when Peter's shadow fell on them.

It's not our pastor, nor our President, nor the friend beside me, "It's *me,* O Lord, standing in the need of prayer."

Prayer:

Our Father, we thank Thee for the privilege of doing errands for Thee, of carrying Thy gifts to other people. Give us grace to find in shadow a hiding place of forgetfulness for life's hurts and losses. Help us to be honest stewards and give back the love and laughter life has so freely given to us.

In Jesus' name and for His sake, Amen.

—From Mrs. B. R. Hoover

Tipping and Tithing

"Now it came to pass on a Day at Noon that the Editor was Guest of a certain rich Man. And the Lunch was enjoyed at a popular Restaurant, And the Waiters were very efficient.

"Now when the End of the Meal was at Hand, the Waiter brought unto the Host the Check And the Host examined it, frowned a bit, but made no Comment.

"But as we arose to depart, I observed that he laid some Coins under the Edge of his Plate. Howbeit, I know not what Denomination the Coins were.

"But the Waiter who stood nearby smiled happily, which being interpreted, means that the Tip was satisfactory.

"Now with such Customs we are all familiar. And this Parable entereth not into the Merits or Demerits of Tipping.

"But as I meditated on the Coins that become Tips throughout our Nation, I began to think of Tips and Tithes. For the proverbial Tip should be at least a Tithe, lest the Waiter or the Waitress turn against you.

"And as I continued to think on these Things, it came unto me that few people who go to Church treat their God as well as they honor their Waiter. For they give unto the Waiter a Tithe, but unto God they give whatsoever they think will get them by.

"Verily, doth Man fear the Waiter more than he feareth God? And doth he love God less than he loveth the Waiter?

"Truly, truly, a Man and his Money is past Understanding!"

—Author Unknown

Information for Shipping Material Relief Goods Through Church World Service

WHAT IS NEEDED: Sound, clean clothing of all kinds for men, women and children, especially sweaters, underwear, socks and stockings (no nylons), coats, trousers, caps (no hats), shirts, blouses, dresses, gloves, mittens; also sheets, blankets, quilts, etc. Men's clothing is especially needed.

HOW TO PACK: The goods which you send should be carefully packed and securely tied. Some prefer to use canvas DUFFEL BAGS holding about 50 pounds. These can be secured free of charge by writing direct to Church World Service, at either of the addresses given below. All relief goods are repacked by Church World Service before sending them overseas.

WHERE TO SEND: Ship your collection prepaid by parcel post or express to the Church World Service Center nearest you. If possible, send 8 cents per pound for every pound of clothing you send to the Center, to defray cost of sorting, baling and transportation to ports for overseas shipment.

BE SURE to place the name and address of the sender, indicating "Presbyterian, U.S." source, so that proper acknowledgement and credit may be given.

ADDRESSES: (Send to one nearest you) Church World Service, New Windsor, Maryland, or Church World Service, 4165 Duncan Avenue, St. Louis 10, Missouri.

DESTINATION OVERSEAS: All goods received by Church World Service will be sent overseas to the people in greatest need. In Europe, Asia, and the Near East, there are hundreds of thousands who have been refugees for years. What little clothing they brought with them has long since worn out. They await your help.

PLEASE **DO NOT** SEND CLOTHING OR PROCESSING COSTS TO THE DEPARTMENT OF OVERSEAS RELIEF AND INTER-CHURCH AID, NASHVILLE, TENNESSEE, AS WE DO NOT HAVE FACILITIES HERE FOR PROCESSING THEM.

Additional copies of this instruction sheet may be had from

Rev. Paul B. Freeland, Secretary

Department of Overseas Relief and Inter-Church Aid

Board of World Missions

Box 330

Nashville, Tennessee

Alcoholic Beverage Expenditures And Church Contributions

The people of the United States spent a total of $10,099,000,000 (source: U. S. Dept. of Commerce) for alcoholic beverages in 1955. During the same period, contributions by 48 Protestant and 2 eastern Orthodox bodies totaled $1,842,-592,260 — the highest in history (source: News Bulletin, National Council of Churches). But the amount spent for liquor was more than five times greater than the amount contributed to the churches. The church member per capita giving reached an all-time high of $53.94. But this is less than the per capita expenditure for the whole population for alcoholic beverages which amounted to $61.48.

Church members do not give as much per capita to their churches as the nation as a whole spends per capita for liquor. It would be interesting, as well as quite an indictment, if it could be ascertained, how much per capita church members spend for alcoholic beverages. Undoubtedly, many of them are spending far more for liquor than they are contributing to the church to which they belong. If every church member in this country were a total abstainer, the liquor traffic would collapse. It is still true "The liquor traffic would destroy the Church if it could, the Church could destroy the liquor traffic if it would."

—The Christian Statesman

Helps To Understanding Scripture Readings in *Day by Day*

By Rev. C. C. Baker

Sunday, February 3, *Psalm* 119:25-32. The whole of Psalm 119 is a prayer. The Psalmist's prayers center around such things as his own spiritual needs (vv.25,28), his desire for spiritual instruction (vv.26-27,29) and the dedication of his heart to the Lord (vv.30-32). Observe the place of the Word of God in his petitions. How does he know he can find help from God to meet his spiritual needs (vv.25,28)? How does he expect to receive spiritual instruction (vv.26-27,29)? As the Psalmist receives strength (v.28b) and understanding from God (v.32a), notice how he expresses his dedication to Him (vv.30-32). The Scriptures are not to be read only that we might receive strength and understanding from them, but also that we might obey their commandments.

Monday, February 4, *Matthew* 10:32-39. An aspect of Christian living that is difficult for many of us to fulfill, but which is imperative in the eyes of Christ, is the giving of oral expression to our faith in Him (vv.32-33). One of the things that hinders us most in our witness for Christ is the fear of disapproval from our family and friends (vv.35-37). The thing that will help us most to begin speaking a word for Christ is the putting of Him before everyone and everything else in our lives (vv.38-39). When He has the proper place in our lives, Christ makes life so worth living that we cannot help talking about Him (v.39). The Christian who speaks a word for Christ out of love for Him in the face of social disapproval can be assured of His heavenly Father's care and keeping (vv.29-32).

Tuesday, February 5, *Ezekiel* 34:1-6. The minister who does not have a shepherd's heart enjoys all the benefits of the ministry (vv.2b,3) but utterly neglects the spiritual needs of his people (v.3b-4). Verse 4b reveals the manner in which he deals with them. God's people are like sheep (v.6). What are the consequences among a flock, if the minister does not have a shepherd's heart (vv.6,8a)? Think of a minister you know who has the positive traits of v.4. Do his people love him? Is his church united and moving forward in its work? When human leadership fails, God Himself shepherds His people (vv.11-12ff). Meditate upon vv.12-15 and think how Christ, your Good Shepherd (John 10:11,14) exemplified the description you find there. A minister can develop a shepherd's heart as the life of Christ, his Shepherd, moulds and controls him.

Wednesday, February 6, *Matthew* 14:22-23. Try to picture yourself with the disciples in the storm-tossed boat (vv.22,24), at night, far from shore (vv.24-25). Would your reactions have been similar to those of the disciples if you had seen something coming toward you on the water (vv.25-26)? How heart-warming the words of v.27 must have been! Upon what basis did Jesus tell the disciples not to be afraid (v.27)? Upon what condition did Peter ask for an invitation to walk out on the water (v.28)? What was it that caused Peter to sink (v.30)? Notice whom Peter instinctively called on when he was in trouble (v.30)? Was this help sufficient (v.31)? How would this experience with Christ strengthen Peter as he sought to serve Him in later years? This same Jesus is with you in all your experiences.

Thursday, February 7, *Luke* 15:3-7. The tax collectors and sinners were coming to Jesus while the religious leaders stood aside in condemnation (vv.1-2). How does the parable Jesus told in vv.3-7 explain His gladness for the closeness of the despised sinners? How does the parable of the lost coin (vv.8-10) and the lost son (vv.11-32) reinforce Jesus' teaching that He can only help those who know they need His help? The criticism of vv.1-2 had been levelled at Jesus before, as in Luke 5:29-30. On that occasion Jesus spoke plainly (5:31-32) the truth He now speaks in parables (c.15). Is Jesus saying that He cannot help the religious leaders because they are already righteousness or because they think they are already righteous (16:15)? Does a sense of self-approval on your part keep Christ from meeting the needs in your life that He would like to fulfill?

Friday, February 8, *Romans* 10:14-15. Trace the number of times the Old Testament is quoted in this chapter (see vv.5,6,8,11,13,16,18, 19,20,21). These are quotations from every section of the Old Testament, Lev., Deut., Psalms, Isaiah, Joel. The questions Paul asks in vv. 14-15 logically follow the conclusion of v.12. How does the quotation of v.13 support v.12? Paul has shown that a person is saved only by faith in Christ (vv.9-11). How do the Old Testament quotations of vv.6,8,11 substantiate verses 9-11)? What, then, is the responsibility of the reader who has a personal faith in Christ (vv.14-15)? How does the quotation of v.15b strengthen this conviction? With what degree of authority does Paul treat the Old Testament? Do the quotations lend authority to Paul's argument? We preach the Gospel to the world, if for no other reason, because Christ has commanded it in the Scriptures.

Saturday, February 9, *II Timothy* 1:1-10. Some people are converted suddenly and dramatically as was Paul (Acts 9), while others, like Timothy, grow up in a home of godly influence (v.5) and perhaps do not even remember the time or place of their conversion. Notice that Paul treated Timothy as a fellow-believer (vv.1-2) and accepted his conversion as completely valid (v.5a). However, Paul did take Timothy to task (tenderly and lovingly, vv.3-4) for certain things that were lacking in his life (vv.6,8). What seemed to be missing in Timothy's experience (vv.6-8)? How did Paul's own testimony set an example for what was lacking (vv.8,12,15-16)? Many of us are like Timothy; we have a valid Christian experience, though we may not be able to remember its beginning, yet we are lacking in a bold witness for Christ.

NEWS
of CHURCHES
around the World

The Rev. Richard Gustavus McLees, D.D.

On December 13, 1956, the Rev. Richard Gustavus McLees, D.D., pastor emeritus of Chatham Presbyterian Church, passed to his heavenly reward, full of years and good works for his Master.

Dr. McLees, who had made his imprint on church work throughout the Southland as an evangelist, was born in Greenwood, S. C., December 4, 1864. He was the eighth and last child of the Rev. John McLees and Mrs. Sarah Cornelia Anderson McLees, both of Scotch-Irish descent.

Blinded in a hunting accident at the age of 14, Dr. McLees was educated at the Academy for the Blind at Macon, Ga. He was licensed to the ministry in 1902 and, prior to accepting a call to become the pastor of the Chatham Presbyterian Church in 1909, he served the Synod of South Carolina as evangelist, carrying the "Glorious Gospel of the Blessed God" to multitudes of people, many of them yielded their lives to Christ.

Dr. McLees was affiliated with the church at Chatham, Virginia, until his retirement in 1940. In recognition of his outstanding ability as a preacher and his service to the church, he was given the honorary degree of D.D. in 1920 by King College in Bristol, Virginia.

His autobiography, entitled "Opening Doors", which was published in 1954*, gained considerable recognition for its literary merits, as well as a recounting of a man's rise over a physical handicap.

Old in years, but progressive in spirit, Dr. McLees was honored, loved and respected by all who knew him. Possessed of many fine qualities and talents, Dr. McLees will probably be remembered above all else for his Christlikeness. He was one of whom it might truly be said, "A Prince and a great man has fallen in Israel".

Dr. McLees was married to Miss Julia Earle Thornwell of Fort Mill, S. C., in 1906. She pre-

The purpose of this announcement of the meeting of the nominating committee is to invite all interested people throughout the assembly to suggest names for the important positions of leadership in the various Assembly Committees. These names should be sent to the chairman, Dr. Joseph M. Garrison, Walker and Mendenhall Sts., Greensboro, N. C. Accompanying each suggestion there should be a brief statement of particular qualifications for the suggested nominations, together with definite addresses in the case of all laymen suggested. It is requested that all suggestions be in the hands of the chairman by February 15th to facilitate preparation for the coming meeting.

ALABAMA

Tuscaloosa—Stillman College received a $40,000 present for Christmas, as the result of the Presbyterian, U.S. Negro Work Campaign.

The money was in the form of a check received by President Sam Burney Hay from an anonymous foundation, in payment of the final portion of a $100,000 conditional grant. The grant was made dependent upon the contributions to Stillman College of a total of $900,000 from the South-wide Negro Work campaign. Terms of the grant were met by the 40th regular proration of funds received in the campaign, when money provided Stillman reached $900,198.81. An earlier check for $60,000 had been sent to Stillman from the foundation, to meet the urgent needs of the school's building program, and in trust that the Church would meet the terms of the grant.

The campaign, conducted in 1952-53, had pledges of more than $2,200,000, to cover a three year period. But by early December 1956, when the 50th proration was made, only $1,861,545.12 had been received. Contributions are still being divided equally between Stillman and the Negro Work Division of the Board of Church Extension, after expenses of the campaign have been deducted.

The payment by the foundation brings to over $1,000,000 the total made available to the Church's Negro college.

Birmingham — Ellis Wanninger, of Huffman Presbyterian Church, has been elected president of the Young Adult Fellowship of the Presbytery of Birmingham. Election was held in connection with the annual Christmas party of the fellowship, and officers were installed by the Rev. Robert L. Williams, pastor of the Wylam Presbyterian Church.

Other officers elected and installed include Pete Hollifield, Ensley Church, vice-president; Mrs. J. D. Smith, Fairfield Highlands Church, corresponding secretary; Miss Sarah Neff, Handley Memorial Church, recording secretary; Eloise Robinson, Third Church, historian, and Buddy Hollifield, Fairfield Church, treasurer.

GEORGIA

Atlanta — Stated clerks of presbyteries and synods throughout the General Assembly have a new address to learn.

Dr. E. C. Scott, Stated Clerk of the General Assembly, has announced a change of address for his office. The Office of the Stated Clerk and Treasurer now is housed in 341-E Ponce de Leon Ave., N.E., Atlanta 8, Georgia. It formerly was housed in 341-A, together with the Board of Women's Work.

The new address is the result of acquisition of property adjacent to the Presbyterian Center here, together with two residences on the property. Purchase was made by the Board of Annuities and Relief, which advanced funds for purchase and holds title to the Center until all indebtedness has been paid off by regular rentals paid by each of the agencies using the facilities of the Center. When the Annuities and Relief Board's investment has been repaid, title to the property will be held jointly by all the agencies using the Center.

KENTUCKY

Louisville—The 1957 Town and Country Pastors' Institute at Louisville Theological Seminary will be held at the seminary's Harbison Memorial Chapel from January 22 to January 25. The seminary-sponsored Instituted will be attended by ministers of Presbyterian Church, U.S. and Presbyterian Church, U.S.A.

LOUISIANA

New Orleans—James S. Mason, an elder in the Carrollton Avenue Presbyterian Church, is the new president of the Protestant Laymen in New Orleans.

Mr. Mason, general agent of the Wabash Railroad, is also treasurer of the Presbyterian Laymen's Association of New Orleans. Milton Van Manen, of the Salem Evangelical and Reformed Church, is vice-president of the Protestant Laymen of New Orleans.

Oak Park Presbyterian Church of New Orleans has just dedicated its new educational building. A special service at 11 a.m. Sunday, Dec. 30 was conducted by the pastor, the Rev. William A. Crosland, and dedicatory sermon was brought by Dr. John S. Land, chairman of the strategy committee of the New Orleans Presbytery.

NORTH CAROLINA

Davidson — Davidson College will award more than 20 major scholarships to entering freshmen this year as part of a $100,000 student aid program.

Dr. S. R. Spencer, Jr., said today that applications from secondary school seniors for the competitive scholarships will be received through Jan. 10. Dr. Spencer is Dean of Students and Chairman of the Scholarship committee.

"We will accept applications for a few days after Jan. 10," he stated, "and will then begin selection of finalists."

Last year 260 high school and preparatory school seniors competed for the top scholarships, which range in value up to $1250 per year. At least that many applications are expected this year.

TEXAS

Fort Worth—First Presbyterian Church here held its first services in its $2,000,000 new church building on Dec. 22. The previous Sunday, Dr. Robert F. Jones, pastor, took special note of the final services in the old sanctuary.

The move from the 5th and Taylor sanctuary to the new location at 1000 Penn marked the end of 68 years of use for the old sanctuary. This period covers all but 15 years of the life of the church that was organized in 1873.

as He read from the book of the prophet Isaiah in the Capernaum synagogue.

The wealth of information in this Bible Atlas is presented in an easy-to-understand way. The many sub-heads and the analytical table of contents enables the reader to find what he is looking for quickly. There is an index of geographical names for both text and maps and a subject index also.

With full appreciation for the fine features of this volume it is regrettable that we have to dissent from some of Dr. Kraeling's presuppositions, especially as related to the Pentateuch. Apparently the editor has adopted the hypotheses of scholars who hold to the liberal documentary ideas of the higher critics. In this respect the Rand McNally Bible Atlas published seventy years ago is a safer guide. Although there are many improvements in the later work, we still intend to keep the original Rand McNally Bible Atlas in our library.

—J.R.R.

PLENTY, PRISCILLA. Helen R. Mann. Eerdman's. $3.00.

This is a moving and sensitive story of love and courage. It vividly sets forth the morally rich life of Puritan New England. Mrs. Mann, who proves her special talent for making the religious foundations of American culture significant and real for the modern reader, writes with great insight into both history and human nature.

Letting her imagination play upon the exciting and inspiring events and people of seventeenth century New England, Mrs. Mann recreates our history in such a way that it has meaning for our present and our future.

The story centers around the lives of Priscilla Appleton, a lovely and vivacious member of one of America's oldest families, and the Rev. Joseph Capen, a young and striking preacher who tries to combat the spirit of materialism that slowly invades the colonists as prosperity and independence beckon them to break their political ties with the Old World and their religious ties with a vital Christian inheritance. This story is a thing of beauty and delight. In it we are called back to the simple elemental Christian virtues that make a nation great.

SEQUELS. Mrs. Henry M. Woods. Marshall, Morgan and Scott.

A prayer meeting in Shanghai on New Year's Day 1924, gave birth to the World-Wide Revival Prayer Movement. A year later during a series of meetings in that same Oriental city, revival broke out. The story of that revival stirred Christian people throughout the world to pray for similar visitations on high. Subsequent publications have continued to stimulate prayer, each being a "sequel" to the last and continuous story of the Lord working through this movement. Mrs. Woods is the founder of this movement and here she retells its history of prayer and its answer.

YOUNG PEOPLE'S DEPARTMENT

(Continued from Page 11)

we can be sure that He will make it known to us. When God makes known His plan for our lives, that is our calling . . . our vocation.

How can we know what God would have us to do with our lives? In the first place, we can pray to be shown His will for us with a willingness on our part to do whatever He indicates. Paul did not learn what God's plan for his life was until he was willing to say on the Damascus road, "Lord, what wilt thou have me do?" If we ask guidance sincerely and with a readiness to go where He leads us, we may be sure that the Lord will reveal His purpose for our lives.

The second way of getting an indication of what the Lord would have us to do with our lives is to take an honest look at the skills and abilities He has given us. God ordinarily calls us into kinds of service which will make the best use of the talents He has given us. This is not an iron-clad rule, but it is certainly worth our consideration. If we are really interested in knowing what our best abilities are, we should take an honest look at our interests and our school marks. Those who want to go into the matter more thoroughly may make an appointment with one of the vocational guidance centers maintained by our church.

Program Leader:

Have you heard the call of the Lord to salvation, to service, and to a particular vocation? If not, have you listened? If so, have you been obedient to the call? A Christian is a person under orders. Have you received and obeyed yours?

The Southern
PRESBYTERIAN
Journal

FEB 1 1957

VOL. XV NO. 40 JANUARY 30, 1957 $3.00 A YEAR

The Vote On Ordination Of Women Elders

Forty-six Presbyteries have reported on their vote on Women Elders.

Nineteen Presbyteries have voted *Yes*. These are Montgomery, Westminster, Brazos, East Hanover, Greenbrier, Lafayette, Louisville, Muhlenberg, New Orleans, Potomac, Potosi, Roanoke, Indian, Winston-Salem, Central Alabama, Transylvania, Albemarle, Columbia and Wilmington.

Twenty-seven Presbyteries have voted *No*. These are Central Mississippi, Concord, Winchester, West Hanover, Memphis, Birmingham, Kanawha, Knoxville, Meridian, North Mississippi, South Carolina, Asheville, Everglades, Atlanta, Suwannee, Paris, Mecklenburg, Cherokee, North Alabama, East Alabama, Florida, Kings Mountain, Ouachita, Savannah, Orange, Holston and Augusta-Macon.

THE SOUTHERN PRESBYTERIAN JOURNAL

Rev. Henry B. Dendy, D.D., Editor....................Weaverville, N. C.
Dr. L. Nelson Bell, Associate Editor....................Asheville, N. C.
Rev. Wade C. Smith, Associate Editor....................Weaverville, N. C.

EDITORIAL

The Preaching of the Cross

In First Corinthians, the Apostle tells us that the preaching of Christ as crucified is the Gospel which God blesses with demonstration of the Spirit and of power to bring sinners to Himself. Similarly in Galatians three, when Christ was pictured as crucified, men received the Spirit and exercised faith. The several congregations to which the Ephesian Letter was sent are reminded that in Him we have redemption through His blood, even the forgiveness of sins, and that this is the Gospel of our salvation which is sealed with the promised Holy Spirit.

The forgiveness of sins is preached in connection with the death of Christ on which it is grounded. "Being now justified by His blood, we shall be saved from wrath through Him," R.5.9. "Being justified freely by His grace through the redemption which is in Christ Jesus, whom God set forth as a propitiation, through faith, in his blood," R.3.22. "Who was delivered up for our offenses, and raised for our justification," R.4.25. By the one act of righteousness, or the one obedience unto death and that the death of the Cross, the many are justified, Rom. 5,18-19, Phil. 2.8. Similarly in Revelation we are told that He loved, or loves us, and washed, or loosed us from our sins, in or by His own blood.

The peace of God comes out of Christ's Cross. When we were enemies of God we were reconciled to God by the death of His Son. R.5.10. God has made peace through the blood of His Cross, Col.1.19. Christ is our Peace in that we Gentiles are made nigh by the blood of Christ. Having slain the enmity on the Cross, He brings both Jew and Gentile in one body to God, Eph.2.13f. God reconciled the world to Himself by making Him who knew no sin to be sin for us and for His sake not imputing to us our sins, that is, making us to be the righteousness of God in him, 2 Cor.5.18f.

The preaching of Christ as our substitute who died to atone for our sins, and of him as our representative who rose from the dead for our justification is the foundation of the Church, I Cor. 3.11. And no man can lay any other foundation. It is for each of us to examine our preaching to make sure that it is building upon this foundation. We are not commissioned to offer forgiveness of sins to men except in the name of Christ. Luke 4.47; Acts 2.38; I John 2.12; I Peter 3.18. We are to offer men the peace of God made by the blood of His Cross.

In His Cross and resurrection Christ triumphed over sin, guilt, death and Satan, over principalities and powers in high places. The victorious Redeemer is now exalted to God's right hand above every power and might and name, both in this age and in that which is to come. Consequently, as the Spirit brings Him into our hearts, the crucified and risen Saviour is "Christ in you the hope of glory." Only as the Church preaches Jesus Christ and him as crucified does she preach in demonstration of the Spirit and of power. —W.C.R.

The Children's Page

The brief sketches of Bible characters appearing on the Children's Page must of necessity be in very simple terms understandable to a child. It is not practicable to include in such a presentation the doctrinal significance implied, nor is it expedient. But there will be references which will evoke questions from a child, which will give the parent or the teacher the opportunity to explain more fully. For instance, in a recent issue in the story of Cain and Abel there is mention of the "blood sacrifice." In this issue, the "ark of safety" a type of the sinner's safety in Christ from the penalty of sin. A child is apt to ask "Why?" This opens the way to explain more fully the beginning of a typology pointing to Jesus Christ and Calvary. Parent (or teacher) and child will both profit by a simple explanation of the Atonement, and it is remarkable how a little child can "take in" these great doctrines of the Christian faith.

—W.C.S.

Faith—and the World We See

There be few indeed who have not wondered bout the universe of which we are a part. Inuiring minds have sought the answer to the ıysteries of life, of matter, of force and of ɔuntless other things which obviously exist.

In increasing numbers scientists are coming) admit that research, experimentation and ɔeculation, regardless of how meticulously ıreful they may be, inevitably lead to a place eyond which there yet remains a mystery — 'here and how did these forces originate? What ; the unseen Power which has originated and :ill controls the universe?

The answer is God. And, we catch a glimpse f God's creative power and acts in a number f places in the Bible.

Hebrews 11:3 is an interesting verse. Let us onsider it in several translations:

:. J. V.—*"Through faith we understand that the worlds were framed by the word of God, so that things which are seen were not made of things which do appear."*

:. S. V.—*"By faith we understand that the world was created by the word of God, so that what is seen was made out of things which do not appear."*

Villiams—*"By faith we understand that the worlds were created, beautifully co-ordinated, and now exist, at God's command, so that the things which we see did not develop out of mere matter."*

hillips —*"And it is after all only by faith that our minds accept as fact that the whole scheme of time and space was designed by God — that the world which we can see is operating on principles that are invisible."*

Facts of science and truth *must* be identical. :ere, in beautiful language, language with hich science cannot rightly find fault, is ex-:essed a truth which must be the basis of our titude towards God.

The word "faith" appears again and again. hese things cannot be demonstrated in the st tube. They cannot be arrived at with the :de rule or the complicated equation. They are beyond human comprehension because they deal with the supernatural — with God and His works.

There is no fault to be found with any man who searches for the hidden mysteries of this world and the forces which control it. But there is definite objection to *anyone* who rules God out and, on this biased (and foolish) pre-supposition, goes on to hypothecate about the universe without reference to the Creator and Ruler of the universe and His place in that universe.

A study of what the Scriptures have to say about creation is a rewarding one. It can contribute one essential link necessary for a right perspective to life.

We are told that "without faith it is impossible to please Him." It is equally true that without faith man can never cross that mysterious wall which separates between that which can be demonstrated and that which must be accepted without the confirmatory proofs of scientifc discovery.

"By FAITH we UNDERSTAND."

—L.N.B.

The Drunkards at Corinth

Yesterday I conducted the communion service. In the sermon I referred to the irreverent participants at Corinth who came to the Lord's table drunk. The Corinthians were pretty wicked. There was also fornication among them such as is not so much as named among the Gentiles.

Of course people today still come to the Lord's Supper thoughtlessly and irreverently. This too is sin. But by and large our sins are not so gross as those of the early Corinthians. When has any one of us seen a drunk at the Lord's table? Fornicators? Well, we like to believe the best.

And yet, is all this respectability pure gain? Or does the absence of wicked people in the church indicate that the church is failing to reach the wicked people?

There are today, as well as in the first century, victims of gross immorality. Yesterday I administered a respectable communion service. This morning I learned of a teenage girl who

The Southern Presbyterian Journal, *a Presbyterian Weekly magazine devoted to the statement, defense, and propagation of the Gospel, the faith which was once for all delivered unto the saints,* published every Wednesday by The Southern Presbyterian Journal, nc., in Weaverville, N. C.

Entered as second-class matter May 15, 1942 at the Postoffice at Weaverville, N. C., under the Act of March 3, 1879. Vol. XV, No. 40, January 30, 1957. Editorial and Business Offices: Weaverville, N. C. Printed in the U.S.A. by Biltmore Press, Asheville, N. C.

ADDRESS CHANGE: When changing address, please let us have both old and new address as far in advance as possible. Allow three weeks after change if not sent in advance. When possible, send an address label giving your old address.

for five years had been forced into incest both by her brother and her father. Our respectability therefore has not been gained by a higher level of morality in the whole community, but rather by a failure to reach these degraded people.

If we could convert a group of modern Corinthians, no doubt our churches would be troubled by disciplinary problems. Respectable people, both in the church and out of the church, would be scandalized. And yet, such disorder would not be all loss, would it?

—G.H.C.

An Active Old-Timer

Rev. Pierre Bernard Hill, D.D., L.L.D., Litt.D., Pastor Emeritus of the San Antonio First Presbyterian Church has recently been appointed by Gov. Allan Shivers to an honorary membership on the Governor's Staff; he has also been made a member of Attorney General John B. Shepperd's staff.

Two years ago the Texas Legislature and Governor Shivers named Dr. Hill, "Poet Laureate of Texas." He is also a member of the American Association for the Advancement of Science, the Victoria Institute of Great Britain, the French Institute of Arts and Letters and the Texas Academy of Science. He is the author of many articles in our church papers, of various pamphlets and sacred songs.

Although he will be fourscore years this coming March 4, he has by no means retired from service. Recently in the absence of the pastor of the First Baptist Church of San Antonio he was invited to substitute for him in the Sunday morning church service. Dr. Hill in the power of the Holy Spirit so challenged that congregation to a rededicated life that more than fifteen hundred people came forward, filling the space in front and the aisles. When should a man get too old to be mightily used of God?

Dr. Hill has a keen sense of humor and can tell many interesting stories. He may have forgotten this one, but told it to the writer many years ago. When he went from Louisville to San Antonio in 1921 on invitation of the First Church to preach a "get-acquainted" sermon, returning North he boarded a train on the K. T. & P. Railway, and telegraphed Mrs. Hill, "Am taking Katy to Oklahoma City tonight." "Katy" of course was the well-known name of that K.T.&P. Flyer. At Oklahoma City he was handed a wire from Louisville, reading: "For mercy sake who is Katy?" —W.C.S.

Our Medical Program In Korea

Part III

By L. Nelson Bell, M.D., F.A.C.S

Editor's Note: This is the third in a series of articles. The first appeared in our issue of January 9th. The second article appeared in our issue of January 23rd.—H.B.D.

In our first article we reported on the Presbyterian Medical Center at Chunju where an advanced program in surgery is maintained as a hospital, clinic and teaching center for internes and residents. In that report (see the *Southern Presbyterian Journal* of January 9th) we inadvertently listed the surgical residents as three when it should have been five. One EENT resident is also under appointment.

Our next article dealt with the outstanding program for patients suffering with tuberculosis (Korea's No. 1 public health problem), at the Graham Memorial Tuberculosis Hospital at Kwangju, under the directorship of Dr. Herbert Coddington, Jr. (See the *Southern Presbyterian Journal* of January 23rd).

In this third and final article we want to tell of the program of our Korea Mission in the field of leprosy and public health.

One of the world's outstanding colonies for the treatment of leprosy is the R. M. Wilson Leprosy Colony situated on a beautiful promontory of land jutting out into the sea at Soonchun.

This colony has about 1,200 patients affected with leprosy and its greatest need (and here is the challenge), is for a doctor who will devote himself to this specialty. At present this work is being supervised by Rev. E. T. Boyer and the professional care of the patients is provided by a Korean physician. These two will be the first to tell you that an American doctor, willing to specialize in leprosy, is the first need.

To clarify the picture it will be necessary for the writer to tell something of the modern concept of leprosy and the marvelous advances which have been made in the diagnosis, treatment and arresting of the disease. These star-

patients offers relief, so the care and treatment of leprosy offers similar hope. Here is a challenge to take up a work for Christ in Korea where thousands of people have leprosy; where new techniques and new medicines open up an un-dreamed of future for these people; and where the reward will be the relief of suffering and the privilege of telling at the same time of the One all men everywhere need.

The writer believes some young doctor will read this report, or have his attention called to it, and as a result say: "Here am I, send me."

We would conclude this report with a reference to yet another plan of our Korea Mission; a plan for an effective Public Health program. The Korean government and local officials, along with the Church leaders, rejoice in our surgical program at Chunju, the tuberculosis work at Kwangju and the leprosy colony at Soonchun. In addition there is a crying need for a program of Public Health instruction. This would include demonstrations and classes in hygiene, pre and post-natal clinics, inoculation schedules, diagnostic clinics for tuberculosis and leprosy, and the other avenues of endeavor associated with Public Health here in America.

A start in this work has been made at Mokpo with a Korean woman doctor in charge and with supervisory help from Mrs. John Somerville, R.N.

This program needs to be strengthened and enlarged in Mokpo and to be extended over the entire area of South Korea in which our Mission is working. Here again there is needed a doctor who has had the specialized training so necessary in such an undertaking. This doctor would not work alone but would associate with himself Korean men and women, doctors and nurses, and he would have a wide-open field in which to make his specialty effective.

Another challenge? Certainly, Korea, as is still true in many parts of the world, needs Christian men and women who have heard the Macedonian call to come over and help. Change and progress are requiring more and more that these men and women have had specialized training. But such training is only a part. Needed are those men and women who have the professional "know how" which are the tools of trade today, but they also must *know Him*, whom to know aright is life everlasting.

The writer only wishes he was forty years younger.

Young Christian doctors and nurses, do you want to invest your lives where there is almost infinite need and opportunity?

Make your decision with Christ — on your knees.

Ad Interim Committee On The Revision of the Book of Church Order

An Address to The Stated Clerks Association, Montreat, N. C., August 17, 1956

By Philip F. Howerton, Elder
Charlotte, N. C.
(Member of the Committee)

The Assembly's Committee on Revision of the Book of Church Order welcomes this opportunity to present to you, the Stated Clerks of our various church courts, this "progress report" of its work. The committee is most appreciative of having a part in this conference. In a very real sense you gentlemen are the "Chairmen" of your courts, since you are the continuing executive officers, and for that reason you can be of real service to our committee and the Church by your advice and counsel during the period of this revision work.

Our discussion will cover briefly these points:

I. The Committee and How It Is Operating
II. The Committee's Purpose
III. The Committee's Progress
IV. The Committee's Request for Assistance

I. The Committee and How It Is Operating

Now that we realize the magnitude of the work assigned, no one could be more aware of inadequacy for a task, nor more aware of the need for God's guidance than the members of this Committee. Our appointment was an honor not sought, but accepted as a responsibility and opportunity for service to our beloved Church. It is now quite obvious that much time will be required to complete our work, so we first ask for your patience and understanding. You may be interested in the personnel of the Committee:

A. The chairman is Dr. Vernon S. Broyles, Pastor of the North Avenue Presbyterian Church, and former Executive Secretary of the Board of Church Extension. His long experience as a pastor and as an executive of one of our Church agencies, as well as his experience as a Presbyter, admirably qualifies him for this responsibility.

Then we have two men who are Seminary professors, Dr. James A. Millard of Austin Theological Seminary, and Dr. John H. Leith of Auburn, Alabama, who has been teaching at Columbia Theological Seminary. Both of these men are scholars, students of church history, and thoroughly familiar with the constitutional history of our Reformed Faith. Additionally, Dr. Millard has rendered notable service to our Church as a member of the Permanent Judicial Committee of The General Assembly.

There are three Elder members, Dean John W. Wade of Vanderbilt University Law School, Dr. Edward D. Grant of Louisiana, and myself. Dean Wade is particularly helpful because of his legal training and his service on the Assembly's Judicial Committee. Dr. Grant has rendered great service to our Church as former Secretary of the Board of Christian Education, and is probably as familiar with the operation of our church courts as any man in our denomination. Because of my own service on the Boards of several Assembly's agencies it must have been felt that I could bring some practical help to the Committee.

Then we have the invaluable presence and aid of Dr. E. C. Scott, our Assembly's Stated Clerk, acting as secretary and as ex-officio member. Dr. Scott is undoubtedly one of the real authorities on Presbyterian law and procedure. During any necessary absence on his part his place is taken by Dr. Archie C. Smith, Assistant Stated Clerk.

B. Meetings—To date the Committee has met four times, the first in October 1955, with meetings already scheduled for September and November. These sessions run generally for two days, with night sessions. We did not realize how mentally fatiguing this work could be, so two days at a time is about all that is profitable. This limitation, as well as other responsibilities of the committee members, will necessarily extend the time required for completion of our task.

C. Method of Work—We are presently working in the Form of Government section of the book. Members of the Committee are assigned the structural work of particular parts in advance and distribute a rough draft sometime prior to each meeting. Then when the committee meets each paragraph is taken up in order, thoroughly discussed, sometimes to the point that fifteen minutes may be taken on the use of a single word. The method is consultative, and the debate full, but patient. The committee has sought advice from some twenty of the best students in our Church, from the heads of our various church agencies, from pastors and professors. To date we have been able to obtain complete agreement on all sections covered, though we often started initial discussion of particular sections with considerable diversity of viewpoint. The committee has co-opted other people in our church to assist, and will continue to do so as the work progresses. We welcome contributions and suggestions from responsible and interested people in our Church. All suggestions receive the most careful consideration and discussion.

II. The Committee's Purpose

This committee was set up by order of the 1955 General Assembly to do a "thoroughgoing revision of the Book of Church Order, with a report of its progress to be made to the 1957 General Assembly." The very title of this commission indicates the nature of the work, and gives some hint of its magnitude.

May we say at the outset that the committee realizes that its work is not to **re-write** the Book of Church Order, but to do a **thoroughgoing revision** of the book—the latter being a large enough task in itself!

Furthermore, the committee recognizes its constitutional limitations: first, that it is a **committee** "appointed to examine, consider and report" (to use the language of the Book itself); and second, that any changes suggested must be carried through

(1) To define powers and the purposes for which they are exercised:

(2) To delegate the powers to the proper agencies which are to exercise them.

We aim to make the Book of Church Order a part of our Constitution in the true sense of that legal view.

A constitution should not go into minute detail. Methodology is a matter of by-laws, of manuals, that may be more easily changed from time to time to meet changing conditions. For example, the Book of Church Order should not pretend to be a manual of operations for a church board such as World Missions or Annuities and Relief, or for that matter of a Session or a Presbytery—these agencies and courts must be guided in their day to day operations by the decisions of responsible people who **represent** particular church courts. It is quite true that their methods must plumb with the Constitution, and it is the business of church courts to determine that this is the case, but the methods should not be spelled out in the Book of Church Order. This approach will decrease the need for so many minor amendments, and it is hoped that in the future amendments to the Book may be suspended insofar as possible—certainly until changing times make such amendments mandatory.

III. The Committee's Progress

To this time our work has been confined to the form of Government section. We have done a tentative draft of the first 100 paragraphs. The committee has set this schedule for its work:

(1) We hope to have a rough draft of the Form of Government section to present to the 1957 Assembly for distribution and comment prior to the 1958 Assembly, with possible first formal action on that section at the 1958 Assembly;

(2) Then a rough draft of the rules of Discipline section for distribution and comment at the 1958 Assembly with first formal action in 1959;

(3) Then a rough draft of the Directory for Worship section for distribution and comment at the 1959 Assembly, with first formal action at the 1960 Assembly, and possible final adoption at the 1961 Assembly, our Centennial Meeting!

IV. The Committee's Request for Assistance

Again may we emphasize our need for your help, for your prayers, and your patience. By all means we must want you to feel free to comment upon our work, to offer suggestions that will guide us, to urge your associates at home to do the same. We wish to enlist you as channels of communication. Please help us by reducing to writing any suggestions you have and sending them to Dr. Vernon Broyles, North Avenue Presbyterian Church, Atlanta.

We are not seven men presuming to re-write the Book of Church Order, but a committee appointed by our highest church court to "examine, consider and report" to that court our best efforts in a "thoroughgoing revision of the Book of Church Order." As such we are servants of the Church and, of our blessed Lord and Saviour Jesus Christ.

Helps To Understanding Scripture Readings in *Day by Day*

Rev. C. C. Baker

Sunday, February 10, *Psalm* 146:5-8. "There is sunshine in the Psalmist's face" as he looks unto the Lord, untroubled by any human problem (vv.1-2). God is the great creator (v.6), yet He is concerned for every need of His creatures (vv.7-9). List the conditions God's creatures must meet if He is to help them (vv.7-9). Are the different peoples mentioned in vv.7-9 helpless to help themselves? Is the Lord's provision for each adequate? The Psalmist has seen the futility of human resources (vv.3-4), and has evidently had God meet some need in his life (vv.1-2). Verse 5 is his testimony. One of the richest experiences a Christian can have is that of coming to God with a specific need and watching God supply that need for him. Do you still rely upon human resources and, therefore, know little real joy in your life?

Monday, February 11, *Philippians* 2:1-4. Many of us never come to the point where we are ready to admit that there is nothing good in ourselves (Gen. 6:5; Jer. 17:9). Thus we are unwilling to humble ourselves before God (v.8) or before others (v.3). All the good that is in the Christian is there because of Jesus Christ (1:6,11), and it is His very life that should inspire humility in us (vv.5-8). If Christ was willing to be broken for our sakes (v.8b), should not the "self" in us be willing to be broken for His sake (v.5)? As Christ is crowned Lord and Master in our lives (vv.10-11), we will be formed more and more into the very likeness of Christ Himself (3:7-10).

Tuesday, February 12, *II Corinthians* 5:11-17. Paul had been made a new creature in Christ (v.17) and now no longer lived for himself but for the Lord (vv.9,15). That which motivated Paul to serve the Lord was what Christ had done for him on the cross (vv.14,21). Seeing that Christ's death was not only for him, but for all (vv.14-15), Paul did not spare himself in sharing with others the Good News (vv.13,18,20). He was moved to a love and service for others that he would not otherwise have had (vv.13b,20b). Paul was also aware that everyone would one day have to give an account of himself before Christ (v.10) and he was, therefore, all the more zealous to persuade men (v.11). Thus the Christian is motivated to service for Christ both by the love of Christ, as revealed in the cross, and by the sure knowledge that there will be a day of accounting.

Wednesday, February 13, *John* 9:24-41. In vv.1-7 Jesus enabled a blind man to see. Notice the conclusion this man came to about Jesus (vv.17,35-38) and what he suffered for his faith (vv.22,34). The Pharisees did everything possible to dissuade him from his belief in Christ (vv.13-17,24-34). Observe how their arguments were based on prejudice and unbelief (vv.16,24, 28-29, 34). The simple, logical answers of the once-blind man were well nigh irrefutable (vv.25; 30-33). His belief in Christ was based upon personal experience (v.25). There may well be times when non-Christians, with these same prejudices and unbelief, will try to undermine your faith in Christ. If your faith is based upon personal experience with Him, no human being can take it away from you (10:28,29).

Thursday, February 14, *Philippians* 2:12-16. In the midst of a world of materialism and secularism (v.15), the Christian is to live in preparation for the day when he will give an account of himself to Christ (v.16b). His primary concern in life, therefore, is to be spiritual rather than material (v.12). In the midst of multiple temptations, it is encouraging for him to be aware that God is actually working in his life (v.13) to make him holy and righteous (vv. 13b,15b). The obedient Christian (v.12) who has an awareness of God's presence in his life (v.13) has something that his worldly-minded non-Christian friends will recognize as drastically missing in their own lives (v.15b). Never has there been a time when Christians needed more to radiate before a pagan society the faith they profess.

Friday, February 15, *Philippians* 4:10-20. Paul had learned to accept his circumstances wherever he was (v.12), to be content at all times (vv.7,9,11). This was possible because Christ lived in his life (v.13). Notice that even while in prison, Paul "bubbled over" with joy (3:1; 4:4,10). What did he do with his potential worries (v.6)? What was his confidence concerning the supply of his needs (v.19)? What was his hope for the future (v.15b)? Upon what did he concentrate his thoughts (v.8)? Paul's whole life was centered in Christ (3:8). Thus his love and concern for other people went deep (4:1). As Christ becomes more a part of your life, the above characteristics will also become more a part of your daily walk.

Saturday, February 16, *Colossians* 1:11-29. Meditate on the facts Paul presents in vv.15-17,19 concerning who Christ is. How are these facts related to the teaching of John1:1-3? How would you state in your own words what God in Christ has done for you (vv.12-14,20)? When you realize who Christ is and what He has done for you, what is your response to Him? What is the purpose of the statements made about Christ in v.18? Does He have the pre-eminence in every phase of your life? How does all this passage teaches about Christ increase your confidence in the power that is available in Him to enable you to live the Christian life (v.11)? It is because of this power that is ours that Paul can pray as he does for his Christian readers (vv.9-10).

SUNDAY SCHOOL Lessons

LESSON FOR FEBRUARY 10

By THE REV. J. KENTON PARKER

The Warning And Invitation Of Jesus

Background Scripture: Matthew 11 and 12
Devotional Reading: Isaiah 61:1-4

If we include the Background Scripture, I feel that we should change the Topic to Warnings and Invitations, for there are several warnings and two invitations in these two chapters.

Since there is such an abundance of material in these chapters, I will only mention one thing in regard to our Devotional Reading. In verse 2 of Isaiah 61 we have the two sides of the Gospel presented: (1) The acceptable year of the Lord, and (2) The day of vengeance of our God. The Gospel contains both an invitation and a warning. As Paul tells us, The Gospel is a savor of life unto life, or of death unto death. There is Salvation, and there is Condemnation: He that believeth shall be saved; he that believeth not shall be condemned. This is the condemnation, that light has come into the world, and men loved darkness rather than light, because their deeds were evil.

Warnings: There are many of these, either expressed or implied. 11:1-15.

1. John the Baptist sends two of his disciples to Jesus, asking the question, Art Thou He that should come, or look we for another? There is some difference of opinion as to John's reason for doing this. (I have just gotten "The New Testament for English Readers," by Alford, and it gives a good discussion of this). Did John do this to strengthen his own faith, or the faith of the disciples of John? John was in prison, soon to be beheaded.

Most of us would be discouraged by such an experience. He had preached Jesus as the Coming One Who would baptize with fire and thoroughly purge His floor. He had also borne witness to Him as the Lamb of God Who would take away the sin of the world. Did John see that the Cross would come before the crown? Did he share the common view that the Messiah would be an earthly Ruler and set up His Kingdom and liberate the Jews from their hated Roman masters? Was he disappointed that Jesus had not done more to establish His Kingdom? It does seem from his question that John's faith had weakened a bit.

Jesus answered the question by telling the disciples to go and show John again those things which ye do see and hear. Then, in verse 6 there seems to be a gentle rebuke and warning: And blessed is he, whosoever shall not be offended in me.

After the disciples departed Jesus pronounced a beautiful eulogy upon John the Baptist, including this remarkable tribute: "Verily I say unto you, Among them that are born of women there hath not risen a greater than John the Baptist." We feel sure that John and his disciples were strengthened and encouraged, and that John trusted even where he did not fully understand, perhaps.

2. "This generation." The people of Jesus' day were dissatisfied with both Jesus and John. These two men were very different, but neither one appealed to "this generation." Jesus compares them to a bunch of dissatisfied children who would not join in the games; who would neither dance nor mourn. They said that John had a devil because he did not eat or drink like ordinary men, and that Jesus was a glutton and winebibber because He did. I think that every generation is very similar to the people of Jesus' time. For instance, God uses today very different types of men in preaching the Gospel, and very different methods. We may have a "Billy Sunday" and a "Quiet Talks Gordon" preaching at the same time, and following each other as they did in Lynchburg, Virginia. Some would criticize "Billy" as being too sensational, and others, Gordon, because he was too quiet. When people do not wish to believe it is easy for them to find fault with the messenger, or the method. There is a warning for us today in these words.

3. The Cities wherein most of His mighty works were done: 21-24.

Chorazin, Bethsaida, and Capernaum witnessed many of Jesus' great miracles. He made

Capernaum His headquarters while He pursued His work around the Sea of Galilee. These cities did not repent or respond as they should to His words or works.

He upbraids them for this unbelief and said that Tyre and Sidon, and even Sodom, would have responded better to such evidence. Suppose we change names a bit and put some of our great cities in their place; New York, Chicago, San Francisco; cities full of churches and preachers. If some of the cities of India or China, or Africa had had the opportunities of American cities, would they have responded better? I am afraid that we have a lot of "Gospel-hardened" cities in America.

4. *The Sabbath Controversy:* 12:1-14.

The Pharisees, who were sticklers for the strict observance of the letter of the Law, but completely ignored its spirit, were quick to seize the opportunity which presented itself in the conduct of Jesus' disciples, and His own conduct, in respect to the observance of the Sabbath. They saw some of the disciples plucking off some of the grain and eating it. They said to Jesus, Behold your disciples are doing what is unlawful to do on the Sabbath. In the eyes of these critics they were reaping and thrashing grain! Jesus defended His disciples by citing two Old Testament examples; David and the priests. The Sabbath was made for man, not man for the Sabbath. The needs of men are superior to some lower law.

The second instance concerned His own act of healing the man with the withered hand. They asked Him, Is it lawful to heal on the Sabbath days? He showed them from their own practice how absurd was their question. A man is much better than a sheep. He then healed the man. The Pharisees went out and took counsel how they might destroy Him. How impossible to convince those who are determined not to be convinced! How prone men are to stress the trivial!

There is a very solemn implied warning in connection with these two incidents. Let us beware of exalting some minor matter to a place of supreme importance. It is so easy to be critical of those who do not follow our particular pattern for living. Jesus gives us a good rule in the Sermon on the Mount; Judge not, that ye be not judged; cast out the beam out of our own eye before we try to cast the mote out of our brother's eye. In these instances, of course, neither Jesus nor His disciples were doing wrong. The Pharisees had a beam of unbelief, of jealousy, of hatred, and even murder. Who were they to criticize others?

5. The *"Unpardonable Sin":* 12:22-37.

This section begins with the healing of the man possessed with a devil, blind and dumb. The people were amazed and said, Is not this the son of David? The Pharisees present a preposterous explanation: This fellow durst not cast out devils, but by Beelzebub the prince of the devils. Jesus answered this amazing statement, and then proceeded with a solemn warning which has been called "The Unpardonable Sin." In these Pharisees we see unbelief in its most stubborn and unreasonable form. They were attributing the works of Christ to Satan and resisting the Holy Spirit. Unbelief is the worst of sins. It is the only sin, in the nature of the case, which cannot be forgiven. When we close our eyes and ears and hearts and refuse to believe we shut the door to salvation.

6. "Master, (Teacher) we would see a sign from thee": 38-45.

How could men be so blind and unreasonable? They had seen miracle after miracle, or, as John calls them, "signs." His life; His words; His works; were all signs. Nicodemus recognized this when he said, No man can do these miracles, (signs), that thou doest, except God be with him. The blind man who was healed presented the same unanswerable argument to the Pharisees. (See John 9:30) Jesus refuses to gratify their curiosity by giving them any special sign, but calls up three Old Testament incidents to rebuke and warn them: Jonah; the men of Nineveh, and the Queen of the South. He then shows them that unbelief is like an evil spirit who takes possession of a man's heart.

II. *Invitations:* 11:28-30; 12:15-21; 12:46-50.

The first of these is one of the most far-reaching and beautiful invitations in the Bible. It follows a prayer of thanksgiving to His Father because He has hidden these things from the wise and prudent and revealed them unto babes. The proud Pharisees were the "wise and prudent," (as the world sees things). They refused to see the evidence and rejected Him. There were others, however, the common people, the sick, the heavy-laden ones, who received Him. Then He utters His Great Invitation; Come unto me all ye that labor and are heavy laden, and I will give you rest. We are somewhat surprised to find it here, in the midst of solemn words of warning, but warning and invitation go together. We must warn men; we must also invite men. These are the two sides of Gospel preaching.

The second selection is not an invitation in words, but an implied one, from a beautiful picture of Jesus which is put between the plot to kill Him and the Unpardonable Sin. What sort of Person is it Who is being rejected by the Pharisees? He is the Great Healer, the One pictured by Isaiah the prophet; Behold my ser-

(Continued on Page 11)

YOUNG PEOPLES Department

YOUTH PROGRAM FOR FEBRUARY 10

By THE REV. B. HOYT EVANS

"*Circles Of Influence*"

Scripture: Matthew 13:31-33

Hymns:

"Jesus, I My Cross Have Taken"
"Lord, Speak To Me That I May Speak"
"Take My Life, And Let It Be Consecrated"

Program Leader:

This is the first of three programs to deal with the witness we bear as Christians. We are to think today of our influence and how it can be used for Christ. We usually speak of influential persons as being those who hold important positions in life or who have attained a large degree of fame. It is true that the influence of such people is weighty, but each of us has influence too, and it is most important. That we have influence is a fact, but the thing that should concern us is whether it is good or bad . . . whether it is being used for Christ or not.

Let us think of some of the areas where our influence is felt. In every circle of friends where we live a part of our life, we leave a mark. We live most of our time at home. We have an influence there. We also are a part of a class at school, at Sunday school, and in the youth fellowship. We make an impression on the people with whom we associate in each of these relationships. How many other formal and informal groups can we name to which we belong and in which we have an influence? (Make a list on a blackboard or a large piece of paper of all the circles of friendship or association in which your young people have part. Ask the group for suggestions and be ready with a list of your own.)

It is probably beginning to dawn on us from this discussion that we have influence in more places than we thought we did. We need now to come back to that all important question which has already been suggested: Is our influence Christian . . . do we use all these opportunities to witness for Christ? Are the people with whom we live made more mindful of Christ because we are among them from time to time? Are our associates encouraged by our example to be more Christ-like in their own way of living? There is no question about our being influential, but are we being influential for Christ?

If we really love Christ, we are surely interested in witnessing for Him wherever we are. How can we go about it? We may influence people consciously and unconsciously, and we witness to them consciously and unconsciously. There are times when we make very obvious and intentional attempts to lead people to Christ, and there are other times when our influence for Him may be felt very strongly without our knowing it at all. Jesus said Christians should be the light of the world and the salt of the earth. Light is not conscious of giving light and salt is not conscious of its saltiness. So it is with us as Christians. When Christ is in us, His light ought to shine forth whether we are aware of it or not. Let us make a list of the conscious and unconscious ways we can be influential for the Lord.

(Using the blackboard or a large piece of paper or cardboard, prepare two columns headed "Conscious" and "Unconscious." In the first column list such items as personal soul-winning, personal invitations to attend church, taking part on programs, etc. In the other column list: the company you keep, the kind of speech you use, your attitude toward other people, etc. Ask the group for suggestions and discussion of them. Be prepared with a list of your own suggestions in case the young people are slow in advancing their ideas. It would be well to close the program with sentence prayers, especially asking the Lord to make our influence stronger for Him.)

SUNDAY SCHOOL LESSON

(Continued from Page 10)

vant, whom I have chosen; my beloved, in whom my soul is well pleased, etc. Read these words and see the blackness of unbelief as shown by these leaders of the Jews.

Our third invitation is also an implied one. His mother and His brethren were without desiring to speak with Him. He answered, Who is my mother? and who are my brethren? And he stretched forth His hands toward His disciples, and said, Behold, my mother and my brethren! For whosoever shall do the will of my Father which is in heaven, the same is my brother and sister and mother. Here is a suggested invitation to become a member of the "Household of Faith." Will we accept that invitation?

CHILDRENS Page

The Flood

The people were very wicked. They forgot God and worshiped idols. But Noah was a good man who obeyed God and worshiped Him. So God sent a flood upon the earth to destroy the wicked people; but He saved Noah and his family. God told Noah to build an ark to live in while the waters would cover the earth, and Noah believed God, even before the rain began to fall, and built the ark on high ground. Then God told Noah to take two of every kind of animal, male and female; also some extra ones for Sacrifice. These all came into the ark, and Noah and his wife, and his three sons and their wives - 8 persons in all - entered the ark, and God shut the door to keep them safe. Then it rained for forty days and nights, until the whole earth was covered by the flood, even the high mountains: and all flesh, every living Creature, perished, except those in the ark.

(To be continued)

In the Year Ahead, May I

1. Be more Christ-like in the Home.
   "To the Church in Thy House." Phil. 1:2
   "Suffer little children to come unto me." Mark 10:14

2. Be more Christ-like in the Church.
   "Christ also loved the Church and gave Himself for it." Eph. 5:25

3. Be more Christ-like in my social contacts.
   "They took knowledge of them that they had been with Jesus." Acts 4:13
   "Speak not evil one of another." James 4:11

4. Be more Christ-like in my business relations.
   "Whatsoever ye would that men should do to you, do ye even so to them." Matt. 7:12

5. Be more Christ-like in my Citizenship.
   "Render unto Caesar the things which are Caesar's and unto God the things that are God's." Matt. 22:21

6. Be more Christ-like in my world vision.
   "Thy Kingdom Come." Matt. 6:10
   "Go ye into all the world, and preach the Gospel to every creature." Mark 16:15

7. Be more Christ-like in my own life
   "For to me to live is Christ." Phil. 1:21
   "Pray without ceasing." I Thes. 5:17

Some Tips for You

Do you know that the number of people who are reaching the 65-year mark is increasing rapidly in this country? This year there are over 13,000,000, and it is estimated that by 1960 there will be 10 per cent of the entire population in this bracket. In the past decade the number of people in the 65-75 age group has increased 33%, and the over 75-year group 45%. Medical science has prolonged the life span. It may be true as the ditty says, in not too well-phrased words:

"How do I know that my youth is spent?
Because my get up and go has got up and went!"

But many people who are in this group, and many who are approaching it are active and interested in life today and have resources that are invaluable to the Church.

Suppose you take the following as some objectives to think through with other women of your church, and seek to find effective ways to minister more fully to the older people in your church and to give them opportunities to serve the Church!

Discover ways of developing a concern for the older people in your church and community.

Discover concerns of older people and those growing old.

Discover ways of helping people prepare for older years (that can and should start with young adults.)

Discover the areas of adjustment that people must face as they grow older, and ways to make the proper adjustments.

Discover the kinds of programs the local church might initiate for older people.

Discover ways to get older people interested in planning programs which they want.

Learn more about the process of aging (some very good books in this area).

Watch the daily papers, the magazines and Church periodicals for articles about older people. Start a file for clippings which relate to this topic. A recent issue of a city's Sunday paper carried an editorial and a feature story about older people. The autobiography of Grandma Moses should be very interesting reading.

Discover the people in your community who are working with older folks, such as the Social Agencies, the Public Health Nurse, the Director of Social Security, and invite them to meet with your group and give some definite information which you need.

And — remember that there can be real meaning in those words of Browning:
"Grow old along with me,
The best is yet to be.
The last of life for which the first was made."

A Psalm of the Helpers

The ways of the world are full of haste and turmoil;
I will sing of the tribe of helpers who travel in peace.

He that turneth from the road to rescue another,
Turneth toward his goal;
He shall arrive in due time by the footpath of mercy,
God will be his guide.

He that taketh up the burden of the fainting,
Lighteneth his own load;
The Almighty will put his arms underneath him,
He shall lean upon the Lord.

He that careth for the sick and wounded,
Watcheth not alone;
There are three in the darkness together,
And the third is the Lord.

Blessed is the way of the helpers;
The companions of the Christ.
Author Unknown

The Christ

In the face of a child, eager, aglow, aglow,
I have seen the Christ—
In the beauty of a starlit night,
In the face of a child, eager, aglow, aglow,
In the purity of fresh fallen snow,
He was there.

I have heard the Christ—
In the rippling brook, as it sings its song,
In the joyous chorus of the birds at dawn,
In the voice of a tiny child at play,
In the melodies, at the close of day.
He was there.
—(Mrs. O. F.) Lilla B. Liner
Greenwood, S. C.

Then Let Our Overwhelming Wonder Be:

"That the Great Angel-blinding light should shrink
His blaze, to shine in a poor Shepherd's eye;
That the unmeasur'd God so low should sinke,
As Pris'ner in a few poore rags to lye,
That from his Mother's Breast he milke should drinke,
Who feeds with Nectar Heav'n's faire family,
That a vile Manger his low Bed should prove,
Who in a Throne of stars Thunders above;
That he whom the Sun serves, should faintly peepe
Through clouds of Infant Flesh! that he, the old
Eternall Word should be a Child, and weepe;
That he who made the fire, should feare the cold,
That Heav'n's high Majesty his Court should keepe
In a clay cottage, by each blast control'd;
That Glories self should serve our Griefs and feares,
And free Eternity submit to years."

—Crenshaw.

NEWS of CHURCHES Around the World

Miss Louise Farrior

Mrs. Mable C. Morley

GEORGIA

Atlanta—Miss Louise Farrior of Richmond, Va., and Mrs. Mable C. Morley, Little Rock, Ark., have moved to Atlanta to join the Board of Women's Work and were formally introduced to staff members of the Board January 4. Miss Farrior will direct the newly created Editorial Department of the Board of Women's Work, and Mrs. Morley comes to head the Board's Leadership Education Department.

Mrs. Morley, a native of Lonoke, Arkansas, comes to Atlanta from Little Rock where she served as Director of Christian Education in the Pulaski Heights Presbyterian Church and in the First Presbyterian Church at North Little Rock.

She attended Ouachita College and the University of Arkansas and is a graduate of the Assembly's Training School, with a degree of Bachelor of Religious Education. She received the Bland-Paisley Scholarship the first year she was at the

the pastor would welcome the opportunity to emergency supply work for vacant pulpits, or an interim supply for a month or two in churches awaiting the arrival of a new pastor.

THE GENERAL FUND AND INTERCHURCH AGENCIES

Statement of Receipts

FOR

Church Year Ended Dec. 31, 1956

Covering Period From

January 15, 1956 - January 15, 1957

The General Fund Agencies ----

Budget for 1956	$ 846,581.00
Received from Jan. 15, 1956 - Jan. 15, 1957	595,855.70
Percentage of annual budget received for the year	70.4
Total amount short of askings	250,725.30

Interchurch Agencies

Budget for 1956	21,495.00
Received from Jan. 15,1956 - Jan. 15, 1957	17,746.69
Percentage of annual budget received for the year	83.00
Total amount short of askings	3,748.31

Missionary News

Nashville, Tenn.—Mr. and Mrs. Everett E. Gourley, Jr., of our West Brazil Mission, announce the arrival of a son, Kevin Armistead, in Brazil on December 25.

Mr. Gourley is a native of Nashville, Tenn. He is a graduate of Vanderbilt University, and a member of the Glen Leven Presbyterian Church in Nashville.

Mrs. Gourley is the former Miss Nancy Armistead, the daughter of the Rev. and Mrs. W. H. Armistead of Montreat, N. C., and now living in Ormond Beach, Fla. She is a member of the Friendship Presbyterian Church in Black Mountain, N. C.

The Rev. and Mrs. Robert H. Camenisch of our West Brazil Mission have announced the arrival of their daughter, Marlena Kay, born December 11, in Brazil.

Mr. Camenisch is a native of Stanford, Ky., and is a member of Transylvania Presbytery. He is a graduate of the University of Kentucky, and Louisville Seminary.

Mrs. Camenisch is the former Miss Martha Davis of Stanford, Ky. She is a member of the Perryville Presbyterian Church of Perryville, Ky.

ARKANSAS

Fayetteville — The annual Town and Country Church Seminary for pastors and interested laymen of town and country churches, will be held at the University of Arkansas, February 12-15.

The seminar is being sponsored by the Arkansas Council of Churches, in cooperation with the University of Arkansas' College of Agriculture and Home Economics, the Agricultural Extension Service, and the General Extension Service.

Southern Presbyterians from the Synods of Arkansas, Missouri, and Oklahoma, will join other denominational groups to hear matters discussed on the general theme, "The Church, The Hub of the Community".

The Town and Country Church Seminar in Arkansas has developed from a Presbyterian Church, U.S., beginning in 1950. Afterwards, for three years, it was a Pan-Presbyterian affair, and in 1955 it became interdenominational.

FLORIDA

Miami—The new $300,000 structure for Westminster Presbyterian Church has been completed and as put into use by the congregation the Sunday before Christmas.

The church was moved to a more residential area after 33 years in its former location.

The unique part of the modified colonial Georgian building is the lace-like white aluminum tower.

The education building is yet to be added to the finished sanctuary, Administration, and fellowship units in order to make the proposed plant complete.

GEORGIA

Atlanta—The Office of the General Assembly has issued a supplement to the 1951 edition of the Ministerial Directory of the Presbyterian Church, U.S., according to a recent announcement made by Dr. E. C. Scott, Stated Clerk of the Assembly.

The supplement, a 104-page mimeographed booklet, contains the names and biographical matter of persons ordained from 1951 to 1956. There have been more than 1,000 persons added to the roll of ministers since publication of the 1951 Ministerial Directory. Most of these have been ordained by presbyteries of the Presbyterian Church, U.S., but many have been received from other denominations.

Publication of the supplement in mimeographed form was the result of a direction of the Permanent Committee on the Office of the General Assembly.

"The same abbreviations are used in this volume as are found in the 1941 and 1951 editions of the Directory, therefore it is important that the owner of this new material have a copy of the 1951 edition which contains the key," said Dr. Scott.

The final five pages of the supplement contain incomplete information about men from whom sketches were not received and complete information on others who sent in material after stencils had already been prepared for the final publication.

The supplement sells for $1.00 per copy. Copies of the 1951 edition of the Directory may also be obtained from the Office of the Stated Clerk, at $3.50 each.

Postage for the supplement will be paid if remittance accompanies order; otherwise, invoice will include postage. Purchasers in the State of Georgia are asked to add 3 cents for state sales tax, and any remittance on a nonpar bank is to have 10 cents added to it.

All orders are to be addressed to Dr. E. C. Scott, Stated Clerk, Office of the General Assembly, 341-E Ponce de Leon Ave., N.E., Atlanta 6, Ga.

Atlanta—A most unusual record in giving, with an increase of 71% within one year, is revealed in statistics on stewardship released by Clairmont Presbyterian Church of Decatur, Ga.

The young church, organized in 1952, began 1956 with 499 members, and closed the year with 625, or a growth of 25.2% within the year.

During the same period, giving to all causes rose $30,543.46—from $43,019.03 in 1955 to $73,562.49 in 1956. This most unusual jump of 71% in a single year came in large measure from increased giving for the building fund of the church, but sizeable increases in current expense and benevolence giving is also shown in the report.

Contributions to current expenses increased only 21% (from $25,719.09 to $29,945.97). But gifts to benevolences shot up four times as fast, with an 89½% increase from $6,186.35 given in 1955 to $11,718.68 given in 1956.

Building fund contributions in the four-year-old church increased from $12,113.68 in 1955 to $51,-897.84 in 1956. This is an increase of 163% in one year.

The Rev. Max Milligan is the pastor.

Augusta — The Cliffwood Presbyterian Church was constituted by the Augusta-Macon Presbytery January 6, 1957, with 106 charter members and Rev. Wm. Robert Floyd as pastor. The Session is composed of Ruling Elders C. A. Young, Rex L. Searson,, F. G. Haines, Tunnie Walden, A. D. Thornhill, H. B. Martin and V. B. Pittman. The Diaconate consists of D. A. Watson, J. I. Weathers, E. C. Horne, Jr., H. V. Ware, R. R. Clifford, W. H. Thomas, J. M. Ray, W. F. McDonald, J. T. Cheeley and W. F. Holderman.

This church is an offspring of the First Church of Augusta. A handsome and attractive brochure has been published giving the history of the organization, an account of the constituting service and a roll of the charter members. It is priced at $2.00, proceeds of the sale to go toward a plaque dedicating the church to the memory of war dead.

Cherokee Presbytery

The Rev. Robert Calvin Pooley, Jr., pastor of the First Presbyterian Church in Summerville, Georgia, has accepted the call of Cherokee Presbytery, to serve as Executive Secretary, starting Feb. 1, 1957. Rev. Pooley has served at his present post three years. He has served as Chairman of the Chattooga County Chapter of the American Red Cross for two years, and as President of the Summerville Little League for two years. He has served as chaplain of Mason-McCauley V.F.W. Post 6688, and is presently the only Air National Guard Chaplain in the State of Georgia, assigned to the 116th Fighter Intercepter Wing, stationed at Dobbins Air Force Base. The Pooleys have four children, the youngest born Dec. 28th, 1956. Mrs. Pooley is the former Fannie Rutledge of Leaksville, N. C. and a graduate of Duke Nursing School. Their residence for the time being will remain Summerville, Ga.

The Stated Winter Meeting of Cherokee Presbytery was held Tuesday at the Calhoun Presbyterian Church. Ruling Elder Oscar Clecker, of Menlo, Ga., moderated the meting. The Rev. David B. Walthall, Regional Director of Christian Education for the Synod of Georgia, was received as a member from Lexington-Ebenezer Presbytery. The Rev.

Robert C. Pooley, pastor of the First Presbyterian Church of Summerville, was installed as Executive Secretary of the Presbytery. Mr. James M. Baird, a student at Columbia Theological Seminary and a member of the Acworth Presbyterian Church, was received as a Candidate for the Gospel Ministry. The pastoral relationship existing between the Rev. H. Paul Currie and the Calhoun Presbyterian Church was dissolved. Rev. Currie has enrolled as a student at Emory University.

The World Mission report, presented by the Rev. John Knight, pastor of the Smyrna Presbyterian Church, featured an address by the Rev. Lachlan Vass, Jr., missionary to the Belgian Congo. The Rev. S. W. Dendy, pastor of the First Presbyterian Church of Dalton and the Rev. W. L. Merrin, pastor of the Bethel, Sardis and Walnut Grove Presbyterian Churches, were elected minister commissioners to the General Assembly. Mr. Will Storey, Ruling Elder of the Beersheba Presbyterian Church and Mr. Will Joe Abbott, Ruling Elder of the Acworth Presbyterian Church were elected Elder Commissioners to the General Assembly. Dr. Harry K. Holland, pastor of the First Presbyterian Church of Marietta, Ga., presented the Rev. Will Rogers, minister to students at the University of Georgia, who presented the cause and challenge of the Campus Christian Program. The Rev. Robert S. Busey, pastor of the Chickamauga Presbyterian Church, was nominated to serve as Moderator at the next Stated Meeting of Presbytery to be held at Cartersville, Ga., May 21st. Cherokee Presbytery will hold an adjourned meeting at the Atcooga Presbyterian Church, Dalton, Ga., Feb. 1st, at 10:30 A.M.

Quitman—The Presbyterian Home in Quitman, supported by the Synod of Georgia, has let a contract for the construction of a $120,000 addition.

Mrs. Elizabeth Monk, one of the guests of the home, and blind, was one of the first persons to make the new addition possible, by the gift of an afghan she crocheted which earned the price of digging the first foundation.

Dr. Frank McElroy, the director of Quitman, considers Mrs. Monk's gift as typical of the feeling of the thirty elderly men and women who live in the Home—they love it so much that they want to see the 23 new bedrooms added so that others may also come to Quitman and know the same happiness. Mrs. Monk, who lost her sight in middle age, crochets afghans from various colored wool yarn that church women send her. She learned to read Braille when she was 60 years old and typing when she was 65.

A bequest of $10,000 from the estate of Miss Sarah Rogers in Cartersville, Ga., has been designated for the new building.

The Home, now a one-story brick building with wings, will have an addition that will include rooms for 23 more guests, a sun porch, a nurses' call room, laundry, a dining room, office and storage space. The site for the Home comprises 33 acres.

Quitman Home was erected in 1949 on land given by the city and Brooks County. Money for the original building came mostly from within Southwest Georgia Presbytery.

Some of the guests pay their own way. Some do not. But most residents have private rooms, even though at the present, until the addition is added, it is crowded.

Change of address:' Rev. O. M. Anderson, D.D., to 265 Sequa Ave., Jackson 9, Mississippi.

NORTH CAROLINA

Graham—Mrs. Ella Bernard Scott of Haw River, N. C., stepmother of the U. S. Senator Kerr Scott from North Carolina, died here December 23. Funeral services were held at Hawfields Presbyterian Church where she was a member and Senator Scott is an elder.

Mrs. Scott was a native of Orange County, N. C. and a graduate of Salem Female Academy, taught school at Hawfields for several years and married the late R. W. Scott in 1915.

Survivors include two sisters, Mrs. W. O. Doggett of Mount Airy, N. C.; Mrs. Jessie Anthony of Burlington, N. C.; four stepdaughters, Mrs. Louise M. Smith, Mrs. C. R. Hudson, both of Raleigh, Mrs. George Carrington, Burlington, and Mrs. Paul Haeseler of New Brunswick, N. J. Five stepsons, besides, Senator Scott, who survive, include former State Senator Ralph H. Scott, Henry A. Scott, and A. Hughes Scott, all of Haw River, and Dr. S. F. Scott of Burlington.

Greensboro—Dr. Joseph M. Garrison, pastor of the Church of the Covenant, Greensboro, N. C., and chairman of the General Assembly's Committee on Nominations, has called for a meeting of the Committee, in Atlanta, Ga., March 4-5.

The purpose of this meeting is to prepare nominations for all committees to be submitted to the 1957 General Assembly.

The Permanent Nominating Committee is made up of the following: (Terms expiring in 1957) Dr. Garrison; the Rev. W. M. Logan, pastor of the University Church, Austin, Texas; and Mrs. R. M. Pegram, Louisville, Ky. Members whose terms expire in 1958 include the Rev. J. Wayte Fulton, pastor of Shenandoah Church, Miami, Fla.; the Rev. R. R. Craig, pastor of First Church, Idabel, Okla.; and Dr. J. R. McCain, president emeritus of Agnes Scott College, Decatur, Ga. Committee members whose terms expire in 1959 include the Rev. Henry P. Mobley, pastor of Oakland Avenue Church, Rock Hill, S. C.; Mr. E. L. Repass, layman from Salem, Va.; and Mr. John B. Salsbery, layman from Donelson, Tenn.

All interested people throughout the Assembly "are invited to suggest names for the important positions of leadership in the various Assembly committees," said Dr. Garrison.

These names should be sent to Dr. Garrison at Walker and Mendenhall Sts., Greensboro, N. C. "Accompanying each suggestion there should be a brief statement of particular qualifications for the suggested nominations, together with definite addresses in the case of all laymen suggested," said Dr. Garrison. It is requested that all suggestions be in the hands of the chairman by February 15th, to facilitate preparations for the committee meeting in Atlanta, in March.

Montreat—One hundred and sixty-one men from throughout the General Assembly took part Jan. 4-6 in the 12th annual session of Assembly Men's Council. This was the largest group ever to attend an AMC meeting.

John J. Deifell of Greensboro, N. C., retiring president, presided during the three-day meeting at which plans were formulated for the year's work in 1700 local men's groups, and officers were elected to lead the men during 1957.

M. Elmer Taylor of Jacksonville, Fla., first vice-president of AMC in 1956 was elected to head the body in 1957. AMC is made up of the presidents of all synod and presbytery men's councils, plus advisors in the field of Christian education. Attending this 12th meeting were every president of every presbytery in the synods of Appalachia, Arkansas, Georgia, Kentucky, Louisiana, Mississippi, Texas and West Virginia. Only 13 of the 85 presbyteries were not represented.

Throughout the three-day meeting attention was given to the plans for the Men's Convention in Miami, Fla., Oct. 10-13. A feature of an evening presentation on the work of the Division of Radio and Television, Board of Church Extension, was the premier showing of "On to Miami" colored, sound movie that will be used throughout the Church to build interest in the convention. More than 10,000 men are expected to attend the Assembly-wide event.

Davidson—Winter religious services at Davidson College Feb. 10-13 will include two addresses by Dr. John S. Whale, prominent British theologian.

Dr. Whale will lecture on "The Nature of God" and "The Nature of History." He will raise the questions "Can God be both cosmic and personal?", and "Does God intervene in human events?"

The services will be held during the morning chapel period, and for the four evenings. The public will be welcome to join with the college community, in Chambers auditorium for morning services and the college church for evening worship.

Mecklenburg Presbytery, in its 125th Stated Session, disapproved of the proposed amendment to the Book of Church Order, Paragraph 31, relative to election of women to the Diaconate or Eldership, and approved the proposed amendment to Chapter 36 of the Confession of Faith, relative to marriage and divorce. Rev. Stuart D. Currie, a Queens College professor, was received from the Presbytery of Atlanta, Rev. Geo. W. Powell was received from the Presbytery of Athens, and a commission was appointed to install him pastor of the Pleasant Hills Church. Also, Rev. T. E. Nelson was received from Fayetteville Presbytery and steps were taken to install him pastor of the Biscoe and Star Churches.

The pastoral relations were dissolved between Dr. Harold D. Hayward and the Providence Church, and he was given a letter of transfer to the Presbytery of Albany, U.S.A. Rev. C. H. McLean was dismissed to Wilmington Presbytery, after the pastoral relations were dissolved between him and the East Monroe and Turner Presbyterian Churches.

Mr. Ernest D. Severs, a member of the Thomasboro Church and a Junior in Columbia Theological Seminary, and Mr. Jas. K. Wilson, a member of the Selwyn Avenue Church and a Junior in Union Theological Seminary, were received as candidates for the ministry.

Presbytery adopted a recommendation of the Sub-committee on Evangelism, of which Rev. S. H. Zealy is chairman, to have a simultaneous campaign of Visitation Evangelism April 7-10. Dr. James Appleby addressed the Presbytery on Evangelism.

Rev. Leighton Ford requested prayer for the Billy Graham New York Crusade. Dr. W. M. Walsh announced the completed plans for the exchange of ministers on February 24th, when there will be emphasis on World Missions. Sixteen commissioners and their alternates were elected to attend the meeting of the General Assembly. Hon. Horace McCall, past president of the Men of Mecklenburg Presbytery, gave a review of the year, in which eight new organizations were chartered.

Beginning February 15th, Miss Virginia Morris is to become Area Worker for Mecklenburg Presbytery.

The Stated Clerk, Rev. Malcolm R. Williamson, was unable to give a complete report on statistics.

The Session was held January 15th in the Selwyn Avenue Presbyterian Church, of which Rev. S. M. Inman is pastor. He gave a history of the origin, growth, and program of the church. Mr. Joe W. McLaney, an Elder of the First Church of Charlotte, retiring moderator, was succeeded by Rev. David Wilkinson, pastor of the Plaza Presbyterian Church. Rev. A. Leslie Thompson and Rev. R. W. Rayburn assisted the Stated Clerk as Assistant Clerk and Permanent Clerk, respectively.

The Presbytery enrolled 83 ministers and 87 Elders. The Council will select the place of the next meeting, to be held on April 16th.

R. H. Stone, Secretary

Report of the Winter Meeting of Winston-Salem Presbytery

The Presbytery of Winston-Salem convened for its Winter Adjourned Meeting at the George W. Lee Memorial Church, Winston-Salem, the Rev. Thomas C. Bryan, Minister, Tuesday, January 15th, 1957, 10:00 A.M. The devotional service was led by the Rev. Archie Jones of Lexington. Presbytery was called to order by the Moderator, Rev. Troy Young; the roll-call showed 22 ministers and 34 Ruling Elders present.

Two ministers were received by transfer: the Rev. I. E. Kirkman from Roanoke Presbytery and the Rev. R. L. Berry from Granville Presbytery. Mr. Kirkman will become the Pastor of the Highland Church, Winston-Salem, and Mr. Berry Pastor of the Sparta and Glade Valley churches.

The Rev. Percy A. Carter, Jr., for the past eighteen months serving the Dellabrook colored Mission in Winston-Salem, was at his own request dropped from the roll of the Presbytery and he was commended to the Rowan Baptist Association.

A Judicial Commission, appointed at the last regular meeting to look into the case of the Rev. L. J. Yelanjian, reported that it had "divested Mr. Yelanjian of his office without censure" for his failure for the past two years to engage in the regular duties of the ministry; this was under provision of paragraph 232 of the Book of Church Order.

A Commission appointed at the last meeting to organize the Dellabrook Mission in Winston-Salem into a church reported that this mission has been performed—the name selected for the church was "Dellabrook"—it serves a Negro section of the city.

The Presbytery voted in favor of the Amendment to the Book of Church Order for the Ordination of Women. It voted against the amendment to the Confession of Faith dealing with Marriage and Divorce.

An interesting popular meeting was held on World Missions; Ruling Elder Robert N. Marshall, Chairman of the Committee on World Missions, gave his report after which the Presbytery heard a very able address by Dr. William Rule of our Congo Mission.

The Revs. Robert A. White, Jr., and G. M. Hollenhead were elected commissioners to the General Assembly with Revs. Troy A. Young and Thomas C. Bryan as alternates. Ruling Elders J. J. Vess (Southminster, Winston-Salem, N. C.) and George Isenhour (Elkin, N. C.) were elected Commissioners to the General Assembly with Ruling Elders Tully D. Blair (Highland, Winston-Salem, N. C.) and Thos S. Boyd (Glendale Springs, N. C.) alternates.

Presbytery accepted an invitation from the Second Church, Lexington to hold its next regular Stated Meeting, May 7, 1957, in that church.

The Presbytery was adjourned after the reading of the minutes, with prayer by the Rev. R. B. Hildebrendt.

J. Harry Whitmore, Stated Clerk

BOOKS

EARLY LATIN THEOLOGY. S. L. Greenslade. Volume V, The Library of Christian Classics. Westminster Press. $5.00.

The fifth volume in this excellent series of the Library of Christian Classics presents selections from Tertullian, Cyprian, Ambrose, and Jerome. The editor has chosen the material to illustrate Latin thought on the life of the church as well as its nature and constitution. A helpful introduction precedes the work of each theologian.

Two selections are given from Tertullian—"The Proscriptions Against The Heretics" and "On Idolatry." Three of Cyprian's writings are presented — "The Unity of the Catholic Church," "The Problem of the Lapsed," and "The Baptismal Controversy."

Eight selections by Ambrose are set forth, all of which show that he was essentially a man of action. The editor reminds us that Ambrose as a writer was concerned above all with edification and then remarks, "He was neither an original thinker of the order of Augustine nor a scholar of the order of Jerome." Yet Dr. Greenslade concedes that Ambrose was a great prince of the church in his own right and it was given to him to help a greater man into the way of truth. It was Ambrose's preaching that showed Augustine how to understand the Old Testament and released him from some of his Manichaean difficulties. It was Ambrose who baptized Augustine into the Christian faith.

Six of Jerome's writings are found in this volume. Jerome is known especially for translating the whole of the Old Testament from Hebrew into Latin. He also translated the New Testament books from the Greek into Latin. Dr. Greenslade tells us that though Jerome was not a philosopher or an original theologian, he was the outstanding scholar of his time. He had the instincts of a scholar, and made contributions in the field of Biblical scholarship. We owe to him the principle that where possible Scripture should be studied in the original tongues but that translations should be used in the church by the people. The editor makes this appraisal on his translation of the Bible: "The version which he produced was, with all its faults, a very good one, far more reliable than anything available up to his own time, and not to be superseded in the West for many centuries. It is still of cardinal importance to the student of the text of the Scriptures, and still the official Bible of a great multitude of Christians."

Volume V is certainly one of the finest in the Library of Christian Classics. It is a work that should be on the library shelf of every theological student. This work should be of interest to all who are interested in the best of theological literature and one of the most fascinating sections of Church history.

—J.R.R.

VOL. XV NO. 41 FEBRUARY 6, 1957 $3.00 A YEAR

IT is something to be a missionary. The morning stars sang together and all the sons of God shouted for joy when they saw the field which the first missionary was to fill. The great and loving God, before whom angels veil their faces, had an only Son, and He was sent to earth as a missionary physician. It is something to be a follower, however feeble, in the wake of the great Teacher and only model missionary that ever appeared among men, and now that He is Head over all things, King of Kings, and Lord of Lords, what commission is equal to that which the missionary holds from Him? May I venture to invite young men of education, when laying down the plan of their lives, to take a glance at that of missionary? For my own part, I never cease to rejoice that God has appointed me to such an office."

DAVID LIVINGSTONE.

The Vote on Amendment to the Book of Church Order to permit Women Elders shows 27 Presbyteries have voted for the Amendment and 41 Presbyteries have voted Against. This leaves 17 Presbyteries yet to report.

THE SOUTHERN PRESBYTERIAN JOURNAL

Rev. Henry B. Dendy, D.D., Editor..........Weaverville, N. C.
Dr. L. Nelson Bell, Associate Editor..........Asheville, N. C.
Rev. Wade C. Smith, Associate Editor..........Weaverville, N. C.

EDITORIAL

"Think On These Things"

The conflicting voices in the world today create a problem of the first order for the Christian. Not only are there opposing ideologies which divide the world into two camps but the free world finds it impossible to maintain a balance of opinion on a multitude of problems.

Even a casual reading of the secular press and secular news magazines will show how many individuals and groups are beating the air in vain attempts to arrive at solutions for ever recurring or entirely new issues which arise.

In recent months there has been an ominous increase in "hate literature" being circulated through the mails. Some of it is certainly justified warning against Communism abroad and at home but through this same channel there is spewing forth a volume of anti-Semitic, anti-Catholic, and anti-EVERYTHING propaganda which can easily disturb, distort and misdirect the thinking of good people who receive it.

The net result of all of this conflict in outlook is to further confuse a world and national situation already seemingly confused to the limit.

Under such circumstances what should Christians do? There *are* certainties on which we can fix our minds; good and lovely things which we can promote; eternal verities which we can believe and which are the polestar of Christian faith and living.

We need Jesus Christ and the assurance of His forgiveness and of His cleansing power. We need the ever present power and blessing of the in-dwelling Holy Spirit. We need the comfort, guidance and wisdom which comes alone from making the Holy Scriptures our daily portion. We need the quiet strength and re-directing grace which comes from an attitude of unending prayer.

In other words, we need to make constant use of God's already provided means of grace. By their use our thinking is clarified, our judgments are settled in Him and His holy will, our attitudes are controlled by Christian love.

Paul, in his letter to the Phillipians, gives an admonition which will solve this problem: *"Finally, brethren, whatsoever things are true, whatsoever things are honest, whatsoever things are just, whatsoever things are pure, whatsoever things are lovely, whatsoever things are of good report; if there be any virtue, and if there be any praise, think on these things."*

—L.N.B.

Investing For Eternity

Investors in the stock market hurriedly turn to the pages of the daily papers to see what has happened to the value of their particular stock. This is the inevitable reaction of those whose affections at least in part center in the material.

What about your investment in World Missions?

Our church has investments in over 500 missionaries, thousands of national workers, many schools and hospitals scattered across the world.

How does their stock stand in God's exchange?

The writer has visited most of our mission fields, met hundreds of national Christians, seen many of our various institutions and had warm fellowship with the majority of our missionaries. Have we invested our money well? Are we getting good returns on our stock?

The answer is an unequivocal YES.

Every member of our church should be thankful for that which God is doing in the fields where we are represented. We should praise Him for the choice representatives we have sent out. They are superior men and women. Most of all they are consecrated, efficient and effective in the work God has given them to do.

But we need more such men and women and there is an alarming lag between the call and the number who are responding each year to that call.

Three things are needed: dedication of life, consecration of money and faithful daily prayer for world evangelization. Every Christian should share in this investment.

How much stock do you hold?

—L.N.B.

"Every Person Is of Infinite Value." ? ? ?

Is this statement true? We are told that it is from the Bible and drawn from a careful study of the Scriptures. What are the passages or texts which support it? No doubt, those who drew up this statement studied the Bible, but did they get this from the Bible? Or did they bring it to the Bible? Ought such a questionable premise be made the basis for a program which the whole Church is asked to promote?

The Scriptures are our rule of faith and practice, but we do not find that the Scriptures teach that every person, or indeed that any merely human person, is of infinite value. The Divine Person, each of the Persons of the Trinity, is infinite; but every human person is finite. Jesus said that a man is of more value than a sheep, and that a disciple is of more value than many birds. He told us to value our eternal life more than the riches of this world. But He did not say man is of infinite value. The Psalmist says that man is made but little lower than the angels. Ps. 8.4; Hebr. 2.7. The psalmist, 103.15, the prophet, Isaiah 40.6 and the apostle, I Peter 1.24, compare man to the grass of the field and his fading glory to that of the flower . . . over against the stability of the Word of God.

If every man were of infinite value God's plan to save man would only be a shrewd program to conserve values. If every man is of infinite value the logical conclusion is universalism. The God of that kind of thinking might be expected to be too smart to allow any infinite value to be lost.

Some even forget the clear line drawn in the Institutes between the infinite Creator and the finite creatures of His hand, Bk. I, chapters xiii and xiv, and ascribe to Calvin the infinite value of every human soul. Following Augustine, Calvin ascribes a value to man at the time of Christ's death for him, and at the time of an individual's conversion. Whatever remains in fallen man that is of God's workmanship still has value, despite the loss that man's sin has brought upon man.

Even in these cases, however, Calvin refers to his fuller treatment of the theme in his Commentary on Ephesians. There he goes back with Paul to the electing love of God focused on man before the foundation of the world. There he shows that God loved not because of any value in man — for man was not. Then He chose man to be holy and without blame before Him, even though He foresaw that man would be unholy and blameworthy — for He chose man in Christ.

In the second chapter of this great Epistle Paul lays before us the sin and wickedness of man. In the face of this portrayal of human iniquity, he asserts that God being rich in mercy — not for the sake of any alleged infinite value in man — but for His own great love wherewith He loved us — made us alive with Christ.

Now there are persons in God's electing love out of every nation and kindred and tribe — every sex and every color. If that be the truth that is aimed at, why not state it in Scriptural language, and on the basis of the Word of God, appeal for Christian conduct towards men of all races?

Instead of the allegedly Biblical principle, why not use the Bible itself, e.g., Rev. 7.9: "After these things I saw and behold a great multitude which no man could number out of every nation, and of all tribes and peoples and tongues, standing before the throne and before the Lamb, arrayed in white robes and with palms in their hands." "These are they which have come out of great tribulation and washed their robes and made them white in the blood of the Lamb." The word of our Lord in the parable of the Good Samaritan moves people in our Church who are not moved by the decision of the U. S. Supreme Court.

—W.C.R.

The Southern Presbyterian Journal, *a Presbyterian Weekly magazine devoted to the statement, defense, and propagation of the Gospel, the faith which was once for all delivered unto the saints,* published every Wednesday by The Southern Presbyterian Journal, Inc., in Weaverville, N. C.

Entered as second-class matter May 15, 1942, at the Postoffice at Weaverville, N. C., under the Act of March 3, 1879. Vol. XV, No. 41, February 6, 1957. Editorial and Business Offices: Weaverville, N. C. Printed in the U.S.A. by Biltmore Press, Asheville, N. C.

ADDRESS CHANGE: When changing address, please let us have both old and new address as far in advance as possible. Allow three weeks after change if not sent in advance. When possible, send an address label giving your old address.

Thus It Is Written

By Ralph Brewer

Matthew presented Jesus as the Messiah, and he, Mark, Luke and John referred often in their gospels to prophesies in the Old Testament which were fulfilled in the life, death and resurrection of Christ. Not only our Lord's birth and ministry but even his dying words were foretold in Psalms 22:1 and 31:5.

The prophets said a king of the line of David would come to rule and bless the world and Joseph and Mary could trace their genealogy back to David. "The Branch" is similar to "Nazareth" and so He became a Nazarene. Isaiah said He would be born of a virgin and Micah fixed the spot as Bethlehem. Hosea predicted the sojourn in Egypt and Isaiah said he would live at Nazareth in Galilee. The messenger to announce Him, Elijah-like John the Baptist, was described by Isaiah and Malachi.

Jeremiah forecast the massacre of children in Bethlehem and Isaiah said He would proclaim a jubilee, His mission would be to the Gentiles and His ministry would be featured by healing. Isaiah and the Psalms prognosticated that He would be rejected, hated and disbelieved but that His entry into Jerusalem would be triumphal. His betrayal for thirty pieces of silver was predicted in Zechariah and in the Psalms, Isaiah said He would die with malefactors and Zechariah pictured the smitten shepherd.

The Psalms, years before it happened, depicted the scene at the Cross when dice were thrown for His garments, and said vinegar and gall would be offered Him, that His side would be pierced but not a bone would be broken. Isaiah said He would be buried by a rich man and Psalms foretold He would rise the third day while Daniel predicted the destruction of Jerusalem.

Thus it is written, tying together the Old and New Testaments. He who believes the Bible accepts Christ, he who accepts Christ believes the Bible. But there is a final and sad note: Matthew, describing the scene in the garden of Gethsemane in the 26th chapter, 56th verse, wrote: "But all this was done that the scriptures of the prophets might be fulfilled. Then all the disciples forsook Him and fled."

The Wise Men and Their Gifts

(A New Year Message)

By Rev. J. Kenton Parker

A great deal has been said and written about these "wise men"; who they were, and where they came from. I will not enter into that discussion. We call them wise men. I believe there were several reasons why they were wise:

They were wise in searching the sky, since they had no Scriptures to search. Nature is one of God's Books; a revelation of His character and glory, as the Psalmist so beautifully expresses it; The heavens declare the glory of God.

They were wise enough not to worship the stars, as some of the Eastern people did, but looked beyond the stars to the God Who made them.

They were wise in following the star, living up to the best light they had, for this was a special star, going in a definite direction, and pointing to a special place.

They were wise in consulting those who had the Scripture. The star had led to Palestine, and there at Jerusalem were men who knew the prophesies concerning the Coming One. The Bible is our clearest revelation of God.

They were wise to fall down and worship the King when they found Him. They did not worship Mary or Joseph, but the Babe in the manger; the King. They opened their treasures and presented their gifts; gold, and frankincense and myrrh.

This leads me to the two questions which I wish to ask: What can we, as a church, give to Him? and What can we as individuals give to Him?

I. *What can we, as a Church,* as a Congregation, give to our King?

Jesus Christ, the Head of the Church is interested in, and concerned about, each particular church and congregation. He makes this very clear in His Letters to the Seven Churches of Asia. Each church, as a distinct group, has a personal relationship to Him. What can we give Him?

I am sure that what we have done in a material way, our new buildings, and our loving care of our church property, is pleasing to Him. I wish to turn from these things, however, and suggest a few very simple, but very important things.

said, Doctor, I am a sick woman; I want you to prescribe for me. He repeated, Go home, and read your Bible. She did, and was a new woman. I am sure there are many of us who need to do the same thing. It will make us well, physically and spiritually. Yes, give Him more of our time.

3. Give Him a firmer Faith. We like people to trust us; to believe in us. About the highest tribute I can give to a friend is to say, I would trust him with my life, and everything else I have. Can we not trust Our Best Friend that way? Let us give Him an unwavering faith. We do not know what is coming in the year ahead, but we do know that He will be there. He wants us to trust Him.

4. Let us *remember to thank Him,* to praise Him, to show our gratitude. Do you think to say, Thank you, Lord, when you have some narrow escape on the highway, or when some unexpected blessing comes your way?

5. Give Him our Homes; rededicate them to Him. If the family altar is broken down, build it again. The family that "prays together, stays together," as you have often heard. Is your family "praying together"?

6. Strive to grow like Him. He loves to see His children grow. To grow up into Him is something which will please Him very much. We are never complete until we are complete in Him.

7. Give Him the testimony of an out and out Christian Life. He needs our testimony. We are His letter of recommendation to a world that is sadly in need of a Saviour.

8. Give Him a deeper Love; a Love that "grows and glows": let our constant prayer be, More love to Thee, O Christ, More love to Thee.

As a Church, a congregation, and as individuals, may we open our treasures this morning and present our gifts to the King!

Helps To Understanding Scripture Readings in *Day by Day*

By Rev. C. C. Baker

Sunday, February 17, *I Peter* 1:3-9. The Christians to whom Peter wrote (vv.1-2) were suffering for their faith (v.6). Yet, he spoke to them in terms of joy (vv.6a,8) and hope (v.3). Where are the true hopes of the Christian placed (vv.3-4)? What advantages does this type of inheritance have over earthly treasures (v.4)? What does "in this you rejoice" (v.6a) refer to? Can you rejoice over your prospects in heaven? The Lord is able to hold steadfast those who wonder if they can be faithful (v.5). What divine purpose is there in the testings of this life (v.7)? What is their relation to our eternal inheritance? What relation does Christ have to the Christian's hope (v.3)? joy (v.8)? All of the truths of vv.3-9 are real for the Christian because of Christ.

Monday, February 18, *Genesis* 1:1-13. Genesis One is not a scientific treatise. It is a poetic hymn that tells the story of how God created the universe. It should be read in a devotional spirit. Discover all the facts you can about God. What relation does He have to the universe? Would He exist if the universe had never been made? Is He aware of what is in the universe? What is His attitude toward it? What do the words "God said . . . and it was so" reveal of God's power? The Christian is filled with awe and wonder as he realizes that the Lord Jesus participated in the creation of the universe (John 1:1-2; Hebrews 1:2). Your attitude toward Christ determines your attitude toward your Creator (John 5:23).

Tuesday, February 19, *John* 1:1-14. Think again of vv.1-3 in terms of the creation story of Genesis One. Who is the Word (v.14)? Jesus, the Son of God (v.14b), became a man in order to make us sons of God (v.12). It is indeed strange that when Christ came to make this Sonship available to men, His own people crucified Him (vv.10-11). All of the glory that John and the disciples beheld in Christ (v.14b), all of the grace and truth that was in Him (v.14a), comes into our lives when we receive Him (v.16). His presence in us is life itself (v.4). Through Christ the Christian is able to enter into the Creator's presence as a son (v.12) and call Him "Father" (Rom. 8:15). As we think of the benefits we have received freely in Christ, our hearts should respond in love to Him.

Wednesday, February 20, *Philippians* 2:5-11. To what in vv.6-8 does the "therefore" of v.9 refer? What is it about the ministry of Christ in v.8b that prompts God the Father to so honor the Son in vv.9-11? The name (v.9) that the Father is bestowing upon the Son for His work on earth is found in v.11. What is going to happen in heaven and on earth some day when the very name of the Lord Jesus is mentioned (vv.10-11)? A preview of that day is given in Revelation 5:6-14. Is the honor that you give to Jesus greater than the honor you give to any other name (v.9)? Is your honor of the lips only, or do you bow to Jesus as Lord in your life (v.11)?

Thursday, February 21, *I Peter* 2:1-10. How spontaneous was Peter's praise to the Lord (1:3a)? How real was his anticipation of heavenly things to come (1:3b-4)? How steady in all circumstances (1:5) and how sincere (1:7) his faith must have been! Do you think his love for Christ was any less an actuality than his love for close human friends (1:8a)? Was there any strain or pretense in the joy he found in the Lord (1:8b)? Could Peter have given the advice of 2:1 if he had not found freedom from these sins in his own life? of 2:2-3 if his own devotional life was no more than a duty? For Peter "witnessing for Christ" (v.9b) was a glad privilege, the whole of his Christian experience (vv.9-10) a wonderful, awe-inspiring miracle. What does this study of Peter's life reveal to you of your need for a living relationship to Christ?

Friday, February 22, *I Cor.* 13. Love is the very essence of the nature of God (I John 4:8). We prove to be Jesus' disciples by loving one another (I John 3:23-24). Notice the place that Paul gives to love in relation to all other Christian virtues (vv.1-3,8-9,13). Observe the descriptions given the greatest of eloquence (v.1), the ultimate in knowledge (v.2a), the maximum of faith (v.2b), and the highest in service (v.3) if love is not there. Read over the qualities of love mentioned in vv.4-7 slowly several times and think of each quality as it is applicable in your life. How do these qualities stand in contrast to your own human nature? Whether or not these qualities are manifested in our lives to any degree determines whether or not God in Christ dwells within our hearts.

Saturday, February 23, *Matthew* 25:31-40. Many times throughout His ministry Jesus spoke of the strong ties that made Him one with His followers. See, e.g., Matthew 12:46-50. How strongly did Christ identify Himself with His spiritual brethren in today's passage (vv.40,45)? Ought the good deed a Christian does for a fellow-believer have a deeper significance than the good deed he does for an unbeliever (Galatians 6:10)? Why (Matt. 25:45)? How serious, how real a thing, must the life of Christ dwelling within the believer be (vv.34, 41,46)? Have you been aware of the gravity of your behavior, physical or spiritual, toward the most insignificant, the "least," of your fellow-Christians? Read Matt. 18:3-6; Luke 10:16; Acts 9:4; I Cor. 8:12.

SUNDAY SCHOOL Lessons

LESSON FOR FEBRUARY 17

By THE REV. J. KENTON PARKER

Parables Of The Kingdom

Background Scripture: Matthew 13
Devotional Reading: Matthew 13:24-30; 36-43

This method of teaching — by parables — is used a great deal by our Master, but seldom elsewhere in the Bible. (See Job 27:1; Psalm 49:4; Psalm 78:2; Judges 9:7; Isaiah 5, Song of the Vineyard). The little girl's definition is a good one: A parable is an earthly story with a heavenly meaning. In these parables Jesus uses the ordinary everyday doings of men to illustrate vital truth concerning the nature of His kingdom. When the disciples asked, Why speakest Thou to them in parables, He replied, Because it is given unto you to know the mysteries of the kingdom of heaven, but to them it is not given. These people had stopped their ears and blinded their eyes and their hearts had become gross. They had no spiritual discernment. They usually failed to see the meaning or apply the lesson. In the case of the wicked husbandmen Mark tells us that they knew He had spoken this parable against them, and they sought to lay hold upon Him. To those who had eyes to see and ears to hear and a heart to respond, the parable meant a great deal. (See verse 16, Blessed are your eyes, etc.). Even the disciples were slow to understand at times and in some cases Jesus explained the meaning to them. Two of the ones in this chapter are explained.

I. *The Parable of the Sower,* (or Soils): Matthew 13:1-23.

The emphasis is upon the Soils. Christ was the greatest of sowers, and certainly no fault can be found with Him. We, too, are sowers of the seed. We may be careless or unfaithful, but not so with Jesus. The Seed is the Word. There can be no fault in the seed; not when sown by the Great Teacher. Now, let us turn to the four kinds of soil. These represent us; men and women.

First, there is the soil called the wayside. This is the hard beaten path. These paths would wind through the field and some of the seed would fall upon them. The preaching of the Gospel makes no impression on some people. The wicked one catches away the seed. I am afraid that there are many such hearers.

Second, the seed that fell upon "stony places." This is shallow soil which barely covers a rocky subsoil. The seed springs up quickly but has no depth of earth and when the sun is up it withers and dies. There are people like this everywhere. What preacher has not seen them? They are easily moved, but forget very soon. Dr. Beecher tells of preaching on board ship. The audience was moved to tears by his eloquent and touching sermon, but the dinner bell rang at the close of the service, and in ten minutes no one remembered the message, and you would not have known that such a service had been held.

The third is very common, I am afraid, in this busy age of ours. This seed fell among thorns and was choked. I knew a man who had a very fertile field, but it was literally covered with locust sprouts. He warned his tenant not to sow this field in grain, but the warning was unheeded and when I saw the field the locust sprouts were as high or higher than the wheat and it was practically impossible to reap any grain. We are living at a time when the cares of this world and the deceitfulness of riches are choking out the grain in many a fertile field.

The fourth is "good ground." It is deep and fertile and free from thorns. Thank God for the good soil! There is some in every community. In my forty years of ministry I could point to men and women who have brought forth, some sixty, some thirty, some even a hundredfold.

There is another encouraging thought. The Holy Spirit can make good soil out of bad. He can take the stony heart away, and give a heart of flesh; He can root out the thorns; He can break up a beaten path. The Word of God, when accompanied by the power of the Spirit, is like dynamite. It is the power of God unto salvation: it is living and active and sharper than a two-edged sword.

II. *Parable of the Tares:* 24-30; 36-43.

This parable, too, is interpreted by Jesus. It is the simple story of a man who sowed good seed in his field, but while men slept, his enemy came and sowed tares among the wheat and went his way. The point of the story is not so much the sowing of the tares, but the question of the servants and the answer given them. The servants wanted to go and gather up the tares at once, but they were told to let both grow until the harvest and the separation would take place then. The danger was, that in pulling up the tares they would pull up some of the wheat.

Jesus explains the parable at the request of the disciples. He that sowed the good seed is the Son of Man; the field is the world; the good seed are the children of the kingdom; but the tares are the children of the wicked one; the enemy that sowed them is the devil; the harvest is the end of the world; the reapers are the angels. The separation will come at the end of the world when the righteous and the wicked shall go to their places. (See Matthew 25:31,32; Revelation 14:14-20). I suppose all of us at times have thought that if all the wicked people could just be "rooted out," this world would be a much better place in which to live. The answer is, Let both grow together until the harvest. This does not mean, I take it, that we are to make boon companions of the wicked and partake of their wickedness. God says, Come out from among them and be separate. Jesus prays that we may be "in the world," but "not of the world." Then again, we are to be His witnesses in a wicked world. It may be that some of the "tares" may be changed into wheat. With God, nothing is impossible: we may snatch some as brands from the burning.

III. *Parable of the Mustard Seed:* 31,32.

This is commonly interpreted as meaning the outward growth of the kingdom from a tiny seed to an herb large enough for the fowls of the air to come and lodge in its branches. When you think of the call of Abraham and the promise God gave to him that his seed should be as the sand and the stars, or when you think of the church at Pentecost and the growth of the Christian Church ever since, you can see that both in the Old Testament and in the New, the Church has grown. I cannot pass this parable, however, without calling your attention to the interpretation which Dr. G. Campbell Morgan puts on this story. He thinks that there is an "unnatural growth" pictured here. For example, the Church after Constantine, became very popular; it developed into a semi-political organization with worldly power but little spirituality: the "birds of the air" — princes and leaders who were devoid of any real religion, took refuge in, and became a part of this worldly church. There is food for thought in this interpretation!

IV. *Parable of the Leaven:* 33.

This parable is usually understood as referring to the inward growth of the kingdom in the heart and life, and also its leavening power in the world. Leaven works quietly, but thoroughly, until the whole is leavened. So the work of God's Spirit changes men and society as a whole. Again, as in the parable of the Mustard Seed, Dr. Morgan has a word of warning. He reminds us that "leaven" is almost always used in the Bible to denote evil, not good. Jesus warns in no uncertain terms about the "leaven of the Pharisees and Sadducees, and Herod," and explains that by leaven He means "teaching." It is entirely possible for a church to become so permeated with this sort of leaven that it becomes powerless and apostate. As a great admirer of Dr. Morgan I feel bound to deeply respect what he says.

V. *Parable of the Treasures* 44.

The most valuable, the most important thing in the world is this "kingdom of heaven." Seek ye first the kingdom of God and His righteousness, and all these things shall be added unto you. When the man in the parable finds the treasure, he sells all that he has and buys the field where he had found the treasure. Do not get confused by minor details. The main point is the supreme value of the kingdom. We are to forsake all that we have, if necessary, and follow Him. The rich young ruler did not realize the value of the treasure upon which he turned his back.

VI. *Parable of the Pearl of Great Price:* 45,46.

The main teaching is similar to the other. The man who found the treasure seemed to come upon it accidentally and was surprised when he found it, while the man in this parable is a pearl merchant, seeking goodly pearls. Salvation seems to come to some when they least expect it, but they recognize its value. There are others who are "seekers after truth." God promises that we shall find Him if we seek for Him with all our heart.

VII. *Parable of the Net:* 47-50.

The point in this parable is very much like the one in the parable of the tares. The net gathers all sorts of fish, some good, some bad. They draw it to shore and there separate the bad from the good. So it shall be at the Judgment.

YOUNG PEOPLES Department

YOUTH PROGRAM FOR FEBRUARY 17

By THE REV. B. HOYT EVANS

The Testimony We Bear

Hymns: "Rejoice, Ye Pure In Heart"
"I'll Go Where You Want Me To Go"
"Blessed Assurance, Jesus Is Mine"

Scripture: I Corinthians 13 and Matthew 23:34-40.

Program Leader's Introduction:

When we identify ourselves with Christ and His church, we claim to be His representatives. Every one of us who believes in Christ and who has united with the church is recognized by the world as one of Christ's people. We say we are Christ's representatives, but does our way of living truly represent Him to the world? What we say and do is our testimony. Is our testimony true to the One Whom we claim to represent? Do people get an accurate idea of Christ Jesus when they hear our words and behold our actions day in and day out? If we are not giving a true picture of Jesus in our living, we are not bearing true testimony.

If we are not always bearing a true witness to our Saviour, what can we do about it? First of all, we can be obedient to His will. We can keep the commandments He has given us. This does not mean a mere grudging, legal obedience, but a willing obedience of the heart. It means obeying God because we want to. It is a matter not only of our words and actions but of the motives and attitudes that underlie all words and actions. God is concerned about our outward conduct, but He is more concerned about the condition of our hearts. What we are at heart determines what we do. A half-hearted observance of all the "Thou shalt nots" of God's law will not produce a true testimony to Christ. A true testimony must be based on right attitudes. Our speakers will help us to see what the right attitudes are.

First Speaker:

Before a person can bear true testimony to Christ, he must have the right attitude toward God. What is that right attitude? The Bible sums it up in one word, "love." If we love God with heart, soul, mind, and strength, then we shall have the right attitude toward Him. If we love God, we shall put Him first in our lives. If we love Him, we shall worship Him in the way He desires. If we love Him, we shall surely reverence His name. If we love Him, we shall keep His day of rest and worship. If we love Him, we are sure to be faithful in our reading of His word and in our prayers. If we love Him, we shall want to be very active in the work and service of His church. If we love Him, we shall want never to miss an opportunity to worship Him and learn of Him in the services of the church. If we really love Him, we shall observe all the "Thou shalt nots" naturally and joyfully.

How do we come to love God? We cannot pass a law which requires everyone to love God. Love does not work that way. If love has to be commanded, it is not really love. We cannot issue an order that we ourselves and other people must love God. How do we love God, and why do we love Him. "We love Him because He first loved us." That is what the Bible says, and that is the true answer. We grow in our love to God, as we become more aware of His wondrous love for us in Jesus Christ. We can lead other people to love God by showing them how God loved them and sent His only-begotten Son to die for their sins. The way to love God is to keep one's eyes fixed on the Cross.

Second Speaker:

If we have the right attitude toward God, we shall also have the right attitude toward other people. If we love God, we must love our brothers also. This is necessary to our bearing a true testimony to Christ. We do not represent Christ Who loved people, unless we love them also.

If we really love our brother, we shall naturally fulfill all the requirements of the law with regard to him. If we love him, we shall be glad to respect whatever authority God has given him over our lives. If we love him, we shall be interested in guarding his life and health. If we love him, we shall respect his character and want to do all we can to make it strong. If we love him, we shall do all we can to safeguard his property. If we love him, we shall respect and protect his reputation. If we really love the world as God loved the world, we shall

(Continued on Page 11)

A One-Minute Message on Stewardship

February

Paul was a man with a missionary passion. He was convinced that the Christ who saved him could also save others. He saw God's gracious purpose of salvation as the purpose reached to all men. It was impossible for men to catch Paul's spirit without becoming men who were possessed by the passion to win others to Christ.

Paul and his converts stood together in a fellowship of prayer. Paul's letters were filled with tender passages in which he reveals the way he bore the burden of the care of the churches in prayer to God. He prayed for the churches. He prayed constantly for his friends as individuals. Through prayer the struggling churches scattered over the Roman Empire were bound into a great fellowship in Christ.

February - Message from "Stewardship in the New Testament Church" by Rolston.

Can we not fellowship with those in the foreign field who have caught His passion for the evangelism of the world? We can become partners with them - indeed partners with God, through our prayers and our gifts. Both may be measured by our love and faith in Him.

Paul said "And God shall supply every need of yours according to his riches in glory in Christ Jesus."

How To Get Along

1. Keep skid chains on your tongue; always say less than you think. Cultivate a low, persuasive voice. *How you say it often counts more than what you say.*

2. Make promises sparingly and keep them faithfully, no matter what it costs you.

3. Never let an opportunity pass to say a kind and encouraging word to or about somebody. Praise good work done, regardless of who did it. If criticism is needed, criticize helpfully, never spitefully.

4. Be interested in others; in their pursuits, their welfare, their homes and families. Make merry with those that rejoice; with those who weep, mourn. Let everyone you meet, however humble, feel that you regard him as one of importance.

5. Be careful. Keep the corners of your mouth turned up. Hide your pains, worries, and disappointments under a smile. Laugh at good stories, and learn to tell them.

6. Preserve an open mind on all debatable questions. Deliberate but do not argue. *It is a mark of superior minds to disagree and yet be friendly.*

7. Let your virtues, if you have any, speak for themselves, and refuse to talk of another's vices. Discourage gossip. Make it a rule to say nothing of another unless it is something good.

8. Be careful of another's feelings. Wit and humor at the other fellow's expense are rarely worth the effort, and may hurt where least expected.

9. Pay no attention to ill-natured remarks about you. Simply live so that nobody will believe them. Disordered nerves and bad digestion are a common cause of back-biting.

10. Don't be too anxious about your awards. Do your work, be patient and keep your disposition sweet, forget self, and you will be rewarded.

—From "TIPS"

The Seed Had Taken Root

The Ybor City Presbyterian Mission celebrated the twentieth anniversary of the Rev. and Mrs. Walter Passiglia's ministry in that community. As part of that week-long celebration, three of us, now ministers, were asked to come back and conduct services during that time. I was asked to deliver the sermon on the Lord's Day.

During the part of the worship hour being conducted by Mr. Passiglia, I glanced at the announcements in the bulletin. One particular notice moved me deeply as I sat there waiting for my part of the service. My eyes fell upon the names of a list of children who had been received into the membership of the church the previous week. Two of these were the children of Manuel Navarro, one of the many young people who had been reached for Christ in the early years of the Mission's work.

For more than fifteen years, Manuel has been one of those "clock-and-calendar-Christians," indispensable, dependable, faithful. For some fifteen years he has been one of the bul-

call upon the name of the Lord shall be saved. How then shall they call on Him in whom they have not believed? and how shall they believe in Him of whom they have not heard? and how shall they hear without a preacher? And how shall they preach, except they be sent? Romans 10:12-14.

It pleased God by the foolishness of preaching to save them that believe. I Cor. 1:21.

And I heard the voice of the Lord saying, WHOM SHALL I SEND? and WHO WILL GO FOR US? Then said I . . . Here am I: SEND ME! Isaiah 6:8.

Go therefore and teach all nations. Matthew 28:19,20.

How beautiful are the feet of them that preach the gospel of Peace and bring glad tidings! Isaiah 52:7; Romans 10:15.

Mrs. Charles J. Knapp
Moultrie, Georgia

YOUNG PEOPLE'S DEPARTMENT

(Continued from Page 9)

do all we can to lead the world to God through faith in Christ.

Just as it is useless to command a person to love God, so it is useless to command him to love his brother. It is only when we see God's love for us and for other people, that we really begin to love them ourselves. We do not really love until the flame is kindled in our hearts by the love of God. If we are concerned about being obedient to God's will, we must learn to love one another. The way to learn this love is to behold increasingly the love which God has for us and for others.

Program Leader:
If we really love God and one another, it will be seen in all our words and deeds, and it will mean that we are bearing a strong and true testimony for Christ.

CHILDRENS Page

The Flood - Continued

Noah and his family and the animals, reptiles, birds and insects were kept safely in the ark while the great flood lasted about five months. All other living beings were drowned in the waters that covered the earth. When Noah began to wonder if the waters were subsiding, he opened the little window and sent out a raven which flew back and forth. Then he sent out a dove and the dove returned. Again he sent out the dove, and this time she brought back an olive leaf in her mouth. So Noah knew the waters were going down. Finally the ark rested on Mount Ararat, and soon afterward the dry ground appeared all around. Then Noah let all the creatures out, while he and his family set up an altar, thanking God for His wonderful care of them. And God put a rainbow in the sky as a sign and a promise that the earth would never again be covered by a flood. (Genesis 8)

G.

NEWS of CHURCHES around the World

Report on Presbyterian Negro Work Campaign

By The Rev. P. D. Miller, D.D.

In May of 1953 an effort was launched to raise $2,000,000 to help finance an advance movement in our Presbyterian Negro Work. Stillman College and the Division of Negro Work were to share equally in the funds raised.

At the time of this report, January 18, 1957, a total of $1,924,020 has been collected from pledges made in the campaign. Late in 1956, Stillman College qualified for the full $100,000 conditional grant made during the campaign by an anonymous Georgia Foundation. Including the Foundation grant, Stillman received through this effort a total of $1,000,290, which puts her just over the goal originally sought.

What this money has meant to our Negro College can be fully understood only by those who knew it before and after the campaign. Two beautiful new buildings have been erected, another has been completely modernized and a substantial addition has been made to the permanent endowment. The faculty has been strengthened and the student body very much enlarged. In 1953 we had at Tuscaloosa a poorly equipped school, undertaking to do college work without accreditation. Today Stillman is a fully accredited four year college.

The Negro Work Division of the Board of Church Extension has received as its part of the campaign $850,140 and has credited $72,963 which was given directly to new building projects in the early days of the campaign. This makes a total of $923,103 raised for the purchase of sites and the erection of Negro churches, in strategic locations. These sites have been chosen in new Negro residential areas, some of them adjacent to large housing developments, and several near the campus of Negro colleges. Twenty-four new churches have been completed at a total of about $825,000, of which $540,559 was appropriated from campaign funds. Eight additional sites have been purchased and appropriations made for three buildings not yet erected. A total of approximately $700,000 has been appropriated from campaign funds for all these new projects. Some thirty-five locations are involved in eleven different Synods.

This work could never have been done without the assistance and over-sight of Church Extension Committees and Executives of white presbyteries. In many cases the white presbyteries are giving financial aid through their regular budgets and encouraging the Negro churches to reach self-support. As a result of all this we have practically doubled the size of our Negro membership and have more than doubled its strength. It is generally conceded that nothing comparable to this has been done by any other denomination in the South. Such an accomplishment is the more remarkable when one considers the stresses and strains of these recent years. Very much remains to be done but a real start has been made.

Gifts to the Negro Work Campaign by Synods are as follows:

Alabama	$122,878	Missouri	$ 35,519
Appalachia	175,307	North Carolina	233,599
Arkansas	62,793	Oklahoma	12,984
Florida	115,848	South Carolina	107,884
Georgia	192,367	Tennessee	98,868
Kentucky	49,669	Texas	222,223
Louisiana	54,821	Virginia	168,510
Mississippi	87,335	West Virginia	68,048

Foundations and individuals outside our Assembly gave $115,367.

Stillman College and the Division of Negro Work unite in thanking God for His blessing upon this missionary effort. Gratitude is here expressed to every individual, organization and congregation which worked and gave to make the campaign of 1953 a success. Additional gifts are still coming in and all of them are needed; however, no further notices concerning pledges will be sent from the campaign office, except upon request.

The Princeton Choir

The Princeton Seminary Group will leave Princeton, New Jersey, on Tuesday, June 4, for its twelfth annual summer tour. During the past eleven summers this group has sung in every state in the Union, every province in Canada except Newfoundland, in Cuba, Mexico, Guatemala, Alaska, Hawaii, Japan and Korea.

This year the choir will visit Puerto Rico and possibly the Dominican Republic and Cuba, as well as Virginia, North Carolina, South Carolina, Georgia, Florida, Alabama, Mississippi, Louisiana and eastern Tennessee. About five weeks will be devoted to the States and three weeks to the islands of the West Indies. As usual, the choir will sing on the average of twice a day for eight weeks.

Invitations from the areas listed above will be considered in the order of their receipt. The group, which is willing to sing in any church, regardless of size, depends entirely for its support upon a free-will offering and entertainment in the homes. The choir sings not only in churches, but often in hospitals, prisons, youth camps, schools, colleges, armed forces bases, business men's clubs, on radio and television and occasionally in factories.

For further information, address David Hugh Jones, Princeton Theological Seminary, Princeton, New Jersey, and a folder explaining all the requirements will be mailed immediately.

Church Extension

REPORT OF DECEMBER 1956

Budget 1956	$1,400,000.00
Receipts to Date	1,070,436.67
Percentage of Annual Budget Received to Date	76.46%
Balance Needed for The Year	329,563.33

G. B. Strickland, Treasurer

FLORIDA

Tampa—Mayor Nick Nuccio of Tampa, assisted by Dr. E. S. Campbell, chairman of the home missions committee of Westminster Presbytery, have broken ground for a new West Tampa Presbyterian Church. The church will cost about $100,000.

GEORGIA

Atlanta—The Rev. Robert C. Pooley, Jr., pastor of the Presbyterian Church of Summerville, Ga., and an Air National Guard chaplain, has been selected secretary of the newly organized Atlanta chapter of the U. S. Military Chaplains Association.

LOUISIANA

Shreveport—Dr. Louis H. Evans, minister-at-large for the Presbyterian Church, U.S.A., will speak on evangelism at the First Presbyterian Church in Shreveport on February 15. Dr. W. L. McLeod is pastor of First Church.

A week of visitation evangelism coupled with a week of preaching services is planned in most of the churches participating in the program of Intra-Synod Exchange of Ministers, March 4 - April 21. Presbyterian ministers in the southern part of the Synod will exchange pulpits with ministers of the northern half of the Synod during part of this period.

The Rev. Arthur Strickland of Tallulah, La., is chairman of evangelism in Red River Presbytery.

Monroe—A Leadership Training School for the Eastern Area of Red River Presbytery will be held Feb. 4-8, at the First Presbyterian Church of Monroe. Leaders to conduct sessions each evening include the Rev. Paul Freeland, Nashville, Tenn.; Miss Florence Bennett, Baton Rouge, La., and Mrs. Marcus Mapp and the Rev. Ben Oliphant, Monroe.

Monroe—A house adjoining the campus of Northeast Louisiana State College has been acquired for the college's Presbyterian Student House. "Westminster House," as it will be known, will be the center of Presbyterian activities until a permanent Westminster Center is built sometime in the future. It is to be the headquarters of Mrs. Marcus Mapp, director of Campus Christian Life at NLSC. Funds for the purchase of Westminster House are expected to come through the 1957-58 campaign for Campus Christian Life in the synod and presbytery.

New Orleans—Dr. John S. Land, pastor of the St. Charles Avenue Presbyterian Church here has been appointed by the Greater New Orleans Federation of Churches to a committee whose purpose is to investigate possible sites for a Protestant Chapel and headquarters for the Federation in downtown New Orleans.

Additional gifts of $38,200 and $1000 have been given anonymously toward the project recently. Dr. A. M. Serex, pastor of the Rayne Memorial Methodist Church, and president of the Federation of Churches said that these amounts added to the more than $60,000 already received, assures the "reality of a dream long possessed by Protestant leaders in Greater New Orleans. The creation of a downtown Protestant center will be accomplished as speedily as possible."

Members of the committee who will serve with Dr. Land include Mrs. L. K. Benson, president of the United Church Women, and a member of the Church of the Covenant (Presbyterian); Richard F. Lawton of the St. Charles Avenue Baptist Church; W. W. Pope of St. George's Episcopal Church; J. W. Reilly Sr. of Rayne Memorial Methodist Church; Dr. J. D. Gray, pastor of the First Baptist Church.

New Orleans—Announcement of the installation of two elders and eight deacons at Canal Street Presbyterian Church here was made by the Rev. Pat Easterling, church pastor.

New elders ordained and installed in January are F. O. Hultberg and Frank King, Sr.

New deacons ordained and installed include Carl Reuning, Jaime Pertuz, Calvin Sanford, Sr., and Stanley Egdorf. Deacons reinstalled are: John Bellott, J. B. Davies, Sr., William Green, and Louis Nick.

MISSISSIPPI

Jackson—A convocation in this city launched the Jackson phase of Belhaven College's $1,500,000 development program which is underway. The Jackson part of the program began January 24.

Among benefits Belhaven College will receive from the development program will be a new $500,000 science building and dormitory.

After Mississippi Synod approved the campaign earlier, the first phase for $250,000 was launched and that quota went over the top.

Following this, a number of Jackson business men set an objective of $250,000 to be raised in the city.

The Board of Trustees of Belhaven has been working and planning for the development program for some time.

A steering committee for the Jackson area has been working since the summer of 1956.

NEW YORK

New York—In the New York offices of the Billy Graham Crusade, announcement was made this week of the resignation of Jerry Beavan, effective as of February 1st. Mr. Beavan has been Public Relations Director of the Billy Graham Evangelistic Association.

Beavan, who has been on a two-month rest vacation, explained that health was the basic factor in the decision, together with the necessity of curtailing the excessive travel which has averaged 100,000 flying miles per year during the past six years.

Evangelist Graham in accepting the resignation "with regret" announced that Beavan would serve in a behind-the-scenes advisory capacity to the Graham staff in the direction of the forthcoming New York Crusade, which organization Mr. Beavan had largely developed during the past year.

NORTH CAROLINA

Charlotte — Queens College has been pledged $100,000 by Trinity Presbyterian Church as a gift in anticipation of the college fund raising campaign which will begin in the fall, Dr. Edwin R. Walker, president of the college, has announced. The Trinity congregation met on the Queens campus from the time it was organized in 1951 until its first building was erected in 1955.

Raleigh—Mrs. Harold J. Dudley, wife of the Executive Secretary of the Synod of North Carolina and Presbyterian minister Dr. Harold J. Dudley, has been elected president of Raleigh Woman's Club.

Mrs. Dudley is a graduate of the Assembly's Training School and a former Director of Christian Education. She has been active in civic and church work all over the Southeast and is one who carries Christian citizenship over into her club life.

Because of Mrs. Dudley's belief in carrying Christian citizenship into civic work, classes in Bible are now offered at the N. C. Woman's Prison, with classes becoming so popular that every one of them is packed, and the third six-week-session is now in progress.

A course in family relations for the prison women is in the planning stage at the present, because of Mrs. Dudley.

Davidson—Gifts to Davidson College in 1956 totaled more than $800,000, an increase of 80 per cent over 1955 contributions.

President John R. Cunningham said today that final 1956 figures showed $839,000 was given to the college. This was an increase of $370,537 over the $468,667 donated in 1955.

Most of the money went into the college endowment fund, and almost $150,000 into plant improvements.

The scholarship endowment is in honor of the late Rev. William McIlwaine Thompson, and his brother, Dr. W. Taliaferro Thompson, Jr., both of Richmond, Va., and both 1934 graduates of Davidson.

Reviewing college finance trends, Dr. Cunningham cited the unprecedented "Program for Harvard," announced by President Nathan M. Pusey. Harvard will seek from 75 to 100 millions, and states in Dr. Pusey's words: "all colleges that are alive are in need."

Dr. Cunningham agreed with Dr. Pusey that "a college or university is rich or poor not in terms of its visible resources, but only as these are set against the variety and extent of its full program and activity, and against its demonstrated capacities and ambitions."

Also included in Davidson's 1956 tabulation was $225,000 from the Ford Foundation, $145,000 for faculty salary endowment and $80,000 as an accomplishment grant. Similar amounts are scheduled to be received from the Foundation in June.

The college's total endowment is now more than $8,000,000. The Board of Trustees have voted to increase enrollment gradually from the current 850 to a maximum 1,000, but to govern the increase with improvement of salaries, plant and other facilities.

Greenville—The Presbytery of Albemarle, consisting of ministers and elder representatives from 53 Presbyterian Churches in Eastern North Carolina, met in its regular winter session at the Plymouth Presbyterian Church, Tuesday, January 15th.

Two important questions confronting the ministers and elders were the widely debated proposed changes in the Book of Church Order and the Confession of Faith passed by the General Assembly last Spring and sent to the Presbyteries for their discussion and action. Albemarle Presbytery voted to approve both of these changes. The first relates to permitting women to be selected elders and deacons in the Church. The other relates to divorce and remarriage.

The Moderator of the Presbytery was Dr. John Hay of Ahoskie; the Recording Clerk, Rev. J. W. B. Brooks of Rocky Mount, and General Secretary, Rev. Thomas M. Davis of Greenville.

The General Secretary reported that gifts of the Churches to Benevolences for General Assembly, Synod and Presbytery work amounted to $120,473 for 1956 and that they had accepted a budget of $140,738 for 1957.

Dr. C. I. Lewis, former pastor of the Tabb Street Presbyterian Church of Petersburg, Virginia, was received and arrangements were made for his installation as pastor of the First Presbyterian Church of Goldsboro.

SOUTH CAROLINA

Columbia — Groundbreaking ceremonies have been held for the new Forest Lake Presbyterian Church, Columbia, and the construction of a sanctuary and Sunday School building is under way. A sanctuary seating 400 persons and Sunday School classrooms for 800 persons will be provided for the congregation that was organized last fall. A larger sanctuary, seating 1,000 people, will be built later. A fellowship hall, which will accommodate 200, is in the present plans.

The church is in contemporary style, of brick and glass, and present construction is expected to be completed by June.

TENNESSEE

Nashville—Mrs. Everett E. Gourley, Jr., missionary for the Presbyterian Church, U.S., to West Brazil, died in Sao Paulo January 14. Funeral services were held January 15.

Mrs. Gourley, the former Miss Nancy Armistead of Montreat, N. C., was the wife of the business manager of the West Brazil Mission, and was herself serving in educational work in the mission.

A son, Kevin Armistead Gourley, was born to the couple on December 25, and another son, Blanton Craig, was born in Brazil, in 1955.

Mrs. Gourley was the daughter of the Rev. and Mrs. W. H. Armistead, formerly pastor of Friendship Presbyterian Church in Black Mountain, N. C., who are now living in Ormond Beach, Fla. Mrs. Gourley held her membership in the Black Mountain Church. She received her education at Bob Jones University, Montreat College, and Queens College.

The Gourleys sailed for Brazil in June 1954, and since 1955 have made their home in Patrocinio.

Mr. and Mrs. Everett E. Gourley, Sr., were visiting the missionaries at the time of the younger Mrs. Gourley's death.

TEXAS

Houston—A groundbreaking service was held January 13, between the two morning worship services as Bellaire Presbyterian Church of Houston began construction of a new sanctuary.

After a brief worship service at the site of the new building, several representatives of the church organizations and activities took formal part in the groundbreaking ceremony, along with invited guests of the church who were: Dr. Charles King of the First Presbyterian Church, Dr. Robert Bullock, the first pastor of the Bellaire Church, Dr. Malcolm Purcell, representing the Presbytery, and others.

Each person who wished to share in the building was invited to turn a spade of dirt.

Dallas—Members of the Wynnewood Presbyterian Church at Dallas were shot at church January 13, according to the church's pastor, the Rev. Daniel A. Baker—shot with health protective Salk anti-polio vaccine, that is.

Some 300 adults and children lined up at the church offices following both morning worship services to take part in the inoculation program.

The plan for the immunization against the disease came from Rev. Mr. Baker, and the doctor-members of the Wynnewood Church volunteered their time free to administer the program. Plans are now being made to administer the remaining two shots which will make the vaccine thoroughly effective. The congregation will receive the other shots at the church on other Sunday mornings.

The doctors who gave their services for the program were Dr. Carol O. Haymes, Dr. J. C. Piranio, and Dr. William D. Crane. Nurses who helped with the shots were Miss Florence Morrell, Mrs. Forrest Ray, and Mrs. S. Swafford, along with three student nurses: Miss Davelyn Pritchett, Miss Connie McGee and Miss Donna Lowery.

A reported 86 children and young people took advantage of the vaccine furnished free by the city for all persons under 20 years of age. The others were charged only for the cost of the vaccine.

Commerce—Two ruling elders were ordained and installed and four deacons were installed, three of them ordained, in the Commerce church in early January. D. C. Abernathy, Jr., and Paul F. Street, former deacons in the congregation, were ordained and installed as elders. Malcolm D. Calhoun, Jr., Kenneth Michels and Grover Sims were ordained and installed deacons at the same time. G. A. Lynch, having been ordained previously, was installed a deacon. Reports to Paris Presbytery for 1956 are among the most encouraging in the history of the church: 39 additions, twenty of these by profession of faith, for a membership, the first time in the life of the congregation, of 200; benevolent contributions almost 40% above presbytery's quota; and completion of air-conditioning of the sanctuary and education building without debt.

Dallas—The Texas Presbyterian Foundation will receive $2,000,000 from the sale of American Liberty Oil Company, it was announced Jan. 9 by Dr. Hubert H. Hopper, Foundation director, and Toddie Lee Wynne, American Liberty President.

This is believed to be the largest single transaction ever to involve the Presbyterian Church, U.S., and its institutions. Of the two million, $600,000 is earmarked for specific purposes, the announcement stated. The remaining $1,400,000 will go into the foundation's endowment fund for improving all the institutions of the Synod of Texas.

Austin College in Sherman will receive $300,000 for a chapel; the Pan-American School in Kingsville, $100,000; MO-Ranch, the Presbyterian conference ground near Hunt, Texas, $100,000; and Hollins College in Virginia, $100,000 for a chapel to be named after Mrs. Wynne's mother, Mrs. Allie Nash Young.

Hollins College is not affiliated with the Presbyterian Church, but the Texas Presbyterian Foundation will administer the $100,000 going to the school, Mr. Wynne explained. Mrs. Wynne's mother, Mrs. Wynne, and the Wynne daughters are all graduates of the college.

The Texas oilman has long taken an important part in the work of the Presbyterians in Texas. It has been his custom to provide a plane each year for the use of Austin Seminary Seniors to make a flying visit to headquarters of the Church in Atlanta, Richmond, and Nashville. During 1956 Mr. Wynne was chairman of the Texas Presbyterians' "Together for Christ" campaign, which raised more than $5,000,000 for the Synod's educational institutions. The Wynnes are members of Highland Park Presbyterian Church in Dallas.

VIRGINIA

Montgomery Presbytery met in its 243rd Stated Meeting in the Presbyterian Church of Buchanan, Virginia, on Tuesday, January 22, 1957, at 10 A.M.

In the absence of the Moderator, Ruling Elder Arthur B. Richardson, Rev. J. L. Coppock acted as the retiring Moderator by conducting the opening devotional service of worship, preaching the opening sermon, on the subject, "First Things First", from the Scripture passage of Matthew 6:24-34 and making the opening prayer. There were present thirty-seven Ministers and forty-five Ruling Elders. Rev. John A. Ricks was elected

Moderator. Rev. Howard C. Leming was granted a letter of dismissal to Bluestone Presbytery that he may accept the call of the First Church of Welch, W. Va., to become its pastor. Rev. John A. Ricks was elected to succeed Rev. H. C. Leming as Assistant Clerk for a term of three years ending with the January Meeting of 1960. Rev. Robert F. Field was received from Winchester Presbytery, and given Evangelistic Powers for one year that he may organize a church in the Colonial Heights section of Roanoke, Va. Rev. Henry L. Willis was received from Greenbrier Presbytery and arrangements were made for him to be installed as pastor of the First Presbyterian Church of Narrows, Va. Rev. Millard M. Stephens was received from East Mississippi Presbytery and arrangements were made for his installation as pastor of the High Bridge Presbyterian Church of Natural Bridge, Va. This was the first meeting of Presbytery after the changed boundaries went into effect. By this change Presbytery lost to West Hanover Presbytery the Churches of: First of Lynchburg, Westminster, Rivermont, Quaker Memorial, Bethesda, Jehovah-Jireh, Academy, Altavista, Castle Craig, Otterwood and Pisgah.

Presbytery also lost to West Hanover Presbytery the following Ministers: E. B. McGukin, E. A. Woods, W. W. Williamson, J. E. Long and F. C. Hutcheson. By the same change of boundaries of Presbytery, we received the following churches: Anderson Memorial, Forest Hills, Irisburg and Kate Anderson. By the same change of boundaries

did great things. They did them by means of a Christian education program which has always been an essential part of the life of our Presbyterian Church. Why do we not do more of these same things?"

Dr. Liston points out the great Reformed tradition in education was well carried on until recent years. He shows that in the 20th century Calvinism has not placed the same emphasis upon education and that our desertion of the great Calvinistic tradition goes beyond the matter of money. The author urges Presbyterians to realize that the maintenance and propagation of the Christian faith at the highest level of intellectual life is a major problem of our time and is at this moment being very seriously neglected by our Presbyterian Church.

The conclusion Dr. Liston reaches is that the Presbyterian Church must show a new earnestness and new courage in the field of educational leadership in the United States. He writes, "The Presbyterian Church stands in a position of peculiar responsibility in the United States holding the tradition of educational leadership for all the modern world. Our branch of Presbyterianism is not the largest but the most compact of American Presbyterianism. Jesus said, 'To whom much is given, of him shall much be required.' "

This volume should cause Presbyterians to have a higher appreciation of their educational heritage and challenge them to promote Christian education that emphasizes the Reformed Faith.

John R. Richardson

A TREASURY OF STORIES. Herbert V. Prochnow. W. A. Wilde Co. $2.00.

The hundreds of interesting items that make up this practical reference book have been carefully selected to be suitable for a wide variety of occasions. Each story, illustration and epigram has many applications. The book is planned to be of value in round table discussions, men's church clubs, women's church organizations and leaders of young adult groups. The author is an officer of a large Chicago bank and has had large experience in church work for many years.

INSPIRING TALKS TO JUNIORS. Marion G. Gosselink. W. A. Wilde Co. $2.50.

This new collection of inspiring talks to boys and girls discusses Biblical and ethical themes. Pastors, Sunday School superintendents who face a weekly deadline in giving a devotional message to children will find helpful material in this volume. Parents who want practical help for the spiritual training of children in the home will also find this work useful.

SHOULD CHRISTIANS DRINK? Everett Tilson. Abingdon Press. $2.00.

Dr. Tilson begins this volume by examining the major source of our Christian faith—the Bible. He holds that a dynamic and functional approach supports abstinence. He points out that literal interpretation alone of the Bible does not forbid drinking. He gives a historical survey of the attitude of the churches on the subject of drinking.

Very clearly the author shows how alcohol has been the destroyer of important spiritual values. Evidence is presented here that the Christian should answer with a positive "No" the question "Should Christians drink?"

WANTED

MEN AND WOMEN, 25-30 YEARS OF AGE, WELL TRAINED

For important work overseas in the service of Christ and His Kingdom. The following jobs are open:

MINISTERS

BRAZIL
- 10 Men or Couples

CONGO
- 10 Men or Couples

IRAQ
- 1 Man or Couple

TAIWAN
- 7 Men or Couples

JAPAN
- 6 Men or Couples
- 1 Man or Couple for work among the Chinese

KOREA
- 4 Men or Couples

MEXICO
- 7 Men or Couples

UNORDAINED EVANGELISTS, BIBLE TEACHERS, RELIGIOUS EDUCATION AND STUDENT WORKERS

BRAZIL
- 1 Evangelistic Woman
- 1 Student Worker
- 2 Christian Education Workers for the evangelistic fields
- 1 Literacy and Religious Education Worker for itineration and Sunday School teacher training

CONGO
- 2 Evangelistic Women

IRAQ
- 1 Evangelistic Woman for Baghdad

JAPAN
- 3 Evangelistic Women
- 1 Evangelistic Woman for Work Among Chinese in Japan

KOREA
- 5 Evangelistic Women
- 1 Student Worker, man or couple (ordained or unordained) short-term or regular for Kwangju

MEXICO
- 1 Bible School Teacher, Man or Couple
- 2 Bible Teachers, Women
- 1 Young People's Worker, Woman

TAIWAN
- 3 Evangelistic Women
- 1 Man or Couple for TMC Work (Youth Work)
- 1 Couple for Leadership Training and Christian Education

AGRICULTURAL, INDUSTRIAL, BUSINESS

CONGO
- 1 Industrial Man or Couple
- 1 Industrial Arts Man or Couple

MEXICO
- 1 Agricultural-Evangelistic Couple
- 2 Couples to Direct Student Homes
- 1 Business Administrator, Man or Couple

TAIWAN
- 1 Business Man or Couple for Treasurer of Mission and Sunday School Association and to help with other business of the Mission

Short Term Worker:
- 1 Business Man for short-term to fill the above place while the permanent couple is learning the language

MEDICAL

BRAZIL
- 1 Medical Doctor or Couple (Brazilian trained) for East Brazil Mission
- 1 Nurse to travel and help missionary families in West Brazil Mission

CONGO
- 1 Medical Doctor or Couple
- 6 Nurses
- 1 Medical Technologist

ECUADOR
- 1 Medical Doctor (couple) with special interest in public health

JAPAN
- 1 Nurse to direct a nursing school at the hospital
- 1 Hospital Administrator, for a short-term at Yodogawa Christian Hospital

KOREA
- 1 Medical Doctor or Couple for Soonchun Leprosy Colony
- 1 Medical Doctor, Surgeon for a three-year term (for emergency at Chunju)
- 1 Institutional nurse
- 4 Public Health Nurses for Mokpo, Kwangju and Chunju

MEXICO
- 2 Nurses
- 1 Medical Technologist for Ometepec Hospital
- 2 Pre-Medical Students to study medicine in Mexico

EDUCATIONAL

BRAZIL
- 6 Primary Principals
- 1 Primary and Secondary Piano Teacher
- 1 Primary Teacher
- 1 Primary Music Teacher. Administrative ability desirable
- 1 Secondary Teacher, woman, for English with administrative experience
- 1 Secondary School Worker, Ordained Couple
- 1 Secondary Teacher for Bible and English
- 1 Secondary and Junior College Home Economics Teacher and Dietician
- 1 Music Teacher for Edward Lane Bible Institute
- 1 Couple for West Brazil

Short Term Worker:
- 1 Teacher of Missionaries' Children, short-term

CONGO
- 5 Men or Couples
- 2 Women
- 1 Teacher of Music (primarily piano) for missionary children

Short Term Workers
- 1 Teacher of Missionaries' Children
- 1 Matron for Central School for Missionary Children

JAPAN
- 2 Couples (Kinjo and Shikoku Colleges)
- 4 Women for Kinjo and Seiwa High School
- 1 Man (single) for Shikoku Christian College

Short Term Workers:
- 1 Woman teacher (single) Kinjo
- 1 Man teacher (single) Shikoku
- 1 Woman teacher of Missionaries' children at the Canadian Academy, Kobe

KOREA
- 2 Educational-Evangelistic Men or Couples (ordained or unordained)
- 1 Teacher of Mathematics and Physics, Taejon College
- 1 Teacher of English Literature, Taejon College
- 1 Teacher of Chemistry, Taejon College
- 1 Teacher, Woman

Short Term Workers:
- 1 Teacher of English in Seminary, Single Man
- 1 Teacher of Missionaries' children

TAIWAN

Short Term Workers:
- 1 Teacher, to teach English and help with Music
- 1 Teacher, Single Man, for Tainan Boys' High School, to teach English and help with religious activities

WILL YOU FILL ONE OF THESE JOBS?

For Information Write:

EUGENE L. DANIEL, Candidate Sec'ty.
BOARD OF WORLD MISSIONS
Presbyterian Church, U. S.
Box 330, Nashville, Tenn.

The Southern
PRESBYTERIAN
Journal

VOL. XV NO. 42 FEBRUARY 13, 1957 $3.00 A YEA[R]

JACKSON, Miss.—Enthusiastic and encouraging support was given to Belhaven College here, [a]s the college began its $1,500,000 development program, a long-range plan.

Pictured above are Dr. Moody McDill, Dr. Guy Snavely, Rex I. Brown, W. Calvin Wells III, Ho[n.] H. L. White, Stuart Irby, Dr. John R. Miller, Marvin Callum and Dr. McFerran Crowe.

Governor Hugh L. White, only living member of Belhaven's original Board of Trustees still activ[e,] turned the first spade of dirt at the proposed site of the new $340,000 science building.

THE SOUTHERN PRESBYTERIAN JOURNAL

Rev. Henry B. Dendy, D.D., Editor....................Weaverville, N. C.
Dr. L. Nelson Bell, Associate Editor....................Asheville, N. C.
Rev. Wade C. Smith, Associate Editor....................Weaverville, N. C.

EDITORIAL

Needed, a Long-Range Policy Based on Right— Not Expediency

Unless our thinking is dominated by the restrictions of partisan politics (and this should never be the case with Christians), we are confronted not so much with the military implications of the Eisenhower policy for the Middle East as we are with the far deeper one of whether our nation is prepared for the moral implications involved.

America is deeply and rightly concerned that the fabulous oil reserves of the Middle East shall not fall into the hands of Russia, thereby greatly increasing Communism's potential for war. There is also the more mundane consideration of keeping that oil under the control of the West for peaceful economic pursuits.

For these two basic reasons it is suggested that we take the calculated risk of war as a deterrent to the potential catastrophe of losing that area to Communistic control.

We believe this risk is justified. Our only regret is that we have not been as forthright in many other parts of the world.

But the underlying problem for America is not so much the willingness to face war as the serious question whether we are conducting our domestic and foreign affairs on other than a basis of expediency. We are willing to risk war for oil and its involved implications, but we are consistently continuing to vascillate on matters of far deeper import.

Let us face this frankly: We have exercised the strongest pressures on France and Britain to withdraw from the Suez area. We even talk of sanctions against Israel because of their reluctance to withdraw from the Gaza strip and the Sinai areas where they have been subjected to constant harrassments.

What about Russia in Hungary? Why have we not exerted even greater pressures against this center of the hydra-headed monster of world Communism? We have even sat by in the United Nations while Russia has hypocritically demanded sanctions against Israel.

There is a serious question whether we are at this time exhibiting anything other than a general policy based on expediency. If this is the case there is little cause for optimism for the future.

It is our conviction that we need a full-dress debate from which partisan politics are completely divorced. The object of this debate to be to establish a policy based on righteousness. Nothing would do more to clarify the world situation and to give heart to those who long for freedom and justice, in the free world, and also in the Communist areas.

The continuing vascillations, the double-standard in vogue both inside and outside the United Nations, the rising influence of Moslem statesmen, all combine to make such an affirmation of paramount importance.

Only America is in a position to take such a stand. Only here are there a sufficient number of free and independent men who still give a semblance of allegiance to the Christian ethic to make such an affirmation a reality.

The developments which range across our vision with such rapidity make it imperative that we stop living by a day-to-day policy and establish certain principles which make our policy self-evident, not only next week but in the months to come.

At present we do not have such a policy.

L.N.B.

It's a Battle

In the parable of the sower and the seed our Lord has given us abundant evidence of the pitfalls which lie before all who hear the Gospel message. There is no reason for smug complacency, for the devices of Satan are just as subtle and just as real today as they have ever been. There is no reason to think that the four kinds of ground described by our Lord do not exist today; they do.

The indifferent and inattentive have the word snatched from their heart before it makes any impression.

The superficial and shallow, possibly the more exuberant "converts," when confronted with affliction or persecution for their new-found faith feel that it is not worth standing up for and hastily reject it for a more comfortable place among those who prefer the plaudits of man to the approval of God.

The third group - how dangerous the situation in which they find themselves! Here we have the obstacles, the enticements, the illusions of this world combining to blunt and then leaden one's Christian profession and testimony.

Who escapes the "cares of this world"? They are about us and press in on us daily. Some of them are trite, some are overpowering in their impact and but for the sustaining presence of the living Christ they can divert our minds and hearts and turn us away from Him.

The "deceitfulness of riches" is not a danger peculiar to those endowed with much of this world's goods. An inordinate desire for material things is an ever recurring temptation. Covetousness can eat like a cancer into the fiber of one's life and our Lord lists it for what it is — a deadly danger.

The lusts of other things — the diversions, the time-consuming activities, the permitting of *anything* to usurp Christ's rightful place becomes a snare which chokes out the things of the spirit and the end result is unfruitfulness as a Christian.

Living as a Christian in a hostile world and amidst the temptations and distractions of the polite paganism which is a characteristic of our generation — and probably has been characteristic of every generation — means that we are in the midst of an unending battle.

But what of those who do succeed; of those who by the grace of God run their course with patience and with success? Our Lord tells us that they hear the word and go on to receive it, having it become a transforming experience and the basis of their outlook on life, going on to bring forth fruit for His glory.

There may be unlimited debate as to what constituted *all* of the fruits to which Christ refers but they certainly include the fruits of the Holy Spirit: love, peace, longsuffering, gentleness, goodness, faith, meekness, temperance.

Self-examination can be a healthy exercise. Has the Gospel been received into our hearts to the place where we know these fruits of God's living presence can be seen? Has our profession of faith been translated into a religion of action? In proclaiming our faith are we at the same time demonstrating good works?

Sit down and read the first twenty-five verses of the fourth chapter of Mark's Gospel. We know we have heard the Gospel. Is it accomplishing in our lives that which Christ intended?

—L.N.B.

Chevalier de l'Ordre de Leopold II

The above is the title of a decoration recently conferred upon two Southern Presbyterians "for Meritorious Service" in the Congo by the King of Belgium.

They are Rev. and Mrs. Carroll R. Stegall, Sr., now of Black Mountain. Mr. Stegall is pastor of the Friendship Presbyterian Church of Black Mountain.

Forty-two years ago, as bride and bridegroom (he was 24) this young couple answered the call to the Congo Mission. Stegall was a layman, but he had technical knowledge that was needed and he installed at Luebo the first "wireless" broadcasting station, through which instant inter - mission - station communication could be established. Radio was only in its infancy at the time. The Stegalls performed almost indispensable service to the Mission for

The Southern Presbyterian Journal, *a Presbyterian Weekly magazine devoted to the statement, defense, and propagation of the Gospel, the faith which was once for all delivered unto the saints,* published every Wednesday by The Southern Presbyterian Journal, Inc., in Weaverville, N. C.

Entered as second-class matter May 15, 1942, at the Postoffice at Weaverville, N. C., under the Act of March 3, 1879. Vol. XV, No. 42, February 13, 1957. Editorial and Business Offices: Weaverville, N. C. Printed in the U.S.A. by Biltmore Press, Asheville, N. C.

ADDRESS CHANGE: When changing address, please let us have both old and new address as far in advance as possible. Allow three weeks after change if not sent in advance. When possible, send an address label giving your old address.

eight years; then returning to America on furlough he was licensed to the ministry by "extraordinary process" and the couple returned to the Congo as full fledged missionaries, giving themselves without stint to most valuable service for 27 more years.

This was not only a successful soul-winning effort, but their services were recognized by the Belgian government as of empire building value, and has now been signalized with the above decoration.

Hungarians Fight for Freedom

By Rev. James O. Reavis, D.D.

We have come to the day when the rulers of Russia seem to have proved that they are the products of materialistic evolution. They have tortured and slain thousands of Hungarians who gave their lives in "their last full measure of devotion to freedom."

The Russians' invasion of Hungary by brute force and beastly cruelty, remind us of a cartoon which "depicts an ape squatting among the topmost branches of a tall tree underneath which men are fighting" to enforce their unjust aggression. The cartoonist would have us imagine that we hear the ape's "Sardonic Comment": "Thank God evolution missed me!"

The courageous Hungarians have not died in vain. They have dealt a heavy blow to Communism and to its "diabolical ideology of hate, fear, and intellectual perversion—designed to impoverish the minds of men and to gnaw at their souls."

"Faith," we are told, "is not belief in spite of evidence; it is life in scorn of consequence." "Try to imagine a world in which no one chose to die for God's sake."

In our day when war is an obsession in the minds of men in many nations, who devote much time, energy and wealth preparing for it — the followers of Christ are comforted and strengthened by the assurance that the "Lord reigneth" and that the "earth will rejoice" when He subdues the world to His righteous will.

Then too, true Christians have confidence in the divine plan for the redemption of the world. Jesus gave to His disciples an outline of this plan and of God's program for the nations. In Matthew 24: 6-14, we read the words of Jesus spoken to His disciples from which we quote: "And ye shall hear of wars and rumors of wars; see that ye be not troubled; for all of these things must come to pass, but the end is not yet. For nation shall rise against nation and kingdom against kingdom; and there shall be famines, and pestilences and earthquakes in

Natures Of Christ

›n Cabaniss, Ph.D.

›f Mississippi

ly, a denial of our salvation, a repudiation of the possibility or the necessity of redemption.

No one claims, of course, that the Chalcedonian formula exhausts the answer to the question, "What think ye of Christ? (Matt. 22:42)." Nor does anyone suppose that it can never be rephrased. But it has weathered the test of time. It protects the true humanity of the Lord: He was conceived, born; He ate, drank, wearied, slept, suffered, died. It also preserves His true Deity: before all worlds He was, His birth of the Blessed Virgin was miraculous, He forgave sins, He raised the dead, and He rose from the grave. The Lord is both God and man in two distinct natures for ever. But He is no monster, a double or a middle being; He is one Person. As Pope Leo I so aptly expressed it: "The selfsame One Who is true God is also true man, and there is no deception in this unity. For in it the lowliness of man and the majesty of God pervade each other perfectly . . . Since the two natures constitute only one Person, we read on one hand that the Son of *man* came down from heaven (John 3:13) . . . , and on the other that *God's* Son was crucified (Matt. 27:54, Mark 15:39) . . . " The Incarnation, Atonement, and Resurrection were therefore real occurrences; the witness of Scripture is true; and we sinners, who need to be saved, can be saved and both have been and are being saved.

This formula, implicit in the Bible and Apostolic tradition, carefully wrought out in successive councils of the ancient church, chanted throughout the Middle Ages (in the Athanasian Creed) as a paean of praise, reaffirmed during the Reformation, still stands as the official belief of the vast majority of the churches of Christendom. Indeed, together with the doctrine of the Holy Trinity, to which it is intimately related, it is the essential dogma of Christianity. From it there may be and have been derived certain useful and instructive analogies. For example, the Bible also has two aspects, the human and the divine, and neither may be stressed to the exclusion of the other. The sacraments, too, have the same aspects, and as the First Scots Confession asserts (spelling modernized), "we utterly damn the vanity of those who affirm sacraments to be nothing else but naked and bare signs . . . And therefore whosoever slanders us that we affirm or believe sacraments to be naked and bare signs does injury to us and speaks against the manifest truth."

Similarly the social organism which we call the "state" has a certain twofoldness as well as unity. See the subtle distinctions involved in such texts as Mark. 12:17 (Matt. 22:21), Rom. 13:1-7, I Pet. 2:17, and Rev. 19:16, as well as in the great imperial acclamation, "Christ reigns, Christ conquers, Christ commands." Although a thoroughly secular and attenuated variation on the Chalcedonian formula, the now famous quip of Defense Secretary Charles E. Wilson is also worth recalling: "What is good for the country is good for General Motors, and what's good for General Motors is good for the country." (Either half of that remark may be untrue, and it is often so misquoted, but the full statement is undeniable.)

Still further, the church is both the body of Christ (Eph. 1:22,23) and an assembly of frail human beings (e.g., I Cor. 14:23). All of these

Helps To Understanding Scripture Readings in *Day by Day*

By Rev. C. C. Baker

Sunday, February 24, John 14:1-7. Jesus knew how much His disciples desired to be with Him (13:33,37). Thus when He told them He was leaving (vv.1-2), He also told them that they would see Him and be with Him again (v.3). Despite the disciples' loyalty, they were still appallingly ignorant of Christ and His ministry (13:36; 14:5,8). How elementary were the questions of Thomas (v.5) and Phillip (v.8)! Upon what basis should Phillip have known who Jesus was (vv.9-11)? Notice in v.4 that Jesus seemed to have assumed that Thomas already knew what he went on to ask in v.5. Observe that Jesus answered each question simply, fully, and gently, without anger or impatience (vv.6-7,9-11). Thus Jesus deals with all who love Him and come to Him needing guidance, help, strength or forgiveness.

Monday, February 25, Matthew 5:43-48. The Pharisees had twisted the judicial principle of v.38 to make it include the realm of daily conduct, and had added the phrase, "and hate your enemies" (v.43) to the Golden Rule (Leviticus 19:18). What principles did Jesus lay down for the social conduct of His followers (vv.39-42,44-46)? How did these contrast with the concepts of the Pharisees (vv.38,46-47)? Jesus taught that the Christian's behavior was not to be modeled after man's standards (v.20) but God's (v.48). Did Jesus fulfill the principles of conduct He taught in His own

ESSON FOR FEBRUARY 24

By THE REV. J. KENTON PARKER

Signs Of The Times

ackground Scripture: Matthew 14:1 - 16:12
evotional Reading: Romans 2:6-16

The Pharisees claimed that they wanted a "sign from heaven." Jesus Himself, His Life, and ords and works, was the greatest and plainest sign that could be furnished. Paul, in Romans 2:16 eaks of the day when God shall judge the secrets of men by Jesus Christ. Even while here a rtain sort of "judgment" was taking place. People were being divided into two groups; the harisees, scribes and chief priests on one side, and His disciples on the other, while many among ie multitude seemed to be "between the two des," partly convinced, but hesitating; at one toment inclined to follow, at another, to stone nd crucify Him.

Our Background Scripture contains a good iany incidents which reveal the nature of the mes in which Jesus lived. These incidents ecome "signs" to those who can see beneath ie surface, not only of those times, but of our mes also. Turn with me now to these incients.

John the Baptist Beheaded: 14:1-12.

Herod had a conscience which was troubling im. When he heard of the fame of Jesus, he id, This is John the Baptist: he is risen from ie dead. Then Matthew proceeds to give us ie account of the death of John. It is a failiar story with a variety of lessons. It is a ign" of the times in which Jesus lived; a time hen weak and wicked men were on the throne, id in places of authority; men like Herod and ilate. They were symbols of a great Empire hich was full of corruption.

The times in which we live are similar. As write these words we are in the midst of vful happenings in the Middle East and in urope, in Hungary and Poland. Wicked rulers id plotters are keeping the world in turmoil id strife. Many men as innocent as John are eing killed and exiled. Can we read these igns of the times"?

. *The Feeding of the Five Thousand* (and Four): 14:13-21; 15:32-39.

In both cases we have a hungry multitude. heir hunger was physical, but beneath this unger of the body was a deeper need of the ul. They were unconscious of this need. If u will read the account of the feeding of the ve thousand as recorded by John and the rmon which Jesus preached the next day, you will see that Jesus was trying to arouse a hunger of heart. He preached on the text; Labor not for the food that perishes but for the food that endures unto life eternal, and presented Himself as the Bread of Life which would satisfy that deeper need and hunger. They were ready to take Him by force and make Him a King because He fed their bodies, but when He spoke of soul hunger, even His disciples said, This is a hard saying; who can hear it?

III. *Jesus Walking on the Water:* 14:22-36.

Three pictures in one! A ship on a stormy sea; a Saviour Who can walk on the angry waves; a man with little faith! Read the story and see the pictures. Transfer the whole scene to our day and make the picture symbolical and it fits perfectly. Our "sea" is as stormy as the Sea of Galilee was on that night. Jesus is still the Master of the sea. We have a little faith, but not enough to carry us through and we cry for help. Is not this lack of faith a "sign" of our times?

IV. *Clean Hands or Clean Hearts:* 15:1-20.

The scribes and Pharisees came to Jesus with one of their trivial complaints and questions: Why do Thy disciples transgress the tradition of the elders? for they wash not their hands before they eat bread. This question reveals the extent of the religion of these leaders of the Jews. It was a religion of washed hands and did not go beneath the surface. Jesus shows them their hypocrisy. Which is more important? a tradition of elders, or a commandment of God? While strictly observing a trifling tradition they were breaking one of the Ten Commandments. Then He proceeds to make plain to his disciples what really defiles a man. It is not unwashed hands, but unwashed hearts. Out of the heart of man proceed all these awful things which defile a man.

This "sign of the times" hardly needs explanation; it is too plain. Our generation is seeking to make a "New World" by washing hands instead of hearts. It is rather impatient with those of us who insist that we must go deeper. The only way to change the world is to change men's hearts and lives. It is from wicked, unwashed hearts that all these jealousies and hatreds arise which are defiling men and the world. The more you scrub a dirt floor the muddier it gets. We are busy scouring the dirt floor when the real need is for a new floor; Except men are "born again" we will never have a new world.

V. *The Woman of Canaan:* 15:21-31.

This woman exhibited a remarkable humility and faith. Jesus rebuffed her at first by not answering her, and when the disciples suggested sending her away, He said, I am not sent but to the lost sheep of the house of Israel. She persisted, however, and came and worshipped Him, saying, Lord, help me. When He replied, It is not meet to take the children's bread and cast it to dogs, instead of becoming insulted or offended, she replied, Truth Lord: yet the dogs eat of the crumbs which fall from their master's table. Then Jesus said, O woman, great is thy faith: be it unto thee even as thou wilt. And her daughter was made whole from that very hour.

We find great faith, persevering, humble faith, sometimes, in unusual people. This woman is an example. Jesus drew out her faith, tested it, and then commended her very highly. I feel sure that there was something in His manner and tone of voice that encouraged her. Today, we find great faith in people of other races who have not had the advantages of people of our land. This woman could well have been a "sign" to the scribes and Pharisees of her time, and also a sign to us in America. Women of other races will rise up in the judgment and condemn the women of America.

VI. *Seeking a Sign:* 16:1-4.

The Pharisees and Sadducees came and tempting Him desired Him that He would show them a sign from heaven. We are not told as to the nature of this sign which they pretended to want. They had seen innumerable "signs." The healing of the sick; the feeding of the five thousand and the four thousand, which are among the most astonishing of all His many miracles. What more could they wish? He used a simple illustration to show them how blind they were. They could read the signs in the sky which told them what sort of weather to expect. (And, by the way, these are still the best of signs.) They could not, because they would not, believe the signs which proved that He was the Son of God and their long-expected Messiah. It was the most unreason-

YOUNG PEOPLES Department

YOUTH PROGRAM FOR FEBRUARY 24

By THE REV. B. HOYT EVANS

"Knowing What We Believe And Knowing How To Express It"

Scripture: I Peter 3:8-16.

Suggested Hymns:
"My Hope Is Built On Nothing Less"
"How Firm A Foundation"
"Stand Up! Stand Up For Jesus!"

Suggestions for the Program Leader:

(It will be advisable to invite an adult who is well informed about the Scriptures and the teachings of the church to lead the discussion for this program. Likely prospects for such a leader are ministers, D.C.E.s, and Adult Advisors. You will need copies of the Shorter Catechism together with Scripture proofs. Ask the minister where to find them. Since you will be asking for suggestions from the young people, it will be helpful to have a blackboard on hand for listing the ideas and definitions they give.)

Leader's Introduction:

This is the third of a series of programs in which we have been discussing the witness we should bear as Christians. One very effective way of bearing witness is being able to tell in clear and simple terms just exactly what we believe. It is always impressive to hear a person testify to his faith in convincing words. On the other hand, a person weakens his testimony no matter how sincere is his devotion, if he is not able to give some expression to his convictions.

The first requirement for expressing our faith is that we have some definite convictions to express. We must know what we believe and have some understanding before we can speak of our faith very convincingly. There can be no witness without convictions, and there can be no convictions without knowledge.

We are not responsible for creating our own beliefs out of imagination. Our beliefs should come through the acceptance of facts which we receive from a reliable source. The Bible is our source of truth. We trust its authority and we believe what it says. It is not enough, however, just to believe that what the Bible says is true without actually knowing what it teaches. We must know and understand what is taught in Scripture.

The Bible is not a book of clear-cut theological definitions. We form our spiritual definitions, the articles of our belief, by bringing together various passages of Scripture which throw light on the same subject. That is what the doctrinal standards of our Presbyterian Church attempt to do. The men who wrote the Confession of Faith and the catechisms of our church set out to make a systematic statement of what the Bible teaches about God and man. In all matters of faith and conduct the Scriptures are our final and highest authority.

These doctrinal standards of our church (the larger and Shorter Catechisms and the Confession of Faith) were written by very scholarly men more than three hundred years ago. Sometimes when we read their words for ourselves we realize that their age and their scholarship makes them hard to understand. That which is difficult to understand is even more difficult to explain. With the help of our guest leader (the minister or some other) we want to look at some of the answers of the Shorter Catechism, comparing them with the Scripture passages from which they were taken. In this way we can come to a clearer understanding of what the Scripture teaches and consequently a clearer understanding of our beliefs. Then, let us try to rephrase these Biblical truths in our own words. When we can do this, we shall be able to bear clear and convincing testimony to our faith.

(It is suggested that for this program you consider questions 4-6 of the catechism on the nature of God, and questions 21-28 on the nature of Christ.)

Helps for Circle Bible Study for March

Nationalism versus Internationalism

**By Rev. Carl W. McMurray, Ph.D.
Marion, N. C.**

The theme assigned for March is "Nationalism versus Internationalism" or a study of "Citizenship Loyalties." Let us approach this study by considering the principles of the Founding Fathers of our nation. Their conception as written into the Constitution of the United States is a worthy commentary on the Christian viewpoint and deserves special attention, for they were God-fearing men who honored the light of God's Word, and our citizenship is held under the government they founded.

The godly men who framed the Constitution carefully defined our multiple citizenship loyalties and made it clear that there are basic loyalties which are properly due to the particular State in which we live, and at the same time without any conflict there are other fundamental loyalties due to the nation, and they also recognized that the individual's first responsibility is unto God and they specified the right of free conscience.

They also made provisions for honorable relationships and faithful dealings with other nations, toward whom our national attitudes should be honest and just and peaceable, without any desire to dominate them but to set an example of national integrity and national self-respect among the nations.

These great constitutional principles embody a rare citizenship heritage which stands in sharp contrast to the policies now in practice in the majority of nations. We recognize that even in our own land these basic principles of our Constitution are under attack. Powerful forces are seeking to nullify the provisions of the Bill of Rights which reserve to the several States all those rights which are not specifically granted by the states to the federal government. The encroachment of the national government upon the rights which it has solemnly guaranteed to the individual States has caused much confusion and dismay.

This tragic trend should lead Christians to pray for a revival of moral conscience in the land which would lead to repentance and to an acknowledgement of the sacredness of the covenant agreements as set forth in the Bill of Rights.

Another dangerous viewpoint is that of those who advocate the subordination of our nation to some international political organization or world government. Through clever propaganda there is a continuing effort to condition the minds of our citizens to an abandonment of our constitutional heritage in favor of some international power to which we would yield the right of taxation and the exclusive right to possess military power, thus enabling it to devise its own laws and to enforce its will upon us.

Those who seek this objective regard the United Nations as the "germ of world government" and are contriving by every possible device to hasten the process of incubation. Let us not overlook the fact that in any world government today the Christian viewpoint would be in the minority. The prevailing majority of the masses of the world constitute a terrible tide of unenlightened and anti-moral passions with deep antagonism toward the Christian gospel upon which our free society is founded. It is unthinkable that those who appreciate the light of freedom, and who cherish the high spiritual mission of the Church to a lost world, should agree to put these precious things in jeopardy by putting ourselves under the yoke of the pagan majorities of the world.

Various brands of "internationalism" are seeking our loyalty today. There is international Communism and international Socialism and both of these are desperately seeking to entrap us. Of course, we recognize that there are proper and necessary relationships between the nations, and our Founding Fathers accepted this responsibility.

There is nothing in the Bible to support modern political schemes for an international power which would demand our loyalties. Let us not be confused by those who cite our Lord's great missionary commission (Acts 1:8; Matthew 28:19-20) in support of political internationalism. It is an error to suggest that Jesus was advocating international political schemes of any kind when He commanded us to preach the redeeming gospel to all nations, or when He taught us to practice neighborly compassion toward all men (Luke 10:30-37), or when He pronounced judgment upon apostate Israel for her rejection of the Messiah and her failure to bring forth the fruits God expected of the chosen people (Matt. 21:33-46; 22:1-14; Luke 19:41-44), or when He taught us to pray: "Thy Kingdom come."

The prophets were men of peace and sought the paths of peace, but they were utterly realistic and warned against false prophets who cried "peace, peace, when there is no peace" (Jer. 6:14; 14:13-14; Ezek. 13:10).

It is pertinent to ask: Why did God divide mankind into separate nations? In Genesis 11:6-8 we learn that mankind at Babel was united in apostasy, and when God saw there was nothing by which they would be "restrained" in their vain imaginations, He confused their language, disrupted their unity, and scattered them abroad. The passage clearly indicates that the division of mankind resulting in separate nations was a judgment of God designed in mercy to "restrain" human society in i's evil course. In Acts 17:26-27, Paul also proclaims the divine purpose in the separation of the nations and tells us that God hath "determined . . . the bounds of their habitation" with this purpose: "that they might seek the Lord."

God's purpose among the nations is further revealed in His founding of Israel as a separate and peculiar nation (see Gen. 12:1-3; Deut. 14:2) to be the custodian of His oracles (Rom. 3:1,2) and the channel through whom He would send the Saviour to redeem a multitude out of every nation (Rom. 9:5; 1:16; Rev. 7:9).

When Jesus the Messiah came, He sought first the "lost sheep of the house of Israel" (Matt. 15:24; 10:6), but they despised and rejected Him (John 1:11; Matt. 21:38-39; 27:22), and for this the nation was judged and appointed to be down-trodden among the nations until the times of the Gentiles be fulfilled (Luke 21:24). The risen Christ gave to His followers the high spiritual mission to preach the gospel to all nations and forewarned them of fierce conflict in this task with the "prince of this world," but assured them of final victory when He shall sit upon the throne of His glory and judge the nations.

Through long centuries the faithful followers of Christ bore their witness and suffered persecution and martyrdom in the midst of political tyranny and ecclesiastical harlotry. Then there came a day in the Providence of God when devout souls fled across the seas to the wilderness of the American continent, and there under the guidance of God they founded a new nation dedicated in the name of God to truth and righteousness and freedom, and this nation blessed of God became the home base of world wide missionary labor.

As custodians of this sacred heritage under God, let us dedicate ourselves as Christian citizens to the following scriptural principles:

1. That the highest patriotism is to devote ourselves to the cause of truth and righteousness. (Prov. 14:34).

(Continued on Page 16)

CHILDRENS Page

Abraham Obeyed God

Abraham and Sarah had only one son, and they loved him very dearly. His name was Isaac. God tested Abraham by commanding him to do a very hard thing. He told him to take Isaac to the mountain and kill him and burn him as a sacrifice. This was a terrible shock to Abraham; but he would obey God, whatever the cost. So he called Isaac to go with him, "to make a sacrifice to God." Two servants went with them and a donkey to carry the camp stuff, for they would be gone a week. Isaac was glad to go on a trip with his father, for he loved his father. Arriving at the foot of the mountain they left the men to make a camp, while the father and son climbed to the top. Isaac carried the wood and Abraham carried the fire and a knife. Isaac wondered why his father did not bring a lamb for the sacrifice, and asked him about it. His father said "God will provide Himself the lamb, my son". He just couldn't tell Isaac yet that he was to be the "lamb"! (To be continued) E.

NEWS of CHURCHES around the World

DISTRICT OF COLUMBIA

Washington — The edifice of the Church of the Pilgrims, a church of the Presbyterian Church, U. S., is pictured in the February issue of **America Illustrated**, the Russian-language magazine which the U. S. Information Agency is distributing in the Soviet Union.

The four-page illustrated article on churches of Washington shows views of numerous Protestant, Roman Catholic, and Orthodox churches in the capital city.

The article describes the various styles of architecture represented and includes the Church of the Pilgrims as an example of the conventional Gothic style. Russian readers are shown that Washington is a city of imposing buildings, among which are its more than 400 churches. "Washington's churches are attended not only by the city's permanent residents but by members of the large diplomatic community and travelers from many parts of the globe," says the article.

This is the third article on religion that **America Illustrated** has carried during the magazine's four months of publication. The first three issues distributed throughout the Soviet Union brought a complete sell-out of the 50,000 copies printed of each issue.

Under a reciprocal agreement Russia is permitted to distribute a similar magazine in America.

GEORGIA

Atlanta — The Rev. Joseph L. Griggs, pastor of Gordon Street Presbyterian Church, Atlanta, has been elected moderator of Atlanta Presbytery. The presbytery also named 16 ministers and elders to represent the presbytery at the General Assembly, to be held in Birmingham in April. Ministers named as commissioners were the Rev. Max Milligan, Clairmont Church, Atlanta; the Rev. John Sadler, Kirkwood Church, Atlanta; the Rev. George Smith, East Point Church; the Rev. E. P. Nichols, Covington Church; the Rev. E. G. Clary, Lloyd Church in LaGrange; Dr. Harry Fifield, First Church in Atlanta; the Rev. J. F. Aiken, Woodlawn Church, Atlanta; and the Rev. Kennedy Smart, Ingleside Church, Scottdale.

Elders elected included: Donald Leslie, First Church, Atlanta; W. A. Housworth, Smyrna Church, Conyers; C. J. Welch, Rehoboth Church, Tucker; L. L. Deck and L. C. Veal, Georgia Avenue Church in Atlanta; Alex Gaines and Paul Brown, Central Church, Atlanta; and Searcy Slack, Decatur Church.

LOUISIANA

New Orleans—The Rev. Walter Langtry, pastor of the Church of the Covenant in New Orleans, was general chairman of the steering committee for the Greater New Orleans religious census, conducted the last of January.

Workers from more than 150 Protestant churches, with members of the Roman Catholic churches cooperating, took part in the first such census since 1948.

Mr. Langtry said the purpose of the census is to gather information to form the basis of evangelistic endeavors. He remarked that the census is the only practical way churches can locate people who have moved into the New Orleans area since 1948. There has been a population increase of 128,495 in the three parishes of Greater New Orleans.

New Protestant congregations were assigned sections of the city in their neighborhoods for taking the census there.

Prior to the census-taking, rallies were held to provide various helpful information to the census takers. The three-parish area was divided into sections and each church participating was responsible for a given section.

New Orleans—Election of two new elders and one deacon at Canal Street Presbyterian Church, took place January 20. The men named were L. O. Reuning and George Miestchovich as new elders, and Herbert Bradshaw as deacon. They were selected for three-year terms.

New Orleans—James S. Mason of Carrollton Avenue Presbyterian Church, New Orleans, has been elected president of the Protestant Laymen of New Orleans. The election took place at the group's annual luncheon in December. Another Presbyterian, Lawrence Stevens, also of Carrollton Church, was among those elected to the executive committee.

Speaker at the annual luncheon meeting was the Rev. William McLean, M.B.E., a Presbyterian minister, and chaplain of the Montreal Sailors' Institute, Montreal, Canada.

NORTH CAROLINA

Davidson — Concord Presbytery, meeting yesterday in the Davidson College Presbyterian Church, elected as Moderator Rev. L. T. Edgerton, Minister of the Poplar Tent Presbyterian Church, Concord. The sermon was preached by Rev. Woodrow McKay, Salisbury, upon the invitation of the retiring Moderator, Dr. Frank McCutchan.

The Presbytery elected as Commissioners to the General Assembly, to meet in the South Highland Presbyterian Church, Birmingham, Alabama, April 25, the following Ministers and Ruling Elders. Ministers: A. B. McClure, Barium Springs, S. C. Farrior, Concord, A. L. Moran, Statesville, R. F. Park, Concord; W. H. Matheson, Marion. Elders: Dr. J. B. Woods, Davidson; Dr. N. P. Sholar, Mooresville; J. A. Poole, Kannapolis; W. E. Harris, Harrisburg; J. L. Gourley, Marion.

Rev. N. R. McGeachy, Statesville, Chairman of the Commission on the Minister and His Work, reported that Rev. R. L. Turner, formerly pastor of the Second Presbyterian Church, Kannapolis, had been dismissed to Orange Presbytery. He also announced that Rev. John S. Cook, formerly minister of Harmony and Tabor Churches, left this field December 31, 1956. Mr. Cook had reached the age of retirement early in 1956 and had been reelected by his congregations for an additional term of service.

Rev. Carl May was received from Orange Presbytery in order that he might become the minister of the Thyatira Church, Salisbury. He will be installed as pastor by a Commission of Presbytery, February 3, 7:30 P. M. Members of the Commission: Rev. Carlyle McDonald, Mooresville; Rev. Milton Faust, Salisbury; Rev. H. Reid Newland, Salisbury; Rev. James R. Phipps, Statesville; Dr. F. L. Jackson, Davidson; Mr. Samuel Sloop, Mt. Ulla.

Rev. Charles S. Spencer was received from Charleston Presbytery in order that he might become the pastor of the Bridgewater, McDowell, Westview and Drusilla Churches. These are churches in a Larger Parish recently organized in Burke and McDowell counties. Mr. Spencer will be installed as pastor by a Commission of Presbytery February 17, 1:30 P. M. at the Bridgewater Church. Members of the Commission: Rev. C. W. McMurray, Marion; Rev. John D. Smith, Morganton; Rev. J. Hector Smith, Morganton; Rev. W. T. Boyle, Lenoir; Rev. T. B. Southall, Statesville; B. F. Pollard, Marion; A. H. Maxwell, Morganton; W. F. Ramseur, Morganton.

Rev. James R. Phipps was received from Wilmington Presbytery in order that he might accept the call of the Concord Church, Statesville. Mr. Phipps will be installed as pastor by a Commission of Presbytery February 10, 11 A. M. The Commission: Rev. A. B. McClure, Barium Springs; Dr. Sidney A. Gates, Salisbury; Rev. J. W. Foster, Statesville; Dr. F. L. Jackson, Davidson; Dr. J. C. Bailey, Davidson.

Rev. John Viser, of Enoree Presbytery and the West Brazil Mission, delivered an address on the work of the church in Brazil. Mr. Viser's special responsibility is piloting the mission plane which transports missionary personnel and supplies to the various stations in this vast area. The plane has been found to be most useful also in propaganda work. It often flies low over large gatherings broadcasting hymns and announcements concerning church meetings. The plane also drops leaflets and tracts.

Dr. F. L. Jackson, Treasurer, reported that the churches gave $263,728.32 to the denominational program of benevolences in 1956. These gifts support the work of World Missions, Church Extension, Christian Education, Educational Institutions, homes for children and the aged and other causes of the Presbytery, Synod and General Assembly. The budget of the Presbytery was $250,000.

Rev. E. P. Moye, Mooresville, reporting for the Committee on Church Extension, stated that there were some 31 churches related to this program. These churches have more than 2,000 members and received some 200 new members each year. Total cost of maintaining this work is almost $150,000. The churches provide two-thirds of this support and the Presbytery gives the balance. Mr. Moye stated that two new churches were organized in 1956, Westview at Morganton and Love Valley, Statesville. He said that the Presbytery is cooperating in a county wide evangelism program led by Dr. H. H. Thompson, Director of Evangelism for the Synod of North Carolina. The Presbyterian churches of Cabarrus county have already made their plans for a county-wide effort.

Mr. Fred Long of Lenoir, Chairman of the Council of the Presbytery, gave his report, underscoring the importance of the service of 104 laymen and 2 ministers who visited the churches in the interest of the program of benevolences during the past fall.

Rev. Walter H. Styles, Lenoir, Chairman of the Camp Grier Committee, stated that some 2,000 campers were enrolled at Camp Grier in the various conferences and retreats for children, young people and adults during 1956. He reported that an attractive residence for the custodian had been completed during the year.

Rev. Robert Turner, Regional Director of Religious Education for the Synod of North Carolina and formerly Executive Secretary of Concord Presbytery addressed the Presbytery briefly on plans for the Men's Convention in Miami, October 10-13, 1957.

The next meeting of Presbytery will be in the Concord Presbyterian Church, Statesville April 23, 9 A. M.

in the program were the Rev. Walter Dickson, pastor at St. Philips Church, and Dr. James E. Bullock, pastor of Second Church.

Music for the program was by the 45-member youth choir of the First Presbyterian Church and was under the direction of Charles Paber.

Dallas—Over 200 Dallas Presbyterians attended the tenth annual laymen's dinner of the Presbyterian Extension Committee of Dallas, held at Highland Park Presbyterian Church in January.

This committee has spent approximately $370,000 toward the organization of ten new Presbyterian churches in the Dallas area during the past ten years. Two of the most recent churches are the Emmanuel Presbyterian Church in Grand Prairie and Covenant Church in Farmers Branch.

Theme for the committee meeting was "The Dallas Story—Yesterday, Today and Tomorrow". Outgoing president, Austin B. Watson spoke on the past and the future of the organization's work, with other speakers on the same topic being the Rev. W. A. Dealey of Churchill Way Church; and the Rev. R. Earl Price who has been engaged in organizing Webb's Chapel Road Church and Walnut Hill Lane Church.

New officers and directors installed at the meeting included G. R. Hollingsworth, president; Field Scovell, vice-president; A. D. Harder, secretary; James H. Rankin, treasurer; and B. T. Erwin, J. B. McHale and J. Harry Wood, Jr., directors.

Kingsville—A gift of $2,000 through Texas Presbyterians' "Together For Christ" Program, and a number of memorial gifts have been presented to the Library fund of the Presbyterian Pan-American School. The $2,000 gift was given by an anonymous donor.

HELPS TO UNDERSTANDING SCRIPTURE READINGS IN DAY BY DAY

(Continued from Page 6)

Thursday, February 28, John 12:1-8. The crucifixion was just a week away (v.1). The Pharisees were stopping at nothing to put an end to Jesus' ministry (11:53,57; 12:10-11), and a traitor was in His midst (12:4). What a wonderful relief and welcome for Him must have been the home in Bethany where He was loved and honored with unstinting hospitality (12:1-3). The pound of ointment (v.3) was worth about sixty dollars (v.5). How illogical was Mary's expression of pure devotion to her Lord! Notice how logical yet ill-purposed, was Judas' objection (vv.4-6). Jesus yet looks for those who with open hearts will abandon themselves in service and love to Him in the midst of a society filled with a cold, respectable concern for religion but indifference to genuine spiritual enthusiasm.

Friday, March 1, Nehemiah 2:17-18. Read chapters 1-2 and notice how Nehemiah looked to God to rebuild Jerusalem's walls. Contrition (1:6-8), earnestness (1:4-6), and faith (1:8-10) marked the prayer of Nehemiah when he heard the news of Jerusalem (1:1-4). As God had been faithful in scattering a rebellious people (1:8), so Nehemiah claims the promise of restoration (1:9-11). Observe how he looked to God (2:4) and acknowledged His hand (2:8b) when the opportunity was given him to open his heart to the king (2:1-8). Notice his continued dependence on God as he exhorted the people to rebuild the walls (2:17-18), as opposition arose (2:19-20) and increased (4:1-9) until the walls were completed 6:15-16). Today Christians can still look to the Lord as they seek to do His work and find Him just as faithful to them as He was to Nehemiah.

Saturday, March 2, Mark 10:32-34. Following the disciples' recognition of who He was (8:29), Jesus began to teach them why He had come (8:31). Jesus repeated the announcement of His crucifixion as they journeyed to Jerusalem and each time the disciples reacted with protests (8:32), bewilderment (9:30-32) and fear (10:32). Notice how deliberately Jesus was teaching them (10:33-34); yet they never really heard Him mention the resurrection until after it has occurred (cf. 10:34b, Luke 24:6-11). What state of mind might have provoked the request of 10:35-37? the argument of 9:33-34? Many of the circumstances through which the Lord leads us may seem bewildering and confusing. If we will but listen to Him, and believe that He knows what He is doing, all matters will work out for the good.

HELPS FOR CIRCLE BIBLE STUDY IN MARCH

(Continued from Page 11)

2. That this nation in subjection to God must not be "unequally yoked" with anti-God or anti-moral or anti-Gospel nations (2 Cor. 6:14).

3. That this nation, founded upon faith in God, should not be ashamed to acknowledge God in our national and international relationships (Ps. 119:46; 33:12; Prov. 3:16).

4. That in this critical hour we should seek patience, and pray for all people and all that are in authority (1 Tim. 2:1-2).

5. That the nation in all its acts and treaties and agreements with other nations should be the protector of the Church and the guardian of the path of the missionaries (Matt. 24:15: 2 Thessa. 1:6; Zech. 2:8). (See Confession of Faith, Chap. 23, Sec. 3).

Letters About Circle Bible Study

Dear Editor:

May I voice my sincere appreciation for the added page to your Journal this year. I refer to the Women's Work and Helps for Circle Bible Study, especially. Being an assistant circle Bible leader, I find your stand on the truth of the Word most gratifying and helpful. Do continue to keep this page and the other fine ones and your Journal forthcoming. Thank you.

Dallas, Texas

Gentlemen:

Kindly let me have a dozen copies of the Journal with the article on the Citizenship study for the Women of the Church. I wish to put a copy in the hands of each of our Bible teachers in the circles.

Warwick, Va.

Dear Dr. Dendy:

Thank you so much for note advising about the delivery of the Journal. We women who receive the Journal and are Bible leaders in the circles are so thankful for Bible study you are giving us now and especially February's lesson. It is splendid. Thank you.

Raleigh, N. C.

My dear Dr. Dendy:

I want to thank you for giving us the most comprehensive set of objectives most of us have ever seen. We are simply thrilled and I for one, have spent the month looking up scripture, underlining first in pencil, then ink and finally, I've gotten down to red crayon, the points I want to bring out. Wish each of my members had a copy and then we could read, look up the references and really have a wonderful time. I only have thirty minutes, so will have to high light it.

You know, it is such a joy to find people who really love the Lord and know His Word. Sometimes we get so thirsty in a land that seems to have gone dry. Thank you and yours for your cooperation.

Columbia, S. C.

Dear Dr. Dendy:

My Journal came yesterday. I am writing you to tell you how pleased I was to find the Women's page, "Helps on Circle Bible Study for February." Now the next question is how to let the women know these helps are available. I will announce it at my Presbyterial Board meeting next Wednesday, January 23rd. I wanted to let you know how delighted I was to see the Helps in the Journal.

Columbia, S. C.

Well, This Is Encouraging!

The Children's Page editor is pleased to have some very gratifying reactions to the Journal's new feature.

Extracts from letters:

Please accept my most hearty thanks for the "Children's Page," the new feature in the Presbyterian Journal.—Lexington, Va.

The new Journal is wonderful; certainly like the format, and the "Children's Page" with Little Jetts to illustrate the story is just Grand!—Jacksonville, Fla.

I like the "Children's Page" very much, and I think it greatly increases the attractiveness of the Journal for the whole family.—Denver, Colo.

I think the Journal is very much more interesting; it is so much easier to read now, and I greatly enjoy that new page for the Children.—Crossnore, N. C.

Dr. McGregor Resigns

Dr. J. Rupert McGregor, President of the Montreat Association, announced his resignation before a called meeting of the Trustees recently. This is to be effective as of June 1, 1957, although in case a successor has not been found, Dr. McGregor indicated that he would continue to give any assistance that might be necessary during the 1957 summer conference season. This year marks the end of the tenth year of outstandingly successful leadership in the work of the Association. The addition of the August Bible Conference and the completion of many needed buildings, as well as the accreditation of Montreat College will be a few of the outstanding achievements by which he will be long remembered. Committees have been appointed to prepare appropriate expressions of appreciaton. The Board of Directors have been asked to concur in approving and implementing the actions taken.

Presbytery Votes on Amendments

The Vote on the Amendment to the Confession of Faith on Marriage and Divorce is already decidedly AGAINST this Amendment. A three-fourths majority is required to change the Confession of Faith.

The Vote on Women Elders now stands at 32 FOR Women Elders and 41 AGAINST Women Elders with 12 Presbyteries yet to report.

BOOKS

COURSE OF EMPIRE. Bowlen. Moody Press. $3.00.

Course of Empire is a historical novel of death and power and deals with one of the most dramatic episodes in the history of our nation. In this volume we see the unfailing work of God in our history. It is a well-told historically authentic story which must cause the unbeliever to ask himself as to whether he is being faithful to the sacred trust which has been committed to him. Though written in mature style, this book will appeal to the heart of American youth. —J.R.R.

WITH CHRIST IN THE UPPER ROOM. Alexander Maclaren. Baker Book House. $2.95.

Alexander Maclaren is still one of the favorites among Christians who appreciate the finest expository literature. This volume contains thirty-four messages based on John 14-16. In these messages Dr. Maclaren takes the reader to the Upper Room so that he may share Christ's teachings to His Apostles. The messages are especially adaptable for Passion Week. This book was formerly published under the title, **The Holy of Holies.**

—J.R.R.

Remember Students of All Lands

Universal Day of Prayer for Students

SUNDAY, FEBRUARY 17, 1957

Pray for students on all campuses—in our Southland, in our nation, and in all countries around the world; for the faculties who teach them; for the institutions they attend.

"Eternal God, whose power upholds Both flower and flaming star
To whom there is no here nor there, No time, no near nor far,
No alien race, no foreign shore, No child unsought, unknown:
O send us forth, Thy prophets true, To make all lands Thine own!

"O God of truth, whom science seeks And reverent souls adore,
Who lightest every earnest mind Of every clime and shore:
Dispel the gloom of error's night, Of ignorance and fear,
Until true wisdom from above Shall make life's pathway clear!

"O God of righteousness and grace, Seen in the Christ, Thy Son,
Whose life and death reveal Thy face, By whom Thy will was done:
Inspire Thy heralds of good news To live Thy life divine,
Till Christ is formed in all mankind And every land is Thine!"

(Hymn 485 in The Hymnbook)

Write the Department of Campus Christian Life, Box 1176, Richmond 9, Virginia for the suggested service of worship prepared for observing the Universal Day of Prayer for Students.

PRESBYTERIAN EDUCATIONAL ASSOCIATION OF THE SOUTH
Box 1176
Richmond 9, Virginia

—EDITORIAL—

Catechising
The Scriptures and the Power of God
The New York Campaign
One Isaiah

Should The Southern Presbyterian Church Withdraw From The National Council?

By Dr. J. P. McCallie

In Partnership With God

By Kenneth S. Keyes

"Christ For Our Time Crusade"

By Walter W. Brown

Helps To Understanding Scripture Readings
Sabbath School Lesson for March 3, 1957
Young People's Department
Children's Page — Women's Work — Church News

THE VOTE ON WOMEN ELDERS

To date 77 of the 85 Presbyteries have reported on their votes. Of this number 35 have voted For Women Elders and 42 have voted Against. There are 8 Presbyteries yet to report.

THE SOUTHERN PRESBYTERIAN JOURNAL

Rev. Henry B. Dendy, D.D., Editor........................Weaverville, N. C.
Dr. L. Nelson Bell, Associate Editor........................Asheville, N. C.
Rev. Wade C. Smith, Associate Editor........................Weaverville, N. C.

CONTRIBUTING EDITORS

Mr. Chalmers W. Alexander
Rev. W. W. Arrowood, D.D.
Rev. C. T. Caldwell, D.D.
Dr. Gordon H. Clark
Rev. R. Wilbur Cousar, D.D.
Rev. B. Hoyt Evans
Rev. W. G. Foster, D.D

Rev. Samuel McP. Glasgow, D.D
Rev. Robert F. Gribble, D.D
Rev. Chas. G. McClure, D.D
Dr. J. Park McCallie
Rev John Reed Miller, D.D.

Rev. J. Kenton Parker
Rev. John R. Richardson, D.D.
Rev. Wm. Childs Robinson, D.D.
Rev. George Scotchmer
Rev. Robert Strong, S.T.D.
Rev. Cary N. Weisiger, III, D.D.
Rev. W. Twyman Williams, D.D.

EDITORIAL

Catechizing

"Let him who is catechized in the Word communicate to him who catechizes in every good thing," Gal. 6.6. This text is used in the article in Kittel's Word Studies in the New Testament to show that the office of catechist was the first one supported by the gifts of the early Church. The Christians did not call these teachers rabbis, though Jesus bore that title, nor philosophers of which there were many. As these men drilled the new converts orally in the great acts of God in Christ and the conduct appropriate to Christian living they were called catechists.

Scholars, like Alfred and Reinhold Seeberg, A. D. Heffern, C. H. Dodd, recognize this place of catechesis in the New Testament Church and some of them speak of "a catechism of primitive Christianity." The oldest extant catechism is perhaps the *Didache* or *Teaching of the Twelve* which probably comes from the First Century.

There was a notable catechetical school in Alexandria from the second century, including such teachers as Pantaenus, Clement and Origen. One of these wrote a book describing Christ as the Pedagogue or Tutor. A bit later, Augustine in the West wrote a catechetical rubic to aid a diligent catechist. Cyril of Jerusalem delivered his catechetical lectures, and Gregory of Nyssa composed the Great Catechism.

At the Reformation, Luther's catechisms taught the Saxon and Scandanavian people the Gospel. The Heidelberg Catechism nerved our Reformed forebears for the agonies of the Thirty Years' War. In Britain, the Anglican Catechism of 1549 and Calvin's Catechism taught the things of Christ to the people before the composition of the Westminster Catechisms. In the Roman Catholic world the Franciscans and the Dominican used a catechism to bring some ten million Mexicans into that Church in the first half century after the conquest of Mexic Francis Xavier used one effectively in Asia abo the same time.

Dr. Charles C. Jones worked out his ow catechism for teaching the Christian faith t the slaves. In a number of these cases, a pr digious memory compensated for a lack of th ability to read the Bible.

Our Presbyterian body is a creedal Churc and two of the creeds to which we officiall subscribe at ordination are catechisms. Mor over, the Book of Church Order directs th ministers of the Word to catechize the childre and youth and declares that the Bible includin the catechisms is to be the center of every cour of instruction.

When any one decries the catechisms of th Church he gives the impression that he exalting the philosophy of John Dewey abo the standards of the Church, or that followin Elliott, *Can Religious Education be Christia* he is making experience primary and Chri secondary.

We rejoice that our own Board of Christia Education is advertising its loyalty to the creed interpretation of the Scriptures and declarin that this is what is wanted taught in our enti educational program. We hope that this avow includes a hearty support of the catechisn which give our interpretation of the Scripture

The Heidelberg Catechism used by the Pre byterians of Continental origin and approve by the Kirk of Scotland in 1590 begins: "M only comfort in life and in death is that I b long to my faithful Saviour Jesus Christ, Wh with His precious blood has fully satisfied f all my sins." The Shorter Catechism begin "Man's chief end is to glorify God and to enjo Him forever." Put the two together and yo have Romans 12.1.

—W.C.R.

The Scriptures and the Power of God

When the Sadducees, the religious leaders who jected the supernatural in our Lord's time, ied to pose an absurd hypothetical case on hich they asked Christ to pass judgment, He plied with these words: *"Do ye not therefore r, because ye know not the Scriptures, neither e power of God."*

Is there a connection between the Scriptures ıd the power of God? We believe that not ıly is there such a connection but that it is ıe vital to a ministry of the Word.

We are not here arguing for man's interpre- tion of the Scripture or any part of it. We 'e not arguing for a particular translation of ıe Bible. We are not concerned over those ɔctrinal differences from which have emerged ıe major denominations.

We believe that we must divest ourselves of isconceptions and preconceptions about the ible. We believe we must subject every in- rpretation of the Scripture to the clear light : the Scripture itself. We believe that there sufficient in any major translation of the ible in any language or dialect to sustain the sertion that it is truly the Word of God. We ırther believe that the doctrinal differences nong Christian churches are very minor, com- ıred to the great verities of the Christian faith ı which true Christians all agree.

But having said all of this we believe that :tween each individual and God and between ıch individual and the Scriptures there is a lationship which has a vital bearing on both s understanding and his power to witness for hrist. This can be summed up in one sentence; ıe's witness as a teacher of the Word, whether : be an ordained minister or a Christian lay- an, depends for its power on the Holy Spirit ıt (and this is from an intensive observation), e Holy Spirit withholds His power from those ho "know not the Scriptures" and therefore ıestion, deny or belittle its importance both r faith and practice.

It is this failure to know God's Word which the basic source of so many powerless sermons ross the land today. Man's opinions and man's ıilosophy may tickle the ear and inflate the o of those who proclaim it and those who hear it but it has no more power to convict and to save and to inspire than has an individual to lift himself by his own boot straps.

Christ put His finger squarely on the weak place in the philosophy of the Sadducees. They rejected the law of Moses as well as the later Old Testament books, putting in their place the fluctuating conclusions of human reason; they rejected the supernatural and the immortality of the soul and affirmed the absolute moral freedom of man. Christ said: *"Do ye not therefore err."* They had no foundation on which to stand. They had no authority for their religion. Theirs was a man-made philosophy and it would go the way of man. Their error centered in their lack of a knowledge of the Scriptures, of a belief in the Scriptures, and of a failure to live in accordance to God's revealed will. Small wonder they did not know the power of God, either in this life or in that which is to come.

Phariseeism is not dead for, today, there are those who set up their own man-made rules and then proceed to attack Christian brothers who live and work outside this narrowed concept.

Sadduceeism is also very much alive. Not only are Moses and the prophets denied but the supernatural, whether in the Old or the New Testament, is explained away.

For both of these deviations from Christianity there is a cure and it is found in a surrender of the will, the mind and the heart to the living Christ. When this takes place He shows forth the truth of His Word and we find the God of righteousness and judgment of the Old Testament is the same God of love and mercy revealed in the New. We find that we cannot deny the integrity of the written word and maintain the perfection of the living Word, for the Christ of the Book and the Christ of human experience *must be the same.*

Unless such is the case it is true of us as of the Sadducees of old:

"Do ye not err, because ye know not the Scriptures, neither the power of God?"

—L.N.B.

The Southern Presbyterian Journal, *a Presbyterian Weekly magazine devoted to the statement, defense, and propagation of the Gospel, the faith which was once for all delivered unto the saints,* published every Wednesday by The Southern Presbyterian Journal, nc., in Weaverville, N. C.

Entered as second-class matter May 15, 1942, at the Postoffice at Weaverville, N. C., under the Act of March 3, 1879. Vol. XV, No. 43, February 20, 1957. Editorial and Business Offices: Weaverville, N. C. Printed in the U.S.A. by Biltmore Press, Asheville, N. C.

ADDRESS CHANGE: When changing address, please let us have both old and new address as far in advance as possible. Allow three weeks after change if not sent in advance. When possible, send an address label giving your old address.

The New York Campaign

We are in receipt of an urgent request that Christians everywhere join in prayer for the campaign which is scheduled to begin in New York on May 15th.

The New York Campaign Committee, composed of a number of that city's leading business men and ministers, has leased Madison Square Garden for *five months*. Whether the meetings will continue that long will depend on a number of circumstances.

Billy Graham is being opposed by the extreme liberals who do not like the Gospel which he preaches. He is being just as vigorously opposed by the extreme fundamentalists who would restrict the preaching of the Gospel to the auspices of only those who meet their concept of Christianity.

Mr. Graham and all associated with him, including the New York Committee and local pastors and Christians, need the prayers of God's people everywhere. Satan does not want the Gospel preached every night in the very heart of the area where he holds sway. Only 7½% of the 8,000,000 people in New York own any affiliation with Protestantism. Only a small per cent of these are active Christians.

This is a situation which calls for earnest prayer, for importunate prayer, for agonizing prayer. A true revival in New York could stir the nation and the world. This *must* be a work of God's Holy Spirit.

There must be an outpouring of spiritual and physical strength, of wisdom and grace, of patience and love, of holy boldness and inspired restraint. God alone can give these to His servants who need them so much.

Let us covenant to PRAY DAILY for the New York Campaign!

—Editor.

One Isaiah

Why bother people with two Isaiahs when most of them don't know there is one?" By such witticism practical-minded D. L. Moody is said to have diverted attacks on the unity of the Book of Isaiah which in his day came in on a rising tide.

The famed evangelist knew, of course, that this playful query did not settle the matter of authorship of a great Bible book. But he refused to be entangled in the meshes of speculation which would hinder his soul winning ministry and tend to weaken the faith of his hearers.

Here is the crux of the matter. To deny the ınity of the Book of Isaiah because of its prelictive elements is to deny the inspiration of his part of the Holy Scriptures.

Furthermore, Christ quotes from both the ixth and the sixty-first chapters without any listinction. New Testament references to Isaiah .re about equally divided between the first and he second part.

Also significant is the fact that in the com›lete Book of Isaiah among the acclaimed Dead ;ea Scrolls, a Scripture portion which antedates the New Testament, there is no hint of any divided authorship.

With Dr. Benander and evangelical students of the Word everywhere we confidently believe that the Book of Isaiah is a collection of messages from God through one man, the Old Testament evangelist Isaiah. And the blessed invitation "Come" which in the first chapter speaks of scarlet-sin lives washed white as snow, speaks as clearly and warmly in the fifty-fifth chapter about water offered freely to thirsty souls. —The Standard.

Should The Southern Presbyterian Church Withdraw From The National Council?

By J. P. McCallie, President
The McCallie School
Chattanooga, Tennessee

Since the transformation of the old Federal :ouncil of Churches into the National Council y bringing into it eight different national hurch organizations, I have been a representaive of our General Assembly in the National :ouncil of the Churches of Christ in America N.C.C.C.A.). I was at its inception in Clevend, Ohio, and its biennial meeting in Denver nd its Department of Foreign Missions assemly in Buck Hill Falls, Pennsylvania, and in ıayton, Ohio. During my 33 years' service on ur former Executive Committee of Foreign lissions, I had attended a number of the meetıgs of the North American Conference of oreign Missions. I have received the publicaons and read extensively their communications ıd I believe I am fairly competent to answer ıe above question: "Should the Southern resbyterian Church Withdraw from the '.C.C.C.A.?"

I have some dear friends who differ with ,e in my clear-cut decision that our church ıould withdraw and no longer be placed in compromising position by being forced to nd the weight of its membership to the politiıl lobbying and the socialistic gospel (which no gospel) continually promulgated by the 'ational Council. I love these friends and will ›ntinue to love them, though I cannot see ›w they reconcile their loyalty to the Lord :sus Christ with their fellowship in the liberal adership of the N.C.C.C.A. I have tried ırnestly to see all that is good in the cooperaon with other Christians, which I firmly be:ve in, and the zeal for Christian living manifest in the Council, which is implied in all that our Lord taught, but the defects to my mind far outweigh these goods, and actually cause us to sin by association with ambitious and designing men and policies that would eventually lead our country into Socialism and towards Communism. This is no foolish fear, for already we can see in the leadership of some of the most influential men in the National Council a definite drift toward Communism.

The foremost leader in the N.C.C.C.A., a former President, has been called before the Congressional Committee on Un-American Activities to answer for his membership in a score or more of fellow-traveler organizations. He admitted that he was the friend and employee of a known Communist theological professor for many years.

More than 100 clergymen, connected with the N.C.C.C.A. or its member denominations, signed the petition to the Supreme Court urging it to declare unconstitutional the act of Congress concerning the security of the nation, a petition which rejoiced the Communist *Daily Worker*. Another great N.C.C.C.A. leader has earnestly advocated our Government sitting in at a "Round Table Conference" with Communist Government leaders to discover a way of coexistence. Leaders of the N.C.C.C.A. are constantly urging America not to stand out against admitting Red China to the United Nations.

The thing I cannot understand at all is the requirement some of our own church leaders, by advocating our membership in the

N.C.C.C.A., would place on all of us to take part in something that is against our conscience and is regarded by many of us as positively sinful. This same group tried to vote us into union with the Presbyterian Church, U. S. A. Fortunately it was that we were saved from that catastrophe, largely by the elders of our church. We shall have to again mobilize our efforts to take us out of the N.C.C.C.A.

The former moderator of the Presbyterian Church, U. S. A., is now President of the N.C.C.C.A. and it is he that fraternized with Communist-appointed church leaders in Moscow, and honored the now-repudiated Communist church leaders of Hungary, present at the World Council of Churches at Evanston several years ago.

A great leader of the World Council is now advocating sending and receiving church delegations between America and Red China. How stupid can advocates of ecumenicity become?

I would answer the question: "Should the Southern Presbyterian Church Withdraw From the National Council of the Churches of Christ in America?" — Yes, by all means. Some of my reasons would be:

1. It is largely under the control of liberals and modernists who do not believe in a fully inspired Bible and do not accept the supernatural element in the Bible. They accept the chief doctrine of Judaism—the Universal Fatherhood of God and Brotherhood of Man.

2. It has such small creedal basis as to permit membership to those who put any construction they please on "Jesus Christ as Lord and Saviour."

3. Its leaders have invariably meddled with politics and advocated passage of actions by Congress without full investigation and in some cases that have little or no religious content.

4. It has emphasized for years the Social Gospel to the neglect of the only true Gospel of the Grace of God through the substitutionary atonement of our Lord Jesus Christ. Of course that has its social implications.

5. The leadership and practices of the N.C.C.C.A. have been condemned by the Laymen's Committee established by the Council itself because of the actions of the Council in political matters.

6. The Presbyterian Church in the U. S. does not need to belong to the N.C.C.C.A. in order to cooperate in Christian work throughout the world. We have been cooperating in missions long before N.C.C.C.A. was established. We are a cooperative church in those things and

IN PARTNERSHIP WITH GOD

By Kenneth S. Keyes, Miami, Fla.

An occasion of great significance is the "President's Breakfast," held each year in the grand ball- ɔom of the Mayflower Hotel in Washington under the auspices of the International Council for 'hristian Leadership.

This year, with Senator Carlson presiding, and with the Vice President, Mr. Nixon, members f the Cabinet and the Supreme Court and large numbers of senators and congressmen and guests ı attendance — some 1,500 in all — the main address was given by Mr. Kenneth Keyes of Miami.

Mr. Keyes has also recently been honored by being made President of the National Association of :eal Estate Boards, the highest honor which can come to one in that business.

Mr. Keyes address is given below: —H.B.D.

One of the words that came to have a real ıeaning to all of us during the last war was ıe word "priority." We learned that things ıost important to the war effort had to be iven the right of way over everything else — ıat they had to come first.

I believe with all my heart, friends, that what ıe world needs most today is for Christians › put first things first. In his sermon on the ıount, Jesus said, "Seek ye *first* the kingdom f God and his righteousness" and He promised ıat if we will do that all things necessary to ur well being will be provided.

When we pause to think about it, the reasons 'hy God *should* have first priority over our lives re very clear and plain:

God is certainly entitled to first claim on our time because he *controls* our time. The years we will spend on this earth are in His hands.

God should have first claim on our energies and our abilities because He gives us our energies and our talents of varying kinds.

And it follows very logically that God should have first claim on our money, for the dollars we earn are but the end product of our God given time, energy and ability.

It isn't really difficult to *recognize* that God clearly *entitled* to first claim on our lives and hat we produce with them but the hard part ɔmes when we try to apply this truth and ıake it work in the busy world in which we live.

Surely, if we are to put God first there must ≥ a portion of each day set aside for the read- ıg of His word and for a vital prayer life. We ıust never be too busy to respond to calls for :rvice in our churches. We must witness for [im in our businesses and professions — and se our energies and abilities to serve Him in ur daily living.

Many of us find it especially difficult to put ·od first in our money making. God wants us to remember *always* that it is *He* who gives us the time, energy and ability to earn the dollars we receive. He gives us in this Book a simple, practical plan that we are to adopt as a constant reminder that all of our blessings come from Him. God asks us to set aside the first *tenth* of our income or profits — the scriptural tithe — to dedicate that tenth to His glory and use it to further His work on earth.

It is interesting to note that when God first organized the Jewish people into a nation he gave them the law of the tithe in these words:

> "And all the tithe of the land, whether of the seed of the land or of the fruit of the tree, *is* the Lord's."

Note that God didn't say, "The tithe should be *given* to the Lord." He said, "The tithe *is* the Lord's." It belongs to God. And centuries later in accusing the people of failing to keep this law, God didn't say — "You haven't been liberal enough" — or "You haven't done your duty on this matter of giving." God said, "Ye have *robbed* me in tithes and offerings."

Our Lord endorsed tithing when He was here on earth. The early Christian church considered it the duty of every Christian to tithe. And the early believers must have considered tithing not only a duty but also a high privilege for history records that St. Cyprian, Bishop of Carthage, once *punished* the people in his congregation by *forbidding* them to bring their tithes and offerings until the ban was lifted.

There are some Christians today who conscientiously believe that the law of the tithe was binding only upon Old Testament believers. I do not hold this view but to me the legal angle is unimportant — especially if we substitute this question: "Should not our love for God, our gratitude to Him for the salvation we have through His son and our appreciation for all the other blessings that He provides so bountifully, prompt *us* to give as much as the Old Testament believer was *commanded* to give under the law?" If we answer this question honestly, surely we must all agree that the tithe is the *minimum* which we as Christians should use for God's honor and glory.

God *usually* blesses financially when we share our incomes liberally with Him. We read in Malachi "Bring ye the whole tithe into my storehouse and prove me now herewith, saith the Lord,—if I will not pour you out a blessing, that there shall not be room enough to receive it." In 20 years of speaking on this subject I have yet to meet a tither who was faithful in giving God His tenth who did not receive a real blessing. Even though the income does not increase God seems to make the 9-10ths go further than the 10-10ths did before.

Here's just one testimony from an automobile dealer in Tennessee: "I have learned that by forming a partnership with Christ and paying more attention to spiritual things and less to material things everything works out much better. I am much better off financially now than I was before I started tithing but even if I had less money I would continue to tithe, for it has been the source of my happiest Christian experience. I have learned that being a partner with Christ and having the privilege of handling a small portion of his business is worth more than all the world has to offer."

If time permitted I could tell you of many leaders of industry and finance who honored God with their tithes — Colgate, Heinz, Hershey, Kraft, Jarman, Kellogg, Penny and Wanamaker are just a few. I could tell you of Coy Langford, a real estate salesman who started tithing when he worked for us in the middle thirties, later established his own office in another city and put 25% of his income into a special bank account in the name "Lord and Langford." Or the story of the North Carolina lumberman who after tithing for many years, increased God's part to 15%, then 20% and finally dedicated 50% of the profits of his planing mill to the Lord. I could tell you about the well-known industrialist who put not 25 — not 50 — but 90% of *all* his assets in a trust for religious and educational purposes and who is still getting along just fine on the 10%.

But I can sum up their experiences in just one short sentence — "We can't outgive God!" The more of our time, our energy, our ability and our money we use to further His work on earth, the more God will pour out his blessings.

But the *financial* blessing that usually comes to the tither is *not* the main consideration. The *spiritual* blessing is far more important.

When we tithe, we have the satisfaction of knowing that God's prior claim is being recognized in this vital part of our lives. With this knowledge comes the realization that we are

"Christ For Our Time Crusade"

"Now is the acceptable time, now is the day of salvation" (II Cor. 6:2)

By Walter W. Brown

For more than a year and a half, in one of e dormitory rooms at Louisville Presbyterian minary, a single topic of conversation held ay almost nightly. These "bull sessions" often tended into the wee hours of the morning. volved in these enthusiastic discussions were ree men, all rising seniors at this institution. he subject that was always central was mass angelism, its motive, philosophy, and value a medium for winning people to Christ.

The men engaged in the nightly discussions ere drawn together in a common bond of llowship by the Holy Spirit. It was not long fore they discovered that they were unified their thinking concerning the very evident end toward a great spiritual revival through ass evangelism. Consequently, as a result of ese long discussions, something new in evanlistic outreach has arisen on the horizon of e Presbyterian Church.

Four months ago, Walter Brown, Jim Billman, d Paul Hopwood agreed that "just talking out" this type ministry had grown to make ch of them spiritually miserable. They found difficult to study, almost impossible to cen- their thoughts on anything else; in fact, en sleep had become a problem. They knew nething had to be done, but were at a loss a solution to the problem so deeply engraved on their hearts.

It was a cold October night, and Billy aham's great Louisville Crusade was drawing its close. Walt, Jim, and Paul were in the all dormitory room at school, the conversan centered upon the same theme as usual, ss evangelism. As the hours wore on into the rning of the next day, each student became reasingly aware of an inner compulsion to something about this thing that had made n so restive for months. The central quesn in each of the three hearts was, "What es God want me to do about this great weight on my conscience?" Finally, each made known fact that words were no longer satisfying d that only action could now answer the estion once for all.

At the hour of one-thirty A. M. the three n, who had made a final decision, quickly essed and rushed downtown, were sitting in lobby of the hotel at which Billy Graham s staying. They had phoned ahead only to learn that Billy hadn't yet checked in for the night.

Shortly, Leighton Ford, one of Graham's associates, checked in, and was stopped by the three students in the hotel lobby. At this unholy hour he listened patiently to their plans for organizing an evangelistic team of their own, offered them sound advice, and prayed with them. As the men were leaving the hotel, Billy Graham, with Mrs. Graham, entered. They had been out to one of the numerous cottage prayer meetings that had been set up to follow the Crusade services each evening. The three students introduced themselves and asked for an appointment for later in the day. Billy was not too tired to show a spark of interest, and agreed to see the men following breakfast.

As a result of counseling with Dr. Graham and his associate, Grady Wilson, the determination to form an evangelistic organization was brought to a head. Both of these men, who are being used of God with such amazing results, offered suggestions and advice of immense value, advice that had as its foundation the vast experience of the Graham organization.

As a result of the Lord's leading in so many ways, the opening of one door after another, "The Christ For Our Time" evangelistic organization is now a reality. From discussion and prayer, to action, to formation, God has led these three men in a marvelous way!

The difficulties in setting up such an enterprise are staggering. The fervent prayer for God's guidance, the actual "leg work" involved in making contacts with those who might be interested in supporting such a venture of faith, and the mechanics of organization, and the planning of a mode of operation demand much in the way of optimistic patience. It is difficult to have a patient mind when God has set the heart on fire! But all of the preliminaries are behind. The "Christ For Our Time Crusade" now looks to the future. Like Abraham, the three men who comprise the evangelistic team are ready to venture forth wherever the Lord might lead. A city-wide, or community-wide, Crusade for Christ is possible for your town or community if the local clergy wishes to use this new organization in an effort to bring about a meaningful revival of the hearts of men, women, and young people. The slogan of the "Christ For Our Time Crusade" is "not to do something local ministers have failed to do, but to assist them as they strive to make 'the Word become flesh' a reality to those who are yet strangers to God."

With singleness of purpose, a zeal for winning the lost for Christ that transcends denominational loyalties, and the fervent hope that God *will* bring true revival in our time, Walt, Jim, and Paul encourage the prayers, support, and understanding of all who love the Lord, Jesus Christ.

The Board of Advisors of the Crusade is made up of clergymen representing five denominations. Presbyterian Advisors are: Dr. William A. Benfield, Dr. William Douglas Chamberlain, and Dr. Andrew K. Rule. From the Methodist Church, Dr. Albert G. Stone, Supt. of the Methodist Board of Church Extension. Rev. Mr. Albert H. Behle of the Evangelical-Reform faith, Dr. Paul S. Stauffer, Christian minister, Dr. John W. Meloy, Chairman, Louisville Council of Churches, and Dr. John S. Chambers, Disciples of Christ. These men, as a result of Billy Graham's Louisville Crusade, have seen the Spirit of God at work through mass evangelism. They have volunteered their help to further the great work that can be done through this medium in the name of Christ.

The Crusade team would like to hear from you. As they look forward with great optimism to venturing forth in this great work of the Kingdom, they need your encouragement. Let them hear from you. Let them know that your hearts, your prayers, are with them. You may address your letter to "Christ For Our Time Crusade," P. O. Box 775, Louisville, 1, Kentucky.

Helps To Understanding Scripture Readings in *Day by Day*

By Rev. C. C. Baker

Sunday, March 3, *Luke* 9:23-27. It was when Christ first began to talk about the cross (v.22), that He also began to talk about the price of discipleship (vv.23-26). He made it very clear, however, that following Him was more worthwhile than anything else in the world (vv.23-27). What does a person gain by following Jesus (vv.24,25,27)? Is the question of v.25 a sensible one? What answer does it demand? Following Christ involves a willingness to die to self and its desires in order to live for Christ (v.24), a willingness to take up one's cross and live each day entirely as unto Him (v.23). See

SUNDAY SCHOOL Lessons

.ESSON FOR MARCH 3

By THE REV. J. KENTON PARKER

The Great Confession

3ackground Scripture: Matthew 16:13 - 17:27
)evotional Reading: John 3:14-21

John 3:14-21 is a fine Introduction for our lesson. It contains the very heart of the gospel. In ɩur lesson we have again the heart of the gospel, for the gospel centers in the Deity and Atonement ɩf Christ, His Glory and His Saving power. When we include the Background Scripture we get our great Truths about our Lord: His Deity; His Sacrifice; His Transfiguration; His ministry to a ɩeedy world.

. *The Deity of our Lord;* or

The Great Question and Answer. 16:13-20.

The disciples had been with Christ for some ime. They had seen His Life; His Miracles, or 'Signs"; had listened to His Words as He aught and preached. It was important — very mportant — that they should *believe something lefinite* about Him. It would not do for them o have a vague, hazy notion of His Person, or ɩf His Work. Let me say that I like Con-essional Churches, churches that have a 'Creed." It is rather the fashion in these days ɩf loose thinking to talk in a disparaging way ıbout creeds. People are fond of saying, I do ɩot have any creed, or, My creed is the Sermon ɩn the Mount, especially the Golden Rule, ɩr the Thirteenth Chapter of First Corinthians.)ne of the first things that the Church did vas to make a Creed: we call it "The Apostles :reed," and many churches repeat it every ;unday. The "Creeds of Christendom" make nteresting and profitable material for study. The word "creed," as we all know, comes from 'Credo"; "I Believe." (Go back and read our)evotional Reading, and note the words, "who-oever believeth.")

Jesus leads up to this personal question by ısking first a rather general question: Whom lo men say that I the Son of man am? They eplied, John the Baptist, or Elijah, or Jere-niah, or one of the prophets. This is what . great many people still say about Him. They onfess that He was a great man, and a good nan, but refuse to go further. This is Uni-arianism. Mohammedans, unbelievers like Renan, and some Jews, are ready to say that esus was a great and good man. This is a adly deficient and unsatisfactory answer. It an never be the basis of saving faith.

He next said to them, But whom say ye that I am? Simon Peter, acting as spokesman for the disciples, said, Thou art the Christ, the Son of the Living God. This answer comes from heaven. It is the revelation from God. Upon this great fact — the deity of Christ — He builds His Church, and the gates of hell shall never prevail against it. It makes the Church a Living Church which cannot die. I do not see how words could be plainer. It forever excludes from the church any and all who do not so believe. In other words, a Unitarian church is not a church. He, the Head of the church, refuses to step down from His position and be only a man. He is the Son of God; very God of very God.

The "keys" mentioned in verse 19 were not given to Peter exclusively, but to all the disciples, and to "two or three." (see 18:18). To "bind" or "loose" means to prohibit or allow. In other words, the Apostles were given authority to govern the Church. Alford gives several examples of this promise being verified to Peter: he was the first to admit both Jews and Gentiles into the Church; he shut the door in the face of Simon Magus, (Acts 8:21); the case of Ananias and Sapphira serves as an eminent example of "binding," and the lame man at the Beautiful gate of the Temple, of "loosing." (See an excellent discussion of this in The New Testament for English Readers, by Henry Alford, Moody Press, Chicago). The old idea of Peter with a bunch of keys in his hand, guarding the gate to heaven, is pure fancy. Jesus commands the disciples not to proclaim this truth at this time.

II. *The Sacrifice of Christ:* 21-26; 17:22,23.

It is one thing to confess Christ as the Messiah and Son of God; it is different, and more difficult, to see Him as the Suffering One and understand the meaning of His death. When Jesus began to talk about His death and resurrection, the very man who had made such a noble confession a few minutes before, becomes a stumblingblock. Peter is not the only one to whom the Cross was and is, an offense. People still talk about "the gospel of the shambles" and count the blood of Christ as something to be ignored and rejected. They stress His example and teaching and ministry, but have no use for "the blood of the everlasting covenant." They do not accept the truth that remission of sins is through His precious blood, and that this blood cleanses from all sin. Men in their stubborn pride do not wish to be saved in this way. When you cut the blood out of the Plan of Salvation you have cut the heart out of it, for the blood is the life of this plan.

In this day of "blood banks" and blood transfusions we ought to be able to understand this. Both Old and New Testament lose all their meaning when we eliminate the blood. From Genesis to Revelation this scarlet thread binds the Bible together. Woe to those who try to discard it! The great multitude whom no man can number are saved and safe because they have washed their robes and made them white in the blood of the Lamb. If you and I are saved it will be because Christ died for our sins according to the Scriptures and rose again.

Let me press this point and ask each one who reads this to examine his own belief on this vital point. What can wash away my sins? nothing but the blood of Jesus. What can make me whole again? nothing but the blood of Jesus.

There is a fountain filled with blood, Drawn from Immanuel's veins; And sinners plunged beneath that flood, Lose all their guilty stains. This belief of the church is expressed in such beautiful hymns, and others like them; When I survey the wondrous cross, Rock of Ages, Alas and did my Saviour bleed, etc.

Such a sacrifice on the part of Christ demands complete surrender to Him. Must Jesus bear the cross alone, and all the world go free? He tells His disciples, If any man will come after Me, let him deny himself, and take up his cross and follow Me. This is the only way a man can save his life, and this life (soul) is more valuable than the whole world. Thus Jesus revealed to His disciples, and continued to reveal to them, (see chapter 17:22,23) this great truth about His cross and the cross each of us is to bear. I am afraid that we fail to understand the full import of His words even as the disciples failed. May the Holy Spirit enlighten our minds and enable us to see the meaning of discipleship, and the challenge of these words to us today.

YOUNG PEOPLES Department

YOUTH PROGRAM FOR MARCH 3

By THE REV. B. HOYT EVANS

"That's Where Our Money Went"

Scripture: Matthew 25:31-40.

Hymns:
"Come, Thou Almighty King"
"We Give Thee But Thine Own"
"Lead On, O King Eternal"

Suggestions for Program Leader:

(Try to secure two maps—one of the world and one of the sixteen states where the Presbyterian Church, U.S., is organized. If these are not readily available in your church, you can trace off rough maps on large pieces of wrapping paper. Make a small sign for each of the thirteen financial objectives that can be pinned to the map at the appropriate place. On the signs print the name of the objective, the dates when it was considered, the amount of money contributed, if known, and the specific materials or services which our gifts purchased. Let a different young person present each objective, first pinning the sign on the map and then telling in his own words what has been accomplished. We are supplying the basic information below, but any additional facts about these projects will make the program more interesting. If your group is small, and you do not have as many people as objectives, then some of the young people may present more than one objective.)

Leader's Introduction:

Those of us who have been active in the Youth Fellowship for a year or more will remember that we have had a number of financial projects which we have sought to support with our gifts. As a matter of fact, Presbyterian young people have been following this practice for more than five years. Have you ever wondered how much money is contributed, and what has been accomplished through the gifts we have made? If you have, this program ought to supply answers to some of your questionings. We are going to make a brief survey of our financial objectives over the past five years.

1. (Place this sign at Durant, Oklahoma.) In 1952 the contributions of the young people were used to provide scholarships for students attending Oklahoma Presbyterian College. Originally this was a two year college for Indian girls, but now it is a four year college for Indian, Mexican, Chinese, and Caucasian students, both boys and girls. We made it possible for some worthy young people to receive an education at this fine institution.

2. (Place this sign at Germany on the world map.) In 1952 and 1953 we helped rebuild the Reformed (Presbyterian) Seminary at Wuppertal in Germany. Many of the buildings of this institution were destroyed by the bombings during World War II. Over a period of two years we gave $2,592.02, and the buildings which we helped reconstruct are now being used in preparing young German students for the ministry.

3. (Pin this sign on one of the mission fields, possibly the Belgian Congo in Africa.) Also in 1952-53 we sought to raise $20,000.00 for a project which we called "Missions on Wheels." We learned that many of our foreign missionaries were being hindered in their work by inadquate transporation. The $20,000.00 was to be used to buy Jeeps for the missionaries. Through this project the services of the missionaries were extended to more people and their lot was made easier.

4. (Pin this sign on any of the states located in the deep South.) In 1933 the Presbyterian young people gave $5,482.55 to the Scrivner Fund. The purpose of this fund is to train young Negro men for the Christian ministry, and through our financial objective we had a part in it.

5. (Pin this sign on Charlotte, N. C., because one of the nurseries was located there.) In 1953-54 our gifts helped to equip Negro Nurseries in several southern cities. These nurseries were provided in order that children of working parents could be left in wholesome, Christian surroundings while their parents were away from home. Our gifts amounted to $5,520.60 over the two years, and the money was used to buy pianos, furniture, and play equipment.

6. (Place this sign on Indonesia.) Indonesia, as you can see on the map, is a string of islands stretching from Australia to the Asian continent. There are about 3,000 of these islands, and they cover about 3,000 miles. In 1954 we gave approximately $3,500.00 to help with youth work in Indonesia. The money was used to set up Christian training schools at several points in the scattered island empire, and to publish a Christian newspaper for young people.

7. (Place this sign at Danville, Ky. One of the guidance centers is located there.) In 1954-55 our gifts went to provide equipment and trained personnel for several Vocational Guidance Centers located at various places throughout our church. These centers serve to discover the skills and aptitudes of young people who are interested in making an intelligent choice of their life work. Contributions to this objective amounted to $3,124.59.

8. (This sign should be pinned on Mexico.) Another objective for 1954-55 was a new mission station at Ometepec, in Mexico. We had reports from the two young couples who opened this station, and we learned of the material needs which our dollars could meet. Over the two year period our gifts were used to buy a plane, equip a clinic, and to build and equip a youth center. The missionaries let the Presbyterian young people name the new clinic, and so it is called "Hospital of Friendship."

(9. (Pin this sign on India.) One of our 1955 objectives was known as "World Youth Project." This was a cooperative venture with other denominations in which we contributed approximately $2,300.00 to a fund which was to be used wherever needed all over the world to provide Christian literature and training for young people. Some of the countries which benefited were India, Korea, Japan, and the Bible lands.

10. (This sign should be pinned on West Brazil.) In 1955-56 we gave funds for the building of a Christian high school in one of the thriving new cities of West Brazil. The money we gave was a great encouragement to the Brazilian Christians, and work on the school has gone steadily forward.

11. (Place this sign at Atlanta, Georgia, the home of the Department of Radio and Television of the Presbyterian Church.) Another 1955-56 objective was to help provide a mobile radio and television studio. The purpose of such a studio is to produce on-the-spot Christian programs in various localities, and to train many people in the proper techniques of producing good Christian programs for radio and television. In 1955 we gave $3,698.32.

12. (Place this sign at Richmond, Virginia, the home of the Presbyterian Board of Christian Education.) In 1956 and again this year we are contributing to a fund which will enable the Board of Christian Education to provide a three month supply of free literature to every new Sunday school which is organized in our church. In one of our programs for this quarter we studied the need for such a project.

13. (Pin this sign on Seoul, Korea.) Another of our 1956 objectives carried over to this year is the reconstruction of the largest Presbyterian Seminary in the world. The Korean Seminary which has so many students is pitifully poor in buildings and equipment. Some of the buildings they did have were destroyed during the Korean War. We have already given some help in meeting a desperate need, and we shall have another opportunity this year.

(The closing prayer could either be led by an individual or could be a season of sentence prayers by members of the group. Give thanks for the progress that has been made, and ask God's continued blessings on these various projects.)

CHILDRENS Page

The Sacrifice

When Abraham and Isaac reached the top of the mountain they began to build an altar. They gathered the stones together, and when the altar was completed Abraham arranged the wood upon it. But something was missing. There was no lamb for the sacrifice. Isaac was expecting God to send the lamb any moment, as his father said He would, but now, the Altar, the wood and fire were ready - and no lamb! Isaac must have thought "Why is God delaying"? Then his father spoke: "my boy, God says you are to be the lamb for the sacrifice"! "What? father, I"? "Yes, my son, God says it, and you know God must be obeyed." Isaac trembled while his father tied his hands and lifted him upon the Altar. As he raised the knife to slay his son, God spoke from heaven: "Abraham, Abraham"! "Here am I." "Do not slay the boy, for now I know you are obedient." And Abraham helped Isaac down from the altar. A noise in the bushes - and there was a ram, caught by it's horns. God had sent it in time to take Isaac's place. And so God sent His beloved son to take our place, that we might be saved from the penalty of our sin and have everlasting Life.

E.

"Is This Your Life?"

Prologue

For every woman in this church
There's work to do, you needn't search,
Just look around, as others do
A million needs spring into view.
Or, if you search, then search your soul
Decide on what will be life's goal.
There's no excuse that's big or small
That's strong enough to halt God's call.
Each woman has a talent she
Should give to God most willingly.
We point today to six who give—
They're only samples, just a few
Of many women whom we knew
Who serve with dignity and grace
Whatever time, whatever place.

No Help At Home

No help at home and yet you do
The work the Lord demands of you.
You raise two children, keep a house
Teach Sunday School with your dear spouse.
You lead a circle, take surveys,
For Bible School on your spare days.
You teach them all the Golden Rule
At our Vacation Bible School.
How easy to have turned aside
The many jobs that you have tried.
But you find time and find a way
To serve the church every day.
Is this **your** life? If not, guess who.
With willingness, it could be you.

Grandmother

You could have said, I'm tired, I'll quit
I'll let the others do their bit.
I've raised four children, seven grand
And soon an eighth will be on hand.
To stewardship I've given time
The nursery is a joy of mine.
I've taught church classes, circles too
I've cheered the old, welcomed new.
I've kept the women's history
For Presbyterial, been V. P.
But no, I won't retire, instead
I'll give myself a quick retread.
Is this your life? If not, guess who.
With enthusiasm it could be you.

Busy With Civic Affairs

Perhaps your mother said, as mine
"For every woman there is time
To serve her family and her church
To help her City and its search
For better living for us all"—
If this is true, you've heard the call,
And answered with your very best
You've done a lot missed by the rest.
The Crippled Children, P. T. A.,
The Scouts, Arts Council shared your day.
Twice you've helped a woman's club
Have been their leader, been their hub.
You've headed circles, taught them too
And even then have passed review
On programs of the W.O.C.
And lessons that you taught Class Three.
Is this your life? If not, guess who.
With civic pride, it could be you.

Mother of Young Children

For you to say "But I have four . . ."
A grand excuse—you need no more.
A busy mother, wife and friend
You start at dawn, some days don't end.
Your circle meets, there're plans to make
You told the boys you'd bake a cake.
Vacation Bible School's begun
There's always things that must be done.
The young folks meet, you chaperone
Remind your husband on the 'phone.
The Christmas Toy Shop needs you now
You take the children, show them how
To do for others, learning too
What Christian living does for you.
Is this your life? If not, guess who.
With planning, then, it could be you.

Professional Member

To face that office, type each day
To work from 8 to 5, then say
"I'll stop at church and help them now
They need us all—there's strength somehow
To type the yearbook, records too
To help some other persons who
Just have no way to get about
No car in which they can get out."
You take them everywhere in town
You've moved them lock and stock and gown,
You've been a circle chairman twice
Given committees good advice.
You've held Class 17th' purse strings
And done a dozen other things.
On holidays and late at night
You've kept an ever-burning light.
Is this your life? If not, guess who.
With effort, then it could be you.

Physical Disadvantage

Of all the burdens on us all
How can you look on your's as small.
And yet make us realize
Above what hardships we can rise.
So richly you have spent your life
In nursing others through their strife.
In healing with your kindly hand
The sicknesses that threaten man.
And yet there has been time for you
To serve your church and circle too.
To go to Sunday School and pray
For strength to work another day.
You fold our News Appeals with care
And help each one at home to share,
88 years of Christian living
Of Christian doing and Christian giving.
Is this **your** life? If not, guess who.
With perseverance, it could be you.

Postlogue

Perhaps you've guessed each woman who
Has shared her life here in review.
But if you do not know them now
It's more important to know how
They have found a peace of mind
By serving God and all mankind.
This life of joy is yours to live
You only need to learn to give
A little of your thought and time
A little of your heart and mind.
Remember, God will ask of you
No more than He knows you can do.

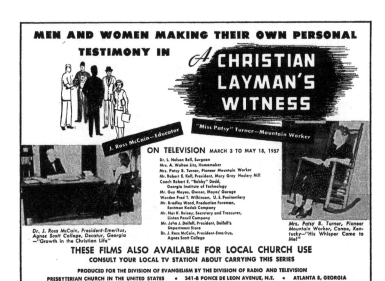

New Homes

Traveling home, on the night train to Pittsburgh, I found myself, quite by accident, sharing a coach with twenty refugees who had arrived in our country that morning on a troop ship. Their destinations varied from Gettysburg, Pennsylvania, to Columbus, Ohio, Indianapolis, Indiana, and on even to Texas. With what eagerness they were approaching their new homes!

They all spoke enough English to be easily understood and explained that they had been studying in the camps in preparation. Most of them were from Germany, from Lutheran or Reformed churches and were fine, intelligent looking people. They were all sponsored by the World Council of Churches and had been met that morning at the pier by Church World Service. The young man who sat with me was an escapee from East Berlin. He had lost contact with his family completely and was alone at the age of twenty-four. He said, "Everyone has been so kind to us. The women are wonderful."

I said "good-bye" to them as I left the train and wished them godspeed. The little ones were curled up on the seats, sleeping soundly. The men were peering out the windows at the large illuminated buildings in wonder. "What were their thoughts? What would happen to them tomorrow?" I wondered. "They believe in Christian ideals and have faith in God's love. That is why they have come to build a new life," I kept reminding myself. "Our work is to introduce them to the finest our country has to offer." The Scripture for the World Day of Prayer service had new meaning for me. "Who shall separate us from the love of Christ? Shall tribulation, or distress, or persecution or famine, or nakedness, or peril, or sword?"

Who, indeed!

—Martha E. McCurdy
Pittsburgh, Pennsylvania

My Methods and Plans of Developing a One Day Conference

When I received a communication from Mrs. J. O. Cobb, of Smyrna, Georgia, asking me to plan a One Day Conference to be held at my church (The Ebenezer Presbyterian) I thought that I would surely faint. However I began making plans and wondering at the same time if they would materialize. I called Mesdames E. Hyer and J. White asking their support (Mrs. Hyer is a recent graduate of the Women's Conference held at Spellman College each year and Mrs. White will graduate next year) both readily agreed . . . this gave me inspiration.

I then called the ladies of my church and other churches. Mrs. J. Howell of the First Presbyterian Church, sent cards to some in nearby cities. All readily agreed to give of their services. Too, Mr. John Howell (son of Mrs. Howell) furnished the music for the first half of our service. All of the above mentioned invited their church members and friends, so we had a very good attendance.

Feeling that we would have plenty of sandwiches and cookies (furnished by the ladies) my thoughts turned to drinks—immediately I called the Coca Cola Plant and asked for the president, Mr. Barron, and told him of our plans and that I would appreciate a donation of drinks. He asked how many I expected. I told him and he immediately put his secretary on the phone to take the order. They were sent out iced and packed to perfection.

We had a wonderful time and a full program, I think.

I learned a wonderful lesson from this experience — people are eager and willing to be of service if they are only asked and it gave me a wonderful feeling of inspiration and a closer contact with our Almighty One.

(Mrs. Robert P.) Alice G. Del Pino
Rome, Georgia

"We Want Bibles"

There has probably never been a greater evidence of the power and need for the Bible than has been shown by the thousands of requests for Scriptures received by the American Bible Society from the desperate and homeless Hungarian people.

"The very first convoy of trucks driving into Budapest found terrible depredation—absence of bread, loss of great stocks of clothing—but the cry was for an adequate supply of Scriptures," according to a report made to the Bible Society by Dr. Franklin Clark Fry, well-known churchman whose information came from an authenticated source.

Immediately the refugees began crossing into Austria all available supplies of Hungarian Scriptures in Western Europe were rushed to Vienna for free distribution. But the several thousand available volumes were not enough for the one hundred thousand refugees. More Bibles were needed. Arrangements were quickly made to ship 60,000 Hungarian Gospels of John from American Bible Society stocks in the United States. Through the cooperation of the Federation of Swiss Bible Societies 100,000 copies each of Luke and John were to be printed in Zurich for delivery by December 15. Before Christmas the Society planned that there would be enough Gospels on hand for free distribution to every refugee so that he could read the Christmas story himself.

Presses in England were already printing 10,000 Hungarian Testaments for the British and Foreign Bible Society and authorization was given to increase the edition to 20,000 volumes. These Testaments will be ready by March 15. And what about whole Bibles? The Bible Society learned that printers in Holland had paper and an available press. Printing of 30,000 Testaments and 15,000 Bibles could begin immediately. Delivery of these books has been promised also for March 15, thanks to the modern method of printing from photo-offset plates prepared from photographs of Bibles and Testaments printed in Hungary in 1955 and shipped to Amsterdam for distribution to Hungarians in Western Europe.

Scriptures are also being supplied for Hungarian refugees arriving in the United States. Secretary Richard H. Ellingson has been meeting the refugees at Camp Kilmer, New Jersey, and personally and with the added help of the Chaplains at the Camp offering them either a Hungarian Bible or a New Testament. These Scriptures have been eagerly received.

A Testimony

I memorized Ephesians last year, and this year I have memorized Philippians, Colossians and Philemon. It is such a blessed experience to know the Bible by heart, to be able to go to bed at night and shut your eyes and read His promises in silence, to wake with His Word in your heart.

Please don't think I could repeat any or all of them without a mistake for I couldn't, but I do know them so that I can go all the way through just for my own enjoyment and without missing any of the content, though I do leave out a word, maybe here and there, or use the wrong article or conjunction of something. I did want to know all the prison epistles and I believe the more one tries to memorize, the easier it is. Ephesians was lots harder than the others, I worked on it the whole year. Philippians, I almost learned in just two weeks.

—From A Woman of Our Church

From Habakkuk 2:4

Oh—God
These times, this world—these wars
We do not understand—
Lift us from despair. Instead
May we know Thy hand
In love rests still upon our head.

Oh—God
Our vision is so short. This strife
And all these horrors seem
So endless—fierce and dark—
The end of every dream
Of liberty and life.

Oh—God
Of thy bounteous strength do give—
Give us that kind of faith
By which, in thy Holy Word
Thou sayest
The just shall live—

(Mrs. W. E.) Mary Patton

NEWS of CHURCHES Around the World

Increased Benevolence Giving

Atlanta—Giving to the benevolence causes of the General Assembly of the Presbyterian Church, U.S., reached an all-time high during 1956. The General Council of the denomination announced today that a total of $6,026,283.26 was contributed by the Church for the eleven benevolence agencies' work. This is the first time the total has passed the $6 million mark, and represents a 14.02% increase over 1955.

The increase from 1955 to 1956 amounted to $736,958, believed to be the largest within a single year in the history of the Church. Even so, giving fell short of the budgeted needs of the benevolence program by $491,295, or 7.54%. This in itself reflects a highly significant gain over 1955, for with a smaller budget for the smaller total membership, giving still fell short of budgeted needs by 15.5% in that earlier year.

Of special significance was the fact that the budget of the Board of World Missions, representing more than half the denomination's total for Assembly benevolences, was over-subscribed for the first time since 1928. The Board actually received $3,332,210, or 101% of its $3,300,000 budget. This record giving has already been reflected in immediate increases in salaries paid to missionaries, made effective Jan. 1, 1957, and voted by the Board in its January meeting. From that date single missionaries will receive $10 more a month, and couples $20 more a month.

The Board of Annuities and Relief also received more than its budget, by 31%, and will thus be able to maintain its increased rate of aid to retired ministers, and the widows and orphans of ministers. Actual receipts of this board totaled $579,537.

With the application of the Equalization Fund, all other benevolence agencies have received 86.325% of their budgeted needs. Actual receipts of all benevolence agencies are as follows:

World Missions	$3,332,210.00
Annuities and Relief	579,537.87
Church Extension	1,070,436.67
Christian Education	430,869.84
Board of Women's Work	92,839.35
The General Council	101,186.61
Assembly's Training School	131,511.41
Montreat	125,393.98
Stillman College	108,623.01
Historical Foundation	16,162.03
American Bible Society	37,512.49
	$6,026,283.26
	92.46% of budget

General William K. Harrison To Head Chicago Evangelical Welfare Agency

Lieutenant General William K. Harrison, soon to retire from the United States Army, has accepted an appointment as executive director of the Evangelical Welfare Agency. The organization is the Chicago subsidiary of the Midwest Region of the National Association of Evangelicals, and its program is the placement of orphaned or deserted children in Christian homes for adoption or foster care.

General Harrison will begin his civilian career March 1, following 40 years of service in the United States Army. He entered military life during World War I. His first assignment was with the First Cavalry at Camp Lawrence J. Hearn, California, and Douglas, Arizona. He was commissioned a Second Lieutenant in the cavalry in 1917.

Following the war, he served on the Army's language detail in France and Spain, after which he did duty at various posts in this country.

In 1954 General Harrison was appointed Commander-in-Chief of the Caribbean area, which position he held until January, 1957, when he returned to the United States pending retirement from active service.

The Evangelical Welfare Agency, chartered in 1950, has its headquarters at 542 South Dearborn Street in Chicago, and is currently aiding 140 children. It serves, on an interdenominational basis, both white and colored children. The agency's activities are governed by an 18 member board whose chairman is a Chicago attorney, Harold B. MacKenzie. The EWA is supported largely by evangelical Protestants.

Having expressed the desire to devote the years following retirement from the army to Christian service, General Harrison will succeed Dr. Harold L. Lundquist, who resigned January 1.

General Harrison has long been noted for his Christian leadership. Throughout his years of military service he was active in aiding his men spiritually, both by private counsel and public speaking in army chapels.

ALABAMA

Tuscaloosa Presbytery—From January 13th-16th, four World Missions Conferences were arranged by the Executive Secretary, Reverend J. David Simpson, to be held in the following Districts of the Presbytery: The First Presbyterian Church, Tuscaloosa, January 13th, to serve District IV; The First Presbyterian Church, Marion, January 14th, to serve District III; The First Presbyterian Church, Demopolis, January 15th, to serve District II; The First Presbyterian Church, Selma, to serve District I.

We were privileged to have Dr. D. J. Cumming, Education Secretary of our Board of World Missions with us during these days, and also, Dr. and Mrs. L. A. McMurray of our Congo Mission in Africa.

Chas. E. (Chuck) Templeton, D.D.

Society of Missionary Inquiry . . . Columbia Seminary

The Society of Missionary Inquiry of Columbia Theological Seminary, Decatur, Georgia, has announced plans for the Fifth World Missions Conference to be held April 5-7, 1957. This year's conference will again be held at Rock Eagle State Park (4-H Club Camp near Eatonton, Georgia.)

Invitations are extended to all Seminary and graduate students, faculty, and medical and nursing students, college students, high school students in the last two years of school, and adult advisors who are interested in learning of the great task that our Church, and the whole Christian Church, faces in presenting Christ to a needy world. The Society of Missionary Inquiry personally urges each and every student to remember this date and make plans to attend.

The program will include addresses by Dr. James Sprunt, pastor of the First Presbyterian Church in Raleigh, N. C., and Dr. S. Hugh Bradley from the Board of World Missions in Nashville, Tenn. Also, on the program will be missionaries directly back from the mission field to give a first-hand account of the mission work and the needs of these people. Our Church is presently sending missionaries to nine different foreign countries. All missionaries and their families who are home on furlough will be extended a special invitation to be at this conference and tell of their experiences on the field.

The purpose of this conference is to present the challenge of the mission program of our church; to meet the great mission leaders of our Church; to get acquainted with missionaries and their work; to have fellowship with hundreds of Christian young people in an atmosphere of renewed spiritual strength and faith.

Last year there were between five and six hundred young people and adults who attended this conference, representing nine states and four foreign countries. Our missionary leaders gave the great challenge that Christ has given to all Christians: "Go ye into all the world and preach the gospel . . ." Our youth of today will be our leaders of tomorrow. They must be presented with this great work of telling to the world the Gospel of Christ. Every Christian, regardless of his calling in life, should be aware of this great need.

Every person certainly is not called by God to go to the mission field, but we all, as Christians, are called by God to support His work throughout the world. This conference is one of the few opportunities our young people will have in getting a first-hand account of our mission work. As a result of a lot of work and prayer last year's conference was a great success. Over forty young people stated that they were seriously considering going into the mission field. It is our hope and prayer that the 1957 conference will be even greater.

The Society of Missionary Inquiry is fortunate in being able to have two such able speakers as Dr. Sprunt and Dr. Bradley.

Dr. James Sprunt received his B.A. degree from Davidson College and Th.M. from Princeton Theological Seminary. He has held several pastorates and is now serving the First Presbyterian Church of Raleigh, N. C. Dr. Sprunt has visited our mission work in Mexico, Brazil, and the Belgian Congo, at his own expense, in an effort to bolster the support of World Missions. He is also a noted speaker in the Presbyterian Church .

Dr. S. Hugh Bradley was born in China of missionary parents. He received his B.A. degree from Davidson College and B.D., Th.M., and Th.D. from Union Theological Seminary. He held several pastorates before he became the Field Secretary of the Board of World Missions, Presbyterian Church, U.S.

Rock Eagle State Park is more than adequate in handling the needs of this conference. It is one of the most modern up-to-date camps of its kind in the South. There are fifty-four cabins, each of which cost approximately ten thousand dollars each. The cabins are of concrete structure and will house 18 people. The auditorium will seat 1200. There is also a modern cafeteria that can serve four different lines simultaneously. This cafeteria will compare favorably with the best on any college campus.

On the camp grounds are facilities for soft ball, volley ball, indoor sports, swimming (swimming pool), and many other types of recreation. Quoting one of last year's missionaries, "It is indeed 'roughing it' in style!"

It is the earnest desire of the Society of Missionary Inquiry that all interested students come and take part in this great undertaking. The date again: April 5-7, 1957. Registrations will be handled by Mr. Bill Shouse, Columbia Seminary, Decatur, Georgia. The cost for each student will be $6.50. The remainder of the cost will be paid by the Society of Missionary Inquiry. Every one who is interested please send your name and registration fee to Mr. Shouse. The registration fee also may be paid upon arrival at the Conference. However, if these matters could be sent in beforehand it would save time and confusion.

Commercial buses run within three miles of Rock Eagle State Park. Transportation will be furnished from this point or from the two towns nearby, Eatonton and Madison. If this transportation is so desired please make a notation on your registration that is sent in.

It is the humble and sincere prayer of the Society of Missionary Inquiry to spread the wonderful news of the saving knowledge of our Lord Jesus Christ around the world. Join them in praying God's blessing upon the conference and those who come.

GEORGIA

The Presbyterian Center in Atlanta, Georgia has announced the purchase of two additional structures which brings the total housing on the property at 341 Ponce de Leon Avenue to six buildings. Cost of the newly acquired buildings was $85,000.

Total footage along Ponce de Leon Avenue is now 417 feet. The property runs 400 feet deep through to North Avenue and 400 feet along North Avenue. Buildings are listed as A, B, C, D, E and F. General Assembly Agencies now located at the Center are: Board of Women's Work, Minister and His Work—in Building A; Board of Church Extension—Building B; General Council, Board of Annuities and Relief—Building C; (Presbyterian Book Store—Building D); Office of the Stated Clerk, recently moved into one of the newly purchased structures—Building E.

Charles J. Currie, Executive Secretary of the Board of Annuities and Relief, which Board manages the Center, states that preliminary planning for one modern structure to house all of these offices is underway. Mr. Currie expressed the hope that the structure will be completed by 1961—the year that marks the 100th anniversary of the Presbyterian Church in the United States.

CHANGE OF ADDRESS: Rev. Vernon Crawford, formerly of Moultrie, Ga., is now Associate Minister at First Presbyterian Church, St. Petersburg, Florida.

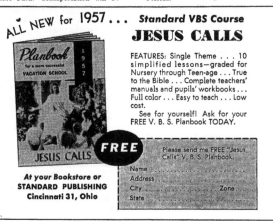

LOUISIANA

Alexandria—The world premiere of the "On to Miami" color movie in sound was held at the Assembly Men's Council meeting at Montreat, N. C., Jan. 4, 5 and 6. The movie, promoting the convention of Presbyterian men at Miami, Fla., Oct. 10-14, was narrated by Dr. S. J. Patterson, Jr., secretary of men's work.

The film was supplied by the Miami Chamber of Commerce and was edited and the sound track attached by the Protestant Radio and TV Center at Atlanta. Dr. John M. Alexander, secretary of the Board of Church Extension, told the council of the work on the Center on the movie and five TV shorts authorized by the convention over-all committee. Thirteen copies of the movie will be available in February to be shown to church groups and will be offered to television stations.

This twelfth annual meeting of A.M.C. was featured by the attendance of ten of the eleven past presidents: Robert F. Kennon, Louisiana, 1946; Everett L. Repass, Virginia, 1947; L. Roy Klein, Texas, 1948; Joseph B. Fraser, Georgia, 1949; Nat K. Reiney, Tennessee, 1950; J. E. Dews, Arkansas, 1951; Emile Deith, Louisiana, 1952; John V. Matthews, Tennessee, 1954; Walter Humphrey, Texas, 1955; John Deifell, North Carolina, 1956. Royall Brown, North Carolina, 1953, was unable to attend.

Officers elected for 1957 were: Elmer Taylor, Jacksonville, Fla., president; J. W. Baldwin, Midland, Tex., T. Mack Blackburn, Knoxville, Tenn., and H. Rives King, Norfolk, Va., vice presidents; James A. Harkins, Oklahoma City, Okla., budget and finance secretary; John M. Myers, Jr., New Orleans, secretary.

Six permanent committe chairmen were named: J. W. Baldwin, program, and J. W. Hyde, Georgia, projects, for three years; Ralph Brewer, Louisiana, publicity, and James A. Harkins, Oklahoma, contact men, two years; H. Rives King, Virginia, men's council training, and T. Mack Blackburn, Appalachia, best practices, one year. Brewer is serving a three-year term, having been originally appointed at Louisville in January, 1956.

More than 165 men attended the meeting and almost 100 recommendations of the six committees were adopted. Representatives of the various boards and agencies of the church addressed the council. Promotion of the Miami convention was stressed throughout the three-day session.

Dr. Marshall C. Dendy installed the officers and members of the executive committee at the Sunday morning services.

Belhaven College

Jackson, Miss. — Enthusiastic and encouraging support was given to Belhaven College here, as the college began its $1,500,000 development program, a long-range plan.

The first phase of the program was a drive for $250,000 to be given by the Presbyterian churches of Mississippi Synod. This drive has already gone over the top.

The Jackson and Hinds County phase of the program began Jan. 24. The goal for this campaign is another $250,000 to be given by the friends of the college in the vicinity of the college community. They hope to match the amount pledged or given by the Presbyterians. The $500,000 will secure for the college a much needed science hall, and a dormitory.

to freedom as we know it on the Western Hemisphere." He affirmed his belief that Belhaven has a "significant and vital, and perhaps unique contribution to make, not only to the denomination which supports it, and the community in which it is located, but also to the State of Mississippi, and to the South." He said that he was glad that Belhaven, in its curricula, in its faculty, and in its executive administration by the tests of scholarship and dynamic Christian faith and purpose, justifies the loyalty of the Christian church and the community."

Dr. G. T. Gillespie, president emeritus, presented the banquet invocation.

NORTH CAROLINA

Davidson — Russell Elway Brown of Lenoir has joined the Davidson College faculty for the spring semester as Visiting Assistant Professor of Economics.

Prof. Brown is on leave of absence from the Lenoir-Rhyne College faculty, and has been completing work during the past year toward his Doctor of Philosophy degree from the University of Chicago.

SOUTH CAROLINA

Columbia—Elected to serve as commissioners to this year's General Assembly, which meets in Birmingham, Ala., on April 25, are the 3 ministers and 3 elders who will represent Congaree Presbytery. They were chosen with their alternates at the January 29 meeting of the Presbytery, which was held at the First Presbyterian Church of Aiken, S. C.

The ministers are: The Rev. Palmer P. Patterson of Eastover, the Rev. Jack M. Kennedy of Aiken, the Rev. Jno. W. Davis of Johnston. Elders chosen are: H. Graham Reynolds of Trenton, Frank Needham of Columbia, and W. W. Zealy, Jr., of North Augusta.

Alternates are the Rev. W. T. King of Bethune, the Rev. Jos. D. Beale of Ridgeway, the Rev. Jno. Pridgen, Jr., of North Augusta; and elders, Gen. W. N. Cork of Columbia, Claude H. Ragsdale, Jr., of Winnsboro, and Jas. Ward of Lugoff.

TEXAS

Texas City—The Rev. David M. Currie, pastor of First Presbyterian Church here, was one of three selected as Texas City's outstanding men of 1956. The honor was given the pastor at the annual banquet of the Chamber of Commerce on Jan. 16. Mr. Currie, Robert Renfroe and W. P. Ludwig, Jr., were praised for "unselfish devotion to duty and contributions to the city during the past year." Renfroe is director of Texas City High School Band, and Ludwig is president of the Texas City Terminal Railroad and Docks.

IN PARTNERSHIP WITH GOD

(Continued from Page 8)

Our country was brought into being under God. We recognize our dependence upon Him in our national motto "In God We Trust." And in spite of the fact that as individuals and as a nation we have at times strayed far from Him, God blessed and prospered us above all the countries on earth. God who controls the destinies of all nations has seen fit to elevate the United States into a position of unquestioned world leadership.

These blessings impose upon us a responsibility which far transcends the mere making of loans or grants of money, food or other national aid to our less fortunate neighbors, helpful as these are. We must impart something of our *spiritual* strength to the peoples of these lands.

May we therefore through God centered Christian statesmanship lead the peoples of the world to recognize—

1st, that America today is in a position to help others primarily because God has blessed our nation whose foundations were laid in trust in Him,

And 2nd, that our help to others is prompted not only by defense considerations but also by a sincere desire to be faithful stewards of the blessings that God has poured out so bountifully upon us.

May we therefore as *individuals* and as a *nation* gratefully acknowledge that all of our blessings come from God and recognize more fully that we have a *responsibility* and indeed, a *challenge*, to administer our stewardship — using our time, energy, ability and money — in ways that will honor God and help our fellow man.

HELPS TO UNDERSTANDING SCRIPTURE READINGS IN DAY BY DAY

(Continued from Page 10)

for our sins that we might behold His love (vv.10,14). Whoever commits Himself to Christ for the forgiveness of his sins finds God's nature abiding in Him (v.15) — and a new life in Christ (v.9). We can recognize this new life by the presence of the Holy Spirit (v.13). As God's nature dwells within, His love must also abide within (vv.12,16). What is the outward evidence in your life that God's nature abides in you (vv.7-8,11,20)? The same love that sent Jesus into the world enables us to love one another (vv.7-8).

Friday, March 8, *I Corinthians* 10:12-13. The Christian who is beginning to feel secure because of the progress he has made in the Christian life must beware lest He fall (v.12). To illustrate this point Paul used the story of the deliverance of the Children of Israel from Egypt (vv.1-2) and their subsequent journeys (vv.3-4, 7-10). With what supernatural blessings did the Lord care for them after their deliverance from Egypt (vv.2-3)? Of what sins did they become guilty (vv.7-10)? What was their fate as a result of their sins (vv.5,9-10)? Look again at the application Paul makes for the Christian from this Old Testament history (vv.11-12)? For the Christian who is concerned that he might stumble, God offers the promise of v.13. Claim this promise for yourself in a very practical way whenever you are tempted to sin.

Saturday, March 9, *Acts* 10:34-43. Because of his willingness to learn new lessons from the Lord (vv.28-29,34-35), new opportunities were given to Peter to preach the Gospel (vv.30-33). Notice how Peter presented the totality of Christ's ministry, from His baptism (v.37) through His final commission (v.42). Are you familiar with all the aspects of Jesus' ministry that Peter mentioned in vv.37-42? What message did Peter proclaim as a result of Jesus' ministry (v.43)? When we present Christ, we are not to neglect any aspect of His ministry, but our main emphasis should be upon the cross and its power (v.43). Such a proclamation of Christ God honors with His presence (v.44) and with lives that are committed to Him (vv.45-48.

LETTERS

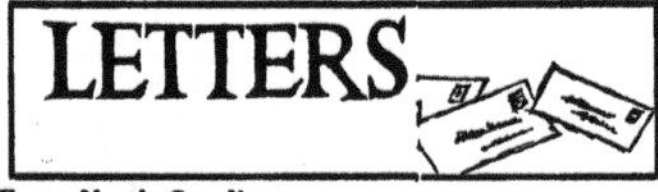

From North Carolina:

"My brother, my sister-in-law, my sister and I are thoroughly enjoying the **Southern Presbyterian Journal**, and feel that it is accomplishing a great deal for us really Southern Presbyterians; although I recently heard it called "the heretic magazine" by a Presbyterian minister's wife. My family and I wish to thank you and the rest of the **Journal** staff for the spiritual help you are rendering."

From Oklahoma:

"In your January 30th issue a mistake. The Missouri, Kansas and Texas, or M.K.&T. is the railroad known as 'The Katy' in Oklahoma (not 'K.T.&P.' as you have it in the article about Dr. P. B. Hill)."

(The editor thanks Oklahoma for setting him straight with "Katy" and is grateful for what Katydid (pardon!) in the matter of assuring us that Oklahoma is reading the **Journal** carefully.)

AN UNCOMPROMISING FAITH

Tertullian, an early Christian leader, said, "Away with all attempts to produce a mottled Christianity of Stoic, Platonic, and diabolic composition. We want no curious disputation after possessing Jesus Christ. With our faith we desire no further belief, for there is nothing we ought to believe besides." Those early Christians knew what they believed, and they were ready to die for their faith. They would rather be burned at the stake than drop a pinch of incense before the statue of the Emperor. They held clearcut distinctions; things were true or false, right or wrong. They knew from bitter experience what paganism could not do; they had come out of all other religions to Jesus Christ, the Saviour of all men. Through Him they had come from darkness to light, from death to life.

Dr. E. Stanley Jones, in one of his books, tells of what may have happened to the Nestorian Church. It was thought it had died of persecution in the early centuries. Then archaeology uncovered a cornerstone of one of their ancient buildings. On it were three symbols. The cross was in the center, a lotus flower (symbol of Buddha) on the left, and another symbol on the right. It had compromised, and died! This is the inevitable result of any compromised Christian Faith that seeks to blend Christianity with other religions in some new eclecticism.

If there is "none other name," if there is only one Saviour, then it is not intolerant to declare that. As James Denney says, "As there is only one God so there can be only one Gospel. If God has really done something in Christ on which the salvation of the world depends, and if He has made it known, then it is a Christian duty to be intolerant of everything which ignores, denies or explains it away. The man who perverts it is the worst enemy of God and men; and it is not bad temper or narrowmindedness which explains such vehement language as Paul's in Galatians 1:8, 'Though we, or an angel from heaven, preach any other gospel unto you than that which we have preached unto you, let him be accursed.' It is the jealousy of God which has kindled in a soul redeemed by the death of Christ a corresponding jealousy for the Saviour. Intolerance like this is an essential element in the true religion. Intolerance in this sense has its counterpart in comprehension: it is when we have the only Gospel, and not till then, that we have the Gospel at all."

THE CHURCH HERALD

THE SOUTHERN PRESBYTERIAN JOURNAL

Rev. Henry B. Dendy, D.D., Editor........Weaverville, N. C.
Dr. L. Nelson Bell, Associate Editor........Asheville, N. C.
Rev. Wade C. Smith, Associate Editor........Weaverville, N. C.

EDITORIAL

Church Discipline—A Matter of Faith as Well as Practice

There is a disturbing number of reports from over the Church having to do with the discipline of ministers, elders or church members for supposed failure to comply with our Book of Church Order.

We are not discussing the merits or otherwise of any particular case. But we are disturbed because there appears to be a growing demand for adherence to the letter of the *government* of our church without a corresponding insistence on the more important matter of the *doctrines* of our church.

A church is strong as her faith is strong. She is also strong as she is faithful to her system of government. That which the church believes is more important than how it administers its affairs should go without saying. But the emphasis today is on administration, and loyalty to it, rather than on doctrine, and faithfulness to it. Furthermore, an increasing number of changes are being made in the Book of Church Order where only a majority of the Presbyteries have to vote approval.

The whole trend of recent years is towards a regimentation of procedure. First the office of elder was degraded so that after a few years service those holding office might be shifted to the side lines. That this has helped situations in certain churches cannot be denied, but the price paid has been the loss of the spiritual insight and experience of age while in many instances men without Presbyterian backgrounds have been rotated into places of leadership.

Then the Commission on the Minister and His Work was established, ostensibly to enable ministers to secure new locations or to help a congregation anxious to secure a change. Unfortunately, local commissions have often acted as ecclesiastical gestapos, forbidding congregations to call a minister of their own choice (although the commission has no such auth ity), or in other cases thwarting the call of individual by passing on unfavorable repo secured by a unilateral procedure.

Then the permanent nominating committ were established on the various levels of chur administration. Being human and also bei subjected to the pressures of personal bias outside friendships, these committees have times failed to represent their constituencies a whole. That, despite these handicaps, t have operated as well as has often been t case is a tribute to the men who have compos these committees.

But, this trend to regimentation; to the pl ing of administrative loyalty above doctrin loyalty; all combine to make one uncertain abo the future.

The life of our church must be infused wi Christian love straight across the board. V need to guard at every step anything which w infringe on love on the one hand and the pur of the church on the other. To do this we mu at all times put first things first. We have Book of Church Order. Let us also rememb that we have the Confession of Faith.

—H.B.D.

Rules Not Laws

Paragraph 58 of our Book of Church Order quite explicit in denying to church courts t authority to make laws, and affirming to the only the power to establish rules for the gover ment, discipline, worship, and extension of t Church. It says this by inference in the ope ing sentence, declaring that the jurisdiction Church courts is only ministerial and decla tive — this means not magisterial nor legis tive. It asserts explicitly in the second senten that "they can make no laws." In the thi sentence it recognizes their power "to establi rules." In the fourth sentence it asserts the right to require obedience to the laws of Chri

The same doctrine is set forth earlier in the ook of Church Order. Par. 9 describes Jesus hrist as THE ONLY LAWGIVER IN ZION id asserts the right of His Majesty to rule and ach the Church through His Word and Spirit, the ministry of men, thus mediately exer- ing His own authority and "enforcing His vn laws." Par. 10 denies any right to add what Christ the King has given to His hurch. Par. 17 describes the function of the hurch as to administer, to proclaim, and to iforce "the law of Christ revealed in Scrip- re." Par. 19 says that the exercise of church ower only has the Divine sanction "when in nformity with the statutes "enacted by Christ e Lawgiver."

A few years ago there was a footnote in the ook of Church Order to the effect that this ook was enacted into law by the General As- mbly. When this erroneous statement was lled to the attention of the Atlanta General ssembly, the phrase *into law* was ordered de- ted by that Assembly. Thus the General As- mbly respects the distinction of paragraph 58.

It is with profound regret that we note this stinction not observed by one of the Assem- y's agencies, namely *The Assembly's Commit- e on the Minister and His Work.* This body is put out a film strip entitled, So Your Church eeds a Minister. Here the script reads, in irt:

> "The Commission must be thoroughly familiar with the Book of Church Order, which contains the laws by which the Presbyterian Church, U. S., is governed."

Now we do not assume that this mistake is made deliberately, but that those who ere responsible were using the word law in me loose sense with some such meaning as olity. But the film strip goes to our eighty ld Commissions on the Minister and His Work each presbytery. Many of these commissions e carrying out their functions in the fear of od with consideration for their brethren and th proper Christian humility. But the will power is in every one of us as the most dis- ictive principle of our fallen nature. The rversion wrought by sin continually asserts elf in the pride which lords it over the breth- n. Some commission will certainly misuse is phrase to make of the details provided in e Book of Church Order laws to bind the nscience of the candidate or of the church.

Augustine properly showed that the fundamental dogma and the fundamental ethic of the Christian faith is humility. He Who was in the form of God took the form of a slave, and being found in human fashion humbled Himself to the obedience of the Cross. By His act of humiliation He wrought our salvation, and on the basis of it He calls us to have in ourselves the mind of Christ. Thus Augustine says that the first mark of the Christian is humility, and the second mark of the Christian is humility, and that the third mark of the Christian is humility.

This clear understanding of the faith presented by Augustine of Hippo was forgotten by Augustine, the lord archbishop of Canterbury. When the old British Christians came to confer with him as to a union of the Christian forces in England, they had privately agreed to yield obedience to him if he showed humility by rising when they entered. He retained his seat and they retained their separate autonomy.

We earnestly trust that each of our presbytery commissions on the Minister and His Work will follow Augustine of Hippo, dealing in humility with the brethren and the churches of their several presbyteries. If not — the Father has committed all judgment to His Son because He is the Son of man. We can and will deal with those who turn their own preferences or details of the Book of Church Order into laws to bind the consciences of their brethren.

Professor A. LeCerf of Paris writes, "Calvinism confines itself to laying down a principle which renders the unity of the Church possible, i.e., that the Church on the one hand and individual Christians on the other, confess from the heart both the distress of the Church and the misery of the Christian man."

"The power of the keys in the Reformed (Presbyterian) Church implies pedagogic tact and Christian love, rather than juridical virtuosity." "Practice of the communion of saints by the individual implies, on Reformed (Presbyterian) principles, humility and filial love, rather than the servile sentiment of juridical obligation." "For Calvinism, the solution of the problem of reconciling the rights of the Church with the duties of the individual lies in the humility shown by both." *An Introduction to Reformed Dogmatics,* pp. 353-355.

—W.C.R.

The Southern Presbyterian Journal, *a Presbyterian Weekly magazine devoted to the statement, defense, and propagation of the Gospel, the faith which was once for all delivered unto the saints,* published every Wednesday by The Southern Presbyterian Journal, nc., in Weaverville, N. C.

Entered as second-class matter May 15, 1942, at the Postoffice at Weaverville, N. C., under the Act of March 3, 1879. Vol. XV, No. 44, February 27, 1957. Editorial and Business Offices: Weaverville, N. C. Printed in the U.S.A. by Biltmore Press, Asheville, N. C.

ADDRESS CHANGE: When changing address, please let us have both old and new address as far in advance as possible. Allow three weeks after change if not sent in advance. When possible, send an address label giving your old address.

Are Some Religious Educators Moving Toward Pelagianism?

For the benefit of the "laymen," Pelagianism is that form of religious thought which gives man rather than God the credit for beginning the work of salvation in man. Pelagianism says that man comes to God of his own will, semi-Pelagianism says that at least he begins the coming. On the other hand, Augustinianism or Calvinism says that man is dead in sins and unable to come until God makes him alive in Christ Jesus.

Have we any business thinking that some religious educators are bringing in that glorifying of man which went under the name of Pelagius in the ancient Church, and which is taught by the philosopher Immanuel Kant in more recent times?

Ere answering this question, we wish to testify again our great pleasure that our Board of Christian Education is advertising:

> "We Presbyterians are a creedal Church. We are Presbyterians because we believe in our interpretation of the Scriptures. It is the basis of what is taught from the pulpit. Naturally it is what we want taught in our entire educational program."

AMEN AND AMEN! It is beginning to look as though the change from "religious education" to "Christian education" were meaningful.

Just because we so heartily want our creedal interpretation taught in our entire educational program we must question what we sometimes hear from some religious educators. Their statements sometimes run about as follows:

> There is in everyone a better man or self, a part of the image of God left despite the fall. This better man begins the turn toward God. Did not Jesus say, "Let the little children come to me, do not hinder them?" And did not the prodigal son first come to himself and then bring himself to the father?

The first part of this statement sounds like the philosopher Kant, who taught that the Son of God was the idea of moral perfection, the intelligent or the better man in each of us who suffers for the empirical or the worse man. The reference to Jesus' invitation to the little children is a case of a text taken out of its context. In the text, Mark 10, the little children are not coming to Him of their own accord as the religious educator implies. Parents were bringing these little children — children so little that He took them up in the crook of His arms, as he laid His hands upon

Our Youth Program

Shall It Be Christian Training or One of Social Science?

We are publishing in full some material with reference to the Senior High Fellowship Spring Rally in one of our Presbyteries.

The name of the Presbytery is being deleted because this secularization of some of our youth programs is a church-wide problem, not a local one.

We are ready to admit that the Christian faith carries with it social implications, but we are strong in our belief that a Church Rally should be a Church Rally, not a school of social science and ethics.

We further question the propriety of having a Jewish Rabbi and a Roman Catholic Priest as scheduled speakers in a rally. Does not Protestantism have a distinctive message to teach our young people? Do not we as Presbyterians have a heritage and a faith that our young people need to have imparted to them?

The right of religious freedom should be defended, but it should be done by qualified leaders of our own church, not by leaders of faiths who would rightly (from their viewpoint), use such an opportunity to present their own religious beliefs, while propriety would make it difficult to call them in question from the viewpoint of our own church's teaching.

Our young people need more of spiritual inspiration and biblical instruction than they are now getting. If the church does not furnish this where are they to get it? If our young people's rallies degenerate into debating grounds for political and social questions something infinitely precious is being lost.

One of the most distressing things about a suggested program such as this is that these dear young people can go out enthused (although only partially instructed), to work for the transformation of society when they themselves have never been transformed by the redeeming work of Christ.

It is our prayer that the publication of this material will lead to a sober reappraisal of all of our young people's programs. It is our confirmed opinion that in a program such as this we are letting our young people down. We are taking entirely too much for granted. That many of them may come from Christian homes does not make them Christians. They need Christ as personal Saviour and then as the Lord of their lives. They need the inspiration of home and world mission programs; of personal and visitation evangelism; of putting Christ at the center of their lives thereby giving them power and victory over the temptations with which they are confronted daily. They need a program of intensive Bible study and of Scripture memorizing.

Let our church become a citadel of training in Christian doctrine and Christian living, then, as time may permit, let programs of secondary importance have a lesser share in the general planning for young people.

Unless we take immediate and complete stock of that which we are doing we can be held accountable: accountable by those who have been denied proper training, and, by the One to Whom we all are ultimately responsible.

—L.N.B.

THE FOLLOWING SPEAKS FOR ITSELF:

Dear Mr. ————

March 17 (Sunday) — 2:30 P. M. — First Presbyterian Church — Senior High Fellowship Spring Rally — Theme:

OPEN HOUSE TO THE WORLD

Enclosed with this letter you will find a schedule of the program for March 17, and some material for the Rally. As you read through the material you probably will notice that this Rally is somewhat different from previous Rallies. As we planned for the Rally we felt it would be necessary to send you the material, so as to give an over all picture of the entire Rally.

In order for this Rally to be effective and to be done, we will need the help of twenty leaders for the Study Groups. We are writing various local Fellowships to make a study in their own community of certain basic rights. At the Rally these Fellowships will give a report on what they found to be true in their community. Following these, a Senior High member who has worked in Mexico, will talk about what she found there to be true in regard to certain basic rights. The young people will then be divided into twenty study groups of not more than twenty persons in each group to study one basic right more completely and fully.

Each Study Group will last forty-five minutes. Any method can be used by the leaders of the various Study Groups. They are for the purpose of deciding if everyone in the community are entitled to these rights, and if they enjoy them? Also what can a young person do about these things in their own community?

As you can probably see that unless the local Fellowships after the Rally do something, then little will be accomplished from this Spring Rally. The purpose of the "So What" Panel is to give a report on what can be done in and through our local Fellowships. We are asking various Study Groups to appoint a reporter (not a member of the Presbytery Council) to give a summary on the "So What" Panel.

We hope you will be able to have the Study Group on the Right to Work. As soon as possible please let me know if you can be a leader of this particular group. I am looking forward to having you at the Spring Rally on the 17th of March.

Serving the Master,

————————

P. S. I would appreciate if you would appoint a member from your class to make a report to the general meeting.

Material for the Spring Rally

Ask four Fellowships to come to the Rally ready to take about ten minutes to tell about their own community in terms of one or more of the basic human rights set forth in the Universal Declaration of Human Rights. (This will take real study on their part. See outline below for study in the local Fellowship.) Be sure these four Fellowships understand they are to be responsible for a five minute report to the entire Rally. Be sure these Fellowships see their report as one large part of the total Rally, and as a background for helping the whole Rally to see our Christian responsibilities to persons in our communities.

Resource for Community Study on Human Rights

Purpose: to study our community in relation to one or more of the basic human rights to discover to what extent it assures all persons in your community of these rights, and what steps might be taken to increase that assurance. The following five human rights are suggested as a basis of study:

(a) Right to "belong" to the community: "All human beings are born free and equal in dignity and rights. They are endowed with reason and conscience and should act toward one another in a spirit of brotherhood." (Art. 1) "Everyone has the right to life, liberty, and the security of person."

(b) Right to health: "Everyone has the right to a standard of living adequate for the health and well-being of himself and his family, including food, clothing, housing and medical care and necessary social services, and the right to security in the event of . . . sickness, disability . . ."

(c) Right to education: "Everyone has the right to education. Education shall be free, at least in the elementary and fundamental stages. Elementary education shall be compulsory . . . .

(e) to freedom of religion:
President of the ministerial association
Secretary of Council of Churches
A Rabbi
A Roman Catholic Priest.

Findings from the observation tours, interviews or panel should be gathered together and compiled in a ten-minute report for the Rally presentation. This report might be in the form of a graph showing the extent to which various rights apply to everyone — or it might be a flip chart, illustrating areas of need for extending these rights; or it might be made against the background of a "Community's Report Card" showing the grades of a community from this test.

This might form part of a unit of study for a Fellowship which would continue then in other vesper meetings to explore ways of making these rights real for even more members of the community.

Ask each of four Fellowships to discover and bring to the Rally someone of another country or another race. Ask them to plan for interviewing that person at the Rally (before the whole group) in regard to their freedom to enjoy the human rights set forth in the Universal Declaration of Human Rights. People of other races or of other countries are in or near almost every community in our Church. This will take some exploration and planning by the local Fellowships who accept this assignment. But it will be worth the effort. See Guidance for these Fellowships below. Be sure these Fellowships see these interviews as opportunities for the Rally to experience a fellowship beyond their own race or nation, and to sense our Christian responsibilities to be concerned for all persons of all countries and races.

Reports from Community Studies on Human Rights:

The leader might introduce these reports as evidence of our need to remind ourselves that as Christians professing a concern for every person made for fellowship with God, there is yet much we may do to see that every person has opportunity to be the person God created him to be. Point out that such surveys and studies might be made by non-Christians and turn up similar needs, but that as Christians we seek to demonstrate the love of Christ in every phase of life and that we should show even greater concern for needs of persons. Say that later on we will attempt to define a World Charter for *Christian* Youth.

Discussion on Reports and World Charter for Christian Youth:

Divide into groups of fifteen or twenty to consider *one* of the five rights. With the guidance of a chairman discuss such questions as: Do we agree everybody in our town is entitled to the "right" assigned to us? Does everybody in our community enjoy it? If not, why not? Can we do anything as individuals about this? As church groups working together? What should be said in a World Charter for Christian Youth to express what we believe and will try to do?

These groups should be allowed about 45 minutes. There should be a recorder for the group and the group should plan to reconvene after the interviews.

"So What?" Panel:

This is to be a panel made up NOT of Presbytery Council members but of reporters from five different groups on the various basic rights. The panel will take 20 minutes to discuss such questions as:

Where could we begin our local Fellowships to put into action these beliefs?

How can these beliefs be demonstrated in the program and study of our local Fellowships?

What can we do in our community to spread such concerns?

It would be helpful to have near the panel *a display of resource material for further study and action by Fellowships.* Each resource should be briefly introduced. *Resource should include* "World Christian Citizenship through United Christian Youth Action," (30 cents); "Seeking to Be Christian in Race Relations," ($1); "What Can We Do," See, (50 cents); *"Now Is The Time," Lillian Smith,* ($2); "Youth Guide on Christ, the Church, and Race," Little, (50 cents); Presbyterian YOUTH outlines (Department of Youth Work, free); "Sense and Nonsense about Race," Alpenfels, 50 cents; "In the Direction of Dreams," Wood, ($1). (All of these will not be available at the Rally.)

The Panel members will need to do some careful preparation, thinking over these questions and thinking in regard to reporting on major significant work.

Education

If the churches are to minister properly to their constituents, they should know something about the conditions which these people experience in their usual occupations. Therefore, when a congregation contains college students, or high school students preparing for college, or college graduates, the minister, the elders, the Sunday School teachers ought to be aware of the factors that influence their thinking.

In American education today, both college and high school education, there are factors that

themselves (vv.18,20,23) to believers (vv.16-17)? How do vv.16-17 answer Judas' question of v.22? By coming to them thus (vv.16-18) Christ provides for His followers not only His companionship (v.18) but also the power to obey his commandments (15:5). What difference in their state of mind will Christ's presence make (vv.16,18,26,27; 15:11)? Power to obey, comfort to dispell fear and joy to fill the heart come to those Christians who sincerely seek to keep Christ's commands.

Tuesday, March 12, *Matthew* 22:15-22. Jesus officially identified Himself as the Messiah when He entered the temple in Jerusalem and took charge (21:12-13). Notice the impact His presence made upon the people (21:14-15,46); upon the religious rulers (21:15,23,45,46; 22:15). Remember as you read 22:15 that the Pharisees were well educated and highly intelligent. Was the compliment of v.16 sincere? How did His use of a coin (v.19) and His question of v.20 increase the effectiveness of Jesus' answer (v.21) to the question of v.17? Jesus momentarily thwarted the Pharisees' efforts (v.22); then He launched His own counter-attack and thoroughly routed them (vv.42-45). The Church today needs preachers who can defeat the false "philosopher" in his own lair, yet speak with an authority and compassion that draws the common people.

Wednesday, March 13, *Matthew* 11:25-30. Much of the generation of Jesus' day was indifferent to His claims (vv.18-19) and, consequently, judgment awaited them (vv.20-24). Notice the great authority the Father had put into the hands of the Son (v.27), yet how the Son employed this authority (vv.28-29). The cities were condemned (vv.21-24) because they refused to acknowledge their sins and repent (v.20); the invitation of v.28 was evidently given to those who were already aware of their sinfulness (v.19) and, therefore, needed grace rather than judgment. What attitude must a person manifest when he comes to Christ (v.25b)? Is there any mention of a person first getting rid of his sins or can he come as he is (v.28)? In Christ Himself is found the fulfillment of all the needs of the soul (v.28).

Thursday, March 14, *I John* 3:13-19. The Church can expect hatred from the world (v.13) but must experience love within its own gates (v.14). Observe that John takes hatred from the world as a matter of course, but hatred within the Church is considered the grossest of crimes (vv.12,15). What does John say is the spiritual condition of unloving church members (vv.14b,15b)? How is the love of Christians for each other to be expressed (vv.17-18)? Notice that God has shown in terms we can see and understand that He loves us (v.16). When the Church loves the world rather than Christ, strife and discord among church members results (I Cor. 3:3). The more Christians keep their eyes centered upon Christ, rather than the world, the more they love one another (v.16).

Friday, March 15, *Luke* 22:39-46. No human being has entered into an experience like that which Jesus went through as He faced the cross (vv.39-46). He was about to accept His Father's cup of wrath upon a sinful and rebellious mankind (v.42). Romans 1:18-32 and Revelation 20:11-15 picture something of the wrath of a holy God upon an utterly ungodly race. We can not imagine the struggle Christ went through as He prayed the prayer of v.42, but we can see visible evidence of something of its intensity (v.44). Only after the wilderness experience was there any mention of angels ministering to Him (v.43; Matt. 4:11). Little wonder Satan (Matt. 4:8-10) tempted Jesus by offering Him the kingdoms of the world without the cross! Compare with Philippians 2:8-11. Remember that it was for you and your sins that Christ died on the cross.

Saturday, March 16, *Romans* 12:1-8. The "mercies of God" (v.1a) refers to all that has been said since 1:16 (our justification and sanctification through God's grace in Christ), and especially the wisdom and mercy of God mentioned in chapter 11. Because of God's mercies, what appeal does Paul make in vv.1-2 to the Roman Christians? Why must they turn from conformity to the world to be holy and acceptable to God? What picture does Paul draw of the place of each member in the body of Christ (vv.4-8)? What should be the relation of Christians to each other (vv.3,9,10)? How do you think the Christian's conduct in vv.3-8 is related to the appeal of vv.1-2? Do you cause notes of discord in your Christian group because of your holding to the ways of the world (v.2) or your self-will (v.1)?

LESSON FOR MARCH 10

By THE REV. J. KENTON PARKER

Unlimited Forgiveness

Background Scripture: Matthew 18 - 20
Devotional Reading: Isaiah 55:6-9

God in His mercy grants "unlimited forgiveness" to sinners who forsake their ways and thoughts and return to Him. Isaiah says, "He will abundantly pardon." God remembers our sins no more against us; He removes them as far as the East is from the West; He hides them in the depth of the sea; He blots them out as a thick cloud. There are still depths in the sea which have not been measured by man. How far is the East from the West? We have all seen the sun blotted out by a thick cloud. There is therefore now no condemnation for those in Christ Jesus. This full, free, unlimited forgiveness comes through Jesus Christ : by this Man is preached unto you the forgiveness of sins. I believe in the forgiveness of sins.

Our lesson centers around the thought of our forgiveness of those who have sinned against us. This section — our Printed Text — is found in 18:21-35. The Background Scripture includes three chapters, 18-20, and contains material which is not directly related to our subject. I wish to briefly go through this material, and then come back to our main lesson.

I. *True Greatness:* 18:1-5; 20:20-29.

This discussion was started by a question of the disciples; Who is the greatest in the kingdom of heaven? This subject was often in the minds of the disciples, and two of them, James and John, asked for the chief places in the kingdom. The idea of an earthly kingdom, with "places of authority," persisted in the thoughts of these men. They did not seem to be able to disabuse themselves of this false conception, and it was not until after the death and resurrection of their Master that the whole truth came to them. They were even discussing this matter just before the keeping of the Passover, and His arrest and crucifixion. (Luke 22:24-27)

Jesus takes a little child and tells them that to enter the kingdom they must be converted and become as this little child. Humility is the first requisite for being great in the sight of God. If we compare this with other passages such as Matthew 20:26-28 you will see that the path of greatness in the kingdom of heaven is the path of humility, service, and sacrifice, as exemplified by Christ Himself, Who came not to be ministered unto, but to minister, and give His life a ransom for many. Well would it have been for the church if this teaching of her Head had been always heeded.

II. *Offences, Occasions of Stumbling:* 18:6-14.

He had used a little child as an illustration of true greatness. He now warns them about causing such a little one to stumble. It were better for such a man to have a millstone hung about his neck and be cast into the sea. I saw two pictures on television just recently which presented this from different angles. How much of our "juvenile delinquency" is caused by older people — often parents — causing children to go wrong! We older people are sinning grievously against the "generation to come," and be sure our sin will find us out, to our sorrow and to the destruction of our nation.

Verse 14 is very comforting to parents who have lost a little one: "Even so it is not the will of your Father which is in heaven, that one of these little ones should perish." Our "Brief Statement" says, "Those who die in infancy, and others who are incapable of exercising choice, are regenerated and saved by Christ through the Spirit, Who works when and where He pleases."

"Around the throne of God in heaven
Thousands of children stand,
Children whose sins are all forgiv'n,
A holy, happy band,
Singing, 'Glory, glory, glory be to God on high'!"

III. *The Question Concerning Divorce:* 19:1-12.

This question, like many of the questions put to Him by the Jewish leaders, was not asked because they wanted to find out the truth, but to make trial of Him, or "tempt" Him, so they could have something against Him whereby they might accuse Him. He referred them to Genesis 1:27 and 5:2. What God has joined together, let not man put asunder. They refer to Moses who allowed a writing of divorcement to be granted. Jesus explains this by saying that it was because of the hardness of their hearts that he allowed this. It was permission granted as the lesser of two evils. The only cause which justifies divorce is fornication which automatically severs the marriage tie and vow.

IV. *He Receives Little Children:* 19:13-15.

These beautiful words of Jesus have always been very precious to us all. They should make us realize the value of little children and the place they have in the heart of Jesus and in the kingdom. In another place, (Mark 10:15), He adds, Verily I say unto you, Whosoever shall not receive the kingdom of God as a little child, he shall not enter therein," and in Matthew 18:3, Except ye be converted and become as little children, ye shall not enter the kingdom of heaven. We have seen His warning about offending one of them.

V. *The Rich Young Ruler:* 19:16-30.

This man had many things in his favor; he was young; he was rich; he was in earnest, not trying to "catch" Jesus by his question; he was reverent; he was a moral man; he asked a very important question; Jesus loved him. Jesus referred him to the Commandments, especially the last half, which point out our duty to our fellowmen. He claimed to have kept all these from his youth. He was not satisfied, however, and asks, What lack I yet? Then Jesus pointed him to the thing which was in his way. He had to make a choice between his wealth and Jesus; sell what you have, give to the poor, come and follow me. Exchange your earthly treasure for heavenly treasure. He went away sorrowful.

Jesus took this opportunity to warn His disciples about the danger of riches. It is hard for a rich man to enter the kingdom of heaven. It is possible, for God can give to a rich man the right kind of heart. We not only have rich men saved, but greatly blessed and greatly honored and used. Abraham was a very wealthy man, but he did not make an idol out of his wealth. He had one thing which he prized much more than his riches; his son, Isaac, but he did not allow even his son to come first, as we see when he was tested in this respect. (See Gen. 22)

Closely related to the above is the question of Peter, We have left all; What shall we have? Jesus makes a great promise to him, and to us all; promise of a rich reward both here and hereafter. Hope of reward is not wrong in a Christian.

VI. *Laborers in the Vineyard:* 20:1-16.

This parable is spoken to rebuke a mercenary spirit which could easily develop from this hope

YOUNG PEOPLES *Department*

YOUTH PROGRAM FOR MARCH 10

By THE REV. B. HOYT EVANS

"*The Church In Southeast Asia*"

Scripture: Isaiah 42:1-12.

Suggested Hymns:
"From Greenland's Icy Mountains"
"Jesus Shall Reign Where'er The Sun"
"O Zion, Haste! Thy Mission High Fulfilling"

(One very interesting way of dealing with this subject would be to invite a well informed person to speak to your young people. If there is a college or university near you, you might inquire if they have any Christian students from the southeast Asian countries. Another possibility would be a missionary who has served in this area. One church had a series of programs presented by sons and daughters of missionaries who are studying in the States. The Women of the Church have made a careful study of southeast Asia this year, and you could probably secure one of their leaders to speak to you on the work of the church there.)

Leader's Introduction:

Of course, Christianity is not new to the continent of Asia. It was in the western part of this continent that Christ lived during His earthly sojourn. We also have reports of missionary activity in India and China in the early Christian centuries. It is tragic to think that the church which had such a prompt start in these great centers of population was allowed to die out. We should take warning from this fact and renew our efforts to be strong and vigorous in our work and witness for Christ. A church which does not grow in spiritual and numerical strength will lose ground and will eventually die.

The work of the church has been renewed in Asia through the modern missionary movement. For this program our attention is focused especially on the countries of southeast Asia and the work of the church there. The church has no easy place in these countries because the opposition of non-Christian religions is strong and thoroughly entrenched. Added to this problem is the added opposition of Communism which has already won the day in China and is making a strong bid for the loyalties of all the Asian peoples. The eyes of the world are turned toward southeast Asia. What the church is able to accomplish there in the next few years will surely determine the future for that area, and to a large extent the future of the eastern world.

First Speaker:

It would probably take quite an expert to name the countries that make up southeast Asia, much less to tell anything significant about all of them. The countries are these: Burma, Taiwan (Formosa), Indochina, Indonesia, Malaya, Philippines, and Thailand. Three of the seven (Taiwan, Indonesia, and the Philippines) are island nations. The other four (Burma, Indochina, Malaya, and Thailand) are on the Asian mainland, south of China and east of India. (The use of a map to point out these countries would be very helpful.) The total area of the seven countries is about three fifths that of the United States, and the total population is more than 180 million, or about 20 million greater than that of the United States.

The principal religion of the Philippines is Roman Catholicism, of Indonesia and Malaya is Islam, and of the other four is Buddhism. The total Protestant population in the seven countries is just over six million, or about three and a half per cent of the total population. Although the church is in such a small minority, it is vigorous and active, and its influence is far greater than its numerical strength.

Second Speaker:

Taiwan (Formosa) is the country on which Presbyterians focus their attention, because it is there that our missionaries are laboring. Taiwan is an island in the Chinese sea, and is the smallest in area of the southeast Asian countries. It is slightly larger than the state of Maryland, but crowded into this small area are nine and a half millions of people. The original inhabitants of the island were fiercely independent people of Malayan extraction. In 1662 the Chinese gained control of the island, and from that time on, a large number of Chinese have lived there. From 1895 to 1945 the Japanese held Taiwan. It was recovered by China in 1945, and now serves as the seat of the Chinese nationalist government. The Chinese nationalist army is stationed on Taiwan, and great numbers of loyal Chinese have fled there for refuge. That which was already a crowded country is even more crowded with the great influx of refugees from the mainland.

Third Speaker:

Until 1945 the only Christian mission work in Taiwan had been done by English and Canadian Presbyterians. After 1945 many different denominational groups rushed into the area, and some of the Formosan Christians became confused. Our Southern Presbyterian missionaries entered Formosa when so many of their own Chinese people left China to take refuge on the island. It was about this time that our missionaries were being systematically pushed out of China by the Communists. Not all of the China missionaries were sent to Formosa, but it was planned to send enough to carry on the work that had been begun with the Chinese Christians.

Fourth Speaker:

Our missionaries have been requested, not only to minister to the Chinese immigrants but to enter the total mission program on the island. This means working with the original inhabitants, or Tribes people, as they are called. The Chinese are located near the cities for the most part, and the Tribes people are in the rugged mountains which run south to north, dividing the island into eastern and western halves. The Presbyterian mission work is divided into three stations: (1) Taipei Station in the north which includes the capital city of Taipei and another city about fifteen miles away; (2) The West Coast Station which includes four cities on the northwest coast; and (3) the East Coast Station which includes Hwalien, the largest city in that area, and another smaller city nearby.

The work on the Taipei Station features: (1) Tent evangelism, which has been very well received by the people and very effective; (2) Distribution of Christian literature through book rooms, libraries, and distribution societies; and (3) Christian student centers for high school and college students in and near the great cities.

The West Coast Station includes: (1) The Presbyterian Bible School in Chu Pei where Christians from the mountain tribes and from the mainland receive further training; (2) Medical work in the Changhua Christian Hospital; and (3) Evangelistic and educational work in the cities and villages.

There are five missionaries working in the East Coast Station. They are serving almost entirely among the Tribes people. Their main responsibility is to guide in the organization of native churches, and to teach the Bible wherever there is an opportunity. The minister missionary works with the pastors and elders of

CHILDRENS Page

Miriam, Moses' Sister

Here is a little girl who used her head and her heart in saving her baby brother. Their parents were God's people, but Hebrew slaves in Egypt. The King of Egypt commanded that all the Hebrew boy babies must be drowned in the river. Moses' mother made a little boat, put Moses in it and pushed it out into tall grass in the river to hide him from the King's soldiers. Then she told Miriam to stay nearby and watch, and she did! Soon, the princess came down with her maidens to the river to swim, and, seeing the little boat in the tall grass, sent a maiden to bring it to her. Little Moses was crying, and the princess felt so sorry for him and wanted to keep him. Then Miriam came out from hiding and told her she knew a Hebrew woman who would nurse the baby for her. The princess said "Run and bring her." So Miriam ran as fast as her little legs could go, and brought her mother, and the princess gave little Moses to his own mother to nurse and keep for her until he would be old enough to come to the palace and be her adopted son. Happy mother, happy little sister and happy little Moses! — E.

Week of Prayer and Self-Denial
For World Missions
February 24 - March 3, 1957

The people of our Church throughout the Assembly are called to unite in prayer for the mission program of our Church around the world during this week.

LET US PRAY

For the strengthening of the Church throughout the world and an increasing sense of fellowship of all Christians around the world.

For a positive witness by all Christians wherever they are remembering the danger and difficulty of such witness in many lands.

For the missionaries of our Church and our work in nine countries overseas.

For the leaders of National Churches as they strive to build strong and increasingly self-supporting congregations.

For Christians who are denied contact with fellow Christians; who suffer persecution; who must go against their families and culture.

For all people who are hungry and ill clad; the multitude of refugees; the sufferers from disaster.

For all people everywhere who do not know the love of God in Christ Jesus.

Whenever we pray, let us pray—
FOR THE WORLD

Under the Study Lamp
A Home or a House—Which?

A few evenings ago I settled myself in a comfortable chair with the intention of reading the Book of Deuteronomy through at a sitting. When about midway of the interesting exercise, however, I bumped against such an arresting sentence that the rest of the agreeable task was suspended for the evening. Here it is: "When thou buildest a new house, then thou shalt make a battlement for thy roof, that thou bring not blood upon thine house, if any man fall from thence." (Chapter 22:8).

Every oriental house had a flat roof where the family and neighbors were accustomed to visit together, usually after sunset. For the protection of visitors as well as of the children the law was that every housetop should be provided with battlements—wall extending about three feet above the roof on every side. The lesson derived therefrom was that every householder was warned against permitting his home in any wise to endanger the well-being of his neighbor or of his own family. It must be an embattled castle, as it were, into which no evil power or influence may gain entrance.

The obligation continues. The Englishman's house is his castle. So runneth the British common law, the idea being that unwarranted invasion of one's property is forbidden. But the Bible goes beyond that, declaring that a house is more than a material structure. It must offer protective defense for the family, and for the community as well.

The word "home" is derived from an old Scandinavian word "heim," meaning a place of refuge. It means therefore for us, of course, that within its sacred precincts nothing should be permitted that might cause injury to the moral and religious interests of the dwellers therein, or to the neighbors thereabouts. In this connection it may be said that entirely too many so-called Christian parents are inexcusably careless in that particular.

Speaking of the Christian home, Roger Babson, the distinguished statistician, declared, "I have not been able to find such a single and useful institution which has not been founded by either an intensely religious man or by the son of a praying father or a praying mother. I have made this statement before the Chambers of Commerce of all the largest cities of the country, and have asked them to bring forward a case that is an exception to this rule. Thus far I have not heard of a single one."

Let it be remembered that the fruitfulness as well as the durability of a house is absolutely dependent upon its battlements. "As for me and my house, we will serve the Lord." So said Joshua the courageous patriot. It is for that reason that the name of Joshua stands in the top bracket of the great men of all time.

—By Dr. William Crowe

(Copies of a booklet containing 34 of these articles may be had from the Brannon Printing Company, Talladega, Alabama.)

"Teen-Beer" for Juveniles

Brewers in certain sections of the country are busy cultivating the crop of war and post-war babies who will become potential customers soon after 1960. To set up the new market they have given a new twist to an old product, pushing a teen-brew that looks like beer, foams like beer, tastes like beer and smells like beer. The new brew is "legal"—it just skirts the law.

One brewing firm provides it in carry-out containers as a "teen-agers" special. It contains one-half of one per cent of alcohol or less, thus avoiding state and federal regulations and taxes. In Wisconsin the teen-beer is called a "cereal beverage." This marks a new low for liquor merchandising and emphasizes the importance of sound and convincing education as to the effect of alcohol upon the body, mind and skills, not only in the public schools and churches but also in the home, both by precept and example.

—Temperance Action

They Want Bibles

By Robert T. Taylor
Secretary American Bible Society

Many Hungarians fleeing from tyranny with empty hands but hearts full of hope are crying out for Bibles.

When the first relief trucks went into ravaged Budapest the people asked not only for food, clothing and medicine but they said

"Please send us Bibles"

Within a week our whole supply of more than 70,000 Hungarian Scriptures had been given away. Another 200,000 were printed at once—more are on the presses.

In the past three years 110 tons of paper which we sent to Hungary had been used to print Bibles, for through the centuries Bible reading men have been liberty loving men.

We acted on faith but if we are to keep on offering Scriptures to every Hungarian refugee—both in the United States and in foreign lands—and if we are to have Scriptures available to send into Hungary, more money is needed right now.

We must continue to meet the needs of Hungary and we must also keep on supplying Scriptures for millions in many lands who wait and struggle for liberty.

Because of this emergency, we are appealing to you for an extra gift which we hope can be over and above your regular gifts to the Bible Society.

It costs about $1.00 to print a Bible. Can they depend on you for at least 5 Bibles?

DUTY

By Mrs. W. T. Kelley
McDonough, Ga.

No matter how much good we've done—
Nor how many battles we may have won—
How great our talents or abilities be—
Our name may be known across the sea;
Our works may be praised by all we meet—
The Ten we may faithfully try to keep;
But when all is said and done—behold!
We must face a fact that never grows old—
Unworthy! Unprofitable!
We have no beauty — —
Lo! We have only done our duty!

Luke 17:10.

In Memory of Mrs. Vernon S. Broyles, Jr.

Bena Broyles has gone home. On December 2, 1956, she silently slipped away and, on angels' wings, was gently borne aloft to her home in Heaven.

In this life God generously endowed her with many admirable traits and qualities: a splendid mind; a true sense of values; a kind, sympathetic and understanding heart; an attractive and engaging personality; a keen sense of humor; a blithe spirit; and above all, with a deep, true and abiding Christian faith.

She loved life. To her, life was not a dark and somber thing to be endured but a bright, cheerful and God-given opportunity for happiness. She did not approach life with hesitant and reluctant step but ran eagerly to meet its challenge. She found that the heavy blows of the sword of sorrow and disappointment could be deflected and parried with the light rapier of understanding and faith and she found her greatest happiness in service to others. She was indeed a blithe spirit! Her touch was ever light and deft and yet in every thought, deed and action she epitomized the happy Christian.

She was an ideal pastor's wife—always patient, understanding and helpful. She was all that a mother should be. She was a true, loyal and understanding friend and a pillar of strength in the work of the Women of the Church.

To know her was to love her and those who knew her best loved her best.

Bena Broyles is not dead and will never die; some part of her will ever live in each of us and in our children and in our children's children and each of us is stronger in the Faith for having known her.

In her untimely passing we feel that the Women of the Church have lost an efficient and loyal worker and a devoted and sincere friend and though we feel that her "going home" leaves an unfilled void, we believe that her kind and gentle soul would have us accept her departure in the spirit of the following words:

"Weep not for me;
Be blithe as wont, not tinge with gloom
The stream of love that circles home,
Light hearts and free!
Joy in the gifts Heaven's bounty lends,
Nor miss my face, dear friends!
I still am near."

Mrs. John L. Tye, Jr., Chairman
Mrs. J. D. Osborne
Mrs. Deloney Sledge

NEWS of CHURCHES around the World

Board of Church Extension

Budget 1957	$1,518,225.00
Receipts to date	38,110.34
% of Annual Budget received to date	2.5%
Balance needed for the year	1,480,114.66

G. B. Strickler, *Treasurer*

Passing of Rev. E. T. Drake, D.D.

Dr. Drake died on January 29th, last, in Orange, Texas. He was 76 years old. He had been pastor of the Lutcher Memorial Presbyterian Church, of Orange, 45 years—1906-1951. He was one of the first graduates from Austin Theological Seminary; was married in 1907 to Miss Mary Sampson, the daughter of the Seminary's first president, Dr. Thornton R. Sampson. He is survived by his wife and one son, John Drake.

General Troup Miller

Brigadier General Troup Miller, U.S.A. (Retired), aged 76, died in Atlanta Hospital, February 2, after a brief illness. General Miller was in action in both World War I and II and received about all the medals and honors accorded to members of the United States Army, including the Distinguished Service Medal in World War II and the Legion of Merit. He was a graduate of U. S. Military Academy at West Point and at one time was instructor to a young cadet by the name of Dwight D. Eisenhower.

Better still, he was an elder in the Southern Presbyterian Church and a diligent soul winner, an earnest Christian whose influence spread into many lives. He and Mrs. Miller who survives him, celebrated their Golden Wedding anniversary in 1953.

Funeral services were conducted by Rev. Vernon Broyles, D.D., of Atlanta, and burial took place in Arlington National Cemetery, Washington, D. C.

ALABAMA

Birmingham—Youth Fellowships of the Presbyterian Churches in Birmingham, both the U.S., and the U.S.A., held a joint banquet meeting at the Independent Presbyterian Church here, in early February.

Hosts for the meeting were the youth groups of the Independent church, and of Birmingham Presbytery. Dr. Ian Stuart, author and lecturer, was the featured speaker.

Members of the planning committee for the meeting, included: Taylor Beard, moderator of the host Presbytery; Marion Stephens, moderator of the Youth of the U. S. Presbytery; John Baggett, vice moderator; and Alice McSpadden, Witness Commission chairman.

Among plans discussed by the group at the banquet was the plan for the annual camp at Oak Mountain State Park, scheduled for the first two weeks in June.

The First Presbyterian Church of Phenix City, Alabama

Organized January 20, 1957

A Commission of the Presbytery of East Alabama organized the First Presbyterian Church of Phenix City on last Sunday aternoon. The Rev. John Milton McKnight accepted a call from the Home Mission Committee of the Presbytery to begin this work and went on the field October 1, 1956. On last Sunday, seventy charter members came together to establish the newest church in our Presbytery. The Commission was composed of Dr. H. E. Russell, minister of Trinity Presbyterian Church, Montgomery, presiding, with the Rev. Merle C. Patterson, Minister of the First Presbyterian Church of Montgomery, conducting the organization of the Church and the installation of the pastor and the charge was delivered by Dr. A. C. Windham of the First Presbyterian Church, Opelika. The charge to the congregation was made by the Rev. A. Patton White, Minister of the First Presbyterian Church of Tuskegee.

The newly elected officers of this Church are:

Elders: Mr. W. F. Massicott, Mr. Richard Nason, Mr. W. E. Soenksen and Mr. J. A. McLean.

Deacons: Mr. A. J. Bartram, Mr. John Drake, Mr. J. W. Gaus, Secretary; Mr. J. W. Murphey, Chairman, and Mr. L. T. Downing, Jr., Treasurer.

GEORGIA

Atlanta—Preliminary planning for one modern structure to house all of the offices located here at the Presbyterian Center is underway.

Charles J. Currie, executive secretary of the Board of Annuities and Relief, which Board operates and manages the Center, says that property recently acquired by the Center fulfills the property need for the projected building, and he expresses the hope that the structure will be completed by 1961—the year that marks the 100th anniversary of the Presbyterian Church in the United States.

The newly acquired lots adjacent to the Presbyterian Center bring holdings in the Center to 417 feet facing Ponce deLeon Ave., a main artery through Atlanta. The property runs 400 feet deep through to North Avenue and 400 feet along North Avenue. Two residences were purchased with the new lots. Office of the Stated Clerk of the General Assembly is now occupying one of these structures, now known as building E.

Other General Assembly Agencies now located at the Center are: Board of Women's Work, The Minister and His Work, in building A; Board of Church Extension, building B; General Council,

The missionary also provides a graphic illustration of some of the differences between American and Japanese agriculture by citing the fact that Mr. Kudo comes from a Japanese farm of 4½ acres, operated by his father and his uncle, and will live on the DeVore farm of 750 acres, also operated by two brothers. Vegetables occupy a good portion of both farms, but the Kudo farm also produces sheep and silkworms. One of the suits the young Japanese will bring with him was made from the back of the sheep to his own, by his mother.

Taking part in the baptism service of Mr. Kudo, in addition to Mr. Boyle, was the Rev. Eiichi Itoh, himself a product of the Presbyterian Church, U.S., mission work.

KENTUCKY

Louisville — Church officers of the Louisville area heard two members of the Louisville Presbyterian Seminary faculty in a series of four Sunday evening classes. Dr. Julian Price Love taught two classes "How We Got Our Bible" on January 20 and January 27. Dr. Andrew K. Rule lectured on "The Christian Doctrine of Salvation" on February 3 and February 10. Enrollment for the series totaled 246.

Eighty-four high school students and twenty-one counselors met at Louisville Presbyterian Seminary on Saturday, February 10, for a consideration of church vocations. The Rev. Marcus J. Priester of Philadelphia made the opening statement about Christian vocation in general and church vocations in particular. Then the young people discussed seven specific areas of church vocations during two discussion periods of one hour each. The Seminary faculty and the churches of the Louisville area provided leadership.

LOUISIANA

Alexandria — The Louisiana Synod Men's Conference to be held at Silliman, Clinton, La., May 25 and 26 will stress "Forward with Christ through Christian Citizenship" as its theme.

John Deifell, Greensboro, N. C., Assembly Men's Council president in 1956 and chairman of the Miami Convention attendance committee, will tell about the convention planned for October 10-13.

"Our Responsibility as Christian Citizens" will be the subject of an address by Dr. Peyton Rhodes, Memphis, Tenn., president of Southwestern.

Clint Harris, Richmond, Va., Department of Church Relations, will speak on "The Credentials of a Christian Citizen."

Rev. George Ricks, Baton Rouge, will preside at the communion service; Dr. Ed Grant, Baton Rouge, will teach the Bible class, and Dr. Walter Courtney, Pastor of the First Church, Nashville, will preach the Sunday morning sermon.

There will be eight clinics on Christian Citizenship.

MISSISSIPPI

The First Presbyterian Church of Canton, Dr. Charles R. McCain, Minister, entertained the Presbytery of Central Mississippi in its quarterly Stated Meeting on January 17th. Rev. E. C. Brasington, Retiring Moderator, brought the opening sermon, on the topic, "Going Forward With Christ," his text being Exodus 14:15.

Dr. John Reed Miller, of the Jackson First Church, Vice-Moderator, was elected Moderator. Dr. R. E. Hough of Jackson was elected Vice-Moderator and as such will be the first nominee at the April meeting.

Four Ministers and four Ruling Elders (and their alternates) were elected as Commissioners to the General Assembly meeting in Birmingham in April: Rev. Hayes Clark, Dr. C. R. McCain, Dr. T. R. Nunan, Dr. John W. Young; Ruling Elders T. Jasper Lowe, Hugh S. Potts, W. Calvin Wells III, W. C. Wells, Jr. Mr. W. Calvin Wells is a son of the late Dr. John M. Wells, who was Moderator of the Birmingham Assembly meeting in 1917. Mr. W. C. Wells, Jr., is a son of "Major" Calvin Wells, who was a Ruling Elder Commissioner from this Presbytery to the 1917 Assembly along with his brother Dr. John Wells who was a Commissioner from Wilmington Presbytery.

Presbytery adopted the recommendation of its Christian Education Committee to put special emphasis upon use of the catchism in 1957. Also, this Committee reported through its Chairman, Dr. C. R. McCain, that the Presbytery now has sixteen ministerial candidates and one lay-worker candidate.

Rev. Hayes Clark was elected Chairman of the Commission on the Minister and His Work; Rev. E. L. Jackson, Chairman of the Church Extension Committee. Other committee chairmanships include Dr. Van. M. Arnold, Stewardship; Rev. B. B. Underwood, Forward With Christ Committee; Dr. R. S. Woodson, World Missions. Rev. D. M. Mounger is Executive Secretary.

The day's meeting was closed with a season of prayer, the Presbyters kneeling for this.

The next Stated Meeting will be held at the Power Memorial Church in Jackson, on April 18th. Invitations are in hand for the July meeting (Westminster Church, Vicksburg) and the October meeting (First Church, Philadelphia, Miss.).

W. A. Gamble, Stated Clerk

NORTH CAROLINA

Raleigh—Mr. J. Neveland Brand, lay leader of Wilmington, N. C., has been elected chairman of the Council of the Presbyterian Synod of North Carolina, succeeding Dr. Frank L. Jackson of Davidson, N. C.

Twenty members of the council, representing the nine Presbyteries of the Synod attended the session in Raleigh when Mr. Brand was elected to the two-year term.

Dr. Jackson, a member of the council since it was organized in 1951, was honored as retiring chairman with a rising vote of thanks.

Brand, a native of Wilmington, is a graduate of the University of North Carolina, and did post graduate work at Columbia in accounting. He is a senior member of the firm of Brand and Perdew, public accountants, Wilmington.

He has been a deacon in the First Presbyterian Church of Wilmington, and is currently a ruling elder and president of the Men's Club of that church. He has been a member of the Synod's Council for five years and has served as a member of the sub-committee on Budget and Finance.

Charlotte — Dr. A. B. Montgomery, the new pastor of the Caldwell Memorial Church in Charlotte, N. C., occupied the pulpit for the first time

"In view of the divergent conditions which exist in the different areas in which our missionaries are now working in Japan, conditions which make one fixed policy impracticable, our individual missionaries are authorized to accept affiliate membership in the Kyodan, or, in the churches of the Presbyterian and Reformed tradition—the particular group where they feel they can best bear their witness for Christ and further the work of the Church in that land.

"It is understood, and here stipulated, that these affiliate relationships of individual missionaries to any national church is subject to be approved by the Mission in the spirit of the above statement. It is recommended further that this action be communicated to the Japan Mission for its advice and for a proposal to the Board of the exact wording of the constitution of the Mission which would set forth this policy."

In Taiwan the new plan of relationship is the result of proposals by the General Assembly of the Taiwanese Presbyterian Church. The Assembly, only two years old, is trying to establish formal bases for cooperation with all Presbyterian groups working in the island. Toward that end it has offered its "Mother Churches" (the Canadian and English Presbyterian Churches which pioneered missionary work there) one type of relationship, and to the others (Presbyterians U.S., and U.S.A., who have worked in the island only since 1949 when China was lost to the communists) it has offered a choice of several possible relationships. The Board of the Southern Church, after discussion with English, Canadian and Taiwanese, in this country, in Canada, and in Taiwan, approved the pattern of cooperation which the Taiwanese Assembly had designated "B-2, Second Kind," which provides:

"**The Second Kind.** The appointment of missionaries and the spending of financial aid shall be under mission control.

"1. Requests for missionaries: Requests shall be from the General Assembly (of Taiwan), after the agreement of the two mother churches has been obtained.

"2. Appointment and Finance: The appointment of missionaries and the sending of financial aid shall be under mission control, but the agreement of the General Assembly must be obtained.

"3. Status. In General Assembly: They may appoint up to one seventh of their membership as corresponding (non-voting) members of the Assembly. If they have fewer than seven members, they may appoint one member.
In Presbytery: They may appoint two members as corresponding members of those presbyteries in which they work.

"4. Mission Council. They shall organize their own mission council or other mission organization.
"5· United Conference: A united conference shall be organized to include all missionaries working under this second kind of relationship and all misionares of the mother churches' council."

Somewhat similar problems of mission-church relationship are shaping up in Korea, where the General Assembly of the Presbyterian Church of Korea has asked a review of the policies under which Presbyterian Churches, U.S., U.S.A., and of Australia, are cooperating with the national church. A special committee of the Board of the Southern Church has already been in conference with representatives of the Northern Church Board, both in New York and in Nashville, and the recommendations from those conferences were approved by the Board as follows:

"1. In view of the fact that there are matters of Church-Mission Relationship in Korea affecting the work of the Presbyterian Churches of Australia, U.S.A., and U.S., it is recommended that a conference be scheduled in Korea April 5-19, 1957, dealing with all aspects of this question, conferees to include representatives of the Presbyterian Church in Korea and the U.S.A., U.S., and Australian Boards of Missions.

"2. It is recommended further, that Dr. S. Hugh Bradley and Dr. D. J. Cumming be the representatives of the Staff in this conference in the name of the Board.

"3. Recommended further, that the Chairman of the Fields Committee, Dr. Jas. A. Jones, be the Board's representative in this conference, with Dr. Elliott, chairman of the Board, and Dr. James E. Bear, as the alternate."

Another outstanding event in the January meeting of the Board was the announcement by Mr. Curry B. Hearn, treasurer, that for the first time since 1928 the Board had received more than its General Assembly—approved budget. Actual receipts from all sources totaled $3,465,000 during 1956 Mr. Hearn reported. Of this, about $132,790 was income from endowments established for specific mission projects, and the remainder, $3,-332,210 were gifts from living donors. This represents a jump of 18% over giving to the Board in 1955, and was immediately reflected in the salary increases voted to all missionaries.

The increase was also reflected in increases in work budgets approved for the mission fields. These increases for 1957 average about 12% for all fields, but were of course dependent in some degree upon the urgency of the needs of projects.

The Rev. Paul B. Freeland, secretary of the Department of Overseas Relief and Inter-Church Aid also presented an encouraging report when he stated that special gifts for the Hungarian relief work have been pouring in from the Church. By Jan. 15 the total had reached $26,197.54, and the total continues to grow. These funds are being put into immediate use through Church World Service and the Inter-Church Aid department of the World Council of Churches, Mr. Freeland stated.

Nashville—During the year we have given you our total receipts from living donors with the percentage of the approved spending budget received.

We now wish to report that for the entire year our receipts from living donors amounted to $3,-332,210.00, or 100.98% of our approved spending budget of $3,300,000.00.

For your further information our receipts from other income, lapsed Annuities, legacies and income from investments, amounted to $133,729.61, bringing our total receipts to $3,465,939.61 as compared to $2,932,052.80 for 1955.

Sincerely,
Curry B. Hearn, Treas.

Nashville—Miss Nan Fulson of our Congo Mission is scheduled to return to the field on March 9 following her furlough in the United States.

Miss Fulson is a native of Atlanta, Ga., and is a member of North Avenue Presbyterian Church in Atlanta.

Anyone who reads this volume will gain a new appreciation of the heritage passed down from the fathers of the flesh and of the faith. Our Southern Presbyterian Church is fortunate in having a man of the stature of Dr. Spence to serve as the director of this Foundation.

—J.R.R.

SOUL-WINNING SERMONS. R. A. Torrey. Fleming H. Revell. $2.50.

The sermons in this volume were used by the Evangelist in his campaign around the world. They were blessed of God in the salvation of many souls. It has been often noted that Dr. Torrey had a vivid manner of expression that made the printed page seem almost like the spoken word. This is especially true of these sermons. One seems to hear them and experience how the Lord used them to reach the souls of the listeners and constrain them to come to Christ. This volume gives us some of Dr. Torrey's greatest heart-warming Gospel messages and reveals his passionate love for the souls of men.

—J.R.R.

HOUSE-IN-THE-WOODS, a biographical sketch of Juliet and Cr by Adams. Kathleen Lemmon. Island Press. $2.75.

Many of our readers will remember Crosby and Juliet Adams and their contributions in the field of music. In 1913, the Adamses came to North Carolina in search of a temperate climate, and in building their quaint "House-in-the-Woods" as a lifetime retreat, they began a mecca for students, composers, teachers, and graduates from all over the world. Miss Lemmon has brought the story of the Adamses together in the form of an intimate biography. The writing is simple and affectionate. It is a successful effort to recapture the lives of two people between book covers and to provide a keepsake for those who treasure their memory.

Miss Lemmon is a math teacher in the Mount Zion High School in Winnsboro and a member of the Zion Presbyterian Church.

—J.R.R.

THE GREAT INVITATION AND OTHER SERMONS. Emil Brunner. Westminster. $3.00.

Dr. Brunner is a controversial theologian. He has his ardent disciples and vigorous opponents. This volume of sermons is free from many of the controversial points found in his theological treatises. They demonstrate a side of the author's character not found in his other writings. Most of these messages could be read with approval by evangelicals. Despite the fact that we must disagree with much of Brunner's theology, one must have respect for him as a brilliant thinker and an able scholar. This volume convinces us also that he is an effective teacher.

The sermons in this book were preached in recent years in the Fraumunster and dedicated to this church on the occasion of the jubilee celebrating its eleven hundred years of history. Brunner writes, "To look back on such a long period of church life makes one realize, with peculiar vividness, that each of us preachers is only one of many hundred links in the chain which binds our present-day worship of God with that of the apostolic communities. May this venerable and beautiful house of God for long be a place where the Word of God is faithfully preached and a believing congregation unites to praise God to its own spiritual fortification and comfort."

It is difficult to reconcile how one who holds to some of his theological views could write this statement showing such reverence for the Word of God.

Readers who find it impossible to understand Brunner's major works will likely find it possible to interpret the messages in this volume of sermons prepared for vocal delivery to laymen.

—J.R.R.

GOD CAN TRANSFORM THE WORLD. Anne S. White. Christopher. $2.00.

The author has had wide experience in Japan, both in teaching and establishing prayer groups. She has spent much time in counseling and praying for the sick in mind, body, and soul. The meditations written during the days of counseling have become the chapters of this manuscript. The aim of this book is to draw laymen into a real and vital friendship with God. The volume closes with the affirmation on Christ's ability to heal today. —J.R.R.

THE BIBLE IN PICTURES FOR LITTLE EYES. Kenneth N. Taylor. Moody Press. $2.95.

The author believes that little children can understand the great truths of the Bible when told to them in simple words. And when pictures are added, indelible impressions are made that can last forever. He maintains that it is important to begin Bible training at the earliest possible age. This book can be read to children of approximate ages of three and a half to six years with great profit. The high aim of this work is to establish in little minds the truths of the Bible that will cause children to trust Christ all the days of their lives. This work is beautifully done.

—J.R.R.

The INTERNATIONAL LESSON ANNUAL (A lesson analysis). Charles M. Laymon, 1957. Roy L. Smith. Abingdon Press. $2.95.

This is the second in a series of annual lesson helps published by the Abingdon Press. This work gives the complete text in the King James Version and the Revised Standard Version, printed in parallel columns for easy comparisons. There is an explanation in each lesson that presents the background for the Bible passage and brings out special meanings which might otherwise be overlooked. Dr. Roy L. Smith tells what the text means in terms of life today. Teaching suggestions by prominent preachers show how to make the lesson clear to the class.

From the standpoint of organization of material, this work must be rated high. Some of the contributors are apparently conservative in their views concerning the Bible. Others are obviously liberal. The indivdual Sunday School teacher should be able to separate the wheat from the chaff.

STUDIES IN FIRST CORINTHIANS. M. R. DeHaan. Zondervan. $2.50.

In these simple studies in I Corinthians, Dr. DeHaan is true to the Bible. He gives most attention to those subjects which are of present-day interest and application. In his discussion of the many subjects contained in this letter, the author allows Scripture to speak for itself and compares text with text. Dr. DeHaan is helpful in discussing the problems of this "problem church."

—J.R.R.

VOL. XV NO. 45 MARCH 6. 1957 $3.00 A YEA

THE MAIL GOES THROUGH! And with it, the SOUTHERN PRESBYTERIAN JOURNAL. Harold D. Bailey, Rural Mail Carrier of Route No. 1, Woodleaf, N. C., finding a newly cut road impassable by automobile, goes on horseback to deliver the mail. Postmaster Oren M. Click and Carrier Bailey believe in service and evidently realize how eager readers are to get THE JOURNAL, for, as you can see, it is on top of the pack. Photograph by John Suther, Jr., Staff Photographer, The Salisbury (N. C.) Evening Post.

THE SOUTHERN PRESBYTERIAN JOURNAL

Rev. Henry B. Dendy, D.D., Editor....Weaverville, N. C.
Dr. L. Nelson Bell, Associate Editor....Asheville, N. C.
Rev. Wade C. Smith, Associate Editor....Weaverville, N. C.

EDITORIAL

The Stone of Destiny

Isaiah speaks of Our Lord as a "foundation stone, a tried stone, a precious corner stone, a sure foundation."

Paul speaks of him as the "foundation" which has been laid, and as the "chief corner stone."

Daniel tells of a stone which destroys the image which he sees in his vision, this stone becoming a mountain and filling the whole earth.

Our Lord, probably referring to both the Psalmist and Isaiah and identifying Himself as the Stone, gives this solemn warning: *"And whosoever shall fall on this stone shall be broken: but on whosoever it shall fall, it will grind him to powder."*

Many today are stumbling over Christ. To do so without subsequent change and repentance means certain breaking. Pride of intellect, of culture, of power; any or all of these can lead men to stumble over Christ. But how utterly foolish for us to put *anything* ahead of Christ. Little wonder that some day such folly will be manifested and the offender broken.

But when Christ's relationship with man becomes punitive, when he falls under His just condemnation and because of his hard and unrepentant heart receives in himself the judgment for his sins which Christ came to bear for him, how true that he shall be ground to powder.

We should never forget that God is love and that He yearns for us to turn to Him. We should also remember that our God is a consuming fire.

We can receive Him as Redeemer, or, we may fall on Him and be broken, or, He may fall on us and grind us to powder.

—L.N.B.

The Christian Century

The Christian Century is the best known and probably the most outspoken organ of modernism in the United States. It is interesting to examine its standards of journalism, its propaganda techniques, and the accuracy of its reporting. A recent issue brings to mind some earlier examples.

In the issue of February 29, 1956, page 261 the Century referred to "the late and unlamented Laymen's Committee." The article asserted "Cut business and politics out of the Christian's religious concern, and you have left faith dangling . . ." and so on for several lines. How true this assertion is! It could not be truer But a turn of the phrase can insinuate more than can be cleared up in a paragraph. Here the impression is given that the Laymen's Committee had advocated that Christians should pay no attention to business or politics. This insinuation is of course utterly false.

There are a great number of shorter examples of biased language. The same issue speaks of "Billy Graham's incredible gaff"; and the previous issue declaimed against the "Creaking McCarran Act."

In reporting the efforts of a Lutheran denomination to maintain its doctrinal standards the Century of February 8, 1956, says, "early departers met a disgruntled visiting minister who had evidently had all he could take of the lecture going on inside. He could not see much sense or make much sense of the speeches." Who was this visiting minister? If he happened to be the Century's reporter, the statement no doubt is absolutely accurate; the Century hardly ever sees sense in maintaining standards of doctrinal purity; but this does not imply that the speeches made no sense. The Century continues, "The preacher pulled out all the stops . . . . The preacher used the communion table like a jury box . . . the whole sorry sequel . . . the desolating near-unanimity."

Unintentionally no doubt, in spite of its pulling out its own stops, the Century lets slip the fact that the speeches made sense to nearly everybody present.

One of the Century's most contemptible articles appeared on February 1, 1956, entitled, *Five Missionaries Die Needlessly*. It states, "The credit that is theirs does not automatically transfer to those who were responsible for sending them to their unnecessary deaths." Of course it is completely true that their credit does not automatically transfer to anybody. But what of the insinuation that someone was responsible for sending them to their unnecessary deaths? Note the continuation. "The greater availability of funds for missionary purposes has resulted in the hasty organization of many 'independent' groups with a real or alleged missionary purpose." Does not this suggest that the board under which these martyrs went out was hastily organized and that its missionary purpose was perhaps only allegedly missionary? No, the Century does not say this; but the Century gives this impression. It continues, "hundreds of poorly trained missionaries . . . has immensely complicated the work of responsible boards . . . so-called Bible or independent churches . . . shallowly conceived . . . hardly more than rackets whose main purpose is to shake loose the dollars of credulous and uninformed people . . . "

Can this biased ranting be considered other than contemptible?

Something not so venomous, in fact something almost ludicrous, occurs in the current issue, February 20, 1957, page 222, column 2. "But what has this hard-core fundamentalism to say concerning Christ? Only that he was born of a Virgin and will reappear in a second coming, and that those two matters and no others are really essential to a valid allegiance to and faith in Jesus Christ as the Son of God. Nothing in his teaching, nothing in his death or resurrection . . . is to be compared in importance to the two articles of the fundamentalist creed about Christ."

Now, this is news indeed. The fundamentalists assert that the death and resurrection of Christ are not fundamentals; the substitutionary atonement and the bodily resurrection are not really essential. Fundamentalists have only two articles of faith: the Virgin Birth and the Second Coming. Well, that is two better than the Christian Century has, anyway.

How can this nonsense be taken? Is it malevolence? Is it abysmal ignorance? Is it irresponsibility? Or is it just the modernist idea of good journalism?

—G.H.C.

Election and Christ: In Calvin

It is quite popular for those who follow in the steps of Karl Barth to describe the place Calvin gives to Christ in election as inadequate. Now all the new light that diligent study can bring forth FROM THE WORD is to be welcomed. But Barth himself once remarked that "Calvin is better than most." In this matter also Calvin is better than most of us are. Accordingly, it is well to see what Calvin does say and examine ourselves to ascertain whether we are saying that much before blaming him for not saying more.

In the first edition of the Institutes Calvin treats of predestination chiefly in relation to the Church. And the connection between the two is grounded in the person and work of Jesus Christ. The Church manifests eternal election only as she is the body of Christ, for election is election in Christ, who is the constant and unchangeable truth of the Father. The mystery of the eternal goodness of God unveiled in Christ leads to the judgment of charity concerning those who are not yet evidently believers.

In the final edition of the Institutes Calvin relates election to Christ as true man, as true God, and as the Mediator. But whereas the emphasis falls for Barth on the true God-true man, it rests for Calvin on the Mediator.

The brightest example of gratuitous election

"The example of Christ ought at least to deter man from carelessly prating concerning this sublime mystery. A mortal man is conceived of the seed of David: to the merit of what virtues will they ascribe his being made, even in the womb, the Head of angels, the only-begotten Son of God, the Image and Glory of the Father, the light of righteousness and salvation of the world? . . . There is the brightest example of gratuitous election in the Head of the Church himself that it may not perplex us in the members; that he did not become the Son of God by leading a righteous life, but was gratuitously invested with this high

The Southern Presbyterian Journal, *a Presbyterian Weekly magazine devoted to the statement, defense, and propagation of the Gospel, the faith which was once for all delivered unto the saints,* published every Wednesday by The Southern Presbyterian Journal, Inc., in Weaverville, N. C.

Entered as second-class matter May 15, 1942, at the Postoffice at Weaverville, N. C., under the Act of March 3, 1879. Vol. XV, No. 45, March 6, 1957. Editorial and Business Offices: Weaverville, N. C. Printed in the U.S.A. by Biltmore Press, Asheville, N. C.

ADDRESS CHANGE: When changing address, please let us have both old and new address as far in advance as possible. Allow three weeks after change if not sent in advance. When possible, send an address label giving your old address.

honor, that he might afterwards render others partakers of the gifts bestowed upon Him." III. xii.1.

The Author of Election

While as man, Christ is the brightest example of gracious election; as God he is at the same time the author of election. Thus, "Though Christ introduces himself in his mediatorial capacity, yet he claims to himself the right of election in common with the Father. 'I speak not of all,' he says, 'I know whom I have chosen' . . . they are distinguished not by the nature of their virtues, but by the decree of heaven . . . Christ represents himself as the author of election . . . God creates whom he chooses to be his children by gratuitous election." III. xxii.7.

The Material Cause and *The Mirror of Election*

Fundamentally, Calvin thinks of Christ as the Mediator in whom the Father has chosen His people and through whom He brings them to Himself. "Paul says that the love which God has for us before the foundation of the world was founded on Christ," Eph.1.4-5, II.xvi.4. "It is beyond all controversy that no man is loved but in Christ . . . the Beloved Son in whom the love of the Father perpetually rests and then diffuses itself from Him to us, as Paul says that we are accepted in the Beloved," Eph.1.6, III.ii.32. "That material cause of eternal election and of the love which is now revealed is Christ the Beloved . . . by whom the love of God is communicated to us," Commentary on Ephesians 1.5. "If we seek the fatherly clemency and propitious heart of God, our eyes must be directed to Christ, in whom alone the Father is well pleased. If we seek salvation, life, and the immortality of the heavenly Kingdom, recourse must be had to no other; for He alone is the Fountain of life, the Anchor of salvation, and the Heir of the kingdom of heaven . . . But if we are chosen in Him, we shall find no assurance of our election in ourselves; nor even in God the Father, considered alone, abstractedly from the Son. Christ therefore is the mirror, in which it behooves us to contemplate our election, and here we may do it with safety. For as the Father has determined to unite to His Son, all who are the objects of His eternal choice, that he may have as his children, all that he recognizes among his members . . . if we have communion with Christ we are written in the book of life . . . Since our highest limit is found in Christ, we betray folly in seeking out of Him, that which we have already obtained in Him, and which can never be found anywhere else." III. xxiv.5.

—W.C.R.

Don't Break the Sequence

The best known verse in all of the Bible is John 3:16. In it is found a sequence and an objective which are minimized or altered to our own loss.

In this verse we see the *love* of God. We are told that it was God's loving and yearning heart which motivated His plan for our redemption: *"For God so loved the world."*

Here we also see the *deity* of our Lord; that He was pre-existent with the Father and the only begotten Son of God: *"that He gave His only begotten Son."*

We also learn here the glorious fact that salvation is God's free gift to *all* who will accept it. The all-inclusive word, "whosoever," means just what it says. God's redeeming work is for *all* if they will but take it: *"that whosoever."*

Again, we learn here the vital place *faith* has in determining man's eternal destiny. This hinges on our accepting in faith that which God has done for us. We can not understand it fully, nor can we adequately explain all that is involved, but God requires of us an act of obedience and trust which is faith: *"believeth."*

Here too is a flat statement that the state, direction and destiny of the unregenerate sinner is to *perish*. In other passages our Lord speaks of this as Hell. He came to rescue us from the certainty of eternal punishment! *"shall not perish."*

Finally, we find in this affirmation of our Lord the glorious hope of an *eternity* to be spent with Him. The hope of eternal life has been played down only too often. Some have failed to see that Christ did not come into the world *primarily* to make the world a better place in which to live. A change and improvement in world conditions is a by-product in the lives of redeemed men. The fruits of the Christian faith are glorious, but they are fruits, *not* the roots. Our Lord's primary objective in coming into this world was to save us from our sins and to thereby give us eternal life: *"but have everlasting life."*

Within this one glorious verse is to be found the very heart of the Gospel message, a message all need to hear, to believe and to live by.

—L.N.B.

Son of Man

By Ralph Brewer

Did you know that Jesus has fifty titles in the Bible? We know Him best as Christ, The Messiah, Son of God, Lord, Redeemer and The Good Shepherd, but these are only a few. Some eople who love Him prefer the Lamb of God, King of Kings or the Bright and Morning Star. Do you know Jesus' favorite name for himself? It was Son of Man, used 80 times in the Gospels. And you will find it in the Old Testament in Daniel 7 and 14.

John the Baptist, the Apostle John, Mark, Peter, Martha and the angel Gabriel all called Him the Son of God. Thirty times he is referred to in the Gospels by this name. He was both Son of God and Son of Man.

Aside from the divine titles, Jesus said of himself: "I am the truth," "I am the way," "I am the door," "I am the bread of life," "I am the resurrection," and it may surprise you, once in John 4:25-26, He admitted He was the Messiah!

"He that hath seen me hath seen the Father," Jesus declared, so Christ, Our Lord, became man to offer mankind forgiveness of sins and He died that we might have life eternal. As . Man, it was this role of Son of Man that He liked best, and both Man and Son of God He chose to offer man the Truth and Bread of Life.

Earth-bound man may not comprehend or understand God or the Holy Spirit, but here was a fellow creature who described himself as Son of Man who mended broken bodies, cured the sick, gave sight to the blind and raised the dead.

The crowds on the dusty roads in Galilee could appreciate miracles even though their little minds often did not understand His words or His ministry. They knew He was a great Teacher and as Son of Man under His everlasting arms He was their brother and protector.

Regardless of the role or title, many did not know His true identity. Today we know. We have no excuse. When He speaks to us it is not necessary for us to act like Paul, crying, "Lord, who art thou?" We know His voice. It is the Master speaking.

The Worker More Than The Work

(Part One)

By Dr. F. L. Chapell
(Late Dean of Gordon Missionary Training School)

Here is expressed a thought which may be new to many of us who think of ourselves as striving Christians, meeting many obstacles in our efforts to be faithful in service to our Master. Some cherished goals we seem to never reach. In the article which follows, Dr. Chapell has offered what I would call "The Antidote to Discouragement." Discouragement can be devastating. Like a black cloud it can obscure the very promises of God. Here is truth that will help to dispel the cloud and let the sun come shining through. It will be divided into two parts. Following is Part One.—W.C.S.

God's purpose in calling us to be laborers together with Him during this present age is not simply that the apparent work which He sets before us may be accomplished. It is rather, that, in the accomplishment of this work, we may be prepared for our chief and ultimate service in the age to come.

But too often men, judging simply from the narrow view of the present time, suppose that the present conquest of evil and the immediate establishment of righteousness in the earth are the main objects God now has in calling us into His service. This they conceive is the work He has given us to do. But if this were the chief thing in view He could more easily accomplish it by other and better agents. He could set His own hand to it more vigorously, and call in more supernatural agents than He now does.

All power is in His hand, and He has but to use it to bring about the result. There is a time coming when He will arise in His might and make short work in the earth. And if the immediate rooting out of sin and the establishment of righteousness were the chief things to be accomplished, He might thus arise at once and speedily work this short and radical work. But evidently this is not His chief aim at present. And unless we discern what the real end is, which He has in view, we wonder as we behold the long and dreary reign of sin, and survey the vast extent of the misery and sorrow that abound in the earth. We are ready to cry, "How long, O Lord!" We wonder why He that hath the keys of death and hell does not turn them in the lock—why He that hath the residue of the Spirit does not pour it out upon the earth. Or, looking at our great Example, we ask: if work were the chief thing, why did He spend the greater part of His life on earth without working? Why did He give only about three of His thirty-three years to work; and why did He allow Himself to be cut off at so early an age, when, apparently, He was best fitted to work? Or, further yet, following the history of the church, why was Stephen, when full of faith and the Holy Ghost, and doing wonderful works, cut off so soon, and why have so many of the rarest workers been cut down so prematurely? Why, then, are all these things as they are?

We do not presume to give all the reasons of God's administration when He Himself does not give account of His matters. But one evident reason we can see. And this one is that *the worker is more than the work*—that character is more than mere deeds—that the doer is more than the things done. It is the character more than the deeds of the church that God now contemplates, since her chief sphere of service is to be in the ages to come. *The present age is disciplinary rather than executive. We are disciples, that is, learners, more than we are workers, at present.* Is it not modern self-importance that has set the name "workers" above that of "disciples"? To be sure we are workers, but this is largely because the work may be necessary to learning, since there are some lessons that can be best learned in work. We are workers in order that we may be learners, in order that we may be fully equipped for the age to come. When our character is perfected our present age work is largely done, even though we may seem to have accomplished so little in the way of pulling down the strongholds of Satan or in building up the cause of God. The Saviour could say, "I have finished the work Thou gavest me to do," even when His whole nation was rejecting Him, and His own chosen apostles were forsaking and denying Him. He was One in whom the Father was well pleased, notwithstanding the world was not won to God. So also, Paul could rejoice when nearly all his fellow-laborers had forsaken him, and apostasy was creeping into all the churches he had founded, for he had *kept the faith. His boast was not what he had achieved in the way of work, but what he had come to be in the way of character.*

(Part II Next Week)

A Modern Approach in Missio

It was a village in north central Korea. large number of children and adults were ga ered about a small truck atop which we megaphones of sound equipment. Hangi from the side of the truck was a large color picture of the outline of a human heart.

Careful examination of the picture reveal within the heart the figure of Satan with spear directed at the drawing of a human e Around Satan were the figures of a peaco a goat, a pig, a turtle, a tiger, a serpent a a toad. At the top of the V of the heart v a picture of a Korean boy, while to the l of his face was an open Bible and to the rig a dove with outspread wings.

The speaker began by pointing to each the figures within the heart outline, explaini that the eye represented the ever-present e of God, the peacock the sin of pride, the gc the sin of lack of restraint, the pig the s of gluttony, the turtle the sin of laziness, t tiger the sin of anger and revenge, the serpe the sin of envy and deception, and the to the sin of filth and gossip. Then he add that the Word of God seeks entrance into t sinful heart, and that when the Word is receiv in sincerity all the types of sin will flee, wi Christ taking up His abode in the heart.

Another picture was then shown, a picture (the heart with all of the animals, the serpen the turtle and the peacock on the outside (the heart, while within appeared a cross, th open Bible, the dove, a pair of opened lips an a clear eye.

The worker was using the famed "Heart (Pak" booklet, one of the most potent aids t missionary work. The little booklet of 24 pag is profusely illustrated with pictures, while th text material very clearly explains the full pla of salvation. The booklets are published an supplied free of charge to missionaries by th Bible Meditation League of Columbus, Ohio.

Our own Joe Hopper in Korea is using hu dreds of thousands of these booklets, and wit their aid has been able to supply his man associates and national workers which has e abled them to win many, many souls to Christ.

Writing to one of his friends a few months ;o, Mr. Hopper stated: "I will write Dr. Fal- :nberg and tell him of our opportunities and :eds. Naturally in the distribution of litera- ıre of this sort the sky is the limit as to how uch we can use, but I will try to show him clearly as possible our needs."

On the same day Mr. Hopper wrote to Dr. ılkenberg, the president of the League, in ırt as follows: "During evangelistic campaigns e received considerable quantities of The eart of Pak booklets from Bob Rice, but they ere really far less than the total needed. Mr. ice is currently having printed for you 200,000 :re in anticipation of the total of 600,000 to : printed for use in this area." (Ed. The eague has now printed more than four million ıpies for Korea.)

Then Mr. Hopper adds: "The area of our ission work covers North and South Chulla :ovinces, South Choon-chung province and heju Island. The total population of this area about seven million. No reliable figures are ˈailable as to how many have been reached ith the Gospel message, but my estimate is ıat perhaps 2% are in active connection with ıe church. I think it is safe to say that at ast five million know virtually nothing of ıe Gospel or have never heard of it at all. ıch of us missionaries is in contact with scores country churches, and leaders throughout ıese provinces come to us with appeals for ıspel literature which we give to them as long we have supplies. I myself am in regular ıntact with about 150 small churches in an ea with a population of about one million, you can see that we can use all of this type material you can supply. The Koreans are eat readers, and will read whatever we can ve them."

Mr. Hopper's comment concerning local Ko- an leaders is most interesting, as probably nety per cent of the services held with the d of "The Heart of Pak" booklets are held nong the five million who "know virtually ıthing of the Gospel or have never heard of at all." The scene described in the opening ıragraphs above was one where a Korean na- ınal Christian was holding the meeting, there- ' supplementing the ministry of the mission- ies.

"The Heart of Pak" story was born for Korea in response to the pleading of an outstanding missionary of that land. From it grew the translation into languages other than Korean. Today it is used in English in many States of our nation, especially in Child Evangelism classes. For South America it is the Spanish "The Heart of Pedro," for Germany "The Heart of Hans," for Japan "The Heart of Jiro," for Indonesia "The Heart of Adjang," and on and on, the total printing in various languages now exceeding ten million copies, all provided free to the Christian workers. The Bible Meditation League, Box 477, Columbus 16, Ohio, has offered to send sample copies to anyone who makes request for same.

Helps To Understanding Scripture Readings in *Day by Day*

By Rev. C. C. Baker

Sunday, March 17, *Acts* 17:1-9. Notice the missionary methods used by Paul and Silas in Thessalonica (vv.1-3). Where did they preach? What message did they proclaim? What was the basis of their authority? Did they appeal to the emotions or to the intellect? How does the list of those who received the Gospel (v.4) stand in contrast to the place where it was preached (v.1)? Notice the extent of the measures the Jews took to stop the preaching of the Gospel (vv.5-7)? What do their charges against Paul and Silas indicate of their attitude toward the Gospel (vv.6-7)? Based upon a presentation of the Gospel that was founded in the Scriptures and centered in Christ, the Christians in Thessalonica, in the face of persecution and without a primarily emotional appeal, formed one of the strongest of the New Testament churches

Monday, March 18, *Amos* 5:11-15. Amos had a difficult task as he proclaimed God's truth to the nation of Israel. What was the people's attitude toward the prophets of God (v.10)? What was their chief purpose in living (6:1-6)? Was there any lack of religious ceremonies among the people (5:21-23)? What did God desire more than the observance of religious services (vv.4,6)? How should their religion have been manifested in their daily lives (vv.11a,12b, 14-15,24)? What was to be the end of those who were interested only in "gracious living" (5:11; 6:1,4,7)? of those who sought the Lord and His ways (vv.14b,15b)? If Amos stood in the pulpit of your church, in what particular aspects would he be likely to proclaim the same message to your congregation that he spoke to the people of Israel?

Tuesday, March 19, *Hebrews* 13:7-16. The author of Hebrews warns his readers of false Jewish teachers who say that a person grows in grace through the eating of certain sacrificial foods taken from the altar (v.9). He states that the altar to which the Christian comes when he approaches God does not contain sacrificial meats, etc., but has been sprinkled by the blood of Christ (vv.11-12). The author is using figurative language as he speaks in terms of the Old Testament tabernacle. A person is strengthened in grace by coming to Christ himself (vv.12-13). The sacrifice that is truly pleasing to God is that of a grateful and giving heart (vv.15-16). Do you seek to grow in grace by engaging or not engaging in certain external practices, or simply by yielding yourself to the living Christ?

Wednesday, March 20, *Luke* 4:16-30. Notice the great miracles Jesus performed everywhere — except in Nazareth where he grew up (vv.16, 23b,31-34). What attitude did the people's reactions (v.22; Matt. 13:54-57) manifest when Jesus read from Isaiah (vv.17-20) and made the pronouncement of v.21? How did the miracles (v.23) and the pronouncement of v.21 produce a concept of Jesus that differed from the picture of the carpenter's son the people were used to (vv.22b, Matt. 13:54-56)? Verses 25-27 tell of one of the few times Jesus deliberately used examples of God's blessings upon Gentiles rather than upon Jews. Notice v.24 and Matt. 13:58 for clues as to why He did this. What was the cause of the unbelief of the people of Nazareth? Have familiar concepts of Christ become so trite to you that you have become blind to the reality that He could be in your life?

Thursday, March 21, *Luke* 10:29-37. Most of Jesus' parables have but one point; the details are usually not to be used as symbols. What question provoked the story of the Good Samaritan (v.29)? With what motive was it asked (v.29)? Notice also the motive behind the question of v.25. What central point did Jesus make in the story of vv.30-36? Do you think Jesus would have used Jewish religious leaders as villians (vv.31-32) and a despised Samaritan as the hero of the story (vv.33-34) if the Jewish lawyer had asked theyquestion of

ESSON FOR MARCH 17

By THE REV. J. KENTON PARKER

The Authority Of Jesus

'ackground Scripture: Matthew 21:12 - 22:46
'evotional Reading: Isaiah 53:10-12

The authority of Jesus is the authority of God, for Jesus is the Second Person of the Trinity, the ɔn of God. He has the authority to teach, to heal, to cast out demons, to forgive sins. In all His ords and works He is speaking and acting with the full authority of God. This truth is fully estab- ɜhed by our lesson material and Background Scripture. It was the stubborn unbelief and refusal : the Jewish leaders to recognize this fact that made their sin so heinous and inexcusable. Much : our Background Scripture is related to the :ntral thought of the lesson: the authority of :sus.

The Triumphal Entry into the City of Jerusalem: 21:1-11.

I wish to include these verses for they make good introduction to our lesson. Jesus sent ɤo of His disciples into the village to make :eparation for this magnificent display of His ıthority as the Coming King. This whole scene ould have been a meaningless pageantry unless ıck of it was His right to thus ride in triumph to the city of the King. He allowed the multi- ıdes to acclaim Him as the Messiah, and shout .eir praise, and spread their garments in His ıth and branches of palm trees. I will not ɲger on this scene, as we have often studied in other lessons, but it very naturally leads ɔ to the other events in these chapters. He ıd the authority, the right, to thus ride into e city; He was their King.

"By what authority doest thou these things?" 12-27.

He went into the temple and cast out all ose who bought and sold. He had done this fore, in the early days of His ministry. (See hn 3:13-22). It does not take men long to back to their old sinful practices. It is ɜy to profane the house of God. In this st case He had been questioned and asked r a sign.

This time, the blind and the lame come to ım, but the proud Pharisees, scribes, and Sad- :cees were "moved with indignation." He :nt back to Bethany to lodge for the night, d in the morning he "curses" the barren ; tree. This was a symbolic act of judgment; act of judicial authority, and pointed to e barren nation of Israel, and the coming dgment upon her, because of her unbelief d fruitlessness.

When He comes again to the temple His enemies are ready with their question, By what authority doest thou these things? They were taken by surprise the day before, but now they begin their barrage of questions which continues for some time. Jesus answers his critics with His usual Heavenly wisdom by asking them a question which He knew they would be afraid to answer : The baptism of John, whence was it? from heaven, or of men? They were shrewd enough to see that either way they answered, they would be caught; so they said, We cannot tell. Then Jesus said, neither tell I you by what authority I do these things. When men are determined not to believe there is no use wasting words upon them. I fear that some of our modern unbelievers are in this class.

Jesus now proceeds with some parables which were directly pointed toward these hardhearted unbelievers and critics.

III. *Some Pointed Parables:* 21:28; 22:14.
1. *Parable of the Two Sons:* 21:28-32.

A certain man had two sons. He came to the first and said, Son, go work today in my vineyard. He answered, I will not; but afterwards repented, and went. When he approached the second son with the same command, he said, I go, sir, and went not. Then He makes them answer the question, Whether of the twain did the will of his father? They say, The first. He then drives home the point of the story; the publicans and harlots would go into the kingdom before these unbelieving and impenitent Pharisees and scribes. There is a lesson for us too in this parable. We who have been brought up in Christian homes and attend church, are prone to say, I will do, or I will say, and then put off the doing and saying, while some great sinner will suddenly change and put us to shame by the earnestness of his endeavors.

2. *Parable of the Wicked Husbandmen:* 21:33-46.

This is a longer story and even more pointed as we see from verse 45 : it penetrated their thick "skulls and skin," and they perceived that He had spoken it against them. It is interesting to compare this parable with the "Song of the Vineyard" as we find it in Isaiah, chapter five. Both tell the story of Israel's history and her departure from God. The householder sent servant after servant — the prophets — and these had been treated shamefully. Now he sends his son, saying, they will reverence my son. The prophets had some authority as the messengers of God; the Son had even greater authority. The reaction of the wicked husbandmen to the Son is more violent: they said, This is the heir; let us kill him and the inheritance will be ours. Back of all the opposition of these Jewish leaders is this feeling of envy and greed. In the Song of the Vineyard it is the character of the fruit — wild grapes — that is stressed; here it is the attitude of the men who had charge of the vineyard. Israel sinned in both ways. Not even these "thick-skinned" scribes and Pharisees could fail to see and feel the point of this parable. It angered them.

Again, He makes them pronounce their own doom. What will He do unto these husbandmen? He asks. They say, He will destroy these wicked men and will let out his vineyard to others. Jesus refers them to an Old Testament prophecy, (Psalm 118:22), and tells them plainly that the kingdom of God will be taken from them and given to a nation bringing forth the fruits thereof. All of us Gentiles realize how truly this prophecy has been fulfilled. One thing amazes me today : the adamant attitude of practically all the Jews even now when Christianity has proved itself. What a glorious day it would be if the veil could be removed from the poor blind Jews and they would accept Christ as their Messiah!

3. *Parable of the Marriage Feast:* 22:1-14.

The kingdom of heaven is often spoken of as a "feast." This was the figure Isaiah used when he cried, Ho, everyone that thirsteth, Come ye to the waters — Come, buy wine and milk without money, etc. Compare this story with Luke 14:15-24. Those invited in Luke made excuses for not coming: These "made light of it and went their ways," and some went so far as to mistreat the messengers. The king destroyed these murderers, and then commands his servants to go out into the highways and bid them come. And the wedding was furnished with guests.

YOUNG PEOPLES Department

'OUTH PROGRAM FOR MARCH 17

By THE REV. B. HOYT EVANS

The Birth Of A Mission

cripture: Acts 1:1-11

uggested Hymns:
"I Love To Tell The Story"
"Where Cross The Crowded Ways Of Life"
"We've A Story To Tell To The Nations"

uggestions for Program Leader:
(It will mean much to your program if you an find someone with first-hand knowledge f the Belgian Congo to present this informa- ion about the new station at Leopoldville. ıny missionaries who are now or were formerly n the Congo, or their close relative, could lead his program for you. Try to have a reasonably ırge map of the Belgian Congo posted before he group so that the speaker or speakers may oint out the location of the older stations in he Kasai region and the new station at Leopold- ille. If you receive a special offering, do it t the end of the program. Whether you receive special offering or set aside a portion of your :gular budget for this financial objective, be ıre to have a prayer of dedication for your ifts.)

.eader's Introduction:
In this program we are considering the second f our 1957 Financial Objectives. This year 'e have five special objectives instead of four, s in former years, so that is the reason for aving two "objective" programs in one quarter.

The purpose of this project is to help with ıe building of new churches in the city of .eopoldville, which is the capital of the Belgian :ongo. Our speakers will tell us something bout this great African city and will explain ıe special reasons for building churches there.

irst Speaker:
Most of you know already that the Presby- :rian Church has a very successful mission work ı the Belgian Congo, which is in the very heart f Africa. If you do know that, it may seem :range to you that we should be making so ıuch fuss about building churches in Leopold- ille which is the capital city of that country. 'ou will notice on the map, however, that our lder mission stations are separated by a con- iderable distance from Leopoldville. Our mis- ion territory has always been the Kaisai region of the Congo, which is very primitive and quite remote from the city life of Leopoldville. City mission work is a new thing for Presbyterians in the Congo.

It may come as a surprise to some that central Africa actually has a large modern city. Leopold- ville is such a city. In many respects it is more up to date than American cities because it has been built more recently. Forty years ago it was about what most of us would expect an African village to be. Today it is a thriving city with 350,000 inhabitants. Most of its citizens are Congolese, with only 22,000 whites living there.

The city was named for King Leopold of Belgium. As you know, the Congo is a Belgian colony, and in contrast to the grave unrest in other African countries, the Congo is relatively peaceful. This is due in large part to wise and fair management by the Belgian government.

Leopoldville is a center of production and transportation for the whole country. The mighty Congo River becomes navigable at Leopoldville, and has long served as the main artery to bring the life of the country into the city. Now new factories are springing up over the city and an airport is under construction which is claimed to be the largest commercial airport in the world. Literally thousands of substantial, low- cost houses are being built as the city grows larger and larger. It is in such a situation that our church opened a new mission work in 1955.

Second Speaker:
Someone may ask if Leopoldville had any Christian mission work before 1955, and if so, why did our church feel constrained to enter the field. In answer to those questions we would have to say that there have been Christian mis- sionaries and Christian churches in Leopoldville for many years. Our church sent some of its missionaries into Leopoldville because the Amer- ican Baptists, who had been there for many years, urged them to come.

Here in our own country we have long been faced with the problem of a shifting population. For years people have been moving from rural areas to the cities, and now they are moving from the centers of the cities to the outskirts. As the people have moved, the church has sought to move with them. That is exactly what is taking place in the Belgian Congo. More and more people are leaving the primitive, tribal villages of the Congo and making their homes in the Congo's most important city, Leopoldville. Education received in the mission schools has fitted many Africans for city employment, and city employment means better wages and higher standards of living. The movement of population to Leopoldville has taken place more rapidly than the Christian workers there could reach the new people. The Presbyterian church responded to the call for help, and we now have eight missionaries assigned to the work in Leopoldville.

Third Speaker:

What can we do to help our missionaries in Leopoldville? Before we answer that question, let us try to get an idea of the size of their task. When the work was first begun, each missionary couple was assigned a territory containing 30,000 unchurched people. Some of these people had received Christian training in interior mission stations, but there were no churches for them in Leopoldville. It is the task of the missionaries to lead out in providing the churches. So far, only temporary structures with open sides and crude benches are available. The crying need is for permanent church buildings and several of them. That is where our gifts come in. The money we give will be used in the construction of church buildings in Leopoldville.

Communism is making a strong bid for the loyalty of all Africans. We have here a wonderful opportunity to claim some of them for Christ and His church. Let us be generous in our giving and faithful in our prayers.

Offering

Prayer of Dedication

CHILDRENS Page

Daniel and the Lions

The King erected a huge idol for all his subjects to worship, but Daniel worshiped the true God of heaven. (This is our God, too.) The King said that Daniel must worship the idol or he would be thrown into the den of lions. Daniel continued to worship the God of heaven, and he was thrown into the lion's den. The lions would quickly kill and eat human beings, but to the surprise of all, they did not bother Daniel at all. That was because he trusted God. Next morning the King came and looked in, and there stood Daniel calmly among the lions. The King said, "O, Daniel, how can this be?" And Daniel answered, "O King, my God hath shut the lions' mouths that they have not harmed me." Then the King commanded that Daniel be taken out and restored to his high position in the Kingdom, and he issued a proclamation in honor of Daniel's God - (and our God). "Commit thy way unto the Lord; trust also in Him, and He shall bring it to pass." (Ps. 37:5) memorize this.

A One-Minute Message on Stewardship

MARCH

"Winning souls to Christ is the business of every Christian laid upon him by his Lord. Evangelism is the "telling of that good news." Bearing witness to the faith is the primary responsibility of *every* Christian. Personal witnessing includes such vital areas as: helping canvass the neighborhood for unchurched people; visiting church prospects to bring to them a testimony of Christian faith and an invitation to church services; distributing tracts as opportunities present themselves.

With Paul our passion and delight must be to spend and be spent in giving all for the sake of Christ and lost souls.

God tells us definitely that He will be with us and fill our lives with divine power through witnessing. Discouragements are a sign that the devil is tempting us to weaken in our zeal to proclaim Christ among the unchurched. Personal soul winning is likely to be difficult for us because we lack a childlike trust in God. We are apt to think that the entire duty is ours and so we easily lose courage and heart. But when we bear in mind that one hundred per cent of the conversion of a sinner to Christ is by the working of the Holy Spirit and that we are but His mouth piece, we will lose our fears and hesitancy. We can give the world the Christ it needs, we cannot give it more, and we dare not give it less, "Let the redeemed of the Lord say so" (Psalm 107:2).

—March talk from "Investing Your Life" by W. J. Werning.

Alcoholism a Disease?

In a recent article by Mrs. Mann, she relates her experiences as an alcoholic. She says, "I well remember when I was hopelessly in the grip of the vicious disease of alcoholism."

We agree that the word "vicious" is correct, but we believe the word "disease" as applied to alcoholism is a misnomer. If alcoholism is a disease:

1. It is the only disease that is contracted by an act of will.

2. It is the only disease that requires a license to propagate it.

3. It is the only disease in which the "germ," alcohol, is bottled and sold as a beverage.

4. It is the only disease that requires nearly 500,000 outlets for its spread to those possessed of a deadly thirst for it.

5. It is the only disease that is habit forming.

6. It is the only disease that produces crime.

7. It is the only disease which places revenue dollars on the eyes of a nation's dead conscience.

8. It is the only disease for which over nine billion dollars is spent to "catch" it.

9. It is the only disease against which woe is pronounced and is classified as a bar to heaven.

10. It is the only disease without a germ or virus cause, and for which there is no corrective medicine.

There is a cure—total abstinence—through the help of God.

—Mrs. M. B. Briggs

My Code for Christian Living as a Homemaker

I choose for the motto of my life: "I have set the Lord always before me; because He is at my right hand, I shall not be moved." Psalms 16:8.

1. *Prayer*—With the waking moments of each day I will commit myself and my loved ones into God's hands for His direction and guidance.

2. *Family Altar*—I will arrange to have a family altar at the time most convenient to my household.

3. *Meditation*—I will endeavor to have for myself a period of quiet meditation and prayer each day.

4. *Practice the Presence of God*—I will endeavor to create for my home a Christian atmosphere where the presence of God becomes a living reality to each member of the family and to everyone who comes within my doors. (I will accomplish this purpose through conversations and attitudes of the family, books and other literature in the home, music, pictures, entertainment, and hospitality.)

5. *Serenity*—I will try to keep myself serene so that my home will be a place of peace and happiness for all.

O tired heart of mine:
When thou art quiet grown,
The wondrous warmth and comfort of her life will steal
Back from the shadowy gates which do but hide
Her face, her form from my despairing eyes.
But that which made her life the poem that it was,
That vital, magic, potent charm, will stay
And fall athwart my path adown the years,
And thou wilt say (is it not so?)
The loveliest part of life, as that of day, is Afterglow!

—E. Grace Updegraff
On the death of her mother

WITNESS

This is in truth the Christ.
I know. For He has closely walked with me.
More surely than the day's light have I known
His presence, near in utmost verity.
I doubt not sunrise when the sun I see,
And this I know: He is the Christ, and He
Is Christ alone.

The Christ, the Son of God.
I, poor in knowledge, can this truth proclaim—
He is the sum of living and of light.
For I have seen Him like a whitening flame
In hearts of those who name His holy Name;
Have seen Him give His healing to the lame,
To blind ones, sight.

Yes, this is He, the Christ.
I saw. This is the record that I bear.
I will not reason with you of His grace;
Nor argue of the why, and when, and where.
This is my record. This I do declare—
I know Him. In my need I found Him there,
And saw His face.

—By Nell Latham

Seedlings of Alcoholism

Declaring that moderate drinkers will never give the support necessary to make a law succeed in eliminating the liquor traffic, Mr. Wilfrid Winterton says, "Moderate drinking that hazardous practice that defies all definition — never will remove the evils of intemperance. Moderate drinkers provide the seedlings and the nursery from which all the consequences of alcoholism grow. These are the people who are responsible for there being a liquor problem. It is for their convenience and in response to their demands that the traffic exists at all. Obviously, it does not exist for the total abstainers, and no state would tolerate it for a single day if all its customers were drunkards."

* * *

You are either a part of the alcohol problem or a part of the answer to the problem — depending upon your attitude.

—Temperance Action

Recommend The Journal To Friends

NEWS of CHURCHES Around the World

World Missions Receipts

Budget for 1957	$3,500,000.00
Receipts to date	86,114.33
Percentage of annual budget received for 1957	2.46%
Balance needed for 1957	3,413,885.67

Curry B. Hearn, Treasurer

Rural Leaders Summer School
Garrett Biblical Institute

The Interdenominational School for Rural Leaders at Garrett Biblical Seminary, Evanston, Illinois, will be held June 24 - July 26, 1957. Two scholarships, providing tuition and room, are available to ministers in the Presbyterian Church, U. S.

Courses and teachers are:

1. Agricultural Economics for Rural Ministers —Dr. Robert Hewlett, Paris, France.

2. Rural Sociology—Dr. Samuel Blizzard, Pennsylvania State University.

3. The Program of the Rural Church—Dr. Rockwell Smith, of the Garrett Biblical Institute faculty.

Any pastors, who are college graduates, who may be interested, should write to me. I am to send our two nominations by May 15th, but an earlier date would be much better.

James M. Carr, Secretary
Town and Country Church Department
341-B Ponce De Leon Avenue, N.E.,
Atlanta 8, Georgia

ALABAMA

Birmingham — South Highland Presbyterian Church here recently had as guest speaker for special weekend services Dr. Theodore Floyd Adams, president of the Baptist World Alliance, and pastor of the First Baptist Church of Richmond, Va.

Dr. Frank Alfred Mathes, pastor of South Highland Church, said that the appearance of Dr. Adams is part of the church's program to bring annually some of America's outstanding ministers and church leaders.

Dr. Adams spoke on the topics: "Freedom's Holy Light," "The Glory of Our Religion," and "Expendable Christians." Dr. Adams also had a special message for Christian ministers of the Birmingham area. At a special luncheon meeting at South Highland church he addressed the ministers on the topic "A Quick Trip Around the World."

Dr. Adams has visited Soviet Russia twice. On his first visit he said that he was not able to talk with the Christians in Russia, but on the last trip he preached in the only Baptist Church in Moscow, a city of over four million people. In discussing the question of religion in Russia, Dr. Adams said that there is today freedom of worship in Russia but not freedom of religion as we in the United States know it.

"Christians in Russia, because they are Christians, are not members of the Communist party, and they, as Christians, enjoy only freedom of worship," Dr. Adams said.

GEORGIA

Atlanta — The Board of Church Extension, numbering twenty-one members, met at the Presbyterian Center in Atlanta February 13-14 and discussed work of the various divisions which make up that board of the Presbyterian Church, U. S.

Announcement was made at the meeting that a total of 38 loans, amounting to $462,500.00 were made to churches in 1956. At the end of 1956 there were 155 outstanding loans, amounting to $1,096,930.00, the report said.

Noting the number of churches damaged in the flood areas recently, the Board authorized the expenditure of funds up to $10,000 to meet the needs for repair of the churches in those areas of the Assembly. These funds will be made from the 1957 receipts of the Board's Division of Home Mission and Negro Work under the leadership of Dr. Claude H. Pritchard who has estimated that about a dozen churches have been damaged in Guerrant and Abingdon presbyteries alone.

Hal Hyde, secretary of the Urban Church Department, reported on plans for the Church's supplemental offering to raise $1 million for building new churches, and a plan whereby each Presbyterian will be asked to give one day's pay or income for this purpose.

The Rev. O. V. Caudill, secretary of the Church Architecture Department, in his report, called attention to the urgency in combating the lack of space and proper facilities within churches. There is a special need for space in many religious education departments, Mr. Caudill said, and the Church Architecture Department head pointed out that some churches were losing members because of this inadequacy.

The Rev. James Alexander, reporting for the Chaplains and Military Personnel Department, announced an increase in Presbyterian military chaplains, placing the present total at 45 chaplains. He also reported that last year there were 24 ecclesiastical endorsements for reservists in the chaplaincy.

The report of the Town and Country Church Department, presented by Dr. James M. Carr, secretary of the department, told of the development

Heres a *gift* that returns you an *income for life!*

Yes, you both give AND receive when you make an Annuity Gift to foreign missions. One of our annuitants, a retired missionary, says this:

> "The Annuity Fund provides an opportunity by which a lover of the Kingdom may be a channel of blessing to benighted souls throughout the earth by the investment of funds that will bring to him an interest which will compare favorably with rates of interest to be secured from the leading business concerns of our country."

This income, paid semi-annually, is not subject to change, is partly tax free, and not a single payment has ever been omitted or deferred in over 50 years operation. The income rate ranges from 3 to 7.4 per cent, depending on age.

If you are interested in this ideal gift and investment combined, write for our informative booklet, *"A Guaranteed Lifetime Investment."* Just address

CURRY B. HEARN, TREASURER
BOARD OF WORLD MISSIONS
PRESBYTERIAN CHURCH IN THE UNITED STATES
POST OFFICE BOX 330, NASHVILLE 1, TENN.
"To Foreign Missions a Share"

MOODY BIBLE INSTITUTE

Dr. William Culbertson, president of Moody Bible Institute, is currently on a six-week tour of Africa where he will minister to missionaries. This trip to Africa is being made in response to the invitation of the Sudan Interior Mission and the Africa Inland Mission to speak at their annual conferences.

While there, Dr. Culbertson will meet Moody alumni at special gatherings that have been arranged. He will also speak in several leading cities of South Africa, and confer with government officials in the Belgian Congo about further use of Moody Institute of Science films in the Congo schools.

Traveling with Dr. Culbertson is the Rev. Harold R. Cook, an Institute faculty member who is studying missions in Africa at first hand. They will return at the end of March.

KENTUCKY

Louisville — Eighty-four high school students and twenty-one counselors met in February at Louisville Presbyterian Theological Seminary to discuss church vocations.

The Rev. Marcus J. Priester of Philadelphia delivered the opening statement in which he discussed the Christian vocation in general, and church vocations in particular.

During two discussion periods which followed, the young people discussed seven specific areas of church vocations. They were aided by advisers from the Seminary faculty, and from the churches of the Louisville area.

Louisville — Strathmoor Presbyterian Church here has extended a hearty welcome to the Garami family of Hungary.

The Garamis arrived in Louisville on January 18, and are presently making their home with Mr. Joe D. Brown. Two days after their arrival, the Garamis attended worship services at Strathmoor Presbyterian Church. Language proved no barrier when they joined in singing "A Mighty Fortress Is Our God," in their own tongue.

Mr. and Mrs. Frank Garami have two children, Frank, who is 12, and Georgia who is 2½. Mrs. Garami's mother, Mrs. Maria Stepco, is also with them in Louisville.

Mr. Garami started working at the American Air Filter Company on January 24. Young Frank is attending Highland Junior High School as an observer and will become enrolled as soon as the family becomes located. Two nights a week the family attends language classes for Hungarian refugees at Ahrens Trade School. The Pioneers and the Boy Scout troop of Strathmoor welcomed young Frank immediately.

Members of the church are helping the Garamis to obtain the needed furnishings so that they may make their own home as soon as a house is found available.

INTRODUCE
THE JOURNAL
TO YOUR FRIENDS

NORTH CAROLINA

Oak Forest Presbyterian Church of the Asheville Presbytery is completing a School of World Missions on the last Sunday night in February. There were five sessions which began with an assembly when there were hymns, Bible reading and prayer. The group was then dismissed to classes to study Southeast Asia with emphasis on Formosa. After which the classes met to view a film or to hear a talk. "Decision in Thailand," "Formosa," and "Recruits for Christ" were seen. A talk was given by Dr. L. Nelson Bell, noted Presbyterian layman of Montreat, retired surgeon of Asheville and editor of the new church magazine, "Christianity Today." Dr. Bell has just returned from a trip to Korea and Japan and spoke on the situation there. Malvern Hills and West Asheville Presbyterian Churches met at Oak Forest to hear the talk. Rev. Stanley L. Bennett, pastor of the Montreat Church and immediate Past-Chairman for Missions of the Council of the Asheville Presbytery, spoke another night on Communism and Christianity.

A round-table talk will be a feature of the supper which will precede classes on the last night of the school. Mr. Edgar Richardson, English instructor at Warren Wilson College, will be in charge. Mr. Richardson is the son of a former missionary to China from the Presbyterian Church, U. S., who is now vice president of Southwestern University in Memphis. The talks will deal with the life of a missionary and the work of the church in a foreign country, by students from Thailand, India and Indonesia.

After supper and classes the assembly will include reports by each class and a film will be shown to end the School of Missions.

In connection with the study of foreign countries and of Missions, warm clothes and blankets were collected to be sent to a center in Maryland to be sent overseas.

Mrs. Milton A. Sullivan,
World Missions Chairman.

Charlotte — A Diamond Jubilee dinner, launching the Presbyterian College development program among alumni in the Charlotte region was held here recently.

Dr. John McSween, former president of Presbyterian College, delivered the main address of the program. Dr. Marshall W. Brown, president of PC, introduced Dr. McSween.

Wilson — First Presbyterian Church of Wilson celebrated its birthday recently with special morning services commemorating the 6th, 72nd, and 104th anniversaries of the church.

February, 1957, marked the 6th year of use for the present church buildings, the 72nd year of the founding of the church, and the 104th year of Presbyterian services in the city of Wilson.

The first known Presbyterian to live in Wilson came to the city in 1853, and two years later services were being conducted among Presbyterians in the area. The church was organized in 1885 with a charter membership of 24. As of January 1, 1957, the church has grown to 710 members.

Recommend The Journal To Friends

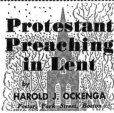

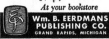

SOUTH CAROLINA

Union — The Rev. Kenneth Pollock of Clinton, S.C., has accepted a call to the Second Presbyterian Church in Union. He served Lydia and Rock Bridge churches at Clinton.

Before going to Clinton, Mr. Pollock was pastor of Cooleemee Presbyterian Church at Cooleemee, N. C.

TEXAS

Commerce—Day of Prayer for Students Around the World was observed in the First Church in Commerce, home of East Texas State Teachers College, in a special service Sunday evening, February 17. James McWilliams, local college junior whose home is Crockett, Texas, led the service, assisted by Frank Street of Commerce. The message was given by Tommie P. Morris, senior in East Texas whose home is Commerce. He spoke on "A Student's Thoughts on Prayer." Other students in the musical leadership of the observance were Myra Erwin, Jo Anne Gray, Genevieve Hogue, and Ann Cox O'Neal. Robert E. Baker, for over twenty-five years a member of the faculty of the local college, ruling elder in the church, an effective leader among youth, led the closing prayer. Carey T. Southall, Jr., member of the education faculty of the college, and Walter Tom White, superintendent of the local light plant, were ordained and installed deacons in the congregation February 24.

VIRGINIA

Narrows — On October 31, Rev. Brown Sperow, pastor of the First Presbyterian Church, Narrows, Virginia, retired after serving the church as pastor for thirteen years, he having reached retirement age. The beloved pastor and his wife will make their home in Johnson City, Tennessee, where he will serve as supply in the Holston Presbytery. They returned to their old home which they left forty years ago.

Mr. and Mrs. Sperow left Johnson City April 1916 and have served pastorates in Georgia, West Virginia, and Virginia. The Rev. Sperow was born on a farm in Berkley County, West Virginia. Graduated in the county schools, he then attended Shepherd College where he took both normal and academic diplomas in four years. In 1904 he was graduated from the University of West Virginia with degree of B. S. C. E., practicing his profession for twelve years chiefly as draftsman in the general offices of C. & O., where he branched out into architectural and steel work and designed the general office building of the company at Erwin, Tennessee.

During these years he became interested in modern Sunday School work and spent his vacation for four years in succession in the International Sunday School Association. July 15, 1908, he married Nelle Kathleen Wade, who has been his constant companion and inspiration ever since. On April 1916 this couple left Johnson City to engage in full time religious service. For two years he was assistant to Rev. J. Sprole Lyons, D. D., pastor of the First Presbyterian Church, Atlanta, Georgia, then for two years assistant to the Rev. Ernest Thompson, D. D., of the First Presbyterian Church, Charleston, West Virginia. During the last two years, Mr. Sperow read under Dr. Thompson and was received into Kanawha Presbytery as a minister and installed as pastor of the Presbyterian Church, Kenova, West Virginia, August, 1919.

Under his leadership the Narrows Church has grown in membership and many improvements have been made in the local church. He not only served the First Church but two mission points. During his thirteen years ministry in the local church he received 259 members into the church, baptisms 97, funerals 52, weddings 143. He and his wife have always been interested in young people, and he was instrumental in organizing a Bible course in the high school at Narrows, Virginia.

Mr. and Mrs. Sperow will not only be missed by the congregation of the church but the community as a whole as they were friends to all, and active in all activities of the community for betterment. Although he has reached the age of retirement and cannot serve as pastor, he and his good wife will be found active in the Master's work wherever they may be.

BOOKS

THE WORTH OF A MAN. Arnold H. Lowe, minister of Westminster Presbyterian Church, Minneapolis. Harper & Brothers. $3.00.

A series of 23 short sermons. Some typical subjects are: What Do We Know About God? The World Has Just Begun, Who Wants Paradise? The Parentheses of Prayer, Getting Something Out of Life, Anger on Calvary, The Worth of a Man, Our Divine Impulses.

Dr. Lowe, out of his long and varied experience, with a heart of compassion for human frailty and sorrow, skillfully plays upon the heart strings to comfort and inspire. With pointed questions, as with a spotlight, he searches out the depths of man's inner self and challenges him to seek God and renew his faith and courage.

However, doctrinally, Dr. Lowe is vague and disappointing. To him, the Virgin Birth, the Inerrancy of the Scriptures and the Physical Resurrection are debatable (p. 169). He feels that "religion is not wholly innocent," when it speaks of

manner. We writes glowingly of the glory and power, the humility and witness of the church and her relation to the Kingdom of God. He closes with the thought that Christians are stewards over the household who wait for the return of their Master. Their prayer is 'Thy Kingdom come'. In this prayer there is both a dedication to service and looking forward to the blessed hope.

We commend this volume as a most excellent help to the interpretation to the Kingdom of God. The minister will find highly suggestive material in each of these chapters that will be of real value in the preparation of sermons dealing with this timely subject.

John R. Richardson

A MAN SENT FROM GOD, The Biography of Robert E. Speer., W. Reginald Wheeler., Fleming H. Revell Company. $3.95.

Robert E. Speer was one of the best known Christian leaders of his generation. He served for forty-six years as the Secretary of the Board of Foreign Missions, Presbyterian Church in the U.S.A. He was a speaker of remarkable ability and the author or editor of sixty-seven books. This biography was written by one who was closely associated with him over a period of years. It gives a documented record of Dr. Speer's fruitful life and devoted service. This biography has been developed with the close cooperation of Dr. Speer's family, friends and associates.

One of the best chapters in this biography is called "His Belief in the Virgin Birth of Christ." Dr. Speer said that he could rejoice with great joy in the miracle of the Virgin Birth. In one of his books Dr. Speer declared, "I believe in the Virgin Birth and the resurrection because I believe the Gospels are true and that they teach unmistakably that our Lord was born of a Virgin and rose from the dead. It is sometimes said that the story of the Virgin Birth is in only two of the Gospels, but it is in both of the Gospels that deal with Jesus's earthly life at all. No one questions the teachings of Jesus because they are not in all the Gospels; the Sermon on the Mount is in only one Gospel; the Prodigal Son and the Good Samaritan are in only one Gospel. . . . Even if John and Paul did not refer to it, if this were the fact, it would not prove that it were not true. Neither one of them refers to the Sermon on the Mount or to most of the events or sayings in the life of Jesus. . . . No language could be plainer than that used by Paul in asserting God's unique Fatherhood of Jesus. He quotes at Antioch the Second Psalm, 'Thou art my Son, this day have I begotten thee,' and immediately connects His unique origin with His unique end and the Resurrection. Both John, in the prologue of his Gospel, and Paul, in the first chapter of Colosians, deal with the pre-existence of Jesus in a way that makes it utterly impossible to think of him as originating and ending in the world as an ordinary human child. In one word, the New Testament in certain books asserts unequivocally the Virgin Birth of Our Lord, and in its other books either assumes it or implies it or says nothing inconsistent with it. Accordingly, if the New Testament's representations of Jesus are trustworthy, the Virgin Birth must be accepted as a fact as reliable as any other fact of the life or character of the Saviour."

One does not have to share all of Dr. Speer's views to appreciate the contribution he made to the cause of Christ during this generation. This biography may not be as brilliant as some that have been written, but it succeeds in giving a graphic picture of Dr. Speer as a man and his prodigious accomplishments.

John R. Richardson

God and a revelation from God was necessary for man to even be able to say, "I know God."

This book will be of special interest to students and teachers of philosophy and religion. It is a provocative treatment of philosophic history.

John R. Richardson

COOPERATION WITHOUT COMPROMISE. James DeForest Murch. Eerdman's. $2.50.

Dr. Murch presents in this volume interesting facts regarding the history and functions of the National Association of Evangelicals. He shows that scriptural ecumenicity is the basis for the existence of the National Association of Evangelicals. We are informed that this organization represents some ten million evangelicals, and the organizational structure is based upon the sound biblical profession of faith that accepts the Bible as the only infallible and authoritative Word of God. The N.A.E. believes that the only ecumenicity authorized by the Bible is the ecumenicity in which the Church is led and guided by the Holy Spirit in cooperative evangelical action at home and abroad. Succinctly stated, the purpose of this book is to portray the only kind of ecumenicity in which evangelicals can cooperate without compromise.

The opening chapters picture the background of this movement and then narrate the thrilling story of the organization of the National Association of Evangelicals and how it functions through its various commissions, agencies, and affiliates.

The term "evangelical" is used frequently in this book. The author points out that it has been in common usage since the Reformation and has been used to designate theological parties claiming that their views constitute "the Gospel." Evangelical Christianity, according to this group, affirms the great essentials of divine revelation contained in the Scriptures such as the fall of man, the necessity of the new birth, the atonement of Christ, and justification by faith.

By 1940, most evangelicals had come to the conclusion that the Federal Council of Churches in America was no longer a fit vehicle for evangelistic cooperation at the national level. Under the circumstances, there was no other alternative left but to perfect their own organization for cooperation and action at the national level.

Dr. Murch is well qualified to tell the story of this organization that is giving a splendid testimony for "the faith once for all delivered to the saints." This book should be of great interest to preachers and Christian laymen. It provides valuable information on the crucial issues in the church today.

John R. Richardson

THE BIBLE AND THE HUMAN QUEST. A. O. Steele. Philosophical Library. $3.75.

The author discusses the subject of Religion in this volume. He holds that Religion is the most powerful force in human life. The Religion, he advocates, however, is not always the Religion of the Bible. For example, on page 60 he writes, "Christ is eternal and has been known in many different ages under many different names. In a sense Christ is the wisdom of the Hebrews, the Logos of Greece, the Krishman of India, the familiar appearing and disappearing God in human form of many lands and peoples. Always he is the divine revealed man." Bible-believing Christians will not be able to follow many of the fatuous ideas set forth in this volume.

John R. Richardson

PROPHETIC REALISM AND THE GOSPEL. John Wick Bowman. Westminster Press. $4.75.

The subtitle of this book is "A Preface to Biblical Theology." The lectures were first given on the James Sprunt Foundation at Union Seminary in 1951. The main thrust of the volume is the right way to view Scripture and its teaching as a whole. The author's point of view is what he calls "prophetic realism." He defines this phrase as "evangelism brought down to date." By this he means evangelism speaking the terminology in the context of modern thought. The author believes that the whole of the Scriptures is prophetic literature in the best sense of the term.

In the formulation of his position the author states that he considers prophetic realism to be another name for revelational theology. He says, "Prophetic realism is the theology of the Spirit and its content is determined by the Spirit." In this sense he maintains that the New Testament is equally prophetic with the Old Testament. He holds to the conviction that the term "Gospel" stands for the entire content of the prophetic revelation.

Dr. Bowmen in Part One discusses the three current positions in Biblical theology. In Part Two the term of Scriptures as prophetic realism is set forth. The content of Scriptures' prophetic realism is the subject of Part III. In the last section the author shows that Christ is the norm of the history of what God must be.

This work is to be commended for pointing out the unity of the Old and New Testaments. We need to recognize the golden thread of redemption that runs through God's revelation from beginning to end.

In reading this volume we have noted certain sections that are disappointing. On page 20 he speaks of Unitarian Calvinists. No honest Calvinist has ever been a Unitarian. Calvinism is Trinitarian from start to finish. His treatment of the fall is not satisfactory. He says that Driver is likely correct in suggesting that the Biblical idea of the fall has been taken from materials commo to many mythologies of primitive man. The theological student can find some of Dr. Bowman' views to be helpful, but the reader will have to realize that the author's theology is not alway the reliable theology of the Westminster Confession of Faith.

John R. Richardson

THE SCHOLASTIC MISCELLANY. Edited by Eugene R. Fairweather. Westminster Press. $5.00.

The bulk of this volume is occupied with works of Anselm of Canterbury, and theologists of the twelfth century. The editor has attempted to illustrate the principal interest of the great scholastic theologians. The work of greatest interest presented in this volume is Anselm's "Why God Became Man." Anselm divided this theme into two short books. The first of these contains the objections of the unbeliever who rejects Christian faith because he regards it as contrary to reason, along with the answers of believers. It ends by proving by necessary reasons that it is impossible for any man to be saved without Christ. In the second book Anselm shows by equally clear reasons that human nature was created in order that hereafter the whole man, body and soul, should enjoy a blessed immortality. It is proved that it is necessary for this purpose for which man was made to be achieved, but only through a Man-God, so that all things we believe concerning Christ must necessarily take place.

Bonaventure has an interesting exposition, "Disputed Questions Concerning Christ's Knowledge." His conclusion is, "But the truth which is absolutely immutable can be clearly seen by those alone who can enter into the innermost silence of the mind, and to this no sinner attains but who is a supreme lover of eternity, and he alone."

This work brilliantly illustrates the theological, ecclesiastical, social, and cultural patterns of the Middle Ages.

John R. Richardson

VOL. XV NO. 46 MARCH 13, 1957 $3.00 A YEA

EDITORIAL

Rules Not Laws — It Is Hard To Grasp

Our Youth Programs, Whither?

Protest Against Youth Program Made by Thirty Elders

A Report That Must Be Read and Faced

MINORITY REPORT

By Members of the Interchurch Relations Committee

Overtures 28, 29, 35, 36, 37 & 50

(See pages 6 to 13)

Sabbath School Lesson for March 24, 1957

Young People's Department

Helps To Understanding Scripture Readings in Day by Day

Women's Work — Bible Study for Circle Bible Leaders on

"Jesus and Citizenship". See pages 18-22.

News of Churches

THE SOUTHERN PRESBYTERIAN JOURNAL

Rev. Henry B. Dendy, D.D., Editor..........Weaverville, N. C.
Dr. L. Nelson Bell, Associate Editor..........Asheville, N. C.
Rev. Wade C. Smith, Associate Editor..........Weaverville, N. C.

EDITORIAL

Rules Not Laws

Editors Note:

We are reprinting this Editorial by Dr. Robinson because of a serious typographical error which we let slip when it was printed in the Feb. 27, 1957 issue. This error occurred in the second paragraph from the end and made the statement in that sentence mean just the opposite of what Dr. Robinson had written. We very much regret this error.

Paragraph 58 of our Book of Church Order is quite explicit in denying to church courts the authority to make laws, and affirming to them only the power to establish rules for the government, discipline, worship, and extension of the Church. It says this by inference in the opening sentence, declaring that the jurisdiction of Church courts is only ministerial and declarative — this means not magisterial nor legislative. It asserts explicitly in the second sentence that "they can make no laws." In the third sentence it recognizes their power "to establish rules." In the fourth sentence it asserts their right to require obedience to the laws of Christ.

The same doctrine is set forth earlier in the Book of Church Order. Par. 9 describes Jesus Christ as THE ONLY LAWGIVER IN ZION and asserts the right of His Majesty to rule and teach the Church through His Word and Spirit, by the ministry of men, thus mediately exercising His own authority and "enforcing His own laws." Par. 10 denies any right to add to what Christ the King has given to His Church. Par. 17 describes the function of the Church as to administer, to proclaim, and to enforce "the law of Christ revealed in Scripture." Par. 19 says that the exercise of church power only has the Divine sanction "when in conformity with the statutes enacted by Christ the Lawgiver."

A few years ago there was a footnote in the Book of Church Order to the effect that this book was enacted into law by the General Assembly. When this erroneous statement wa called to the attention of the Atlanta Genera Assembly, the phrase *into law* was ordered deleted by that Assembly. Thus the General Assembly respects the distinction of paragraph 58

It is with profound regret that we note thi distinction not observed by one of the Assembly's agencies, namely *The Assembly's Committee on the Minister and His Work.* This bod has put out a film strip entitled, So Your Churc Needs a Minister. Here the script reads, i part:

> "The Commission must be thoroughly familiar with the Book of Church Order, which contains the laws by which the Presbyterian Church, U. S., is governed."

Now we do not assume that this mistak was made deliberately, but that those wh were responsible were using the word law ir some loose sense with some such meaning a polity. But the film strip goes to our eight odd Commissions on the Minister and His Worl in each presbytery. Many of these commission are carrying out their functions in the fear o God with consideration for their brethren an with proper Christian humility. But the wil to power is in every one of us as the most distinctive principle of our fallen nature. Th perversion wrought by sin continually assert itself in the pride which lords it over the brethren. Some commission will certainly misus this phrase to make of the details provided ir the Book of Church Order laws to bind th conscience of the candidate or of the church.

Augustine properly showed that the fundamental dogma and the fundamental ethic of th Christian faith is humility. He Who was ir the form of God took the form of a slave, an being found in human fashion humbled Himself to the obedience of the Cross. By Hi act of humiliation He wrought our salvation and on the basis of it He calls us to have ir ourselves the mind of Christ. Thus Augustin ıys that the first mark of the Christian is umility, and the second mark of the Christian humility, and that the third mark of the hristian is humility.

This clear understanding of the faith presented by Augustine of Hippo was forgotten by ugustine, the lord archbishop of Canterbury. Vhen the old British Christians came to con-r with him as to a union of the Christian rces in England, they had privately agreed yield obedience to him if he showed humility y rising when they entered. He retained his at and they retained their separate autonomy. Ve earnestly trust that each of our presbytery ommissions on the Minister and His Work ill follow Augustine of Hippo, dealing in umility with the brethren and the churches of ıeir several presbyteries. If not — the Father as committed all judgment to His Son because Ie is the Son of man, Who can and will deal ith those who turn their own preferences or etails of the Book of Church Order into laws bind the consciences of their brethren.

Professor A. LeCerf of Paris writes, "Calvinm confines itself to laying down a principle hich renders the unity of the Church possible, e., that the Church on the one hand and inividual Christians on the other, confess from ıe heart both the distress of the Church and ıe misery of the Christian man." "The ower of the keys in the Reformed (Presbyrian) Church implies pedagogic tact and hristian love, rather than juridical virtuity." "Practice of the communion of saints y the individual implies, on Reformed (Presyterian) principles, humility and filial love, ıther than the servile sentiment of juridical bligation." "For Calvinism, the solution of the roblem of reconciling the rights of the Church ith the duties of the individual lies in the umility shown by both." *An introduction to eformed Dogmatics*, pp. 353-355.

—W.C.R.

It Is Hard To Grasp

The Creator of the World came down to die the hand of and for His creatures! The Lord Glory came down to bear a cross! The King Kings came into the world to wear a crown thorns!

The implications of these thoughts stagger the imagination and should force us to bow in humility and in wonder.

Involved is the overwhelming fact that it is the eternal Son of God who came into this world. Also coupled with it is a sense of the enormity of sin which made such a sacrifice necessary. At the same time we are awed by the price necessary to free us from the guilt and penalty of sin.

As we consider these things we are confronted with our complacency in the face of that which God has done for us, We almost act like we deserved such love and consideration from Him.

In a past generation far more was made of a conversion experience than is true today. Of course, there are many of us who were raised in Christian homes and who grew up with the knowledge of Christ such a reality that it is hard for us to say, *That* day I was saved. But again, even a Christian home and environment may lead to a clearly experienced and well remembered day when we passed from death to life.

On the other hand, there are thousands who have never known a Christian home or a childhood environment under the influence of the Church. This does not mean that the conversion experience shall be emotional, or spectacular, but it should mean that conversion denotes a confession of sin and a surrender to the living Christ as both Savior and Lord, rather than merely joining of the Church.

Here in America Church membership is so easy. There is no stigma attached to the name Christian because the nominal and true Christian are often hardly distinguishable. Few of us have suffered for our faith or for our Church affiliations. Such is not the case in many other countries where to become a Christian demands a standing against odds of every sort.

There are times when introspection and contemplation can be of great profit. One of these is when we think WHO it is that came to die for us; WHY it was necessary for Him to come; and, WHAT He did for us.

When the tremendous implications of these truths break in on our souls we will cry out like Job of old: *"I have heard of thee by the hearing of the ear: but now mine eye seeth thee. Wherefore I abhor myself, and repent in dust and ashes."*

—L.N.B.

The Southern Presbyterian Journal, *a Presbyterian Weekly magazine devoted to the statement, defense, and propagation of the Gospel, the faith which was once for all delivered unto the saints*, published every Wednesday by The Southern Presbyterian Journal, nc., in Weaverville, N. C.

Entered as second-class matter May 15, 1942, at the Postoffice at Weaverville, N. C., under the Act of March 3, 1879. Vol. XV, Io. 46, March 13, 1957. Editorial and Business Offices: Weaverville, N. C. Printed in the U.S.A. by Biltmore Press, Asheville, N. C.

ADDRESS CHANGE: When changing address, please let us have both old and new address as far in advance as possible. Allow three 'eeks after change if not sent in advance. When possible, send an address label giving your old address.

Our Youth Programs—Whither?

Last week this *Journal* carried an editorial on some of the programs being arranged for Spring Youth Rallies and reproduced in detail one of these programs.

At that time we did not mention the Presbytery in which this particular program was scheduled because we felt it to be symptomatic and indicative of the general trend in our youth work, away from Christian instruction and toward a program primarily socio-political in nature.

However, this matter has been brought to a head in this particular Presbytery, — Wilmington — by a meeting of elders in that Presbytery and by a ringing protest signed by a large group of them. This protest is printed below with names of its signers appended.

In writing about this, Mr. Dallas Herring, elder in the Rose Hill Presbyterian Church and prominent in educational circles in the State of North Carolina where he is a member of the State Board of Education and was recently appointed by Gov. Hodges to the State Board of Higher Education, has this to say: "You are aware, I am sure, that in the history of the Scottish Church on numerous occasions the elders found it necessary in the defense of the faith to hold such meetings and to enter into covenants wherein they pledged each other to certain articles of faith which our Church throughout the centuries has held sacred. The meeting in Wallace, in my humble opinion, was no less significant, for we also entered into a solemn covenant wherein we agreed upon our stand in this matter. It is there for all to see in the context of our own times, which are no less free of heresy than were the times of the Scottish Covenanters.

"The appended paper has been sent to every elder and minister in Wilmington Presbytery and the entire matter is being handled in an open and Christian way. As one elder wrote: "If we are unwilling to stand up and be counted on this issue, we have no right to be elders. . . . The Scottish Covenanters took their action at the risk of their lives. Surely we can risk the displeasure of the brethren with whom we honestly disagree."

During the frank discussions which took place at the Wallace meeting a leader of prominence admitted that the program "stinks," but he defended the right of the young people to have it and stated that it would be wrong to censor them in any way.

This *Journal* earnestly questions the philosophy outlined above. Are our young people free to carry on a program within the church without guidance or control? Has the rightful lead-

cometh through Judaism, Buddhism, Babism or Unitarianism or any other false doctrine or worldly philosophy that rejects Him for what He claimed to be.

We do not understand why our young people must be confused on this essential truth in the name of tolerance, in the Church itself, and by its leaders. We assert that it is a shameless sin. May God forgive us.

We, therefore, pledge to each other this solemn

COVENANT

We in no wise accept the teaching that any man, having once accepted Christ as his personal Saviour, has a God-given right to reject Him and to change his belief — much less that the Church should defend such a right. We in no wise accept the teaching that the Church's mission is to foster partisan, economic and social theories and to urge its members, young and old, to adopt a program for action in the furtherance of these theories.

We pledge ourselves to oppose any and all measures devised for these purposes in the Church and we respectfully call upon Wilmington Presbytery to take whatever measures may be necessary to assure that our young people will no longer be led into confusion on these vital issues.

Signed at Wallace, North Carolina, this the 24th day of February, 1957.

Hyman Hall, Rose Hill, N. C.
W. B. Wheeler, Mt. Olive, N. C.
Frank Wilson, Jacksonville, N. C.
G. E. Maultsby, Jacksonville, N. C.
George S. Beatty, Harrells, N. C.
H. S. Wiggins, Jacksonville, N. C.
Wayland W. Cobb, Mt. Olive, N. C.
G. E. Fisler, Ivanhoe, N. C.
J. C. Southerland, Willard, N. C.
Leon Corbett, Burgaw, N. C.
Ben G. Fussell, Willard, N. C.
T. J. Bradshaw, Burgaw, N. C.
E. S. Williams, Wallace, N. C.
William Loftin, Mt. Olive, N. C.
Marion Wilson Eubank, Jacksonville, N. C.
Edward F. Johnston, Wallace, N. C.
David N. Henderson, Wallace, N. C.
A. C. Hall, Sr., Wallace, N. C.
R. L. Smith, Burgaw, N. C.
Angus C. Pate, Wilmington, N. C.
J. D. Turner, Wallace, N. C.
T. T. Murphy, Burgaw, N. C.
Melvin G. Cording, Wallace, N. C.
DeLeon Wells, Sr., Wallace, N. C.
J. K. Blanchard, Wallace, N. C.
Dallas Herring, Rose Hill, N. C.
L. B. Huie, Warsaw, N. C.
A. C. Newkirk, Magnolia, N. C.
John B. Boney, Wallace, N. C.
N. P. Farrior, Pink Hill, N. C.

A Report That Must Be Read and Faced

In this issue we are carrying the minority report of the Interchurch Relations Committee. It is our sincere hope that it will be read in its entirety.

Any discussion of the activities of the National Council of Churches is so apt to generate such strong reactions that it is difficult to secure an impartial hearing. But, in this case we would urge our readers, whether they are for or against the Council, to read this report and evaluate it on the basis of its contents, not on the basis of prejudice one way or the other.

There are those who are so blindly opposed to the National Council that they will admit neither a need of nor a potential usefulness inherent in an organization which might speak with a united voice on some matters of mutual concern to Protestantism.

There are others who are so blindly loyal to the National Council that to even suggest that it has weaknesses and that it has gone and does go beyond the limits consistent with its designed place in the Church, constitutes in their mind a form of *lese majeste*.

We believe that both positions are wrong. We believe that there are times when a united voice is needed for Protestantism. We believe there are activities in which all denominations have a common cause and for which a central agency is desirable and necessary.

At the same time, whenever we read pronouncements by the National Council of Churches in which there is usually inserted the parenthetical explanation that they represent 34,000,000 Protestants, there immediately rises in one's mind and heart a resentment which is itself based on our Protestant heritage.

The problem facing our church is whether a reformation can be effected from within the organization or whether there is needed a jolt (such as the withdrawal of our church), which would tilt the scales in favor of a thoroughgoing reorganization of the Council and a change of policies and objectives.

Such a jolt is needed and can be most salutary. From sources which we are not at liberty to divulge we know that all is not well within the National Council. Some of its former supporters are highly critical of some of the leadership and some of the activities of the Council.

While vigorously disclaiming the allegation that it is in any way a super-church, and offering documentary proof of this disclaimer, the

Minority Report

By members of the
Interchurch Relations Committee

in answer to
Overtures 28, 29, 35, 36, 37, 50.

The Ninety-Sixth General Assembly of the Presbyterian Church in the United States instructed the Permanent Committee on Interchurch Relations to:

a. Investigate the specific charges made or implied in Overtures 28, 29, 35, 36, 37, 50, submitted to the 1956 General Assembly, and other specific charges of a related nature submitted to the Permanent Committee on or before November 15, 1956;

b. Make a further study of the advantages and disadvantages of membership of the Presbyterian Church, U.S., in the National Council of Churches and the World Council of Churches.

c. Submit to the 1957 Assembly a complete report of such investigations and study with its recommendations.

As we have examined the tremendous amount of material which is available from the official records and activities of the National Council of Churches, and other sources, we have been amazed at the abundance of documented facts which substantiate the specific charges made and implied in the overtures from six presbyteries to last year's General Assembly. We shall summarize these findings and facts as briefly as possible.

Leadership

Your Committee has been unable to find in its examination of the record of any particular volume of evidence to show that the National Council of Churches has deviated from policies followed by its predecessor, the Federal Council of Churches. Indeed there is a considerable body of evidence to show that the National Council has broadened the scope of the old Federal Council and intensified many of its policies and programs.

The primary reason so many members of our church are convinced that we should withdraw from the National Council of Churches is because of the grave difference in doctrinal matters between our Confession of Faith and the practically creedless doctrinal basis of the Council, between what our church believes, and what very evidently the leaders of the Council do not believe. The theological beliefs of some Council leaders are responsible for their radical economic, social, racial, and political opinions. The off-color vagaries of these leaders on the practical affairs of life are due to off-color theology. What we believe about God and His Son Jesus and the Bible's teaching about man and his nature affect enormously what we think about our life and its purpose, about history and man's place in it, about our relationship one to another, to property, to money, to race, and to society in general.

The National Council of Churches through most of its pronouncements has either openly, or by inference, stated the false doctrine of the Universal Fatherhood of God and the Universal Brotherhood of Man. In large measure, this ideology is responsible for their teaching on economics, race relations, social measure, and political pressures. Since this false doctrine considers *every man on earth as our spiritual brother,* one can easily see how this unscriptural premise leads the National Council into all sorts of *radical ideas* on economics, (such as collectivism and the sin of the profit motive and free enterprise), and on race relations (such as non-segregation everywhere, in church, school, employment, and society in general), and on politics (such as pressure groups and socialism), and on social measures (such as socialized medicine, socialized insurance, and social planning.)

The leadership of an organization determines its character. When the National Council leaders speak, even in their personal writings and utterances, they clearly show what they are trying to accomplish through the National Council.

Actually instead of the churches using the National Council to promote their interests, the National Council is using the churches to promote its program. Still more accurately, a handful of extreme liberals are using the Council to promote through the churches their socialistic ideas and programs. Three basic errors lie at the root of the Council's teaching and activities and threaten the very foundations of our Church and State, namely:

1. Its unscriptural political activity that violates the separation of Church and State.

2. Its unscriptural social principle that undermines our social and national peace and safety.

3. Its un-American economic program that threatens our system of free enterprise.

Its Political Activity

First, as to its political activity, the Council is not merely a passive agency carrying out the instructions given it by the denominations which it represents: It is an active and very aggressive political machine promoting a program of its own. Its political organization is very intricate and far-reaching. It works through the various denominational boards, particularly the Boards of Religious Education, Social Service and Christian Relations, down into every church activity. It recommends sermon topics to pastors. It promotes the organization of Youth Councils, Men's Councils, and Women's Councils in the churches. It advocates the holding of seminars, and open forums, conferences and retreats, especially for the youth, for the teaching of its principles.

It promotes the setting up of Social Service Boards and Christian Relations Commissions in the denominations for the carrying out of its policies. It has developed its own Youth Council on an international scale. It officially promotes the organization of City, County, and State Councils of Churches, which are now in practically all of the 48 states. They are continually promoting the union of various agencies of the denominations dealing with Religious Education, Missions, and Youth Work.

The Council maintains in Washington, D. C., an office which it characterizes as a "listening-post" for the purpose of keeping the churches informed regarding legislation which affects them. Actually, this office serves as a *lobby to bring political pressure* to bear upon members of Congress, congressional committees, and all governmental agencies, and even the President. Dr. Liston Pope, the Chairman of its Commission on Industrial Relations, declared on July 4, 1946: "Not until the Protestant Churches *are willing to function in pressure-group fashion* will they be able to make an impact on the social problems of today." By weight of numbers and by force of its powerful political machine, the Council seeks to influence legislation and governmental action favorable to its programs, not only in city, state and national governments, but also in foreign nations and international organizations. This is a very wide departure from the spiritual method recommended to the Church by the Apostle Paul, when he wrote: "The weapons of our warfare are not carnal, but are mighty through God to the pulling down of strongholds." (II Cor. 10:4).

In the name of the churches, the Council has *officially endorsed* and *has brought political pressure to bear for the enactment* of the following legislation, though the list is far from complete: Anti-Poll Tax Bill, Anti-Lynching Bill, FEPC, Fair Employment Bill, Minimum

sey. Following Mr. Hall's activities with the CIO in the South and his leadership in setting up the Pittsburgh conference, news came in July, 1947, that he had been promoted to be the head of the Federal Council's new Department of the Church and Economic Life. Rev. Charles C. Webber was appointed Chaplain to Organized Labor. Mr. Webber was at the same time a Methodist minister and head of the CIO Industrial Council of Virginia and President of the CIO Political Action Committee.

The writers of this report deem it wise that in comments herein offered on the practices and policies of the National Council of Churches that the writers themselves disclaim any intent to speak for or against either capital or labor. We are citing the record to point out the danger of official church pronouncements where men's minds and consciences differ so widely. We concede to the advocates of the respective positions taken on both capital and labor their conscientious sincerity, but it is the opinion of the writers of this report that any pronouncements on the subject by official church bodies should be made only after the most careful scrutiny, if at all. We contend on the other hand that there is ample work for the church in the building of moral character. When this has been done the individual may be left to follow the dictates of his conscience.

How the *CIO leaders* are using the National Council of Churches *as a propaganda front,* and *to lobby for legislation which they favor,* is clearly revealed in a letter sent to the leaders of local labor unions throughout the country on November 10, 1952, *on the official stationery of the National Council of Churches and signed by three top CIO officials.*

NATIONAL COUNCIL OF THE
CHURCHES OF CHRIST
in the United States of America

Division of Christian Life and Work

DEPARTMENT OF THE CHURCH
AND ECONOMIC LIFE

The Rt. Rev. Henry Knox Sherrill, President
Rev. Samuel McCrae Cavert, General Secretary
Charles P. Taft, Department Chairman
Rev. Cameron P. Hall, Dept. Director

Dear Sirs and Brothers:

We who are writing you *are not only active in the CIO but have also worked closely with* the Department of the Church and Economic Life of the National Council of Churches.

Labor and the Churches should stand shoulder to shoulder in the fight for justice and brotherhood in industrial and economic life.

We are glad to report the real contribution to this cause being made by the Department of the Church and Economic Life *with which we have had* close personal contact. *As illustrations of the activities of this interdenominational church body we cite —*

Its Labor Sunday Message which commended unions for assisting "free unions in Europe, Asia and other areas to organize and raise living standards of working people and to oppose the efforts of Communists to gain control of the unions of workers in free democratic nations."

Its strong public statements in support of "an unsegregated church in an unsegregated society" and *in opposition to universal military training.*

Its denunciation of "the attempt to enforce conformity or to silence people by character assassination, guilt by association, or the use of unfounded charges."

Its continuing promotion of study among the churches of the problems of inflation, its evils and injustices.

Its important conference on the Christian and his Daily Work, the chairman of which was Al Whitehouse of the United Steelworkers. The conference had its delegates and speakers from Labor, industry, farmers, consumers and the churches.

Each year Rev. Cameron P. Hall, Director of the Department, *brings ministers to CIO Conventions* to hear its speakers and *get acquainted with its leaders.*

As a labor union always in the thick of the fight for justice and brotherhood, we feel sure you will want to make a contribution to this work which is entirely dependent upon voluntary support. Some internationals are contributing $100, with one at $500; some councils and locals are giving $50 or more; others $25; and some smaller amounts. Whatever you can send from your treasury will be deeply appreciated. *Please use the enclosed envelope and make checks payable to the National Council of Church.*

Sincerely yours,

Walter P. Reuther, Pres., UAW-CIO.

John G. Ramsay, Public Relations Director, Organizing Committee CIO

Ted F. Silvey, Secretary, National Community Services Committee.

— — — — C O P Y — — — —

In July 1954, CIO President, Walter P. Reuther, announced a gift of $200,000 to the National Council of Churches by the CIO's Philip Murray Memorial Foundation, stating,

"This money will be used by the National Council on behalf of the *practical application of religious principles* to the everyday world of economic life." "The trustees of the Philip Murray Memorial Foundation," said Reuther, *"are most favorably acquainted with the work of the National Council and especially the excellent work it is doing in the field of the church and economic life."*

This gift, as might be expected, *brought forth certain results.* The following appeared in the daily newspapers June 22, 1956.

"NEW YORK — The National Council of the Churches of Christ in the United States authorized the issuance of a 14-page statement *disapproving 'right-to-work' laws already passed by 18 states* and being pushed in 15 additional states by the National Right-to-Work Committee headed by former Rep. Fred Hartley (R., N. J.)

"The statement, authorized for distribution by the National Council's General Board, was adopted by a 16 to 3 vote of its *Division of Christian Life and Work.* Noting that 'the recognition of Protestant Churches of labor unions as an important form of social organization *has been made clear' by previous declarations* of the National Council of Churches in 1912, 1932, and 1940, the *new statement on union membership as a condition of employment reaffirmed this stand."*

The constitution of our church states, (Chapter IV, Paragraph 17, The Book of Church Order):

"The sole functions of the Church as a kingdom and government distinct from the civil commonwealth, are to proclaim, to administer, and to enforce the law of Christ revealed in the Scriptures."

No one can deny the fact that the official records of the Federal Council of Churches and the World Council of Churches show beyond any question or doubt that the membership of the Southern Presbyterian Church in the National Council of Churches, has made it possible for the liberal and modernistic leaders of the Council, to commit the Southern Presbyterian Church to many activities and objectives that are *contrary to the constitution of the Southern Presbyterian Church.*

Its Economic Program

Its third error is its un-American economic program that threatens our system of free enterprise. This is clearly stated in its Social Creed. The Council refuses to adopt a doctrinal creed with the exception of a simple statement requiring acceptance of "Jesus Christ as Divine Lord and Saviour," *which the Council allows each Church to interpret as it pleases.* Yet it adopted in 1932 a long and detailed "Social Creed for the Churches." This indicates where its major emphasis lies. This Creed states: *"The Churches should stand for:*

"I. Practical application of the Christian principle of social well-being to the acquisition and use of wealth; subordination of speculation and the profit motive to the creative and co-operative spirit.

"II. Social planning and control of the credit and monetary system and economic processes for the common good."

The Creed continues: "The Christian ideal calls for hearty support of a planned economic system in which maximum social values shall be sought. It demands that co-operation shall supplant competition as the fundamental method."

Think of the Church being called upon to advocate "social planning and control of credit and monetary systems and economic policies for the common good"! *Here is a system of collectivism which is diametrically opposed to our American system of free enterprise.* It is in complete accord with the Russian Constitution. Yet this creed is adhered to by the Council and *forms the basis for its social programs.*

The seriousness of these activities and programs of the leaders of the National Council of Churches can best be illustrated by a report from the National Lay Committee of the National Council of Churches of Christ in the United States of America. This was a committee composed of 190 outstanding Christian laymen from all denominations which worked from March 28, 1951 to June 30, 1955 with top leaders of the clergy in the National Council of Churches. These leaders *permitted* this 190-person laymen's committee to be *dissolved because of the Committee's opposition to their political, social, and economic programs.* This committee's final report was published in the February 3, 1956 issue of the U. S. NEWS & WORLD REPORT, with a circulation of more than 775,000 under the heading "Laymen and Clergy at Odds on Role of Church in Politics." A group of laymen in the Southern Presbyterian Church were so concerned about this matter that they mailed 12,000 reprints of this article to every minister and approximately 8,000 elders in our church .

The article in the U. S. NEWS & WORLD REPORT brings out the following facts from the Laymen's Committee's Report:

"A conflict has been boiling up within the Protestant Church over the question of whether the clergy should take sides in political controversies. This dispute, going on beneath the surface for five years, has come out into the open now with the final report of a laymen's

tive security, reduction of armaments, technical assistance to underdeveloped countries, refugees.

In his report Mr. Pew says the following are *"typical"* of the comments he received from committee members in the late months of 1954:

"Greater concentration and attention than ever is being given economic and political questions; I thought that this was a religious organization. The *majority* of the General Board decisions are made *without proper consideration* and *far too little research.* Questions that Congress must take *months to decide* are disposed of in the General Board *inside a half hour."*

In another effort to persuade the National Council to avoid taking sides in public issues, the Pew committee adopted a "lay affirmation" in September, 1954, by a vote of 115 to 15. The key paragraph read:

"Our Committee believes that the National Council of the Churches impairs its ability to meet its prime responsibility when, sitting in judgment on current secular affairs, *it becomes involved in economic or political controversy having no moral or ethical content,* promoting division where unity of purpose should obtain, *nor do we believe that the National Council has a mandate to engage in such activities."*

No one can deny that this National Lay Committee which worked with the top ecclesiastical leaders of the Federal Council of Churches for four years has failed to present a clear and accurate picture of the activities, policies, and programs of the National Council of Churches. The official records of the National Council substantiate the charges of this committee in every detail.

Many more activities of the National Council are causing the members of our church great concern such as their constant efforts to get the National radio networks to *eliminate all paid religious broadcasts* and allot free time under the supervision of the National Council of Churches. This would eliminate such well-known evangelical programs as Billy Graham's Hour of Decision, the Old Fashioned Gospel Hour, and the Lutheran Hour and give the liberal leaders of the National Council complete control as to the type of religious programs which would be heard over the National networks.

MEMBERSHIP IN THE FEDERAL AND NATIONAL COUNCIL OF CHURCHES HAS CAUSED MUCH DIVISION IN THE SOUTHERN PRESBYTERIAN CHURCH.

Our church first entered the Federal Council in 1912. The Minutes of our General Assembly of 1915 show that it was necessary for our Assembly to enter its protest against actions taken by the Council which were in violation "to the historic and scriptural position of our Church." Continuing, our General Assembly of 1915 stated that in some instances the actions taken by the Council were "contrary to the doctrine of the separation of the Church and the State" and that in other instances the actions of the Council were "wholly extraneous to the recognized mission of the Church on earth." In entering its protest to certain actions of the Council, our General Assembly of 1915 stated:

"Troublous times such as these caused that action in the Presbyterian Church which necessitated the birth of the Church South; should we not, then, most carefully guard again the age tendencies which are turning the forces of the Church into so many side channels and so weakening the force of her one supreme call to save men for time and eternity?" (See page 30, Minutes of General Assembly of 1915).

In the Minutes of the General Assembly of 1919, page 55, we read the following:

"(a) That the Assembly note with special care that fact that in the Resolutions adopted by the said Federal Council at its meeting May 6-8, 1919, in Cleveland, Ohio, the Council repeats the acts again which the Assembly protested so vigorously in 1915 and 1916;

(b) that the Assembly now utter its most emphatic protest against the Council's repeating the objectional acts and *violating its own agreement of* 1916, touching the making of deliverances on political, industrial and other such objects;

(c) that this Assembly ask that this protest be entered on the records and published with the proceedings of the Council. The objectional acts of the Council passed May 6-8, 1918, *violating its own former agreement,* were its representing and affirming, as the belief of the churches connected with it, certain views on political relations, international relations, labor and capital problems, wage questions and working days, woman's work, race problems, the making of laws and the enforcement of same, treaties with foreign countries, women's full political and economic equality, and similar questions.

At long last, after a series of promises and the breaking of those promises on the part of the Federal Council, our General Assembly in 1931 adopted the minority report of the Standing Committee on Foreign Relations *by a vote of* 175 *to* 79 *and withdrew from the Federal Council of Churches.*

Our church re-entered the Council in 1941. A minority report declining to re-enter was defeated 160 to 109. An amendment to the minority report providing that the Presbyteries be given an opportunity to vote on the ques-

majority of the members of the Southern Presbyterian Church.

SUMMARY AND RECOMMENDATIONS

Overtures 28, 29, 35, 36, and 37 make the following specific charges:

1. Continued membership gives tacit approval of public prononuncements and resolutions that have been widely circulated, which do not express the convictions of the majority of the total membership.

Your committee finds that continued membership in the National Council gives tacit approval to the pronouncements of the National Council and its representatives, which pronouncements have been and are being given publicity. Many of these pronouncements conflict directly with the Constitution of the Presbyterian Church in the United States and with the convictions of the majority of its membership.

2. The National Council has accused those not in agreement with their social, economical and political views as unchristian.

On this question your committee finds in the affirmative. We cite one case in point. In an Associated Press story, date line New York, published in the Sumter, S. C. Daily Item, Friday, February 4, 1955, the following news story was carried. We quote:

"The National Council of Churches says that anyone who condones or practices racial prejudice of any kind 'sins against God.'

"In one of the strongest church denunciations yet of color line discrimination, the council of 30 Protestant and Orthodox denominations declared yesterday: 'Racial prejudice in any and all forms is contrary to the will and design of God. It is not merely bad, unfortunate, unrighteous — it is sin.' "

The church leadership of the Southern Presbyterian Church has declared that there is room for a wide variety of beliefs on this subject.

3. That the leadership of both associations above referred to (The National Council and the World Council) openly envision the ultimate goal as organic union of all Protestant churches in one world church.

A reading of the pronouncement of many of the leaders of these organizations indicates that this is their ultimate goal. We cite only one case, selected out of many, in evidence of this point. From a release by the Religious News Service and published in a Greensboro, N. C. paper Sunday, January 20, 1957, we quote:

"In a recent statement, Dr. John Baillie of Edinburgh, Scotland, a president of the World Council of Churches, declared that the ultimate goal of the council and the ecumenical movement is that there be only one Christian church.

" 'But,' he stressed, 'this goal is still far off and not to be reached quickly. Nor,' he added 'is it the business of the World Council to promote specific forms of unity, since this is a responsibility that rests with the churches themselves.' "

All of the above Overtures, with the exception of 36, request either:

A. That the question of withdrawal be submitted to the Presbyteries

or

B. That the question of withdrawal be conducted in accordance with properly constituted authority.

In view of the failure of our efforts, after repeated protest and patient effort over many years to remedy these defects, *we hold that our Church is impotent to correct these vital defects of the National Council from within.* The conditions now complained of have existed for years *and continue to increase instead of decrease. Our protests have been of no avail for the purging of the Council.* The continued membership of our Church in the National Council is one of the greatest hindarances of harmony and concord that exists throughout our Church.

Now, therefore, for the reasons herein set forth; and for the cause of peace and harmony within our beloved Church; and for the advancement of the cause of a true Gospel and a clear and authoritative Scriptural Message to a lost world, we hereby recommend to this Ninety-Seventh General Assembly of the Presbyterian Church in the United States that our Church withdraw from the National Council of the Churches of Christ in the United States of America.

John H. Martin
G. T. Gillespie
U. S. Gordon
Clarence E. Piephoff

January 22, 1957.

LESSON FOR MARCH 24

By THE REV. J. KENTON PARKER

Woes To Hypocrites

Background Scripture: Matthew 23
Devotional Reading: Isaiah 29:11-16

Isaiah, in our Devotional Reading, gives a picture of a religious hypocrite which is quoted by Christ in Matthew 15:8 and Mark 7:6,7: "Forasmuch as this people draw near me with their mouth, and with their lips do honor me ; but have removed their heart far from me, and their fear of me is taught by the precept of men." Webster gives this definition of a hypocrite: one who plays a part on the stage; one who feigns to be other or better than he is; a false pretender to virtue or piety. Charles Dickens has made the hypocrite live in his character of Pecksniff. Jesus uses the word over and over again to describe the Pharisees and scribes.

The Greeks had their actors on the stage who pretended to be other persons, and we, today, see plenty of these "hypocrites" on our TV programs. All of us know that these men and women are acting a part. There is no deception intended, for we are told who the actors actually are, and also the characters they represent. Like so many other words this word, "hypocrite" has been transferred to the moral and spiritual realm and its meaning altered. It is used in these realms to denote someone who tries to fool his fellowmen by an outward life which appears good while the heart and inner life is corrupt. This pretense to piety is put on for the purpose of deceiving other people.

Men outside the church often give as their excuse for not becoming Christians, "There are so many hypocrites in the church." I feel that very often these critics are confusing a weak Christian with a hypocrite. There are many weak Christians who fall sometimes into sin. They are not pretending to be better than they are. They know they are weak, and confess their sins. They are not trying to deceive anyone. For instance, I knew a man many years ago who was a member of the church, and I believe, a real Christian, but once in a while he would get drunk. When he was over his "spree" he would shed tears of repentance, and confess his sin to the Session. He was not a hypocrite, but a weak brother in Christ. So, let us not be too prone to say, There are so many hypocrites in the church. Let us restore our weak brother in the spirit of meekness considering ourselves lest we be tempted.

The scribes and Pharisees were real hypocrites. They wanted to fool people and make them believe that they were paragons of virtue while their hearts were full of sin. In this chapter we have very severe words used by our Saviour in condemnation of these pretenders to piety. As we study these verses may we pray the prayer of the Psalmist: Search me and try me and see if there is any wicked way in me. It is easy for us, too, to draw near to God with our lips and our words, while our minds and hearts are far away. It is so easy to go through the form of worship and not have our hearts in it. Oh that all of us who lead our people in worship, handle sacred things, and stand in sacred places, would remember this!

Instead of trying to divide the lesson into sections, suppose I take up some of the words of Jesus, and looking at them, try to get a picture of a hypocrite.

"For they say and do not." As long as they quote Scripture and follow Moses we can listen, but we must not copy their deeds. You may hear a sermon in what they say, but you will never see a sermon in what they do. Most of us would rather see a sermon than hear one. These men may talk about loving our neighbors as ourselves, but you will never find them doing it; instead they will bind heavy burdens on men's shoulders, and not try to lift them.

"But all their works they do to be seen of men." I am afraid that sometimes we try to "put on a show" for men to see rather than worship God in spirit and in truth. We like to be called Father, or Doctor, or Reverend, and take pride in our position and almost bow to the audience and say, "Thank you." We feel that we have given a good performance. To be seen of men can become a trap for us as it was to the Pharisee.

"For ye shut up the kingdom of God against men." They shut themselves out, and they shut others out. One of the greatest stumbling-blocks

prayer with which it closes, Search me, O God, and know my heart: try me, and know my thoughts: and see if there be any wicked way in me, etc.

"Because ye build the tombs of the prophets." The hypocrite is apt to be a persecutor of God's messengers. This was true in the Old Testament times. It was true when Jesus was here, for His enemies were these Pharisees and scribes. It has been true in all ages of the church. What led to the terrible persecution of Protestants? It was an apostate, hypocritical church, wearing a mask and pretending to be a saintly church. The Reformers tore off that mask of sham and pretense and hypocrisy, and they were burned at the stake and suffered all the horrors of the Inquisition. Hypocrites put the prophets to death; their children crucified the Christ; and their children have followed in the steps of their fathers.

When we think about this awful record we are not surprised at the stern words of Jesus as He pronounces these "Woes upon Hypocrites": Ye serpents, ye generation of vipers, how can ye escape the damnation of hell? Here is sin at its worst and blackest. When you put this sin alongside of the so-called "grosser" sins of the publicans and sinners you can understand why He told them that these despised classes would enter the kingdom before the Pharisees and scribes. In verse 34 He gives the bloody record. It was a record that condemned them as murderers and persecutors. This terrible account comes to a climax with "this generation" — the generation to which He was speaking. Judgment, long delayed, was about to fall upon them. We know from history how this prophecy was fulfilled. About forty years later Titus came and Jerusalem was destroyed. Historians tell us of the crucifixion of thousands of Jews. It was a terrible but just judgment upon a generation of hypocrites.

There is a note of grief and tender love in the lament over the city in verses 37-39. We know from other references, (Luke 19:41) that there were tears in His eyes as He spoke these words. The responsibility is put where it belongs; upon them: "How often would I . . and ye would not." The stubborn hearts and wills of men resist the loving entreaties of God. God's heart yearns over His disobedient children; O Ephraim, How can I give thee up? How sad it is that this same hardness of heart persists in the Jews of today. Let us pray that this veil of unbelief may be lifted and that the Jews may come to the light. What a glorious day that would be for the church and for the world!

Recommend The Journal To Friends

By THE REV. B. HOYT EVAN

"What Is Death?"

Scripture: Genesis 3:19; Ecclesiastes 12:7;
I Corinthians 15:52-58.

Suggested Hymns:
"The Lord Is My Shepherd"
"Rock of Ages"
"Jesus, Lover Of My Soul"

Suggestions to Program Leader:
(This is the first of two programs on the subject of death. If you desire to have a discussion among the members in connection with these programs, you should ask your minister to be present. In discussing the meaning of death it is easy to become involved in very difficult questions. There are abroad quite a few unreliable and superstitious ideas about death, and some of them are likely to be mentioned in a discussion. Your minister can help you find the right answers to perplexing questions.)

Leader's Introduction:
A young man had just completed his freshman year at college. He was enjoying being at home for the summer vacation. As he was walking along the street of his home town, he very suddenly collapsed on the sidewalk. All his friends and acquaintances were shocked by his immediate death. He was the victim of an incurable disease which he had not known that he had. He was not the athletic type, but he took part in all normal activities, and not even his closest friends suspected that his life would end so soon.

Death is a universal experience, and incidents such as the one just cited show why it is important even for young people to give serious consideration to it. It is an experience which comes to everyone sooner or later, and there is no way of predicting with certainty when it will come to us. Statistical tables which show that the average man lives so many years are not very meaningful to the family and friends of the college freshman.

Death is not only a universal experience, it is a dreaded and disturbing one. It disturbs us because it is so final and so mysterious. It was this mysteriousness about death which made Hamlet say:

"the dread of something after death,
The undiscovered country from whose bourn
No traveller returns, puzzles the will,
And makes us rather bear those ills we have
Than fly to others that we know not of."

It is indeed an experience from which no o returns. We have, however, a source of info mation about death which is more reliabl than the witness of any mortal man. We hav the word of God contained in the Scripture Included in the word of God is the testimon of His Son, Christ, Who did die and rise agai What God says about death is more trustworth than what any man could say. Our speake will set forth some of the truths of the Bibl concerning death.

First Speaker:
According to the Scriptures, death is essentially the separation of the body from the soul The Lord God said to Adam, "In the sweat o thy face shalt thou eat bread, till thou return unto the ground; for out of it wast thou taken for dust thou art, and unto dust shalt thou return." Genesis 3:19. In Ecclesiastes 12:7 we read these words, "Then shall the dust return to the earth as it was; and the spirit shall return unto God who gave it." It is quite obviou that the physical body sees corruption at death but men have never been content to believe that the spirit disintegrates as does the body Even pagan people believe in the continued existence of the soul after death. In the sixteenth chapter of Luke, Jesus teaches that botl good men and evil men have a conscious existence after death.

Second Speaker:
The Bible tells us that death is a punishmen for sin. "The wages of sin is death." Roman 6:23. "Wherefore, as by one man sin entered into the world, and death by sin; and so deatl passed upon all men, for that all have sinned.' Romans 5:12. It seems most reasonable tha death should come to those who are still in their sins, but what about those for whom Chris has died? We believe that Christ bore ou guilt and punishment when He died on the cross. Why then are we punished for sins fo which He has already paid? In the first place

Does the shallowness of your spiritual life result from your holding on to the sin of religious pride, to the desire to be admired by others (v.21)?

Monday, March 25, II Corinthians 5:17-21. The person who has become a Christian is brand new inside (v.17). God is the initiator of this newness (v.18a), having accomplished it through Christ (v.18) through the marvelous message of v.21. What new motive for living does the Christian have (vv.9,15)? What responsibility is laid on the Christian concerning this message of Christ (vv.18b,20)? Notice how seriously Paul took this responsibility and how much he endured for the sake of Christ (6:4-10). Has the message of the cross (v.21) become stale to you? Has the transforming power of Christ (v.17) made an appreciable difference in your life? To the extent that we are aware of the fact that Christ died for us personally, to the extent that we are aware of His presence in us, to this extent we love and serve Him.

Tuesday, March 26, II Timothy 2:1-10. Timothy was the spiritual son of Paul (v.1). What Paul himself had gone through (vv.9,10) he now called upon Timothy to be willing to endure (v.3). Analyze the three illustrations of vv.4-6 in their relation to v.3. How does each illustrate the principle of complete dedication? of willingnesss to endure what is necessary to accomplish the task? How does v.4b summarize the Christian's purpose? Indeed these are serious matters to think over (v.7). Notice the complete abandon of Paul to those whom he served (v.10), and his confidence in the triumph of the Gospel (v.9b). Always remember it is in the power of Christ that the Christian serves (v.1). Do you desire to abandon yourself to Christ (vv.3-6) and have Him work through you (v.1)?

Wednesday, March 27, Acts 4:5-22. The religious leaders, the same ones who condemned Christ less than two months before (cf.v.6, John 18:12-14), seized the apostles (vv.1-2) and conducted an investigation of their activities (v.7). Their preaching had produced dynamic results (v.4). Why had the apostles been arrested (v.2)? Recall Peter's cowardly denial of Christ previous to the crucifixion (John 18:25-27). Notice the boldness of Peter's sermon (vv.8-12). What statements did he make about Christ (vv.10-12)? Observe his reply in vv.19-20 to the prohibition of v.18. Would Peter's remarks in vv.8-12,19-20 have tended to pacify his investigators? How do vv.8a, 2:1-4 account for the change in Peter in just two months? Christ, in the power of the Holy Spirit, can take the weakness and defeat out of your life, replacing it with a bold, meaningful witness for Him.

Thursday, March 28, *Acts* 8:26-40. Read through the story of the Ethiopian eunuch and notice the kind of man he was. What facts about his official capacity indicate that he was a capable and dependable person (v.27)? For what purpose had he traveled to Jerusalem (v.27b)? How interested was he in spiritual things (vv.28,31-33)? Notice what vv.34,36 reveal of his eagerness to follow Christ. What facts in the story of vv.26-40 show the hand of Providence in the conversion of this eunuch? Many feel that the Christian Church in Ethiopia was begun by the Ethiopian eunuch. God is still looking for capable men and women who will wholeheartedly dedicate themselves to seeking Him and serving Him as His Ambassadors.

Friday, March 29, *Acts* 8:4-25. Great multitudes responded to the preaching of the Gospel in Samaria (vv.4-8). What visible evidence did Simon (v.9) see of God's power (vv.7,13,17-18)? Observe the success of his practice of magic (vv.9-11). Notice his opinion of himself (v.9a). How did the people regard him (v.10)? Do you think Simon's reaction to the Gospel was genuine (v.13)? What statement did Peter make about the condition of Simon's heart (vv.2 23)? What incident provoked Peter to mak such a strong statement (vv.18-20)? What woul you say was the sin in Simon's heart? The wor "simony," which means "sordid traffic i church offices and dignitaries," can be trace back to this person. The work of the Churc is hopelessly crippled when it allows individua who are interested in using the Church for the own ends to gain positions of leadership.

Saturday, March 30, *Acts* 9:10-19. Anani never became famous as a missionary or prea er, but he was a faithful Christian. Of wh Old Testament call does v.10 remind yo (Isaiah 6:6-8)? Did God ask Ananias to d anything he was not capable of doing (vv.11-12) What obstacles were in the way (vv.13-14) Do you have a tendency to balk at difficultie or dangers in the Lord's work? Does the Lord' reply to Ananias in vv.15-16 answer his objection? What do the responses of Ananias i vv.10b,13-14,17-18 reveal of his basic attitud toward Christ? Do you reveal this same attitud of submission and trust in similar circumstances

WOME

Bible Study for Circle Bible Leaders on "Jesus and Citizenship"

Prepared by Morton H. Smith, Belhaven College, Jackson, Miss.

(Approved by the Board of the Synodical of Mississippi, and sent free of charge to Circle Bible Teachers in Mississippi, upon request.)

Lesson 4 The Things Which Are Caesar's

Introduction:

In our last lesson we dealt with the question of "Nationalism versus Internationalism." From Genesis 11 we found that the nations were established by God as a part of His gracious dealing with man so as to prevent the united apostacy of mankind that had led to the judgment of the flood. When we recognize this, we find an even greater motive for seeking to determine our relation to the nation in which we live, than if we held that nations were merely some chance evolutionary product of human culture. God has established the nations, and that for a purpose; and He has placed us within specific nations, and this also for a purpose. "And He has made of one every nation of men to dwell on all the face of the earth, having determined their appointed seasons, and the bounds of their habitation; that they should seek God . . . " Acts 17:26-27a)

It shall be our purpose in this lesson to examine our relation to the state under which we live. Again, just as we did in our last lesson, we shall need to go beyond the words found in the Gospels to see the teaching of the whole Scripture on this important matter. Jesus does enunciate the great and important principle regarding our duties to God and to the state when He says: "Render unto Caesar the things that are Caesar's and unto God the things that are God's." It is this basic principle that we shall seek to examine. There are a number of other passages that deal with this matter, such as, Romans 13:1-7; I Peter 2:13-14; I Timothy 2:1-2; John 19:11; Jeremiah 27:6-11; 29:7. The fullest statement is found in Romans 13:1-7, which seems to be a commentary on the principle as enunciated by our Lord. It shall be our purpose in this lesson to examine first of all the principle as given by Jesus Himself, and then to consider more fully the commentary of Paul in Romans together with any particular points to be found in the other passages.

I. *Mark* 12:12-17 *Considered*

A. Context of the Question.

As we look at the context in which our text is found we find that it was an answer of Jesus

have cause to accuse Him before Pilate of conspiracy against Rome.

B. The Answer of Jesus.

Jesus, seeing their hypocrisy, very wisely secures from His interrogators the acknowledgement of the actual factuality of the historic situation, namely, that Rome was recognized by the Jews themselves as their earthly ruler. This was seen in the very coins they used in their daily business. Wherever a man's coins are used, there his influence is recognized. Once this was acknowledged by the Jews, it was obvious that they recognized the actual situation of the time involved a separation between church and state. True, it may not have been the ideal state of Israel, yet it was the God ordained situation, as prophesied in the Old Testament, due to the sinfulness of Israel. As Calvin points out, Jesus is saying, in effect, "The money attests that Caesar rules over you; so that by your own silent consent, the liberty to which you lay claim is lost and gone." (Commentary on the Harmony of the Evangelists).

Having obtained this admission from the Jews themselves, Jesus then answers, "Render unto Caesar, that which is Caesar's and unto God that which is God's". In this answer we find Him making a clear-cut distinction between the spiritual and the civil governments. Yet, this does not mean that there is necessarily a conflict between the two. It is not necessarily Caesar or God, but rather it is Caesar and God. The "outward subjection does not prevent us from having within us a conscience free in the sight of God." (Calvin). Rather in the obedience to the God ordained civil authorities there is actually obedience to God.

The fact is that above the sphere of civil government lies the over-all rule of God, and thus the rendering of the obligations in the one realm is a fulfilling of duty in the other as well. "Dependence on God does not exclude, but involves, not only personal duties, but the various external and providential relations of dependence in which the Christian may find himself placed." (Godet, *Commentary on Luke*).

Or as Rudolph Stier so strikingly paraphrases the principle: "Seek and maintain the true unity in your duty and obligation toward God and man! Serve Caesar for God's sake, who has placed him over you, as once He did Nebuchadnezzar over your fathers." The two duties are perfectly compatible with one another, so long as the duty to man is recognized as part of the duty to God, and so long as we ultimately serve God in exercising our duty to man. Stier goes on to bring out a rather interesting contrast between the two realms of duty. The duty to man lies in the realm of the physical and material, even as there was a physical image of Caesar on the coin, whereas the duty to God is spiritual and involves the whole man, just as God's image is spiritually implanted upon man himself. "Caesar is satisfied with money and goods, obedience and honour rendered in the outward act; but God requires the whole man, the entire heart in every act." (Stier, *Words of the Lord Jesus*).

Having seen the basic teaching of Jesus on this subject, let us now examine the further passages of Scripture dealing with this question, especially noting the comments of Paul in Romans 13:1-7.

II. Romans 13:1-7.

A. Analysis of the Text — Principle - Let every soul be in subjection to the higher powers, v.1.

I. Ground - there is no power but of God v.1.

a. Consequence - all powers that be are ordained of God v.1.

b. Application - to resist the power is to oppose God v.2.

II. Design of Civil Government - for good, not evil vs. 3-4.

a. Consequence - Civil Government - ordained of God, a minister, an avenger for wrath to evil doers v. 4.

b. Christian is to obey, not only as expediency, but as a matter of conscience v. 3-5.

III. Applications - vs. 6-7.
a. Tribute - taxes v. 6.
b. Tribute, custom, fear, honor - v. 7.

B. Exposition of Romans 13:1-7.

"Let every soul be in subjection to the higher powers."

As an exhortation addressed to Christians, we would understand from the opening words, that this applies to every Christian in every nation and under every situation. The use of the term "soul" is an intensive form, and may even carry with it some implication as to the nature of the proper sort of subjection, namely, a sincere subjection on the part of the inner man.

The duty that is incumbent on every Christian is that of being in subjection to higher powers. By this latter expression we find that Paul, as he expands the subject, is speaking of civil authorities. Peter in I Peter 2:13-14 points out the fact that the subjection is due to all those in authority, no matter what their rank. "Be subject to every ordinance of man for the Lord's sake: whether to the king as supreme; or unto governors as sent by him . . . "

"For there is no power but of God."

Having indicated the duty of every Christian, Paul then displays the grounds upon which

of the country, and does the things that are good, he will have no reason to be afraid of the government. If called to suffer for Christ's sake, he has no need to fear."

This whole question of a government which persecutes the Christian faith brings us to the major exception to the rule that every Christian is to be in subjection to the civil powers that are over him. This exception is that of a conflict between the requirement of the civil power and the clear teaching of the Word of God.

The Christian is governed by the principle that he "must obey God rather than men." (Acts 5:29). The disciples themselves set such an example. Yet despite this exception the Christian is still to be subject to the powers over him. It may be that he shall have to disobey the particular law of the civil government, but he must be ready to pay the penalty that the government exacts.

The Israelites were told to seek the peace of the nation Babylon which was to take them captive. See Jeremiah 29:7. Two special cases of obedience to God rather than men are seen in the book of Daniel. The one is that of Daniel himself, in his refusal to obey the tyrannical ruling about prayer. He submits to the subsequent punishment of being cast into the lion's den, and by the power of God was delivered.

The result was a proclamation on the part of the king in recognition of the God of Daniel. We never can tell, when God may be putting us to the test in order to glorify His own name when we pass the test. (See Daniel 6.) So also with the three friends of Daniel, Shadrach, Meshach and Abed-nego, who refused to bow before the king's idol. These too were subjected to the punishment of the state for their religious convictions, but apparently submitted willingly. Though they were miraculously delivered from the fiery furnace, they did not presume that God would have to deliver them, and yet they were ready and willing to suffer the punishment. They acknowledged the possibility that God could deliver them, but if not they would still not serve the idol in opposition to God's Word. (See Daniel 3, especially verses 17-18.) Would that we too were willing to stand firmly in the face of death as these men were! The early Christian martyrs also followed this pattern of obedience to God first, and then submitting to the heathen government that persecuted them for this.

We shall not deal with the matter of the exercise of the power of the sword by the state at this time, since that shall be treated more fully under the next lesson, but this is one of the main texts that bears on this fact. We should note that the power has been given, not just for show, but to be used.

In verse 5 Paul returns to the exhortation with which he had begun, namely, that we should be in subjection to the authorities. He points out that this subjection should be recognized as our moral duty. It is not to be done just as a matter of expediency to avoid punishment by the state, but rather should be done as part of our duty to god. Paul puts it as duty "for conscience' sake" whereas Peter makes it even stronger "for the Lord's sake" (I Pet. 2:13).

Paul concludes the passage with two verses of practical application of the principles that he has set forth. He starts with the most practical matter of paying taxes. Since the civil authorities are God's ministers, who are attending to His work, they should be properly supported by our taxes. Of course, for us today, this involves the matter of honest tax returns. In the 7th verse he repeats the matter of taxation, and then moves on to the matter of fear and honor. Thus our duty as citizens involves not only taxation, but also proper honor and respect to all who have authority over us.

In addition to these practical applications Paul teaches in I Timothy 2:1-2 that we should pray for those who are over us. "I exhort therefore first of all, that *supplications, prayers, intercessions, thanksgivings,* be made for all men; for kings and all that are in high place; that we may lead a tranquil and quiet life in all godliness and gravity."

III. Summation.

In summation we shall just list some of the basic implications of the passages that we have studied. Individual circle members might expand this list.

1. The Christian has the moral duty, imposed by God's Word, to be in subjection to whatever authority he may find himself under.

2. As a people who have been granted right of self rule we should recognize the t design of civil government as indicated in Word of God. It is not to be used for the s faction of the desires of a few, but rather the good of society as a whole. In our vot and in offices we may be called on to h we should keep this in mind.

3. When a government opposes God's W the Christian must obey God rather than m and if need be to pay the penalty exacted that government for such action.

4. When we find our government out accord with what is right, we as Christians h the duty of seeking to correct our nation's s through whatever properly constituted chan we may have. We do not have the right revolution in such situations.

5. As to the practical duties we need har mention them. They include the payment taxes, obeying the laws of the land, voti serving our country in public office when cal to do so, etc.

6. Perhaps one of the most important dut that we as Christians have to our country that of I Timothy 2:1-2, namely, praying our nation and all those who govern us.

7. As we observe our proper duty toward o nation it should always be done as part of o duty to God, and with the ultimate goal seeking His glory. It is this that will ultimate give the citizenship of the Christian a differe quality from that of the non-Christian. It this that makes the Christian the salt of t earth and the light of the world. May God gi us grace to live in accord with His Word this most important sphere of our lives!

NEWS of CHURCHES around the World

Dr. Jno. R. Cunningham Resigns as President of Davidson

Davidson, N. C., Feb. 20—Dr. John R. Cunningham today presented his resignation as president of Davidson College to the Davidson Board of Trustees.

The Trustees "regretfully accepted," and praised his leadership in establishing Davidson as "one of the nation's finest church colleges, strong in faculty and student body."

Dr. Cunningham's resignation becomes effective Sept. 1. He will then become Executive Director of the Presbyterian Foundation, which will have its headquarters in Charlotte and will centralize fund-raising activities of the entire Presbyterian Church in the United States.

Officers Elected for Consolidated Presbyterian College

Lumberton, N. C.—A team of top administ tion personnel has been selected by the trustees the consolidated Presbyterian college, which w be established in Laurinburg through the merg of Flora Macdonald College, Peace College, a Presbyterian Junior College. Dr. Marshall Sc Woodson, president of Flora Macdonald Colleg Red Springs, has accepted the appointment as a ing president. He will also be a permanent vi president. Dr. William C. Pressly, president Peace College, Raleigh, has been offered a post vice-president(but he has not yet announced l decision. Dr. Louis C. LaMotte, president of Pr byterian Junior College, Maxton, has been a pointed a permanent vice-president. Dr. Willia

man of the Committee on the Minister and His Work. Judge John A. Fulton of Louisville, Ky., was named vice-chairman and the Rev. J. Clyde Plexico, pastor of First Presbyterian Church, Cartersville, Ga., was selected as the other member of the Committee's executive group. Each was elected for a term of one year.

The Committee took three additional major actions during its meeting. It negotiated a comity agreement with the Department of Ministerial Relations of the Presbyterian Church, U.S.A. The U.S.A. Presbyterian offices are in Columbus, Ohio.

The Committee voted to have Synod conferences, instead of regional conferences, on the Minister and His Work each year; and the group commended the filmstrip, "So Your Church Needs a Ministers" to commissions on the Minister and His Work and to nominating committees of pastorless churches. The filmstrip, fifteen minutes long, is accompanied with one long-playing record. Copies of the filmstrip may be obtained from the Office of the Committee on the Minister and His Work at 341-A Ponce de Leon Ave., N. E., Atlanta 8, Ga.

NORTH CAROLINA

Concord Presbytery—The Rev. John L. Fain, Jr., pastor of the First Presbyterian Church in Kannapolis, North Carolina, has accepted a call to serve as co-pastor in Fort Lauderdale, Florida's Bethany Presbyterian Church — famed for its World Missions and evangelistic emphasis. Along with the present pastor of Bethany, Rev. Larry Love, Mr. Fain will divide responsibility as pastor and field worker. Mr. Love, who has launched a remarkable missionary program with support of forty-six missionaries and an annual offering of approximately $100,000, will continue to serve as director of Bethany's Missionary program which includes an Annual World Missions Conference in Bethany, as well as a wide ministry in foreign lands.

Mr. Fain, well known in the Southeast for his ministry of evangelism in a large number of Presbyterian churches and in various schools (having held approximately fifty meetings during his eight-year pastorate in Kannapolis), plans to continue his work in this capacity.

Bethany of Fort Lauderdale sponsors a weekday school and an outpost. They have a membership of 850 and a winter congregation of over 1100 on Sunday mornings.

Kannapolis First Church has received 268 members under Mr. Fain's ministry. The church has assumed partial support of seven missionaries in three fields of Presbyterian World Missions — Korea, Brazil, Africa. Five young people of the congregation are in training for full-time Christian service; four of them are now in Presbyterian Colleges and Seminaries. The building fund has reached one-third of its goal of $300,000 for a new church building. Mr. Fain has been a strong supporter of the Bible teaching program in this area in the public schools of Kannapolis and in the County, having given much of his time personally to teaching the children.

The Fains have four girls, 3, 6, 9, 12. Mrs. Fain is the former Mary Lee Caldwell of Salisbury, North Carolina; while Florida is the native state of Mr. Fain, where he begins, March 1, his third pastorate.

VOL. XV NO. 47 MARCH 20, 1957 $3.00 A YEAR

—EDITORIAL—

The Vote On The Ordination Of Women Elders

Eighty-four Presbyteries have reported on their vote on Women Elders.

Forty Presbyteries have voted "Yes".

Four-four Presbyteries have voted No".

Abingdon Presbytery is yet to vote in April.

THE SOUTHERN PRESBYTERIAN JOURNAL

Rev. Henry B. Dendy, D.D., Editor....Weaverville, N. C.
Dr. L. Nelson Bell, Associate Editor....Asheville, N. C.
Rev. Wade C. Smith, Associate Editor....Weaverville, N. C.

EDITORIAL

Our Presbyterian Heritage and Mission

The Centennial of our Church is 1961 and the theme for that year is set as OUR PRESBYTERIAN HERITAGE AND MISSION. The Assembly has directed that the occasion be celebrated by emphasizing primarily our heritage and mission as a member of the great family of Presbyterian and Reformed Churches throughout the world. It is to be a time in which we become more conscious of our common tradition in doctrine, polity, worship and practice in our own Calvinistic confessional group.

If this can be properly carried out, it will be eminently worthwhile and appropriate. In 1861 our Church showed its consciousness of its ecumenical outlook by addressing a Letter to All the Churches of Jesus Christ Throughout the World. The position of our First General Assembly and of our Book of Church Order on the Headship and Kingship of Christ ought to be seen in the light of W. A. Visser t'Hooft's *The Kingship of Christ.* Our 1861 recognition of the Great Commission as the end of the Church's organization and the condition of our Lord's promised blessing ought to be read in the light of the current outreach of World Missions and the resulting Ecumenical Church. Thornwell's recognition of giving as an act of worship, and his emphasis on the high function of ruling elders and deacons ought to be evaluated in terms of current stewardship. The effort of our people to keep all the agencies of the Church directly under the control of the General Assembly as simply hands of the Church ought to be appreciated in view of efforts in sundry places to set up semi-independent boards or institutions. But the look back ought to be used to give us today a new sense of our present responsibility and our future service. The founding fathers were men of faith, of vision and of hope. They sought for charity between sister Presbyterians despite the national conflict.

Many of their positions and problems a issues are not ours. But the romance of yesterdays can and should become the real of our tomorrows. Whatever of sin and er marred their records we ought to reject a repent of. Whatever of courage, vision, tru guided their steps beckon us onward. See we also are compassed about with so grea cloud of witnesses to Christ and His salvati let us run with patience the race that is before us. We look not primarily to the fou ing fathers, but to Jesus the author and finisher of our faith.

—W.C.R

When Do Judgments Have God's Sanction? Not Ourselves But Christ Jesu As Lord

II *Corinthians* 4:5.

The Apostle reminds us that we preach r ourselves but Christ Jesus as Lord and o selves your servants for Christ's sake. Elsewh he bids us freely subject ourselves to one anot in the fear of Christ, holding Him up in humiliation for our example in the several lations of the home and of business. Our Lc taught that the rulers of the Gentiles lc it over them, but that it shall not be so amo His disciples. Though He was in the form God, He took the form of a slave and humbl Himself to the death of the Cross that He mig minister to and save us. Thus He left us example that we should follow in His steps.

Ecclesiastical rulers took control of the li of the lower clergy and of the laity in t middle ages. The Reformation restored t priesthood of all believers. Luther hurled t church law into the flames and made the Bil alone the rule of faith and practice. Our We minster Confession declares that God alone the lord of conscience and has left it free fr the commandments of men which are eit contrary to His Word or beside it in matter faith or worship.

In the middle of the eighteenth century in :otland, the Moderate Machine set aside this ear mandate of the Confession, in the interest their majority rule. When Mr. Andrew Richdson was presented to the parish of Inver-:ithing by the patron, the parishioners rejected m. The Presbytery of Dumferline hesitated proceed but were ordered by the Commission the General Assembly to do so. Principal 'illiam Robertson, the Moderate leader, dermined to make an example of those who)jected by requiring the lower judicatory dictly to install him. Among others, Rev. homas Gillespie declined so to act, and was :posed from the ministry for contumacy. The :nerable man replied, "I rejoice that to me given, in behalf of Christ, not only to believe ı Him but also to suffer for His sake."

To prevent the occurrence of such man made rdships in American Presbyterianism, Dr. John 'itherspoon wrote into the Preliminary Prinples of Presbyterianism:

> That all church power, whether exercised by the body in general, or in the way of representation by delegated authority, is only ministerial and declarative; that is to say, that the Holy Scriptures are the only rule of faith and manners: that no church judicatory ought to pretend to make laws, to bind the conscience in virtue of their own authority; and that all their decisions should be founded upon the revealed will of God.

Under the pressure of the tension of Reconruction these great principles were forgotten. he volume in the Harvard Historical Series ı the Presbyterian Churches and the Federal nion, 1861-69, by Professor Vander Velde ows just two names shining through those fficult days with the light of Christ clearly)on them. Those two are Charles Hodge of :inceton and S. B. McPheeters of St. Louis. 'hen the latter was removed from his pastore, the former wrote:

> Less than one-fifth of that Presbytery (of St. Louis), knowing that the majority would not attend, came together the 3rd of June to dissolve the pastoral relations between the Pine Street Church and the Rev. S. B. McPheeters, D.D., without being requested to do so either by the pastor or the Church, and against the known wishes and judgment of the great majority of the Presbytery . . . That such a man should be dismissed from his church and forbidden to preach in its pulpit by a mere fragment of the Presbytery to which he belongs who knew him and all the circumstances of the case, seems to us an injustice which has few, if any, parallels in the history of our church.

Clearly Dr. Hodge did not regard the action taken by St. Louis Presbytery as having Divine sanction. Quite the contrary, it led to a sharp split in Missouri Presbyterianism as a result of which a large segment came into the Southern Presbyterian Church.

To avoid just such acts as those against Dr. Thomas Gillespie and against Dr. S. B. McPheeters in which their brethren set themselves up as their lords, our Book of Church Order expressly declares that Christ is the only Lawgiver in Zion, that church courts cannot make laws, that nothing is to be regarded as an offense the proper object of judicial censure except what can be shown to be such by the Word of God.

Yet one hears of acts taken by dominant persons against a weaker brother that leave one wondering. Do certain of these acts have the Divine sanction? Are they in accord with the laws enacted by Christ the Lawgiver, or are they merely according to the inclination of the highly placed member? Is the living God carrying out these decrees, or is He blessing some ministers or congregations that have been excluded from the Presbytery's fellowship thus calling in question (or even setting aside) the claim that the action has the Divine sanction?

A judicial act which seems not to have the Divine sanction ought nevertheless to be obeyed as a matter of order—unless it is contrary to the Word of God. But for those who make such a decision it is only their word and these judges need the admonition of the Lord: Judge not, and ye shall not be judged; for with what measure ye meet, it shall be measured unto you again. Let us take heed lest we take judgment into our own hands and judge according to our own wills.

When the responsibility for judging properly devolves upon us, we stand on holy ground and must act in the fear of Christ. Only as our judgments are authentic echoes of His to Whom the Father has committed all judgment do they have the Divine sanction.

—W.C.R.

The Southern Presbyterian Journal, *a Presbyterian Weekly magazine devoted to the statement, defense, and propagation of the Gospel, the faith which was once for all delivered unto the saints,* published every Wednesday by The Southern Presbyterian Journal, 'nc., in Weaverville, N. C.

Entered as second-class matter May 15, 1942, at the Postoffice at Weaverville, N. C., under the Act of March 3, 1879. Vol. XV, No. 47, March 20, 1957. Editorial and Business Offices: Weaverville, N. C. Printed in the U.S.A. by Biltmore Press, Asheville, N. C.

ADDRESS CHANGE: When changing address, please let us have both old and new address as far in advance as possible. Allow three weeks after change if not sent in advance. When possible, send an address label giving your old address.

He Is Able!!!!

A Christian's security is founded on God himself and every believer should rejoice in that which He has promised and in the fact that He is able.

Near the end of his ministry the Apostle Paul exulted: *"I know whom I have believed, and am persuaded that he is able to keep that which I have committed unto him against that day."*

Christians can rejoice because God is able to *"do abundantly above all that we ask or think."*

Sustained as we are by His grace. Kept and saved by His grace, we are told that he is *"able to make all grace abound toward you; that ye, always having all sufficiency in all things, may abound to every good work."*

Living among temptations and constantly subject to them we are told that God is *"able to succor them that are tempted."*

Another glorious asset of the Christian is the overwhelming fact that our Lord prays for us. We are told that He is *"able to save them to the uttermost that come to God by him, seeing he ever liveth to make intercession for them."*

But our blessings do not stop here. We are told that the Lord Jesus Christ is, *"able to keep you from falling, and to present you faultless before the presence of his glory with exceeding joy."*

In each of these assurances the significant word is *"able."* We are told further that it is He, *"Who shall change our vile body, that it may be fashioned like unto his glorious body, according to the working whereby he is able even to subdue all things unto himself."*

It is not for us to question these assurances but rather to believe them and act on them by faith. On one occasion two blind men came to Jesus begging for a restoration of their sight. Jesus said to them: *"Believe ye that I am able to do this."* On their assurance that they did believe He said to them: *"According to your faith be it unto you,"* and immediately their sight was restored.

We Christians, heirs of God's mercy and grace and recipients of eternal life through faith in His Son, so often live like spiritual paupers. Like Peter of old we see the waves and hear and feel the winds of adversity and take our eyes off of Jesus and begin to sink.

Let us consider anew Who has promised and what He has promised. He is ABLE. Let our faith take hold of this fact and then let us step out on His promises. He cannot and will not let us down.

L.N.B.

parted from the common Christian faith, start with man.

The ancient philosophy began with the universe, the modern with man; the Christian thinking — Paul — Augustine — Luther — Calvin — begins with God.

God has given us His own revelation that we may and ought to start with God's point of view. God has placed us in Christ Jesus and made Him unto us wisdom, I Cor. 1.29. We must start where we are, but the believer has been graciously placed in Christ. Start, then, intellectually where God has graciously placed you. Read the truth of God and of man, of salvation and service, of nature and the Bible from the revelation God has made of Himself in Jesus Christ. Begin with the light of the knowledge of the glory of God as it shines in the face of Jesus Christ. Here is the distinction between Bultmann and Tillich on the one hand and of Barth and Cullmann on the other. The last two strive to begin with the revelation God has made of Himself in the Incarnation and Crucifixion and Resurrection of Jesus Christ. And that makes theirs a Christian theology, not a mere philosophy of religion. (For the detailed presentation of the truth and the vagaries in Barth cf C. G. Berkouwer's *The Triumph of Grace in the Theology of K. Barth.)*

But let us come to Calvin. The following summary of Calvin's view is made in Professor Fuhrmann's *God Centered Religion* and endorsed by Professor John T. McNeill in his *Calvinism:*

> Calvin's true legacy is, indeed, not a system but a method, the method of striving to see everything — man, Christ, faith, the world, the Bible, religion, life . . . not from man's point of view but from the viewpoint of God.

—W.C.R.

When Life Is Impossible

A prominent mid-Western lawyer once praised the *New York Times Magazine.* He claimed that anyone who read it regularly would get a liberal education. If one has scruples about a Sabbath newspaper, let him read this supplement during the week. It can be good devotional reading, however, for Dr. Emile Cailliet of Princeton has pointed out that the "committed" Christian can make any literature devotional reading.

The February 24, 1957, issue of this magazine has a number of articles through which a theme sounds that even the able editors probably did not anticipate when they planned the contents. The lead article finds the Secretary of State in an impossible job. He has to have a complete rapport with the man above him; i.e., the President. He must supervise the 15,000 members of the State Department and Foreign Service. His relations with Congress, especially the Senate, and with the United States press and public are of critical importance. Delicate, too, are his dealings with foreign governments and peoples, so that he must be honest, precise, courageous, tactful, and tough at the same time. All of this adds up to a superhuman assignment.

Article No. 2 in the magazine is about the much-maligned Marine drill instructors. These men have been in a pitiless glare ever since Staff Sgt. Matthew C. McKeon ordered recruits to make a night march in a tidal swamp which resulted in six drownings. The drill instructors, says the article, "are up against an almost impossible job."

The magazine in the third article leads us to the troubled Near East. It tells us that Iraq, the land of the Tigris and Euphrates, is trying "Operation Bootstrap." By oil revenues and public works, the Iraqi government is seeking a way out of destitution for most of its 5 million inhabitants. The task seems hopeless.

Probably each generation thinks its responsibilities are the heaviest the world has ever known, but we may lay claim to living in a time when the pressures of a vast world population and the complications of interrelatedness are unprecedented. It seems impossible to rear children wisely, to find justice and a Christian way for all races and groups, to run a business, a labor organization, a hospital, a school, a church efficiently and without nagging frustrations.

The best answer to life's impossibilities fell from the lips of One who came to deal savingly and justly with all generations of men in all the world. Commenting on the salvation of the self-sufficient, Jesus said, "With men this is impossible; but with God all things are possible" (Matthew 19:26). The only wise course for a Christian is to accept the assignment God has given him and to do each day's work leaning hard on divine guidance, grace and power.

—C.N.W. III

The Worker More

(PART

By Dr. F. L.
Late Dean of Gordon Missi

The Antidote to Discouragement. If now we inquire what are the elements that God is seeking in the worker, we may say that the first is *godliness,* that is, a proper appreciation of God — such a vivid apprehension of Him as will keep us constantly thoughtful of Him and reverent toward Him. Ungodliness — that is, inappreciation of God, is the marked manifestation of the wicked, especially in the last days. Of the wicked, the Psalmist said, "God is not in all their thoughts." *But the true disciple learns to realize and recognize God in all things and at all times. He prays without ceasing because God is such a constant reality to him.* The prayerfulness of Jesus is a marked witness to this fact. His prayer at the tomb of Lazarus is eloquent in this regard, showing not only His own constant communion with the Father, but also His desire that the bystanders should learn to recognize God as the source of the power about to be so signally displayed. And if our work gives us a vivid apprehension of God, and brings us into communion with Him, it largely accomplishes its end, whether it seems to be largely "successful" in the eyes of the world or not. The high priestly prayer of Jesus just as He was being rejected by the world illustrates this point. He knew God most thoroughly, whether He had led the world to know Him or not. Blessed is that work, however appearing to the public, that makes us know God.

Another element in the character of the worker is *submission to the will of God.* This, perhaps, is a greater acquisition than the mere appreciation of God. It is blessed to have the mighty God bend to aid us in our work; but if He shall will that we suffer rather than that we achieve, we must be very closely attached to Him if we say with sweet submission, "Not my will, but Thine, be done." This, apparently, was the finishing touch in the career of Jesus when he bowed in Gethsemane and uttered this supreme submissive petition. Often in the exigencies of our work, we are brought into the holy hush of profound submission.

But there is another sense in which the worker needs to become submissive to the will of God, not so much passively as actively. The will or the purpose of God is sometimes far beyond what we ask or think. *He purposes larger than we plan,* and we must be led to comply with His purposes rather than with our plans.

Return they did! A very small part of the audience was townspeople; nearly all were students at Yale. One was greatly impressed by the simplicity of the program which began promptly at 7 p.m. each evening. An opening congregational hymn was followed by a call to worship, invocation, and the Lord's Prayer. An anthem by one of the glee clubs followed, and then Mr. Graham spoke for 45 minutes. The address on Tuesday night was "The Challenge of the Cross." Using Galatians 6:14 as his text, Mr. Graham said that the cross signified at least three things: (1) It is an expression of human iniquity; (2) it signifies the love of God, and (3) it is the only means of salvation or it reveals the finality of redemption.

DEFINES SIN

Under his first point Mr. Graham masterfully defined sin by showing what was the sin of those who sent Christ to the cross: Caiaphas, Pilate, Herod, Judas and those who sat watching. The sins of those men were most skillfully applied to the men of Yale in the 20th Century, showing that, as Mr. Graham said, "We all had a part in the death of Christ." Under the second point, Mr. Graham was careful to make clear that the love of God as shown in and through the cross is a holy love—the love of a judge. In the third place Mr. Graham showed that conscience and sincerity are not enough.

One was encouraged that Mr. Graham pointed out that coming to Christ will not automatically solve every problem; there is growth involved. It is easy to die for Christ, but it is hard to live for Christ. He stated that in the challenge of the cross there are four possible reactions: Ridicule, rejection, neglect, or acceptance. The message received careful and thoughtful attention.

Mr. Graham then asked all those who were interested in learning more about Christ and becoming a Christian to remain and for the rest to leave quietly. It was a thrilling surprise to see about 500 remain behind. The how of becoming a Christian was carefully, lucidly, and briefly explained. Those who knew very definitely that they wanted to accept Christ as Lord and Saviour were asked to stand quietly and then sit down. It was a joy to see close to 100 college men rise to their feet with one accord. Mr. Graham waited in silence for any others that might want to stand, and some 15 or 20 more stood in the few minutes he waited. He then urged them to do four things, explaining each: Read their Bible, pray, witness and attend church and become active in it.

Wednesday evening Mr. Graham spoke on "The Mystery of Conversion," using Matthew 18:3 as his text. He defined "conversion" by showing, first of all, that it is used in nearly every realm of human experience — banking, mathematics, law, psycho-analysis; so also in the spiritual and moral realms. "Conversion" is "a changing of directions." He then said, "I want to ask you a question straight out. Have you been converted?" He paused and the vast hall was completely silent. He went on to speak of the heart as the symbol of the total man and to tell how God looks upon the heart, drawing heavily from Biblical passages which were carefully explained and illustrated. He continued by showing that there are at least three elements in the process of conversion: Repentance, faith and regeneration. Each of these elements was clearly expounded and illustrated.

Once again those interested were invited to remain. On Wednesday evening 700 to 800 remained. Not so many stood to make decisions (probably 75 or 80); but interest was there, and that could not be doubted. The topic on the final evening was to have been "The Cost of the Christian Commitment." We returned to Princeton thrilled and warmed by our experiences at Yale; however, we should like to make some observations before leaving Yale.

The students at the Yale Divinity School were, in general, either aloof or hostile towards Mr. Graham and his method, if not his message. We found four or five hours spent with the men there most rewarding and stimulating. A few openly admitted a change in attitude towards Mr. Graham specifically and towards evangelism in general. Here, indeed, is an impact which cannot possibly be measured in terms of the number who stand to make a "decision for Christ."

A number of the resident missioners in each of the 10 colleges of the university were ministers of the New Haven area. Some frankly stated that their ministry had already been transformed from participating in the 1957 mission at Yale. Effects such as these may have far greater impact than even the men who stood, not that we would in the least detract from the thrill of seeing college men come to Jesus Christ.

What is Mr Graham like in a situation like that at Yale? One would perhaps expect him to have less emphasis on "the Bible says" in a university mission than in a city-wide campaign. This, however, is not the case. He used Scripture freely, but it was used so that it was made relevant to those there. We were also impressed with the simplicity, skillfulness, and aptness of his illustrations. His rate of delivery was much slower than usual; in fact, he was almost deliberate in places. He used pauses well and frequently. His messages were simple and to the point. They were not intellectual; neither were they antiintellectual. There was no emotionalism or pleading for decisions at any time.

eaven Be
e Stages?

W. Cousar, D.D.

Drop down a little over half way between Calvary and ourselves, and see a man of great Christian proportions. Observe one who profoundly influenced peasants, Popes and Kings — a true saint of the Middle Ages, Bernard of Clairvaux. Is it sacrilegious to say that this French giant of piety lived in heaven here below? Listen to him as he sings:

"Jesus, Thou joy of loving hearts
Thou Fount of life, Thou light of men.
From the best bliss that earth imparts
We turn unfilled to Thee again."

Heaven Number Two

State number two is a blessed condition in eternity but only partially revealed in the Word of God. Notice carefully our Lord's statement in the fourteenth of John, "In my Father's house are many mansions . . . I go to prepare a place for you, — I will come again and receive you unto myself." Scholars are divided on the reference to our Lord's words. "I will come again." The tense is actually present. Some think it refers to death, others to the Parousia, or second coming in glory. Whichever the case, in Philippians (1:23) we read, "Having a desire to depart, and to be with Christ, which is far better." Again in II Cor. 5:8, "We are confident, I say, and willing rather to be absent from the body and to be present with the Lord."

The Christian's promotion and change at death are indeed great. Then with unveiled faces and Divinely opened eyes he will behold his Lord whom he loved. That One Whom he has seen only by the eye of faith, he shall see as a friend sees friend. With all weaknesses of the body removed and with, "The spirits of just men made perfect," there is the immediate commencement of an unfettered, joyous fellowship and service. Someone has well said, "We will never get thoroughly relaxed until we get to heaven." By the same token, we will never be fully girded for effective service till then.

Heaven Number Three

The third stage commences both at and after our Lord's return. Undoubtedly the saints in heaven today, as well as those upon earth, look forward to the Resurrection. Then spirit and body will be reunited. At the judgment, full rewards will be received for deeds done in the body. Heaven will then be completely garnished with the precious stones of a life more abundant. Someone has aptly commented, "Heaven is a prepared place for a prepared people." To see clearly the picture of our full and final heaven, one must carefully examine the 21st and 22nd chapters of Revelation. There and only there is found a complete picture of heaven after Judgment Day. If we may use a common-place illustration, it is similar to the purchase of a Pullman ticket, weeks or months before you board the train, for your expected trip. The room or berth is yours the moment you purchase it and yet you can't rest there until the porter announces everything is "ready." "Come ye blessed of my Father, inherit the kingdom 'prepared' for you from the foundation of the world." (Matt. 25:34). "I go to 'prepare' a place for you."

As we ponder this matter further, the New Testament seems to focus a great spotlight of blessing upon the Second Advent. Great things happen to the believer then. First, note the change in his resurrected body. "Who shall change our vile body (the body of our humiliation), that it may be fashioned like unto His glorious body." (Phil. 3:21). We could not ask for more than the stupendous change indicated. "For this corruptible must put on incorruption and this mortal must put on immortality."

The next change is in either our status or relationship as sons of God. Listen to John's breathless words. He is not quite sure as he sees it all from a great distance. "Beloved, now are we the sons of God and it doth not yet appear what we shall be: but we know that when He shall appear we shall be like Him for we shall see Him as He is." (John 3:3).

As far as we know the believer never becomes just like Christ until this blessed occasion. To point this up, may we say it with the greatest of reserve, although John the beloved apostle has been in the glory land 1857 years, or thereabouts, he has not yet experienced this great change indicated by his own words. Paul, great pastor that he was, looked forward to a marvelous perfection in character for his yet undeveloped parishioners, at the Parousia. That perfection he expected at that particular time. "To the end He may establish your hearts unblamable in holiness before God even our Father, at the coming of our Lord Jesus Christ, with all His saints." (I Thess. 3:13). This thought seems to be prominent in his mind, for as he closes his letter he utters a prayer with the exact same objective as he expresses above, "And the very God of peace sanctify you wholly: and I pray God your whole spirit and soul and body be preserved blameless unto the coming of our Lord Jesus Christ (I Thess. 5:23).

LESSON FOR MARCH 31

By THE REV. J. KENTON PARKER

The Last Judgment

Background Scripture: Matthew 24 and 25
Devotional Reading: Matthew 24:32-44

I would like to enlarge the Topic and call it, The Second Coming of Christ and the Judgment. Most of the Background Scripture concerns the Coming of our Lord. The two subjects are closely related as stated in the Apostles' Creed: "from thence He shall come to judge the quick, (living), and the dead." His Second Coming will be followed by the resurrection and the Judgment. The Topic naturally divides itself into, (1) His Coming, (2) Some Parables, and (3) The Judgment Scene.

There have been many preliminary judgments. The Flood was a terrible judgment upon a wicked world. The confusion of tongues at Babel was another; the destruction of Sodom and Gomorrah, a third, the Captivity, another, and we believe that there have been many more. The destruction of Jerusalem was to be a severe judgment and part of our Scripture points to this.

I. *The Second Coming of Christ:* Chapter 24.

This subject was brought up by the disciples when Jesus said to them, as they showed Him the buildings of the Temple, See ye not all these things? Verily I say unto you, there shall not be left here one stone upon another, that shall not be torn down. They went out to the Mount of Olives, and the disciples asked Him, Tell us, when shall these things be? and what shall be the sign of thy coming, and of the end of the world? This question has three parts, (1) the destruction of the Temple and city of Jerusalem, (2) His Coming, and, (3) the end of the world (or age). In our Background Scripture all three of these are discussed.

Verses 15 - 28 seem to refer especially to the first of these parts, When shall these things be? and gives us an account of the destruction of Jerusalem and the temple which occurred about forty years after these words were spoken. Since we are not studying this event, I wish to confine myself to the second part of the question, What shall be the sign of Thy Coming? It is interesting to compare what Jesus says in this "Olivet Discourse" with the visions of John in Revelation as he saw the opening of the Seven Seals, the blowing of the Seven Trumpets, and the pouring out of the Seven Vials. The language in Revelation is couched in symbols while the words of Jesus are simple statements. These throw light upon the symbols. As we compare the two we get a striking picture of the world from the time of Jesus to the present. John describes it in pictures; Jesus gives simple facts. I wish to take up some of these statements of Jesus. Many of these things, I believe, are being enacted under our very eyes today.

1. "For many shall come in my name, saying, I am Christ, and shall deceive many." How strikingly these words have been and are being fulfilled. We have had many false Christs and we have them today. There are three or four men in our land right now who are practically claiming this, and their followers are numbered by the thousands.

2. "Ye shall hear of wars and rumors of wars." I do not have to cite any proofs of the truth of these words. Our histories are mainly accounts of one war after another. We have volumes on the Decisive Battles of the World. Ever since I finished Seminary there have been wars. We live now when half a dozen small wars are raging, when the "Cold War," as we call it, threatens to become a "Hot War" at any moment. There are "trouble spots" all over the world. Our own nation has soldiers in the majority of the countries and airplane bases everywhere. In fact, the whole world is divided into two armed camps, and the larger nations are trying to outdo each other in the invention and improvement of deadly weapons of every kind. We have our A-Bombs and our H-Bombs and our guided missiles. We will spend a million dollars to rescue victims of an accident, and turn right around and spend a hundred million to perfect some machine which will kill thousands. Our "ways" do not "make sense." We seem to want peace, but are "war crazy."

3. "They shall deliver you up to be afflicted, and shall kill you." This has been the experience

of Christians from the time of the apostles to the present. Even as I write these words many are suffering for the sake of Christ and there have been periods of terrible persecution.

4. "Many false prophets shall arise." These, along with the false Christs will deceive many. Think of how many millions have been deceived by the prophet Mohammed, and the hundreds of millions of Mohammedans. In our country we have at least three prominent false prophets right now, and their fanatical followers support them in luxury. In verse 24 we have the false Christs and false prophets grouped together. They work hand in hand, but at times there is rivalry and, like gangsters, they fight one another.

5. "This gospel of the kingdom shall be preached in all the world for a witness unto all nations." (Compare with the "White Horse" in the vision of John). The Missionary Movement, halted for a time because the Church went to building cathedrals instead of preaching the gospel, and hindered by the worldliness of a corrupt church, has been revived and nearly all the world has been reached to some extent. Great Bible Societies have printed the Bible in almost all the languages of mankind, and have distributed the Word in every land.

6. "For as the lightning cometh out of the East, and shineth even unto the West: so shall the coming of the Son of Man be." We had a visitor some time ago who claimed that the world had come to an end years ago, and we were ignorant of the fact. This verse assures us that we shall all know when He comes. It will be in clouds of glory, and every eye shall see Him.

7. Verses 29-35 seem to describe certain supernatural phenomena which will be evident just before He comes. Compare this with the vision of the Sickle in Revelation 14:14-20.

8. His Coming will be unexpected. The world will not be ready. Conditions will be similar to those at the time of the Flood: "For as in the days that were before the flood they were eating and drinking . . . and knew not until the flood came: . . . so shall also the coming of the Son of man be."

9. Our duty is to Watch: "Watch therefore: for ye know not what hour your Lord doth come." In order to emphasize and impress this upon them He now turns to

II. *Three Parables:* 24:43 - 25:30.

1. The first parable illustrates this command to "Watch." If the master of the house had known what hour the thief would come, he would have watched and not suffered his goods to be stolen. The coming of Christ will be as unexpected as the coming of a thief. The faithful and wise servant is one who watches and is faithful in performing the duties of a servant. Woe be to the servant who thinks that his lord delays his coming and mistreats his fellow-servants.

2. The Parable of the Ten Virgins stresses the thought of being ready. The story is familiar and the lesson so plain that no one can fail to see it. Are we ready? Are we watching? Are we keeping our lamps filled with oil? If He should come tonight could we go forth to meet the Bridegroom, or would we have to go and buy some oil? It will help us to remember the lesson of this parable.

3. Parable of the Talents. We are to be watching! we are to be ready; we are to be working, using faithfully the talents given to us, whether it be five, or two, or one. A good and faithful servant will use every talent he has for the glory of his master. What a lesson for us all! Most of us have but few, perhaps but one, talent. The temptation to do as the man with the one talent did is apt to be our temptation. The law of the kingdom is: "Use or lose."

III. *The Judgment:* 25:31-46.

This is but one of the many pictures of the Judgment and is not meant to give a complete account of that Great Day — the Day of the Lord. To complete the picture we will have to turn to other places in the Bible. One of these is Revelation 20:11-15; the Judgment of the Great White Throne: "And I saw the dead, small and great, stand before God; and the books were opened : and another book was opened, which is the book of life: and the dead were judged out of those things which were written in the books, according to their works."

The judgment is a time of final separation. He had already taught this in the parable of the Tares, and of the Net. Here the "sheep" are separated from the "goats." The ground of condemnation, or of commendation is, "Inasmuch as ye did it not", (condemnation), or "Inasmuch as ye did, (commendation) our works are evidence of our faith.

The real Christian is busy ministering to the needs of men. It is good to minister to the bodies and physical needs of mankind; it is even better to minister to their spiritual needs; to feed their souls; to liberate from slavery of sin. Be sure we minister "in His Name."

YOUNG PEOPLES Department

YOUTH PROGRAM FOR MARCH 31

By THE REV. B. HOYT EVANS

"If I Should Die Before I Wake"

Scripture: Philippians 1:21-24; II Timothy 4:6-8

Suggested Hymns:

"Blessed Assurance, Jesus Is Mine"

"Lord, Speak To Me That I may Speak"

"O Jesus, I Have Promised"

Leader's Introduction:

A high school student and his girl friend were driving home after a school function. There was an automobile accident, and both of them suddenly and unexpectedly experienced death. Everyday occurrences, such as this one, reveal the importance of considering death. We thought about the meaning of death last week. In this program we shall consider what needs to be done to make preparation for dying.

Many of us as children learned the prayer which begins, "Now I lay me down to sleep." That prayer closes with these words, "If I should die before I wake, I pray Thee, Lord, my soul to take." It may be that we have never thought about those words very seriously. We have probably never expected to die before morning light, nor do we expect to die this night. The two high school students did not expect to die so soon, but they did. The Boy Scouts have as their motto "Be Prepared." We ought always to be prepared for death. It may seem morbid to be talking this way, but it is realistic. How can young people be always prepared to die?

First Speaker:

The best way to make preparation for death is to be sure that we have been born again spiritually. "Except a man be born again, he cannot see the kingdom of God." John 3:3. The Bible tells us that even though we are alive physically, we are dead spiritually because of our sins. When we believe in Christ as our Saviour, He gives us new life. "And you hath he quickened, who were dead in trespasses and sins." Ephesians 2:1. "He that believeth on the Son hath everlasting life: and he that believeth not the Son shall not see life; but the wrath of God abideth on him." John 3:36.

Sin is the thing that makes death so formidable, because once death comes, there is no longer an opportunity to have our sins forgiven. He whose sins are not forgiven must endure spiritual death as well as physical death. The sting of death is removed for those who trust in Christ, because He is the one "Who his own self bare our sins in his own body on the tree, that we, being dead to sins, should live unto righteousness, by whose stripes ye were healed." I Peter 2:24.

It is written of God, "For he hath made him to be sin for us, who knew no sin; that we might be made the righteousness of God in him." II Corinthians 5: 21. Christ took the place of sinners, and those who by faith accept His substitution are spared spiritual death and destruction. It has been said that those who are born only once, must die twice (physically and spiritually), while those who are born twice, die only once (physically). Paul said, "I know whom I have believed, and am persuaded that he is able to keep that which I have committed unto him against that day." II Timothy 1:12. The person who has committed his life to Jesus Christ has made the essential preparation for death. There is no substitute for it. "There is none other name under heaven given among men, whereby we must be saved." Acts 4:12.

Second Speaker:

We are not saved from spiritual death by trying to be good, but if we have been saved by faith in Christ, we ought to try to be good. John Calvin said, "It is faith alone which justifies, but faith which justifies can never be alone." If we have received the righteousness of Christ by faith, then we ought to be producing works of righteousness in our lives. It would be embarrassing, to say the least, if death came to us and we had accomplished nothing for the Lord. The Bible tells us that we shall have to give an account of our lives. "For we must all appear before the judgment seat of Christ; that everyone may receive the things done in his body, according to that he hath done, whether it be good or bad." II Corinthians 5:10.

(Continued on Page 24)

Jonah and the Whale

Jonah tried to run away from God. How foolish that was! God told him to go and preach to the people of Nineveh but Jonah did not want to do it, so he got on a ship sailing in another direction. A great storm came up and the ship was about to sink. So the sailors, when they learned that Jonah was trying to run away from God, suspected that he was the cause of the storm. Jonah thought so, too, and begged them to toss him into the sea, which they did, and the storm ceased immediately. A great big fish came along and swallowed Jonah, and Jonah prayed inside, confessing his sin. God answered his prayer by causing the fish to vomit up Jonah on the shore. Then Jonah went and preached to Nineveh as God had commanded, which he should have done at first. Never try to run away from God. It only brings trouble.

Seek Him in the Morning

Seek Him in the morning,
While the day is fresh and sweet;
It will make the world seem brighter,
Just to kneel at Jesus' feet.

With His presence ever near us,
Need we fear each coming day?
Just take our hand in Thine dear Lord,
And lead us all the way.

When temptations round us gather,
And the way seems hard to meet;
Give us faith to wholly trust Thee,
And humbly sit at Thy dear feet.

When our earthly life is over,
And we lay our burdens down;
Oh the joy of that reunion,
When we too receive our crown.

(Mrs. O. F.) Lilla B. Liner.
Greenwood, S. C.

Christian Witnessing

For many years I have taught a Women's-Bible class. When I began to teach years ago, in a church in North Carolina, I was concerned primarily in the subject material that I would present each Sunday. I studied hard and felt that I was accomplishing great things as my class grew and I seemed to be very "popular" with the women. After a period of this kind of teaching, I began to realize that even mature, educated, cultured women who had been professing Christians for years needed *more* than just an "interesting and entertaining" lesson each Sunday. I wondered if they could be truly hungry for a soul-stirring experience that I had thought only the unsaved needed.

So my teaching began to change, and I began to feel a deep sense of responsibility toward the *souls* of those women. I found myself making every lesson as evangelistic and as practical as I could; as the months went on, it became evident to me that only by witnessing for Him every Sunday morning as earnestly and strongly as possible could I hope to satisfy the needs of those women and my own great urgency to win souls to Christ.

I teach a large class and every week I am thrilled over the great opportunity that is mine, not only to teach the Gospel but to witness in a very practical way by reaching women who have never made a complete committal to Christ before. Seven of these women, regular attenders for months, joined the church this past year. There are six others on the roll for whom I am working and whom the Holy Spirit is touching and reaching; there are others constantly joining the class. I am deeply grateful for this opportunity. Please help me pray that I will have sense enough to grasp every opening I may have, and that I may reach more and more women for Christ by the power of the Holy Spirit.

—Ethel Witherspoon

Getting Myself Ready for . . .

Public worship can be a good time to you—

Providing you get up in time to get ready without having a heart attack.

Providing you use your Christian judgment in how you spend Saturday night.

Providing you have at least a small yearning for fellowship with God's people.

Providing you have a sense of need to hear the Gospel of healing for you and for yours.

Providing you can forget your worries long enough to lean on the Lord a little.

Providing you can forgive your neighbor so his face will not stand between you and God.

Providing you bring enough money to be sure your share of the labor of the Gospel isn't being carried by some widows, with a mite.

Report of Texas Synodical

Listen closely, my friends, and you shall hear
Of seven General Fund Agencies. Is that clear?
One fund for seven agencies or seven in one,
That is the way that the work is done.

General Assembly's Training School
in Richmond, Virginia,
Trains the lay student for services today,
For missionary work both at home and abroad
The training of these we are glad to applaud.
1,503 now belong to ATS Auxiliary.
Three projects plus one have been lately done,
Using the money from this mebership fund.

Montreat is the home of General Assembly,
A summer conference ground and retreat for the church family.
The mountains majestic, the air sweet and cold,
Lifts to supreme heights the mind and the soul.
Twenty-six conferences this summer were held,
Eighteen hundred young people the recreation hall swelled.

Negro boys and girls their education obtain
At the one and only institution Presbyterians maintain.
At Tuscaloosa, Alabama, *Stillman* is its name,
A four year accredited college, we are proud to acclaim.

The W. O. C. Birthday Gift of 1952,
Helped to build many school buildings, and a library, too.

The American Bible Society sheds a light on the way,
By translating and printing the Scriptures,
'Tis truly a great display.
For peoples, black, white, yellow, brown, and red,
Throughout all the world the Bibles are spread.
The Scriptures are distributed in our U. S. A.
In 85 languages; an accomplishment, I'd say.

The Board of Women's Work with its staff so clever,
Is eager to help us in every endeavor.
It interprets for us the work of the church,
And there many fine helps you will find in your search.
Thirty-three hundred and eight churches have W. O. C.,
Mrs. McCutchen, the new leader, for you and for me.

The Historical Foundation our treasures does store,
Relics, and books, and histories galore.
Chalices, tokens, and hymnals of past ages,
Are sure to be there with the works of the sages.
The micro film and photostatic center,
Is a new project that now we may enter.

Like a lighthouse the *General Council gleams,*
Gives directions to churches by the very best means,
Through budgets and research, publicity, and programs,
Five boards work together with few problems or jams.

In '57 the month of emphasis is June,
The askings of Texas is one hundred eleven thousand, seven hundred and two.

My term of office is at an end,
Been a privilege and joy I'm confessing,
And now a new chairman this office will tend,
May she receive in her work the Lord's blessing.
—(Mrs. Karl H.) Gertrude B. Oelfke
Houston, Texas, 1956

Helps To Understanding Scripture Readings in *Day by Day*

By Rev. C. C. Baker

Sunday, March. 31, John 17:1-5. How much is wrapped up in the little phrase, "The hour has come" (v.1). Jesus had finished the teaching and training of the twelve (v.6); He had completed the work God had given Him to do in His ministry of preaching and healing (v.4). The hour for His betrayal (18:1-11), arrest 18:12-14), trial (18:19-24ff), and crucifixion (19:17ff) had come. For what in vv.1-2,5 did Jesus pray in this hour? How was His concern for His disciples manifested (vv.15,17-19)? His concern for the future of the church (vv.20-23)? As you glance through vv.1-23 do you find any sign of Jesus engaging in self-pity? The example of Jesus presents a challenge to all of His followers who face an hour of trial and distress —to pray that God will be glorified in them and to remember the needs of others.

Monday, April 1, *John* 17:4-8. Jesus had accomplished the task that God had given Him to do with His disciples (v.4). How had the disciples reacted to the words of Christ (vv.6,8)? Do Jesus' statements in vv.6,8 amaze you in the light of all of the failings of the disciples during their time with Him? Notice, for example, their slowness to understand the most basic facts about Christ even after three years (13:36; 14:5,8). What one central fact had Jesus gotten across to His disciples (17:7, 8b)? Though they were slow to learn, the disciples' basic attitude toward Christ was expressed in Peter's remark of 13:37. (See Mark 14:21). Even among Christians who sincerely love Christ, spiritual growth often seems exceedingly slow and stumbling. Christ's example of patience with His disciples teaches us to be patient with others and with ourselves in spiritual growth.

Tuesday, April 2, *John* 17:9-11. As far as human means were concerned, the success of the Christian Gospel following Jesus' ascension would depend entirely upon the disciples (v.11a). Thus Jesus earnestly prayed for them in His last hours (vv.9-11ff). Why could He pray to God for the disciples with confidence (vv.9b-10)? List the requests mentioned in His prayer on their behalf (vv.11b,13b,15,17). Upon what basis were they to be sanctified, i.e., made holy (v.17)? What relationship to evil would this sanctification produce (v.15)? to the world (v.15)? to each other (v.11b)? What should be characteristic of their inner lives (v.13)? How would you summarize the fellowship of the apostles that Jesus prayed for? Would He be truly glorified in them (v.10b)? Is Christ glorified through your fellowship with

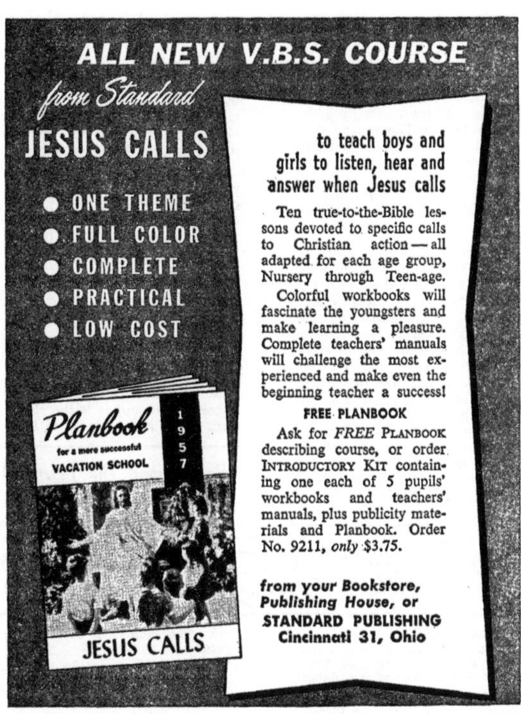

'ellow-believers? He is dependent upon Chris- ian people like you for the advance of the Gospel today.

Wednesday, April 3, John 17:12-14. Notice he attitude of the world toward the disciples ven while Jesus was on earth (v.14). Why vas this attitude manifested (vv.14,16)? Have ou ever experienced hatred on the part of he world because of your likeness to Christ 15:18-21)? How adequately had Jesus watched ver and protected His disciples (v.12)? What oes He offer to compensate for the adversities he Christian encounters (v.13b)? Hatred from he world (v.14), but tender concern (vv.9-11) nd abundant provision (v.19) from their Lord the lot of all who really know Jesus Christ v.3). Jesus has declared in Scripture that no ıan shall be able to pluck us out of His hand John 10:28-29).

Thursday, April 4, John 17:15-19. Read through the first 19 verses of this chapter and notice how much of Christ's prayer to the Father was taken up with the welfare of the disciples. In spite of His varied activities during the three years of His ministry, Jesus seemed to give Himself primarily to the training of the twelve (v.19). What did Jesus desire to see in His disciples as He spent Himself in their behalf (vv.17,19)? Read John 1:41-42; 13:37-38; 21:15-19 and observe the development of Peter, the leader of the twelve. It was Christ's prayer for Peter (Luke 22:31-32) that preserved his faith when he denied his Lord (19:15-18,25-27). Do you give yourself unstintingly in prayer for those whom God has entrusted into your hands?

Friday, April 5, John 17:20-23. Christ's prayer extended beyond the disciples to the church of every age (vv.20ff). He prayed for the same oneness in the church (vv.20,22) that He sought among the apostles (v.11b). To what end did He pray for this unity (vv.21b,23b)? What example was to set the pattern for the church's unity (v.21)? What was to be the source of this oneness (v.22)? What do you see in vv.22-23 that reminds you of Jesus' teaching on "abiding in Him" in 15:1-5? The perfect oneness (v.23) for which Christ prays cannot possibly be achieved through human organization or effort; only as Christ's presence, and with His presence His love, abides in the hearts of believers will man-made barriers be removed (vv.22-23).

Saturday, April 6, *John* 17:24-26. According to the titles given the Father in vv.11,25, what do you think is the reason that the world has not known Him (v.25)? What relationship to the world, therefore, can be expected from those who come to know God (v.14)? How is Christ able to sustain those who come to know God through Him (v.26)? What does v.24 say as to the nature of the future joys of Christ's followers? Does this chapter teach that Christians must separate themselves entirely from the things of the world (v.15)? Does it mean anything to you that you will be able to see Christ someday as He really is (v.24)? Do you find your deepest pleasures in the things of the world or in the Person of Christ?

What Is Faith?

By Ralph Brewer

Faith is not obtained by intellectual training or technical knowledge. Faith is attained only by the communication of the Holy Spirit with man's mind. Faith is right relationship with God; by faith we accept the super-natural; it is the product of Divine Grace.

Scripture is the storehouse of faith. It tells you (1) Have faith in God, (2) Faith hath made thee whole, (3) Thy faith hath saved thee. We walk in faith, stand fast in faith and it "worketh by love." Faith cometh by hearing and what is not of faith is sin. Jesus is the author and finisher of our faith, which is the substance of things hoped for. Therefore, "have great boldness in faith," it sanctifies and justifies.

Faith is given by the Spirit, it is "in Christ," and leads to salvation, producing peace and joy. It has power to overcome the world, blessings are received through it, miracles are performed by it and it is the shield of the Christian. Faith is confidence in God.

NEWS of CHURCHES around the World

ARKANSAS

Presbytery of Ouachita—According to a Standing Rule adopted at the fall meeting of 1956, Ouachita Presbytery will hold its spring meetings on the Tuesday after the first Sunday in May, which will be May 7 this year. The meeting is at 2:30 P.M., and is to be in May, which will be May 7 this year. The meeting is at 2:30 P.M., and is to be held at Malvern.

John T. Barr, St., Stated Clerk

GEORGIA

Rome — For the second successive year, a Presbyterian layman from the First Presbyterian Church in Rome has been honored as "Young Man of the Year." This year the award was given to Mr. George Griffin, a deacon in the church.

This year Mr. Griffin is head of the every member canvass for the church, and is an active churchman in every part of the church's program.

Mr. Griffin, president of the Griffin Foundry in Rome, is well known for his work in the community as well as the church. He is the grandson of a former moderator of the General Assembly, Dr. George Goetchius, who also was a former minister of the First Church in Rome.

Mrs. Griffin is the niece of Dr. Pit Van Dusen, president of Union Theological Seminary in New York. The couple has four children, Paul, Lucy, George, Jr., and Nancy.

Atlanta — Peachtree Road Presbyterian Church here has recently concluded a deal to purchase 10 acres of land for a new church site, almost on the 40th anniversary of the purchase of the present site.

The cost was approximately $141,450. The new church to be erected in the near future, together with the land, will cost about one million dollars, according to Duncan Peek, trustee of the church. The new sanctuary plans call for a seating capacity of 1,200, or about twice that of the present sanctuary. Church membership exceeds 1,600, according to Dr. Eugene T. Wilson, pastor.

Atlanta — Four outstanding churchmen of the Methodist, Presbyterian, U.S., and Presbyterian, U.S.A., Churches will be featured speakers at the 6th annual Pre-Assembly Evangelism Conference, which will be held April 24 through 25 at South Highland Presbyterian Church, in Birmingham, Ala.

Dr. John F. Anderson, Jr., pastor of the First Presbyterian Church, Dallas, Texas, outstanding leader in church and community work, will deliver three addresses: "The Whole Church—Winning"; "The Whole Gospel—Warning"; and "The Whole World—Yearning".

He added that ne was convinced not all faith healers are frauds, but in many cases, he declared, the "healing" is really a psychological matter.

Dr. Boggs is the author of a recently published book, "Faith Healing and the Christian Faith."

Davidson—Salaries of the Davidson College faculty will be raised by five per cent beginning March 1.

The increase was authorized by the college Board of Trustees, following the recommendations of President John R. Cunningham. Dr. Cunningham's resignation, effective Sept. 1, was "regretfully accepted by the Trustees last week."

The salary increase was the second in as many years granted to the faculty, and is termed by Dr. Cunningham as a part of a long-range program designed to continually strengthen the teaching group.

NORTH CAROLINA

Raleigh — Consecration services for the new church building were held in February at the First Presbyterian Church of Fairmont, N. C.

The building program, at a total cost of $125,000, includes a sanctuary, educational building, and a manse.

At the special morning worship service the Rev. L. A. McLaurin of Kings Mountain was guest speaker. Following the service, the congregation participated in the placing of the cornerstone. Open house was held in the afternoon for the friends and members of the church.

The evening service featured Dr. Walker Healy of the First Presbyterian Church in Fayetteville, N. C., as guest speaker.

TEXAS

Dallas — Sunday, February 24, was another high day for Presbyterian Extensionism in the city of Dallas. At 2:00 P. M. groundbreaking ceremonies were held by the Covenant Church congregation for the first unit of their church plant. Providing a chapel and educational space this unit has a contract price of $71,380. Organized in November, 1955, this congregation under the ministry of Rev. Joseph O. Rand, Jr., has been meeting in the Farmers Branch elementary school and eagerly anticipates occupation of their building within 90 days.

At 3:00 P. M. a Commission of the Presbytery of Dallas effected the organization of the Chapel Hills Presbyterian Church. Rev. R. Earl Price came from the Woodlawn Church, Corpus Christi, and under the employ of Presbytery's Committee on Church Extension initiated services in the David G. Burnett School on Sunday, December 2, 1956. A thorough community survey was made by Mrs. Ellen P. Weaver, Church Extension visitor, assisted by Rev. and Mrs. Nelson R. Hawkins. Just prior to organization date a program of visitation evangelism was held by Mr. Price, and a group of interested men from the community, aided by a number of teams supplied by Presbytery's Committee on Evangelism. A congregation which well nigh filled the school auditorium was thrilled as fifteen adults came forward for reception upon profession of faith. Three came by reaffirmation, and forty-six by certificate of transfer from other churches. Twenty-two of these members came from seven other Presbyterian U. S. churches in Dallas. The others came from various churches in nine different states.

Officers elected to serve this congregation are Elders Tom Keese, Wm. F. Haden, Jr., Richard Skinner, R. S. Houck; Deacons John Gilmore, Harold Jones, Chas. Donahue, Ralph Major, Joe Poore, Lewis Boyd.

Cecil H. Lang
Stated Clerk

Houston — Dr. and Mrs. Charles L. King were honor guests at a recent celebration at the First Presbyterian Church here, marking Dr. King's 25th anniversary of service as the church's pastor.

A 30-minute service of prayer and thanksgiving was followed by a reception in the fellowship hall. The Rev. William L. Van Auken, and the Rev. Herbert A. Miller, assistant pastors, conducted the service.

In the time since Dr. King came to First Presbyterian Church from Grace Covenant Church in Richmond, Va., the congregation has grown from 1,400 to 3,600, and with only two exceptions has contributed to the development of 13 new churches and rehabilitation of 8 others in the Houston area.

Dr. King has been moderator of the General Assembly, twice moderator of the Texas Synod, delegate at three world church conferences, and denomination chairman of the committee on union with the U. S. A., and United Presbyterian Churches during the past 25 years.

VIRGINIA

Richmond—More than $73,000 has been appropriated by the Board of Christian Education at its February session for use in 1957 challenge funds to stimulate higher education activities.

Improvement of teaching and libraries will be the main areas for the College Challenge Fund. A total of $20,000 is to be used for grants-in-aid to faculty members at Presbyterian colleges, five graduate fellowships to professors at Presbyterian colleges for obtaining Ph.D. degrees, and ten graduate scholarships for prospective college teachers.

The College Challenge Fund will pay $1,000 to any senior college supported by Presbyterians which adds $2,000 to its budget for buying new library books. For junior colleges, $500 will be paid for adding $1,000 to its book budget.

The Seminary Challenge Fund will consist of $12,500. From this total, $2,500 will be allotted to each of the four Presbyterian seminaries and to the General Assembly's Training School. To meet the challenge conditions, the supporting synods of the seminaries and the General Assembly must raise $2,500 beyond the budget benevolence support for the institutions.

Money from the Seminary Challenge Fund is to be used for visiting lecturers, guest professors, faculty study, and to improve libraries and recruiting programs for Church vocations.

Emphasis in the Campus Christian Life Challenge Fund will shift this year toward improving personnel standards. This fund will have $7,500 to match funds from the various synods to raise salary levels of all full-time local staff members to established minimums. Within three years the synods should assume the entire cost of salary increases.

A total of $14,600 will be used to match equal funds from synods in starting Campus Christian Life programs on 15 campuses in the following 8

because the Bible is basic to Presbyterian Educational Materials

we use them in our Church schools

The Bible is the basic book in the Christian education program of our Church. As the inspired Word of God it holds the central place in all the Church's teachings. Our Presbyterian educational materials help students and teachers interpret Bible truths and translate them into action. They guide children, youth, and adults, each at his own level, to an increasing knowledge, understanding, and love of the Bible. The materials do not stand between the student and his Bible, but lead him to his Bible to learn those things which will be of particular value to his needs and to deepen his spiritual growth. Each lesson is brought within the understanding of the student and interpreted in accord with the theological system of our Church. We use Presbyterian educational materials because they make the Bible most meaningful to our people.

Board of Christian Education
Presbyterian Church U. S.
Box 1176, Richmond 9, Va.

THE MIDDLE EAST — ITS RELIGION AND CULTURE. Edward J. Jurji. Westminster Press. $3.00.

Dr. Jurji at the present time is professor of Islamics and Comparative Religion at Princeton Theological Seminary. He has written this book to illuminate a passion-clouded issue.

Since the Middle East has captured the headlines and still holds world attention this book should be of great interest. What the author has to say is peculiarly relevant for it touches upon man's immediate predicament and his quest for peace. In seeking relief for Middle East tensions the author advocates a return to first principles.

The Middle East and world peace the author believes to be one and the same. He tells us what serves the enlightened policies of the free world should shape the Middle East future.

In his discussions, the author gives us close up views of regional Islam, Christianity, and Judaism. We may not accept all of the conclusions of the author but any reader will have to acknowledge that he has done a fine piece of work in analyzing objectively both the background and the present situation in that area of the world we call the Middle East.

CASE HISTORIES From the Files of Dr. Luke. Paul N. Varner. Wartburg Press. $2.50.

The author's ministry has majored in the field of psychotherapy. He has devoted a great deal of his time to pastoral and marriage counseling. In this department of life he has seen the need for The Great Physician. The author shows how the resources of Scripture are applicable to human needs and are of value for both sick people and well people.

In this volume the author attempts to make Dr. Luke speak in the language of today. He conceives of Luke as a consecrated Christian physician who had practical experiences in company with Paul, the greatest of apostles and knew intimately the Lord Jesus Christ. The author says, "We cannot conceive of one who has such a remarkable insight into the heart of the Saviour hesitating for a moment to bear eloquent testimony to Him and His healing powers for sin-cursed lives." At all times the reader is directed to Christ, the Great Physician, the same yesterday, today, and forever. He puts into the mouth of Dr. Luke these words, "I record these case histories with the hope and the prayer that when Jesus Christ, your Lord and Saviour, your Great Physician, looks through your eyes into your very soul, you will not draw away from Him as some of the people in His day did but will accept His healing for body and for soul and walk with Him from day to day every step of the way."

COMMENTARY ON THE EPISTLE TO THE ROMANS. Martin Luther. J. Theodore Mueller. Zondervan. $2.95.

Just as the great church father, Augustine, finally chose Christianity and committed his heart and mind to Christ after reading Romans, so Luther began the course that led to the Reformation after reading Romans. It was the glorious truth of Romans 1:17 that finally gave to Luther the peace of mind and heart which he had sought for in vain in the doctrines, relics and monasteries of the medieval church.

The easy-to-read translation by Dr. J. Theodore Mueller of Concordia Theological Seminary presents explanatory notes and headings. Here you will find surprisingly fresh and edifying insights into the whole problem of law and grace, of works and faith. Luther's comments are always stimulating, practical and within the grasp of every Christian man. The devotional character of this commentary makes it an ideal one to place into the hands of student, pastor, teacher and layman.

WHY I AM A PRESBYTERIAN. Park Hayes Miller. Westminster Press. $2.75.

Dr. Miller is a member of the Presbyterian Church, U.S.A., and has written primarily for Presbyterians. He delineates some of the historical views of the Presbyterian Church. and shows how this Church is administered today.

Dr. Miller says that Presbyterians believe in a sound interpretation of the Scriptures and significantly adds "they try to discover what the words were **meant** to say."

In Chapter 4 the subject is, "What Do Presbyterians Believe?" The author tells us that no one can answer this question for many answers could be given. He follows this statement with a better one: namely, "The Presbyterian Church is doctrinal and it has an official statement of its beliefs. This is found in the **Confession of Faith** which is part of the Constitution and in the Catechisms."

This book was written primarily for the author's own communion. Presbyterians, other than Presbyterians, U.S.A., would profit by the reading of the 14 chapters.

John R. Richardson

COMMENTARY ON THE ACTS OF THE APOSTLES. J. A. Alexander. Zondervan. Unabridged Edition—2 volumes in one. $1.25.

Joseph Addison Alexander is one of the great luminaries of Princeton Theological Seminary. He served first in the Chair of Church History and in 1859 became professor of New Testament literature. He is rightly appraised as one of America's finest exegetes. This work on Acts is one of the best standard works ever published. Zondervan has reissued it in the "Classic Commentary Library Series."

This volume meets the peculiar needs of ministers and adult Sunday School teachers. If the Bible student is looking for the best single volume on the Acts of the Apostles he should seriously consider the acquisition of Alexander's Commentary.

A SURVEY OF THE OLD TESTAMENT. W. W. Sloan. Abingdon Press. $3.50.

The author is Professor of Bible and Religious Education at Elon College. For eighteen years he has taught Old Testament courses to college freshmen. He has made eleven trips abroad and has been around the world twice. He has an extensive knowledge of conditions in the Near East.

In this volume the author proposes to give a synopsis of the Old Testment in readable style. He has written to stimulate the investigative point of view. The book has been designed for classroom use, and there are supplemental reading lists and assignments at the end of each chapter.

The author espouses the radical higher critical views. Conservative views are ignored. In the closing paragraph the author concludes that the Bible is divinely inspired and truly the Word of God. He even affirms, "It is infallible." His idea of infallibility, however, is not the same as that of this reviewer's.

John R. Richardson

THE CHRISTIAN LIFE. Lelia Boring Lassiter. Greenwich Book Publishers, Incorporated. $2.50.

The author wrote a book of daily devotions entitled **Search Me, Oh God.** She recently has recast a number of these devotional messages and published them under the title of **The Christian Life.** The purpose of this volume is to enable the reader to live the Christian life more effectively. She discusses such subjects as "Growing Through Prayer", "Christian Stewardship", "Christian Home", "The Christian and His Church", and "The Christian Mission." Each message is practically written from a common sense point of view.

CYRIL OF JERUSALEM AND NEMESIUS OF EMESA, VOL. IV LIBRARY OF CHRISTIAN CLASSICS. Edited by William Telfer. The Westminster Press. $5.00.

The influential writings of two Eastern churchmen in the latter part of the Fourth Century, A.D. are embodied in this volume. They include large selections from twelve of the eighteen "Catechetical Lectures" of Cyril, Bishop of Jerusalem and a letter from Cyril addressed to the Emperor Constantius "concerning the portent of the cross of light that appeared in the sky and was seen from Jerusalem."

"A Treatise on the Nature of Man" by Nemesius, Bishop of Emees and Syria, is here translated into English for the first time on the basis of the Greek text. Although little is known of Nemesius, his writings indicate that he was a man of liberal Greek education, widely read in philosophy and also medicine. The editor describes his treatise on the nature of man as "the fruits of the vast deal of human thinking in a very small space."

Complete introductions to each section of the volume giving the background of the writers and the settings of the writings can be read with interest and profit. Students of Church history and theology will appreciate Volume IV in the Library of Christian Classics.

John R. Richardson

MAN IN THE PROCESS OF TIME. J. Stafford Wright. Eerdmans. $3.00.

In this volume Dr. Wright, the Principal of Tyndale Hall of Bristol, England, discusses the Biblical view of man, revelation and inspiration, and the Perfect Man, Jesus Christ, in whom God came down to redeem fallen humanity and restore man to fellowship with his Maker. The volume may be summarized as a Christian assessment of the powers and functions of human personality.

The author is a profound student of the Bible. He observes that there are no more difficulties in the Bible than in God's other book of Creation. He comments, "The Bible, of course, needs to be read and applied intelligently: it is not a mere nest of promises which we may dip into at random, but we are persuaded that the Bible is indeed the Word of God and we do not find the need of regarding it merely as containing the Word of God." Although the writer recognizes that there is a distinction between revelation and inspiration, he tells us that in practice the two are interlocked: "one cannot conceive of an abstract revelation waiting to be received nor of an inspiration to receive nothing at all. For those who believe that God can reveal fresh truths to man in an infallible form and not merely give flashes of insight to be worked out in a right or wrong way, the distinction between inspiration and revelation is merely academic. It is primarily because of the attitude of Jesus Christ to the Bible of His day that we may accept the full inspiration and accuracy of the Bible. He corrected the rabbis on many of their beliefs but it is clear from the gospels that He agreed with them in their belief about the Bible which was that of full inspiration and accuracy. His immediate followers who claimed to have been instructed by Him held a similar view as the Epistles show. Those who criticize Evangelicals for obscurantism and God-dishonoring views of the Old Tesament are in effect criticizing the Lord Jesus Christ. He apparently made no distinction between the God of the Old Testament and the Father of whom He spoke."

This book contains a vast field of valuable knowledge and amazing facts. It is packed full of sound philosophy in a common sense style.

—John R. Richardson

500 SELECTED SERMONS—Volumes III - IV. T. DeWitt Talmage. Baker Book House. $4.50.

Dr. Talmage ranked high among such contemporaries as Henry Ward Beecher, Phillips Brooks and Matthew Simpson. One of the most far-reaching features of his ministry was his printed sermons. They were printed weekly by as many as 3,500 newspapers and they were read by more than 25 million readers.

Dr. Talmage once said, "A preacher should start out with the idea of helping someone. Everyone wants help except a fool." These sermons reflect that point of view. Dr. Clarence Macartney said of Dr. Talmage, "Like most great preachers, he preached to the heart. He made it the aim in his preaching always to help somebody." These messages are Scriptural, practical, warm and dramatic.

MAKINGS OF MEETINGS. Flora E. Breck. W. A. Wilde Publishing Co. $1.75.

The material in this book should provide a starting point for programming and planning worship services by inexperienced young people. The book will even be found helpful by young, inexperienced ministers. Applying its suggestions should make the leadership of meetings a joy instead of an anxiety.

COMMENTARY ON THE EPISTLE TO THE ROMANS. F. L. Godet. Zondervan. $6.95.

The author of this volume was born in Switzerland October 25, 1812. He studied in Germany and majored in philosophy and theology. He is well known among Bible students as an eminent expositor.

In his commentary, Dr. Godet examines critically the original text and discusses the doctrines involved. This method adds much to the value of the work for homiletic purposes. This work has survived through two generations and it still speaks to us with a fresh voice in the "Classic Commentary Library."

BEYOND THE KIKUYU CURTAIN. H. Virginia Blakeslee. Moody Press. $3.75.

Here is a graphic account of a veteran missionary who labored for many years in Africa. She shows how the fiery trials and awful atrocities have served to purify and strengthen the true stalwarts of the Christian faith. The reader will learn from this volume that there are great values in missionary labors despite both uprisings and atrocities. This work will bring new courage and hope to God's servants who are called upon to undergo fiery trials.

NOT ASHAMED. V. Raymond Edman. Scripture Press. 75c.

This is a book of devotions that has to do with what the Bible teaches concerning shame. The Bible has much to say about the possibility of our being ashamed and in this little volume Dr. Edman traces God's provision for our confidence from the first statement of innocence in Genesis 2:25 to the last reference of assurance in I John 2:28. We are warned of the subtlety and sting of shame.

THE GREATEST THING IN THE WORLD. Henry Drummond. Fleming H. Revell. $1.00.

This is a republication of Drummond's well-known book about love. In I Corinthians 13, Drummond shows that love is the greatest thing in the world. He points out how Paul contrasts and analyzes it and defends it as the supreme gift.

THE CHANGED LIFE. Henry Drummond. Fleming H. Revell. $1.00.

No man can change himself, Henry Drummond says. We are changed. The author's aim is to help starved humanity burst into a fuller life. In these pages Drummond shows the steps along the higher road to a more beautiful life.

INVESTING YOUR LIFE. W. J. Werning. Zondervan. 75c.

Life presents one long and continuous series of situations in which man must make decisions as to how he will invest his time, his ability his money, indeed, his entire life. The author believes that men everywhere are interested in making good investments. This little book gives to Christians guidance in the living of the stewardship of life.

THE GOSPELS, AN EXPANDED TRANSLATION. Kenneth S. Wuest. Eardman's. $3.50.

The author has written a number of popular books on word studies in the Greek New Testament. This volume is a diligent attempt to give a literal translation of the Greek. It excels in accuracy. It reproduces much of the freshness and vigor of the original.

In the author's earlier books, he maintained that the word-for-word variety of translation fails to bring out the riches of the original text. This work on the Gospels has as its major objective the setting forth of what was in the author's mind. Dr. Wuest has the ability to make values found in the original Greek available for students who have never studied the Greek language. This expanded translation of the 4 Gospels is a delight to read.

VOL. XV NO. 48 MARCH 27, 1957 $3.00 A YEAR

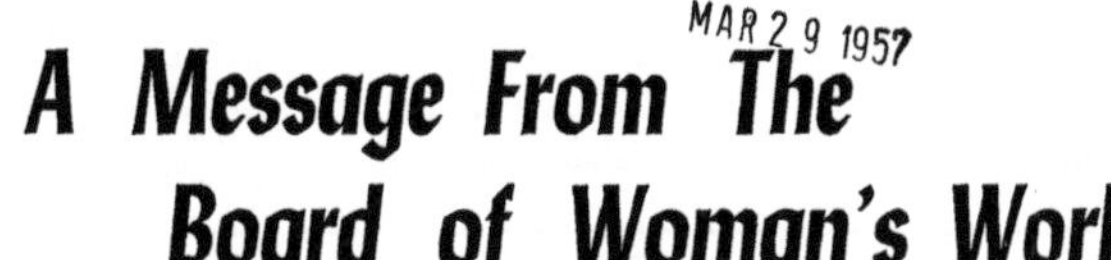

A Message From The Board of Woman's Work

Giving Church papers an official sanction in our Church, the General Assembly has set April 21-27 as Independent Church Paper Week. Through wide experience, active Christians have found that an informed Christian is a more effective Christian. The Church papers offer an avenue through which news, editorials, current issues of concern, and inspiration can reach the church. The independent Church papers perform a vital service to both home and Church in providing church members with such information.

As the name indicates, these papers can speak independently thus giving a channel of expression to all voices in the Church. This is a healthy situation and one to be cherished. The Church papers also serve as an effective instrument in promoting all phases of the Church's work both at home and abroad.

Church papers which broaden our field of vision contribute to the growth and enrichment of the Church as a whole.

Make Your Plans Now to help Introduce The Southern Presbyterian Journal to other Members of Your Church at this Season.

THE SOUTHERN PRESBYTERIAN JOURNAL

Rev. Henry B. Dendy, D.D., Editor........Weaverville, N. C.
Dr. L. Nelson Bell, Associate Editor........Asheville, N. C.
Rev. Wade C. Smith, Associate Editor........Weaverville, N. C.

EDITORIAL

Hiding Christ From a Weeping World?

"And they say unto her, Woman, why weepest thou? She saith unto them, Because they have taken away my Lord, and I know not where they have laid him."

The Christian longs for a close fellowship with the living Christ and this longing can never be satisfied with anything less than Christ himself.

The unbeliever needs this same Christ and peace will never come to his soul until he finds Him and becomes His own.

There is nothing which can take the place of preaching about Christ Himself. He and His truth are inexhaustible sources from which there can be preached sermons a life-time will not be adequate to enjoy.

Mary stood without the empty tomb weeping. The resurrection was not within her grasp at this time. She did not realize that she was looking for the living among the dead. The extent of her thinking was that the One she loved had been carried away and buried in another place. Her one desire was to go and find Him.

But her love was genuine and her heart was open and at that second she saw Christ. At first He was not recognized but when he uttered her name the dimness of her eyes was taken away and she saw and recognized her risen Lord.

Across the world today there are hungry hearts; yes, even weeping hearts. They long to know Someone who can take away the burden of sin, the sense of guilt, the hopelessness of the present and the darkness of the future.

The Church has the message of this Someone — the Son of God, the Lord Jesus Christ, the Saviour. God forbid that we should squander away such a glorious Message for a mess of ethical and social pottage.

Ethics and social action have their place but they are useless until motivated by men and women who have been transformed by the living Christ and who are truly new creatures in Him.

The eyes of many are weeping today because they have sought the Lord and He is not where they expected to find Him. There are many counterparts of the Greeks of old who say: "Sir, we would see Jesus."

Are they seeing Him in our lives?

Are they seeing Him in our churches?

Are they hearing about Him in our sermons?

Are they directed to Him by our own personal witnessing?

—L.N.B.

Babel — Again

During the CBS news broadcast on Sunday morning, March 17th, the announcer said: "And now we will take you to what many people hope will some day be the capital of the world —United Nations Headquarters."

Some twenty minutes later, in a different broadcast entitled, "Religion in the News," it was announced that the National Council of Churches has approached the Council of Catholics and Jews suggesting that they unite in sponsoring a program "emphasizing spiritual values without reference to individual religious beliefs; beamed to the unchurched."

While the above remarks came from different sources they reflect a philosophy abroad — the Philosophy of Babel — which can have deadly consequences for the nation and for the church.

We believe every form of legitimate international cooperation possible should be fostered but we also believe that our national integrity must be preserved at the same time, not only for national survival but also because the world needs nations with the spiritual and moral ideals which are a part of our American heritage.

This effort to belittle patriotism and national pride and to submerge our interests in an international organization where we would no longer be the master of our own destiny, or able to exercise our influence according to the dictates of our own judgment, is nothing less than pernicious. The idealism of the one-worlders (if "idealism" is the correct word) simply does not make sense. America does not have to surrender her God-given position in order to exercise the best possible influence on the world. A philosophy which would lower all decisions to the one most acceptable to the largest number of nations possible is nothing less than a philosophy of national suicide.

But this philosophy is not restricted to the political or international level. There are some within the Church who have become so enamored with the idea of "brotherhood" that they would emphasize it to the loss of Christian truth itself.

What "unchurched" person will be impressed by a religious program arrived at by mutual consent among Protestants, Catholics and Jews? Sinners need more than a watered down message which has nothing better than an ethical content. It is this shallowness of so much that is presented in the name of "religion" which is the tragedy of contemporary effort on the part of some churchmen.

Let the Jew have his radio programs and let him present his faith with all the earnestness and fervor possible.

Let the Roman Catholic continue his efforts to reach the masses with the Gospel as he conceives it to be the Gospel.

And, let the Protestant preach the Gospel of God's redeeming love and the power of the living Christ with all of the earnestness which his faith should engender.

Presented in its purity and its power, and under the blessing of the Holy Spirit, we have no fear but that the vital message of Christianity which is a part of this historic Protestant tradition will attract hearers, convict sinners and strengthen saints.

We write with earnestness and because we are sick and tired of the attempts of some of the leadership within Protestantism which would dilute the very heart of Christianity itself to make it palatable to an already unbelieving world.

As an American we believe that our national integrity must be preserved at all cost. We must not surrender our sovereign rights and power to alien hands. Rather we should remember that the world itself needs the example of a nation whose God, at least nominally, is the Lord and which honestly tries to exercise her power in the best interests of the entire world.

As a Protestant we protest any and every effort to squander the Protestant heritage and tradition in a watered down and emasculated gospel which has no power to save and which but adds to the world's confusion.

To take this position does not preclude the fullest cooperation in international affairs. Actually it increases our influence for good.

To take such a position does not preclude the fullest cooperation in every effort for righteousness. But it may help preserve the faith many have died for rather than to recant, and it does lift up a banner for Christ the King and for the Church He died to make possible.

This philosophy of Babel can be a deadly thing. May God deliver us from it.

—L.N.B.

"Out of the Mouth of Babes"

A few months ago the *Journal* reported an incident aboard an airplane when a little fellow (4 years old) rebuked two women cigarette smokers sitting in the seat next behind him. He first said to them, "Jesus doesn't like that," and when they asked him "Why?" he replied, "Because it will give you a dirty heart." This little fellow does an amazing amount of mature thinking, for which his limited vocabulary is inadequate. His latest outburst occurred in his bedtime prayer at his mother's knee one night recently, showing his concern for the future of his baby brother, Robert. " . . . and, Lord, please let Robert grow up to be a good man and be a *menace in a big church.*"

—W.C.S.

The Southern Presbyterian Journal, *a Presbyterian Weekly magazine devoted to the statement, defense, and propagation of the Gospel, the faith which was once for all delivered unto the saints,* published every Wednesday by The Southern Presbyterian Journal, Inc., in Weaverville, N. C.

Entered as second-class matter May 15, 1942, at the Postoffice at Weaverville, N. C., under the Act of March 3, 1879. Vol. XV, No. 48, March 27, 1957. Editorial and Business Offices: Weaverville, N. C. Printed in the U.S.A. by Biltmore Press, Asheville, N. C.

ADDRESS CHANGE: When changing address, please let us have both old and new address as far in advance as possible. Allow three weeks after change if not sent in advance. When possible, send an address label giving your old address.

Testimonial Banquet for Dr. William Childs Robinson

Professor of Church History and Polity,

Columbia Theological Seminary,

Decatur, Georgia

On Monday, March 11, a large number of Presbyterian elders and ministers met in a downtown dining room in Jackson, Mississippi, to honor one of the great scholars of the Presbyterian Church, U.S., Dr. William Childs Robinson. Dr. Robinson was in Jackson to deliver the Christian Lecture Series at Belhaven College, and a large number of his friends decided to use this occasion to show their high regard for, and appreciation of, Dr. Robinson.

Mr. Russ M. Johnson, Executive Vice-President of the Deposit Guaranty Bank of Jackson, was master of ceremonies and expressed on behalf of the laymen the appreciation which they have for the great contribution which Dr. Robinson has made toward the training of our ministry and in the wider field of evangelical Christianity. Mr. Chalmers Alexander, one of the Commissioners of the City of Jackson, presented Dr. Robinson with a certificate of citizenship. The pastor of the First Presbyterian Church, Dr. John Reed Miller, read the testimonial to Dr. Robinson. After mentioning the many positions of leadership which he has held and commenting upon a number of the important books of which he has been the author, Dr. Miller continued:

"Dr. Robinson has been a conspicuous figure in that goodly company of scholars who have followed and adorned the noble traditions of Scottish, English and American Presbyterianism. He has carried himself with dignity through periods of controversy as well as in times when the theological climate was more calm. He has never met the arguments of others with ridicule nor has he ever descended to the use of cheap methods of making his points. Like a mighty river flowing powerfully toward its appointed destination, he has pursued his course; and his convictions, like the current of the river, have carried others along the way toward a maturer and firmer faith in the eternal verities.

Like the wise man in the parable of our Lord, he has built the house of his beliefs upon a sure foundation — the impregnable rock of Holy Scripture. His studious habits have taken him to the root of things. Painstaking research and careful preparation have been characteristic of his work. His scholarship has been of the very soundest order. Again and again he has evidenced to his students, and to those who have read his books and articles, an amazing familiarity with the whole body of scripture as

ll his colleagues and companions. Nobody could nderstand how the most learned man of his me could find in his faith those restful cer- ιinties on which he so calmly and surely re- osed . . . He never closed his eyes at any agment of truth; he never divided his mind ιto watertight compartments; he never shrank om the approach of a doubt. He saw life hole . . . He moved for fifty years amidst he speculations of science, whilst, in his soul, he certainties that cannot be shaken were sing- ıg their deathless song. Like a coastguard who, anding on some tall cliff, surveys the heaving aters, he stood, with his feet upon the rock, ooking out upon a restless sea of surmise and onjecture . . .

This, my friends, can be truly said of Dr. William Childs Robinson, scholar and minister of Jesus Christ. His convictions are rooted deep in the eternal verities; therefore, the winds of contrary opinion have not detained him nor diverted him from the course which his convictions have directed. True to the beliefs and traditions of our Reformed faith he stands today as one of our church's most notable scholars and most able exponents. Columbia Seminary, the ministry of our great Assembly, and the whole body of our beloved Presbyterian Church is blessed by his presence and leadership among us. Therefore, in obedience to the word of the scripture, that we give "honor to whom honor is due," we are privileged to show our high regard for this Christian friend and fellow-minister today."

—J.R.M.

Visitation Witnessing

By Rev. R. W. Cousar, D.D.

"NEVER IN THE HISTORY OF CHRIS- ENDOM HAS THERE BEEN A GREATER IEED FOR A SPIRITUAL AWAKENING HAN TODAY." So begins Dawson Bryan's ook on "A Workable Plan of Evangelism." tatistics, both as to men and money, show ıat we are, apparently, in an extremely healthy osition just now. Yet, one cannot help but onder if all is well. Is the heart of the average hristian brimming with love for the Master nd love for His straying people? What pro- ortion of modern Christians are willing to ollow the total program of the Church, much ss full abandonment to the will of our Ieavenly Father? How many of our entire ıembership are actually striving to win the nsaved and to reach the unchurched all about s?

Bryan Green has stated a bold fact, when he ιys, "Unfortunately there are Christians — nd Christians. Some who profess to follow the Iaster exhibit no active interest in the mis- onary task of the Church nor any zeal to in others to Christian discipleship. No one ould wish to question the sincerity of their hristian faith nor their practice of Christian fe, but it is a fact that they show no keenness spread the Gospel. There is, however, a ıinority of Christians who see the duty to vangelize as a great privilege and a pressing eed."

The program of men winning men for Christ here followed is a thrilling part of our modern hurch life. Someone has well said "Never in the Christian centuries has there been a more effective means for the revival of men than the method of lay evangelism which is now being used in American Protestantism." Let us make the most of it for folks, both within and without the Christian fellowship.

May a few suggestions be offered to help keep our efforts on an even keel.

I. LET US KEEP CLOSE TO THE MEANING OF REGENERATION.

There seems to be, today, an over-weaning emphasis upon the great word, "commitment." We are to secure as many "commitments" to Christ as possible. This is done with the finest of intentions, but without, apparently, any adequate understanding of what is involved in this great word. Obviously, in a short visit, a team can only say a few things. Much that is important will naturally, be left unsaid. Without being "preachy," one can state very humbly that he knows that for himself, he is only a great sinner. He is, however, also, at the same time assured that because of Christ's death he knows he is forgiven. He can lean very heavily upon that glorious word in (Ephesians 2:8) "For by grace are ye saved through faith; and that not of yourselves: it is the gift of God." Here the emphasis can well be laid upon God's part and God's gift which we accept in humble faith, with no merit or goodness on our part.

Again realizing the limitations of a single conversation, the visitor may find the appropriate moment to place some emphasis upon "Repentance." Our Lord, in close step with John the Baptist, commenced His ministry upon this same high plane. While He did not use the word "Repentance" in every interview, yet He was constantly urging men to turn from something poor to something good, from something better to something that is best. A man may be walking towards the bleak north, he is invited to turn around and go to the sunny south. The woman at the well of Samaria was lured on, by our Lord, from her present sordid existence to one incomparably more beautiful, if she would only drink of the water of life. "Taste and see that the Lord is good, blessed is the man that trusteth in Him," (Psalm 34:8). Maybe the visitor is timid in the use of Scripture, but what is more beautiful than Isaiah's musical but earnest invitation that has been ringing like a bell down the centuries, "Seek ye the Lord while He may be found; call ye upon Him while He is near. Let the wicked forsake his way and the unrighteous man his thoughts and let him return unto the Lord and He will have mercy upon him and to our God for He will abundantly pardon." (Isa. 55:7).

When they have turned their weary selves towards the uplifted Saviour then we may seek to introduce them to some of the marvels of the new Birth. If you cannot explain it do not be too much discouraged, — Jesus never explained it to Nicodemus. He urged the necessity; He declared the agent, the Spirit, but He never made clear precisely what happens in the process. Born again, or born from above is truly in the realm of the miraculous yet it must occur in every soul that enters the Kingdom of God. Realizing keenly your own deficiencies, you can always resort to those blessed words, "Therefore if man be in Christ Jesus, he is a new creature, old things are passed away, behold, all things are become new." (II Cor. 5:17).

II. LET US KEEP CLOSE TO THE IDEA OF WITNESSING.

After all, we are first and last witnesses. "Ye shall be witnesses unto me," is a must for all times. Some men have had a conversion that is good newspaper "copy." Their "change" had within it "explosive" qualities. Night turned into day all in a moment. With them, like Augustine, chains immediately dropped off, vile habits were gone, brand-new practices were established. Their souls were flooded with a great sense of release and forgiveness. They loved what they once hated, and hated what they once loved. Such an experience is thrilling and is often worth more than a dozen ordinary sermons and that many conversations besides. Thank God for such!

On the other hand, a definite impression was registered, recently, from the words of a

ESSON FOR APRIL 7

By THE REV. J. KENTON PARKER

Jesus Faces The Cross

ackground Scripture: Matthew 26:1 - 27:10
evotional Reading: Isaiah 53:1-9

As we read Matthew 26 and 27 and Isaiah 53 we can easily see that both the prophet and the gospel riter are describing the same Person and the same event, — His sufferings and death. Isaiah gives n explanation as to why He suffered and died; He was wounded for our transgressions and bruised or our iniquities, etc. Matthew does not fully explain what it meant, but gives us the facts, the tragic vents of those days and nights. He does give some explanation. Jesus' words in 26:28, "For this my blood of the new testament, (covenant) hich is shed for many for the remission of ns," agrees with Isaiah, and explains pretty illy the meaning of His death. Then, His ormer words, "even as the son of man came ot to be ministered unto, but to minister, and ive His life a ransom for many." Jesus knew nat He came to die. It was not a sort of second best" as some would have us believe. le did ride into the city as a King, and He reached the coming of the Kingdom, but He iced the cross all along. When the Greeks sked to see Him, He said, Verily, verily, I ly unto you, Except a corn of wheat fall into ie ground and die, it abideth alone: but if die, it bringeth forth much fruit": "Now is iy soul troubled; and what shall I say? Father, ve me from this hour: for this cause came I nto this hour."

It remained for the apostle Paul, the inspired ieologian of the New Testament, to fully ex- lain the Atonement, and give the full meaning f the Cross.

In our lesson today — the Background Scrip- ıre — the events leading up to His death are :lated. As we read and ponder may the Holy pirit enable us to see and feel the tragedy and orrow and agony of this awful experience, and lso the glory of it, for it is in the Cross of hrist that we glory. It was the hour of dark- ess and suffering, but it was also the hour of lis triumph and glory.

The Plot to Kill Jesus: 26:1-5.

His enemies were plotting to kill Him, but ot on the feast day, lest there be an uproar f the people. God's plan was that He should e crucified at the Passover season. Jesus him- :lf said, "after two days is the feast of the assover, and the son of man is betrayed to e crucified." It was most fitting that "Christ, ur Passover" be crucified at the passover season. It was to take place at the time of God's appointment, not when his enemies said.

II. *The Anointing in Bethany:* 6-13.

This beautiful incident, showing the love that Mary of Bethany had for Jesus, and also showing that she seemed to have a deeper insight into what was coming, is given in two other places, Mark 4 and John 12. We have here the sharp contrast between the devotion of a soul like Mary's and the black heart of a man like Judas. In the church we sometimes see such contrasts even in our day. Every now and then some thief, or covetous man, gets his hands on some of the money meant for the work of the Lord. There are those who make a "racket" out of religion. On the other hand we have devoted men and women who give their most precious possessions to the Lord. The words of Jesus, "Wheresoever this gospel shall be preached in the whole world, there shall also this, that this woman hath done, be told for a memorial of her," have been gloriously fulfilled. All over the world men and women have been inspired to "go and do likewise."

III. *Judas' Bargain with the Chief Priests:* 14-16.

Perhaps the rebuke to Judas — for he was the principal one back of the criticism—may have made Judas hasten to carry out his plan. He covenanted with these enemies of Jesus for thirty pieces of silver. In Zechariah 11:12 we have the prophecy: "So they weighed for my price thirty pieces of silver." We see again how minutely these prophecies were fulfilled.

IV. *The Passover and the Lord's Supper:* 17-30.

Jesus was careful to observe this feast for it was the one that pointed to His redemptive work. This was the last time that He would keep it with His disciples. They asked Him; Where wilt thou that we prepare for thee to eat the passover? Comparing this account with the ones in Mark 14 and Luke 22 we see what His full instructions were. It was to be a momentous occasion for Him and for His disciples.

As they were eating, He said, Verily I say unto you, that one of you shall betray me. They were exceeding sorrowful and began to say unto Him, Lord, is it I? Turn to John 13:21-30 and find more told us of just what took place at the table that night. Combining all the accounts we are convinced that Judas had ample warning about what he was going to do, and its awful consequences: "Woe unto that man by whom the Son of man is betrayed! it had been good for that man if he had not been born." Judas was, as Jesus said, a "devil," to have pursued relentlessly his evil course in the face of such warnings.

He then institutes the Lord's supper. How such a simple and beautiful Sacrament could have become such a battleground of controversy and cause so much confusion and hard feelings in the Church, is hard to see. It shows how Satan works, his "wiles" and "devices," by which he seeks to hinder the work of the church. The very institution which ought to connote the unity of Christians and their love for each other has become a stumbling block, splitting the Church into opposing groups. It is a symbol of division rather than fellowship even when our Ecumenical Conferences are held.

V. *Warning to Peter:* 31-35.

Judas had been warned and had not heeded the warning. Peter is now warned, but in his self-confidence he, too, goes on to deny his Master. How little heed we give to the warnings of the Bible! Then, too late, we "go out and hang ourselves," or go "out to weep bitter tears." What a lesson for us in His words to Peter! Our spirits may be willing, but the flesh is weak. The warning was for all the disciples, but all of them seemed as confident as Peter. While they did not deny Him, they all forsook Him and fled.

VI. *In Gethsemane:* 36-46.

This is a very familiar passage. We have become used to these words, and I am afraid we miss seeing the real meaning and message:

> Into the woods my Master went,
> Clean for-spent, for-spent;
> Into the woods my Master came,
> For-spent with love and shame.

The burden was getting so heavy that He could hardly stand up under it. Those pathetic words, "My soul is exceeding sorrowful, even unto death," give us a vision of the breaking

YOUNG PEOPLES Department

YOUTH PROGRAM FOR APRIL 7

By THE REV. B. HOYT EVANS

The Theological Seminary Of The Presbyterian Church Of Korea

Scripture: II Timothy 2:11-16

Suggested Hymns:
"Break Thou, The Bread Of Life"
"The Church's One Foundation"
"I Love Thy Kingdom, Lord"

Program Leader:
In this program we are considering the third of our five financial objectives for 1957, the rebuilding of the Presbyterian Seminary in Korea. You will remember that this is the second year that our gifts have been sent to this work. In 1956 the young people of our entire denomination contributed $2667.65 to this project, and our dollars have already gone to work for us.

It is possible that we may have forgotten some of the things we learned about the seminary a year ago. In order to refresh our memories, our speakers will describe the seminary, its usefulness to the Korean Church, and its continuing needs.

First Speaker:
The largest Presbyterian Seminary in the United States is Princeton, with slightly less than five hundred students. The Presbyterian Seminary of Korea, located in the city of Seoul, can still claim to be the largest Presbyterian Seminary in the world, because last year it enrolled 616 students. This institution is jointly supported by the Korean Presbyterian Church, the Presbyterian Church, U.S.A., and our church, the Presbyterian Church, U.S. This means that both financial aid and teachers are provided from all three churches.

The students from the seminary come from all parts of Korea. Some of them are Christians who have fled from Communism in North Korea. Others are former members of the Communist army who were converted to Christianity while in prisoner of war camps, and now they have heard the call to serve the Lord in the ministry. Still others come from the many churches and communities of South Korea.

The arrangement of courses at the Korean seminary differs considerably from the normal course of study in an American seminary. There is a two year preparatory course for students who have completed high school. It includes the study of Bible, English, science, philosophy, and other courses. Last year 246 students were enrolled in the preparatory course. The three year course includes Bible, theology, Hebrew, Greek, church history, religious education, and music. It is open to students who have completed the preparatory course, or who have a college education equivalent to it. This is called the regular course. Three year training is also open to special students who have had five years experience as evangelists or who have graduated from a Bible school. Special students are given an entrance examination to determine whether or not they are sufficiently prepared for the seminary course.

Second Speaker:
The seminary at Seoul is vital to the life of the Presbyterian Church of Korea. It is the only institution which can train ministers for almost half a million Korean Christians. Korea is one of the few countries in the world where Presbyterianism is the dominant Christian church. There are more Presbyterians in Korea than all other Christian groups combined. There are 105 Presbyterian churches in the city of Seoul, more than in any city of the Southern Presbyterian Church. We do not cite these facts to be boasting, but to show how great is the opportunity and responsibility of the Presbyterian Church in Korea, and to show how important it is to have a strong seminary.

Before the Korean War, the southern part of the country (which is now free Korea) was largely agricultural. Cities have grown tremendously since the war, but many, many of the Christian people and the Christian churches are still located in the rural areas. These smaller churches and their faithful members are in desperate need of trained leadership. Only the seminary at Seoul can provide ministers for these country churches.

There is a wonderful opportunity for Christian schools and colleges in Korea. Many such institutions are already in operation, and more are needed. Bible and religion teachers for these schools must be properly trained, and the seminary is the only place to train them. There can be no doubt about the usefulness of the Korean seminary.

Third Speaker:

If we remember last year's program, we learned that this seminary which is so rich in students is very poor in buildings and equipment. The classes are too large (100 to 140 in each class). Often two classes will sit back to back in the same large room, with only a six foot screen separating them. Others meet in flimsy rooms divided from the world and each other only by glass doors. Heating and lighting are rarely adequate or certain. At present the physical plant consists of two repaired buildings, a chapel and an administration building, and two war-damaged buildings, which serve as dormitories. The immediate need is for a library and a dormitory. As soon as these can be provided, a second dormitory and a recitation building must be had.

Mention was made of the need for a library. This includes books as well as the building. The first speaker told us that Princeton Seminary is smaller than the Korean Seminary by more than a hundred students, but the Princeton library contains 500,000 books and pamphlets, while the library in Seoul contains only 4,000 books. American theological students are not usually able to read Korean, but most Koreans can read English. The 4,000 books they do have are printed in English for the greater part, and they would be glad to receive more from us. Any Christian books we can collect, especially commentaries, etc., would be greatly appreciated. They should be sent in care of Dr. Bruce Cummings, one of our missionaries who is now serving on the faculty of the seminary.

There can be no question but that our gifts are sorely needed, but there is another perhaps more important thing we can do for the Presbyterian Seminary in Seoul. We can pray for it. We can pray for the students, many of whom are making great sacrifices in order to prepare themselves to minister the word of God. We can pray for those who teach there, both missionaries and Korean teachers. We can pray for the graduates of the seminary as they go out into Korea to proclaim the Gospel of Christ to twenty million people who seem eager to receive it. This is a great work. We can be thankful to have a share in it.

(Whether or not you receive an offering for this objective at this program, be sure to have a prayer of dedication for your gifts.)

The Minor Prophets
II

By Rev. R. W. Cousar, D. D.

PROPHECY A FRUITFUL STUDY

We must remember that prophecy, first, "forth-telling" and secondly, "fore-telling," speaks directly to us. It is personal as well as social. The thrill and the challenge of its message should result in better personal, community as well as national life. More and more we are impressed how its words come to grips with the vital matters of faith, obedience and true worship. The living God in prophecy lets us know how He feels about us and our present wayward conduct.

PROPHETS KNEW THREE THINGS

The prophets knew the people, their manner of life, their failures, their disobedience, their longings, their hopes, and their fears. Again the prophets knew the infinite God and possessed vivid and deep-seated personal convictions as to His character, His redemption, and His providence. Finally they knew God's purposes. They were the purveyors of His awful judgments, His mercy and the knowledge of a coming King and His Kingdom. Habakkuk, Zechariah, Malachi form our center of interest, now, as the last half of the Circle Bible Study.

HABAKKUK

Someone has called Habakkuk, "The Philosopher Prophet." Nothing is definitely known about the man himself. If the name was derived from the Assyrian tongue it probably means, "a heartener, or one who takes another to his heart and his arms, as one soothes a poor weeping child, telling it to be quiet." He was probably a resident of Jerusalem and therefore was thoroughly conversant with the local situation both political and religious.

HISTORICAL SITUATION

Apparently the Chaldeans or the Babylonians were on the march although there is no evidence that they had, as yet, conquered little Judah, the Southern Kingdom. Nineveh the capital of Assyria had fallen; the Egyptians had been defeated at Carchemish and now Nebuchadnezzar of Babylon was master of the world. Josiah King of Judah had effected a blessed reformation, or revival, a few years before, but it seemed to be all too superficial to halt the nation in its course of rebellion, ending in ultimate destruction.

PROBLEMS

Rather than furnish an outline by chapters we shall attempt to state the "problems," or deep concerns, of the prophet. Remember Habakkuk is called the "Philosopher prophet." He would like to know the "why" and the "wherefore" of Jehovah's dealings.

First, among his problems was, why does Jehovah permit such gross evils? Why does He not hear the prophet's prayer? As someone has well said, "He does not complain AGAINST God, but TO God." This complaint is to be found along with Jehovah's answer, in the first eleven verses of chapter one. We leave the leader to search for himself, or herself, what the answer really is. It is most satisfying to the soul.

Second, among his problems, Why should Jehovah, the Holy God, use a cruel nation like the mighty Chaldeans to execute judgment on His Chosen people? From chapter one, verse twelve, on through chapter two, verse one, he grapples with this dark question, involving, or questioning, the Divine providence. As he climbs his watch tower, however, the far and the near stand out in clear outline. God doeth all things well! Look at chapter two, verses one through four and we behold the patient unfolding of the Divine answer. The prophet is to write the vision on tablets so plainly, "that he may run that readeth it." Surely it will take time, but in the end the righteous and not the wicked will survive. God deals righteously and fairly with all men.

EXCITING DISCOVERY

May we pause and bow in reverence before one GREAT BIG SIGNIFICANT FACT! Let's not miss it, for there is perhaps nothing nobler in Habakkuk, or in any of the other prophets, "The just shall live by faith." (2:4). Prof. George Robinson puts it thus, "It was not Luther, nor Augustine, nor even Paul who first taught this great principle, but Habakkuk." Evangelical Christianity owes everything to this prophet for being the earliest preacher of so precious a truth. To him it meant not only trust, but loyalty, steadfastness, persistence, and endurance. Here we find the registered fact of one who traveled far from a nagging irritating doubt to a living faith that trusted God in the midst of calamity and dire distress.

You have heard it over the radio:

"Oh what a beautiful morning
Oh what a beautiful day
Oh what a beautiful feeling
Everything is going my way."

But everything was NOT going his way as is often the case with us. In spite of this the prophet declares a glorious fact, "Although the fig tree shall not blossom neither shall fruit be in the vines, the labor of the olive shall fail — yet I will rejoice in the Lord, I will joy in the God of my salvation." (3:17).

ZECHARIAH

Zechariah is known as, "The Seer." His mission was to induce the Jewish exiles in Persia to rebuild the temple in Jerusalem. It is thought that he lived to see it completed in 516 B. C. His book contains a great deal more, however. The strong Messianic flavor is frequently discovered, — that is, predictions concerning the coming of our Lord.

To get back to the temple idea, 42,360 Jews had returned to Jerusalem under the leadership of Zerubbabel and Joshua. The construction work on the temple had commenced. Opposition from their neighbors, however, had caused them to stop the work. They were discouraged and depressed because they had not been able to re-establish beautiful Zion. The foundations had been laid but there was no super-structure.

The words of Zechariah were electrifying in their effect. How often we have all heard them quoted, "Not by might, nor by power, but by my Spirit saith the Lord of hosts." (3:6). Again he says, as God's spokesman, "For who has despised the day of small things?" (3:10). The people responded. They had a mind to complete the work which they had commenced. In building churches and missions, what an encouragement, what an inspiration! We may go forward, no matter how great the discouragements, since God is with us.

ANALYSIS AND CONTENTS

It is quite easy to oversimplify this book. Apparently it falls into two broad divisions, (I) Chapters 1-8. This is composed of three messages which could have been delivered on different occasions. The sublime call to repentance in the first six verses of the first chapter is considered one of the strongest of its kind and one of the most spiritual in all of the Old Testament. Read it for yourself. Following this is a series of eight symbolic night-visions all of which, with the possible exception of one, spell encouragement and hope for the rebuilding of the temple, the forgiveness of God's people and His protecting providence. A climax is reached in a coronation scene (6:9-15) in which Joshua the high priest is crowned and is apparently made typical of the Coming One who will be Branch, Messiah, Priest, and King. This is one of the most complete portraits of Him, who is all-glorious, found in Old Testament scriptures. The temple-idea reaches out into a distant future and incorporates into itself what He will accomplish in the golden days ahead. We cannot refrain from quoting these blessed words, "Even He shall build the temple of the Lord; and He shall bear the glory, and shall sit and rule upon His throne; and He shall be a priest upon His throne; and the counsel of peace shall be between them both." (6:13). The visit of the Bethel deputation closes this section. The turning of their fasts into feasts, which is the answer, portrays the great and glorious days yet ahead.

Division (II) chapters 9-14 is concerned with two "burdens," or oracles. The first in chapters 9-11 is the promise of a land to which they would return with many temporal blessings and much inward strength. Woven in with these messages there is a bright scarlet thread, the hope of the Coming King. What lovely words, these, "Rejoice greatly, O daughter of Zion; shout O daughter of Jerusalem: behold thy King cometh unto thee: He is just and having salvation; lowly and riding upon an ass, and upon a colt the foal of an ass." (9:9).

The last part of this second section is concerning the future of Israel, purified and redeemed as the center of the nations. "The bells of the horses," shall bear the name, "HOLINESS UNTO THE LORD" and "the pots in the LORD'S house shall be like the bowls before the altar." The whole concept is tremendous and involves all nations. It is difficult to confine this simply to Israel restored. What an uplift to read in the great closing climactic chapter, "And the Lord shall be King over all the earth: in that day shall there be one Lord, and His name one." (14:9).

MALACHI

Nothing is known about the person of this the last book of the Old Testament prophets. The same meaning, "My Messenger," may have been an official title referring especially to his prophetic office.

The prophet's message is most vigorous and courageous. One is naturally led to believe that he has a colorful character and strong in the faith. As a prophet in the time of Israel's exile and return he was probably a contemporary of Ezra and Nehemiah.

CONDITIONS IN ISRAEL

The temple had been rebuilt and dedicated by those Jews who had returned to Palestine. The sacrifices had been restored, but serious abuses had crept into Israel's conduct and life;

the priests had become lax and subject to fees; inferior animals were offered for sacrifice; the tithe was being neglected; divorces were prevalent; the covenant was neglected, and the nation was skeptical of the fact that they were the chosen people of God.

CONTENTS

The writer begins with a very strong statement of the love of God for wayward Israel. What better start could he make? The main thrusts of this important book of four chapters are two in particular, — first one against the priests, and secondly another against the people. Both needed to take heed to themselves. This order is important and timely for this and every age. The priests had corrupted the covenant of the Lord, that sacred bond, sealed in blood at Sinai. They would not give glory unto the name of Jehovah. Fees were sought for every little thing they did, — "Who is there even among you that would shut the doors for nought? neither do you kindle fires upon mine altar for nought." (1:10). Instead of being sincere leaders and helpers in worship they were actual hindrances and were the generators of spiritual darkness. What solemn words, "But ye are departed out of the way; ye have caused many to stumble at the law; ye have corrupted the covenant of Levi, saith the Lord of hosts. (2:8).

Secondly, "Like people like priests." In days of spiritual declension, and we hate to say it, revival must begin with the ministers of the living God. As for the people they brought sacrificial animals that were both lame and blind. Some of these animals were actually sick or wounded. Polluted bread was offered upon the altar. Not only did the people in effect despise the worship of Jehovah but they despised the ways of righteousness in every day living. A sad, long, realistic list of offenses is chalked up against them, — sorcery, adultery, lying, oppression of labor and meanness towards the widows, orphans and strangers.

The tithe, through a neglect of the same, shines out in classic words so familiar and yet so often neglected in our time, "Will a man rob God? Yet ye have robbed me — in tithes and offerings — Bring ye all the tithes into the storehouse, — and prove me now herewith — if I will not open you the windows of heaven and pour you out a blessing, that there shall not be room enough to receive it." (3:8-10). Some writers think there were three tithes, — two every year and a third one every third year for the poor.

CLIMAX

Chapters three and four provide the beautiful vista of a coming Lord and Redeemer. Thrilling indeed are the opening words of chapter three, "Behold I will send my messenger, and He shall prepare the way before me; and the Lord whom ye seek shall suddenly come to His temple." Chapter four, the closing words, provide us the hopeful streaks of dawn before the rising of the sun. "But unto you that fear my name shall the Sun of righteousness arise with healing in His wings." Four more centuries and the Babe of Bethlehem would appear.

"Brightest and best of the Sons of the morning
Dawn on our darkness and lend us Thine aid;
Star of the East, the horizon adorning,
Guide where our infant Redeemer is laid.

Say, shall we yield Him, in costly devotion,
Odors of Edom and offerings divine,
Gems of the mountain and pearls of the ocean
Myrrh from the forest, and gold from the mine?

CHILDRENS Page

She Told It

This is about a little Hebrew girl who was used in saving the life of a Syrian general. Her name is not given, but her act has a place in the record of God's Word. She had been taken from her home by the Syrian soldiers and was serving as a maid to the general's wife. He was a great man but he was a leper. Leprosy is a terrible disease, and the doctors could not cure him. The little maid said to her mistress, "There is a prophet of my God in Israel who can heal the general's disease" and some one told the general; So he got in his chariot and went to the prophet, who told him to dip seven times in the river Jordan. This he did, and came out of the river a healed man. He said to the prophet, Behold now I know there is no other God but Israel's God, and I will worship Him instead of idols. Thus a little girl who believed in God and loved Him, was used to help another to know and love Him, though she was a slave and far away from home and family.

2. Kings 5 - Acts 1:8

NEWS of CHURCHES
around the World

World Missions Receipts

Budget for 1957	$3,500,000.00
Receipts to date	236,581.38
Percentage of Annual Budget received for 1957	6.75%
Balance needed for 1957	3,263,418.62

Board of Church Extension

Report of February 1957

Budget 1957	$1,518,225.00
Receipts to date	82,292.93
Percentage of Annual Budget received to date	5.4%
Balance needed for the year	1,435,932.07

G. B. Strickler, Treasurer

Report of the Centennial Committee to the General Assembly

The committee met in Atlanta on Thursday, March 7, and organized, with President Wallace M. Alston as chairman.

The committee carefully reviewed and discussed the action of the 1956 Assembly in connection with its authorization of the observance of 1961 as the Centennial year of the Presbyterian Church in the United States.

It was decided to organize the work of the committee under the following five heads:

1. Celebrations. This includes all programs of special observance from the local church to the General Assembly.

2. Goals. Certain goals will be recommended to the Assembly and other agencies and groups will be encouraged to set their own.

3. Special Literature. It is contemplated that certain books and shorter works will be produced in connection with the Centennial.

4. Communications. The production of a film and possible use of television, radio, and other audio-visual aids is envisioned.

5. Publicity.

A sub-committee was appointed for each of these areas.

It was the judgment of the committee that the theme of the Centennial should be: "Our Presbyterian Heritage and Mission." In agreement with the action of the 1956 General Assembly, this committee is of the conviction that the effect of the observance will depend largely on the spirit and manner in which it is carried out. Accordingly it proposes that the Centennial program be designed primarily to point the Church forward. While our appreciation for the abiding values in our heritage should be deepened, we should be chiefly concerned to clarify our vision of our future rule and receive fresh stimulus in the service of our Lord. Furthermore, the committee hopes to fashion a program which will enlarge our horizons and vivify our sense of fellowship with all other Presbyterian and Reformed Churches throughout the world, both those which are older and those which have come into being as a result of the missionary enterprise. Our common traditions in doctrine, polity, worship and practice will be presented in such a way as to strengthen our sense of unity with the Calvinistic Family, and through it with the Ecumenical Church.

Recommendations:

1. That the Assembly adopt the following as the theme of the Centennial: "Our Presbyterian Heritage and Mission."

2. That the committee answer Dr. Scott's request regarding finances by stating that the estimated expenses for 1957 and 1958 are $7,500 and that there will be further expenses which will be dependent upon the nature of the program to be adopted later by the General Assembly.

3. That the budget finally to be adopted by the General Assembly of 1958 for the observance of the Cetennial to be referred to the General Council with the request that they recommend a procedure for financing it.

—Wallace M. Alston, Chairman

ALABAMA

Birmingham — Third Presbyterian Church in Birmingham has begun a campaign for $150,000 for a new educational building to be called the Brother Bryan Memorial Christian Education Building, in memory of the late Rev. James A. Bryan, known as "Brother Bryan."

"Brother Bryan" was pastor of Third Church for 52 years.

The new unit of Third Presbyterian Church will adjoin the present church sanctuary, and will have a fellowship hall with kitchen facilities, classrooms for Sunday School sessions, a library, choir room, a pastor's office and office for the director of education.

James H. Bryan, the son of the late "Brother Bryan," is general chairman of the building committee. Also serving on the committee are Bryan A. Chace, co-chairman; Mrs. Walter F. Quattlebaum, secretary; Wincent A. Graham, treasurer; and Fred G. Moran, David L. Rawls, Mr. and Mrs. O. Z. Collins, Mrs. T. N. Blake, Miss Jeanette Cruse, Miss Dona Hubbard, Roy L. Waddell, Robert McBrayer, Mrs. C. A. Weaver, and W. G. Hightower.

GEORGIA

Atlanta — Rev. Robert D. Alexander has been appointed by the moderator to fill the unexpired term of office of the Stated Clerk of the Synod of Georgia, having been held by the Rev. L. B. Gibbs.

The next stated meeting of the Synod of Georgia is to be held June fourth and fifth. The meeting is to take place at the Druid Hills Presbyterian Church in Atlanta. Dr. Thomas Fry is the host pastor.

Atlanta — The Rev. Albert E. Dimmock, Associate Secretary of the Division of Evangelism of the Board of Church Extension, in Atlanta, has been elected secretary of that Division, succeeding Dr. William H. McCorkle. Dr. McCorkle resigned last year in order to assume the pastorate at First Presbyterian Church, Bristol, Tenn.

Atlanta — Dr. Eugene R. Kellersberger, for thirty years a medical missionary to the Belgian Congo from the Presbyterian Church, U. S., was here recently to receive his third decoration from the Belgian government for outstanding work in the tropics. Dr. Kellersberger is one of the nation's foremost authorities on leprosy.

Latest award received by Dr. Kellersberger is the Croix de l'Officier de la Couronne, one of Belgium's highest honors, which was presented to the former Presbyterian missionary by Robert S. Sams, Atlanta lawyer and de jure consul for the Belgian government.

Dr. Kellersberger had already received the Chevalier Royal Order of the Lion and the Chevalier Royal Order of the Crown, high awards of the Belgian government.

While he was in the Congo, Dr. Kellersberger treated more than 55,000 natives who were suffering from leprosy, sleeping sickness and other tropical diseases. He helped establish the first government-financed leprosy colony in the Belgian Congo.

The Kellersbergers are now living in Melbourne, Fla. Dr. Kellersberger, past general secretary of the American Leprosy Missions, Inc., still treats occasional cases of leprosy.

Atlanta — Mrs. Leighton McCutchen, Executive Secretary of the Board of Women's Work, Mrs. A. L. Devarieste of New Orleans, field worker for the Board, and Miss Mary Crawford, returning missionary to the Belgian Congo, have left for the Congo.

Miss Crawford has been on her regular furlough in the States. Mrs. McCutchen and Mrs. Devarieste will remain in the Congo long enough to attend meetings there and view the work of the Presbyterian missions.

Mrs. McCutchen is to attend a Congolese women's conference on March 25-27, at Kakinda, where she will speak. The conference will be the first of its kind ever held. She will also attend synod and youth meetings in the Congo, and at the invitation of the Presbyterian Church, U. S. A., will visit Douala and Yaounde in French Cameroons. She will visit Brussels, Rome, Geneva, Paris, and Leopoldville, Luluabourg and Brazzaville in the Congo before returning to the States.

Mrs. Devarieste and Mrs. McCutchen will return together to this country on April 10.

NORTH CAROLINA

Davidson — Davidson College has renamed a dormitory in honor of the late J. Archie Cannon of Concord.

Mr. Cannon, at the time of his death last July, was vice-president of the Davidson College Board of Trustees, a position he had held for the preceding 20 years.

President John R. Cunningham announced that West dormitory had been renamed "J. Archie Cannon" dormitory. The renaming was unanimously approved by the Board of Trustees.

The dormitory was completely renovated last summer, receiving new flooring and ceilings and baths. The exterior will be refinished this spring.

Mr. Cannon served as chairman of the Buildings and Grounds committee of the trustees during the entire administration of Dr. John R. Cunningham, which began in 1941. During that time seven major buildings were constructed, the older dormitories were renovated and the grounds landscaped.

Mr. Cannon served as president of the Concord Rotary Club and of the Cabarrus Country Club, and as chairman of the trustees of the Presbyterian Orphan's home at Barium Springs.

Laurinburg — The committee on curriculum of the Consolidated Presbyterian College met in Laurinburg today and, following lunch, spent the afternoon in a conference as to ways and means to proceed in drafting a curriculum. The consensus of opinion of the committee was that a thorough-going study should be made seeking to determine exactly what a Christian college aims to do, and also as to what means should be devised for the realization of these aims.

Because of the importance of such a study to Christian Higher Education in general, and particularly in the launching of the new college, the committee planning to seek funds to finance a study which will enable the consolidated college in the launching of its academic program to have the guidance of the careful thinking of a number of the outstanding educators in America.

TEXAS

Dallas—The Tenth Annual Church Extension Seminar for local chairmen of Church Extension in the Women of the Church of the Presbytery of Dallas was held on Thursday, February 28, 1957, at the Highland Park Church, in Dallas. Representatives from the churches heard the work of Church Extension presented from the standpoint of evangelism with a discussion period led by Rev. Lyndon M. Jackson, member of the Committee's Division on Evangelism. He emphasized particularly the need for follow-up evangelism in every church, and more thorough preparation for church membership.

The work of the Division of Christian Relations and Radio-Television was presented jointly by Rev. G. H. Slusser, chairman of the Division of Christian Relations. The scope of this work was presented through the showing of a film recording the life and work of Mrs. Patsy B. Turner, well known mountain missionary, together with the tape recording entitled "Mile Away Mission." The film of Mrs. Turner is being offered for use on television stations throughout the territory embraced by our church, and the tape recording is being offered for use by local radio stations.

Helps To Understanding Scripture Readings in *Day by Day*

Sunday, April 7, *Mark* 6:32-42. Surely Jesus' "public" ministry has been rightly named! Notice the demands the public continually made upon him — at every time of day (1:32-33,35-37), wherever He went, even in His home (1:45; 2:1-2,13; 5:21; 6:54-56), pushing, jostling, reaching mob proportions (3:9; 4:1), always demanding His attention and energy (1:32,40; 2:3; 3:10; 5:22-23,30), thoughtless of His own weariness (6:31-34a) or sorrow (6:25-33). Notice in these verses the verbs that reveal Jesus' response to the people: healed, cast out (demons), preached, forgave, taught, fed. Before we can minister to people as Jesus ministered to them, we have to be filled with the compassion with which Jesus was filled, i.e., with the ability to "suffer with" those we try to serve.

Monday, April 8, *Matthew* 14:13-21. The compassion with which Jesus viewed the multitudes expressed itself in His ministering to both their physical (14:14,16) and spiritual (Mark 6:34) needs. It was a driving force that constrained Him to take the most practical, strategic steps to get the job done (Matt. 9:36,38; 10:1,5-8). It affected not only the deed He did, but the manner and attitude in which He did them. Notice, for example, the way He touched the loathsome leper (Mark 1:41) and His thoughtfulness in attending to the needs of Jairus' daughter (Mark 5:43). How much of His compassion can Christ express through your life? Does your concern for others take in all their needs? Is it a practical concern? Is it a tender, loving concern?

Tuesday, April 9, *Matthew* 15:29-32. Sit down beside Jesus in the hills of Galilee (v.29) and watch the different classes of people as they were brought to Him (v.30). It seems that none of those who needed Jesus' help were able to get to Him by themselves (v.30). Others did the only thing they could — brought them to the place where Jesus was and simply laid them at His feet (v.30). There is only one class of people that can be seen returning from the presence of Jesus — people who are well and happy (v.31,39). What was the twofold reaction of the multitude to all of this (v.31)? There is no thrill that can compare with that of watching Christ's transforming touch upon a deformed body or soul, unless it is the thrill of having had some part yourself in bringing the deformed one to the Lord.

Wednesday, April 10, *I Kings* 17:8-16. Ahab was one of the most evil of the kings of Israel (16:30-33). Against him God raised up a prophet, Elijah, to speak the word of the Lord (17:1-2ff). What was the purpose of the sign Elijah performed in v.1 (see 18:21,38-39)? Observe God's faithfulness in hearing Elijah's prayer (17:1-7) and supplying His needs in a supernatural manner (vv.3-10), guiding him step by step during the drought (vv.3,9), protecting him from all his adversaries (18:7-10), and blessing those with whom he came in contact (vv.10-16). It was when human resources came completely to an end that God stepped in (vv.7-8,12-14). What evidences do you see in vv.3-16 of Elijah's child-like trust in God? When human resources fail and the adversary is strong, can you look to God to be your unfailing source of supply?

Thursday, April 11, *James* 2:14-17. The problem of the relationship of faith and works has ever existed in the history of the Christian Church. What particular problem is James facing in this passage? What concept of faith do those to whom James refers in v.14 have? Is James denying the need or place of faith in salvation? Does he say that a man can be saved by works? What, then, is the relationship between faith and works (vv.17,18b)? See Ephesians 2:8-10. Are there times when you become so concerned about your faith or your inner spiritual life that you neglect the admonitions of vv.15-16? Do you attempt to perform good works in the energy of the flesh? See John 15:4-5.

Friday, April 12, *John* 6:1-14. What drew the attention of the crowds to Jesus (6:2)? What attitude did they manifest toward Him (vv.14-15)? Yet, what did Jesus say was their real motive in seeking Him (v.26)? Jesus then began to speak in language they could not understand (vv.35,41-42,52). Even some of His own disciples were offended (vv.60,66)? What insights did Peter and the Twelve have into the nature of Jesus' ministry that was lacking in the others (vv.68,69)? Was the understanding of the Twelve complete (vv.5-7, 8-9)? Though we make much of our profession of Christianity, if we follow Christ with wrong motives, as did the crowds in v.26, He will not associate Himself with us (v.15). But if we follow Christ sincerely, even though we do not understand everything about Him (5,7,8-9), He will graciously reveal Himself to us (v.16-21).

Saturday, April 13, *Luke* 10:30-37. The story of the Good Samaritan is known to most by heart. What prompted its telling (vv.25-29)? According to Matthew 23:23-24, what was basically lacking in the religion of the religious leaders of Israel? Like the Pharisee, the lawyer who came to Jesus was familiar with the Scriptures (10:25-27). What point did Jesus make to him about the Scriptures (v.28)? What was the central point of the story as far as the lawyer was concerned (vv.36-37)? Do you think Jesus displayed a good deal of tact and patience as He dealt with the lawyer's needs in v.25-37? Though you are active in the Church and know your Bible well, would Jesus point out a similar need in your life?

MANUAL ON SOUL WINNING. M. W. Downey. Baker Book House. 40c.

This booklet is a condensation of 10 lessons from the author's book, "The Art of Soul Winning". This manual is designed to serve as a handbook for students in short-term Bible study courses. The review questions at the end of each lesson are helpful.

Missionary Truths in Isaiah

By George S. Lauderdale

Isaiah preached to religious people; men everywhere today are religious, but need the gospel. God punished His people because of their sin: "They have cast away the law of the Lord of Hosts, and despised the word of the Holy One of Israel." Isaiah 5:24,25. These religious persons also despised Jesus Christ, God's Word made flesh, but God used their opposition to cause Gentiles to hear His message.

* * *

Jesus' Name, "Immanuel," teaches us to trust in Him alone: "Cease ye from man, whose breath is in his nostrils: for wherein is he to be accounted of?" Isaiah 2:22. "Sanctify the Lord of hosts himself; and let him be your dread." Isaiah 8:13. The Lord promised that after Israel was punished, a remnant would "no more again stay upon him that smote them; but shall stay upon the Lord, the Holy One of Israel, in truth." Isaiah 10:20. May God grant that the church now will be that remnant; Jesus Christ is all we need!

Until the Spirit of God is poured out from on high, all is barrenness, but He changes the wilderness into a fruitful field. What folly it is, therefore, to grieve the Holy Spirit and trust in Egypt, or worldly wisdom! "Now the Egyptians are men, and not God; and their horses flesh, and not spirit. When the Lord shall stretch out his hand, both he that helpeth shall fall, and he that is helped shall fall down, and they shall all fall together." Isaiah 31:3.

It is *daring* to become a Christian and thus a target of Satan, but it is *fatal* to forsake the fountain of living waters for leaky cisterns which can hold nothing. Immanuel means "God with us"; He is sufficient!

* * *

Listen to this promise to all who witness for the Lord Jesus Christ: "Thou wilt keep him in perfect peace, whose mind is stayed on thee: because he trusteth in thee." Isaiah 26:3. By abiding in Christ we bring forth fruit and are filled with His joy; joy includes perfect peace, and abiding in Christ having one's mind stayed on Him! But peace is promised *only* to those who keep God's commandments: "There is no peace, saith the Lord, to the wicked." Isaiah 48:22.

God wants you to repent: "O that thou hadst hearkened to my commandments! then had thy peace been as a river." Isaiah 48:18. Obey the Lord's charge to evangelize the nations: "And the work of righteousness shall be peace; and the effect of righteousness, quietness and assurance for ever." Isaiah 32:17.

The wars and rumors of wars, the bickering among political leaders, even in small towns, give Christians a chance to prove that God does keep His people in perfect peace.

* * *

God says to idols, "Show the things that are to come hereafter, that we may know that ye are gods: yea, do good, or do evil, that we may be dismayed, and behold it together." Isaiah 41:23. Only when an idol inspires a man to write an accurate book like "Revelation," or any other Bible prophecy, will we be excused from not evangelizing the nations of idol-worshippers.

There is danger in putting a picture, supposed to look like the Lord Jesus Christ while He was on earth, at the front of a church or room for worship, flanked by candles, draperies, placed above Bibles, offering plates, and other things. Faith's eyesight looks on Jesus Christ in the Word, and bodily eyes cannot see Him now at God's right hand. Let us not be in the number of those who reject the Holy Spirit because we cannot see Him!

Bibles for Oklahoma Children

In the Southwestern District a total of 97,241 New Testaments were circulated, more than in any district in any previous year. Secretary Langham concluded that this could only have been done by effective cooperation. Mr. W. R. Lence of Oklahoma was one man who cooperated wholeheartedly. He wrote the Society recently:

"In my home city of Enid there is an association of churches which undertakes to teach the children the Bible along with the other regular studies of the public schools. Three years ago the manager of the Association came to me for help in supplying Bibles and New Testaments. The Association gave special attention to the fifth grade. I agreed to furnish New Testaments with the children's names stamped on the cover if the names were furnished. The first year of the program was such a grand success that I extended my offer to nine counties in Oklahoma, and two in Missouri. I have a small income and invest nearly all of it in this way. During the past three years I have distributed nearly 10,000 New Testaments to children with their names stamped in gold on the cover. I have received between 2,500 and 3,000 letters from children, parents and teachers, thanking me for the Testaments."

—From American Bible Society Report

Refugees

Today the steadily increasing tide of refugees, already numbered in the millions, forces us to realize that the whole pattern of our world life has been changed. The ministries of relief and reconstruction must be recognized as an integral part of the churches' life and witness along with, and in addition to, home and foreign missions. The need is vast. Our churches are bound by the gospel of Jesus Christ to help these suffering people, His brethren and ours.

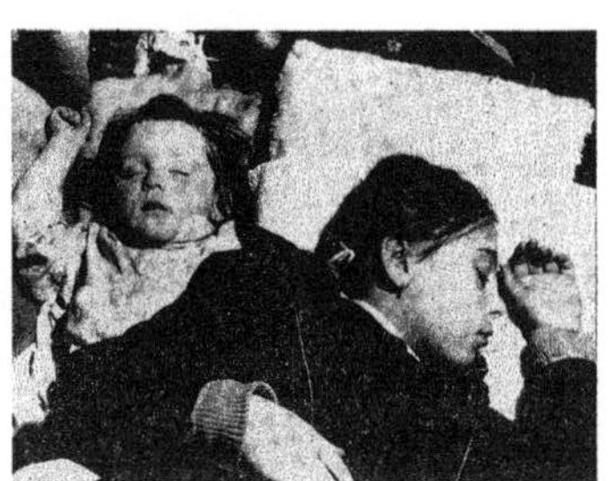

Refugees-
All Over the World
Are in Need.

You Can Send Help
"Give Through Your Church"

THE EASTER OFFERING

APRIL 21, 1957

For Work Not Included In The Budget Of

OVERSEAS RELIEF AND INTER-CHURCH AID

BOARD OF WORLD MISSIONS • BOX 330 • NASHVILLE, TENN.

THE SOUTHERN PRESBYTERIAN JOURNAL

Rev. Henry B. Dendy, D.D., Editor....Weaverville, N. C.
Dr. L. Nelson Bell, Associate Editor....Asheville, N. C.
Rev. Wade C. Smith, Associate Editor....Weaverville, N. C.

EDITORIAL

How Do We Meet This Test?

According to the Scriptures love is an outstanding characteristic of a Christian; love for God and love for our fellow men.

As we realize more and more from what we have been saved, and the privileges and hope which are ours, this love for God and His Christ must deepen.

And as the Holy Spirit works in our hearts there must also develop an increasing love for others; for other Christians as brothers in Christ and for the unsaved as men and women who need Him.

By the standards laid down in the Bible how do we rate? Is love an obvious and outstanding characteristic of our lives? The writer is writing to himself more than any one else. How pitifully we fail in this *basic* requirement!

John writes: *"We know that we have passed from death unto life, because we love the brethren."* Do we have this witness in our hearts?

Love is the first Christian grace mentioned as a fruit of the indwelling Spirit. It was love which motivated God's redemption of man through His Son.

It is love in our lives which will commend the Gospel we profess. An unbelieving world may be totally unimpressed by theological or ecclesiastical arguments but love will break down the barriers of indifference and help win men to Christ.

The problem of race relations has been immeasurably harmed by trying to solve it primarily on a legal basis. Christian love in one's heart and a genuine appreciation of the feelings of others will do more to solve this problem than all court decisions or church pronouncements combined.

The love about which the Bible talks has nothing in common with the maudlin sentiment usually associated with the word "love" today. The love which comes only as Christ captivates and fills the heart is described by the apostle Paul in I Corinthians 13 and our own self-esteem shrivels up and we stand naked and condemned as we realize how utterly we fail to exemplify this in our own lives.

We believe a new emphasis on the *fruits* of the Holy Spirit is needed; an emphasis which recognizes that where there is fruit there must first be a root and that this is found in the possession of one's heart and life by the Holy Spirit.

Our Church has been beset with internal problems for years. Too often we have tried to solve them in a spirit having little in common with the work of the Holy Spirit.

All around us there are men and women who do not know Christ. Again and again we fail them — and in failing them we are failing our Lord — because we do not approach them in a spirit of love and genuine concern.

Within society as a whole there is needed the softening and transforming power of a Christ-inspired love. How often we approach our community or our national life with the mailed fist rather than with a spirit of Christian love!

Take the New Testament and underscore the word love wherever it occurs. It rests at the very heart of the Christian profession and of daily living for Christ. But do we exemplify it in our lives as we should?

Love is not a natural state but a Christian grace, the evidence of the transforming power of the indwelling Holy Spirit. It is a grace which can be cultivated by exercise and which is a rewarding evidence of a continued growth in our knowledge of and love for our Saviour and Lord.

Our constant prayer should be for the opening of our hearts to the Holy Spirit that He

Who alone can bring about this transformation and inspire this new quality in our lives may have His righteous way.

Not only will it make us new creatures but it will make others want the One who brings about the transformation.

—L.N.B.

Not Apostate: Sometimes Wrong.

The other day a Presbyterian college student asked me whether the Presbyterian Church USA was apostate. His father is the leading officer in such a congregation. He was converted in it, but he had been told that it as a part of the USA Church was apostate. My question in reply, "Does this congregation preach the Gospel?" "Yes, indeed," he responded, "perhaps more vigorously than the nearby US Church." "Then it is not apostate," was my answer.

This whole thing of labeling a denomination apostate is not Protestant, but Roman Catholic. The Protestant measuring rod is not the denominational organization. The marks of the Church are the Word truly preached and the sacraments rightly administered.

When John Calvin was put out of Geneva, preaching deteriorated, discipline became lax, and the work of the deacons lagged. His friends wrote him that the Church was apostate and that they had ceased attending. He wrote them back by all means to go to Church, that those who deserted the Church were themselves traitors to God. Where the Gospel is preached in its substantial integrity there is the Church and there those who would have God as their Father are to worship.

The Reformers never labeled even the Roman Catholic Church in all its parts as apostate. They rejected the Papal cancer, while affirming the body of Christ. They affirmed that there were true Churches even among the papists, that is, wherever the Gospel was preached among them.

When the Kirk of Scotland under the domination of the Moderates put out such men as Thomas Gillespie, John Witherspoon held the machine up to ridicule in his *Arcana* or *Ecclesiastical Characteristics,* but he never deserted the Church nor described it as apostate. In due time he came to Princeton to teach sound theology in America and organize the first General Assembly in the United States.

When St. Louis Presbytery removed Dr. S. B. McPheeters, Dr. Charles Hodge denounced it as an injustice with few parallels in the history of the Church. But Dr. Hodge never left the Church nor his charge at Princeton, though Oxford Presbytery denounced him for his fearless condemnation of the wrong done Dr. McPheeters.

It is my opinion, that the USA Church was wrong in deposing from the ministry that heroic defender of the faith, J. Gresham Machen under a decree that has no citation of nor any reference to Scripture in it. After this act, Dr. Machen continued to preach the glorious Gospel of the Blessed God with his lips and his pen. Consequently, I do not agree that the act of deposition from the ministry of the Word had the Divine sanction.

In all such cases, if wrong has been done, we can leave the wrong to the Son of God to judge and deal with as He alone is able to do in wisdom, understanding, love, righteousness, grace — speaking to the wrongdoers in judgment and in forgiving grace. We do not have to take judgment into our hands, nor put ourselves on Roman Catholic ground and decry the denomination as apostate.

Have such wrongs been done also in the Presbyterian Church, US? Under the leadership of J. H. Thornwell and his successors we have written into our Book of Church Order that an offense, the proper object of ecclesiastical discipline, is only that which the Holy Scriptures, the law of Christ, the only Lawgiver, condemns as sinful, cf. par. 179. "Nothing ought to be considered by any court as an offense, or admitted as a matter of accusation, which cannot be proved to be such from Scripture as interpreted in these Standards." Further charges ought not to be received on slight grounds, 224, and errors ought to be considered whether they strike at the vitals of religion or are not likely to do much injury, 227. Wherever these or other sections of our Book have been disregarded and injury has been done to a minister of the Gospel by his brethren the higher court ought to redress the error. In the final analysis, if wrong has been done in our Church and the highest appeal has not righted the wrong, then as a Christian receive the wrong as Christ received so many wrongs for our sakes . . . and leave the righting of the wrong to Him Whose eyes are as a flame of fire.

—W.C.R.

The Southern Presbyterian Journal, *a Presbyterian Weekly magazine devoted to the statement, defense, and propagation of the Gospel, the faith which was once for all delivered unto the saints,* published every Wednesday by The Southern Presbyterian Journal, Inc., in Weaverville, N. C.

Entered as second-class matter May 15, 1942, at the Postoffice at Weaverville, N. C., under the Act of March 3, 1879. Vol. XV, No. 49, April 3, 1957. Editorial and Business Offices: Weaverville, N. C. Printed in the U.S.A., by Biltmore Press, Asheville, N. C.

Address Change: When changing address, please let us have both old and new address as far in advance as possible. Allow three weeks after change if not sent in advance. When possible, send an address label giving your old address.

BOOK REVIEW

By Rev. John R. Richardson, D. D.

God, Gold and Government

Howard E. Kershner. Prentice Hall, Inc. $2.95.

Why has America developed a standard of living never before approached by any other people? What is the reason for the miracle of America? What is the explanation for the fact that 7% of the world's people produce nearly half of its industrial wealth? What is the reason for this astonishing performance? Such penetrating questions are raised in this volume and convincing answers are given.

Dr. Kershner contends that the true explanation of the miracle of America lies in the spiritual rather than in the material realm. Other countries have large natural resources. America has no monopoly on natural wealth. The author points to "the worship of God and the willingness to observe His laws and follow His leadership as the greater part of the explanation of the miracle of America."

The Profit Motive

Despite the fact that many today are castigating the profit motive in business, Dr. Kershner devotes Chapter 5 to the nature of profit and its legitimacy. On this subject Dr. Kershner avers, "Profit is the corn not used for food that is carefully saved, in order that a bigger crop may be grown next year; it is the dollars not used for payroll, raw materials, taxes, payment for the use of capital and other expenses, that can be re-invested for plant expansion and better equipment in order that future production may be greater; it is the fertilizer that quickens the imagination of men, spurring them to ever new and greater efforts. Profit is the reward that comes to those who are most successful in supplying human wants — who deliver better goods and services than others are offering; it might be said to be a commission on the service an entrepreneur is able to render to the public. Profit will inspire more men and women to make extraordinary efforts than any other known motive; since it comes from rendering better service or producing better merchandise at lower prices, it is a result, or by-product of service rendered to the public. The fact of profit is proof that service has been rendered. Profit is probably only a fraction of one per cent of the benefit accruing to the public but small as it is, it caused that benefit.

"Some there are who regard profit with disdain and contempt and speak of producing goods for use and not for profit. They do no[t] seem to realize that unless goods are widel[y] used, there will be no profit, and that if ther[e] is no profit, equipment cannot be maintaine[d,] assembly lines expanded nor production i[n]creased. Profit is the proof that there has bee[n] use — extensive use. Business must be profitabl[e] or it will not and cannot continue to suppl[y] goods and services to the people."

Dr. Kershner denies that profit in busines[s] is a drag or a handicap or an expense to th[e] people. Profits are prima facie evidence, h[e] says, that someone has succeeded in renderin[g] better service to the public than anyone els[e] has been able to render. A number of illustr[a]tions are employed to make clear the essentia[l] and beneficial nature of profit. Summarizin[g] these examples he concludes, "Profit has give[n] us hospitals, museums, libraries, churches, orchestras, operas, schools and colleges. It contributes in a thousand ways to the material cultural and spiritual progress of our people. It might truthfully be said that the amount of profit earned within a nation is a measure of the progress that is being made. Destroy profit, or confiscate it by excessive taxation, and advance in all these many directions will cease. The status quo could not even be maintained and regression toward primitive times would set in."

People who would eliminate profit from business seldom propose a sensible alternative. Recognizing this fact, Dr. Kershner declares, "Maybe capable men could be persuaded to perform such miracles by some incentive other than large salaries but, for most men, and excepting only a few great souls, no other inducement has proved so effective. Some are not reconciled to face the facts but continue to complain that men ought to be motivated by more worthy considerations. Try as we will to change them, nevertheless, we must work with men as we find them.

"Our Lord was sparing in his criticism of men and declared that ' . . . the laborer is worthy of his hire . . . ' (Luke 10:7). He commended those who were industrious and used such capital as they possessed to earn profit, and the larger the profit the more he entrusted them with larger responsibilities.

"There is nothing wrong with profit earned in honest enterprise. It is essential as a means

"We need a law, say some, to make employers pay higher wages; we need a law, say others, to compel the workers to give a fair day's labor; we need laws, say many, to force a redistribution of wealth through the medium of taxation and a bigger government bureaucracy.

"Listen again to Jesus' reply to all this clamor: ' . . . who made me a judge or a divider over you? . . . ' ' . . . Take heed and beware of covetousness . . . '

"Thus Jesus silenced the propaganda and refused to have any part in the distribution of wealth and equalization of income.

"Although the poor were much in Jesus' mind, and He had great sympathy for them, He nevertheless saw clearly that the way to help them was not to give them the possessions of others, but to nurture in them the seeds of character and integrity which would make them more useful members of society, and so bring to them more adequate incomes. As Paul Harvey puts it, 'You never hear of Jesus worrying about moving people out of the slums. He walked the squalid streets from end to end . . . and getting the slums out of the people.' "

Limited Government

Chapter 7 will make a strong appeal to Southerners who still believe in the 10th amendment to the Constitution. This chapter is called "Limited Government." The author holds that our ancestors knew that if they were to remain free men in control of their government and not to become its slaves they must greatly limit its power. Our federal government was established on the basis that it would do nothing which the states and the people were able to do for themselves. Little by little this has been reversed until we are approaching a condition wherein the states and the people will do nothing which they hope to get the federal government to do for them. "Today," says Dr. Kershner, "when difficulty of any kind arises, the ready answer is 'more government.' "

Citing the early history of our country, Dr. Kershner shows that the Pilgrim Fathers tried communism when they founded the Plymouth colony in Massachusetts. All grain was put in a common pool from which each received his portion. The experiment failed. The author quotes Governor Bradford's comment on this attempt at collectivism: " 'It was found to breed much confusion and discontent and retard much employment that would have been to their benefit and comfort. For the young men that were most able and fit for labor and service did repine that they should spend their time and strength to work for other men's wives and children without any recompense. The strong or men of parts had no more in division of victuals and clothes than he that was weak and not able to do a quarter the others could; this was thought injustice.'

"Governor Bradford goes on to explain how this experiment showed the falsity of the belief that, ' . . . the taking away of property and bringing in community into a commonwealth would make them happy and flourishing if they were wiser than God.'

"The able men, Governor Bradford explains, ' . . . thought it some indignity and disrespect to be ruled and equalized in labor and victuals, clothes, etc., with the meaner and younger sort and for men's wives to be commanded to do service for other men as dressing their meat, washing their clothes, etc., they deemed it a kind of slavery, neither could many husbands well brook it.'

"At the end of two years of collectivism, the Pilgrims were starving. They held a council to devise means of staying alive. As usual under such circumstances, they decided it would be each man for himself. In Governor Bradford's own words, the Pilgrims ' . . . began to think how they might raise as much corn as they could and obtain a better crop. . . . At length after much debate of things, the Governor with the advice of the chiefest among them gave way that they should set corn every man for his own particular and in that regard trust to themselves . . . '

"The decision having been made, the Governor assigned to every family a fair share of ground. This move he reports, ' . . . had very good success; for it made all hands very industrious, so as much more corn was planted than otherwise would have been by any means the Governor or any other could use, and saved him a great deal of trouble, and gave far better content. The women now went willingly into the fields and took their little ones with them to set corn, which before would allege weakness and disability; whom to have compelled would have been thought great tyranny and oppression.'

"In the autumn of 1623, six months after the end of the communist experiment, the first Thanksgiving celebrated the abundance resulting from private enterprise. In Governor Bradford's words: 'By this time the harvest was come and instead of famine now God gave them plenty and the face of things was changed to the rejoicing of the hearts of many for which they blessed God. And the effect of their particular planting was well seen, for all had, one way and another, pretty well to bring the year about, and some of the abler sort and more industrious had to spare, and sell to others, so as any general want or famine hath not been amongst them since this day.' "

When the government is limited to a few functions, the people can understand and con-

and in government — will never submit to an all powerful state. Upon the ministers of the Christian religion rests the responsibility of proclaiming the living Gospel that will command the whole allegiance of men. They must arouse our citizens to the danger that threatens them and bring them to a willingness to pledge their lives, their fortunes and their sacred honor to the perpetuation of our free, Christian civilization."

Dr. Kershner does not pretend to write from a neutral state of mind. He believes that the time has come for Americans to make definite decisions. His final appeal is, "Our fathers bequeathed to us this pearl of great price. Shall we preserve it and pass it on to posterity, or must our remote descendants, through renewed martyrdom and toil in centuries to come, retrace the bloody steps leading to a new age of peace and freedom wherein men will have another opportunity to achieve the destiny for which God created them?"

This book should be circulated and read widely through our church by both laymen and ministers. The church has much at stake in the field of Christian economics. Dr. Kershner is an able counselor on this subject. We are grateful for his courageous presentation in this forthright discussion expressed in "God, Gold and Government."

Where Are The Un-Wed Fathers?

By Mrs. Leland Barbee

Scattered across America are many homes established by men and women with the love of Christ in their hearts; homes where unfortunate girls are received, protected and cared for. One such home is Faith Cottage in Asheville, N. C., a home where Christ is magnified and where many of those who come under its roof also come to know the Saviour.

The author of this article wrote it for one of our national magazines but has graciously permitted us to print it. Herein is food for thought. —The Editor

"Often the illegitimate offspring of a harlot or betrayed daughter carries through life the stigma which should rightfully have been carried by him who did the wilful sin. Unfair world that it is, one goes entirely free and clear so far as man can see, and the other, sometimes crushed, carries the shame alone."

("The Pilgrim from the Hills"
by Grace E. Green)

This is to you, un-wed fathers, wherever you may be.

Do you know where the unwed mother of your child is? Do you *care* what has become of her and your child or did you lose interest when you learned there was to be a child? Did you cast her aside unfeelingly and deny your responsibility for her condition? When your conscience began to prick you, did you try to silence it after the fashion of Adam who hesitated not at all to lay the blame for his disobedience on Eve? Did you consider yourself the innocent victim of a woman's wiles? Since when could any woman—may she be ever so wily—force herself on an unwilling man? On the other hand, you have only to read the newspapers and listen to the radio to learn of the many women who have fallen victims to some man's evil passions.

In Nathaniel Hawthorne's *The Scarlet Letter,* you remember that Hester Prynn was made to wear a scarlet "A" exposed so that all could see it. The world today doesn't go quite that far, but its un-Christian and inhuman treatment of what it calls a "fallen woman" is none the less cruel. That cruelty is deliberate and wicked.

It was my privilege recently to spend a day by invitation in Faith Cottage in Asheville, North Carolina. Strange to say, I had to be told that Faith Cottage is a home which has been open to unwed expectant mothers for fifty years. During that time more than a thousand girls have been looked after there and equally that many have been turned away because of lack of room accommodation for more than twenty girls at one time. The waiting list is also alarmingly long.

The girls who are so fortunate as to be admitted to Faith Cottage find there three wise and good women who mother them, bind up their spiritual wounds as best they can and see to their religious training. Each girl is, as a rule, permitted to stay until her baby is four weeks old. Some provision is usually made for her future before she leaves. If she wants to keep her baby, she may. Otherwise it is taken to "Eliada" ("one whom God cares for"), an orphanage established by Mr. Compton who conceived and carried out the plans for Faith Cottage.

That day at Faith Cottage stirred up in me all kinds of emotions. There was deep sympathy for those unfortunate girls and great admiration for what was being done with and for them. But when I met them in assembly room for evening devotions and saw how very young they were and how sweet and ladylike, just like other girls we all know, indignation gripped me. Why should they have to leave their homes and families and friends and be isolated to a certain extent—from choice, I was told—when the fathers of their expected babies went scot-free? I turned to Miss Jesperson and her sister and Miss Anderson, the three dedicated women who have charge of Faith Cottage, and asked, "Where are the unwed fathers of these expected babies?" They answered that they had often wondered.

So, *where are you?* Carrying on the kind of life, a normal life, such as all people have a right to enjoy? Living in such a way that those with whom you come in contact trust you, like you and haven't the slightest idea that in all justice you should be wearing a big scarlet "A" where every one could see it! Or that you should be confined for a time in a home for unwed fathers?

Now I'm going to tell you about a little girl who, I'm sure, is not the one who bore your child, for no man in his right mind would have brought shame and sorrow to one so young.

Helen, we will call her, was only thirteen years old when she was admitted to Faith Cottage. She was wearing her entire wardrobe which barely covered her pathetically thin body. Her childish face was pale and pinched and her suffering eyes seemed too large for their setting. When Miss Anderson took her to her room to freshen up, she found that what meager flesh covered her bones was black and blue from the beatings which, Helen later admitted, were given by her parents. Miss Anderson also learned later that the child had been underfed and had been obliged to sleep on the floor.

Proper clothes, good nourishing food, good treatment and pleasant surroundings soon did wonders for Helen and she began to enjoy life in a real home such as she had never known before. She dreaded the time when she would have to leave it all . . . for what?

Soon after her baby was born, Miss Jesperson found her sobbing her little heart out. Miss Jesperson put her arms around her, gave her a good hug and said, "Helen, baby, what is the matter? You can tell me, can't you?"

"Oh, Miss Jesperson," Helen cried out, "Can't I stay here? Can't I? I don't want to leave. If you will let me stay, I'll be no trouble at all. I'll do everything I can to help everybody that needs help — I really will. May I stay — *please?*" That pleading voice and the desperate look in those big eyes would have won over a heart much harder than Miss Jesperson's which is noted for its tenderness.

So Helen was permitted to stay and she more than lived up to the promises she made. She not only made herself useful in the usual ways but she improvised some of life's little extras as glad surprises.

Shortly before I spent that memorable day at Faith Cottage, Helen left to become the "daughter" of a childless couple in one of our eastern states. She is twenty-three years old.

You have now had a glimpse of some of the things which go on in Faith Cottage. Bow your head in thankfulness, unwed father, for the many "Faith Cottages" in our glorious country which do everything humanly possible to erase the harmful effects of your deliberate sins. Won't you try from now on to take pride in your manhood instead of in your malehood? There is a difference, you know.

ESSON FOR APRIL 14

By THE REV. J. KENTON PARKER

Jesus Praised And Condemned

'ackground Scripture: Matthew 21:1-11
'evotional Reading: Hebrews 2:9-18

Public opinion is very uncertain and unreliable. A mob may shout "Hosanna" one day, and Crucify," the next. I have seen something of the sort here in our country. A man may be a public ero one week and "in the doghouse" the next. We do not know just how many of the people who iouted and sang the praises of Jesus on Palm Sunday were in the crowd that yelled, "Crucify Him," n Black Friday, but no doubt there were some of the same people. A mob is easily swayed by a :w skillful leaders, and it was this small group f chief priests, scribes, and others who stirred p the multitude to call for the release of arabbas and the crucifixion of Jesus.

In Hebrews 2:9-18 we see the twofold nature f this scene at the cross: "But we see Jesus, ho was made a little lower than the angels ır the suffering of death, crowned with glory ıd honor." There is the "shame of the cross," ıd the "glory of the cross." In the eyes of ıe world a cross is a shameful thing, the symbol : death because of some crime : in the eyes of od, and of those who realize that He was ying for sinners, the cross of Christ is a mbol of glory, so that Paul could boast in , and say, "God forbid that I should glory ve in the cross of Jesus Christ," and we Chrisans can sing, In the cross of Christ I glory.

In our lesson today we see Jesus both praised ıd condemned.

Jesus Praised: 21:1-11; 27:19,23,24; 27:54.

Matthew 21:1-11 gives the account of the Trinphal Entry into Jerusalem. Jesus made :eparation for this by sending two of His sciples into the village to get the colt upon hich He was to ride. This was in fulfillment Zechariah 9:9. The meekness of the King as emphasized. He does not ride upon a ancing warhorse but upon the lowly colt of ı ass.

He was placed upon the colt and a great ultitude spread their garments in the way hile others cut down branches from the trees ıd strewed them in the way. He was in the idst of the throng; and both those going bere and those following cried, saying, Hosanna the son of David : Blessed is he that cometh the name of the Lord : Hosanna in the ghest. So great was the demonstration that e whole city of Jerusalem was moved and asked, Who is this? The multitude said, This is Jesus the prophet of Nazareth of Galilee. We see from this that they had not grasped the truth about Him, that He was the Son of God, although their words implied that He was their King and they were acclaiming Him as such. The religious leaders in Jerusalem were greatly disturbed by this outburst of public approval and wanted Him to rebuke His disciples, but He answered, "I tell you that, if these should hold their peace, the stones would immediately cry out." (Luke 19:40). It was the day of His triumph and nothing could stop it. The mob that only a few days later cried out, "Crucify" may have been composed of different people, people from the city itself, but no doubt there were some of the same crowd.

In Matthew 27:19 we have the words of Pilate's wife who wrote, Have thou nothing to do with that just man. She had suffered many things in a dream because of Him. Then, in verses 23 and 24 we have the words of Pilate himself as he asks the question, Why, what evil hath he done? He called for a basin of water and washed his hands before them, saying, I am innocent of the blood of this just person. If he had only the courage to refuse the demands of the Jews he might have gone down in history as a hero instead of a coward. The blood of Jesus on his hands could not be washed off with water. The answer of the people, as they said, His blood be on us and on our children, is to be kept in mind as we read the history of the Jews since that day. There is only one way for this blood to be removed : when they cry out Blessed is He that cometh in the name of the Lord, and accept Him as Saviour and King.

Matthew tells about the two thieves, but does not tell of the conversion of one of them. We find this in Luke 23:39-43. This thief saw the truth and believed with a most remarkable faith, a faith that saw the King in His glory in Christ on the cross by his side, and knew that He would come in his kingdom.

In Matthew 27:54 we have the reaction of the centurion who had charge of the soldiers, and the soldiers themselves as they feared greatly, saying, Truly this was the Son of God.

Not all of those who "sitting down they watched him there," were scoffing and jeering. Some saw His glory; some praised Him; others, like the women, were beholding afar off and grieving. There was praise mixed with condemnation; glory with shame; faith in the midst of unbelief.

II. *Jesus Condemned:* 27:11-54.

This chapter is mainly an account of His unjust trials and condemnation and the shameful proceedings which accompanied these. I am afraid that our very familiarity with these words has a tendency to harden our hearts, and we read them without much feeling. We ought to pray for tender hearts as well as understanding hearts as we "think on these things." Someone reading this chapter for the first time could hardly keep back the tears. May we feel as well as see.

1. *Jesus and Pilate:* 11-26.

Who could imagine Caesar Augustus being tried by a governor of a minor province of the empire? Yet, a far greater than Caesar is here; the King of Kings and Lord of Lords. The Just Judge of all the earth is being tried by an unjust judge : the Innocent is standing before the guilty; the Holy One before the immoral and impure Pilate.

It is no wonder that the judge is afraid of his Prisoner. Pilate marveled as Jesus answered never a word; he was troubled by the message of his wife; he well knew that Jesus was innocent.

He is more afraid of the Jews. He wanted to keep his position and knew that they could stir up all sorts of trouble for him politically. So many crimes are committed because politicians are afraid of what the people will do. His pathetic attempts to get rid of Jesus, (see John's Gospel) make us almost pity him as he tries all sorts of ways, except the right way, to avoid passing sentence upon Him. The determined leaders of the Jews thwart every move made by Pilate to release Him, and at last he takes the basin of water and goes through the ceremony of washing his hands, saying, I am innocent of the blood of this just person. However, no amount of washing with water could cleanse those guilty hands, or relieve that guilty conscience. Pilate condemns himself rather than his Holy Prisoner.

YOUNG PEOPLES Department

YOUTH PROGRAM FOR APRIL 14

By THE REV. B. HOYT EVANS

Can A Christian Be A Soldier?

Scripture: Romans 12 and Ephesians 6:10-18

Suggested Hymns:
"Who Is On The Lord's Side?"
"A Mighty Fortress Is Our God"
"Lead On, O King Eternal"

Suggestions for Program Leader:

(In the minds of most young people there is little question about the propriety of being both a Christian and a soldier. If they are already convinced that Christians are justified in wearing a military uniform and bearing arms, they at least ought to give some thought to being good Christian soldiers. Many of the boys in youth meetings today will be in the military service in a few years or less. In this program you want to determine how a Christian can be a soldier and what kind of soldier a Christian can be. After you, as leader, make your introductory remarks, have two of the young people to present the arguments usually advanced by pacifists and non-pacifists. Following their reports, ask the young people for their comments. You can usually start a discussion of this kind by asking questions of specific individuals.)

Program Leader:

It would never have occurred to most of us to ask this question, "Can a Christian be a soldier?" We have assumed that he could. The great majority of Christians have always felt the same way. This is especially true of our own church. The War for American Independence was spoken of in the British Parliament as "that Presbyterian rebellion." For many years, however, there have been some Christians who refused to bear arms on moral grounds. It is a violation of their religious conscience to be members of a military organization. Most notable among these in our own country are the Friends (Quakers) and the various Mennonite bodies. Our government has always honored the convictions of these bodies and of other individuals who believe as they do. No person who conscientiously objects to taking up arms is required to enter the military service. Other types of service may be required of them at times in lieu of military service.

Many of the boys among us will be called into military service before long. Every Christian must be convinced that this kind of service is consistent with his faith before he enters upon it, and he ought to give serious thought to the kind of soldier a Christian should be. Through the points our speaker presents and through the discussion which follows we hope to bring out some ideas which will be helpful to those who are contemplating military life.

First Speaker:

People who are conscientiously opposed to bearing arms are usually called pacifists. Their lot is not easy. They are often accused of being cowardly or "yellow." Sometimes they are abused. These are some of the arguments they advance to uphold their position.

1. The Bible says, "Thou shalt not kill." This law admits no exceptions, even in cases of self defense. It is better to die than to kill. It is better to let our loved ones be killed than to kill in order to defend them.

2. Christ said not to resist evil. (Read Matthw 5:38-39). This rules out all self-defense, and establishes the idea of non-resistance to evil. Some pacifists are not opposed to catching and punishing criminals in our own society, although, when perfectly consistent, they refuse to resist evil of any kind.

3. Wars often create as many or more problems than they solve. Most pacifists doubt that war solves anything.

4. While it is very difficult to avoid all involvement in a war effort, pacifism bears witness to the principle of love.

Second Speaker:

Non-pacifists do not deny that there is much of evil in war, or that wars may create as many problems as they solve, but they do have some very definite ideas as to why a Christian can and should do military service.

1. The Bible never expressly condemns war, but it does tell us to be loyal to our government. (Read Romans 13:1-7.)

2. War may be evil, but there are greater evils. To have religion blotted out would be worse than death. Failure to resist such an effort would be to condone it. If we fail to resist a killer, we condone his killing. In Old Testament times God commanded His people to go out and make war against the godless.

3. Taking up arms to defend it is one way of witnessing to the importance of that in which we believe.

4. Non-resistance is not always the truest expression of love. A parent punishes the wrongdoing of his child because he loves him. Some pacifists think it wrong to correct their children. God has used war to punish evil nations.

5. Every citizen of a nation contributes to the military establishment whether he wears a uniform or not. Every taxpayer is involved in military service. The only sure way of escaping a contribution to the war effort, would be to renounce one's citizenship and leave the country altogether. Refusal to join a military organization is in reality just a gesture.

6. On many occasions Paul likened Christians to soldiers. Surely he would not have used this figure if it had been contrary to God's will for Christians to be soldiers.

(Have a general discussion of the ideas presented at this point.)

Program Leader:

We must not forget that our chief calling is to be soldiers of Christ in the war against Satan. In this war victory is assured, but the battle must be completed. There will never be any lasting peace on earth or any true freedom from evil as long as Satan has control of the lives of men. The best way of destroying Satan's soldiers is to win them to Christ. Our strategy is to preach the Gospel which is the power of God unto salvation. If Christians before us had been more faithful in this kind of warfare, there would be less need for worry about the warfare of guns, tanks, planes, and bombs, and the place of the Christian in it all.

Helps To Understanding Scripture Readings in *Day by Day*

By Rev. C. C. Baker

Sunday, April 14, *Luke* 19:28-40. It had been prophesied in the Old Testament that the Messiah would ride into Jerusalem on an ass (Matt. 21:5; Zech. 9:9). It was on a colt that had never been ridden that Jesus entered Jerusalem (Luke 19:30). It is quite possible that Jesus knew the owners of the colt (vv.30-33). It should also be noted that He promised that it would be returned (Mark 11:3). Who was it that acclaimed Christ as He rode into Jerusalem (Lk. 19:37)? Upon what basis did they feel He was worthy of acclaim (v.37b)? List the titles given Him (v.38). See also John 12:13. How were the circumstances of

over feast (v.15). When would they next celebrate the Lord's Supper together (vv.16,18)? Yet, even in these sacred moments there was the presence of the traitor (vv.21-23). Strife arose among the disciples (vv.24-27). There was the knowledge that His own disciples would forsake Him (vv.31-34). He, Himself was about to die a horrible death for the sins of the world (vv.17-20). Yet, through it all (vv.14-34) notice how calm and patient Jesus was. Have you learned the secret of love for men and confidence in God that can keep you unruffled in such situations?

Friday, April 19, *John* 12:27-36. No experience of suffering that we endure can compare to the suffering of Christ on the cross, but there are lessons we can learn from the way in which He met His "hour" to help us in our own times of trial. Are feelings of perplexity or distress necessarily wrong, i.e., necessarily a sign of a lack of trust in God (v.27)? Do you think that such feelings are wrong when dwelt upon or pampered (v.27)? What ought the one purpose of all our suffering be (v.28a)? The Christian who trusts His heavenly Father does not need a sign to prove that He is near, but is anxious that others know that God is glorifying Himself, working out His purpose (v.27b), through their suffering (vv.28b-30).

Saturday, April 20, *Matt.* 27:62-66. Notice the extreme precautions (vv.65-66) taken by the religious leaders to see that no rumor of a fictitious resurrection be started (vv.62-66). Notice, on the other hand, the rapid spread of the true report of a real resurrection (28:1-10, 16-20; the Book of Acts). How futile seem all the petty plots of men (27:62-66) to halt the irresistible working of the power of God (28:1-4). In their helplessness, the religious leaders were forced to take the very measures they had been trying to prohibit (28:11-15). Think a little about the power and majesty of God as revealed in the resurrection (28:1-10,16-17). Can any earthly force keep His purpose for the world (28:18-20) or for your life (John 15:4,8) from being accomplished?

NEWS of CHURCHES Around the World

Honorary Degrees

At a recent convocation celebrating the centennial of Queens College, Charlotte, North Carolina, Mrs. W. Murdoch MacLeod, general director of United Church Women, received the degree of Doctor of Humanities. Mrs. MacLeod was presented by President Edwin R. Walker as "the woman whose post of religious service is perhaps the highest within the ranks of the Christian women of America." Mrs. MacLeod also holds the honorary degree of Doctor of Religious Education, conferred in 1954 by Southwestern University, Memphis.

Dr. Rachel Henderlite, of the faculty of the General Assembly's Training School, Richmond, Virginia, and Miss Myrtle Williamson, of the faculty of Stillman College, Tuscaloosa, Alabama, also received honorary degrees at the convocation. Dr. Henderlite, who holds the Ph.D. degree in Christian ethics from Yale Divinity School, led the Bible hour each morning at United Church Women's 1955 Cleveland Assembly.

—From *The Church Woman*

ALABAMA

Birmingham — Men of the Birmingham Presbytery, Presbyterian Church, U. S., recently had as guest speaker at a dinner meeting, Dr. E. C. Scott, stated clerk of the General Assembly. The meeting was held March 12 at the Fairfield City Hall, with the Fairfield Presbyterian Church as host.

FLORIDA

Tampa — The Senior High School Fellowship of First Presbyterian Church here recently held a public show featuring the old art of rug hooking. A contest was open to any Tampan who wished to submit an entry, and an added attraction were the 16 floral arrangements, done by Tampa garden circles, to coordinate with the individual rugs.

Many of the members of the Senior High Fellowship are rug-hookers themselves, including Miss

Martha Dickson, daughter of Dr. and Mrs. John B. Dickson, who has been hooking rugs since she was ten years old. Dr. Dickson is pastor of the First Church.

Miami — Dr. L. Nelson Bell, noted Presbyterian medical missionary of Montreat, N. C., recently preached at Shenandoah Presbyterian Church here to wind up the week of self-denial and prayer for world missions.

GEORGIA

Atlanta — Two major recommendations from ad interim committees of a former General Assembly have been knocked down by votes of the presbyteries within the Assembly. Announcement of results which killed the two recommendations was officially made today by Dr. E. C. Scott, Stated Clerk of the denomination. Of the total 85 presbyteries called upon to ratify the Assembly's recommendations, all but two have officially reported.

By a narrow margin — only 39 to 44 votes — presbyteries failed to approve a recommendation of the 1956 General Assembly that would permit the ordination of women as elders and deacons on a permissive basis within local churches. A change in the Book of Church Order — necessary before any alteration in the status of officers can be put into effect — needed only a majority vote to become valid.

Earlier, another recommendation placed by the 1956 Assembly, was killed in an overwhelming vote of 29 - 54. This recommendation would make changes in the Confession of Faith which would have deleted certain paragraphs dealing with the Church's stand on divorce and remarriage. The proposal called for decisions on remarriage following divorce to be left to the discretion of a committee and the minister within each local church.

In order to change the Confession of Faith, an affirmative vote of three-quarters of the presbyteries is mandatory.

LOUISIANA

New Orleans — A special service commemorating the 110th anniversary of the Third Presbyterian Church of New Orleans was conducted in the sanctuary of the church on March 7 at 7:45 P. M. Dr. C. Penrose St. Amant, professor of Church History at the New Orleans Baptist Theological Seminary and now presently engaged in writing a history of the Presbyterian Church in Louisiana, delivered the historical address on the subject, "Eleven Decades of Grace and Labor."

The session of the present church is composed of C. A. Bader, W. F. Delotues, Vernon R. Kennedy, F. E. Nance, M. A. Quartararo, E. L. Ridlen, C. B. Thomas, George S. Thomas, Joseph C. White and J. T. Young. The Board of Deacons is composed of A. S. Aitken, W. E. Bader, W. C. deBrueys, M. L. Edgett, C. P. Edmonds, C. G. Flaig, O. H Hastings, H. L. Hitt, J. C. Kirkwood, O. C. McNeese John Montgomery, Raymond Nolan, Phillip Quar tararo, H. A. Ridlen, and Arthur Shank. Othe leaders include George Broten, president of th Men of the Church; Mrs. Albert Hurwich, presi dent of the Women of the Church; Mr. George S Thomas, superintendent of the Sunday School Henry Weber, president of the Senior High Fel lowship, Linda Brandt, president of the Pionee Fellowship, and Mrs. Edith M. Flynn, Director o Christian Education.

MISSISSIPPI

Jackson — The engagement of Miss Lenoir Mer cer Williams, daughter of Isham Bowland William of Dunn, N. C., to the Rev. Leslie Campbel Tucker, Jr., pastor of the First Presbyterian Churc in Dunn, was announced here recently. The wed ding is planned for April 27.

Laurel — Mrs. J. Curtis Crane, wife of Dr. J Curtis Crane, recently gave a brief lecture for he many friends here, and illustrated her lecture wit her own paintings.

Dr. and Mrs. Crane, the former Florence Hed dleston, came back to the United States last fal from the mission field in Korea. Mrs. Crane i recognized as an authority on Korean flowers an plants, and has illustrated a book on the flowers.

NORTH CAROLINA

Charlotte — The Rev. Charles E. Kirkpatrick ha accepted a call to become pastor of Forest Cit Presbyterian Church. He was formerly pastor o the Presbyterian Church in Lowrys, S. C. He at tended Presbyterian College and Columbia Theo logical Seminary.

Davidson — Nine Davidson College seniors hav been elected to Phi Beta Kappa, highest academi honor the college bestows.

They are Milton F. Campbell of Taylorsville, Da S. LaFar, Jr., of Gastonia, William W. Daniel o Jacksonville, Fla., and Philip F. Kukura of Delan Fla.

Also, three Tennesseans, John C. Gilmer of Bri tol, F. Leon Howell, Jr., of Copperhill, and Emo Kimbrough, Jr., of Clarksville; Basil Price Sha of Marlinton, W. Va., and Edwin S. Young Louisville, Ky.

Selection is based upon excellence in "gener scholarly attainments," and is limited to not mo than twelve and one-half percent of the seni class. All selected have an average of B plus better.

The selectees are outstanding student leaders well as scholars. LaFar is student body preside Young is editor of the yearbook, Campbell a

Sharp are varsity athletes, Kimbrough and Kukura are honorary fraternity leaders, Daniel is president of his social fraternity and Gilmer is battalion commander in the ROTC unit.

Howell is associate editor of the student newspaper and holds a Union Carbide and Carbon Co. scholarship.

NORTH CAROLINA

Laurinburg — Dr. S. H. Fulton, pastor of the Laurinburg Presbyterian Church, led in a prayer of dedication on the site of the Consolidated Presbyterian College at a ceremony which marked the beginning of service as President of the Board of Trustees of the college for Dr. Marshall S. Woodson, and the beginning of term as vice-president for Dr. Louis C. LaMotte.

A temporary office has been opened in the educational building of the Laurinburg Presbyterian Church.

Lumberton — The annual retreat of the Directors of Christian Education in the Synod of North Carolina was held recently in the First Presbyterian Church of Lumberton. Minister of the host church is Dr. R. F. Sloop, and the Director of Christian Education at the Church is Miss Helen Tillinghast, retiring president of the organization.

Principal speakers for the approximately 115 D.C.E.s in the Synod were Dr. Henry DuBose, former president of Assembly's Training School, and Dr. Sara Little, professor at the Richmond school. Dr. Dubose was the Bible teacher, and Miss Little conducted Group Dynamics at the conference whose theme this year was "Unity in Christ."

SOUTH CAROLINA

Greeleyville — Mr. and Mrs. Ira McLees Moore, missionaries in the Belgian Congo, are in Greeleyville on furlough, and plan to speak at various churches all over the state this month.

Kingstree — Central Presbyterian Church of Kingstree held groundbreaking ceremonies recently for a new church at the present site. The pastor, the Rev. Russell W. Park, Jr., lead the service. Members of the building committee are H. M. Brown, Mrs. Minnie S. Kellehan, Mrs. J. L. Brown, Jack Scott, E. D. Ward, R. C. Rogers, and R. I. Snowden. Treasurer of the building fund is W. N. Kellehan.

TENNESSEE

Nashville — The Rev. and Mrs. Lardner C. Moore of our Japan Mission announce the arrival of a son, Lardner Charles, Jr., in Osaka, Japan, on February 26.

The Rev. and Mrs. John Folta of our Korea Mission announce the arrival of a son, Paul Humes, in Chunju on February 14.

The Rev. and Mrs. Robert Hoffman of our Korea Mission announce the birth of a son, Frank Timothy, in Chunju, on February 21.

The Rev. and Mrs. Herbert Meza and family of our Portugal Mission are scheduled to arrive in the United States on March 23 on an emergency health furlough.

The Rev. and Mrs. Marshall Guthrie and son, of our East Brazil Mission, arrived in the United States February 21 for furlough. They proceeded to Indiana on arrival.

Mr. and Mrs. Walter Shepard of our Congo Mission announce the arrival of their daughter, Charline Anne. She was born on February 21 in the Congo.

Board of World Missions

Nashville — In a record-setting action, 20 missionaries were appointed to service in seven Presbyterian Church, U. S., foreign fields, by the Board of World Missions in its March session here. This was the largest number of candidates for missionary service ever to be approved during a single session of the Board.

Of the 20 new appointees, nine will be engaged in educational work, eight in evangelistic, two in industrial and one in medical work. Brazil's three fields will get seven of the 20, and the Belgian Congo six, Japan and Korea three each, and Mexico one.

At the same time, however, the Board regretfully accepted the resignation of three missionaries, and the retirement of two others. Miss Eliza Gonzales, missionary to Brazil, resigned to be married to Mr. Henry L. Pierre of New York City, and Dr. and Mrs. Wm. W. Beckner, appointed missionaries to Africa, were forced to resign because of ill health. The retirement of Dr. and Mrs. S. H. Wilds, medical missionaries to the Congo, was accepted with expressions of "warm and affectionate appreciation for their service."

In another action, the Board approved a formal statement of policy concerning the marriage of missionaries to nationals of the countries in which they are serving, and another concerning assignment of children of missionaries, should these children later volunteer for missionary service.

The Department of Overseas Relief and Interchurch Aid presented the Board with a comprehensive report of the part played by the Presbyterian Church, U. S., in the world wide relief work of Church World Service. The Rev. Paul B. Freeland, secretary of the department, reported that actual expenditures, plus the estimated value of clothing and surplus foods contributed through the denomination to CWS relief work of all types totaled an amazing $2,485,356.50 in 1956.

"The Presbyterian Church, U. S., ranked fifth among the 35 cooperating denominations within Church World Service, in weight of used clothing provided for relief," Mr. Freeland reported. "Our Church sent to CWS centers 178,293 pounds of clothing. Total receipts of 3,781,664 pounds of clothing by CWS was 23.7% in 1955, itself a record year."

The total value of surplus food distributed through CWS, as reported to the Board, was $27,423,944, or 186,834,717 pounds.

"The cost of distribution to needy in 34 countries was only $734,000," Mr. Freeland said, pointing out this meant that each dollar of the $54,500 provided for surplus food shipment by the Southern Church, paid for distributing 254 pounds of food.

The Board was also told that gifts continue to be received for use on Hungarian relief. Since January 15, $8,049 has come in, Mr. Freeland stated. The total thus far received by the Department for aid to the Hungarians is $34,247. The full load of Hungarian relief very soon must be carried by religious groups, Mr. Freeland warned, since the Red Cross and other secular agencies pulling out within a few weeks, even though mo than 70,000 refugees remain in camps in Austri

The policy statements concerning marriage nationals is as follows:

"General Statement:

"The World Mission enterprise of our Chur should be essentially an expression of the mi sionary purpose and devotion of our own peop and must be sustained primarily by the dedicatio of life and means of our own membership. It to be expected, therefore, that the Board will co tinue as in the past to look chiefly to the your men and women of our own communion for tl personnel needed to carry this enterprise forwa in the world.

"This policy of the Board does not preclude tl enlistment as missionaries of qualified and ded cated persons from other denominational bac ground who are in harmony with the principl and the declared faith of the Presbyterian Chur in the United States, though it is recognized desirable that such persons, wherever willing, shou transfer their membership to our Church in tl interest of the fullest possible identification bo with the sending constituency and the co-worke on the field.

"Nor does the policy of the Board preclude tl appointment as missionaries of qualified natio of other lands, provided they are willing to acce

Appointed to Mexico: Miss Helen Blanch Tannehill, of Dallas, Texas, and Richmond, Va., where she is a student in Assembly's Training School; to go as an educational missionary.

Appointees to Korea:

Mr. and Mrs. Clarence Elmer Prince, Jr., of Dallas, Texas, where he is research assistant in the Department of Electrical Engineering, Southern Methodist University; to go to Taejon College, Korea, as educational missionaries.

Mr. Homer Tyndale Rickbaugh, of New Castle, Pa., and Louisville, Ky., where he is a student in Louisville Seminary; to the Presbyterian Seminary, Seoul, Korea, as an educational missionary for a term of three years.

Appointees to Japan:

Mr. and Mrs. Merle Irwin Kelly of Apopka, Fla., and Richmond, Va., where he is a student in Assembly's Training School; to Nagoya, Japan, and educational missionaries in music at Kinjo College.

Miss Katherine Clements Womeldorf, of Richmond, Va., where she is a student in Assembly's Training School; as an educational missionary to Japan.

LETTERS

From Georgia—"Before I took the JOURNAL, I was warned that 'it was dangerous reading' (a year ago that was). Now it is something I would not want to be without. Enclosed is check for renewal. God 'bless and increase' you."

From Virginia—"I wish to express my gratitude for 'something new' we are having in the JOURNAL's Women of the Church Department — special treatment of the Minor Prophets and the material for Circle Bible study. Let me assure you of my continued prayers for God's guidance in your important work for our Church. Thank your staff of workers for the blessing I have received from the pages of the JOURNAL in the past."

From West Virginia—"I loaned my JOURNAL to one of our members, and after reading it she said, 'When they sent me sample magazines and literature to recommend to my Christian friends, I wonder why they did not include the JOURNAL as the kind of literature to have in the house'?"

From Georgia—"My wife was substituting for an absent teacher in the Women's Bible Class last Sunday, and held in her hand a copy of the JOURNAL, to which she referred during the lesson discussion. At the close of the lesson three ladies (see names and addresses on list enclosed) handed her the subscription price and asked her to send for it. Herewith enclosed check for $9.00 to cover."

From North Carolina—"I do enjoy your paper. It is passed on at once to others who also get inspiration from it."

From North Carolina—"The JOURNAL is a real blessing to me. I teach a Sunday school class and get so much help from its pages. In my opinion it is the best of all our religious papers."

BOOKS

CHRISTIAN PERSONAL ETHICS. Carl F. H. Henry. Wm. B. Eerdmans. $6.95.

The study of ethics is not a new form of intellectual exercise. The ancient Greeks had much to say on this subject. They defined it as the study of forms of human behavior for the purpose of discovering their worth and efficacy as means to the perfection of life. Through the centuries serious thinkers have engaged in trying to reach definite conclusions as to just which acts may be called good and which bad.

Christian ethics goes beyond philosophical ethics. It is the study of human behavior in relation to its approval or disapproval in the light of the Biblical revelation. Dr. Henry believes that the time is ripe for a renewed study of Christian ethics. He says that his studies and reflections on this subject during the years have brought about two major convictions in his mind. The first is the impotence and sterility of speculative ethics which are segregated from the ethics of revelation. The second conviction is that Christian ethics becomes impoverished when unrelated to the problems of secular morality to which the man of the world seeks an answer. These two convictions are dealt with in a masterly fashion and applied in the sphere of Christian personal ethics.

The contents of this volume are divided into two sections. Section I discusses speculative philosophy and the moral quest. Various types of naturalism, idealism, and existentialism are examined in this section.

Section II comes to grips with the redemption of the moral life as interpreted by Christianity and its moral revelation. There are 22 chapters in this section dealing with the distinctive views

tian ethics and the atonement are inextricably bound together. To deplore the atonement, whether it be simply dismissed as superfluous or decried as barbarous, is to deplore Christian ethics. There is no Christian ethics that does not flow directly from the atonement."

Anyone desiring to obtain a comprehensive and constructive guide to Christian living will find this volume to be highly satisfactory. The exhaustive documentation and the penetrating analyses will earn for this monumental work a place of enduring importance among students of Christian ethics. Ministers are expected to give authoritative guidance on life's situations and problems. This volume will assist in this ministry.

J.R.R.

ESCAPE FROM A KILLER

By Lowell Saunders

Moody Bible Institute, Chicago

One of the most vicious threats to human life during cold weather is carbon monoxide gas poisoning. This gas attacks its victim without warning and frequently results in death, comments the Illinois State Medical Society.

The exhaust from an automobile is the most common source of carbon monoxide gas. During cold weather, people often keep the car windows tightly closed. The exhaust fumes seep into the car where they are inhaled. Because of the odorless, colorless and tasteless quality, persons breathing the fumes are unaware of the gas until symptoms develop.

Symptoms may progress from a headache and dizziness to muscular weakness, loss of memory, unconsciousness and finally death. By the time the victim becomes aware of his danger, he may be unable to save himself because of induced muscular weakness.

Sin sometimes reacts upon a person's soul in much the same way carbon monoxide affects his body. Sin in its many guises may seem to be inoffensive, unobjectionable, even harmless. But sooner or later sin makes itself known. "Be sure your sin will find you out" (Numbers 32:23). And sin kills. "The wages of sin is death" (Romans 6:23).

Happily there is one great difference between sin poisoning and carbon monoxide poisoning. The victim of gas may recognize his plight too late to save his life; the victim of sin once made aware of his peril assuredly may be saved, regardless of how far advanced is his condition. The way is simple, but it works every time. "Believe on the Lord Jesus Christ, and thou shalt be saved" (Acts 16:31).

CHILDRENS Page

God Chooses A Man

This man was fighting against God. But one day he met Jesus and was changed to become one of God's greatest servants. He had a warrant from the high priest to go to Damascus and hale men and women Christians to prison and to death. This was Saul of Tarsus, afterwards known as Paul, the Apostle. On the way suddenly a great light shone round him, and he fell to the ground; and Jesus said "Saul, Why are you persecuting me"? Saul was blinded by the light, and he said "Who art thou, Lord"? The Lord said "I am Jesus, the One you are persecuting". And Saul said, "Lord, what do you want me to do"? Jesus told him to go into Damascus and wait there for instructions, and he did. Saul was blind now and had to be led by one of his men. A servant of God came to him in Damascus and told him God had chosen him for a special purpose. Saul made a complete surrender to Jesus and became one of His greatest servants. Read Acts 22:1-16

E.

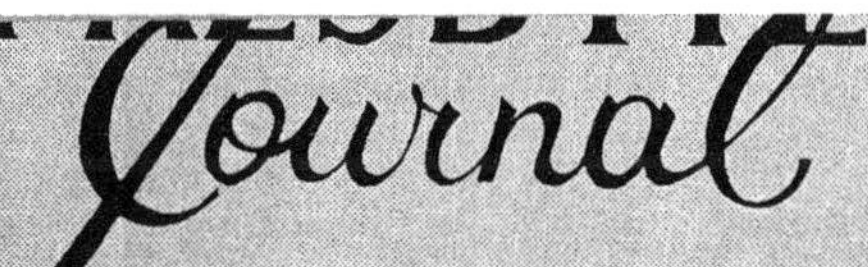

VOL. XV NO. 50 APRIL 10, 1957 $3.00 A YEAR

For The Relief of Human Suffering

"GIVE THROUGH YOUR CHURCH"

To The

EASTER OFFERING

APRIL 21, 1957

Administered By

DEPT. OF OVERSEAS RELIEF AND INTER-CHURCH AID

BOARD OF WORLD MISSIONS · BOX 330 · NASHVILLE, TENNESSEE

THE SOUTHERN PRESBYTERIAN JOURNAL
Rev. Henry B. Dendy, D.D., Editor....Weaverville, N. C.
Dr. L. Nelson Bell, Associate Editor....Asheville, N. C.
Rev. Wade C. Smith, Associate Editor....Weaverville, N. C.

EDITORIAL

One Reason for Our Lack of Enthusiasm for the Councils

The spectacle of church leaders from the iron curtain countries being welcomed at the Evanston assembly of the World Council and given places of responsibility in its work, the tour of Soviet churchmen under National Council sponsorship are some of the reasons why many Southern Presbyterians lack confidence in these organizations under their present leadership.

Hungarian refugees denounced all five Hungarian delegates to the WCC as collaborators of the Communists and specifically accused Bishop Peter, the leading representative in the delegation, of being in the employ of the detested secret police. Information was laid before a Congressional committee to the effect that Bishop Peter had lured his brother-in-law from Cairo to Budapest, where he was then executed.

In spite of all of these things came a report from the WCC's section on social questions expressing confidence that church leaders who cooperate with Communist regimes are loyal to Christ.

The spontaneous action of the Hungarians when Nagy had his few days of power in ousting despised collaborators from places of religious leadership shows how fallacious WCC thinking was.

There are signs that it is at last being realized by some of the council leaders that you cannot do business with any Communists whatsoever, even with those who wear clerical garb. The lesson is being learned terribly late. The effort to establish a wider and wider front for the WCC has cost this organization dearly.

It does not make for respect to be guilty of fatuous thinking. And that, to state it in the kindest possible way, is exactly what the Council leaders have been guilty of in their eager desire to draw the Red religionists into the Council deliberations. —R. S.

Yesterday, Today and Tomorr

In reading D'Aubigny's *History of the Re mation* — a most interesting and reward book — one is struck by the spontaneity which reaction to Romish superstition br out over all Europe at the same time. It comes very clear that although God had cho Luther to lead, it was God and not Lut who awakened the people from their medie slumbers.

A century before, Huss had preached the pel and a few people responded; but there no wide-spread enthusiasm, and Huss treacherously executed. Fifty years before Hu Wycliffe in England preached the gospel a met with some evident success; but oppositi increased as he grew old, and when he di his movement collapsed.

In contrast with these somewhat localized forts largely under the stimulus of one m when Luther sounded the trumpet of justifi tion by faith, he found that nearly everywh people had been thinking the same thougl Zwingli was beginning to preach in Zuri the sister of the King of France had learr of grace; there were stirrings again in Engla — no thanks to Henry VIII; the memory Huss still lingered in Bohemia; somebody Hungary had read the Scriptures; and ev in Italy, in addition to the Waldensians, th were now longings and aspirations. This d not detract from Luther's greatness; he was leader; but the Reformation was the work God, not of Luther.

Will God do anything like this for us tod: May we hope for a great outpouring of grac

At various times faithful servants of the L have arisen to call men to repentance. Th work has not been in vain, for some peo have always responded. Jonathan Edwards a George Whitefield, to mention evangelists an earlier day, saw the results of their lab But the results did not outlast their own liv

Chere was no widespread, spontaneous out- ıreak of true religion. Are today's efforts also ocally restricted to the efforts of one man, or ; there evidence of God's working indepen- .ently in many hearts?

Sober judgment forces us to admit that there ; little evidence of any great reformation; and et on a smaller scale and within a narrower rea there seem to be independent effects of ;od's power. Two instances, in fact.

First, the Southern Presbyterian Church de- isively defeated a merger that would have reatly diminished its testimony to the gospel. Chis was not the work of any one man or any mall group. To be sure, there was a small roup opposed to union from the beginning; ıut their highest expectations were to carry he fourth of the Presbyteries. When to the mazement of everyone, union was defeated by majority vote, when ministers and elders who ad no connection with the smaller group oted against union, the hand of God was dis- ernible above the hands of men. It was a pontaneous and independent awakening.

Now, second, the proposal to ordain women as been defeated. This action was even more pontaneous and independent. No group was rganized to defeat it. Possibly a group should ave been so organized, but it was not. The esult was produced by the desire of widely cattered individuals to obey the commands of ;od. The Scriptures plainly forbid the ordina- ion of women, and the majority decided that ıe church should obey.

This action may be thought to be inconse- uential; this does not have the conventional :appings of a revival; but obedience to God never a trivial matter. On the contrary, this ›ontaneous resolve to conduct ecclesiastical af- iirs in accordance with God's explicit com- ıands may be the herald of greater obedience › come. And if so, one may in faith expect, erhaps not a world-wide or even a nation-wide :formation, but one may in faith expect God's ch blessing to be poured out on the Southern resbyterian Church in the days to come.

—G.H.C.

A Needed Perspective

Life should be lived in the light of eternity. or the unbeliever this is impossible; for the hristian it is often forgotten. How can such a perspective be arrived at and how can it be maintained?

Life should be lived in the light of a *past event*. The greatest event of all history is that which took place on the cross of Calvary. When the Christ of Calvary becomes our Saviour then time and eternity assume their proper places in our thinking, planning and living and this tremendous event becomes the focus of our changed lives.

Life should also be lived in the light of a *present fact*. It is not enough to accept Christ as Saviour from sin for He must also become the Lord of our lives. One of the tragedies of contemporary life is that so many who name the name of Christ show so little evidence of being new creatures in Him. This comes from accepting Christ as a theological concept but failing to admit Him into the heart as the Lord of daily living.

Life must also be lived in the light of *coming judgment*. For the Christian this judgment is past, having been executed on the Cross of Calvary. But for all others its certainty is a matter of paramount import. Hell and judg- ment are no longer popular subjects but they are *realities* and because they are, Christ died for sinners.

In this need for living in a right perspective to time and eternity we find Christ at the heart of the answer, His Cross the center of its power and His living presence the pledge of its everlasting hope.

—L.N.B.

Sky-Pie

Anon there echoes the fling of scornful de- rision at the Church and Christianity: "Pie in the sky bye and bye." Enough truth lies in the solecism to invite study. When either des- perate need of hungry men, or stark material- ism, meets a caricature of the Faith, or thinks to judge Christianity's true nature by its be- trayal on the part of "nominal" Christians, one can but sympathize on the one hand, and decry fake Christianity, on the other. Yet either ma- levolence or plain ignorance lies at the base of the criticism of the pie.

Now it is true that the Scripture advises: " . . . therewith to be content." It is also

The Southern Presbyterian Journal, *a Presbyterian Weekly magazine devoted to the statement, defense, and propagation of the Gospel, the faith which was once for all delivered unto the saints,* published every Wednesday by The Southern Presbyterian Journal, Inc., in Weaverville, N. C.

Entered as second-class matter May 15, 1942, at the Postoffice at Weaverville, N. C., under the Act of March 3, 1879. Vol. XV, No. 50, April 10, 1957. Editorial and Business Offices: Weaverville, N. C. Printed in the U.S.A., by Biltmore Press, Asheville, N. C.

ADDRESS CHANGE: When changing address, please let us have both old and new address as far in advance as possible. Allow three weeks after change if not sent in advance. When possible, send an address label giving your old address.

true that Christianity has been the greatest incentive to enterprise, the chiefest lever of beneficence, the major reliever of human ills, the greatest comforter of sad hearts. Does one quote: "Lay not up for yourselves treasures upon earth?" Add, does the same person, to be simply consistent, play down capitalism and forego all attempts at saving money for a rainy day, or refuse to make attractive investment? Does he reflect on the fact that capitalism has been the fount out of which sweet charity has filled its cup of blessing, and from which beneficence has replenished its cornucopia?

History and experience combine to show that "Godliness is profitable unto all things, having promise of the life that now is and of that which is to come." It is possible that those sympathetic with the sky-pie taunt, have not reflected upon the fact that honesty, integrity and fair dealing, while not by any means limited to Christianity, are, in Christianity absolute. And again do such folk know that the bases of society and government, along with security and peace, are most consonant with revealed religion? Facts indeed show that it is not *true Christianity* that can be charged with the sky-pie doctrine. In no small measure is it due to our holy Faith, the gift of God, that there is any pie at all, anywhere! And Christianity is abundantly worth all that it costs the Christian, and that even if there were no beyond, or, supposititiously, even if Hell were the end of the believer! That Christianity has the greater treasure in the promise regarding the life which is to come, simply makes the Christian religion the more desirable, if not indeed in such light, altogether necessary. Therefore, all this and heaven too, is not to be lightly despised.

The unspeakable value of Christianity to all men, directly and indirectly, is seen in the other quotation: "If in this life only, we have hope in Christ, we are of all men most miserable." This is the great point. Christianity does not deny, but the rather distinctly affirms, that *here* is pie indeed, — and all-important. But what if one gets all *here,* and loses *that!* Yes, so great, so glorious, so unspeakable, according to the Christian revelation, is the future, that the very best which this life affords is neglible by contrast. Men may not believe this; but their unbelief cannot nullify the fact.

Say then that Christianity does not prevent calamity, — say also that Christianity was given to a world already in calamity. Say that Christianity does not prevent disease, — say also that under its aegis, that which has been done for disease, has been done. Say that Christianity does not obviate thievery, — say in addition, that where real Christianity is actually embraced, there are no thieves.

—R.F.G.

"Stand up, speak up, and then shut up," is our advice.

Dr. Luke reports that you are a thin little man, bald, frequently sick, and always so agitated over your churches that you sleep very poorly. He reports that you pad around the house praying half of the night. A healthy mind in a robust body is our ideal for all applicants. A good night's sleep will give you zest and zip so that you will wake up full of zing.

We find it best to send only married men into foreign service. We deplore your policy of persistent celibacy. Simon Magus has set up a matrimonial bureau at Samaria where the names of some very fine widows are available.

You wrote recently to Timothy that "you had fought a good fight." Fighting is hardly a recommendation for a missionary. No fight is a good fight. Jesus came, not to bring a sword but peace. You boast that "I fought with wild beasts at Ephesus." What on earth do you mean?

It hurts me to tell you this, Brother Paul, but in all my twenty-five years experience, I have never met a man so opposite to the requirements of our Foreign Mission Board. If we accepted you, we would break every rule of modern missionary practice.

Most sincerely yours,

J. FLAVIUS FLUFFYHEAD,
Secretary Foreign Mission Board

—From *Famous Unwritten Letters,* by Henden M. Harris, II. Used by permission of the *Baptist Bulletin.*

LESSON FOR APRIL 21

By THE REV. J. KENTON PARK

Jesus' Victory And Commission

Background Scripture: Matthew 27:55 - 28:20
Devotional Reading: I Cor. 15:12-23

In our Devotional Reading the apostle Paul is showing us the importance — the vital necessity of the Resurrection. The phrase, "Logic on fire," which was used to describe the preaching Charles G. Finney, is applicable in a greater degree to the writings of Paul, the theologian. In t first part of I Corinthians 15 Paul states the Fact of the Resurrection, and in the last part of th chapter, the Nature of the Resurrection, and in these verses, 12-23, he pauses to note the dire con quences which would follow, if the Resurrection were not true. There were some who were saying — the Sadducees were of this group — that there is no resurrection. If there is no resurrection, Paul reminds us, then, (1) Christ is not risen, and if He is not risen, (2) our preaching is vain. There is no gospel — no Good News — if Christ is still in the tomb; only sad and distressing news for a world without hope. (3) Your faith is vain. Jesus said to Martha, after He had spoken those great words, I am the resurrection and the life, etc., Believest thou this? The very foundation of faith is here. (4) We are found false witnesses. This was the very message which the church proclaimed: HE IS RISEN. They had seen Him alive and had walked and talked and eaten with Him. Had they been lying when they faced imprisonment and death because they preached what they knew to be true? (5) Ye are yet in your sins. He died for our sins, but He was raised to prove that His atoning death was accepted; that He had conquered death, our last great enemy. The sting of death is sin. He took away sin, and He lives to make intercession for us. (6) They who are fallen asleep in Christ are perished. We will see our dead no more if Christ is still dead. (7) We are of all men most pitiable. Why? Because they had suffered persecution — the loss of all things — for Him.

In verse 20 breaks the sad refrain and exclaims triumphantly; But now is Christ risen from the dead, and become the firstfruits of them that are asleep. In Adam, all die; in Christ, all are made alive. Christ is the firstfruits, and then they that are Christ's at His coming. From this part on he explains and expounds the Nature of the resurrection.

I. *The Burial of Jesus:* 27:55-66.

There are several groups of people who had a part in His burial. First, there were the faithful women who had been watching from afar the crucifixion, and now were continuing watch and see where they laid Him. The plan was to come and bring spices as soon the Sabbath was past. The second group w composed of two men, Joseph and Nicodem (Matthew only mentions Joseph as he is t more prominent). He begged the body of Jes and when he had taken it, wrapped it in clean linen cloth and laid it in his own tom rolling a stone to the door. Isaiah had sa in his prophecy, "and with the rich in death." Joseph was a rich man, a secret discipl as was Nicodemus who came to Jesus by nigh At last they came forward to show openly som thing of their faith and love. The third grou were His enemies who came and asked th: the sepulchre be made sure since He had sai that He would rise again. Pilate said, Mak it as sure as ye can. So they went, sealed tł stone, and set a watch.

II. It has been said that the women wei "last at the cross and first at the sepulchre These women showed their loyalty and lo far better than the men. Even their faith ha not grasped the whole truth, and they wei expecting to find a dead body, not a livin Saviour. None of these devoted women denie or betrayed Him. They had stood as heartbroke spectators at His crucifixion, and now they a rive early in the morning with the spices the had prepared for His body.

One of the facts which clearly proves tł reality of the resurrection is this; none of tł disciples, not even these women, were expectin to find Him alive. All were completely take by surprise, and it was hard for them to belie it. Mary of Bethany, who sat at His feet an listened to His words, seemed to grasp the fa that He was to die, but even she had not take in the further truth that He would rise o the third day. The disciples "wondered what h meant by rising from the dead." This fact di

of the scoffers had said, Let Him come down from the cross, and we will believe Him. To come up from the grave is a greater miracle than to come down from the cross, but they have no idea of believing. Their only thought is to explain away, if they can, what they will not believe. Their hatred of Christ was so strong that they would not even try to see the truth. There is all the difference in the world between a "Doubting Thomas" and these men. God has great patience with an honest doubter who is seeking the truth — or rather, an honest seeker after the truth — and people who deliberately close their eyes and ears and harden their hearts in spite of the most convincing evidence.

IV. *The Great Commission:* 16-20.

Even when they saw Him, some doubted. This is another simple proof of the resurrection. It took time and much evidence to convince all the disciples. Turn to John and read about Thomas, (see John 20:24-29), and also the account of the two disciples on the road to Emmaus, (see Luke 24:13-25), and the verse, "O fools, and slow of heart to believe all that the prophets have spoken."

Let us look at several interesting statements which we find in these concluding verses of Matthew's gospel. First, as a foundation for the Commission, "All power (authority) is given unto me in heaven and in earth." He assumes His rightful place as the Head of the Church and Captain of our salvation. He had power, (authority) on earth to forgive sins; He has the authority to issue these "marching orders" for His followers.

"Teach (make disciples of) all nations." While on earth He had limited His mission largely to the lost sheep of the house of Israel. He made His first appeal to His own peculiar people. It is useless to speculate on what would have been the result if they had accepted instead of rejecting Him. His death was a part of God's plan for saving the world. The "good news" was now to be taken to all men.

This is to be followed by "teaching them to observe all things whatsoever I have commanded you. As His disciples we are to grow, and teaching is necessary for the development of Christian life and service. We are to go on to perfection.

The Commission ends with a word of encouragement: "Lo, I am with you alway".

By THE REV. B. HOYT EVAN

Christ Lives Through Me

Scripture: I Cor. 15:3-8; 12-22; and Col. 3:1-4.

Suggested Hymns:
"The Day of Resurrection"
"Christ, The Lord, Is Risen Today"
"Lord, Speak To Me, That I May Speak"

Program Leader:

Even though we are still young people, we have known many people who have lived and died. Perhaps some of them have been close friends or even members of our families. Whoever these acquaintances were who died, we know that they are still dead . . . they remain under the power of death. In the history of humanity all those who have experienced death are held in its grip, with one notable exception. Christ is that exception. He lived a normal life, He died a very real death, but He rose from the dead and has continued to live ever since. In Revelation 1:18 He says, "I am he that liveth, and was dead; and, behold, I am alive forever more." This fact is important to us not merely because it is unique in history, but even more so because it has a very profound significance for us today. On this Easter day let us give thought to the meaning of the resurrection to our own personal lives.

First Speaker:

An old Negro lady, who worked as a cook in a college boarding house, asked some of the college students to teach in a Sunday School she had organized for the colored children who lived around her home. On an Easter Sunday afternoon one of the students was trying to present some of the rational arguments which are given to prove the resurrection. The old woman listened very patiently, but when the student had finished his discourse she said, "I don't need to have anyone prove to me that Christ rose from the dead. I know He rose, because He lives in my heart."

The resurrection is significant to us for this very reason . . . Christ lives in us today. Jesus said, "Lo, I am with you alway, even unto the end of the world." Matt. 28:20. For Him to make and keep that promise the resurrection was necessary. Because He rose from the dead, and because He continues to live, He can be with us and in us at all times. There is no need for a Christian to be lonely, because Chri is always with Him. There is no reason for Christian to be wanting for wisdom or guidanc because the wisdom of Christ is at hand. Thei is no need for a Christian to be lacking in powe because the One to whom all power in heave and earth has been given is immediately avai able. The Christian has no call to be weighe down with sorrow and discouragement, becau the sympathetic Christ is always at his side. the hymn states it, "Yea, all I need in The I find," and He is always with us because H arose from the dead and continues to live.

Second Speaker:

There is a great contrast in the way that di ferent people respond to the experience of deat when it comes into their homes and to thei loved ones. It is always a cause for sorrow. Fo some it is an agonizingly mysterious thing whicl calls for hysterical expressions of grief. Fo Christians it is an interlude of separation befor the realization of a blessed hope. That hope o restoration and reunion in eternity is based o the resurrection of Christ. Jesus said, "Becaus I live, ye shall live also." John 14:19. He i spoken of as "the first fruits of them that slept" (I Cor. 15:20) meaning that our bodies shall b raised from the grave and reunited with ou spirits even as it was with Him. The Christia hope involves more than the on-going of th soul, it includes the restoration of our bodie for eternity. The resurrection of Christ is th guarantee and demonstration of our hope. Th Bible tells us that when Christ appears we shal be like Him. I John 3:2. This is another im portant way in which the resurrection of Chris has meaning for us today.

Third Speaker:

Jesus said, "Let your light so shine befor men, that they may see your good works, an glorify your Father which is in heaven." Matt 5:16. This command could not be carried ou without the resurrection of Christ from the dead The only light we have to let shine is th spiritual light of Him who said, "I am the ligh of the world." John 8:12. The only light w have in the reflected light of Christ. If He ha

(Continued on Page 18)

Bible Study for Circle Bible Leaders on "Jesus and Citizenship"

Prepared by Morton H. Smith,

Belhaven College, Jackson, Mississippi

Lesson 5: "WAR AND PEACE"

Introduction:

Upon the suggestion of one of our readers, we are going to present a brief epitome of the lesson at the beginning, in which we shall seek to set forth the essentials that should be presented by the Bible teacher to her Circle. Then, following our previous practice, we shall give a detailed treatment of the more difficult aspects of the lesson, so that the Bible teacher may have a full background for discussion and questions.

I. *The Essence of the Lesson*

The problem of war is ultimately theological, not political. In James 4:1-2 we find a clear statement to the effect that wars arise because of the sinful nature of men. Warfare among nations is but the manifestation of the sinfulness of the people who make up the nations. This sinfulness ultimately involves enmity of man against God. Jesus spoke very plainly of this when He told the Jews that as sinners they are the children of Satan. "Ye are of your father the devil . . . " (John 8:44). If this was true of the physical seed of Abraham, how much more is it true of the Gentiles! Paul in Ephesians 2:11-22 speaks of the fact that Christ is our peace. He is the One who has come to establish peace, first of all, between God and men, and then between men. Outside of the Gospel, then, there is no peace, either between God and men or between man and man. But within the Gospel of Christ, we have a peace that passeth all understanding (Phil. 4:7), because we have peace with God our Maker (Rom. 5:1-11).

Permanent peace can be attained only in an acceptance by the whole world of Jesus Christ as Saviour and King. Our task as Christian citizens is to stand for the truth of the Gospel and to proclaim it to the world. We have the answer to the needs of the world in the Gospel of Jesus Christ. "What folly it is, then, for the Church to neglect her real, God-given mission, which is that of delivering souls from the bondage of sin through the preaching of faith in Christ and His finished work, and to embark on programs calling for the reformation of the world through national disarmament and kindred social and political movements." (Boettner, L., *The Christian Attitude Towards War,* Wm. B. Eerdmans, Grand Rapids, 1942.)

As citizens of our nation, it is also our duty to support our government in its efforts to preserve peace and security. We should, of course, encourage our leaders to maintain the integrity of our nation, by the use of just and upright means of preserving peace and security. Since it is God Himself who has given the power of the sword to the State, the Christian should not stand against the use of this power for the preservation of peace and security. (See Rom. 13:1-7.) The State has the task of preserving order in a sinful world, and it must at times use the power of the sword to do so. This is the case with all law enforcement that involves the threat of punishment. When a nation is called upon to wage war to preserve its freedom and security it is simply exercising this same power at the international level. (We shall seek to deal with the problem of war more fully in the detailed portion of our study.)

Until the whole world comes to a recognition of Christ as Saviour and King, we cannot expect to be without crimes or wars. In the light of the terrible destructiveness of modern warfare the Church should be stirred to the utmost to spread the Gospel of Christ, the only means of establishing a real peace. Our own Southern Presbyterian Church, which came into being during a period of war, recognized this in its first historic deliverance. In a letter addressed to all other Churches of Jesus Christ across the world, the Headship and Kingship of Jesus Christ was recognized, together with His Great Commission as the "end of the Church's organization and the condition of the Lord's promised blessing." If we are really interested in Christian citizenship and its relation to the matter of war and peace in the world, then we should examine ourselves and our Church in regard to our obedience to the Great Commission of Christ our King. Are we as faithful in this duty to Him as we ought to be? May God give us a vision of the field, white unto the harvest, and may be each be more faithful in the spread of the Glorious Gospel of Jesus Christ, the Gospel of Peace and Life.

II. *The Lesson in Detail*

Having seen the basic Christian teaching of the subject of "War and Peace," let us now consider in more detail the Biblical teaching on this subject. We shall study especially the question of what the Bible teaches about war, looking at both the Old and New Testaments for a full understanding of the subject.

A. *Teaching of the Old Testament Concerning War.*

There are at least thirty-five references in the Old Testament in which God commanded the use of armed force to carry out His Divine purposes. Loraine Boettner concludes his study of war in the Old Testament with these words: "There is absolutely no question but that in the Old Testament wars were sanctioned as a means of gaining righteous ends. Sometimes wars were used to destroy the enemies of Jehovah. At other times they were used as severe disciplinary measures against the Israelites themselves when they went off into apostasy . . . " (Op. Cit. p. 24).

Following the deliverance from Egypt and the destruction of the Egyptian army in the Red Sea, Moses sang, "Jehovah is a man of war, Jehovah is His name" (Ex. 15:3). In Numbers 33:50-56 we find Him giving the instructions to Israel to go into the Land and to drive out all those who dwelt therein. In the victories of Israel over her enemies it is made clear that God Himself gave them their victory in war. For example, consider Jericho, or Gideon and the Midianites, or David and Goliath. The Battle of Jericho is especially interesting in this connection, for the instructions for that battle, including the instructions to destroy all that were in the city, came to Joshua directly from the Prince or Captain of the Hosts of God. Many commentators see in this theophany none other than the Second Person of the Trinity.

Difficulties Answered

1. That the God of the Old Testament was unjust.

It is irrefutable that the God of the Old Testament is represented as the God who commanded war and who gave victory to His own. Many have questioned the justice of the command of God to the Israelites to destroy the Canaanites. Let us remember, however, that God never acts in a way which is not proper. He does not have to answer to our sense of justice or mercy. Actually, He would have been completely justified if He had cast all of humanity into hell for all eternity, when we sinned against Him. The fact that He has shown His mercy on any is entirely a matter of grace, of unmerited favor. Who are we to find fault with God in dealing with a segment of the human race by means of war to destroy them from the face of the earth? This can be more easily understood when we recognize the utter depravity of the Canaanite culture. Their religion involved a sex-cult which included all sorts of lewd practices. They sacrificed their

It has been argued that in Mt. 5:39 He taught against the Old Testament. "Whosoever smiteth thee on thy right cheek, turn to him the other also." In seeking to understand any Scriptural text, we must always remember that it can only be understood properly in the light of its context. This particular passage occurs in the midst of the Sermon on the Mount. This is a Sermon descriptive of the Kingdom of God, its Citizens, and its Demands. In this particular section He has been expounding the law. He has used the formula, "Ye have heard it was said, . . . but I say unto you . . . " three times earlier. Again this expression must be understood in context. It might be construed to mean that Jesus was changing the old Law. Actually He began this exposition of the Law by affirming that He has not come to destroy it, but to fulfill. Jesus is not changing the Law or setting it aside, but giving the true interpretation of the Law. The thing that He is setting aside is the false interpretation of the Jews. This is seen quite clearly in the earlier cases of murder and adultery. The Jews taught that it was only the open sin that was wrong, whereas the attitude of heart did not matter. Jesus insists that the Law was and is spiritual, and that the intents of the heart is included under the Law. Thus not only is the open act sinful, but all that leads to the act, or even contemplates sin, is sinful.

He is doing the same thing in the passage before us. The Jews had taken the Old Testament prescription that applied to the courts, and applied it to individual personal revenge. "They thought that they did no wrong, provided they were not the first to make the attack, but only, when injured, returned like for like." (Calvin). Christ teaches that it is not the right of the individual to take revenge into his own hands, but rather that he must bear patiently the injuries which he receives.

The injunction not to resist him that is evil is not to be construed as teaching that we are to encourage evil by not standing against that which is wrong. Rather, it is the command to the individual not to resist evil with violence, but to overcome evil by good (Rom. 12:21).

"Turn the other cheek"

Having seen that the whole context of this passage is dealing with the individual, and the matter of personal revenge, it becomes clear that Jesus is not teaching us pacifism in this verse. This is but a further example urging that the individual should be patient, and he should even be prepared for further injury. Jesus Himself did not interpret His teaching literally when He was struck. He gave a rebuke to the man who struck Him, though we may be sure that He was prepared for the further injuries inflicted upon Him that night and the next day. See John 18:22-23, and also Paul in Acts 23:2-3.

It is significant to see that Jesus, in the last discourse, told His disciples to prepare themselves to go forth with the Gospel in these words: "But now, he that hath a purse, let him take it, and likewise a wallet; and he that hath none, let him sell his cloak and buy a sword" (Luke 22:36). In His earlier commissioning of the disciples to go only to the house of Israel they had no need for purse or sword, but now that they are to go into the Gentile world they are to be prepared, both financially and also with means of self-defense. This was a virtual necessity for the traveler of that day. The fact that Peter misused his sword a little later and was rebuked for it does not in the least invalidate this earlier command. Notice that he is not told to dispose of the sword, but to put it up. Due to the danger of man's seeking to rest upon his own strength, Jesus does point out that those who seek to live by the sword shall perish by the sword. Thus the Christian is to learn to put his trust in the Lord, though He does expect us to use the normal and ordinary means that He has provided for our protection, just as He expects us to use means to grow and prepare food for sustenance of life. Our normal means of protection today is found in our police force, which is no less a use of the power of the sword than that of the individual in the first century.

3. Civil Government and the Power of the Sword in the New Testament.

The teachings of Jesus that we have examined have dealt with the individual and not the nations. They can hardly be considered as determinative for the civil actions of nations. Perhaps the most important passages of the New Testament, dealing with the subject of war, are those which set forth the principles of civil government and the power of the sword as granted to civil magistrates. Romans 13:1-7, which we dealt with last month, is the clearest passage on this subject.

"For he is a minister of God to thee for good. But if thou do that which is evil, be afraid; for he beareth not the sword in vain; for he is a minister of God, an avenger for wrath to him that doeth evil." Rom. 13:4.

In this passage we find that the civil magistrate is divinely appointed. He is God's minister. Further, God has given him the power of the sword. This is in contrast to the power of the Church, which is spiritual, namely, ministerial and declarative of the Word. The State has external, physical power, the power of the sword. This power is seen in the police power of a nation or state to enforce its law. This same police power may be exercised legally and properly by one nation against another, when the latter is acting the part of a criminal nation. "As it is sometimes necessary for kings and nations to take up arms for the infliction of such

Week of Spiritual Enrichment

April 14-21, 1957

This pre-Easter Week should be a high week in the Christian experience of women. The chairman of Spiritual Growth and the local presidents plan the observance of this week with the pastor, and enlist the help of the whole Executive Board in the promotion of it. Here are some suggestions for the observance of the Week of Spiritual Enrichment. Local leaders will select from these suggestions that which they feel can be used most profitably for the enrichment of their women. It is believed that all groups will give special promotion to items 1, 2 and 5—

1. Attendance upon all the services of the local church this week.

2. Every woman begin each day with the use of the "For Personal Use" leaflet which has for its theme "Steps Toward Christian Growth." It is hoped that every woman — business women, shut-ins, and inactive women as well as the active women of the church — will be provided a copy of this leaflet before April 14, price 1 cent, from Board of Women's Work. The leaflet is arranged so that it may be mailed without envelope, if it is not delivered through circle visitation program.

3. A poster to be made by the local group giving date and theme of Week of Spiritual Enrichment, to be displayed beginning March 15. An effective poster can be made by putting each word of the theme, STEPS TOWARD CHRISTIAN GROWTH, on a step leading up to a picture of Sallman's "Head of Christ." A copy of this picture will be found in almost every church. If it is framed, the poster may be cut out to let the picture appear in recess. On the opposite side of the picture and slightly lower than the picture would be the words "Pre-Easter Week, Week of Spiritual Enrichment, April 14-21, 1957, for all women of the Church."

4. A day of "house-to-house" visitation to invite women of the community without a church home in the community to become a part of the local church fellowship; and to make contact with the inactive women of the church within their homes.

5. Every woman personally called to set in motion one new operation that will be continued through 1957, designed to strengthen the Christian life and fellowship, such as:

a. Visiting absentees.

b. Serving neighbors to make possible their attendance upon church meetings.

c. Studying with shut-ins some book of the Bible or some subject.

d. Using my home for God, inviting friends I'd like to reach to come into my home for coffee and Christian fellowship.

e. Reading an inspirational book a month, and a Gospel a month in different translations.

f. Memorizing a hymn a month. (Suggested "Hymn for the Home" in PRESBYTERIAN WOMEN.)

g. Recording each night the evidences of God's love and power seen through the day.

6. Special Bible study used by the groups that feel this is the best time. Local leaders are urged to plan the observance of the week, arranging for that which they feel will lead the women to experience some growth. Every woman is urged to plan to put into this week Bible reading, meditation, the reading of stimulating religious books, prayer and service that will make the week different and themselves and others know that our thoughts are on the Risen Living Present Lord of Life.

Helps To Understanding Scripture Readings in *Day by Day*

By Rev. C. C. Baker

Sunday, April 21, *Luke* 24:1-11. For weeks before Jesus' last entry into Jerusalem He had been telling His followers that He would rise from the dead (cf v.6-7 with 9:22; 18:31-33). Notice that it was the women who followed Jesus to the cross (23:49), observed His burial (23:55) and came to the tomb early on Easter morning (24:1-10). The twelve disciples had completely forsaken Him (Matt. 26:56). Contrast the reactions of the women (vv.6-8) and the disciples (vv.10-11) when they heard the news of the resurrection. How did the twelve receive the news (vv.8-10)? Though it was the twelve who became the famous apostles of the early church, it was the obscure women who saw Jesus through His darkest hours and who first learned the news of the resurrection. It is often the obscure saint who shows the greatest loyalty and receives the greatest manifestation of Christ's presence.

Monday, April 22, *Mark* 16:1-8. It is sometimes difficult to fit together all the details of the resurrection story as it is found in the four Gospels. Compare the accounts in Mark 16:1-8 and in yesterday's passage, Luke 24:1-12. In what ways are they alike? Do they differ in any of their details? Why did the angel say, "and Peter" in Mark 16:7? Notice 14:66-72. Read the touching story in John 21:1-23 of Jesus' manifesting Himself to Peter after the resurrec-

the questions? Must a teacher know what the feelings and thoughts of His students are before he can really teach them? Is good rapport important to good teaching? Following these questions, Jesus began to teach them directly (vv.25-27). How did they come to recognize the risen Christ (vv.30-31)? Is it more effective for a person to discover truth for himself than to simply tell it to him? The Holy Spirit similarly teaches us, using our experiences and opening to us the Scriptures.

April 27, *Colossians* 1:15-23. Meditate seriously on each of the phrases in vv.15-20 that describe Jesus Christ. What is said about His relationship to God? to creation? to the Church? to you? These are not simply abstract facts but actual realities of the Person who "made Himself of no reputation and was obedient unto death" (Phil. 2:8). While realizing that our hearts are hard, sinful and rebellious (v.21), we must remember that Christ died on the cross (v.22a) for the specific purpose of making us holy and pure (v.22b). Remember that Christ, being who He is (vv.15-20) can do in your life what you cannot do (v.22b). The cross is the evidence of His desire to change our lives if we will but stop trying to be good and look to Him to make us good.

NEWS of CHURCHES Around the World

The Proposed General Assembly Budget

Atlanta — The 1957 General Assembly will be asked to approve a record budget for Assembly benevolences, of $7,403,175.00, when it meets in Birmingham, April 25, and officially receives the report of the General Council.

The Council, at its semi-annual meeting in Atlanta, March 5 - 6, approved the record 1958 budget. It would mark a 6.41 per cent increase, or $446,279.00 more than the 1957 budget called for.

The addition came in part as a result of Presbyterians breaking their own record in benevolence giving in 1956, when members gave a total of $6,026,283 to General Assembly benevolences. This topped 6,000,000 for the first time in the Church's history and represented a 14.2 per cent increase within the year.

If approved by the General Assembly in April, more than half — $3,775,000 — of the 1958 budget will go to World Missions. Next largest amount $1,623,304 — goes to the Board of Church Extension for work in the homeland, through its four divisions. A total of $613,000 is earmarked for the Board of Christian Education. The Board of Annuities and Relief will receive $444,817. The eight General Fund Agencies, plus administrative expenses of this Fund, will get $933,459 The five Interchurch Agencies are to receive a total of $23,595.

Included in the budget were funds for additional Board funds to develop the church-wide use of the Every Family Plan for the Presbyterian Survey, official magazine of the denomination.

Dr. C. E. Mount, chairman of the Committee to Study Reorganization, recommended that the Division of Christian Relations, now under the Board of Church Extension, be made a separate agency reporting directly to the General Assembly and that it be supported by all the other agencies of the Assembly. The report further recommended that the Council of Christian Relations become a permanent committee of the General Assembly. These recommendations will be presented to the 1957 General Assembly for approval before they become effective.

The special committee studying the possibility of establishment of a "Central Treasurer for Assembly's Causes" was reported on by chairman Thomas A. Fry, Jr., and was in answer to a directive to the Council by the 1956 Assembly through an overture of Mid-Texas. The committee recommended a negative answer to the overture calling for the organizational change. The committee warns that the Assembly "should be reluctant to recommend any change in procedure when things are going so well unless it has overwhelming proof that such a change would increase dramatically the effectiveness, efficiency and appeal of the benevolence causes."

Council members accepted the Program Committee's recommendation that the 1960 emphasis for the Church's program be on the theme "Understanding the Bible." A change in the Church Calendar would move Church Extension Season from the fall to spring, beginning in 1959. The first year for the change places the Week of Prayer and Self-Denial for Church Extension from May 17 to 24 and provides for Church Extension Season to be observed during the entire month of May.

The Council accepted the Executive Committee's recommendations which included promotion of Bluford B. Hestir, director of Publicity, to the status of Publicity Secretary of the General Council.

Dr. J. Farra Van Meter, Lexington, Ky., physician and chairman of the Council, presided over the spring meeting.

The fall session of the Council will be held in Miami, October 9 and 10, for the first Council meeting to be held outside of the environs of Atlanta.

TEXAS

Dallas — Highland Park Presbyterian Church has inaugurated a new mid-week program. The planners of the new program stress it is designed for all members of the Church, youth and adult, single persons and families.

After much consideration and prayer a special mid-week program committee appointed by the session of the Highland Park Presbyterian Church presented a new mid-week service program to the session of the Church where the plan was unanimously adopted without delay and on March 13th the first of the new series was conducted by the Church.

According to the chairman of the Committee, Dr. L. H. Quinn, the Committee concerned itself primarily with planning a program for the mid-week service which would attract the Youth of the Church as well as the adults. Heretofore, the regular mid-week service was attended by an average of 200 members and it had long been felt that this was entirely inadequate for the large membership of Highland Park. Because of the desire to attract the single person as well as the entire families, and the youth as well as the adult alike a program of necessity had to be varied in many ways.

Program Begins With Buffet Supper

One of the outstanding features of the new mid-week service is the feature of enabling the entire family to attend the mid-week service together and to have supper together at Church — something never before realized in Highland Park. At 6:00 p.m. promptly supper is served at a very nominal charge of $.75 for the adults, $.50 for those from six to twelve years old and for those under six, there is no charge. In order to assure an outstanding buffet supper each week a special chef has been obtained to prepare and direct the preparation of the dinner and the menu will be attractive and varied from week to week.

A Brief "Capsule" Devotional Service Follows Dinner

The carefully planned time schedule calls for the brief devotional service to begin promptly at 6:50 p.m. with the audience participating in very familiar hymns led by the Minister of Music of the Church. Each week there will be special music presented by the many choirs of the Church and this will be followed by a "capsule" devotional by one of the Ministers of the Church, Dr. Wm. M. Elliott, Dr. Arthur V. Boand, or Dr. Edwin H. Mohns. This devotional portion of the evening's program will be concluded at 7:15 p.m. promptly, and at this time all will retire to the respective groups and classes for the remainder of the evening which concludes at 8:00 p.m. promptly.

Unusual Classes and Groups Offered

The Church's Nursery and Kindergarten facilities are in full operation for this mid-week program and the mothers and fathers bring their children with full confidence that the children are in good hands, while they the parents are enjoying the mid-week programs.

The children of Primary age have a full schedule of events planned including film strip, cartoons, Bible stories, records, as well as many other appealing programs in which they will take an active part themselves.

The Junior, Pioneer and Senior Group of the Church will have equally attractive programs and these are announced from week to week as they develop.

Unusual Feature is Study Hall for Those Who Want to Study

Realizing that many children would have to stay away from this mid-week service because of necessity of school lessons, arrangements have been made to have as many supervised study halls as necessary to accommodate those who would like to come to church on that evening and still be able to prepare their lessons. The study halls are supervised by qualified persons who can actually

urdays, with a joint choir singing on Sundays. An average attendance of 1,500 voices per night is expected to fill the west end of the vast Madison Square Garden Arena. Approximately 600 trained ushers will be required to staff the tiers of seats in the vast 19,000 seat arena and more than 2,000 churchmen have been recruited for this task.

Auxiliary programs to augment the Madison Square Garden meetings are already under way including the program for young people and the program for college and university students under the direction of Paul Little, former Inter-Varsity Christian Fellowship staff member, and now a member of the Graham staff. An enlarged staff of associate evangelists will join with Evangelist Graham in meeting the need for scores of daily auxiliary meetings including Grady Wilson and Leighton Ford of the Graham team, the Rev. Joseph Blinco and the Rev. Stephen Olford of London, England, Dr. Paul S. Rees of the First Covenant Church, Minneapolis, Minnesota, and Howard Butt, layman evangelist from Corpus Christi, Texas. Special speakers to head a program of pastors' workshops will include Dr. L. David Cowie of the University Presbyterian Church of Seattle, Washington, Dr. Robert Boyd Munger of First Presbyterian Church, Berkeley, California, the Rev. John Stott of All Souls' Church, Langham Place, London, England, and the Rev. Tom Allan, organizer of the "Tell Scotland" movement in Glasgow, Scotland.

Extensive use of radio and television will feature the New York Crusade to a degree that the Graham team has never known previously. Plans call for a night-time telecast over a New York City station to begin with the start of the Crusade meetings and arrangements are also under way for a nation-wide telecast direct from Madison Square Garden over one of the major television networks.

Group reservations from churches throughout the area, as well as from distant cities, have reached a new high in the New York plans. Chartered trains, planes and buses have already been arranged from such distant points as Oklahoma City; Houston, Texas; Nashville, Tennessee; Richmond, Virginia; Louisville, Kentucky; Detroit, Michigan, and Toronto, Canada. An extensive staff is required to handle requests for group reservations which continue to pour into the Crusade headquarters.

Immediate plans for the Crusade call for meetings to continue only from May 15 to June 30, but the availability of Madison Square Garden during July and August have made the continuation of the Crusade a prime subject of earnest prayer on the part of the hundreds of thousands of prayer partners across America and around the world.

Facing the challenge of New York City has forced Mr. Graham and his staff to come to the world's greatest metropolis "literally, on our knees." Billy Graham has often asked for New York to become "the most prayed for spot on the face of the earth."

(It is the hope of this *Journal* that our readers will make this Crusade an object of earnest daily prayer.)

Series on Personal Witnessing To Be Broadcast

Lorne C. Sanny, president of The Navigators, will be guest speaker each Friday from April through June on the worldwide Back to the Bible Broadcast. His series of thirteen messages will deal with the subject, "Individual Witnessing."

In response to the widespread demand for practical know-how in person-to-person witnessing for Christ, Theodore H. Epp, director of Back to the Bible Broadcast, requested Sanny to give the series.

The 36-year-old Christian leader brings to the radio audience a wealth of practical experience in the field of personal evangelism, having worked for fifteen years alongside his predecessor Dawson Trotman in the ministry of The Navigators. Since 1951 Sanny has trained personal counselors and directed follow-up for every major Billy Graham Crusade. Assisted by Charles Riggs, now New York Crusade Director, he trained 8800 church people as personal counselors for the 1954-55 London and Glasgow crusades, and an additional 40,000 throughout Great Britain by means of tape-recorded counselor classes.

Titles of some of the broadcast messages will be, "You Can Witness Effectively," "How To Lay the Groundwork," "The Power for Witnessing," and "Telling the Story."

An outline of the contents of the thirteen messages is available to individual listeners from Back to the Bible Broadcast. The outline includes personal study suggestions for those who wish to follow the series as a course.

Local newspapers will carry time and station for release of the Friday broadcasts.

Brigadier General Troup Miller, Christian Soldier - Christian Layman

With feelings of deepest regret, the Session of North Avenue Presbyterian Church of Atlanta, Ga., must record the passing of one of its most distinguished and useful Elders, who died on January 26th, 1957.

General Miller graduated from West Point in 1902. His first assignment was with the Seventh Cavalry at Chicamauga, Ga. He was a General Staff Officer during World War I, and was awarded the Distinguished Service Medal.

He became a member of North Avenue Presbyterian Church on December 2nd, 1945 by letter from the Fifth Avenue Presbyterian Church of New

CHILDRENS Page

The Prodigal Son

The boy was tired of home and wanted to see the big outside world. He persuaded his father to give him money, and left his home. It was a bad mistake. He met with evil companions and spent his money freely. He lived only for pleasure and soon his money was all gone. His companions deserted him and he was hungry and ragged and miserable. No one cared for him. He went out in the Country and found a farmer who hired him to tend the hogs, As he watched the hogs munching their sloppy food he was so hungry that he wished he could eat with them. Then he thought about his father. He said to himself, "I know my father would forgive me if I go back and tell him I am sorry". And he got up and went. His old father was wishing he would come, and as he looked down the road and saw the boy Coming, he ran out to meet him and put his arms around him and kissed him and forgave him. Jesus told this story to show how our Heavenly Father will forgive us, if when we do wrong, we are sorry and tell him so. Now read the story in Luke 15: 11-32. E.

The Southern
PRESBYTERIAN Journal

VOL. XV NO. 51 APRIL 17, 1957 $3.00 A YEAR

THE SOUTHERN PRESBYTERIAN JOURNAL

Rev. Henry B. Dendy, D.D., Editor........Weaverville, N. C.
Dr. L. Nelson Bell, Associate Editor........Asheville, N. C.
Rev. Wade C. Smith, Associate Editor........Weaverville, N. C.

EDITORIAL

Subjection to Our Brethren in the Lord

The Fourth, or the Fifth— Not the First—Ordination Vow

In our ordination vows we promise subjection to our brethren in the Lord. But this is the fourth vow for the minister and the fifth for the ruling elder. It is not the first ordination vow. Our vows are arranged in proper order both logically and chronologically. Accordingly, this fourth or fifth vow is understood in the structure, order, or framework in which it is taken. The candidate takes this vow only *after* he has taken the first three or four vows, so that this one presupposes the earlier vows, and it is not a pledge to violate any one of the prior vows at the direction of the brethren.

Our first ordination vow sets forth the Scriptures as the Word, of God, the only infallible rule of faith and practice. These Scriptures teach, *inter alia*, "the LORD is our judge, the LORD is our lawgiver, the LORD is our King; He will save us," Isaiah 33.22. And conversely it warns, "In vain do they worship me, teaching as their doctrines the precepts of men," Matt. 15.9. It is my conviction that the Word of God is against women elders. Suppose I were in a presbytery in which my brethren were all in favor of women elders, and they directed me on the ground of my fourth ordination vow to vote for women elders so that the presbytery might have a unanimous action. Or suppose some ruling elder is told by his pastor and session to vote for a divorcee as a ruling elder, when said elder understands I Tim 3.2; Tit. 1.6 as forbidding the election as an elder of a man having two living wives. Now neither my understanding of the Bible on women elders, nor the ruling elder's understanding of the bishop's being the husband of one wife is infallible for everyone else. But it is the Word of God as each understands it, and under our system of doctrine and government we can properly an swer, "We must obey God rather than men."

Or suppose I were in a "liberal" presbyter in which the brethren tried to use the fourt vow to require me to vote for the acceptanc of a minister who could not accept the bodil resurrection, or the virgin birth of Christ, c that He offered up himself a sacrifice to satis divine justice and reconcile us to God — eac of which is taught in our standards and d clared by our General Assembly to be involve in our ordination vows. I could properly repl that my fourth ordination vow was taken su sequent to and subject to my second vow an could not set aside my second vow. Furthe more, under our second ordination vow the sy tem of doctrine taught in Scripture include the proclamation that God alone is the Lord c conscience and has left it free from the con mandments of men which are either contrar to or in addition to it in matters of faith an worship.

Or read carefully the third ordination vov This is not a vague acceptance of somethin that somebody fancies is Presbyterianism, c representative republicanism, or majority ru church government. By the third vow eve ordained minister and ruling elder has solemn subscribed to the government and disciplir of the Presbyterian Church in the United State This government and discipline is anchored i our Lord Jesus Christ as Head and King of th Church, "the only Lawgiver in Zion." "It b longs to His Majesty to rule and teach th Church through His Word and Spirit by th ministry of men, thus mediately exercising H own authority and enforcing His own laws Thus the exercise of Church power has God sanction only when it is in conformity with th laws enacted by Christ the Lawgiver, that i when the courts of the Church limit their de inition of an offense to that which is plain contrary to the Word of God, BCO, 8,9,19,5 179. Accordingly, before a Presbytery, its Con mission, or a Session depose a minister or a elder for failing to obey his brethren in th

Lord, it is the duty of the court to make sure that the court itself is acting entirely in accord with the third ordination vow. It is its duty to assure itself that the charge against the brother is *an offense* according to par. 179 of our Book of Church Order. "Nothing ought to be considered by any court as an offense, or admitted as a matter of accusation which cannot be proved to be such from Scripture." The court ought to take scrupulous care that every right guaranteed by the government and discipline of the Presbyterian Church, U.S., be preserved to the defendant throughout the whole disciplinary process.

The Reformers listed the marks of the Church in the following order: first, the Word, secondly the sacraments; and discipline only in the third place. Accordingly, Protestants object when separatists, under the name of a Twentieth Century Reformation, reverse the order and treat discipline as the first mark of the Church, and declare every denomination in which there is not adequate doctrinal discipline as apostate.

Similarly, Presbyterians U. S. object when in the name of Presbyterianism the order of the ordination vows in our Book of Church Order is reversed, and the fourth or the fifth treated as though it were the first.

Subjection to our brethren IN THE LORD means obedience to the Word of the Lord, by the grace of His Spirit, in the fellowship of His family, in the spirit of meekness or gentleness, under the example of Him Who being in the form of God took the form of a slave that He might be obedient even unto the death of the cross — and so give Himself a ransom for many. This kind of subjection does not exalt any brother or group as bishop or overlords. It keeps before all that Jesus Christ ALONE is the Lord and the Head and the King and the Lawgiver in the Church. —W.C.R.

A Layman Looks at the Resurrection

By L. Nelson Bell, M.D., F.A.C.S.

Breaking through the gloom of death and hovering over the seeming finality of the grave there abides the certainty of the resurrection morning; of a morning centuries ago when two men in dazzling robes stood in an empty tomb and exclaimed, *"Why seek ye the living among the dead: He is not here, but is risen: . . ."*, and, the certainty of a yet future morning when, *" . . . The Lord himself shall descend from heaven with a shout, with the voice of the archangel, with the trump of God: and the dead in Christ shall rise first: . . . and so shall we ever be with the Lord."*

The true significance of the Cross is inexorably linked with the empty tomb, for while the Cross is the central event of all history the reality of man's redemption is validated by the resurrection.

Without the resurrection our Lord's death on the Cross would have been the symbol of a lost cause. But because He arose from the dead the Christian faith and eternal life combine into one glorious hope.

Without the resurrection there is no Gospel to preach. Because of Christ's victory over death and the grave the Gospel is a message of life and victory for everyone who believes.

The Necessity of the Resurrection

As the plan of God's redemptive work for sinful man unfolds, the resurrection emerges as an absolute necessity. Prior to any resurrection there must have been death, and we know that death came into this world because of sin. If Christ's work of redemption was to be effective then He must triumph over all the results of sin. The resurrection therefore becomes living proof of His power as Saviour.

The curse of sin not only has passed from man to man and from generation to generation but the ground itself was a partaker of the curse: . . . *"thorns and thistles shall it cause to bud."* The crown of thorns worn at Calvary was not merely a symbol of the derision of His tormentors. Rather we believe it to be a divinely ordained symbol of His bearing in His body the penalty of sin, — in man and in nature.

The Southern Presbyterian Journal, *a Presbyterian Weekly magazine devoted to the statement, defense, and propagation of the Gospel, the faith which was once for all delivered unto the saints,* published every Wednesday by The Southern Presbyterian Journal, Inc., in Weaverville, N. C.

Entered as second-class matter May 15, 1942, at the Postoffice at Weaverville, N. C., under the Act of March 3, 1879. Vol. XV, No. 51, April 17, 1957. Editorial and Business Offices: Weaverville, N. C. Printed in the U.S.A., by Biltmore Press, Asheville, N. C.

ADDRESS CHANGE: When changing address, please let us have both old and new address as far in advance as possible. Allow three weeks after change if not sent in advance. When possible, send an address label giving your old address.

Isaiah, writing of the ultimate triumph of the Gospel, tells of a day when: *"Instead of the thorn shall come up the fir tree, and instead of the brier shall come up the myrtle tree: and it shall be to the Lord for a name, for an everlasting sign that shall not be cut off."*

In the light of the unfolded Gospel, revealing as it does God's love for man and the redemption which He had planned in and through His Son in the councils of eternity, the resurrection becomes an absolutely necessary part of the whole.

The Fact of the Resurrection

That our Lord arose physically and visibly from the dead is one of the best attested facts of all history. Remove the resurrection story from the historical records, — in the gospels, in the history of the early Church as given us in the Acts of the Apostles, in the Pauline and others letters, and in the book of the Revelation, and the crowning proof of Christ as Saviour, and of the immortality of the soul, vanishes from sight.

The evidence is so overwhelming, and the effect so transforming, that a study of the record brings with it the certainty of the resurrection. It was first ignored, then disbelieved and finally accepted as the crowning proof of the Christian faith.

The scriptural record is one of internal evidence beyond the realm of collusion. The disciples never understood our Lord's frequent references to his death and resurrection. After He had risen from the dead they still doubted. Only as they were confronted with *"many infallible proofs"* was their unbelief and hopelessness transformed into a burning assurance. Only then did they know that the One they had seen die on the cross and then knew had been buried in a near-by tomb was alive.

They *knew* this same Jesus was alive.
They *saw* Him.
They *heard* Him speak.
They *touched* Him.
They *ate with* Him.

They were aware of the amazing fact that while in some way He was changed He had the *same body* for they saw the scars in His hands and feet and at least one of them was invited to end his persistent doubts by thrusting his hand into the wound in His side.

In the succeeding days they frequently enjoyed the fellowship of the risen Lord. His miraculous powers were still in evidence and His command to them to go out, after they had received the power of the Holy Spirit, and make disciples of all nations was an impelling commission which turned timid and ignorant men into flaming evangels of whom it was said that they

A final impelling truth: his disciples were confused and dull of understanding when He referred to His coming death and resurrection; they frankly admit that they did not at first believe the resurrection story; collusion for the removal of the body would have been impossible; then, they saw, and touched, and heard and lived with the risen Lord:

It Transformed Their Lives

Because the resurrection was crowning and *visible* evidence of the power of God to these disciples; unlearned and ignorant men; fearful and scattered as sheep without a shepherd; yet these same men were completely transformed.

To the end of their days evidence of a lack of formal education remained with them. But the educated and the powerful were amazed in their presence and *"took knowledge of them, that they had been with Jesus."*

These same disciples who had fled before the torch-lit mob headed by Judas; (one of whom had cursed and sworn that he knew not the Christ), — these same disciples stood unafraid and unabashed before the murderers of Jesus and said: *"Be it known unto you all, and to all the people of Israel, that by the name of Jesus Christ of Nazareth, whom ye crucified, whom God raised from the dead, even by him doth this man stand here before you whole."* And, when ordered not to preach in His Name and threatened with dire punishment should they do so, they prayed — not for protection but for courage: *"And now Lord, behold their threatenings: and grant to thy servants, that with all boldness they may speak thy word . . . "*

Weak in faith and turning again to their fishing nets in their disillusionment, these same disciples were suddenly transformed by the blinding light of a new faith, a knowledge that the Lord they thought to be decaying in a tomb was alive — that He had triumphed over death and the grave — *and this realization completely transformed their lives.* Instead of returning to a quest for the fish of Galilee, they went out to preach the Gospel of redemption and a new life in their risen Lord: *"Whom God hath raised up, having loosed the pains of death: because it was not possible that he should be holden of it."*

Nothing less than the visible, bodily resurrection of the Lord Jesus Christ; a fact beyond any possible doubt; a transforming event which itself became *a doctrine to be preached;* nothing less than the infallible proofs which they themselves had seen and experienced could account for the transformation of these men.

How Has the Resurrection Affected You?

The Christian religion is a supernatural religion and it has a supernatural effect on those who believe. It is folly to try to confine God to the natural realm. We the creatures can but humbly bow in the presence of the Creator.

In God's plan of redemption the supernatural is seen on every hand. Our Lord, the eternal Son of God, is a supernatural Person. That He emptied Himself and came into this world was itself a supernatural act and it was accomplished in a supernatural way — His virgin birth. His life showed His supernatural powers and His death accomplished a supernatural redemption for those who will accept it. His resurrection, while a supernatural event was but the natural consequence of both His person and His power.

Therefore, faith in the resurrection of our Lord and the assurance that believers have immortality and will spend eternity with Him is an absolutely necessary corollary of the Christian faith. He lives and we who believe in Him will live too.

Our faith is not in a dead man but in a living Saviour and Redeemer. The resurrection story and its effect on the hearts and minds of believers is the crowning evidence of God's saving grace. Prove it? Talk with Him today and He will make His living presence a reality in your life.

Faith in the resurrected Lord transformed a group of timid and unlearned men so that they went out and established the early Church against seemingly impossible odds. Has faith in Him and His resurrection power made any difference in your life?

These disciples of old went out to preach: *"This Jesus hath God raised up, whereof we are witnesses."* They did this because He had poured out His Holy Spirit upon them and they went in the wisdom and in the power of that Spirit.

That which God did through His disciples nineteen hundred years ago He wants to do through you and me today. Paul saw this same risen Lord and He transformed him. Later he was able to make this profound affirmation: *"I am crucified with Christ; nevertheless I live; yet not I, but Christ liveth in me: and the life which I now live in the flesh I live by the faith of the Son of God, who loved me, and gave himself for me."*

Brothers . . . *That* is LIVING!

LESSON FOR APRIL 28

By THE REV. J. KENTON PARKE

The Book Of Beginnings

Background Scripture: Genesis 1 and 2
Devotional Reading: Psalm 104:1-13

We begin today our "Studies in Genesis." In some ways Genesis is the most important book i the Bible. Dr. Campbell Morgan says that every important doctrine, or truth, of the Bible, is foun in this book. The book is called "Genesis" because it records the beginning or generation of things It sets forth several beginnings: that of the world, of life, of domestic relations, of the moral order of sin and its consequences, of the scheme of Redemption, of nations, and of the Messianic nation This statement makes clear two facts: "The design of the Bible is to reveal the Divine plan of redemption in Jesus Christ, and the other, that the understanding of the Bible requires a knowledge of the Book of Genesis." (New Analytical Bible).

In Psalm 104 we have a very lovely description of Creation and God's Providential care of the earth. In verses 6-13 His "Watering System" for the world is described. Men spend countless millions of dollars and constant effort to water a city like New York. With what ease does God water the earth from His chambers! The vapor rises from the ground, the rain and snow come down from the clouds, springs burst from the sides of mountains, streams run among the hills, great rivers rush on to the seas, and these waters are restrained and controlled by Him. When we think of all His wondrous works, "Our meditation of Him will be sweet."

In our study today we have the creative work of God with special emphasis upon the creation of man.

I. *The Beginning of the Material Universe:* 1:1-19.

First there was the creation of the heaven and the earth. The earth was without form and darkness was upon the face of the earth. Then the Spirit of God moved upon the face of the waters. Light came at the command of God, Let there be light. Thus the Day and Night were made. Then came the "expanse" in the midst of the waters, and God called this expanse heaven. The waters were then separated and the dry land appeared. And God said, Let the earth bring forth grass, the herb and the fruit tree, and it was so. Then came the greater light to rule the day and the lesser light to rule the night, and the stars. Thus, in perfect order, and natural order, the material universe, the mineral and vegetable kingdoms, were brought into being.

II. *The Beginning of "Living Creatures":* 20-25

We have the Hebrew word to "create" use again in verse 21 as it had been used in verse 1 A new development came as God created grea whales and every living creature that movet in the water and in the air. In verses 24-2 we have the other part of the animal kingdom the beasts of the earth. Wonderful as the vege table and mineral kingdoms are, the anima kingdom is even more varied and marvelous When we consider all the insects and bird and fish and land animals of every description we begin to realize something of the wonders He hath wrought.

III. *The Beginning of Man:* 26-31.

In verse 27 we have the word "create" used a third time in this chapter. When God comes to the creation of man the wording is changed: "Let us make man in our image, after our likeness: and let them have dominion over the fish of the sea, and over the fowl of the air, and over the cattle, and over all the earth." Man was to be ruler, king, of all the othei creation. So God created man in His own image We believe this to be moral and spiritual like ness, and that knowledge, righteousness, and holiness were the distinctive marks of humanity Man was created male and female, and com manded to be fruitful and multiply and replen ish the earth and subdue it. He was to have a vegetable diet, but meat was added later (See Genesis 9:3).

In Genesis 2 we have several important de tails added:

1. The resting of God on the seventh day He blessed this day and sanctified it. This reason for keeping the Sabbath is given in Exodus 20:10 and 11. In Deuteronomy 5:15 an additional reason is stated, that God had brought them out of Egypt. When Christ rose from the dead on the First day of the week the church gradually changed their day of rest

and worship to the First instead of the Seventh. We can see this plainly if we read the book of Acts, the Epistles and Revelation. Upon the first day of the week let each one lay by in store, says Paul in I Cor. 16:2. In Revelation 1:10 it is called the "Lord's Day." It commemorates the resurrection. So, in thinking of the Christian Sabbath, or Lord's Day, we can combine three great ideas: Creation, Redemption, Resurrection. Business and Pleasure are both trying to rob us of our Sabbath. It is still true that "A Sabbath well spent, brings a week of content." When we give our Lord His Day and spend it in worship, rest and in doing works of necessity and mercy, it will be "well spent." It was made for man, and rightly used by man will be a glorious blessing.

2. In verse six there is an indication that the earth was at first watered in a very gentle manner by a mist that went up from the ground. When the Flood came everything was disrupted; the fountains of the great deep were broken up, the windows of heaven opened, and there seems to have been a cataclysmic change. Paul speaks of the whole creation groaning together waiting for our redemption. Some geologists believe that the climate of the world underwent a most radical change, and there is much evidence to support that view in fossil ivory found in Siberia and in the broken strata of the earth. Those of us who do not enjoy terrible storms wish that we could get back to the original method of watering the earth. Perhaps when we have the "new earth" this will be true.

3. The Garden of Eden. There has been a great deal of discussion as to just where it was located, but it is generally conceded that the Euphrates and Tigris rivers give the general location. Four rivers are mentioned in verses 10-14. Eden is a synonym for an ideal home, a real Paradise. This Paradise was lost but will be regained when the new heavens and earth are made.

The man was not to live a life of idleness; he was to dress and keep the garden. I can think of nothing more delightful, for I have always loved a garden. We often see on television the garden of some wealthy man with its flowers and trees. Suppose we had a garden where there were no pests nor diseases nor weeds nor briers, would it not be a delight to "keep" such a place? We enjoy keeping a garden even though we have to fight all its varied enemies. Work itself is not a curse or hardship. The thorns and thistles the pests and diseases, are part of the curse that came when man fell into sin.

Man was to eat of every tree of the garden except one; the tree of the knowledge of good and evil; "For in the day that thou eatest thereof thou shalt surely" (Hebrew, dying thou shalt die"). Man was to be tested to see whether he would obey the will and command of God. Our Catechism says that mankind being left to the freedom of their wills, fell from the estate in which he was created.

4. The making of "an helpmeet for him." This does not conflict with the simple statement of chapter one, but tells how God did it. Matthew Henry makes the well-known comment: woman was not taken from man's head that she might rule over him, nor from his feet that he might trample upon her, but from his side that he might love and protect her. In this beautiful way God made the woman to be a companion to the man, and populate the earth. When Jesus was questioned about divorce He made it plain that God created man male and female and that they should be one flesh, loving each other and helping each other.

We have here the beginning of a real home. When God's plan and purpose in marriage is carried out home becomes the nearest thing to heaven that we will know while on this old earth. When God's plan is changed and corrupted we find that home becomes a place of jealousy, hatred, immorality, and utter confusion. There is nothing more beautiful than one man and one woman living together in love; there is nothing uglier than some of the relationships we call home. Our multitudes of broken homes are a shame and scandal to our nation. As a pastor I find more heartaches and tears in such homes than anywhere else. What a wonderful and beautiful plan God had for our homes! What a mess sinful man has made of it! In our next lesson we begin to see what havoc sin made of the home.

Verses 19-20 tell of the naming of the beasts and fowls of the air. We get an inkling of the "knowledge" that Adam must have had. He named them all and God accepted his names. I do not believe that even Solomon could have been put to a more severe test. Adam is no "cave man" with horridly ugly features and unkempt hair as we see him portrayed in some of our books, even textbooks in schools. No! Our First Parent was a kingly man, made in the image of His God. Let us refuse to be misled and insulted by the fancies of ignorant men. Let us rely upon the Word of God to give us a true picture of the first man.

By THE REV. B. HOYT EVAN

"How Do I Know It's Love?"

Scripture: I Corinthians 13

Hymns:
"Love Divine, All Loves Excelling"
"Jesus, Thou Joy of Loving Hearts"
"More Love to Thee, O Christ"
"O Perfect Love"

(This is the first of a unit of three programs on courtship and preparation for marriage. Some groups have found it very helpful to invite a young married couple from the church to be on hand for programs of this type to answer questions. The most satisfactory arrangement would be to announce each program the week before it is to be presented, ask the young people to write out their questions, and then let your resource couple study the questions and give their answers the following Sunday. The questions need not be signed.)

Program Leader:

We are probably living in a time when more is being said about love with less understanding than ever before. With all the talk and advertisement about love, it is only natural for us to want to know what constitutes real love. It is certainly a matter of concern for Christians because all love finds its source in God. "God is love." It will be helpful to know how to weed out the false from the genuine in all our relations of love, and especially in our boy-girl relations.

We need to realize that the attraction which boys and girls feel for each other is perfectly natural. It is a part of God's plan for the happiness and welfare of the human race. Dating is a normal and useful outgrowth of this natural feeling of attraction. Dating, when it is done wisely, helps young people grow in genuine love and prepares them for marriage. In this program we want to discover how we, through our dating, can know when love is real.

First Speaker:

One question which nearly always comes up for consideration when we think about courtship is the matter of going steady with one boy or one girl. Many young people feel there are advantages. It is comforting to think that someone cares for you particularly. There is a sense of security in knowing that you have a companion for every party and every ball game. There are also disadvantages to steady datin and it seems that they may well out-weigh t advantages. Going steady is very likely to lim your associations with other young people, bot boys and girls, at a time when you need to kno a number of people in order to make compar sons. It is difficult to recognize real love unle you have other relationships and associations t which you can compare it. Steady dating als flirts with the danger of getting young peop emotionally involved far beyond their physica financial, and social maturity. Practically a authorities agree that it is normally better t include several boys and girls in your datin for some time before settling down with "steady."

Second Speaker:

True love takes time to develop and t be discovered. There is certainly an eleme of romance and glamour connected with fallin in love, it it is often over played in fiction an in the movies. Love which is built altogethe on "high-pressure" courtship of expensive en tertainment, artificial glamour, and excitemen is in for a rude awakening when it discover that life is not like that. Love that require all these "shots in the arm" to keep it goin is not real love. "Low-pressure" courtship where people enjoy each other even withou any artificial props, are more likely to gro into real love. It sounds very un-glamorou but someone has said that successful marriag is about seventy-five per cent practicality. I you want to know whether or not love is th real thing, put it to the test of practicality. D you enjoy doing simple things together, lik working and studying, as well as exciting ac tivities? Life offers more of the former tha the latter. Love had better be able to flouris on a "low-pressure" basis.

Third Speaker:

Some of the happiest couples you will fin today are those whose courtship was carrie on in connection with the church and churc activities. One man who is still very muc in love tells of joining in the family prayer at the home of his girl friend after he ha walked her home from church on Sunday eve

(Continued on Page 14)

Strengthening Our Prayer Life

Believing Prayer to be the proper undergirding of Christian growth and achievement, the Spiritual Growth Committee looked about for ways of strengthening the prayer life of the women of First Presbyterian Church.

Feeling that a Home Circle member has a unique opportunity in her "quiet times" for real service in intercessory prayer, we have asked by letter each (as many as are able) to be prayer partner to a member of the Board and to join the Assembly Wide Fellowship of Prayer. One member already has expressed appreciation and enthusiasm.

The Bible Leaders were asked to organize each circle as a prayer group, and individual circles then adopted various plans for prayer partners and group prayers. Since Bible Leaders rotate among the circles, we are organized as prayer partners within our group.

For closer contact between the committee and individual circle members, each circle chairman was asked to appoint a Spiritual Growth Representative who will meet with the Bible Leaders for Bible study under our Pastor (Dr. Charles L. King) and share the privilege and inspiration of hearing him teach.

Her duties will be: first, to take back to her circle mimeographed outlines of the Bible lesson for further personal study, reminding members to study for next month the lesson in Work books and Bible.

Second, she will remind her circle to pray for each other and will receive requests from members for prayer by the circle (this has proven wonderfully helpful in several groups.)

Third, she will meet with the board next month and take charge of Let's Talk About in the circle meeting.

Fourth, she will remind members of the monthly Prayer Objectives (which will include the special Church Emphasis and Let's Talk About topic each month) and of special days or weeks of prayer, distributing pertinent printed material on occasion.

These prayer objectives are published each month in our local Church paper which goes to every home. For January we printed:

"WOMEN OF THE CHURCH."

"Will each of you clip the following Prayer Objectives and tuck them into a corner of your mirror where you'll be reminded at least once a day to join the rest of us in prayer? Prayer works wonders.

"1. Pray for the strengthening of our Faith in and our use of Prayer in matters of personal and public interest.

"2. Pray that in 1957 we may so relate our personal lives to Christ that it will be reflected in our relations to others in the community.

"3. Pray that we may so use this Year that we may, next December 31, feel that we have grown in grace, and in the knowledge of our Lord and Saviour Jesus Christ!" (2nd Peter 3:18).

Mrs. Milton Breckland
Chairman Spiritual Growth
First Presbyterian Church,
Houston, Texas

A New Book on Prayer

A Simple Guide to Prayer by Stephens

Here is an enjoyable book for personal reading and spiritual profit. The author makes a fresh approach to old truths. His language arrests attention, while his treatment of the subject opens up vistas for new and developing ideas in the mind of the reader, concerning man's relationship to God and God's relationship to man.

While the treatment of the subject earns the title "A *Simple* Guide to Prayer," it is at the same time sublime in its simplicity, stimulating to thought, and pictorial in its expressional structure.

The book is in itself a testimony to the author as a man who *knows* God. It gives the reader confidence that the treatment is by one who has spent a lifetime in communion with God and in contemplating the privilege and the wonder of His fellowship which is open and available to every man of faith and humility.

A Simple Guide to Prayer is recommended for reading in the Week of Spiritual Enrichment because of what it will do to lead the reader forward in spiritual adventuring for God.

The book may be ordered from the Presbyterian Book Stores: Box 6127, Atlanta 8, Georgia; Box 1020, Dallas 21, Texas; Box 1176, Richmond, Virginia. The price is $2.00.

VICTORIOUS PRAYING. Alan Redpath. Fleming H. Revell. $2.00.

The eleven sermons in this volume are all based on the Lord's Prayer. They were first given from the pulpit of Moody Memorial Church of Chicago. They evoked such enthusiastic appreciation that the congregation requested their publication. The author brings out some of the unfathomable depths of the Lord's Prayer and shows how it is a pattern for the spirit of all who would pray acceptably to God.

It is interesting to note that Dr. Redpath demonstrates how the Lord's Prayer is full of Christ from the beginning to end, even though it does not mention Him by name. This book is deeply devotional and will lead the Christian to new heights of Christian experience.

—J.R.R.

Jesus Is There

There is never a load too heavy,
Nor a hill too hard to climb,
When we have a wonderful Saviour
Who is always walking behind.
There is never a day of darkness,
When we feel we have lost the way,
For the shadows will turn into sunlight
And our Saviour will show us the way.
So whether it's darkness or sunlight,
Our burdens grow heavy to bear;
Stop, and listen behind for the footsteps —
For Jesus must surely be there.

—Mrs. Ruby R. Thompson,
McDonough, Ga.

NEWS of CHURCHES around the World

ALABAMA

Birmingham — "Minister for a day," a new program at the University Hospital under the sponsorship of the Birmingham Ministers Association, got underway in March with the Rev. James Cantrell, pastor of the Third Presbyterian Church of Birmingham as the first pastor on duty.

The "Minister of the Day" visits with patients in the hospital to offer his friendship and to give spiritual comfort. More than 60 Birmingham ministers have volunteered to give one afternoon of every 60 days to help with this service. If a patient expresses a desire to see his or her own pastor, then the minister of the day and the hospital attendants cooperate in notifying the requested pastor. Several ministers of different denominations have agreed to answer any calls where patients express a denomination preference.

The program is a volunteer service by various religious groups in Birmingham, and one of the projects carried on for the welfare of the patients and their families.

ARKANSAS

Fayetteville — Some three hundred people are expected to attend the fourth Southwest Conference of Christian World Missions, to be held here June 30 - July 5, at Mt. Sequoyah, near Fayetteville.

Presbyterians from Arkansas, Missouri, Oklahoma and Texas will make up most of the total attendance.

Among conference speakers are Dr. Henry Smith Leiper of the World Council of Churches, who will bring the opening address on Sunday evening, June 30, and each morning will teach a course on the Ecumenical Church; Dr. J. Carter Swaim, Director of the Department of English Bible Division of the National Council of Churches, who will present a Bible meditation each morning and teach a Bible class later in the morning; and Mrs. Rosa Page Welch, who will direct vespers every evening. Three years ago, Mrs. Welch went around the world on a Christian witnessing mission, under the sponsorship of the United Church Women, and Presbyterian and Disciples of Christ women's groups.

FLORIDA

High Springs — A complaint, taken by Rev Arthur A. Froehlich and Rev. Thompson L. Casey Jr., against an action of the Synod of Florida, i coming before the General Assembly in April.

The complaint is against an action of the Com mission on the Minister and His Work of St John's Presbytery and the Synod's action in no sustaining the complaint of the Maitland Churc taken against this action of the Presbytery's Com mission.

On the night of May 17th, 1956, the Commission on the Minister and His Work of St. John's Presbytery dissolved the Pastoral Relationship between Rev. Arthur A. Froehlich and the Maitland Presbyterian Church and the official relationships between the Elders and Deacons and the church.

September 10th, following the last meeting of the Synod of Florida, the Rev. Arthur Froehlich and the four Elders of the Maitland Church were deposed from their respective offices. An appeal to the Synod of Florida has been taken by them against this action.

Thompson L. Casey, Jr.
First Presbyterian Church
High Springs, Florida

Jacksonville — From a chicken coop to a church in seven months and ten days — that's a dramatic story of conversion in any language, but for a small group of Presbyterians in Jacksonville it particularly means the result of much prayer, hard work, and generous giving.

It all began in the spring of 1956 when Suwannee Presbytery's Home Missions Committee purchased a ten-acre chicken farm in a rapidly growing residential area of southwest Jacksonville.

The few buildings on the newly acquired property — a bungalow, a brooder house, and several chicken houses — made up all the physical facilities of what was the beginning of a new Presbyterian Church. The Rev. William T. Baker, who for more than eight years was the Visiting Minister at Jacksonville's Riverside Church, one of the sponsoring churches of the project, was called to lead the growth and development of the little building chapel. Other Presbyterian churches in Jacksonville, besides Riverside — Lake Shore, St. Johns, and Murray Hill — joined in the plan.

The new group — later to be known as the St. Andrew's Presbyterian Church — got its organized beginning under the guidance of St. Andrew's Chapel Committee. This committee was headed by Mr. Baker, chapel minister, and was composed of an elder from each of the sponsoring churches; the Rev. Joseph W. Conyers, executive secretary of Suwannee Presbytery; and three members of the chapel .

With an investment of $1,400 in materials, the brooder house was soon converted into a chapel worth $6,000. All of this was done by volunteer work by the Men of the Church of sponsoring churches, under the direction of Howard Kaufold, an elder in the Murray Hill Church and member of the Home Missions Committee. The first service was held at St. Andrew's on June 10, 1956.

Only slightly over seven months later — on January 20, 1957 — a Commission of Suwannee Presbytery formally organized St. Andrew's into a self-supporting church with 85 charter members.

Today the $6,000 building will accommodate 150 persons. Friends and members have given $5,000-worth of items, including a Hammond spinet organ, an electric refrigerator, and a silver Communion Service. The 1957 budget totals $8,412.00.

LOUISIANA

New Orleans — The Adult Work Institute for the Presbytery of New Orleans was held March 17 at the First Presbyterian Church of New Orleans. The guest leader for the institute was Miss Louanna Roach from the Department of Adult Education of the Board of Christian Education in Richmond, Va. Miss Roach interpreted a new piece of material — "Coordinating the Adult Program in a Local Church."

New Orleans — Dr. Ray D. Fortna marked the 25th anniversary of his pastorate of the Carrollton Presbyterian Church in New Orleans in March. He and Mrs. Fortna were honored in a brief program at the church, followed by a reception in the Bible school building. Dr. John S. Land, pastor of the St. Charles Ave. Presbyterian Church, was the principal speaker at the ceremonies.

New Orleans — Dr. Oswald J. Smith, whose name, according to evangelist Billy Graham, "symbolizes worldwide evangelism," was principal speaker for the first annual mission conference held at the Carrollton Presbyterian Church in New Orleans.

Other speakers included Dr. William Rule, III, medical missionary to the Congo, the Rev. and Mrs. George Hudson of the Taiwan mission, and the Rev. and Mrs. Frank Soules, and Mr. and Mrs. John W. Davis, newly appointed missionaries of our church.

Services were conducted March 27-31, with an additional Sunday morning service, and a special service aimed at the young people on Saturday afternoon. Purpose of the conference, according to Dr. Ray D. Fortna, pastor of the host church, is "that under the power of prayer, the spell of the Word of God, and the inspiration of fellowship with Christian leaders, our hearts may be gripped by an imperative world vision, and that we may do something about it."

Other features of this first conference included sound films of actual scenes from the mission fields; special music by the choir of the Carrollton Church, and exhibits showing some of the highlights of missionary work in foreign fields.

NORTH CAROLINA

Mecklenburg Presbytery met in a called session in the Covenant Presbyterian Church on March the 5th. There were received into the Presbytery: Rev. A. B. Montgomery, D.D., from Abingdon Presbytery, and a Commission has been appointed to install him pastor of the Caldwell Memorial Presbyterian Church; Rev. Frank S. Jones was received from Orange Presbytery, and a Commission was appointed to install him pastor of the Bethlehem Presbyterian Church; Rev. J. A. Sanders was received from Holston Presbytery, and he becomes pastor of the Benton Heights Presbyterian Church, Monroe. Piedmont Presbytery transferred to Mecklenburg Presbytery Rev J. E. Stowe, and a Commission was appointed to install him pastor of the Central Steele Creek Presbyterian Church.

R. H. Stone, Secretary

TENNESSEE

Nashville — Mr. and Mrs. William C. Worth of our Congo Mission have arrived in the United States on an emergency health furlough. They reached New York in March.

Mr. Worth, a layman, was born of missionary parents in China. He is a graduate of Davidson College and has had two years of post-graduate work at Cornell University, Ithaca, N. Y., in agriculture. Mr. Worth first went to Congo in 1926. Both his brother, Charles, and his sister, Ruth, became missionaries, originally serving in China.

His sister has now transferred to the Belgian Congo where she serves as a medical technician.

Mrs. Worth is the former Miss Martha Brand of Staunton, Va. She attended Mary Baldwin College, White's Bible School, and is a graduate of the Assembly's Training School. She is a member of the Tinkling Spring Presbyterian Church of Staunton, Virginia. The Worths have three children. Mrs. Worth has served since 1926 in the educational work in the Belgian Congo, while her husband worked with the building program of the Mission.

VIRGINIA

Richmond — Miss Bettie Currie, formerly the Associate in the Department of Youth Work, Board of Christian Education, has been named Director of the Department, succeeding the Rev. John Spragens, now in Dallas, Texas.

Miss Currie, who has had the responsibility for the Senior Program with the Youth Department since 1949, has been acting director since Mr. Spragens accepted the position of minister of education at Dallas' First Presbyterian Church. Her appointment as director was announced by the Board.

Ruth

Ruth was born and reared in a home that did not know God, but she married a man who came with his mother, Naomi, from the land of Israel. They knew and loved God, the only true God, the God whom we love. Ruth learned from them how to know and to love the true God, and when her husband died and Naomi decided to return to Israel, her homeland, Ruth went with her, saying she wanted to live and die with the people of God. Arriving in Bethlehem with Naomi, Ruth went out into a field to gather the fragments of grain which were left by the reapers, and there she met Boaz, the owner of the field. Boaz loved Ruth at first sight, and soon afterward he married her and she was very happy. Naomi was happy, too. Then a little boy baby was born and they named him Obed. Obed became the father of Jesse, and Jesse the father of David. So this little girl, Ruth, who was born and reared in a heathen home came to be in the line of our Lord's human ancestry. Now read the beautiful story of Ruth in the Bible. G.

yoke upon themselves (vv.29-30). Our burdens are often the result of our being yoked to pride or self-centeredness, hurt feelings, anger, resentment or an unwillingness to accept our circumstances. How is a willingness to learn of Christ who is meek and lowly in contrast to these sins (v.29a)? Notice again what one finds in Christ's yoke (vv.29b-30). We do not come to Christ after we are rid of our sin and troubles; we come as we are (v.28) — with a willingness to turn these things over to Him and have Him as the one who rules our lives. Does an unwillingness to accept a meek and lowly place with Christ (v.29) keep you from coming to Him with your burdens?

Thursday, May 2, James 5:13-16. The rich of vv.1-6 are the persecutors of the Christians (vv.7-11). What hope of deliverance is presented to these Christians (vv.7-9)? What Christian attributes must they develop in preparation for the day of Christ's return (vv.7,8,9,)? What illustrations are given of the development of these virtues (vv.10-11)? How is Job especially appropriate (v.11)? Are you willing to rest the reasons for your suffering with God until He shows you His purposes in His own time? Prayer was the only recourse these Christians had for changing things (vv.13-18). Notice in vv.13-18 the variety of conditions that can be affected by prayer. Which of these are not subjects of your prayer life? Do you honestly believe that God does alter things as a result of earnest prayer (vv.16b-18)?

Friday, May 3, Joshua 1:7-9. Years before, God had promised Abraham, Isaac and Jacob (Gen. 13:14-17; 26:1-4; 28:13) that their descendants would inherit the land of Palestine. As the Israelites stood on the edge of the Promised Land, God repeated this promise to His people (vv.1-4). By what power or by what means were the people to take the land (vv.5,9)? What was expected of the people in relation to the Lord (vv.7-8)? Why would they need not be afraid of the obstacles that faced them (vv.7,9)? There are repeated promises and exhortations in the New Testament for the Christian to enter into the new life that is available to him in Christ (e.g., Heb. 3:12-14; 4:1-11). It is God who opens up the way and gives us the strength to live this new life (II Cor. 3:5; 12:9).

Saturday, May 4, II Corinthians 5:17-21. God, for some mysterious reason, has chosen us, who were once in rebellion against Him, to proclaim His message of redemption (vv.18b-20). However, it is still God who works through us in this ministry (v.20). It is His love that motivates us (v.14). It is His power and life in us that enables us (vv.17-18). It is His speaking through us the message of redemption (vv.20-21) that wins men to Himself. Thus it is incumbent upon us to be willing instruments to make known the good news (vv.13-15). This gospel message was made possible only through the life-blood of God's only Son (vv.19a, 21). We who have been the objects of God's love will be held responsible for how we have revealed it to others (vv.10-11).

YOUNG PEOPLE'S DEPARTMENT

(Continued from Page 8)

nings. There is no special magic that causes true happiness and love to result from such a courtship as this. It is perfectly reasonable. When two people share a common devotion to Christ, they are bound together spiritually whether there is any other attraction between them or not. Persons who fall in love and who share a love for Christ, build their love on the surest foundation of all. People who think they love each other but who do not have Christ in common, are lacking one of the strongest guarantees for the durability of their love.

ERS

ending the *Journals*. I have
bers whom I hope we might
g subscribers. Please send me
of March 13 issue which has
k" for April.

eling of appreciation to the
on "Jesus and Citizenship."
the *Journal*, but I want all
eaders and their substitutes

---

getown, S. C., March 13, 1957

tery through its Evangelism
ing a "Your Community for
ctober 20-27 at Camp Har-
eyville, S. C. We are in des-
ymnals For Christian Wor-
use during this meeting, as
amps and Conferences, Men
Rallies, and other meetings
eds. Would you sound the

Sincerely,

Ace L. Tubbs
Chairman of Evangelism

---

na:

njoy your "Children's Page"
that they are so good and
en that I am saving them to
k for some little boy or girl.

Last Will and Testament
BOARD OF WORLD MISSIONS

In your will, remember Him!

Many Christian men and women have found satisfaction in leaving part of their earthly goods to advance the work of God's kingdom.

Your Board of World Missions is one favorite medium for thus aiding the cause of Christianity after one's earthly activities have ended. You simply name the Board in your will, for whatever you wish to give.

All you have to do is consult your lawyer regarding your bequest. The suggested wording is contained in our pamphlet "Have you, too, forgotten . . . in your will?" which we will be glad to send you on request. Just write

CURRY B. HEARN, TREASURER
BOARD OF WORLD MISSIONS
PRESBYTERIAN CHURCH IN THE UNITED STATES
POST OFFICE BOX 330, NASHVILLE 1, TENN.
"To Foreign Missions a Share"

THE SOUTHERN PRESBYTERIAN JOURNAL

Rev. Henry B. Dendy, D.D., Editor....Weaverville, N. C.
Dr. L. Nelson Bell, Associate Editor....Asheville, N. C.
Rev. Wade C. Smith, Associate Editor....Weaverville, N. C.

EDITORIAL

This Thing Called Greatness

" . . . but whosoever will be great among you, let him be your minister; and whosoever will be chief among you, let him be your servant." Matt. 20:26,27.

Lurking within each heart there lie some aspirations to greatness. To distinguish between that which God considers great and that which attracts the plaudits of the world is not always easy. In fact, it is difficult to ascertain at times and it is doubly difficult to reach.

Because man looks on the outward appearance it is easy to confuse tinsel with gold, the false for the true, the temporary for the lasting.

Every Christian should aspire to true greatness, not only because it is the Lord's will for him but also because in these qualities he magnifies the Gospel which he professes. One of the great shortcomings of contemporary Christianity is that too few of us commend the faith we profess by the lives we live each day in our dealings with others.

In the Bible, by example, by precept, by command we learn many things which should characterize truly great people.

They are *people of service.* The natural man serves himself and his own personal interests before anything else. The regenerate man should serve others. Paul expressed it this way: *"Look not every man on his own things, but every man also on the things of others."* This entails a conecrn for the welfare of others and this concern must be translated into action where necessary.

Greatness involves *discipline.* These are days when self-gratification is far more prevalent than discipline of any kind. Our own actions, our habits, our deliberate choices are so often the very antitheses of those Christ would have us make. Paul recognized the danger of such a lack of discipline and wrote: *"But I keep under my body, and bring it into subjection: lest that by any means, when I have preache[d to] others, I myself should be a castaway."* St[ern] stuff? Yes, and how few of us attain to greatness!

True greatness means a *dedicated heart*[, an] eye single to God's service regardless of the [con]sequences. Such dedication often involv[es a] clear-cut choice of a path we know is ne[ither] attractive nor easy, but in that way lies the [road] to greatness by God's standards.

Again, the greatness about which Christ t[aught] means a *surrendered will.* To separate this [from] a dedicated heart is neither easy nor neces[sary.] But what is required is an act of the will w[here]by we renounce the right to say yes to self [and] say yes to Christ. It is a volitional act and we must make ourselves.

Another sign of Christian greatness is [an] *enriched mind*, one trained and also filled [with] worth-while things. *"Whatsoever things are [true,] whatsoever things are honest, whatsoever th[ings] are just, whatsoever things are pure, whatso[ever] things are lovely, whatsoever things are of g[ood] report: if there be any virtue, and if there [be] any praise, think on these things"* . . . a [phil]osophy of other-worldly idealism? No, a p[rac]tical road to true earthly greatness through [the] enriching of the mind.

Faithfulness is another characteristic of [the] truly great. It is not the greatness of the [task] but the faithfulness with which *any* task is [car]ried out which honors the Lord and makes greatness of character. Faithfulness does [not] require supervision, nor does it measure su[ccess] by human acclaim. It is not a trait best ex[em]plified in an emergency; rather it is someth[ing] which enables us to carry to its rightful [con]clusion a work which may become wearin[g to] the extreme.

The most convincing evidence of true g[reat]ness is seen in the lives of those Christians [who] day by day show the *fruits of the Holy S[pirit]* in their contacts with others. The world [does] not associate love, joy, peace, longsuffe[ring] gentleness, goodness, faith, meekness, temperance with greatness, but God does. In this catalogue of Christian graces nothing is said about power, influence, prestige, organization, intellect, money, position and other things rated high by the world. All of these may have their legitimate place and rightful usage, but there are things which are infinitely more important and it is ours to either choose or reject them.

Paul chose the road of greatness by willingness to be weak that Christ's power might be manifested in him. He chose the same road when he determined that the faith of his hearers should be founded in the power of God and not in enticing words of men's wisdom. Far from being an anti-intellectual in this attitude he demonstrated for all generations to follow that the greatest are those who give their all to glorify and magnify the crucified Saviour.

—L.N.B.

A Christian Philosophy . . . The Safeguard to Education

From its beginning the Church has exercised a leading influence in education. As Christianity has spread, knowledge and a thirsting for knowledge have spread with it; educational institutions have been established with resulting cultural changes and progress.

Secular advantages are a natural corollary of education and the world has hurried to take advantage of the material benefits so that the Church no longer has a monopoly on the training of the minds of men, but in large measure has lost the educational field and it has become a secular enterprise.

True, the churches still maintain schools usually at the college level, but in the world at large education is no longer primarily protected or controlled by the Church. It is the state which dominates the educational scene.

With the change in sponsorship there has obviously come a change in emphasis. The atmosphere of the educational field is now secular, not religious, and because it is secular religion is largely ignored and the mind, not the spirit of man, is given priority.

This transition has had its tragic results. Ignoring God, and man's responsibility to and need for God, secular education has only too often sharpened the tools of the devil. That which should be the handmaiden of righteousness has become the valet of the most monstrous evil of all — indifference to God Himself.

Secularization of once God-centered educational institutions is also a demonstrable fact. Most of America's great independent centers of learning were founded by Christian men and in their beginning were maintained with dedicated money and for a specific objective — to strengthen faith in God and to further the cause of Christianity. That the express wishes of the original benefactors have been violated and that these institutions are no longer conducted for their original purpose is open for all to see.

There is a growing demand for education today. The once backward peoples of Russia are demonstrating an amazing emphasis on education, particularly in the field of the sciences. Japan is one of the most literate nations in all the world. Germany has excelled in academic learning for years. The so-called "backward nations" are feverishly absorbing knowledge.

It should be obvious to all that secular learning is not in itself sufficient. Raise the I. Q. of every member of a nation, give each individual a broad basic education, and even advanced specialized training in one or more of the amazing new fields of learning, and there is yet lacking something of infinite and essential worth. What of the spirit of man? What of his responsibility to God? What of life in the light of eternity? What of this world in the light of coming judgment?

When we consider education in the light of the eternal verities we begin to realize how far short we have come to God's ideal and how dangerous are both present omissions and continuing trends.

Man does not live by bread alone, nor is there true wisdom apart from God. "The fear of the Lord is the beginning of wisdom" runs counter to much in the modern philosophy of education. That man's life must first be properly oriented to God before it can be properly adjusted to his fellow men, and therefore to contemporary life, is a concept almost totally absent in our present-day theory of teaching. Cultured pagans, erudite agnostics, godless scientists, will never solve the problems of their

The Southern Presbyterian Journal, *a Presbyterian Weekly magazine devoted to the statement, defense, and propagation of the Gospel, the faith which was once for all delivered unto the saints,* published every Wednesday by The Southern Presbyterian Journal, Inc., in Weaverville, N. C.

Entered as second-class matter May 15, 1942, at the Postoffice at Weaverville, N. C., under the Act of March 3, 1879. Vol. XV, No. 52, April 24, 1957. Editorial and Business Offices: Weaverville, N. C. Printed in the U.S.A., by Biltmore Press, Asheville, N. C.

ADDRESS CHANGE: When changing address, please let us have both old and new address as far in advance as possible. Allow three weeks after change if not sent in advance. When possible, send an address label giving your old address.

own personal lives, much less the destiny of the world. Where then is there hope? Has the trend of a secular and godless education become finalized until there is no solution? Shall the Christian retreat into a shell of frustration and defeat? Just the opposite!

In the realm of eternal truth the most ignorant Christian is wiser than the most learned agnostic. Only the Church and the Christians of which it is composed have the perspective which is the basis for true wisdom. Only the Christian knows where he stands and in Whom his hope of eternity rests. Only the Christian knows his essential responsibilities to his fellow man. It is the adjustment of perspective which must be the basis of education if it is to glorify God and to advance His Kingdom.

The Christian perspective must therefore be the philosophical presupposition on which education is predicated if it is to be a blessing to society and not a curse. The staggering technological advances, the discoveries of science by which life is made longer and its living more pleasant, the yet un-charted and unrealized progress to be made in the realm of advanced science, all are the result of education, but none of them contribute one whit to lessen man's dependence on or responsibility to God. Where this knowledge of, and faith in God and His Christ are lacking, there stands the stark and pitiful comparison of man surrounded by things and helpless to transport them into spiritual values or make them relevant to eternity itself.

The need of this generation is a new vision of education which gives God His rightful place in His universe and recognizes Him as the source of all things — including eternal life for repentant sinners. Who but the Church can give this renewed emphasis? Who but Christians can implement such a program? Immediately we are faced by the sober fact that the majority of advanced educators; the majority of those responsible for our scientific and technological advances, are not themselves committed to God, certainly to the extent that they give Him priority in either thought or practice.

The obvious alternative then is reaching men and women, boys and girls, with the Gospel of Jesus Christ in all of its implications and at all levels, national and international, apart from our present educational systems. This restores to the home and the Church a responsibility only too often neglected.

Reverential trust in God must be basic. The recognition of Him as sovereign and supreme in all of His creation must be instilled in the minds and lives of men. The Gospel is not a complicated theological formula; it is a simple message that changes the hearts and lives of those who accept it.

and in humility of mind looking upon the things of others, v. 3. The context on the other side, v. 8, speaks of Christ humbling Himself to the obedience of death, the death of the cross. This mind of humility is inculcated in the whole passage, accordingly it seems best to interpret *emptied* as an emptying of all self-consideration. We could imitate such a psychological emptying, but we could not heed a call to empty ourselves of Deity — since we are not gods. Throughout this as other passages there is one Person who is the subject of the whole story, cf. 2 Cor. 8.9; Rom. 8.3; Hebr. 5:8-10; Jno. 1:1-18.

Luke 2.52 clearly refers the increase in wisdom as the increase in stature to Jesus' human nature. He advanced in wisdom as in stature, that is in both cases, in his human growth from a child to a man. The other passages may both also refer to our Lord's human limitations of knowledge, and this notwithstanding the use of the term the or a Son. Our Confession well states, "By reason of the unity of the person that which is proper to one nature, is sometimes in Scripture attributed to the Person denominated by the other nature." So when it is asserted that though he was a Son yet learned he obedience by the things which he suffered, we can understand the development in the human life experiences of our Saviour. The most difficult word is concerning the Son's not knowing the hour of his Coming in Glory. Perhaps, there is here an analogy to the statement that Christ died. The Person died but he could not and did not die in his Divine nature — God cannot die. He Who is God took a full human nature and therein died for us and for our salvation. Similarly, God the Word took as a part of his truly human nature a human mind, to which the Father communicated those things He wished the Saviour to reveal to us as our final Prophet. Those things did not include the day or the hour of his Coming in Glory.

There are other passages in the Gospels which assure us that the Son knows the Father completely, that as he knows the Father so he knows his sheep, that he knew what was in man, that he knows all things and that the Father has given all things into his hands. In such passages the Divine mind shines forth.

And that brings us to the third objection to kenosis. It does not do justice to the fundamental revelation which God has seen fit to make of Himself in Jesus of Nazareth. It assumes that we have an adequate conception of God apart from Christ and by this assumed adequate knowledge of God are able to say that in order to be incarnate God had to empty himself of most or part of his Deity. How do we get such an adequate revelation of God? The real revelation of the living God is one that has its climax and culmination in Jesus Christ. This is set forth by Paul, by the epistle to the Hebrews, and by the Fourth Gospel as well as inferentially by the other New Testament books. The Apostle says that Christ is the image of God, Col.1.14, Rom.8.29, in whom all fullness dwells, Col. 1.19, that in Him the mystery of the Godhead is revealed and all wisdom and knowledge is hidden, Col.2.2-3; I Cor. 1.29. In Hebrews, God has finally revealed Himself in one who is Son, who is the outshining of the Father's glory and the reiteration of the Father's being. In the Fourth Gospel, he is the Word who came bearing unquenched clouds of Divine glory, full of grace and truth, for God's only-begotten who dwells in the bosom of the Father has exegeted him, I. 14,18. "He that has seen me has seen the Father," 14.9. He that believes on me, believes on him that sent me; he that sees me sees him that sent me, 12.44-45. The quotations from Malachi and Isaiah with which the synoptic account begins, Mark 1, point in the same direction. Those who are taking seriously the revelation of God in Christ, such as Professor Karl Barth, are thoroughly opposed to the kenosis doctrine on this theological ground.

Somewhat as John Calvin showed that in our idea of God, unless we are thinking of the triune God, we are not thinking of the living God at all, so these theologians are saying that unless we are thinking of the God who became incarnate in Jesus Christ we are not thinking of the living God at all. The idea of a God than which a greater cannot be thought is the idea of the living God who can and did open his fellowship to us by coming into our lot and life in Jesus of Nazareth.

If there were space it might be pointed out that there are also metaphysical difficulties with kenosis. Can the unchangeable God change himself into that which is not God? Can his substance of Godhead exist apart from the attributes which properly distinguish this substance? But we prefer not to get into such abstractions. By the light of the Word we are unable to accept the kenotic theory. For any who may be interested, our views on the Person of Christ are set forth more fully in the chapter, *The Word Became Flesh,* in the book, CHRIST: THE BREAD OF LIFE.

—W.C.R.

THE FIRST PRESBYTERIAN CHURCH IN AUGUSTA, GEORGIA

By Rev. Robert Strong, S.T.D.
Pastor

"The thrill of that hour is upon me now. The house was thronged—galleries and floor. The meagre person of the intellectual athlete (Dr. James Henley Thornwell) occupied a small space in the front of the pulpit, and so near as to gain from its framework a partial support, for even now he felt the approach of fatal disease. Every eye was upon him, and every sound was hushed as by a spell, while for forty historic minutes this Calvin of the modern Church poured forth such a stream of elevated utterance as he of Geneva never surpassed, his arguments being as unanswerable as they are logically compact."

Thus Rev. Joseph Ruggles Wilson, pastor of First Presbyterian Church, Augusta, Ga., during the Civil War years, described the opening session of the First General Assembly of the Southern Presbyterian Church. To this day the fact of greatest moment and inspiration in its 153 years of history is that First Church, Augusta, was the birthplace of our denomination.

Let us briefly review the circumstances that led to this historic hour. On April 12, 1861 Fort Sumter was fired on by the Charleston batteries. The General Assembly met in May in Philadelphia. Over the opposition of Dr. Charles Hodge and 56 other commissioners the Assembly adopted the resolutions offered by Dr. Gardner Spring of New York that had the effect of making loyalty to the federal government a test of church membership. Dr. Hodge termed the resolutions a denial of the Kingship of Christ. The Southern commissioners saw no course but to withdraw from the Assembly. Meeting in Atlanta they called a new General Assembly, which was convened in First Church, Augusta, December 4, 1861.

High emotion there was in the meeting, but testimony abounds that the sessions of that first assembly were marked by rare calmness and dignity and by the absence of rancor and bitterness. Dr. Benjamin Palmer of New Orleans was elected Moderator: the massive pulpit chair he used as presiding officer has been preserved as a memento of those great days. Rev. Dr. J. N. Waddell was stated Clerk, and the host pastor, Dr. Wilson, served as Permanent Clerk, an office he was to hold for more than 25 years.

Dr. Wilson was minister of First Church from 1858 to 1870. Thus when the Wilson family left Augusta, Woodrow Wilson was 14. There can be no doubt that the years in Augusta had a large formative influence upon the boy. What he saw during the Civil War and the Reconstruction

Strong

contributed to his deep hatred of war and bloodshed, later to find expression in his effort as President to keep the United States out of World War I. He would have seen, in September of 1863, after the frightful struggle at Chickamauga, the church building turned into an emergency ward for the Confederate wounded. Grimy, dirty, blood-stained men in ragged grey uniforms were taken into the old church, located as it was near the railroad tracks, and placed in the broad aisles and between the pews, where they were nursed by the women of Augusta. At the same time he would have stared wide-eyed at the Yankee soldiers held under guard in the large, fenced-in churchyard, which was used as a temporary prisoner of war camp. Likely he was in his pew, the second from the front in the right of the center aisle when one Sunday his father announced: "A great battle is raging today in Virginia and the forces of the Confederacy are suffering from lack of ammunition. This congregation must do its duty. Immediately at the close of these services, men and women will repair to the arsenal to help with the cartridges.

You will now rise and sing the Doxology and be dismissed."

It was in these years that Woodrow Wilson learned the Shorter Catechism by heart and the foundation was laid for that Christian conviction which would in later years find utterance in such a statement as "I do not see how any man can go through life without faith in the Lord Jesus Christ", and the sentiment he expressed when President that he regarded it as a higher honor to serve as an elder in the Presbyterian Church, which he did during his years in Washington, than to occupy the White House.

First Church was more than pleased to be selected as the place where the City of Augusta would observe the Woodrow Wilson Centennial, December 9, 1956.

First Church was organized in 1804. In 1750, 17 years after Oglethorpe made his first settlement in Georgia, 15 years after Augusta was founded, a church had been built under the jurisdiction of the Church of England. The building was destroyed early in the Revolutionary War. After the war a new church was erected for the use of all denominations, episcopacy having fallen into disfavor. In 1804 the Presbyterians of the flock worshiping in St. Paul's organized themselves into a church and called Rev. Washington McKnight as pastor. For some years the only services of public worship in Augusta were Presbyterian in character. Session records show that budgets were truly modest in those days. For 1808, for example, the following items appear: pastor's salary $800., clerk of the church $100., sexton $50., music director $100.

In 1809 in the pastorate of Rev. John R. Thompson of New York, ordained in Augusta by the Presbytery of Hopewell in 1807, it was decided that a Presbyterian Church should be built. The Legislature gave title to the trustees of the Presbyterian Church to a large lot on the Commons of Augusta. Construction was then begun.

As the building neared completion two members of the committee were discussing the important question of finances. One remarked "I think you and I must make up the deficit." "How much is it?" inquired his friend. The first held up the fingers of one hand. The friend agreed to do his part, but when his obligation was put before him in writing he became panic-stricken, for he found himself bound to contribute half of $5000. "Thousands, thousands!" he exclaimed. "I thought you meant hundreds!" Whether he rose to the occasion we do not know, but the church was finished and opened for worship. May 17, 1812 was a great day in Augusta: about 700 people attended the service of dedication, and the "publick prints" report that "no congregation was ever more seriously attentive."

When it is considered that there were only 50 members on the roll to undertake the building program, it can be seen that those early Presbyterians

One of the happiest seasons in the history of the church was the week of the sesquicentennial celebration in May, 1954. From the opening service, attended by more than 700, to the reception that concluded the proceedings a spirit of joy, good will, and devotion prevailed; it was like a "fellowship revival," some said. Former First Church ministers came back to make addresses; the moderators of general assembly, synod, and presbytery brought greetings in person. The heritage of the church was reviewed. The ancient foundations were re-appraised. A new commitment was given that First Church, Augusta, would continue to seek to be unswervingly loyal to the Westminster Confession of Faith and to sound forth with all her strength the blessed Gospel of Christ in terms of that noblest creedal expression of the whole counsel of God.

Helps To Understanding Scripture Readings in *Day by Day*

By Rev. Clinton C. Baker

Sunday, May 5, *Psalm* 145:1-9. Praise is upon the lips of the Psalmist because of God's greatness and mercy (vv.1-3). Read through the Psalm thinking of what it says about God in terms of Christ. How do vv.8-9 describe the compassion God has revealed to us in Christ? What do we know of the kingdom that Christ will establish that parallels the description of vv.10-13? See Revelation 5:9-13; 19:1-9. What words of Jesus can you recall that parallel the truths about God presented in vv.14-20? According to vv.14-20, is the Lord adequate for all the needs of His children? The Psalmist did not have Christ in mind when he wrote this, but the God he worshipped is the same God that is revealed to us in Christ? Can you praise God for the reasons that are presented in this Psalm?

Monday, May 6, *Psalm* 8. The Psalmist gives praise to God for His creation (Genesis one). In this Psalm we behold the work of creation from man's point of view and in Genesis one from God's point of view. How did God look upon His creation (Gen. 1:31)? Try to imagine what was involved in each act of creation (Gen. 1:4, 10,12,16-18,21,25). As the Psalmist beholds all the wonders of God's creation, what thoughts come to his mind (v.4)? What position was given man in relation to God's other creation (Gen. 1:26; Psalm 8:6-8)? A "little lower than the angels" means "a little lower than God." Do you sometimes feel insignificant and fearful, alone in the vastness of the universe? Do you realize the greatness of your importance to the Creator? Have you made your peace with Him?

Tuesday, May 7, *Psalm* 62. There comes a time in the life of most people when circumstances force them to look to God alone for help and strength (vv.1,5-6). What figure is used in v.9 to picture the futility of trusting in the arm of man? What attitude toward wealth is advocated (v.10)? List the words in the Psalm that describe what the Lord will be to those who wait before Him. What relation will He assume to them? Is He adequate for their needs? What two characteristics of God mentioned in vv.11-12 make this relationship and this care possible? What do the words "alone" (vv.1,5) and "only" (v.2) add? In the midst of the pressures of this life (vv.3-4,e.g.) it is a grand thing for the Christian to have such a God, one to whom he can "pour out his heart" (v.8).

Wednesday, May 8, *Psalm* 23. The twenty-third Pslam can be especially meaningful for the Christian as he thinks of it in terms of Christ. Read through John 10:7-18, 27-30. Everything Psalm 23 promises to the Old Testament saint can be found by the believer in Jesus Christ. How does John 10:9-10 correspond to vv.2-3 of Psalm 23? What does the number of personal pronouns in the Psalm point up about the author's relation to the Lord? Compare this with John 10:14,27. How would the fact that Jesus mentions about Himself in John 10:11,15,17 apply the truth of v. 4 of Psalm 23 concerning death? How is the security of the believer paralled in John 10:28-30 and Psalm 23:5-6? With Christ as our shepherd we "shall not want."

Thursday, May 9, *Mark* 10:17-22. The man who ran up to Jesus (v.17) was the rich young ruler of Luke 8:18. The attitude of his question (v.17) must have been quite different from that of the Pharisees (v.2). Notice Jesus' attitude toward him (v.21) when the ruler made the reply of v.20. Do you think the man was sincere? How did Jesus' regard for him differ from His attitude toward the Pharisees (v.5)? What do you think was the purpose of Christ's statement of v.21? Which one of the Ten Commandments does v.22 reveal that the young man was really breaking? He went away sorrowful (v.22), yet he went away. Does the desire for ease and comfort keep you from following Christ?

Friday, May 10, *Psalm* 100. How complete is God's claim to our lives (v.3)? Surely we ought to serve and worship Him (v.2), render our thanks and praise to Him (v.4), as a matter of course, as the fulfillment of our most basic obligations. Notice,however, what vv.1,2,4 do to the concept that man's duty to God is a dull, burdensome thing. How many words can you find in these verses that speak of man's relationship to God as a thing of glowing and spontaneous joy? What is it that accounts for the Christian's joy (v.5)? Is the poet's attention in this Psalm centered upon the duties he

LESSON FOR MAY 5 — **By THE REV. J. KENTON PARKER**

God's Plan And Man's Response

Background Scripture: Genesis 1:27,28; 3 - 9
Devotional Reading: Psalm 90:1-12

Psalm 90, which is, "A Prayer of Moses the Man of God," is often read at funerals. It reminds us of the everlasting character of God and the frailty of man. Due to his sins, man's days are not long upon the earth — threescore years and ten, or fourscore — and are filled with labor and sorrow. He prays that God will teach us to number our days that we may apply our hearts unto wisdom. (Or, "get us a heart of wisdom"). It takes heavenly wisdom to enable man to live as he should upon earth. He closes the psalm with the plea that God will satisfy us early with His mercy, make us glad, let His beauty be upon us, and establish our work.

In our lesson today we study about God's Plan for man when He created him, and man's response to that plan. The Background Scripture includes a number of important and interesting events which marked the early days of man upon the earth. I am selecting a verse, or phrase, from each chapter which illustrates some of these responses.

In 1:27,28, we have the simple statement about God creating man and blessing him, saying to him, Be fruitful and multiply and replenish the earth and subdue it: and have dominion over all the earth. He made man in His image, and His plan was for this man to have dominion; to be a king. In chapters 3-9 we see how man responded to this plan of his Creator.

I. *Chapter* 3: *"Where art thou?"*: The Fall of Man; Sin Comes.

God comes into the Garden and calls to them, "Where art thou?" Why were Adam and Eve hiding? What had happened? Why was their fellowship broken? This chapter gives the story of the Fall of Man. Satan, under the form of the serpent, came to tempt Eve. He comes with a question; "Hath God said, Ye shall not eat of every tree of the garden?" Then he tells Eve that, "Ye shall not surely die; but be as gods." Eve partook of the forbidden fruit and gave to her husband and he ate.

Sin had come. Our first parents failed to stand the test; they had disobeyed, and a feeling of guilt and shame had come, and they were hiding from God. God pronounced a curse upon them, and upon the serpent, and upon the ground which should thenceforth bring forth thorns and thistles. They were driven from their beautiful home, the garden of Eden. In this short chapter we see the beginning of sin and also the beginning of salvation in verse fifteen; the promise that the seed of the woman should bruise the serpent's head.

II. *Chapter* 4: *"Cain rose up against his brother and slew him";* First murder; Sin is now spreading into the Family and the Home.

Dr. Alexander Whyte with his vivid imagination, sees Eve with her firstborn son, saying, I have gotten a (or,the) man from the Lord, as thinking that this boy was to be the "Seed" that should bruise the serpent' head. If she had such a thought she was to be bitterly disappointed, for, instead of being the Saviour, he was to be the first murderer.

Cain and Abel brought their offerings to the Lord. God was pleased with Abel and his offering from the flock, and had respect to it, but He did not have respect for the offering of Cain, which consisted of the fruits of the ground. In Hebrews we are told that it was "by faith" that Abel offered a more excellent sacrifice than Cain. No doubt there had been more revealed to man as to the way He was to worship, and the need for "blood" as an atonement for sin. Of one thing we are sure; there was something lacking in Cain's offering, something very important, and God was justly displeased with it. In Abel's offering there appears to be a recognition of sin and faith in the promise of God, while in Cain's offering there was a lack of faith. Thus early we see that "without shedding of blood there is no remission of sins."

It is well to remember that when we approach God we should be sure that we come in a way that pleases Him. Man sometimes "rushes in where angels fear to tread," and I fear that there is sometimes undue familiarity and lack of reverence in our approach to the throne of grace. We fail to see our need of our Great High Priest Who has gone into the presence of God to make intercession for us. There is only One Way to God, and that "Way" is Christ; "I am the way . . . no man cometh unto the Father but by Me."

We have the third question in the Bible when God asks Cain; Where is Abel thy brother? Cain answers by another question, Am I my brother's keeper? In these two questions we see something of our responsibility for others. What a difference between Cain's answer, Am I my brother's keeper? and the noble answer of the apostle Paul, "I am debtor, both to the Greeks, and to the Barbarians, both to the wise and the unwise." What sort of answer are we giving to the question, Where is Abel, thy brother?

We are then told of the punishment of Cain, and something as to his immediate descendants. A third son is born to Adam, and "then began men to call upon the name of the Lord." Mankind is separating into two groups; those who believed, and those who believed not.

III. *Chapter* 5: *"And he died";*
Eight times in this chapter; Death Comes.

This is the monotonous refrain that runs through this record of these men who lived so long, had so many sons and daughters, and then died. The only exception to the rule is in the case of Enoch; "And Enoch walked with God : and was not; for God took him." Again the book of Hebrews tells us that it was "by faith" that Enoch walked with God. It takes a high degree of faith to walk with God when most men were walking the other direction, walking according to their own desires. This chapter, as well as the universal experience of men ever since, proves that God was speaking the truth when He said, In the day that thou eatest thereof thou shalt surely die, (or, Dying, ye shall surely die). Satan had said, "Ye shall not surely die." He is well named "the father of lies," and "a murderer from the beginning." (John 8:44) Paul tells us that death passed upon all men, for that all have sinned. (Romans 5:12).

IV. *Chapter* 6: *"And it grieved him at his heart"*:
Judgment, the Flood, came.

What was it that grieved God at his heart? The wickedness of mankind. Sin had now spread until we have this awful description; "every imagination of the thoughts of his heart was only evil continually." Notice how Moses piles up the words : every imagination - heart - only evil - continually - corrupt before God - filled with violence, (These last two in verse 11). These expressions describe the awful condition of the world prior to the Flood, a condition which demanded Judgment. God revealed to

YOUNG PEOPLES Department

YOUTH PROGRAM FOR MAY 5 | **By THE REV. B. HOYT EVANS**

"*What Difference Does It Make*"

Scripture: Ruth 1:12-17 and Ephesians 5:31

Suggested Hymns:
"Stand Up, Stand Up For Jesus"
"More Love To Thee, O Christ"
"Take My Life, And Let It Be Consecrated"

'(Again, as last week, we suggest that you have a resource couple or person on hand to answer questions which may arise from the consideration of this subject. The young people might state their questions more freely, if they were allowed to write them on slips of paper and hand them in. In case they want to submit questions for next week, the matter for discussion then will be early marriages and the factors involved in marriage for those who are very young.)

Program Leader:

We discovered last week that there is a large percentage of practicality in true love and sucessful marriage. We admire Ruth's high purose in going with her mother-in-law to a trange land and forsaking her own family and ackground. Ruth's attitude is sometimes cited s the ideal for marriage, but we need to recogize that in real life it is very hard to forsake ne's background and family ties as she did. oung people who are caught in the swell of omance often ask "What difference does it ake?" when it is pointed out to them that here are serious differences between their own ackgrounds and those of their intended husands or wives. Family background is one of he very important practical factors in love nd marriage. It makes a great deal of difference hether the family and home life of two young eople is very similar or not. Because it does ake a difference, this subject demands our erious consideration.

irst Speaker:

The wisest course to follow is to take a careful ook at a person's family before we become oo deeply involved with him or her. This oes not mean that we shall adopt a superior, nooty, critical attitude, but that we are simply illing to face facts that will have an important earing on our friendship.

How does the pattern of their family life ompare with yours? Some families are very lose-knit and others are not. One young bride was very upset because her husband nearly always ate lunch with his mother, leaving his wife at home alone. She had a reason to be provoked, but she might have been better prepared if she had looked at her husband's family a bit more carefully before the wedding. In that home loyalty to the family came before everything else.

The idea of the rich boy marrying the poor girl or vice versa is very romantic, but in real life it is a situation that can be full of problems. It can be very trying for a boy or girl to have to "live up" to a standard far higher than that of his own family. Also, the attitude of the family toward finances is ordinarily passed on to the family members. A girl from a home where money is spent freely as long as it lasts may think her boy friend is terribly stingy, if he tries to practice the thrift which has been taught in his home.

A lack of similarity between social and cultural background can be a cause of conflict. If drinking, dancing, and petty gambling have never been allowed in your home, you had better be very careful about becoming seriously involved with a person in whose home these practices are considered both desirable and acceptable.

It is also a good idea to know what values in life your boy or girl friend's family considers most important. A woman whose family had emphasized comfortable material living (plenty of stylish clothes, etc., etc.) was rather resentful of her husband's interest in books, scholarship, and education. Had she given the matter much thought, she would have seen that intellectuality was a strong family characteristic.

Much has been said about the danger of marriages between persons of different faiths (Catholics, Jews, and Protestants). We can hardly overemphasize the importance of this matter, but there is another phase to the problem. There can be almost as much conflict between people who belong to the very same church when one is very devout and faithful and the other is a merely nominal member. It is most important to know how your families compare as to their attitude toward religion and church life.

(Continued on Page 16)

Acting a Lie

It's an awful thing to tell a lie. And did you know a person can lie without saying a word? A man did that and God struck him dead. Ananias promised to sell his land and give all the money to God; but he changed his mind and brought only a part of it and laid it at the apostles' feet, pretending it was all. He did not say it was all; just let them think it was all. But Peter said, "Ananias, why hath Satan filled thine heart to lie to the Holy Ghost and to keep back part of the price of the land? Thou hast not lied unto men, but unto God"! And Ananias dropped dead right there. And they carried his body out and buried it. The Bible, God's Word, says no liar shall enter Heaven. Read it in Revelation 21:8 & 27. And read about Ananias in Acts 5:1-11. Make up your mind you will always tell the truth, both in word and in act, no matter what it costs. "Lying lips are abomination to the Lord; but they that deal truly are His delight" Proverbs 12:22.

Christian Love

By Rev. James O. Reavis, D.D.

The book of Hosea brings to our attention the beautiful example of Hosea's Christian love and the revelation of the "wonderful love of God that will not let man go."

Hosea was called of the Lord to be a prophet. Apparently, Hosea spoke of Israel's unfaithfulness before he experienced domestic tragedy of his own. In obedience to the will of God, Hosea married Gomer. The marriage seems to have been a "happy fellowship until it was ruined by the outbreak of Gomer's harlot spirit."

As Hosea reflected on his tragic domestic experience he could "recognize in it a type of the Lord's broken fellowship with His bride Israel." It is believed that Hosea and Gomer separated and that he dismissed her. Yet, he still loved her. He felt incomplete without her. Though Gomer had been faithless and was not worthy of his love, Hosea could not discontinue loving her. In substance God seems to have said to Hosea: "Continue loving, thou art allowed to love Gomer, thou must love her—so do I, the Lord, love Israel."

Hosea was "constrained even against his own judgment to restore the old marriage relationship," though to redeem Gomer he must discipline her. "If Hosea under the compulsion of love was constrained to redeem his erring wife, how much more must the Lord yearn to restore His erring people to the old covenant relationship."

Gomer did not deserve Hosea's merciful treatment. Nor did Israel merit the mercy and the love of God. Israel's redemption from sin and shame was an act of God's grace and of His "love that would not let His faithless people go."

Israel and all other sinful nations and men deserve God's condemnation and destruction, but in His infinite love He has provided redemption in Christ His only begotten Son, who died on the cross, that "whosoever believeth in Him should not perish, but have everlasting life."

We are indebted to Dr. Harold Cooke Phillips for his scholarly Exposition in the "Interpreters Bible"—Volume VI—(pages 593-95), in which he discusses helpfully the difference between divine love and human love.

Says Dr. Phillips: "There is a great difference between divine love and human love. Hosea discovered it; Christ revealed it; the Church must preach it. The difference is seen when we recall that in English we have only one word for love and we use this for all objects. Thus we might say: "I love my friend," "I love music," "I love God." In Greek, however, there are three different words. Two of them concern us now. One is "Eros," a word which never occurs in the New Testament, though constantly used in classical Greek. The other is Agape, a word which is never used in classical Greek but is used almost exclusively in the New Testament.

In classical Greek if one should say, "I love you," he would use the word Eros, designating the love of natural affection, human love. But in the New Testament if one should say, "I love you," he would use the word Agape, symbol of divine love. It is the divine love that Hosea discovered and Christ made known. "Human love, Eros, is evoked by something loveable in the object loved." "Divine love is evoked without any merit in the loved object."

"Christ gave His life to reveal and amplify Agape love—not Eros, human love. The love of the Cross, Agape love, was not to those who merited or deserved it." " But God commendeth His love toward us in that while we were yet sinners Christ died for us." Romans 5:7, 8.

"Hosea was the first to discover that the divine love goes out to us not because we are worthy of it, but because God is love, so that when we say that God loves man, we are not told what man is like, but what God is like. And this is the message which Christ, who died on the Cross, proclaims."

In Luke 6:27, we read Christ's words: "Love your enemies."

But says someone: "I cannot do that. I can see nothing lovable in my enemies. There is nothing in them to evoke my Eros love."

"But to love one's enemies is not impossible with divine Agape love. In this love there is nothing sentimental. Divine love is understanding, redeeming, creative. It is a fixed disposition of resolute good will." Agape love is compassionate "persistence of good will in Christ."

Christ does not demand that we "resolve to like everybody, but rather that we act in good will from God toward those we like and those we do not like."

In Luke 2:14, we read the precious words: "On earth peace, good will toward men." In this war-torn world we cannot have "peace on earth" until the followers of Christ show the divine Agape love to all men everywhere. "He that dwelleth in love dwelleth in God and God in him." I John 4:16.

"If ye love them which love you, what reward have ye, more than others." Matt. 5:46, 47. We cannot love our neighbors as ourselves merely with Eros human love. Many of our neighbors do not evoke our human love. But we can and must love our neighbors with Agape love, which is a fixed disposition of resolute good will toward them and all men, and the outgoing of our hearts in goodness, kindness and compassion to them.

Our Agape love seeks not its own, takes no account of evil, "beareth all things," "believeth all things," "hopeth all things."

With this love to our neighbors goes the hatred of our sins and their sins. We love their souls with a fixed disposition of resolute good will in Christ in spite of our sins and their sins.

With all our heart we must try to love in all men what God loves in them with His infinite Agape love and to hate in them what He hates. The night before Edith Cavell, the devoted English nurse, was put to death by the enemies of her country, she said, "Patriotism is not enough. I must not have in my heart any bitterness or hatred toward anyone."

Christian Agape love, the symbol of God's love, must have no bitterness and no hatred toward any human being.

With Agape love we are to "love the Lord our God with all our heart, with all our soul, and with all our mind and with all our strength" and to "love our neighbor as ourselves."

YOUNG PEOPLE'S DEPARTMENT

(Continued from Page 13)

Second Speaker:

Our first speaker has urged that differen in background be recognized before marri and preferably before we become too serio attached to a person. When the differences recognized both boy and girl, or man a woman, must reach an agreement as to how deal with them. This calls for a willingness the part of both to compromise. There is set way of working out these problems, beca no two couples will find the same solution : isfactory. If it is found that the differences too great and too numerous to be compromis then it is good to know about them before is too late.

Some marriages and friendships have s ceeded beautifully in spite of serious differen in many areas, but wherever they have s ceeded it was when the couples had their e wide open to the differences, and when th WORKED hard at resolving them. As we c served last week, a common faith in Christ a strong stabilizer for any marriage, and t strong foundation on which every home shou be built.

NEWS of CHURCHES around the World

The Vacation Fund

The Vacation Fund is made up each year from voluntary contributions by Presbyterians and Presbyterian Church organizations. The Fund has no place in the budget and has never asked to be included. It results entirely from gifts of persons who desire to help provide some periods of rest and inspiration to a considerable number of our ministers whose regular income would hardly permit them to spend a week at Montreat, Massanetta Springs or Mo-Ranch.

Attention is called to this now because summer is approaching and the Vacation Fund treasury is about empty. A list is being made of those who might well be helped to get away for short periods in July or August. The number who can be assisted will depend upon t contributions received for this purpose in t next few weeks. No minister applies to t Fund and no one knows he is to be helped un notice is sent to him. Of course, this shou be done as early as possible if his plans are be made and reservations obtained at one the conference centers. Hence the need f prompt response from those who plan to hel The Fund does not make promises until t money is in hand.

Any person who desires to have a part in tl quiet ministry of helpfulness is asked to se his contribution to Mrs. Ira D. Holt, Treasur Box 358, Montreat, North Carolina. The r sponse to this request will determine how ma ministers can be helped during the coming v cation and conference period.

The General Fund and Interchurch Agencies Statement of Receipts

Jan. 16 - Mar. 30, 1957

The General Fund Agencies

BUDGET for 1957	$893,259.00
Receipts to date	80,001.15
Percentage of annual budget received to date	8.96%
Balance needed for the year	$813,247.85

Interchurch Agencies

Budget for 1957	$23,595.00
Receipts to date	2,472.10
Percentage of Annual Budget received to date	10.48%
Balance needed for the year	$21,122.90

Standing Committee Chairmen—1957 General Assembly

Bills and Overtures — Rev. William Logan, pastor, University Presbyterian Church, Austin, Texas.

Judicial Business — Judge MacSwinford, layman from Cynthiana, Ky.

Office of the General Assembly — Rev. R. L. St. Clair, pastor, Second Presbyterian Church, Staunton, Va.

The General Council — Rev. James E. Cousar, pastor, Independent Presbyterian Church, Savannah, Ga.

World Missions — Rev. James L. Fowle, pastor, First Presbyterian Church, Chattanooga, Tenn.

Church Extension — Rev. Andrew R. Bird, Jr., pastor, First Presbyterian Church, Huntington, W. Va.

Christian Education — Rev. Harry G. Goodykoontz, Professor of Religious Education at Louisville Presbyterian Seminary, Louisville, Ky.

Annuities and Relief — Mr. Julian B. Fenner, layman from Rocky Mount, North Carolina.

Women's Work — Rev. J. P. F. Stevenson, pastor, First Presbyterian Church, Clarksdale, Miss.

Interchurch Relations — Rev. Joseph M. Garrison, pastor, Church of the Covenant, Greensboro, N. C.

Christian Relations — Colonel Francis Pickens Miller, layman from Charlottesville, Va.

The Minister and His Work — Rev. C. Newman Faulconer, pastor, First Presbyterian Church, Greenville, S. C.

Presbyterian Survey — Dr. Milton Carothers, layman from Florida State University.

Christianity and Health — Rev. C. D. Wardlaw, pastor, First Presbyterian Church, Lake Charles, La.

Stillman College

The naming of three major buildings on the campus of Stillman College was accomplished at a semi-annual meeting of the Board of Trustees.

The beautiful new women's dormitory which was the first construction project of $1,000,000 in funds from the 1953 Presbyterian Negro Work Campaign, was given the name of **Geneva Hall** taken from the Swiss cradle of Presbyterianism.

The men's dormitory, which had a modern annex provided by the Negro Work Campaign, was named **John Knox Hall** after one of the the great founding fathers of our Church.

The building housing the dining room and student center, which was completely modernized from the Negro Work Campaign Funds, was named **Student Union.** This building serves as the central gathering point for all of the campus life of the College.

Other major buildings making up the new campus at Stillman College had been previously named. The beautiful new library is called the **William Henry Sheppard Library** in memory of the illustrious alumnus of Stillman who served our Church with Samuel Lapsley as a pioneer missionary to the Congo and explorer in Africa. For his distinguished service he was awarded by the British government a Fellow of the Royal Geographic Society.

Birthright Building is the **auditorium-gymnasium** and is named in honor of Charles H. Birthright and his wife, Bettie, who were ex-slaves. They bequeathed two fine Missouri cotton farms to Stillman and this now forms a valuable portion of the income producing endowment of the College.

Older campus buildings are a women's dormitory, **Winsborough Building,** which bears the name of Mrs. Hallie Winsborough who founded the Woman's Auxiliary, now the Women of the Church (Presbyterian).

Snedecor Hall, the science building, is named for Dr. J. G. Snedecor and his wife, Emily Estes Snedecor, both of whom were devoted and heroic laborers for Stillman and our Church for years.

A new campus proudly stands where an old rundown Stillman once existed. The rally of Presbyterians to the call for help through the Negro Work Campaign, and through the General Fund where Stillman receives its church support, is responsible for this advance into something of which our entire Church can justly be proud!

GEORGIA

Decatur — Students, alumnae, and friends of Agnes Scott College in Decatur honored at a luncheon the last week of March Dr. Samuel Gerry Stukes who will retire in June after more than 40 years at the college.

The guest of honor was taken by surprise when the students put on a "This Is Your Life" skit for him, and when he was given a new automobile.

Dr. Stukes said of the surprise party in his honor, "I am completely stunned by all of it—and profoundly grateful."

MISSISSIPPI

Bay St. Louis—On Sunday, March 31, 1957, the First Presbyterian Church of this city was organized. The Commission appointed by Meridian Presbytery for the purpose, was composed as follows: Ministers—L. A. Beckman Jr., Superintendent of Home Missions; Morton H. Smith, Prof. of Bible in Belhaven College, Jackson; G. Thomas Preer, Minister to Students, Mississippi Southern College, Hattiesburg; H. Edward Morren, Pastor at Poplarville, and Supply at Bay St. Louis; and Ruling Elders, W. L. Rigby, H. R. Barber, D. A. McCandliss, all of First Church, Gulfport.

Service was held at 11 A.M. Mr. Beckman, as Chairman, presided. Rev. Mr. Smith, who is present Moderator of Presbytery, preached a very helpful and appropriate sermon. There were thirty charter members received into the organization.

The officers elected to serve the congregation are: Ruling Elders—C. L. Reab, W. P. McCutchon, T. T. Reboul Jr., Dr. W. C. Russo; and Deacons—P. S. Finn Jr., W. G. Wingo, C. G. Schaefer, and Earl F. Gates.

The Church was started as a preaching mission in a home by Mr. Beckman. Later a house and lot was purchased by the Home Mission Committee, and the house used for services. They will continue to hold services and Sunday School there until a house of worship can be erected.

It is interesting to note that this is the first Presbyterian Church to be established in Hancock County. And it is the eighth new church to be organized in Meridian Presbytery in the past nine years.

Jackson — Miss Rosemary Thompson, daughter of Mr. and Mrs. J. L. Thompson of Ackerman, Mississippi, has been elected president of the Belhaven College Christian Association for the 1957-58 school year.

Newly elected president of Belhaven student body is Miss Mary Elizabeth Richardson, daughter of Dr. and Mrs. John R. Richardson of Atlanta, Ga. Dr. Richardson is pastor of the Westminster Presbyterian Church in Atlanta.

NEW YORK

New York — Confederate General Thomas J. ("Stonewall") Jackson, who was a deacon at the Lexington, Va. Presbyterian Church, will be honored on May 19 when a memorial of Jackson will be entered in New York University's Hall of Fame.

The southern Presbyterian leader will take his stand beside a number of other great Americans honored by placement in the institution's Hall of Fame since it began in 1900. Additions are entered every five years.

TEXAS

Austin — Dr. Eugene McDanald of John Sealy Hospital, and the Titus Harris Clinic, Galveston, Texas, is the new staff psychiatrist at Austin Seminary. Dr. McDanald succeeds Dr. William B. Adamson who began the program of psychiatric counseling last year. Dr. Adamson has accepted a position in Pennsylvania.

Under the direction of clinical psychologist Dr. Carl F. Hereford of the Austin Guidance Center, all entering students are required to take comprehensive psychological tests. After Dr. Hereford checks and evaluates these tests, he passes them on to Dr. McDanald who then holds a personal conference with each student. Dr. McDanald has additional visits throughout the year with those students who may need or desire further con sultation. All of the seminary students are given an opportunity to confer with Dr. McDanald.

According to President David L. Stitt, this service aims at enabling the student to understand himself more completely thereby to better understand the many people he is likely to meet during his ministry.

"Having realistic attitudes toward human behavior makes a minister more effective in helping his congregation when problems occur," said Dr. Stitt.

VIRGINIA

Staunton—Dr. Samuel Reid Spencer, Jr., 37-year-old former dean of students at Davidson College in North Carolina, has been named president of Mary Baldwin College, Presbyterian affiliated college, in Virginia.

Dr. Spencer's acceptance was announced by Edmund D. Campbell, Washington attorney, and president of the Mary Baldwin Board of Trustees. He begins his duties August 1.

Dr. Spencer earlier served as assistant to former Davidson president, Dr. John R. Cunningham.

THIS IS THE DAY. Nell Warren Outlaw. Zondervan. $2.50.

Crowded full and brimming over with its wealth of discerning insights into Christian living, this thoroughly stimulating volume conveys to us many great devotional thoughts on the special days in the year.

Books can have a mighty influence for good or evil. They have the capacity to guide or misguide. Here is a book that guides us safely and steers us in the right direction. Mrs. Outlaw is a great Christian as well as a gifted writer. Her counsel is sane and trustworthy.

The 25 chapters in this volume cover all of the days that receive national recognition or those of special personal significance. Her primary purpose, however, is to show that every day is the Lord's and can be made to count for Him. She counsels, "Every day is the Lord's day. For that reason alone it should be a time of rejoicing. He is at the helm. He made the day. He, if allowed, will see it through to a victorious culmination."

The day that merits first place in our thinking, says Mrs. Outlaw, is the Lord's day. "Always," she remarks, "it holds first place in each week, and how blessed are mortals to have it as a day of preparation for the following six."

Illustrating the fact that God will have His own, either given in glad obedience to His will or taken as His just due, she cites an experience that occurred during World War II in England. She tells of an English minister who said to the English people that their desperate condition was due to the disregard of the Lord's day. He told his congregation, says Mrs. Outlaw, "that they had used this sacred day to throng the beaches in search of pleasure and now at all times those beaches were bare because of the fear of bombs. They had used their autos for fun-mad Sunday trips; now there was no fuel. They had ignored the bells calling them to worship; now the bells were silent. They had left their beautiful churches empty; now many of them were in ruins. They had held back money which should have gladly been laid on the altar on the Lord's Day; now that money had to go for extra taxes and the high cost of living. They had held back from the Heavenly Father His rightful service; now they were conscripted for all forms of military service and defense. They had refused to give joyfully of themselves in worship and work for the Lord and, like many other nations before them, were learning the hard way."

Then Mrs. Outlaw applies this principle to ourselves. "It would seem that America would be able to read the handwriting upon the wall and take stock before it is too late. The pages of history constantly reveal that no nation has ignored God's Day and ultimately survived. Will this beloved land be forced to have a severe jolt in order to reawaken to its divine obligation and privilege?

"There was a day when Bible-school teachers dreaded the rainy Sunday because it kept pupils at home. Today they have every reason to dread the pleasant one because it sends forth upon the highway hundreds who should be in God's House worshipping and serving Him. Wake up, beloved land! Give His day its rightful place before it is too late and America is weighed and found wanting!"

This volume should make a wide appeal as it carries a vital message to every age and every major occasion in life. It speaks to the romantic on "Valentine's Day". It speaks to the disconsolate on "The Dark Day". It speaks to mothers on "Mother's Day". It speaks to children on "Back-to-School Day". It speaks to the Christian believer on "Today" reminding him "that nothing can come into the life of the believer which does not first pass through the will of God."

In the publication of "For These Days" the author of "Voiceless Lips" and "For Love for Life" has sustained her reputation as a writer of remarkable versatility and an authority on the inner life of the Christian. Mrs. Outlaw has brought to this book the warmth of her consecrated life and the finished product is a means of grace to the thoughtful reader.

John R. Richardson

THE CHRISTIAN AND HIS AMERICA. Bishop Gerald Kennedy. Harper & Brothers. $3.00.

To Dr. Kennedy, the youngest bishop of the Methodist Church, true Americanism is a spiritual quality based on faith in God and Christ. America's strength lies in its faith; its weakness, in its material resources apart from faith.

The book is in three divisions: I, Delusions; II, Designations; and III, Demands. The delusions are "The Myth of the Superman", "The Delusion of Power" and "The Mass Mind". In the second section, he describes the Christians as Pilgrims, Priests, Prophets, Pioneers, Pastors, and Perfectionists. The Demands in the third section are "To Become", "To Bring Forth", and "To Advance."

The style is lucid, thought-provoking, and inspiring. The illustrations are appropriate and impressive. The presentation is more experimental than theological, and indicates a widespread knowledge of human nature and world events, flowing from a great mind and heart. One is sometimes confused by suggestions of a broad inclusivism as to what constitutes real Christianity and many will differ as to some of his applications, particularly as to the race issue, where he holds that our very survival depends on prompt desegregation; but altogether the book points out the weaknesses and dangers confronting America and the true Christian qualities and character needed to overcome them.

V.W.P.

THE UNFOLDING OF THE AGES, Paul R. Alderman, Jr. Zondervan Publishing House. $2.00.

A series of studies in prophecy, arranged for Bible classes with outlines, Scripture references, and clear expositions. The author holds the premillennial, pre-tribulation rapture interpretation that was taught by such teachers of prophecy as A. C. Gaebelein, Jas. M. Gray, C. I. Scofield, A. T. Pierson, and R. A. Torrey. The book is especially valuable as a concise summary of the teachings of this great school, who formulated their interpretations mainly from the Scriptures alone, before the disasters of World Wars I and II practically silenced post-millennialism and brought into prominence a millennialism and mid- and post-tribulations.

V.W.P.

THE SEVEN DEADLY SINS. Billy Graham. Zondervan. $2.00.

The seven deadly sins with which this book deals are: pride, anger, envy, impurity, gluttony, avarice, and slothfulness. In the Sixth Century Pope Gregory the Great categorized these seven sins as deadly. Since that time a number have preached a series of sermons on them.

The author brings these seven sins before us in the light of the Bible and exposes them before our eyes. Graham believes that during the last few years we have been putting a deceptive label on sin. He says, "We've called it 'error,' 'negative action' and 'inerrant fault.' But it is high time that we put a poison label back on the poison bottle and not be afraid to be as plain as the Bible is about the tragic consequences of sin."

The best feature of these simple messages is that they not only expose sin but show that there is a cure for it. At all times Graham lets us see that where "sin did abound grace does much more abound."

Here is a volume that should be circulated and those who read it can do so with profit. It is a pleasure to commend this volume to our readers.

—J.R.R.

THE SEVEN WORDS FROM THE CROSS. Ralph G. Turnbull. Baker Book House. $1.50.

Christ's words from the cross have eternal relevance. This fact will come to mind with striking clarity as we read Dr. Turnbull's messages on these utterances. The author's aim is to expound these words with reverence and devotion. Anyone who is looking for a fresh approach to these timeless messages will appreciate this volume.

—J.R.R.

UNDER THE STUDY LAMP. William Crowe, Sr. Brannon Printing Co. $1.00.

Friends of Dr. Crowe know that when he takes up his pen to express himself he has something valuable to communicate. And this communication, as Matthew Arnold would say, is always in the grand style. Dr. Crowe is a master of the English language and has the ability to impart great truths with remarkable charm and lucidity.

This slender volume is described by the author as "A Melange of Meditations." They began to reach the public about twelve years ago through the medium of the **Talladega News.** These pithy messages grew in popularity and today they are published in 34 newspapers embracing a potential readership of 276,000 persons.

A passage of Scripture is selected as the basis for each meditation. A striking subject is given, followed by the overflow of a vigorous mind and a great soul.

Dr. Crowe is perhaps our oldest living preacher in the active pastorate today. He is still going strong and preaching with phenomenal power. In one of these messages Dr. Crowe observes, "As long as one dreams of something that he can do tomorrow, whether the undertaking be large or small, he may be assured that he is holding his own with God, with his fellowmen, and with the passing years." It is not difficult to detect an autobiographical aroma in this sentence.

"They shall bring forth fruit in old age," said the Psalmist. This promise is validated in this "Melange of Meditations," produced "Under the Study Lamp."

Lightning Source UK Ltd.
Milton Keynes UK
UKHW020756011218
333087UK00005B/72/P